A GUIDE
TO
IRISH BIBLIOGRAPHICAL MATERIAL

A GUIDE
TO
IRISH
BIBLIOGRAPHICAL
MATERIAL

A Bibliography of Irish Bibliographies
and Sources of Information

Alan R. Eager, F.L.A., F.L.A.I.
Librarian, Royal Dublin Society

Second revised and enlarged edition

LONDON
THE LIBRARY ASSOCIATION

For
Alison
and in grateful acknowledgement
to
Jill

First published 1980

British Library Cataloguing in Publication Data

Eager, Alan Robert
A guide to Irish bibliographical material.
– 2nd ed., revised and enlarged.
1. Bibliography – Bibliography – Ireland
2. Ireland – Bibliography
I. Title   II. Library Association
016.0169415   Z2031

ISBN 0 85365 931 1

CONTENTS

The work of compiling a Dictionary of Irish Biography, and of collecting and editing into comprehensive volumes the various works extant on Irish bibliography might well furnish someone with a life's work.

Charles Anderson

A bibliography in any field is always a labour of love, for it seldom receives appreciation commensurate with the long and tedious labour involved.

Ida Kaplan Langman

Information in hand, however imperfectly presented, is more important to the user than the promise of an ideally compiled work which may never be completed.

Sir Frank Francis

Items differ widely in value and no attempt has been made to discriminate between them as it is impossible to anticipate the needs of users of this bibliography.

Bryan P. Beirne

Probably no bibliography has ever been compiled without some errors; it remains for me now to ask pardon for any which may be found in this one, and to thank, in advance, those critics who will point them out.

Allan Wade

INTRODUCTION

Kenneth Povey, in his fine survey of bibliographies of interest to the historian, printed in 1939, states in effect 'that there is no bibliography of Ireland as a whole — there is no great comprehensive work — the nearest substitutes are the catalogues of the large libraries'. Ireland, in short, remained unrepresented by a published work in the field of national bibliography.

The first edition of this work, published in 1964 was an attempt to fill this gap in some measure. This second edition is almost three times as long and my hope is that it will be that much more effective as a bibliographic index covering this still otherwise unexplored field.

My endeavour is to provide a bibliographic index covering Irish enumerative bibliography and aims to serve as a quick reference guide to all who are interested in Irish studies and research work. Both an author and subject index are provided for ease of reference. This edition has been updated and extended to include topics which were not covered in the original edition and should serve as a starting point for all who are engaged in research work on Ireland. It should be used in conjunction with the extensive bibliographies (Nos. 49-50) compiled by Richard J. Hayes which appeared during the period 1965-70.

The arrangement of subjects is based roughly on the Dewey Decimal Classification and material included covers the following:

1. Catalogues
2. Bibliographies completely devoted to Irish material
3. Bibliograhies appended to books and articles
4. General bibliographies which include Irish material to a greater or lesser degree
5. Bibliographies printed in Ireland, but which are not Irish in character
6. Periodicals and indexes
7. Unpublished material and work in progress
8. Other primary sources

In order to give balance to the work as a whole I have included works which are not bibliographies *per se* but are standard or representative. Articles of value which appeared in periodicals and newspapers and are often overlooked because they are not generally catalogued separately also find a place.

I wish to pay tribute to the help I received from the staffs of the undermentioned libraries where the bulk of the research work was undertaken:

British Museum, London
Central Catholic Students Library
Government Departmental Libraries
Irish Central Library for Students
Irish Folklore Commission
Maynooth College Library
National Library, Dublin
Pearse Street Public Library, Dublin
The Representative Church Body
Royal Dublin Society

Royal Irish Academy
Trinity College, Dublin
University College, Dublin

By means of correspondence I have included material from the remaining important Irish libraries, including the county libraries, and have written to the chief libraries in England and America for details of special Irish collections.

In attempting to cover so broad a canvas it was impossible to specialise, but it is hoped that the work will be judged for the utility and value of the material included rather than for what has been omitted or overlooked.

My thanks are also due to all those interested persons who made suggestions for inclusion in this work, and particularly to John Hurst and Pádraig O Táilliúir who both understood what I had set out to do originally, and put pen to paper in support.

I am indebted to Charles Ellis and David Pratt of the Library Association for their help and expertise in seeing the work through the press at a time when communication is down to almost zero due to the prolonged Irish postal strike.

Especial thanks are due to my secretary, Jill Condon, who kindly offered and accomplished most of the work of typing at home in her spare time. The fact that the book is now appearing is mainly due to Jill's enthusiasm and assistance.

Alan Eager
June, 1979

ABBREVIATIONS

Admin. Administration
Adv. Sci. Advancement of Science.
Agr. Hist. Rev. Agricultural History Review
Agr. Prog. Agricultural Progress
Amer. Book. Coll. American Book Collector
Amer. J. Leg. Hist. American Journal of Legal History
Amer. Mus. Nat. Hist. Bull. American Museum of Natural History Bulletin
Amer. Phil. Soc. Proc. American Philosophical Society Proceedings
Amer. Phil. Soc. Trans. American Philosophical Society Transactions
Anal. Bolland. Analecta Bollandiana
Anal. Hib. Analecta Hibernica
Anglesey Hist. Soc. Trans. Anglesey Historical Society Transactions
Anglo Ir. Stud. Anglo Irish Studies
Ann. Annual
Ann. Sci. Annals of Science
Arch. Hib. Archivium Hibernicum
Arch. J. Archaeological Journal
Archives. Archives: the journal of the British Records Association
Arts Ir. The Arts in Ireland
Aslib. Association of Special Libraries and Information Bureaux
Assoc. Geog. Teach. Ir. J. Association of Geography Teachers of Ireland Journal
Belfast Nat. Fld. Cl. Belfast Naturalists' Field Club
Belfast Nat. Hist. Phil. Soc. Proc. Belfast Natural History and Philosophical Society Proceedings and Reports
Bibliog. Bibliography or Bibliographical
Bibliog. Reg. Bibliographical Register
Bibliog. Soc. Bibliographical Society, London
Bibliog. Soc. Amer. Bibliographical Society of America
Bibliog. Soc. Ir. Bibliographical Society of Ireland Publications
Bibliog. Soc. Univ. Virginia. Bibliographical Society of the University of Virginia
Biog. Mem. R. Soc. Biographical Memoirs of the Royal Society
Bod. Lib. Rec. Bodleian Library Record
Book Auct. Rec. Book Auction Records
Book Coll. The Book Collector
Book Coll. Qtr. Book Collector's Quarterly
Bot. Soc. Br. Isl. Proc. Botanical Society of the British Isles Proceedings
Breifne. Breifne: Journal of Breifne Historical Society
Breifny Antiq. Soc. J. Breifny Antiquarian Society Journal
Bristol Univ. Spel. Soc. Proc. Bristol University, Proceedings of the Speleological Society
Brit. & Col. Print. British and Colonial Printer and Stationer
Brit. Bryol. Soc. Trans. British Bryological Society Transactions
Brit. Museum (Nat. Hist.) Bull. Zool. Bulletin of the British Museum (Natural History), Zoology
Brit. Print. The British Printer
Brit. Soc. Fran. Stud. British Society of Franciscan Studies
Build. Cont. J. Ir. Building and Contract Journal for Ireland
Bull. Bibliog. Bulletin of Bibliography
Bull. Inst. Hist. Rec. Bulletin of the Institute of Historical Research
Bull. Pres. Hist. Soc. Ir. Bulletin of the Presbyterian Historical Society of Ireland
Camb. Bibliog. Soc. Cambridge Bibliographical Society
Camb. Mod. Hist. Cambridge Modern History
Camb. Univ. Lib. Bull. Cambridge University Library Bulletin
Cap. Ann. Capuchin Annual
Cart. J. Cartographic Journal
Cath. Hist. Rev. Catholic History Review
Cath. Univ. Bull. Catholic University of America Bulletin
Cave Res. Group News. Cave Research Group of Great Britain Newsletter
Celt. Mag. Celtic Magazine
Chart. Surv. Chartered Surveyor
Chem. Ind. Chemistry and Industry
Chicago Fld. Mus. Nat. Hist. Chicago Field Museum of Natural History
Church Qtr. Rev. Church Quarterly Review
Clogher Rec. Clogher Record
Colby Lib. Qtr. Colby Library Quarterly
Coll. Fran. Collectanea Franciscana
Comm. Dublin Inst. Adv. Stud. Geophys. Bull. Communications of the Dublin Institute of Advanced Studies, Geophysical Bulletin

Comp. Compiler
Cork Hist. Arch. Soc. J. Cork Historical and Archaeological Society Journal
Donegal Ann. Donegal Annual
Donegal Hist. Soc. J. County Donegal Historical Society Journal
Down Con. Hist. Soc. J. Down and Connor Historical Society Journal
Dublin Hist. Rec. Dublin Historical Record
Dublin Mag. Dublin Magazine
Dublin Pen. J. Dublin Penny Journal
Dublin Qtr. J. Med. Sci. Dublin Quarterly Journal of Medical Science
Dublin Rev. Dublin Review
Dublin Univ. Law Rev. Dublin University Law Review
Econ. Geog. Economic Geography
Econ. Hist. Rev. Economic History Review
Econ. Soc. Hist. Economic and Social History
Ed. Edition or editor(s)
Edinburgh Bibliog. Soc. Pub. Edinburgh Bibliographical Society Publications
Eire-Ir. Eire-Ireland
Empire Sur. Rev. Empire Survey Review
Eng. J. Engineers Journal
English Hist. Rev. English Historical Review
Enl. Enlarged
Entomol. Entomologist
Entomol. Gaz. Entomological Gazette
Etudes Celt. Etudes Celtiques
Eur. Teach. European Teacher
Farm Econ. Farm Economist
Folklore Soc. Pub. Folklore Society Publications
For. Affairs. Foreign Affairs
Forgnan. Forgnan: Journal of the Building Centre, Dublin
Fran. Stud. Franciscan Studies
Furrow. The Furrow
Gael. J. Gaelic Journal
Galway Arch. Hist. Soc. J. Galway Archaeological and Historical Society Journal
Garden J. Garden Journal
Geneal. Mag. Genealogical Magazine
Geog. Mag. Geographical Magazine
Geol. Assoc. Proc. Geologists Association Proceedings
Geol. Soc. Amer. Geological Society of America.
Geol. Soc. Dublin J. Geological Society of Dublin Journal
Geol. Soc. J. Journal of the Geological Society
Geol. Soc. Proc. Proceedings of the Geological Society
Geol. Surv. G. B. Bull. Bulletin of the Geological Survey of Great Britain
Geol. Surv. Ir. Bull. Geological Survey of Ireland Bulletin
Geol. Surv. Ir. Info. Circular. Geological Survey of Ireland Information Circular
Harpers Mag. Harpers Magazine
Harvard Hist. Stud. Harvard Historical Studies
Hist. J. Historical Journal
Hist. MSS. Comm. Rpts. Royal Commission on Historical Manuscripts Reports
Hist. Stud. Historical Studies
Hist. Today. History Today
Hon. Ulst. The Honest Ulsterman
Index Soc. Pub. Index Society Publications
Inst. Civ. Eng. Ir. Trans. Transactions of the Insitution of Civil Engineers of Ireland
Inst. Hist. Res. Bull. Institute of Historical Research Bulletin
Ir. Ancest. Irish Ancestor
Ir. Arch. Bull. Irish Archival Bulletin
Ir. Bibliog. Pamph. Irish Bibliographical Pamphlets
Ir. Bld. Irish Builder
Ir. Bld. & Engineer. Irish Builder and Engineer
Ir. Book. Irish Book
Ir. Booklore. Irish Booklore
Ir. Book Lov. Irish Book Lover
Ir. Cath. Hist. Comm. Proc. Irish Catholic Historical Committee Proceedings
Ir. Coll. Phys. Surg. J. Journal of the Irish Colleges of Physicians and Surgeons
Ir. Comm. Hist. Sci. Bull. Irish Committee of Historical Sciences Bulletin
Ir. Def. J. Irish Defence Journal (*An Cosantoir*)
Ir. Dept. Agric. J. Ireland, Department of Agriculture Journal
Ir. Dept. Agric. Fish., Fish. Leaflet. Ireland, Department of Agriculture and Fisheries, Fishery Leaflet
Ir. Eccles. Gaz. Irish Ecclesiastical Gazette
Ir. Eccles. Rec. Irish Ecclesiastical Record
Ir. Econ. Soc. Hist. Irish Economic and Social History
Ir. Folk Song Soc. J. Irish Folk Song Society Journal
Ir. Geneal. Irish Genealogist
Ir. Geog. Irish Geography
Ir. Georg. Soc. Qtr. Bull. Irish Georgian Society Quarterly Bulletin
Ir. Hib. Iris Hibernia
Ir. Hist. Stud. Irish Historical Studies
Ir. J. Ed. Irish Journal of Education
Ir. J. Med. Sci. Irish Journal of Medical Science
Ir. J. Psychol. Irish Journal of Psychology
Ir. Jurist. Irish Jurist
Ir. Lib. Bull. Irish Library Bulletin
Ir. Lit. Inquirer. Irish Literary Inquirer
Ir. Mag. Irish Magazine
Ir. Mon. Irish Monthly
Ir. Nat. Irish Naturalist
Ir. Nat. J. Irish Naturalists Journal
Ir. Num. Irish Numismatist
Ir. Qtr. Rev. Irish Quarterly Review
Ir. Rail. Rec. Soc. J. Irish Railway Record Society Journal
Ir. Spel. Irish Speleology
Ir. Theol. Qtr. Irish Theological Quarterly
Ir. Times. Irish Times
Ir. Today. Ireland Today
Ir. Univ. Rev. Irish University Review
Ir. Wel. Ireland of the Welcomes
Ir. Writing. Irish Writing
Iver. Soc. J. Journal of the Ivernian Society
J. Journal
J. Beckett Stud. Journal of Beckett Studies
J. Butler Soc. Journal of the Butler Society

J. Cons. Int. Explor. Mer. Journal du Conseil International pour l'exploration de la mer
J. Document. Journal of Documentation
J. Ir. Lit. Journal of Irish Literature
J. J. Qtr. James Joyce Quarterly
J. Mod. Hist. Journal of Modern History
J. Old Athlone Soc. Journal of the Old Athlone Society
J. Proc. Arts Crafts Soc. Ir. Journal and Proceedings of the Arts and Crafts Society of Ireland
J. Welsh Bibliog. Soc. Journal of the Welsh Bibliographical Society
Kerry Arch. Mag. Kerry Archaeological Magazine
Kerry Arch. Hist. Soc. J. Kerry Archaeological and Historical Society Journal
Kildare Arch. Soc. J. County Kildare Archaeological Society Journal
Kilkenny S.E. Ir. Arch. Soc. J. Kilkenny and South-East of Ireland Archaeological Society Journal
An Leab. An Leabharlann: the Journal of Cumann na Leabharlann
An Leab. An Leabharlann: the Journal of the Library Association of Ireland
Leeds Phil. Lit. Soc. Lit. Hist. Sec. Proc. Leeds Philosophical and Literary Society, Literary and History Section Proceedings
Lib. Assoc. Rec. Library Association Record
Lib. Qtr. The Library Quarterly
Lib. Rev. Library Review
Limerick Fld. Cl. J. Limerick Field Club Journal
Louth Arch. J. County Louth Archaeological Journal
Mag. Nat. Hist. The Magazine of Natural History
Manchester Rev. Manchester Review
Manp. App. Psychol. Manpower and Applied Psychology
Marine Biol. Assoc. J. Marine Biological Association Journal
May. Rev. Maynooth Review
Mem. Memoirs
Minutes Proc. Inst. Civ. Eng. Minutes and Proceedings of the Institution of Civil Engineers
Mod. Phil. Modern Philology
Monthly Mag. Monthly Magazine
Mus. Assoc. Proc. Musical Association Proceedings
Mus. Bull. Museum Bulletin
Mus. Lett. Music and Letters
Mus. Times. Musical Times
N. & Q. Notes and Queries
New Ser. New series
Nat. Lit. Soc. J. National Literary Society Journal
New Camb. Bibliog. Eng. Lit. New Cambridge Bibliography of English Literature
New Ir. Rev. New Ireland Review
New Sci. New Scientist
New York Pub. Lib. Bull. Bulletin of the New York Public Library
Nth. England Inst. Min. Mech. Eng. Trans. North of England Institute of Mining and Mechanical Engineering Transactions
Nth. Ir. Leg. Qtr. Northern Ireland Legal Quarterly
Nth. Munster Antiq. J. North Munster Antiquarian Journal
Old Kilk. Rev. Old Kilkenny Review
Old Wexford Soc. J. Journal of the Old Wexford Society
Oxford Bibliog. Soc. Proc. Oxford Bibliographical Society Proceedings
p. page
pp. pages
pamph. pamphlet or pamphlets
Philol. Soc. Trans. Philological Society Transactions
Pol. Qtr. Political Quarterly
Post. Hist. Soc. Bull. Postal History Society Bulletin
Prehist. Soc. Proc. Proceedings of the Prehistoric Society
Proc. R. Soc. Med. Proceedings of the Royal Society of Medicine
pt. part
pub. publication
Qtr. J. Forestry. Quarterly Journal of Forestry
R. Arch. Inst. Royal Archaeological Institute
R. Coll. Surg. Ir. J. Royal College of Surgeons in Ireland Journal
R. Dublin Soc. Econ. Proc. Royal Dublin Society Economic Proceedings
R. Dublin Soc. Sci. Proc. Royal Dublin Society Scientific Proceedings
R. Geol. Soc. Ir. J. Royal Geological Society of Ireland Journal
R. Hist. Arch. Soc. Ir. J. Royal Historical and Archaeological Society of Ireland Journal
R. Hist. Soc. Royal Historical Society
R. Inst. Arch. Ir. Journal of the Royal Institution of Cornwall
R. Ir. Acad. Proc. Royal Irish Academy Proceedings
R. Ir. Acad. Trans. Royal Irish Academy Transactions
R. Phys. Soc. Edinb. Proc. Royal Physical Society of Edinburgh Proceedings
R. Soc. Antiq. Ir. J. Royal Society of Antiquaries of Ireland Journal
R. Soc. Edinburgh Proc. Royal Society of Edinburgh Proceedings
R. Soc. N. & R. Notes and Records of the Royal Society of London
R. Soc. Obit. N. Obituary Notices of the Royal Society of London
Ray Soc. Pub. Ray Society Publications
ref. references
Rep. Report
Rep. D. K. Pub. Rec. Ir. Reports of the Deputy Keeper of the Public records in Ireland
Rep. Nov. Reportorium Novum
Rev. Celt. Revue Celtique
Rev. d'hist. litt. relig. Revue d'histoire et de littétature religieuses
Rev. Eng. Lit. Review of English Literature
Rice Univ. Stud. Rice University Studies
S.O.C. Rev. Sean O'Casey Review
Sci. Amer. Scientific American
Science Lib. Bibliog. Ser. Science Museum Library Bibliographical Series
Sean Ard. Seanchas Ardhmaca
Sec. Section
Ser. Series

Smithsonian Inst. Misc. Coll. Smithsonian Institution Miscellaneous Collection
Soc. Bibliog. Nat. Hist. J. Society for the Bibliography of Natural History Journal
Soc. Dairy Technol. J. Journal of the Society of Dairy Technology
Soc. Geol. Mineral. Bretagne Bull. Societé Géologique et Minéralogique de Bretagne Bulletin
Soc. Stud. Social Studies
Sociol. Rev. Sociological Review
Spl. Special
Stat. Social Inq. Soc. Ir. J. Statistical and Social Inquiry Society of Ireland Journal
Stud. Bibliog. Studies in Bibliography
Stud. Celt. Studia Celtica
Supp. Supplement
T.C.D. Ann. Bull. Friends of the Library of Trinity College, Dublin, Annual Bulletin
Technol. Ir. Technology Ireland
Thomond Arch. Soc. Fld. Cl. Thomond Archaeological Society and Field Club
Times Lit. Suppl. Times Literary Supplement
Toronto Univ. Qtr. Toronto University Quarterly
Trans. Transactions
Trans. Inst. Min. Met. Transactions of the Institution of Mining and Metallurgy
Trans. R. Inst. Nav. Arch. Transactions of the Royal Institute of Naval Architects
U.S. Nat. Mus. Proc. United States National Museum Proceedings
Ulster Arch. Her. Soc. Ulster Architectural Heritage Society
Ulster Folk. Ulster Folklife
Ulster J. Arch. Ulster Journal of Archaeology
Univ. Cal. Lib. Bull. University of California Library Bulletin
Univ. Rev. University Review
Vol. Volume or volumes
Waterford S.E. Ir. Arch. Soc. J. Waterford and South-East of Ireland Archaeological Society Journal
Wise. Rev. Wiseman Review
Yacht. Boat. Week. Yachting and Boating Weekly
Yale Hist. Pub. Misc. Yale Historical Publications Miscellaneous
Zeit. für celt. philol. Zeitschrift für Celtische Philologie

A GUIDE TO IRISH BIBLIOGRAPHICAL MATERIAL

GENERAL WORKS

Communications

1 COMMUNICATIONS DIRECTORY AND YEARBOOK, 1973–, Dublin: 1973–. Published annually.

2 THE IRISH MEDIA. *Management*, vol. 19, no. 3, 1972, 41–43. First of an annual checklist of the communications media in Ireland, including newspapers, radio and television, provincials, weekly publications, periodicals and directories in Northern Ireland and the Republic.

Bibliography

3 THE BIBLIOGRAPHICAL SOCIETY OF IRELAND. [Publications.] Dublin: vols. 1–6, 1918–58.

4 THE BOOK ASSOCIATION OF IRELAND. Bibliography and miscellaneous literature [book list]. *Ir. Lib. Bull.,* 6, 1945, 142–3.

5 COLE, GEORGE W. An index to bibliographical papers published by the Bibliographical Society and the Library Association, London: 1877–1932. Chicago: 1933. (*Bibliog. soc. America spl. pub.*)

6 DIX, E.R. MCCLINTOCK. Chronological list of contributions to Irish bibliography, compiled by Eugene Carberry. *In* Printing in Dublin prior to 1601 . . . 2nd ed. Dublin: 1932, pp. 34–41.

7 — Irish bibliography: the use and need of its study. *Dublin Pen. J., new ser.,* 1, 1902–3, 200–2; 217–18.

8 — Irish librarians and Irish bibliography. *An Leab*., 1, 1905, 28–34. Reprinted *An Leab*., 11, 1953, 107–10.

9 — Irish pirated editions. *An Leab*., 2, 1906, 67.

10 — Suggestions for Irish book collectors. *Ir. Book Lov*., 1, 1909–10, 144–6.
E.R. McC. Dix (1857–1936), founder and first president of the Bibliographical Society of Ireland (1919), was one of the pioneer workers in the field of Irish bibliography, listing the publications of printers throughout Ireland, town by town. His most important work is his *Catalogue of early Dublin-printed books, 1601–1700*. He also gave valuable assistance in compiling *A catalogue of the Bradshaw collection of Irish books in the University Library, Cambridge.*

11 GILBERT, JOHN T. Irish bibliography; two papers by the late Sir John T. Gilbert, with an introduction, notes and appendices by E.R. McC. Dix. *R. Ir. Acad. Proc., Sec. C,* 25, 1904–5, 117–42. Reprinted in part in Lady Gilbert's *Life of Sir J. T. Gilbert, 1905,* pp. 437–42; another ed., with notes by Desmond Clarke, *An Leab*., 12, 1954, 37–41, 49. See also *The Gilbert and local collections of the Dublin municipal libraries*, by P.B. Glynn. *An Leab*., 10, 1949–52, 181–5, 192.

12 GREAT IRISH BOOK COLLECTORS, with notes on the sales of their libraries. 1. Dr. John Murphy, Bishop of Cork; 2. William Chadwick Neligan; 3. William Horatio Crawford; 4. Sheffield Grace; 5. Canon Jeremiah Murphy; 6. William Monck Mason; 7. Dr. Sheehan, Bishop of Waterford. *Ir. Book Lov*., 7, 1915–16, 1–3, 21–3, 38–9, 59–60, 89–90, 107–8, 125–6, 180–1.

13 HEWSON, M. and POLLARD, M. Bibliography in the Republic of Ireland, 1963. *Ir. Book*, vol. 3, no. 1, 1964, 23–25.

14 THE IRISH BOOK. Dublin, Bibliographical Society of Ireland. Vols. 1–3, 1959–64.

15 THE IRISH BOOK LOVER. Dublin: vols. 1–32, 1909–57. Index to vols. 1–31, 1909–51, compiled by Eugene Carberry, in typescript in the National Library, Dublin.

16 IRISH BOOKLORE. Belfast, vol. 1, no. 1– 1971–. Edited by Jim Gracey and Aiken McClelland.

17 MACLOCHLAINN, ALF. Irish books reviewed, 1970. *An Leab*., vol. 29, 1971, 11–13, 15–17, 14–20, 22–23, list of books and pamphlets reviewed in the *Irish Independent*, *Irish Press*, *Irish Times* and *Hibernia*.

18 MACMANUS, M.J. Some unexplored fields in Irish bibliography. *Ir. Book Lov*., 22, 1934, 32–7.

19 MINOGUE, CARMEL. Notes on Irish book collectors, 1957. Typescript: thesis for Fellowship of the Library Association of Ireland.

20 POWER, JOHN. Irish literary inquirer; or notes on authors, books, and printing in Ire-

land, biographical and bibliographical, notices of rare books, memoranda of printing in Ireland, biographical notes of Irish writers, etc. London: nos. 1–4, 1865–6. For note on Power and his bibliographical works see *Ir. Book Lov*., 1, 1909–10, 2–4.

General Bibliographies

21 BESTERMAN, THEODORE. A world bibliography of bibliographies, and of bibliographical catalogues, calendars, abstracts, digests, indexes and the like. 4th rev. enl. ed. Societas Bibliographica. Lausanne: 1966. 4 vols.

22 BIBLIOGRAPHIC INDEX. New York: vol. 1–, 1937–42–.

23 THE BRITISH NATIONAL BIBLIOGRAPHY. London; The Library Association, 1950– Published weekly and cumulated annually.

Anonyms and Pseudonyms

24 CUSHING, WILLIAM. Anonyms: a dictionary of revealed authorship. Hildesheim: 1967. Reprint of Cambridge (Mass.) ed. 1889.

25 — Initials and pseudonyms: a dictionary of literary disguises. Hildesheim: 1967. 2 vols. Reprint of New York and London ed: 1886–88.

26 HALKETT, SAMUEL and LAING, JOHN. Dictionary of anonymous and pseudonymous English literature. New enl. ed. Edinburgh: 1926–62. 9 vols.

27 STONEHILL, CHARLES A. *and others*. Anonyma and pseudonyma, by C.A. Stonehill, Andrew Black, and H.W. Stonehill. London: 1926–7. 4 vols. Limited ed. of 324 copies.

National Bibliographies

28 ARBER, EDWARD. The term catalogues, 1668–1709 A.D., with a number for Easter term 1711 A.D. London: 1903–6. 3 vols. Privately printed.

29 BOOKS IRELAND: a monthly review. Ballinteer (Dublin): no. 1.–, March, 1976–. Includes list of Irish interest books in print.

30 BRISTOL PUBLIC LIBRARIES. A catalogue of books in the Bristol reference library, printed in England, Scotland and Ireland, and of English books printed abroad, 1641–1700. Bristol: 1958.

31 COURTNEY, WILLIAM PRIDEAUX. A register of national bibliography, with a selection of the chief bibliographical books and articles printed in other countries. London: 1905–12. 3 vols.

32 THE CUMULATIVE BOOK INDEX. New York: 1898–. From 1929 has attempted to be a world list of books in the English language.

33 THE ENGLISH CATALOGUE OF BOOKS. London:1835–.

34 IRISH PUBLISHING RECORD, 1967–. Dublin: 1968–. Compiled by members of the School of Librarianship it includes material published both in the Republic and Northern Ireland and comprises books, pamphlets, the first number of new periodicals, yearbooks, musical scores and works on music, also government publications of general interest; from 1969 it has been compiled on behalf of the Irish Association for Documentation and Information Services.

35 KING, JEREMIAH, Dictionary of Ireland [including King's *Irish Bibliography*]; persons, places and subjects of historic interest. 2nd ed. Wexford: 1917–24. Three separately paged sections, the latter being titled *Leabar Lemair Eireann*. *Irish Bibliography* first published London and Dublin: 1903.

36 LONDON, STATIONERS' COMPANY. Records of the Courts of the Stationers' Company, 1602–40. Edited by William A. Jackson. London: Bibliographical Society, 1957.

37 — A transcript of the registers . . . 1554–1640 A.D., edited by Edward Arber. London: 1875–94. 5 vols. Privately printed.

38 — A transcript of the registers . . . 1640–1708 A.D. London: 1913–15.3 vols. Privately printed.

39 LOWNDES, W.T. The bibliographer's manual of English literature. New ed. by H.G. Bohn. London: 1857–64. 6 vols.

40 NATIONAL LIBRARY OF IRELAND. National bibliography, and Dictionary of Irish biography. In preparation on cards. For details see *Report of the trustees . . . National library*, 1953–4, pp. 5–6; also *Irish national bibliography,* by R.J. Hayes, *An Leab*., 18,

1960, 5–13.

41 POLLARD, ALFRED W. and REDGRAVE, G.R., (Compilers). A short-title catalogue of books printed in England, Scotland and Ireland, and of English books printed abroad, 1475–1640. 2nd rev. ed. London. vol. 2. I–Z, 1976. Vol. 1 to be published in 1980.

42 RAMAGE, DAVID, (Compiler). A finding list of English books to 1640 in libraries of the British Isles based on the numbers in Pollard and Redgrave's *Short-title catalogue* . . . Durham: 1958.

43 WATT, ROBERT. Bibliotheca Britannica; or, a general index to British and foreign literature. Edinburgh: 1824. 4 vols.

44 WHITAKER'S CUMULATIVE BOOK LIST. London: 1924–.

45 WING, DONALD. Short-title catalogue of books printed in England, Scotland, Ireland . . . and of English books printed in other countries, 1641–1700. New York: 1945–51. 3 vols.

46 — Bibliographia Hibernica: additions to Wing, by John Eliot Alden. Charlottesville. Bibliog. Soc. Univ. of Virginia, 1955. Contains approximately 215 entries of Irish material, either in addition or correction to Wing.

Subject Bibliographies

47 AITCHSON, CHRISTOPHER. Irish librarian: a manuscript compilation forming a bibliography of works relating to Ireland from the earliest times. 5 vols. In National Library, Dublin, *Mss. collection nos.* 185–8. Material included covers civil history, jurisprudence, ecclesiastical history, heraldry, peerage, family history, biography, natural history, archaeology, population, morals and manners, education, agriculture, literary history and philology.

48 CASAIDE, SEAMUS UA. Bibliographies of Irish subjects: a classified list of bibliographies, arranged under subject, author and reference. *Ir. Book Lov.*, 3, 1911, 22–3.

49 HAYES, RICHARD J. *ed.* Manuscript sources for the history of Irish civilisation: articles in Irish periodicals. Boston (Mass.): 1965. 11 vols.

50 — Sources for the history of Irish civilisation: articles in Irish periodicals. Boston (Mass.): 1970. 9 vols. Reviewed by A.R. Eager in *Ir. Booklore*, vol. 1, no. 2, 1971, 271–4.

51 HISTORICUS, *pseud.* (*i.e.*, R. Barry O'Brien). The best hundred Irish books, with annotated index. Dublin: 1886. Reprinted from *The Freeman's Journal*.

52 HOWARD-HALL, T.H. Bibliography of British literary bibliographies. Oxford: Clarendon Press, 1969. (*Index to British literary bibliography*, vol. 1.)

53 HUMPHREYS, ARTHUR LEE. A handbook to county bibliography; being a bibliography of bibliographies relating to the counties and towns of Great Britain and Ireland. London: 1917. Includes all systematic bibliographies, also source books, indexes, etc., of local history or topographical material, including printing and archaeology.

54 LEWANSKI, RICHARD C., (Compiler). Subject collections in European libraries; a directory and bibliographical guide. New York: 1965.

55 MALCLES, L.–N. Les sources du travail bibliographique. Geneva: 1950. 3 vols. in 4.

56 MASON, WILLIAM SHAW. Bibliotheca Hibernicana: or, a descriptive catalogue of a select Irish library collected for the Right. Hon. Robert Peel [1st edition reprinted] with an essay by Norman D. Palmer. Shannon: 1970. Photolithographic facsimile of the first 1823 Dublin edition. See also *Ir. Book Lov.*, 7, 1916, 117–8; also *Sir Robert Peel's select Irish library*, by Norman D. Palmer, *Ir. Hist. Stud.*, 6, 1948–9, 101–13.

57 O'REILLY, EDWARD. A chronological account of nearly four hundred Irish writers with a descriptive catalogue of their works; introduction by Gearoid MacEoin. Shannon: 1970. Reprint of first Dublin edition, 1820.

58 PEDDIE, ROBERT A. Subject index of books published before 1880. London: 1933. 2nd ser., 1935; 3rd ser., 1939; new ser., 1948.

59 QUEEN'S UNIVERSITY. Institute of Irish Studies. Theses on subjects relating to Ireland presented for higher degrees, 1950–1967. Belfast: 1968. 28 leaves.

60 A SELECTED, ANNOTATED BIBLIOGRAPHY ON IRELAND, by the editor. *Liturgical Arts*, 29, 1961, 109–20.

61 SONNENSCHEIN, WILLIAM SWAN. The best books. 3rd ed. reprinted. Detroit: 1969. 6 vols.

Microforms

62 IRISH MICROFORMS LTD. [Catalogue] 1975 — Spring 1976. Dublin: 1975. Catalogue of books, newspapers, photographs and prints available on microfiche or reel microfilm.

General Catalogues

63 BANDINEL, BUCKLEY. Catalogus librorum impressorum bibliothecae Bodleianae in academica Oxoniensi. Oxonii: 1843. 3 vols.

64 BELFAST. ASSEMBLY'S COLLEGE. Catalogue of books in theology and general literature. Belfast: 1912.

65 BELFAST CITY PUBLIC LIBRARIES. Bibliographic Department. Finding list of books added to the stock of the Irish and local history collection before 1956. Belfast: 1964. Section 1. Main author and title entries arranged alphabetically. Section 2. Main author and title entries arranged in classified order.

66 BELFAST LIBRARY AND SOCIETY FOR PROMOTING KNOWLEDGE (Linen Hall Library). General catalogue, compiled by G. Smith. Belfast: 1896.

67 — Catalogue of the books in the Irish section. Belfast: 1917.

68 BELFAST PUBLIC LIBRARIES. Catalogue. Belfast: 1831.

69 — Catalogue of the reference department, compiled by George Hall Elliott. Belfast: 1896.

70 — Catalogues of the public libraries, 1888–1945. [Printed catalogues of the central, lending and branch libraries, *c.* 1902–20, and printed lists of additions to 1945.] Belfast Public Libraries hope to publish in the future a catalogue of their Irish material of approximately 30,000 vols and over 20,000 pamphlets including the Crone collection.

71 BIGGER, FRANCIS JOSEPH. Catalogue of books and bound Mss. of the Irish historical, archaeological and antiquarian library of F.J. Bigger. Belfast: 1930. Collection is now in Belfast Public Library.

72 BLACKWOOD, FREDERICK TEMPLE HAMILTON. Catalogue of the library of Helen's Tower, belonging to the Marquess of Dufferin and Ava. Belfast: 1901.

73 BOSTON PUBLIC LIBRARY. A list of books on modern Ireland in the public library of the city of Boston. Boston: 1921.

74 BRITISH MUSEUM. List of bibliographical works in the Reading Room of the British Museum. 2nd rev. ed. London: 1889.

75 — Catalogue of books in the library of the British Museum printed in England, Scotland and Ireland, and of books in English printed abroad, to the year 1640. London: 1884. 3 vols.

76 — Catalogue of printed books: Ireland. 1891. Forms part of the General Catalogue printed between 1881–1900.

77 — General catalogue of printed books. Photolithographic ed. to 1955. London: British Museum, 1960–1966. 263 vols. Compact ed. New York: Readex Microprint Corp., 1967. 27 vols. Supplements, 1956–70. 7 vols.

78 — Subject index of the modern works added to the library . . . 1881–1900. London: vol. 1–, 1902–. See also the following: *The catalogues of the British Museum: printed books*, by F.C. Francis. London: 1952; *The catalogues of the manuscript collections in the British Museum*, by T.C. Skeat. London: 1953. *A list of catalogues, guide books and facsimiles* . . . London: 1956.

79 CAMBRIDGE, MASS., PUBLIC LIBRARY. List of books in the Cambridge Public Library, Cambridge, Massachusetts, on Ireland and the Irish people. [Cambridge, Mass.]: 1920.

80 CAMBRIDGE, UNIVERSITY LIBRARY. A catalogue of the Bradshaw collection of Irish books in the University Library, Cambridge, edited by C.E. Sayle. Cambridge: 1916. 3 vols.
Vol. 1: Books printed in Dublin by known printers, 1602–1882; list of printers and booksellers in Dublin, pp. 681–90.

Vol. 2: Books printed in Dublin of which the printer is not known . . . Irish provincial printing . . . works of Irish authors printed elsewhere . . . books printed elsewhere which relate to Ireland . . . Appendix, consisting of the catalogue of the collection of books presented by the Rev. R.J. McGhee . . . A second appendix containing the list of books added to the collection by purchase . . . amongst these are two volumes of ballads. The collection of ballads formed by Sir Frederick Madden has been indexed with these . . . addenda and corrigenda.
Vol. 3: Index.
See also *Cambridge Univ. Lib. Bull, extra ser*. The Henry Bradshaw Irish collection, presented in 1870 and 1886. Cambridge: 1909, and The Bradshaw collection, Cambridge, and additions made to it since 1916, by J.J. Hall. *Ir. Booklore*, vol. 2, no. 1, 1972, 22–28.

81 CARNEGIE UNITED KINGDOM TRUST, book repository. Catalogue of the books in the repository, compiled by Christine Keogh. Dublin [1924].

82 CATALOGUE OF BOOKS PRINTED IN IRELAND, and published in Dublin from 1700; alphabetically and classically arranged. Dublin: 1791. Copy in Trinity College Library, Dublin.

83 CHICAGO PUBLIC LIBRARY. Leabhair gaedhilge: Irish books in the Chicago Public Library. [Chicago: 1942.]

84 CLONMEL MECHANICS' INSTITUTE. Catalogue of the books in the Clonmel Mechanics' Institute. Clonmel: 1856.

85 CLOUGH, E.A. A short-title catalogue, arranged geographically, of books printed and distributed by printers, publishers and booksellers in the English provincial towns and in Scotland and Ireland up to and including the year 1700. London: 1969.

86 COMYN, DAVID. A catalogue of the books and Mss. in the language, history and archaeology of Ireland from the library of the late David Comyn, presented to the National Library of Ireland as the Comyn bequest. Dublin: 1907.

87 CORK LIBRARY SOCIETY. Catalogue of books of the Cork Library Society, to which is prefixed a list of subscribers. Cork: 1801.

88 CORK UNIVERSITY COLLEGE. Catalogue of the Irish library, University College, Cork. Cork: 1914.

89 CROFTON, AILEEN. Catalogue of the pamphlets from Bibliotheca Earberiana, presented to the library of Trinity College. Dublin: 1955. Typescript of 216 pp.

90 DUBLIN LIBRARY SOCIETY. Catalogue of books belonging to the Dublin Library Society, to which are prefixed the laws of the institution, and a list of subscribers. Dublin: 1792.

91 — Catalogue of books . . . Dublin: 1810.

92 — Catalogue of the library of the Dublin Library Society and Hibernian Athenaeum. Dublin: 1857. For a note on the Society, see *Bibliog. Soc. Ir.*, vol. 2, 1921–5, 121–31.

93 FALKINER, CAESAR LITTON. Catalogue of the library formed by the late Caesar Litton Falkiner, M.A. 1909. Copy in the Bigger collection, Belfast Public Library.

94 FISKE, W. Books printed in Ireland, 1578–1844: a supplement to the British Museum catalogue. Florence: 1886. 2nd and 3rd supplements. Florence: 1889–90.

95 GALWAY UNIVERSITY COLLEGE. Alphabetical catalogue of the library of Queen's College, Galway, by J.H. Richardson. Dublin: 1864.

96 — Alphabetical catalogue of the books . . . arranged according to departments, by D'Arcy W. Thompson. Galway: 1877.

97 — Catalogue of the library of University College, Galway, compiled by V. Steinberger. 1913.

98 GLASGOW PUBLIC LIBRARIES. Union catalogue of additions to the libraries, classified, annotated and indexed. Glasgow. Pt. 1–, 1929–.

99 — Catalogue of additions, 1915–49. Glasgow, 1959–60. 2 vols. Vol 1: Classified; vol. 2: Index.

100 HALLIDAY, BERNARD. Catalogue of a special collection of books on Ireland, and a remarkable collection of original Mss. and deeds from 1500–1850, relating to the principal families of Ireland, mostly from the collection of the Rev. J. Graves. Leicester: 1904.

101 HYDE, DOUGLAS, and O'DONOGHUE, D.J. Catalogue of the books and manuscripts comprising the library of the late Sir John T. Gilbert. Dublin: 1918. This collection is now in Pearse Street Public Library, Dublin.

102 IRISH OFFICE LIBRARY. List of the pamphlets in the library of the Irish Office, by T.P. Le Fanu. London: 1913.

103 LECKY, W.E.H. Catalogue of the Lecky collection, The Library, Trinity College, Dublin. [1955.] Typescript of 265 pp.

104 LIBRARY OF CONGRESS. A catalogue of books represented by Library of Congress printed cards issued to July 1942. Ann Arbor: 1942–6. 167 vols.
Supplement, 1948, 42 vols; author catalogue, 1953, 24 vols.

105 LONDON LIBRARY. Subject index . . . vol. 1–, 1909–.

106 LOWELL, MASS., CITY LIBRARY. Ireland: a list of books relating to Ireland in the Lowell City Library. Lowell, Mass: 1910.

107 LOYAL NATIONAL REPEAL ASSOCIATION OF IRELAND. Catalogue of the library comprising many works on Ireland and Irish affairs. 1848.

108 MAGEE COLLEGE, LONDONDERRY. Catalogue of the library. Dublin: 1870. First Supplement. Dublin: 1872.

109 — Pamphlet catalogue. 1887.

110 MARSH'S LIBRARY, DUBLIN. An account of Archbishop Marsh's Library, Dublin, with a note on autographs. Dublin: 1926. Swiftiana in Marsh's Library (reprinted and revised from *Hermathena*, 1901) pp. 20–30.

111 — A catalogue of books in the French language, printed in or before 1715 A.D., remaining in Archbishop Marsh's Library, Dublin, with an appendix relating to the Cashel Diocesan Library, by N.J.D. White. Dublin: 1918.

112 — French Renaissance books: an exhibition, June 1959, Marsh's Library, Dublin. 1959. Typescript of 144 entries.

113 — Notes on a visit to Archbishop Marsh's Library, Dublin. *Edinburgh Bibliog. Soc. pub.*, vol. 6, 1906, 133–40.

114 — Short catalogue of English books in Archbishop Marsh's Library, Dublin, printed before 1641 . . . By N.J.D. White. 1905. (*Bibliog. Soc. catalogue of English books, no. 1.*)

115 MORROW, VERONICA M.R. Bibliotheca Quiniana: a description of the books and bindings in the Quin collection in the library of Trinity College, Dublin. Accepted for Diploma in Librarianship, University of London, October 1969– September 1970.

116 NATIONAL LIBRARY OF IRELAND. Supplemental catalogue of books . . . added . . . from 1874–9. Dublin. Supplemental catalogues . . . 1880–93. These catalogues are supplemental to the catalogues of the Royal Dublin Society Library, the greater part of the library being transferred to the Crown under the Science and Art Museum Act of 1877 to become the National Library of Ireland.

117 — Subject index of books added, 1894–1903. Dublin: 1911. Subject index of books added, 1904–15, and of those in the general collection prior to 1894. Dublin: 1926.

118 — List of publications deposited under the terms of the Industrial and Commercial Property (Protection) Act, 1927. Nos. 1–5, 1927–36. Dublin: 1930–8.

119 — Select list of books relating to Ireland. Dublin: 1942.

120 — Books on Ireland: list compiled by National Library of Ireland. Dublin, Cultural Relations Committee, 1953.

121 — William O'Brien Collection: a catalogue. Dublin: 1969.

122 NEW YORK PUBLIC LIBRARY. List of works in the New York Public Library relating to Ireland, the Irish language and literature, etc. New York: 1905. Reprinted from the *New York Pub. Lib. Bull.*, March–July 1905.

123 NEWMAN HOUSE, ST. STEPHENS GREEN, DUBLIN. Catalogue of the library. 2 vols. Not published. First entry made in 1858. Arranged by authors and written in bound volumes, with thumb index. The collection is now in the library of University College, Dublin.

124 NEWRY FREE LIBRARY. Catalogue of the . . . library, reference and lending department,

compiled by Francis C. Crossle and Adah M. Armstrong. Newry: 1897.

125 Nitrigen Eireann Teoranta, Library. List of catalogued books in library of Nitrigin Eireann Teoranta, together with a list of current periodicals. Arklow: 1971.

126 O'Hegarty, Patrick Sarsfield. Catalogue of books in the library of P.S. O'Hegarty, 1958. 4 vols. Typescript in the Library, Trinity College, Dublin.

127 Philadelphia, Cathedral Total Abstinence Society. Irish literature: catalogue of books in the Irish library . . . Philadelphia: 1884.

128 Queen's University, Belfast. Catalogue of the books in the library of Queen's College, Belfast; with supplements. Belfast: 1859–78.

129 — Catalogue of books in library of Queen's College, Belfast. Belfast: 1897. For complete list of catalogues see *Queen's Belfast, 1845–1949*, by T.W. Moody and J.C. Beckett. London, 1959, vol. 2, pp. 898–9.

130 Royal Dublin Society. Catalogue of books in the library of the Dublin Society. Dublin: 1796.

131 — Catalogue of books in the library classed under proper heads. Dublin: 1807.

132 — Catalogue of pamphlets in the Royal Dublin Society's Library. Dublin: 1838. Ms. folio.

133 — Catalogue of the library: catalogue 1731–1839, by J.F. Jones, 1839; supplement, 1839–49, by J.F. Jones, 1850; supplement, 1849–59, Edward Richard Purefoy Colles. Dublin: 1860. Bound in 1 vol.

134 — Alphabetical index to the first 80 vols. of the Royal Dublin Society's collection of pamphlets (printed from the Ms. made in 1840). In Catalogue of the library . . . supplement, 1850, pp. 169–95.

135 — General catalogue of the library to June 1895 not including scientific periodicals and the publications of learned societies. Dublin: 1896. Subsequent vols in this series were published in 1900, 1905, 1910 and 1915.

136 — Library list of accessions. Dublin: 1924–.

137 Royal Irish Academy. Catalogue of Haliday 8vo pamphlets . . . compiled under the direction of J.T. Gilbert, 1870. Manuscript copy in 8 vols chronologically arranged; author, subject and title catalogue on cards in preparation, with index of printers and place of publication.

138 — Catalogue of tracts. 21 vols. In manuscript covering period 1578–1879. For fuller description of catalogues see The library of the Royal Irish Academy, by C. Bonfield and A. Farrington, *An Leab*., 8, 1941–5, 10–16.

139 Shirley, Evelyn Philip. Catalogue of the library at Lough Fea, in illustration of the history and antiquities of Ireland. London: 1872. Privately printed. See also The Shirley Library at Lough Fea, Carrickmacross in Co. Monaghan, Ireland. *Book Coll. Qtr*., 6, 1932, 1–9.

140 Stanford University. The library catalogue of the Hoover Institution on war, revolution and peace. Boston: 1970. 85 vols. Includes the James A. Healy Collection on Irish history, especially during the twentieth century.

141 Trinity College, Dublin. Catalogus librorum impressorum qui in bibliotheca Colegii, sacrosanctae et individuae Trinitatis, Reginae Elizabethae, juxta Dublin adservantur. Dublin: 1864–87. 9 vols.

142 — A catalogue of the books in the lending library . . . Dublin: 1861. Other editions in 1872 and 1879. Supplement 1880–97, with appendix. Dublin: 1898.

143 — A short list of Elizabethan books in the library, by Ian MacPhail. *T.C.D. Ann. Bull*., 1958, 3–7. For further description of catalogues and their contents see *The Book of Trinity College, Dublin, 1591–1891*, by T.K. Abbott. Belfast: 1892, pp. 147–81.

144 Ware, James. Librorum manuscriptorum in bibliotheca Jacobi Waraei, equitis catalogus. Dublin: 1648.

145 Wigan Public Library. Ireland and the Irish: a catalogue of works relating to Ireland in the Reference Department of the Wigan Public Library. Wigan: 1896.

146 Wise, Thomas James. The Ashley Library: a catalogue of printed books, manuscripts and autograph letters collected by T.J. Wise.

London: 1922–36. 11 vols. 200 copies privately printed.

Booksellers' and Sales' Catalogues

147 BENNETT and SON, *booksellers*. Catalogue of an important and comprehensive library of Irish literature . . . to be sold . . . by direction of the administrator of the late Rev. Michael P. O'Hickey (formerly Professor of Irish at Maynooth College). Dublin: 1917.

148 BIBLIOTHECA BRANDIANA: a catalogue of the unique, scarce, rare, curious and numerous collections of works on antiquity, topography, and decayed intelligence of Great Britain and Ireland, early poetry, classics, belles lettres and miscellaneous, etc., being the entire library of the late Rev. John Brand, sold by auction by Mr. Stewart, May 6 and thirty-six following days. London: 1807.

149 BIBLIOTHECA PUTLANDIA SIVE CATALOGUS LIBRORUM IN BIBLIOTHECA JOHANNIS PUTLANDIA ARM. Dublin: 1749, 3 vols.

150 BIBLIOTHECA PUTLANDIA: Catalogue of the Library of George Putland . . . sold by auction by George Sharpe on Monday, July 19, [1847]. Dublin: 1847.

151 BOOK ASSOCIATION OF IRELAND. Catalogue of books published in Ireland since 1938 and still in print. London: 1945.

152 BYRNE, D.J. The Rev. D.J. Bryne, C.C., deceased: catalogue of an important and interesting library . . . Andrew J. Keogh, bookseller, Dublin: 1926.

153 CATALOGUE OF RARE AND SCARCE BOOKS (the library of an eminent Divine) with additions; also about 500 volumes of early printed Belfast books from the library of a celebrated collector. 1892. In the Bigger collection, Belfast Public Library.

154 CATALOGUE OF TWELVE THOUSAND TRACTS, pamphlets and unbound books, in all branches of literature. Parts 1–7 . . . comprising three thousand in biography, county history, Scotland, Wales, Ireland, America, West and East Indies, history and politics . . . to be had at Thomas Rodd's. London: 1819.

155 COLLECTION OF CATALOGUES OF IRISH BOOKS, Mss., maps, etc., on sale by John O'Daly and Thomas Connolly, booksellers in Dublin, 1854–76. In the British Museum.

156 CONWAY, FREDERICK WILLIAM. Catalogue of the valuable library of the late Frederick William Conway. Dublin: 1854.

157 CORK UNIVERSITY PRESS. Select list of publications, 1956. Cork: [1956].

158 CROKER, THOMAS CROFTON. Catalogue of the greater part of the library of the late Thomas Crofton Croker, consisting chiefly of works interesting to the archaeologist and antiquary, and to the student of Irish history . . . which will be sold by auction, by Messrs. Puttick and Simpson, December 18, 1854. London: 1854.

159 — [Another copy] with memoir and catalogue of a . . . collection of antiquities formed by . . . Thomas Crofton Croker, which will be sold by auction . . . December 21, 1854. London: 1854.

160 DALY, DENIS. A catalogue of the library of the late Rt. Hon. Denis Daly, which will be sold . . . on May 1, 1792. Dublin: 1792.

161 DUBLIN BOOKSELLERS' ASSOCIATION. Catalogue of books published in Ireland during 1927. Dublin: [1928]. Continued as a quarterly list for 1928 only.

162 DUNDALGAN PRESS. Various books of value, 1859–1959, printed and published by Dundalgan Press (W. Tempest) Ltd. Dundalk: 1959.

163 GILL, M.H. and SON LTD. Book list, 1959. Dublin:1959.

164 AN GUM. Leabhair arna bhfoilsiu, 1955. Baile Atha Cliath: [1955].

165 GUERNSEY BOOKS. Ireland — Union to Free State: a collection of over 3,000 original pamphlets together with thousands of press-cuttings illustrative of struggles in Ireland from the Union to the Free State, with an introduction by Prof. F.S.L. Lyons. St. Peter Port (Guernsey): 1973.

166 HARDIMAN, JAMES. Catalogue of the library of the late James Hardiman, comprising many very rare and valuable works illustrative of Irish history and antiquities; a collection of Irish manuscripts . . . including the library of the late James F. Ferguson, to be sold by auction by John F. Jones . . . 1856.

Dublin: 1856.

167 HOARE, JOSEPH. Catalogue of the library of valuable . . . books in classic bindings . . . works on liturgy and canon law . . . volumes relating to Ireland . . . to be sold by auction . . . 1927. Dublin [1927].

168 HODGES FIGGIS and Co. LTD. Various catalogues for period 1926–52.

169 — A catalogue of books relating to Ireland. Dublin: 1953. (New Ser. no. 10).

170 — Books relating to Ireland in the seventeenth century. Dublin: 1956. (New ser. no. 11.)
Pt. 1: Seventeenth-century printings with a few earlier examples.
Pt. 2: Later printings relating to the seventeenth century.

171 — Books relating to Ireland: literature since 1800. Dublin: 1957. (New ser. no. 12.)

172 — Philology, linguistics, literature to 1800, place names, mythology and folk-lore relating to Ireland, Scotland, Cornwall, Isle of Man and Brittany. Dublin: 1958. (New ser. no. 13.) Title on cover: Celtic philology.

173 — Books relating to Ireland: history and topography. Dublin: 1959. Contents: History and topography, pp. 9–144; atlases and maps, pp. 147–54; the Irish revolution, 1916–23, pp. 155–78. (New ser. no. 14.)

174 — Bibliographia Hibernica: a quarterly list of new and forthcoming publications relating to Ireland. Dublin: no. 1–, 1957–.

175 — Books relating to Ireland: Literature before 1800. Dublin: [1961] (New ser. catalogue 15).

176 — Books relating to Ireland: Literature before 1850. Dublin [1964] (New ser. catalogue 18).

177 — Books relating to Ireland: Anglo-Irish literature, Dublin [1967].

178 HOE, ROBERT. Catalogue of the library of Robert Hoe of New York: illuminated manuscripts, incunabula, historical bindings, early English literature, rare Americana, French illustrated books, eighteenth-century English authors, autographs, manuscripts, etc., to be sold by auction beginning on Monday, April 24, 1911, by the Anderson Company. New York: 1911, 4 pts. Includes first editions of Goldsmith, Swift, Moore, etc.

179 IRISH UNIVERSITY PRESS. Catalogue to the IUP Library of fundamental source books. Shannon: 1968.

180 — Catalogue. 1974. Dublin: 1974.

181 JONES, JOHN. A general catalogue of books in all languages, arts and sciences that have been printed in Dublin from the year 1700 to the present time; the whole alphabetically and classically arranged under the several branches of literature with their sizes and prices. Dublin: 1791.

182 KELLY, DENNIS H. Sale catalogue of the library of Dennis H. Kelly, containing rare books and Mss. on the history, antiquities, etc. of Ireland. Sold by John Fleming Jones. Dublin: 28 October 1875.

183 KELLY, THOMAS HUGHES. The library of the late Thomas Hughes Kelly, New York, including his renowned collection of books about Ireland, together with some prints including mezzotints by S. Arlent Edwards . . . public sale, October 24–25, 1934. New York: American Art Association, Anderson Galleries Inc., 1934.

184 KEOGH, BRIAN. Catalogue[s] nos. 1–6. Princes Risborough (Bucks): 1974 and 1977. Books in these catalogues are all related to Ireland.

185 LAWLOR, BRISCOE and Co. Catalogue of the choice library of the late Rev. Walter MacDonald, D.D., Librarian, St. Patrick's College, Maynooth . . . also the library of the late Very Rev. Thomas Byrne, P.P., St. Audeon's (sic), High Street, Dublin.

186 LOWDERMILK, W.H., and Co. Bibliotheca Hibernica: a collection of scarce and valuable works on . . . Ireland and the Irish people. Washington: 1890.

187 MADDEN, RICHARD ROBERT. Catalogue of the library of R.R. Madden . . . to be sold by Charles Sharpe . . . January 13, 1847. Dublin: 1846.

188 — Catalogue of the library of Dr. R.R. Madden . . . to be sold by John F. Jones, November 20. Dublin: 1865.

189 — Catalogue of the valuable library of the

late Dr. R.R. Madden, to be sold by auction . . . December 8, 1886, by Messrs. Bennett and Son. Dublin: [1886].

190 Marsh's Library, Dublin. Bibliotheca Marsiana: catalogue of books, the duplicate copies of the public library, Dublin, founded by the Most Rev. Narcissus Marsh . . . which are to be sold by auction on . . . May 8, 1833, and following days by Charles Sharpe at Anglesea Street. Dublin: 1833.

191 Mason, William Monck. Catalogue of the literary collections and original compositions of William Monck Mason, in the department of Irish history and general philology, with a descriptive note. Sold by Sotheby's, March 29–31, 1858. London: 1858. Comprises books, Mss., newspapers, maps and broadsides. For an account of Mason and his library see *Ir. Book Lov.*, 7, 1915–16, 125–6.

192 Murphy, John. Catalogue of the sixth and final portion of the library of Dr. John Murphy, Bishop of Cork. Sold by Sotheby's, December 18, 1848. London: 1848. The Irish items are in this portion. The library was described as 'the largest ever formed by a private individual.'

193 O'Lochlainn, Colm. Books and booklets printed and published by Colm O'Lochlainn. Dublin: 1948.

194 Phillipps, Thomas. Bibliotheca Phillippica: list of Irish Mss. and other items from the sale of the library of Sir Thomas Phillipps, June 1910, and April 1911. *Ir. Book Lov.*, 1, 1909–10, 164–5; 3, 1911–12, 10–11.

195 — The catalogues of manuscripts and printed books of Sir Thomas Phillipps, by A.N.L. Munby. Cambridge: 1951. (*Phillipps Studies* no.1.)

196 — The dispersal of the Phillipps library, by A.N.L. Munby. Cambridge: 1960. (*Phillipps Studies* no. 5.)

197 Quaritch, Bernard. Catalogue of the literature and history of the British Islands. London: 1899–1900, 7 pts. Pt. 4, pp. 334–56, Ireland: literature, history, language.

198 Quinn, John. Complete catalogue of the library of John Quinn sold by auction in five parts (with printed prices). New York: Anderson Galleries. 2 vols. Sale from November 12, 1923 to March 20, 1924.

199 Richardson, S.J. Catalogue of an extensive and valuable collection of books relating to Ireland formed by S.J. Richardson of New York, to be sold at auction, Tuesday, June 3 and following days by Merwin Sales Co. New York: 1913.

200 Sullivan, John W., *bookseller*, 8 D'Olier Street, Dublin. Catalogue of books including a portion of the valuable library of a collector . . . Dublin: [1896].

201 — Catalogue of the valuable libraries of the late Rev. Frederick J.L. Dowling . . . Dublin: 1889.

202 — Catalogue of the library of the Rev. M.B. Kelly, P.P., Naul, Balbriggan. Dublin: 1882.

203 — Catalogue of the valuable library of the late Rev. Charles Macauley, D.D., Professor of Sacred Scripture and Hebrew, St. Patrick's College, Maynooth. Dublin: 1890.

204 — Catalogue of the valuable library of the late Rev. P.A. Murray, D.D., prefect of the Dunboyne establishment, and Professor of dogmatic and moral theology, St. Patrick's College, Maynooth, Dublin: 1883.

205 — Catalogue of the libraries of the Rev. Frederick Tymons, M.A., Cloghran, Co. Dublin, the late Denis Shine Lawlor, Esq., Grenagh, Co. Kerry, and of the late John Taaffe, Esq., J.P., D.L., Smarmore Castle, Co. Louth. Dublin: 1893.

206 — Catalogue of the libraries of the late Rev. P.A. Yorke, C.C., M.R.I.A., and of a divine recently deceased . . . Dublin: 1888.

207 Ware, John. A catalogue of books in several faculties and languages being the library of that learned and ingenious gentleman, Thomas Scudamore . . . consisting of a curious collection of the most valuable books of divinity, law, physick, philosophy, cosmography, history, mathematicks, philology, chronology, &c. in the Hebrew, Latin and other tongues. To be sold . . . on November 14, 1698. Dublin: 1698.

208 — A catalogue of books in several faculties and languages: consisting of a choice collection of divinity, philosophy, philology, physick, cosmography, history, mathematicks, chronology; together with a

large collection of civil, canon and common-law books, as also a curious collection of the new pamphlets bound and stich't, to be sold by way of auction . . . May 1699. Dublin: 1699.

209 WEALE, JAMES. Sale catalogue of the library of James Weale, relating to the history, literature and antiquities of Ireland. Sold by Evans, London, February 5–11, 1840. Collections of Mss. in the Irish language, proclamations, etc.

210 WHITE, LUKE. The complete Dublin catalogue of books in all arts and sciences (printed in Ireland) from the beginning of the century to the present time. Dublin: 1786.

211 WILLIS, THOMAS. Sale catalogue of the library of Dr. Thomas Willis, senior, containing a remarkable collection of Mss., books, maps, ballads, etc., relating to Ireland. Sold by John Fleming Jones, Dublin. November 22, 1876. Dublin: 1876.

Booksellers and Catalogues: Aids and Guides

212 CATALOGUES OF DUBLIN BOOKSELLERS. *Ir. Book Lov.*, 6, 1914–15, 42–3.

213 DIX, E.R. MCCLINTOCK. Some eighteenth-century catalogues of books printed in Ireland and for sale in Dublin by booksellers. *Bibliog. Soc. Ir.*, 3, 1926–9, 81–2.

214 DUNTON, JOHN. *The Dublin Scuffle*, 1699, edited by J. Nichols. London: 1818. Contains notices of book auctions and booksellers of Dublin at the end of the seventeenth century.

215 EARLY BOOK AUCTIONS IN IRELAND. *Ir. Lit. Inquirer*, edited by John Power, no. 3, 1865, 29–30.

216 LIST OF IRISH BOOKSELLERS BEFORE 1800. *N. & Q.*, 10th ser., 5, 1906, 243; 11th ser., 1, 1910, 424.

217 O'KELLEY, FRANCIS. Irish book-sale catalogues before 1801. *Bibliog. Soc. Ir.*, vol. 6, no. 3, 1953.

Librarianship

218 BURTON, MARGARET and VOSBURGH, MARION E. *compilers*. A bibliography of librarianship: classified and annotated guide to the library literature of the world . . . London: Library Association, 1934.

219 CANNON, H.G.T. Bibliography of library economy: a classified index to the professional periodical literature in the English language relating to library economy, printing, methods of publishing, copyright, bibliography, etc., from 1876 to 1920. Chicago: American Library Association, 1927.

220 — Library literature, 1921–32–,: a supplement to Cannon's *Bibliography* . . . compiled . . . under the editorship of Lucile M. Morsch. Chicago: 1934–. See also *Library Science Abstracts,* London, vol. 1–, 1950–.

221 FOLEY, DERMOT. A Minstrel boy and a satchel of books. *Ir. Univ. Rev.*, vol. 4, no. 2, 1974, 204–217. Reminiscences of life as a librarian in Co. Clare.

222 IRISH LIBRARY NEWS. Dublin, No. 1.–1977–.

223 AN LEABHARLANN: the journal of Cumann an Leabharlann. vol. 1–3, 1905–9. Author, title and subject index, compiled by Hilda Tuohy, for Fellowship of the Library Association of Ireland.

224 AN LEABHARLANN: the journal of the Library Association of Ireland. vol. 1–, 1930–.

225 MINTO, JOHN. A history of the public library movement in Great Britain and Ireland. London: 1932. Appendix 1: Bibliog. pp. 343–4; Appendix 2: Conspectus of the various acts of parliament relating to public libraries, museums and gymnasium, by James Hutt.

225a NORTHERN IRELAND LIBRARIES. (Belfast): vol. 1–9, 1960–1971. From 1972 amalgamated with *An Leabharlann*.

226 O'BYRNE, MAIRIN. Libraries and librarianship in Ireland. *Admin.* vol. 16, 1968, 148–154.

227 TAYLOR, PETER J. Library and information studies in the United Kingdom and Ireland, 1950–1974: an index to theses. London : Aslib, 1976.

228 WALKER, T. MACCALLUM. Libraries and librarianship in Northern Ireland. *Libri*, 4, 1954, 315–329.

229 WHITE, NEWPORT J.D. Elias Bottherau of La Rochelle, first public librarian in Ireland. *R.*

Ir. Acad. Proc., Sec. C., 27, 1908–9, 126–158.

Libraries

230 ASLIB DIRECTORY: a guide to sources of information in Great Britain and Ireland. London: 1957, 2 vols.

231 — Amendment list. [No.] 1, 1960–61. [London, 1961.]

232 FEISENBERGER, H.A.: The libraries of Newton, Hooke and Boyle. *R. Soc. N. and R.*, vol. 21, no. 1, 1966, 42–55. Originally published in *Ivory Hammer*, 3, London: 1965.

233 HURST, F.J.E. University Libraries in Eire. *Lib. World*, 65, 1964, no. 766, 331–335.

234 KAUFMAN, PAUL. Community lending libraries in eighteenth century Ireland and Wales. *Lib. Qtr.*, vol. 33, 1963, 299–312.

235 THE LIBRARIES, MUSEUMS AND ART GALLERIES YEAR BOOK. Cambridge: 1976. Republic of Ireland, pp. 210–6.

236 LIBRARY ASSOCIATION. Libraries in the United Kingdom and the Republic of Ireland: a complete list of public library services and a select list of academic and other library addresses. 6th ed., London: 1974.

237 — Northern Ireland Branch. Directory of Northern Ireland Libraries. 2nd ed., edited by W.R.H. Carson and A. Morrow. [Belfast]: 1977.

238 NEYLON, MAURA and HENCHY, MONICA. Public libraries in Ireland. Dublin: 1966. (*School of librarianship publication*). Table of statutes applicable to public libraries, pp. 26–27: bibliog., pp. 28–34. Traces the development of public libraries with particular reference to the acts under which they were established and administered.

239 O'NEILL, THOMAS P. and CLARKE, DESMOND J. Libraries in Ireland: an historical outline. Dublin. Reprinted from *Lib. Assoc. Rec.*, vol. 58, no. 2, 1956.

240 RYAN, MICHAEL J. Some notes on the libraries and book trade of Dublin. *Book Auct. Rec.*, vol. 4, pt. 4, 1907, xlv–xlix.

241 STEPHENSON, P.J. Early Dublin public libraries. *Ir. Lib. Bull.*, new ser., 12, 1951, 27–33.

242 WHEELER, W.G. Libraries in Ireland before 1855: a bibliographical essay. Submitted for the Academic Postgraduate Diploma in Librarianship and in Archive Administration, University of London. 1957.

Individual Libraries

(See also General Catalogues)

243 ARMAGH COUNTY MUSEUM. Weatherup, D.R.M. Armagh County Museum — The Reference Library. *Ir. Book*, vol. 2, no. 1, 1972, 44–53.

244 ARMAGH PUBLIC LIBRARY. Simms, G.O. The founder of Armagh's public library: Primate [Richard] Robinson among his books. *Ir. Book*, vol. 1, no. 2, 1971, 139–149; vol. 2, no. 1, 1972, 150–1.

245 — WEATHERUP, D.R.M. The Armagh public library, 1771–1971. *Ir. Book*, vol. 2, no. 2, 1976, 269–299.

246 CENTRAL CATHOLIC LIBRARY. Brown, Stephen J. A Catholic library for Dublin. *Studies*, vol. 11, 1922, 307–312.

247 CHESTER BEATTY LIBRARY. [Hayes, R.J.] The Chester Beatty Library. Dublin: 1958. List of publications. pp. 33–6.

248 — MCHUGH, JAMES N. The Chester Beatty Library and Gallery of Oriental Art. *Ir. Wel.*, vol. 25, no. 6, 1976, 21–26.

249 — WILKINSON, J.V.S. The Chester Beatty Library. *An Leab.*, 14, 1956, 111–117.

250 CORK LIBRARY. Coleman, James. The Cork Library in 1801 and 1820. *Cork Hist. Arch. Soc. J.*, 11, 1905, 82–93.

251 CREAGH, PIERS. Mooney, Canice. The Library of Archbishop Piers Creagh. *Rep. Nov.*, vol. 1, no. 1, 1955, 117–39.

252 CURRAN, CONSTANTINE. Kain, Richard M. The Curran library. *Eire-Ir*, vol. 7, no. 4, 1972, 135–6.

253 KING, WILLIAM. Matterson, Robert S. Archbishop William King's Library: some discoveries and queries. *Longroom*, no. 9. 1974, 7–16.

254 MARSH'S LIBRARY. McCarthy, Muriel. Archbishop Marsh and his library. *Dublin Hist. Rec.* vol. 29, no. 1, 1975, 2–23.

255 — Swift and the primate of Ireland: Marsh's Library in the early eighteenth century. *Dublin Hist. Rec.*, vol. 17, no. 3, 1974, 109–112.

256 NATIONAL LIBRARY. Allberry, E. Hilda. The National Library of Ireland, 1890–1970. *Ir. Build. Eng.*, 103, 1971, 63–65, 69–72.

257 — Henchy, Patrick. The National Library of Ireland. *An Leab.*, 26, 1968, 44–49.

258 ROYAL IRISH ACADEMY. Bonfield, C. and Farrington, A. The Royal Irish Academy and its library: a brief description. Dublin: 1964.

259 ST. CANICE'S LIBRARY. Woodworth, *The Rev.* David. St. Canice's Library. *Old Kilk. Rev.*, no. 22, 1970, 5–10; no. 23, 1971, 15–22.

260 UNIVERSITY COLLEGE GALWAY. Townley, Christopher J. University College, Galway, and its library. *An Leab.*, vol. 22, 1964, 39–43, 57.

261 USSHER, RICHARD JOHN. Barnard, T.C. The Purchase of Archbishop Ussher's library in 1657. *Longroom.*, no. 2, 1970, 9–14.

262 — LAWLOR, HUGH JACKSON. Primate Ussher's library before 1641. *R. Ir. Acad. Proc., 3rd Ser.*, 6, 1900–02, 216–64.

Reference Books

263 MINTO, JOHN. Reference books: a classified and annotated guide. London: 1929. Supplement, 1931.

264 WALFORD, A.J. *ed.* Guide to reference material. London: 1973–77. 3 vols.

Children's Books

265 LIBRARY ASSOCIATION. Youth Libraries Group., Northern Ireland Branch. Ireland. Birmingham: 1972. (*Storylines no.* 8). Children's stories with an Irish theme.

Information

266 INSTITUTE FOR INDUSTRIAL RESEARCH AND STANDARDS. Technical information Division. Sources of Scientific and Technical information in Ireland. Dublin: 1972. Prev. ed. 1969.

Encyclopaedia

267 ENCYCLOPAEDIA OF IRELAND. Dublin: Figgis, 1968. Includes bibliogs.

Essays, Theses

268 ASLIB INDEX TO THESES accepted for higher degrees in the universities of Great Britain and Ireland. Vol. 1–, 1950–1–. London: 1953–.

269 ESSAYS AND GENERAL LITERATURE INDEX. Vol. 1–, 1900–33–. New York: 1934–.

270 RETROSPECTIVE INDEX TO THESES OF GREAT BRITAIN AND IRELAND. 1716–1950; Roger R. Bilboal (ed), Frances L. Kent (Associate ed). Santa Barbara and Oxford. 5 vols.
Vol. 1. Social Sciences and Humanities. 1976.
Vol. 2. Applied Sciences and Technology. 1976.

Periodicals

271 BELFAST PUBLIC LIBRARIES. List of current periodicals in Belfast libraries. Belfast: 1931. 4th ed. Belfast: 1937.

272 BOWEN, B.P. Dublin humorous periodicals of the nineteenth century [with bibliog.]. *Dublin Hist. Rec.*, 13, 1952–4, 2–11.

273 BRITISH HUMANITIES INDEX [no. 1]— 1962— London. Supersedes the *Subject Index to Periodicals* which was published from 1915 with the exception of the years 1923–25.

274 BRITISH MUSEUM. Catalogue of printed books . . . periodical publications. 2nd ed. London: 1899–1900. 2 vols. Periodicals are entered under place and there is a title index.

275 BRITISH UNION CATALOGUE OF PERIODICALS: a record of the periodicals of the world, from the seventeenth century to the present day, in British libraries. London: 1955–9. 4 vols. Supplement, 1962.

276 CASAIDE, SEAMUS UA. A history of the periodical literature of Cork from the beginning up to A.D. 1900. 1943. Typescript in National Library, Dublin. Appendices list holdings of Carnegie Free Library, Cork; National Library, Dublin; Trinity College, Dublin; British Museum, London; Cambridge University

Library, Cambridge, and the compiler's own library.

277 CRONE, J.S. Some rare Dublin periodicals. *Ir. Book Lov.*, 12, 1921, 104–6.

278 DIX, E.R. McC. An early Dublin occasional journal or newsletter. *Ir. Book Lov.*, 8, 1916–17, 51–2.

279 — The earliest periodical journals published in Dublin. *R. Ir. Acad. Proc.*, 3rd ser., 6, 1900, 33–5.

280 — Rare ephemeral Dublin magazines of the eighteenth century. *Ir. Book Lov.*, 1, 1909–10, 71–3.

281 — Some rare Dublin magazines of the eighteenth century. *Ir. Book Lov.*, 8, 1916–17, 25–8.

282 FORAS TALUNTAIS. List of periodicals and serials, 1969. Dublin: 1969.

283 HANLY, THE REV. JOHN. Two rebel Meath journals [*Sinn Fein — The Oldcastle Monthly Review* and *The Irish Peasant*]. *Riocht na Midhe*, vol. 3. no. 4. 1966, 359–384.

284 HAYLEY, BARBARA. Irish periodicals from the Union to the *Nation*. *Anglo-Ir. Stud.*, 2, 1976, 83–108.

285 HOUGHTON, WALTER EDWARDS. *ed.* The Wellesley index to Victorian periodicals. 1824–1900. Toronto, and London: Vol. 1. 1966; Vol. 2. 1972.

286 IRISH ASSOCIATION FOR DOCUMENTATION AND INFORMATION SERVICES. Union list of current periodicals and serials in Irish Libraries, 1974. Dublin: 1974. 2 vols. Previous eds. 1955, 1960, 1963, [supp.] 1966.

287 IRISH MAGAZINES. Bibliog. *Camb. Bibliog. Eng. Lit.*, 2, 1940, 687–8.

288 KAIN, RICHARD M. Irish periodical literature: an untilled field. *Eire-Ir.*, vol. 7, no. 3, 1972, 93–99.

289 MADDEN, RICHARD ROBERT. History of Irish periodical literature. London, 1867. 2 vol. Reprinted New York, Johnson Reprint Co. 1968. Notes for a third vol, covering period 1800–40, are in manuscript in Pearse Street Public Library, Dublin.

290 NINETEENTH CENTURY READERS GUIDE TO PERIODICAL LITERATURE. New York: vol 1–, 1944–.

291 NORTHERN IRELAND LIBRARY ADVISORY COUNCIL. Union list of current periodicals and serials in Northern Ireland Libraries, compiled by A.K. Megan. Belfast: Belfast Public Libraries, 1966.

292 O'CONNAILL, SEAN. Roman Catholic periodicals in Ireland. *Focus*, 8, 1965, 77–78.

293 PERIODICAL PRESS OF GREAT BRITAIN AND IRELAND. Edinburgh: 1824.

294 POOLE'S INDEX TO PERIODICAL LITERATURE, 1802–1906. Boston, Mass: 1888–1908. 7 vols.

295 POWER, JOHN. List of Irish periodical publications (chiefly literary) from 1729 to the present time. London: 1866. 250 copies printed: appeared originally in part in *N. & Q.*, March–April 1866 and *Ir. Lit. Inquirer*, no. 4, 1866, with additions and corrections.

296 ROUPELL, MARION G. Union catalogue of the periodical publications of the university libraries with their respective holdings. London: 1937. Excludes titles in *World list of scientific periodicals*.

297 ROYAL IRISH ACADEMY: Committee for the study of Anglo-Irish Language and Literature. Irish and Anglo-Irish periodicals [a list]. Dublin: 1970.

298 SUBJECT INDEX TO PERIODICALS. London: Library Association, 1915–61. Published annually except for period 1923–5. Superseded by *British Humanities Index*, 1962–.

299 ULRICH'S PERIODICALS DIRECTORY. 17th ed. New York: 1977.

300 UNITED STATES EMBASSY, LONDON. Checklist of periodicals published in the Republic of Ireland, including newspapers, but excluding annuals. U.S. Dept. of State: 1952. Typescript. Copies in National Library, Dublin, and Royal Dublin Society.

301 WALL, THOMAS. Catholic periodicals of the past.
1. The Catholic Penny Magazine, 1834–1835. *Ir. Eccles. Rec.* 5th ser. vol. 101, 1964, 234–244.
2. The Catholic Book Society and the Irish Catholic Magazine. *ibid.*, vol. 101, 1964, 289–303.

3. Philip Barron's Ancient Ireland, 1835. *ibid*., vol. 101, 1964, 375–388.
4. The Catholic Luminary, 1840–41. *ibid*., vol. 102, 1964, 17–27.
5–6. Duffy's Irish Catholic Magazine, 1847–1848. *ibid*., vol. 102, 1964, 86–100, 129–147.
7. The Catholic University Gazette, 1854–1856. *ibid*., vol. 102, 1964, 206–223.

302 WARD, WILLIAM S. Index and finding list of serials published in the British Isles, 1789–1832. Lexington, Univ. of Kentucky: 1953. Includes bibliog.

Individual Periodicals

303 ALL IRELAND REVIEW. Sullivan, Daniel J. Standish James O'Grady's All Ireland Review. *Stud. Hib*., 9, 1969, 125–136.

304 BALLYHULAN REGISTER. Maffett, R.S. Two old Monaghan journals [*Ballyhulan Register* and *The Retaliater*]. *Ir. Book Lov*., 28, 1941–2, 80–3.

305 THE BELL. Index, vol. 1–19, 1940–54. Completed for Fellowship of the Library Association of Ireland, by Miss V. Grogan and Miss E.Murray.

306 — Holzapfel, Rudi, *compiler*. An index of contributors to *The Bell*. Blackrock: 1970.

307 BONAVENTURA. Index, vols. 1–4, 1937–41. Completed for Fellowship of the Library Association of Ireland, by Patrick Daly and C. O'Rourke.

308 THE CORK FREEHOLDER. Casaide, Seamus ua. *The Cork Freeholder*: an eight-day magazine [1813–42]. *Ir. Book Lov*., 25, 1937, 32–7.

309 THE CORK MAGAZINE. Holland, M. *The Cork Magazine* and its writers. *Iver. Soc. J*., 7, 1914–15, 142–6.

310 DUBLIN MAGAZINE [1923–1958]. An index of contributors to the Dublin Magazine. Dublin: 1966 (*Dublin Bibliographical series no. 1*)

311 — HOLZAPFEL, RUDI. A note on *The Dublin Magazine* [1923–1958]. *Dublin Mag*., 4, 1965, 18–27.

312 — PRESSLEY, STUART. The Archives of *The Dublin Magazine*, 1923–58. *Longroom*, 7, 1923, 27–32.

313 DUBLIN REVIEW. *Dublin Review*, 1836–1936; centenary number, April 1936. Includes complete list of articles published during period May 1836 to April 1936.

314 THE DUBLIN SPY. Glynn, P.B. The Dublin Spy: an eighteenth-century Dublin periodical. *Dublin Hist. Rec*., vol. 14, 1955–58, 20–25.

315 DUBLIN UNIVERSITY MAGAZINE. Index vols. 1–55, 1833–1860. Manuscript index compiled by Mr. Haig, Kings Inns Library, is in the Library of the Royal Irish Academy. See *Ir. Book Lov*., vol. 6, no. 6, 1915, 103–4.

316 — Sadleir, Michael, *Dublin University Magazine*: its history, contents and bibliography. *Bibliog. Soc. Ir*., 5, 1933–8, 59–81.

317 — DUBLIN UNIVERSITY MAGAZINE [an article]. *Ir. Book Lov*., 10, 1918–19, 75–9.

318 THE HONEST ULSTERMAN. *Eire-Ir*., vol. 11, no. 2, 1976, 157–8.

319 IRISH METROPOLITAN MAGAZINE. O'Hegarty, P.S. *The Irish Metropolitan Magazine* [1857–8]. *Ir. Book Lov*., 29, 1943–5, 15–18.

320 IRISH REVIEW. Index, vol. 1–3, 1936–8, and index to *Ireland To-day,* vol. 1–4, 1911–14. Completed for Fellowship of the Library Association of Ireland, by Miss C. Griffin.

321 THE LEADER. Callan, Patrick. D.P. Moran, founder editor of *The Leader. Cap. Ann*., 1977, 274–287.

322 LOUGHREA JOURNAL. O'Farrell, Thomas T. *The Loughrea Journal. Ir. Book Lov*., 19, 1931, 172–3.

323 STUDIES. An Irish quarterly review. Dublin: vol. 1–, 1912–. Index, vols. 1–20, compiled by E.M. Kerrigan. Typescript. In four sections: author, title, poetry in Irish and English, reviews. Copies in University College, Dublin, and the Central Catholic Library, 76 Merrion Square, Dublin.

324 — General index of vols 1–50, 1912–1961. Compiled by Fr. Aloysius O'Rahilly. Ros Cre. (Roscrea): 1966. Includes indexes of authors, subjects, poems and books reviewed.

Societies

325 BERRY, HENRY F. A history of the Royal Dub-

lin Society. London: 1915.

326 DE VERE WHITE, TERENCE. The Story of the Royal Dublin Society. Tralee [1955].

327 O'CONNOR, CHARLES. Origins of the Royal Irish Academy. *Studies*, vol. 38, 1949, 325–337.

328 PETTIT, S.F. The Royal Cork Institution: a reflection of the cultural life of a city. *Cork Hist. Arch. Soc. J.*, 81, 1976, 70-90.

Newspapers

329 BOWEN, B.P. *The Comet Newspaper* [1831–33]. *Ir. Book Lov.*, 28, 1941–2, 120–7.

330 BRITISH LIBRARY, NEWSPAPER LIBRARY. Microfilms of newspapers and journals for sale. London: The British Library [1976]. Lists 160 Irish newspapers available for purchase.

331 BRITISH MUSEUM. Catalogue of printed books: Newspapers published in Great Britain and Ireland, 1801–1900. London: 1905. Newspapers prior to 1801 are listed in *Catalogue of the printed books . . . periodical publications*. 1899–1900.

332 BROWN, STEPHEN J. The Dublin newspaper press: a bird's-eye view, 1659–1916. *Studies*, 25, 1936, 109–22.

333 BUCKLEY, JAMES. The first Irish newspaper—*The Irish Monthly Mercury*, Cork, 1649. *Cork Hist. Arch. Soc. J., 2nd ser.*, 3, 1897, 136–43.

334 — A study of some old [Dublin] newspapers. *New Ir. Rev.*, 16, 1901, 110–21.

335 BUTLER, M. Ramsey's *Waterford Chronicle* for 1814. *Bibliog. Soc. Ir.*, vol. 2, no. 1, 1921, 21–2.

336 CAMPBELL, A.A. Belfast newspapers, past and present. Belfast: 1921. Reprinted from *The Belfast Telegraph*.

337 — Early Strabane newspapers and magazines. *Ulster J. Arch.*, 7, 1901, 176–7.

338 CARROLL, F. Irish newspapers in 1798. *Ir. Book Lov.*, 32, 1952–7, 65–6.

339 CASAIDE, SEAMUS UA. A guide to old Waterford newspapers. Waterford: 1917.

340 — Newspapers of Ireland in 1819. *Ir. Book Lov.*, 19, 1931, 90–1.

341 COLLINS, D.C. A handlist of news pamphlets, 1590–1610. London: 1943.

342 COLLINS, JOHN T. Gleanings from old Cork newspapers [1738–54]. *Cork Hist. Arch. Soc. J.*, 62, 1957, 95–101.

343 — Gleanings from old Cork newspapers [1754–5]. *ibid*, 63, 1958, 95–102.

344 COUNTY GALWAY NEWSPAPERS AND PERIODICALS OF THE PAST. Galway Reader, vol. 1, no. 3, 1948, 30–32.

345 CRANE, R.S. and KAYE, F.B. A census of British newspapers and periodicals, 1620–1800. (*Studies in philology*, vol. 24, no. 1), North Carolina: 1927. Reprinted 1963, Johnson Reprint Corporation, New York.

346 CRICK, BERNARD R. and DALTROP, ANNE. List of American newspapers up to 1940, held by libraries in Great Britain and Ireland. [London], 1958. (*British Association for American Studies bulletin supp.*). Typescript.

347 CUNNINGHAM, TERENCE P. Gustavus Tuite Dalton (1811–1879): first editor of *The Anglo Celt* [1846–47]. *Breifne*, vol. 4, no. 15, 1972, 438–449.

348 DIX, E.R. McC. Bibliography of Irish newspapers, 1660–1700. *Ir. Independent*, January 18–20, 1905.

349 — Eighteenth-century newspapers. *Ir. Book Lov.*, 1, 1909–10, 39–41.

350 — The first Irish newspapers: a bibliographical note. *Ir. Book Lov.*, 4, 1912–13, 97–8.

351 — Irish bibliography; tables relating to some Dublin newspapers of the eighteenth century, showing what vols, etc., of each are extant and where access to them can be had in Dublin. Dublin: 1910.

352 — Notes on some early Dublin newspapers (1707–8). *Bibliog. Soc. Ir.*, vol. 2, no. 5, 1923, 87–91.

353 DUBLIN NEWSPAPERS BEFORE 1800. *Ir. Times*, 3rd March 1881.

354 FFOLLIOTT, ROSEMARY. The surprising newspapers of Ennis. *Ir. Ancest.*, vol. 6, no. 2, 1974, 98–101. The *Ennis Chronicle* and the *Clare Journal*.

355 FREEMAN'S JOURNAL. Dublin: 1763–1924. At present being indexed by long-term prisoners of good education in Portlaoighise prison. Entries on cards are being made on behalf of the National Library of Ireland for inclusion in the National Bibliography.

356 GRACEY, J.W. Newspaper collections and the Linen Hall Library. *Northern Ireland Libraries*, vol. 9, no. 1, 1971, 6–10.

357 HAMMOND, JOSEPH W. The Dublin Gazette, 1705–1922. *Dublin Hist. Rec.*, 13, 1952–4, 108–17.

358 HANLEY, JOHN. The beginnings of Meath's first weekly [The Meath Herald, 1845] *Riocht na Midhe*, vol. 4, no. 1, 1967, 55–60.

359 HAYES, J.C. History of Tipperary newspapers. 1960. Typescript of 79 p.; presented to the Library Association of Ireland.

360 HORGAN, JOHN J. A Cork centenary [*The Cork Examiner*].*Studies*, 30, 1941, 571–579.

361 IRISH DAILY PAPERS, 1801–1900. *Camb. Bibliog. Eng. Lit.*, 3, 1940, 808–9.

362 IRISH NEWSPAPER PRESS DIRECTORY, including newspapers, periodicals, trade and technical, advertising agencies, printers and publishers, photo-engravers and blockmakers, radio and television, paper makers, and box makers and bookbinders. Dublin: 1962.

363 IRISH NEWSPAPERS, 1660–1800. *Camb. Bibliog. Eng. Lit.*, 2, 1940, 733–9.

364 KAVANAGH, P.J. Carlow newspapers, 1828–1841. *Carloviana*, vol. 2. no. 24, 1975, 26–28.

365 KEESING'S CONTEMPORARY ARCHIVES: weekly diary of world events. Bristol, 1931–.

366 KENEALY, MARY. *Finn's Leinster Journal. Old Kilk. Rev., new ser.*, vol. 1, no. 5, 1978. 332–348. Afterwards *The Leinster Journal* and from 1830 was known as *The Kilkenny Journal*.

367 McCLELLAND, AIKEN. An unknown Fermanagh newspaper [*Newtownbutler Herald* dated 14 August 1894]. *Ir. Booklore*, vol. 2. no. 1, 1972, 162. Acquired by Ulster Folk Museum.

368 McKENNA, KATHLEEN. The *Irish Bulletin* [1919–21]. *Cap. Ann.*, 1970, 503–527.

369 McTERNAN, JOHN C. Sligo newspapers. *An Leab.*, 16, 1958, 5–9. From *A bibliography of Sligo*, which was accepted as thesis for Fellowship of the Library Association of Ireland.

370 MADDEN, R.R. Bibliographical note on Limerick newspapers. In his *History of Irish periodical literature*, vol. 2, 1867, 202–6.

371 MUNTER, Robert L. A handlist of Irish newspapers , 1685–1750. (*Camb. Bibliog. Soc. monograph*, no. 4.) London: 1960.

372 — The History of the Irish newspaper, 1685–1760. Cambridge: 1967. Bibliog., pp. 192–207.

373 NEWSPAPER PRESS OF IRELAND. *Monthly Mag., new ser.*, vol. 4, 1827, 337–44.

374 NINETEENTH-CENTURY GALWAY NEWSPAPERS. *Galway Reader*, vol. 1. no. 4, 1949, 40–41.

375 SHERIDAN, NIALL. The First Sinn Fein paper. *Riocht na Midhe*, vol. 4. no. 4. 1970, 54–57. Reprinted from *Cap. Ann.*, 1968, 140–144.

376 THE TIMES. Palmer's Index to *The Times*. Corsham (Wilts.): 1790–1943.

377 — The official Index to *The Times*. London: 1906–.

378 TUTTY, MICHAEL J. *The Dublin Evening Post*, 1826. *Dublin Hist. Rec.*, vol. 24. no. 2. 1971, 15–24.

379 UNIVERSITY MICROFILMS. Irish newspapers prior to 1750 in Dublin libraries, now available for purchase in positive microfilm form. Ann Arbor, Michigan: 1950.

380 — Irish Newspapers, II: *The Dublin Journal, Freeman's Journal*. Ann Arbor, Michigan: 1959.

381 WEED, KATHERINE KIRTLEY and BOND, RICHMOND PUGH. Studies of British newspapers and periodicals from their beginnings to 1800: a bibliography. Chapel Hill, Univ. of North Carolina: 1946. (*Studies in philology, extra ser.*)

382 WILLIGAN, WALTER LUKE. A bibliography of the Irish-American press, 1691–1835. Photostat copy of an original typescript of 21 pages in the National Library, Dublin.

383 WILLING'S PRESS GUIDE. London: 1874–.

Journalism

384 BROWN, STEPHEN J. The press in Ireland: a survey and a guide. Dublin: 1937.

385 — The press in Ireland. Pt. 2: Some Catholic periodicals. *Studies*, 25, 1936, 428–42.

386 INGLIS, BRIAN. The freedom of the press in Ireland, 1784–1841. (*Studies in Irish history*, vol. 6). London: 1954. Bibliog., pp. 236–48.

387 MCCLELLAND, AIKEN. The Ulster press in the eighteenth and nineteenth centuries. *Ulster Folk.*, 20, 1974, 89–99.

Directories and Almanacs

388 BOWEN, B.P. Old Moore's *Almanack. Dublin Hist. Rec.*, 3, 1940–1, 26–37.

389 CASAIDE, SEAMUS US. Irish almanacks. *Ir. Book Lov.*, 3, 1912, 128–9.

390 DENNAN, JOSEPH. The first hundred years of the Dublin Directory. *Bibliog. Soc. Ir.*, vol. 1, no. 7, 1920. Covers period 1751–1851.

391 DIX, E.R. McC. A Dublin almanack of 1612. *R. Ir. Acad. Proc., Sec. C*, 30, 1912–13, 327–30.

392 — Early almanacs printed in Ireland. *Ir. Book Lov.*, 18, 1930, 38.

393 — An early Dublin almanack [1636]. *R. Ir. Acad. Proc., Sec. C*, 33, 1916–17, 225–9.

394 — Early Dublin-printed almanacs (seventeenth century). *Bibliog. Soc. Ir.*, vol. 1, no. 2, 1918.

395 EVANS, EDWARD. Historical and bibliographical account of almanacks, directories, etc., published in Ireland from the sixteenth century; their rise, progress, and decay, with jottings of their compilers and printers. A book for the antiquary as well as the general reader. Facsimile ed. with an introduction by Dr. Thomas Wall. Blackrock: 1976. First published Dublin: 1897.

396 GUINNESS, H.S. Dublin directories, 1751–60. *Ir. Book Lov.*, 14, 1924, 84–6.

397 HAMMOND, JOSEPH W. The founder of *Thom's Directory*, [Alexander Thom]. *Dublin Hist. Rec.*, 8, 1945–6, 41–56.

398 HENDERSON, G.P. *compiler*. Current British directories: a guide to the directories published in Great Britain, Ireland, the British Commonwealth and South Africa. Beckenham (Kent): CBD Research Ltd. 1973–74, edited by I.G. Anderson, 1973.

399 IRISH PROVINCIAL DIRECTORIES, 1788. Lucas, Richard. A general directory of the Kingdom of Ireland. *Ir. Geneal.* vol. 3. no. 10, 1965, 392–416. Includes the counties of Carlow, Kildare, Kilkenny, Queens County, Waterford, Wexford and Wicklow.

400 — The Cork Directory, 1787 [and a General Directory of the Kingdom of Ireland, 1788. Ennis. Co. of Clare] by Richard Lucas, *Ir. Geneal.*, vol. 4, no. 1, 1968, 37–46.

401 LUCAS, RICHARD. The Cork Directory for the year 1787. *Cork Hist. Arch. Soc. J.*, 72, 1967, 135–157.

402 LYNCH, PATRICK. An historical account of Irish almanacks. *Ir. Mag.*, 1810, 330, 378, 476, 524; 1811, 36.

403 NESBIT, J.N.H. *compiler*. A bibliography of Ulster directories. Typescript, compiled October 1959, containing seventy items, for competition held by Northern Branch of the Library Association.

MUSEUMS

404 GROGAN, L.S. The case for a Dublin [municipal] museum. *Dublin Hist. Rec.*, 1, 1938–39, 97–107.

405 HAYES-MCCOY, G.A. Museums and our national heritage. *Cap. Ann.*, 1971, 128–135.

406 INSTITUTE OF PROFESSIONAL CIVIL SERVANTS. Museum Service for Ireland. [Dublin: Inst. of Prof. Civil Servants, 1973].

407 INTERNATIONAL COUNCIL OF MUSEUMS. Irish National Committee of ICOM. Directory of local museums and local societies in Ireland. [Dublin: 1976].

408 LUCAS, A.T. The National Museum: its place in the cultural life of the nation. *Oideas*, 1. 1968, 40–50.

409 MURRAY, DAVID. Museums, their history and use; with bibliography and list of museums in the United Kingdom. Glasgow: 1904. 3 vols.

410 MUSEUMS AND ART GALLERIES IN GREAT BRITAIN AND NORTHERN IRELAND. London:

Index Publishers, 1960–. Published annually.

411 MUSEUMS ASSOCIATION. Directory of museums and art galleries in the British Isles, compiled by S.F. Markham. London: 1948.

MANUSCRIPTS

412 AINSWORTH, J. Manuscripts at the Royal Hospital, Kilmainham. *Anal. Hib.*, 23, 1966, 311–312.

413 — Manuscript collections in private keeping: reports in National Library. *Anal. Hib.*, 23, 1966, 371–387.

414 ARCHIVIUM HIBERNICUM. Irish historical record. Maynooth. Catholic Record Society of Ireland. vol. 1–, 1912–.

415 ARMAGH PUBLIC LIBRARY. Catalogue of manuscripts . . . compiled by James Dean. Dundalk: [1928].

416 ARTHURS, J.B. A catalogue of Irish Mss. in Ulster libraries. In preparation. See *Ulster J. Arch., 3rd ser.*, 13, 1950, 106–7.

417 BIELER, LUDWIG. Manuscripts of Irish interest in the libraries of Scandinavia: a general survey. *Studies*, 54, 1965, 252–258.

418 BINDON, SAMUEL H. Catalogue of the Mss. relating to Ireland in the Burgundian Library at Brussels. *R. Ir. Acad. Proc.*, 3, 1847, 477–502.

419 — Some notices of manuscripts relating to Ireland in various languages now to be found in the Burgundian Library at Brussels . . . Dublin: 1848.

420 BRITISH MUSEUM. Catalogue of Irish manuscripts in the British Museum, by Standish Hayes O'Grady and Robin Flower. Oxford: 1926–53. 3 vols.

421 — Catalogue of Mss. in the Cottonian Library, British Museum. London, 1802.

422 — Catalogue of the Lansdowne Mss . . . London, 1812. 2 pts.

423 — Catalogue of the Harleian Mss . . . London, 1808–12. 4 vols.

424 — Catalogue of the Stowe Mss . . . London, 1896.

425 — Catalogue of additions to the Mss . . . (including Sloane collection), 1836–99. London: 1901.

426 — The Irish Mss. in the British Museum, by Robin Flower. *Philol. Soc. Trans.*, 1911–14, 118–22.

427 BULL, PHILIP. The William O'Brien Mss. in the library of University College, Cork. *Cork Hist. Arch. Soc. J.*, 75. 1970, 129–141. William O'Brien (1852–1928), journalist, writer and politician.

428 BURKE MSS. AT MOUNT MELLERAY ABBEY. *Ir. Geneal.* vol. 4, no. 4, 1971, 363. The manuscript notes, documents and books of Canon W.P. Burke, author of the *History of Clonmel* (1907).

429 CAREW MSS. Calendar of the Carew Mss. preserved in the Archiepiscopal Library at Lambeth, 1515–1600, edited by J.S. Brewer and William Bullen. London: 1867–9. 6 vols.

430 CARTE MSS. Report upon the Carte and Carew papers in the Bodleian and Lambeth libraries, 1863, by Sir Thomas Duffus Hardy and J.S. Brewer. London: 1864.

431 — The Carte manuscripts in the Bodleian Library, by C.W. Russell and J.P. Prendergast; a report presented to . . . the Master of the Rolls. London: 1871.

432 CASAIDE, SEAMUS UA. Sean O Mathghamhna's [John O'Mahony] Irish Mss. [a list]. *Ir. Book Lov.*, 18, 1930, 80–4. Preserved in the Presbyterian private library, Philadelphia.

433 CATALOGI LIBRORUM MANUSCRIPTORUM ANGLIAE ET HIBERNIAE . . . CUM INDICE. Oxonii. 1696–7. 2 vols.
Vol 1: Catalogues of the Mss. in the Bodleian and other libraries of the universities of Oxford and Cambridge.
Vol. 2: Catalogues of the cathedral libraries, etc., of England and Ireland.

434 CATALOGUE OF IRISH MSS. and such as relate to Irish affairs in the Lambeth Palace Library. *Monthly Museum*, 1, 1814, 440–1.

435 CRICK, BERNARD R. and ALMAN, MIRIAM, *eds*. A guide to manuscripts relating to America in Great Britain and Ireland. London: British Association for American Studies, 1961.

436 CURTIS, EDMUND. Irish Mss. in Sheffield. *Ir.*

Book Lov., 22, 1934, 91.

437 D'ALTON, JOHN. John D'Alton's Ms. collections relating to Ireland. Bibliog. notes by William MacArthur and others. *Ir. Book Lov*., 7, 1915–16, 75, 101, 116.

438 — John D'Alton's manuscripts, by S.U. Casaide. *Ir. Book Lov*., 16, 1928, 16–19. D'Alton's Mss. are now in Chicago University Library.

439 DE BRUN, PADRAIG. Chuasaigh de Lamhscribhinni Gaeilge: Treoirliosta. *Stud. Hib*., 7, 1967, 146–181.

440 — Lamhscribhinn Ghaeilge O Thaisceart Chiarrai. *Stud. Hib*., 4, 1964, 197–208.

441 — Two Breifne manuscripts. *Breifne*, vol. 4, no. 15, 1972, 426–437.

442 — Some Irish Mss with Breifne associations *Breifne*. vol. 3. no. 12. 1969. 552–561.

443 DIETZ, BRIAN. A survey of manuscripts of Irish interest for the period 1715–1850 in the House of Lords' Record Office. *Anal. Hib*., 23, 1966, 225–243.

444 DILLON, MYLES *and others*. Catalogue of Irish manuscripts in the Franciscan Library, Killiney, by Myles Dillon, Canice Mooney and Padraig de Brun. Dublin: Dublin Institute for Advanced Studies, 1969.

445 DIX, E.R. MCCLINTOCK. A recent bibliographical acquisition: rare Irish pamphlets. *Ir. Book Lov*., 1, 1909–10, 53–4.

446 DRAAK, MAARTJE. Construe marks in Hiberno-Latin manuscripts. Amsterdam: 1957. (*Mededelingen der Koninklijke Nederlandse Akademie van Wetenschappen, Afd. Letterkunde, nieuwe reeks, deel*, 20, no. 10)

447 EARLY IRISH MANUSCRIPTS OF MUNSTER. *Cork Hist. Arch. Soc. J., 2nd ser*., 14, 1908, 83–92.

448 EDWARDS, ROBERT DUDLEY. The work of the Irish Manuscripts Commission. *Studies*, 27, 1937, 481–8.

449 ESPOSITO, M. Notes on Hiberno-Latin manuscripts in Belgian libraries. *Arch. Hib*., 3, 1914, 203–9.

450 FITZGERALD, GERALDINE. Manuscripts in the Representative Church Body Library. *Anal. Hib*., 23, 1966, 307–309.

451 GILBERT, JOHN T. The manuscripts of the former College of Irish Franciscans, Louvain. *Hist. Mss. Comm. Rpts*., no. 4, pt. 1, 1874, 599–613.

452 GILBERT, JOHN T. The manuscripts of Charles Haliday . . . acts of the privy council in Ireland, 1556–71. *Hist. Mss. Comm. Rpts*., no. 15, 1897, appendix III.

453 — Facsimiles of national manuscripts of Ireland. London: 1874–84. 4 pts. in 5 vols.

454 — Account of facsimiles of the national Mss. of Ireland to 1719. London: 1884. An introduction to *The facsimiles of the national manuscripts of Ireland*.

455 GIUSEPPI, M.S. A guide to the manuscripts preserved in the Public Record Office [London]. London: 1923–4. 2 vols.

456 GOUGAUD, LOUIS. The remains of ancient monastic libraries. In *Feil-sgribhinn Eoin mic Neill* . . . Dublin: 1940, pp. 319–34. Manuscripts written in, or belonging to, the ancient Irish monasteries.

457 — Répertoire des facsimiles des manuscrits irlandais. *Rev. Celt*., 34, 1913, 14–37; 35, 1914, 415–30; 38, 1920, 1–14.

458 GWYNN, EDWARD. The manuscript known as the *Liber Flavus Fergusiorum. R. Ir. Acad. Proc*., 26, Sec. c, 1906–7, 15–41.

459 HAYES, RICHARD J. *ed*. Manuscript sources for the history of Irish civilisation. Boston (Mass.): 1965. 11 vols.

460 HILLIGARTH, J.N. Visigothic Spain and early Christian Ireland. *R. Ir. Acad. Proc*., 62, Sec. C, no. 6, 1962. Early Spanish Mss. in Ireland.

461 HISTORICAL MANUSCRIPTS COMMISSION. A guide to the reports on collections of Mss. of private families, corporations, and institutions of Great Britain and Ireland.

Pt 1: Topographical [index]. London: 1914. Pt 2: Index of persons. London: 1935–8. 2 vols.

462 HOGAN, JAMES. The Irish Manuscripts Commission. Cork: 1954. (*Irish historical ser*., no. 1). Lists works published and forthcoming, also contents of *Analecta Hibernica*, nos. 1–19.

463 IRISH MANUSCRIPTS COMMISSION. Analecta Hibernica, including the reports of the Irish

Manuscripts Commission. Dublin: no. 1–, 1930–.

464 — Catalogue of publications issued and in preparation, 1928–1966. Dublin: Stationery Office, 1966.

465 LESLIE, JAMES B. Catalogue of manuscripts in possession of the Representative Church Body . . . Dublin, collected by the Ecclesiastical Records Committee. Dublin: 1938.

466 LHUYD, EDWARD. A catalogue of Irish Mss. In his *Archaeologia Britannica*, Oxford: 1707. vol. 1, pp. 435–6.

467 LIST OF BOOKS containing facsimiles of Irish Mss. In Best's *Bibliography of Irish philology* . . . Dublin: 1913, pp. 63–8.

468 LOWE, E.A. (ed). Codices Latini antiquiores: a palaeographical guide to Latin manuscripts prior to the ninth century. Oxford: 1934–5. 2 pts. Bibliog. pt. 2, pp. 45–53.

469 LUARD, H.R. *ed*. Catalogue of the Mss. preserved in the library of the University of Cambridge. Cambridge: 1856–67. 6 vols.

470 MACAODHAGAIN, PARTHALAN. Irish Mss. in the Vatican. *Ir. Book. Lov*., 32, 1952–7, 61–2.

471 MAC GIOLLA IASACHTA, EAMONN (*i.e*., Edward MacLysaght). Roinn na Laimhscribhinn sa Leabharlann Naisiunta. *Galvia* 1, 1954, 11–14.

472 MCGOVERN, J.B. Some Irish Mss. and books in the John Rylands Library, Manchester. *Bibliog. Soc. Ir*., 2, 1921–5, 13–15.

473 MACKINNON, DONALD. A descriptive catalogue of Gaelic manuscripts in the Advocates' Library, Edinburgh, and elsewhere in Scotland. Edinburgh: 1912.

474 MACLOCHLAINN, AILFRID. Irish manuscripts at Liverpool. *Celtica*, 4, 1958, 217–38.

475 MACSWINEY, MARQUIS. Notes on the history of the *Book of Lecan. R. Ir. Acad. Proc., ser. C*, 38, 1928–9, 31–50.

476 MADDEN, P.J. and CLARKE, DESMOND. The manuscripts of Ireland: an introduction to Irish palaeography. Pt. 1. *An Leab*., 13, 1955, 119–39.

477 MOORE, MARGARET F. Two select bibliographies of mediaeval historical study.
no. 1: A classified list of works relating to the study of English palaeography. London: 1912.
No. 2: Contains no Irish material.

478 NATIONAL LIBRARY OF IRELAND. Reports of the Council of Trustees.
1930–31: Appendix, pp. 15–27. The Phillipps collection of Irish Mss.
1938–39: Appendix, pp. 16–36. Manuscripts in the Irish language.
1949–50: pp. 9–120. List no. 1 of manuscripts relating to Ireland in the Bibliothèque Nationale, Paris.
1950–51: pp. 10–124. List of manuscripts relating to Ireland copied on microfilm and photostat.
1951–52: pp. 10–103. List no. 2 of manuscripts relating to Ireland copied on microfilm.

479 — Gaelic manuscripts. Manuscript catalogue which includes the collections of Sir Thomas Phillipps, David Comyn, and the Joly collection.

480 NICHOLLS, K.W. The Register of Clogher. *Clogher Rec*., vol. 7, no. 3, 1971–2, 361–431.

481 O'CONOR, CHARLES. Rerum Hibernicarum scriptores veteres. Tom. 1. Continens epistolam nuncupatoriam quae codicum vetustissimorum Hibernensium notiliam et rerum chronologiam complectitur: item prologomena ad annales, partibus II. Quarum prima vetustissimorum de Hibernia testimonia historica, secunda annalium et carminum Hibernensium catalogus comprehendit. Buckingham: 1814.

482 — Bibliotheca Mss. Stowensis: a descriptive catalogue of the manuscripts in the Stowe Library. Buckingham: 1818. vol. 1, pt. 2. Irish Mss., pp. 21–232. Now deposited in the Royal Irish Academy.

483 O'CURRY, EUGENE. Lectures on the manuscript materials of ancient Irish history, delivered at the Catholic University of Ireland, in 1855 and 1856. Dublin: 1861. Reissued 1873.

484 O'DONOVAN, JOHN. The lost and missing Irish manuscripts. *Ulster J. Arch*., 9, 1861–2, 16–28.

485 OMONT, HENRI. Catalogue des manuscrits celtiques et basques de la Bibliothèque Nationale. *Rev. Celt.*, 11, 1890, 389–433. Includes 29 Irish items.

486 O MORDHA, SEAMUS P. Irish manuscripts in St. McCarten's seminary, Monaghan. *Celtica*, 4, 1958, 279–87.

487 — Lamhscribhinni Gaeilge i gColaiste Phadraig [Dromchonrach, Baile Atha Cliath]. *Studia Hibernica*, 1, 1961, 172–94.

488 O'SHEA, P.J. Irish manuscripts in the Museum, College Square, Belfast. *Ulster J. Arch.*, 1, 1895, 106–10.

489 O'SULLIVAN, WILLIAM. The Irish manuscripts in case H in Trinity College Dublin: catalogues by Matthew Young in 1761. *Celtica*, 2, 1976, 229–250.

490 PEDDIE, ROBERT A. Mss. relating to Ireland in the libraries of France. *Ir. Book Lov.*, 1, 1909–10, 86–7.

491 PHAIR, P.B. [Sir William] Betham and the older manuscripts. *R. Soc. Antiq. Ir. J.*, 92, 1962, 75–8.

492 — Sir William Betham's manuscripts. *Anal. Hib.*, 27, 1972, 1–99.

493 PHILLIPPS, THOMAS. Bibliotheca Phillippica: list of Irish Mss. and other items from the sale of the library of Sir Thomas Phillipps, June 1910, and April 1911. *Ir. Book Lov.*, 1, 1909–10, 164–5; 3, 1911–12, 10–11.

494 PLUMMER, CHARLES. On the colophons and marginalia of Irish scribes. London: British Academy, 1927.

495 POWER, PATRICK. Irish Mss. in the library of St. John's College, Waterford. *Gael. J.*, 14, 1904, 572, 584, 606–7, 632–3.

496 — Irish Mss. in Waterford. *Gael. J.*, 14, 1904, 647–9, 692–5, 707–9, 728–9.

497 RECORD, P.D. The bibliography of palaeography [an article]. *J. Document.*, 6, 1950, 1–5.

498 REEVES, WILLIAM. Descriptive catalogue of a collection of manuscripts formerly belonging to and mainly the handiwork of William Reeves, Lord Bishop of Down and Connor and Dromore. Belfast: 1899.

499 ROYAL IRISH ACADEMY. Catalogue of Irish manuscripts in the Royal Irish Academy. Dublin: 1926–70. Fasciculi 1–28. Index, compiled by Kathleen Mulchrone, Elizabeth Fitzpatrick and A.I. Pearson. Dublin: 1948–58. 2 vols. See also *Collection and care of manuscript material in the library of the Royal Irish Academy*, by C. Bonfield. *An Leab.*, 10, 1949–52, 175–80.

500 SCOTT, JOHN RUSSELL. Catalogue of the Mss. remaining in Marsh's Library, Dublin, edited by Newport J.D. White. Dublin: 1913.

501 SHEAGHDHA, NESSA NI. Catalogue of Irish Manuscripts in the National Library of Ireland. Dublin.
Fasciculus 1. Mss. G1–G14. 1967.
Fasciculus 2. Mss. G15–G69. 1961.

502 SHEEHY, MAURICE P. *The Registrum Novum:* a manuscript of Holy Trinity Cathedral: the medieval charters. *Rep. Nov.*, vol. 3, no. 2, 1963–64, 249–281.

503 SHEFFIELD CITY LIBRARIES. Guide to the manuscript collections . . . Sheffield: 1956. Contains Irish material.

504 SKULRUD, OLAI. Catalogue of Norse manuscripts in Edinburgh, Dublin and Manchester. Christiana: 1918.

505 TALLON, MAURA. An Irish medieval manuscript in Wexford Cathedral chained library. *Ir. Book.*, vol. 3, no. 1, 1964, 26–29.

506 TODD, JAMES H. On the Irish Mss. in the Bodleian, Oxford. *R. Ir. Acad. Proc.*, 5, 1853, 162–76.

507 TORNA, *pseud*. Canon Lyons Mss. *Iver. Soc. J.*, 7, 1914–15, 24–31, 103–10, 168–77. Preserved in the library of the Presbytery, St. Mary's Cathedral, Cork.

508 — Canon Murphy Mss. *Iver. Soc. J.*, 7, 1914–15, 224–32.

509 TRINITY COLLEGE, DUBLIN. ABBOTT, T.K. Catalogue of the manuscripts in the library of Trinity College, Dublin, to which is added a list of the Fagel collection of maps in the same library. Dublin: 1900.

510 — ABBOTT, T.K. and GWYNN, E.J. Catalogue of the Irish manuscripts in the library of Trinity College, Dublin: 1900.

511 — DOUGAN, R.O. A descriptive guide to twenty Irish manuscripts in the library of Trinity College, Dublin, with an appendix of five early Irish manuscripts in the Royal Irish

Academy. 2nd rev. ed. Dublin: 1955. 1st edition *Guide to the Irish manuscripts exhibited* . . . 1953.

512 — MURRAY, ROBERT HENRY. A short guide to some manuscripts in the library of Trinity College, Dublin. London: 1920 (*Helps for students of history, no. 32*.)

513 WALSH, PAUL. Catalogue of Irish manuscripts in Maynooth College Library. Pt. 1: Contents of Murphy manuscripts 1–10. Magh Nuadhat, Cuallacht Chuilm Chille. 1943. No further pts. published.

514 WARE, JAMES. A manuscript of James Ware: British Museum Additional 4788, by Kathleen Hughes. *R. Ir. Acad. Proc., ser. C*, 55, 1952–3, 111–16.

Book Rarities and Illustrations

515 CHAMBRE, JEAN M. A guide to the literature on the Book of Kells. Bibliography submitted in part requirement for University of London Diploma in Librarianship. 1962.

516 DIRINGER, DAVID. The illuminated book: its history and production. London, 1958. Bibliog. pp. 199–202.

517 DOUGAN, R.O. Catalogue of a loan collection of Western illuminated manuscripts from the library of Sir Chester Beatty exhibited in the library of Trinity College, Dublin, 1955. Dublin: 1955.

518 DUFT, JOHANNES, and MEYER, PETER. The Irish miniatures in the abbey library of St. Gall. Berne and Lausanne: 1954. Includes bibliogs; limited edition of 600 copies.

519 HENRY, FRANÇOISE. Les débuts de la miniature irlandaise. *Gazette des Beaux Arts*, 37, 1950, 5–34.

520 HENRY, FRANÇOISE and MARSH-MICHELI, G.L. A century of Irish illumination (1070–1170). *R. Ir. Acad. Proc., Sec. C*, vol. 62, no. 5, 1962, 101–164.

521 LESLIE, SHANE. The script of Jonathan Swift and other essays. London and Philadelphia, 1935. Includes section on the rarest Irish books.

522 LUCE, A.A. The Book of Kells and the Gospels of Lindisfarne — a comparison. *Hermathena*, 79, 1952, 61–74; 80, 1952, 12–25.

523 MCGURK, J.J.N. The Celtic School of manuscript illumination. *Hist. Today*, 16, 1966, 747–755.

524 OSKAMP, H.P.A. Notes on the history of *Lebor na hUidre* [The Book of the Dun Cow]. *R. Ir. Acad. Proc., Sec. C*, vol. 65, no. 6, 1967, 117–137.

525 RADIO TELIFIS EIREANN. Great Books of Ireland. Dublin 1967. (*Thomas Davis Lectures series*). Bibliog. pp. 105–6.
The Book of Durrow, by Liam de Paor; The Book of Kells, by William O'Sullivan; The Lindisfarne Gospels, by R.L.S. Bruce-Mitford; The Stowe Missal, by Prof. Francis John Byrne; The Book of Armagh, by Dr. Ludwig Bieler; Leabhar na hUidhre [The Book of the Dun Cow], by Prof. David Greene; The Book of Ui Mhaine [The Book of Hy Many] by R.A. Breathnach; The Annals of the Four Masters, by Fr. Cathaldus Giblin.

526 RYNNE, ETIENNE. The art of early Irish illumination. *Cap. Ann.*, 1969, 201–222.

527 SIMMS, G.O. The Book of Kells: a selection of pages reproduced with a description and notes. Dublin: 1961. Bibliog. p. xiv.

528 SULLIVAN, EDWARD. The Book of Kells; described and illustrated with twenty-four plates in colour. 3rd ed. London: 1927.

529 SWEENY, JAMES JOHNSON. Irish illuminated manuscripts of the early Christian period. London: 1965.

Incunabula

530 ABBOTT, T.K. Catalogue of fifteenth-century books in the library of Trinity College, Dublin, and in Marsh's Library, Dublin, with a few from other collections. Dublin: 1905.

531 DUFF, E.G. Catalogue of books in the John Rylands Library, Manchester, printed in England, Scotland, and Ireland, and of books in English printed abroad to the end of the year 1640. Manchester: 1895.

532 GROSJEAN, PAUL and O'CONNELL, DANIEL. A catalogue of incunabula in the library at Milltown Park, Dublin. Dublin: 1932. The books formed part of the collection of William O'Brien. 175 copies printed.

533 HAIG, JAMES D. A list of books printed in England prior to the year MDC., in the library of . . . the King's Inns, Dublin. Dublin: 1858.

534 TALLON, MAURA. A catalogue of incunabula in Irish libraries. In preparation.

Binding

535 CRAIG, MAURICE J. Irish bookbindings, 1600–1800. London: 1954.

536 — Irish bookbinding. *Apollo*, 84, 1966, 322–325.

537 DIX, E.R. McC. Irish bookbinding: primary introduction to its study. *Dublin Pen. J., new ser.*, 1, 1902–3, 344.

538 [FOYLE, W. and G., LTD.] An exhibition of Irish bindings from the seventeenth to the twentieth centuries, September 29–23 October, 1954. London: Foyle's Art Gallery, 1954.

539 MCCRINNON, BARBARA. The Binding of The Book of Kells. *Book Coll.*, 24, 1975, 603.

540 SULLIVAN, EDWARD. Decorative bookbinding in Ireland: a paper read before *Ye Sette of Odde Volumes*, 28 February 1911 at the Hotel Capitol (Oddenino's). Letchworth: Arden Press, 1914. Limited edition of 133 copies for private circulation only.

Bookplates

541 DAY, ROBERT. Notice of bookplates engraved by Cork artists. *R. Hist. Arch. Soc. Ir. J.*, 4th Ser., 7, 1885–6, 10.

542 GRACEY, JIM. Irish book-plates and other marks of ownership in books. *Ir. Booklore*, vol. 2, no. 1, 1972, 174–7.

Censorship

543 ADAMS, MICHAEL. Censorship: the Irish experience. Dublin: Scepter Books, 1968. Bibliog. pp. 256–260.

544 CENSORSHIP BOARD. Books prohibited in the Irish Free State under the *Censorship of Publications Act, 1929*. Dublin: 1935–.

545 — Register of prohibited publications. Dublin: Stationery Office, 1973.

546 CLARKE, HAROLD. Censorship in Ireland. *Bookseller*, no. 3761, 1978, 234–237.

547 COMYN, ANDREW F. Censorship in Ireland. *Studies*, 58, 1969, 42–50. Review article of Michael Adams *Censorship: The Irish experience*.

548 ST. JOHN-STEVAS, NORMAN. Obscenity and the law. London: 1956. Bibliog. pp. 264–73. Chapter 8, The Irish censorship.

PHILOSOPHY

General

549 FURLONG, E.J. Philosophy in Trinity College 1866–. *Hermathena*, 115, 1973, 98–115.

550 LAIRD, JOHN. Ulster philosophers. *Belfast Nat. Hist. Phil. Soc. Proc., session* 1921–2, 4–26. Includes philosophers who are not natives but have slight Ulster connections, and embraces the following: Duns Scotus, Johannes Scotus Erigena, Bishop Jeremy Taylor, William King, Archbishop of Dublin, Janus Julius Toland, Bishop Berkeley, Frances Hutcheson, John Young, William Cairns, James M'Cosh and William James.

Individual

551 BERKELEY, GEORGE. Catalogue of manuscripts, books and Berkeleiana exhibited in the library of Trinity College . . . [Dublin, 1953.]

552 — Berkeley Newsletter. Dublin: Trinity College. No. 1–, 1977–.

553 — BERMAN, DAVID. Mrs. Berkeley's annotation in her interleaved copy of *An account of the life of George Berkeley* (1776). *Hermathena*, 122, 1977, 15–28.

554 — BERMAN, DAVID. Some new Bermuda Berkeleiana, *Hermathena*, 110, 1970, 24–31.

555 — BRACKEN, HARRY M. Berkeley. London: 1974.

556 — FURLONG, E.J. Some puzzles in Berkeley's writings. *Hermathena*, 120, 1976, 63–73.

557 — FURLONG, E.J. The Berkeley window in Trinity College; with an account of Berkeleian studies in the College, 1830–1900. *Hermathena*, 114, 1972, 70–87.

558 — JESSOP, T.E. A bibliography of George Berkeley; with inventory of Berkeley's manuscript remains, by A.A. Luce. 2nd rev. ed. The Hague: Martinus Nijhoff, 1973. 1st ed. Oxford: 1934.

559 — JOHNSON, JOSEPH. Bishop Berkeley's *Querist* in historical perspective. Dundalk: Dundalgan Press, 1970.

560 — LAMEERE, J. *and others*. Supplement, 1934–53, to Jessop. *Revue Internationale de philosophie*, vol. 7, 1953.

561 — LUCE, A.A. Some unpublished Berkeley letters with some new Berkeleiana. *R. Ir. Acad. Proc., Sec. C*, 41, 1932–4, 141–61.

562 — LUCE, A.A. Another look at Berkeley's notebooks. *Hermathena*, 110, 1970, 5–23.

563 — LUCE, A.A. The dialectic of immaterialism: an account of the making of Berkeley's *Principles*. London: 1963.

564 — and JESSOP, THOMAS EDMUND. The works of George Berkeley, Bishop of Cloyne. London: 1948–57. 9 vols. Bibliog., vol. 9.

565 — Berkeleian studies in America and France, with an appendix on a new letter about Berkeley's father. *Hermathena*, 90, 1960, 39–55.

566 — MEAD, H. RALPH. A bibliography of George Berkeley, Bishop of Cloyne. *Univ. Cal. Lib. Bull.*, no. 17, 1910.

567 — TIPTON, I.C. Berkeley: the philosophy of immaterialism. London: 1974.

568 — ZEIDAN, M.F. The development of Berkeley's philosophy, 1708–10. *Hermathena*, 97, 1963, 36–56.

569 JOHANNES SCOTTUS ERIUGENA. Bieler, Ludwig. Some recent works on Eriugena [Johannes Scottus]. *Hermathena*, 115, 1973, 94–97.

570 — O'MEARA, JOHN J. and BIELER, LUDWIG. The mind of Eriugena. Dublin: 1970.

PSYCHICAL RESEARCH

571 SOCIETY FOR PSYCHICAL RESEARCH. Library catalogue. *Society for Psychical Research proc.*, vol. 37, pt. 104, 1927.

Ghosts and Witchcraft

572 BYRNE, PATRICK F. Ghosts of old Dublin. *Dublin Hist. Rec.*, vol. 30 no. 1, 1976, 26–36.

573 — Irish ghost stories. Cork.
Book 1, 1966.
Book 2, 1971.

574 — Witchcraft in Ireland. Cork: 1967.

575 DUNNE, JOHN J. Haunted Ireland: her romantic and mysterious ghosts. Belfast: 1977.

576 SEYMOUR, ST. JOHN D. Irish witchcraft and demonology. Wakefield: 1972. Facsimile reprint of 1st ed., Dublin and London: 1913.

577 — and NELIGAN, HARRY L. True Irish ghost stories. 2nd enl. ed. Dublin and London: 1926. First published 1914.

578 UNDERWOOD, PETER. A gazetteer of Scottish and Irish ghosts. London: 1973.

Divining

579 THE IRISH DIVINER. Quarterly journal of the Irish Society of Diviners. Dublin. vol. 1, no. I–, 1977–.

Prophecies

580 O'KEARNEY, NICHOLAS. The prophecies of Ss. Columbkille, Maeltamlacht, Ultan, Seadhna, Coireall, Bearcan, Malachy, etc. together with the prophetic collectanea, or gleanings of several writers who have preserved portions of the now lost prophecies of our saints, with literal translation and notes. New York: 1861. See also *The sources for the early history of Ireland*, vol. 1, *Ecclesiastical*, by James F. Kenney. New York: 1929.

581 THE PROPHECIES OF ST. MALACHY AND ST. COLUMBKILLE: with forewords by H.E. Cardinale and W. Coslett Quin. Gerrards Cross: 1969. 'The prophecies of Saint Malachy' has an introduction and commentary by Peter Baker. 'The prophecies of Saint Columbkille' has an introduction by Tom Marriott and notes written in 1855 by Nicholas O'Kearney.

Astrology

582 EVANS, EDWARD. Historical and bibliographical account of almanacks, directories, etc., etc., published in Ireland from the sixteenth century: their rise, progress and decay; with jottings of their compilers and

printers. Facsimile ed., with an introduction by Thomas Wall. Blackrock (Co. Dublin): 1976. Originally published: Dublin: The Irish Builder, 1897. Astrological almanacks, 1587–1844.

583 GATTEY, CHARLES NEILSON. They saw tomorrow: seers and sorcerers from Delphi till today. London: 1977. Chapter 7, 'Cheiro', i.e. William John Warner: b. Bray, Co. Wicklow, 1866.

Neurosis and Anxiety

584 LYNN, RICHARD. National differences in anxiety. Dublin: 1971. (*Economic and Social Research Institute paper no. 59*) Topics include vehicle accidents, suicide, calorie intake, hospitalised mental illness, atherosclerosis and coronary heart disease, alcoholism, cigarette consumption, ulcers, celibacy, hypertension, and murder.

Temperance and Alcoholism

585 COOMBES, THE REV. JAMES. Europe's first Total Abstinence Society [Skibbereen, Co. Cork] *Cork Hist. Arch. Soc. J.* 72, 1967, 52–57.

586 McCARTHY, BRIAN *ed*. Alcoholism: a study of the problem of alcoholism and drugs in Ireland today. Dublin: 1971.

587 LONGMATE, NORMAN. The Waterdrinkers: a history of temperance. London: 1968. Includes an account of the work of Father Theobald Mathew. Bibliog., pp. 293–312.

RELIGION

General

588 CYCLOPAEDIA BIBLIOGRAPHIA: a library manual of theological and general literature, and guide to books for authors, preachers, students, and literary men; analytical, bibliographical and biographical, by James Darling. London: 1854–9, 2 vols.

589 RICHARDSON, ERNEST CUSHING, *compiler*. An alphabetical subject index and index encyclopaedia to periodical articles on religion, 1890–9. New York: 1907.

Libraries — General

590 DIGAN, PADRAIG. The Seminary Library. *Furrow*, 13, 1962, 703–711.

591 FENNING, HUGH. The Library of a preacher of Drogheda: John Donnelly, O.P. (d. 1748). *Coll. Hib*., no. 18–19, 1976–77, 72–104.

592 MS MATERIAL FOR DIOCESAN AND PAROCHIAL HISTORY: report on collection of sources.
No. 1: The library of the Representative Church Body, Dublin. *Seanchas Ardmhaca*, vol. 1, no. 1, 1954, 202–5.
No. 2: The collection of the Irish Folklore Commission. *ibid*., vol. 1, no. 2, 1955, 223–6.
No. 3: The National Library of Ireland, Dublin. *ibid*., vol. 2, no. 1, 1956, 227–8.

593 TALLON, MAURA. Church of Ireland diocesan libraries. Dublin: 1959. Reprinted from *An Leab*., 17, 1959, 17–27, 45–63. Includes index of founders and benefactors, and covers the following libraries which are not listed below: Christ Church Cathedral Library, Dublin; the Representative Church Body Library, Dublin; Kilmore See House Library, Co. Cavan; Ross Cathedral Library, Cork.

Individual

594 ARMAGH. Armagh Diocesan Library. Catalogue of Mss. 1928.

595 CASHEL. Catalogue of the library of the Dean and Chapter of Cashel. Dublin: 1873.

596 — Catalogue of pamphlets in Cashel Diocesan Library. Typescript in National Library Mss. collection no. 346.

597 — Alderson, Frederick. Cashel Cathedral. *Book Coll*., 17, 1968, 322–330.

598 — JACKSON, ROBERT WYSE. The ancient library of Cashel. *Cork Hist. Arch. Soc. J., 2nd ser*., 52, 1947, 128–34.

599 — POWER, PATRICK. Rare books in Cashel Diocesan Library. *Cork Hist. Arch. Soc. J. 2nd ser*., 43, 1938, 122–4.

600 — TIERNEY, MARK. Cashel Diocesan Archives: a short survey of the papers preserved in Archbishop's House, Thurles. *Ir. Eccles. Rec*. 108, 1967, 29–37. Archives for years 1740–1902 are available on microfilm in the

National Library (negative nos. 5698–5712 and positive nos. 5998–6013).

601 — WHITE, NEWPORT J.D. A catalogue of books in the French language, printed in or before A.D. 1715, remaining in Archbishop Marsh's library, Dublin; with an appendix relating to the Cashel Diocesan Library. Dublin: 1918.

602 CLOGHER. The Clogher Library including the Moffett Library, Monaghan. 1916.

603 — Catalogue of the books in the library of the diocese of Clogher (Church of Ireland), The Board Room, Clones, Co. Monaghan. Typescript of 64 pages. Copy in the Representative Church Body Library, Dublin.

604 CORK. St. Fin Barr's Library catalogue. Typescript of 72 pages, copied in June 1958 from copy loaned by the Dean of Cork, for Representative Church Body Library, Dublin.

605 DERRY. A catalogue of the books in the library of the diocese of Derry. Londonderry: 1848.

606 — Catalogue of Derry Diocesan Library. 1933.

607 —S. Columb's Cathedral, Londonderry, Chapter House Library. Short-title catalogue, pt. 1. Printed books and pamphlets. [By R.G.S. King.] Derry: 1939.

608 DOWN. Down, Connor and Dromore Diocesan Library. Catalogue of books in the diocesan collection and of the books in the Bishop Reichel Memorial Library; with a descriptive catalogue of the Mss. in Bishop Reeves' collection. 1899.

609 OSSORY. Catalogue of St. Canice's Cathedral Library, Kilkenny. 1895. Typescript copy in the Representative Church Body Library, Dublin.

610 RAPHOE. Raphoe Diocesan Library. Catalogue. Dublin: 1868.

611 TUAM. Tuam Cathedral Library. Catalogue. Dublin: 1886.

612 — Catalogue of the books added to the Henry Library in Tuam Cathedral, including nearly one hundred volumes purchased in February 1914 which embrace many of the latest and best books of the present day writers. Dublin: 1917.

613 — Supplementary catalogue of the Henry Library, 1926, in connection with St. Mary's Cathedral, Tuam, Galway. 1926.

614 WATERFORD. Lismore Diocesan Library. A catalogue of the books in the diocesan library of Lismore. Dublin: 1851.

615 — List of books compiled in 1957 from a set of cards lent to the library of the Representative Church Body, Dublin. Typescript of 93 pages.

616 — DIX, E.R. McC. Report on the Waterford Diocesan Cathedral Library. *Bibliog. Soc. Ir.*, vol. 2, no. 1, 1921, 5–6.

Bible

617 COTTON, HENRY, *Dean of Lismore.* Editions of the Bible and parts thereof in English from the year MDV to MDCCCL (1505 to 1850): with an appendix containing specimens of translations, and bibliographical description. 2nd rev. ed. Oxford: 1852.

618 DOYLE, P. The text of St. Luke's Gospel in the Book of Mulling. *R. Ir. Acad. Proc., Sec. C,* 71, no. 6, 1973, 177–200.

619 DUMVILLE, D.N. Biblical Apocrypha and the early Irish: a preliminary investigation. *R. Ir. Acad. Proc., Sec. C,* 73, no. 8, 1973, 299–338.

620 JOHNSTON, G.P. Notices of a collection of Mss. relating to the circulation of the Irish Bibles of 1685 and 1690 in the Highlands, and the association of the Rev. James Kirkwood therewith. *Edinburgh Bibliog. Soc.*, 6, 1906, 1–18.

621 MACGURK, PATRICK. Latin gospel books from A.D. 400 to A.D. 800. Brussels and Amsterdam, 1961. Includes section on Ireland and Irish manuscripts in other countries.

622 MCNAMARA, MARTIN. The Apocrypha in the Irish church. Dublin: 1975.

623 — Psalter text and Psalter study in the early Irish Church. (A.D. 600–1200). *R. Ir. Acad. Proc., Sec. C.,* 7, 1973, 201–298.

624 MINNIS, A.J. 'Authorial intention' and 'literal sense' in the exegetical theories of Richard Fitzralph and John Wyclif: an essay in the medieval history of Biblical hermeneu-

tics. *R. Ir. Acad. Proc. Sec. C*, vol. 75, no. 1, 1975, 1–31.

625 Newcome, W. An historical view of the English Biblical translations . . . Dublin: 1792. A list of various editions of the Bible, and various editions of the Psalms in English for the years 1505 to 1765, pp. 387–426.

626 Proceedings Of The Irish Biblical Association. Dublin: Dominican Publishers.
No. 1: Biblical Studies: the medieval Irish Contribution, edited by Martin McNamara. 1976. Includes: The Latin Bible in Ireland: its origins and growth, by Peter Doyle, pp. 30–45; Catalogue of the Latin exegetical literature, both Hiberno-Latin and that showing Irish influence, up to the beginning of the ninth century, by Dr. Bernhard Bischoff. pp. 95–160; Bibliography of Hiberno-Latin Biblical texts, by Joseph F. Kelly, pp. 161–4.

627 Roscoe, S. Early English, Scottish and Irish Thumb Bibles (with chronological checklist). *Book Coll.*, 22, 1973, 189–207.

628 Seymour, St. John D. Notes on Apocrypha in Ireland. *R. Ir. Acad. Proc. Sec. C*, 37, 1924–7, 107–17.

629 Trinity College, Dublin. Catalogue of Bibles added to the library since the year 1872. [Dublin: 1904.] For Bibles added prior to 1872 see *Catalogus librorum impressorum* . . .

630 Weingreen, J. *Hermathena* and Old Testament Studies. *Hermathena*, 115, 1973, 20–25.

Hagiography Saints — General

631 Bieler, Ludwig. Recent research on Irish hagiography. *Studies*, 35, 1946, 230–8; 536–44.

632 Butler, Hubert. Ten thousand saints: a study in Irish and European origins. Freshford (Co. Kilkenny), 1972. Bibliog. pp. 333–4.

633 Grosjean, Paul. Catalogus codicum hagiographicorum latinorum bibliothecarum Dubliniensium. *Anal. Bolland.*, 46. 1928, 81–148.

634 Hennig, John. Ireland's place in the tradition of the Cistercian menology. *Ir. Eccles. Rec.*, 95, 1961, 306–17.

635 Holweck, F.G. A biographical dictionary of the Saints, with a general introduction to hagiology. London: 1924.

636 Lehane, Brendan. The quest of three abbots: pioneers of Ireland's golden age. London: 1968. St. Patrick, St. Brendan and St. Columbanus (Columban). Bibliog., pp. 229–232.

637 Mould, Daphne D.C. Pochin. The Irish saints: short biographies of the principal Irish saints from the time of St. Patrick to that of St. Laurence O'Toole. Dublin and London: 1964. Bibliog., pp. 303–308.

638 Neeson, Eoin. The book of Irish saints. Cork: 1967.

639 O'Hanlon, John. Lives of the Irish saints, compiled from calendars, martyrologies and various sources. Dublin: 1875–1903. 10 vols.

640 O'Riain, Padraig. The composition of the Irish section of the calendar of Saints. *Dinnseanchas*, vol. 6, no. 3, 1975, 77–92.

641 O'Suilleabhain, The Rev. Padraig. The early Dublin editions of Butler's *Lives of the Saints*. *Ir. Eccles. Rec.*, 100, 1963, 240–244.

642 Plummer, Charles. Bethada Naem nErenn: lives of Irish saints . . . Oxford: 1922. 2 vols. Bibliog., vol. 1, pp. xli–xliv.

643 — A tentative catalogue of Irish hagiography. *Subsidia Hagiographica*, vol. 15: *Miscellanea Hagiographica Hibernica, Bruxelles, Société des Bollandistes*, 1925, pp. 171–288.

644 Stokes, Whitley. Lives of saints from the *Book of Lismore*. Oxford: 1890.

Saints – Individual

645 Brigid, Saint. Curtayne, Alice. St. Brigid of Ireland. Dublin: 1933. Bibliog., pp. 159–63.

646 — Brigit, Saint Of Kildare. Mould, D.D.C. Pochin. Saint Brigid. Dublin and London: 1964.

647 — O hAodha, Donncha. The early life of Saint Brigit. *Kildare Arch. Soc. J.*, vol. 15, no. 4, 1974–5, 397–405.

648 Carthage, Saint. Carthage, Father. The

story of St. Carthage, otherwise St. Mochuda (seventh century). Dublin: 1937.

649 COLUMBA, SAINT. ADOMNAN, SAINT. Life of Columba, edited with translation and notes by Alan Orr Anderson and Marjorie Ogilvie Anderson. London: 1961. Bibliog., pp. xv–xxiii.

650 — ANDERSON, MARJORIE O. Columba and other Irish Saints in Scotland. *Hist. Stud.*, 5, 1965, 26–36.

651 — BYRNE, FRANCIS J. The Ireland of St. Columba. *Hist. Stud.*, 5, 1965, 37–58.

652 — MENZIES, LUCY. Saint Columba of Iona: a study of his life, his times and his influence. London: 1920. Bibliog., pp. 220–3.

653 — RYAN, JOHN. St. Columba of Derry and Iona. *Studies*, 52, 1963, 37–51.

654 — SIMPSON, DOUGLAS. The Historical Saint Columba. 3rd ed. Edinburgh and London: 1963. Includes analytical catalogue of all the church sites bearing or said to bear his invocations.

655 COLUMBAN, SAINT. CONCANNON, MRS. THOMAS. The life of St Columban (St. Columbanus of Bobbio): a study of ancient monastic life. Dublin:1915. Bibliog., pp. xxvii–xxxii.

656 — DUBOIS, MARGUERITE-MARY. Un pionnier de la civilisation Occidentale: St. Columban (*c.* 540–615). Paris: 1950. Bibliog., pp. 217–30.

657 — English edition with additional notes by James O'Carroll. Dublin: 1961.

658 — MACMANUS, FRANCIS. Saint Columban. Dublin and London: 1963.

659 FINBARR, SAINT. O'BUACHALLA, LIAM. Commentary on the life of St. Finbarr. *Cork Hist. Arch. Soc. J.*, 70, 1965, 1–6.

660 — The homeplace of St. Finbarr. *Cork Hist. Arch. Soc. J.*, 68. 1963, 104–106.

661 — O'RIAIN, PADRAIG. St. Finbarr: a study in a cult. *Cork Hist. Arch. Soc. J.*, 82, 1977, 63–82.

662 MALACHY, SAINT. LAWLOR, H.J. Notes on St. Bernard's *Life of St. Malachy*, and his two sermons on the passing of St. Malachy. *R. Ir. Acad. Proc., Sec. C*, 35, 1918–20, 230–64.

663 MARTIN, SAINT. GWYNN, THE REV. AUBREY. The cult of St. Martin in Ireland. *Ir. Eccles. Rec.*, 105, 1966, 353–364.

664 MICHAEL, SAINT. ROE, HELEN M. The cult of St. Michael in Ireland. *In* Folk and Farm, edited by C. O'Danachair. 1976, pp. 251–264. Includes Gazeteer (!) of descriptions of the Archangel Michael in Ireland.

665 MOCHAOI, SAINT. TOWILL, EDWIN S. Saint Mochaoi and Nendrum, [with bibliog.] *Ulster J. Arch.*, 27, 1964, 103–120.

666 MOGUE, SAINT. O'CONNELL, PHILIP. Sources for the life of St. Mogue. *Breifne*. vol. 1, no. 2, 1959, 118–33.

667 PATRICK, SAINT. BIELER, LUDWIG. Codices patriciani latini: descriptive catalogue of Latin manuscripts relating to St. Patrick. Dublin: 1942.

668 — The life and legend of St. Patrick: problems of modern scholarship. Dublin: 1949. Bibliog., and notes, pp. 126–42.

669 — Patrician studies in the 'Irish Ecclesiastical Record'. *Ir. Eccles. Rec.*, 5th ser., 102, 1964, 359–366.

670 — The works of St. Patrick and *Hymn of St. Patrick*, by St. Secundinus, translated and annotated by L. Bieler. Westminster (Maryland) and London: 1953. (*Ancient Christian writers ser., no. 17*)

671 — BINCHY, D.A. Patrick and his biographers: ancient and modern. *Stud. Hib.*, 2, 1962, 7–173.

672 — St. Patrick's 'First Synod'. *Stud. Hib.*, 8, 1963, 49–59.

673 — BURY, J.B. The life of St. Patrick and his place in history. London: 1905. Bibliog. sources and notes, pp. 225–391.

674 — CARNEY, JAMES. The problem of St. Patrick. Dublin: 1961. Bibliog., pp. 190–3.

675 — CHICAGO PUBLIC LIBRARY. List of books and magazine articles on St. Patrick in the Chicago Public Library. Chicago: 1910.

676 — DIXON, V.F. Saint Patrick of Ireland and the dramatists of golden-age Spain. *Hermathena*, 121, 1976, 142–158.

677 — GAFFNEY, J.E., *compiler*. Books about St. Patrick. *An Leab.*, 2, 1932, 46–8.

678 — GALLICO, PAUL. The steadfast man: a life of St. Patrick. London: 1958. Bibliog., pp. 231–4.

679 — HANSON, R.P.C. Saint Patrick: his origins and career. Oxford: 1968. Bibliog., pp. 230–5.

680 — The D-text of Patrick's *Confession*: original or reduction. *R. Ir. Acad. Proc., Sec. C*, vol. 77, no. 8, 1977, 251–256.

681 — KEEGAN, THE REV. DESMOND J. The writings of St. Patrick. *Ir. Eccles. Rec.*, 106, 1966, 204–226.

682 — MACGIOLLA PHADRAIG, BRIAN. St. Patrick; his crozier, his writings. *Dublin Hist. Rec.*, vol. 24, no. 1, 1970, 189–199.

683 — MACNEILL, EOIN. Saint Patrick. Edited by John Ryan. With a memoir by Michael Tierney, and a Bibliography of Patrician Literature, by F.X. Martin. Dublin: 1964.

684 — MARSH, ARNOLD. Saint Patrick and his writings: a modern translation with introduction. Dundalk: 1966.

685 — NERNEY, D.S. A study of St. Patrick's sources. *Ir. Eccles. Rec.*, vol. 71, 1949, 497–507; vol. 72, 1949, 14–26, 97–110, 265–280.

686 — O'FIAICH, TOMAS. Record of Patrician publications. *Seanchas Ardmhacha*, 1961–2, pp. 192–204. Special issue devoted to the Patrician Year.

687 — O'RAIFEARTAIGH, T. The life of St. Patrick: a new approach. *Ir. Hist. Stud.*, 16, 1968–69, 119–137.

688 — St. Patrick's twenty-eight days' journey. *Ir. Hist. Stud.*, 16, 1968–69, 395–416.

689 — O'SUILLEABHAIN, PADRAIG. Sermons on St. Patrick on the Continent. *Ir. Eccles. Rec.*, 101, 1964, 170–171.

690 — SCHOFIELD, A.N.E.D. St. Patrick at Glastonbury. *Ir. Eccles. Rec.*, 107, 1967, 345–361.

691 —RYAN, JOHN. St. Patrick, apostle of Ireland. *Studies*, vol. 50, 1961. The documents on which historians rely, pp. 113–20.

Devotional

692 BRADY, JOHN. The Catechism in Ireland: A survey. *Ir. Eccles. Rec.*, 83, 1955, 167–76.

Hymns and Writers

693 ALEXANDER, CECIL FRANCES. McMahon, Sean. All things bright and beautiful. *Eire-Ir.*, vol. 10, no. 4, 1975, 101–109. On her hymns and poems.

694 CRAWFORD, GEORGE ARTHUR, and EBERLE, JACOB AMANDUS. Church hymnal: biographical index. Dublin: 1876. 3rd ed., 1878.

695 HAYDEN, ANDREW J. and NEWTON, ROBERT F. British hymn writers and composers: a check-list giving dates and places of birth and death. Croydon: The Hymn Society of Great Britain, 1977.

696 LINDSAY, T.S. *and others*. The Church's song: a companion to the Church Hymnal. 2nd edition, Dublin: 1920. First published, 1908. Irish hymns, pp. 174–197.

Liturgy

697 CUNNANE, JOSEPH. Recent writings on the liturgy of the sick [with bibliog]. *Furrow*, 11, 1960, 607–21.

698 GOUGAUD, LOUIS. The Celtic liturgies historically considered [with bibliog]. *Cath. Hist. Rev.*, 16, 1930–1, 175–82. See also *Dictionnaire d'archaeologie chrétienne et de liturgie, t.* II, *pt.* 2, 1910, *cols.* 2969–3032. Celtic liturgies [with bibliog.].

699 HAWKES, WILLIAM. The liturgy in Dublin, 1200–1500: manuscript sources. *Rep. Nov.*, 2, 1957–8, 33–67.

700 WHITE, NEWPORT B., *compiler*. The Watson collection: prayer books and related liturgical works given by Edward John Macartney Watson; a catalogue. Dublin: 1948. The collection is in the Representative Church Body Library, Dublin.

CHURCH HISTORY

Bibliographies

701 BRANDRETH, HENRY R.T. Union and reunion: a bibliography. 2nd ed. with supplement. London: 1948.

702 COMMISSION INTERNATIONALE d'HISTOIRE ECCLESIASTIQUE COMPAREE. Bibliographie de la Reforme, 1450–1648; ouvrages parus de 1940 à 1955. Deuxième fascicule. Leiden:

1960. Irelande, sous la direction du R.P. Aubrey Gwynn. pp. 51–61. 196 items.

703 — British Sub-Commission. The Bibliography of the Reform, 1450–1648, relating to the United Kingdom and Ireland for the years 1955–70, edited by Derek Baker; compiled by D.M. Loades, J.K. Cameron, Derek Baker, for the British Sub-Commission. Oxford: 1975.

704 DODD, ROMUALD. Vatican archives: instrumenta miscellanea; documents of Irish interest. *Arch. Hib.*, 19, 1956, 135–40.

705 GIBLIN, CATHALDUS, *ed.* Vatican library. Mss. Barberini Latini: a guide to the material of Irish interest on microfilm in the National Library, Dublin. *Arch. Hib.*, 18, 1955, 67–144.

706 KENNEY, JAMES. F. The sources for the early history of Ireland: an introduction. New York: 1929. Vol. 1. Ecclesiastical. No more published. Reprinted New York and Dublin: 1966.

707 MCNEILL, CHARLES. Publications of Irish interest published by Irish authors on the continent of Europe prior to the eighteenth century. *Bibliog. Soc. Ir.*, 4, 1930, 3–41. Index . . . compiled by Rosalind M. Elmes, *ibid.*, pp. 45–8.

708 MOONEY, CANICE. Short guide to the material of interest for the student of Irish church history in the Franciscan Library, Killiney. Co. Dublin. Killiney: 1954.

709 PIN, LOUIS ELLIES DU. Bibliothèque des auteurs ecclésiastiques. Paris: 1701–4. 46 vols.

710 — [Another edition] Dublin: 1722–4, 3 vols.

Calendars and Registers

711 BERNARD, J.H. Calendar of documents contained in the chartulary commonly called *Dignitas Decani* of St. Patrick's Cathedral. *R. Ir. Acad. Proc., Sec. C*, 25, 1904–5, 481–507.

712 CONLAN, PATRICK. A short-title calendar of Hibernia 1 (1706–1869), in the General Archives of the Friars Minor, Rome. *Coll. Hib.*, nos. 18–19, 1976–77, 132–183.

713 LAWLOR, H.J. Calendar of the *Liber Ruber* of the diocese of Ossory. *R. Ir. Acad. Proc., Sec. C*, 27, 1908–9, 159–208.

714 — A Calendar of the *Liber Niger* and *Liber Albus* of Christ Church, Dublin. *ibid.*, 27, 1908–9, 1–93.

715 — A Calendar of the Register of Archbishop Sweteman [1368–71]. *ibid.*, 29, 1911–12, 213–310.

716 — A Calendar of the Register of Archbishop Fleming. *ibid.*, 30, 1912–13, 94–190. Covers first half of fifteenth century and is supplementary to the *Register of Archbishop Sweteman*.

717 MCNEILL, CHARLES, *ed.* Calendar of Archbishop Alen's Register, *c.* 1172–1534; being the extra volume of the Royal Society of Antiquaries of Ireland for 1949. Dublin: 1950.

718 TIERNEY, MARK. A short-title calendar of the papers of Archbishop James Butler II in the Archbishop's House, Thurles. Pt. I, 1764–86. *Coll. Hib.*, nos. 18–19, 1976–77. 105–131.

General Church History

719 ARCHIVIUM HIBERNICUM, or Irish historical records. Maynooth, Record Society, St. Patrick's College. Vol. 1–, 1912–.

720 BETHELL, DENIS. English monks and Irish reform in the eleventh and twelfth centuries. *Hist. Stud.*, 8, 1971, 111–135.

721 BIELER, LUDWIG. Ireland: harbinger of the Middle Ages. London: 1963. Bibliog., p. 145; first published in German, 1961.

722 BOSSY, JOHN. The Counter-Reformation and the people of Catholic Ireland, 1596–1641. *Hist. Stud.*, 8, 1971, 155–169.

723 BOWEN, DESMOND. Souperism: myth or reality — a study in souperism. Bibliog., pp. 235–248. Cork: Mercier Press, 1970. Special attention is paid to . . . proselytisers who tried to take advantage of the terrible suffering in the west by establishing missionary colonies in Dingle and Achill.

724 BRADY, W.M., *ed.* State papers concerning the Irish Church in the time of Queen Elizabeth. London: 1868.

725 CURTIN, SISTER BENVENUTA., *ed.* Irish material in Fondo Santa Sede, Madrid. [1570–1827] *Arch. Hib.*, 26, 1963, 40–49.

726 Duke, John A. The Columban Church. Oxford: 1932. Bibliog., pp. 171–89.

727 Fenning, Hugh. Some problems of the Irish Mission, 1733–1774: documents from Roman archives. *Coll. Hib*., 8, 1965, 58–109.

728 Giblin, Cathaldus, *ed*. Miscellaneous papers. *Arch. Hib*., 16, 1951, 62–98.

729 — Catalogue of material of Irish interest in the collection *Nunziatura di Fiandra*, Vatican archives: Pt. 4, vols. 102–122, *Coll. Hib*., 5, 1964, 1–130.

730 — Catalogue of material of Irish interest in the collection *Nunziatura di Fiandra*, Vatican Archives: Pt. 6, vols. 133–135Gg. *Coll. Hib*., 10, 1967, 72–138.

731 — Catalogue of material of Irish interest in the collection *Nunziatura de Fiandra*, Vatican Archives: Pt. 7, vols. 135Hh–137. *Coll. Hib*., 11, 1968, 53–90.

732 — Catalogue of material of Irish interest in the collection *Nunziatura di Fiandra*, Vatican Archives: Pt. 8, vols 137A–147C. *Coll. Hib*., 12, 1969, 62–101.

733 — Catalogue of material of Irish interest in the collection *Nunziatura di Fiandra*, Vatican Archives: Pt. 9, vols. 148–152. *Coll. Hib*., 13, 1970, 61–99.

734 — Catalogue of material of Irish interest in the collection *Nunziatura di Fiandra*, Vatican Archives: Pt. 10, vols. 153–153D. *Coll. Hib*., 14, 1971, 36–81.

735 — Catalogue of material of Irish interest in the collection *Nunziatura di Fiandra*, Vatican Archives: Pt. 11, vols. 154–207. *Coll. Hib*., 15, 1972, 7–55.

736 Gougaud, Louis. Modern research with special reference to early Irish ecclesiastical history; lectures delivered at University College, Dublin, April 1929. Dublin: 1929. See also The historical work of Louis Gougaud, *Ir. Hist. Stud*., 3, 1942–3, 180–6.

737 Haddan, A.W. and Stubbs, William. Councils and ecclesiastical documents relating to Great Britain and Ireland. Oxford: 1869–78. 3 vols in 4. Covers period to A.D. 870.

738 Hardinge, Leslie. The Celtic church in Britain. London: 1972. Bibliog., pp. 235–257.

739 Hart, Richard. Ecclesiastical records of England, Ireland, and Scotland to the Reformation. Cambridge: 1836. 2nd ed. 1846.

740 Holloway, Henry. The Reformation in Ireland: a study of ecclesiastical legislation. London, 1919. (*Studies in church history*). Bibliog., pp. 234–5.

741 Hughes, Kathleen. The church in early Irish society. London: 1966. Bibliog., pp. 284–292.

742 Hurley, Michael. The Irish School of Ecumenics. *Month*, vol. 231. no. 1245, 1971, 147–8.

743 — The Irish School of Ecumenics. *Cap. Ann*., 1972, 77–80.

744 Irish Catholic Historical Committee Proceedings. Dublin. No. 1–, 1955–.
1955, pp. 18–27: Irish historical material (mainly ecclesiastical) in archives in France and Spain.
1956, pp. 17–31: Irish ecclesiastical history and the Papal archives.
1958, pp. 1–10: The letters of Innocent III as a source for Irish history, by the Rev. P.J. Dunning.
1958, pp. 11–15: Papal letters of the fifteenth century as a source for Irish history, by Rev. Urban Flanagan.

745 Jennings, Brendan, *ed*. Miscellaneous documents.
1: 1558–1634. *Arch. Hib*., 12, 1946, 70–200.
2: 1625–40. *Arch. Hib*., 14, 1949, 1–49.
3: 1602–1715. *Arch. Hib*., 15, 1950, 1–73.

746 Killen, W.D. The ecclesiastical history of Ireland. London: 1875. 2 vols.

747 Lanigan, John. An ecclesiastical history of Ireland to the beginning of the thirteenth century. Dublin: 1822. 4 vols. 2nd ed., 1829.

748 Lydon, J.F. The Irish Church and taxation in the fourteenth century *Ir. Eccles. Rec*., 103, 1965, 158–165.

749 McEvoy, Brendan. Father James Quigley, priest of Armagh and United Irishmen. *Sean. Ard*., vol. 5. no. 2. 1970, 247–268.

750 MacNaught, John Campbell. The Celtic Church and the See of Peter. Oxford: 1927. Bibliog., pp. v–viii.

751 McNeill, John T. The Celtic churches: a

history, A.D. 200 to 1200. Chicago and London: 1974. Bibliog., pp. 273–279.

752 MARTIN, F.X. Friar Nugent: a study of Francis Lavalin Nugent (1569–1635) agent of the counter-Reformation. Rome and London: 1962. (*Bibliotheca Seraphico-Capuccina cura instituti historici ordinis. Fr. Min. Capuccinorum 21*). Bibliog., pp. XI–XXVII.

753 MEISSNER, JOHN L.G. The Celtic Church in England after the Synod of Whitby. London: 1929. Bibliog., pp. 226–30.

754 MILLETT, BENIGNUS. Calendar of vol. 1 (1625–68) of the Collection *Scritture riferite nei congressi, Irlanda* in Propaganda Archives. *Coll. Hib*., 6–7, 1963–64, 18–211.

755 — Catalogue of vol. 294 of the *Scritture originale riferite nei congressi generali* in the Propaganda Archives. *Coll. Hib*., 8, 1965, 7–37.

756 — Catalogue of Irish material in fourteen vols. of the *Scritture originale riferite nelle congregazioni generali* in Propaganda Archives. *Coll. Hib*., 10, 1967, 7–59.

757 — Catalogue of Irish material in vols. 129–131 of the *Scritture originali riferite nelle congregazioni generali* in Propaganda Archives. *Coll. Hib*., 11, 1968, 7–18.

758 — Catalogue of Irish material in vols. 132–139 of the *Scritture originali riferite nelle congregazioni generali* in Propaganda Archives. *Coll. Hib*., 12, 1969, 7–44.

759 — Catalogue of Irish material in vols. 140–143 of the *Scritture originali nelle congregazioni generali* in Propaganda Archives. *Coll. Hib*., 13, 1970, 21–60.

760 — Calendar of vol. 2 (1669–71) of the *Scritture riferite nei congressi, Irlanda*, in Propaganda Archives: Pt. I, ff. 1–401. *Coll. Hib*., 16, 1973, 7–47; Pt 2, ff. 402–803. *ibid*. no. 17. 1974–5, 17–68.

761 — Calendar of vol. 3 (1672–5) of the *Scritture riferite nei congressi, Irlanda*, in Propaganda Archives: Pt. I, ff. 1–200. *Coll Hib*., 18–19, 1976–77, 40–71.

762 MOULD, D.C. POCHIN. Ireland of the Saints. London: 1953. Bibliog., pp. 171–2.

763 MURPHY, THE REV. IGNATIUS. Some attitudes to religious freedom and ecumenism in Pre-Emancipation Ireland. *Ir. Eccles. Rec*., 105, 1966, 93–104.

764 OLDEN, THE REV. MICHAEL. Counter-Reformation problems: Munster. *Ir. Eccles. Rec*., 104, 1965, 42–54.

765 O'SUILLEABHAIN, PADRAIG. Sidelights on the Irish Church, 1811–38. *Coll. Hib*., 9, 1966, 71–78.

766 RONAN, MYLES V. The Reformation in Dublin, 1536–58 (from original sources). London: 1926. Bibliog., pp. xxix–xxxii.

767 — The Reformation in Ireland under Elizabeth, 1558–80 (from original sources). London: 1930. Bibliog., pp. xxix–xxxii.

768 SEYMOUR, ST. JOHN D. The Puritans in Ireland (1647–61). Oxford: 1921. (*Oxford historical and literary studies*, vol. 12.) Bibliog., pp. xiii–xiv.

769 SHEEHY, MAURICE P. Pontificia Hibernica: medieval papal chancery documents concerning Ireland, 640–1261. Dublin: 1962–65. 2 vols.

770 STUDIA HIBERNICA. Dublin: no. 1– 1961–.

771 WALKER, THE REV. BREIFNE. Blessed Oliver Plunkett and the Popish plot in Ireland. *Ir. Eccles. Rec*., 109, 1968, 313–330.

772 WATT, J.A. The Church and the two nations in medieval Ireland. Cambridge: 1970. (*Cambridge studies in medieval life and thought*, 3 ser. vol. 3).

773 WATT, JOHN. The Church in medieval Ireland. Dublin: 1972. (The Gill History of Ireland; General eds: James Lydon, Margaret Mac Curtain.,) Bibliog., pp. 221–225.

774 WILKINS, DAVID. Concilia Magnae Britanniae et Hiberniae. 446–1717. Londini: 1737. 4 vols.

775 WOODS, C.J. Ireland and Anglo-papal relations, 1880–85. *Ir. Hist. Stud*., vol. 18, no. 69, 1972, 29–60.

776 ZIMMER, HEINRICH. The Celtic Church in Britain and Ireland, translated by A. Meyer. London: 1902. Bibliog., pp. xi–xiv.

Christianity

777 BIELER, LUDWIG. Christianity in Ireland during the fifth and sixth centuries: a survey and

evaluation of sources. *Ir. Eccles. Rec.*, 101, 1964, 162–7.

778 CASE, S.J., *ed.* A bibliographical guide to Christianity . . . Chicago; 1931.

779 CROSS, F.L., *compiler.* The Oxford dictionary of the Christian Church. London: 1957.

780 DOTTIN, GEORGES. Notes bibliographiques sur l'ancienne littérature chrétienne de l'Irlande. *Rev. d'hist. litt. relig.*, 5, 1900, 162–7.

781 GOUGAUD, LOUIS. Christianity in Celtic lands . . . London: 1932. Bibliog., pp. xvii–lv; sources for liturgy, pp. 313–16.

782 — Gaelic pioneers of Christianity: the work and influence of Irish monks and saints in continental Europe (sixth-twelfth century). Dublin: 1923. Bibliog., pp. ix–x.

783 HERON, JAMES. The Celtic Church in Ireland: the story of Irish Christianity to the Reformation. London: 1893.

784 O'BRIAIN, FELIM. The expansion of Irish Christianity to 1200: an historiographical survey. *Ir. Hist. Stud.*, 3, 1942–3, 241–66; 4, 1944–5, 131–63.

Church Furnishings and Related Articles

785 GOGAN, L.S. The Ardagh Chalice: a description of the ministral chalice found at Ardagh in County Limerick in the year 1868, with a note on its traditional conformity to the Holy Grail of legend and story. Dublin: 1932.

786 ODDY, W.A. and MCINTYRE, L.M. St. Mel's Crozier — technical examination and report on conservation and restoration in 1971–2. *R. Soc. Antiq. Ir. J.*, 103, 1973, 35–46.

Personal Holy Wells

787 MACBRIDE, PATRICK. Saint Patrick's Purgatory in Spanish literature. *Studies*, 25, 1936, 277–291.

788 O'DANACHAIR, CAOIMHIN. The Holy Wells of Co. Limerick. *R. Soc. Antiq. Ir. J.*, 85, 1966, 193–217.

789 — The Holy Wells of North County Kerry. *R. Soc. Antiq. Ir. J.*, 88, 1958, 153–163.

790 RYAN, PATRICK. Saint Patrick's Purgatory. *Studies*, 21, 1932, 443–460.

Sermons

791 O'SUILLEABHAIN, PADRAIG. Catholic sermon books printed in Ireland, [1700–1850]. *Ir. Eccles. Rec.*, 99, 1963, 31–36.

Church and Social Problems

792 DALY, CATHAL B. Violence in Ireland and Christian conscience. Dublin: 1973.

Penance and Confession

793 BIELER, LUDWIG, *ed.* The Irish Penitentials; with an appendix, by D.A. Binchy. Dublin: 1963. (*Scriptores Latini Hiberniae vol. 5.*).

Missions

794 BROWN, STEPHEN J. Foreign missions: a survey. *Studies*, 15, 1926, 105–120.

795 COLGAN, *The Rev.* JOHN. Irish missionaries in South Africa. *Studies*, 20, 1931, 611–626.

796 CONCANNON, HELENA. Irish missionaries in Liberia. *Studies*, 36, 1947, 431–438.

797 DORR, DONAL. The theology of the Irish Missionary Union. *Furrow*, 22, 1971, 210–221.

798 GIBLIN, CATHALDUS. St. Oliver Plunkett, Francis MacDonell, O.F.M., and the mission to the Hebrides. *Coll. Hib.*, 17, 1974–5, 69–102.

799 GWYNN, AUBREY. The first Irish priests in the new world. *Studies* 21, 1932, 213–228.

800 HALLY, CYRIL. A hundred years of Irish missionary effort. *Furrow*, 22, 1971, 335–349.

801 SHANAHAN, JOSEPH. LEEN, EDWARD. A great Irish missionary: Bishop Joseph Shanahan, C.S. Sp., 6 June 1871–25 December 1943. *Studies*, 33, 1944, 145–157.

802 ARINZE FRANCIS. The Great Apostle of Southern Nigeria. *Furrow*, 22, 1971, 316–319.

803 — CORKERY, SEAN. Missionary with an Irish accent. *ibid.* 22, 1971, 319–335.

Liturgy Public Worship

804 BURKE-SAVAGE, ROLAND. The growth of

devotion to the Sacred Heart in Ireland. *Ir. Eccles. Rec.,* 110, 1968, 185–208.

805 CREHAN, JOSEPH H. The liturgical trade route: east to west. *Studies,* 65, 1976, 87–99.

806 O'DWYER, PETER. Devotion to Mary in Ireland, A.D. 700–1100. Dublin: 1976.

807 PYLE, HILARY. You can say that again: common prayer in the Church of Ireland. Dublin: 1977.

Religious Communities

808 McCREARY, ALF. Corrymeela: the search for peace. Belfast; 1975.

Diocesan History

809 BARROW, LENNOX. Glendalough and St. Kevin. Dundalk: 1972. Bibliog., pp. 49–50.

810 BOLSTER, EVELYN. A history of the Diocese of Cork from the earliest times to the Reformation. Shannon: 1972. Bibliog., pp. 505–528.

811 BRADY, J., *ed.* Documents concerning the diocese of Meath. *Arch Hib., new ser.,* 8, 1941, 203–43.

812 BRADY, W.M. Clerical and parochial records of Cork, Cloyne, and Ross, taken from parish registers, Mss. in the principal libraries and public offices of Oxford, Dublin and London, and from private or family papers. Dublin: 1863–4. 3 vols.

813 COMERFORD, M. Collections relating to the dioceses of Kildare and Leighlin. Dublin: [1883–6] 3 vols.

814 CURRAN, M.J. Dublin diocesan archives. *Rep. Nov.,* 2, 1957–8, 1–5.

815 FENNING, HUGH. A guide to eighteenth-century reports on Irish Dioceses in the archives of Propaganda Fide. *Coll. Hib.*, 11, 1968, 19–35.

816 FLOOD, W.H. GRATTAN. The diocesan manuscripts of Ferns during the rule of Bishop Sweetman (1745–86). *Arch. Hib.,* 1913, 100–6; 3, 1914, 113–23.

817 GLEESON, DERMOT F. A history of the diocese of Killaloe. Dublin: 1962. Pt. I. The early period, by The Rev. Aubrey Gwynn. Pt. 2–4 The Middle Ages, by Dermot F. Gleeson. Bibliog., pp. 537–544.

818 GWYNN, AUBREY, *ed.* Documents relating to the medieval diocese of Armagh. *Arch. Hib.,* 13, 1947, 1–29.

819 IRISH CATHOLIC HISTORICAL COMMITTEE PROCEEDINGS, 1957, pp. 31–7. A handlist of Irish diocesan histories.

820 — 1957, pp. 25–30. Sources for the history of the clergy of the diocese: seventeenth-century Clogher, by The Rev. Patrick Gallagher.

821 MACNAMEE, JAMES J. History of the diocese of Ardagh. Dublin: 1954. Bibliog., pp. 801–12.

822 O'SHEA, KIERAN. Bishop [Francis] Moylan's *relatio status,* 1785. *J. Kerry Arch. Hist. Soc.,* 7, 1974, 21–36. *Relatio status* is an episcopal report of the material and spiritual state of a diocese. This is the earliest known for Kerry.

823 SILKE, J.J. A preliminary guide to Irish diocesan and local history. In preparation for Irish Catholic Historical Committee.

824 SOURCES RELATING TO THE HISTORY OF A DIOCESE: Armagh. *Ir. Cath. Hist. Comm. Proc.,* 1955, 1–17.

Parish Histories

825 CHAVASSE, CLAUDE. The story of Baltinglass: a history of the parishes of Baltinglass, Ballynure and Rathbran in County Wicklow. Lemybrien, (Co. Wexford): 1920.

826 CLARKE, J.W. The Parish of St. Olave. *Dublin Hist. Rec.,* 11, 1949–50, 116–123.

827 CREAN, CYRIL P. *ed.* Parish of the Sacred Heart, Donnybrook. Dublin, [1966].

828 DONNELLY, N. A short history of some Dublin parishes. Facsimile ed., with an introduction by Thomas Wall. Facsimile reprint of 1st ed. Dublin: 1905. Pt. 1– 1977–.

829 DUFFICY, MAURICE. The story of St. James's church, James's Street, Dublin. *Dublin Hist. Rec.,* vol. 29, no. 2, 1976, 66–69.

830 ELLISON, *The Rev.* C.C. Early 19th century lists of Protestant parishioners in the diocese of Meath. *Ir. Ancest.,* vol. 5, 1973, 37–53.

831 NICHOLLS, K.W. Rectory, vicarage and parish in the western Irish dioceses. *R. Soc.*

Antiq. Ir. J., 101, 1971, 53–84.

832 O'SUILLEABHAIN, PADRAIG. Documents relating to Wexford friary and parish, 1773–98. *Coll. Hib.,* 8, 1965, 110–128.

833 POYNTZ, S.G. St. Ann's: the church in the heart of the city. [Dublin: 1976].

834 YOUNG, CANON E.J. St. Michan's parish in the eighteenth century. *Dublin Hist. Rec.*, 3, 1940–41, 1–7.

Archbishops and Bishops

835 BALE, JOHN, *Bishop of Ossory*. Davies, W.T. A bibliography of John Bale. *Oxford Bibliog. Soc. Proc.,* 5, 1940, 201–79.

836 BOLSTER, EVELYN. The Moylan Correspondence in Bishops House, Killarney: Pt. 1. *Coll. Hib.,* 14, 1971, 82–142. Francis Moylan, Bishop of Cork.

837 BONNER, BRIAN. Reamann O Gallachair, Bishop of Derry, [1569–1601]. *Donegal Ann.,* vol. 11, no. 1, 1974, 41–52.

838 BRADY, WILLIAM MAZIERE. The episcopal successions in England, Scotland and Ireland, A.D. 1400 to 1875. [1st. ed. reprinted] with a new introduction by A.F. Allison. Farnborough: 1971. 3 vols. Facsimile reprint of 1st ed. Rome, 1876–77.

839 BROWNE, THE REV. P.W. Irish bishops in Newfoundland (1794–1893). *Studies,* 20, 1931, 49–66.

840 CAMPBELL, ANDREW. Andrew Campbell, Bishop of Kilmore, 1753–1769; introduction by The Rev. Patrick J. Campbell. *Louth Arch. J.,* vol. 18, no. 4, 1976, 296–7. *See also* Andrew Campbell, Bishop of Kilmore, 1753–1769: student days in Spain, by Micheline Walsh. *ibid.,* 298–303.

841 CHART, D.A., *ed.* The Register of John Swayne, Archbishop of Armagh and Primate of Ireland, 1418–39, with some entries of earlier and later archbishops. Belfast: 1935. (*Northern Ireland Record publication.*)

842 COEN, MARTIN. The Post-Reformation Catholic bishops of Kilfenora. *Nth. Munster Arch. J.,* 12, 1969, 53–62.

843 COOMBES, THE REV. JAMES. The life and times of Archbishop Denis O'Driscoll (1600–1650). *Cork Hist. Arch. Soc. J.,* 70, 1965, 108–119.

844 CORNISH, PATRICK J. *ed.* Bishop Wadding's Notebook. *Arch. Hib.,* 29, 1970, 49–114.

845 D'ALTON, JOHN. The memoirs of the archbishops of Dublin. Dublin: 1838.

846 ELLISON, C.C. Bishop Dopping's Visitation Book. 1682–86. *Riocht na Midhe* vol. 5. no. 1. 1971, 28–39; no. 2., 1972, 3–13; no. 3., 1973, 3–11; no. 4., 1974, 98–103; vol. 6. no. 1., 1975, 3–13.

847 FEENEY, JOHN. John Charles McQuaid: the man and the mask. Dublin and Cork: 1974.

848 GATHORNE-HARDY, ROBERT, and WILLIAMS, WILLIAM PROCTOR. A bibliography of the writings of Jeremy Taylor to 1700, with a section of Tayloriana. Dekalb, (Illinois): 1971.

849 GIBLIN, CATHALDUS, *ed.* The nomination of Denis Moriarty for the see of Ardfert, 1697–1747. *Arch. Hib.,* 29, 1970, 115–132.

850 GILBERT, JOHN T. 'Crede Mihi': the most ancient register of the archbishops of Dublin before the Reformation. Dublin: 1897.

851 GREEN, E.R.R. Thomas Percy [Bishop of Dromore, 1782–1811]. *Ulster Folk.*, 15–16, 1970, 224–232.

852 HEGARTY, MAUREEN. Dr. Richard Pococke [Bishop of Ossory]. *Old Kilk. Rev.,* 15, 1963, 48–54.

853 HOWLETT, LIAM. Saint Laurence O'Toole, Archbishop of Dublin. *Cap. Ann.,* 1971, 373–386.

854 KNOX, R. BUICK. James Ussher, Archbishop of Armagh. Cardiff: 1967. Bibliog., pp. 194–201.

855 LANIGAN, MRS. K.M. Richard de Ledrede, Bishop of Ossory [1280–1360]. *Old. Kilk. Rev.,* 15, 1963, 23–29.

856 LYSAGHT, MOIRE. Daniel Murray. Archbishop of Dublin 1823–1852. *Dublin Hist. Rec.*, vol. 17, no. 3, 1974, 101–108.

857 MACCARTHY, R.B. A regency prelate [Dr. Joseph Stock] in Ireland. *Church Qtr. Rev.,* 165, 1964, 449–460.

858 MCELLIGOTT, THOMAS. Recall to a pioneer: John England, Bishop of Charleston. *Ir. Eccles. Rec.,* 105, 1966, 173–179.

859 MacGiolla Phadraig, Dr. Brian. Dr. John Carpenter, Archbishop of Dublin, 1760–1786. *Dublin Hist. Rec.,* vol. 30, no. 1, 1976, 2–17.

860 Meagher, Claude. Calendar of the papers of Dr. Bray, Archbishop of Cashel and Emly (1792–1820). *Cork Hist. Arch. Soc. J.*, 73, 1968, 81–113; 74, 1969, 40–70, 157–183; 75, 1970, 58–92.

861 Meagher, John. Edmond Byrne (1656–1723), Archbishop of Dublin. *Rep. Nov.,* vol. 3, no. 2, 1963–64, 378–386.

862 Mohan, Christopher. Archbishop Richard Robinson, builder of Armagh. *Sean. Ard.*, vol. 6, no. 1, 1971, 94–130.

863 O'Brien, A.F. Episcopal elections in Ireland, *c.* 1254–72. *R. Ir. Acad. Proc.* 73, Sec. C, no. 5. 1973, 129–176.

864 O'Donnell, James Louis. O'Connell, Philip. Dr. James Louis O'Donnell (1737–1811), first bishop of Newfoundland. *Ir. Eccels. Rec.,* 103, 1965, 308–324.

865 O'Dwyer, *Sir* Michael F. The Adventures of Bishop Edmund O'Dwyer, 1641–1654. *Studies*, 32, 1933, 12–28.

866 Purcell, Mary. Archbishop John Thomas Troy (1739–1823). *Dublin Hist. Rec.,* vol. 31, no. 2. 1978, 42–52.

867 Renehan, Laurence F. Collections on Irish Church history from the Mss. of the late V. Rev. L.F. Renehan, president of Maynooth College. Edited by The Rev. Daniel McCarthy.
Vol. 1: Irish archbishops. [Dublin: 1861.]
Vol. 2: Irish bishops. Dublin: 1874.

868 Rennison, *The Rev.* William H. *compiler.* Succession list of bishops, cathedral and parochial clergy of the dioceses of Waterford and Lismore, from the earliest times, together with some hitherto unpublished records. [Waterford: 1920]. Bibliog., pp. v–x.

869 Savage, Roland Burke. The Church in Dublin: 1940–1965: study of the achievement and of the personality of the Most Reverend John Charles McQuaid, D.D., silver jubilee of his episcopate. *Studies,* 54, 1965, 297–346.

870 Seaver, George. John Allen Fitzgerald Gregg, archbishop. London and Dublin: 1962. Archbishop of Dublin and afterwards Archbishop of Armagh.

871 Silke, John J. The Irish Peter Lombard [Archbishop of Armagh, 1601–25] *Studies*, 64, 1975, 143–155.

872 Talbot, Peter. Primatus Dublinensis: the primacy of the See of Dublin . . . Translated by W.E. Kenny. Dublin: 1947.

873 Tallon, Maura. A famous patriot bishop of Kildare and Leighlin. [Dr. James Warren Doyle]. *Kildare Arch. Soc. J.,* vol. 14, no. 2, 1966–67, 254–261.

874 Theiner, Augustin. Vetera monumenta Hibernorum et Scotorum historiam illustrantia, 1216–1547. Rome: 1864. Contains valuable collection of papal letters to bishops of Ireland.

875 Tierney, Mark. Croke of Cashel: the life of Archbishop Thomas William Croke, 1823–1902. Dublin: 1976.

876 — A short-title calendar of the papers of Archbishop Thomas William Croke in Archbishop's House, Thurles. Pt. 1, 1841–1885. *Coll. Hib.,* 13, 1970, 100–138.

877 Traynor, Owen F. Dr. James Magauran, Bishop of Ardagh [1815–29]. *Breifne,* vol. 4, no. 15, 1972, 336–344.

878 — Dr. Eugene McParlan: candidate for the Bishopric of Kilmore. *Breifne*, vol. 4, no. 15, 1972, 450–1.

879 Valkenberg, Augustine. Walter Wellesley, bishop of Kildare, 147?–1539. *Kildare Arch. Soc. J.,* vol. 14, no. 5, 1970, 518–543. See also *ibid,* 544–563. The tomb of Bishop Walter Wellesley, at Great Connell Prior, Co. Kildare.

880 Ware, James. Depraesulibus Hiberniae commentarius. Dublin, 1665. History of the bishops of Ireland, translated by Walter Harris, in *Whole Works of James Ware,* vol. 1. Dublin: 1739: reprinted 1764. One of the best general works on Irish bishops.

881 Whelen, Patrick. Anthony Blake, Archbishop of Armagh, 1758–1787. *Sean Ard.,* vol. 5, no. 2, 1970, 289–323.

882 Woods, C.J. The politics of Cardinal McCabe, Archbishop of Dublin, 1879–85. *Dublin Hist. Rec.*, vol. 26, no. 3, 1973, 101–110.

Personal Religion

883 LESLIE, SHANE. Saint Patrick's purgatory: a record from history and literature. London: 1932. Bibliog., pp. 195–215.

884 O'DANACHAIR, CAOIMHIN. The holy wells of Corkaguiney, County Kerry. *R. Soc. Antiq. Ir. J.,* 90, 1960, 67–78.

885 — The holy wells of County Dublin [and supplement]. *Rep. Nov*., 2, 1957–60, 68–87; 233–5.

Monasticism, Religious Orders, Education

886 ANSON, P.F. The religious orders and congregations of Great Britain and Ireland. Worcester: 1949.

887 ARCHDALL, MERVYN. Monasticon Hibernicum. Dublin: 1786. Another edition, edited by P.F. Moran. 1873–6. 2 vols.

888 BOYLE, PATRICK. The Irish college in Paris from 1578 to 1901. London: 1901. Bibliog., pp. xiii–xv.

889 BRADSHAW, BRENDAN. The dissolution of the religious orders in Ireland under Henry VIII. London: 1974.

890 BRADY, JOHN. The Irish colleges in the Low Countries [documents from the San Clemente archives relating to the Irish colleges in Flanders]. *Arch. Hib*., 14, 1949, 66–91.

891 — The Irish colleges at Douai and Antwerp [documents]. *Arch. Hib*., 13, 1947, 45–66.

892 BROWNE, MICHAEL. Irish College at Salamanca. *Furrow*, 22, 1971, 697–702.

893 CUNNINGHAM, T.P. and GALLOGLY, *The Rev.* DANIEL. St. Patrick's College and the earlier Kilmore Academy: a centenary history. Cavan: 1974.

894 DEGNAN, M. BERTRAND. Mercy unto thousands [life of Mary Catherine McAuley, founder of the Sisters of Mercy]. Dublin: 1958. Bibliog., pp. 383–5.

895 DIRECTORY OF RELIGIOUS ORDERS, Congregations and Societies of Great Britain and Ireland. Glasgow: 1972.

896 FINEGAN, FRANCIS. The Irish College of Poitiers, 1674–1762. *Ir. Eccles. Rec.*, 104, 1965, 18–35.

897 — Rectors of the Irish College of Salamanca, 1705–67. *Ir. Eccles. Rec*., 110, 1968, 231–241.

898 GLANCY, MICHAEL. The Primates and church lands of Armagh. *Sean. Ard.*, vol. 5, no. 2, 1970, 370–396.

899 GWYNN, AUBREY and HADCOCK, R. NEVILLE. Medieval religious houses in Ireland: with an appendix to early sites. London: 1970. Bibliog., pp. 15–19.

900 HANLY, JOHN. Sources for the history of the Irish College, Rome. *Ir. Eccles. Rec*., 102, 1964. 28–34.

901 JENNINGS, BRENDAN, *ed*. Documents of the Irish colleges at Douai. *Arch. Hib*., 10, 1943, 163–210.

902 — Reports on Irish colleges in the Low Countries, 1649–1700. *Arch. Hib.*, 16, 1951, 1–39.

903 JONES, FREDERICK M. Documents concerning the Collegium Pastorale Hibernicum at Louvain, 1624. *Arch. Hib*., 16, 1951, 40–61.

904 LIST OF IRISH MONASTIC CHARTULARIES. In Richard Sims' *Manual for the genealogist* . . . 1856, p. 27.

905 MOULD, DAPHNE D.C. POCHIN. The Monasteries of Ireland: an introduction. London: 1976. Bibliog., pp. 184–8.

906 O'FIAICH, TOMAS. The Monastic life in early Christian Ireland. *Cap. Ann*., 1969, 116–134.

907 REEVES, WILLIAM. The culdees of the British islands. Dublin: 1864. Also appeared in *R. Ir. Acad. Trans*., 24, 1873, 119–263.

908 RYAN, JOHN. Irish monasticism: origins and early development [Photolitrographic facsimile of 1st ed. with new introduction] Shannon: 1972. Bibliog., pp. 415–481.

909 SILKE, *The Rev. J. ed.* The Irish College, Seville [sources and history]. *Arch. Hib*., 24, 1961; 103–147.

910 STEELE, FRANCESCA M. The convents of Great Britain. London and Dublin: 1902.

911 TIPTON, CHARLES L. The Irish Hospitallers during the schism. *R. Ir. Acad. Proc.*, Sec. C, vol. 69, no. 3, 1970, 33–43.

912 WALSH, T.J. Some records of the Irish col-

leges at Bordeaux. *Arch. Hib.*, 15, 1950, 92–141.

913 — Nano Nagle and the Presentation Sisters. Dublin: 1959. Bibliog., pp. 419–22.

914 WHITE, NEWPORT B. *ed.* Extents of Irish monastic possessions, 1540–1, from manuscripts in the Public Record Office, London. Dublin, Irish Manuscripts Commission, 1943.

Ecumenical Movement

915 IRISH EPISCOPAL CONFERENCE. Directory on ecumenism for Ireland. Dublin: 1976.

Cistercians

916 BUTLER, CONSTANCE MARY, and BERNARD, JOHN HENRY. The charters of the Cistercian abbey of Duiske in the county of Kilkenny. *R. Ir. Acad. Proc., Sec. C*, 35, 1918–20, 1–188.

917 CONWAY, COLUMCILLE *ed.* The Irish Cistercian documents in Octavian's Register, Armagh. *Seanchas Ardmhaca*, vol. 2, no. 2, 1957, 269–94.

918 — Sources for the history of the Irish Cistercians, 1142–1540. *Ir. Cath. Hist. Comm. Proc.*, 1958, 16–23.

919 — The story of Mellifont. Dublin: 1958. Bibliog., pp. 304–9.

920 HARTRY, MALACHY. Triumphalia chronologica monasterii S. Crucis (Co. Tipperary). De Cisterciensium Hibernorum viris illustribus. Edited with a translation by Denis Murphy. Dublin: 1895.

921 MACNIOCAILL, GEAROID. Na Manaigh Liatha in Eirinn, 1142–*c.* 1600. Dublin: 1959. Bibliog., pp. 223–8.

922 O'DWYER, BARRY. The Conspiracy of Mellifont, 1216–1231: an episode in the history of the Cistercian order in medieval Ireland. Dublin: Dublin Historical Association, 1970. (*Medieval Irish History series, no. 2*.) Appendix I. List of Cistercian monasteries in medieval Ireland, by Fr. Colmalle Conway.

923 — Gaelic monasticism and the Irish Cistercians, *c.* 1228. *Ir. Eccles. Rec.*, 108, 1967, 19–28.

924 THOMPSON, A. HAMILTON *and others*. The Cistercian order in Ireland, by Prof. A. Hamilton Thompson, A.W. Clapham, and H.G. Leask. *Archaeol. J.*, 88, 1931, 1–36.

Benedictines

925 COOMBES, *The Rev.* J. The Benedictine priory of Ross. *Cork Hist. Arch. Soc. J.*, 73, 1968, 152–160.

Dominicans

926 CURRAN, ARTHUR. The Dominican order in Carlingford and Dundalk. *Louth Arch. J.*, vol. 16, no. 3, 1967, 143–60.

927 DE BURGO, THOMAS. Hibernia Dominicana: sive historia provinciae Hibernae ordinis praedicatorum. Colon, 1762–72. Though bearing the imprint of Cologne, was executed by Edmund Finn, at Kilkenny, under Burgh's own direction; reprinted with a new introduction by Thomas Wall. Farnborough: 1970.

928 FENNING, HUGH. The Athenry House-Chronicle, 1666–1779. *Coll. Hib.*, 11, 1968, 36–52. 'The chief objective has been to include every item of Dominican interest'.

929 — The Book of Receptions and Professions of SS Sixtus and Clement in Rome, 1676–1792. *Coll. Hib.*, 14, 1971, 13–35.

930 — The Dominicans of Mullingar, 1622–1654. *Riocht na Midhe*, vol. 3, no. 4, 1966, 299–314.

931 — The Dominicans of Mullingar, 1667–1696. *Riocht na Midhe*, vol. 4, no. 2, 1968, 20–32.

932 — The Dominicans of Trim, 1713–1883. *Riocht na Midhe*, vol. 2, no. 4, 1962, 21–32. Includes 'Bibliographical Directory of priests affiliated to Donore, 1720–1833.

933 — A list of Dominicans in Ireland, 1817. *Coll. Hib.*, 9, 1966, 79–82.

934 — The Vestiary-book of the Irish Dominicans in Rome, 1727–1796. *Coll. Hib.*, 10, 1967, 60–71.

935 KEARNS, CONLETH, *ed.* Archives of the Irish Dominican College, San Clemente, Rome: a summary report. *Arch. Hib.*, 18, 1955, 145–9.

936 MOULD, D.C. POCHIN. The Irish Dominicans. Dublin: 1957. Bibliog., pp. 267–71.

937 O'SULLIVAN, B. The Dominicans in mediaeval Dublin. *Dublin Hist. Rec.*, 9, 1946–8, 41–58.

938 QUETIF, JACOBUS and ECHARD, JACOBUS. Scriptores ordinis praedicatorum recensiti, notisque historic et criticis illustrati. Inchoavit Jacobus Quetif absolvit Jacobus Echard. Lutetiae Parisiorum, 1719–21. 2 vols.

939 — Editio altera . . . ad hanc nostram aetatem perducta curis et labore Fr. Remigii Coulon [Antonin Papillon]. Parisiis, 1910–34.

940 VALKENBURG, AUGUSTINE. The Ven. Peter Higgins, Dominican, 1601?–1642. *Kildare Arch. Soc. J.*, vol. 15, no. 3, 1973–4, 284–309.

941 WALSH, DERMOT. The Dominicans of Arklow. *Rep. Nov.*, vol. 3, no. 2, 1963–64, 307–323.

Franciscans

942 COLEMAN, JAMES. A mediaeval Irish monastic library catalogue [Franciscan friary at Youghal]. *Bibliog. Soc. Ir.*, 2, 1921–5, 111–20.

943 CONLON, PATRICK. Franciscan Ireland: the story of seven hundred and fifty years of the Friars Minor in Ireland . . . with notes on all the major sites associated with the friars . . . and a brief description of the other members of the Franciscan family in Ireland. Dublin and Cork: 1978. Bibliog., pp. 115–6.

944 EGAN, BARTHOLOMEW. An eminent Franciscan of the emancipation era [William Aloysious O'Meara]. *Cork Hist. Arch. Soc. J.*, 76, 1971, 21–23.

945 — Franciscan Limerick: the order of St. Francis in the city of Limerick. Limerick: 1971.

946 — Some Irish theses in The Hague. *Col. Hib.*, 8, 1965, 43–46. Refers to priests who were connected with the Irish Franciscan College at Louvain in Belgium.

947 — Superiors of the Franciscan Friaries at Adare, Askeaton and Limerick. *Nth. Munster Antiq. J.*, 14, 1971, 41–45.

948 FAULKNER, ANSELM. Liber Dubliniensis: chapter documents of the Irish Franciscans, 1719–1875. Killiney: 1978.

949 FITZMAURICE, E.B. and LITTLE, ANDREW GEORGE, *compilers*. Materials for the history of the Franciscan Province of Ireland, A.D. 1230–1450. Farnborough (Hants): 1966. Fascimile reprint of 1st ed., Manchester: 1920.

950 GIBLIN, CATHALDUS. The Franciscan ministry in the diocese of Clogher. *Clogher Rec.*, vol. 7, no. 2, 1970, 149–203.

951 — Irish Franciscan mission to Scotland, 1619–1646: documents from Roman archives. Dublin: 1964.

952 — Liber Lovaniensis: a collection of Irish Franciscan documents, 1629–1717. Dublin: 1956.

953 — A list of personnel of the Franciscan Province of Ireland, 1770. *Coll. Hib.*, 8, 1965, 47–57.

954 — Papers relating to Meelick Friary, 1664–1731. *Coll. Hib.*, 16, 1973, 48–88.

955 GILBERT, JOHN T. The manuscripts of the former College of Irish Franciscans, Louvain. London: 1874. *4th report of the Royal Commission on Historical Manuscripts. Pt. 1. Report and Appendix C.* pp. 599–613.

956 HICKS, ERIC. Unique library of history and Celtic studies. [Franciscan House of Celtic study and Historical Research, Killiney] *Hibernia*, vol. 29, no. 11, 1965, 11, 17.

957 HISTORICAL MANUSCRIPTS COMMISSION. Report on Franciscan manuscripts preserved at the convent, Merchant's Quay, Dublin. Dublin: 1906. See also *The Franciscan Library, Merchant's Quay, Dublin*, by the Rev. Canice Mooney, *An Leab.*, 8, 1941–5, 29–37.

958 JENNINGS, BRENDAN. Brussels Ms. 3947: Donatus Moneyus de Provincia Hiberniae S. Francisci. *Anal. Hib.*, 6, 1934, 12–138.

959 — Documents from the archives of St. Isidore's College, Rome. *Anal. Hib.*, 6, 1934, 203–47.

960 — Documents of the Irish Franciscan College at Prague. *Arch. Hib.*, 9, 1942, 173–294.

961 — The Irish Franciscans at Boulay [documents]. *Arch. Hib*., 11, 1944, 118–53.

962 — The Irish Franciscans in Poland [documents]. *Arch. Hib*., 20, 1957, 38–56.

963 — *ed*. Louvain papers, 1606–1827; prepared for publication and indexed by Cathaldus Giblin. Dublin: 1968. Consists almost exclusively of the documents which constitute the archives of the College of St. Anthony which was founded at Louvain by the Irish Franciscans in 1606.

964 KELLY, R.J. The Irish Franciscans in Prague (1629–1786): their literary labours. *R. Soc. Antiq. Ir. J.*, 52, 1922, 169–74.

965 MILLETT, BENIGNUS. The Irish Franciscans, 1651–1665. Rome: 1964. (*Analecta Gregoriana* vol. 129. *Series Facultatis Historiae Ecclesiasticae: sectio B*, n. 22). Bibliog., pp. xi–xviii.

966 MOLONEY, JOSEPH. Brussels Ms. 3410: a chronological list of the foundations of the Irish Franciscan province. *Anal. Hib*., 6, 1934, 192–202.

967 MOONEY, CANICE. Devotional writings of the Irish Franciscans, 1224–1950. Kilkenny: 1952. Edition limited to 300 copies.

968 — Franciscan Library, Killiney, Co. Dublin: a short guide for the student of Irish Church history. *Arch. Hib*., 18, 1955, 150–6.

969 — Irish Franciscan relations with France, 1224–1850. Killiney: 1951.

970 — The Franciscans in Waterford. *Cork Hist. Arch. Soc. J*., 69, 1964, 73–93.

971 — The Friars of Broad Lane: the story of a Franciscan friary in Cork, 1229–1977; revised and extended by Bartholomew Egan. Cork: 1977. Collector's ed. of 305 numbered copies.

972 — Irish Franciscans and France [2nd ed.], Dublin and London: 1964. Previous ed. published as *Irish Franciscan relations with France 1224–1850*. 1951.

973 O'CONNELL, W.D. Cork Franciscan records (1764–1831). Cork: 1942. (*Historical and archaeological papers, ser. no. 3*.)

974 RYAN, MARTIN. The Franciscan houses of Thomond in 1616. *Nth. Munster Antiq. J*., 10, 1966–67, 112–115.

975 WADDING, LUKE. Father Luke Wadding and St. Isidore's College, Rome: biographical and historical notes and documents. A contribution to the tercentenary celebrations. 1625–1925, by Gregory Cleary. Rome: 1925.

976 — Guide to material for a biography of Father Luke Wadding, by Benignus Millett. In *Father Luke Wadding: commemorative volume*, edited by the Franciscan Fathers. Dublin: 1957, pp. 229–62.

977 — The writings of Father Luke Wadding, O.F.M., by Canice Mooney. *Fran. Stud*., 18, 1958, 225–39.

978 WALSH, KATHERINE. Franciscan friaries in pre-Reformation Kerry. *Kerry Arch. Hist. Soc. J*., 9, 1976, 16–31.

Capuchins

979 CAPUCHIN ANNUAL. Dublin: 1930–77.

980 MARTIN, FRANCIS X. Sources for the history of the Irish Capuchins. *Coll. Fran*., 26, 1956, 67–79.

981 O'DONOVAN, CONRAD. The Capuchins in Dublin. *Cap. Ann*., 1972, 171–200.

982 — The Irish Capuchins in the United States of America. *Cap. Ann*., 1973, 249–289.

983 O'SHEA, TIMOTHY P. The Irish Capuchins in Capetown and Zambia. *Cap. Ann*., 1975, 267–313.

Augustinians

984 BATTERSBY, WILLIAM J. A history of all the abbeys, convents, churches, and other religious houses of the Order, particularly of the Hermits of St. Augustine in Ireland, from the earliest period to the present time; with biographical sketches of the bishops, provincials, priors, etc. of that holy institute. Dublin: 1856.

985 HACKETT, F.X. The Tirry documents in the Augustinian general archives. *Arch. Hib*., 20, 1957, 98–122.

986 MARTIN, FRANCIS X. Archives of the Irish Augustinians, Rome: a summary report. *Arch. Hib*., 18, 1955, 157–63.

987 — and MEIJER, A. DE. Irish material in the Augustinian archives, Rome, 1354–1624. *Arch. Hib.*, 19, 1956, 61–134.

988 — The Tirry documents in the Archives de France, Paris. *Arch. Hib.*, 20, 1957, 69–97. William Tirry, O.S.A., executed 1654.

Jesuits

989 BACKER, AUGUSTIN, and BACKER, ALOIS DE. Bibliothèque des écrivains de la Compagne de Jesus. Liege: 1853–61. 7 vols.

990 BATTERSBY, WILLIAM J. The Jesuits in Dublin or, brief biographic sketches of those deceased members of the Society of Jesus who were born or who laboured in the Irish metropolis: with an account of the parish of St. Michan, their ancient residence . . . Dublin: 1854.

991 FINNEGAN, FRANCIS. The Jesuits and Athlone in the seventeenth and eighteenth centuries. *J. Old Athlone Soc.*, vol. 1, no. 2, 1970–1, 77–83.

992 HOGAN, EDMUND J. Chronological catalogue of the Irish members of the Society of Jesus, from 1550 to 1814. [Half title only.] n.p., n.d. [with index]. In National Library of Ireland, Dublin. Forms Appendix to Henry Foley's Records of the English Province of the Society of Jesus, vol. 7, pt. 2. 1883.

993 THE MANUSCRIPTS OF THE JESUITS IN IRELAND. *Hist. Mss. Comm. Rpt.*, no. 10, Appendix 5, pp. 340–79.

994 OLIVER, GEORGE. Collections towards illustrating the biography of the Scotch, English and Irish members, S.J. Exeter: 1838.

995 RIBADENEIRA, PEDRO DE. Bibliotheca scriptorum Societatis Iesu, a Petro Ribadeneira, Philippo Alegambe, Nathanaele Sotvello. (1st ed. reprinted), with a new introduction by A.F. Allison. Farnborough: 1969. 1st ed. Rome: 1676.

Carmelites

996 O'DWYER, *The Rev.* PETER. The Carmelite order in pre-republican Ireland. *Ir. Eccles. Rec.*, 110, 1968, 350–363.

997 O'MAHONY, S.C. Discalced Carmelites in Ireland, 1641. *Coll. Hib.*, 17, 1974–5, 7–16.

Vincentians

998 KELLY, JOSEPH P. Rev. Thomas McNamara, C.M. 1808–1892. *Riocht na Midhe*, vol. 5, no. 4, 1974, 60–67.

999 PURCELL, MARY. The story of the Vincentians: a record of the achievements in Ireland and Britain of the priests and lay-brothers of the Congregation of the Mission founded by St. Vincent de Paul. Dublin: 1973.

Sisterhoods

1000 LEADEN, A.H. The Sisters of Mercy in Kilmore, 1868–1968. *Breifne*, vol. 3, no. 12, 1969, 562–582.

1001 MARY GENEVIEVE, *Sister*. Mrs. Bellew's family in Channel Row. *Dublin Hist. Rec.*, 22, 1968, 230–241. Story of the Dublin Dominican community of nuns, 1717–1808.

Roman Catholic Church

1002 ALLISON, A.F., and ROGERS, D.M. A catalogue of Catholic books in English printed abroad or secretly in England, 1558–1640. Bognor Regis: 1956. 2 pts.

1003 BELLESHEIM, ALPHONS. Geschichte der Katholischen Kirche in Irland. Mainz, 1890–1. 3 vols. Includes good bibliogs.

1004 BIOGRAPHICAL STUDIES, 1534–1829. Vol. 1–, 1951–. Sub-title: Materials towards a biographical dictionary of Catholic history in the British Isles from the breach with Rome to Catholic emancipation, edited by A.F. Allison and D.M. Rogers.

1005 BLANCHARD, JEAN. Le droit ecclésiastique contemporain d'Irlande. Paris: 1958. Bibliog., pp. 163–6.

1006 BLANSHARD, PAUL. The Irish and Catholic power: an American interpretation. London: 1954. Bibliog., pp. 357–60.

1007 BLISS, W.H. Calendar of entries in the Papal Registers relating to Great Britain and Ireland. London: vol. 1–, 1893–. First 12 vols. cover period 1198–1471.

1008 — Petitions to the Pope. vol. 1. A.D. 32–1419. 1896. No further volumes published.

1009 BOYLAN, P. *ed.* The Book of the Congress Dublin, 1932. Wexford: 1934.

1010 **Brown, Stephen J.** Catholic mission literature: a handlist. Dublin: 1932. (*Catholic bibliog. ser.*, no. 3.)

1011 — An introduction to Catholic book-lore. London: 1933. (*Catholic bibliog. ser.*, no. 4.)

1012 — Catholic juvenile literature: a classified list, compiled . . . with the assistance of Dermot J. Dargan. London: 1935. (*Catholic bibliog. ser.*, no. 5.)

1013 — Libraries and literature from a Catholic standpoint. Dublin: 1937. (*Catholic bibliog. ser.*, no. 6.)

1014 — *and* **McDermott, Thomas.** A survey of Catholic literature, rev. ed. Milwaukee: 1949. First published 1944.

1015 **Burke, O.J.** The history of the Catholic archbishops of Tuam from the foundation of the See to the death of the Most Rev. John MacHale, D.D., A.D. 1881. Dublin: 1882.

1016 **Burke, William P.** The Irish priests in the penal times (1660–1760), from the State Papers in H.M. Record Offices, Dublin and London, the Bodleian Library and the British Museum. Waterford: 1914. Privately printed. Reprinted 1969 by Irish Univ. Press with an introduction by Mgr. Patrick Corish.

1017 **Catholic Emancipation.** Bibliog. in *Camb. Mod. Hist.*, 10, 1907, 860–6.

1018 **Catholic Encyclopaedia.** New York: 1907–22. 17 vols.

1019 **Catholic Truth Society.** Booklets and books [a list, Dublin]. 1952.

1020 — First fifty years: golden jubilee record, 1899–1949. [Dublin, 1952.] Includes complete list of booklets published by the society since 1900.

1021 **Ceillier, Remy.** Histoire générale des auteurs sacrés et ecclésiastiques. Paris: 1858–68. 14 vols. and 2 index vols.

1022 Corish, Patrick J. *General ed.* A history of Irish Catholicism. Dublin.

1023 Vol. I, no. 1. St. Patrick and the coming of Christianity, by Ludwig Bieler. 1967.

1024 Vol II, no. 2. The Monastic Institute, by John Ryan.
[and] 3. The Christian mission, by Patrick J. Corish. 1972.

1025 Vol. II, no. 1. The twelfth-century reform, by Aubrey Gwynn, 1968.

1026 Vol. II, no. 3. The Church in English lordship, 1216–1307, by Geoffrey Hand.
[and] no. 4. Anglo-Irish Church Life, fourteenth and fifteenth centuries, by Aubrey Gwynn. 1968.

1027 Vol. III, no. 2. The first impact of the Reformation, by Canice Mooney.
[and] no. 3. The Counter-reformation, by Frederick M. Jones. 1967.

1028 Vol. III, no. 7. Survival and reorganisation, 1650–1695, by Benignus Millett.
[and] no. 8. The origins of Catholic nationalism, by Patrick J. Corish. 1968.

1029 Vol. IV, no. 2. The church under the penal code, by John Brady and Patrick J. Corish.,
[and] no. 3. Irish exiles in Catholic Europe, by Cathaldus Giblin. 1971.

1030 Vol. V, no. 2. Political problems, 1850–60, by John H. Whyte.
[and] no. 3. Political problems, 1860–78, by Patrick J. Corish. 1967.

1031 Vol. V, no. 6. Primary education, by Ignatius Murphy; Secondary education, by Seamus V. O'Suilleabhain; The University question, by Fergal McGrath. 1971.

1032 Vol. V, no. 7. The Church since the emancipation: 1970. Church reorganisation, by Terence P. Cunningham.
[and] no. 8. Church building, by Thomas P. Kennedy.,
[and] no. 9. Ecclesiastical learning, by John Corkery.,
[and] no. 10. Epilogue: Modern Ireland, by Peter McKevitt.

1033 Vol. VI, no. 1. Great Britain: England and Wales, by Denis Gwynn; Scotland, by James E. Handley. 1968.

1034 Vol. VI, no. 2. The United States of America. 1970. The Irish Clergyman, by Thomas T. McAvoy; The Irish layman, by Thomas N. Brown.

1035 Vol. VI, no. 3. Canada, by Arthur P. Monahan.,
[and] no. 4. South Africa, by Francis B. Doyle.,
[and] no. 5. South America, by Anthony M. Canning. 1971.

1036 Vol. VI, no. 6. Australia, by J.J. McGovern and Patrick J. O'Farrell., [and] no. 7. New Zealand, by Eileen Duggan. 1971.

1037 Vol. VI, no. 8. The missions: Africa and the Orient, by Joseph McGlade. 1967. All published.

1038 CUNNINGHAM, PATRICK. The Catholic Directory for 1821. *Rep. Nov.*, 2, 1957–60, 324–63.

1039 DUBLIN EUCHARISTIC CONGRESS BIBLIOGRAPHY. By R. A[ylward], and S.J. B[rown]. *Ir. Book Lov.*, 20, 1932, 136.

1040 DUFFY, JAMES and Co. Catalogue of standard Catholic publications, authorised Catholic prayer books, works relating to Ireland and works of history and fiction. Dublin: 1903.

1041 EDWARDS, ROBERT DUDLEY. Church and state in Tudor Ireland: a history of penal laws against Irish Catholics, 1534–1603. London: 1935. Bibliog., pp. 313–32. Reprinted, New York: 1972.

1042 EGAN, PATRICK K. The Influence of the Irish on the Catholic Church in America in the nineteenth century. Dublin: 1968.

1043 EUCHARISTIC LITERATURE: a short list of books suitable for reading in connection with the Eucharistic Congress, Dublin, June 1932. *An Leab.*, 2, 1931–2, 39–41.

1044 FENNELL, DESMOND *ed*. The Changing face of Catholic Ireland. London: 1968.

1045 FINEGAN, FRANCIS. The Irish *Catholic Convert Rolls. Studies*, 38, 1949, 73–82.

1046 THE FURROW, Maynooth. Vol. 1–., 1950–. General Index of vols I–XVII, 1950–1966. 1968.

1047 GIBLIN, CATHALDUS. Material relating to Ireland in the Albani Collection of Mss. in the Vatican archives. *Ir. Eccles. Rec.*, 101, 1964, 389–396. Period covered, 1690–1721.

1048 GILLOW, JOSEPH. A literary and biographical history, or bibliographical dictionary of the English Catholics from the breach with Rome, in 1534, to the present time. London [1885–1903]. 5 vols.

1049 GUIDE TO CATHOLIC LITERATURE. 1888–1940: an author-subject-title index in one straight alphabet of books and booklets, in all languages, on all subjects, by Catholics or of particular Catholic interest, published or reprinted during the fifty-two years, 1888–1940, with more than a quarter of a million biographical, descriptive, and critical notes, each with complete reference to its authoritative sources for further reference, reading and study. Detroit, Michigan. Vol. 1–, 1940–.

1050 HAMELL, PATRICK J., *compiler*. Maynooth students and ordinations, 1795–1895: Index, *Ir. Eccles. Rec.*, 109, 1968, 28–40, 256–264. 110, 1968, 84–99, 173–182, 277–288, 381–386.

1051 IRISH CATHOLIC DIRECTORY, 1836–. Dublin: 1836–.

1052 IRISH ECCLESIASTICAL RECORD. Dublin. vol. 1–110, 1864–1968.

1053 — Index to the articles and papers which have appeared in it from 1865 to 1922, compiled by Thomas J. Shaw. London: 1925.

1054 — Documents, 1864–1917: index [and] Subject and author index, 1864–1917: articles, correspondence, notes and queries (theology, canon law, liturgy), compiled by the Rev. P.J. Canon Hamell. Dublin: Brown and Nolan [1960]. Appeared originally in *Irish Ecclesiastical Record*.

1055 — Indexes . . . 1864–1963, compiled by Rev. P.J. Canon Hamell. Dublin: Brown and Nolan [1964]: Contents: 1864–1917, documents, articles, etc., reviews. 1917–1963, articles; appeared originally in *Irish Ecclesiastical Record.*

1056 HOEHN, MATTHEW. *ed*. Catholic authors: contemporary biographical sketches, 1930–47. Newark, St. Mary's Abbey: 1948.

1057 HOWARD, LEONARD. The Penal laws in County Clare, 1677–1685. *Nth. Munster Antiq. J.*, 13, 1970, 30–36.

1058 — The Penal laws in Limerick, 1670–1684. *Nth. Munster Antiq. J.*, 12. 1969, 41–52.

1059 — The Penal laws in North Kerry, 1677–1685. *Nth. Munster Antiq. J.*, 14, 1971, 49–52.

1060 HUNTER, ROBERT J. Catholicism in Meath, *c*.1622. *Coll. Hib.*, 14, 1971, 7–12.

1061 **Hurter**, H. Nomenclator literarius recentioris theologiae Catholicae, theologos exhibens aetate, natione, disciplinis distinctos. Innsbruck: 1899. 6 vols.

1062 **McCarthy, Michael** J.F. Priests and people in Ireland. Dublin and London: 1902.

1063 **McKiernan, Francis** J. Parish priests of Kilmore [a list, 1398–1973]. *Breifne*, vol. 4, no. 15, 1972, 370–405.

1064 **Madden, Richard** C. Dublin priests at Charleston, South Carolina, in the eighteenth century. *Rep. Nov*., vol. 3, no. 2, 1963–4, 361–367.

1065 **Martin**, F.X. *ed*. Provincial rivalries in eighteenth-century Ireland: an Irish Augustinian document. *Arch. Hib*., 30, 1972, 117–135.

1066 **Mey, John**. Registrum Johannis Mey: the Register of John Mey, Archbishop of Armagh, 1443–1456, edited by W.G.H. Quigley and E.F.D. Roberts. Belfast: H.M.S.O., 1972. 'Present volume contains a general discussion of the series of medieval registers at Armagh and an analysis of the nature of the Register of Archbishop Mey.'

1067 **Miller, David** W. Church, State and Nation in Ireland, 1898–1921. Dublin: 1973. Bibliog., pp. 561–567.

1068 — The Roman Catholic Church in Ireland: 1898–1918. *Eire-Ir*., vol. 3, no. 3, 1968. 75–91.

1069 **Murphy** J.A. The support of the Catholic clergy in Ireland, 1750–1850. *Hist. Stud*., 5, 1965, 103–121.

1070 **O'Gallchobhair, The Rev**. P. Clogherici: a dictionary of the Catholic clergy to the diocese of Clogher (1535–1835). *Clogher Rec*. Vol. 1. no. 3, 1955, 66–87, no. 4, 1956, 137–160; Vol. 2. 1957–59, 170–191, 272–279, 504–511; Vol. 4. 1960–62, 54–94; Vol. 6. 1966–68, 126–136, 379–387, 578–596; Vol. 7. 1969–72, 89–104, 514–528; Vol. 8. 1973–75, 93–103, 207–220, 271–280; Vol. 9. 1976, 67–75.

1071 **O'Neill**, T.P. Sources for a history of Catholic life in Ireland, 1780–1850. *Ir. Cath. Hist. Comm. Proc*., 1959, 19–23.

1072 **O'Riordan**, W.M. A list of seventeenth century Dublin diocesan priests. *Rep. Nov*., 2, 1957–60, 109–19, 257–68.

1073 **O'Suilleabhain, Padraig**. Catholic books printed in Ireland, 1740–1820, containing list of subscribers. *Coll. Hib*., 6–7, 1963–4, 231–233.

1074 — The Library of a parish priest of the penal days [John Wickham, of Templeshannon and Edermine, Co. Wexford]. *Coll. Hib*., 6–7, 1963–64, 234–244.

1075 **Pollen, John Hungerford**. Sources for the history of Roman Catholics in England, Ireland, and Scotland from the Reformation period to that of emancipation, 1533–1795. London: 1921. (*Helps for students of history, no*. 39.)

1076 **Reynolds, James** A. The Catholic emancipation crisis in Ireland. 1823–29. New Haven: 1954. (*Yale Hist. Pub. Miscell. no. 60*)

1077 **Ronan, Myles** V. An apostle of Catholic Dublin: Father Henry Young. Clonskeagh: 1944.

1078 — The Irish martyrs of the penal laws. London: 1935. Bibliog., pp. 189–97.

1079 **Silke, John** J. The Roman Catholic Church in Ireland, 1800–1922: a survey of recent historiography. *Stud. Hib*., 15, 1975, 61–104.

1080 **Survey Of Catholic Clergy And Religious Personnel**, 1971: research carried out by the Research and Development Unit, Catholic Communications Institute of Ireland. *Soc. Stud*., 1, 1973, 137–234.

1081 **Traynor**, *The Very Rev*. **Owen Francis**. Kilmore clergy list of 1723. *Breifne*, vol. 3, no. 12. 1969. 481–491.

1082 **Wall, Maureen**. The Catholic merchants, manufacturers, and traders of Dublin, 1778–82 [with list]. *Rep. Nov*., 2, 1957–60, 298–323.

Church of Ireland

1083 **Akenson, Donald Harman**. The Church of Ireland: ecclesiastical reform and revolution, 1800–1885. New Haven and London: 1971. Bibliog. pp. 379–408.

1084 **Association For Promoting Christian Knowledge**. Catalogue of Church of Ireland prayer books, hymnals, psalters, and chant books [and] general books. Dublin [1963].

1085 B., H.A. Full account of the periodicals issued in connection with the Church of Ireland. *In* About newspapers, chiefly English and Scottish; with an appendix containing an account of the periodical publications issued in connection with the Anglican communion in Great Britain and Ireland. Edinburgh: 1888.

1086 BEALE, ANGELA. Church of Ireland records in Tralee, Co. Kerry. *Ir. Arch. Bull.*, 5, 1975, 23–24.

1087 BOLTON, F.R. The Caroline tradition of the Church of Ireland with particular reference to Bishop Jeremy Taylor. London: 1958. Bibliog., pp. 328–9.

1088 CAREY, F.P. The Medieval parish of St. Stephen. *Dublin Hist. Rec.*, 6, 1943–44, 63–73.

1089 CARPENTER, ANDREW. William King and the threats to the Church of Ireland during the reign of James II. *Ir. Hist. Stud.*, vol. 18, no. 69, 1972, 22–28.

1090 CHRIST CHURCH CATHEDRAL, DUBLIN. Acts, charters and other documents and extracts relating to the Cathedral, covering the period *c.* 1170–1793. 2 vol. In *National Library Mss. Collection, nos.* 97–8.

1091 — LEWIS-CROSBY, E.H. The ancient books of Christ Church Cathedral, Dublin. Dublin [1947]. (*Christ Church series, no. 4.*)

1092 COGHLAN, VALERIE. Protestant periodicals published in Dublin and Belfast between 1830 and 1900. Thesis accepted for Fellowship of the L.A.I, 1975.

1093 COOTE, MICHAEL H. *ed.* A short history of Taney Parish; research by R.C.H. Townshend. Dublin [1969].

1094 CROCKFORD'S CLERICAL DIRECTORY ... 1858–. London: 1858–.

1095 ELLISON, THE REV. C.C. Early 19th century lists of protestant parishioners in the Diocese of Meath. *Ir. Ancest.*, 5, 1973, 37–53, 113–126.

1096 HURLEY, MICHAEL, *ed.* Irish Anglicanism, 1869–1969: essays on the role of Anglicanism in Irish Life presented to the Church of Ireland on the occasion of its disestablishment, by a group of Methodist, Presbyterian, Quaker and Roman Catholic scholars. Dublin: 1970.

1097 IRISH CHURCH DIRECTORY. 1862–. Dublin 1862–.

1098 JOHNSTON, THOMAS J. *and others*. A history of the Church of Ireland, by the Rev. T.J. Johnston, Ven. John L. Robinson and Rev. Robert Wyse Jackson. Dublin: 1953.

1099 LAWLOR, HUGH JACKSON. The Fasti of St. Patrick's, Dublin ... Dundalk: 1930. Bibliog., pp. 299–305.

1100 LESLIE, JAMES B. Ardfert and Aghadoe clergy and parishes: being an account of the clergy of the Church of Ireland in the diocese of Ardfert and Aghadoe from the earliest period, with historical notices of the several parishes, churches, etc. Dublin: 1940.

1101 — Armagh clergy and parishes ... Dundalk: 1911. Bibliog., pp. xv–xxii. Supplement ... continuation of the biographical succession lists of the clergy of Armagh diocese up to 1947 with additions ... Dundalk: 1948.

1102 — Clogher clergy and parishes. Enniskillen: 1929.

1103 — Derry clergy and parishes ... Enniskillen: 1937.

1104 — *and* Swanzy, H.B. Biographical succession lists of the clergy of the diocese of Down. Enniskillen: 1936.

1105 — Ferns clergy and parishes ... Dublin: 1936.

1106 — Ossory clergy and parishes from the earliest period. Enniskillen: 1933.

1107 — Raphoe clergy and parishes. Enniskillen: 1940.

1108 MCDOWELL, R.B. The Church of Ireland, 1869–1969. London and Boston: 1975. *(Studies in Irish History, 2nd Ser. vol: 10)* Bibliog., pp. 147–152.

1109 MCKENNA, *The Rev*. J.J. The Church of Ireland clergy in Cork: an analysis of the 1615 Royal visitation. *Cork Hist. Arch. Soc. J.*, 77, 1972, 117–123.

1110 MANT, RICHARD. History of the Church of Ireland from the Reformation to the Revolution with a preliminary survey of the papal usurpation in the 12th century to 1st legal abolition in the 16th century. London: 1840. 2 vols.

1111 MILNE, KENNETH. The Church of Ireland: a history. Dublin: 1966.

1112 MURPHY, JOHN A. The Politics of the Munster Protestants, 1641–49. *Cork Hist. Arch. Soc. J.*, 76, 1971, 1–20.

1113 O'DUILL, GREAGOIR. Church records after disestablishment. *Ir. Arch. Bull.*, 5, 1975, 10–22.

1114 OLDEN, THOMAS. The Church of Ireland. London: 1892. Bibliog., pp. 430–432.

1115 PHILLIPS, WALTER ALISON. History of the Church of Ireland from the earliest times to the present day. London: 1935. 3 vols. Bibliogs., vol. 1. The Celtic church, pp. 403–13; vol. 2. The movement towards Rome, the medieval church and the Reformation, pp. 631–46; vol. 3. The modern church, pp. 459–72; list of the succession of bishops of the Church of Ireland, pp. 433–58.

1116 ROBINSON, H.W. A study of the Church of Ireland population of Ardfert, Co. Kerry: 1971. *Econ. Soc. Rev.*, vol. 4, no. 1, 1972, 93–139.

1117 ROBINSON, JOHN L. On the ancient deeds of the parish of St. John, Dublin, preserved in the library of Trinity College. *R. Ir. Acad. Proc. Sec. C*, 33, 1916–17, 175–224.

1118 STOKES, GEORGE THOMAS. Some worthies of the Irish Church: lectures delivered in the school of the University of Dublin. Edited, with preface and notes, by Hugh Johnson Lawlor. London: 1900. Contents: Richard Lingard, D.D.; Dudley Loftus, D.C.L; Narcissus Marsh, D.D. [with account of Marsh's Library]; William King, D.D; St. Colman of Lindisfarne and Innisbofin; the sources of local history.

1119 SWANZY, H.B. Succession lists of the diocese of Dromore, edited by J.B. Leslie. Belfast: 1933.

1120 TWISS, HENRY F. Some ancient deeds of the parishes of St. Catherine and St. James, Dublin, 1296–1743. *R. Ir. Acad. Proc. Sec. C*, 35, 1918–20, 265–81.

1121 — Some ancient deeds of St. Werburgh, Dublin, 1243–1676, *ibid*, vol. 35, 1918–20, 282–315.

1122 WEBSTER, CHARLES A. The diocese of Ross and its ancient churches [with bibliog.]. *R. Ir. Acad. Proc. Sec. C*, 40, 1931–2, 255–95.

1123 WHEELER, H.A. St. Michael's parish. *Dublin. Hist. Rec.*, vol. 15, 1958–60, 97–104.

1124 WILSON, W.G. How the church of Ireland is governed. Dublin: 1963.

Huguenots

1125 CARRE, ALBERT. L'Influence des Huguenots francais en Irlande aux XVIIe et XVIIIe siècles. Paris: 1937. Bibliog., pp. 143–51.

Huguenot Society of London publications:

1126 No. 7: Registers of the French conformed churches of St. Patrick and St. Mary, Dublin, edited by J.J.D. la Touche. Dublin: 1893.

1127 No. 14: Registers of the French nonconformist churches of Lucy Lane and Peter Street, Dublin, edited by T.P. Le Fanu. London: 1901.

1128 No. 18: Letters of denization and acts of naturalization for aliens in England and Ireland, 1603–1700, edited by W.A. Shaw. Lymington: 1908.

1129 No. 19: Registers of the French church of Portarlington, edited by T.P. Le Fanu. London: 1908.

1130 No. 27: Letters of denization and acts of naturalization for aliens in England and Ireland, 1701–1800, edited by W.A. Shaw. Manchester: 1923.

1131 No. 41: Dublin and Portalington veterans, by T.P. Le Fanu and W. Manchee. Frome: 1946.

1132 JOURDAN, G.V. Huguenot gleanings. *Hermathena*, 91, 1958, 55–69.

1133 KNOX, S.J. Ireland's debt to the Huguenots. Dublin: 1959.

1134 LEE, GRACE LAWLESS. The Huguenot settlements in Ireland. London: 1936. Bibliog., pp. 265–7.

1135 O'MULLANE, BRIGID. The Huguenots in Dublin. *Dublin Hist. Rec.*, 8, 1945–6, 110–34.

1136 POWELL, JOHN STOCKS. The Huguenots of Portarlington, *Studies*, 61, 1972, 343–353.

1137 REAMAN, G. ELMORE. The Trial of the Huguenots in Europe, the United States, South Africa and Canada. London: 1964.

1138 SMILES, SAMUEL. The Huguenots, their settlements, churches in England and Ireland. 6th ed., London: 1889. 1st ed., London: 1867.

Presbyterians

1139 BARKLEY, J.M. Francis Makemie. *Donegal Ann.*, vol. XI, no. 1, 1974, 3–21. Presbyterianism in Donegal and America.

1140 — Irish Presbyterian magazines, 1829–1840, *Bull. Pres. Hist. Soc. Ir.*, December 1970, 4–8.

1141 — A short history of the Presbyterian church in Ireland. Belfast, [1959]. Bibliog., pp. 125–127.

1142 BECKETT, J.C. Protestant dissent in Ireland, 1687–1780. London: 1948. Bibliog., pp. 150–4.

1143 CAMPBELL, A.A. Irish Presbyterian magazines, past and present: a bibliography. Belfast: 1919.

1144 — The historian of the Presbyterian Church in Ireland [The Rev. William Thomas Latimer], with a bibliography. *Ir. Book Lov.*, 6, 1915, 173–5.

1145 CARSON, JOHN T. God's river in spate: the story of the religious awakening of Ulster in 1859. Belfast: 1958. Bibliog., pp. 134–5.

1146 EVANS, GEORGE EYRE. Vestiges of Protestant dissent, being lists of ministers, sacramental plate, registers, antiquities, etc. Liverpool: 1897. Ireland, pp. 273–306.

1147 MCCONNELL, J., and MCCONNELL, S.G. Fasti of the Irish Presbyterian Church, 1613–1840. Belfast: Presbyterian Historical Society, 1936–51. 16 pts.

1148 REID, J.S. History of the Presbyterian Church in Ireland; new ed. with additional notes by W.D. Killen. Belfast: 1867. 3 vols.

1149 STEWART, DAVID. The Seceders in Ireland with annals of their congregations. Belfast: 1950. Secession authors, pp. 427–30.

1150 WITHEROW, THOMAS. Historical and literary memorials of Presbyterianism in Ireland (1623–1731) . . . London: 1879.

Baptists

1151 ASSOCIATION RECORDS OF THE PARTICULAR BAPTISTS OF ENGLAND, WALES AND IRELAND TO 1660. London: Baptist Historical Society. Pt. 2. The West Country and Ireland, edited by B.R. White: 1973. Indexes, compiled by K.N.H. Howard, 1977.

1152 IRISH BAPTIST MAGAZINE. Belfast: vol. 1–, 1877–.

1153 WHITLEY, WILLIAM THOMAS, *compiler*. A Baptist bibliography; being a register of the chief materials for Baptist history, whether in manuscript or in print, preserved in Great Britain, Ireland and the Colonies. London: 1916–22. 2 vols. Vol. 1: 1526–1776; vol. 2: 1777–1837, and addenda from 1613.

Methodists

1154 COLE, R. LEE. A history of Methodism in Dublin. Dublin: 1932.

1155 CROOKSHANK, C.H. History of Methodism in Ireland. Belfast. 1885–8, 1960. 4 vol. Vol. 4. One Methodist Church, 1860–1960, by R. Lee Cole. Bibliog., pp. 189–91.

1156 FREEMAN, T.W. John Wesley in Ireland. *Ir. Geog.*, 8, 1975, 86–96.

1157 GREEN, RICHARD. Anti-Methodist publications issued during the eighteenth century: a chronologically arranged and annotated bibliography of all known books and pamphlets written in opposition to the Methodist revival during the life of Wesley, together with an account of replies to them, and of some other publications; a contribution to Methodist history. London: 1902.

Quakers

1158 BARBOUR, HUGH and ROBERTS, ARTHUR O. *eds*. Early Quaker writings, 1650–1700. Grand Rapids (Michigan): 1973. Bibliographical Index, pp. 505–616.

1159 COMERFORD, PATRICK. The early Society of Friends and their history in Kilkenny. *Old.*

Kilk. Rev., 25, 1973, 68–75.

1160 DOUGLAS, J.M. Early Quakerism in Ireland. *J. Friends' Hist. Soc.*, 48, 1956, 3–32.

1161 GOODBODY, OLIVE C. Irish Quaker diaries. *J. Friends' Hist. Soc.*, vol. 50, no. 2, 1962, 51–64.

1162 — Guide to Irish Quaker Records, 1654–1860. With contribution on Northern Ireland Records, by B.G. Hutton. Dublin: Irish Manuscripts Commission, 1967.

1163 — Quaker inventories. *Ir. Ancest.*, 3, 1970, 52–62.

1164 — Quakers in Wexford. *Old Wexford Soc. J.*, vol. 3, no. 1, 1970, 36–41.

1165 GREEVES, J.R.H. Quaker families. *Belfast Nat. Hist. Phil. Soc. Proc.*, 8, 1964–70, 50–57.

1166 — The Records of the Society of Friends. *Ir. Geneal.*, 2, 1943–55, 177–179.

1167 GRUBB, GEOFFREY WATKINS. The Grubbs of Tipperary: studies in heredity and character. Cork: 1972. Bibliog., pp. 229–231.

1168 GRUBB, ISABEL. Quakers in Ireland, 1654–1900. London: 1927. Bibliog., pp. 149–52.

1169 IRISH MANUSCRIPTS COMMISSION. Quaker records, Dublin: abstracts of wills, edited by P. Beryl Eustace and Olive C. Goodbody. Dublin: 1957. Irish Quaker records dating from 1650 are preserved at 6 Eustace Street, Dublin.

1170 MORTIMER, R.S. Biographical notices of printers and publishers of Friends' books up to 1750: a supplement to Plomer's *Dictionary*. *J. Document.*, 3, 1947. 107–25.

1171 MYLERS, ALBERT COOK. Quaker arrivals in Philadelphia, 1682–1750. [Facsimile reprint of 1st ed.] Baltimore: Genealogical Pub. Co. 1969. Originally published Philadelphia: 1902.

1172 NEWHOUSE, NEVILLE H. The Founding of Friends' school, Lisburn. *R. Soc. Antiq. Ir. J.*, 98, 1968, 47–55.

1173 — John Hancock, Junior, 1762–1823. *R. Soc. Antiq. Ir. J.*, 101, 1971, 41–52. Throws an interesting light on the Ulster Quakerism of his day.

1174 SMITH, JOSEPH. A descriptive catalogue of Friends' books or books written by the Society of Friends commonly called Quakers, from their rise to the present time. London: 1867. 2 vols. Supplement. London: 1893.

1175 — Biblioteca Anti-Quakeriana; or, a catalogue of books adverse to the Society of Friends. London: 1873.

1176 SOCIETY OF FRIENDS. Catalogue of the library of the Institute of the Society of Friends, Eustace Street, Dublin: 1853.

1177 — Alphabetical catalogue of the lending library belonging to Dublin monthly meeting of the Society of Friends at their meeting house, Eustace Street, printed in 1860; with a supplement including works since added, and a list of books suitable for young people. Dublin: 1877.

1178 — Library catalogue of the Dublin Friends' Institute, 35 Molesworth Street, Dublin: 1893. The historical collection of printed books and manuscripts of the Society of Friends is at present being compiled into a dictionary catalogue by Miss N. Hardiman and Miss Hicks.

Non-Christian

1179 BONWICK, JAMES. Irish Druids and old Irish religions. London: 1894. Bibliog., pp. 325–8.

1180 CHADWICK, NORA K. The Druids. Cardiff: 1966.

1181 CRAWFORD, O.G.S. The Eye Goddess. London: 1957. Bibliog., pp. 150–7.

1182 DALTON, G.F. The tradition of blood sacrifice to the goddess Eire. *Studies*, 63, 1974, 343–354.

1183 KENDRICK, T.D. The Druids: a study in Keltic prehistory. London: 1927. Reprinted 1966. Bibliog., pp. vii–ix.

1184 NEW YORK PUBLIC LIBRARY. Druids and Druidism: a list of references, by G.F. Black. New York: 1920.

1185 PIGGOTT, STUART. The Druids. London: Thames and Hudson, 1968. *(Ancient peoples and places series, vol. 63)* Bibliog., pp. 197–203.

Jews

1186 BUTLER, KATHERINE. Synagogues of old Dublin. *Dublin Hist. Rec.*, vol. 27, no. 4, 1974, 118–130.

1187 HYMAN, LOUIS. The Jews of Ireland from earliest times to the year 1910. Shannon: Ir. Univ. Press, 1972. Bibliog., pp. 352–366.

1188 ROTH, CECIL. Magna Bibliotheca Anglo-Judaica: a bibliographical guide to Anglo-Jewish history: new rev. and enl. ed. London: Jewish History Society of England, 1937.

1189 SHILLMAN, BERNARD. A short history of the Jews in Ireland. Dublin: 1945. Bibliog., pp. 150–1.

Mythology

1190 LUCAS, A.T. The sacred trees of Ireland [with bibliog.] *Cork Hist. Arch. Soc. J.*, 68, 1963, 16–54.

1191 MACCANA, PRIONSIAS, Celtic mythology. London: 1970.

1192 MACCULLOCH, JOHN ARNOTT. Celtic mythology. Boston: 1918. *(The Mythology of all races, edited by L.H. Gray,* vol. 3.) Bibliog., pp. 365–88.

1193 ROSS, ANNE. Pagan Celtic Britain: studies in iconography and tradition. London and New York: 1967. Bibliog., pp. 388–399.

SOCIOLOGY

1194 DARLING, VIVIENNE. Development of social work in the Republic of Ireland. *Soc. Stud.*, 1, 1972, 24–37.

1195 ECONOMIC AND SOCIAL RESEARCH INSTITUTE. Register of research projects in the social sciences in progress in Ireland. Dublin: 1972.

1196 — Research projects in the social sciences: Ireland: January 1973: a periodic register prepared for the Economic and Social Research Institute, Dublin, by Maria Maher. *Econ. Soc. Rev.*, vol. 4. no. 3. 1973, 395–420.

1197 — Social Research in progress in Ireland: the Economic and Social Research Institute Research projects in the social sciences in progress in Ireland — January 1973. *Soc. Stud.*, 2, 1973, 179–193.

1198 FOGARTY, MICHAEL P. Future social research in Ireland. *Stat. Social Inq. Soc. Ir. J.*, vol. 22 pt. 1, 1968–69, 56–77.

1199 FRIIS, HENNING. Development of social research in Ireland: a report. Dublin: Institute of Public Administration, 1965.

1200 NIC GHIOLLA PHADRAIG, MAIRE. Bibliography of demography, human geography, migration, rural and urban sociology in Ireland. *Soc. Stud.*, 1, 1972, 597–622.

1201 — Bibliography of Socio-economic studies in Ireland. *Soc. Stud.*, 1, 1972, 699–717.

1202 — Bibliography of the social aspects of the legal system, politics, administration in Ireland. *Soc. Stud.*, 1, 1972, 480–498. Draft section of the Bib. of the Social Services in Ireland.

1203 — Select bibliography of social problems and social services in Ireland. *Soc. Stud.*, 1, 1972, 94–111.

1204 O'DONNELL, EDWARD EUGENE. Northern Irish stereotypes. Dublin: College of Industrial Relations, 1977. Study to examine stereotypes as a way of understanding intense personal conflict particularly between Protestant and Roman Catholic.

1205 RECENT SOCIOLOGY. Section I. Theoretical: dynamic sociology, by Michael Peillon. *Soc. Stud.*, 3, 1974, 528–537. Section II. Population loss and social decline in County Leitrim, by Seamus Grimes. *ibid.*, 3, 1974, 538–547.

1206 ROSEINGRAVE, TOMAS. Sociology in Ireland [with bibliog.] *Admin.*, 11, 1963, 207–223.

1207 SOCIAL STUDIES: Irish journal of sociology. (Maynooth). vol. 1–, 1972–.

Ecology and Community

1208 BYRNE, GEORGE. A librarian looks at environmental studies [with bibliogs.] *Oideas*, no. 4, 1970, 53–65.

1209 HANNAN, DAMIEN. Rural exodus; a study of the forces influencing the large scale migration of Irish rural youth. Dublin and London: 1970.

1210 O'HARE, PATRICK J. Ecology and modern man. *Cap. Ann.*, 1974. 229–241.

Environment and Pollution

1211 GRAHAM, T.R. Water pollution control, with particular reference to Northern Ireland [with bibliog]. *Water Pollution Control*, vol. 66, no. 6, 1967, 583–92.

1212 INSTITUTE FOR INDUSTRIAL RESEARCH AND STANDARDS: Chemical Engineering Department. National survey of air and water pollution, 1974. Dublin: 1975.

1213 LANG, JOHN TEMPLE. Conservation of the environment in Ireland. [with comment by Fergus J. O'Rourke]. *Studies*, 59, 1970, 279–300.

1214 MCMANUS, T. *ed.* Air pollution: proceedings of a symposium held in Dublin on 22 March 1972 organised by IIRS. Dublin: 1973.

1215 — Sulphur dioxide concentrations over Dublin. *Technol. Ir.*, vol. 7, no. 8, 1975, 33–35. Maps showing isopleths of sulphur dioxide concentrations.

1216 O'CONNOR, R. Economics and the environment. *R. Ir. Acad. Proc.*, vol. 77. Sec. C, no. 4. 1977, 193–211.

1217 TONER, P.F. and O'SULLIVAN, A.J. Water pollution in Ireland: a review of the existing situation, current investigations and future research needs. Dublin: National Science Council, 1977.

The Community

1218 BOAL, F.W. Territoriality and class: a study of the residential areas in Belfast. *Ir. Geog.*, vol. 6, no. 3, 1971. 229–248.

1219 BROWNE, IVOR. Why community participation? *Admin.*, vol. 21, no. 1, 1973, 41–44.

1220 WARD, CONOR K. Living in a new community: a summary of results of a social survey. *Stat. Social Inq. Soc. Ir. J.*, vol. 22, pt. 1, 1968–69, 30–55.

Rural Communities

1221 AALEN, F.H.A. *compiler*. Enclosures in Eastern Ireland: report of a symposium held in Dublin on 23 September 1964. *Ir. Geog.*, vol. 5, no. 2, 1965, 29–39.

1222 — and BRODY, HUGH. Gola: the life and last days of an island community. Cork: 1969. Island off Donegal.

1223 ARENSBERG, CONRAD M. The Irish countryman: an anthropological study. London: 1937.

1224 — and KIMBALL, SALON T. Family and community in Ireland. 2nd ed. Cambridge (Mass.); 1968. 1st ed., 1940.

1225 BERESFORD, MAURICE and HURST, JOHN G. *eds*. Deserted medieval villages: studies. London: 1971. Pt. 4: Ireland. Contents: The study of deserted medieval settlements in Ireland (to 1968), by R.E. Glasscock. Gazetteer of deserted towns, rural boroughs, and nucleated settlements in Ireland [and] select bibliography, Ireland, by R.E. Glasscock.

1226 BUCHANAN, R.H. Rural change in an Irish townland, 1890–1955. *Adv. Sci.*, 14, 1957–8, 291–300. Study of Sheeplands, Co. Down.

1227 — Tradition and change in rural Ulster. *Folk Life.*, 3, 1965, 39–45.

1228 CONNELL, K.H. Irish Peasant society: four historical essays. Oxford; 1968. Contents: I. Illicit distillation; II. Illegitimacy before the Famine; III Ether-drinking in Ulster; IV Catholicism and marriage in the century after the famine. Earlier versions of I and III appeared in *Hist. Stud.* III, and the *Quarterly Journal of Studies on Alcohol*.

1229 DEENY, JAMES. Fanad [Co. Donegal]: a situational analysis. *Admin.*, vol. 21, no. 1, 1973, 45–79.

1230 EVANS, E. ESTYN. Rural settlement in Ireland and Western Britain [reprint of a symposium] *Adv. Sci.*, 15, 1958–59, 333–345. Ireland, by V.B. Proudfoot. pp. 336–338.

1231 FAHY, E.M. Early settlement in the Skibbereen area. *Cork Hist. Arch. Soc. J.*, 74, 1969, 147–156.

1232 GABRIEL, TOM. An Anthropological perspective on land in Western Ireland. *Anglo-Ir. Stud.*, 3, 1977, 71–84. Fieldwork undertaken in a north Mayo parish, 1973–74.

1233 HANNAN, DAMIEN. Kinship, neighbourhood and social change in Irish rural communities. *Econ. Soc. Rev.*, vol. 3, no. 2, 1972, 163–188.

1234 HUGHES, T. JONES. Society and settlement in nineteenth century Ireland. *Ir. Geog.*, vol. 5, no. 2, 1965, 79–96.

1235 MACCURTAIN, MARGARET. Pre-famine peasantry in Ireland: definition and theme. *Ir. Univ. Rev.*, vol. 4, no. 2, 1974, 188–198.

1236 O'FARRELL, PATRICK N. The urban hinterlands of New Ross and Enniscorthy. *Ir. Geog.*, vol. 5, no. 2, 1965, 67–78.

1237 SMYTH, WILLIAM J. Continuity and change in the territorial organisation of Irish rural communities. *Maynooth Rev.*, vol. 1, no. 1, 1975, 51–78, vol. 1, no. 2, 1975, 52–101.

Towns and Cities

1238 BRADY, J. and PARKER, A.J. The factorial ecology of Dublin: a preliminary investigation. *Econ. Soc. Rev.*, vol. 7, no. 1, 1975, 35–54.

1239 BUTLIN, R.A., *ed.* The development of the Irish town. London and Totowa, (N.J.): 1977.

1240 GRANLUND, JOHN. Coumeenole, Dunquin (Co. Kerry) and other townlands. In *Folk and Farm*, edited by C. O Danachair. 1976., 72–89.

1241 HUMPHREYS, ALEXANDER J. New Dubliners: urbanisation and the Irish family. London: 1966. Bibliog., pp. 280–284.

1242 SPENCER, A.E.C.W. Urbanisation and the problem of Ireland. *Month*, vol. 233, no. 1264, 1972, 355–362. Assesses the cultural and social structural features of urbanisation.

Undeveloped areas

1243 CONGESTED DISTRICTS BOARD FOR IRELAND. Dublin. Annual reports nos. 1–27, 1891–1920. The congested districts embraced the following counties: Donegal, Leitrim, Sligo, Roscommon, Mayo, Galway, Kerry and West Cork.

1244 MICKS, WILLIAM L. An account of the constitution, administration, and dissolution of the Congested Districts Board for Ireland from 1891 to 1923. Dublin: 1925.

1245 O'FARRELL, F. The congested districts of Ireland and how to deal with them. *Stat. Social. Inq. Soc. Ir. J.*, 65, 1887, 153–163.

The Sexes and their Relations

1246 BIRCH, PETER. The Irish family in modern conditions. *Soc. Stud.*, vol. 2, no. 5, 1973, 485–497.

1247 THE FAMILY, *Soc. Stud.*, vol. 2, no. 6, 1973. Papers of the Council for Social Welfare's Seminar on the family, Glencolumcille, Ulster, 1973.

1248 FENNELL, NUALA. Irish marriage – how are you! Dublin and Cork: 1974.

1249 FINLAY, PETER. Divorce in the Irish Free State. *Studies*, 13, 1924, 353–362.

1250 FOGARTY, MICHAEL P. *and others*. Men and women: the next frontiers, by M.P. Fogarty with Rhona and Robert Papoport. *Econ. Soc. Hist.*, vol. 6, no. 1, 1974, 5–25. Position of women and men in contemporary society.

1251 HEALY, JAMES. Abortion: some references and questions. *Soc. Stud.*, vol. 3, no. 3, 1974, 317–331.

1252 MCCANN, SEAN. The Irish in love. Dublin: 1972.

1253 MCGRATH, PATRICK J. Marriage annulments: A second look. *Maynooth Rev.*, vol. 1, no. 2, 1975, 45–51. See also Marriage annulments, by Maurice Dooley. *Furrow*, vol. 26, no. 4, 1975, 211–219.

1254 MARKET RESEARCH BUREAU OF IRELAND. Religious practice and attitudes towards divorce and contraception among Irish adults. *Soc. Stud.*, 3, 1974, 276–285. This survey was commissioned by R.T.E. 7 days. [Television programme]

1255 O'HIGGINS, KATHLEEN. Marital desertion in Dublin: an exploratory study. Dublin: 1974. Bibliog., pp. 181–3.

1256 ROHAN, DORINE. Marriage Irish style. Cork: 1969.

1257 VINEY, MICHAEL. No birthright: a study of the Irish unmarried mother and her child.

Dublin: 1964. First appeared as articles in the *Irish Times*.

1258 WALSH, NOEL. In defence of the unborn [abortion]. *Studies*, 61, 1972, 303–314.

Racial and Ethnic Origins

1259 CURTIS, L. PERRY, JR. Apes and angels: the Irishman in Victorian caricature. Newton Abbot: 1971. Bibliog., pp. 118–122.

Itinerants

1260 GMELCH, SHARON. Tinkers and travellers. Dublin: 1975. Bibliog., pp. 142–3.

1261 — and GMELCH, GEORGE. The itinerant settlement movement: its policies and effects on Irish travellers. *Studies*, 63, 1974, 1–16.

1262 IRELAND, REPORT OF THE COMMISSION ON ITINERANCY. Dublin: 1963.

Social Stratification by Religion

1263 AUNGER, EDMUND A. Religion and occupational class in Northern Ireland. *Econ. Soc. Rev.*, 7, 1975, 1–18.

1264 BELL, GEOFFREY. The Protestants of Ulster. London: 1976.

1265 BOWEN, DESMOND. The Protestant crusade in Ireland, 1800–70: a study of Protestant-Catholic relations between the Act of Union and Disestablishment. Dublin and London: 1978. Bibliog., pp. 390–402.

1266 CANAVAN, JOSEPH E., *S.J.* The Future of Protestantism in Ireland. *Studies*, 34, 1945, 231–240. Review article of pamphlet *Irish Protestantism today and tomorrow* by the Rev. R.P. McDermott and D.A. Webb. (Dublin: 1945).

1267 LOWE, W.J. The Lancashire Irish and the Catholic Church, 1846–71: the social dimension. *Ir. Hist. Stud.*, vol. 20, no. 78, 1976, 129–155.

1268 MCKENNA, J.J. Young Protestants in the community – the way forward. *Soc. Stud.*, vol. 3, no. 2, 1974, 158–162.

1269 NIC GIOLLA PHADRAIG, MAIRE. Bibliography of the sociology of religion in Ireland. *Soc. Stud.*, 1, 1972, 246–260.

1270 O'DONOGHUE, DONAL. Religious gaps in Ireland — a sociological approach. *Soc. Stud.*, 1, 1972, 505–516.

Social Conflicts

1271 BLEAKLEY, DAVID. Peace in Ulster. London and Oxford: 1972.

1272 ELLIOTT, R.S.P. and HICKIE, JOHN. Ulster: a case study in conflict theory. London: 1971.

1273 FEENEY, VINCENT E. The civil rights movement in Northern Ireland. *Eire-Ir.*, vol. 9, no. 2, 1974, 30–40.

1274 HARRIS, ROSEMARY. Prejudice and tolerance in Ulster: a study of neighbours and 'strangers' in a border community. Manchester: 1972. Bibliog., pp. 226–7.

1275 MACGREIL, MICHAEL. Prejudice and tolerance in Ireland; based on a survey of intergroup attitudes of Dublin adults and other sources. Dublin: 1977.

Surveys

1276 AALEN, F.H.A. Rural surveys and the role of local development associations: a case-study in West Wicklow. *Development*, 15, 1967, 109–127.

1277 CLARKE, DESMOND J. Dublin Society's statistical surveys. *An Leab.*, 15, 1957, 47–54.

1278 CULLEN, L.M. Townlife, by L.M. Cullen with the collaboration of George Morrison. Dublin: Gill and MacMillan: 1973. (*Insights into Irish History*).

1279 AN FORAS FORBARTHA. Urban and regional research projects in Ireland, 1973–74: an annotated list. Dublin: 1974.

1280 — Urban and regional research projects in Ireland, 1975: an annotated list, prepared for the United Nations Economic Commission for Europe, Committee on Housing, Building and Planning, Group of Experts on Urban and Regional Research. Dublin: 1976.

1281 AN FORAS TALUNTAIS. West Donegal resource survey. Dublin.
Pt. 1. Soils and physical resources. 1969.

Pt. 2. Some aspects of production — crops, livestock and fisheries. 1969.
Pt. 3. Economic demographic and sociological aspects. 1969.
Pt. 4. Summary, conclusion and some development proposals for agriculture. 1969.

1282 HANLY, DAITHI. Planning report on the Galway Gaeltacht. Dublin: Foras Forbartha. 1971.

1283 HAUGHTON, J.P. Local rural surveys. *Admin*, vol. 11, no. 1, 1963, 46–53.

1284 JACKSON, JOHN A. Report on the Skibbereen Social Survey. Dublin: 1967.

1285 MOGEY, JOHN M. Rural life in Northern Ireland: five regional studies made for the Northern Ireland Council of Social Services. London: 1947. Bibliog., pp. 235–6.

1286 NEWMAN, *The Rev.* JEREMIAH. *ed.* The Limerick rural survey, 1955–64. Tipperary: 1964. Originally published as interim reports, 1960–64.

1287 TREADWELL, VICTOR. The survey of Armagh and Tyrone, 1622. *Ulster J. Arch.*, 23, 1960, 126–37; 27, 1964, 140–154.

1288 UNIVERSITY COLLEGE, GALWAY. Social Sciences Research Centre. An tSuirbheireacht ar Ghaeltacht na Gaillimhe: The Galway Gaeltacht Survey/Social Sciences Research Centre. University College, Galway [on behalf of the National Institute for Physical planning and Construction Research]; Director: Brendan S. MacAodha. 1969. 2 vols. Irish and English text.

1289 WHELAN, MARY. Reflections on a community survey. *Soc. Stud.*, vol. 3, no. 1, 1974, 3–11. A suburban community which in the interests of anonymity has been given the fictitious name of Castle Cross.

Church and Society

1290 WATERFORD COUNTY LIBRARIES. Catholic social teaching: a guide to books available in the County Waterford Libraries; introduction by Feargus MacMurchadha; comment by Dr. Alfred O'Rahilly. Athlone [1951].

Statistics

1291 CENTRAL STATISTICS OFFICE, DUBLIN. Select list [of publications]. Dublin [1956].

1292 — Irish trade journal and statistical bulletin. vol. 1–, 1925–. From 1964 *Irish Statistical Bulletin*.

1293 — Statistical abstract of Ireland. vol. 1–, 1931–.

1294 — Agricultural statistics, 1934–56. Dublin: 1960.

1295 COUSENS, S.H. The regional variation in mortality during the great Irish Famine. *R. Ir. Acad. Proc. Sec. C.*, vol. 63 no. 3, 1963, 127–149.

1296 CURTIN, J.V. A guide to regional statistics. Dublin: 1972.

1297 DRAKE, MICHAEL. The Irish demographic crises of 1740–41, *Hist. Stud.*, 6, 1968, 101–124.

1298 ELWOOD, J.H. Geographical distribution of fatal congenital malformations in Ireland. *Ir. J. Med. Sci.*, 7th Ser. 1968, 517–521.

1299 — A demographic study of Tory Island and Rathlin Island, 1841–1964. *Ulster Folk.*, 17, 1971. 70–80.

1300 — Tory Island, 1841–1964. Pt. 1 and 2. *Ir. J. Med. Sci.*, 7th ser. vol. 1. no. 1. 1968, 19–24, 63–72. Trends in population size.

1301 FROGGATT, P. The demographic work of Sir William Wilde. [with bibliog.] *Ir. J. Med. Sci.*, 6th Ser. no. 473, 1965, 213–230.

1302 GRIMSHAW, THOMAS WRIGLEY. Facts and figures about Ireland. Pt. I. Comprising a survey and analysis of the principal statistics of Ireland for the fifty years, 1841–1890. Pt. 2. Comprising comparative statistics of Irish counties; with tables of the principal statistics of the contents for each of the six decennial census years 1841–1891, and a summary analysis. Dublin: 1893.

1303 — On some comparative statistics of Irish counties, compiled from the returns obtained during the late census and the census of 1841, and other publications issued by the General Register Office of Ireland. *Stat. Social Inq. Soc. Ir. J.*, Pt. 61, 1883, 444–458.

1304 — A statistical survey of Ireland from 1840 to 1888; being the opening address for the session 1888–89. *Stat. Social Inq. Soc. Ir. J.*, Pt. 68, 1888, 321–361.

1305 IRELAND, DEPARTMENT OF INDUSTRY AND COMMERCE. Agricultural statistics, 1847–1926: report and tables. Dublin: 1928. Also vol. covering period 1927–33.

1306 LESER, C.E.V. Recent demographic developments in Ireland. *Stat. Social Inq. Soc. Ir. J.*, vol. 21, pt. 3, 1964–65, 179–204.

1307 MCGILVARY, JAMES. Social statistics in Ireland: a guide to their sources and uses. Dublin: Institute of Public Administration, 1977.

1308 MEGHEN, P.J. Statistics in Ireland. Dublin: Institute of Public Administration, 1970.

1309 MORGAN, VALERIE. Mortality in the Magherafelt, County Derry, in the early eighteenth century. *Ir. Hist. Stud.*, vol. 19. 1974, 125–135.

1310 NORTHERN IRELAND, MINISTRY OF FINANCE. Digest of statistics. Belfast, no. 1–, 1954–.

1311 O'GRADA, CORMAC. Seasonal migration and post-famine adjustment in the West of Ireland. *Stud. Hib.*, 13, 1973, 48–76.

1312 WALSH, BRENDAN M. Ireland's demographic transformation, 1958–70. *Econ. Soc. Rev.*, 3, 1972. 251–275.

1313 — Post-war demographic developments in the Republic of Ireland. [with bibliog]. *Soc. Stud.*, 1, 1972, 309–317.

1314 — Religion and demographic behaviour in Ireland, with appendix, Migration between Northern Ireland and the Republic of Ireland. Dublin: 1970. (*Economic and Social Research Institute paper no. 55*).

Population Census

1315 BUTLIN, R.A. The population of Dublin in the late seventeenth century. *Ir. Geog.*, vol. 5, no. 2, 1965, 51–66.

1316 CARNEY, F.J. Pre-famine Irish population: the evidence from the Trinity College estates. *Ir. Econ. Soc. Hist.*, 2, 1975, 35–45.

1317 CENTRAL STATISTICS OFFICE. Census of population of Ireland: 1971. Dublin: Stationery Office. vol. 1–, 1972–.

1318 CHRISTIANSON, GALE EDWARD. Population, the potato and depression in Ireland, 1800–1830. *Eire-Ir.*, vol. 7, no. 4, 1972, 70–95.

1319 COMPTON, P.A. and BOAL, F.W. Aspects of the intercommunity population balance in Northern Ireland. *Econ. Soc. Rev.*, vol. 1. no. 4. 1970, 455–476.

1320 CONNELL, K.H. The population of Ireland, 1750–1845. Oxford: 1950. Bibliog., pp. 276–86.

1321 CORCORAN, MOIRA. A Drogheda census list of 1798. *Louth Arch. J.*, vol. 17, no. 2, 1970. 91–96.

1322 COUSENS, S.H. Population trends in Ireland at the beginning of the twentieth century. *Ir. Geog.*, vol. 5, 1964–68, 387–401.

1323 CULLEN, L.M. Population trends in seventeenth century Ireland. *Econ. Soc. Rev.*, 6, 1975, 149–165.

1324 CURTIN, D. Population growth and other statistics of middle-sized Irish towns. Dublin: 1976. (*Economic and Social Research Institute paper no. 85*)

1325 DE BRUN, PADRAIG. A census of the parish of Ferriter, January 1835. *J. Kerry Arch. Hist. Soc.*, 7, 1974, 37–70.

1326 — A census of the parishes of Prior and Killenlagh, December 1834. *J. Kerry Arch. Hist. Soc.*, 8, 1975, 114–135.

1327 FROGGATT, PETER. The census in Ireland of 1813–15. *Ir. Hist. Stud.*, vol. 14, no. 55, 1965, 227–235.

1328 HORNER, A.A. Future population change in the Dublin region. *Ir. Geog.*, 7, 1974, 120–6.

1329 — The pre-famine population of some Kildare towns, with an additional note on the population of some rural areas. *Kildare Arch. Soc. J.*, 14, no. 4, 1969, 444–451.

1330 HUNTER, J.A. Population changes in the Lower Roe valley, 1831–1861. *Ulster Folk.*, 17, 1971, 61–69.

1331 JOHNSON, JAMES H. Population changes in Ireland, 1951–1961. *Geog J.*, 129, 1963, 167–174.

1332 — Population change in Ireland, 1961–66. *Ir. Geog.*, 5, 1964–68, 470–477.

1333 — Rural population changes in nineteenth

century Londonderry. *Ulster Folk.*, 15–16, 1970, 119–136.

1334 KELLY, EDMOND WALSH. Extracts from the census of 1821: Barony of Iverk, County of Kilkenny, contributed by Kathleen Kelly. *Ir. Geneal.*, vol. 5, no. 5, 1976, 383–393.

1335 KELLY, KATHLEEN. Extracts from the census of the city of Waterford, 1821. *Ir. Geneal.* vol. 4, no. 2, 1969, 17–24, 122–130.

1336 KENNEDY, ROBERT E., JR. The Irish: emigration, marriage and fertility. Berkeley and London: 1973.

1337 MCCARTHY, MICHAEL D. Some Irish population problems. *Studies*, vol. 56, 1967, 237–247.

1338 MORGAN, VALERIE. The Church of Ireland registers of St. Patrick's, Coleraine, as a source for the study of a local pre-famine population. *Ulster Folk.*, 19, 1973, 56–67.

1339 NORTHERN IRELAND, GENERAL REGISTER OFFICE. Census of population, Northern Ireland, 1961. Belfast: 1961–65. 10 vols.

1340 — Census of population, 1966. Preliminary report, 1967.

1341 O'BRIEN, GEORGE. The coming crisis of population: the future population of Ireland. *Studies*, vol. 25, 1936, 567–580.

1342 O'FERRALL, FERGUS. The population of a rural pre-famine parish, Templebredin, counties Limerick and Tipperary in 1834. *Nth. Munster Antiq. J.*, 17, 1975, 91–101.

1343 ROMAN CATHOLIC CHURCH, Archdiocese of Cashel and Emly. Pobal Ailbe — Cashel and Emly census of population, 1841–1971. Durlas [Thurles] (*Teach an Ardeaspaig*, Durlas Eile, Co. Tipp.) 1975.

1344 WALSH, BRENDAN. An empirical study of the age structure of the Irish population. *Econ. Soc. Rev.*, 1, 1970, 259–279.

1345 — Ireland's population prospects. *Soc. Stud.*, 3, 1974, 254–260.

1346 — Marriage rates and population pressure: Ireland 1871 *and* 1911. *Econ. Hist. Rev.*, 23, 1970, 148–162.

1347 — A perspective on Irish population patterns. *Eire-Ir.*, vol. 4. no. 3, 1964, 3–31.

1348 — Some Irish population problems reconsidered. Dublin: 1968. (*The Economic and Social Research Institute paper no. 42*)

1349 — Trends in the religious composition of the population in the republic of Ireland, 1946–1971. *Econ. Soc. Rev.*, 6, 1975, 543–555.

1350 WATERMAN, STANLEY. Some comments on standard distance: a new application to Irish population studies. *Ir. Geog.*, vol. 6, no. 1, 1969, 51–62.

POLITICAL SCIENCE

Sources

1351 MCCULLOCH, J.R. The literature of political economy: a classified catalogue of select publications in the different departments of that science, with historical, critical and biographical notices. London: 1845. Reprinted by the London School of Economics, 1938.

1352 PALGRAVE, R.H. INGLIS. Dictionary of political economy; new edition edited by Henry Riggs. London: 1923–6. 3 vols.

1353 RASHID, S. Political economy in the *Dublin University Magazine*, 1833–40. *Longroom*, 14–15, 1976–77, 16–19.

1354 UNITED NATIONS EDUCATIONAL, SCIENTIFIC AND CULTURAL ORGANISATION. International bibliography of political science. vol. 1– [Works published in 1952], 1953–. Paris: 1954–.

History

1355 AYEARST, MORLEY. The Republic of Ireland: its government and politics. London and New York: 1971. Bibliog., pp. 229–233.

1356 BOYCE, D.G. Englishmen and Irish troubles: British public opinion and the making of Irish policy, 1918–22. London: 1972. Bibliog., pp. 207–216.

1357 CHUBB, BASIL. The government and politics of Ireland; with a historical introduction, by David Thornley. Stanford and London: 1970.

1358 DICEY, A.V. England's case against home rule; new introduction by E.J. Feuchtwanger. Richmond (Surrey): 1973 (*English political history ser.*) Facsimile reprint of 1st ed. London: 1886.

1359 JOHNSTON, EDITH M. Great Britain and Ireland, 1760–1800: a study in political administration. Edinburgh and London: 1963 (*St. Andrew's Univ. pub.* 55) Bibliog., pp. 409–417.

1360 O'DAY, ALAN. The English face of Irish nationalism: Parnellite involvement in British politics, 1880–86. Dublin and Toronto: 1977.

1361 O TUATHAIGH, GEAROID. Nineteenth-century Irish politics: the case for 'normalcy'. *Anglo-Ir. Stud.*, 1, 1975, 71–81.

1362 RAVEN, JOHN *and others*. Political culture in Ireland: the views of two generations, by John Raven, C.T. Whelan, Paul A. Pfretzschner and Donald M. Borock. With an introduction by John H. Whyte. Dublin: 1976.

1363 WHYTE, JOHN H. The Tenant League and Irish politics in the eighteen-fifties. Dundalk, 1963. (*Ir. history ser. no.* 4)

Civics

1364 BLUEPRINT: a source magazine for teachers of civics and allied subjects. Dublin. vol. 1–, 1975–.

Periodicals

1365 HOWARD, PAULA. Irish sectarian periodicals. Brighton: 1973.

Nation and Territory

1366 ANDREWS, J.H. The papers of the Irish Boundary Commission. *Ir. Geog.*, 5, 1964–68, 477–481.

1367 EMPEY, C.A. The cantreds of medieval Tipperary. *Nth. Munster Antiq. J.*, 13, 1970, 23–29.

1368 IRISH BOUNDARY COMMISSION. Report of the Irish Boundary Commission, 1925; introduction by Geoffrey J. Hand. Shannon: 1969.

1369 O RIAIN, PADRAIG. Boundary association in early Irish society. *Stud. Celt.*, 7, 1972, 12–29.

Church and State

1370 BELL, P.M.H. Disestablishment in Ireland and Wales. London: 1969. Bibliog., pp. 330–336.

1371 LARKIN, EMMET. Church and state in Ireland in the nineteenth century. *Church Hist.*, 31, 1962, 294–306.

1372 — Economic growth, capital investment, and the Roman Catholic church in nineteenth century Ireland. *Amer. Hist. Rev.*, 72, 1967, 852–884.

1373 NATIONAL GALLERY OF IRELAND. Church disestablishment, 1870–1970; centenary exhibition commemorating the disestablishment of the Church of Ireland in 1870. Dublin: 1970. 180 items.

1374 NORMAN, E.R. The Catholic church and Ireland in the age of rebellion, 1859–1873. London: 1965. Bibliog., pp. 463–476.

1375 NOWLAN, KEVIN B. The Catholic clergy and Irish politics in the eighteen thirties and forties. *Hist. Stud.*, 9, 1974, 119–135.

1376 SCHMITT, DAVID E. Catholicism and democratic political development in Ireland. *Eire-Ir.*, vol. 9, no. 1, 1974, 59–72.

1377 TIERNEY, MARK. Correspondence concerning the disestablishment of the Church of Ireland, 1862–1869. *Coll. Hib.*, 12, 1969, 102–191.

1378 WHYTE, J.H. Church and state in modern Ireland, 1923–1970. Dublin: 1971. Bibliog., pp. 433–448.

Nationalism

1379 ALTER, PETER. Symbols of Irish nationalism. *Stud. Hib.*, 14, 1974, 104–123. Includes material on the anthem, flag, festivals and the O'Connell monument.

1380 CELTIC NATIONALISM, by Owen Dudley Edwards, Gwynfor Evans, Ion Rhys and Hugh MacDiarmid. London: 1968.

1381 CONWAY, THOMAS G. Women's work in Ireland. *Eire-Ir.*, vol. 7, no. 1, 1972, 10–27. Women's service in the cause of nationalism.

1382 KEE, ROBERT. The green flag: a history of Irish nationalism. London: 1972. Bibliog., 823–839.

1383 MCCAFFREY, LAWRENCE J. Daniel Corkery and Irish cultural nationalism. *Eire-Ir.*, vol. 8, no. 1, 1973, 35–41.

1384 O'CONNELL, BERNARD. Irish nationalism in Liverpool, [1873]– 1923. *Eire-Ir.*, vol. 10. no. 1, 1975, 24–37.

1385 PINSON, KOPPEL S. A bibliographical introduction to nationalism. New York: Columbia Univ. Press, 1935.

1386 RUMPF, E. and HEPBURN, A.C. Nationalism and socialism in twentieth century Ireland. Liverpool: 1977. Bibliog., pp. 250–260.

1387 STEELE, E.D. Cardinal Cullen and Irish nationality. *Ir. Hist. Stud.*, vol. 19, no. 75, 1975, 239–260.

1388 SYNDERGAARD, REX. The Fitzwilliam crisis and Irish nationalism. *Eire-Ir.*, vol. 6, no. 3, 1971, 72–82. Lord William Fitzwilliam, Lord Lieutenant.

1389 TIERNEY, MICHAEL. Origin and growth of modern Irish nationalism. *Studies*, 30, 1941, 321–336.

1390 — Nationalism: a survey. *ibid.*, 34, 1945, 474–482.

The State and the Individual

1391 ELLIS, P. BERRESFORD. A history of the Irish working class. London: 1972. Bibliog., pp. 336–339. Deals with the struggle for national and social freedom.

1392 KELLY, JOHN MAURICE. Fundamental rights in the Irish law and constitution. Dublin: 1961. Bibliog., pp. 268–9. 2nd ed. Dublin, 1967. Contains no bibliog.

Emigration and Immigration

1393 ADAMS, WILLIAM FORBES. Ireland and Irish emigration to the new world from 1815 to the Famine. New Haven and London: 1932. (*Yale Hist. Pub. Misc. no.* 23). Bibliog., pp. 429–38. Reprinted New York: Russell and Russell, 1967.

1394 BURKE, NICHOLAS R. Some observations on the migration of labourers from the south of Ireland to Newfoundland in pre-famine times. *Cork Hist. Arch. Soc. J.*, 76, 1971, 95–109.

1395 COLEMAN, TERRY. Passage to America: a history of emigrants from Great Britain and Ireland to America in the mid-nineteenth century. London: 1972. Sources and bibliog., pp. 251–286.

1396 COWAN, HELEN I. British emigration to British North America, 1783–1837. Toronto, 1928 (*University of Toronto studies, history and economic ser.*)

1397 DAVIS, R.P. Irish immigrant culture in New Zealand. *Threshold*, 20, 1966–7, 47–61.

1398 DICKSON, R.J. Ulster emigration to colonial America, 1718–1775. London: 1966 (*Ulster-Scot historical ser., no.* 1) Bibliog., pp. 298–311.

1399 ELLIS, EILISH. State-aided emigration schemes from crown estates in Ireland, *c.* 1850. *Anal. Hib.*, 22, 1960, 331–94. Includes lists of emigrants.

1400 GEARY, R.C. and HUGHES, J.G. Internal migration in Ireland; with Appendix: County migration, an alternative approach, by C.J. Gillman. Dublin: 1970. (*Economic and Social Research Institute, paper no.* 54)

1401 GREEN, E.R.R. *ed.* Essays in Scotch-Irish history. London and New York: 1969. Essays of Irish interest are: Ulster emigration, 1783–1815, by Maldwyn A. Jones; The Scotch-Irish: their culture, adaptation, and heritage in the American Old West, by E. Estyn Evans; Ulster emigrants' letters, by E.R.R. Green.

1402 HEINBERG, AAGE. Danske i England, Skotland og Irland. Denmark: 1934.

1403 IRELAND, DEPARTMENT OF SOCIAL WELFARE. Commission on emigration and other population problems, 1948–54: reports. Dublin: 1955.

1404 JUPP, PETER. Genevese exiles in County Waterford. *Cork Hist. Arch. Soc. J.*, 75, 1970, 29–35.

1405 KEEP, GEORGE REX CROWLEY. The Irish migration to Montreal, 1847–67. Rochester, N.Y: Univ. of Rochester Press, 1956. 4 cards

7½× 12½ cm. Microcard F1054.5.M8.

1406 MORRISSEY, PATRICK J. Working conditions in Ireland and their effect on Irish emigration: an industrial relations study. New York: 1958. Bibliog., pp. 76–9.

1407 O DANACHAIR, CAOIMHIN. Emigration from County Clare. *Nth. Munster Antiq. J.*, 17, 1975, 69–76.

1408 O'FARRELL, PATRICK. Emigrant attitudes and behaviour as a source for Irish history. *Hist. Stud.*, 10, 1976, 109–131.

1409 SCHRIER, ARNOLD. Ireland and the American emigration, 1850–1900. Minneapolis: Univ. of Minnesota, 1958. Reprinted New York: Russell and Russell, 1970.

1410 TAYLOR, PHILIP. The distant magnet: European emigration to the U.S.A. London: 1971. Bibliog., pp. 283–309.

Foreign Affairs

1411 BECKETT, J.C. Irish-Scotch relations in the seventeenth century. *Belfast Nat. Hist. Phil. Soc. Proc., 2nd ser.*, 7, 1961–64, 38–49.

1412 BOND, M.A. A German view of Anglo-Irish relations in 1800: Friedrich von Gentz on the Act of Union. *Eire-Ir.*, vol. 8, no. 1, 1973, 13-20.

1413 BROMAGE, MARY C. Churchill and Ireland. Nôtre Dame: Univ. of Nôtre Dame, 1964.

1414 BUTLIN, ROBIN. Ireland in an international world. *Geog. Mag.*, 49, 1977, 430–437.

1415 CALKIN, HOMER L. The United States Government and the Irish: a bibliographical study of research materials in the U.S. national archives. *Ir. Hist. Stud.*, 9, 1954–5, 28–52.

1416 DWYER, T. RYLE. Irish neutrality and the USA, 1939–47. Dublin and Totowa (N.J.): 1977.

1417 FOREIGN AFFAIRS BIBLIOGRAPHY: a selected and annotated list of books on international relations, 1919–32–. New York and London: 1933–.
1919–32: edited by W.L. Langer and H.F. Armstrong. 1933.
1932–42: edited by R.G. Woolbert. 1945.
1942–52: edited by H.L. Roberts and others. 1955.
1952–62: edited by H.L. Roberts. 1969.
1962–72: edited by J.A. Kreslins. 1976.

1418 HACHEY, THOMAS E. The British Foreign Office and new perspectives on the Irish issue in Anglo-American relations, 1919–1921. *Eire-Ir.*, vol. 7, no. 2, 1972, 3–13.

1419 — The Irish question: the British Foreign Office and the American political conventions of 1920. *ibid.*, vol. 3, no. 3, 1968, 92–106.

1420 HARKNESS, D.W. The restless dominion: the Irish Free State and the British Commonwealth of Nations, 1921–31. London: 1969. Bibliog., pp. 273–280.

1421 HARRISON, HENRY. Ireland and the British Empire, 1937: conflict or collaboration? A study of Anglo-Irish differences from the international standpoint, with statistics prepared by the intelligence branch of *The Economist*. London: 1937.

1422 KEATINGE, PATRICK. The formulation of Irish foreign policy. Dublin: 1973. Bibliog., pp. 303–305.

1423 — Ireland and the League of Nations. *Studies*, 49, 1970, 133–147.

1424 — A place among the nations: issues of Irish foreign policy. Dublin: 1978. Bibliog., pp. 272–275.

1425 LIBRARY OF CONGRESS. Brief list of recent references on the Irish-English question. Washington: 1921. 2nd ed., 1922.

1426 LYNCH, JOHN M. The Anglo-Irish problem. *For. Affairs*, 50, 1972, 601–617.

1427 MANSERGH, NICHOLAS. The Irish question, 1840–1921: a commentary on Anglo-Irish relations and on social and political forces in Ireland in the age of reform and revolution. 3rd ed., London: 1975. Bibliog., pp. 326–332. 1st ed. *Ireland in the age of reform and revolution*, pub. London: 1940.

1428 MITCHELL, ARTHUR. Ireland and the Soviet Union. *Cap. Ann.*, 1975, 163–168.

1429 NOWLAN, KEVIN B. The politics of repeal: a study in the relations between Great Britain and Ireland, 1841–50. London and Toronto: 1965. (*Studies in Irish history, 2nd ser.*, vol. 3.) Bibliog., pp. 232–241.

1430 O'FARRELL, PATRICK. Ireland's English question: Anglo-Irish relations, 1534–1970. London: 1971. Bibliog., pp. 308–327.

1431 PRILL, FELICIAN. Ireland, Britain and Germany, 1871–1914: problems of nationalism and religion in nineteenth-century Europe. Dublin and New York: 1975. Bibliog., pp. 189–192.

1432 SNODDY, OLIVER. Bungling British diplomacy: notes on Irish, Cypriot, Egyptian and Indian history. *Cap. Ann*. 1973, 337–356.

1433 WOODS, C.J. The secret mission to Ireland of Captain Bernard MacSheehy, an Irishman in French service, 1796. *Cork Hist. Arch Soc. J*., 78, 1973, 93–108.

PARLIAMENT

Sources

1434 ADAM, MARGARET I. *and others*. Guide to the principal parliamentary papers relating to the Dominions, 1812–1911, by M.I. Adam, John Ewing, and James Munro. Edinburgh: 1913.

1435 CHUBB, BASIL, *ed*. A source book of Irish government. Dublin: 1964.

1436 FARRELL, BRIAN, *ed*. The Irish parliamentary tradition; with three essays on the Treaty debate, by F.S.L. Lyons. Dublin and New York: 1973.

1437 FORD, P. and FORD, G. A breviate of parliamentary papers, 1900–1916. Shannon: 1969. 1st published, Oxford: 1957.

1438 — A breviate of parliamentary papers, 1917–1939. Rev. ed., Shannon: 1969. 1st published, Oxford: 1951.

1439 — A breviate of parliamentary papers, 1940–1954. Oxford: 1961.

1440 — Hansard's Catalogue and breviate of parliamentary papers, 1696–1834 [1837]: reprinted in facsimile with an introduction . . . Oxford: 1953. Reprinted also as Index I of Irish University Press series of British parliamentary papers. Shannon: 1971.

1441 GABINE, B.L., *compiler*. A finding list of British royal commission reports, 1860–1935. Cambridge, Mass: 1935.

1442 GREAT BRITAIN, HOUSE OF COMMONS. A bibliography of parliamentary debates of Great Britain. London: 1956. (*House of Commons Library documents*, no. 2.) Appendix VI: The parliament of Ireland, pp. 49–52.

1443 — General index to the bills, reports and papers printed by order of the House of Commons and to the Reports and Papers presented by command, 1900 to 1948–9. London: 1960.

1444 IRIS OIFIGIUIL. Dublin: no. 1–, 1922–. Includes list of government publications.

1445 IRISH UNIVERSITY PRESS. Checklist of British parliamentary papers in the Irish University Press 1000 vol. series, 1801–1899. Shannon: 1972.

1446 — Short-title catalogue of the first 520 volumes (of the British parliamentary papers 'Blue Books'.) Shannon: 1970.

1447 MALTBY, ARTHUR. The government of Northern Ireland, 1922–72: a catalogue and breviate of parliamentary papers. Dublin: 1974.

1448 NEALON, TED. Ireland, a parliamentary directory, 1973–74. Dublin: 1974.

1449 — Guide to the 21st Dail and Seanad, written in association with Frank Dunlop. Dublin: 1977.

1450 QUEENS UNIVERSITY OF BELFAST LIBRARY. British and Irish government publications in the Queens University Library, prepared by Frieda Brown. Belfast: 1973. 28pp.

1451 STATIONERY OFFICE, DUBLIN. Consolidated list of government publications issued by the Stationery Office. Dublin: 1922–25–. Supplements published at frequent intervals.

1452 UNITED NATIONS EDUCATIONAL, SCIENTIFIC AND CULTURAL ORGANISATION. Etudes des bibliographies courantes des publications officielles nationales. (A study of current bibliographies of national official publications): guide sommaire et inventaire; rédacteur: Jean Meyriat. Paris: 1958.

Parliament and Politics

1453 BECKETT, J.C. The Irish parliament in the eighteenth century; with an appendix on

British legislation for Ireland between *the Sixth of George I* and its repeal, by J.C. Beckett and A.G. Donaldson. *Belfast Nat. Hist. Soc. Proc., 2nd ser.*, 4, 1955, 17–37.

1454 BOLAND, JOHN. Irishman's day: a day in the life of an Irish M.P. London: 1944. Bibliog., pp. 170–1.

1455 BRADSHAW, BRENDAN. The opposition to the ecclesiastical legislation in the Irish Reformation parliament. *Ir. Hist. Stud.*, 16, 1968–69, 285–303.

1456 CLARKE, AIDAN. The policies of the 'Old English' in parliament, 1640–41. *Hist. Stud.*, 5, 1965, 85–102.

1457 — *and* FENLON, DERMOT. Two notes on the parliament of 1634. *R. Soc. Antiq. Ir. J.*, 97, 1967, 85–90. For previous articles see *ibid.*, 93, 1963, 161–7; 94, 1964, 159–175.

1458 COMERFORD, MAIRE. The first Dail, January 21st 1919. Dublin, 1969.

1459 EDWARDS, R. DUDLEY. The Irish Reformation parliament of Henry VIII, 1536–7. *Hist. Stud.*, 6, 1968, 59–84.

1460 FARRELL, BRIAN. The founding of Dail Eireann: parliament and nation building. Dublin: 1971.

1461 — Dail deputies: 'The 1969' generation. *Econ. Soc. Rev.*, vol. 2, no. 3, 1971, 309–327.

1462 GARVIN, THOMAS. The Irish Senate. Dublin: 1969.

1463 JOHNSTON, E.M. Members of the Irish parliament, 1784–7. *R. Ir. Acad. Proc., Sec. C*, 71, 1971, 139–246.

1464 JUPP, P.J. Irish M.P.s at Westminster in the early nineteenth century. *Hist. Stud.*, 7, 1969, 65–80.

1465 LAWLESS, MICHAEL. The Dail electoral system. *Administration*, vol. 5, no. 1, 1957, 57–74.

1466 LYONS, F.S.L. The Irish parliamentary party, 1890–1910. London: 1951. (*Studies in Irish history*, vol. 4.) Bibliog., pp. 265–74.

1467 MALCOMSON, A.P.W. John Foster and the speakership of the Irish House of Commons. *R. Ir. Acad. Proc., Sec. C*, 72, 1972, 271–303.

1468 MANSERGH, NICHOLAS. The Irish Free State, its government and politics. London: 1934. Bibliog., pp. 335–9.

1469 MOODY, T.W. The Irish parliament under Elizabeth and James I: a general survey. *R. Ir. Acad. Proc., Sec. C*, 45, 1938–40, 41–81.

1470 MOUNTMORRES, HERVEY REDMOND MORRES, *Viscount*. The history of the principal transactions of the Irish parliament, from the year 1634 to 1660. [1st ed. reprinted]; introduction by Dermot Englefield. Shannon: 1971. 2 vols.

1471 O'SULLIVAN, DONAL JOSEPH. The Irish Free State and its Senate: a study in contemporary politics. London: 1940. Bibliog. footnotes.

1472 RICHARDSON, H.G. and SAYLES, G.O. The Irish parliament in the Middle Ages. 2nd ed., Philadelphia: 1964.

1473 — Parliament in medieval Ireland. Dundalk; 1964. (*Dublin Historical Association, Medieval Irish history ser., no.* 1.)

1474 — Parliaments and councils of medieval Ireland. Dublin: Irish Manuscripts Commission. vol. 1. 1947. Bibliog. information in introduction.

1475 ROBINSON, MARY T. The role of the Irish parliament. *Admin.*, vol. 22, no. 1, 1974, 3–25.

1476 SIMMS, J.G. The Irish parliament of 1713. *Hist. Stud.*, 4, 1963, 82–92.

1477 — The Jacobite parliament of 1689. Dundalk; 1966. (*Dublin Historical Association, Irish history ser., no.* 6)

1478 SMYTH, JOHN MCGOWAN. The Houses of the Oireachtas. 3rd rev. ed., Dublin: 1973.

1479 — Seanad Eireann. *Admin.*, 15, 1967, 301–7; 16, 1968, 56–63.

1480 SNODDY, CLIODNA. Some notes on parliament and its Limerick members (1767–1771). *Nth. Munster Antiq. J.*, 9, 1962–65, 165–181.

1481 TREADWELL, V. The Irish parliament of 1569–71. *R. Ir. Acad. Proc., Sec. C*, 65, 1966, 55–89.

1482 WARD, ALAN J. Parliamentary procedures and the machinery of government in Ireland. *Ir. Univ. Rev.*, 4, 1974, 222–243.

Political Parties

1483 BUCKLAND, PATRICK. Irish unionism. Dublin and New York.
Vol. 1. The Anglo-Irish and the new Ireland, 1885–1922. 1972.
Vol. 2. Ulster unionism and the origins of Northern Ireland, 1886-1922. 1973.

1484 — Irish unionism, 1885–1923: a documentary history. Belfast: 1973.

1485 FARRELL, BRIAN. Labour and the Irish political party system. *Econ. Soc. Rev*., vol. 1, no. 4, 1970, 477–502.

1486 FIANNA FAIL. Iubhaile orga: Fianna Fail, the republican party, 1926–76: the first fifty years. [Dublin: 1976.]

1487 HAYTON, DAVID. Tories and Whigs in County Cork, 1714. *Cork Hist. Arch. Soc. J*., 80, 1975, 84–88.

1488 MCALLISTER, IAN. The Northern Ireland Social Democratic and Labour Party. London: 1977. Bibliog., pp. 191–4.

1489 MANNING, MAURICE. Irish political parties: an introduction. Dublin: 1972. (*Studies in Irish political culture no*. 3) Bibliog., pp. 119–120.

1490 MITCHELL, ARTHUR. The Irish labour movement and the foundation of the Free State. *Cap. Ann*., 1972, 362–374.

1491 — Labour in Irish politics, 1890–1930: the Irish labour movement in an age of revolution. Dublin: 1974. Bibliog., pp. 299–305.

1492 — Thomas Johnson, 1872–1963: a pioneer labour leader. *Studies*, 58, 1969, 396–404.

1493 — William O'Brien, 1881–1968, and the Irish labour movement. *Studies*, 60, 1971, 311–331.

1494 MOSS, WARNER. Political parties in the Irish Free State. New York: 1933. Biographies of politicians, pp. 222–7.

1495 PYNE, PETER. The Third Sinn Fein party. *Econ. Soc. Rev*., 1, 1970, 29–50, 229–257.

1496 SACKS, PAUL MARTIN. The Donegal Mafia: an Irish political machine. New Haven and London. 1976. An account of Neil Blaney's political activities.

Elections

1497 BUSTEED, M.A. and MASON, HUGH. The 1973 general election in the Republic of Ireland. *Ir. Geog*., 7, 1974, 97–106.

1498 D'ALTON, IAN. Cork unionism: its role in parliamentary and local elections, 1885–1914. *Stud. Hib*., 15, 1975, 143–161.

1499 JUPP, PETER. British and Irish elections, 1784–1831. Newton Abbot and New York: 1973.

1500 — County Down elections, 1783–1831. *Ir. Hist. Stud*., vol. 18, no. 70, 1972, 177–206.

1501 — Irish parliamentary elections and the influence of the Catholic vote, 1801–20. *Hist. J*., 10, 1967, 183–196.

1502 KNIGHT, JAMES and BAXTER-MOORE, NICOLAS. Northern Ireland: the elections of the twenties; the general elections for the House of Commons of the Parliament of Northern Ireland, May 1921 and August 1925, by the system of proportional representation, by the single transferable vote in multi-member constituencies, and May 1929 by the X-vote in single member constituencies. London: 1972.

1503 — Republic of Ireland: the general elections of 1969 and 1973; with a foreword by Garret Fitzgerald. London [1974].

1504 LAWRENCE, R.J. *and others*. The Northern Ireland general elections of 1973, by R.J. Lawrence, S. Elliott, and M.J. Laver. London: 1975.

1505 MORAN, JOHN. Local elections in Cork city (1929–1967). *Cork Hist. Arch. Soc. J*., 78, 1973, 124–133.

1506 MURRAY, PATRICK. Irish elections: a changing pattern. *Studies*, 65, 1976, 193–209.

1507 NIHILL, J.J. The election manifesto. *Ir. Booklore*, vol. 1. no. 1, 1971, 92–95.

1508 PADDISON, R. The revision of local electoral areas in the Republic of Ireland: problems and possibilities. *Ir. Geog*., 7, 1974, 116–120.

1509 SACKS, PAUL M. Bailiwicks, locality, and religion: three elements in an Irish Dail constituency election [Donegal north-east]. *Econ. Soc. Rev*., vol. 1, no. 4, 1970, 531–554.

1510 WALKER, BRIAN M. A county Dublin election poll book. *Longroom*, 5, 1972, 21–2.

1511 — Irish election poll books, 1832–72. Pt. 1. *Ir. Booklore*, vol. 3, no. 1, 1976, 9–13.

1512 — The Irish electorate, 1868–1915. *Ir. Hist. Stud.*, vol. 18, no. 71, 1973, 359–406. Includes tables listing number of electors, M.P.s, population in parliamentary boroughs and counties for the period.

ECONOMICS

Sources

1513 BLACK, R.D. COLLISON. A catalogue of pamphlets on economic subjects published between 1750 and 1900 and now housed in Irish libraries. Belfast: 1969.

1514 — Guide to archive sources in the history of economic thought and policy since 1750. In preparation.

1515 — A selective bibliography of economic writings by members of Trinity College, Dublin. *Hermathena*, 66, 1945, 55–68.

1516 BOOK ASSOCIATION OF IRELAND. Economic, legal and political questions [book list]. *Ir. Lib. Bull.*, vol. 6, no. 5, 1945, 109–11.

1517 CHALONER, W.H. and RICHARDSON, R.C., *compilers*. British economic and social history: a bibliographical guide. Manchester: 1976.

1518 ECONOMIC AND SOCIAL RESEARCH INSTITUTE. Abstracts of published papers, 1961–1969. Dublin: 1969.

1519 ECONOMIC HISTORY REVIEW. London: vol. 1–, 1927–8–. Includes *List of books and articles on the economic history of Great Britain and Ireland*.

1520 FITZPATRICK, PAUL J., and CLETUS, F. DIRKSEN. Bibliography of economic books and pamphlets by Catholic authors, 1891–1941. Washington, Catholic Univ. of America: 1941.

1521 HALL, HUBERT. A select bibliography for the study, sources and literature of English mediaeval economic history. London: 1914.

1522 HANSON, L.W. Contemporary printed sources for British and Irish economic history, 1701–1750. Cambridge: 1965.

1523 HIGGS, HENRY. Bibliography of economics, 1751–75. Cambridge: 1935. Important source for agriculture, shipping, navigation, manufactures, commerce, colonies, finance, transport, and social conditions.

1524 IRISH ECONOMIC AND SOCIAL HISTORY. Dublin, vol. 1–, 1974–. Includes annual select bibliography of publications in Irish economic and social history.

1525 KRESS LIBRARY OF BUSINESS AND ECONOMICS. Catalogue covering material published through 1776 with data upon cognate items in other Harvard libraries. Boston, Mass: 1940.

1526 LEWIS, PETER R. The literature of the social sciences: an introductory survey and guide. London: 1960.

1527 LONDON BIBLIOGRAPHY OF THE SOCIAL SCIENCES; being the subject catalogue of the British Library of Political and Economic Science . . . compiled under the direction of B.M. Headicar and C. Fuller. London: 1931–2. 4 vols; supplements, vol. 5–, 1934–.

1528 NORTHERN IRELAND. Public Record Office. Exhibition of Irish economic documents. Belfast: 1967. 79 documents covering overseas trade, expansion of communications, management of landed estates, the linen industry, and development of Belfast.

1529 [O] RAHILLY, ALFRED. A guide to books for social students and workers. Cork and Dublin: 1916. (*Univ. and labour ser.*, no. 1.)

1530 PRENDEVILLE, P.L. A select bibliography of Irish economic history. Reprinted from *Econ. Hist. Rev.*, 3, 1931, 274–92, 402–16; 4, 1932, 81–90.

1531 STATISTICAL AND SOCIAL INQUIRY SOCIETY OF IRELAND. Historical memoirs of the . . . society, by S. Shannon Millin. Dublin: 1920. Includes index to publications of the society for period 1847–1919.

1532 — Centenary volume, 1847–1947; with a history of the society by R.D. Collison Black and indexes to the Transactions of the society. Dublin: 1947. Biographical sketches, pp. 48–85.

1533 STURGES, R.P., *compiler*. Economists' papers, 1750–1950: a guide to archives and other manuscript sources for the history of British and Irish economic thought. London: 1975. Includes Charles Francis Bastable, Edmund Burke, Isaac Butt, William Neilson Hancock, John Kells Ingram, Thomas Edward Cliffe Leslie and Richard Whately.

1534 UNITED NATIONS EDUCATIONAL, SCIENTIFIC AND CULTURAL ORGANISATION. International bibliography of economics. Paris: vol. 1 (Works published in 1952), 1955; vol. 2–, 1955–.

1535 — World list of social science periodicals. 2nd rev. and enl. ed.; prepared by the International Committee for Social Sciences Documentation. Paris: 1957. 1st ed., 1954. Text in French and English.

Statistics

1536 MCGILVRAY, JAMES. Irish economic statistics. Dublin: 1968. Chapters on population, manpower, agriculture, industrial production, foreign trade, national income and expenditure, and distribution.

Economic History

1537 BARRY, J.G. Sir Robert Kane and national development. *Manp. App. Psychol*. vol. 2, no. 1, 1968, 20–25.

1538 BLACK, R.D. COLLISON. Economic studies at Trinity College, Dublin. No. 1: *Hermathena*, 70, 1947, 65–80; no. 2: *ibid*, 71, 1948, 52–63.

1539 — Economic thought and the Irish question, 1817–70. Cambridge, 1960. Bibliog., pp. 249–92.

1540 — Theory and policy in Anglo-Irish trade relations, 1775–1800. *Stat. Social Inq. Soc. Ir. J*., 18, 1949–50, 312–26.

1541 — Trinity College, Dublin, and the theory of value, 1832–63. *Economica, n.s*., 12, 1945, 140–8.

1542 BRISTOW, J.A. and TAIT, A.A., *eds*. Economic policy in Ireland. Dublin: 1968.

1543 CHARLTON, KENNETH. The state of Ireland in the 1820s: James Cropper's plan. *Ir. Hist. Stud*., 17, 1970–1, 320–339.

1544 CHART, D.A. An economic history of Ireland. Dublin: 1920.

1545 CULLEN, L.M. An economic history of Ireland since 1660. London: 1972. Bibliog. note, 188–195.

1546 — *ed*. The formation of the Irish economy. Cork: 1969. (*Thomas Davis lectures ser*.) Contents: The Irish economy in the eighteenth century, by L.M. Cullen; The rise of the linen industry, by W.H. Crawford, Catholics in economic life, by Maureen Wall; Capital in the Irish economy, by Joseph Lee; Population and the Irish economy, by Michael Drake; The railways in the Irish economy, by Joseph Lee; Industrial decline in the nineteenth century, by E.R.R. Green; The industrialisation of the North-East, by J.M. Goldstrom; Irish economic history: fact and myth, by L.M. Cullen.

1547 — and SMOUT, T.C., *eds*. Comparative aspects of Scottish and Irish economic and social history, 1600–1900. Edinburgh: 1977.

1548 FREEMAN, T.W. Pre-famine Ireland: a study in historical geography. Manchester: 1957. Bibliog., pp. 318–340.

1549 GIBSON, NORMAN J. and SPENCER, JOHN E., *eds*. Economic activity in Ireland: a study of two open economies. Dublin: 1977.

1550 JOHNSON, DAVID S. The economic history of Ireland between the wars. *Ir. Econ. Soc. Hist*., 1, 1974, 49–61.

1551 HUTCHINSON, BERTRAM. On the study of non-economic factors in Irish economic development. *Econ. Soc. Rev*., vol. 1, no. 4, 1970, 509–529.

1552 LEE, JOSEPH. The dual economy in Ireland, 1800–50. *Hist. Stud*., 8, 1971, 191–201.

1553 LYONS, F.S.L. The economic ideas of Parnell [with bibliog.] *Hist. Stud*., 2, 1959, 60–78.

1554 MCGOVERN, P.D. Northern Ireland: people with a purpose. *Geog. Mag*., 38, 1965–6, 505–520.

1555 MEENAN, JAMES. The Irish economy since 1922. Liverpool; 1970. Bibliog., pp. 409–418.

1556 MURIE, ALAN. Spatial aspects of unemployment and economic stress in Northern Ireland. *Ir. Geog*., 7, 1974, 53–67.

1557 O'BRIEN, GEORGE. The economic history of Ireland in the seventeenth century. Clifton, New Jersey: 1972. (*Reprints of economic classics*). 1st ed., Dublin: 1919.

1558 — The economic history of Ireland in the eighteenth century. Dublin: 1918.

1559 —The economic history of Ireland from the Union to the Famine. London: 1921.

1560 O GADHRA, NOLLAIG. The economic development of the Gaeltacht. *Eire-Ir.*, vol. 8, no. 1, 1973, 124–130.

1561 O'HAGAN, J.W. The economy of Ireland: policy and performance. Dublin: 1975. Select bibliog., p. 245.

1562 O'MAHONY, DAVID. The Irish economy: an introductory description. New rev. ed., Cork: 1967. 1st ed., Cork: 1964.

1563 O'NEILL, HELEN B. Spatial planning in the small economy: a case study of Ireland. New York, Washington and London: 1971. (*Praeger special studies in international economics and development*).

1564 O'SULLIVAN, WILLIAM. The economic history of Cork City from the earliest times to the Act of Union. Cork and Dublin: 1937. Bibliog., pp. 363–82.

1565 PETTY, WILLIAM. Hoppen, K. Theodore. Sir William Petty: polymath, 1623–1687. *Hist. Today*, 15, 1965, 126–134.

1566 — HULL, CHARLES HENRY, *ed.* The economic writings of Sir William Petty, together with the observations upon the bills of mortality, more probably by Capt. John Graunt. Cambridge, 1899. 2 vols. Bibliog. of the printed writings of Petty, pp. 633–52; supplement, pp. 653–7; bibliog. of the natural and political observations, pp. 658–60; list of books and manuscripts used, pp. 661–72.

1567 — A bibliography of Sir William Petty, F.R.S., and of 'Observations on the bills of mortality' by John Graunt, F.R.S. Oxford: 1971.

1568 — MASSON, IRVINE, and YOUNGSON, A.J. Sir William Petty, F.R.S. [with bibliog.]. *R. Soc. N. & R.*, 15, 1960, 79–90.

1569 — STRAUSS, E. Sir William Petty: portrait of a genius. London: 1954. Bibliog., pp. 233–6.

1570 ROBBINS, LIONEL. Robert Torrens and the evolution of classical economics. London: 1958. Bibliog., pp. 259–353.

1571 STEELE, E.D. J.S. Mill and the Irish question: *The principles of political economy*, 1848–1865. *Hist. J.*, vol. 13, no. 2, 1970, 216–236.

1572 VAIZEY, JOHN, *ed.* Economic sovereignty and regional policy: a symposium on regional problems in Britain and Ireland. Dublin: 1975.

1573 WAKEFIELD, EDWARD. An account of Ireland, statistical and political. London. 1812. 2 vols.

Employment, Labour

1574 AGNEW, JOHN A. Manpower policy. *Stat. Social Inq. Soc. Ir. J.*, vol. 21, pt. 6, 1967–68, 31–50.

1575 BLACK, WILLIAM and JEFFERSON, CLIFFORD W. Regional employment patterns in Northern Ireland. Dublin: 1974. (*Economic and Social Research Institute paper no.* 73)

1576 CLARKSON, J. DUNSMORE. Labour and nationalism in Ireland. New York, 1952. (*Columbia Univ. studies in history, economics and public law*, vol. 120.) Bibliog., pp. 479–91.

1577 DEENY, JAMES. The Irish worker: a demographic study of the labour force in Ireland. Dublin: 1971. (*Institute of Public Administration research ser. no.* 4)

1578 DUBLIN, UNIVERSITY COLLEGE. Dept. of Social Science. Manpower in a developing community: a pilot survey in Drogheda; abridged report by Conor K. Ward. Dublin: 1967.

1579 GARMANY, J.W. A survey of manpower: Londonderry, Coleraine, Limavady and Strabane — a case study. *Stat. Social Inq. Soc. Ir. J.*, vol. 21, 117*th session*, 1963–64, 55–66.

1580 GEARY, R.C. and DEMPSEY, M. A study of schemes for the relief of unemployment in Ireland; with Appendix by E Costa. (*Economic and Social Research Institute broadsheet no.* 14) Bibliog., pp. 143–147.

1581 — and HUGHES, J.G. Certain aspects of non-agricultural unemployment in Ireland. Dublin: 1970. (*Economic and Social*

Research Institute paper no. 52)

1582 HENRY, E.W. Production functions for 14 subsectors of Irish industry, 1960–68, for the purpose of estimating employment. *Econ. Soc. Rev*., vol. 3, no. 2, 1971, 189–213.

1583 INSTITUTE OF PUBLIC ADMINISTRATION. Report on the Placement and Guidance Service. Dublin: 1968.

1584 KENNEDY, KIERNAN A. and DOWLING, B.R. Productivity, earnings and the composition of labour: Irish manufacturing industries, 1953–1966. *Econ. Soc. Rev*., vol. 1, no. 2, 1970, 215–228.

1585 LYNN, RICHARD. The Irish brain drain. Dublin: 1968. (*Economic and Social Research Institute paper no*. 43)

1586 MARSH, ARNOLD. Full employment in Ireland. Dublin: 1945.

1587 NATIONAL INDUSTRIAL ECONOMIC COUNCIL. Report on full employment. Dublin: 1967.

1588 NORTON, DESMOND. Unemployment and public policy. *Studies*, 65, 1976, 1–16.

1589 O hEIDEAIN, E.M. Galway labour survey. *Admin*., 14, 1966, 20–23.

1590 O'HERLIHY, C.S.J. Economic studies in Northern Ireland labour statistics. *Stat. Social Inq. Soc. Ir. J*., vol. 21, 117*th session*, 1963–64, 145–175.

1591 O'MUIRCHEARTAIGH, COLM A. Absenteeism in Irish industry. Dublin: 1975. (*Irish productivity centre, Human sciences in industry study no*. 12) Bibliog., pp. 160–164.

1592 O'REILLY, A.P. Manpower for offshore oil and gas. *Technol. Ir*., vol. 6, no. 6, 1974, 33–38.

1593 REDFORD, ARTHUR. Labour migration in England, 1800–50. Manchester: 1926. (*Manchester Univ. pub. econ, hist. ser*., no. 3.) Bibliog., pp. xv–xvi.

1594 SMITH, LOUIS P.F. Cooley Peninsula [Co. Louth] manpower survey, 1967. Dublin: 1969.

1595 TAYLOR, F. ISABEL. A bibliography of unemployment and the unemployed. London: 1909.

1596 WALSH, BRENDAN M. Aspects of labour supply and demand with special reference to the employment of women in Ireland. *Stat. Social Inq. Soc. Ir. J*., vol. 22, pt. 3, 1970–71, 88–123.

1597 — and O'TOOLE, ANNETTE. Women and unemployment in Ireland: results of a national survey. Dublin: 1973. (*Economic and Social Research Institute paper no*. 69).

Income

1598 BEHREND, HILDE, *and others*. Views on income differentials and the economic situation; findings from a national sample survey, by Hilde Behrend, Ann Knowles and Jean Davies. Dublin: 1970. (*Economic and Social Research Institute paper no*. 57)

1599 COWLING, KEITH. Determinants of wage inflation in Ireland. Dublin: 1966. (*Economic and Social Research Institute paper no*. 31)

1600 MCGINLEY, MICHAEL. Pay negotiation in the public service. *Admin*., vol. 24, no. 1, 1976, 76–95.

1601 WALSH, BRENDAN. Wages and labour mobility: an inter-industry study. *Econ. Soc. Rev*. vol. 1, no. 4, 1970, 555–566.

Housing

1602 COLIVET, M.P. The Housing Board, 1932–44. *Admin*., vol. 2, no. 3, 1954, 83–6.

1603 CRAFT, MAURICE. The development of Dublin: background to the housing problem. *Studies*, vol. 59, 1970, 301–313.

1604 CUNNINGHAM, ANTHONY C. New homes: housewives' likes and dislikes. Dublin: 1971. (*University College, Dublin, Dept. of Business Administration, Faculty of Commerce, Business research report, no*. 3)

1605 FAUGHNAN, PAULINE. Depressed housing. *Soc. Stud*., vol. 1, no. 5, 1972, 565–575.

1606 HOGAN, R.N. Some aspects of housing in Ireland. *Inst. Civ. Eng. Ir. Trans*., 67, 1940–41, 51–93.

1607 KAIM-CAUDLE, P.R. Housing in Ireland: some economic aspects. Dublin: 1965. (*Economic and Social Research Institute paper no*. 28)

1608 McCULLOUGH, JOSEPH. The Ballymun project. *Inst. Civ. Eng. Ir. Tran.*, 94, 1967–8, 69–78.

1609 MEGHEN, P.J. Housing in Ireland. Dublin: 1963. (*Institute of Public Administration, guides to the public services*: 1)

1610 MUIRE, A.S. An index of housing conditions for Ireland. *Soc. Stud.*, vol. 1, no. 3, 1972, 318–324.

1611 PFRETZSCHNER, PAUL A. The dynamics of Irish housing. Dublin: 1965. Bibliog., pp. 131–133.

1612 UNIVERSITY COLLEGE, DUBLIN. Dept. of Social Sciences. New homes: a pilot social survey; report by Mary J. Galligan, Margaret E. Glynn and Conor K. Ward. Dublin: 1968. Report was carried out in association with The Irish Housebuilders Association and An Foras Forbatha.

1613 WARD, CONOR K. New homes for old: report by Conor K. Ward. Research by Mary J. Galligan, Margaret E. Glynn, and Katherine M. Hodkinson. Dublin: 1969. (*Irish National Productivity Committee, Human science in industry, study no.* 3)

Industrial Relations

1614 DALY, GEORGE F. Industrial relations: comparative aspects with particular reference to Ireland. Cork: 1968.

1615 FROGGATT, P. One-day absence in industry. *Stat. Social Inq. Soc. Ir. J.*, vol. 21, pt. 3, 1964–65, 166–178.

1616 GOSS, JOHN. Industrial relations and moves towards industrial democracy in Ireland. Brighton: 1973. (*Univ. of Sussex, Centre for contemporary European studies, research papers no.* 4.)

1617 IRISH MANAGEMENT INSTITUTE. Industrial democracy: a symposium. Dublin: 1969. Bibliog., pp. 144–148.

1618 KAIM-CAUDLE, P.R. *and others*. Irish pension schemes, 1969, by P.R. Kaim-Caudle and J.G. Byrne, assisted by Annette O'Toole. Dublin: 1971. (*Economic and Social Research Institute broadsheet no.* 5)

1619 KELLY, AIDAN and HILLERY, BRIAN. Bargaining for productivity. *Studies*, 62, 1973, 221–232.

1620 McAULEY, D.J. Collective bargaining and industrial disputes in Ireland. *Stat. Social Inq. Soc. Ir. J.*, vol. 21, pt. 5, 1966–67, 125–150.

1621 NORTHERN IRELAND. Dept. of Manpower Services. Industrial relations in Northern Ireland; report of the Review Body, 1971–74. Belfast: 1974. Chairman: Dr. W.G.H. Quigley.

1622 RYAN, ANDREW F. College of Industrial Relations. *Development*, 15, 1967, 128–137. Originally known as The Catholic Workers' College.

Trade Unions

1623 BOYD, ANDREW. The rise of the Irish trade unions, 1729–1970. Tralee: 1972. Bibliog., pp. 142–144.

1624 D'ARCY, FERGUS A. The trade unions of Dublin and the attempted revival of the guilds: an episode in mid-nineteenth century Irish labour history. *R. Soc. Antiq. Ir. J.*, 101, 1971, 113–127.

1625 HILLERY, BRIAN. The Irish Congress of Trade Unions. *Admin.*, 21, 1973, 460–469.

1626 — *and others*. Trade union organisation in Ireland, by Brian Hillery, Aidan Kelly and A.I. Marsh. Dublin: 1975. (*Irish Productivity Centre, Human sciences in industry study no.* 11)

1627 HORN, PAMELA L.R. The National Agricultural Labourers' Union in Ireland. *Ir. Hist. Stud.*, 17, 1970–1, 340–352.

1628 IRISH TRANSPORT AND GENERAL WORKERS UNION. Library, Information Section. Some information sources and literature of relevance to trade unions. 1976. Typescript.

1629 McCARTHY, CHARLES. The decade of upheaval: Irish trade unions in the nineteen sixties. Dublin [1974].

1630 — Trade unions in Ireland, 1894–1960. Dublin: 1977. (*Institute of Public Administration, Direct reproduction ser.* 1). Bibliog., pp. 640–647.

1631 O'CONNELL, T.J. History of the Irish National Teachers' Organisation, 1868–1968. Dublin [1969]

1632 O'HIGGINS, RACHEL. Irish trade unions and politics, 1830–50. *Hist. J.*, 4, 1961, 208–217.

1633 SHILLMAN, BERNARD. Trade unionism and trade disputes in Ireland. Dublin: 1960.

1634 WEBB, SIDNEY and WEBB, BEATRICE. The history of trade unionism. London: 1894. Bibliog., prepared by Robert A. Peddie, pp. 499–543.

Strikes

1635 CURRICULUM DEVELOPMENT UNIT, DUBLIN. Divided city: portrait of Dublin, 1913. Dublin: 1978. Chronicles the events before and during the 'lock-out' of 1913.

1636 KEOGH, DERMOT. The 'New Unionism' and Ireland: Dublin coal porters' strikes, 1890: war of attrition. *Cap. Ann*, 1975, 64–70.

1637 — William Martin Murphy and the origins of the 1913 lock-out. *Cap. Ann.*, 1977, 130–158.

1638 NEVIN, DONAL, *compiler*. 1913: Jim Larkin and the Dublin lock-out. Dublin: 1964.

1639 WRIGHT, ARNOLD. Disturbed Dublin: the story of the great strike of 1913–14, with a description of the industries of the Irish capital. London: 1914.

Finance

1640 BARROW, G.L. The emergence of the Irish banking system, 1820–1845. Dublin: 1975. Bibliog., pp. 231–244.

1641 — Some Dublin private banks. *Dublin Hist. Rec.*, vol. 25, no. 2, 1972, 38–53.

1642 — Kilkenny private banks. *Old Kilk. Rev.*, 23, 1971, 36–40.

1643 COYNE, EDWARD J. Report of the Banking Commission. *Studies*, 27, 1938, 394–406.

1644 FLANAGAN, FINDLA. The Central Bank of Ireland. *Admin.*, 13, 1965, 53–58.

1645 FOGARTY, MICHAEL P. Report of banks inquiry: report on dispute of 1970 between the Associated Banks and the Irish Bank Officials' Association, and recommendations as to what action might be taken to avoid the risk of closures through industrial action in the future. Dublin: 1971.

1646 GREAT BRITAIN. House of Commons, Committee on the condition of the Irish currency, 1804. The Irish pound, 1797–1826; a reprint of the report of the committee of 1804 of the British House of Commons on the condition of the Irish currency, with selections from the minutes of evidence presented to the committee, and an introduction by Frank Whitson Fetter. London: 1955. Bibliography of contemporary publications on Irish money, banking and exchange, 1797–1820, pp. 125–8.

1647 HALL, F.G. The Bank of Ireland, 1783–1946, with an architectural chapter by C.P. Curran, and biographical notes by Joseph Hone; edited by George O'Brien. Dublin and London: 1949. Bibliog., pp. 409–22.

1648 HEIN, JOHN. Institutional aspects of commercial and central banking in Ireland. Dublin: 1967. (*Economic and Social Research Institute paper, no.* 36).

1649 INTERNATIONAL ASSOCIATION FOR RESEARCH IN INCOME AND WEALTH. Bibliography on income and wealth, vol. 1, 1937–47–, New York: 1948–. vol. 1. Edited by Daniel Creamer.

1650 IRELAND. Department of Agriculture and Technical Instruction. Report of the departmental committee on agricultural credit in Ireland. London: 1914. Bibliog., pp. 387–90, which covers: joint stock banks, post office and trustee savings banks, moneylenders, Loan Fund Board system, co-operative credit and agricultural co-operation, state loans and grants for agricultural purposes, land registration and mortgage credit, agricultural labourers, and Irish rural industries.

1651 — Department of Finance. Commission of inquiry into banking, currency, and credit, 1938. Dublin: 1938. 3 vols.
Vol. 1–2: Memoranda and minutes of evidence. [3]: Reports.

1652 KIERNAN, THOMAS JOSEPH. History of the financial administration of Ireland to 1817. London: 1930. Bibliog., pp. 341–7.

1653 LANG, JOHN TEMPLE. The new Irish bank lending system. *Dublin Univ. Law Rev.*, 2, 1970–1, 102–110.

1654 MILNE, KENNETH. A history of the Royal Bank of Ireland Limited. Dublin: 1964. Bibliog., pp. 107–9.

1655 MOYNIHAN, MAURICE. Currency and central banking in Ireland, 1922–1960. Dublin: 1975.

1656 MURRAY, ALICE EFFIE. A history of the commercial and financial relations between England and Ireland from the period of the Restoration. London: 1903. Bibliog., pp. 445–67.

1657 O'BRIEN, JOHN B. Sadleir's Bank (The Tipperary Joint Stock Bank, 1838–56). *Cork Hist. Arch. Soc. J.*, 82, 1977, 33–38.

1658 O'CONNELL, J.B. The financial administration of Ireland, new ed. Dublin [1960]. Previous ed. published as *The financial administration of Saorstat Eireann*. 1934.

1659 O'KELLY, EOIN. The old private banks and bankers of Munster. Pt. 1. Bankers of Cork and Limerick cities. Cork: 1959. Bibliog., pp. 161–6.

1660 O'NUALLAIN, LABHRAS. Ireland, finances of partition. Dublin: 1952. Bibliog., pp. 194–6.

1661 O'SULLIVAN, M.D. Italian merchant bankers in Ireland in the thirteenth century. Dublin: 1962. Bibliog., pp. 140–154; the Cistercian houses in Ireland: a family tree, p. 139.

1662 SIMPSON, J.V. An estimate of the profits of banking in Northern Ireland. *Stat. Social Inq. Soc. Ir. J.*, 119*th session*, 1965–66, 43–66.

1663 SIMPSON, NOEL. The Belfast bank, 1827–1970: 150 years of banking in Ireland. Belfast: 1975.

1664 THOM, D. RODNEY. Money, interest and economic activity in Ireland. *Econ. Soc. Rev.*, vol. 5, no. 2, 1974, 201–211.

1665 WAGNER, HENRY R. Irish economics, 1700–1783: a bibliography with notes. New York: 1969. (*Reprints of economic classics*). First published London, 1907; deals mainly with banking.

1666 WALDRON, J.J. The Irish customs and excise. *Administration*, vol. 5, no. 4, 1957–8, 35–53.

1667 WESTROPP, M.S. DUDLEY. Notes on Irish money weights and foreign coin current in Ireland. *R. Ir. Acad. Proc., Sec. C*, 23 1916–17, 43–72.

Usury, Moneylending

1668 GIBBON, PETER and HIGGINS, M.D. The Irish 'Gombeenman': reincarnation or rehabilitation. *Econ. Soc. Rev.*, 8, 1977, 313–320.

1669 — Patronage, tradition and modernisation: the case of the Irish 'Gombeenman'. *Econ. Soc. Rev.*, 6, 1974, 27–44.

1670 KENNEDY, LIAM. A sceptical view on the reincarnation of the Irish 'gombeenman'. *Econ. Soc. Rev.*, 8, 1977, 213–222.

Taxation

1671 DOWLING, BRENDAN R. The income sensitivity of the personal income tax base in Ireland, 1947–1972. Dublin; 1977. (*Economic and Social Research Institute paper no.* 86).

1672 JUDGE, NORMAN E. Value-added tax in Ireland. Dublin: 1972.

1673 KELLY, F.N. and CARMICHAEL, K.S. Irish income tax and corporation tax. 9th ed., London: 1976.

1674 MORIARTY, THOMAS F. The Irish absentee tax controversy of 1773: a study in Anglo-Irish politics on the eve of the American Revolution. *Amer. Phil. Soc. Proc.*, vol. 118, no. 4, 1974, 370–408.

1675 REAMONN, SEAN. The philosophy of the corporate tax. Dublin: 1970. Bibliog., pp. 265–269.

Excise

1676 IRELAND. Revenue Commissioners. Customs and excise tariff of Ireland in operation on 1st January 1976. Dublin: 1975.

Estate Inheritance

1677 HACCIUS, CHARLES. An introduction to the Irish death duties. Dublin: 1969.

Land and Land Tenure

1678 AALEN, F.H.A., *compiler*. Enclosures in Eastern Ireland: report of a symposium held in Dublin on September 23, 1964. *Ir. Geog.*, vol. 5, no. 2, 1965, 29–39.

1679 **Alexander**, D.J. Farm land mobility and adjustments in farming in Northern Ireland. *Stat. Social Inq. Soc. Ir. J.*, vol. 21, pt. 3, 1964–65, 1–14.

1680 **Arnold, Lawrence** J. The Manor of Lucan and the Restoration Land Settlement, 1660–1688. *Dublin Hist. Rec.*, 21, 1966–67, 139–143.

1681 **Attwood**, E.A. Some economic aspects of land use policy in Ireland. *Stat. Social Inq. Soc. Ir. J.*., vol. 21, pt. 3, 1964–65, 143–165.

1682 **Baker, Alan** R.H. and **Butlin, Robin** A. *eds.* Studies of field systems in the British Isles. Cambridge: 1973. Field systems of Ireland, by R.H. Buchanan, pp. 580–618.

1683 **Bateman, John**. The great landowners of Great Britain and Ireland. 4th ed. reprinted with an introduction by David Spring. Leicester, 1971. Facsimile reprint of 4th ed., London: 1883.

1684 **Bottigheimer, Karl** S. English money and Irish land: the 'Adventurers' in the Cromwellian settlement of Ireland. Oxford: 1971. Bibliog., pp. 216–221.

1685 — The Restoration Land Settlement in Ireland: a structural view. *Ir. Hist. Stud.*, vol. 18, no. 69, 1972, 1–21.

1686 **Buchanan, Ronald** H. Common fields and enclosure: an eighteenth-century example from Lecale, Co. Down. *Ulster Folk.*, vol. 15–16, 1970, 99–118.

1687 **Buckley**, K. The records of the Irish Land Commission as a source of historical reference. *Ir. Hist. Stud.*, 8, 1952–3, 28–36.

1688 **Case**, H.J. *and others*. Land use in Goodland Townland, Co. Antrim, from neolithic times until today, by H.J. Case, G.W. Dimbleby, G.F. Mitchell, M.E.S. Morrison and V.B. Proudfoot. *R. Soc. Antiq. Ir. J.*, 99, 1969, 39–53.

1689 **Christianson, Gale** E. Landlords and land tenure in Ireland, 1790–1830. *Eire-Ir.*, vol. 9, no. 1, 1974, 25–58.

1690 **Clark, Sam**. The social composition of the Land League. *Ir. Hist. Stud.*, vol. 17, no. 69, 1971, 447–469.

1691 **Crawford**, W.H. Landlord-tenant relations in Ulster, 1609–1820. *Ir. Econ. Soc. Hist.*, 2, 1975, 5–21.

1692 **Currie**, E.A. Land tenures, enclosures and field patterns in Co. Derry in the eighteenth and nineteenth centuries. *Ir. Geog.*, 9, 1976, 50–62.

1693 **De Burgh**, U.H. **Hussey**. *Compiler*. The landowners of Ireland: an alphabetical list of the owners of estates of 500 acres or £500 valuation and upwards in Ireland, with the acreage and valuation in each county; and also containing a brief notice of the education and official appointments of each person, to which are added his town and county addresses and clubs. Dublin [1878].

1694 **Denman**, D.R. *and others*. Bibliography of rural land economy and landownership, 1900–47: a full list of works relating to the British Isles and selected works from the United States and Western Europe, by D.R. Denman, J.F.Q. Switzer, and O.H.M. Sawyer. Cambridge: 1958.

1695 **The Dispossessed Landowners Of Ireland**, 1664. *Ir. Geneal.*, vol. 4, no. 4, 1971, 275–302; *ibid.*, no. 5, 1972, 429–449. Lists given to the Duke of Ormonde to select his nominees for restoration.

1696 **Donnelly, James** S., **Jr**. Landlord and tenant in nineteenth century Ireland. Dublin, 1973. (*Insights into Irish history*)

1697 **Drudy**, P.J. Land use in Britain and Ireland. *Anglo-Ir. Stud.*, 1, 1975, 105–116.

1698 **Duffy, Patrick** J. Irish landholding structures and population in the mid-nineteenth century. *May. Rev.*, vol. 3, no. 2, 1977, 3–27.

1699 **Fisher, Joseph**. The history of landholding in Ireland. London: 1877. The expansion of a paper which was published in *R. Hist. Soc. Trans.*, 5, 1877, 228–326.

1700 **Food And Agriculture Organization Of The United Nations**. Bibliography on land tenure [compiled by Sir Bernard Binns. Rome, 1955]. Irish section, pp. 192–3; works on Northern Ireland included with United Kingdom of Great Britain.

1701 **Fox**, J.R. Kinship and land tenure on Tory Island. *Ulster Folk.*, 12, 1966, 1–17.

1702 **Gebbie, John** H. An introduction to the

Abercorn letters (as relating to Ireland, 1736–1816). Omagh: 1972. Correspondence of the Duke of Abercorn's family relating to their estates in Ireland.

1703 GREAT BRITAIN. Parliament. Landowners in Ireland: return of owners of land of one acre and upwards, in the several counties, counties of cities, and counties of towns in Ireland . . . to which is added, a summary for each province and for all Ireland. Dublin: 1876.

1704 HARDIMAN, JAMES. Ancient deeds and writings chiefly related to landed property, from the twelfth to the seventeenth century, with translations, notes and a preliminary essay. Dublin: 1826.

1705 HILL, GEORGE. An historical account of the Plantation in Ulster at the commencement of the seventeenth century, 1608–1620. [1st ed. reprinted with] introduction by John G. Barry. Shannon: 1970. Facsimile reprint of 1st ed., Belfast: 1877.

1706 HORNER, ARNOLD. Land transactions and the making of Carton Desmesne. *Kildare Arch. Soc. J.*, vol. 15, no. 4, 1974–5, 387–396.

1707 HUNTER, R.J. The English undertakers in the Plantation of Ulster, 1610–41. *Breifne*, vol. 4, no. 16, 1973–5, 471–499.

1708 KOLBERT, C.F. and O'BRIEN, T. Land reform in Ireland: a legal history of the Irish land problem and its settlement. Cambridge: 1975.

1709 LARGE, DAVID. The wealth of the greater Irish landowners. *Ir. Hist. Stud.*, 15, 1966, 21–47.

1710 LIST OF PRIMARY VALUATION BOOKS IN SAORSTAT EIREANN. Typescript in Trinity College Library, Dublin; includes each of the twenty-six counties, with notes of the unions and baronies.

1711 LYNE, GERARD J. Dr. Dermot Lyne: an Irish Catholic landholder in Cork and Kerry under the penal laws. *Kerry Arch. Hist. Soc. J.*, 8, 1975, 45–72.

1712 MACAODHA, BREANDAN S. Clachan settlement in Iar-Chonnacht. *Ir. Geog.*, vol. 5, no. 2, 1965, 20–28.

1713 MCCOURT, EILEEN. The management of the Farnham estates [Co. Cavan] during the nineteenth century. *Breifne*, vol. 4, no. 16, 1973–5, 531–560.

1714 MACNIOCAILL, G., *ed*. The Red Book of the Earls of Kildare. Dublin: Irish Manuscripts Commission, 1964. A cartulary containing documents relating to the lands of the Leinster Fitzgeralds in Ulster, Munster and Connaught from the twelfth to the sixteenth century.

1715 MAGUIRE, W.A. The Downshire estates in Ireland, 1801–1845: the management of Irish landed estates in the early nineteenth century. Oxford: 1972. Bibliog., pp. 265–270.

1716 MASTERSON, HAROLD T. Land use patterns and farming practice in County Fermanagh, 1609–1845. *Clogher Rec.*, vol. 7, no. 1, 1969, 56–88.

1717 MONTGOMERY, W.E. The history of land tenure in Ireland. Cambridge: 1889.

1718 MOODY, T.W. Anna Parnell and the Land League. *Hermathena*, 117, 1974, 5–17.

1719 O GRADA, CORMAC. The investment behaviour of Irish landlords, 1850–75: some preliminary findings. *Agr. Hist. Rev.*, vol. 23, pt. 2, 1975, 139–155.

1720 O'LOAN, J. The Manor of Cloncurry, Co. Kildare, and the feudal system of land tenure in Ireland. *Ir. Dept. Agric. J.*, 58, 1961, 14–36.

1721 POMFRET, JOHN E. The struggle for land in Ireland, 1800–1923. [1st ed. reprinted] New York: Russell and Russell, 1969. 1st ed. Princeton, New Jersey: 1930. Bibliog., pp. 315–26.

1722 ROBINSON, OLIVE. The London companies and tenant-right in nineteenth-century Ireland. *Agr. Hist. Rev.*, vol. 18, pt. 1, 1970, 54–63.

1723 SIMMS, J.G. Mayo landowners in the seventeenth century. *R. Soc. Antiq. Ir. J.*, 95, 1965, 237–247.

1724 SMYTH, W.J. Estate records and the making of the Irish landscape: an example from County Tipperary. *Ir. Geog.*, 9, 1976, 29–49.

1725 SOLOW, BARBARA LEWIS. The land question and the Irish economy, 1870–1903.

Cambridge (Mass.): 1971. Bibliog., pp. 236–242.

1726 STEELE, E.D. Irish land and British politics: tenant-right and nationality, 1865–1870. London: 1974. Bibliog., pp. 351–356.

1727 — Tenant-right and nationality in nineteenth-century Ireland. *Leeds Phil. Lit. Soc. Lit. Hist. Sec. Proc.*, vol. 15, pt. 4, 1973, 75–111.

Conservation

1728 DARLING, F. FRASER. The economics of conservation. *Studies*, 59, 1970, 127–132.

1729 AN FORAS FORBARTHA (The National Institute for Physical Planning and Construction Research). The protection of the national heritage: a report addressed to the Minister for Local Government, through An Foras Forbartha, by the Nature and Amenity Conservation and Development Committee of An Foras Forbartha. Dublin: 1969.

1730 LANG, JOHN TEMPLE. Conservation of the environment in Ireland [with comment by Fergus J. O'Rourke]. *Studies*, 59, 1970, 279–300.

1731 AN TAISCE (National Trust for Ireland). The Hill of Howth: a conservation study, by Anthony O'Neill. Dublin: 1971.

Energy, Fuel

1732 BOOTH, J.L. Fuel and power in Ireland. Dublin: Economic Research Institute.
Pt. 1. Energy consumption in 1970. 1966. (*Paper no.* 30)
Pt. 2. Electricity and turf. 1966. (*Paper no.* 34)
Pt. 3. International and temporal aspects of energy consumption. 1966. (*Paper no.* 35)
Pt. 4. Sources and uses of energy. 1967. (*Paper no.* 37)

1733 BUNYAN, RICHARD. Ireland and natural gas. Dublin: United Dominions Trust (Ireland) Ltd., 1974. Bibliog., p. 183.

1734 COULTER, B.S. Nuclear power station at Carnsore Point. Dublin: An Foras Taluntais, 1977.

1735 HENRY, E.W. Energy conservation in Ireland, 1975–85. Dublin: 1976.

1736 — and SCOTT, S. A national model of fuel allocation: a prototype. Dublin: 1977. (*Economic and Social Research Institute paper no.* 90)

1737 LALOR, E. Ireland — the energy future. *Studies*, 65, 1976, 17–29.

1738 MCMULLAN, JOHN T. *and others*. Energy in Northern Ireland, by John T. McMullan, Roger Morgan and Robert B. Murray. *Technol. Ir.*, vol. 8, nos. 4–5, 1976, 41–44.

1739 ROBINSON, K.W. and RIDDIHOUGH, R.P. Ireland — oil and gas exploration. Dublin: Geological Survey of Ireland, 1975. (*Information circular no. 8*)

Water Economics

1740 FOOD AND AGRICULTURE ORGANIZATION OF THE UNITED NATIONS. Groundwater legislation in Europe; prepared by Legislation Research Branch in collaboration with Land and Water Development Division. Rome: 1964. Ireland, pp. 78–81, 167.

1741 GRIBBON, H.D. The history of water power in Ulster. Newton Abbot: 1969. Bibliog., pp. 267–291.

1742 INSTITUTE FOR INDUSTRIAL RESEARCH AND STANDARDS. The development of the marine resources of Ireland, 22–23 June, 1971. Proceedings. Dublin: 1971.

1743 MCKENNA, T. Our territorial sea. *Ir. Defence J.*, vol. 34, 1974, 103–105. Extent of areas and fishing limits.

1744 O'RIORDAN, J.A. The exploitation of water power in Ireland. *Studies*, 35, 1946, 513–522.

Co-operation

1745 BOLGER, PATRICK. The Irish co-operative movement: its history and development. Dublin: 1977.

1746 CO-OPERATIVE WHOLESALE SOCIETY LTD. Dublin: a handbook of the forty-ninth co-operative congress, Whitsuntide, 1914 compiled by the Handbook Committee. Manchester: 1914.

1747 DUBLIN CO-OPERATIVE REFERENCE LIBRARY BULLETIN, vol. 1, 1915, 321–43. Selected bibliography of co-operative literature. For list of publications see *The Co-operative Reference Library, Dublin: an explanation and an appeal*, by R.M. Fox. Dublin: 1925.

1748 HORACE PLUNKETT FOUNDATION. Agricultural co-operation in Ireland: a survey. London: 1931.

1749 — Yearbook of agricultural co-operation . . . 1927–. London: 1926–. Each volume contains a bibliography of agricultural co-operation, those appearing in the yearbooks for 1937, 1947 and 1954 being particularly comprehensive.

1750 IRELAND. Department of Industry and Commerce, Committee on Co-operative Societies. Report. Dublin: 1964.

1751 NORTHERN IRELAND. Ministry of Agriculture. Agricultural co-operation in Northern Ireland: a report on the place of co-operation in the future of Northern Ireland [prepared by Professor J.R. Parkinson]. Belfast: 1965.

1752 SMITH-GORDON, LIONEL, and O'BRIEN, CRUISE. Co-operation in Ireland. Manchester: 1921. Bibliog., pp. 85–6.

1753 — Co-operation for farmers. London: 1918. Bibliog., pp. 235–40.

1754 VALKO, LASZLO. International handbook of co-operative legislation. Washington: 1954. Bibliog., pp. 266–73; also gives a list of acts of parliament [1893–1946] under which the Irish co-operative movement operates.

Free Trade

1755 BELFAST PUBLIC LIBRARIES, Bibliographic Department. The Common Market and European free trade: a select list of books and periodical articles. [Belfast], 1961. Typescript of 5 p.

1756 COMMISSION OF THE EUROPEAN COMMUNITIES. The European Community: a brief reading-list. London: 1977.

1757 HILLERY, P.J. Ireland and Britain in the European Community. *Admin*., vol. 24, no. 1, 1976, 1–11.

1758 IRELAND. OIREACHTAS. Free trade area agreement and related agreements, exchanges of letters and understandings [with British Government]. Dublin: 1965.

1759 — Membership of the European communities: implications for Ireland. Dublin: 1970.

1760 MURRAY, C.H. Ireland and the European free trade area: *Administration*, vol. 5, no. 2, 1957, 25–42.

1761 NATIONAL FARMERS' ASSOCIATION. Irish agriculture in the Common Market. Dublin: 1961. (*N.F.A. pub*., no. 21.) Title on cover: 'The Common Market and the Irish Farmer'.

1762 NEVIN, EDWARD. The Irish tariff and the E.E.C.: a factual survey. Dublin: 1962. (*Economic Research Institute paper no*. 3)

Guilds

1763 BERRY, HENRY F. Existing records and properties of the old Dublin city gilds. *R. Soc. Antiq. Ir. J*., 35, 1905, 338–41.

1764 CLUNE, GEORGE. The medieval gild system. Dublin [1943]. Bibliog., pp. 281–5.

1765 DALY, M.H. A few notes on the gild system. *Dublin Hist. Rec*., 11, 1949–50, 65–80.

1766 DIXON, F.E. The Dublin tailors and their hall. *Dublin Hist. Rec*., 22, 1968–9, 147–159.

1767 GROSS, CHARLES. The gild merchant: a contribution to British municipal history. Oxford: 1890. 2 vols. Bibliog., vol. 1, pp. 301–22.

1768 MACLOCHLAINN, ALF. The Guild of Saint Luke [records deposited in the National Library, Dublin]. *Ir. Book*., 2, 1963, 61–62. Guild of St. Luke the Evangelist, Dublin, or Fraternity of Cutlers, Painter-Stainers and Stationers.

1769 SNODDY, OLIVER. The charter of the Guild of St. Luke, 1670. *R. Soc. Antiq. Ir. J*., 98, 1968, 79–87.

1770 SWIFT, JOHN. History of the Dublin bakers and others. Dublin [1948].

1771 WEBB, JOHN J. The guilds of Dublin. Dublin: 1929. Bibliog., p. [viii].

Natural Resources

1772 CRANLEY, MARTIN J. The natural resources of Ireland. *Admin*., vol. 24, no. 1, 1976, 50–75.

1773 KANE, ROBERT. The industrial resources of Ireland. 2nd ed.,[reprinted]. Shannon, 1971. Facsimile reprint of 2nd ed., Dublin: 1845.

1774 McCONNELL, BRIAN. Ireland's resources: a statistical survey of the resources of Ireland — people, land, minerals, forests, bogs, rivers and the sea. *Management*, vol. 18, no. 5, 1971, 49–54.

1775 ROYAL DUBLIN SOCIETY. The natural resources of Ireland: a series of discourses delivered before the Royal Dublin Society, April 12–14, 1944, in commemoration of the centenary of the publication by the Society of Sir Robert Kane's *The industrial resources of Ireland*. Dublin: 1944. Bibliog. of Sir R. Kane, pp. 41–2; fuel resources, pp. 53–4; mineral resources, p. 61; water power, pp. 68–9; fisheries since 1900, pp. 79–80; forestry, p.90.

INDUSTRIAL PRODUCTION

(See also Economic History)

Bibliography

1776 JOHNSTONE, ANN. Irish industry since 1950: contributions to a bibliography [1976]. Accepted as thesis for Fellowship of the Library Association of Ireland.

General

1777 BLACK, W. *and others*. Costs and prices in transportable goods industries, by W. Black, J.V. Simpson, and D.G. Slattery. Dublin: 1969. (*Economic and Social Research Institute paper no*. 51)

1778 BURKE, JOHN F. Outlines of industrial history of Ireland. Dublin: 1940.

1779 CENTRAL STATISTICS OFFICE, DUBLIN. Irish trade journal and statistical bulletin. vol. 1–, 1925–.

1780 FARLEY, NOEL J.J. Determinants of established size in Irish manufacturing industries: some notes on the Irish case, 1931–1972. *Econ. Soc. Rev*., vol. 6, no. 2, 1975, 187–213.

1781 FENNELL, ROSEMARY. Industrialisation and agricultural development in the congested districts. Dublin: 1962. (*The Agricultural Institute, Economy research series no*. 2) Typescript.

1782 FLANAGAN, PATRICK. Some notes on Leitrim industry. *Breifne*, vol. 4, no. 15, 1972, 406–425.

1783 FOGARTY, M.P. Irish entrepreneurs speak for themselves. Dublin: 1973. (*Economic and Social Research Institute, broadsheet no*. 8)

1784 GLASS, J. COLIN. Technical change in Northern Ireland manufacturing, 1950–1968: a comment. *Econ. Soc. Rev*., vol. 6, no. 4, 1975, 483–5.

1785 IPEC TECHNICAL SERVICES CORPORATION. An appraisal of Ireland's industrial potentials. New York: 1952. Also reproduced by photo-lithography by Alex Thom and Co. Ltd., Dublin, for Stationery Office, Dublin.

1786 INDUSTRIAL DEVELOPMENT AUTHORITY. Overseas-sponsored companies. Dublin: 1972. A complete list of all the grant-aided overseas firms in Ireland.

1787 INDUSTRIAL DEVELOPMENT AUTHORITY. *Admin*. (Special issue), vol. 20, no. 1, 1972.

1788 INDUSTRIAL ESTATES IN IRELAND. *Management*, vol. 24, no. 4, 1977, 37–55. Estates listed by county.

1789 IRELAND. Committee on Industrial Organisation. A synthesis of reports by survey teams on 22 industries. Dublin: 1964.

1790 — General report. Dublin: 1973.

1791 — Survey of grant-aided industry: survey teams' report, October, 1967. Dublin: 1968.

1792 IRISH INTERNATIONAL EXHIBITION, 1907. Home industries section. Irish rural life and industry with suggestions for the future. Dublin: 1907. Contents include lace and crochet manufacture, hand-tufted carpets, woollen industry, Connemara curtain making, shirt making, underclothing industry, hosiery manufacture, bootmaking, straw-hat making, glove making, manufacture of cutlery, art embroidery, art metal work, Connemara marble and pebble cutting, bulb farming, tobacco growing; paper on The Housing of the Irish artisan, by R. Brown, and The Arts and Crafts Society of Ireland, by G.N. Count Plunkett.

1793 IRISH INDUSTRY. DUBLIN. Vol. 1–, 1932–.

1794 JEFFERSON, C.W. Capital statistics for Irish manufacturing industry. Dublin: 1971. (*Economic and Social Research Institute paper no. 60*)

1795 KENNEDY, KIERAN A. Growth of labour productivity in Irish manufacturing, 1953–1967. *Stat. Social Inq. Soc. Ir. J.*, vol. 22, pt. 1, 1968–69, 113–154.

1796 LUCEY, DENIS I.F. and KALDOR, DONALD R. Rural industrialization: the impact of industrialization on two rural communities in Western Ireland. Dublin: 1969. Bibliog., pp. 199–201; study deals with Tubbercurry, Co. Sligo, and Scarriff, Co. Clare.

1797 MCALEESE, DERMOT. Industrial specialisation and trade: Northern Ireland and the Republic. *Econ. Soc. Rev.*, 7, 1976, 143–160.

1798 MCCULLOUGH, A. Technical change in Northern Ireland manufacturing, 1950–1968. *Econ. Soc. Rev.*, 5, 1974, 181–197.

1799 MURIE, A.S. A survey of industrial movement in Northern Ireland between 1965 and 1969, by A.S. Murie, W.D. Birrell, P.A.R. Hillyard, and D.J.D. Roche. *Econ. Soc. Rev.*, 4, 1972, 231–244.

1800 NEVIN, EDWARD. The cost structure of Irish industry, 1950–60. Dublin: 1964. (*Economic Research Institute paper no.* 22)

1801 O'FARRELL, P.N. Regional industrial development trends in Ireland, 1960–1973. Dublin: 1975. Bibliog., pp. 65–66.

1802 O'MALLEY, PATRICK. Irish industry: structure and performance. Dublin and New York: 1971. Bibliog., pp. 136–8.

1803 O'NEILL, E.R. Re-organisation and adaptation of industry: the role of the Industrial Re-Organisation Branch of the Department of Industry and Commerce. *Admin.*, vol. 12, no. 1, 1964, 48–54.

1804 QUISH, JOHN A. The growth of technology and science based industry in the South-West. *Technol. Ir.*, vol. 9, no. 11, 1978, 18–23.

1805 STEWART, J.C. Foreign direct investment and the emergence of a dual economy. *Econ. Soc. Rev.*, 7, 1976, 173–197. Analyses a sample of manufacturing firms in the Limerick mid-west region.

1806 SUTTON, JOHN. Productivity, prices, and factor shares in Irish manufacturing industry, 1953–70. *Econ. Soc. Rev.*, 6, 1975, 237–260.

1807 TARRANT, JOHN R. Industry in South-East Ireland: a study in industrial location. *Ir. Geog.*, 5, 1964–68, 440–458.

Agriculture

1808 ATTWOOD, E.A. Agricultural developments in Ireland, North and South. *Stat. Social Inq. Soc. Ir. J.*, vol. 21, pt. 5, 1966–67, 9–14.

1809 — Ireland and the European agricultural market. Dublin: 1963. (*An Foras Taluntais, Rural Economy Division, Economic Research series no.* 8). Typescript.

1810 BAILLIE, I.F. and SHEEHY, S.J. Irish agriculture in a changing world. Edinburgh: 1971.

1811 BARRINGTON, RICHARD M. The prices of some agricultural produce and the cost of farm labour for the past fifty years. *Stat. Social Inq. Soc. Ir. J.*, 65, 1887, 137–153.

1812 CROTTY, RAYMOND D. Irish agricultural production: its volume and structure. Cork: 1966.

1813 EDWARDS, CHRISTOPHER J.W. Farm enterprise systems in east Co. Londonderry. *Ir. Geog.*, 7, 1974, 29–52.

1814 FAHY, EDWARD. Irish agriculture in the 1970s: maximizing the profits — and the risks. *Studies*, 64, 1975, 121–131.

1815 GILLMOR, DESMOND A. The spatial structure of agricultural output in the Republic of Ireland. *Econ. Soc. Rev.*, 8, 1977, 127–142.

1816 GREENE, J.N. A survey of Irish agriculture with special reference to its interdependence with British agriculture. *Adv. Sci.* 14, 1957–8, 374–380.

1817 LIVERSAGE, V. The approach to farm planning in Northern Ireland. *Agr. Prog.*, 45, 1960, 18–23.

1818 O'BRIEN, J.T. Aspects of farming in Northern Ireland. *Chart. Surv.*, 100, 1967, 131–134.

1819 O'BRIEN, JOHN B. Agricultural prices and living costs in pre-famine Cork. *Cork Hist. Arch. Soc. J.*, 82, 1977, 1–10.

1820 O'CONNOR, R. and BRESLIN, M. An input-output analysis of the agricultural sector of the Irish economy in 1964. (*Economic and Social Research Institute paper no*. 45)

1821 SCULLY, JOHN J. Agriculture in the West of Ireland: a study of the low farm income problem. Dublin, 1971.

1822 — and SWANSON, EARL R. Inter-area resource productivity comparisons in Irish agriculture. *Farm Econ*., vol. 10, no. 7, 1964, 284–295.

1823 STUART, H. VILLIERS. Prices of farm products in Ireland from year to year for thirty-six years, illustrated by diagrams, with observations on the prospects of Irish agriculture, including the substance of letters addressed to the Rt. Hon. W.E. Gladstone, M.P. in February and March of this year. Dublin and London: 1886.

Agricultural Machinery

1824 IRELAND. COMMITTEE ON INDUSTRIAL ORGANISATION. Report on survey of the agricultural machinery manufacturing industry. Dublin: 1965.

Fertilisers

1825 FERTILISERS PRICES ADVISORY BODY. Report of enquiry into the fertiliser industry. Dublin: 1976.

1826 GOWAN, COLM. Establishing a major fertiliser plant [Nitrigin Eireann Teoranta]. *Technol. Ir*., vol. 8, no. 3, 1976, 27–30.

1827 IRELAND. COMMITTEE ON INDUSTRIAL ORGANISATION. Report on survey of the fertiliser industry. Dublin: 1963.

1828 PARKES, J.W. The fertiliser industry in Ireland. *Adv. Sci*., 14, 1957–8, 336–8.

Crops

1829 ATTWOOD, E.A. and O'DWYER, T. Economics of wheat and barley production. Dublin: 1964. (*An Foras Taluntais, Rural Economy Division, Economic Research series, no*. 15)

1830 BOURKE, P.M. AUSTIN. The average yields of food crops in Ireland on the eve of the Great Famine. *Ir. Dept. Agric. J*., 66, 1969, 26–39.

1831 — The Irish grain trade, 1839–48. *Ir. Hist. Stud*., vol. 20, no. 78, 1976, 156–169. Includes tables of statistics.

1832 DUNNE, W. The grain market in Ireland: an analysis of the components of grain production, processing and utilisation. Dublin: 1976. (*An Foras Taluntais, Rural Economy Division, Economic Research series, no*. 21)

1833 FENNELL, ROSEMARY. Grain in Europe. Dublin: 1963. (*An Foras Taluntais, Rural Economy Division, Economic Research series, no*. 11) Typescript.

1834 GREEN, E.R.R. History of the Belfast grain trade. *Belfast Nat. Hist. Phil. Soc. Proc*., 8, 1964–70, 38–45.

Garden Crops

1835 IRELAND. COMMITTEE ON INDUSTRIAL ORGANISATION. Report on survey of the processing of fruit and vegetables and the manufacture of jams, marmalades and other preserves, etc. industry (*sic*). Dublin: 1965.

Tomatoes

1836 GIBBONS, E.T. *and others*. The Irish tomato industry, by E.T. Gibbons, M.J. Harkin and F.K. O'Neill. Dublin: 1970.

1837 O'NEILL, F.K. Economics of tomato production. Dublin: 1963. (*An Foras Taluntais, Rural Economy Division, Economic Research series, no*. 7) Typescript.

Glasshouses

1838 IRELAND. DEPARTMENT OF AGRICULTURE AND FISHERIES. Report of the survey team established by the Minister for Agriculture and Fisheries on the glasshouse industry. Dublin: 1966.

Livestock

1839 ATTWOOD, E.A. and FITZGERALD, S. Economic factors in cattle production. Dublin: 1964. (*An Foras Taluntais, Rural Economy Division, Economic Research series, no*. 13)

1840 **Baker, Terence J.**, *and others*. A study of the Irish cattle and beef industries, by Terence J. Baker, Robert O'Connor and Rory Dunne. Dublin: 1973. (*Economic and Social Research Institute paper no*. 72)

1841 **Bord na gCapall/Irish Horse Board.** Yearbook of the Irish horse. Tallaght, Co. Dublin: [vol. 1–] 1974– Deals mainly with the economic history of the horse.

1842 **Kennedy, Patrick J.** Livestock sales in Co. Galway at the close of the 18th century. *Galway Reader*, vol. 3, no. 3, 1951, 66–70.

1843 **Ireland. Department Of Agriculture And Fisheries.** Report of the store cattle study group, appointed by the Minister for Agriculture and Fisheries. Dublin: 1968.

1844 **MacCormac, Michael.** The Irish racing and bloodstock industry: an economic analysis. Dublin: 1978. Bibliog., [317–322]. Commissioned by the Turf Club.

1845 **O'Donovan, John.** The economic history of livestock in Ireland. Dublin: 1940. Bibliog. footnotes.

1846 **Ross, M.D.** Economics of pig production. Dublin: 1962. (*An Foras Taluntais, Rural Economy Division, Economic Research series, no*. 6)

Poultry

1847 **Gillmor, Desmond A.** The changing location of fowl production in the Republic of Ireland. *Ir. Geog*., 5, 1964–68, 484–491.

1848 **Ireland. Central Statistics Office.** Poultry inquiry, 1960–61: report. Dublin: 1964.

1849 **O'Carroll, Barbara M.** Poultry and eggs in Europe. Dublin: 1963. (*An Foras Taluntais, Rural Economy Division, Economic Research series no*. 12). Typescript.

Dairy Produce

1850 **Boal, F.W.** and **MacAodha, B.S.** The milk industry in Northern Ireland. *Econ. Geog*., 37, 1961, 170–180.

1851 **Ireland. Department Of Agriculture And Fisheries.** Irish dairy industry organisation, by Hugh L. Cook and Gordon W. Sprague. Dublin: 1968.

1852 — Report of the Survey Team established by the Minister for Agriculture on the dairy products industry. Dublin: 1963.

1853 **Northern Ireland. Ministry Of Agriculture.** The dairy industry in Northern Ireland. Belfast: 1963.

1854 **O'Carroll, Barbara M.** The dairy industry in Europe. Dublin: 1963. (*An Foras Taluntais, Rural Economy Division, Economic Research series no*. 10) Typescript.

1855 **Robinson, J.A.** The liquid milk and fresh cream industry in Northern Ireland. *Soc. Dairy Technol. J*., 17, 1964, 18–26.

1856 **Walshe, M.J.** The growth and future development of the dairy industry in the Republic of Ireland. *Soc. Dairy Technol. J*., 21, 1968, 190–199.

Butter

1857 **Donnelly, James S., Jr.** Cork Market: its role in the nineteenth century Irish butter trade. *Stud. Hib*., 11, 1971, 130–163. *See also* The decline of the Cork Butter Market: a comment, by Liam Kennedy. *ibid*., 16, 1976, 175–7.

1858 **Nolan, Peter.** Records of the Cork butter market and a note on the Great Famine. *Cork Hist. Arch. Soc. J*., 66, no. 204, 1961, 117–25.

Fisheries

1859 **Barry, Michael D.** Irish oyster industry. *Technol. Ir*., vol. 7, no. 10, 1976, 13–15.

1860 **Crowley, M.** Irish mussel industry, 1971–1972. Dublin: 1972. (*Ireland, Department of Agriculture and Fisheries, Fisheries Division, Fishery Leaflet no*. 40.)

1861 **Gibson, F.A.** The Irish shellfish industry (1948–1967). Dublin: 1969. (*Ireland, Department of Agriculture and Fisheries, Fisheries Division, Fishery Leaflet, no*. 17)

1862 — A review of the Irish lobster fishery. Dublin: 1969. (*Ireland, Department of Agriculture and Fisheries, Fisheries Division, Fishery Leaflet, no*. 5)

1863 **Hughes, J.L.J.** The Dublin Fishery Company, 1818–1830. *Dublin Hist. Rec*., 12, 1951, 34–46.

1864 HUGHES, P.H. An examination of the Northern Ireland sea fishing industry. *Stat. Social Inq. Soc. Ir. J.*, vol. 21, pt. 6, 1967–68, 174–200.

1865 — The sea fishing industry of Northern Ireland: an economic study. Belfast: 1970.

1866 KENNEDY, T.D. The herring fisheries on the north-west and west coasts, 1970 and 1971. Dublin: 1971. (*Ireland, Department of Agriculture and Fisheries, Fisheries Division, Fishery Leaflet no*. 29)

1867 MCNALLY, KENNETH. The sun-fish hunt. Belfast: 1976. On the Achill Island basking shark fishery.

1868 MERCER, JOHN P. Scientific research and development within the fishing industry. *Technol. Ir.*, vol. 7, no. 2, 1975, 35–39.

1869 MOLLOY, J.P. The herring fisheries on the south and south-west coasts, 1970–71. Dublin: 1971. (*Ireland, Department of Agriculture and Fisheries, Fisheries Division, Fishery Leaflet, no*. 28)

1870 — Herring fisheries on the south and south-west coasts, 1972–73. Dublin: 1973. (*Ireland, Department of Agriculture and Fisheries, Fisheries Division, Fishery Leaflet, no*. 55).

1871 — South coast (Waterford and Cork) herring fishery, 1968–69. Dublin: 1969, (*Ireland, Department of Agriculture and Fisheries, Fisheries Division, Fishery Leaflet, no*. 7)

1872 — and KENNEDY, T.D. The winter herring fishery of the north-west coast of Ireland, 1968–69. Dublin: 1969. (*Ireland, Department of Agriculture and Fisheries, Fisheries Division, Fishery Leaflet, no*. 12)

1873 O'CONNOR, R. and WHELAN, B.J. Economic evaluation of Irish salmon fishery. Dublin, Economic and Social Research Institute.
1. The visiting anglers. 1973. (*Paper no*. 68)
2. The Irish anglers, by R. O'Connor, B.J. Whelan and A. McCashin. 1974. (*Paper no*. 75)
3. The commercial fishermen, By B.J. Whelan, R. O'Connor and A. McCashin. 1974. (*Paper no*. 78)

1874 O'DONNELL. SEAN. Poor relations [fishing industry]. *Eire-Ir.*, vol. 10, no. 4, 1975, 116–119.

1875 WENT, ARTHUR E.J. Salmon fishing as an ancient Irish industry. *Technol. Ir.*, vol. 7, no. 1, 1975, 42.

Insurance

1876 IRELAND. DEPARTMENT OF INDUSTRY AND COMMERCE. Committee of inquiry into the insurance industry: interim report on motor insurance. Dublin: 1972.

Air Travel

1877 O'DONOGHUE, M. A cost/benefit evaluation of Irish airlines. *Stat. Social Inq. Soc. Ir. J.*, vol. 22, pt. 1, 1968–69, 153–180. An attempt to measure the economic contribution which Aer Lingus and Aer Linte make to the economy.

Chemicals

1878 IRELAND. COMMITTEE ON INDUSTRIAL ORGANISATION. Report on survey of the chemical industry. Dublin: 1963.

Oil

1879 HANSON, T.J. and GERAGHTY, D. Estimation and significance of Ireland's offshore production potential. *Technol. Ir.*, vol. 7, no. 11, 1976, 12–15.

1880 INSTITUTE FOR INDUSTRIAL RESEARCH AND STANDARDS, TECHNICAL INFORMATION DIVISION. Suppliers to the offshore industry: Ireland. Dublin: 1975.

Pharmaceuticals

1881 BOYD, DONALD W.P. History of the Irish pharmaceutical industry — a memoir. *Technol. Ir.*, vol. 2, no. 7, 1970, 7–11.

1882 TIMONEY, R.F. The pharmaceutical industry and industrial development in Ireland. *Technol. Ir.*, vol. 2, no. 7, 1970, 16–25.

Engineering

1883 COE, W.E. The engineering industry of the north of Ireland. Newton Abbot: 1969. Bibliog., pp. 218–221.

1884 HANNON, PAUL. Discarding the sow's ear. *Technol. Ir.*, vol. 9, no. 11, 1978, 15–17. An account of the engineering industry.

Electrical

1885 IRELAND. COMMITTEE ON INDUSTRIAL ORGANISATION. Report on survey of the electrical equipment and apparatus industry. Dublin: 1963.

1886 — Report on the wireless, television and telecommunications industry. Dublin: 1963.

1887 O'CONNOR, T.P. The Irish electronics industry. *Technol. Ir.*, vol. 6, no. 10, 1975, 9–10.

1888 POOLE, MICHAEL A. Rural domestic electricity expenditure in the republic of Ireland: an exploratory case-study in consumption geography. *Ir. Geog.*, vol. 6, no. 2, 1970, 113–135.

1889 RYDER, R.W. A survey of electrical energy development in Ireland. *Energy International*, vol. 2, no. 6, 1965, 8–11.

Mining

1890 GRIMES, T.A. Base metal production and the Irish economy. *Central Bank of Ireland Annual Report*, 1977, 99–128.

1891 TECHNOLOGY IRELAND. vol. 9, no. 6, 1977. Issue devoted to the mining industry in Ireland.

Motor Cars

1892 JACOBSON, D.S. The political economy of industrial location: the Ford Motor Company at Cork, 1912–26. *Ir. Econ. Soc. Hist.*, 4, 1977, 36–55.

Food

1893 THE FOOD INDUSTRY IN IRELAND. *Technol. Ir.*, vol. 8, nos. 4–5, 1976, 22–38.

1894 FORAS TALUNTAIS. Into Europe — the challenge to the food industry, edited by E.J. Wymes. Dublin: 1971.

1895 FOY, MICHAEL. The sugar industry in Ireland. Dublin: 1976. Bibliog., pp. 157–8.

1896 MACSWEENEY, PADRAIG. Food and dairying in the Munster region. *Technol. Ir.*, vol. 4, no. 8, 1972, 32–37.

Milling

1897 IRELAND. DEPARTMENT OF AGRICULTURE AND FISHERIES. Report of the Survey team established by the Minister for Agriculture and Fisheries on the flour milling industry. Dublin: 1965.

Confectionery

1898 IRELAND. COMMITTEE ON INDUSTRIAL ORGANISATION. Report on the cocoa, chocolate and sugar confectionery, and chocolate crumb industry. Dublin: 1963.

Sugar

1899 FOOD AND AGRICULTURE ORGANISATION OF THE UNITED NATIONS, ROME. The world sugar economy in figures. [1961.] (*Commodity reference ser.*, no. 1.)

Meat

1900 IRELAND. DEPARTMENT OF AGRICULTURE. Report of the survey team established by the Minister of Agriculture on the bacon and pigmeat industry. Dublin: 1963.

1901 — Report of the survey team established by the Minister of Agriculture on the beef, mutton and lamb industry. Dublin: 1963.

1902 LYNCH, T.J. The meat industry: quality control, research and development. *Ir. Dept. Agric. J.*, 61, 1964, 97–106.

1903 ORGANISATION FOR EUROPEAN ECONOMIC CO-OPERATION, European Productivity Agency. Organisation of the wholesale meat markets in Europe [by J. O'Mahony]. Project no. 5/31–31A. (*Documentation — Food and Agriculture, 1961 ser.*, no. 42.)

Clothing

1904 IRELAND. COMMITTEE ON INDUSTRIAL ORGANISATION. Report on the hosiery and knitwear industry. Dublin: 1963.

1905 — Report on the men's and boys' outerwear clothing industry. Dublin: 1965.

1906 — Report on survey of the men's protective clothing industry. Dublin: 1965.

1907 — Report on the survey of the miscellaneous clothing and accessories industry. Dublin: 1965. Includes gloves, neckties, Irish poplin, scarves, handkerchiefs, church vestments, umbrellas, slide fasteners, braces, habits and coffin drapery; also includes list of firms surveyed.

1908 — Report on survey of the women's readymade clothing industry (other than the mantles and gowns sector). Dublin: 1963.

Millinery

1909 BOYLAN, LENA. Lady Louisa Connolly's chip hat factory. *Kildare Arch. Soc. J.*, vol. 15, no. 5, 1975–6, 468–472.

Printing

1910 IRELAND. COMMITTEE ON INDUSTRIAL ORGANISATION. Report on survey of the printing industry. Dublin: 1964.

Advertising

1911 ALLEN, W.E.D. David Allens: the history of a family firm, 1857–1957. London: 1957. Bibliog. footnotes. Includes Ulster history in the nineteenth century.

Retailing

1912 DAWSON, J.A. Capital expenditure in retailing in Northern Ireland. *Ir. Geog.*, vol. 6, no. 3, 1971, 249–262.

1913 — The development of self service and supermarket retailing in Ireland. *Ir. Geog.*, vol. 6, no. 2, 1970, 194–199.

1914 MURPHY, DONAL. Packaging in Ireland. *Technol. Ir.*, vol. 8, no. 3, 1976, 9–11.

Brewing

1915 CORRAN, STAN. The Irish brewing industry. *Technol. Ir.*, vol. 6, no. 10, 1975, 46.

1916 GUINNESS, A., SON and CO. (DUBLIN) LTD. Guinness Harp (*afterwards* The Harp). Dublin. vol. 1–. 1958–.

1917 — LYNCH, PATRICK, and VAIZEY, JOHN. Guinness's brewery in the Irish economy, 1759–1876. London: 1960. Bibliog., pp. 255–9.

1918 — MALONE, ANDREW E. A great Irish industry: Messrs. Arthur Guinness, Son and Co. Ltd. *Studies*, 15, 1926, 441–453; *ibid.*, 16, 1927, 115–126, 465–476.

1919 — MOORE, DESMOND F. The Guinness saga. *Dublin Hist. Rec.*, 16, 1960–61, 50–57.

1920 O'LEARY, J.J. Developments in the brewing industry. *Technol. Ir.*, vol. 4, no. 8, 1972, 38–42.

1921 POWELL, THOMAS. An economic factor in the Wexford rebellion of 1798. *Stud. Hib.*, 16, 1976, 140–157. Malt trade and brewing in Co. Wexford.

Distilling

1922 BARNARD, ALFRED. The whisky distilleries of the United Kingdom. [Reprint of 1st ed. with a new introduction by I.A. Glin]. Newton Abbot: 1969. 1st ed., London: 1887; contains accounts of 28 Irish distilleries.

1923 HOLMES, JOHN. Monasterevan Distillery: a brief outline of its history and background. *Co. Kildare Arch. Soc. J.*, vol. 14, no. 4, 1969, 480–487.

1924 KENNEDY, K.A. *and others*. The demand for beer and spirits in Ireland. *R. Ir. Acad. Proc., Sec. C.*, vol. 73, no. 13, 1973, 669–711.

1925 MCGUIRE, E.B. Irish whiskey: a history of distilling, the spirit trade and excise controls in Ireland. Dublin and New York: 1973. Bibliog., pp. 444–452.

1926 SHIPKEY, ROBERT. Problems in alcoholic production and controls in early nineteenth-century Ireland. *Hist. J.*, vol. 16, no. 2, 1973, 291–302.

Tobacco

1927 ALFORD, B.W.E. W.D. and H.O. Wills and the development of the U.K. tobacco industry, 1786–1965. London: 1973. Wills in Ireland, pp. 385–397.

Iron

1928 ANDREWS, J.H. Notes on the historical geography of the Irish iron industry. *Ir. Geog.*, vol. 3, no. 3, 1956, 139–49.

1929 MCCRACKEN, EILEEN. Charcoal-burning ironworks in seventeenth and eighteenth century Ireland [with bibliog]. *Ulster J. Arch.*, 3rd ser., 20, 1957, 123–38. Includes comprehensive list of sites of ironworks.

1930 — Supplementary list of Irish charcoal-burning ironworks. *ibid.*, 28, 1965, 132–136.

Steel

1931 GILLMOR, DESMOND A. The Irish steel industry. *Ir. Geog.*, vol. 6, no. 1, 1969, 84–90.

Plastics

1932 PLASTICS INDUSTRIES ASSOCIATION [and] CONFEDERATION OF IRISH INDUSTRY. Plastics in Ireland, 1974: present status and future prospects. A study commissioned for the Plastics Industries Association. Dublin: 1974.

1933 ROTHERY, BRIAN. Pressures in the plastics industry. *Technol. Ir.*, vol. 7, no. 11, 1976, 33–37.

Leather

1934 DWYER, D.J. The leather industries of the Irish Republic, 1922–55: a study in industrial development and location. *Ir. Geog.*, vol. 4, no. 3, 1961, 175–89.

1935 IRELAND. COMMITTEE ON INDUSTRIAL PROGRESS. Report on footwear industry. Dublin: 1972.

1936 — Report on tanning and dressing of leather industry. Dublin: 1971.

1937 IRELAND. COMMITTEE ON INDUSTRIAL ORGANISATION. Report on the leather footwear industry. Dublin: 1963.

1938 — Report on the leather industry. Dublin: 1965.

1939 LEATHER AND FOOTWEAR JOURNAL. Dublin: vol. 1–, 1952–.

1940 O'BRIEN, D. The future of Irish leather. *Technol. Ir.*, vol. 3, no. 9, 1971, 12–13.

Textiles

1941 COTTON AND LINEN MANUFACTURE. (*Industrial history, no*. 3) *Technol. Ir.*, vol. 8, no. 3, 1976, 43–44. Reprinted from the Irish Trade Journal, February, 1926.

1942 DWYER, D.J., and SYMONS, L.J. The development and location of the textile industries in the Irish republic. *Ir. Geog.*, 4, 1959–63, 415–431.

1943 GEARY, MICHAEL. Development in the textile industry. *Technol. Ir.*, vol. 4, no. 8, 1972, 19–22.

1944 LOCKHART, DOUGLAS G. Dunmanway, County Cork, 1746–9. *Ir. Hist. Stud.*, vol. 20, no. 78, 1976, 170–5. An important centre of textile manufacturing in the eighteenth century.

1945 LONGFIELD, ADA KATHLEEN. History of tapestry-making in Ireland in the 17th and 18th centuries. *R. Soc. Antiq. Ir. J.*, 68, 1938, 91–105.

1946 — Prosperous, 1776–1798. *Kildare Arch. Soc. J.*, vol. 14, no. 2, 1966–67, 212–231. Account of Robert Bourke's project of developing a cotton manufacture at his property at Prosperous, Co. Kildare.

Linen

1947 BEACHAM, A. The Ulster linen industry. *Economica*, 11, 1944, 199–209. Bibliog. footnotes.

1948 CARTER, WILLIAM. A short history of the linen trade. Belfast: 1952. 2 vols. Bibliog., vol. 1, p. 19.

1949 CHARLEY, WILLIAM. Flax and its products in Ireland. London: 1862.

1950 CRAWFORD, W.H. The origins of the linen industry in North Armagh and the Lagan valley. *Ulster Folk.*, 17, 1971, 42–51.

1951 GILL, CONRAD. The rise of the Irish linen industry. Oxford: 1925. Reprinted Oxford: 1965. Bibliog., pp. 344–9.

1952 HORNER, JOHN. The linen trade of Europe during the spinning-wheel period. Belfast: 1920. Ireland. pp. 15–213.

1953 LINEN HALL LIBRARY. General catalogue, compiled by George Smith. Belfast: 1896. Contains a large number of works on the linen industry.

1954 — Supplementary catalogue of books added, 1903 and 1904, compiled by George Maxwell. 1904–5.

1955 — Catalogue of the books in the Irish section. Belfast: 1917.

1956 LINEN INDUSTRY RESEARCH ASSOCIATION. Library catalogue, 1919–54. Lambeg, Antrim: 1955. Material arranged under the following main headings: agriculture, biology, bleaching, building, chemistry, colloids, dyeing, economics, engineering, fibres, finishing, general information, humidity, instrumentation and measurements, knitting, laundering and dry cleaning, making up and embroidery, mathematics, microscopy and photography, mill and factory problems, physics, printing, spinning, standardisation, technology, testing, utilisation of materials, and weaving.

1957 LONGFIELD, ADA KATHLEEN. History of the Irish linen and cotton printing industry in the eighteenth century. *R. Soc. Antiq. Ir. J.*, 67, 1937, 26–56. Includes list of printers on linen and cotton.

1958 — Irish linen for Spain and Portugal: James Archbold's letters, 1771–79. *R. Ir. Acad. Proc., Sec. C.*, vol. 76, no. 2, 1976, 13–22.

1959 SMYTH, WILLIAM J. Locational patterns and trends within the pre-famine linen industry. *Ir. Geog.*, 8, 1975, 97–110.

Wool

1960 CUNNINGHAM, W. The repression of the woollen manufacture in Ireland. *English Hist. Rev.*, 1, 1886, 277–294.

1961 IRELAND. DEPARTMENT OF AGRICULTURE AND FISHERIES. Report of the Committee on Wool Improvements. Dublin: 1966.

1962 IRELAND. COMMITTEE ON INDUSTRIAL ORGANISATION. Report on survey of the woollen and worsted industry. Dublin: 1965.

1963 OLDHAM, CHARLES H. The woollen industry of Ireland. Dublin: 1909.

Timber

1964 McCRACKEN, EILEEN. The Irish timber trade in the 18th century. *Qtr. J. Forestry*, 61, 1967, 42–51.

Needlework

1965 ANDERSON, MISS. Notes on the Irish lace and crochet industry. *Ir. Dept. Agric. J.*, 14, 1913–14, 53–58.

1966 BOYLE, ELIZABETH. The Irish flowerers. Belfast: 1971. History of the Irish embroidery and lace industries since 1600.

1967 BRENAN, JAMES. The modern Irish lace industry. *J. Proc. Arts Crafts Soc. Ir.*, 1898, 69–103.

1968 WRIGHT, THOMAS. The romance of the lace pillow . . . with some account of the lace industries of Devon and Ireland. Chicheley (Bucks.): 1971. Facsimile reprint of 1st ed., 1919; bibliog., pp. 263–266.

Poplin

1969 CAMPION, MARY. An old Dublin industry—poplin. *Dublin Hist. Rec.*, vol. 19, no. 1, 1963, 2–15.

Ceramics

1970 IRELAND. COMMITTEE ON INDUSTRIAL ORGANISATION. Report on survey of the pottery, china, and earthenware industry. Dublin: 1963.

Furniture

1971 CORR, FRANK. The Irish furniture industry now. *Technol. Ir.*, vol. 6, no. 11, 1975, 15–17.

1972 HANNON, PAUL. A brief statistical review of the Irish furniture industry. *Technol. Ir.*, vol. 9, no. 11, 1970, 54–55.

1973 IRELAND. COMMITTEE ON INDUSTRIAL ORGANISATION. Report on survey of the wood and metal furniture industry. Dublin: 1964.

Building

1974 DAVIES, A.C. Roofing Belfast and Dublin, 1896–98: American penetration of the Irish market for Welsh slate. *Ir. Econ. Soc. Hist.*, 4, 1977, 26–35.

1975 KELLY, PATRICK. Aspects of the construction industry in Irish economic development. *Chart. Surv.*, 100, 1967, 135–142.

1976 MURPHY, P. The building industry in Cork. *Technol. Ir.*, vol. 4, no. 8, 1972, 29–31.

Films

1977 IRELAND. DEPARTMENT OF INDUSTRY AND COMMERCE. Report of the Film Industry Committee. Dublin: 1968.

Tourism

1978 AALEN, F.H.A., and BIRD, J.C. Tourism in

Ireland — East: guidelines for development. A survey commissioned by the Eastern Regional Tourism Organisation Ltd. Dublin: 1969.

1979 BORD FAILTE. RESEARCH AND PLANNING DEPARTMENT. Tourism plan, 1973–1976: a four-year working document for the Irish tourist industry. Dublin: 1973.

1980 — Tourism plan, 1974–1977: a four-year working document for the Irish tourist industry. Dublin: 1974. Supplementary to the Tourism Plan, 1973–1976, and should be read in conjunction with it.

1981 CORNFORTH, JOHN. Tourism and Irish houses. *Country Life*, vol. 159, no. 4114, 1976, 1154–56.

1982 CUNNINGHAM, A.C., and QUIRKE, T. Bord Failte Eireann as seen from the smaller hotel. Dublin, University College: 1971. (*Business Research Report no*. 2)

1983 HENEGHAN, PHILIP. The tourist industry in Ireland, 1960 to 1975. *Studies*, 65, 1976, 225–234.

Small Firms

1984 DAWSON, J.A., and WATKIN, D.G. The small shop in the urban retail economy: a case study in Northern Ireland. *Ir. Geog*., 9, 1976, 76–88.

Economic Expansion, Regional Development

1985 BARRINGTON, T.J. Organisation for development. *Admin*., vol. 21, no. 1, 1973, 3–15.

1986 — Some problems of regional development. *ibid*., 16–26.

1987 BRISTOW, J.A. State enterprise and economic planning in the Irish republic. *Stat. Social Inq. Soc. Ir*., vol. 21, pt. 3, 1964–5, 77–95.

1988 BROCK, C. The C.I.O. Survey. *Stat. Social Inq. Soc. Ir*., vol. 21, pt. 2, 1963–64, 176–188. Committee on Industrial Organisation.

1989 CAMBLIN, GILBERT. Economic planning and regional development. *Chart. Surv*., 100, 1967–8, 65–79.

1990 CHADWICK, J.W. *and others*. Ballina: a local study in regional economic development, by J.W. Chadwick, J.B. Houston and J.R.W. Mason. Dublin: 1972. Bibliog. pp. 172–6.

1991 CURRAN, R.G. Confidence — Ulster's key weapon. *Geog. Mag*., 45, 1972, 92–95.

1992 DEENY, JAMES. Regional development. *Soc. Stud*., vol. 2, no. 3, 1973, 205–222.

1993 DONALDSON, LORAINE. Development planning in Ireland. New York and London: 1966. Bibliog., pp. 149–156.

1994 DRUDY, S.M. and DRUDY, P.J. Problems of development in remote rural regions: case studies in Britain and Ireland. *Anglo-Ir. Stud*., 3, 1977, 56–70.

1995 FITZGERALD, GARRET. Planning in Ireland: a PEP study. Dublin: Institute of Public Administration; London: Political and Economic Planning; 1968.

1996 — The role of Development Centres in the Irish economy. *Admin*., 12, 1964, 171–180.

1997 AN FORAS TALUNTAIS (THE AGRICULTURAL INSTITUTE) West Donegal resource survey. Dublin: 1969. 4 pts.

1998 GIBSON, NORMAN. Economic conditions and policy in Northern Ireland. *Econ. Soc. Rev*., vol. 4, no. 3, 1973, 349–364.

1999 GLASS, J.C., and KIOUNTOUZIS, E. Linear programming models for development planning in Northern Ireland. *Econ. Soc. Rev*., vol. 7, no. 2, 1976, 121–141.

2000 HOARE, ANTHONY G. Spheres of influence and regional policy: the case of Northern Ireland. *Ir. Geog*., 9, 1976, 89–99.

2001 IRELAND. DEPARTMENT OF INDUSTRY AND COMMERCE. Science and Irish economic development; report of the Research and Technology Survey Team appointed by the Minister for Industry and Commerce in November, 1963. Dublin: 1966. 2 vols.

2002 KENNEDY, KIERAN A. Productivity and industrial growth: the Irish experience. Oxford: 1971. Bibliog., pp. 272–6.

2003 — and DOWLING, BRENDAN R. Economic growth in Ireland: the experience since 1947. Dublin and New York: 1975. Bibliog., pp. 303–9.

2004 **Leser**, C.E.V. Problems of industrialisation in developing countries and their implications for Ireland. *Stat. Social Inq. Soc. Ir. J.*, vol. 21, pt. 6, 1967–68, 1–30.

2005 **Lichfield, Nathaniel**. Limerick regional plan: interim report on the economic, social and technical problems of the planning of the Limerick City/South Clare/Shannon industrial estate complex. Dublin: 1965.

2006 **National Planning Conference**. National planning and reconstruction: the official handbook of the National Planning Conference. Dublin: 1944.

2007 **O'Farrell, Patrick** N. Regional development in Ireland: the economic case for a regional policy. *Admin.*, 18, 1970, 342–362.

2008 **Roche, Desmond**. An outline of the regional situation in Ireland, Britain, France, Italy. *Admin.*, 21, 1973, 27–40.

2009 **Scully, John** J. The development of Western Ireland. *Ir. Geog.*, vol. 6, no. 1, 1969, 1–13.

2010 — The pilot area development scheme. *Stat. Social Inq. Soc. Ir. J.*, vol. 21, pt. 6, 1967–68, 51–71. Region comprises eight seaboard counties from Donegal to Cork, and four inland counties — Cavan, Roscommon, Longford and Monaghan.

2011 **Symposium On Science And Irish Economic Development**. *Stat. Social Inq. Soc. Ir. J.*, vol. 21, pt. 5, 1966–67, 35–47. Contributions by D.I.D. Howie, T.E. Nevin, A.V. Vincent and Dr. M.D. McCarthy.

2012 **Tait**, A.A. and **Bristow**, J.A., *eds*. Ireland: some problems of a developing economy. Dublin and New York: 1972.

Consumption of Wealth

2013 **Harrison**, M.J., and **Nolan**, S. The distribution of personal wealth in Ireland — a comment. *Econ. Soc. Rev.*, 7, 1975, 65–78. Comment on Patrick M. Lyons's paper.

2014 **Hughes**, J.G. The functional distribution of income in Ireland, 1938–70. Dublin: 1972. (*Economic and Social Research Institute paper no*. 65)

2015 **Lyons, Patrick** M. The distribution of personal wealth in Northern Ireland. *Econ. Soc. Rev.*, 3, 1972, 215–225.

2016 **Walsh, Brendan** M. and **Walsh, Dermot**. Economic aspects of alcohol consumption in the Republic of Ireland. *Econ. Soc. Rev.*, 2, 1970, 115–138.

Poverty

2017 **O'Neill, Timothy** P. Clare and Irish poverty, 1815–1851. *Stud. Hib.*, 14, 1974, 7–27.

2017a — Poverty in Ireland, 1815–45. *Folk Life*, 11, 1973, 22–33.

2018 **Social Studies**, vol. 1, no. 4, 1972. This issue is devoted to the Conference on Poverty held in Kilkenny, 19–21 November 1971; papers include: The concept of poverty, by James Kavanagh; The extent of poverty in Ireland, by Seamus O Cinneide; Families in poverty, by Peter Birch; Rural poverty, by Eileen Kane.

2019 **Walsh, Brendan**, *compiler*. Poverty in Ireland: research priorities. Account of one-day conference held in ESRI, 18 April 1972. Dublin: 1972. (*Economic and Social Research Institute, broadsheet no*. 7)

LAW

General Bibliographies

2020 **Hepple**, B.A. and others. A bibliography of the literature on British and Irish labour law, by B.A. Hepple, J.M. Neeson, and Paul O'Higgins. London: 1975.

2021 **A Legal Bibliography Of The British Commonwealth Of Nations**. Vol. 4. Irish law to 1956, compiled by Leslie F. Maxwell and W. Harold Maxwell. 2nd ed. London: 1957. 1st ed., 1936.

2022 **Marvin**, J.G. Legal bibliography, or a thesaurus of American, English, Irish and Scotch law books. Philadelphia: 1847.

2023 **United Nations Educational, Scientific And Cultural Organisation**. A register of legal documentation in the world, prepared by the International Association of Legal Science and the International Committee for Social Sciences Documentation. 2nd rev. and enl. ed. Paris: 1957. Text in both English and French.

2024 UNIVERSITY OF LONDON. INSTITUTE OF ADVANCED LEGAL STUDIES. Finding list of primary source materials for British and Irish law held by London libraries. London: 1974. Typescript.

2025 — Supplement. London: 1975. Typescript.

Catalogues

2026 DUBLIN CASTLE. LAW LIBRARY. Catalogue of books. Not published; includes alphabetical lists of law reports and tables of abbreviations used in law reports and text books.

2027 INCORPORATED LAW SOCIETY OF IRELAND. Colley, Thomas B. *compiler*. Catalogue of books in the library . . . with index of subjects. Dublin: 1937.

2028 — EVANS, S.W. *compiler*. Catalogue of the books in the library. Dublin: 1909.

2029 — GAVAN-DUFFY, COLUM. *compiler*. Catalogue of the Incorporated Law Society. In preparation.

2030 KING'S INNS, DUBLIN. Catalogue. Dublin: 1834.

2031 — CONNOR, HENRY. *compiler*. Juridicial catalogue of the library. Dublin: 1846.

2032 — [DUHIGG, BARTHOLOMEW THOMAS] *compiler*. A catalogue of the library . . . to Trinity term 1801. Dublin: 1801.

2033 — HAIG W. *compiler*. List of books printed in England prior to the year 1600, in the library . . . Dublin: 1858.

2034 O'REILLY, EDWARD. An essay on the subject proposed by the Royal Irish Academy, viz: An essay on the nature and influence of the ancient Irish institutes, commonly called the Brehon Laws . . . with an appendix, containing a catalogue of the principal ancient Irish laws to be found in the Mss. library of Trinity College and other libraries; a prize essay. *R.Ir. Acad. Trans.*, 14, 1825, 141–226.

Periodicals

2035 GAVAN-DUFFY, COLUM, *compiler*. List of journals and law reports in Dublin libraries as at 1 January 1958. Typescript.

2036 O'HIGGINS, PAUL. A bibliography of periodical literature relating to Irish law. Belfast: 1966.

2037 — 1st supplement. Belfast: 1973.

History

2038 BINCHY, D.A. Ancient Irish law. *Ir. Jurist*, vol. 1, no. 1, 1966, 84–92.

2039 — Irish history and Irish law. *Stud. Hib.*, 15, 1975, 7–36; 16, 1976, 7–45.

2040 BRYANT, SOPHIE. Liberty, order and law under native Irish rule: a study in *The Book of the ancient laws of Ireland*. London: 1923. Bibliog., p. xxiii.

2041 CLARKE, AIDAN. The history of Poynings' Law, 1615–41. *Ir. Hist. Stud.*, vol. 18, no. 70, 1972, 207–222.

2042 COSGRAVE, LIAM. The King's Inns. *Dublin Hist. Rec.*, 21, 1966–67, 45–52.

2043 DE BREFFNY, BRIAN. Magistrates of Co. Clare in 1837. *Ir. Ancest*, 7, 1975, 99–101.

2044 DELANY, V.T.H. The administration of justice in Ireland, edited by Charles Lysaght. 4th rev. ed., Dublin: 1975. Bibliog., pp. 100–101.

2045 — Legal studies in Trinity College, Dublin, since the foundation. *Hermathena*, 89, 1957, 3–16.

2046 DONALDSON, ALFRED GASTON. Some comparative aspects of Irish law. Durham, N.C.,: 1957. (*Duke Univ. Commonwealth-Studies center pub.*, no. 3.) Bibliog., pp. 270–82.

2047 HAND, G.J. English law in Ireland, 1290–1324. Cambridge: 1967. Bibliog., pp. 251–261.

2048 MCDOWELL, R.B. The Irish courts of law, 1801–1914. *Ir. Hist. Stud.*, 10, 1956–7, 363–91.

2049 MACLYSAGHT, E. Reports of Fenian trials in Oireachtas library. *Anal. Hib.*, 23, 1966, 299–301.

2050 MACNIOCAILL, GEAROID. Aspects of Irish law in the late thirteenth century. *Hist. Stud.*, 10, 1976, 25–42.

2051 NEWARK, F.H. Notes on Irish legal history. Belfast: Queen's Univ., 1960. Revised ed. of paper which first appeared in the *Northern Ireland legal quarterly*, 1947.

2052 O'BUACHALLA, LIAM. Some researches in ancient Irish law. *Cork Hist. Arch. Soc. J., 2nd ser.*, 52, 1947, 41–54, 135–48; 53, 1948, 1–12, 75–81.

2053 O'FLANAGAN, J. RODERICK. The lives of the Lord Chancellors and Keepers of the Great Seal of Ireland. [Reprinted] Clifton (N.J.), 1972. 2 vols. (*Reprints of legal classics*)

2054 O'HIGGINS, PAUL. A select bibliography of Irish legal history. *Amer. J. Leg. Hist.*, 4, 1960, 173–80.

2055 — WILLIAM SAMPSON (1764–1836). *Dublin Univ. Law Rev.*, vol. 2, no. 1, 1970, 45–52.

2056 — WILLIAM RIDGEWAY (1765–1817) — law reporter. *Nth. Ir. Leg. Qtr.*, 18, 1967, 208–222.

Acts and Statutes

(Arranged chronologically)

2057 BERRY, HENRY F. *ed.* Statutes and ordnances, and acts of the parliament of Ireland, King John to Henry V.[1199–1422.] Dublin: 1907.

2058 ROBBINS, N. An exact abridgement of all the Irish statutes [1275–1735]. Dublin: 1736.

2059 APPENDIX TO THE LATE KING JAMES'S ACTS . . . to which is added, a catalogue of the . . . acts . . . [1603–88]. Dublin: 1740.

2060 OULTON, ANDREW NEWTON. Index to the statutes at present in force or affecting Ireland, from the year 1310 to 1835 inclusive. Dublin: 1836.

2061 — Chronological table of the statutes . . . with reference to the Index to these statutes. Dublin: 1837.

2062 — Annual supplements to the Index. Dublin: nos. 1–13, 1836–49.

2063 STATUTES AT LARGE, passed in the parliaments held in Ireland. Dublin: 1765. 8 vols. Rev. ed. by J.G. Butler, Dublin: 1786–1801. 20 vols. Covers period 1310–1800.

2064 QUINN, DAVID. The bills and statutes of the Irish parliaments of Henry VII and Henry VIII. *Anal. Hib.*, 10, 1941, 73–169.

2065 INDEX TO ACTS EXTENDING AND RELATING TO IRELAND, from the Union 41 Geo. 3, 1801, to end of the session 3 Geo. 4. [1801–23.] London: 1826.

2066 STATUTE LAW OF THE IRISH FREE STATE (Saorstat Eireann), 1922 to 1928, reviewed and indexed by the Hon. Mr. Justice Hanna, assisted by A. Denis Pringle. Dublin: 1929.

2067 GAVAN DUFFY, GEORGE, *compiler*. A calendar of the Statute Roll for twenty-one years in force exhibiting a complete, alphabetical table of the Public General Acts, promulgated since the 6th day of December, 1922, and remaining operative on New Year's Day, 1944, with a record of every repealed section — prefaced by the heads of the Constitution. Dublin: 1944.

2068 INDEX TO STATUTORY RULES AND ORDERS (EIRE) 1922–47. Dublin, 1944–55. 3 vols.

2069 INDEX TO THE LEGISLATION PASSED BY THE OIREACHTAS in the years 1922–1932. Dublin: 1934.

2070 GROGAN, VINCENT, *compiler*. Index to the statutes 1922 to 1948; with chronological tables showing their effect on Pre-Union Irish statutes, British statutes, Saorstat Eireann statutes, and Acts of the Oireachtas. Dublin [1950].

2071 INDEX TO THE LEGISLATION PASSED BY THE OIREACHTAS . . . 1922–1953. Dublin: 1955.

2072 INDEX TO EMERGENCY POWERS ORDERS. Dublin: 1943–54. 3 vols.

2073 INDEX TO THE STATUTES 1922–1958, with chronological tables. Dublin [1959].

2074 INDEX TO THE STATUTES 1922–1968, with chronological tables. Dublin: 1970.

2075 INDEX TO THE STATUTES 1922–1975, with tables and 1976 supplement. Dublin: 1977.

Digests

(Arranged chronologically)

2076 FINLAY, JOHN. A digest and index of all the Irish reported cases in law and equity, from the earliest period to the present time, and also of the reported cases in ecclesiastical and criminal law. Dublin: 1830.

2077 BRUNKER, T. Digest of cases of Superior and

other courts of common law in Ireland and Courts of Admiralty from Sir John Davies reports to 1865. Dublin: 1865.

2078 GAMBLE, R.W. and BARLOW, W. Index to all reported cases in the Courts of Equity in Ireland from 1838 to 1867. Dublin: 1868. 2 vols.

2079 MURRAY, R.D. and DIXON, G.Y. Digest of cases reported in the Irish Reports from 1867 to 1893. Dublin: 1899.

2080 STUBBS, W.C. Digest of the *Irish Law Times Reports* from 1867 to 1893. Dublin: 1895.

2081 MAXWELL, T.H. Digest of all cases reported in the *Irish Reports* and *Irish Law Times Reports* from 1894 to 1918. Dublin: 1921.

2082 RYLAND, R.H. Digest of cases decided by the Superior and other Courts in Ireland from 1919 to 1928. Dublin: 1930.

2083 — Digest of cases decided by the Superior and other Courts in Ireland from 1929 to 1938. Dublin: 1941.

2084 HARRISON, R.A. Digest of cases decided by the Superior and other Courts in Ireland from 1939 to 1948. Dublin: 1952.

2085 FALCONER, JOHN, *publisher*. Annual digest of cases published by the *Irish Law Times* to Superior and other Courts in Ireland. Dublin: 1949–.

2086 RYAN, EDWARD F. *compiler*. Notes of Irish cases, reported in the *Irish Reports*, the *Northern Ireland Reports*, the *Irish Law Times Reports*, and the *Irish Jurist Reports* 1949–58. Cork: 1960.

2087 — Notes of Irish cases reported in the *Irish Reports*, the *Northern Ireland Reports*, and *Irish Law Times Reports*, and the *Irish Jurist Reports* 1959–1968. Cork: 1970.

Private Law

2088 CALENDAR OF THE JUSTICIARY ROLLS OR PROCEEDINGS in the Court of the Justiciar of Ireland preserved in the Public Record Office of Ireland, XXIII to XXXI year of Edward I. [1295–1303.] Edited by James Mills. Dublin: 1905. Pt. 2. XXXIII to XXXV years [1305–7.] London: 1914.

2089 — CALENDAR OF THE JUSTICIARY ROLLS OR PROCEEDINGS in the Court of the Justiciar of Ireland, I to VII years of Edward II. [1308–14], prepared under the direction of the Deputy Keeper of the Public Records, by Herbert Wood and Albert E. Longman and revised by Margaret C. Griffith. Dublin: 1956. For periods 1295–1377, 1378–1620 see *Rep. D.K. Pub. Rec. Ir.*, 26, 1894, 57–68; 28, 1896, 41–56.

2090 CALENDAR OF THE PATENT AND CLOSE ROLLS OF CHANCERY IN IRELAND, edited by James Morrin. Dublin: 1861–3. 3 vols.

2091 FERGUSON, JAMES FREDERICK. A calendar of the contents of the *Red Book of the Irish Exchequer. Kilkenny and Sth. E. Arch. Soc. Proc. and Trans.*, 3, 1854–5, 35–52. See also *Rep. D.K. Pub. Rec. Ir.*, 24, 1892, 96–9.

2092 SHATTER, ALAN JOSEPH. Family law in the Republic of Ireland. Dublin: 1977.

2093 WYLIE, J.C.W. Irish land law. London: 1975. Invaluable bibliographical footnotes.

Constitution

2094 ARNOLD, BRUCE. Bipartisanship and the Constitution. *Studies*, 66, 1977, 1–7.

2095 CHUBB, BASIL. The Constitution of Ireland. Dublin: 1963. (*Introduction to public administration ser., no.* 5.) Bibliog., pp. 41–42.

2096 MCCOLGAN, JOHN. Implementing the 1921 treaty: Lionel Curtis and constitutional procedure. *Ir. Hist. Stud.*, vol. 20, no. 79, 1977, 312–333.

Criminal Law

2097 O SIOCHAIN, P.A. The criminal law of Ireland. 6th ed., Dublin: 1977.

Social Law

2098 SCANNELL, YVONNE. The law and practice relating to pollution control in Ireland. London: 1976.

Commercial Law

2099 CHARTERED INSTITUTE OF SECRETARIES. The Companies Act, 1963: part of a series of lectures and discussions arranged by the College of Commerce, Rathmines, in conjunction with the Chartered Institute of Secretaries. London: 1965.

2100 CROWLEY, T. PEARSE. A guide to the Companies Act, 1963. [Reprinted] Dublin: 1977. 1st ed., Dublin: 1965.

2101 SCOTT, W.R. The constitution and finance of English, Scottish, and Irish joint-stock companies to 1720. Cambridge: 1910–12. 3 vols. Bibliog. vol. 1, pp. xxvii–lvi.

2102 WALLER, GEORGE. A general index to the several statutes from the 33rd of George the Second relating to the revenue of Ireland. Dublin: 1778.

Judiciary

2103 BARTHOLOMEW, PAUL C. The Irish judiciary. Dublin: 1971.

2104 BETH, LOREN P. The development of judicial review in Ireland, 1937–1966. Dublin: 1967.

2105 O'DONOVAN, JOHN. The Irish judiciary in the 18th and 19th centuries. *Eire-Ir.*, vol. 6, no. 3, 1971, 51–56; *ibid.*, no. 4, 1971, 17–22.

Northern Ireland

2106 BOYLE, KEVIN, *and others*. Law and state: the case of Northern Ireland, by Kevin Boyle, Tom Hadden and Paddy Hillyard. London: 1975. (*Law in Society ser.*)

2107 CALVERT, HARRY. Constitutional law in Northern Ireland: a study in regional government. London and Belfast: 1968.

2108 MAXWELL, T.H. Northern Ireland supplement to the United Kingdom Index of statutes, being the index to the imperial statutes in force relating to Northern Ireland to the end of the session, 31 December 1922. Belfast: 1925.

2109 NARAIN, B.J. Public law in Northern Ireland: a study in autochthony and statecraft and an exercise towards harmonisation of the western legal conceptual framework. Muckamore [Antrim]: 1975.

2110 — Index to the statutes in force affecting Northern Ireland covering the legislation to 31 December 1963. 11th ed. Belfast: 1964.

2111 NORTHERN IRELAND, STATUTES. Chronological table and index of the statutes affecting Northern Ireland. Belfast: 1930–.

2112 — Index to the statutes in force affecting Northern Ireland covering the legislation to 31 December 1954. 8th ed, Belfast: 1957.

2113 UNITED NATIONS EDUCATIONAL, SCIENTIFIC AND CULTURAL ORGANISATION. A bibliographical guide to the law of the United Kingdom, the Channel Islands and the Isle of Man. London: 1956. Select bibliog on Northern Ireland, pp. 62–4.

ADMINISTRATION

2114 ADMINISTRATION: journal of the Institute of Public Administration of Ireland. vol. 1–, 1953–. Dublin: 1953–. Index, vol. 1–5. [1958.]; Cumulative index, vol. 1–15, 1969. Source for material on adult education, central government, Central Statistics Office, civil aviation, civil service, customs and excise, Electricity Supply Board, Gaeltacht, local government, management, shipping, housing and fisheries.

2115 GALE, PETER. An inquiry into the ancient corporate system of Ireland. London: 1834. A general sketch of municipal history, with a valuable appendix of charters and other documents.

2116 GREAT BRITAIN. Commisioners on municipal corporations in Ireland. First report and appendices of the commissioners appointed to inquire into the municipal corporations in Ireland. Presented to both Houses of Parliament by command of His Majesty. London: 1835–6. 3 vol. and appendix. (*Parliament, House of Commons sessional papers*, 23–5, 27–8, 1835; 26, 29, 1836.

2117 GROGAN, VINCENT. Administrative tribunals in the public service. Dublin [1961].

2118 GROSS, CHARLES. A bibliography of British municipal history including gilds and parliamentary representation. 2nd ed. with a preface by G.H. Martin. Leicester: 1966. 1st ed., New York: 1897.

2119 INDEX to *Liber Munerum Publicorum Hiberniae*. *Rep. D.K. Pub. Rec. Ir.*, 9, 1877, append., pp. 21–58.

2120 INSTITUTE OF PUBLIC ADMINISTRATION, DUBLIN. Library catalogue. Dublin: 1958.

2121 IRELAND. DEPARTMENT OF THE PUBLIC SERVICES. State directory, 1977. Dublin: 1977. Published annually; contents include details of members of the government, parliamentary secretaries, government secretariat, Dail Eireann, Seanad Eireann, register of political parties, government departments, civil service pay and allowances, and personnel.

2122 KING, FREDERICK CHARLES. *ed.* Public administration in Ireland: a series of lectures delivered under the auspices of the Civics Institute of Ireland to candidates for the Diploma of Public Administration of Dublin University. Dublin: 1944–53. 3 vols.

2123 McDOWELL, R.B. The Irish administration, 1801–1914. London: 1964. (*Studies in Irish history, 2nd ser.*, vol. 2.) Bibliog., pp. 302–315.

2124 MARTIN, G.H. and MACINTYRE, SYLVIA. A bibliography of British and Irish municipal history. Leicester: vol. 1, General works, 1972. Excludes titles cited in Gross's Bibliography.

2125 O'LOAN, J. Nineteenth century administrators: William Thomas Mulvany. *Administration*, vol. 8. no. 4, 1960, 315–332. Mulvany's primary interests were drainage and navigation.

2126 RICHARDSON, H.G. and SAYLES, G.O., *eds.* The administration of Ireland, 1172–1377. Dublin: 1963. Bibliog., pp. ix–xiii.

2127 SAINTY, J.C. The secretariat of the chief governors of Ireland, 1690–1840. *R. Ir. Acad. Proc., Sec. C*, vol. 77, no. 1, 1977, 1–33.

Civil Service

2128 DOONEY, SEAN. The Irish civil service. Dublin: 1976. Bibliog., pp. 184–197.

2129 IRELAND. DEPARTMENT OF FINANCE. Report of public services organisation review group, 1966–1969. Dublin: 1969. Chairman of group: Liam St. J. Devlin.

2130 O BROIN, LEON. Joseph Brennan, civil servant extraordinary. *Studies*, 66, 1977, 25–37.

2131 THE OFFICE OF PUBLIC WORKS. ITS ORIGIN AND DEVELOPMENT. *Oibre*, 2, 1965, 23–25; 4, 1966, 22–24; 6, 1968, 23–25.

2132 SCIENTIFIC SERVICE: journal of the Institute of Professional Civil Servants. Dublin, vol. 1–, 1930–.

Finance

2133 DI BUITLEIR, DONAL. Problems of Irish local finance. Dublin: 1974.

2134 GOLDEN, T.P. Local authority accounting in Ireland. Dublin: 1977.

2135 KIERNAN, THOMAS JOSEPH. History of the financial administration of Ireland to 1817. London: 1930. Bibliog., pp. 341–7.

2136 LYDON, JAMES F. Survey of the Memoranda Rolls of the Irish Exchequer, 1294–1509. *Anal. Hib.*, 23, 1966, 51–134.

2137 O'CONNELL, J.B. The financial administration of Ireland; new ed. Dublin [1960]. Previous ed. published as *The Financial administration of Saorstat Eireann*, 1934.

2138 WALKER, DAVID. Local government finance in Ireland: a preliminary survey. Dublin: 1962. (*Economic Research Institute paper no.* 5)

2139 — Local government finance and county incomes. Dublin: 1964. (*Economic Research Institute paper no.* 18).

Government

2140 CHUBB, BASIL. The Government: an introduction to the cabinet system in Ireland. Dublin, Institute of Public Administration, 1961. (*Introduction to public administration ser.*, no. 3.) Bibliog., pp. 44–5.

2141 — A source book of Irish government. Dublin, Institute of Public Administration, 1964.

2142 COLLINS, JOHN. Local government. Dublin: 1954. Bibliog., pp. 119–26; first appeared in *Administration*, vol. 1, no. 4, 1953–4; new edition, 1963.

2143 FARRELL, BRIAN. Chairman or chief? — the role of Taoiseach in Irish government. Dublin: 1971. List of members of the Cabinet from 1922 onwards, pp. 88–110.

2144 FENNELL, DESMOND. Studies of the new Ireland. Galway: Association for the Advancement of Self-Government, 1973.

2145 LAWRENCE, R.J. Local government in Northern Ireland: areas, functions and finance. *Stat. Social Inq. Soc. Ir. J.*, vol. 21, pt. 4, 1965–66, 14–23.

2146 LOUGHRAN, G.F. The problem of local government in Northern Ireland. *Admin*, 13, 1965, 35–38.

2147 McKINSEY and Co. INC. Strengthening the local government service : a report prepared for the Minister for Local Government by McKinsey and Co. Inc. Dublin: 1972.

2148 MALCOMSON, A.P.W. The Newton Act of 1748: revision and construction. *Ir. Hist. Stud.*, vol. 18, no. 71, 1973, 313–344.

2149 MANSERGH, NICHOLAS. The government of Northern Ireland: a study in devolution. London: 1936. Bibliog., pp. 325–30.

2150 MEGHEN, P.J. Local government: a guide for the citizen. 2nd rev. ed. Dublin: 1964. (*Guide to public administration ser*: 1.)

2151 O'BRIEN, KATHLEEN. A select list of Irish government reports, 1960–1972, with chairman or author index and title index. Dublin: Radio Telefis Eireann, 1974. Typescript, 58p.

2152 O'DONNELL, JAMES D. How Ireland is governed. Dublin: 1965. Bibliog. pp. 154–5.

2153 O'GADHRA, NOLLAIG. The future development of the Oireachtas. *Eire-Ir.*, vol. 7, no. 4, 1972, 111–3.

2154 O MUIMHNEACHAIN, M. The functions of the department of the Taoiseach. Dublin: Institute of Public Administration, 1960.

2155 SHANNON, CATHERINE B. The Ulster liberal unionists and local government reform, 1885–98. *Ir. Hist. Stud.*, vol. 18, no. 71, 1973, 407–423.

2156 SHEARMAN, HUGH. How Northern Ireland is governed: central and local government in Northern Ireland. 2nd ed. Belfast: 1963.

2157 SMYTH, J.C. The Houses of the Oireachtas. Dublin: 1961. (*Introduction to public administration ser.*, no. 1.)

Police

2158 BLYTHE, EARNAN P. The D.M.P. (The Dublin Metropolitan Police). *Dublin Hist. Rec.*, 20, 1965–66, 116–126.

2159 BRADY, CONOR. Guardians of the peace. Dublin and London: 1974. A history of the Garda Siochana. Bibliog., pp. xiv–xvi.

2160 BREATHNACH, SEAMUS. The Irish police from earliest times to the present day. Tralee and Dublin: 1974. Bibliog., pp. 221–3.

2161 BROEKER, GALEN. Rural disorder and police reform in Ireland, 1812–36. London and Toronto: 1970. (*Studies in Irish history, 2nd ser.*, vol. 8.)

2162 COX, LIAM. Constabulary employed in the district of Moate, Co. Westmeath in 1876. *Ir. Ancest.*, vol. 7, 1975, 35–38.

2163 GAUGHAN, J. ANTHONY. Memoirs of Constable Jeremiah Mee, R.I.C. Dublin: 1975. Bibliog., pp. 366–374; first-hand account of life in the R.I.C. from 1910 to 1920.

2164 HEZLET, SIR ARTHUR. The 'B' specials: a history of the Ulster Special Constabulary. London: 1972. Bibliog., p. 242.

2165 JUBILEE YEAR TRIBUTE TO GARDA SIOCHANA. *Ir. Def. J.*, 32, 1972, 201–230.

2166 O'CEALLAIGH, TADHG. Peel and police reform in Ireland, 1814–18. *Stud. Hib.*, 6, 1966, 25–48.

MILITARY HISTORY

(See also History)

2167 The barracks and posts of Ireland [1] [Introductory], by Capt. Martin D. Bates. *Ir. Def. J.*, 25, 1965, 19–24.

2168 2. Marlborough (McKee) barracks; 1888–1892, by Lieut.-Col. Olaf MacNeill. *ibid.*, 25, 1965, 59–64.

2169 3. A history of Columb barracks, Mullingar, by Comdt. M.J. O'Donnell. *ibid.*, 25, 1965, 109–115.

2170 4. The story of Islandbridge barracks [now Clancy barracks], by Capt. P.D. O'Donnell. *ibid.*, 25, 1965, 197–207.

2171 5. Collins barracks, Cork, by Comdt. B.M. O'Brien. *ibid.*, 25, 1965, 219–227.

2172 6. History of Sarsfield barracks, by Lieut. T.F. Drohan. *ibid.*, 25, 1965, 343–348.

2173 7. A history of Haulbowline, base to the naval service, by Lt. Commander D.N. Brunicardi. *ibid.*, 25, 1965, 375–384, 460–466.

2174 8. Clonmel barracks, by Col. Eoghan O'Neill. *ibid*., 25, 1965, 483–489.

2175 9. Templemore military barracks, by Paul Walsh. *ibid*., 26, 1966, 161–166.

2176 10. The Royal Hospital, Kilmainham, by E. Tobin. *ibid*., 26, 1966, 417–426.

2177 11. Arbour Hill, by E. Tobin. *ibid*., 26, 1966, 486–506.

2178 12. The Royal Military Infirmary: Department of Defence and Army Headquarters, by E. Tobin. *ibid*., 28, 1968, 17–22.

2179 13. Dunree and the Inishowen forts, by Lt. Col. J.P. Kane *ibid*., 28, 1968, 37–39.

2180 14. Collins barracks, Dublin. Pt. 1, by Col. Michael Hefferon. *ibid*., 28, 1968, 129–136.

2181 15. Portobello barracks, Dublin. Pt. 1, by Comdt. P.D. O'Donnell. *ibid*., 28, 1968, 319–325; Pt. 2, by Comdt. P.D. O'Donnell, *ibid*., 29, 1969, 37–47.

2182 16. Collins barracks, Pt. 2. by Col. Michael Hefferon. *ibid*., 29, 1969, 126–129.

2183 17. Royal Hospital, Kilmainham, by Col. Michael Hefferon. *ibid*., 30, 1970, 1–4.

2184 18. Military barracks, Dundalk. Pt. 1, The British era, by Comdt. P.D. O'Donnell, *ibid*., 31, 1971, 137–140; Pt. 2, The Irish era, by Comdt. P.D. O'Donnell. *ibid*., 31, 1971, 276–282.

2185 [19] The Curragh of Kildare. (Curragh commemorative issue) *ibid*., 32, no. 5, 1972.

2186 20. Templemore military barracks, by Comdt. Paul Walsh. *ibid*., 32, 1972, 220–224.

2187 21. Collins barracks, Pt. 3, by Comdt. P.D. O'Donnell. *ibid*., 33, 1973, 48–52.

2188 22. Royal, or Collins barracks Pt. 4, by Comdt. P.D. O'Donnell. *ibid*., 33, 1973, 266–276.

2189 [23] Dun ui Mhaoiliosa [Renmore barracks, Galway], by Comdt. P.D. O'Donnell. *ibid*., 34, 1974, 181–196.

2190 24. Sean Connolly barracks, Longford, by Joseph O'Dwyer. *ibid*., 36, 1976, 43–51.

2191 BELFAST MUSEUM AND ART GALLERY, publication no. 120: A guide to the Irish volunteer, yeomanry and militia relics (eighteenth and nineteenth centuries). Belfast: 1938. Documents. pp. 41–3; bibliog., p.44.

2192 BOURKE, F.S. A contribution towards a bibliography of the volunteers of 1782. *Ir. Sword*, 2, 1954–6, 352–7. See also note, by N.W. English, *ibid*., vol. 8, no. 30, 1967, 71.

2193 CARGILL, DAVID C. Irishmen in Scottish census records. *Ir. Ancest*., 4, 1972, 8–14. Lists concern the Royal Artillery and the 13th Light Dragoons, 1851.

2194 COSTELLO, C. Historic recruiting posters. *Ir. Def. J*., 34, 1974, 408–411.

2195 DE COURCY IRELAND, JOHN. Notes on Civil war Irish seamen. *Eire-Ir*., vol. 6, no. 1, 1971, 8–10.

2196 FORDE, FRANK. The Liverpool Irish volunteers. *Ir. Sword*, vol. 10, no. 39, 1971, 106–123.

2197 — The Royal Irish Artillery, 1755–1801. *Ir. Sword*, vol. 11, no. 42, 1973, 32–38.

2198 — The South African Irish regiment. *Ir. Def. J*., 27, 1967, 295–301.

2199 GLASGOW, TOM. The Elizabethan navy in Ireland (1558–1603). *Ir. Sword*, vol. 7, no. 29, 1966, 291–307.

2200 HARDY, EVELYN. Survivors of the Armada. London: 1966. Experiences of Spanish survivors in Ireland.

2201 HARRIS, HENRY. The Royal Irish Fusiliers (The 87th and 89th Regiments of Foot). London, 1972. (*Famous regiments series*)

2202 HAYES-MCCOY, G.A. Twenty-five years of Irish military history. *Ir. Sword*, vol. 12, no. 47, 1975, 90–97. Account of military history societies and publications of the *Irish Sword*, 1949–1975.

2203 A HISTORY OF THE IRISH BRIGADES. A manuscript history of 512 pages on the Irish Brigades in the French and Spanish services, 1692–1815, presented by Thomas J. Mullen, Jr., to the library of Trinity College, Dublin, where it is available for consultation by scholars. See note in *Ir. Sword*, vol. 12, no. 46, 1975, 67.

2204 THE IRISH SWORD: the journal of the Military History Society of Ireland. vol. 1–, 1949–53–.

2205 KERRIGAN, PAUL M. The defences of Ireland. 1793–1815: [1][Introductory]. *Ir. Def. J.*, 34, 1974, 107–9.

2206 2. The Martello towers. *ibid.*, 34, 1974, 148–9.

2207 3. The Signal towers. *ibid.*, 34, 1974, 225–7.

2208 4. The Dublin area and the Wicklow mountains. *ibid.*, 34, 1974, 285–290.

2209 5. Shannon estuary. *ibid.*, 34, 1974, 310–4.

2210 6. The Shannon – Portumna to Shannon Harbour. *ibid.*, 35, 1975, 59–63.

2211 7. Shannonbridge. *ibid.*, 35, 1975, 398–403. Included in greater detail in *Ir. Sword*, vol. 11, no. 45, 1974.

2212 8. Athlone. *ibid.*, 37, 1977, 150–3.

2213 KILFEATHER, T.P. Ireland: graveyard of the Spanish Armada. Tralee: 1967.

2214 LINEHAN, D., *compiler*. Index to the Mss. of military interest in the National Library of Ireland. *Ir. Sword*, 2, 1954–6, 33–9.

2215 MCANALLY, HENRY W. Irish militia, 1793–1816: social and military study. Dublin: 1949. Bibliog., pp. 291–314.

2216 MCCARTHY, WILLIAM P. The Irish army list, 1671. *Ir. Sword*, 9, 1969–70, 278–282.

2217 MCDONALD, CAPT. THOMAS. The defence forces' history outlined. *Ir. Def. J.*, 27, 1967, 608–616.

2218 MCKENNA, CAPT. T. 'Thank God we're surrounded by water.' *Ir. Def. J.*, 33, 1973, 103–123.

2219 — Vessels of marine and naval service, 1939–1972., *ibid.*, 33, 1973, 161–168.

2220 MACSWINEY, MARQUIS. Notes on some Irish regiments in the service of Spain and of Naples in the eighteenth century. *R. Ir. Acad. Proc., Sec. C*, 57, 1924–7, 158–74.

2221 MARTIN, COLIN. Full fathom five: wrecks of the Spanish Armada. London: 1975. Bibliog., pp. 280–3.

2222 MEEHAN, JOHN. The 11th (Dublin Infantry Battalion). *Ir. Def. J.*, 34, 1974, 403–6.

2223 MORTON, R.G. Naval activity on Lough Neagh, 1558–1603. *Ir. Sword*, 8, 1967–8, 288–293.

2224 MURRAY, KEVIN. Loughlinstown Camp. *Dublin Hist. Rec.*, 7, 1944–45, 22–34.

2225 O'DONNELL, P.D. Dublin military barracks. *Dublin Hist. Rec.*, 25, 1971–2, 141–154.

2226 — How to research a barrack history. *Ir. Def. J.*, 37, 1977, 278–279.

2227 O'DONNELL, SEAN. Our Armada wreck sites. *Eire-Ir.*, vol. 11, no. 2, 1976, 129–132.

2228 — Technology of the Spanish Armada. *Technol. Ir.*, vol. 7, no. 10, 1976, 32–37.

2229 O'DUIBHIR, POL. The French are on the sea . . . a military history of Killiney Bay from 1793 to 1815. *Ir. Sword*, vol. 12, no. 46, 1975, 55–61.

2230 O'SNODAIGH, PADRAIG. Notes on the volunteers, militia, yeomanry and Orangemen of Co. Louth. *Louth Arch. J.*, vol. 18, no. 4, 1976, 279–293.

2231 — Notes on the volunteers, militia, yeomanry and fencibles of Kerry. *Kerry Arch. Hist. Soc. J.*, 4, 1971, 48–70.

2232 OTWAY-RUTHVEN, JOCELYN. Royal service in Ireland. *R. Soc. Antiq. Ir. J.*, 98, 1968, 37–46. Includes list of Proclamations of Royal Service, 1212–1480.

2233 PATERSON, T.G.F. The Volunteer companies of Ulster, 1778–1793. *Ir. Sword*, 7, 1965–66, 90–116, 204–230, 308–312; 8, 1967–68, 23–32, 92–97, 210–217.

2234 PIVKA, OTTO VON. The armies of Europe today. Reading: 1974. The Republic of Ireland, pp. 180–7; includes details of uniform and badges.

2235 QUANE, MICHAEL. The Royal Hibernian Military School, Phoenix Park, Dublin. *Dublin Hist. Rec.*, 18, 1962–3, 15–23, 45–55.

2236 SHIELS, JOSEPH. Captain Luke Ryan of Rush. *Dublin Hist. Rec.*, 24, 1971–2, 25–40.

2237 SIMMS, KATHARINE. Warfare in the medieval Gaelic lordships. *Ir. Sword*, vol. 12, no. 47, 1975, 98–108.

2238 SNODDY, OLIVER. Notes on the volunteers, militia, yeomanry, Orangemen and fencibles of Co. Limerick. *Ir. Sword*, vol. 10, no. 39, 1971, 125–140.

2239 — Notes on volunteers, militia, yeomen, and Orangemen of Co. Donegal. *Donegal Ann.*, vol. 8, no. 1, 1969, 49–73.

2240 — Notes on the volunteers, militia, Orangemen, and yeomanry of Co. Roscommon. *Ir. Sword*, vol. 12, no. 46, 1975, 15–35.

2241 — The volunteers, militia, yeomanry, and Orangemen of Co. Kildare in the 18th century. *Kildare Arch. Soc. J.*, vol. 15, no. 1, 1971, 38–49.

2242 — The volunteers, militia, yeomanry, and Orangemen of Co. Waterford. *Ir. Def. J.*, 35, 1975, 319–322, 341–347.

2243 VAN BROOK, F.W. A proposed Irish regiment and standard, 1796. *Ir. Sword*, vol. 11, no. 45, 1974, 226–233.

2244 VERNEY, PETER. The Micks: the story of the Irish Guards [1900–1970]. London, 1970.

2245 WALSH, MICHELENE. Unpublished Admiral Brown documents in Madrid. *Ir. Sword.*, vol. 3, no. 10, 1957, 17–19.

2246 WALTON, CLIFFORD. History of the British standing army, A.D. 1660 to 1700. London: 1894. Bibliog., pp. 859–66. Covers campaign of 1689–91.

2247 WHITE, ARTHUR S. A bibliography of regimental histories of the British Army. London: 1965.

2248 YOUNG, CAPT. PETER. Military archives in the defence forces. *Ir. Def. J.*, 37, 1977, 274–5.

Decorations and Medals

2249 O'RYAN, WILLIAM D. and GAYNOR, ROBERT M. Irish recipients of awards for bravery in the United States armed forces (1863–1963). *Ir. Def. J.*, 28, 1968, 263–5.

2250 O'TOOLE, E.H. Decorations and medals of the Republic of Ireland. London: 1972.

2251 WENT, ARTHUR E.J. The medals of the Royal Irish Ordnance Corps. *Ir. Num.*, 37, 1974, 27–28.

Battles

2252 BUTLER, GEORGE. The battle of Piltown [Co. Kilkenny], 1462. *Ir. Sword*, vol. 6, no. 24, 1964, 197–212.

2253 — The battle of Affane [Co. Waterford]. *Ir. Sword*, vol. 8, no. 30, 1967, 33–47.

2254 — The battle of Affane. *J. Butler Soc.*, vol. 1, no. 5, 1973–4, 320–7.

2255 GREEN, HOWARD. Guide to the battlefields of Britain and Ireland. London: 1973. Includes the Boyne (1690), siege of Limerick (1690), and siege of Cork (1690).

2256 HAYES-MCCOY, C.A. Irish battles. London: 1969. Includes Clontarf, Dysert O'Dea, Knockdoe, Farsetmore, Clontibret, the Yellow Ford, Moyra Pass, Kinsale, Benburb, Rathmines, the Boyne, Aughrim, Arklow, with bibliogs. for each chapter.

2257 JOHNSON, D. NEWMAN. A contemporary plan of the siege of Caher Castle, 1599, with some additional remarks. *Ir. Sword*, vol. 12, no. 47, 1975, 109–115.

2258 MCCLELLAND, AIKEN. The battle of Garvagh [Co. Londonderry]. *Ulster Folk.*, 19, 1973, 41–49. Immortalised in a ballad.

2259 MACIOMHAIR, DIARMUID. The battle of Fochart [Co. Louth], 1318. *Ir. Sword*, vol. 8, no. 32, 1968, 193–209.

2260 MILLER, AMOS C. The battle of [New] Ross: a controversial military event. *Ir. Sword*, vol. 10, no. 39, 1971, 141–158.

Arms

2261 BOSTON, NOEL. Old guns and pistols. London: 1958. List of British gunsmiths, pp. 103–141.

2262 CAREY, A. MERWYN. English, Irish, and Scottish firearms makers: when, where, and what they made, from the middle of the sixteenth century to the end of the nineteenth century. 2nd British ed., London: 1967. Bibliog., pp. 120–1.

2263 CARROLL, F., *compiler*. Irish gunsmiths and sword cutlers. *Ir. Sword*, vol. 3, no. 10, 1957, 39–43.

2264 GLENDINNING, IAN. British pistols and guns, 1640–1840. 2nd ed. reproduced in facsimile from the original edition published in 1951. London: 1967.

2265 HARBISON, PETER. Native Irish arms and armour in medieval Gaelic literature, 1170–1600. *Ir. Sword*, vol. 12, 1976, 173–199, 270–284.

2266 HAYES-MCCOY, G.A. The early history of

guns in Ireland. *Galway Arch. Hist. Soc. J.*, 18, 1938, 43–65.

2267 — The first guns in Ireland. *Ir. Def. J.*, 34, 1973, 3–7.

2268 WESTROPP, M.S. DUDLEY, *compiler*. Irish gunsmiths and sword cutlers. *Ir. Sword*, 1, 1949–53, 181–187, 352. For supplementary list by F. Carroll see no. 2263.

Uniforms

2269 HUDSON, JOHN M. and THOMPSON, F. GLENN. A survey of the uniforms and insignia of the defence forces [1915–1975]. *Ir. Def. J.*, 35, 1975, 147–194.

2270 McDONNELL, JOSEPH. Military heraldry in Ireland. *Ir. Def. J.*, 27, 1967, 375–381. Includes uniforms, cap and collar insignia, rank insignia and shoulder flashes.

CHARITIES

2271 CORRIGAN, FRANK. Dublin workhouses during the Great Famine. *Dublin Hist. Rec.*, vol. 29, no. 2, 1976, 59–65.

2272 DALY, *Mrs*. JAMES F. An 18th century charity – Simpson's Hospital. *Dublin Hist Rec.*, 15, 1958–60, 74–85.

2273 DELANY, V.T.H. The law relating to charities in Ireland. Dublin [1956]. Bibliog., pp. 243–8.

2274 DUBLIN CHARITIES; being a handbook of Dublin philanthropic organisations and charities, including benevolent and educational organisations, shelters, refuges, orphanages, hospitals, reformatories, industrial schools, etc., in or applicable to Ireland. Compiled by G.D. Williams, and published by the Association of Charities. Dublin: 1902.

2275 MACTHOMAIS, EAMONN. The South Dublin Union. *Dublin Hist. Rec.*, vol. 26, no. 2, 1973, 54–61.

2276 O'SULLIVAN, HAROLD. Ardee dispensary minute book, 1813–1851. *Louth Arch. J.*, vol. 16, no. 1, 1965, 5–27.

2277 POWELL, MALACHY. The workhouses of Ireland [with bibliog.]. *Univ. Rev.*, vol. 3, no. 7, 1965, 3–16.

2278 STRAIN, R.W.M. Belfast and its Charitable Society: a story of urban social development. London: 1961. Bibliog., pp. 321–2.

2279 TIGHE, JOAN. The Mendicity Institution. *Dublin Hist. Rec.*, 20, 1965–66, 100–115.

2280 TUTTY, M.J. Dublin's oldest charity [The United Charitable Society for the Relief of the Sick and Indigent Roomkeepers of the city of Dublin]. *Dublin Hist. Rec.*, 16, 1960–61, 73–85.

HEALTH SERVICES

2281 BURKE, AIDAN P. Prognostications on the economics of health in the 1970s. *Admin.*, 14, 1966, 139–170.

2282 HANNON, E. Regionalisation of the health services and the hospital matron. *Admin.*, 21, 1973, 80–86.

2283 IRELAND. DEPARTMENT OF HEALTH. The health services and their further development. Dublin: 1966.

2284 JESSOP, W.J.E. Health services: a critical appraisal. *Stat. Social Inq. Soc. Ir. J.*, vol. 21, pt. 1, 1962–63, 81–108.

2285 MURPHY, THOMAS. A survey of industrial health services. *Management*, vol. 15, no. 4, 1968, 28–33.

2286 O'REILLY, KENNETH A. Development of services to hospitals in Ireland. *Technol. Ir.*, vol. 6, no. 11, 1975, 19–20.

2287 PADDISON, R. Reorganisation of hospital services in Ireland. *Ir. Geog.*, vol. 6, no. 2, 1970, 199–204.

WELFARE SERVICES

2288 CLIFFORD, J.D. The public, the client and the social services: a study in an Irish town. *Soc. Stud.*, 3, 1974, 457–498.

2289 CUMANN CROISE DEIRGE NA HEIREANN [The Irish Red Cross Society]. *Ir. Def. J.*, 34, 1974, 270–273.

2290 DARBY, JOHN and WILLIAMSON, ARTHUR *eds*. Violence and the social services in Northern Ireland. London: 1978. Bibliog., pp. 195–200.

2291 DILLON, T.W.T. The social services in Eire. *Studies*, 34, 1945, 325–336.

2292 FARLEY, DESMOND. Social insurance and social assistance in Ireland. Dublin: 1964.

2293 IRELAND. DEPARTMENT OF SOCIAL WELFARE. Summary of social insurance and social assistance services. Dublin: 1977.

2294 KAIM-CAUDLE, P.R. The future of social services in the Irish Republic. *Admin.*, 15, 1967, 340–354.

2295 — Dental services in Ireland. Dublin: Economic and Social Research Institute, 1969. (*Broadsheet no.* 1.)

2296 — Ophthalmic services in Ireland, by P.R. Kaim-Caudle, assisted by Kathleen O'Donoghue and Annette O'Toole. Dublin: Economic and Social Research Institute, 1970. (*Broadsheet no.* 4.) Bibliog., pp. 98–99.

2297 — Social policy and social work. *Soc. Stud.*, 3, 1974, 445–456.

2298 — Social policy in the Irish Republic. London: 1967. Bibliog., pp. 116–120.

2299 — Social security in Ireland and Western Europe [with bibliog.]. Dublin: The Economic Research Institute, 1964. (*Paper no.* 20).

2300 VARAH, CHAD *ed.* The Samaritans in the '70s: to befriend the suicidal and despairing. 2nd rev. ed. London: 1973. List of branches of the Samaritans in the United Kingdom and Eire, pp. 218–239.

Drugs, Alcohol

2301 BLANEY, ROGER. Alcoholism in Ireland: medical and social aspects. *Stat. Social Inq. Soc. Ir. J.*, vol. 23, pt. 1, 1973–4, 108–124.

2302 COONEY, J.G. Alcohol and the Irish. *Ir. Coll. Phys. Surg. J.*, vol. 1, no. 2, 1971, 50–54, 70.

2303 DRUGS OF DEPENDENCE IN IRELAND.
1. Drug control in Ireland, by James G. Coleman.
2. The evidence for adolescent drug abuse in Ireland, by C.W.M. Wilson.
In The pharmacological and epidemiological aspects of adolescent drug dependence: proceedings of the Society for the Study of Addiction, London, 1 and 2 September 1966, edited by C.W.M. Wilson. London: Pergamon Press, 1968.

2304 FITZPATRICK, JOYCE. Drinking among young people in Ireland. *Soc. Stud.*, vol. 1, no. 1, 1972, 51–60.

2305 O'CALLAGHAN, SEAN. Drug addiction in Britain. London: 1970. The drug menace in Ireland, pp. 166–181.

2306 O'CONNOR, JOYCE. Methodology of a cross-cultural study. *Soc. Stud.*, vol. 2, no. 2, 1973, 147–157. Deals mainly with alcoholism.

2307 — The young drinkers: a cross-national study of social and cultural influences. London: 1978. Bibliog., pp. 288–305; drinking behaviour and customs . . . special attention is paid to the comparative study of two ethnic groups – the English and the Irish – whose drinking habits are generally believed to be very different.

2308 O'ROURKE, A. *and others*. Smoking, drugs and alcohol in Dublin secondary schools, by A. O'Rourke, K. Wilson-Davies and Cora Gough. *Ir. J. Med. Sci.*, 140, 1971, 230–241.

2309 STIVERS, RICHARD. A hair of the dog: Irish drinking and American stereotype. University Park and London: Pennsylvania State Univ. Press, 1976.

2310 TIMMS, M.W.H. *and others*. A factor analytic study of drug abuse in adolescents, by M.W.H. Timms, P.A. Carney and R.D. Stevenson. *Ir. J. Psychol.*, vol. 2, no. 2, 1973, 86–95.

Mentally Retarded

2311 IRELAND. DEPARTMENT OF LOCAL GOVERNMENT AND PUBLIC HEALTH: COMMISSION OF INQUIRY ON MENTAL HANDICAP. Report. Dublin: 1965.

2312 SCALLY, B.G. and MACKAY, D.N. The special care service in Northern Ireland: origins and structure, *Ir. J. Med. Sci.*, 6th ser., no. 462, 1964, 267–270. Describes briefly the provisions which exist for mentally retarded persons.

2313 WILLIAMSON, ARTHUR. The beginnings of state care for the mentally ill in Ireland. *Econ. Soc. Rev.*, vol. 1, no. 2, 1970, 281–290.

Deaf

2314 **National Association For The Deaf.** The young adult hearing impaired population of Ireland: a general survey. Dublin: 1973.

Poor

2315 **O Cinneide, Seamus.** The development of the Home Assistance service. *Admin.*, 17, 1969, 284–308. Deals with poor law and the relief of poverty.

2316 — A law for the poor: a study of home assistance in Ireland. Dublin: Institute of Public Administration, 1970. (*Research ser. no.* 3).

Aged

2317 **Gormley, M.** The case of the aged in Ireland. *Admin.*, 12, 1964, 297–324.

2318 **Reeves, Anthony J.** The social and medical needs of old people in Ireland, with comments by Dr. Brian Pringle, Sister M. Campion, Dr. John Fleetwood and Thomas J. Scully. *Studies*, 55, 1966, 341–362.

Legal Aid

2319 **Ireland. Committee On Civil Legal Aid And Advice.** Report. Dublin: 1978. Chairman: A. Denis Pringle.

Children

2320 **Bourke, Geoffrey J.** *and others*. Dublin hospital paediatric study, by Geoffrey J. Bourke, J.A. Coughlan and J.W. McGilvray. Dublin: Medical Research Council of Ireland, 1969.

2321 **Care — Campaign For The Care Of Deprived Children.** Children deprived: the CARE memorandum on deprived children and children's services in Ireland. Dublin: 1972.

2322 **Meenan, F.O.C.** *ed*. The Children's Hospital, Temple Street, Dublin, centenary book, 1872–1972. Dublin: 1973. Contains short note on Cappagh Orthopaedic Hospital.

2323 **Tuairim. London Branch Study Group.** Some of our children: a report on the residential care of the deprived child in Ireland. London: 1966. (*Tuairim pamphlet no*. 13).

Other Social Services

2324 **Flannery, Michael.** Sanitation, conservation and recreation services in Ireland. Dublin: Institute of public administration, 1976.

CRIME

2325 **Bacon, Peter, and O'Donoghue, Martin.** The economics of crime in the Republic of Ireland: an exploratory paper. *Econ. Soc. Rev*., vol. 7, no. 1, 1975, 19–34.

2326 **Casey, Daniel J.** Wildgoose Lodge: the evidence and the lore. *Louth Arch. Hist. Soc. J.*, vol. 18, no. 2, 1974, 140–163; *ibid*., no. 3, 1975, 211–231.

2327 **Cullen, L.M.** The smuggling trade in Ireland in the eighteenth century. *R. Ir. Acad. Proc., Sec. C.*, vol. 67, no. 5, 1969, 149–175.

2328 **Cumming, John.** A contribution towards a bibliography dealing with crime and cognate subjects. London: 1935.

2329 **Hurst, James W.** Disturbed Tipperary, 1831–1860. *Eire-Ir*., vol. 9, no. 3, 1974, 44–59. An analysis of unrest in Co. Tipperary in an effort to clarify the nature and extent of crime.

2330 **James, F.G.** Irish smuggling in the eighteenth century. *Ir. Hist. Stud*., 12, 1960–61, 299–317.

2331 **O'Hanlon, Terence.** The highwayman in Irish history. Dublin: 1932.

2332 **Skehan, John.** Who stole the Crown Jewels? *Ir. Wel*., vol. 25, no. 2, 1976, 26–29.

Penal System, Prisons

2333 **Byrne, John.** Mountjoy Prison and the Irish penal system. *Soc. Stud*., 1, 1972, 289–308.

2334 **Davitt, Michael.** Leaves from a prison diary; or lectures to a 'solitary' audience. [Facsimile reprint of 1st ed.] with an introduction by T.W. Moody. Shannon: Irish Univ. Press, 1972. 1st ed. pub. in 2 vols, London: 1885.

2335 **Hart, Ian.** A survey of some delinquent boys in an Irish industrial school and reformatory. *Econ. Soc. Rev*., 1, 1970, 185–214.

2336 HEANEY, HENRY. Ireland's penitentiary, 1820–1831: an experiment that failed. *Stud. Hib.*, 14, 1974, 28–39.

2337 KELLY, TIM. Ennis County jail. *Nth. Munster Antiq. J.*, 16, 1973–4, 66–69.

2338 KILMAINHAM JAIL RESTORATION SOCIETY. Kilmainham: the bastille of Ireland. Dublin: 1961.

2339 — Ghosts of Kilmainham. Dublin: 1963.

2340 NOWLAN, A.J. Kilmainham jail. *Dublin Hist. Rec.*, 15, 1958–60, 105–115.

2341 SHAW, A.G.L. Convicts and the colonies: a study of penal transportation from Great Britain and Ireland to Australia and other parts of the British Empire. London: 1966. Bibliog., pp. 369–390.

2342 OSBOROUGH, NIAL. Borstal in Ireland: custodial provision for the young adult offender, 1906–1974. Dublin: 1975. Bibliog., pp. 173–177.

2343 PRISON STUDY GROUP. An examination of the Irish penal system. [Dublin], 1973.

SOCIETIES

2344 DEWAR, THE REV. M.W. *and others*. Orangeism: a new historical appreciation, by the Rev. M.W. Dewar, the Rev. John Brown and the Rev. S.E. Lang. Belfast, [1967].

2345 GRAY, TONY. The Orange order. London: 1972. Bibliog., pp. 283–5.

2346 POLLARD, H.B.C. The secret societies of Ireland: their rise and progress. London: 1922.

2347 SENIOR, HEREWARD. Orangeism in Ireland and Britain, 1795–1836. London, 1966. (*Studies in Irish history, 2nd ser.*, vol. 4.) Bibliog., pp. 285–297.

2348 SIMMS, SAMUEL. The Orange Society: a select bibliography. *Ir. Book Lov.*, 25, 1937, 2–9, 85–90.

2349 WILLIAMS, T. DESMOND, *ed*. Secret societies in Ireland. Dublin and New York: 1973. Notes and bibliog., pp. 191–207.

Rotary

2350 DUNCAN, TERENCE S., *compiler*. The hub of the wheel: the story of the Rotary movement in Ireland: district 116 (earlier 5, 6, and 16), 1911–1976. [Belfast]: 1976.

Masonry

2351 CAHILL, E. Freemasonry and the anti-Christian movement. Dublin: 1929. Bibliog., pp. xiii–xx.

2352 DRING, EDMUND HUNT. English masonic literature before 1751, with a tentative list of English references to, and works on freemasonry before 1751. London: 1913.

2353 HISTORY OF THE GRAND LODGE OF FREE AND ACCEPTED MASONS OF IRELAND. Dublin: Lodge of Research, 1925, 1957. 2 vols. Vol. 1, by John Heron Lepper and Philip Crossle; vol. 2, by R.E. Parkinson.

2354 TUDOR-CRAIG, ALGERNON *compiler*. Catalogue of manuscripts and library at Freemasons' Hall in the possession of the United Grand Lodge of England. London: 1938. 3 vols. Vol. 1: Museum catalogue; vol. 2: Portraits and prints.

EDUCATION

Bibliography

2355 BELL, ROBERT *and others, eds*. Education in Great Britain and Ireland: a source book, edited by Robert Bell, Gerald Fowler and Ken Little. London and Boston: 1973.

2356 COLVIN, CHRISTINA EDGEWORTH and MORGENSTERN, CHARLES. The Edgeworths: some early educational books. *Book Coll.*, 26, 1977, 39–43.

2357 CORCORAN, T. Selected texts on education systems in Ireland from the close of the Middle Ages. Dublin: 1928.

2358 JACOBS, PHYLLIS M. Registers of the universities, colleges and schools of Great Britain and Ireland. *Bull. Inst. Hist. Res.*, 37, 1964, 185–232.

2359 MCGEOWN, VINCENT. Comprehensive education: a bibliography. *Education Times*, vol. 1, no. 19, 1973, 14.

2360 MURPHY, MICHAEL W. A list of theses on educational topics completed at University College, Cork. *Ir. J. Ed.*, 2, 1968, 136–138.

2361 NIC GHIOLLA PHADRAIG, MAIRE. Bibliography of the sociology of education in Ireland. *Soc. Stud.*, 1, 1972, 350–366.

2362 POWER, ELLEN. Education in Ireland: a bibliography. *Oideas*, 1, 1968, 57–63.

2363 RAVEN-HART, H. Bibliography of the registers (printed) of the universities, inns of court, colleges and schools of Great Britain and Ireland. *Inst. Hist. Res. Bull.*, 9, 1931–2, 19–30, 65–83, 154–70; addenda and corrigenda, *ibid*, 10, 1932–3, 109–13.

2364 TANSEY, P.J. and UNWIN, DERICK. SAGSET: simulation and gaming in education, training and business: a bibliography. Coleraine: 1969.

2365 TEACHERS GUILD OF GREAT BRITAIN AND IRELAND. Catalogue of the library. London: 1887.

2366 — Catalogue of the pedagogic portion of the library. London: 1900. Supplement, 1902.

Periodicals

2367 UNIVERSITY COLLEGE LIBRARY, DUBLIN. List of current periodicals in education and related subjects. 2nd ed., Dublin: 1972. First published in 1969 as *List of current periodicals in the Education Library*.

Directories

2368 THE IRISH EDUCATION AND TRAINING DIRECTORY — a compendium of almost 1300 courses leading to a wide range of careers for which specialised education or training is required, compiled by Tom Casey and Tommy Murray. 2nd ed., Claremorris. [Co. Mayo]. 1976. 1st ed. published in 1973 as *Education and Training Directory*, by the Irish Management Institute.

Research

2369 EDUCATIONAL RESEARCH IN IRELAND: work in progress or projected. *Oideas*, 2, 1969, 56–60.

2370 NATIONAL FOUNDATION FOR EDUCATIONAL RESEARCH IN ENGLAND AND WALES, publications series, no. 1. A list of researches in education and educational psychology, presented for higher degrees in the universities of the United Kingdom, Northern Ireland, and the Irish Republic, from 1918 to 1948; classified according to a modification of the Dewey decimal system by A.M. Blackwell . . . London: 1951.

2371 — A second list . . . in the years 1949, 1950 and 1951. London: 1952.

2372 — Supplement 1: 1952 and 1953. 1954. Supplement 2: 1954 and 1955. [1956.] Future lists to appear biennially.

2373 NORTHERN IRELAND COUNCIL FOR EDUCATIONAL RESEARCH. Register of research in education, Northern Ireland. vol. 1, 1945–70. [1977].

2374 UNIVERSITY COLLEGE LIBRARY, DUBLIN. List of research work in education and educational psychology presented at University College, Dublin, 1912–1968; a provisional list. Dublin: 1969.

2375 — Appendix covering period 1969–1972.

History

2376 AKENSON, DONALD H. The Irish education experiment: the national system of education in the nineteenth century. London and Toronto, 1970. (*Studies in Irish history, 2nd ser.*, vol. 7). Bibliog., pp. 403–424.

2377 — A mirror to Kathleen's face: education in independent Ireland, 1922–1960. Montreal and London, 1975. Bibliog., pp. 207–220.

2378 ATKINSON, NORMAN. Irish education: a history of educational institutions. Dublin: 1969. Bibliog., pp. 218–240.

2379 AUCHMUTY, JAMES JOHNSTON. Irish education: a historical survey. Dublin and London: 1937. Bibliogs. appended to each chapter.

2380 DOWLING, P.J. A history of Irish education: a study in conflicting loyalties. Cork: 1971. Bibliog., pp. 184–189.

2381 DURCAN, THOMAS JOSEPH. History of Irish education from 1800 (with special reference to manual instruction). Bala (North Wales): Dragon Books: 1972.

2382 EDUCATION IN COUNTY GALWAY. *Galway Reader*, vol. 1, no. 2, 1948, 24–28; *ibid.*, no. 3, 1948, 39–45.

2383 EDUCATION, TODAY AND TOMORROW. *Ir. Hib.*, vol. 4, no. 4, 1961.

2384 FFOLLIOTT, ROSEMARY. Some schoolmasters in the diocese of Killaloe, 1808. *Nth. Munster Antiq. J.*, 11, 1968, 57–63.

2385 GOLDSTROM, J.M. Richard Whately and political economy in school books, 1833–80. *Ir. Hist. Stud.*, vol. 15, no. 58, 1966, 131–146.

2386 GRAHAM, HUGH. The early Irish monastic schools: a study of Ireland's contribution to early medieval culture. Dublin: 1923. Bibliog., pp. 195–206.

2387 HAMMERSTEIN, HELGA. Aspects of the continental education of Irish students in the reign of Queen Elizabeth I. *Hist. Stud.*, 8, 1971, 137–153.

2388 HYLAND, W.J. Education and Irish society – with special reference to informational needs. *Stat. Social Inq. Soc. Ir. J.*, vol. 22, pt. 3, 1970–71, 69–87.

2389 KENNEDY, DAVID. Popular education and the Gaelic tradition in north-east Ulster. *Studies*, 30, 1941, 273–286.

2390 — The Ulster academies and the philosophies. *Bonaventura*, vol. 3, no. 3, 1939–40, 117–128.

2391 McELLIGOTT, T.J. Education in Ireland. Dublin: Institute of Public Administration, 1966. Bibliog., pp. 186–188.

2392 MORTON, R.G. Mechanics' Institutes and the attempted diffusion of useful knowledge in Ireland, 1825–79. *Ir. Booklore*, vol. 2, no. 1, 1972, 59–74; vol. 2, no. 2, 1976, 308–9.

2393 MOORE, H. KINGSMILL. An unwritten chapter in the history of education; being the history of the Society for the Education of the Poor of Ireland, generally known as the Kildare Place Society, 1811–31. London: 1904. Publications of the Kildare Place Society, pp. 214–64.

2394 MURPHY, MICHAEL W. *ed.* Education in Ireland. Cork.
1. Now and the future. 1970.
2. What should students learn? 1971.
3. To lease the potential. 1972.

2395 O BUACHALLA, SEAMAS. Permanent education in the Irish context. *Studies*, 63, 1974, 355–365.

2396 O'CATHAIN, SEAN. Secondary education in Ireland. Dublin: 1958. (*Questions of the day*, no. 4.) First appeared as articles in *Studies*, 1951–7.

2397 O CEALLAIGH, TADHG. Disestablishment and church education. *Stud. Hib.*, 10, 1970, 36–69.

2398 O'FLYNN, GRAINNE. Aspects of concern in the Religious Society of Friends with education in Ireland, 1627–1812. *Cap. Ann.*, 1975, 320–336.

2399 — Some aspects of the education of Irish women through the years. *Cap. Ann.*, 1977, 164–179.

2400 O HEIDEAIN, EUSTAS. National school inspection in Ireland: the beginnings. Dublin: 1967. Includes account of the influence of the Kildare Place Society in national inspection.

2401 O'MEARA, JOHN J. Education in the Republic of Ireland. London: Encyclopaedia Britannica Ltd., 1965. (*Advisory guide for parents series*).

2402 ORGANISATION FOR ECONOMIC CO-OPERATION AND DEVELOPMENT. Reviews of national policies for education: Ireland. Paris: 1969.

2403 O'RIORDAN, BRENDA. The documentation of the Irish Labour Party on education, 1922–1975. *Studies*, 66, 1977, 122–134.

2404 O'SULLIVAN, HAROLD. The emergence of the national system of education in Co. Louth. *Ir. Eccles. Rec.*, 110, 1968, 209–230.

2405 OUTLINE OF THE HISTORY OF AGRICULTURAL EDUCATION IN IRELAND UP TO 1900. *Ir. Dept. Agric. J.*, 49, 1952–3, 3–28.

2406 PARKES, SUSAN M. Irish education in the British Parliamentary Papers in the nineteenth century and after, 1801–1920. [Cork and Leicester]: History of Education Society in association with Cork University Press: 1978.

2407 PETTIT, PHILIP. Reflections on an Irish education. *Anglo-Ir. Stud.*, 1, 1975, 37–49.

2408 QUANE, MICHAEL. Aspects of education in Ireland, 1695–1795. *Cork Hist. Arch. Soc. J.*, 73, 1968, 120–135.

2409 ORGANISATION FOR EUROPEAN ECONOMIC CO-OPERATION, European Productivity Agency. The professional training of teachers in vocational agricultural schools. Project no. 6/14–IV. (*Documentation, 1961 series, Food and Agriculture*, no. 38.) Ireland, pp. 153–65.

Educational Sociology

2410 CULLEN, KATHLEEN. School and family: social factors in educational attainment. Dublin: 1969. Bibliog., pp. 199–204.

Teaching

2411 DALY, J.P. Aids in advisory work. *Ir. Dept. Agric. J.*, 53, 1956–7. Publications on advisory methods, audio-visual aids and photography, pp. 101–2.

Students

2412 BLOCK, GEOFFREY D.M. Jewish students at the universities of Great Britain and Ireland — excluding London, 1936–9: a survey. *Sociol. Rev.*, 34, 1942, 183–97.

Textbooks

2413 DIX, E.R. McC. School books printed in Dublin from the earliest period to 1715. *Bibliog. Soc. Ir.*, vol. 3, no. 1, 1926.

2414 NORTHERN IRELAND, MINISTRY OF EDUCATION. List of books recommended for use by teachers of elementary schools. Belfast: 1926.

2415 — List of books in history, citizenship and economics approved for use in public elementary schools. Belfast: 1936.

2416 RYAN, M.J. A list of Greek and Latin classics printed in Dublin down to 1800. *Bibliog. Soc. Ir.*, vol. 3, no. 2, 1926.

Examinations

2417 MAGUIRE, WILLIAM J. Helps for students: book lore. Key to the primary, intermediate and leaving certificate courses of the Department of Education (Primary and Secondary branches). Dublin: 1936.

Schools

2418 BRENAN, MARTIN. Schools of Kildare and Leighlin, A.D. 1775–1835. Bibliog. footnotes; contains *Full text of parochial school returns, 1824, of Kildare and Leighlin*, supplemented by summaries drawn from *The Second Report of Commissioners of Irish education inquiry, 1826*.

2419 DOWLING, PATRICK JOHN. The Hedge schools of Ireland. Dublin. [1935]. Bibliog., pp. 162–9.

2420 FITZPATRICK, J.D. Edmund Rice, founder and first superior general of the Brothers of the Christian schools of Ireland . . . Dublin: 1945. Bibliog., pp. 353–5.

2421 IRELAND. DEPARTMENT OF EDUCATION. List of national schools arranged alphabetically according to location. Dublin: 1974.

2422 — Liosta de mheanscoileanna aitheanta, 1976–77. Dublin: 1977. List of recognised secondary schools.

2423 JOHNSTON, JOHN I.D. Hedge schools of Tyrone and Monaghan [with bibliog.]. *Clogher Rec.*, vol. 7, no. 1, 1969, 34–55.

2424 KERR, THE REV. DONAL. Dr. Quinn's school and the Catholic university, *Ir. Eccles. Rec.*, 108, 1967, 89–101.

2425 QUANE, MICHAEL. Quaker schools in Dublin [1677–1844]. *R. Soc. Antiq. Ir. J.*, 94, 1964, 47–68.

2426 RONAN, MYLES V. Catholic schools of old Dublin [with bibliog.]. *Dublin Hist. Rec.*, 12, 1951, 65–82.

2427 SADLEIR, T.U. The Register of Kilkenny school, 1685–1800. *R. Soc. Antiq. Ir. J.*, 54, 1924, 55–67, 152–69.

2428 SCHOOLS: a directory of the schools in Great Britain and Northern Ireland, arranged in order of their counties and towns; including statistical information regarding recognised public schools for boys, sections for tutors and career training courses, and schools on the continent of Europe. 56th ed. London: 1979. Published annually.

2429 THE SCHOOLS OF ENGLAND, WALES, SCOTLAND and IRELAND: a book of reference for parents, principals, and students, with scholarships, careers, and Continental sections and a directory of schools and colleges. London: 67th ed., 1978. Published annually.

Individual

2430 Crowe, W. Haughton. In Banbridge town: a history of Banbridge Academy, and of the social circumstances that led to its foundation. Belfast: 1964.

2431 Cunningham, The Rev. Terence P. Students of Kilmore Academy, 1839–1874. *Breifne*, vol. 4, no. 16, 1973–5, 501–530. Also known as St. Augustine's College.

2432 Figgis, T.F. and Drury, T.W.E. Rathmines School: the school roll from the beginnings of the school in 1858 till the close in 1899. Dublin: 1932.

2433 Jameson, John. The history of the Royal Belfast Academical Institution, 1810–1960. Belfast: 1959. Bibliog., pp. 216–22.

2434 McClelland, Aiken. The early history of Brown Street primary school[Belfast]. *Ulster Folk*, 17, 1971, 52–60.

2435 O Donnabhain, Diarmaid. The Munster Academy, 1772–1792. *Cork Hist. Arch. Soc. J.*, 69, 1964, 101–112.

2436 Quane, Michael. Athlone classical school, founded by William Handcock, and Athlone English school, founded by Arthur St. George. *J. Old Athlone Soc.*, vol. 1, no. 2, 1970–1, 90–99.

2437 — Ballitore School. *Kildare Arch. Soc. J.*, vol. 14, no. 2, 1966–67, 174–209.

2438 — Banagher Royal School. *Nth. Munster Antiq. J.*, 10, 1966–67, 116–142.

2439 — Bishop Foy School, Waterford. *Cork Hist. Arch. Soc. J.*, 71, 1966, 103–122.

2440 — The Borough School, Swords. *Dublin Hist. Rec.*, 15, 1958–60, 21–32.

2441 — Castledermot Charter School. *Kildare Arch Soc. J.*, vol. 13, no. 19, 1963, 463–487.

2442 — Castleisland Charter School. *Kerry Arch. Hist. Soc. J.*, 6, 1968, 25–40.

2443 — Cavan Royal School. *R. Soc. Antiq. Ir. J.*, 100, 1970, 39–66.

2444 — Celbridge Collegiate School. *Kildare Arch. Soc. J.*, vol. 14, no. 4, 1969, 397–414.

2445 — Dr. Jeremy Hall Endowed Schools, Limerick. *Nth. Munster Antiq. J.*, 11, 1968, 47–56.

2446 — Drogheda Blue School. *Louth Arch. J.*, vol. 16, no. 3, 1967, 163–168.

2447 — Drogheda Grammar School. *Louth Arch. J.*, vol. 15, no. 3, 1963, 207–248.

2448 — Dundalk Grammar School. *Louth Arch. J.*, vol. 16, no. 2, 1966, 91–102.

2449 — Ennis Grammar School. *Nth. Munster Antiq. J.*, vol. 10, no. 1, 1966, 27–46.

2450 — The Erasmus Smith School, Ardee. *Louth Arch. J.*, vol. 17, no. 1, 1969, 10–18.

2451 — The Feinaiglian Institution, Dublin. *Dublin Hist. Rec.*, 19, 1963–4, 30–43.

2452 — The Free School of Clonmel. *Cork Hist. Arch. Soc. J.*, 69, 1964, 1–28.

2453 — The lands of the Free School of Clonmel — a chapter of famine history. *ibid.*, 70, 1965, 36–54.

2454 — Hewetson's Endowed School, Clane. *Kildare Arch. Soc. J.*, vol. 14, no. 1, 1964–5, 56–85.

2455 — The Hibernian Marine School, Dublin. *Dublin Hist. Rec.*, 21, 1966–67, 67–78.

2456 — Meath Diocesan School. *Riocht na Midhe*, vol. 4, no. 5, 1971, 40–59.

2457 — Monasterevan Charter School. *Kildare Arch. Soc. J.*, vol. 15, no. 2, 1972, 101–121.

2458 — Preston Endowed School, Navan. *Riocht na Midhe*, vol. 4, no. 2, 1968, 50–78.

2459 — Ranelagh Endowed School, Athlone. *J. Old Athlone Soc.*, vol. 1, no. 1, 1969, 23–34.

2460 — Raphoe Royal School. *Donegal Ann.*, vol. 7, no. 2, 1967, 148–211.

2461 — Viscount Limerick Grammar School, Dundalk. *Louth Arch. J.*, vol. 16, no. 1, 1965, 32–41.

2462 — Waterford School in the opening decades of the nineteenth century. *R. Soc. Antiq. Ir. J.*, 101, 1971, 141–145.

2463 — Wicklow Free School. *R. Soc. Antiq. Ir. J.*, 98, 1968, 171–190.

2464 — Zelva School, Valentia Island. *Cork Hist. Arch. Soc. J.*, 72, 1967, 10–19.

2465 Sheldon, Ester K. The Hibernian Academy: an eighteenth-century group experiment in modern education. *Longroom*, 10, 1974, 23–34.

Vocational Guidance

2466 CHURCH OF IRELAND BOARD OF EDUCATION. Careers in Ireland. 2nd ed., Dublin: 1969. Bibliography of careers guidance publications, p. 203.

2467 — The Sparsely Populated Areas Commission. Careers in Ireland. [Dublin: 1959.]

2468 CORK SCIENTIFIC COUNCIL. Careers. Tralee: 1963.

2469 INDEPENDENT NEWSPAPERS LTD. Guide to careers. New ed., Dublin: 1968.

2470 JENKS, RICHARD E. The Youth Employment Service — why, what and how. *Stat. Social Inq. Soc. Ir. J.*, vol. 21, pt. 1, 1962–63, 71–80. On the Northern Ireland Youth Employment Service Board.

2471 NEWMAN, J. *and others*. Attitudes of young people towards vocations, by Mgr. J. Newman, Liam Ryan and Conor K. Ward. *Soc. Stud.*, vol. 1, no. 5, 1972, 531–550. Part of a survey commissioned by the Irish hierarchy.

2472 SHEEHAN, MARGARET. The influence of family background in choice of careers. *Soc. Stud.*, vol. 3, no. 1, 1974, 25–33.

Education of Special Classes

2473 O CUILLEANAIN, T.A. Special education in Ireland. *Oideas*, no. 1, 1968, 5–17. Appendix: List of schools for handicapped children recognised by the Department of Education.

Elementary

2474 CALLAN, JAMES. The scope of the junior cycle curriculum, 12–15 years; primary-secondary education: a contribution. *May. Rev.*, vol. 2, no. 2, 1976, 47–64.

2475 IRELAND. DEPARTMENT OF EDUCATION. Primary school curriculum: teachers handbook. Dublin: 1971. 2 pts.

2476 KELLY, SEAN G. Teaching in the city: a study of the role of the primary teacher. Dublin and London: 1970. Bibliog., pp. 169–175.

2477 MACNAMARA, JOHN. Bilingualism and primary education: a study of Irish experience. Edinburgh: Edinburgh Univ. Press. 1966. Bibliog., pp. 151–161.

Secondary

2478 O SUILLEABHAIN, SEAMUS V. Second level education: dimensions and directions. *May. Rev.*, vol. 1, no. 1, 1975, 3–16.

2479 RANDLES, SISTER EILEEN. Post-primary education in Ireland, 1957–1970. Dublin: 1975. Bibliog., pp. 368–372.

Adult Education

2480 ASPECTS OF ADULT EDUCATION. *Administration*, vol. 1, no. 2, 1953, 13–61. Contents: (1) The contribution of the vocational schools, by M. Sheehy; (2) The Cork university extension courses, by D.L. Whyte; (3) The public libraries, by D. Foley; (4) Agricultural education, by Joseph Johnston; (5) The broadcast technique, by Michael Dillon; (6) As Muintir na Tire sees it, by P.J. Meghen; (7) The farmers' view, by H.M. Fitzpatrick; (8) The workers' education movement in Ireland, by Ruaidhri Roberts; (9) In Northern Ireland, by Brian Trainer.

2481 IRELAND. DEPARTMENT OF EDUCATION. Adult education in Ireland: a report of a committee appointed by the Minister for Education. Dublin: 1973.

2482 — National adult education survey: interim report. Dublin: 1970. Con Murphy, chairman of advisory committee.

2483 NORTHERN IRELAND. MINISTRY OF EDUCATION. Adult education in Northern Ireland: report of the committee appointed by the Minister of Education in March 1963. Belfast: 1964.

Religious Education

2484 CORCORAN, T. The Clongowes record, 1814– to 1932; with introductory chapters on Irish Jesuit education, 1564 to 1813. Dublin: 1932.

2485 DUFFY, PATRICK S. The lay teacher: a study of the position of the lay teacher in an Irish Catholic environment. Dublin: 1967. Bibliog., pp. 105–109.

2486 FULTON, JOHN F. Some reflections on Catholic schools in Northern Ireland, *Studies*, 58, 1969, 341–356.

2487 GREER, J.E. Sixth form religion in Northern Ireland: religious belief, religious practice and moral judgement in a sample of Protestant boys and girls [with bibliog.]. *Soc. Stud.*, vol. 1, no. 3, 1972, 325–340.

2488 HOWARD, LEONARD. Irish Catholic education, 1669–85. *Studies*, 58, 1969, 191–205, 309–321.

2489 O MORDHA, SEAN C.O. The origin of the written examination in religious knowledge in Irish secondary schools. *Ir. Eccles. Rec.*, 105, 1965, 278–285.

2490 O SUILLEABHAIN, PADRAIG. Maynooth's first Professor of Scripture [Thomas Clancy, 1748–1814]. *Ir. Eccles. Rec.*, 103, 1965, 88–92.

2491 QUANE, MICHAEL. Quaker schools in Dublin [1677–1844]. *R. Soc. Antiq. Ir. J.*, 94, 1964, 47–68.

Higher Education

2492 FAHY, PETER. Psychological aspects of student wastage. *Studies*, 62, 1973, 195–204. Students who fail to acquire a degree.

2493 FENTON, DAVID F. Regional technical colleges in Ireland. *Eur. Teach.*, 11, 1976, 21–23.

2494 IRELAND. DEPARTMENT OF EDUCATION: Commission on higher education, 1960–67. Report. Dublin: 1967. 2 vols.

2495 LICHFIELD, NATHANIEL, and ASSOCIATES. Higher education in the Limerick, Clare and Tipperary (N.R.) region: report commissioned by the Higher Education Sub-Committee of the Limerick, Clare and Tipperary (N.R.) Regional Development Organisation. London: 1969.

2496 McCAFFREY, PATRICIA. The Wyndham university scheme, 1903–4. *Ir. Eccles. Rec.*, 110, 1968, 329–349. George Wyndham, chief secretary.

2497 McCARTNEY, DONAL. Lecky and the Irish university question. *Ir. Eccles. Rec.*, 108, 1967, 102–112.

2498 McGRATH, FERGAL. Newman's university: idea and reality. Dublin: 1951. Bibliog., pp. 512–22.

2499 McHENRY, FRANCIS. The university dilemma: a world problem in an Irish context. Limerick: 1970.

2500 McHUGH, ROGER J. *ed*. Newman on university education. Dublin: 1944. Bibliog., pp. 165–7.

2501 NEVIN, MONICA. A study of the social background of students in the Irish universities. *Stat. Social Inq. Soc. Ir. J.*, vol. 21, pt. 6, 1967–68, 201–255.

2502 O CATHAIN, SEAN. University selection in Ireland. *Studies*, 53, 1964, 47–56.

2503 TIERNEY, MARK. Catalogue of letters relating to the Queen's Colleges, Ireland, 1845–50, in the papers of Archbishop Michael Slattery at Thurles. *Coll. Hib.*, 9, 1966, 83–120.

Universities and Colleges

2504 HOLY CROSS COLLEGE, CLONLIFFE, DUBLIN. College history and centenary record [1859–1959]. Dublin: 1962.

2505 MAYNOOTH COLLEGE. BRADY, *The* REV. JOHN. Origins of Maynooth College. *Studies*., 34, 1945, 511–514.

2506 — HAMELL, PATRICK J. Maynooth students and ordinations, 1795–1895: index. *Ir. Eccles. Rec.*, 109, 1968, 335–340; 407–416.

2507 — HAMELL, PATRICK J. Maynooth students and ordinations, 1795–1895: index, pt. 2. Maynooth: 1973.

2508 — MEEHAN, DENIS. Window on Maynooth. Dublin: 1949. Bibliog., pp. 167–79.

2509 NATIONAL UNIVERSITY OF IRELAND. Calendar. 1911–. From 1922 includes *List of published works and theses submitted for doctorate degrees*.

2510 — Graduate and sessional lists, 1952– Published every three years.

2511 — The National University handbook, 1908–32. Dublin: 1932. Academic publications by the teaching staff, and other graduates holding higher degrees of the National University, pp. 175–270.

2512 — Summary of progress for the seven years, 1932–1939: a supplemental issue to the University Handbook of 1932. Dublin: 1939.

2513 QUEEN'S UNIVERSITY, BELFAST. MOODY, T.W. and BECKETT, J.C. Queen's, Belfast, 1845–1949: the history of a university. London: 1959. 2 vols. Bibliog., vol. 2, pp. 869–936.

2514 — REA, DESMOND. A discussion on social class background with special reference to students at Queen's University, Belfast [with bibliog.]. *Stat. Social Inq. Soc. Ir. J.*, vol. 21, pt. 6, pp. 152–173.

2515 ST. KIERAN'S COLLEGE. BIRCH, P. St. Kieran's College, Kilkenny. Dublin: 1951. Bibliog., pp. 332–7.

2516 TRINITY COLLEGE, DUBLIN. Dublin University Calendar, 1840–. From 1931–2 includes *List of recent publications by members of the staff*.

2517 — Register of the alumni of Trinity College, Dublin. 9th ed. Dublin: 1970.

2518 — BURTCHAELL, G.D., and SADLEIR, T.U. Alumni Dublinenses: a register of students, graduates and provosts of Trinity College in the University of Dublin. 2nd ed. Dublin: 1935. 1st ed., 1924.

2519 — DAGG, T.S.C. College Historical Society: a history (1770–1920). [Tralee, 1969]. Appendix: notes and pen-portraits, pp. 374–425. Edition limited to 25 numbered copies; copies in Trinity College, Dublin, and the Royal Dublin Society.

2520 — FURLONG, E.J. The story of the College baths: a study in action and reaction. *Hermathena*, 98, 1964, 97–110.

2521 — MAXWELL, CONSTANTIA. A history of Trinity College, Dublin. 1591–1892. Dublin: 1946. Bibliog., pp. 281–9.

2522 — MURPHY, HAROLD LAWSON. A history of Trinity College, Dublin from its foundations to 1702. Dublin: 1951. Bibliog. pp. 203–5.

2523 — SADLEIR, T.U., and WATSON, HELEN M. A record of seventeenth-century alumni. *Hermathena*, 89, 1957, 54–8.

2524 — STUBBS, JOHN WILLIAM. The history of the University of Dublin, from its foundation to the end of the eighteenth century; with an appendix of original documents which, for the most part, are preserved in the college. Dublin and London: 1889.

2525 — Treasures of Trinity College, Dublin: [catalogue of] an exhibition chosen from the college and its library, at Burlington House, London, January 12 — March 5, 1961. Dublin [1961].

2526 — WEBB, D.A. *ed*. Of one company: biographical studies of famous Trinity men. Dublin: 1951.

2527 UNIVERSITY COLLEGE, DUBLIN. Calendar, 1910–11–.

2528 — Fathers of the Society of Jesus, *compilers*. A page of Irish history: story of University College, Dublin, 1883–1909. Dublin: 1930. Publications connected with the college, pp. 271–322.

2529 — MACHALE, JOSEPH P. University entry requirements: limitation of entry to University College, Dublin. *Studies*, 60, 1971, 284–294.

2530 — MEENAN, JAMES, *ed*. Centenary history of the Literary and Historical Society of University College, Dublin, 1855–1955. Tralee [1956]. Bibliog. footnotes.

2531 — NEVIN, MONICA. A study of the social background of students in University College, Dublin. *Stat. Social Inq. Soc. Ir. J.*, vol. 21, pt. 5, 1966–67, 62–95.

National Supervision and Control

2532 AKENSON, DONALD H. Education and enmity: the control of schooling in Northern Ireland, 1920–50. Newton Abbot and New York: 1973. Bibliog., pp. 274–281.

National and State Aid

2533 CANNON, PATRICK F.G. Symposium on investment in education. *Stat. Social Inq. Soc. Ir. J.*, 119th session, 1965–66, 67–98. Contributions by Charles McCarthy, Dr. K. Milne, and C.OhEocha.

2534 O'BRIEN, TERENCE and MACAIRT, DR. JUSTIN. Finance and school meals: the financial aspect of providing an integrated school-meals system for Irish children. *Soc. Stud.*, vol. 3, no. 1, 1974, 63–73.

2535 TUSSING, A. DALE. Irish educational expenditure — past, present and future. Dublin: Economic and Social Research Institute, 1978.(*Paper no*. 92).

COMMERCE

2536 CULLEN, L.M. Anglo-Irish trade, 1660–1800. Manchester, 1968. Bibliog., pp. 221–242.

2537 GREEN, E.R.R. The Lagan Valley, 1800–50: a local history of the industrial revolution. London: 1949. Bibliog., pp. 164–76.

2538 HENDERSON, G.P., *compiler*. Current British directories: a comprehensive guide to the local, trade and professional directories of the British Isles. London [1955]. 4th ed. London: 1962.

2539 HULTMAN, CHARLES. Ireland in world commerce. Cork: 1969. (*Mercier original paperback*) Bibliog., pp. 158–160.

2540 INSTITUTE FOR INDUSTRIAL RESEARCH AND STANDARDS. TECHNICAL INFORMATION DIVISION. Ireland: products and services. Dublin.
Pt. 1. Engineering. 1971.
Pt. 2. Textiles, furniture and household goods. 1972.
Pt. 3. Non metallic materials. 1972.
Pt. 4. Printing and packaging paper and paper products. 1973.
Pt. 5. Food, drink and tobacco. 1973.

2541 LESTER, C.E.V. A study of imports. Dublin: Economic and Social Research Institute, 1967. (*Paper* no. 38).

2542 LONGFIELD, ADA KATHLEEN. Anglo Irish trade in the sixteenth century. London: 1929. Bibliog., pp. 227–32.

2543 MASSIE, JOSEPH. Bibliography of the collection of books and tracts on commerce, currency and poor law (1557 to 1763) formed by Joseph Massie (died 1784), transcribed from Lansdowne Manuscript mxlix, with historical and bibliographical introduction by William A. Shaw. London: 1937. Author index only.

2544 MURRAY, ALICE EFFIE. A history of the commercial and financial relations between England and Ireland. London: 1903. Bibliog., pp. 445–67.

2545 NORTHERN IRELAND. MINISTRY OF COMMERCE. Who makes what in Northern Ireland . . . 6th ed., Belfast: 1968.

2546 PINKERTON, WILLIAM. Contributions towards a history of Irish commerce. *Ulster J. Arch*., 3, 1855, 177–99.

2547 UNITED STATES, Bureau of foreign and domestic commerce. Irish Free State, by Hugh D. Butler. 1928. (*Commercial and industrial handbooks*.)

2548 UNIVERSITY COLLEGE, DUBLIN. HISTORICAL SOCIETY. Survey of business records in Dublin. *Ir. Arch. Bull*., vol. 3, no. 2, 1973, 10–13.

Exports

2549 ABSTRACTS OF IMPORTS AND EXPORTS FROM DUBLIN for the years 1764–1823. 24 vols. fol. *In* National Library Mss. collection, nos. 353–76.

2550 CORAS TRACHTALA (the Irish Export Board), Dublin. Annual report no. 1–, 1952–3–. Exporters Newsletter (*afterwards* Exporters Review). vol. 1–, 1955–.

2551 — The Irish export handbook, 3rd. ed., 1977. In loose-leaf form so that additional material can be added and obsolete data removed. See also Coras Trachtala Teo, *Administration*, vol. 3, no. 1, 1955, 29–36.

2552 COYNE, EDWARD J. Ten years of export trade, 1924–1933. *Studies*, 24, 1935, 459–472, 654–669; *ibid*., 25, 1936, 473–489.

POSTAL SERVICES

2553 BUTLER, BEATRICE BAYLEY. John and Edward Lees, secretaries of the Irish Post Office, 1774–1831. *Dublin Hist. Rec*., 13, 1952–54, 138–150.

2554 DIXON, F.E. Irish postal history. *Dublin Hist. Rec*., vol. 23, no. 4, 1970, 127–136.

2555 FARRUGIA, JEAN YOUNG. The letter box: a history of post office pillar and wall boxes. Fontwell (Sussex): 1969.

2556 FELDMAN, DAVID, and KANE, WILLIAM. Handbook of Irish postal history to 1840. Dublin: 1975.

2557 GREAT BRITAIN, GENERAL POST OFFICE. Post offices in the United Kingdom and the Irish Republic excluding the London postal area. London: 1961.

2558 JACKSON, T.V. The Irish post office, 1638–1703 [with bibliog.]. *Post. Hist. Soc. Bull*., 100, 1959, 33–6.

2559 MEGHEN, P.J. Anthony Trollope and the Irish post office. *Admin*., 11, 1963, 163–172.

2560 SMYTH, T.S. Postal history: a story of progress. Dublin: 1941. Supplement, 1942.

2561 WATSON, EDWARD. The Royal Mail to Ireland, or an account of the origin and development of the post between London and Ireland, through Holyhead, and the use of the line of communications by travellers. London: 1917. Bibliog. notes. pp. 237–44.

Philately

2562 [BACON, EDWARD DENNY.] A bibliography of the writings general, special and periodical, forming the literature of philately; divided into two parts. (1) Authors and titles; (2) Periodicals. Aberdeen: 1911. (*Bibliotheca Lindesiana*, vol. 7.)

2563 BUCHALTER, M. DON, *compiler*. Hibernian specialised catalogue of the postage stamps of Ireland, 1922–1972. Dublin: Hibernian Stamp Co. 1972.

2564 FELDMAN, DAVID. Handbook of Irish philately. Dublin: 1968. Deals with all aspects of philately and fills a growing need for a definitive work of this nature.

2565 — Price list of items in 'Handbook of Irish philately'. Dublin: 1968.

2566 MACKAY, JAMES A. Eire: the story of Eire and her stamps. London: Philatelic Publishers Ltd., 1968. Bibliog., pp. 149–150.

2567 MILLER, LIAM. Ireland in the world of stamps. *Ir. Today*, 886, 1976, 1–5.

2568 O'NEILL, C.P. Newspaper stamps of Ireland. [Enniskillen, 1978].

TRANSPORT AND COMMUNICATION

2569 BLACKWELL, JOHN. Transport in the developing economy. Dublin: Economic and Social Research Institute, 1969. (*Paper no*. 47).

2570 CORAS IOMPAIR EIREANN, DUBLIN. Annual report no. 1–, 1950–1–.

2571 CORAS IOMPAIR EIREANN. *Admin*, vol. 16, no. 4, 1968, 331–439. Special issue.

2572 CORCORAN, MICHAEL. Six decades of Irish road transport. *Cap. Ann*, 1977, 325–339.

2573 FLANAGAN, PATRICK. Transport in Ireland, 1830–1910. Dublin: Transport Research Association, 1969. Illustrated with photographs from the Lawrence collection of the National Library of Ireland. Bibliog., p. 180.

2574 AN FORAS FORBARTHA. Transportation in Dublin: an advisory report. Dublin: 1973.

2575 IRELAND, DEPARTMENT OF INDUSTRY AND COMMERCE. Report on transport in Ireland, 1948 [by J. Milne]. Dublin: 1948.

2576 — Committee of inquiry into internal transport, 1957. Report. Dublin: 1957.

2577 LYNCH, PATRICK. Irish transport in the 1950s and 1960s. *Forum* (CIE), vol. 1, no. 4, 1971, 3–19.

2578 MCKINSEY and COMPANY INC. Defining the role of public transport in a changing environment: a report prepared for – Department of Transport and Power, Department of Finance, Coras Iompair Eireann. Dublin: 1971.

2579 NOWLAN, KEVIN B. Travel and transport in Ireland. Dublin and New York: 1973.

2580 O'SULLIVAN, PATRICK. Transport networks and the Irish economy. London: 1969. (*London School of economics and political science*, *Geographical papers*, no. 4).

2581 WALLACE, PATRICK F. The organisation of pre-railway public transport in counties Limerick and Clare. *Nth. Munster Antiq. J.*, 15, 1972,34–58.

Marine and Inland Waterways

2582 ANDERSON, ERNEST B. Sailing ships of Ireland; being a record of Irish sailing ships of the nineteenth century. Dublin: 1951.

2583 COOKE, SHOLTO. The Maiden City and the Western Ocean: a history of the shipping trade between Londonderry and North America in the nineteenth century. Dublin [1960]. Bibliog. note in foreword.

2584 DE COURCY IRELAND, J. Some notes on Wexford maritime affairs in the Middle Ages and Renaissance. *Old Wexford Soc. J.*, vol. 3, no. 1, 1970, 51–55.

2585 HORNELL, JAMES. British coracles and Irish curraghs . . . London: Society for Nautical Research, 1938. Bibliog. footnotes.

2586 LAWLOR, ANTHONY T., *compiler*. Irish maritime survey: a guide to the Irish maritime world, 1945. Dublin: 1945.

2587 LITTLE, GEORGE A. The Ouzel galley. 2nd. rev. ed. Dublin: 1953. First published by the

Old Dublin Society as a special issue of the *Dublin Historical Record*, (vol. 3, no. 2, 1940).

2588 McNEILL, D.B. Coastal passenger steamers and inland navigations in the North of Ireland, Belfast [1960]. (*Belfast museum and art gallery transport handbook*, no. 3.)

2589 — Irish passenger steamship services. Newton Abbot.
Vol. 1. North of Ireland. 1969.
Vol. 2. South of Ireland. 1971.

2590 MATHIAS, P. and PEARSALL, A.W.H. Shipping: a survey of historical records. Newton Abbot: 1971. Includes details of Belfast Steamship Co. Ltd. and Coast Lines Ltd.

2591 PETERSON, BASIL. Turn of the tide: an outline of Irish maritime history. Dublin and Cork, 1962. Bibliog., p. 185.

2592 ROGERS, MARY. The navigation of Lough Erne [with bibliog.]. *Ulster Folk.*, 12, 1966, 97–103.

Canals

2593 CANALIANA: the annual bulletin of Robertstown Muintir na Tire. 1965–

2594 D'ARCY, GERARD. Portrait of the Grand Canal. Dublin: Transport Research Association, 1969. Bibliog., p. 106.

2595 DELANY, RUTH. The County of Kildare Canal. *Kildare Arch. Soc. J.*, vol. 15, no. 3, 1972, 122–135.

2596 — The Grand Canal of Ireland. Newton Abbot: 1973.

2597 DELANY, V.T.H. and DELANY, D.R. The canals of the south of Ireland. Newton Abbot: 1966. (*The canals of the British Isles series*) Bibliog. notes, pp. 218–227.

2598 DENHAM, PETER. Waterways of Ireland. *Geog. Mag.*, 39, 1966–67, 773–782.

2599 FLANAGAN, PATRICK. The Ballinamore and Ballyconnell Canal. Newton Abbot: 1972. (*Inland waterways histories*). Links the rivers Erne and Shannon.

2600 HUNT, J.M. New life for an Irish waterway [the Grand Canal]. *Country Life*, 140, 1966, 312–314.

2601 McCUTCHEON, W.A. The canals of the North of Ireland. Dawlish and London, 1965. (*Canals of the British Isles*).

2602 — The Newry navigation: the earliest inland canal in the British Isles [with bibliog.]. *Geog. J.*, 129, 1963, 466–480.

2603 PHILLIPS, HENRY. Early history of the Grand Canal. *Dublin Hist. Rec.*, 1, 1938–39. 108–119.

2604 RYNNE, STEPHEN. The Irish Grand Canal. *Countryman*, vol. 67, no. 1, 1966, 90–99.

Railways

Bibliography

2605 OTTLEY, GEORGE, *compiler*. A bibliography of British Railway history. London: 1965. Ireland, pp. 126–140.

General

2606 AHRONS, E.L. Locomotive and train working in the latter part of the nineteenth century; edited by L.L. Asher. vol. 6: Great Southern and Western Railway; Waterford, Limerick and Western Railway; Dublin, Wicklow and Wexford Railway; Midland Great Western Railway; Great Northern Railway (Ireland). Cambridge: 1954. Reprinted from *The Railway Magazine*.

2607 ARNOLD, R.M. NCC Saga; being a story of the LMS (Northern Counties Committee) where the enginemen were the heroes, and the villain, the diesel engine. Newton Abbot: 1973.

2608 — Steam over Belfast Lough: a look at the railways to Bangor and Larne and especially the work of the locomotives. Lingfield (Surrey): 1969.

2609 BAKER, MICHAEL H.C. Irish railways since 1916. London: 1972. Bibliog., p. 218.

2610 — The Railways of the Republic of Ireland: a pictorial survey of the G.S.R. and C.I.E., 1925–75. Truro (Cornwall): 1975.

2611 BOOCOCK, C.P. Irish railway album. London: 1968.

2612 CASSERLEY, H.C. Outline of Irish railway history. Newton Abbot: 1974.

2613 CONROY, J.C. A history of railways in Ireland. London: 1928. Bibliog. footnotes.

2614 COTTERELL, S. A handbook to various publications, connected with the rise and development of the railway system, chiefly in Great Britain and Ireland, to be sold by Edward Baker. Birmingham: 1893. Very full list particularly for the earlier period.

2615 CREEDON, C. The Cork and Macroom direct railway: a short history. [Cork]: 1961.

2616 CURRIE, J.R.L. The Northern Counties Railway, Newton Abbot.
Vol. 1. Beginnings and development, 1845–1903. 1973.
Vol. 2. Heyday and decline, 1903–1972. 1974.

2617 — The Runaway train: Armagh (1889). Newton Abbot: 1971. Bibliog., p. 142.

2618 DAY-LEWIS, SEAN. Bulleid, last giant of steam. London: 1964. Account of Bulleid's work on the modernising of Irish railways in the present century.

2619 FAYLE, HAROLD. Narrow gauge railways of Ireland. [1st ed. reprinted] with a new introduction by K. Mellor. Wakefield: 1970. 1st ed., London: 1964.

2620 — The Waterford and Tramore railway. 2nd ed. Newton Abbot: 1972. 1st ed. 1964.

2621 FLANAGAN, PATRICK J. The Cavan and Leitrim railway. Newton Abbot: 1966.

2622 GAMBLE, NORMAN E. Belfast Central Railway reopening. *Ir. Geog*., 9, 1976, 109–112.

2623 HAJDUCKI, S. MAXWELL. A railway atlas of Ireland. Newton Abbot: 1974. Bibliog., xxix–xxxi.

2624 HEMANS, GEORGE WILLOUGHBY. On the railway system in Ireland, the Government aid afforded, and the nature and results of county guarantee. *Minutes Proc. Inst. Civ. Eng*., 18, 1858–59, 24–50.

2625 IRISH RAILWAY RECORD SOCIETY. Journal, no. 1–, 1947–.

2626 — An index to the Journal of the Irish Railway Record Society. Vols. 1–9, 1947–1970, compiled by Thomas F. Wall. Dublin: 1973. (*Occasional papers, no*. 1).

2627 — A list of Irish railways, with a classification of railway material, by Joseph J. Leckey. Dublin: 1973. (*Occasional papers*, no. 2).

2628 — Nineteenth-century railway politics in the Belfast-Dublin-Enniskillen triangle, with a note on sources, by Joseph J. Leckey. Dublin: 1973. (*Occasional papers*, no. 3).

2629 KIDNER, R.W. Narrow gauge railways of Ireland. 3rd ed. Lingfield: 1960. (*Light railway handbooks*, no. 4.)

2630 LECKEY, JOSEPH J. A classification of Irish railway records. *Ir. Arch. Bull*., vol. 3, no. 2, 1973, 5–9.

2631 MCCORMICK, W.P. The railways of Northern Ireland and their locomotives. 2nd ed. [Belfast, 1946.]

2632 MCCUTCHEON, ALAN. Ireland. Newton Abbot: 1969. (*Railway History in pictures*), 1969–70. 2 vols.

2633 MCGRATH, WALTER. Some industrial railways of Ireland (and other minor lines). Cork: 1959.

2634 MURRAY, KEVIN. The Atmospheric railway to Dalkey. *Dublin Hist. Rec*., 5, 1942–3, 108–120.

2635 — Dublin's first railway. *Dublin Hist. Rec*., 1, 1938–9, 19–26, 33–40. The Dublin and Kingstown Railway.

2636 — The Great Northern Railway (Ireland). Dublin, 1944.

2637 — and MCNEILL, D.B. The Great Southern and Western Railway. Dublin: Irish Railway Record Society, 1976.

2638 NEWHAM, A.T. The Cork and Muskerry light railway. Lingfield (Surrey): 1968. (*Locomotion papers no*. 39)

2639 — The Cork Blackrock and Passage railway. Lingfield (Surrey): 1970.

2640 NORTHERN IRELAND. MINISTRY OF HOME AFFAIRS. Northern Ireland railways: report by Henry Benson. Belfast: 1963.

2641 O'CUIMIN, PADRAIG. The Baronial lines of the Midland Great Western Railway: the Loughrea and Attymon light railway [and] the Ballinrobe and Claremorris light railway. Dublin: Transport Research Association, 1972.

2642 O'DONNELL, SEAN. The evolution of our railways. *Technol. Ir*., vol. 9, no. 2, 1977, 13–15.

2643 PATTERSON, EDWARD M. The Ballycastle

Railway. Newton Abbot: 1965. (*A history of the narrow-gauge railways of North-East Ireland, pt. 1.*) Bibliog., pp. 149–150.

2644 — The Ballymena lines. Newton Abbot: 1968. (*A history of the narrow-gauge railways of North-East Ireland, pt. 2.*) Bibliog., pp. 195–6.

2645 — The Belfast and County Down railway. Lingfield (Surrey): 1958. (*Oakwood library of railway history.*) Bibliog., p. 50.

2646 — The Clogher Valley Railway. Newton Abbot: 1972. Bibliog., pp. 261–263.

2647 — The County Donegal railways. London: 1962. (*A history of the narrow-gauge railways of North-West Ireland, pt.1.*) Bibliog., pp. 148–150.

2648 — The Londonderry and Lough Swilly Railway. Dawlish and London: 1964. (*A history of the narrow-gauge railways of North-West Ireland, pt. 2*). Bibliog., pp. 182–184.

2649 — The Great Northern Railway of Ireland. Lingfield (Surrey): 1962. Bibliog., pp. 180–182.

2650 PEDDIE, R.A. Railway literature, 1556–1830: a handlist. London: 1931.

2651 PENDER, BRENDAN and RICHARDS, HERBERT. Irish railways today. Dublin: Transport Research Association, 1967.

2652 ROWLANDS, DAVID G. The Tralee and Dingle railway. Truro (Cornwall): 1977. Bibliog., p. 96.

2653 RYAN, J.H. The Galway and Clifden Railway. *Inst. Civ. Eng. Ir. Trans.*, 28, 1902, 203–235.

2654 SHEPHERD, W. ERNEST. The Dublin and South Eastern Railway. Newton Abbot: 1974. Bibliog., 226–7.

2655 SPRINKS, N.W. Sligo, Leitrim and Northern Counties Railway. Billericay (Essex): Irish Railway Record Society, 1970.

2656 WHISHAW, FRANCIS. The Railways of Great Britain and Ireland (1842). 2nd ed. rep., Newton Abbot: 1969. New introduction by C.R. Clinker; Dublin and Kingstown Railway, pp. 62–71; Ulster Railway, pp. 430–437.

2657 WHITEHOUSE, P.B. Narrow gauge album. London: 1957. Bibliog., p. 134.

2658 — On the narrow-gauge. London: 1964. Accounts of West Clare Railway, Tralee and Dingle, Cavan, Leitrim and Roscommon light railway, Londonderry and Lough Swilly Railway, County Donegal Railways, Strabane and Letterkenny Railway.

Internal Transport

2659 CORAS IOMPAIR EIREANN. The C.I.E. report on internal public transport. Dublin: 1963. 2 pts.

2660 FLANAGAN, P.J. and MAC AN tSAOR, C.B. Dublin buses. Dublin: 1968.

2661 LENNAN, L.K. An economic examination of traffic congestion in towns. *Admin.*, vol. 20, no. 2, 1972, 50–61.

2662 REYNOLDS, D.J. Inland transport in Ireland: a factual survey. Dublin: The Economic Research Institute, 1962. (*Paper no.* 10).

2663 SEXTON, J. Road freight transport in Ireland. *Stat. Social Inq. Soc. Ir. J.*, vol. 21, pt. 5, 1966–67, 96–124.

2664 THOMPSON, G.R. Primitive land transport of Ulster. Belfast, 1958. (*Belfast museum and art gallery transport handbook*, no. 2.) Bibliog., pp. [33–34].

Roads

2665 ADMINISTRATION vol. 10, no. 2, 1962. [Roads Survey Issue]. Contents: Some current road problems, by M. Flannery; Roads administration, by E.T. Sheehy; The Economics of roads, by James McGilvray; Economic aspects of road improvements in Ireland, by Peter J. O'Keeffe; Road services for a county [Antrim] by T.A.N. Prescott; Main roads, by Peter J. O'Keeffe; The development of modern techniques of road making, by J.D. Hally; Productivity and road engineering, by M. Dee; The need for further research in road pavements, by C.D. O'Donoghue.

2666 ANDREWS, J.H. Road planning in Ireland before the railway ages [with bibliog,] *Ir. Geog.*, vol. 5, no. 1, 1964, 17–41.

2667 BALLEN, DOROTHY. Bibliography of road-making in the United Kingdom. London: 1914.

2668 IRISH ROADS CONGRESS. Record of proceedings, Dublin, 1910. Dublin: 1910.

2669 — The second Irish road congress, Dublin, 1911. Dublin: 1911.

2670 MCCUTCHEON, ALAN. Roads and bridges [in Northern Ireland] *Ulster Folk*., 10, 1964, 73–81.

2671 O'KEEFFE, PETER J. The development of Ireland's road network. Dublin: Institution of Engineers of Ireland, 1973. Bibliog. pp. 55–60.

2672 O'LOCHLAINN, COLM. Roadways in ancient Ireland. *In* Essays and studies presented to Prof. Eoin MacNeill ... edited by John Ryan. Dublin: 1940, pp. 465–474.

2673 O'LUING, SEAN. Richard Griffith and the roads of Kerry. *J. Kerry Arch. Hist. Soc*., 8, 1975, 89–118; 9, 1976, 92–124.

Harbours

2674 BRUNICARDI, D.N. Notes on the history of Haulbowline. *Ir. Sword*, vol. 7, no. 26, 1965, 19–33.

2675 — Haulbowline, Spike and Rocky Islands in Cork Harbour. Cork: Cork Historical Guides Committee, 1968.

2676 CORRY, GEOFFREY. The Dublin Bar — the obstacle to the improvement of the port of Dublin. *Dublin Hist. Rec*., vol. 23, no. 4, 1970, 137–152.

2677 FOX, CHRISTOPHER. Skerries harbour: a short history. Dublin: Three Candles Ltd., [1970].

2678 HAMPTON, F.W.P. History of Belfast Harbour. *Belfast Nat. Hist. Phil. Soc. Proc*., 8, 1964–70, 5–11.

2679 HAYES-MCCOY, MARGARITE. The port of Galway. *Galway Reader*, vol. 2, nos. 1–2, 1949, 38–45.

2680 MOORE, DESMOND F. The port of Dublin. *Dublin Hist. Rec*., 16, 1960–61, 131–143.

2681 MURRAY, KEVIN. Old Dunleary harbour. *Dublin Hist. Rec*., 7, 1944–5, 150–153.

2682 O'SULLIVAN, J.B. Cork harbour development. *Technol. Ir*., vol. 4, no. 8, 1972, 14–16.

2683 SANDERLIN, WALTER S. Galway as a transatlantic port in the nineteenth century. *Eire-Ir*., vol. 5, no. 3, 1970, 15–31.

2684 SWAN, ALLAN B. The port of Dundalk. *Louth Arch J*., vol. 17, no. 2, 1970, 66–78.

2685 TWOHIG, A.J. O'BRIEN. Developments in the port of Dublin, 1903–1962. *Trans. R. Inst. Nav. Arch*., 104, 1962, 493–500.

Tramways

2686 FAYLE, HAROLD AND NEWHAM, A.T. The Dublin and Blessington Tramway. Lingfield, (Surrey), 1963.

2687 FLEWITT, R.C. Dublin tramways. *Ir. Rail. Rec. Soc. J*., 5, 1960. 252–66, 324–34.

2688 — The Hill of Howth tramway. Dublin: Transport Research Association, 1968.

2689 JOHNSTON, DENIS. The Dublin trams [with bibliog.]. *Dublin Hist. Rec*., 12, 1951, 99–113.

2690 JOYCE, J. *ed*. Tramway memories. London: 1967. Dingle to Dun Laoghaire, by A.T. Newham, pp. 4–18; gives an account of Irish tramways.

2691 — Tramway twilight; the story of British tramways from 1945 to 1962. London: 1962. Bibliog., p. 112. Last cars, Dublin to Dalkey, 9 July 1949. Last cars, Hill of Howth, 31 May 1959.

2692 KILLEEN, MICHAEL J. The Dublin and Blessington steam tramway. *Dublin Hist. Rec*., vol. 30, no. 2, 1977, 42–50.

2693 NEWHAM, A.T. The Schull and Skibbereen Tramway and light railway. Lingfield, (Surrey): 1964.

2694 — The Dublin and Lucan Tramway. Lingfield: 1965. (*Locomotion papers*, no. 29).

Air Transport

2695 AER LINGUS, DUBLIN. Reports and accounts. 1948–.

2696 CIVIL AVIATION. *Administration*, vol. 3, no. 4, 1955–6.

2697 TURNER, PAUL ST. JOHN. U.K. and Eire commercial airports, Hounslow, (Middlesex): 1974.

COSTUME AND DRESS

2698 COSTUME INDEX: a subject index to plates and to illustrated text; edited by Isabel Monro and Dorothy E. Cook. New York: 1937. Supplement. New York: 1957.

2699 DANAHER, KEVIN. The dress of the Irish, by Caoimhin O Danachair. *Eire-Ir.*, vol. 2, no. 3, 1967, 5–11.

2700 FFOLLIOTT, ROSEMARY. Children's clothes, 1679–1867. *Ir. Ancest.*, 2, 1970, 19–22.

2701 — Men's clothes in Ireland, 1660–1850. *Ir. Ancest.*, 4, 1972, 89–93.

2702 — Women's dress in Ireland, 1680–1880. *Ir. Ancest.*, 3, 1971, 85–89.

2703 HILER, HILAIRE, and HILER, MEYER, *compilers*. Bibliography of costume: a dictionary catalogue of about eight thousand books and periodicals. New York: 1939.

2704 LUCAS, A.T. Footwear in Ireland. *Louth Arch. J.*, 13, no. 4, 1956, 309–94. Main theme is the use of soleless stockings.

2705 MCCLINTOCK, H.F. Old Irish and Highland dress and that of the Isle of Man; 2nd enl. ed. Dundalk: 1950. References in contemporary English and continental writings, pp. 74–94.

2706 PRICE, ANNE. The Irish way of dress. *Country Life*, vol. 148, no. 3823, 1970, 318–9.

CUSTOM AND TRADITION

2707 DANAHER, KEVIN. Bunratty Folk Park. *Ir. Wel.*, vol. 14, no. 1, 1965, 27–30.

2708 EVANS, EMYR ESTYN. Irish folk ways. London: 1957. Bibliog., pp. 307–12.

2709 GOMME, A.B. The traditional games of England, Scotland and Ireland, with tunes, singing rhymes and methods of playing according to the variants extant and recorded in different parts of the kingdom. London: 1894–8. 2 vols.

2710 JENKINS, GERAINT *ed*. Studies in folk life: essays in honour of Iorwerth C. Peate. London: 1969. Irish material includes: Once upon a time [an Sean O'Conaill], by Seamus O Duilearga; Sod and turf houses in Ireland, by E. Estyn Evans; Representation of houses on some Irish maps of *c*. 1600, by Caoimhin O'Danachair.

2711 MCCLELLAND, AIKEN. Folklife miscellanea from eighteenth and nineteenth-century newspapers. *Ulster Folk.*, 17, 1971, 92–95; 19, 1973, 68–72.

2712 REES, ALWYN and REES, BRINLEY. Celtic heritage: ancient tradition in Ireland and Wales. London: 1961. Bibliog. notes, pp. 352–413.

2713 THOMPSON, G.R. Estyn Evans and the development of Ulster Folk Museum. *Ulster Folk.*, 15–16, 1970, 233–238.

Burial Customs

2714 O SUILLEABHAIN, SEAN. Caitheamh Aimsire ar Thorraimh. Baile Atha Cliath: 1961. Bibliog., pp. 155–62. A monograph on 'wakes'.

Public and Social Customs

2715 DALY, *Mrs*. MARGIE. Entertainment in 18th century Dublin. *Dublin Hist. Rec.*, 22, 1968, 288–295.

2716 DANAHER, KEVIN. The year in Ireland. Cork: 1972. Bibliog., 268–272.

2717 IRELAND, COMMISSION INTO PUBLIC HOLIDAYS AND BANK HOLIDAYS, 1965. Report, Dublin: 1965.

2718 LUCAS, A.T. Washing and bathing in ancient Ireland. *R. Soc. Antiq. Ir. J.*, 95, 1965, 65–114.

2719 MASON, THOMAS H. St. Brigid's Crosses. *R. Soc. Antiq. Ir. J.*, 75, 1945, 160–166. Crosses made of straw or rushes, usually placed over entrance door on 1 February, St. Brigid's Day.

2720 O'DEA, LAURENCE. The Fair of Donnybrook. *Dublin. Hist. Rec.*, vol. 75, 1958–60, 11–20.

2721 SMITHSON, *Miss* A.M.P. Christmas in old Dublin. *Dublin Hist. Rec.*, 6, 1943–4, 1–7.

Food and Drink

2722 FITZGIBBON, THEODORA. Food in Ireland in the eighteenth century. *Kildare Arch. Soc. J.*, vol. 14, no. 4, 1969, 452–456.

2723 — More eighteenth-century food. *Kildare Arch. Soc. J.*, vol. 15, no. 2, 1972, 168–9.

2724 MOTT, GEORGE. Eating and drinking habits in Ireland two hundred years ago. *Ir. Ancest.*, 5, 1973, 7–11.

Games

2725 BRADY, EILIS. All in! All in!: a selection of Dublin children's traditional street games with rhymes and music. Dublin: 1975.

2726 DAIKEN, LESLIE. Out goes she: Dublin street rhymes, collected and with a commentary. Dublin: Dolmen Press 1963. Contains bibliog. of author.

2727 GOMME, ALICE BERTHA. The traditional games of England, Scotland and Ireland, with tunes, singing-rhymes and methods of playing according to the variants extant and recorded in different parts of the Kingdom. Introduction by Dorothy Howard. New York: 1964. 2 vols. 1st ed. London: 1894–8.

Women

2728 CONCANNON, MRS. THOMAS. Daughters of Banba. Dublin: 1922. History of the women of Ireland.

2729 WOMEN IN IRELAND: a special issue for International Women's Year 1975. *Admin.*, 23, no. 1, 1975, 1–102.

FOLKLORE

Sources

2730 BIBLIOGRAPHY OF IRISH TALES, SAGAS, etc. In Best's *Bibliography of Irish philology and of printed literature*. Dublin: 1913, pp. 78–126.

2731 BOLTE, JOHANNES and POLIVKA, GEORG. Anmerkungen zu den Kinder u. Hausmarchen der Bruder Grimm v. Leipzig: 1932. *Preliminary sketch for a bibliography of Irish and Scottish-Gaelic folktales*, by Reidar Th. Christiansen, pp. 52–64.

2732 BRIGGS, KATHERINE M. A dictionary of British folk-tales in the English language, incorporating the F.J. Norton Collection. London: 1970. 2 vols. Bibliog., pp. 11–34.

2733 CHRISTIANSEN, REIDAR TH. Towards a printed list of Irish fairy tales *Bealoideas*, 7, 1937, 3–14; 8, 1938, 97–105.

2734 — Further notes on Irish folktales. *Bealoideas*, 22, 1953, 70–82.

2735 — Studies in Irish and Scandinavian folktales. Copenhagen and Dublin: 1959.

2736 CORMIER, RAYMOND J. Tom Peete Cross: an American Celticist (1879–1951). *Eire-Ir.*, vol. 5, no. 4, 1970, 112–115.

2737 CROSS, TOM PEETE. Motif-index of early Irish literature. Bloomington, Indiana: 1952. (*Indiana univ. pub. folklore ser.*, no. 7.)

2738 CROSS, TOM PEETE and SLOVER, CLARK HARRIS, *eds*. Ancient Irish tales; with a revised bibliography by Charles W. Dunn. Dublin: 1969. First published, 1936. Bibliog., pp. 601–606.

2739 DORSON, RICHARD M. British folklorists: a history. London: 1968. Ireland, pp. 431–439; bibliog., 442–460.

2740 INTERNATIONAL ARTHURIAN SOCIETY. Bibliographical bulletin, no. 1–, 1949–.

2741 MCCORMACK, W.J. Mairtin O Cadhain as folklorist: a bibliographical note. *Hermathena*, 113, 1972, 35–39.

2742 MULLER-LISOWSKI, KATE. Contributions to a study in Irish folklore: traditions about Donn. *Bealoideas*, 18, 1948, 142–99.

2743 NATIONAL BOOK LEAGUE, LONDON. Irish folklore: stories, mythologggy. 1956. (*Book information bureau book list*.)

2744 O RUADHAIN, MICHAEL. Birds in Irish Folklore [with bibliog.]. *Acta XI Congressus Internationale Ornitholigici, Basel*: 1954, pp. 669–76.

2745 O'SULLIVAN, SEAN. A handbook of Irish folklore, by Sean O'Suilleabhain. Introductory note by Seamus O'Duilearga. Hatboro (Pa.) and London: 1963. Facsimile reprint of 1942 ed.

2746 — Story telling in Irish tradition. Cork: 1973. Published for the Cultural Relations Committee of Ireland.

2747 — and CHRISTIANSEN, REIDAR TH. The types of the Irish folktale, [a catalogue]. Helsinki: Academia Scientiarum Fennica, 1963. (*FF Communications, 188*). Bibliog., pp. 10–26.

2748 THOMAS, N.W. Bibliography of folklore, 1905. *Folklore Soc. Pub.*, vol. 57, 1906.

2749 — The bibliography of anthropology and folklore ... containing works published within the British Empire; published for the joint committee of the Royal Anthropological Institute and the Folklore Society, 1906–7. London: 1907–8. 2 vols.

2750 THOMPSON, STITH. Motif-index of folk-literature ... Bloomington, Indiana, 1932–6. 6 vols. New ed. Indiana, 1955–8. 6 vols.

2751 — The types of the folktale: a description and bibliography. Translated and enlarged by Stith Thompson for Antii Aarne's *Verzeichnes der Marchentypen*. Helsinki: 1961. (*FF Communications*, 184).

2752 ULSTER FOLKLIFE SOCIETY, BELFAST. Ulster folklife. [vol. 1–], 1955–. Index, vols. 1–10, 1965.

2753 VOLKSKUNDLICHE BIBLIOGRAPHIE, STRASSBURG. 1917–18. *Continued as* International Folklore bibliography, 1939–41–(1949–).

General Publications

2754 BRUFORD, ALAN. Gaelic folk-tales and mediaeval romances: a study of the early modern Irish 'Romantic Tales' and their oral derivatives. Dublin: 1969. Bibliog., pp. 250–275; originally published as vol. 34 of *Bealoideas*, 1966.

2755 CURTIN, JEREMIAH. Irish tales by Jeremiah Curtin in *The New York Sun, Sunday supplements*, 1892–3. *Bealoideas*, 4, 1933, 93–5; 11, 1941, 196.

2756 — A list of works by Jeremiah Curtin, by Seamus O Duilearga. *Bealoideas, appendix*, 12, 1942, 165–6.

2757 — Myths and folklore of Ireland [Reprint of 1st ed.] Detroit: 1968. First published Boston, 1890.

2758 DILLON, MYLES. The cycles of the Kings. London: 1946. Bibliog., pp. 122–4.

2759 — *ed*. Irish sagas. Dublin: 1959. (*Thomas Davis lecture series*.)

2760 FOSTER, JEANNE COOPER. Ulster folklore. Belfast: 1951. Bibliog., pp. 138–9.

2761 GREGORY, ISABELLA AUGUSTA, LADY. Gods and fighting men: the story of the Tuatha de Danaan and of the Fianna of Ireland ... with a preface by W.B. Yeats. 2nd ed., and a foreword by Daniel Murphy. Gerrards Cross: 1970. (*Coole ed*. vol. 2.) Bibliog., pp. 362–4.

2762 — Visions and beliefs in the west of Ireland, with two essays and notes by W.B. Yeats, 2nd ed., with a foreword by Elizabeth Coxhead. Gerrards Cross: 1970. (*Coole ed*. vol. 1.)

2763 HEIST, WILLIAM W. The Fifteen signs before Doomsday. East Lansing, Michigan: 1952. Bibliog., pp. 215–23.

2764 HULL, ELEANOR, *ed*. The Cuchullin saga in Irish literature: being a collection of stories relating to the hero Cuchullin. Trans. from the Irish by various scholars; compiled and edited with introduction and notes by Eleanor Hull. London: 1898.

2765 JACKSON, KENNETH HURLSTONE. The oldest Irish tradition: a window on the Iron age. Cambridge: 1964. On the legend of Cuchullainn.

2766 JACKSON, JOSEPH. Celtic fairy tales; being the two collections *Celtic fairy tales* and *More Celtic fairy tales*. London: 1970. Originally published separately 1891 and 1894.

2767 MACEOIN, GEAROID. On the Irish legend of the origin of the Picts. *Stud. Hib*., 4, 1964, 138–154.

2768 MURPHY, MICHAEL J. Folktales and traditions from County Cavan and South Armagh. *Ulster Folk*., 19, 1973, 30–37.

2769 —Now you're talking ... folk tales from the North of Ireland. Belfast: 1975.

2770 O DUILEARGA, SEAMUS. Leabhair Sheain I Chonaill, sgealta agus seanchas o Ibh Rathach. Baile Atha Cliath: 1948. Bibliog., pp. 397–413.

2771 O'RAHILLY, CECILE, *ed*. The Stowe version of Tain Bo Cuailnge. Dublin: 1961.

2772 O'SULLIVAN, SEAN. The folklore of Ireland. London: 1974. Bibliog., pp. 179–181.

2773 — Folktales of Ireland. London: 1966. Bibliog., pp. 293–297.

2774 SWAN, HARRY PERCIVAL. Romantic stories and legends of Donegal. Belfast: 1965.

2775 THUENTE, MARY HELEN. A bibliography of W.B. Yeats's sources for *Fairy and folk tales of the Irish peasantry* and *Irish fairy tales*. *Ir. Book*., vol. 3, no. 1, 1976, 43–49.

2776 YEATS, WILLIAM BUTLER, *ed*. Fairy and folk tales of Ireland. Gerrards Cross: 1973. Foreword by Kathleen Raine; this volume contains *Fairy and folk tales of the Irish peasantry*, first published in 1888, and *Irish fairy tales*, first published in 1892.

2777 WOOD-MARTIN, WILLIAM GREGORY. Traces of the elder faiths in Ireland. [1st ed. reprinted]. London: 1970. 2 vols. 1st ed. London: 1902.

Superstitions

2778 WILDE, JANE FRANCESCA, *Lady*. Ancient legends, mystic charms, and superstitions of Ireland, with sketches of the Irish past; to which is appended a chapter on 'The ancient race of Ireland', by the late Sir William Wilde. Galway: 1971. Reprint of 1888 ed.

Places, Beings and Animals

2779 BRIGGS, K.M. The fairies in tradition and literature. London: 1967. Bibliog., pp. 241–250.

2780 DANAHER, KEVIN. A short guide to the little people. *Ir. Wel*., vol. 13, no. 1, 1964, 21–25.

2781 — Birds in Irish tradition and folklore. *Ir. Wel*., vol. 12, no. 5, 1964, 9–12.

2782 EVANS, GEORGE EWART and THOMPSON, DAVID. The leaping hare. London: 1972. The Irish hare, pp. 41–49.

2783 FOSTER, JOHN WILSON. Certain set apart: the Western island in the Irish Renaissance. *Studies*, 66, 1977, 261–274. The Western Island, real and mythical.

2784 FRAZER, W. On Hy Brasil: a traditional island off the west coast of Ireland, plotted in a Ms. map, written by Sieur Tassis, geographer royal to Louis XIII. *R. Dublin Soc. Proc*., 2, 1878–80, 173–176. Includes map drawn *c*. 1640.

2785 MACKIE, HENRY. Fairies and leprechauns. *Ulster Folk*., 10, 1964, 49–56.

2786 MACMANUS, D.A. The middle kingdom: the faerie world of Ireland. Gerrards Cross: 1973. Originally published London, 1960.

2787 PREMNAY, JOHN. Small tales of the little people. *Country Life*, vol. 153, no. 3961, 1973, 1472–3.

Chap Books

2788 GAILEY, ALAN. A missing Belfast chap book: the Christmas Rime or the Mummers' own book. *Ir. Book*., vol. 2, no. 1, 1972, 54–58.

2789 HARVARD CHAP BOOKS: a bibliographical note on the Irish items in *The Catalogue of the chap books and broadsides in the library of Harvard University*. *Ir. Book Lov*., 2, 1910–11, 35–6.

2790 MARSHALL, JOHN J. Irish chap books. *Ir Book Lov*., 1, 1909–10, 157–9.

Proverbs

2791 BONSER, WILFRID. Proverbs literature: a bibliography of works relating to proverbs; compiled from materials left by the late T.A. Stephens. London: 1930. *Folklore Soc. Pub*., vol. 89.

2792 O MAILLE, TOMAS S. Sean-fhocla Chonnacht. Baile Atha Cliath, 1948–52. 2 vols. Bibliog., vol. 1, pp. xi–xiv.

2792a O'RAHILLY, THOMAS F. *ed*. A miscellany of Irish proverbs. Dublin: 1922. Bibliog., pp. 147–158.

2793 TAYLOR, ARCHER. An introductory bibliography for the study of proverbs. *Mod. Phil*., 30, 1932–3, 195–210.

Riddles

2794 HULL, VERNAM, and TAYLOR, ARCHER. A collection of Irish riddles. Berkeley and Los Angeles: 1955. (*California univ. pub. folklore stud*., no. 6.).

PHILOLOGY

General

2795 ADAMS, G.B. Aspects of monoglottism in Ulster. *Ulster Folk*., 22, 1976, 76–87.

2796 — The 1851 language census in the north of Ireland. *Ulster Folk*, 20, 1974, 65–70.

2797 — Language census problems, 1851–1911. *Ulster Folk*., 21, 1975, 68–72.

2798 — Language in Ulster, 1820–1850. *ibid*., 19, 1973, 50–55.

2799 BAUMGARTEN, ROLF. Alf Sommerfeld's proposals for an Irish linguistic survey, 1941. *Stud. Hib*., 14, 1974, 124–139.

2800 CLERY, ARTHUR E. The Gaelic League, 1893–1919. *Studies*, 8, 1919, 398–408.

2801 CORKERY, DANIEL. The Fortunes of the Irish language. Dublin: 1954. (*Irish life and culture series*).

2802 COMHAIRLE NA GAEILGE. Towards a language policy. Dublin: 1971. Text in English and Irish.

2803 DE FREINE, SEAN. The great silence. Dublin: 1965. Bibliog., pp. 265–275; decline of the Irish language in the nineteenth century.

2804 DOTTIN, GEORGES. Manuel d'irlandais moyen. Paris: 1913. 2 vols. Bibliog., vol. 2, pp. xi–xxvi.

2805 FRENCH, R.B.D. J.O. Hannay and the Gaelic League. *Hermathena*, 102, 1966, 26–52.

2806 GREENE, DAVID. The Irish language. Dublin: 1966. (*Irish life and culture series*).

2807 — Robert Atkinson and Irish studies. *Hermathena*, 102, 1966, 6–15.

2808 HENRY, P.L. A linguistic survey of Ireland: preliminary report [with bibliog.]. *Lochlann*, 1, 1958, 49–208.

2809 KENNY, IVOR. The future of the Gaeltacht. *Admin*., vol. 20, no. 3, 1972, 3–15.

2810 O'CATHAIN, SEAN. The future of the Irish language. *Studies*, 62, 1973, 303–322.

2811 O'CUIV, BRIAN, *ed*. A view of the Irish language. Dublin: 1969.

2812 O'LUING, SEAN. Douglas Hyde and the Gaelic League. *Studies*, 62, 1973, 123–138.

2813 O'SE, LIAM. The Irish language revival: Achilles Heel. *Eire-Ir*., vol. 1, no. 1, 1965–66, 26–49.

2814 PARKER, A.J. 30,000 Gaeltacht Irishmen. *Geog. Mag*., 45, 1972, 126–134.

2815 POKORNY, JULIUS. Keltologie. *In* Karl Honn's Wissenschaftliche Forschungsberichte Geisteswissenschaftliche Reihe, Bd. 2. Bern: 1953. (*Allgemeine und Vergleichende Sprachwissenschaft Indogermanistik*).

2816 POWER, PATRICK. The Gaelic Union: a nonagenarian retrospect. *Studies*, 38, 1949, 413–418. Forerunner of the Gaelic league.

2817 STOKES, WHITLEY and STRACHAN, JOHN. *eds*. Thesaurus Palaeohibernicus: a collection of old-Irish glosses, scholia prose and verse. Cambridge: 1901–3. 2 vols. Supplement [Errata and additions]. Halle a S. 1910.

2818 TIERNEY, MICHAEL. What did the Gaelic League accomplish, 1893–1963? *Studies*, 52, 1963, 337–347.

Bibliography

2819 ANNUAL BIBLIOGRAPHY OF ENGLISH LANGUAGE AND LITERATURE. Edited for the Modern Humanities Research Association. Cambridge, vol. 1–, 1920–.

2820 BAUMGARTEN, ROLF, *compiler*. Irish studies theses — 1975. *Eigse*, vol. 16, pt. 3, 1976, 239–242. A list of 46 theses, including theses in progress.

2821 BEST, RICHARD IRVINE. Bibliography of Irish philology and of printed Irish literature. Dublin: National Library of Ireland, 1913.

2822 — Bibliography of Irish philology and manuscript literature: publications, 1913–1941. [Fascimile reprint of 1st ed.,] Dublin: Dublin Institute for Advanced Studies, 1969. 1st ed., 1942.

2823 — On recent Irish studies in the Academy. *R. Ir. Acad. Proc*., *Sec. C*, 51, 1945–8, 15–34.

2824 BIBLIOTHECA CELTICA: a register of publications relating to Wales and the Celtic peoples and languages ... Aberystwyth, National Library of Wales, vol. 1–, 1924–.

2825 BRAMSBACK, BIRGIT. Irish studies — Celtic Languages. *Acta Universitatis Upsaliensis, Uppsala University, 500 years*, 6, 1976, 11–74.

2826 DUBLIN INSTITUTE FOR ADVANCED STUDIES. Publications of the school of Celtic studies, revised to 30 June 1948. Dublin: 1948.

2827 — Publications of the Dublin Institute for Advanced Studies. *Lochlann*, 1, 1958, 305–6.

2828 HODGES FIGGIS and Co. LTD. Philology, linquistics, literature to 1800, place names, mythology and folklore relating to Ireland, Cornwall, Isle of Man, and Brittany. Dublin: 1958. (*Catalogue, new ser.* 13.)

2829 INSTITIUID TEANGEOLAIOCHTA EIREANN /LINGUISTICS INSTITUTE OF IRELAND. Register of research: language and linguistics. Dublin: 1977.

2830 MALCLES, L.-N. Les sources du travail bibliographique. Langue et littérature celtique, vol. 2, 1952, pp. 345–8.

2831 O'DEIRG, IOSOLD. Language and linguistic theses in Irish University Libraries, July 1977. [Compiled by] Iosold ni Dheirg [Dublin]: Institiuid Teangeolaiochta Eireann, 1977. (*Publication no. 10*).

2832 PERMANENT INTERNATIONAL COMMITTEE OF LINGUISTS. Linguistic bibliography . . . Utrecht and Cambridge. vol. 1–, 1949–.

2833 QUIN, E.G. Irish studies in *Hermathena*, *ibid*., 115, 1973, 41–44.

2834 REID, JOHN. Bibliotheca Scoto-Celtica; or, an account of all the books which have been printed in the Gaelic language, with bibliographical and biographical notices . . . Glasgow: 1832.

2835 WOOLLEY, J.S. Bibliography for Scottish linguistic studies. Edinburgh: 1954. (*Edinburgh univ. linguistic survey of Scotland*). Ireland, with special reference to Ulster. pp. 23–4.

2836 YEAR'S WORK IN MODERN LANGUAGE STUDIES . . . vols. 1–7, 1930–6. Oxford and Cambridge: 1931–7. Includes section on Irish studies, by Myles Dillon.

Periodicals

2837 CELTICA, Dublin, vol. 1–, 1946–.

2838 EIGSE. Dublin, vol. 1–, 1939–.

2839 ERIU. Dublin, vol. 1–, 1904–. Index, vol. 1–10, compiled by Eleanor Knott, in vol. 10, 1928, pp. 194–207.

2840 ETUDES CELTIQUES. Paris, vol. 1–, 1936–. Table des volumes 1–10, (1936–1963). *ibid*., vol. 10., fasc. 3, 1964–65.

2841 INDOGERMANISCHES JAHRBUCH IM AUFTRAG INDOGERMANISCHEN GESELLSCHAFT. Strassburg, vol. 1–, 1913–.

2842 IRISLEABHAIR NA GAEDHILGE (The Gaelic Journal). Dublin: vols. 1–19, 1882–1909. Classified list of the principal articles, vols. 1–13, by Georges Dottin. *Rev. Celt*., 31, 1910, 368–76.

2843 — Index to Irisleabhar na Gaedhilge . . . 1882–1909, by E.M. ni Chiaragain. Dublin: 1935.

2844 LOCHLANN: a review of Celtic studies. Oslo, vol. 1–, 1958–.

2845 REVUE CELTIQUE. Paris.
Tables des six premiers volumes . . . by Georges Dottin, vol. 7, 1886.
Tables des volumes 7–12 . . . by Louis Duvau, vol. 14, 1893.
Tables des volumes 13–18 . . . by P. Le Nestour, vol. 19, 1898.
Tables des volumes 19–24 . . . vol. 26, 1905.
Tables des volumes 25–30 . . . vol. 32, 1911.

2846 STUDIA CELTICA. vol. 1–, 1966–.

2847 WATTS, GARETH O. A list of books, articles, etc., concerning various aspects of the Celtic languages, received at the National Library of Wales, Aberystwyth, during 1967. *Stud. Celt*., vol. 3, 1968, 141–146. Appears annually.

2848 ZEITSCHRIFT FÜR CELTISCHE PHILOLOGIE, Halle a S. vol. 1–, 1897–.

Dialects

2849 ADAMS, G.B. An introduction to the study of Ulster dialects [with bibliog.]. *R. Ir. Acad. Proc., Sec. C*, 52, 1948–50, 1–26.

2850 ENGLISH DIALECT SOCIETY. A bibliographical list of works that have been published or are known to exist in Mss. illustrative of the various dialects of English including those prevalent in Scotland and Ireland, compiled by members of the English Dialect Society, edited by W.W. Skeat and J.H. Nodal. London: 1877. Ireland, by William H. Patterson, pp. 155–6.

2851 EVANS, EMRYS. The Irish dialect of Urris, Innishowen, Co. Donegal, [with bibliog.]. *Lochlann*, 4, 1969, 1–130.

2852 HENRY, P.L. An Anglo-Irish dialect of North Roscommon: phonology, accidence and syntax. Dublin: 1957. Bibliog., pp. 9–14.

2853 — A linguistic survey of Ireland: preliminary report [with bibliog.] *Lochlann*, 1, 1958, 49–208.

2854 HOLMER, NILS M. The dialects of Co. Clare. 2 pts. *R. Ir. Acad. Todd lecture ser.*, vols. 19–20, 1962–65.

2855 — — The Irish Language in Rathlin Island, Co. Antrim. *R. Ir. Acad. Todd lecture ser.*, vol. 18, 1942.

2856 MHAC AN FHAILIGH, EAMONN. The Irish of Ennis, Co. Mayo. Dublin: Dublin Institute for Advanced Studies, 1968. Bibliog., pp. 258–9.

2857 MACLOCHLAINN, ALF. The Irish language in Clare and North Tipperary, 1820: Bishop Mant's enquiry. *Nth. Munster Antiq. J.*, 17, 1975, 77–82.

2858 O'CASAIDE, SEAMUS. The Irish language in Belfast and Co. Down, A.D. 1601–A.D. 1850. *Down Con. Hist. Soc. J.*, 2, 1969, 4–59.

2859 O'CUIV, BRIAN. The Irish of West Muskerry, Co. Cork: a phonetic study. Dublin: Dublin Institute for Advanced Studies, 2nd ed., 1968. 1st ed., 1944.

2860 O'DANACHAIR, CAOIMHIN. The Irish language in County Clare in the 19th century. *Nth. Munster Antiq. J*, 13, 1970, 40–52.

2861 O'RAHILLY, THOMAS F. Irish dialects past and present with chapters on Scottish and Manx. Dublin: Dublin Institute for Advanced Studies 1972. Mainly a photographic reprint of the 1st edition (Dublin, 1932) with the addition of extensive indexes.

2862 ULSTER FOLK MUSEUM. Ulster dialects: an introductory symposium. Holywood: 1964.

2863 WAGNER, HEINRICH. Linguistic atlas and survey of Irish dialects. Dublin: Dublin Institute for Advanced Studies.
vol. 1 Introduction, 1958.
vol. 2. The dialects of Munster, 1964.
vol. 3. The dialects of Connaught, 1966.
vol. 4. The dialects of Ulster and the Isle of Man, specimens of Scottish Gaelic dialects [and] phonetic texts of East Ulster Irish, by Heinrich Wagner and Colm O'Baoill, 1969. For review by Gordon W. MacLennan, see *Stud. Celt.*, 7, 1972, 49–62.

Dictionaries

2864 ATKINSON, ROBERT. Irish lexicography: an introductory lecture. *R. Ir. Acad. Todd lecture ser.*, vol. 2, pt. 1, 1885.

2865 DE BHALDRAITHE, TOMAS. English-Irish dictionary. Baile Atha Cliath: 1959.

2866 DINNEEN, PATRICK STEPHEN. Irish-English dictionary; being a thesaurus of the words, phrases and idioms of the modern Irish language; new rev. ed. Dublin: 1927.

2867 IRISH DICTIONARIES. *Freeman's Journal*, 21 October 1904.

2868 LANE, TIMOTHY O'NEILL. Larger English-Irish dictionary; new rev. ed. Dublin: 1916.

2869 O'DONAILL, NIALL. Focloir Gaeilge-Bearla. Baile Atha Cliath. [1978].

2870 O'REILLY, EDWARD. Irish-English dictionary . . . a new edition . . . with a supplement, containing many thousand words, with their interpretations in English, collected throughout Ireland, and among ancient unpublished manuscripts, by John O'Donovan. Dublin: 1864.

2871 ROYAL IRISH ACADEMY. Dictionary of the Irish language, based mainly on old and middle Irish materials. Dublin: 1913–76. Appeared over the years in parts, some with the title *Dictionary of the Irish language*, the remainder as *Contributions to a dictionary of the Irish language*.

2872 VENDRYES, J. Lexique etymologique de l'irlandais ancien. Dublin and Paris: 1959–. Letters published to date – A, MNOP, RS.

Study and Teaching

2873 HERMATHENA. no. 121, 1976. Modern language teaching in Trinity College, Dublin, 1776–1976. [Special issue].

Grammar

2874 BYRNE, JAMES, *Dean of Clonfert*. Ms. list of grammars, books on language, etc., left by him. [1897.] In Trinity College Library, Dublin.

2875 DE BLACA, SEAMAS. Aims in the study of modern Irish; materials available for self-instruction in Irish: an annotated list. *An*

Feinisc, vol. 1, 1968–69, 39–45. Published by the New York Gaelic Society.

2876 DILLON, MYLES and O CROININ, DONNCHA. Teach yourself Irish. London: 1961. (*Teach yourself books ser.*)

2877 MALONE, SYLVESTER. Recent books on Irish grammar. *Ir. Eccl. Rec., 3rd ser.* 4, 1883, 504–8; 5, 1884, 95–105, 315–22.

2878 THURNEYSEN, RUDOLF. A grammar of old Irish; translated from the German by D.A. Binchy and Osborn Bergin, rev. and enl. ed. Dublin: 1946. Bibliog., pp. xix–xxi.

English

2879 ALDUS, JUDITH BUTLER. Anglo-Irish dialects: a bibliography; enlarged version. *Regional Language Studies*, 7, 1976. Prev. ed. 1969. Contains 238 items and seeks to include most of the published writings on the English language in Ireland and those dealing with Irish English in other areas where it exists.

2880 DOUGLAS, ELLEN. A socio-linguistic study of Articlave, Co. Londonderry — a preliminary report. *Ulster Folk.*, 21, 1975, 55–67.

2881 HOGAN, JEREMIAH J. The English language in Ireland. [Reprint of 1st ed] Maryland: McGrath Publishing Company, 1970. 1st pub. Dublin: Educational Co. of Ireland, 1927.

2882 IRWIN, PATRICK J. Ireland's contribution to the English language. *Studies*, 22, 1933, 637–652.

2883 TRAYNOR, MICHAEL. The English dialect of Donegal: a glossary (incorporating the collections of H.C. Hart (1847–1908)). Dublin: 1953. Bibliog., pp. xv–xvi.

Latin

2884 DRAAK, MAARTJE. The higher teaching of Latin grammar in Ireland during the ninth century. *Mededelingen der Koninklijke Nederlandse Akademie van Wetenschappen, afd. Letterkunde, nieuwe reeks*. Deel 30, no. 4, 1967, 109–144.

Reading

2885 GREANEY, VINCENT. *ed*. Studies in reading. Dublin: The Educational Company of Ireland Ltd. 1977.

Philologists

2886 BERGIN, OSBORN.
BINCHY, D.A. Osborn Bergin. Dublin: Univ. College, 1970. (*Osborn Bergin Memorial Lecture no. 1*).

2887 BEST, RICHARD IRVINE. Bibliography of the publications of Richard Irvine Best. *Celtica*, 5, 1960, v–x.

2888 DILLON, MYLES.
BAUMGARTEN, ROLF. Myles Dillon (1900–1972), a bibliography. *Celtica*, 11, 1976, 1–14. Vol. 11 is a memorial volume for Myles Dillon.

2889 DINNEEN, PATRICK STEPHEN.
O CONLUAIN, PROINSIAS, *and* O CEILEACHAIR, DONNCHA. An Duinneneach: an tAthair Padraig O Duinnin, a shaol, a shaotar agus an re inar mhair se. Baile Atha Cliath: 1958. A shaotar litoartha . . . pp. 269–375.

2890 LYNEGAR, CHARLES.
RISK, M.H. Charles Lynegar, Professor of the Irish Language, [Trinity College, Dublin] 1712. *Hermathena*, 102, 1966, 16–25.

2891 MCNEILL, EOIN.
MacNeill papers: catalogue of an exhibition of manuscript letters from the collection of the late Eoin MacNeill [held in University College, Dublin]. Dublin: 1959. Material mainly confined to the Gaelic League and the Irish language.

2892 MEYER, KUNO.
BEST, RICHARD IRVINE. Bibliography of the publications of Kuno Meyer. *Zeit. fur celt. philol.*, 15, 1924, 1–65.

2893 — SCHULZE, WILHELM. Kuno Meyer, 1858–1919. *Studies*, 9, 1920, 291–297.

2894 MURPHY, GERARD.
O'C[UIV], B[RIAN]. Bibliography of the publications of Gerard Murphy, connected with Irish studies. *Eigse*, vol. 10, pt. 1, 1961, 2–10.

2895 POKORNY, JULIUS.
Beitrage zur Indogermanistik und Keltologie: Julius Pokorny zum 80. Geburtstag gewidmet. Herausgegeban von Wolfgang Meid. *Innsbrucker Beitrage zur Kulturwissenschaft*. Bd. 13, 1967. Bibliographie der

wissenchaftlichen Veroffentulichungen von Julius Pokorny, zusammengestellt von Hans Schmeja. pp. 323–332.

2896 — Julius Pokorny (1887–1970): obituary, by C.R.C. *Celtica*, 9, 1971, 343–5.

2897 — Julius Pokorny (1800 (sic)–1970) obituary, by T. Arwyn William. *Stud. Celt.*, 6, 1971, 195–6.

2898 QUIGGIN, E.C.
Poems from *The Book of the Dean of Lismore*, by E.C. Quiggin. Cambridge: 1937. Publications of E.C. Quiggin, pp. xi–xii.

2899 STOKES, WHITLEY.
BEST, RICHARD IRVINE. Bibliography of the publications of Whitley Stokes. *Zeit. fur celt. philol.*, 8, 1911, 351–406. The Whitley Stokes Library on Celtic philology is in University College Library, London.

2900 STRACHAN, JOHN.
MEYER, KUNO. John Strachan [with list of publications]. *Eriu*, 3, 1907, 202–6.

2901 THURNEYSEN, RUDOLF.
HEIERMEIER, A. Bibliographie der Wissenschaftlichen Veroffentlichungen Rudolf Thurneysen. *Deutsche Gesellschaft für Celtische Studien, Schriftenreibe* (no. 10). Halle (Salle): 1942.

2902 — RYAN, JOHN. Rudolf Thurneysen: 1857–1940. *Studies*, 29, 1940, 583–590.

2903 VENDRYES, J.
LOICA, J. Bibliographie de J. Vendryes: complement pour 1952–1960. *Etudes Celt.*, 20, 1963, 349–353. Includes a note of previous bibliographies.

2904 WILLIAMS, SIR IVOR.
DAVIES, ALUN EIRUG. Sir Ivor Williams: a bibliography. *Stud. Celt.*, 4, 1969, 1–55. Sir Ivor Williams (1881–1965) is generally acknowledged as one of the outstanding Celtic scholars of his age.

2905 ZIMMER, HEINRICH.
LEWIS, TIMOTHY. A bibliography of the published works of the late Dr. Heinrich Zimmer, professor of Celtic philology in the University of Berlin. Reprinted from *J. Welsh Bibliog. Soc.*, vol. 1, pt. 2, 1911. For *Addenda*, by R.I. Best, see *Zeit. fur celt. philol.*, 8, 1912, 593–4.

SCIENCE

Bibliography

2906 BIBLIOTHECA CHEMICO-MATHEMATICA: catalogue of works in many tongues on exact and applied science, with a subject index . . . London: 1921. 2 vols. First supplement, 1932; second supplement, 1937, 2 vols.; third supplement, 1952.

2907 QUEEN'S COLLEGE LIBRARY, BELFAST. Department of mathematics and natural philosophy. Catalogue of books. Belfast: 1856.

2908 QUEEN'S UNIVERSITY OF BELFAST, SCIENCE LIBRARY. Guide to subject literature. 2nd ed.: 1970. (*Information bulletin no*. 1).

2909 ROYAL DUBLIN SOCIETY LIBRARY. General index to the printed proceedings of the Dublin Society in 50 volumes. Dublin: 1814. Covers period 1764–1813; another edition, covering the first 61 volumes. Dublin: 1826, for period 1764–1825.

2910 — Index to the Scientific Proceedings and Transactions of the Royal Dublin Society from 1877 to 1898 inclusive. Dublin: 1899.

2911 — Index to the Scientific Proceedings and Transactions . . . from 1898 to 1909 inclusive. Dublin: 1910.

2912 — Index to the Scientific Proceedings . . . new ser. from 1910 to 1949 inclusive. Dublin: 1958.

2913 — Index to the Scientific Proceedings . . . new ser. from 1950 to 1957 inclusive. Dublin 1961.

2914 — A bibliography of the publications of the Royal Dublin Society from 1731 to 1951, 2nd rev. ed. with index. Dublin: 1953. A comprehensive list dealing with publications of the Society which did not appear in the Scientific Proceedings or Transactions.

2915 ROYAL IRISH ACADEMY. An index to the Transactions of the Royal Irish Academy from 1786 to the present time, by N. Carlisle. London: 1813. An index to the Proceedings, vols. 1–7, 1836–61, compiled by William Reeves, is contained in vol. 7, 1861.

2916 — List of papers published in the Transactions, Cunningham Memoirs and Irish Mss. series . . . 1786–1886, compiled by Robert MacAlister. 1887.

2917 — Index to . . . Transactions, Proceedings, Cunningham Memoirs, Todd Lecture series [and Irish Mss. series] from 1786 to 1906. Dublin: 1912.

2918 — Index to the serial publications . . . from 1907 to 1932. Dublin: 1934.

2919 — Index to the serial publications . . . from 1932 to 1953. Dublin: 1959.

2920 ROYAL SOCIETY OF LONDON. Catalogue of scientific papers, 1800–1900. London: 1867–1925. 19 vols.

2921 ST. PATRICK'S COLLEGE, MAYNOOTH. Souvenir catalogue [of an] exhibition illustrating some Irish contributions to the progress of the arts and science. 1953. Supplement, 1954. Typescript.

2922 — Third Tostal display souvenir catalogue, 1955. Typescript; revised and enl. ed. of the previous catalogues.

2923 SCIENCE MUSEUM LIBRARY. List of science library bibliographical series. London: 1955. Typescript, covering nos. 1–757, 1930–57; a list and index to nos. 1–555, by Samuel Baig, appears in *New York P.L. Bull.*, 46, 1942, 707–31.

2924 — Select references on Irish science. n.d. (*Science Library bibliog. ser.* no. 42.) Period covered 1882–1931.

Periodicals

2925 BRITISH UNION CATALOGUE OF PERIODICALS: a record of the periodicals of the world, from the seventeenth century to the present day in British libraries. London: 1955–9. 4 vols. Supplements to date.

2926 IRISH ASSOCIATION FOR DOCUMENTATION AND INFORMATION SERVICES. Union list of current periodicals and serials in Irish libraries, 1974, compiled by Larairiona Duignan, Dublin: 1974. 2 vols.

2927 KIRKPATRICK, T. PERCY C. The periodical publications of science in Ireland. *Bibliog. Soc. Ir.*, vol. 2, no. 3, 1921.

2928 NATIONAL LIBRARY OF IRELAND. List of scientific and technical periodicals in Dublin libraries: 1929. Lists holdings of eighteen special libraries.

2929 ROYAL DUBLIN SOCIETY LIBRARY. Catalogue of scientific and technical periodicals, containing the publications of learned societies and institutions in the natural, physical, mathematical, and medical sciences, and in technology, to the end of the year 1907. Dublin: 1909.

2930 — List of current periodicals and serials. Dublin: 1953. Typescript.

2931 SCUDDER, SAMUEL H. Catalogue of scientific serials of all countries including the transactions of learned societies in the natural, physical and mathematical sciences, 1633–1876. Cambridge: Mass., 1879. (*Library of Harvard Univ. special pub.*, no. 1.)

2932 UNITED NATIONS EDUCATIONAL, SCIENTIFIC AND CULTURAL ORGANIZATION, Department of natural sciences. List of scientific and technical periodicals published in Ireland currently received in the Royal Irish Academy, Dublin: 1953. (Ref. 280/3416.)

2933 WORLD LIST OF SCIENTIFIC PERIODICALS, published in the years 1900–1960; 4th ed., by Peter Brown and George B. Stratton. London: 1964.

Teaching

2934 WALLACE, JUSTIN. Science teaching in Irish Schools, 1860–1970. *Ir. J. Education*, vol. 6, no. 1, 1972, 50–64.

2935 WILLIAMS, W.J. The Shannon scheme and the teaching of science: a plea for realism in education [with comments by the Rev. Edward Leen, John J. Nolan, and Hugh Ryan]. *Studies*, 15, 1926, 177–192.

Research Information

2936 INSTITUTE FOR INDUSTRIAL RESEARCH AND STANDARDS, TECHNICAL INFORMATION DIVISION. Sources of scientific and technical information in Ireland. Dublin: Institute for Industrial Research and Standards, 1972.

2937 NATIONAL SCIENCE COUNCIL. Research and development in Ireland, 1969, by Diarmuid Murphy and Donal O'Brolchain. Dublin: Stationery Office, 1971.

2938 — Register of Scientific research personnel, compiled by Diarmuid Murphy and Donal

O'Brolchain. 2nd ed. Dublin: Stationery Office, 1971. Produced in conjunction with the Royal Irish Academy; 1st ed. published by the Royal Irish Academy, 1968.

2939 — Ireland, background report on Science and Technology, compiled by Diarmuid Murphy. Dublin: 1972. Prepared as one of the basic documents for the Review of Irish Science Policy being conducted jointly by the National Science Council (on behalf of the Irish Government) and the Organisation for Economic Co-operation and Development (OECD) in 1972.

2940 — Fellowships and scholarships available to Irish scientists and technologists, compiled by Diarmuid Murphy and Michael Fitzgerald. Dublin: 1973.

2941 — Scientific and Technical Information in Ireland: a review. Dublin. Supplement I. Manpower developments in Scientific Information and Documentation Services, 1970 and 1975; a comparative analysis, 1977. List of Publications of the National Science Council [1969–1977] pp. 31–32.

2942 — Scientific and Technical Information in Ireland: financial resources devoted to S.T.I.D. in Ireland, 1975; a report presented to the Documentation Co-ordinating Committee of the National Science Council, by Ross Cooper and Norman Wood. Dublin: 1978.

2943 — Scientific and technical information in Ireland: the findings of the national documentation use study — a report presented to the Documentation Co-ordinating Committee of the National Science Council, by Barre Carroll and Norman Wood. Dublin: 1978. 2 vols.

History

2944 BARNARD, T.C. The Hartlib circle and the origins of the Dublin Philosophical Society. *Ir. Hist. Stud*., 19, 1974, 56–71.

2945 — Miles Symner and the new learning in seventeenth century Ireland. *R. Soc. Antiq. Ir. J*., 102, 1972, 129–142.

2946 BARRETT, W.F. A historical sketch of the Royal College of Science from its foundation to the year 1900. Dublin: 1907.

2947 BARRY, VINCENT. The place of the Academy in contemporary Ireland. *R. Ir. Acad. Presidential Address*, 1970.

2948 CLARKE, DESMOND. The contribution of the Royal Dublin Society to science and technology in Ireland. *Admin*., 15, 1967, 25–34.

2949 — An outline of the history of science in Ireland. *Studies*, 62, 1973, 287–302.

2950 HALLIWELL, JAMES ORCHARD. Collection of notes on the early history of science in Ireland. *R. Ir. Acad. Proc*., 2, 1840–44, 66–73.

2951 HOPPER, K. THEODORE. The Common scientist in the seventeenth century: a study of the Dublin Philosophical Society, 1683–1708. London: 1970. Bibliog., pp. 212–228.

2952 — The Hartlib circle and the origins of the Dublin Philosophical Society. *Ir. Hist. Stud*., 20, 1976, 40–48.

2953 KELHAM, BRIAN B. The Royal College of Science for Ireland (1867–1926). *Studies*, 56, 1967, 297–309.

2954 KIERNAN, COLIN. Swift and Science. *Hist. J*., 14, 1971, 709–722. On Swift's opposition to Newtonian Science.

2955 MCLAUGHLIN, *The* REV. PATRICK J. A century of science in the I.E.R.: Monsignor [Gerald] Molloy, and Father [Henry V.] Gill. *Ir. Eccles., Rec*., 102, 1964, 251–261.

2956 O'hEOCHA, C. New moves in Irish Science. *Eire-Ir*., vol. 8, no. 3, 1973, 95–103. Reprinted from *Nature*, 243, 1973, 132–134.

2957 WHITE, J.H. BANTRY. History of the science and art institutions. *Mus. Bull*., vol. 1, pt. 4, 1911, 7–34; vol. 2, 1912, 41–44.

Biography

2958 GILLESPIE, CHARLES COULSTON. *ed*. Dictionary of scientific biography. New York: Charles Scribner's, 1970–72. 6 vols.

2959 O'DONNELL, SEAN. Early Irish scientists. *Eire-Ir*., vol. 11, no. 1, 1976, 122–26. Short account covering John Duns Scotus Erigena, Archbishop James Ussher, Robert Boyle, George Berkeley, Richard Lovell Edgeworth, Richard Kirwan, William Higgins, Peter Woulfe, Adair Crawford, William James MacNevin.

2960 O'DONNELL, SEAN. Famous Irish Scientists. 1. Robert Boyle, the first chemist. *Technol. Ir.* vol. 7, no. 7, 1975, 47–48.

2961 2. R.L. Edgeworth — the learned squire. *ibid*., vol. 7, no. 9, 1975, 43–44.

2962 3. Kirwan and Higgins — the emergent natives. *ibid*., vol. 7, no. 10, 1975, 47–48.

2963 4. [William James] MacNevin and [Josias Christopher] Gamble. *ibid*., vol. 7, no. 12, 1976, 47–48.

2964 5. Nicholas Callan — the electrician priest. *ibid*., vol. 8, no. 2, 1976, 47–48.

2965 6. Sir Robert Kane — resources pioneer. *ibid*., vol. 8, no. 6, 1976, 39–40.

2966 7. William Rowan Hamilton: mathematician supreme. *ibid*., vol. 8, no. 9, 1976, 51–2.

2967 8. William of Rosse: the gifted amateur. *ibid*., vol. 8, no. 11, 1977, 55–56.

2968 9. George Gabriel Stokes — viscosity pioneer. *ibid*., vol. 9, no. 1, 1977, 55–56.

2969 10. Kelvin — the supreme mechanist. *ibid*., vol. 9, nos. 4–5, 1977, 51–2.

2970 [11]. John Joly — geological pioneer. *ibid*., vol. 9, no. 6, 1977, 47–48.

2971 [12]. Tyndall's light effect. *ibid*., vol. 9, no. 8, 1977, 43–44. John Tyndall of Carlow, 1820–1893.

2972 [13]. The Engineering revolution of Robert Mallet. *ibid*., vol. 9, no. 10, 1978, 31.

2973 QUEEN'S UNIVERSITY OF BELFAST. Science Library. Catalogue to the 1st exhibition of Irishmen in science and engineering . . . 1973. Lord Kelvin, Sir William Rowan Hamilton, George Johnstone Stoney. Catalogue to the 2nd exhibition . . . April, 1974. William Parsons, John Joly, Robert Boyle. Catalogue to the 3rd exhibition . . . November, 1974. Sir John MacNeill, John B. Dunlop, Harry Ferguson. Catalogue to the 4th exhibition . . . February, 1976. George Francis Fitzgerald, Francis Beaufort, John Phillip Holland. Catalogue to the 5th exhibition . . . Robert Lloyd Praeger [and] Sir Hans Sloane. [Compiled by Sheila Landy]. 1977.

2974 SPENCER, JOHN E. The Scientific work of Robert Charles Geary. *Econ. Soc. Rev*., 7, 1976, 233–241. Published works of R.C. Geary. *ibid*., 243–247.

MATHEMATICS

2975 BALL, ROBERT.
BALL, W. VALENTINE. *ed.* Reminiscences and letters of Sir Robert Ball. London: 1915. *Catalogue Raisonné of Sir Robert Ball's mathematical papers,* by E.T. Whittaker, pp. 388–96.

2976 BOOLE, GEORGE.
— Celebration of the centenary of *The Laws of Thought*. [10 papers.] *R. Ir. Acad. Proc. Sec. A*, 57, 1954–6, 63–130.

2977 — BARRY, PATRICK D. George Boole: a miscellany. Cork: 1969.

2978 — CYPRUS, JOEL HOWARD. Optimal synthesis of the Boolean functions of four variables with majority logic. [with bibliog.] *Rice Univ. Stud*., vol. 50, no. 2, 1964, 1–110.

2979 — GRIDGEMAN, N.T. In praise of Boole. *New. Sci*., 24, 1964, 655–657.

2980 — LAITA, LUIS M. The Influence of Boole's search for a universal method in analysis on the creation of his logic. *Ann. Sci*., 34, 1977, 163–176.

2981 EDGEWORTH, F.Y.
BOWLEY, A.L. F.Y. Edgeworth's contribution to mathematical statistics. London, Royal Statistical Society, 1928. Annotated bibliog., pp. 129–39.

2982 GRAVES, JOHN THOMAS.
DORLING, ALISON R. The Graves Mathematical Collection in University College, London. *Ann. Sci*., 33, 1976, 307–309. Includes 14,000 items collected by John Thomas Graves (1808–1870).

2983 HAMILTON, WILLIAM ROWAN.
— CONWAY, A.W. The influence of the work of Sir William Rowan Hamilton on modern mathematical thought. *R. Ir. Acad. Proc., new ser*., 20, 1930–3, 125–8.

2984 — GRAVES, ROBERT PERCEVAL. Life of Sir William Rowan Hamilton . . . including selections from his poems, correspondence, and miscellaneous writings. Dublin and London, 1882–9. 3 vols. Bibliog., vol. 3, pp. 645–58.

2985 — LANCZOS, C. William Rowan Hamilton — an appreciation. *Univ. Rev*., vol. 4, no. 2, 1967, 151–166.

2986 — McCONNELL, DR. A.J. William Rowan Hamilton. *Adv. Sci*, vol. 14, no. 56, 1958, 323–332.

2987 — MACLAUGHLIN, *The* REV. P.J. Centenary of the discovery of quaternions. *Studies*, 32, 1943, 441–456.

2988 McCONNELL, A.J. The Dublin Mathematical School in the first half of the nineteenth century; an address delivered in the Academy at the Quaternion centenary meeting, 8 November 1944. *R. Ir. Acad. Proc. Sec. A*, 50, 1944–5, 75–88.

2989 MACFARLANE, ALEXANDER. Bibliography of quaternions and allied systems of mathematics. Dublin: 1904. (*International Association for promoting the study of quaternions and allied systems of mathematics*.)

2990 PARKE, NATHAN GRIER. Guide to the literature of mathematics and physics including related works on engineering science. New York and London: 1947.

2991 RONAYNE, PHILIP.
Dickson, David. Philip Ronayne and the publication of his *Treatise of Algebra* [1717 and 1727 eds.]. *Longroom*, 8, 1973, 13–18. [Ronayne, b. in Co. Cork, 1683].

Calculators, Computers

2992 FOSTER, F.G. *and others*. Computers in Ireland, by F.G. Foster assisted by F. Land, J.A. Moynihan and M.G. Tutty. Dublin: Economic and Social Research Institute, 1971. (*paper no*. 58).

2993 RANDELL, BRIAN. Ludgate's analytical machine of 1909. *Univ. of Newcastle upon Tyne. Computing Laboratory, Technical Report Series, no. 15*. Also appeared in *Computer journal*, vol. 14, 1971: contains a bibliographical account of Percy E. Ludgate.

ASTRONOMY

2994 BEESLEY, D.E. Formation of the Irish Astronomical Association. *Ir. Astron. J.*, vol. 12, nos. 5–6, 1976, 216–7.

2995 CROWE, DOLORES. Thomas Romney Robinson (1792–1882), Director of Armagh Observatory (1823–1882) [with bibliog.]. *Ir. Astron. J.*, vol. 10, no. 3, 1971, 93–101.

2996 DIXON, F.E. Dunsink observatory and its astronomers. *Dublin Hist. Rec.*, 11, 1949–50, 33–50.

2997 ESPOSITO, MARIO, *ed*. An unpublished astronomical treatise by the Irish monk Dicuil. *R. Ir. Acad. Proc., Sec. C*, 26, 1906–7, 378–446.

2998 GREW, SHEELAGH. Eamon de Valera and Armagh Observatory. *Ir. Astron. J.*, vol. 12, nos. 5–6, 1976, 204–5.

2999 HOUZEAU, J.C. and LANCASTER, H. Bibliographie genérale de l'astronomie. Bruxelles: 1882–9. 2 vols.

3000 IRISH ASTRONOMICAL JOURNAL. Vol. 1–, 1950–. For suggestions for a bibliography of Irish astronomy and astronomers, see editorial, vol. 5, 1958–9, 217.

3001 IRISH ASTRONOMICAL JOURNAL, vol. 12, nos. 3–4, 1975. Memorial issue to Eric Mervyn Lindsay (1907–1974); includes list of his publications.

3002 MCKENNA, SUSAN M.P. Astronomy in Ireland from 1780, [with bibliog.], *In* Vistas in astronomy, edited by Arthur Beer. vol. 9, 1968, 283–296.

3003 MCLAUGHLIN, PATRICK J. The 'prelections' of Nicholas Callan (1799–1864). *Ir. Astron. J.*, 6, 1963–64, 249–252.

3004 MOORE, PATRICK. Armagh Observatory: a history, 1790–1967. Armagh: 1967. Bibliog., pp. 58–61.

3005 — The Astronomy of Birr Castle. London: 1971. Bibliog., pp. 79–81.

3006 MURPHY, FRANK. Sir Robert Ball, royal astronomer. *Dublin Hist. Rec.*, vol. 26, no. 4, 1973, 147–153.

3007 O'CONCHEANAINN, THOMAS. The scribe of the Irish astronomical tract in R.I.A. B II 1, *Celtica*, 11, 1976, 158–167.

3008 O'CONNOR, F.J. Solar eclipses visible in Ireland between A.D. 400 and A.D. 1000 (with tables). *R. Ir. Acad. Proc. Sec. A*, 55, 1952–3, 61–72.

3009 OPIK, ERNEST JULIUS. *Irish Astronomical Journal*, vol. 10, *Special Issue*, 1972. Includes biographical account, by E.M. Lindsay, and a classified list of astronomical papers, by Opik, for period 1912–1969.

3010 PARSONS, LAURENCE MICHAEL HARVEY, *6th Earl of Rosse*. William Parsons, 3rd Earl of Rosse. *Hermathena*, 107, 1968, 5–13.

3011 WAYMAN, P.A. Notes on the history of Dunsink Observatory.
1. Henry Ussher at Dunsink, 1783 to 1790.
2. The visitation book of Dunsink Observatory, 1791–1924.
3. The Arnold clocks. *Ir. Astron. J.*, 10, 1971–2, 121–128, 135–141, 275–281.

3012 — Parson's telescope. (Industrial History — 6). *Technol. Ir.*, vol. 8. no. 10, 1977, 38–40.

SURVEYING, GEODESY

3013 EDEN, PETER, *ed.* Dictionary of land surveyors and local cartographers of Great Britain and Ireland, 1550–1850, compiled from a variety of sources by Francis Steer, John Andrews, Peter Eden, Sean McMenamin, Avril Thomas, and others. London: pt. 1–, 1975–.

3014 HORNER, ARNOLD. The mapping of Ireland. *Ir. Def. J.*, vol. 34, no. 11, 1974, 363–366.

3015 — Some examples of the representation of height data on Irish maps before 1750, including an early use of the spot-height method. *Ir. Geog.*, 7, 1974, 68–80.

3016 IRELAND. Ordnance Survey.
ANDREWS, JOHN H. A paper landscape: the Ordnance Survey in nineteenth-century Ireland. Oxford: 1975. Appendix G. Select list of maps and plans; Appendix H. Published Annual Reports of the Ordnance Survey. For review by J.B. Harley see *Ir. Geog.*, 9, 1976, 137–142.

3017 — CARBERRY, EUGENE. The Irish Ordnance Survey. *An Leab.*, 2, 1931–2, 67–9; 3, 1933, 11–16.

3018 — Notes on a bibliography of the Irish Ordnance; paper read before the *Bibliog. Soc. Ir.*, 27 February 1933.

3019 — CLOSE, CHARLES. The early years of the Ordnance Survey. Newton Abbot: 1969. A reprint with new introduction by J.B. Hartey and with an index added. 1st published Chatham: 1926. Includes account of the Down Survey.

3020 — EDWARDS, R. DUDLEY. Ordnance Survey manuscripts: preliminary report. *Anal. Hib.*, 23, 1966, 279–296.

3021 — GROGAN, DICK. The Ordnance Survey: 150 years on. *Technol. Ir.*, 6, no. 11, 1975, 31–34.

3022 — MACNEILL, NIALL. The Ordnance Survey of Ireland. *Admin.*, 14, 1966, 1–19.

3023 — MADDEN, P.G. The Ordnance Survey of Ireland. *Ir. Sword*, vol. 5, no. 20, 1962, 155–163.

3024 — The geodetic levelling of Ireland. *Eng. J.*, 16, 1963, 338–340.

3025 — MEW, G.H. The work of the Ordnance Survey of the Irish Free State. *Empire Sur. Rev.*, January, 1932.

3026 O'HANLON, JOHN. A general index of the Ordnance Survey records of Irish counties. *R. Soc. Antiq. Ir. J.*, vol. 4–9, 1856–67. See also article on Eugene O'Curry, by the Rev. Timothy Lee, *Limerick Fld. Cl. J.*, vol. 1, no. 3, 1899.

3027 MURPHY, THOMAS. A vertical force magnetic survey of the counties Roscommon, Longford, Westmeath and Meath, with parts of the adjacent counties of Galway, Cavan, Louth and Dublin [with bibliog.]. Dublin: 1955. (*Dublin Institute for Advanced Studies, School of cosmic physics, geophysical bull.*, no. 11.)

3028 — The gravity base stations for Ireland. Dublin: 1957. (*Dublin Institute for Advanced Studies, School of cosmic physics, geophysical bull.*, no. 14.)

3029 PETTY, WILLIAM. A catalogue of the maps of the 'Down Survey' (arranged under counties) and the barony maps copied by General Vallancey. *Pub. Rec. Ir. 3rd ann. rpt.*, 1813, *supp.*, pp. 502–39.

3030 — The History of the Survey of Ireland commonly called 'The Down Survey', edited by T.A. Larcom. Dublin: Irish Archaeological Society, 1851.

3031 — The maps of the Down Survey [with list of baronies and maps], by Sean O Domhnaill. *Ir. Hist. Stud.*, 3, 1942–3, 381–92. For earlier account of the maps of the Down Survey made by Sir William Petty, and the barony maps of General Vallancey, see *The Monthly Museum*, Dublin, vol. 1, p.489; vol. 2, p. 141, 1814; also *Rep. D.K. Pub. Rec. Ir.*, no. 34, 1902, 22–9.

3032 **Riddihough**, R.P. An analysis of daily magnetic variation in Ireland. *Comm. Dublin Inst. Adv. Stud. Geophys. Bull., Ser. D*, no. 28, 1970.

3033 — A magnetic anomaly map of the area 51°–55°N, 10°–16°W. *ibid.*, no. 34, 1975. Includes Irish Continental Shelf, Porcupine Sea-Bight, Porcupine Bank and adjacent position of Rockall Trough.

3034 — Magnetic map of the Ardara granite and Southern County Donegal. *ibid.*, no. 27, 1969.

3035 — A magnetic map of the continental margin west of Ireland, including part of the Rockall Trough and the Faeroe Plateau. *ibid.*, no. 33, 1975.

3036 — Magnetic surveys off the north coast of Ireland. *R. Ir. Acad. Proc., Sec. B*, vol. 66, no. 3, 1968, 27–41.

3037 **Taylor**, W.R. The Ordnance Survey of Northern Ireland: an outline of the history and present mapping tasks. *Cart. J.*, vol. 6, no. 2, 1969, 87–91.

3038 **Young**, D.G.G. The gravity anomaly map of County Donegal. *Comm. Dublin Inst. Adv. Stud. Geophys. Bull., Ser. D*, no. 26, 1969.

3039 — and **Bailey**, R.J. A reconnaissance magnetic map of the continental margin west of Ireland. *ibid.*, no. 29, 1973.

CARTOGRAPHY, MAPS

3040 **Aalen**, F.H.A. and **Hunter**, R.J. The estate maps of Trinity College: an introduction and annotated catalogue. *Hermathena*, 98, 1964, 85–96.

3041 — Two early seventeenth century maps of Donegal. *R. Soc. Antiq. Ir. J.*, 94, 1964, 199–202.

3042 **Andrews**, **John** H. Baptista Boazio's map of Ireland. *Long Room*, 1, 1970, 29–36.

3043 — Charles Vallancey and the map of Ireland. *Geog. J.*, 132, 1966, 48–61.

3044 — Charles Vallancey and the map of Ireland. *Ir. Def. J.*, vol. 34, no. 11, 1974, 367–370.

3045 — Christopher Saxton and Belfast Lough. *Ir. Geog.*, vol. 5, no. 2, 1965, 1–6.

3046 — An early map of Inishowen. *Long Room*, 7, 1973, 19–25.

3047 — An Elizabethan map of Kilmallock. *Nth. Munster Antiq. J.*, 11, 1968, 27–35.

3048 — Ireland in maps: an introduction, with a catalogue of an exhibition mounted in the Library of Trinity College, Dublin, 1961, by the Geographical Society of Ireland in conjunction with the Ordnance Survey of Ireland. Dublin: 1961. See also Bibliographical postscript in *Ir. Geog.*, vol. 4, no. 4, 1962, 234–243.

3049 — Ireland in maps. *Ir. Wel.*, vol. 13, no. 5, 1965, 19–22. Includes reproduction of John Speed's Map of Ireland.

3050 — The maps of the escheated counties of Ulster, 1609–10. *R. Ir. Acad. Proc., Sec. C*, vol. 74, no. 4, 1974, 133–170. Includes counties Fermanagh, Cavan, Armagh and parts of Londonderry and Louth.

3051 — Medium and message in early six-inch Irish ordnance maps: the case of Dublin city. *Ir. Geog.*, vol. 6, no. 5, 1973, 579–593.

3052 — Patrick Gerard Madden: obituary. *Ir. Geog.*, 7, 1974, 127–8. Cartographer attached to the Ordnance Survey of Ireland.

3053 — Two maps of eighteenth-century Dublin and its surroundings by John Rocque. Lympne Castle [Kent]: 1977.

3054 **Andrews**, **Michael** C. The map of Ireland, A.D. 1300–1700. *Belfast Nat. Hist. Phil. Soc. Proc.*, 1922–3 *session*, pp. 9–33.

3055 **Blake**, **Martin** J. A map of part of the county of Mayo in 1584; with notes thereon, and an account of the author [John Browne], and his descendants. *Galway Arch. Hist. Soc. J.*, 5, 1907–8, 145–58.

3056 **Bowen**, B.P. John Rocque's maps of Dublin. *Dublin Hist. Rec.*, 9, 1946–8, 117–27.

3057 **Catalogue Of Maps And Plans** relating to Ireland in H.M. State Paper Office, Whitehall, London. *Ulster J. Arch.*, 3, 1855, 272–6.

3058 **Chubb**, **Thomas**. The printed maps in the atlases of Great Britain and Ireland: a bibliography, 1579–1870. [Facsimile reprint]. London: 1974. 1st published London: 1927.

3059 **Corry**, **Somerset** R. **Lowry**, *Earl of Bel-*

more. Ancient maps of Enniskillen and its environs. *Ulster J. Arch*., 2, 1896, 218–43.

3060 — Descriptive notes on the Irish historical atlas, 1609. Belfast: 1903.

3061 DAVIS, A.G. Notes on Sir Richard John Griffith's geological maps of Ireland. *Soc. Bibliog. Nat. Hist. J*., vol. 2, pt. 6, 1950, 209–11. Contains a list of the 'issues' of Griffith's *Geological map of Ireland*. See also *R. Geol. Soc. Ir. J., new ser*., vol. 5, 1877–80, 132–48.

3062 DUNLOP, ROBERT. Sixteenth-century maps of Ireland [in the British Museum, Public Record Office, Trinity College, Dublin, and elsewhere]. *English Hist. Rev*., 20, 1905, 309–37.

3063 EWART, LAVENS M. Belfast maps: a record of plans of the town chronologically arranged, with a copy of Ms. plan of Belfast [A.D. 1680] in the British Museum [1660–1894]. *Ulster J. Arch*., 1, 1895, 62–9, 99–105.

3064 FORDHAM, HERBERT GEORGE. Handlist of catalogues and works of reference relating to carto-bibliography and kindred subjects for Great Britain and Ireland, 1720–1927. Cambridge: 1928.

3065 — Notes on British and Irish itineraries and road books. Hertford: 1912.

3066 — The road books and itineraries of Ireland, 1647 to 1850: a catalogue. *Bibliog. Soc. Ir*., vol. 2, no. 4, 1923, 63–76.

3067 FREY, J. A catalogue of the eighteenth and early nineteenth century estate maps in the Antrim Estate Office, Glenarm, Co. Antrim. *Ulster J. Arch., 3rd ser*., 16, 1953, 93–103.

3068 GREAT BRITAIN. Public Record Office. Maps and plans in the Public Record Office. London. 1. British Isles, *c*. 1410–1860. 1967. Ireland, pp. 547–593.

3069 GREEN, E.R.R. A catalogue of the estate maps, etc., in the Downshire Office, Hillsborough, Co. Down. *Ulster J. Arch., 3rd ser*., 12, 1949, 1–25. Includes Down, Wicklow, Kildare, and King's County (Offaly).

3070 HARDIMAN, JAMES. A catalogue of maps, charts, plans, etc., in the library of Trinity College, Dublin. *R. Ir. Acad. Trans*., 14, 1825, 57–77.

3071 HAYES-MCCOY, G.A. *ed*. Ulster and other Irish maps, *c*. 1600. Dublin, 1964. 23 maps, 15 dealing mainly with areas in Ulster, 6 of places in Munster, 1 of part of the Outer Hebrides and a plan of Dublin Castle, and includes 12 maps of Richard Bartlett or Barthelet.

3072 HORE, HERBERT F. Notes on a facsimile of an ancient map of Leix, Ofaly, Irry, (sic) etc., in the British Museum. *Kilkenny S. E. Ir. Arch. Soc. J*., 7, 1863, 345–72.

3073 HORNER, ARNOLD. New maps of Co. Kildare in the National Library of Ireland. *Kildare Arch. Soc. J*., vol. 15, no. 5, 1975–6, 473–489.

3074 HUGHES, T. JONES. The six inches to the mile ordnance survey townland map. *Assoc. Geog. Teach. Ir. J*., 1, 1964, 11–17.

3075 HULL, EDWARD. Palaeo-geological and geographical maps of the British Islands and the adjoining parts of the continent of Europe. *R. Dublin Soc. Sci Trans., ser*. 2, vol. 1, 1877–83, 257–96.

3076 IRELAND. Ordnance Survey. Catalogue of the maps and plans and other publications of the Ordnance Survey of Ireland. London: 1862.

3077 — Catalogue of the county maps and town plans and other publications of Ireland, of the Ordnance Survey of the United Kingdom, to January 1908. London: 1908.

3078 — Catalogue of the maps and other publications of the Ordnance Survey Department, Dublin, at 30 June 1927. Dublin: 1927.

3079 — Catalogue of the maps and other publications of the Ordnance Survey of Saorstat Éireann. Dublin: 1933.

3080 — Catalogue of the maps and Ordnance Survey publications. rev. ed., 1949. Dublin: 1949.

3081 — Catalogue of the large-scale maps with dates of survey and latest revision shown on the indexes to each county. Dublin: 1964.

3082 — Catalogue of small scale maps and charts, 1968. Dublin: 1968.

3083 KERRY, *earl of*. The Lansdowne maps of the Down Survey. *R. Ir. Acad. Proc., Sec. C*, 35, 1918–20, 385–407.

3084 LETT, H.W. Maps of the mountains of Mourne. *Ulster J. Arch.*, 8, 1902, 133–7.

3085 LYNAM, EDWARD. Baptista Boazio's Irish maps: appendix to 'English maps and map makers of the sixteenth century'. *Geog. J.*, 116, 1950, 23–5.

3086 MACCARTHY, C.J.F. Maps and plans of Cork interest. *Cork Hist. Arch. Soc. J.*, 73, 1968, 72–3.

3087 MCCROSSAN, J.L. Notes on some Dublin city maps. *Ir. Book Lov.*, 26, 1938–9, 2–8.

3088 MACGIOLLA PHADRAIG, BRIAN. Speed's Plan of Dublin. *Dublin Hist. Rec.*, 10, 1948–9, 89–105.

3089 MAPS OF IRELAND. See lists in 'Sale catalogue of the library of William Monck Mason', March 29, 1858, p. 71, etc.; and 'Catalogue of the library of Dr. Thomas Willis', sold by John Fleming Jones, Dublin, November 22, 1876, pp. 99–105; also 'Notes on old Irish maps', *Ulster J. Arch.*, 4, 1856, 118–27.

3090 MURPHY, THOMAS and RYAN, ROISIN. The latitudes and longitudes of the six-inch sheet maps of Ireland [with bibliog.]. Dublin: 1906. (*Dublin Institute for Advanced Studies, School of cosmic physics, geophysical bull.*, no. 13.)

3091 NORTHERN IRELAND. Ordnance Survey. The ordnance maps of Northern Ireland, rev. ed. Belfast: 1962.

3092 — Map catalogue. Belfast: 1968.

3093 NORTHERN IRELAND. Public Record Office. How to use the Record Office. [Belfast, *c.* 1969].
Leaflet no.
11. Maps and plans, *c.* 1570–*c.*1830, Co. Antrim.
12. Maps and surveys, *c.*1600–*c.*1830, Co. Armagh.
13. Maps and plans, *c.*1600–*c.*1830, Co. Down.
14. Maps and plans, *c.* 1590–*c.*1830, Co. Fermanagh.
15. Maps and plans, *c.*1600–*c.*1830, Co. Londonderry.
16. Maps and plans, *c.*1580–*c.*1830, Co. Tyrone.
17. Maps and plans, *c.*1570–*c.*1860, Belfast.
18. General maps of Ireland and Ulster, *c.*1538–*c.*1830.

3094 ORPEN, GODDARD H. Ptolemy's map of Ireland. *R. Soc. Antiq. Ir. J.*, 24, 1894, 115–28.

3095 ROBINSON, ARTHUR H. The 1837 maps of Henry Drury Harkness. *Geog. J.*, 121, 1955, 440–50.

3096 RODGERS, E.M. The large scale county maps of the British Isles, 1596–1850. 2nd ed., Oxford: 1972. 1st ed., Oxford: 1960.

3097 ROYAL IRISH ACADEMY. John O'Donovan, 1806–61; Eugene O'Curry, 1794–1862; centenary celebration, September 12 to October 7, 1961 [exhibition catalogue]. Dublin, 1961. Nos. 1–16, Bibliographical and personal material; nos. 17–37, The Ordnance Survey; nos. 38–46, O'Donovan and O'Curry as scribes; nos. 47–58, Historical and editorial work; nos. 59–61, Letters; no. 62, A display of publications by or concerning O'Donovan and O'Curry.

3098 SKELTON, R.A. County atlases of the British Isles, 1579–1850: a bibliography. London. vol. 1, 1579–1703. 1970.

3099 SMITH, THOMAS R. and THOMAS, BRADFORD L. Maps of the 16th to 19th centuries in the University of Kansas Libraries: an analytical carto-bibliography. 1963. (*Univ. Kansas pub., library ser.*, no. 16) Ireland, pp. 103–111.

3100 SWANTON, WILLIAM. Maps of Carrickfergus. *Ulster J. Arch.*, 2, 1895, 2–3.

3101 TAYLOR, GEORGE and SKINNER, ANDREW. Maps of the roads of Ireland. 2nd ed. photolithographic facsimile; introduction by J.H. Andrews. Shannon: 1969. Reprint of 2nd ed., London: 1783.

3102 TRENCH, W.F. *and others*. Notes on the pictorial map of Galway. *Galway Arch. Hist. Soc. J.*, 4, 1905–6, 41–8, 133–60.

3103 ULSTER MUSEUM. Three hundred years of Irish printed maps [exhibition catalogue]. Belfast: 1972.

3104 WARD, FRANCIS A. National Library of Ireland: exhibition of Irish maps. *Ir. Lib. Bull., new ser.*, 10, 1949, 65–8.

3105 WESTROPP, THOMAS JOHNSON. Early Italian maps of Ireland from 1300 to 1600 with notes on foreign settlers and trade. *R. Ir. Acad. Proc., Sec. C*, 30, 1912–13, 361–428.

3106 WHITAKER, HAROLD. The Harold Whitaker collection of county atlases, road-books and maps presented to the University of Leeds: a catalogue. Leeds: 1947.

PHYSICS

3107 DUBLIN INSTITUTE FOR ADVANCED STUDIES, School of Theoretical Physics. Books acquired for the library up to June 1950. Typescript; supplements issued at frequent intervals.

3108 — Fifteen Year report, 29 October 1940 to 31 March 1955. Appendix 1. Publications; Appendix 2. Biographies.

3109 — SYNGE, J.L. The Dublin Institute for Advanced Studies. *Nature*, vol. 218, no. 5144, 1968, 838–840.

3110 McLAUGHLIN, P.J. Some contemporaries of Faraday and Henry. *R. Ir. Acad. Proc., Sec. A*, vol. 64, no. 2, 1964, 17–35. Dr. Patrick Murphy, Frederick William McClintock, Robert Kane, Robert Mallet, James William McGauley, Frederick William Mullins, Nicholas Joseph Callan.

3111 ST. PATRICK'S COLLEGE, MAYNOOTH, Museum. Third Tostal display souvenir catalogue, 1955. Pt. 40: Irish contributions to the development of electromagnetism.

Physicists

3112 CALLAN, NICHOLAS J.
HEATHCOTE, NIELS H. DE V. N.J. Callan, inventor of the induction coil. *Ann. Sci.*, 21, 1965, 145–167.

3113 — McLAUGHLIN, P.J. Nicholas Callan, priest-scientist, 1799–1864. Dublin: 1965.

3114 — MURPHY, PATRICK A. Nicholas Callan — his work and times. *Ir. Eccles. Rec.*, 101, 1964, 404–406.

3115 CONWAY, ARTHUR WILLIAM.
McCONNELL, JAMES. *ed.* Selected papers of Arthur William Conway. Dublin: 1953.

3116 — WHITTAKER, EDMUND T. Arthur William Conway, 1875–1950. Reprinted without change of pagination from *Obituary notices of the Royal Society*, vol. 7, 1951. Bibliog., pp. 339–40.

3117 FITZGERALD, GEORGE FRANCIS.
LARMOR, JOSEPH *ed*. The scientific writings of the late George Francis Fitzgerald . . . Dublin and London: 1902.

3118 KELVIN, *Baron*.
Glasgow University. Kelvin papers: index to the manuscript collection of William Thomson, Baron Kelvin, in Glasgow University Library. Glasgow: 1977. 'Unless stated otherwise the letters are addressed to Thomson'.

3119 — University of Cambridge Library. Catalogue of the manuscript collections of Sir Gabriel Stokes and Sir William Thomson, Baron Kelvin of Largs, in Cambridge University Library, compiled by David B. Wilson. Cambridge: 1976.

3120 MURPHY, *Dr*. PATRICK.
McLAUGHLIN, P.J. The Irish inventor of the dynamo. *Studies*, 37, 1948, 179–188.

3121 STONEY, GEORGE JOHNSTONE.
O'HARA, J.G. George Johnstone Stoney, F.R.S., and the concept of the electron. *R. Soc. N. & R.*, vol. 29, no. 2, 1975, 265–276.

3122 SYNGE, J.L.
O'RAIFEARTAIGH, L. General relativity: papers in honour of J.L. Synge. Oxford: 1972. Bibliog. of J.L. Synge, pp. 257–265.

3123 THOMSON, JAMES, *Jr*.
O'DONNELL, SEAN. Thomson and Reynolds — the physicists of flow. *Technol. Ir.*, vol. 9, no. 11, 1978, 64–65. James Thomson, Jr., and George Osborne Reynolds; also includes short account of Thomas Andrews and his chemical work.

CHEMISTRY

3124 ANNOTATED BIBLIOGRAPHY OF HISTORY OF CHEMISTRY EXHIBITION. Held at Trinity College, Dublin, 1977 and to be published by the Royal Dublin Society. See Report of the Council for the year 1977, p. 48.

3125 BOLTON, HENRY CARRINGTON. A select bibliography of chemistry, 1492–1892. *Smithsonian Misc. Coll.*, vol. 36, 1893.

3126 — First supplement, *ibid*, vol. 39, 1899. Covers period 1492–1897.

3127 — Second supplement, *ibid*, vol. 44, 1904.

Covers period 1492–1902.

3128 DAVIES, W.J. In praise of Irish chemists: some notable nineteenth-century chemists. *R. Ir. Acad. Proc., Sec. B*, vol. 77, no. 19, 1977, 309–316. Sir Robert Kane, Thomas Andrews, Sir Charles Cameron, Cornelius O'Sullivan and James Emerson Reynolds.

3129 DILLON, THOMAS. The relation of chemical research to the development of our industries. *Studies*, 32, 1943, 45–57.

3130 — A history of Institiud Ceimici na hEireann. [The Institute of Chemistry of Ireland]. *Orbital*, 2, 1966, 40–44; 2, 1967, 21–31.

3131 FERGUSON, JOHN. Bibliotheca chemica: a catalogue of the alchemical, chemical and pharmaceutical books in the collection of the late James Young of Kelly and Durris . . . Glasgow: 1906. 2 vols.

3132 INSTITUTE OF CHEMISTRY OF IRELAND. From 1923–1936 the Chemical Association of Ireland; afterwards the Irish Chemical Association, 1936–1949, and from 1950 the Institute of Chemistry. *Irish Chemical Association Journal*, 1946–49. *The Institute of Chemistry Journal*, vols. 1–4, 1950–56. *Orbital*: official journal of the Institute of Chemistry of Ireland, 1965–.

3133 LETTS, E. A. and BLAKE, R. F. The carbonic anhydride of the atmosphere. *R. Dublin Soc. Sci. Proc., new.ser.*, 9, 1899–1902. Bibliog., pp. 230–70.

3134 MCLAUGHLIN, P. J. The Kirwanian Society (1812–18?). *Studies*, 43, 1954, 441–50. Includes *Some papers read or presented to the Society*, also a list of members.

3135 REILLY, DESMOND. Three centuries of Irish chemists, by Deasmumhan O'Raghallaigh. Cork: 1941. First appeared in *Cork Hist. Arch. Soc. J., 2nd ser.,* 46, 1941, 25–54.

3136 SINGER, DOROTHEA WALEY. Catalogue of Latin and vernacular alchemical manuscripts in Great Britain and Ireland dating from before the sixteenth century. Bruxelles: Union Academique Internationale, 1928–31. 3 vols.

Chemists

3137 ANDREWS, THOMAS
MACKLE, HENRY, and WILSON, CECIL L. Thomas Andrews, (1813–1885). *Endeavour*, vol. 30, no. 109, 1971, 8–10.

3138 OBITUARY OF THOMAS ANDREWS. *R. Ir. Acad. Min. Proc., ser. 2. Pol. Lit. Antiq.*, vol. 2, 1877–80, 131–2.

3139 — RIDDELL, HENRY. Dr. Thomas Andrews: the great chemist and physicist. *Belfast Nat. Hist. Phil. Soc. Proc., session* 1920–21, 107–138.

3140 BLACK, JOSEPH.
MCKIE, DOUGLAS, *ed.* Notes from Doctor Black's lectures on chemistry, 1767/8, by Thomas Cochrane. Wilmslow (Cheshire): Imperial Chemical Industries, 1968. Private circulation.

3141 — On Thos. Cochrane's Ms. notes of Black's chemical lectures, 1767/8. *Ann. Sci.*, 1, 1936, 101–110.

3142 — On some Ms. copies of Black's chemical lectures. *ibid.*, 15, 1959, 65–73; 16, 1960, 1–9; 18, 1962, 87–97; 21, 1965, 209–255; 23, 1967, 1–33.

3143 — and KENNEDY, DAVID. On some letters of Joseph Black and others. *Ann. Sci.*, 16, 1960, 129–170. Mainly consists of letters of Joseph Black to his brother Alexander.

3144 — RIDDELL, HENRY. The great chemist, Joseph Black, his Belfast friends and family connections. *Belfast Nat. Hist. Phil. Soc. Proc., session* 1919–20, pp. 49–88.

3145 BOYLE, ROBERT.
BOAS, MARIE. Robert Boyle and seventeenth century chemistry. London: 1958. Bibliog., pp. 233–5.

3146 — HALL, MARIE. Robert Boyle. *Sci. Amer.*, vol. 217, no. 2, 1967, 97–102.

3147 — MADDISON, R.E.W. Boyle's Hell. *Ann. Sci.*, 20, 1964, 101–110. The preparation of mercuric oxide by calcination.

3148 — O'BRIEN, JOHN J. Samuel Hartlib's influence on Robert Boyle's scientific development. *Ann Sci.*, 21., 1965, 1–14, 257–276.

3149 DAVY, EDMUND.
BARKER, WILLIAM. Memoir of the late Professor Davy. *R. Dublin Soc. J.*, 1, 1856–57, 419–425. Enumerates his most important publications.

3150 HIGGINS, WILLIAM
REILLY, J., and MACSWEENEY, D.T. William Higgins, a pioneer of the atomic theory. *R. Dublin Soc. Sci. Proc., new ser.*, 19, 1928–30, 139–57.

3151 — WHEELER, THOMAS S. William Higgins, chemist (1763–1825). Dublin: 1954. *Reprinted from Studies*, 43, 1954, 78–91, 207–18, 327–38.

3152 — WHEELER, THOMAS., and PARTINGTON, J.R. The life and work of William Higgins, chemist (1763–1825), including reprints of *A comparative view of the phlogistic and antiphlogistic theories*, and *Observations on the atomic theory and electrical phenomena*. Oxford and London: 1960. Includes bibliog. notes and indexes.

3153 MACNEVEN, WILLIAM JAMES.
REILLY, DESMOND. An Irish-American chemist, William James MacNeven, 1763–1841. Reprinted from *Chymia* (Univ. of Pennsylvania), 2, 1949, 17–26.

3154 SIMPSON, MAXWELL.
REILLY, DESMOND. Contributions of Maxwell Simpson (1815–1902), to aliphatic chemical synthesis. Reprinted from *Chymia* (Univ. of Pennsylvania), 4, 1953, 159–70.

3155 TYNDALL, JOHN.
MCMILLAN, N. On John Tyndall's contribution to chemistry and biochemistry. *Orbital*, 1, 1978, 46-53.

GEOLOGY

Bibliography

3156 BRUCK, P. M. Bibliography of the Irish Lower Palaeozoics including the Bray Group. Geological Survey of Ireland. (*Information Circular no. 7*). In preparation.

3157 CHARLESWORTH, J. KAYE. Recent progress in Irish geology [papers published 1924–36]. *Ir. Nat. J.*, 6, 1936–7, 266–74.

3158 — Recent progress in Irish geology [papers published 1937–50]. *Ir. Nat. J.*, 10, 1950–2, 61–71.

3159 — Recent progress in Irish geology [papers published 1950–9]. *Ir. Nat. J.*, 13, 1959, 49–65.

3160 — Recent progress in Irish Geology, 1959–1971. Special supplement to *Irish Naturalists' Journal*, 1972.

3161 COLE, GRENVILLE A. J. Recent papers relating to Irish geology [1900–2]. *Ir. Nat.*, 12, 1903, 1–12.

3162 DAVIES, GORDON L. HERRIES. The earth sciences in Irish serial publications, 1787–1977, [with bibliog.] *J. Earth Sci. R. Dublin Soc.*, 1, 1978. 1–23.

3163 GARDINER, P.R.R. and LUNSEN, H. VAN. Bibliography of Irish carboniferous geology. Geological Survey of Ireland. (*Information Circular no. 3*). In preparation.

3164 — and REEVES, T.J. Bibliography of unpublished theses relating to the geology of Ireland (including those due for completion in 1969. Dublin: Geological Survey of Ireland, 1969. (*Information Circular no.1*).

3165 GEOLOGICAL SOCIETY, LONDON. Geological literature added to the Geological Society's library ... 1894–1934, London: 1895–1935. Published annually with author and subject indexes.

3166 GEOLOGICAL SOCIETY OF AMERICA, WASHINGTON. Bibliography and index of geology exclusive of North America. vol. 1–, 1934–.

3167 GEOLOGICAL SOCIETY OF DUBLIN. Titles of papers read before the ... Society ... 1832–53. *Geol. Soc. Dublin J., appendix*, vol. 5, 1850–3.

3168 HORNE, RALPH R. *compiler*. Bibliography of radiometric ages of Irish rocks (to December, 1970). Dublin: Geological Survey of Ireland, 1971. (*Information Circular no.4*).

3169 IRELAND. Department of Agriculture and Technical Instruction. List of memoirs, maps, sections, &c., published by the Geological Survey of Ireland to July 1915. Dublin[1916].

3170 — Geological Survey. Catalogue. Comprehensive author and subject catalogue on cards is at present being compiled.

3171 — Catalogue of the publications of the Geological Survey of the United Kingdom: Ireland. London: 1884.

3172 — Geological Heritage Inventory. An inventory of sites of geological interest is being compiled by the Geological Survey of Ireland and An Foras Forbartha in association with the Irish Geological Association, which is intended to form part of the National Heritage Inventory at present being compiled by An Foras Forbartha (The National

Institute for Physical Planning and Construction Research).

3173 PEARL, RICHARD M. Guide to geologic literature. New York: 1951.

3174 ROYAL GEOLOGICAL SOCIETY OF IRELAND. Catalogue of the library, corrected to January 31, 1865. Dublin: 1865.

3175 SEYMOUR, HENRY J. Papers relating to Irish geology published during the years 1903, 1904 and 1905. *Ir. Nat.,* 15, 1906, 6–11.

3176 SYNGE, F.M. Bibliography of Irish quaternary geology. Geological Survey of Ireland. (*Information Circular no. 5.*) In preparation.

History

3177 CHARLESWORTH, J. KAYE. The geology of Ireland: an introduction. Edinburgh and London: 1953. Bibliog., pp. 262–6.

3178 — Historical geology of Ireland. Edinburgh and London: 1963. Bibliog., pp. 500–530.

3179 DAVIES, G. The Geological Society of Dublin and the Royal Geological Society of Ireland, 1831–1890. *Hermathena*, 100, 1965, 66–76.

3180 HORNE, R.R. and GARDINER, P.R.R. The Geological Survey of Ireland. Geological Survey of Ireland. 1973 (*Information Circular no. 2*).

3181 SEYMOUR, HENRY J. The centenary of the first Geological Survey made in Ireland. *R. Dublin Soc. Econ. Proc.*, 3, 1936–50, 227–48.

3182 SWEET, JESSIE M. Robert Jameson's Irish journal, 1797: excerpts from Robert Jameson's 'Journal of my tour in 1797'. *Ann. Sci.*, 23, 1976, 97–126. Jameson (1774–1884) was Professor of National History in the University of Edinburgh (1804–1854) and his account includes a description of the Leskean Museum in Dublin and his meeting with George Mitchell, Richard Kirwan and others.

3183 WATERHOUSE, G. Sir Charles Giesecke's autograph albums. *Proc. R. Ir. Acad., Sec. C.* 70, 1970, 1–2.

3184 WHITTOW, J.B. Geology and scenery in Ireland. Harmondsworth: 1974.

Biography

General

3185 SCIENCE MUSEUM LIBRARY. A bibliography of British geologists who died between 1850 and 1900. 1972. (*Science Museum Library Bibliographical Series no. 801*).

Geologists

BELL, ROBERT.

3186 STENDALL, J.A.S. Robert Bell, geologist: a biographical sketch. Belfast: 1938.

CHARLESWORTH, JOHN KAYE.

3187 WILSON, H.E. John Kaye Charlesworth, 1889–1972 (obituary). *Ir. Nat. J.,* vol. 17, no. 7, 1972, 209–10.

CLOSE, MAXWELL HENRY.

3188 Maxwell Henry Close, M.A. [obituary notice and bibliog.]. *Ir. Nat.,* 12, 1903, 301–6.

FITTON, W.H.

3189 MANNING, P.I., and MANNING, J.M.E. The centenary of a pioneer Irish geologist, W.H. Fitton, 1780–1861. *Ir. Nat. J.,* 13, 1961, 242–4.

HUDSON, ROBERT GEORGE.

3190 JACKSON, J.S. Robert George Spencer Hudson, 1895–1965. [with bibliog.]. *R. Dublin Soc. Sci. Proc., Ser. A*, vol.2, nos. 16–19, 1966, i–ix.

3191 HULL, EDWARD.
Bibliog., *Ir. Book Lov.*, 9, 1917–18, 63.

JUKES, JOSEPH BEETE.

3192 BAYLISS, ROBERT A. The travels of Joseph Beete Jukes, F.R.S. *R. Soc. Lond. N. & R.*, 32, 1978, 201–212. Local director of Geological Survey in Ireland in the 1850's.

KINAHAN, GEORGE HENRY.

3193 CLARK, R. George Henry Kinahan [obituary and bibliog. notes]. *Ir. Nat.*, 18, 1909, 29–31.

Maps

3194 DAVIES, GORDON L. The oldest surviving geological map of Ireland. *Ir. Nat. J.*, vol.17, no. 12, 1973, 397–399.

3195 DAVIS, A.G. Notes on Sir Richard John Griffith's geological maps of Ireland. *Soc. Bibliog. Nat. Hist. J.*, vol. 2, pt. 6, 1950, 209–11. Contains a list of the 'issues' of Griffith's *Geological map of Ireland*. See also *R. Geol. Soc. Ir. J., new series.*, 5, 1877–80, 132–48.

3196 HULL, EDWARD. Palaeo-geological and geographical maps of the British Islands and the adjoining parts of the continent of Europe. *R. Dublin Soc. Sci. Trans., ser. 2*, vol. 1, 1877–83, 257–96.

3197 JUDD, J.W. The earliest geological maps of Scotland and Ireland. *Geol. Mag., n.s., Decade IV*, vol. 5, no. 4, 1898, 145–9.

3198 WILLS, L.J. A palaeogeographical atlas of the British Isles . . . London: 1951. Bibliog., p. 64.

3199 WOODWARD, H.B. Stanford's Geological atlas of Great Britain and Ireland, 4th ed. London: 1920.

Physical Geology

3200 HULL, EDWARD. The physical geology and geography of Ireland, 2nd rev. ed. London and Dublin: 1891. Bibliog., pp. 309–12.

Geomorphology

3201 CLAYTON, KEITH M. *ed.* A bibliography of British geomorphology; compiled by members of the British Geomorphology Research Group. London: 1964. (*Occasional publication, no. 1*). No entries after 1962 are included as these are covered in the journal *Geomorphological Abstracts*.

3202 DAVIES, GORDON L. The earth in decay: a history of British geomorphology, 1578–1878. London: 1969. Bibliog., pp. 357–374.

3203 — From flood and fire to rivers and ice – three hundred years of Irish geomorphology. [with bibliog.] *Ir. Geog.*, vol.5, no.1, 1964, 1–16.

3204 DREW, D.P. A preliminary study of the geomorphology of the Aillwee area, Central Burren, Co. Clare. *Bristol Univ. Spel. Soc. Proc.*, vol.13, no. 2, 1973, 227–244. Includes a note of caves in the area.

Volcanic

3205 EMELEUS, C.H. and PRESTON, J. The Tertiary volcanic rocks of Ireland. Belfast: 1969. Bibliog., pp. 67–70.

3206 STILLMAN, C.J. Palaeozoic volcanism in Great Britain and Ireland. *Geol. Soc. J.*, 133, 1977, 401–411.

3207 — and MAYTHAM, D.K. The Ordovician volcanic rocks of Arklow Head, Co. Wicklow. *R. Ir. Acad. Proc., Sec. B*, vol. 73, no. 4, 1973, 61–77.

3208 STROGEN, P. Brecciated lavas from County Limerick, Ireland, and their significance. *Geol. Mag.*, 110, 1973, 351–364.

Regional Geology

3209 BRANDON, A. and WILSON, H.E. The geology of the Templepatrick area, Co. Antrim, N. Ireland. *Geol. Surv. G.B. Bull.*, 51, 1975, 41–56.

3210 BRINDLEY, J.C. The Geology of the Irish Sea area. *Ir. Nat. J.*, 15, 1965-67, 245–249.

3211 CHARLESWORTH, J. KAYE. *ed.* The geology of North-East Ireland [with bibliog.]. *Geol. Assoc. Proc.*, 71, 1960, 429–59.

3212 COBBING, E.J. The Geology of the district north-west of Clifden, Co. Galway. [with bibliog.] *R. Ir. Acad. Proc., Sec. B*, vol. 67, no. 14, 1969, 303–325.

3213 COLE, GRENVILLE A.J. County Dublin, past and present. *Ir. Nat.*, 1, 1892, 9–14, 31–6, 53–7, 73–6, 90–5.

3214 — *and others*. The Geology of Clare Island, Co. Mayo, by G.A.J. Cole, J.R. Kilroe, T. Hallissy and E.A. Newell Arben. London: 1914. (*Memoirs of the Geological Survey of Ireland*).

3215 CRUSE, M.J.B. and LEAKE, B.E. The Geology of Renvyle, Inishbofin and Inishshark, North-west Connemara, Co. Galway. *R. Ir. Acad. Proc., Sec. B*, 67, 1968, 1–36.

3216 CURRALL, A.E. The geology of the S.W. end of the Ox Mountains, Co. Mayo. [with bibliog.] *R. Ir. Acad. Proc., Sec. B*, 63, 1963–4, 131–165.

3217 EVANS, B.W. and LEAKE, B.E. The Geology of the Toombeola district, Connemara, Co.

Galway. [with bibliog.] *R. Ir. Acad. Proc., Sec. B*, 70, 1970, 105–139.

3218 **Flatrés, Pierre.** La péninsule de Corran, comte de Mayo, Irlande; étude morphologie. *Soc. Geol. Mineral. Bretagne. bull. new. ser.* 1, 1957. Bibliog., pp. 57–61.

3219 **Gardiner, Piers** R.R. and **Robinson,** K.W. The geology of Ireland's Eye: the stratigraphy and structure of a part of the Bray group. [with bibliog.] *Geol. Surv. Ir. Bull.*, 1, 1970, 3–22.

3220 **Hardman, Edward** T. *compiler*. List of papers published on the geology of the North of Ireland, and adjoining districts. Dublin: Geological Society of Ireland, 1872. Includes also counties of Galway, Leitrim, Longford, Louth, Mayo, Meath, Roscommon, Sligo and Westmeath.

3221 **Institute of Geological Sciences.** The geology of the South Irish Sea, by M.R. Dobson, W.E. Evans and R. Whittington. London: 1973. Bibliog., pp. 34–35.

3222 **Lamplugh,** G.W. *and others*. The Geology of the country around Belfast (Explanation of the Belfast Colour-Printed Drift Map), by G.W. Lamplugh, J.R. Kilroe, A. McHenry, H.J. Seymour, W.B. Wright and H.B. Muff. Dublin: 1904. (*Memoirs of the Geological Survey of Ireland*). Bibliog., pp. 153–160 for the period 1790–1903.

3223 — *and others*. The Geology of the country around Cork and Cork harbour, (Explanation of the Cork Colour-Printed Drift Map), by G.W. Lamplugh, J.R. Kilroe, A. McHenry, H.J. Seymour, W.B. Wright and H.B. Muff. Dublin: 1905. (*Memoirs of the Geological Survey of Ireland*) Bibliog., pp. 127–130.

3224 — The Geology of the country around Dublin. (Explanation of Sheet 112). by G.W. Lamplugh, J.R. Kilroe, A. McHenry, H.J. Seymour and W.B. Wright. Dublin: 1903. (*Memoirs of the Geological Survey of Ireland*) Bibliog., pp. 148–155.

3225 — The Geology of the country around Limerick, by G.W. Lamplugh, S.B. Wilkinson, J.R. Kilroe, A. McHenry, H.J. Seymour and W.B. Wright. Dublin: 1907. (*Memoirs of the Geological Survey of Ireland*) Bibliog., pp. 111–114.

3226 **McHenry, Alex.** Sketch of the geology of Antrim [with bibliog]. *Geol. Assoc. Proc.,* 14, 1895–6, 129–47.

3227 **Northern Ireland, Geological Survey.** Geology of Belfast and the Lagan Valley, by P.I. Manning, J.A. Robbie, and H.E. Wilson; with contributions by J.R. Hawkes, M.J. Hughes, J. Pattison, G. Warrington, G.J. Wood and J.S.V. McAllister. 2nd ed. of explanatory memoir by E. Hull, J.L. Warren and W.B. Leonard. Belfast: 1970. Bibliog., pp. 184–192.

3228 — Geology of the country around Ballycastle (one-inch geological sheet 8), by H.F. Wilson and J.A. Robbie; with contributions by W. Butterwell [and others], 2nd ed. of explanatory memoir by Richard G. Synes, F.W. Egan and Alex McHenry. Belfast: 1966.

3229 **Patterson,** E.M. A bibliography of Donegal geology [1887–1963]. *Donegal Ann.*, vol.6, no. 1, 1964, 69–76.

3230 — Donegal geology: a further bibliography. *ibid.*, vol.7, no. 3, 1968, 319–323.

3231 **Pitcher, Wallace** S. and **Berger, Anthony** R. The Geology of Donegal: a study of granite enplacement and unroofing. New York and London: 1972. Bibliog., pp. 377–412; with a geological map compiled by Margaret O. Spencer.

3232 — and **Spencer, Margaret Olive.** The geology of north-west and Central Donegal – a bibliography. *Geol. Soc. Proc.*, 1645, 1968, 332–337. Contains 109 items for period 1930–1967.

3233 **Portlock,** J.E. Report on the geology of the county of Londonderry, and of parts of Tyrone and Fermanagh. Dublin and London: 1843. Review of the work of preceding writers, pp. 22–82.

3234 **Riddihough,** R.P. and **Max,** M.D. A geological framework for the continental margin to the west of Ireland. *Geol. J.,* vol. 11, pt. 2, 1976, 109–120.

3235 **Seymour, Henry** J. Recent geological work in the county of Waterford. *Ir. Nat.,* 7, 1898, 44–7.

3236 **Smyth, Louis** B., *and others*. The geology of South-East Ireland, together with parts of Limerick, Clare, and Galway. *Geol. Assoc. Proc.,* 50, 1939, 287–351. Includes bibliogs.

3237 WILKINSON, S.B. *and others*. The Geology of the country around Londonderry, by S.B. Wilkinson, A. McHenry, J.R. Kilroe and H.J. Seymour. Dublin: 1908. (*Memoirs of the Geological Survey of Ireland*) Bibliog., pp. 101–102 for period 1726–1908.

3238 WILSON, H.E. Regional geology of Northern Ireland. Belfast: 1972. (*Ministry of Commerce, Geological Survey of Northern Ireland*). Bibliog., pp. 96–103.

3239 WRIGHT, SAMUEL. Rathlin Island: extracts from a diary written during a scientific tour of Co. Antrim. *Ir. Book*., vol.1, no. 1, 1971, 40–43.

3240 WRIGHT, W.B. The Geology of the Ballycastle Coalfield, Co. Antrim, with chapters on the palaeontology of the field, by E.A. Newell Arben and L.B. Smyth. Dublin: 1924. (*Memoirs of the Geological Survey of Ireland*), Bibliog., pp. 4–21.

3241 — The Geology of Killarney and Kenmare, with an introduction and petrological notes by Grenville A.J. Cole; and a chapter on soils and agriculture, by T. Hallisy Dublin: 1927. (*Memoirs of the Geological Survey of Ireland*). Bibliog., pp. 102–103 for period 1756–1922.

Speleology

3242 BAKER, ERNEST A. Accounts of Michelstown caves. *Ir. Nat.,* 15, 1906, 35–6.

3243 BRISTOL UNIVERSITY. Speleological Society Proceedings, vol. 1–, 1919–. Rich in Irish material.

3244 — Speleological Society Proceedings, vol. 12, no. 1, Jubilee issue, 1919–1969. Includes the Society in Ireland by J.C. Coleman; caving expedition to Sligo, by H. McShea and J. McShea; Poll-Ballynahown, Co. Clare, by P.A. Standing.

3245 — The Caves of North-West Clare, Ireland, edited by E.K. Tratman. Newton Abbot [1969]. Bibliog., by T.R. Shaw, pp. 237–250.

3246 CASSELY, I.H. Pollballing [Co. Clare]; the 1974 extension. *Bristol Univ. Spel. Soc. Proc.,* 1977, 14, 269–275.

3247 COLEMAN, J.C. Irish cave excavation. *R. Soc. Antiq. Ir. J.,* 77, 1947, 78–80.

3248 — and DUNNINGTON, N.J. The Pollnagollum cave, Co. Clare [with bibliog.]. *R. Ir. Acad.Proc., Sec. B,* 50, 1944–5, 105–32.

3249 — The Caves of Ireland. Tralee: 1965.

3250 — Speleology in Ireland, 1965–1969 [a bibliography]. *Ir. Spel*., vol. 2, no. 1, 1969, 2–9.

3251 COLLINBRIDGE, B.R. *and others*. Poulnagollum – Poulelva caves, Slieve Elva, Co. Clare, Eire, [with bibliog]. *Bristol Univ. Spel. Soc. Proc*., vol.9, no. 3, 1962, 212–271. Paper was constructed from a number of separate reports by various authors on individual sections of the cave.

3252 CULLINGFORD, C.H.D., *ed*. British caving: an introduction to speleology. London: 1953. Bibliogs., pp. 123–35: British caving regions; pp. 234–46: selected bibliography [archaeology and palaeontology] and list of museums housing cave material; pp. 282–3: cave fauna and flora; pp. 298–9: cave-dwelling bats. 2nd ed. London: 1962; see also review in *Ir. Nat. J*., vol. 14, 1962, 82–3.

3253 DEVOY, E. and GILHUYS, D. Cavetown, Co. Roscommon: an interim report. *Ir. Spel*., 3, 1969, 8–9.

3254 DIXON, JOHNSTON. Two recent discoveries in County Leitrim (Fernagh Cave and Badger Pot). *Ir. Spel*., vol.2, no. 4, 1975, 14–17.

3255 DREW, D.P. Ballyglunin Cave, Co. Galway and the hydrology of the surrounding area. *Ir. Geog*., vol.6, no. 5, 1973, 610–617.

3256 — McGanns Cave, Ballycahill, Co. Clare. *Bristol Univ. Spel. Soc. Proc.,* vol.13, no.3, 1974, 361–367.

3257 — McGanns Cave, The Burren, Co. Clare. *Ir. Spel*., vol.2, no. 4, 1975, 18–20.

3258 DUNNINGTON, N.J. and COLEMAN, J.C. Dunmore cave, Co. Kilkenny [with bibliog.]. *R. Ir. Acad. Proc.,Sec. B*, 53, 1950–1, 15–24.

3259 FINCHAM, A. Speleological surveys in Co. Sligo and Co. Leitrim, Eire. *Leeds Phil. Lit. Soc. Proc., Sci. Sec*., vol.8, pt. 10, 1962, 225–242.

3260 GILHUYS, DONAL. Pollskeheenarinky. *Ir. Spel*., vol.2, no. 4, 1975, 26–31.

3261 — Potholes in counties Sligo and Leitrim. *Ir. Spel*., vol.2, no. 4, 1975, 8–9.

3262 [GLENNIE, E.A.] Bibliographical notes relating to caves and caving regions in Ireland, including Eire and Northern Ireland. *Cave Res. Group News*., no. 81, 1959, 14–17.

3263 HANNA, F.K. The Cave of the Wild Horses, Kilcorney, Co. Clare. *Bristol Univ. Spel. Soc. Proc*., vol.3, no. 11, 1967–68, 287–291.

3264 HOBBS, D.P.S. and NICHOLSON, F.H. Vigo Cave and neighbouring potholes, Co. Clare, Eire. *Bristol Univ. Spel. Soc. Proc*., vol.10, no. 1, 1962–63, 70–77.

3265 HOLGATE, H.F. and MCLAUGHLIN, D. Speleological developments in county Fermanagh:Arch Cave, near Derrygonnelly. *Ir. Nat. J*., vol.14, no. 6, 1963, 109–113.

3266 IRISH SPELEOLOGY: journal of the Speleological Society of Ireland. [Dublin] vol. 1, no. 1–, 1965–.

3267 JONES, GARETH LLWYD. The caves of Fermanagh and Cavan. Enniskillen: 1974. Bibliog., pp. 111–113.

3268 LLOYD, OLIVER C. Doolin Cave extensions [Co. Clare] *Bristol Univ. Spel. Soc. Proc*., vol. 13, no. 2, 1973, 285–290.

3269 — Poulomega, Co. Clare, Eire. *ibid*., vol.10, no. 1, 1962–63, 65–69.

3270 MARTEL, E.–A. Irlande et cavernes anglaises. Paris: 1897. Bibliog., pp. 16–18.

3271 PEAT, R. and SUTHERLAND, J.K. Upper Callaun 2, Co. Clare, Ireland, *Bristol Univ. Spel. Soc. Proc*., vol.14, no. 3, 1977, 263–267.

3272 PERRATT, N.N. and TRATMAN, E.K. The Hydrology of the Coolagh River catchment and its caves, Co. Clare, Ireland. *Bristol Univ. Spel. Soc. Proc*., vol.14, no. 1, 1975, 83–105.

3273 PRAEGER, ROBERT LLOYD. Derc-Ferna: the cave of Dunmore [with bibliog.]. *Ir. Nat.,* 27, 1918, 148–58.

3274 — Irish caves [with bibliog.]. *Ir. Nat.,* 5, 1896, 123–4.

3275 SCHARFF, R.F. Some notes on Irish caves [with bibliog.]. *Ir. Nat.,* 4, 1895, 57–9.

3276 SHAW, T.R. Bibliography of the caves of Co. Clare. [1961]. Not published. University of Bristol Speleological Society.

3277 SMART, C.C. The Formoyle East Cave, Co. Clare, Ireland. *Bristol Univ. Spel. Soc. Proc.,* vol.13, no. 3, 1974, 369–374.

3278 — Formoyle East Cave, Co. Clare. *Ir. Spel*., vol.2, no. 4, 1975, 21.

3279 SQUIRE, R. and SQUIRE, J.E. Caves in the Tralee area, Co. Kerry, Eire. *Bristol Univ. Spel. Soc. Proc*., vol.10, no. 2, 1963–64, 139–148.

3280 STANDING, P.A. Poll Kilmoon East, Co. Clare, Ireland. *Bristol Univ. Spel. Soc. Proc*., vol.3, no. 11, 1967–68, 297–299.

3281 TRATMAN, E.K. A flash flood in the cave of Northwest Clare, Ireland. *Bristol Univ. Spel. Soc. Proc*., vol.3, no. 11, 1967–68, 292–296.

3282 — The Kilcorney depression and its caves, Co. Clare, Ireland. *ibid*., vol.3, no. 11, 1967–68, 284–287.

3283 WILKINS, A.G. *and others*. The Fergus River Cave, Co. Clare, Ireland, by J.D. Wilkins, J.D. Walford and A. Boycott. *Bristol Univ. Spel. Soc. Proc*., vol.13, no. 1, 1972, 119–128. Alternative names Ballycasheen Cave, Poll-na-Cloch, Greanta, Roughaun Cave.

3284 WILLIAMS, P.W. and WILLIAMS, R.B.G. The deposits of Ballymihil cave, Co. Clare, Ireland, with particular reference to non-marine mollusca, [with bibliog.]. *Bristol Univ. Spel. Soc. Proc*., vol.11, no. 1, 1965–66, 71–82.

Earthquakes

3285 MALLET, ROBERT and MALLET, JOHN WILLIAM. The Earthquake catalogue of the British Association, with the discussion, curves and maps, etc. [with bibliog.]. London: 1858. From *The Transactions of the British Association for the Advancement of Science, 3rd and 4th reps*., 1852–8. Covers period 1606 B.C. to A.D. 1842.

Bog Flows

3286 COLHOUN, ERIC A. The Debris-flow at Glendalough, Co. Wicklow, and the bog flow at Slieve Rushen, Co. Cavan, January 1965. [with bibliog.]. *Ir. Nat. J*., vol.15, no. 7, 1966, 199–206.

3287 — *and others*. Recent bog flows and debris slides in the North of Ireland, [with bibliog.], by E.A. Colhoun, R. Common and M.M. Cruickshank. *R. Dublin Soc. Sci. Proc., Ser. A*, vol. 2, no. 10, 1965, 163–174. Includes a list of 32 recorded bog flows in Ireland for period 1640–1965.

3288 PRIOR, D.B. and DOUGLAS, G.R. Landslides near Larne, Co. Antrim, 15–16th August, 1970. *Ir. Geog*., vol.6, no. 3, 1971, 294–301.

Meteorites

3289 SEYMOUR, HENRY J. On a recent addition to the collection of Irish meteorites in the National Museum, Dublin. *R. Dublin Soc. Sci. Proc., new ser*., 24, 1945–8, 157–64.

3290 — Catalogue of the examples of meteoritic falls in Irish museums. *R. Dublin Soc. Sci. Proc*., 25, 1949–51, 193–199.

Mineralogy

3291 BISHOPP, D.W. A short review of Irish mineral resources. Dublin, Department of Industry and Commerce, 1943. (*Geological Survey of Ireland, emergency period pamphlet*, no. 1.) Bibliog., pp. 19–20.

3292 COLE, GRENVILLE A.J. Memoir and map of locations of minerals of economic importance and metalliferous mines in Ireland. Dublin: 1922. (*Memoirs of the Geological Survey of Ireland — Mineral Resources*).

3293 FIRSOFF, V. ALEX. Gemstones of the British Isles. Edinburgh: 1971. Ireland, pp. 53–67; bibliog., pp. 146-148.

3294 GARDINER, PIERS R.R. and HORNE, RALPH R. A current profile of Irish mineral resources. *Technol. Ir*., vol.10, no. 3, 1978, 19–32.

3295 GREG, ROBERT PHILIPS. Manual of the mineralogy of Great Britain and Ireland, by Greg and Lettsom [1st ed. reprinted]; with supplementary lists of British minerals by L.J. Spencer, and a fourth supplementary list (1977) together with foreword by Peter G. Embrey. Broadstairs (Kent): Lapidary Publications, 1977. Facsimile reprint of 1st ed. London: 1858.

3296 HALLISSY, T. Barytes in Ireland, Dublin: 1923. (*Memoirs of the Geological Survey of Ireland, Mineral resources*).

3297 O'BRIEN, MURROGH V. Irish mineral resources and some related engineering operations [with discussion]. *Inst. Civ. Eng. Ir. Trans*., 93, 1966–7, 135–149.

3298 O'DONNELL, SEAN. Ireland – a new mineral province. *New Sci*., vol.60, no. 878, 1973, 910–912.

3299 REEVES, T.J. Gold in Ireland, [with bibliog.] *Geol. Surv. Ir. Bull*., vol.1, no. 2, 1971, 73–85.

3300 RUDLER, F.W. A handbook to a collection of the minerals of the British Islands, mostly selected from the Ludlam collection, in the Museum of Practical Geology, Jermyn St., London: 1905. Minerals of Ireland [with bibliog.], pp. 222–232.

Oceanography

(See also Marine Biology)

3301 BARY, B. McK. Oceanography in Ireland: a new university department in Galway. *Studies*, 60, 1971, 169–179.

3302 BIBLIOGRAPHY OF HYDROLOGY, IRELAND, for the years 1934 to 1949 (both inclusive). Dublin, International Council of Scientific Unions, International Union of Geodesy and Geophysics, International Association of Scientific Hydrology, National Committee for Geodesy and Geophysics. 1953.

3303 BOWDEN, K.F. Physical oceanography of the Irish Sea. London: 1955. (*Fishery investigations, ser.* 2, vol. 18, No. 8.)

3304 BOWEN, E.G. The Irish Sea in the age of the Saints. *Stud. Celt*., 4, 1969, 56–71.

3305 BULLERWELL, W. and MCQUILLIN, R. Preliminary report on the seismic reflection survey in the Southern Irish sea, July 1968. London: 1969. (*Institute of Geological Sciences, Report no. 69/2*).

3306 EMERY, K.O. and SEARS, MARY, *compilers*. An international dictionary of oceanographers, 3rd ed. Washington: National Academy of Sciences, 1960. Eire, pp. 29–30.

3307 GROGAN, DICK. The *Glomar Challenger* and the deep sea drilling project. *Technol. Ir*., vol.6, no. 6, 1974, 39–40.

3308 LEE, ARTHUR. Hydrographical observations in the Irish Sea, January–March 1953 [with bibliog.]. London: 1960. (*Fishery investigations, ser.* 2, vol.23, no. 2.)

3309 LEWIS, H. MABEL. The physical and chemical oceanography of the Irish Sea: a bibliography. *J. Cons. Int. Explor. Mer.,* 9, 1934, 87–92.

3310 NATURAL ENVIRONMENT RESEARCH COUNCIL. Institute of Geological Sciences. Irish Sea investigations, 1969–70, [with bibliog.]. by J.E. Wright, J.H. Hull, R. McQuillin and Susan E. Arnold. London: 1971.

3311 WENT, ARTHUR E.J. Ireland's contribution to the work of the International Council for the Exploration of the Sea, Pt. 1, 1902 to 1927; Pt. 2, The second quarter of century, (1927–1952). *Ir. Dept. Agric. J.*, 71, 1974, 21–28; *ibid.* 73, 1976, 5–13.

Glacial Geology

3312 CHAPMAN, R.J. The late-Weichselian glaciations of the Erne basin, [Co. Fermanagh]. *Ir. Geog*., vol.6, no. 2, 1970, 153–161.

3313 CHARLESWORTH, J. KAYE. Some observations on the glaciation of north-east Ireland [with bibliog.]. *R. Ir. Acad.Proc., Sec. B*, 45, 1938–40, 255–95.

3314 CLOSE, MAXWELL H. Notes on the general glaciation of Ireland. *R. Geol. Soc. Ir. J.,* 1, 1864–7, 207–42.

3315 COLHOUN, ERIC A. The deglaciation of the Sperrin Mountains and adjacent areas in Counties Tyrone, Londonderry and Donegal, Northern Ireland, [with bibliog.]. *R. Ir. Acad. Proc., Sec. B*, vol. 72, no. 8, 1972, 91–147.

3316 — The Glacial stratigraphy of the Sperrin mountains and its relation to the glacial stratigraphy of North-West Ireland. *ibid., Sec. B*, vol. 71, no. 2, 1971, 37-52.

3317 — Late Weichselian periglacial phenomena of the Sperrin mountains, Northern Ireland. *ibid., Sec. B*, vol. 71, no. 3, 1971, 53–71.

3318 — On the nature of the glaciations and final deglaciation of the Sperrin Mountains and adjacent areas in the North of Ireland. *Ir. Geog*., vol. 6, no. 2, 1970, 162–185.

3319 FARRINGTON, A. The last glaciation in the Burren, Co. Clare. *R. Ir. Acad. Proc., Sec. B*, vol. 64, no. 3, 1964, 33–39.

3320 — The last glacial episode in the Wicklow mountains, [with bibliog.]. *Ir. Nat. J.*, 15, 1965–7, 226–229.

3321 — and MITCHELL, G.F. Some glacial features between Pollaphuca and Baltinglass, Co. Wicklow. *Ir. Geog*., vol.6, no. 5, 1973, 543–560.

3322 HOARE, P.G. Glacial meltwater channels in County Dublin, [with bibliog.]. *R. Ir. Acad. Proc., Sec. B*, vol. 76, no. 12, 1976, 173–185.

3323 LEWIS, COLIN A. The glaciations of the Dingle Peninsula, Co. Kerry. *R. Dublin Soc. Sci. Proc., Ser. A*, vol. 5, no. 13, 1974, 207–235.

3324 — The Knockmealdown Mountains: a glacial nunatak. *Ir. Geog*., 9, 1976, 18–28.

3325 MCCABE, A.M. The Glacial stratigraphy of eastern counties Meath and Louth. [with bibliog.] *R. Ir. Acad. Proc., Sec. B*, vol. 73, no. 21, 1973, 355–382.

3326 — The Glacial deposits of the Maguiresbridge area, County Fermanagh, Northern Ireland. *Ir. Geog*., vol.6, no. 1, 1969, 63–77.

3327 PRAEGER, ROBERT LLOYD. A bibliography of Irish glacial and post-glacial geology. *Belfast Nat.Fld. Cl. Proc., appendix,* vol. 2, no. 6, 1895–6, 237–316.

3328 SOLLAS, W.J. A map to show the distribution of eskers in Ireland [with bibliog.]. *R. Dublin Soc. Sci. Trans., ser.* 2, 5, 1893–6, 782–822.

3329 SYNGE, FRANCIS M. The Glacial deposits of Glenasmole, County Dublin, and the neighbouring uplands, [with bibliog.]. *Geol. Surv. Ir. Bull*., vol. 1, no.2, 1971, 87–97.

3330 — The Glaciation of South Wicklow and the adjoining parts of the neighbouring counties. *Ir. Geog*., vol. 6, no. 5, 1973, 561–569.

3331 — The Glaciation of the Nephin Beg range, County Mayo, [with bibliog.]. *ibid*., 4, 1959–63, 397–403.

3332 — The glaciation of west Mayo. *ibid*., 5, 1964–68, 372–386.

3333 WATTS, W.A. Interglacial deposits at Baggotstown, near Bruff, Co. Limerick, [with bibliog.]. *R. Ir. Acad. Proc., Sec. B*, 63, 1963–64, 167–190.

3334 — The pattern of glaciation of County Dublin, [with bibliog.]. *ibid., Sec. B*, vol. 75, no. 9, 1975, 207–224.

METEOROLOGY

3335 BILHAM, E.G. Climate of the British Isles. London: 1938.

3336 BOURKE, AUSTIN. The climate of Ireland as a natural resource. *Admin.*, vol. 21, no. 3, 1973, 365–383.

3337 CAMERON *Captain* (*ed*). Meteorological observations taken during the years 1829 to 1852 at the Ordnance Survey Office, Phoenix Park, Dublin; to which is added a series of similar observations made at the principal trigonometrical stations, and at other places in Ireland. Dublin: 1856.

3338 DIXON, F.E. Climatic change? *Technol. Ir.*, vol. 7, no. 10, 1976, 9–11. Diagrams give mean temperatures for winters in Dublin for period 1795–1975.

3339 — Meteorology and the community. *Stat. Social Inq. Soc. Ir. J.*, 19, 1956–7, 81–103.

3340 — Some Irish meteorologists. *Ir. Astron. J.*, 9, 1969–70, 113–119.

3341 More Irish meteorologists. *ibid.*, 9, 1969–70, 240–245.

3342 — Weather in old Dublin [with bibliogs.]. *Dublin Hist. Rec.*, 13, 1952–4, 94–107; vol. 15, no. 3, 1959, 65–73.

3343 GREAT BRITAIN. Meteorological Office. British rainfall: on the distribution of rain over the British Isles. Vol. 1–, 1860–.

3344 HOUGHTON, JOHN G. and O'CINNEIDE, S. Distribution and synoptic origin of selected heavy preciptation storms over Ireland, [with bibliog.]. *Ir. Geog.*, 9, 1976, 1–17.

3345 HUGHES, N.J. Rainfall and rainfall measurement: a select bibliography. Dublin: 1974.

3346 — Water evaporation: a bibliography. Dublin: 1974.

3347 IRELAND, DEPARTMENT OF TRANSPORT AND POWER. Meteorological Service. Aeronautical climatological summaries, Shannon Airport, 1961–1970, and descriptive meteorological memorandum. Dublin: 1972.

3348 — Air temperature in Ireland, 1931–1960. Dublin: 1971.

3349 — Degree-days above and below various base temperatures in Ireland, 1961–1970. Dublin: 1973.

3350 — Monthly and annual averages of rainfall for Ireland, 1941–1970, by H.B. Doherty and J.J. Logue. Dublin: 1977.

3351 — Rainfall in Ireland, 1931–1960. Dublin: 1973.

3352 — Monthly seasonal and annual, mean, and extreme values of duration of bright sunshine in Ireland, 1931–1960. Dublin: 1971.

3353 IRISH RAINFALL ASSOCIATION, DUBLIN. Annual reports, nos. 1–27, 1918–46.

3354 LAMB, H.H. British Isles weather types and a register of the daily sequence of circulation patterns, 1861–1971. London: 1972.

3355 LLOYD, HUMPHREY. Notes on the meteorology of Ireland, deduced from the observations made in the year 1851 under the direction of the Royal Irish Academy. *R. Ir. Acad. Trans.,* vol. 22, pt. 1, 1855, pp. 411–98. Also contained in *Miscellaneous papers connected with physical science*, by Humphrey Lloyd, London: 1877, pp. 317-80. Includes monthly rainfall tables for period 1841–51.

3356 LOGUE, J.J. The annual cycle of rainfall in Ireland. Dublin: 1978.

3357 — Extreme rainfalls in Ireland. Dublin: 1975. Covers period 1941–1970.

3358 — Extreme wind speeds in Ireland for periods ending in 1974. Dublin: 1975.

3359 — Rain intensity – amount – frequency relations in Ireland. Dublin: 1971. Rain records for period 1950–69.

3360 LONG, JOHN. Daily observations on the weather, and on the rise and fall of the Shannon, during the years 1846, 1847 and 1848, made at Athlone. *R. Ir. Acad. Proc.*, 4, 1850, *Appendix no*. VI, lxix–lxxiv.

3361 LYSTER, JOSEPH. The shadow on the lake: a memory of 'the long frost' of fifty years ago [*c.*1896] *J. Old Athlone Soc.*, vol. 1, no. 4, 1974–5, 283–4.

3362 MORLEY, T.J. and BOLSTER, K. The climate of Dublin city: extremes of temperature, rainfall, sunshine and wind speed. *Comm. Dublin Inst. Adv. Stud. Geophys. Bull.*, 30, 1973. 5 tables for years 1948–1972.

3363 — Wind in Dublin city. *ibid.*, 24, 1969.

3364 PERRY, A.H. Spatial and temporal characteristics of Irish precipitation. *Ir. Geog.*, vol.6, no.4, 1972, 428–442.

3365 POLLAK, L.W., and MORLEY, T.J. The climate of Dublin city. No. I. Rainfall at Trinity College [1904–53]. Dublin: Dublin Institute for Advanced Studies, 1956. *(School of cosmic physics, geophysical bulletin*, no. 12.)

3366 — The climate of Dublin. No. II. Temperature at Trinity College, by T.J. Morley. Dublin: 1964. *ibid.*, 23.

3367 RACKLIFF, P.G. Summer and winter indices at Armagh, [1880–1962]. *Weather*, 20, 1965, 38–44.

3368 ROHAN, P.K. The climate of North Ulster. Dublin: 1968.

3369 — The climate of Ireland. Dublin: 1975.

3370 ROYAL METEOROLOGICAL SOCIETY. Bibliography of meteorological literature. London: vols. 1–6, 1922–50.

3371 SOME CONTRIBUTIONS TO METEOROLOGICAL SCIENCE. *In* St. Patrick's College, Maynooth. Museum third Tostal display souvenir catalogue. 1955, pt. 49.

3372 UNDERWOOD, JOHN. A diary of the weather and the state of vegetation at the botanic garden of the Dublin Society for the year[s] 1801–[08]. *R. Dublin Soc. Trans.*, vols. 2–6, 1802–10.

3373 YEATES, GEORGE. Meteorological journal commencing 1st January 1843 and ending 31st December 1843. *R. Ir. Acad. Proc.*, 2, *Appendix no.* 5, 1840–44. Continued in subsequent vols. covering period 1844–49.

Geochemistry

3374 CRONAN, D.S. Geochemistry of recent sediments from the central north-eastern Irish Sea. London: 1970. (*Institute of Geological Sciences, Report no.* 70/17).

3375 KIELY, P.V. and FLEMING, G.A. Geochemical survey of Ireland: Meath-Dublin area. *R. Ir. Acad. Proc., Sec. B*, vol.68, no. 1, 1969, 1–28.

PALAEONTOLOGY

3376 ADAMS, A. LEITH. On the recent and extinct Irish mammals. *R. Dublin. Soc. Proc., new series., 2,* 1880, 45–86.

3377 — Report on the history of Irish fossil mammals. *R. Ir. Acad. Proc., 2nd ser.,* 3, 1877–83, 89–100.

3378 ARBER, E.A. NEWELL. Contributions to our knowledge of the floras of the Irish carboniferous rocks. Pt. 1. The Lower Carboniferous (carboniferous limestone) flora of the Ballycastle coalfield, Co. Antrim [with bibliog.]. *R. Dublin Soc. Proc., new series.,* 13, 1911–13, 162–76.

3379 BALL, V. On the collection of the fossil mammalia of Ireland in the Science and Art Museum, Dublin. *R. Dublin Soc. Sci. Trans., 2nd ser.,* 3, 1883–7. Fossil mammalia of Ireland bibliog., pp. 345–8.

3380 BASSLER, R.S., and MOODEY, MARGARET W. Bibliographic and faunal index of Paleozoic Pelmatozoan echinoderms. *Geol. Soc. Amer. special papers*, no. 45, 1943.

3381 — Faunal lists and descriptions of Paleozoic corals. *Geol. Soc. Amer. Mem.,* no. 44, 1950.

3382 CAMP, C.L. *and others*. Bibliography of fossil vertebrates, 1928–33. *Geol. Soc. Amer. special papers,* no. 27, 1940.

3383 — Bibliography of fossil vertebrates, 1934–8. *Geol. Soc. Amer. special papers,* no. 42, 1942.

3384 — Bibliography of fossil vertebrates, 1939–43. *Geol. Soc. Amer. Mem.,* no. 37, 1949.

3385 — Bibliography of fossil vertebrates, 1944–8. *Geol. Soc. Amer. Mem.,* no. 57, 1953.

3386 — Bibliography of fossil vertebrates, 1949–1953. *Geol. Soc. Amer. Mem.,* no. 84, 1961.

3387 — Bibliography of fossil vertebrates, 1954–1958. *Geol. Soc. Amer. Mem.*, no. 92, 1964.

3388 — Bibliography of fossil vertebrates, 1959–1963. *Geol. Soc. Amer. Mem.*, no. 117, 1968.

3389 DAVIES, GORDON, L. The Palaeontological collection of Lord Cole, third earl of Enniskillen (1807–1886), at Florence Court, Co. Fermanagh. *Ir. Nat. J.*, vol.16, no. 12, 1970, 379–381.

3390 DEAN, W.T. The Trilobites of the Chair of Kildare Limestone (Upper Ordovician) of Eastern Ireland. London: (*Palaeontographical Society Monographs*). Pt. 1, 1971. Bibliog., [pp. 61–64].

3391 GODWIN, H. The history of the British flora: a factual basis for phytogeography. Cambridge: 1956. Bibliog., pp. 356–66.

3392 JESSEN, KNUD and FARRINGTON, A. The bogs at Ballyhetagh, near Dublin, with remarks on late-glacial conditions in Ireland [with bibliog.]. *R. Ir. Acad. Proc., Sec. B,* 44, 1937–8, 205–60.

3393 — Studies in late quaternary deposits and flora-history of Ireland [with bibliog.]. *R. Ir. Acad. Proc., Sec. B,* 52, 1948–50, 85–290.

3394 McHENRY, A. and WATTS, W. Guide to the collections of rocks and fossils belonging to the Geological Survey of Ireland, arranged in the Curved Gallery of the Museum of Science and Art, Dublin. Dublin: 1898.

3395 MITCHELL, GEORGE FRANCIS, *and others*. A correlation of Quaternary deposits in the British Isles. London: Geological Society of London, 1973. (*Special report no. 4*). Ireland by G.F. Mitchell, E.A. Colhoun, N. Stephens and F.M. Synge, pp. 67–80; bibliog., pp. 81–99.

3396 — The Quaternary deposits between Fenit and Spa on the north shore of Tralee Bay, Co. Kerry. *R. Ir. Acad. Proc., Sec. B*, 70, 1970, 141–162.

3397 THE QUATERNARY HISTORY OF THE IRISH SEA, edited by C. Kidson and J. Tooley. Liverpool: 1977. (*Geological Journal special issues no. 7.*)

3398 REED, F. COWPER. Revision of certain Ordovician fossils from County Tyrone [with bibliog.]. *R. Ir. Acad. Proc., Sec. B*, 55, 1952–3, 29–136.

3399 ROMER, ALFRED SHEWOOD, *and others*. Bibliography of fossill vertebrates exclusive to North America, 1509–1927. *Geol. Soc. Amer. Mem.*, no. 87, 1962.

3400 SAVAGE, R.J.G. Irish Pleistocene mammals, [with bibliog.]. *Ir. Nat. J.*, vol.15, no. 5, 1966, 117–130.

3401 SIZER, C.A. Remains of the Irish giant deer in Leicestershire. *Trans. Leicester Lit. Phil. Soc.*, 56, 1962, 24–27.

3402 SMYTH, LOUIS B. The carboniferous rocks of Hook Head, Co. Wexford [with bibliog.]. *R. Ir. Acad. Proc., Sec. B*, 29, 1929–31, 523–66.

3403 — On the index fossil of the Cleistopora zone [with bibliog.]. *R. Dublin Soc. Sci. Proc.,* 18, 1924–8, 423–31.

3404 STUDIES IN IRISH QUATERNARY DEPOSITS, by G.F. Mitchell, *and others*. No. 1: Some Lacustrine deposits near Dunshaughlin, Co. Meath [with bibliog.]. *R. Ir. Acad. Proc., Sec. B*, 46, 1940–1, 13–37.

3405 — No. 2: Some Lacustrine deposits near Ratoath, Co. Meath [with bibliog.]. *ibid.*, pp. 173–82.

3406 — No. 3: The reindeer in Ireland [with bibliog.]. *ibid.*, pp. 183–8.

3407 — No. 4: The exploration of some caves near Castletownroche, Co. Cork [with bibliog.], by A.M. Gwynn, G.F. Mitchell, and A.W. Stelfox. *ibid.*, 47, 1941–2, 371–90.

3408 — No. 5: Two inter-glacial deposits in south-east Ireland. *ibid.*, 52, 1948–50, 1–14.

3409 — No. 6: The Giant Deer in Ireland [with bibliog.], by G.F. Mitchell and H.M. Parkes. *ibid.*, pp. 291–314.

3410 — No. 7: Studies in Irish quaternary deposits: supplements Jessen's paper, 1949. *ibid.*, 53, 1950–1, 111–206.

3411 — No. 8: Further identifications of macroscopic plant fossils from Irish quaternary deposits, especially from a late-glacial deposit at Mapastown, Co. Louth [with bibliog.]. *ibid., Sec. B*, 55, 1952–3, 225–81.

3412 — No. 9: A pollen-diagram from Lough Gur, Co. Limerick [with bibliog.]. *ibid., Sec. C*, 56, 1953–4, 481–8.

3413 — No. 10: The Mesolithic site at Toome Bay, Co. Londonderry [with bibliog.]. *Ulster J. Arch.,* 18, 1955, 1–16.

3414 — No. 11: Post-boreal pollen-diagrams from Irish raised bogs [with bibliog.]. *R. Ir. Acad. Proc., Sec. B,* 57, 1954–6, 185–251.

3415 WRIGHT, H.E. and FREY, DAVID G. International studies on the Quaternary. 1965.

Geol. Soc. Amer. special papers. no. 84. Includes paper on Littleton Bog, Tipperary: an Irish vegetational record, by G.F. Mitchell.

ANTHROPOLOGY

3416 ASHBEE, PAUL. The Bronze Age round barrow in Britain: an introduction to the study of the funerary practice and culture of the British and Irish single-grave people of the second millenium B.C. London: 1960. Appendix and bibliog., pp. 202–14.

3417 BLOXAM, GEORGE W. Index to the publications of the Anthropological Institute of Great Britain and Ireland [1843–91] including *The Journal and Transactions of the Ethnological Society . . . The Anthropological Review, and The Journal of the Anthropological Institute*. London: 1893.

3418 CASEY, ALBERT E. and FRANKLIN, ROBERTA B. Cork-Kerry Irish compared anthropometrically with 139 modern and ancient peoples [with bibliog.]. *Ir. J. Med. Sci., 6th ser.,* no. 429, 1961, 409–15.

3419 HOOTON, EARNEST A., and DUPERTUIS, C. WESLEY. The physical anthropology of Ireland; with a selection on the west coast Irish families, by Helen Dawson. Cambridge, Mass.: 1955. *Papers of the Peabody Museum of Archaeology and Ethnology, Harvard Univ.,* vol. 30, nos. 1–2. Bibliog., pp. 303–4.

3420 INTERNATIONAL BIBLIOGRAPHY OF SOCIAL AND CULTURAL ANTHROPOLOGY. Paris, United Nations, Educational, Scientific and Cultural Organisation, vol. 1–, 1957–.

3421 MESSENGER, JOHN C. Man Of Aran revisited: an anthropological critique, [with bibliog.]. *Univ. Rev.*, vol. 3, no. 9, 1966, 15–47.

3422 MOGEY, J.M. The peoples of Northern Ireland. *Belfast Nat. Hist. Phil. Soc. Proc., 2nd ser.,* vol. 1, pt. 4, 1938–9, 14–18.

3423 RIPLEY, WILLIAM Z. Selected bibliography of the anthropology and ethnology of Europe. Boston: 1899. Prepared as a supplement to *The Races of Europe*. London: 1900.

Ethnography

3424 BROWNE, CHARLES R. The ethnography of Ballycroy, Co. Mayo. *R. Ir. Acad. Proc., 3rd ser.,* 4, 1896–8. Bibliog., pp. 110–11.

3425 — The ethnography of Carna and Mweenish in the parish of Moyruss, Connemara. *ibid.*, 6, 1900–2, 503–34.

3426 — The ethnography of Clare Island and Inishturk, Co. Mayo. *ibid.,* 5, 1898–1900. Bibliog., p. 72.

3427 — The ethnography of Inishbofin and Inishshark, Co. Galway. *ibid.,* 3, 1893–6. Bibliog., pp. 369–70.

3428 — The ethnography of The Mullet, Inishkea Islands and Portacloy, Co. Mayo. *ibid.*, 3, 1893–6. Bibliog., pp. 648–9.

3429 HADDON, A.C. and BROWNE, CHARLES R. The ethnography of the Aran Islands, Co. Galway. *R. Ir. Acad. Proc., 3rd ser.,* 2, 1891–3. Bibliog., pp. 827–9.

Ethnology

3430 CRESSWELL, ROBERT. Une Communaute rurale de l'Irlande. 1969. (*Université de Paris, travaux et mémoires de l'institute d'ethnologie*, 74).

3431 DANAHER, KEVIN. A bibliography of Irish ethnology and folk tradition. 2 vols. Available in the Library of the Folklore Department, University College, Dublin. See also no. 9508.

3432 EVANS, E.E. Some problems of ethnology: the example of plowing by the tail. In *Folk and Farm*, edited by C.O Danachair, 1976, pp. 30–39.

3433 FRANKCOM, G. and MUSGRAVE, J.H. The Irish giant [Patrick Cotter, alias O'Brien]. London: 1976.

3434 GAILEY, ALAN. Towards an Irish ethnological atlas? *Ulster Folk.*, 18, 1972, 121–125.

NATURAL HISTORY

Bibliography

3435 BELFAST NATURAL HISTORY AND PHILOSOPHICAL SOCIETY. Centenary volume, 1821–1921, edited by Arthur Deane. Belfast: 1924. Memoirs, pp. 62–117; list of papers with authors' names, pp. 118–63.

3436 CURLE, RICHARD. The Ray Society: a bibliographical history. London: 1954. Includes publications nos. 1–137, 1844–1953.

3437 IRISH NATURALIST, DUBLIN. vols. 1–33, 1892–1924. Index, vols. 1–25, compiled by Alice Scharff, *ibid*., 25, 1916, 173–235; author index, vols. 26–33, appears as supplement to vol. 33, 1924. For continuation see *Irish Naturalists Journal*.

3438 IRISH NATURALISTS JOURNAL, BELFAST. vol. 1–, 1925–. Species index to vols. 1–12, 1925–1958. Bibliog. pp. ii–iii.

3439 SMART, JOHN and TAYLOR, GEORGE, *ed*. Bibliography of key works for the identification of the British fauna and flora. 2nd ed. London: Systematics Association (British Museum), 1953. 1st ed., 1942.

3440 SOCIETY FOR THE BIBLIOGRAPHY OF NATURAL HISTORY (British Museum). Journal, vol. 1–, 1936–.

Nomenclature

3441 IRELAND [DEPT. OF EDUCATION] AN ROINN OIDEACHAIS. Ainmneach plandai agus Ainmhithe/Flora and fauna nomenclature. Baile Atha Cliath: 1978.

History

3442 O RUADHAIN, MICHAEL. The position of nature protection in Ireland in 1956 [with bibliog.]. *Ir. Nat. J.,* 12, 1956, 81–104.

3443 PRAEGER, ROBERT LLOYD. Natural history of Ireland, [1st ed. reprinted], with a new introduction by Raymond Piper. Wakefield (Yorkshire): 1972. Bibliog., pp. 295–321. 1st ed. London: 1950.

3444 — Recent views bearing on the problem of the Irish flora and fauna [with bibliog]. *R. Ir. Acad. Proc., Sec. B*, 41, 1932–3, 125–45.

3445 — Ten years' work of the Fauna and Flora Committee [with list of papers]. *Ir. Nat.,* 12, 1903, 124–31. See also special number of *Ir. Nat. J.,* vol. 11, no. 6, 1954, for account of Praeger's work.

3446 SHARROCK, J.T.R. *ed*. The Natural History of Cape Clear Island. Berkhamsted [Herts.]: 1973.

Regional

3447 ADAMS, J. On the division of Ireland into biological sub-provinces. *Ir. Nat.,* vol. 17, 1908. Bibliog., pp. 150–1.

3448 ARMSTRONG, J.I. *and others*. The ecology of the mountains of Mourne with special reference to Slieve Donard [with bibliog.], by J.I. Armstrong, J. Calvert, and C.T. English. *R. Ir. Acad. Proc., Sec. B,* 39, 1929–30, 440–51.

3449 BATTARBEE, R.W. Observations on the recent history of Lough Neagh and its drainage basin. [with bibliog.]. *Phil. Trans. R. Soc. London, Ser. B*., 281, 1977–78, 303–345.

3450 DE VALERA, MAIRIN. Notes on interdital ecology in Ireland [with bibliog.] *Ir. Nat. J.,* 12, 1956–8, 182–7.

3451 FAHY, EDWARD. Fauna and flora of a thermal spring at Innfield (Enfield), Co. Meath. *Ir. Nat. J*., vol.18, no. 1, 1974, 9–12.

3452 — The biology of a thermal spring at Enfield, Co. Meath, with some observations on other Irish thermal springs. *R. Ir. Acad. Proc. Ser. B.*, vol. 75, no. 3, 1975, 111–123. Includes map showing distribution of thermal springs in Ireland.

3453 HARVEY, J.R. Contributions towards a fauna and flora of the county of Cork, read at the meeting of the British Association held at Cork in the year 1843.
The Vertebrata, by Dr. Harvey. – The Mollusca, Crustacea and Echinodermata, by J.D. Humphreys. – The Flora by Dr. [Thomas] Prior. London and Cork: 1845.

3454 THE IRELAND WE LIVE IN: OUR FLORA AND FAUNA. Contents: The Plants, by Mary J.P. Scannell. – The fauna of Ireland, by Fergus J. O'Rourke. – The Insects of Ireland, by Edward Fahy.– Our larger sport fish, by Desmond Brennan.– Our bogs, by Thomas A. Barry.– Our woods and trees, by Timothy McEvoy. *Cap. Ann*., 1973, 145–214.

3455 MACDONALD, R. and MCMILLAN, NORA F. The natural history of Lough Foyle, North Ireland [with bibliogs.]. *R. Ir. Acad.Proc., Sec. B*, 54, 1951–2, 67–96.

3456 MOULD, DAPHNE D.C. POCHIN. The Burren down on Galway Bay. *Geog. Mag*., 49, 1977, 450–456.

3457 O'CONNELL, GERALD, *ed*. The Burren: a guide. Limerick [1970].

3458 REES, COLIN B. Notes on the ecology of the

sandy beaches of North Donegal [with bibliog.]. *R. Ir. Acad. Proc., Sec. B*, 45, 1938–40, 215–29.

3459 ROYAL IRISH ACADEMY PROCEEDINGS, vol. 31, 1911–15. 3 pts. A biological survey of Clare Island in the county of Mayo, Ireland, and of the adjoining district. Includes extensive bibliogs; see also *The Clare Island Survey* [list of reports], by R.F. Scharff. *Ir. Nat.*, 24, 1915, 179–80.

3460 UNIVERSITY COLLEGE OF NORTH WALES, MARINE SCIENCE LABORATORIES. Survey of environmental conditions in the Liffey estuary and Dublin Bay. [Dublin]: 1976. 8 vols. Survey was carried out on behalf of the Dublin City Corporation, Dublin Port and Docks Board, and the Electricity Supply Board.

Aquatic Life

3461 WOODS, CEDRIC S. Freshwater life in Ireland: keys to the more easily identified Irish freshwater plants and animals and checklist for most groups. Dublin: 1974.

Naturalists — General

3462 PRAEGER, ROBERT LLOYD. Some Irish naturalists: a biographical notebook. Dundalk: 1949.

Individual

ARCHER, WILLIAM.

3463 FRAZER, WILLIAM. William Archer, F.R.S. [biographical note and bibliog.]. *Ir. Nat.,* 6, 1897, 253–7.

BARRINGTON, RICHARD M.

3464 MOFFAT, C.B. List of the scientific writings of R.M. Barrington. *Ir. Nat.,* 24, 1915, 203–6.

CLEALAND, JAMES D.R.

3465 MACDONALD, R. and MCMILLAN, N. James Dowsett Rose Clealand (Cleland): a forgotten Irish naturalist. *Ir. Nat. J.,* 13, 1959, 70–2.

3466 — and MCMILLAN, N.F. James Dowsett Rose-Cleland (1767–1852): some further notes. *ibid*., vol.18, no. 2, 1974, 30–32.

GREEN, WILLIAM SPOTSWOOD.

3467 Obituary and bibliog. notes. *Ir. Nat.,* 28, 1919, 81–4.

HART, HENRY C.

3468 BARRINGTON, RICHARD M. Henry Chichester Hart [obituary notice]. *Ir. Nat.,* vol. 17, 1908. Bibliog., pp. 253–4.

HARVEY, JOSHUA REUBENS.

3469 CULLINANE, JOHN P. Joshua Reubens Harvey. *Ir. Nat. J.,* vol. 17, no. 7, 1972, 223–225.

KNOWLES, WILLIAM JAMES.

3470 Obituary and bibliog. *Ir. Nat.J.,* 1, 1925–7, 257–8.

MCLEAN, GEORGE HUGH.

3471 Obituary. *Ir. Nat. J*., vol.17, no. 5, 1972, 146–7.

MACNEILL, NIALL.

3472 Niall MacNeill, 1889–1969 [and] Tribute to Colonel MacNeill as an entomologist, by Cynthia Longfield. *Ir. Nat. J*., vol. 16, no. 10, 1970, 289–291.

MOFFAT, CHARLES B.

3473 KENNEDY, P.G. *and others*. Charles Bethune Moffat, 1859–1945 [obituary and bibliog.]. *Ir. Nat.J.,* 8, 1942–6, 351–70.

MORE, ALEXANDER GOODMAN.

3474 List of the scientific writings of the late A.G. More. *Ir. Nat*., 4, 1895, 113–16.

3475 — MOFFAT, C.B., *ed*. Life and letters of Alexander Goodman More, with selections from his zoological and historical writings; with a preface by Frances C. More. Dublin: 1898. List of the scientific writings of the late A.G. More, pp. 618–623.

O'REILLY, JOSEPH PATRICK.

3476 COLE, GRENVILLE A.J. and SEYMOUR, HENRY J. Joseph Patrick O'Reilly [obituary and bibliog.]. *Ir. Nat*., 14, 1905, 45–50.

PATERSON, T.F.G.

3477 Obituary. *Ir. Nat. J*., vol.17, no. 5, 1972, 145–6.

READE, THOMAS MELLARD.

3478 HINCH, J. DE W. Obituary and bibliog. *Ir. Nat.,* 18, 1909, 221.

STELFOX, ARTHUR WILSON.

3479 Obituary notice. *R. Ir. Acad. Ann. Rpt*., 1972–73, 4–5.

3480 — Stelfox memorial number. *Ir. Nat. J*., vol. 17, no. 9, 1973, 285–320.

3481 — RIDDOLLS, ANTHEA and TYRRELL,

EILEEN M. The New University of Ulster Stelfox collection. *Ir. Nat. J.*, vol. 18, no. 8, 1975, 246–248.

STENDALL, J.A.S.

3482 J.A.S. STENDALL, (1887–1973). *Ir. Nat. J.*, vol. 18, no. 1, 1974, 8–9.

TEMPLETON, JOHN.

3483 MCMILLAN, N.F. John Templeton – some notes. *Ir. Nat. J.*, 15, 1965–67, 266–7.

USSHER, RICHARD JOHN.

3484 BARRINGTON, RICHARD M. Richard John Ussher [obituary and bibliog.]. *Ir. Nat.*, vol.22, 1913. Bibliog., pp. 225–7.

WARREN, ROBERT.

3485 NICHOLS, A.R. List of the late Robert Warren's more important writings. *Ir. Nat.*, 25, 1916, 41–4.

WILLIAMS, EDWARD.

3486 Obituary and bibliog. *Ir. Nat.*, 15, 1906, 21–6.

Marine Biology

3487 ALLEN, E.J. A selected bibliography of marine bionomics and fishery investigation. *J. Cons. Inter. Explor. Mer.,* vol. 1, nos. 1–2, 1926. Continued as *Current bibliography*, published thrice yearly in *J. Cons. Inter. Explor. Mer.*, vols. 1–24, 1926–58.

3488 FOOD AND AGRICULTURE ORGANIZATION OF THE UNITED NATIONS. Current bibliography for fisheries science [*afterwards*] Current bibliography for aquatic sciences and fisheries. Rome, vol. 1–, 1958–.

3489 MARINE BIOLOGICAL ASSOCIATION OF THE UNITED KINGDOM. List of publications recording results of researches carried out under the auspices of the . . . Association . . . in their laboratory or on the North Sea, 1886–1913. *Marine Biol. Assoc. J., new ser.*, 10, 1913, 143–76.

3490 — List of publications . . . 1886–1927. *ibid*., 15, 1928, 753–828.

3491 — Classified list of publications, vols. 16–29 of the Journal . . . and other publications recording the results of researches carried out at the Plymouth Laboratory from 1928 to 1950. *ibid*., 30, 1951–2, 589–672.

3492 WENT, ARTHUR E.J. Four late nineteenth century [marine] expeditions organised by the Royal Irish Academy. *R. Soc. Edinburgh Proc. Sec. B*, vol.72, 1972, 305–309.

Plankton

3493 BOYD, R.J. The relation of the plankton to the physical, chemical and biological features of Strangford Lough, Co. Down [with bibliog.]. *R. Ir. Acad. Proc. Sec. B*, vol.73, no. 20, 1973, 317–353.

3494 — A survey of the plankton of Strangford Lough, Co. Down. [with bibliog.]. *R. Ir. Acad. Proc. Sec. B.*, vol.73, no. 15, 1973, 231–267.

INVESTIGATIONS OF THE PLANKTON OF THE WEST COAST OF IRELAND.

3495 — Vol. I. Pelagic Cnidaria of the Galway Bay area 1956–72, with a revision of previous records for these species in Irish inshore waters, by R.J. Boyd, P. O'Ceidigh and A. Wilkinson. *R. Ir. Acad. Proc. Sec. B*, vol. 73, no. 22, 1973, 383–403.

3496 — Vol.II. Planktonic copepoda taken off Co. Galway and adjacent areas in plankton surveys during the years 1958–1963, [with bibliog.], by Julie M. Fives. *ibid*., vol.67, no. 10, 1969, 233–259.

3497 — Vol. III. *Calanus finmarchicus* (Gunn) and *Calanus helgolandicus* (Claus) in the plankton of Killeany Bay, Aran Islands, by B.F. Keegan. *ibid*., vol.68, no. 9, 1969, 137–147.

3498 — Vol. IV. Larval and post-larval stages of fishes taken from the plankton of the west coast in surveys during the years 1958–1966. [with bibliog.], by Julie M. Fives. *ibid*., 70, 1970, 15–93.

3499 — Vol. V. Chaetognatha recorded from the inshore plankton off Co. Galway. [with bibliog.] by Julie M. Fives. *ibid*., 71, 1971, 119–138.

3500 O'BRIEN, F.I. The relationship between temperature, salinity and Chaetognatha and the west coast of Ireland. [with bibliog.]. *Proc. R. Ir. Acad., Sec. B*, vol. 77, no. 14, 1977, 245–252.

3501 SOUTHERN, R., and GARDINER, A.C. The Phytoplankton of the River Shannon and Lough Derg [with bibliog.]. *R. Ir. Acad. Proc., Sec. B*, 45, 1938–40, 89–124.

BOTANY

Bibliography

3502 BOTANICAL SOCIETY OF THE BRITISH ISLES. Proceedings. London, vol. 1–, 1954–. Includes *Abstracts from Literature.*

3503 DUBLIN. SCIENCE AND ART MUSEUM, Botanical Department. Catalogue of books: author index. 1906. General catalogue on sheaves including Irish material; there is also an author and subject catalogue on cards which is comprehensive with regard to Irish botany.

3504 HENREY, BLANCHE. British botanical and horticultural literature before 1800, comprising a history and bibliography of botanical and horticultural books printed in England, Scotland and Ireland from the earliest times until 1800, Oxford: 1975. 3 vols.

3505 INTERNATIONAL BIBLIOGRAPHY OF VEGETATION MAPS. Edited by A.W. Kuchler. vol. 2. Vegetation maps of Europe. Compiled by A.W. Kuchler, 1966. (*Univ. Kansas Pub. library ser.* 26). British Isles, compiled by Frank A. Barnes. pp. 89–148.

3506 JACKSON, B.D. Guide to the literature of botany; being a classified selection of botanical works, including nearly 6,000 titles not given in Pritzel's *Thesaurus*. London: 1880. (*Index. Soc. pub.* vol. 8.)

3507 LINNEAN SOCIETY OF LONDON. Catalogue of printed books and pamphlets, new ed. London: 1925.

3508 MITCHELL, M.E. Irish botany in the seventeenth century. *Proc. R. Ir. Acad., Sec. B*, vol. 75, no. 13, 1975, 275–284.

3509 MORE, A.G. List of papers relating to the flora of Ireland, published from 1865 to 1872. *R. Ir. Acad. Proc., 2nd ser.,* 1, 1870–4, 291–3.

3510 O'SULLIVAN, A.M. A partially annotated bibliography of the Irish flora, 1960–1972. Dublin: An Foras Taluntais, 1973. (*Irish vegetation studies, no. 3*).

3511 PRAEGER, ROBERT LLOYD. Bibliography of Irish topographical botany. *R. Ir. Acad. Proc.,* 7, 1901, xcix–cxlvii.

3512 — Supplement, 1901–5. *ibid., Sec. B*, 26, 1906–7, 13–45.

3513 ROYAL DUBLIN SOCIETY. Bi-centenary celebrations, 1931. Official Handbook. Dublin; 1931. Publications illustrating the development of pure and applied botany in Ireland, 1650–1931, pp. 15–21. [Includes The Botanic Gardens, Glasnevin].

3514 SIMPSON, N.D. Bibliographical index of the British flora. [Bournemouth]: 1960. Ireland, pp. 391–429.

3515 SMART, JOHN, and TAYLOR, GEORGE, *eds*. Bibliography of key works for the identification of the British fauna and flora. 2nd ed. London: Systematics Association (British Museum), 1953. 1st ed.: 1942.

Flora, Regional Botany

3516 ADAMS, J. A students' illustrated Irish flora. Ashford: Kent, 1931. Bibliog., pp. 1–8.

3517 ALLIN, THOMAS. The flowering plants and ferns of the County Cork. Weston-Super-Mare: 1883.

3518 BELFAST NATURALISTS' FIELD CLUB. A preliminary report on the survey of the County Armagh flora, 1965–1967. 1968. (*Occasional publication no. 1*)

3519 BOOTH, EVELYN. M. and SCANNELL, MARY J.P. The Flora of county Carlow. Dublin: [1979]. Bibliog., pp. 157–162.

3520 BRUNKER, J.P. Flora of the county Wicklow; flowering plants, higher cryptogams and characeae. Dundalk: 1950. Bibliog., pp. vii–x.

3521 CARVILL, P.H. and CURTIS, T.G. New plant records for County Wicklow. *Ir. Nat. J.*, vol.17, no.11, 1973, 386–388.

3522 — Additional plant records for County Wicklow. (H 20). *Ir. Nat. J.*, vol.18, no. 3, 1974, 90.

3523 COLGAN, NATHANIEL. Flora of the county Dublin; flowering plants, higher cryptogams and characeae. Dublin: 1904.

3524 — Supplement ... Dublin, National Museum of Ireland: 1961.

3525 CONNOLLY, G. The vegetation of Southern Connemara [with bibliog.]. *R. Ir. Acad. Proc., Sec. B,* 39, 1929–30, 203–31.

3526 DICKIE, G. Flora of Ulster and botanist's guide to the North of Ireland. Belfast; 1864. Includes parts of Leitrim, Sligo and Mayo.

3527 DICKSON, C.H. *and others*. Some microhabitats of the Burren, their microenvironments and vegetation, by C.H. Dickson, M.C. Pearson and D.A. Webb. [with bibliog.]. *Proc. R. Ir. Acad., Sec. B*, vol.63, no. 16, 1964, 261–302.

3528 FARRELL, L. New plant records for Co. Monaghan. *Ir. Nat. J*., vol.17, no. 10, 1973, 355.

3529 FERGUSON, I.K. Notes on the flora of Co. Waterford. *Ir. Nat. J*., vol.16, no. 4, 1968, 94–97.

3530 — Further notes on the flora of Co. Waterford. *Ir. Nat. J*., vol.18, no. 3, 1974, 85–87.

3531 GAIDOZ, H. Flora Celtica. *Rev. Celt*., 7, 1886, 162–70.

3532 HARRON, JOHN. Plant records for some Irish counties. *Ir. Nat. J.,* vol. 18, no. 3, 1974, 88–90.

3533 — Recent records of plant distribution for the north-east of Ireland. *Ir. Nat. J*., vol.16, no. 12, 1970, 365–369.

3534 HART, HENRY CHICHESTER. Flora of the County Donegal: or, list of the flowering plants and ferns and their localities and distribution. Dublin and London: 1898.

3535 — The flora of Howth. Dublin: 1887. Bibliog. notes in introduction.

3536 — A list of plants found in the islands of Aran, Galway Bay. Dublin: 1875.

3537 HASS, ERIC. A magical island [Garnish Island, Co. Cork]. *Garden J*., vol.21, no. 3, 1971, 66–72.

3538 IVIMEY-COOK, R.B. and PROCTOR, M.C.F. The plant communities of the Burren, Co. Clare. [with bibliog.]. *R. Ir. Acad. Proc. Ser. B*., vol.64, no. 15, 1966, 211–301.

3539 KERTLAND, M.P.H. The Flora of Ulster. *Belfast Nat. Hist. Phil. Soc. Proc*., vol.8, 1964–70, 46–49.

3540 LUDI, WERNER, *ed*. Die Pflanzenwelt Irlands. (The flora and vegetation of Ireland). Bern: 1952. *Veröffentlichungen des Geobotanischen Institutes Rubel in Zurich, heft* 25. Includes bibliogs.

3541 MCCLINTOCK, D. *and others* Some new plant records for Co. Louth, (H. 31) by D. McClintock, W.E. Harrison and J. Harron. *Ir. Nat. J*., vol.18, no. 3, 1974, 87.

3542 MCMULLEN, R.M. A report on the flora of N. Tipperary (H 10). *Ir. Nat. J*., vol.17, no. 7, 1972, 215–218.

3543 MOORE, JOHN J. A re-survey of the vegetation of the district lying south of Dublin (1905–56) [with bibliog.]. *R. Ir. Acad. Proc. Sec. B*, 61, 1960, 1–36.

3544 MORE, A.G. Contributions to Cybele Hibernica . . . founded on the papers of the late Alexander Goodman More. By N.Colgan and Reginald W. Scully. 2nd ed. Dublin: 1898. Bibliog., pp. xix–xxxvi.

3545 MURPHY, EDWARD. Contributions towards a Flora Hibernica; being a list of plants not before observed wild in Ireland; together with new locations for a few of the more rare ones. *Mag. Nat. Hist*., 1, 1829, 436–438.

3546 PERRING, F.H. New plant records for Co. Mayo. *Ir. Nat. J*., 15, 1965–67, 236–240.

3547 POWER, THOMAS. The Botanist's guide for the County of Cork, in contributions towards the fauna and flora of Cork. Cork: 1845.

3548 PRAEGER, ROBERT LLOYD. The botanist in Ireland. East Ardsley, Wakefield: 1974. Facsimile reprint of 1934 ed.

3549 — Additions to Irish topographical botany in 1901. *Ir. Nat.,* 11, 1902, 1–8; 1902, *ibid*., 12, 1903, 23–40; 1903, *ibid*., 13, 1904, 1–15; 1904, *ibid*., 14, 1905, 21–9; 1905, *ibid*., 15, 1906, 47–61; 1906–7, *ibid*., 17, 1908, 28–37; 1908–12, *ibid*., 22, 1913, 103–10.

3550 — Report on recent additions to the Irish fauna and flora . . . *R. Ir. Acad. Proc., Sec. B*, 39, 1929, 1–94.

3551 — A further contribution to the flora of Ireland. *R. Ir. Acad. Proc., Sec. B*, 45, 1938–40, 231–54.

3552 — Additions to the knowledge of the Irish flora, 1939–45. *R.Ir.Acad.Proc.,Sec.B*,51, 1945–8, 27–51. See also nos: 3511–12.

3553 SCANNELL, MARY J.P. and SYNNOTT, DONAL M. Census catalogue of the flora of Ireland: a concise conspectus of the Irish Pteridophyta, Gymnospermae and Angiospermae including all the native plants and established aliens known to occur in Ireland with the distribution of each species. Dublin: 1972. Bibliogs., pp. xiii–xvi.

3554 SCULLY, R.W. Flora of the county Kerry including flowering plants, ferns, characeae, etc. Dublin: 1916. Bibliog., pp. lxxiii–lxxxi.

3555 SINGH, G. and SMITH, A.G. Post-glacial vegetational history and relative land- and sea-level changes in Lecale, Co. Down. *R. Ir. Acad. Proc. Sec. B*, vol.73, no. 1, 1973, 1–51.

3556 STEWART, S.A. and CORRY, T.H. A flora of the north east of Ireland . . . 2nd ed. Belfast: 1938. Bibliog., pp. liv–lix. 1st ed: 1888.

3557 SYNNOTT, DONAL M. County Louth wild-flowers. Dundalk; 1970.

3558 WEBB, D.A. An Irish flora. 6th rev. ed. Dundalk: 1977. Bibliog., pp. xvii–xviii.

3559 — Noteworthy plants of the Burren: a catalogue raisonné. *R. Ir. Acad. Proc. Sec. B*, 62, 1962, 117–134.

3560 — AND HODGSON, J. The flora of Inishbofin and Inishshark. *Bot. Soc. Br. Isl. Proc*., 7, 1968, 345–363.

3561 — AND GLANVILLE, E.V. The vegetation and flora of some islands in the Connemara lakes. *R. Ir. Acad. Proc., Sec. B*, 62, 1962, 31–54.

3562 WHITE, J.M. The fens of North Armagh [with bibliog.]. *R. Ir. Acad. Proc., Sec.B*, 40, 1931–2, 233–83.

Nomenclature

3563 CAMERON, J. The Gaelic names of plants (Scottish, Irish and Manx) collected and arranged in scientific order, with notes on their etymology, uses, plant superstitions, etc . . . new. rev. ed. Glasgow, 1900. 1st ed. London: 1883.

3564 HOGAN, F.E. *and others*. Luibhleabhran: Irish and Scottish Gaelic names of herbs, plants, trees, etc., by F.Edmund Hogan, John Hogan, and John C. MacErlean. Dublin: 1900.

Botanic Gardens

3565 BESANT, J.W. Botanic gardens [Glasnevin, Dublin]: origin, history and development. *Ir. Dept. Agric.J.*, 33, 1935, 173–82.

3566 BRADY, AIDAN. The origins and development of the national Botanic Gardens. *Cap. Ann*., 1974, 187–203.

3567 DOYLE, J. The place of a national Arboretum in the Irish economy; with notes by H.M. Fitzpatrick and T. Clear. *R. Dublin Soc. Sci. Proc. Ser. B*., 1, 1960–66, 83–92.

3568 FANNING, JOHN. The National Botanic Gardens and the public. *Ir. Dept. Agric. J*., 61, 1964, 234–241.

3569 HACKNEY, PAUL. Notes on the vascular plant herbarium of the Ulster Museum. *Ir. Nat. J*., vol.17, no. 7, 1972, 230–233.

3570 MCCRACKEN, EILEEN. The Arboretum, Dublin Botanic Garden, 1795–1878. *Qtr. J. Forestry*, 63, 1969, 242–253.

3571 — The origins of the library at Glasnevin Botanic Garden. *Ir. Booklore*, vol.2, no. 1, 1972, 82–88.

3572 — The Palm House and Botanic Garden, Belfast. Belfast: 1971. Bibliog., pp. 64–65.

3573 — Some nineteenth century horticulturists. *Ir. Booklore,* vol.1, no. 2, 1971, 179–185. Supplementary material to Praeger's *Some Irish Naturalists*. Entries relate solely to personnel connected with Irish Botanic Gardens.

3574 MOORE, DAVID. Guide to the Royal Botanic Gardens, Glasnevin; rev. and enl. with Prof. W.R. M'Nab. Dublin: 1885. 1st ed. 1850.

3575 WILLIAMS, J.T. Plant collections in the British Isles: a preliminary index. Kew: 1974.

Botanists

3576 DESMOND, RAY. Dictionary of British and Irish botanists and horticulturists, including plant collectors and botanical artists. London: 1977. 1st pub. 1893 under the title *A biographical index of British and Irish botanists*. London; 2nd ed. London: 1931. Lists Irish botanists chronologically, pp. 701–2.

3577 LETT, THE REV. CANON H.W. Botanists of the North of Ireland. *Ir. Nat. J*., 22, 1913, 21–33.

Individual

CLINCH, PHYLLIS.

3578 Award of the Boyle medal to Phyllis E.M. Clinch, D.Sc., M.R.I.A. [with bibliog.]. *R. Dublin Soc. Sci. Proc., Ser. A*, vol. 1, no. 7, 1961.

COLGAN, NATHANIEL.

3579 PRAEGER, R. LLOYD. List of the principal papers published by Nathaniel Colgan, other than those in *The Irish Naturalist. Ir. Nat.*, 28, 1919, 125–6..

HARVEY, WILLIAM HENRY.

3580 WEBB, D.A. William Henry Harvey, 1811–1866, and the kingdom of systemic botany. *Hermathena*, 103, 1966, 32–45.

HEATON, RICHARD.

3581 WALSH, LAURENCE. Richard Heaton of Ballyskenagh, 1601–1666. Roscrea: Parkmore Press 1978. On cover: First Irish botanist. Bibliog., pp. 101–104.

TEMPLETON, JOHN.

3582 KERTLAND, M.P.H. Bi-centenary of the birth of John Templeton, A.L.S., 1766–1825. (with a note on the discovery of part of his herbarium). *Ir. Nat. J.*, vol.15, 1965–67, 229–231.

THRELKELD, CALEB.

3583 MICHELL, M.E. The sources of Threlkeld's *Synopsis Stirpium Hibernicarum*. *Proc. R. Ir. Acad. Sec. B*, vol.74, no. 1, 1974,1–6.

WADDELL, COSSLETT HERBERT.

3584 FITZGERALD, J.W. and FITZGERALD, R.D. Gleanings among the Waddell Mss. *Ir. Nat.J.*, vol.13, no. 10, 1961, 227–31.

Physiologic and Structural

3585 JOHNSON, T. and HENSMAN, R. Agricultural seeds and their weed impurities: a source of Ireland's alien flora [with bibliog.]. *R. Dublin Soc. Sci. Proc., new series*, 12, 1909–10, 446–62.

3586 PRAEGER, R. LLOYD. Hybrids in the Irish flora: a tentative list. *R. Ir. Acad. Proc., Sec. B*, 54, 1951–2, 1–14.

Economic

3587 JACKSON, B.D. Vegetable technology: a contribution towards a bibliography of economic botany, with a comprehensive subject-index. London: 1882. (*Index Soc. pub.*, vol. 11.)

3588 JUDE, *pseud.* Medicinal and perfumery plants and herbs of Ireland: a possible great natural Irish industry suitable to the Gaeltacht. Dublin: 1933. Bibliog., p. xxiii.

Trees

(See Forestry, nos. 4295–4334)

Leguminosae

3589 ARDAGH, J. The Shamrock: a bibliography. *Ir. Book Lov.*, 21, 1933, 37–40.

3590 COLGAN, N. The Shamrock in literature: a critical chronology. *R. Soc. Antiq. Ir. J.*, 26, 1896, 211–26, 349–61. See also R.L. Praeger's *The Way that I went*, Dublin and London, 1937, pp. 265–9.

3591 EVERETT, T.H. Some facts and fallacies about the shamrock. *Garden J.*, vol.21, no. 1, 1971, 24–26.

Rosaceae

3592 WATSON, W.C.R. Handbook of the rubi of Great Britain and Ireland. Cambridge: 1958. Bibliog., pp. 265–6.

Saxifrageae

3593 WEBB, D.A. Notes preliminary to a revision of the Irish dactyloid saxifrages. *R. Ir. Acad. Proc., Sec. B*, 51, 1945–8, 233–59.

Compositae

3594 LAMBERT, D.S. and HACKNEY, P. Taraxacum records from Ireland. *Ir. Nat. J.*, vol.18, no. 10, 1976, 310–2.

Orchidales

3595 ETTLINGER, D.M. TURNER. British and Irish orchids: a field guide. London: 1976.

Bryophyta

3596 LETT, H.W. Census report on the mosses of Ireland [with bibliog.]. *R. Ir. Acad. Proc., Sec. B*, 32, 1913–16, 65–166.

3597 MCARDLE, D. A list of Irish *hepaticae* [with bibliog.]. *R. Ir. Acad. Proc., Sec. B*, 24, 1902–4, 387–502.

3598 MOORE, D. List of books and papers relating to the mosses of Ireland. *Appendix to* A Synopsis of the mosses of Ireland. *R. Ir. Acad. Proc., 2nd ser.*, 1, 1870–4, 467–9.

3599 RYAN, GEORGE, R. The Irish mossers of Scituate [Massachusetts]. *Eire-Ir.*, vol.1, 1965–66, no. 1, 7–17.

3600 SCIENCE MUSEUM LIBRARY, LONDON. Carrageen, Irish moss. *Science Lib. bibliog. ser.*, no. 98, 1933.

3601 — Another edition. *ibid.*, no. 416, 1938.

3602 — Supplement to no. 416. *ibid.*, no. 752, 1957.

3603 SMITH, A.J.E. The moss flora of Britain and Ireland. Cambridge: 1978. Bibliog., pp. 685–6.

3604 TAYLOR, F.J. Bryophyte county floras, no. 2: Scotland and Ireland. *British Bryol. Soc. Trans.*, 2, 1955, 539–51.

Lichens

3605 ADAMS, J. The distribution of lichens in Ireland [with bibliog.]. *R. Ir. Acad.Proc., Sec. B*, 27, 1907–9, 193–234.

3606 BAILEY, R.H. Some Irish lichen records. *Ir. Nat. J.*, vol.17, no. 11, 1973, 392–4.

3607 DUNCAN, URSULA K. Introduction to British lichens. Arbroath: 1970. Bibliog., pp. 231–274.

3608 FENTON, A.F.G. The Lichens of Northern Ireland. [with bibliog.] *Ir. Nat. J.*, vol. 16, no. 5, 1969, 110–127. Includes a brief summary of the history of Irich lichenology.

3609 HAWKSWORTH, DAVID LESLIE and SEWARD, M.R.D. Lichenology in the British Isles, 1568–1975: an historical and bibliographical survey. Richmond (Surrey): 1977.

3610 KNOWLES, M.C. The lichens of Ireland [with bibliog.]. *R. Ir. Acad. Proc., Sec. B*, 38, 1928–9, 179–434.

3611 — The maritime and marine lichens of Howth [with bibliog.]. *R. Dublin Soc. Sci. Proc., new series*, 14, 1913–15, 79–143.

3612 MITCHELL, M.E. A bibliography of books, pamphlets and articles relating to Irish lichenology, 1727–1970. Galway: 1971. Ed. limited to 350 copies.

3613 PORTER, L. The lichens of Ireland (supplement). *R. Ir. Acad. Proc., Sec. B*, 51, 1945–8, 347–86.

3614 SEAWARD, M.R.D. Contributions to the lichen flora of South-East Ireland. *Proc. R. Ir. Acad., Sec. B*, 75, 1975, 185–205; 77, 1977, 119–134.

Mycology, Fungi

3615 ADAMS, J., and PETHYBRIDGE, G.H. A census catalogue of Irish fungi [with bibliog.]. *R. Ir. Acad. Proc., Sec. B*, 28, 1909–10, 120–66.

3616 DICKSON, C.H. and DOOLEY, M. Fungi associated with Irish peat bogs. *Proc. R. Ir. Acad. Sec. B*, vol.68, no. 8, 1969, 109–135.

3617 HASSELL, F.C. The early Irish mycologists, 1726–1900. *Ir. Nat. J.*, 12, 1956–8, 116–20.

3618 MUSKETT, A.E. Mycology and plant pathology in Ireland. *Proc. R. Ir. Acad., Sec. B*, vol.76, no. 27, 1976, 393–472.

3619 — *and others*. Contributions to the fungus flora of Ulster [with bibliog.], by A.E. Muskett, E.N. Carrothers, and H.Cairns. *R. Ir. Acad. Proc., Sec. B,* 40, 1931–2, 37–55.

3620 O'CONNOR, P. A contribution to knowledge of the Irish fungi. *R. Dublin Soc. Sci. Proc., new series*, 21, 1933–38, 381–417.

3621 — A further contribution to knowledge of the Irish fungi. *ibid., new series.*, 25, 1949–51, 33–53.

Algae

3622 ADAMS, J. A list of synonyms of Irish algae, with some additional records and observations [with bibliog.]. *R. Ir. Acad. Proc., Sec. B*, 28, 1909–10, 167–214.

3623 — A synopsis of Irish algae, freshwater and marine. *R. Ir. Acad. Proc., Sec. B*, 27, 1907–9, 11–60.

3624 BLACKER, H. An algal survey of Lough Foyle, North Ireland [with bibliog.]. *R. Ir. Acad. Proc., Sec. B*, 54, 1951–2, 97–139.

3625 BRENNAN, A.T. Notes on some common Irish seaweeds. Dublin: 1950.

3626 CHAPMAN, V.J. Seaweeds and their uses. 2nd ed., London: 1970. Sel. bibliog., pp. 262–285.

3627 COLINVAUX, LLEWELLYN HILLIS. A partially annotated bibliography of the algae of Ireland. *Ir. Nat. J.*, vol. 15, no. 4, 1965, 88–95.

3628 CULLINANE, JOHN P. Irish seaweeds: early Irish collectors. *Cap. Ann.*, 1974, 212–216.

3629 — Records of the distribution of the genus *Vaucheria* in the county of Cork. *Ir. Nat. J.*, 18, 1974–76, 218–9.

3630 — Phychology of the South coast of Ireland. Cork: 1973. Lists species recorded in the literature for Counties Limerick, Kerry, Cork and Waterford.

3631 Dixon, Peter S. *and others*. The Distribution of benthic marine algae: a bibliography for the British Isles, by Peter S. Dixon, David E.G. Irvine, and James H. Price. *Br. Phycological Bull*., vol.3, no. 1, 1966, 87–142.
Supplement 1. *ibid*., vol.3, no. 2, 1967, 305–315.
Supplement 2. *Brit. Phycological J*., vol.5, no. 1, 1970, 103–142.
Supplement 3. *ibid*., vol.10, 1975, 299–307.

3632 Guiry, Michael D. A consensus and bibliography of Irish seaweeds. Vaduz: 1978. *Bibliotheca Phycologica*, Bd. 44.

3633 Kertland, M.P.H. Some early algae collections in the Queen's University Herbarium [with bibliog.] *Ir. Nat. J*., vol.15, no. 12, 1967, 346–349.

3634 — The specimens of Templeton's algae in the Queen's University Herbarium. *Ir. Nat. J*., vol.15, no. 11, 1967, 318–322.

3635 O'Neill, Timothy P. Some Irish techniques of collecting seaweed. *Folklife*, vol.8, 1970, 13–19.

3636 Parke, Mary and Dixon, Peter S. A revised check-list of British marine algae. [with bibliog.]. *J. Mar. Biol. Ass. U.K*., 44, 1964, 499–542. Contains a complete list of the algae recorded as occurring on the coasts of Britain and Ireland or in adjacent waters.

3637 — Check-list of British marine algae – second revision. [with bibliog.] *ibid*., vol.48, 1968, 783–832.

3638 — Check-list of British marine algae – third revision. *ibid*., vol.56, 1976, 527–594.

3639 Parkes, Hilda M. Records of *Codium* species in Ireland. *Proc. R. Ir. Acad., Sec. B*, vol.75, no. 4, 1975, 125–134.

3640 — and Scannell, M.J.P. A list of marine algae from the Wexford coast. [with bibliog.]. *Ir. Nat. J*., vol.16, no. 6, 1969, 158–162.

3641 Pilcher, B. The algae of John Templeton in the Ulster Museum. [with bibliog.]. *Ir. Nat. J*., vol.15, no. 12, 1967, 350–353.

3642 Scannell, M.J.P. Unpublished records of marine algae made mainly in County Wexford by Thomas Johnson and Matilda Knowles. *Ir. Nat. J*., vol.16, no. 7, 1969, 192–198.

3643 Third International Seaweed Symposium. Galway: August 13–19, 1958. Abstracts. Galway: 1958.

ZOOLOGY

3644 Agassiz, Louis. Bibliographia zoologiae et geologiae: a general catalogue of all books, tracts, and memoirs on zoology and geology: corrected, enl. and edited by H.E. Strickland. London: Ray Society, 1848–54, 4 vols. The Ray Society intended to issue a supplement including subject index but this was never published.

3645 Beirne, Bryan P. The origin and history of the British fauna. London: 1952. Bibliog., pp. 153–5.

3646 Forbes, Alexander Robert. Gaelic names of beasts (*mammalia*), birds, fishes, insects, reptiles, etc., in two parts. 1: Gaelic-English:2:English-Gaelic ... with Gaelic, other English names, etymology, Celtic lore, prose, poetry, and proverbs referring to each ... Edinburgh:1905.

3647 Gatenby, J. Bronte. The history of zoology and comparative anatomy in Trinity College, Dublin. *Ir. J. Med. Sci., 6th ser*., 417, 1960, 395–407.

3648 O'Gorman, Fergus and Wymes, Enda. The future of Irish wildlife – a blueprint for development. Dublin: An Foras Taluntais, 1973. Proceedings of a conference held in the Great Southern Hotel, Killarney, February 19–21, 1970.

3649 O'Riordan, C.E. Some notes on the 'Flying Falcon' expedition of 1888, off the southeast coast of Ireland. [with bibliog.]. *Proc. R. Ir. Acad. Sec. B*, vol. 65, no. 17, 1967, 373–384.

3650 Sawyer, F.C. Books of reference in zoology, chiefly bibliographical. *Soc. Bibliog. Nat. Hist.J.*, vol.3, pt. 2, 1955, 72–91. Very good list, including brief topographical index of countries.

3651 Scouler, John. Notice of animals which have disappeared from Ireland during the period of authentic history. *J. Geol. Soc. Dublin*, 1, 1838, 224–231.

3652 SHEPPARD, T. List of papers bearing upon the zoology, botany and prehistoric archaeology of the British Isles during 1919 (1920–5). In *Reports of the British Association for the Advancement of Science*, 1920–6.

3653 SMART, JOHN and TAYLOR, GEORGE, *eds*. Bibliography of key works for the identification of the British fauna and flora. 2nd ed. London: Systematics Association (British Museum), 1953. 1st ed.: 1942.

3654 ZOOLOGICAL RECORD. London: Zoological Society of London, vol.1–, 1864–.

3655 ZOOLOGICAL SOCIETY OF LONDON. Catalogue of the library. 5th ed. London: 1902. Previous ed. published in 1854, 1864, 1872, 1880 and 1883.

Zoological Gardens

3656 ROYAL ZOOLOGICAL SOCIETY OF IRELAND. Animals of Dublin Zoo. Dublin: 1977.

3657 WENT, ARTHUR E.J. Albert Tower and its foundation stone in the Dublin Zoo. *Dublin Hist. Rec.*, vol.25, no. 4, 1972, 133–5.

3658 — Breeding of lions in the Dublin Zoo (1857–1962). *R. Dublin Soc. Sci. Proc.*, Ser. B, vol.1, no. 8, 1963. 67–81.

3659 — The Dublin Zoo. *Dublin Hist. Rec.*, 24, 1970–71, 101–111.

Zoologists

AUGUSTINE.

3660 SCHARFF, R.F. The earliest Irish zoologist [Augustine]. *Ir. Nat.*, 30, 1921, 128–32.

BARRETT-HAMILTON, G.E.H.

3661 MOFFAT, C.B. List of the scientific writings of G.E.H. Barrett-Hamilton. *Ir. Nat.*, 23, 1914, 88–93.

HALIDAY, ALEXANDER HENRY.

3662 WRIGHT, E. PERCEVAL. Naturalists in Ireland: 1–. Alexander Henry Haliday: a bibliography. *Ir. Nat.*, 11, 1902, 197–99.

KANE, WILLIAM FRANCIS DE VISMES.

3663 HALBERT, J.N. List of the more important writings of W.F. de Vismes Kane. *Ir. Nat.*, 27, 1918, 101–3.

MASSY, ANNE L.

3664 MOFFAT, C.B. Obituary notice and bibliog. *Ir. Nat.J.*, 3, 1930–1, 215–17.

RUSS, PERCY.

3665 BEIRNE, BRYAN P. Biographical note [with bibliog.]. *Ir. Nat. J.*, 8, 1942–6, 208–10.

3666 SOUTHERN, ROWLAND
Rowland Southern, 1882–1935: obituary and bibliog. *Ir. Nat. J.*, 6, 1936–7, 42–5.

STRINGER, ARTHUR.

3667 FAIRLEY, J.S. Arthur Stringer, a little known Ulster mammalogist. *Ir. Nat. J.*, vol.18, no. 7, 1975, 211–215.

Distribution

3668 CRICHTON, MARY, *ed*. Provisional distribution maps of amphibians, reptiles and mammals in Ireland. Dublin: 1974.

3669 — and LAMHNA, EANNA NI, *ed*. Provisional atlas of the butterflies in Ireland, part of the European Invertebrate Survey. Dublin: 1975.

3670 FLORA EUROPAEA, edited by T.G. Tutin, V.H. Heywood, N.A. Burges, M.D. Moore, D.H. Valentine, S.M. Walters [and] D.A. Webb. Cambridge. vol.I. Lycopodiceae to Platanaceae. 1964. vol. II. Rosaceae to Umbelliferae. 1968. vol. III. Diapensiaceae to Myoporaceae. 1972. vol. IV. Plantaginaceae to Compositae (and) Runiaceae. 1976. Fifth and final volume to appear on the Monocotyledones.

Marine Biology

LITTORAL AND BENTHIC INVESTIGATIONS ON THE WEST COAST OF IRELAND.

3671 1. (Section A: faunistic and ecological studies) The sponge fauna of Kilkieran Bay and adjacent areas, by G. Konnecker. *Proc. R. Ir. Acad. Sec. B*, vol.73, no. 26, 1973, 451–472.

3672 2. (Section B: shellfish investigations) The occurrence of *Palinurus Mauritanicus* Gruvel, 1911, on the west coast of Ireland. (Decapoda, Palinuridae) [with bibliog.] *by* J.P. Mercer. *ibid.*, vol. 73, no. 25, 1978, 445–449.

3673 3. (Section A: faunistic and ecological studies) The Bivalves of Galway Bay and Kilkerrin Bay. by B.F. Keegan. *ibid.*, vol. 74, no. 4, 1974, 85–123.

3674 4. (Section A: Faunistic and ecological studies). Some shores in Counties Clare and Galway. by J.S. Ryland and A. Nelson-

Smith. *ibid*., vol. 75, no. 11, 1975, 245–266.

3675 5. (Section A: Faunistic and ecological studies). A contribution to the biology of the leopard-spotted goby *Thorogobius ephippiatus* (Lowe) (Pisces: Teleostei: Gobiidae), by James Dunne. *ibid*., vol. 76, no. 8, 1976, 121–132.

3676 6. (Section A: Faunistic and ecological studies). Annotated bibliographies of the genus *Tapes* (Bivalvia; veneridae), by J.K. Partridge. Pt. I. *Tapes decussatus* (L) Pt. II. *Tapes semidecussatus* Reeve. *ibid*., vol. 77, no. 1, 1977, 1–64. Bibliography consists of 225 references arranged according to author.

3677 7. (Section A: Faunistic and ecological studies) The biology of the shanny *Blennius pholis L* (Pisces) at Carna, Connemara, by J. Dunne. *ibid*., vol.77, no. 12, 1977, 207–226.

Invertebrates

3678 FAHY, E. Variation in invertebrate community structure in three freshwater habitats in Ireland, as described by an index of species diversity. *R. Ir. Acad. Proc. Sec. B*., vol.76, no. 20, 1976, 315–321.

3679 LANSBURY, I. Notes on the Hemiptera, Coleoptera, Diptera and other invertebrates of the Burren, Co. Clare and Inishmore, Aran Islands. [with bibliog.]. *R. Ir. Acad. Proc. Sec. B*., vol.64, no. 7, 1965, 89–115.

3680 MORIARTY, CHRISTOPHER. Distribution of freshwater macroinvertebrates in Ireland, 1967–1972. *Ir. Nat. J*., vol.17, no. 12, 1973, 409–412.

3681 SCHARFF, R.F. On the Irish names of invertebrate animals [with bibliog.]. *Ir. Nat.,* 25, 1916, 140–52.

Sponges

3682 STEPHENS, JANE. The fresh-water sponges of Ireland [with bibliog.]. *R. Ir. Acad. Proc., Sec. B*, 35, 1919–20, 205–52.

3683 — Report on the sponges collected off the coast of Ireland by the dredging expeditions of the Royal Irish Academy and the Royal Dublin Society [with bibliog.]. *R. Ir. Acad. Proc., Sec. B*, 34, 1917–19, 1–15.

3684 VOSMAER, GUALTHERUS CAREL JACOB. Bibliography of sponges, 1551–1913: edited by G.P. Bidder and C.S. Vosmaer-Roell. Cambridge: 1928.

Sea Anemones

3685 HADDON, ALFRED C. A revision of the British *Actiniae*. Pt. 1: Introduction [with bibliog.]. *R. Dublin Soc. Trans., 2nd ser.,* 4, 1888–92, 297–361. Pt. 2: The *Zoantheae*, by A.C. Haddon and A.M. Shackleton. *ibid*., pp. 609–72.

3686 STEPHENS, JANE. A list of Irish *Coelenterata* including *Ctenophora* [with bibliog.]. *R. Ir. Acad. Proc., Sec. B*, 25, 1904–5, 25–92.

3687 STEPHENSON, T.A. On certain *Actiniaria* collected off Ireland by the Irish Fisheries Department, during the years 1899–1913 [with bibliog.]. *R. Ir. Acad. Proc., Sec. B*, 34, 1917–19, 106–59.

Hydrozoa

3688 DUERDEN, J.E. The *Hydroids* of the Irish coast [with bibliog.]. *R. Dublin Soc. Sci. Proc., new series.,* 8, 1893–8, 405–20.

Echinodermata

3689 MASSY, ANNE L. The *Holothurioidea* of the coasts of Ireland [with bibliog.]. *R.Dublin Soc. Sci. Proc., new series.,* 16, 1920–2, 37–62.

3690 NICHOLS, A.R. A list of Irish *Echinoderms*, being a report from the Fauna and Flora Committee [with bibliog.]. *R. Ir. Acad. Proc., Sec. B*, 24, 1902–4, 231–67.

Molluscs

3691 ANDERSON, R. Mapping non-marine mollusca in North East Ireland. *Ir. Nat. J*., vol.19, no. 2, 1977, 29–38.

3692 BISHOP, M.J. The Mollusca of acid woodland in West Cork and Kerry. *R. Ir. Acad. Proc. Sec. B*., vol.77, no. 13, 1977, 227–244.

3693 BROWN, THOMAS. Illustrations of the recent conchology of Great Britain and Ireland, with the descriptions and localities of all species, marine, land, and freshwater. 2nd ed., London: 1844.

3694 COLGAN, NATHANIEL. List of the principal books and papers relating to the *Opisthobranch* fauna of Co. Dublin. *Ir. Nat*., 23, 1914, 164–6.

3695 — The marine Mollusca of the shores and shallow waters of Co. Dublin [with bibliog.]. *R. Ir. Acad. Proc., Sec. B*, 39, 1929–30, 391–424.

3696 McMillan, Nora F. The Mollusca of the Wexford gravels (Pleistocene), South East Ireland. [with bibliog.]. *R. Ir. Acad. Proc. Sec. B.*, vol.63, no. 15, 1964, 265–289.

3697 Massy, Anne L. Mollusca (Pelecypoda, Scaphopoda, Gastropoda, Opisthobranchia) of the Irish Atlantic Slope, 50–1500 fathoms. *R. Ir. Acad. Proc., Sec. B*, 39, 1929–30, 232–342.

3698 Nichols, A.R. A list of the marine mollusca of Ireland. *R. Ir. Acad. Proc. Ser. 3.*, 5, 1898–1900, 477–662. Bibliog., pp. 480–491.

3699 Stelfox, Arthur Wilson. A list of the land freshwater mollusks of Ireland; bibliography, by R.J. Welch. *R. Ir. Acad. Proc., Sec. B*, 29, 1911–12, 136–158.

3700 — On references by W.E. Leach to Irish land and freshwater shells. *Ir. Nat.*, 23, 1914, 35–6.

3701 Turk, Stella M. Recording scheme for marine mollusca. *Ir. Nat. J.*, vol.15, no. 1, 1974, 21–23.

Gastropoda

3702 Eales, N.B. Revision of the world species of *Aplysia* (*Gastropoda, Opisthobranchia*) [with bibliog.]. *Brit. Museum* (*Nat. Hist.*) *Bull.Zool.*, vol. 5, no. 10, 1960.

3703 Ellis, Arthur Erskine. British snails: a guide to the non-marine gastropoda of Great Britain and Ireland, pleistocene to recent. Oxford: 1969. Lithographic reprint of 1st (1926) ed. Bibliog. and supp. bibliog. 283–293.

3704 Kennedy, C.R. Studies on the Irish Tubificidae. [with bibliog.]. *R. Ir. Acad. Proc., Sec. B*, vol.63, no. 13, 1964, 225–237.

3705 Quick, H.E. British slugs (*Pulmonata, Testacellidae, Arionidae, Limacidae*) [with bibliog.]. *Brit. Museum* (*Nat. Hist.*) *Bull. Zool.*, vol. 6, no. 3, 1960.

3706 Scharff, R.F. The slugs of Ireland [with bibliog.]. *R. Dublin Soc. Sci. Trans., 2nd ser.*, 4, 1888–92, 513–58.

Cephalopoda

3707 Massy, Anne L. The *Cephalopoda* of the Irish coast [with bibliog.]. *R. Ir. Acad. Proc., Sec. B*, 38, 1928–9, 25–37.

Tunicata

3708 Hopkinson, John. A bibliography of the *Tunicata*, 1469–1910. London: 1913. (*Ray Soc. pub.*, no. 94.)

Vermes

3709 Friend, Hilderic. Irish *Enchytraeids* in the Faroes: light on the question of distribution [with bibliog.]. *Ir. Nat.*, 31, 1922, 112–14.

3710 — Notes on Irish *Oligochaeta* [with bibliog.]. *Ir. Nat.*, 25, 1916, 22–7.

3711 Southern, Rowland. Contributions towards a monograph of the British and Irish *Oligochaeta* [with bibliog.]. *R. Ir. Acad. Proc., Sec. B*, 27, 1907–9, 119–77.

3712 — *Turbellaria* in Ireland [with bibliog.]. *R. Ir. Acad. Proc., Sec. B*, 41, 1932–3, 43–72.

Crustacea

3713 Carpenter, George H. On some *Pycnogonida* from the Irish coasts [with bibliog.]. *R. Dublin Soc. Sci. Proc., new ser.*, 8, 1893–8, 195–204.

3714 Gordan, Joan. A bibliography of the order *Mysidacea. Amer. Mus. Nat. Hist. Bull.*, vol. 112, pt. 4, 1957, 279–394.

3715 Norman, A.M. Irish *Crustacea Ostracoda* [with bibliog.]. *Ir. Nat.*, 14, 1905, 137–55.

3716 Southern, Rowland and Gardiner, A.C. The diurnal migrations of the *Crustacea* of the plankton in Lough Derg [with bibliog.]. *R. Ir. Acad. Proc., Sec.B*, 40, 1931–2, 121–59.

Isopoda

3717 Pack Beresford, Denis R. and Foster, Nevin H. The woodlice of Ireland: their distribution and classification [with bibliog.]. *R. Ir. Acad.Proc., Sec.B*, 29, 1911–12, 165–89.

Decapoda

3718 Gurney, Robert. Bibliography of the larvae of *Decapod Crustacea*. London: 1939. (*Ray. Soc. pub.* no. 125.)

3719 O'Ceidigh, Padraig. A list of Irish marine

decapod crustacea. Dublin: 1963. Bibliog., pp. 21–24.

3720 — The Marine Decapoda of the counties Galway and Clare. [with bibliog.]. *R. Ir. Acad. Proc., Sec. B*, vol.62, no. 11, 1962, 151–174.

Acarina

3721 GROVES, JOAN R. A synopsis of the world literature on the fruit tree red spider mite *Metatetranychus ulmi* (C.L. Koch, 1835), with a brief review of the problem, by A.M. Massee. London: Commonwealth Institute of Entomology, 1951.

3722 HALBERT, J.N. The *Acarina* of the seashore [with bibliog.]. *R. Ir. Acad.Proc.Sec.B*, 35, 1919–20, 106–49.

3723 — List of Irish fresh-water mites (*Hydracarina*) [with bibliog.]. *R. Ir.Acad.Proc.,Sec.B*, 50, 1944–5, 39–104.

Phalangida

3724 PACK BERESFORD, DENIS R. A list of the harvest-spiders of Ireland [with bibliog.]. *R.Ir.Acad.Proc.,Sec.B*, 37, 1924–7, 125–40.

Araneida

3725 CARPENTER, GEORGE H. A list of the spiders of Ireland. *R.Ir.Acad.Proc.,3rd ser.,* 5, 1898–1900, 128–210.

3726 LOCKET, G.H. and MILLIDGE, A.F. British spiders. London: Ray Society. Vol. I. 1951 (*Publication ser. no.* 135). Vol.II. 1953 (*Publication ser. no.* 137). Vol. III. 1974, by G.H. Locket, A.F. Millidge and P. Merrett. (*Publication ser. no.* 149).

3727 MACKIE, D.W. The distribution of some Irish spiders and harvestmen. *Ir. Nat. J.*, vol.17, no. 7, 1972, 234–237.

3728 PACK BERESFORD, DENIS R. A supplementary list of spiders of Ireland [with bibliog.]. *R. Ir. Acad. Proc., Sec. B*, 27, 1907–9, 87–118.

Pseudoscorpions

3729 KEW, H. WALLIS. A synopsis of the false-scorpions of Britain and Ireland [with bibliog.]. *R. Ir.Acad.Proc.,Sec. B*,29, 1911–12, 38–63.

3730 — Supplement. *ibid*., 33, 1916–17, 71–85.

Myriapoda

3731 BRADE–BIRKS, HILDA K. and BRADE–BIRKS, S. GRAHAM. Notes on *Myriapoda* [with bibliog.]. *Ir. Nat.*, 27, 1918, 27–9; *ibid*., 28, 1919, 4–5.

3732 FOSTER, NEVIN H. Bibliography of the Irish *Myriapoda*. *Ir. Nat.,* 25, 1916, 134–5.

3733 PETERSEN, A.C. A review of the distribution of Irish millipedes (*Diploda*) [with bibliog.]. *R. Ir. Acad. Proc., Sec. B*, vol.75, no. 30, 1975, 569–583.

Entomology

3734 BEIRNE, BRYAN P. A bibliography of Irish entomology. Ontario, Canada [1957]. Typescript; copies deposited in the Royal Irish Academy and the National Museum, Dublin.

3735 CARPENTER, GEORGE H. Injurious insects and other animals observed in Ireland during the year[s 1901–18]. Appeared periodically in *R. Dublin Soc. Econ. Proc*., vol. 1–2, 1899–1935.

3736 HAGEN, HERMANN AUGUST. Bibliotheca Entomologica: the complete literature of entomology up to the year 1862. Leipzig: 1862–3. 2 vols.

3737 KLOET, G.S., and HINCKS, W.D. A check list of British insects. Stockport: 1945. Bibliog., pp. xxxv–lv.

3738 STEPHENS, JAMES FRANCIS. A systematic catalogue of British insects . . . containing also the references to every English writer on entomology, and to the principal foreign authors. London: 1829.

Poduridae

3739 WOMERSLEY, HERBERT. The *Collembola* of Ireland [with bibliog.]. *R. Ir. Acad. Proc., Sec. B*, 39, 1929–30, 160–202.

Odonata

3740 HAMMOND, CYRIL O. The dragonflies of

Great Britain and Ireland; with enlarged illustrations of all British species in colour by the author and an illustrated key to the equatic larval stages by the late A.E. Gardner. London: The Curwen Press, 1977.

Neuroptera

3741 KING, JAMES J.F.X. and HALBERT, J.N. A list of the *Neuroptera* of Ireland [with bibliog.]. *R.Ir.Acad.Proc.,Sec. B*, 28, 1909–10. 29–112.

Hemiptera

3742 HALBERT, J.N. A list of the Irish *Hemiptera (Heteroptera* and *Cicadina)* [with bibliog.]. *R. Ir. Acad. Proc., Sec.B*, 42, 1934–5, 211–318.

3743 MACNEILL, N. A revised and tabulated list of the Irish hemiptera-heteroptera. Pt. I. Geocorisae. *R. Ir. Acad. Proc., Sec. B*, vol. 73, no. 3, 1973, 57–60.

3744 MORRIS, M.G. Auchenorhyncha (Hemiptera) of the Burren, with special reference to species-associations of the grasslands. *R. Ir. Acad. Proc., Sec. B*. vol. 74, no. 2, 1974, 7–30.

Coleoptera

3745 JOHNSON, W.F. and HALBERT, J.N. A list of the beetles of Ireland [with bibliog.]. *R. Ir. Acad. Proc., Sec. B, 3rd ser.*, 6, 1900–2, 535–827.

3746 MORRIS, M.G. New vice–county records of Irish weevils (Coleoptera, Curculionoidea) [with bibliog.]. *Ir. Nat. J.*, vol. 17, no. 4, 1971, 136–139.

3747 — Weevils (Coleoptera, Curculionoidea) and other insects collected in North West Clare, with special reference to the Burren region. [with bibliog.]. *R. Ir. Acad. Proc., Sec. B*, vol. 65, no. 16, 1967, 349–371.

Adephaga

3748 BROWNE, FRANK BALFOUR. Bibliography of literature relating to water-beetles taken in the six south-eastern counties [of Ireland]. *Ir. Nat.*,21, 1912, 16.

Diptera

3749 CHANDLER, P.J. An account of the Irish species of two-winged flies (Diptera) belonging to the families of larger Brachycera (Tabanoidea and Asiloidea) *R. Ir. Acad. Proc., Sec. B*, vol.75, no. 2, 1975, 81–110.

3750 — Dung flies and their allies in Ireland. (Diptera, Scatophagidae). *Ir. Nat. J.*, vol. 18, no. 4, 1974, 109–114.

3751 — The Irish species of flat-footed flies (Diptera: Platypezidae). *Ir. Nat. J.*, vol.18, no. 10, 1976, 289–293.

3752 — New records of Irish gnats (Diptera: Mycetophliae). *Ir. Nat. J.*, vol. 19, no. 1, 1977, 12–16.

3753 FAHY, E. A preliminary account of the Simuliidae (Diptera) in Ireland, with observations on the growth of three species. *R. Ir. Acad. Proc., Sec. B*, 72, 1972, 75–81.

3754 GRIFFITHS, G.C.D. Agromyzidae (diptera) from Ireland [with bibliog.] *R. Ir. Acad. Proc., Sec. B*, vol. 67, no. 2, 1968, 37–61.

3755 GRIMSHAW, PERCY H. A guide to the literature of British *Diptera*. *R. Phys. Soc. Edinb. Proc.*, 20, 1917, 78–117.

3756 IRWIN, A.G. and NASH, R. Recent records of Parasite flies (Diptera: Tachinidae) from Northern Ireland). *Ir. Nat. J.*, vol. 17, no. 11, 1973, 390–1.

3757 — A provisional list of soldier flies (Diptera: Stratiomyidae) from Co. Antrim and Down. *Ir. Nat. J.*, vol.17, no. 11, 1973, 388–390.

Siphonaptera

3758 CLAASSENS, A.J.M. and O'ROURKE, F.J. The Distribution and general ecology of Irish *Siphonaptera. R. Ir. Acad. Proc., Sec. B*, no. 23, 1966, 413–463.

Lepidoptera

3759 BAYNES, E.S.A. Irish lepidoptera: some recent discoveries. *Ir. Nat. J.*, vol.15, no. 1, 1965, 13–16.

3760 — A Revised Catalogue of Irish macrolepidoptera (butterflies and moths). Hampton: (Middlesex): 1964. Supplement to a Revised Catalogue . . . Hampton: 1970.

3761 — A list of Irish butterflies. Dublin: National Museum of Ireland, 1960. Bibliog., p. 10.

3762 BEIRNE, BRYAN P. The distribution and origin of the British Lepidoptera [with bibliog.]. *R. Ir. Acad. Proc., Sec. B*, 49, 1943–4, 27–55.

3763 — A list of the *Microlepidoptera* of Ireland [with bibliog.]. *R. Ir. Acad. Proc., Sec. B*, 47, 1941–2, 53–147.

3764 BRADLEY, J.D. *and others*. British Tortricoid moths: Cochylidae and Tortricoidae: Tortricinae, by J.D. Bradley, W.G. Tremewan and Arthur Smith: Ray Society, 1973. (*Publication ser. No. 147*). Bibliog., pp. 236–245.

3765 — and PELHAM–CLINTON, E.C. The lepidoptera of the Burren, Co. Clare, W. Ireland. *Entomol. Gaz*., 18, 1967, 115–153.

3766 DONOVAN, C. A catalogue of the *Macrolepidoptera* of Ireland. Cheltenham: 1936. Privately printed.

3767 — A list of the lepidoptera of County Cork. *Entomol*., 35, 1902, 10–14.

3768 EMMET, A.M. Lepidoptera in West Galway. *Entomol. Gaz*., 19, 1968, 45–58.

3769 — More lepidoptera in West Galway. *ibid*., 22, 1971, 3–18.

3770 HEATH, JOHN. The moths and butterflies of Great Britain and Ireland. London: Blackwell. Vol. I. Micropterigidae-Heliozelidae. 1976. To be completed in 10 vols by about 1982.

3771 JOHNSON, W.F. The distribution of *Argynnis Aglaia* in Ireland [with bibliog.]. *Ir. Nat*., 30, 1921, 44–6.

3772 LISNEY, ARTHUR A. A bibliography of British Lepidoptera, 1608–1799. London [1960]. Further volumes in preparation.

3773 MERE, R.M. and PELHAM–CLINTON, E.C. Lepidoptera in Ireland, 1963, 1964, and 1965. *Entomol. Gaz*., vol.17, 1966, 163–182.

3774 PETERS, JOHN V. The Butterflies of Northern Ireland. *Ir. Nat. J*., vol.14, no. 2, 1962, 21–32.

3775 WRIGHT, W. STUART. The Macrolepidoptera of Northern Ireland. [a catalogue]. Belfast: Ulster Museum, 1964. (*Publication no. 169*).

Hymenoptera

3776 MOLLER, G.J. A list of Irish sawflies (*Hymenoptera: Symphyta*) in the Ulster Museum, including a new Irish record and a note on a teratological specimen of *Hemichroa* Steph. *Ir. Nat. J*., vol.18, no. 5, 1974, 133–136.

3777 STELFOX, ARTHUR WILSON. A list of the *Hymenoptera Aculeata (Sensu Lato)* of Ireland [with bibliog.]. *R. Ir. Acad. Proc., Sec. B*, 37, 1924–7, 201–353.

3778 — A list of the Irish species of *Toxares* and *Ephedrus (Hymenoptera: Aphidiidae)* with descriptions of those which include three species new to science [with bibliog.]. *R. Ir. Acad. Proc., Sec. B*, 46, 1940–1, 125–42.

3779 — A list of the *Proctotrupinae* found in Ireland (*Hymenoptera*). *R. Ir. Acad. Proc., Sec. B*, vol.64, no. 28, 1966, 529–540.

Formicidae

3780 COLLINGWOOD, C.A. A survey of Irish *Formicidae* [with bibliog.]. *R. Ir. Acad. Proc., Sec. B*, 59, 1957–8, 213–19.

3781 O'ROURKE, FERGUS J. The distribution and general ecology of the Irish *Formicidae* [with bibliog.]. *R. Ir. Acad. Proc., Sec. B*, 52, 1948–50, 383–410.

Vespidae

3782 CARPENTER, GEORGE H., and PACK BERESFORD, DENIS R. The relationship of *Vespa Austriaca* to *Vespa Rufa* [with bibliog.]. *Ir. Nat*., 12, 1903, 221–38.

Pisces

(See also Fisheries, nos. 4416–4467)

3783 CHRISTY, MILLER. A catalogue of local lists of British mammals, reptiles and fishes, arranged under counties: Ireland [fishes]. *Zoologist, 3rd ser*., 17, 1893, 262–3. Includes the counties of Antrim, Cork, Down, Dublin and Wexford.

3784 **Farran**, G.P. Local Irish names of fishes [with bibliog.]. *Ir. Nat. J.*, 8, 1942–6, 344–7; 370–6; 402–8; 420–33.

3785 **Netboy, Anthony**. The Atlantic salmon: a vanishing species? London: 1968. Ireland's salmon treasure, pp. 274–313; bibliog., pp. 391–408.

3786 **Roberts, Jonathan**. Salmon: does like breed like? *Country Life*, vol.144, no. 3742, 1968, 1330–1. Short account of the work of the Salmon Research Trust of Ireland in the region of Clew Bay, Co. Mayo.

3787 **Went**, A.E.J. and **Kennedy**, M. List of Irish fishes. 2nd ed. Dublin: National Museum of Ireland, 1969.

3788 — Supplement to *List of Irish Fishes. Ir. Dept. Agric. Fish., Fish. Leaflet. 50, 1973.*

3789 — Irish sea trout, a review of investigations to date. [with bibliog.]. *R. Dublin Soc. Sci. Proc. Ser. A.*, vol.1, no. 10, 1962, 265–296.

3790 — The pursuit of salmon in Ireland. *R. Ir. Acad. Proc., Sec. C*, vol.63, no. 6, 1964, 191–244.

3791 — A review of the investigations on salmon of the River Foyle. [Dublin: 1964].

3792 **Wheeler**, A. and **O'Riordan**, C.E. Type material of fishes from the 'Challenger' expedition in the National Museum of Ireland. *R. Ir. Acad. Proc., Sec. B*, 68, 1969, 89–100.

Amphibians and Reptiles

3793 **Arnold**, E.N. and **Burton**, J.A. A field guide to the reptiles and amphibians of Britain and Europe. London: 1978.

3794 **Christy, Miller**. A catalogue of local lists of British mammals, reptiles and fishes, arranged under counties: Ireland [reptiles]. *Zoologist, 3rd ser.*, 17, 1893, 251. Includes the counties of Antrim, Cork, Down and Wexford.

3795 **Scharff**, R.F. On the Irish names of reptiles, amphibians, and fishes [with bibliog.]. *Ir. Nat.,* 25, 1916, 106–19.

3796 **Taylor**, R.H.R. The distribution of amphibians and reptiles in England and Wales, Scotland and Ireland and the Channel Isles: a revised survey. *Brit. J. Herpetol.*, 3, 1963, 95–115.

Aves

3797 **Barrington, Richard**, M. The migration of birds as observed at Irish lighthouses and lightships, including the original reports from 1888–97, now published for the first time, and an analysis of these and of the previously published reports from 1881–87. Together with an appendix giving the measurements of about 1600 wings. London and Dublin [1900]. Includes list of Irish lights. pp. xi–xxi.

3798 **Benson, Charles William**. Our British song birds. 2nd ed. Dublin: 1901. Bibliog., p. 206.

3799 **Braidwood**, J. Local bird names in Ulster – a glossary. *Ulster Folk*, 11, 1965, 98–135; 12, 1966, 104–107.

3800 — Local bird names in Ulster: some additions. *ibid.*, 17, 1971, 81–84.

3801 **British Ornithologists' Union**. The status of birds in Britain and Ireland. Prepared by the Records Committee of the British Ornothologists' Union, and edited by D.W. Snow. Oxford: 1971.

3802 **Cabot, David**. Results from a bird ringing station in West Mayo, 1963–1973. *Ir. Nat. J.*, vol. 18, no. 1, 1974, 1–8.

3803 — The Slobs of Wexford. *Ir. Welcomes*, vol.24, no. 3, 1975, 10–16.

3804 **Christy, Miller**. A catalogue of local lists of British birds. *Zoologist, 3rd ser.*, 14, 1890, 247–67. Also published separately, London, 1891; Irish section includes the counties of Antrim, Cork, Donegal, Down, Dublin, Mayo and Waterford.

3805 **Coues, Elliott**. Fourth instalment of ornithological bibliography; being a list of faunal publications relating to British birds. *U.S. Nat. Mus. Proc.*, 2, 1879 (1880), 359–499. Period covered 1666–1880, and includes references to periodical literature.

3806 **Cramp, Stanley**. The Seabirds of Britain and Ireland. London: 1974. Bibliog. pp. 266–284.

3807 **Durman, Roger**, *ed*. Bird Observatories in Britain and Ireland. Berkhamsted: 1976.

Cape Clear, Ireland, by Tim Sharrock, pp. 66–80.

3808 EDWARDS, T.K. The Capeland bird observatory. *Belfast Nat. Hist. Phil. Soc. Proc.*, 2nd Ser. vol.7, 1961–64, 50–58.

3809 HILLIS, J.P. Sea-birds scavenging at trawlers in Irish waters. *Ir. Nat. J.*, vol. 17, no. 4, 1971, 129–132.

3810 IRISH ORNITHOLOGISTS' CLUB, DUBLIN, Irish bird report, 1–23, 1953–1975; from 1977 *Irish Birds*. Includes list of papers on or relating to Irish birds.

3811 IRISH WILDBIRD CONSERVANCY. The birds of Dublin and Wicklow, edited by C.D. Hutchinson. Dublin: 1975.

3812 — Birds of Galway and Mayo, compiled and edited by Tony Whilde. [Galway]: 1977.

3813 IRWIN, RAYMOND. British bird books: an index to British ornithology, A.D. 1481 to A.D 1948. London: 1951.

3814 KENNEDY, P.G. *and others*. The birds of Ireland: an account of the distribution, migration and habits observed in Ireland, by P.G. Kennedy, Robert Ruttledge, C.F. Scroope, assisted by G.R. Humphreys. Edinburgh and London: 1954.

3815 — An Irish sanctuary: birds of the North Bull. Dublin: 1953.

3816 LISTER, MICHAEL. The bird watcher's reference book. London: 1956. Includes good bibliography, directory including periodicals, bird observatories, institutions, and ringing stations and schemes.

3817 MORIARTY, CHRISTOPHER. A guide to Irish birds. Cork: 1967. A beginner's book covering all the birds of Ireland.

3818 MULLENS, WILLIAM HERBERT and SWANN, H. KIRKE. A bibliography of British ornithology from the earliest times to the end of 1912, including biographical accounts of the principal writers and bibliographies of their published works. London: 1917.

3819 — Supplement: a chronological list of British birds, by H.K. Swann. London: 1923.

3820 — A geographical bibliography of British ornithology from the earliest times to the end of 1918 arranged under counties; being a record of printed books, published articles and records. London: 1920.

3821 NATIONAL MUSEUM OF IRELAND. A list of the birds of Ireland. [new ed.] by Robert F. Ruttledge. Dublin: 1975.

3822 NICOLAISEN, W.F.H. *compiler*. A short comparative list of Celtic bird names of the British Isles. *In* The Birds of the British Isles, by David Armitage Bannerman, 12, 1963, pp. 405–423.

3823 PERRY, KENNETH W. The Birds of the Inishowen Peninsula: their distribution and habitats. [Warringstown; Craigavon, 1975].

3824 — and WARBURTON, STEPHEN W. The birds and flowers of the Saltee Islands. [Northern Ireland: The authors, 1977].

3825 RUTTLEDGE, ROBERT F. A list of the birds of the counties Galway and Mayo, showing their status and distribution. *R. Ir. Acad. Proc., Sec. B*, 52, 1948–50, 315–81.

3826 — Ireland's birds: their distribution and migrations. London: 1966.

3827 SCHARFF, R.F. On the Irish names of birds [with bibliog.]. *Ir. Nat.*, 24, 1915, 109–29.

3828 SHARROCK, J.T.R. *compiler*. The Atlas of breeding birds in Britain and Ireland. Tring (Hertfordshire): British Trust for Ornithology [and] Irish Wildlife Conservancy. 1976.

3829 — Scarce migrant birds in Britain and Ireland. Berkhamsted: 1974.

3830 — Rare birds in Britain and Ireland: Berkhamsted: 1976.

3831 STRONG, REUBEN MYRON. A bibliography of birds with special reference to anatomy, behavior, biochemistry, embryology, pathology, physiology, genetics, ecology, aviculture, economic ornithology, poultry culture, evolution and related subjects. *Chicago Fld. Mus. Nat. Hist. Zool. Ser.* 25, 1939–59, pts. 1–4.

Mammalia

3832 CHRISTY, MILLER. A catalogue of local lists of British mammals, reptiles and fishes arranged under counties: Ireland [mammals]. *Zoologist, 3rd ser.*, 17, 1893, 215–216. Includes the counties of Antrim, Cork, Donegal, Down, Dublin, Wexford and Wicklow.

3833 CORKE, D. *and others*. Notes on the distribution and abundance of small mammals in

South-West Ireland. by D. Corke, R.A.D. Cowlin and W.W. Page. *J. Zool.*, 158, 1969, 216–221.

3834 FAIRLEY, J.S. An Irish beast book: a natural history of Ireland's furred wildlife. Belfast: 1975. Bibliog., pp. 189–194 (207 references).

3835 —Irish wild mammals: a guide to the literature. Galway: 1972. Privately printed; edition limited to 400 copies.

3836 MOFFAT, C.B. The mammals of Ireland [with bibliog.]. *R. Ir. Acad. Proc., Sec. B*, 44, 1937–8, 61–128.

3837 O'ROURKE, FERGUS J. The Fauna of Ireland: an introduction to the land vertebrates. Cork: 1970. Bibliog., pp. 161–170.

3838 SCHARFF, R.F. On the Irish names of mammals [with bibliog.]. *Ir. Nat.*, 24, 1915, 45–53.

Cetacea

3839 SCHARFF, R.F. A list of the Irish *Cetacea* (whales, porpoises, and dolphins) [with bibliog.]. *Ir. Nat.*, 9, 1900, 83–91.

Cervidae

3840 MOLLOY, FERGAL. Ireland's deer. *Ir. Welcomes*, vol.23, no. 6, 1974, 15–22.

3841 SCHARFF, R.F. The Irish red deer [with bibliog.]. *Ir. Nat.*, 27, 1918, 133–9.

Bovidae

3842 WHITEHEAD, G. KENNETH. The wild goats of Great Britain and Ireland. Newton Abbot: 1972. Bibliog., pp. 165–176.

Felidae

3843 STELFOX, A.W. Notes on the Irish 'Wild Cat'. *Ir. Nat. J.*, vol.15, no. 3, 1965, 57–60.

Canidae

(See also Dogs, nos. 4394–4405)

3844 SCHARFF, R.F. On the breeds of dogs peculiar to Ireland and their origin. *Ir. Nat.*, 33, 1924, 77–95.

3845 — The wolf in Ireland. *Ir. Nat.*, 31, 1922, 133–6.

USEFUL ARTS

Standards

3846 INSTITUTE FOR INDUSTRIAL RESEARCH AND STANDARDS, DUBLIN. Annual report, no. 1–, 1947–. Information sheet, no. 1–, 1949–. Irish standard specifications, no. 1–, 1949–. Irish standards handbook. Dublin: 1954.

3847 MCKEE, J.D.F. Irish standard mark scheme. *Technol. Ir.*, vol. 5, no. 11, 1974, 31–34.

Technology

3848 BRITISH TECHNOLOGY INDEX: a current subject guide to articles in British technical journals. London: Library Association, vol. 1–, 1962–.

3849 TECHNOLOGY IRELAND. Dublin: Institute for Industrial Research and Standards. vol. 1–, 1969–.

Patents, Invenstions

3850 DE COURCY IRELAND, JOHN. Two great maritime inventors: John Philip Holland and Charles Algernon Parsons. *Ir. Wel.*, vol. 24, no. 1, 1975, 31–34.

3851 MURDOCH, HENRY J.P. Invention and the Irish patent system. Dublin: 1971. Bibliog., p. 105; for review by Peter F. Kelly see *Technol. Ir.*, vol. 4, no. 2, 1972, 29–32.

Exhibitions

3852 BENCE–JONES, MARK. Ireland's great exhibition [Dublin, 1853]. *Country Life*, vol. 153, no. 3951, 1973, 666–668.

3853 DIXON, F.E. Dublin exhibitions [of arts and industries]. *Dublin Hist. Rec.*, 26, 1973, 93–100, 137–146.

Industrial Archaeology

3854 DICK, WILLIAM. Industrial archaeology in Ireland – a personal view. *Technol. Ir.*, vol. 5, no. 11, 1974, 44–46.

3855 GREEN, E.R.R. The industrial archaeology

of County Down. Belfast: 1963. Bibliog., pp. 81–87.

3856 HUDSON, KENNETH. A guide to the industrial archaeology of Europe. Bath: 1971. Ireland, pp. 31–37.

3857 IRISH SOCIETY FOR INDUSTRIAL ARCHAEOLOGY. A selection of articles on industrial archaeology as recently published in *Technology Ireland* . . . specially prepared for the Royal Dublin Society Scientific and Technical Exhibition, February 1973. Dublin: 1973.

MEDICINE

General

3858 IRELAND. Census of Ireland for the year 1851. Dublin: 1856. vol.1, pt. 5. The history of epidemic pestilences in Ireland [with full bibliog. notes], pp. 1–40; table of cosmical phenomena, epizootics, epiphitics, and pestilences in Ireland, pp. 41–235; 257–333; the last general potato failure and the great famine and pestilence of 1845–50, pp. 235–56.

3859 PAULY, ALPHONSE. Bibliographie des science médicales: bibliography, history, epidemics, endemics, history of schools and hospitals, medical literature, professional history. London: 1954. Originally published Paris: 1874.

Directories, Yearbooks

3860 THE HOSPITALS AND HEALTH SERVICES YEAR BOOK and directory of hospital suppliers: an annual record of hospitals and health services of Great Britain and Northern Ireland . . . 1977. London: 1977.

3861 IRISH MEDICAL AND HOSPITAL DIRECTORY. Edited by Morgan Crowe. Dublin: 1974.

3862 LIBRARY ASSOCIATION. Directory of medical libraries in the British Isles. London: 1957.

3863 THE MEDICAL REGISTER OF IRELAND, printed and published under the direction of the Medical Registration Council, in pursuance of *The Medical Practitioners Act*, 1927, comprising the names and addresses of medical practitioners registered under *The Medical Practitioners Act*, 1927, *The Medical Practitioners Act*, 1951, and *The Medical Practitioners Act*, 1978. Dublin: 1978.

Journals

3864 COUNCIL FOR POSTGRADUATE MEDICAL AND DENTAL EDUCATION. Guide to the major Irish medical and dental library resources. Edited by Sile M. Nevin, Dublin: 1978. Section 1. Location list of indexing and abstracting services. Section 2. Location list of current journal titles. Section 3. Directory of medical and dental library information services.

3865 HISTORY OF PERIODIC MEDICAL LITERATURE IN IRELAND, including notices of the Medical and Philosophical Society of Dublin. *Dublin Qtr. J. Med. Sci.*, 1, 1846, i–xlviii.

3866 KIRKPATRICK, T.P.C. The Dublin medical journals. *Ir. J. Med. Sci.*, 1932, pp. 243–60.

3867 — List of medical periodicals preserved in the libraries of Ireland. [Dublin, Royal College of Physicians of Ireland, 1912.]

3868 MEDICAL RESEARCH COUNCIL OF IRELAND. List of medical periodicals available in Dublin libraries, compiled by Mary Semple. Dublin: 1938.

3869 — [Another ed.] Revised list, compiled by Marie D. O'Sullivan. Dublin: 1957. Journals in the Veterinary College of Ireland, pp. 96–8.

3870 ROWLETTE, ROBERT J. *The Medical Press and Circular*, 1839–1939: a hundred years in the life of a medical journal. London: 1939.

3871 WIDDESS, J.D.H. An unrecognised medical periodical – *Collectanea Hibernica Medica*. *Ir. J. Med. Sci., 6th ser.*, 1955, 377–9.

Exhibitions

3872 SWIFT, JONATHAN. The legacy of Swift: a bi-centenary of St. Patrick's Hospital, Dublin. Dublin: 1948. Short catalogue of the exhibition, pp. 49–70, includes books and manuscripts.

3873 WIDDESS, J.D.H. Catalogue of books from College of Surgeons, exhibited in Dublin, 1948. *Ir. J. Med. Sci., 6th ser.*, 1948, 228–32.

Study and Teaching

3874 BLAYNEY, A.J. Medical education and otolaryngology. *Ir. J. Med. Sci., 6th ser.*, no. 472, 1965, 177–187.

3875 FLEMING, J.B. The teaching of midwifery in the University of Dublin. *Hermathena*, 103, 1966, 66–82.

3876 JESSOP, W.J.E. Medical research in Ireland. *Hermathena*, 99, 1964, 27–41.

3877 MCCOLLUM, STANLEY T. Surgical training contrasted in Ireland, Sweden, Holland, Belgium and France. *J. Ir. Coll. Phys. Surg.*, vol. 7, no. 1, 1977, 19–24.

3878 MEENAN, F.O.C. The Catholic University School of Medicine. *Studies*, 66, 1977, 135–144.

3879 MOORE, NORMAN. The history of the study of medicine in the British Isles; the Fitz-Patrick lectures for 1905–6 delivered before the Royal College of Physicians of London. Oxford: 1908.

3880 WIDDESS, J.D.H. The French schools of surgery and the Royal College of Surgeons in Ireland. *J. Ir. Coll. Phys. Surg.*, vol. 1, no. 1, 1971, 16–23.

3881 — Newman's medical school and the Royal College of Surgeons. *R. Coll. Surg. Ir. J.*, vol. 5, no. 3, 1970, 95–96.

3882 — The Royal College of Surgeons in Ireland and its medical school, 1784–1966. 2nd ed., Edinburgh and London: 1967. Bibliog., pp. 124–5.

Hospitals, Libraries

3883 BROWNE, O'DONEL T.D. The Rotunda Hospital, 1745–1945. Edinburgh: 1947. Includes bibliogs.

3884 CAMERON, CHARLES A. History of the Royal College of Surgeons in Ireland and of the Irish schools of medicine, including a medical bibliography and a medical biography. 2nd ed. rev., Dublin, London and Edinburgh: 1916. First ed. 1886.

3885 DE BHAL, SILE. A Dublin voluntary hospital: the Meath. *Dublin Hist. Rec.*, vol. 27, no. 1, 1973, 27–37.

3886 KIRKPATRICK, T. PERCY C. The book of the Rotunda hospital: an illustrated history of the Dublin Lying-in Hospital from its formation in 1745 to the present time; edited by Henry Jellett. London: 1913. Bibliog., pp. 195–200.

3887 — The history of Dr. Steevens' Hospital, Dublin, 1720–1920. Dublin: 1924. Bibliog., pp. 384–8.

3888 —History of the medical teaching in Trinity College, Dublin, and of the School of Physic in Ireland. Dublin: 1912. Bibliog., pp. 340–8.

3889 — Sir Patrick Dun's Library. *Bibliog. Soc. Ir.*, vol. 1, no. 5, 1920. Includes note of publications of early Fellows.

3890 — Sir Patrick Dun's library (in the Royal College of Physicians of Ireland). *Dublin J. Med. Sci.*, 149, 1920, 49–68.

3891 — The Worth Library, Steevens' Hospital, Dublin. *Bibliog. Soc. Ir.*, vol. 1, no. 3, 1919.

3892 LEE, GERARD A. The leper hospitals of Leinster. *Kildare Arch. Soc. J.*, vol. 14, no. 2, 1966–67, 127–151.

3893 — The leper hospitals of Munster. *Nth. Munster Antiq. J.*, vol. 10, no. 1, 1966, 12–26. Includes short account of leprosy in Ireland.

3894 — The leper hospitals of the Upper Shannon area. *J. Old Athlone Soc.*, vol. 1, no. 4, 1974–5, 222–229.

3895 MCCARTHY, MURIEL. Dr Edward Worth's library in Dr. Steevens' Hospital. *J. Ir. Coll. Phys. Surg.*, vol. 6, no. 4, 1977, 141–145.

3896 MACWILLIAM, A. The Lying-in Hospital Library [Rotunda Hospital]. *Bibliog. Soc. Ir.*, vol. 2, no. 5, 1923.

3897 O'DEA, LAURENCE. The hospitals at Kilmainham. *Dublin Hist. Rec.*, 20, 1964–65, 82–99.

3898 SOMERVILLE-LARGE, L.B. Dublin's eye hospitals in the 19th century. *Dublin Hist. Rec.*, 20, 1964–65, 19–28.

3899 WIDDESS, J.D.H. A Dublin school of medicine and surgery: an account of the Schools of Surgery, Royal College of Surgeons, Dublin, 1789–1948. Edinburgh: 1949. Bibliog., p. 97.

3900 — A history of the Royal College of Physicians of Ireland, 1654–1963. Edinburgh and London: 1963. Bibliog., pp. 245–247.

Finance

3901 HARGADON, O.P. Irish hospital finances. *Administration*, vol. 4, no. 3, 1956, 13–36.

3902 O'SHEEHAN, J., and DE BARRA, E. Oispideil na hEireann: Ireland's hospitals, 1930–55. Dublin: Hospitals Trust Ltd. [1956]. Irish Hospitals' Sweepstakes official account of money raised for hospitals; includes photographic supplement.

History

3903 BROWNE, A.D.H. The role of the Royal Academy of Medicine in Ireland in Irish medical life. *Ir. J. Med. Sci.*, 145, 1976, 147–155.

3904 COLLIS, W.R.F. The state of medicine in Ireland. Dublin: 1943. (*Carmichael prize essay*).

3905 CUMMINS, N. MARSHALL. Some chapters of Cork medical history. Cork: 1957. Bibliog., p. 117.

3906 FLEETWOOD, JOHN. History of medicine in Ireland. Dublin: 1951. Bibliog., pp. 384–99.

3907 KIRKPATRICK, T.P.C. An index to the papers on the history of medicine that have been published in *The Dublin Journal of Medical Science* from its commencement to August 1916. *Dublin J. Med. Sci.*, 1916, pp. 302–10. For continuation see *An Index to the biographical notices* . . . by J.D.H. Widdess. (No. 3922).

3908 LYONS, JOHN B. Medicine and literature in Ireland. *J. Ir. Coll. Phys. Surg.*, vol. 3, no. 1, 1973, 3–9.

3909 — Some Irish contributions to medicine. *Studies*, 64, 1975, 35–48.

3910 MEENAN, F.O.C. The Victorian doctors of Dublin – a social and political portrait. *Ir. J. Med. Sci., 7th ser.*, vol. 1, 1968, 311–320.

3911 QUINN, JAMES LELAND. The impact of nuclear medicine on Irish medical discoveries. *J. Ir. Coll. Phys. Surg.*, vol. 3, no. 1, 1973, 21–25.

Collected Biography

3912 HAYES, RICHARD. Some notable Limerick doctors. *Nth. Munster Antiq. J.*, 1, 1936–9, 113–23.

3913 KIRKPATRICK, T.P.C. An index to the biographical notices that have appeared in *The Dublin Journal of Medical Science* since its commencement in March 1832. *Dublin J. Med. Sci.*, 1916, pp. 110–18.

3914 LE FANU, W.R. Two Irish doctors in England in the seventeenth century [Edmund O'Meara and Bernard Connor]. *Ir. J. Med. Sci., 6th ser.*, no. 463, 1964.

O'BRIEN, EOIN T. Dublin masters of clinical expression.

3915 1. John Cheyne (1777–1836). *J. Ir. Coll. Phys. Surg.*, vol. 3, no. 3, 1974, 91–93.

3916 2. Robert Adams (1791–1875). *ibid.*, vol. 3, no. 4, 1974, 127–129.

3917 3. Sir Dominic Corrigan (1802–1880). *ibid.*, vol. 4, no. 2, 1974, 67–69.

3918 4. William Stokes (1804–1877). *ibid.*, vol. 4, no. 3, 1975, 100–105.

3919 5. Robert Graves (1796–1853). *ibid.*, vol. 4, no. 4, 1975, 161–163.

3920 ROYAL COLLEGE OF SURGEONS. Inauguration of the Department of the History of Medicine. *J. Ir. Coll. Phys. Surg.*, vol. 4, no. 4, 1975, 175–177. Includes list of publications by J.D.H. Widdess, Stokeseana, and selected publications by Irish medical authors.

3921 SCHMID, LUDVIK. Irish doctors in Bohemia. *Ir. J. Med. Sci., 7th ser.*, vol. 1, 1968, 497–504. Includes list covering period 1678–1778.

3922 WIDDESS, J.D.H. An index to the biographical notices, papers on the history of medicine, and reviews of books on that subject, which have appeared in *The Irish Journal of Medical Science* from September 1916 to December 1954. *Ir. J. Med. Sci.*, 1955, 186–91;238–41; 280–6; 329–35.

3923 — An index to the biographical notices . . . from January 1955 to December 1959. *Ir. J. Med. Sci.*, 1960, 193–7.

3924 — The Royal College of Physicians of Ireland and some of its famous personalities.

Proc. R. Soc. Med., 60, 1967, 580–588.

3925 WILSON, D.J. Napoleon's doctors on St. Helena – the Irish five [Barry Edmond O'Meara, James Verling, Walter Henry, George Henry Ruttledge and Francis Burton]. *Ir. J. Med. Sci*., 140, 1971, 30–44.

Individual Biography

ALCOCK, BENJAMIN.
3926 O'RAHILLY, RONAN. Benjamin Alcock: the first professor of anatomy and physiology in Queen's College, Cork. Cork: 1948. (*Centenary Ser*., no. 2.) Bibliog., pp. 36–7.

BIRMINGHAM, AMBROSE.
3927 HOOPER, A.C. Ambrose Birmingham (1864–1905). *Ir. J. Med. Sci*., 140, 1971, 274–282.

CAMERON, CHARLES A.
3928 MAC THOMAIS, EAMONN. Sir Charles A. Cameron (1803–1921). *Dublin Hist. Rec*., vol. 22, no. 2, 1968, 214–224.

COLLES, ABRAHAM.
3929 FALLON, MARTIN. Abraham Colles, 1773–1843: surgeon in Ireland. London: 1972. Publications of Colles, pp. 222–3; bibliog., pp. 226–33.

CORRIGAN, DOMINIC.
3930 DIXON, EILEEN. Sir Dominic Corrigan. *Dublin Hist. Rec.,* 8, 1945–6, 28–38, 67–76.

3931 MULCAHY, RISTEARD. Sir Dominic Corrigan [with bibliog.]. *Ir. J. Med. Sci*., 1961, 454–63.

ELLIOTT, WILLIAM.
3932 HARTFORD, D.M. William Elliott of Richmond Place (1810–1891), who brought orthopaedics to Dublin. *R. Coll. Surg. Ir. J*., vol. 6, no. 4, 1971, 111–113.

GREATRAKES, VALENTINE.
3933 ARNOLD, LAWRENCE, J. Valentine Greatrakes: a seventeenth-century 'touch-doctor'. *Eire-Ir*., vol. 11, no. 1, 1976, 3–12.

KIRKPATRICK, T.P.C.
3934 BOURKE, F.S. Chronological handlist of Dr. Kirkpatrick's published work. *Ir. J. Med. Sci*., 1954, 371–4.

LABATT, SAMUEL BELL.
3935 MCCABLE, A.M.E. Samuel Bell Labatt (1770–1849): pioneer in preventive medicine in Ireland. *Ir. J. Med. Sci., 6th ser*., no 435, 1962, 97–105.

MCARDLE, JOHN STEPHEN.
3936 DOOLIN, WILLIAM. John Stephen McArdle [surgeon]. *Studies*, 17, 1928, 245–256.

MACNEVEN, WILLIAM JAMES.
3937 DICKSON, CHARLES. William JamesMacNeven, M.D., (1763–1841). *Ir. J. Med. Sci., 6th ser*., no. 466, 1964, 439–441.

MOSSE, BARTHOLOMEW.
3938 FLEMING, J.B. The mysteries concerning the last illness, death and burial of Bartholomew Mosse, founder and first master of the Dublin Lying-in Hospital, (1712–1759). *Ir. J. Med. Sci., 6th ser*., no. 436, 1962, 147–163.

O'CONNOR, JAMES MULCAHY.
3939 HARMAN, JOHN W. The biological significance of O'Connor's general theory of regulation of metabolism and temperature. *Ir. J. Med. Sci., 6th ser*., no. 491, 1966, 558–562. Includes list of publications of Prof. J.M. O'Connor, 1912–1965.

O'HALLORAN, SYLVESTER.
3940 LYONS, J.B. Sylvester O'Halloran. *Ir. J. Med. Sci., 6th ser*., no. 449, 1963, 217–232; *ibid*., no. 450, 279–288.

OSBORNE, JONATHAN.
3941 LITTLE, JAMES. Jonathan Osborne, M.D.; and a chronological list of his published writings, by T.P.C. Kirkpatrick. *Dublin J. Med. Sci.,* 1915, 164–72.

QUINLAN, JAMES.
3942 CURTIN, J. MCAULIFFE. James Quinlan, formerly surgeon-general to the Czar of Russia, 1826. *Ir. J. Med. Sci., 6th ser*., no. 493, 1967, 7–15.

SMYTH, WILLIAM.
3943 RANKIN, MARY. Dr. William Smyth, heroic Donegal doctor. *Donegal Ann*., vol. 11, nos. 2–3, 1975–6, 126–130.

STEARNE, JOHN.
3944 KIRKPATRICK, T.P.C. John Stearne, M. and J.U.D.; an address delivered in the Royal College of Physicians of Ireland on the three hundredth anniversary of his birth, November 26, 1924. Dublin: 1925.

WILDE, WILLIAM.
3945 FROGGATT, P. Sir William Wilde, 1815–1876 – a centenary appreciation: Wilde's place in medicine. *R. Ir. Acad. Proc., Sec. C*, vol. 77, no. 10, 1977, 261–278.

3946 — LYONS, J.B. Sir William Wilde, 1815–1876. *J. Ir. Coll. Phys. Surg.*, vol. 5, no. 4, 1976, 147–152.

WILSON, HENRY.

3947 CURTIN, J. MCAULIFFE. Henry Wilson, M.D., F.R.C.S.I., surgeon to St. Mark's Hospital, Lincoln Place, Dublin, and teacher of opthalmascopy at the house in Industry Hospital; natural son of Sir William Wilde, M.D., F.R.C.S.I., 1838–1877. *Ir. J. Med. Sci.*, 7th ser., 2, 1969, 369–378.

WOODS, ROBERT.

3948 BREATHNACH, C.S. Sir Robert Woods, an early Irish biophysicist. *J. Ir. Coll. Phys. Surg.*, vol. 2, no. 2, 1972, 48–51.

Health Resorts

3949 HENCHY, PATRICK. A bibliography of Irish spas. *Bibliog. Soc. Ir.* vol. 6, no. 7, 1958.

Personal Hygiene

3950 LUCAS, A.T. Washing and bathing in ancient Ireland. *R. Soc. Antiq. Ir. J.*, 95, 1965, 65–114.

Dietetics

3951 BURKITT, DENIS P. Diet and disease: a plea for potatoes. *J. Ir. Coll. Phys. Surg.*, vol. 4, no. 4, 1975, 141–145.

3952 DOYLE, J. STEPHEN. Nutrition and the Irish: an historical and contemporary review. *J. Ir. Coll. Phys. Surg.*, vol. 4, no. 4, 1975, 133–140.

3953 IRELAND. Department of Health. National nutrition survey. Dublin, 1949–52. 7 pts.

3954 LUCAS, A.T. Irish food before the potato. *Gwerin*, vol. 3, no. 2, 1960, 8–43.

3955 THOMPSON, W.H. The food value of Great Britain's food supply [with bibliog.]. *R. Dublin Soc. Econ. Proc.*, 2, 1910–35, 168–220.

Public Health

3956 DRUM, J.A. The composition of Irish drinking waters, with special reference to the distribution and significance of fluoride. *R. Dublin Soc. Sci. Proc.*, 25, 1949–50, 85–92.

3957 FLUORIDATION IN IRELAND. The spadework, by Sean MacEntee. The Fluorine Consultative Council, by Thomas Murphy. The legal issue in the fluoridation case, by John Kenny. The fluoridation case in Ireland – legal and scientific evaluations, by Seamus MacNeill. The progress of fluoridation in Ireland, by Seamus O'Hickey. Special studies on dental caries and fluorides in progress in the Republic of Ireland, by C.K. Collins and D.M. O'Mullane. *J. Ir. Dent. Assoc.*, 18, 1972, 48–82.

3958 GAFFEY, LAWRENCE J., and BOWLES, GEORGE F. Guide to food hygiene: an authoritative reference work to *The Health Act (1947)* as it applies to food and drink under the food hygiene regulations, 1950. Published under the auspices of the Health Inspectors Association of Ireland. Dublin [1952].

3959 HENSEY, BRENDAN. The health services of Ireland. 3rd rev. ed., Dublin: 1979. Bibliog., pp. 269–71. 1st ed. Dublin: 1959.

3960 MCKAY, C. A survey of drinking waters of Northern Ireland with particular references to their fluoride content [with bibliog.]. *R. Dublin Soc. Sci. Proc.*, vol. 3, no. 17, 1974, 221–249.

3961 O'NEILL, TIMOTHY P. Fever and public health in pre-famine Ireland. *R. Soc. Antiq, Ir. J.*, 103, 1973, 1–34.

Specific Diseases

3962 LOGAN, PATRICK. Pestilence in the Irish wars: the earlier phase. *Ir. Sword*, vol. 7, no. 29, 1966, 279–290.

3963 LONGMATE, NORMAN. King cholera: the biography of a disease. London: 1966. Bibliog., pp. 248–258. Includes account of cholera in Ireland.

3964 SINGER, D.W. and ANDERSON, ANNIE, *compilers*. Catalogue of Latin and vernacular plague texts in Great Britain and Eire in manuscripts written before the sixteenth century. Paris, Académie Internationale d'Histoire des Sciences, and London: 1950. Typescript.

3965 ZIEGLER, PHILIP. The black death. London: 1969. Bibliog., pp. 302–312; chapter 12 – The Welsh borders, Wales, Ireland and Scotland.

Trichinosis

3966 CORRIDAN, JOHN P. Trichinosis in Cork. *Ir. J. Med. Sci.*, 1, 1968, 109–113.

Air Pollution

3967 CAREY, G.C.R. Air pollution in Belfast. *Stat. Social Inq. Soc. Ir. J., 120th session*, vol. 21, pt. 5, 1966–67, 48–61.

3968 CRONIN, J.A. A study of pollution by some lead-emitting industries in the Dublin area. *R. Ir. Acad. Proc., Sec. B*, vol. 77, no. 31, 1977, 403–410.

3969 DAWSON, F.E. Air pollution in Ireland. *Administration*, vol. 6, no. 2, 1958, 128–50.

3970 DE WYTT, CAROLYN, and KEVANY, J.P. Air pollution in Ireland [with bibliog.]. *Ir. J. Med. Sci.*, 140, 1971, 108–117. Covers period 1963–69 for cities of Dublin and Cork.

3971 DUBLIN CORPORATION. Atmospheric Pollution Unit. Dublin city: air pollution monitoring stations, 1973–. Dublin: 1973–. On cover: Air Pollution Report. Issued annually.

3972 INDUSTRIAL DEVELOPMENT AUTHORITY. A survey of pollution in Ireland. Dublin: 1976.

3973 LEONARD, A.G.G. and MCVERRY, BRIDGET P. Atmospheric pollution in Dublin during the year 1938. *R. Dublin Soc. Sci. Proc.*, 22, 1938–42, 83–93.

3974 — Atmospheric pollution . . . during the year 1939, by A.G.G. Leonard, B.P. McVerry, and D. Crowley. *ibid.*, 22, 1938–42, 257–265.

3975 — Atmospheric pollution . . . during the year 1940, by A.G.G. Leonard, B.P. McVerry, and D. Crowley. *ibid.*, 22, 1938–42, 399–404.

3976 — Atmospheric pollution . . . during the year 1941, by A.G.G. Leonard, B.P. McVerry, and D. Crowley. *ibid.*, 23, 1942–44, 10–17.

3977 — Atmospheric pollution . . . during the year 1942, by A.G.G. Leonard, B.P. McVerry, and D. Crowley. *ibid.*, 23, 1942–44, 164–170.

3978 — Atmospheric pollution . . . during the years 1944 to 1950, by A.G.G. Leonard, D. Crowley and J. Belton. *ibid.*, 25, no. 12, 1950, 166–7.

Soil and Water Pollution

3979 CARROLL, D.M. Oil pollution identification service. *Technol. Ir.*, vol. 6, no. 11, 1975, 28–29. Identification by chemical analysis.

3980 FAHY, EDWARD. A review of the radioactive build-up in the Irish Sea. *Ir. Nat. J.*, vol. 18, no. 10, 1976, 312–3.

3981 MAUCHLINE, J. and TEMPLETON, W.L. Dispersion in the Irish Sea of the radioactive liquid effluent from Windscale Works of the U.K. Atomic Energy Authority. *Nature*, 198, 1963, 623–626.

Fire Safety

3982 WHITEHEAD, TREVOR. Dublin fire fighters: a history of fire fighting, rescue and ambulance work in the city of Dublin. Dublin: 1970.

Travel Safety

3983 ELDER, MICHAEL. For those in peril: the story of the life-boat service. London: 1963. Includes Ballycotton (Co. Cork), pp. 37–42; Newcastle (Co. Down), pp. 71–74; Portrush (Co. Antrim), pp. 111–116.

3984 WILSON, T.G. The Irish lighthouse service. Dublin: 1968. Bibliog., pp. 147–8.

Pharmacology

3985 KAIM-CAUDLE, P.R. *and others*. Pharmaceutical services in Ireland, by P.R. Kaim-Caudle, assisted by Kathleen O'Donoghue and Annette O'Toole. Dublin: 1970. (*Economic and Social Research Institute broadsheet, no.* 3).

3986 KERR, JAMES J. Notes on pharmacy in old Dublin. *Dublin Hist. Rec.*, 4, 1941–2, 149–59.

3987 KIRKPATRICK, T.P.C. The Dublin Pharmacopoeias. Dublin: 1921. Bibliog., pp. 19–20.

3988 MCWALTER, JAMES CHARLES. History of the Worshipful Company of Apothecaries in the city of Dublin. Dublin: 1916.

Blood Transfusion

3989 BUCKLEY, CLIONA McDONALD. Robert McDonnell (1828–1889). *J. Ir. Coll. Phys. Surg.*, vol. 3, no. 2, 1973, 66–69.

3990 WIDDESS, J.D.H. Robert McDonnell – a pioneer of blood transfusion, with a survey of transfusion in Ireland, 1832–1922. *Ir. J. Med. Sci.*, 1952, 11–20.

Folk Medicine

3991 HAND, WAYLAND D. Folk curing; the magical component. *Bealoideas*, 39–41, 1971–73, 140–156.

3992 LOGAN, PATRICK. Making the cure: a look at Irish folk medicine. Dublin: 1972.

3993 MALONEY, BEATRICE. Traditional herbal cures in County Cavan. *Ulster Folk*, 18, 1972, 66–79.

Radiology

3994 RYAN, MAX. The challenge of radiology. *J. Ir. Coll. Phys. Surg.*, vol. 3, no. 2, 1973, 47–53. An historical account of radiology in Ireland.

Heart

3995 FORAS TALUNTAIS, Health Advisory Committee. The prevention of coronary heart disease, compiled by Dr. J.F. Connolly. Dublin: 1977.

3996 HICKEY, NOEL and MULCAHY, RISTEARD. The significance of changes in certified coronary heart disease mortality rates in Ireland. *Ir. J. Med. Sci.*, 3, 1970, 163–168.

3997 MULCAHY, RISTEARD. The uses of prospective and retrospective population surveys in the study of coronary heart disease – with a note on Ireland's suitability for epidemiological studies. *Ir. J. Med. Sci., 6th ser.*, no. 499, 1967, 299–309.

3998 — The views of the 19th century Irish cardiologists on coronary artery disease. *Ir. J. Med. Sci., 6th ser.*, no. 445, 1963, 35–44.

Gastroenteritis

3999 MEDICAL RESEARCH COUNCIL OF IRELAND. Report of the gastroenteritis survey, Dublin city, 1964–1966. Dublin: 1970.

Dermatology

4000 BARRY, DR. J.M. Industrial dermatitis in Ireland. *Technol. Ir.*, vol. 6, no. 1, 1974, 35–37.

4001 FROGGATT, P. An outline, with bibliography, of human piebaldism and white forelock. *Ir. J. Med. Sci.*, 1959, 89–94.

Neurology

4002 MARTIN, EDWARD A. Irish neurological books, 1724–1894. *Ir. J. Med. Sci., 6th ser.*, no. 488, 1966, 347–350. Records the content of an exhibition held in the Library of Trinity College, Dublin, November 1965.

Multiple Sclerosis

4003 LYONS, J.B. Multiple sclerosis in Ireland. *Ir. J. Med. Sci.*, 3, 1970, 153–162.

Parasitic Diseases

4004 LANE, VICTOR. Bilharziasis in Dublin – report of three cases. *R. Coll. Surg. Ir. J.*, vol. 5, no. 2, 1969, 55–56.

Cancer

4005 IRISH JOURNAL OF MEDICAL SCIENCE. *8th ser.*, vol. 3, no. 2, 1970. Special issue devoted to cancer research. Contents: St. Luke's Hospital. Cancer research at St. Luke's Hospital, by R.A. O'Meara. St. Luke's cancer research fund: a review of cancer deaths in Ireland, by Malachy Powell. The National Radiation Monitoring Service.

4006 IRISH RADIUM COMMITTEE. Reports . . . 1924–43. *R. Dublin Soc. Sci. Proc. new ser.*, vols. 18–23, 1924–44.

4007 STEVENSON, WALTER C. Report of one year's radium work carried out in 1925. *R. Dublin Soc. Sci. Proc., new ser.*, 18, 1924–8, 307–27. Appendix: monographs describing technique, dosage, and apparatus used by the writer.

4008 WICKEN, A.J. Environmental and personal factors in lung cancer and bronchitis mortality in Northern Ireland, 1960–2: a report.

London: 1966. (*Tobacco Research Council research paper no.* 9).

Tuberculosis

4009 DILLON, T.W.T. Tuberculosis: a social problem. *Studies*, 32, 1943, 163–174.

4010 NATIONAL TUBERCULOSIS SURVEY, 1950–3. Tuberculosis in Ireland. Dublin: 1954. Includes bibliogs.

4011 PRICE, LIAM, *ed.* Dr Dorothy Price: an account of twenty years' fight against tuberculosis in Ireland. Oxford: 1957.

Surgery

4012 MACGOWAN, WILLIAM A.L. Irish surgery – retrospect and prospect. *R. Coll. Surg. Ir. J.*, vol. 5, no. 1, 1970, 77–86.

4013 MOGG, RICHARD A. The world of surgery – the Irish influence. *J. Ir. Coll. Phys. Surg.*, vol. 2, no. 4, 1973, 99–105. Deals mainly with urologists.

Regional Surgery

4014 INTERNATIONAL CONGRESS ON INJURIES IN RUGBY FOOTBALL and other team sports, Dublin, April 15th–18th, 1975; collected papers and discussions with chapters on first aid, etc., compiled by Thos. C.J. 'Bob' O'Connell. Dublin: 1976.

4015 LYONS, J.B. Irish contributions to the study of head injury in the eighteenth century. *Ir. J. Med. Sci.*, 1959, 400–12.

Dentistry

4016 IRISH DENTAL REVIEW. Dublin, vol. 1–, 1955–. Published quarterly.

4017 KEITH, J.E. The future of orthodontics in Ireland. *Ir. J. Med. Sci., 6th ser.*, no. 463, 1964, 291–297.

4018 LEE, JOHN B. The history of the Irish Dental Association, 1922–1972. [Dublin: 1972].

Opthalmology

4019 SOMERVILLE-LARGE, L.B. The development of opthalmology in Ireland [with bibliog.]. *Ir. J. Med. Sci.*, 1960, 98–129.

Rheumatic Fever

4020 WARD, O.C. and DEASY, P.F. Rheumatic fever: a ten-year review of patients admitted to an Irish children's hospital. *Ir. J. Med. Sci.*, 3, 1970, 307–319, 415–425.

ENGINEERING

General

4021 LEAHY, P. History of engineering training in Ireland. *Engineers J.*, vol. 15, no. 4, 1962, 147–51.

4022 ROBB, COLIN JOHNSTON. A unique collection of books on engineering and architecture. *Ir. Bld. and Engineer*, 88, 1946, 532. Description of some volumes of Irish connection for period 1578–1839, in collection of 700 works in possession of the Robb family.

Biography

4023 BELL, S.P. A biographical index of British engineers in the 19th century. New York and London: 1975.

4024 DELANEY, RUTH. John Trail – Grand Canal engineer. *Kildare Arch. Soc. J.*, vol. 14, no. 5, 1970, 626–630.

4025 EMERSON, L.J. Professor Robert Crawford of Ballyshannon. [Civil Engineer] *Donegal Ann.*, vol. 6, no. 1, 1964, 77–82. Extract from *The Biographer*, London, January 1901.

4026 LOEBER, ROLF. Biographical dictionary of engineers in Ireland, 1600–1730. *Ir. Sword*, vol. 30, no. 50, 1977, 30–44.

4027 TRINITY COLLEGE DUBLIN: School of Engineering. A record of past and present students. Dublin: [1960].

Street Furniture

4028 O'CONNELL, DERRY. The Antique pavement: an illustrated guide to Dublin's street furniture. Dublin: 1975. Includes lamp-standards, manholes, setts, paving, post boxes, bollards, public lavatories, seats, horse troughs.

4029 LUCAS, A.T. Decorative cobbling: examples from Counties Limerick, Wexford and Cork. *R. Soc. Antiq. Ir. J.*, 106, 1976, 31–72.

Hydraulic Power

4030 BOWIE, GAVIN. Watermills, windmills and

stationery steam engines in Ireland, with special reference to problems of conservation. [Thesis abstract]. *Ir. Econ. Soc. Hist.*, 3, 1976, 80–82.

4031 BOYLAN, LENA. The mills of Kildrought. *Kildare Arch. Soc. J.*, vol.15, no. 2, 1972, 141–155; no. 4, 1974–5, 359–375.

4032 DIXON, F.E. Dublin windmills. *Technol. Ir.*, vol. 7, no. 2, 1975, 46.

4033 MCCUTCHEON, W.A. The Corn mill in Ulster. *Ulster Folk.*, 15–16, 1970, 72–98.

4034 — Water-powered corn and flax scutching mills in Ulster. [with bibliog.]. *Ulster Folk.*, 12, 1966, 41–51.

Electrical

4035 DAVIES, GORDON, L. The Turlough Hill pumped-storage project, Co. Wicklow. *Ir. Geog.*, vol.6, no. 2, 1970, 204–6.

4036 ELECTRICTY SUPPLY BOARD. Annual Report and Accounts. no. 1–, 1927/28–. From 1935–36 includes Report on Shannon Fisheries.

4037 — Report on rural electrification. Dublin [1945].

4038 LAWLER, EDWARD A. The Electricity Supply Board – 40th anniversary. *Studies*, 56, 1967, 406–413.

4039 MURPHY, J. Hydro-electric undertaking at Bandon. *Inst. Civ. Eng. Ir. Trans.*, 51, 1926, 19–59.

4040 O'RIORDAN, J.A. Turlough Hill pumped-storage project. [with discussion and bibliog.] *Inst. Civ. Eng. Ir. Trans.*, 93, 1966–7, 6–24.

4041 QUANEY, JOSEPH. A penny to Nelson's Pillar. Portlaw (Co. Wexford): 1971. A biography of Kerr (Kyran) Quaney, electrical engineer who provided the electric tramcar service in Ireland.

4042 WORK ON SHANNON SCHEME. *Technol Ir.*, vol.7, no. 11, 1976, 51–2. Reprinted from the *Irish Trade Journal*, January 1926.

Telegraphy

4043 O'DONNELL, SEAN. The Trans-Atlantic telegraph. *Technol. Ir.*, vol.7, no. 6, 1975, 13–17.

4044 RUSSELL, W.H. The Atlantic Telegraph (1865). Newton Abbot: 1972. Facsimile reprint of 1st ed. London: 1865.

Solar Energy

4045 LEWIS, J. OWEN. Current Irish work in solar energy. *Technol. Ir.*, vol.10, no. 3, 1978, 46–51.

4046 NATIONAL SCIENCE COUNCIL. Solar energy for Ireland: a preliminary analysis of the basic data with tentative proposals for a programme of research and development; report to the National Science Council by Eamon Lalor. Dublin: 1975.

Mining

4047 CATALOGUE OF THE SEVERAL LOCALITIES IN IRELAND where mines, or metalliferous indications have hitherto been discovered, arranged in counties according to their respective towns. Dublin: [1854].

4048 DEADY, JOHN and DORAN, ELIZABETH. Prehistoric copper mines, Mount Gabriel, Co. Cork. *Cork. Hist. Arch. Soc. J.*, vol.77, 1972, 25–27.

4049 GARDINER, P.R.R. and HORNE R.R. Present day mining in Ireland. (*Geol. Surv. Info. Circular, no. 6*). In preparation.

4050 HARBISON, PETER. Mining and metallurgy in Early Bronze Age Ireland. *Nth. Munster Antiq. J.*, vol.10, no. 1, 1966, 1–11.

4051 KEARNS, KEVIN C. Some contributions of Irish base metal mining. *Ir. Geog.*, 8, 1975, 126–131.

4052 MACLAREN, J. MALCOLM. The occurrence of gold in Great Britain and Ireland [with bibliog. covering period 348 B.C.–A.D. 1901]. *Nth. England Inst. Min. Mech. Eng. Trans.*, 52, 1902–3, 437–510.

4053 O'BRIEN, M.V. Mining revival at Avoca, Co. Wicklow. *Inst. Civ. Eng. Ir. Trans.*, 71, 1945, 73–107.

4054 — Review of mining activities in the Republic of Ireland. *Trans. Inst. Min. Met. Ser. A*, 75, 1966, 70–84.

4055 O'SULLIVAN, M.D. The exploitation of the mines of Ireland in the sixteenth century. *Studies*, 24, 1935, 442–452.

4056 PRIOR–WANDESFORDE, R.C. Coal-mining in the Castlecomer area: a short account. *Carloviana*, vol.2, no. 24, 1975, 33–34, 38.

4057 TECHNOLOGY IRELAND. vol. 3, no. 7, 1971. Special issue on mining. Contents: How a mine operates, by J. Platt. Mines are where you find them, by C. Morley. Irish minerals industry, by A.P. Carroll. Mining in Ireland, by J.S. Jackson. Mining developments in Northern Ireland, by H.E. Wilson. Mining in the national economy, by J. Murray. The Allihies Copper Mine, Co. Cork, by K.A. Mawhinney.

4058 TUOHY, J. Offshore, Ireland ... 1974? *Technol. Ir.*, vol.4, no. 8, 1972, 9–13. Mining at sea.

Marine

4059 BULLOCK, SHAN F. Thomas Andrews, shipbuilder. Dublin: 1912. Employed with Messrs. Harland and Wolff, representing the firm on the *Titanic* and went down with the ship.

4060 CARTER, R.W.G. and RIHAN, C.L. The River Bann mouth bar. *Ir. Geog.*, 9, 1976, 121–123.

4061 DE COURCY IRELAND, J. John Phillip Holland: pioneer in submarine navigation. *Nth. Munster Antiq. J.*, 10, 1966–67, 206–212.

4062 — Robert Halpin and the Great Eastern. *Technol. Ir.*, vol.5, no. 8, 1973, 29–31.

4063 DUNN, LAURENCE. Famous liners of the past, Belfast built. London: 1964.

4064 FLOOD, DONAL T. William Petty and 'The Double Bottom'. *Dublin Hist. Rec.*, vol.30, no. 3, 1977, 96–110. On Petty's twin-hulled boat.

4065 HORNELL, JAMES. Water transport: origins and early evolution. Newton Abbot: 1970. Originally published 1946; the curraghs of Ireland, pp. 133–148.

4066 JOHNSTONE, PAUL. The Bantry boat. [with bibliog.]. *Antiquity*, 38, 1964, 277–284.

4067 LENNOX, HUGH. Shipbuilding in Dublin. *Admin.*, vol. 2, no. 4, 1954–5, 51–5.

4068 MARTIN, P.G. The development of shipbuilding in Cork Harbour. *R. Inst. Nav. Arch. Trans.*, 105, 1963, 91–106.

4069 SMELLIE, JOHN. Shipbuilding and repairing in Dublin: a record of work carried out by the Dublin Dockyard Co., 1901–23. Glasgow: 1935.

4070 WILSON, ALEC. The shipbuilding industry in Belfast. *Belfast Nat. Hist. Phil. Soc. Proc.*, session 1915–16, pp. 5–29.

Fortifications

4071 DONNELLY, MORWENNA. A Napoleonic fort in Donegal. *Country Life*, vol.158, no. 4082, 1975, 748–9. Knockalla Fort, restored in recent years by the author.

4072 FORDE-JOHNSON, J. Castles and fortifications of Britain and Ireland. London: 1977. Bibliog. p. 188.

4073 KERRIGAN, PAUL M. The Fortifications of Kinsale, Co. Cork. *Ir. Defence J.*, vol.32, no. 12, 1972, 239–245. Includes James Fort and Charles Fort.

4074 — The Shannonbridge fortification. *Ir. Sword.*, vol.11, no. 45, 1974, 234–245.

4075 MCKAY, RUSSELL. The Fortifications of Lough Swilly and Lough Foyle: temporary expedients, 1798–1800. *Donegal Ann.*, vol.12, no. 1, 1977, 40–48.

4076 O'BRIEN, B.M. Martello Towers. *Ir. Defence J.*, 25, 1965, 329–336.

4077 SUTCLIFFE, SHEILA. Martello Towers. Newton Abbot: 1972. Bibliog., pp. 168–170.

Ordnance

4078 BELL, J. BOWYER. The Thompson submachine gun in Ireland, 1921. *Ir. Sword.*, vol.8, no. 31, 1967, 98–108.

4079 FOX, S.E. First use of gun powder in Irish history. *Ir. Sword.*, vol.11, no. 44, 1974, 193–4.

4080 SHARPE, MITCHELL R. Robert Emmet and the development of the war rocket. *Eire-Ir.*, vol.5, no. 4, 1970, 3–8.

Lighthouses

4081 DOYLE, P. New Kish lighthouse takes shape at Dun Laoghaire. *Engineers J.*, 16, 1963, 482–485.

4082 HANSEN, FRODE. Design and construction of Kish Bank Lighthouse. *Inst. Civ. Eng. Ir. Trans.*, 92, 1965–66, 248–299.

4083 TURNER, J.S. Kish Bank lighthouse: major advance in durable marine structures. *Build. Cont. J. Ir.*, vol. 1, no. 51, 1965, 11–14.

Civil Engineering

4084 CROSS, R. ERNEST. Presidential Address [Towards a history of public works in Ireland]. *Inst. Civ. Eng. Ir. Trans.*, 92, 1965–66, 1–29.

4085 INSTITUTION OF CIVIL ENGINEERS OF IRELAND. Index to transactions, vol. 1–76, 1844–1950. Author and subject indices.

4086 MULLINS, M.B. An historical sketch of engineering in Ireland. *Inst. Civ. Eng. Ir. Trans.*, 6, 1863, 1–186. Includes inland navigation covering Carlingford Lough, The Lagan, The Nore, Limerick, The Upper Shannon, River Boyne, The Grand Canal, Royal Canal, Ballinasloe Canal, The Ulster Canal, and the following harbours, Howth, Kingstown, Drogheda, Ardglass, Belfast, Carrickfergus, Ballycastle, Cork, Wexford; lighthouses, roads, bridges in Dublin including Carlisle Bridge and Lucan Bridge, surveys and reports on bog improvement, River Shannon, arterial drainage, water-wheels, the steam engine and railways.

Structural Engineering

4087 UNIVERSITY COLLEGE, DUBLIN. Department of Civil Engineering. Concrete practice in Ireland, 1975; proceedings of a symposium held at University College, Dublin, in September 1975. Dublin, [1976].

4088 — Structural steelwork in Ireland, 1967. Dublin: University College, 1967. Proceedings of a symposium held in January 1967.

Bridges

4089 MALLAGH, J. City bridges over the Liffey: present and future. *Inst. Civ. Eng. Ir. Trans.*, 65, 1938–39, 225–253.

Railway Engineering

4090 ELLIS, HAMILTON. Railway carriages in the British Isles from 1830 to 1914. London: 1965.

4091 MCCUTCHEON, W.A. Ulster railway engineering and architecture. *Ulster J. Arch.*, 27, 1964, 155–165. Includes station buildings, bridges, viaducts and tunnels.

4092 MARSHALL, JOHN. A biographical dictionary of railway engineers. Newton Abbot: 1978.

4093 ROWLEDGE, J.W.P. The Turf Burner: Ireland's last steam locomotive design. Essex: Irish Railway Record Society, 1972.

Road Surfaces

4094 CAMERON, I.B. Sources of aggregate in Northern Ireland. 2nd ed. by E.N. Calvert–Harrison. 1977. (*Institute of Geological Sciences report no. 77/1*)

Inland Waterways

4095 MILLER, A. AUSTIN. River development in Southern Ireland. *R. Ir. Acad. Proc., Sec. B*, 45, 1938–39, 321–354.

Flooding

4096 RYDELL, L.E. River Shannon flood problem; final report. Dublin [1957].

Drainage

4097 DAVIES, GORDON L. and WHITTOW, JOHN B. A reconsideration of the drainage pattern of counties Cork and Waterford. *Ir. Geog.*, 8, 1975, 24–41.

4098 GALVIN, L.F. Land drainage survey. *Ir. J. Agric. Res.*, vol. 5, 1966, 79–88; *ibid.* 8, 1969, 1–18. A countrywide land drainage survey is in progress since 1964.

4099 O'BRIEN, GEORGE. Arterial drainage in Ireland. *Studies*, 30, 1941, 555–570.

4100 O'LOAN, J. Origin and development of arterial drainage in Ireland and the pioneers. [John Fox Burgoyne, Richard Griffith, William Thomas Mulvany and Thomas Aiskey Larcom]. *Ir. Dept. Agric. J.*, 59, 1962, 46–74.

4101 SHEEHAN, ANNE MARIE. Dublin drainage scheme. *Technol. Ir.*, vol. 5, no. 8, 1973, 36–88.

4102 SMITH, J. CHALONER. Some notes on the prospects of a revival of arterial drainage work in Ireland. *Inst. Civ. Eng. Ir. Trans.*, 50, 1925, 2–26.

Water Supply

4103 FLANAGAN, P.J. and TONER, P.F. A report on water quality: the national survey of Irish rivers. Dublin: An Foras Forbartha, 1972.

4104 IRELAND, MINISTRY FOR LOCAL GOVERNMENT. Inter-departmental Group on Air and Water Pollution. Report on water pollution to the minister for local government. Dublin: 1973.

4105 JACKSON, V. The inception of the Dodder water supply. *Dublin Hist. Rec.*, 15, 1958–60, 33–41.

4106 — The Limerick watercourse. *Dublin Hist. Rec.*, 9, 1946–8, 37–40.

4107 O'CARROLL, BARBARA M. Some aspects of the economic and social factors in the supply of piped water to rural areas. Dublin: An Foras Taluntais, 1962. (*Economic Research series no. 3*).

4108 O'KELLY, MICHAEL J. Wooden water mains at South Terrace, Cork. *Cork. Hist. Arch. Soc. J.*, 75, 1970, 125–128.

4109 WATERMAN, D.M. The water supply of Dundrum Castle, Co. Down. *Ulster J. Arch.*, 27, 1964, 136–139.

Aeronautics

4110 ARGENT, FRANK R. Early days at Baldonnel. *Ir. Defence J.*, vol. 34, no. 9, 1974, 316–8.

4111 BROCKETT, PAUL. Bibliography of aeronautics. *Smithsonian Inst. Misc. Coll.,* vol. 55, 1910.

4112 CONNOLLY, *Lt. Col.* JAMES. The 'Brennan' flight. *Ir. Defence J.,* 38, 1978, 67–70.

4113 DIXON, F.E. Ballooning in Dublin. *Dublin Hist. Rec.*, 14, 1955–58, 2–11.

4114 KELLY-ROGERS, *Capt.* J.C. Aviation in Ireland – 1784 to 1922. *Eire-Ir.*, vol.6, no. 2, 1971, 3–17.

4115 KOEHL, HERMANN *and others*. The three musketeers of the air: their conquest of the Atlantic from east to west, by Hermann Koehl, James C. Fitzmaurice and Baron Guenther von Huenefeld. New York and London: 1928.

4116 MCCABE, HUGO. Meath's place in aeronautical history. *Riocht na midhe*, vol. 5, no. 3, 1973, 91–2.

4117 MULLEN, THOMAS J. 'Mick' Mannock – the forgotten ace. *Ir. Sword.*, vol.10, no. 39, 1971, 77–86.

4118 O'DONNELL, P.D. Flight into the unknown: from Baldonnell (sic) to the Ford Museum, Greenfield Village. *Ir. Defence J.*, vol. 29, no. 5, 1969, 147–153.

4119 ROBERTSON, B. and GIBBINS, B. Military aviation in Ireland: a fifty year history. *Flight*, 84, 1963, 544–6.

4120 TIMMONS, S.V., *translator*. Report from Greenly Island: an account of the first east-west Atlantic crossing. *Ir. Defence J.*, 28, 1968, 307–311. Trans. from *Junkers-Nachrichten*, official organ of the Junkers Aircraft Company, issue no. 2, 1966; James Fitzmaurice was a member of the three man crew.

Bicycles

4121 MOORE, D.F. The bicycle: a study of efficiency, usage and safety. Dublin: An Foras Forbartha Teoranta: 1975. Bibliog., pp. 35–37.

AGRICULTURE

Bibliography

4122 ASLIN, M.S., *compiler*. Library catalogue of printed books and pamphlets on agriculture between 1471–1840. 2nd ed. Harpenden: Rothamsted Experimental Station, 1940.

4123 — Supplement . . . list of additions [1580–1840]. 1949.

4124 DREW, J.P. List of publications on agricultural subjects. *An Leab.*, 1, 1930–1, 104.

4125 FORAS TALUNTAIS. The published word: research results published by An Foras Taluntais and its staff, 1959–1961. *Farm Research News*, 2, 1961, 72–74. Includes papers on soils, peatland, plant sciences, crop history, horticulture, fishing, annual production and rural economy.

4126 — Scientific publications by staff of An Foras Taluntais, August 1958 – December 1967. [Dublin, 1968].

4127 — Index to publications of An Foras Taluntais, compiled by V. Reilly. Dublin: 1972.

4128 FUSSELL, G.E. Chronological list of early agricultural works in the library of the Ministry of Agriculture and Fisheries [London]. London: 1930.

4129 — The old English farming books from Fitzherbert to Tull, 1523 to 1730. London: 1947.

4130 — More old English farming books from Tull to the Board of Agriculture, 1731 to 1793. London: 1950.

4131 INTERNATIONAL ASSOCIATION OF AGRICULTURE LIBRARIANS AND DOCUMENTALISTS. World directory of agricultural libraries and documentation centres, edited by D.H. Boalch. Harpenden: 1960.

4132 MACDONALD, DONALD. Agricultural writers from Sir Walter of Henley to Arthur Young, 1200–1800 . . . to which is added an exhaustive bibliography. London: 1908.

4133 ORGANISATION FOR ECONOMIC CO-OPERATION AND DEVELOPMENT. Catalogue of agricultural films. Paris: 1961. (*O.E.C.D. documentation in food and agriculture*, no. 37.) 1097 films: "will assist agricultural advisers and teachers, particularly those working in the countries in the process of economic development, to become more fully informed of the types and sources of films suitable to their requirements." – Foreword.

4134 PERKINS, W.F. British and Irish writers on agriculture. 3rd ed. Lymington: 1939. 1st ed. 1929.

4135 PORTER, JOSHUA. Catalogue of books on agriculture and rural affairs, being part of the stock of Joshua Porter, agricultural bookseller, 72 Grafton Street, Dublin. n.d. Porter registered in business for period 1830–65.

4136 ROYAL AGRICULTURAL SOCIETY OF ENGLAND. General index to the Journal. 1st ser., vols. 1–25, 1839–64; 2nd ser., vols. 1–25, 1865–89; etc.

4137 ROYAL DUBLIN SOCIETY. Agriculture: a selective bibliography of modern books in the library of the Royal Dublin Society. [2nd ed.]. Dublin: 1954.

4138 UNITED STATES DEPARTMENT OF AGRICULTURE, WASHINGTON. Bibliography of agriculture. vol. 1–, 1942–.

Rural Life

4139 BOOK ASSOCIATION OF IRELAND. List of books on rural life. *Ir. Lib. Bull.*, vol.5, no. 2, 1944.

4140 GAILEY, ALAN. The Ballyhagan inventories, 1716–1740. *Folk Life*, 15, 1977, 36–64. Illuminates the pattern of domestic and rural life in mid Ulster.

4141 LUCAS, A.T. Bog wood: a study in rural economy. *Bealoideas*, 23, 1954, 71–134.

Atlases

4142 STAMP, L. DUDLEY. The Agricultural atlas of Ireland. London: 1931.

Periodicals

4143 CAMBRIDGE UNIVERSITY, SCHOOL OF AGRICULTURE. Agricultural periodicals of the British Isles, 1681–1900, and their location. Compiled by F.A. Buttress. Cambridge: 1950.

4144 ERBAND DEUTSCHER AGRARJOURNALISM (German Association of Agricultural Journalists). Übersichte über die Agrarpresse der OECE Lander. (Agricultural press in OEEC member countries). [Hamburg, 1958.]. Typescript. Copy in Dept of Agriculture, Dublin.

4145 FUSSELL, G.E. Early farming journals. *Econ. Hist. Rev.*, 3, 1931–2, 417–22.

4146 IRELAND, DEPARTMENT OF AGRICULTURE. List of scientific and technical periodicals in the library of the Department of Agriculture, Ireland. Addenda [to 1944]. Typescript.

4147 ORGANISATION FOR EUROPEAN ECONOMIC CO-OPERATION. List of agricultural press and periodicals in OEEC member countries, rev. ed. Paris, 1960. (*European Productivity Agency, Food and agriculture documentation ser.*, no. 28.) 1st ed. 1959.

Societies, Government Departments

4148 HOCTOR, D. The department's story – a history of the Department of Agriculture. Dublin: Institute of Public Administration, 1971. (*Administrative history series, no. 1*).

4149 IRELAND. Department of Agriculture, Dublin. Annual report. vol.1–, 1900–. From 1956–7 includes section *Scientific papers published by officers of the department during the year under review*.

4150 — Journal. vol. 1–, 1900–. Index to vol. 1–22 in vol. 22.

4151 IRISH AGRICULTURAL ORGANISATION SOCIETY, DUBLIN. Annual report. 1894–.

4152 LIST OF THE LOCAL AGRICULTURAL SOCIETIES IN IRELAND, extracted from the correspondence of the Agricultural Society of Ireland. Dublin: 1835.

Advisory Work

4153 IRELAND, DEPARTMENT OF AGRICULTURE AND FISHERIES. A review of the Irish Agricultural Advisory Service: report by W. Emrys Jones and Albert J. Davies. Dublin: 1967.

4154 KEENAN, P. A study of agricultural advisory work in Ireland. *Agr. Prog*., 39, 1964, 77–88.

4155 ORGANISATION FOR ECONOMIC CO-OPERATION AND DEVELOPMENT. Agricultural advisory services: development in OECD member countries. Paris, OECD: 1969. Ireland, pp., 267–272.

4156 SPAIN, HENRY. Community development and agriculture extension services [with bibliog]. *Ir. Dept. Agric. J*., 60, 1963, 137–157.

4157 WOODS, J.C.H. The Advisory Service in Northern Ireland and the Pilot Farm Scheme. *Agr. Prog*., 35, 1960, 13–17.

Co-operative Agriculture

4158 HUGHES, P.H. The beginnings of the Irish Agricultural Organisation Society. *In* Year Book of Agricultural Co-operation, 1974, 124–147.

4159 KNAPP, JOSEPH. An appraisement of agricultural co-operation in Ireland. Dublin: 1964.

Teaching

4160 MCKILLEY, J. WESLEY and STERLING, W. SALTERS. Gurteen College [Co. Tipperary]; a venture of faith. Omagh: 1976.

4161 MOORE, T. Agricultural education in Northern Ireland. *Agr. Prog*., 44, 1969, 157–159.

4162 UNIVERSITY COLLEGE, DUBLIN. Albert Agricultural college: centenary souvenir, 1838–1938. Dublin: [1938].

Research

4163 COMMONWEALTH AGRICULTURAL BUREAUX. List of research workers, 1972, in the agricultural sciences in the Commonwealth and in the Republic of Ireland. Farnham Royal: 1972.

4164 FOOD AND AGRICULTURE ORGANIZATION OF THE UNITED NATIONS. Index of agricultural research institutions in Europe concerned with animal production and their principal lines of investigation. Rome: 1953. Typescript.

4165 — Index of agricultural research institutions in Europe, prepared by Truman F. Peebles and G. de Bakker. Rome: 1957. 2 vols. Ireland, vol. 2, pp. 11–20.

4166 AN FORAS TALUNTAIS (The Agricultural Institute), Dublin. Farm research news. vol. 1–, 1960–.

4167 — Irish journal of agricultural research. vol. 1–, 1961–.

4168 — *Administration*, vol. 21, no. 2, 1973. Special issue: An Foras Taluntais.

History

4169 AGRICULTURAL HISTORY REVIEW. vol. 1–, 1953–. Published annually and includes *List of books and articles on agricultural history;* from 1955 includes section *Work in progress*.

4170 ANCIENT AGRICULTURE IN IRELAND AND NORTH–WEST EUROPE [a symposium]. *Adv. Sci*., vol.14, no. 56, 1958, 365–373. Contributors include Dr. V.B. Proudfoot and Pierre Flatres.

4171 ATTWOOD, E.A. The future development of Irish agriculture. *Studies*, 58, 1969, 240–255.

4172 — Trends in agricultural development in

Europe and Ireland. *Stat. Social Inq. Soc. Ir. J.*, 116th session, vol.21, pt. 1, 1962–63, 31–49.

4173 BARRINGTON, RICHARD M. The Drought of 1887, and some of its effects on Irish agriculture. *Stat. Social Inq. Soc. Ir. J.*, 67, 1888, 223–247.

4174 BEAUFORT, *Dr.* D.A. *compiler*. Materials for the Dublin Society agricultural survey of County Louth, edited by C.Ç. Ellison. *Louth Arch. Hist. Soc. J.*, vol.18, no. 2, 1974, 121–131; no. 3, 1975, 187–194; no. 4, 1976, 304–309.

4175 BLACK, WILLIAM. Agriculture and regional development in Northern Ireland. *Agr. Prog.*, 44, 1969, 123–131.

4176 BLACKER, WILLIAM. Past and present state of agriculture in Ireland. *R. Agr. Soc. England J.*, 4, 1843, 437–452.

4177 BUTLIN, R.A. Agriculture in County Dublin in the late eighteenth century. *Stud. Hib.*, 9, 1969, 93–108.

4178 CAMPBELL, MARY. Agriculturalist in the age of reason: Arthur Young in Ireland. *Country Life*, vol.160, no. 4123, 1976, 110–111.

4179 CONRY, MICHAEL. Kilkenny's 'Golden Vein': its soils, land-use and agriculture. *Ir. Geog.*, 7, 1974, 19–28.

4180 DONNELLY, Jr., JAMES S. The Irish agricultural depression of 1859–64. *Ir. Econ. Soc. Hist.*, 3, 1976, 33–54.

4181 DUIGNAN, MICHAEL. Irish agriculture in early historic times. *R. Soc. Antiq. Ir. J.*, 74, 1944, 124–145.

4182 AN FORAS TALUNTAIS (The Agricultural Institute), Dublin. The state of Irish agriculture, 1960–1. Typescript.

4183 — Our contribution to Irish agriculture, 1958–1968. [Dublin: 1968].

4184 GILLMOR, DESMOND A. The Agricultural regions of the Republic of Ireland. *Ir. Geog.*, vol.5, no. 4, 1967, 245–261.

4185 — Agriculture in the Republic of Ireland. Budapest: 1977. Hungarian Academy of Sciences, Research Institute, (*Geography of world agriculture*, 7). Bibliog., pp. 195–202.

4186 — Aspects of agricultural change in the Republic of Ireland during the 1960s. *Ir. Geog.*, vol.6, no. 4, 1972, 492–498.

4187 GREENE, DR. J.N. A survey of Irish agriculture with special reference to the interdependence with British agriculture. *Adv. Sci.*, vol.14, no. 56, 1958, 374–380.

4188 HETZEL, FRITZ. Die Irischen Agrarfragen: Inaugural-dissertation zur Erlangung der Staatswissenschaftlichen Doktorwurde einer Hohen Philosophischen Fakultat der Ruprecht-Karls-Universität zu Heidelberg. Heidelberg: 1929. Bibliog., pp. 142–50.

4189 HUNTER, J.A. Farming on Tory Island. *Donegal Ann.*, vol.10, no. 1, 1971, 19–26.

4190 JOHNSON, JAMES H. Agriculture in Co. Derry at the beginning of the nineteenth century. *Stud. Hib.*, 4, 1964, 95–103.

4191 JOHNSTON, JOSEPH. Irish agriculture in transition. Dublin and Oxford: 1951. Bibliog., pp. 181–2.

4192 KERRY COUNTY COMMITTEE OF AGRICULTURE. County Kerry agricultural resource survey. Tralee: 1972. List of authors, 272–4.

4193 LANE, PADRAIG G. An attempt at commercial farming in Ireland after the famine. *Studies*, 61, 1972, 54–66.

4194 MCCRACKEN, EILEEN. Two eighteenth-century surveys at Castlefin. [Co. Donegal] *Donegal Ann.*, vol.7, no. 3, 1968, 313–318.

4195 [MAGUIRE, S.J.] Farming in Galway before the famine. *Galway Reader*, vol.3, no. 3, 1951, 75–88.

4196 MITCHELL, G.F. Littleton bog, Tipperary: an Irish agricultural record [with bibliog.]. *R. Soc. Antiq. Ir. J.*, 95, 1965, 121–132.

4197 MORRIS, E.A.M. A brief survey of Irish agriculture with some statistical notes on agriculture in the Irish Free State. *Ir. Dep. Agric. J.*, 23, 1923–4, 236–251, 341–3.

4198 MOYLES, M.G. and DE BRUN PADRAIG. Charles O'Brien's agricultural survey of Kerry, 1800. *Kerry Arch. Hist. Soc. J.*, 1, 1968, 73–80.

4199 [O'BRIEN, CHARLES] A view of the state of agriculture in the county of Kerry. 1800. *Kerry Arch. Hist. Soc. J.*, 1, 1968, 81–100.

4200 O COMHRAIDHE, E. The Land Commission.

Administration, vol. 4, no. 3, 1956, 37–47.

4201 O'GRADA, CORMAC. Supply responsiveness in Irish agriculture during the nineteenth century. *Econ. Hist. Rev., 2nd ser.*, vol. 28, no. 2, 1975, 312–317.

4202 O'LOAN, J. A history of early Irish farming. *Ir. Dept. Agric. J.*, 60, 1963, 178–219; 61, 1964, 242–284; 62, 1965, 131–197.

4202 PROUDFOOT, V.B. Farms and fields in Northern Ireland. [with bibliog.]. *Agr. Prog.*, 35, 1960, 24–33.

4204 SEYMOUR, J. Back to Donegal. *Geog. Mag.*, vol.45, no. 14, 1968, 1217–1224. Account of Father McDwyer's work in Glencolumbkille.

4205 SHEEHAN, JEREMIAH. South Westmeath: farm and folk. Tallaght: Blackwater Press, 1978. Bibliog., pp. 445–454.

Economics, Statistics

4206 CENTRAL STATISTICS OFFICE, DUBLIN. Agricultural statistics, 1934–56. Dublin: 1960.

4207 FOOD AND AGRICULTURE ORGANIZATION OF THE UNITED NATIONS. Technical conversion factors for agricultural commodities. Rome: 1960. Ireland, pp. 149–53.

4208 GAUGHAN, JOAN, *and others*. Farm management survey, 1967–68, by Joan Gaughan, B.C. Hickey and J.F. Heavey. Dublin: 1970.

4209 HEAVEY, JOHN F. The Farm management survey, 1966 to 1969. *Stat. Social Inq. Soc. Ir. J.*, vol.22, pt. 4, 1971–72, 143–155.

4210 — *and others*. Farm management survey 1972–75: four year report by J.F. Heavey, M.J. Harkin, R. Power, L. Connolly and M. Roche. Dublin: 1973.

4211 — *and others*. Farm management survey, 1977, by J.F. Heavey, M.J. Harkin, L. Connolly and M. Roche. Dublin: 1978.

4212 IRELAND. Department of Industry and Commerce. Agricultural statistics, 1847–1926. Reports and tables. Dublin: 1928. Also volume covering period 1927–33.

4213 O'MUIREADHAIGH, REAMONN. Farm account books, 1802–1860, from Gaulstown, Monasterboice. *Louth Arch. J.*, vol.17, no. 4, 1972, 235–249.

4214 PAKENHAM–WALSH, A.A. Work study on the farm. London: 1961. Bibliog., p. 75.

4215 STAEHLE, HANS. Statistical notes on the economic history of Irish agriculture, 1847–1913. *Stat.Social.Inq.Soc.Ir.J.,104th session*, vol. 18, 1950–1, 444–71.

Structures

4216 CONBOY, M. The old farmhouse. *Old Wexford Soc. J.*, vol.3, no. 1, 1970, 81–2.

4217 O'DANACHAIR, CAOIMHIN. Farm and field gates. *Ulster Folk.*, 11, 1965, 76–79.

4218 O'FARRELL, F. The farm dwelling: a handbook on the layout of the home. Dublin: 1974.

Fences, Hedges

4219 ROBINSON, PHILIP. The spread of hedged enclosure in Ulster. *Ulster Folk.*, 23, 1977, 57–69.

Agricultural Tools

4220 GAILEY, ALAN. Irish iron-shod wooden spades. *Ulster J. Arch.*, 31, 1968, 77–86.

4221 — and FENTON, ALEXANDER, *eds*. The spade in Northern and Atlantic Europe. Belfast: Ulster Folk Museum, 1970. Includes the typology of the Irish spade, pp. 35–48; The use of the spade in Ireland, by Caoimhin O'Danachair; Paring and burning in Ireland, by A.T. Lucas, pp. 99–147; and Slanes: Irish peat spades, by John C. O'Sullivan, pp. 221–242.

4222 KELLY, MARTIN J. Some ploughs of County Kildare. *Kildare Arch. Soc. J.*, vol.15, no. 4, 1974–5, 419–424.

4223 O'DANACHAIR, CAOIMHIN. The spade in Ireland. *Bealoideas*, 31, 1963, 98–114.

Land, Soil

4224 ANDREWS, J.H. The French School of Dublin land-surveyors. *Ir. Geog.*, vol.5, no. 4, 1967, 275–292.

4225 **Bibliography of Soil Science.** Harpenden. 1931–4, 1934–7, 1937–40, 1940–4, 1944–7, 1947–50. In progress.

4226 **Bunting,** B.T. *ed.* An annotated bibliography of memoirs and papers on the soils of the British Isles. London. Pt. I. The classification, morphology, distribution and reclamation of British soils, 1964.

4227 **Collins,** J.F. *and others* A comparative study of three limestone-derived soils in Co. Kildare, by J.F. Collins, D.F. Frayne, and M.J. Conroy. *R. Ir. Acad. Proc., Ser. B*, vol.75, no. 31, 1975, 585–597.

4228 **Conroy,** M.J. The soils of County Carlow. *Ir. Geog.*, vol.5, no. 3, 1966, 204–213.

4229 — Irish Plaggen soils – their distribution, origin and properties. [with bibliog.]. *J. Soil Sci.*, 22, 1971, 401–416.

4230 — and **O'Shea,** T. Soils of the Annascaul pilot area. [West Kerry] Dublin: An Foras Taluntais, 1971. (*National Soil Survey of Ireland*).

4231 — and **Ryan, Pierce.** Soils of Co. Carlow. Dublin: An Foras Taluntais. 1967. (*National Soil Survey of Ireland*).

4232 — *and others*. Soils of County Kildare, by M.J. Conroy, R.F. Hammond and T. O'Shea. Dublin: Agricultural Institute, 1970.

4233 **Cruickshank, James** G. A reconnaissance soil survey of county Fermanagh. *Ir. Geog.*, vol. 4, no. 3, 1961, 190–201.

4234 —Soils and changing agricultural land values in part of Londonderry. *Ir. Geog.*, vol.6, no. 4, 1972, 462–479.

4235 — Soils of the northern and central parts of County Armagh. *ibid.*, 8, 1975, 63–71.

4236 **Culleton,** E.B. and **Mitchell,** G.F. Soil erosion following deforestation of the early Christian period in South Wexford. *R. Soc. Antiq. Ir. J.*, 106, 1976, 120–3.

4237 **Finch,** T.F. Soils of County Clare. Dublin: An Foras Taluntais, 1971. (*National Soil Survey of Ireland*).

4238 — and **Ryan, Pierce.** Soils of Co. Limerick. Dublin: An Foras Taluntais, 1966. (*National Soil Survey of Ireland*).

4239 **Food and Agriculture Organization of the United Nations.** Bibliography on land utilization and conservation in Europe, by C.H. Edelman and B.E.P. Eeuwens. Rome: 1935.

4240 — Supplement. Rome: 1959.

4241 **Foras Taluntais,** County Leitrim resource survey. Dublin. Pt. 1. Land use potential (soils, grazing capacity and forestry), 1973. Pt. 2. Some aspects of production: drainage machinery use, grass production and utilisation, farming systems, animal health, fisheries, 1975. Pt. 3. Demography, sociology and economics, 1975.

4242 — Soil survey bulletin. no. 1–, 1964–.

4243 — Soil survey of An Foras Taluntais Farms at Kilpatrick and Derrybrennan, Lullymore, Rathangan, Co. Kildare, and cut-over peatland experimental area at Derrybrennan, by R.F. Hammond and J. Bouma. Dublin. An Foras Taluntais, 1973. (*Soil Survey Bulletin No. 28*).

4244 **Gardiner, Michael** J. The National Soil Survey [with bibliog.] *Ir. Geog.*, 4, 1959–63, 442–453.

4245 — and **Ryan, Pierce.** Soils of Co. Wexford. Dublin: An Foras Taluntais, 1964. (*National Soil Survey of Ireland*).

4246 — A new generalised soil map of Ireland and its land use interpretation. *Ir. J. Agric. Res.*, 8, 1969, 95–109.

4247 **Geary,** R.C. The National Farm Survey. *Administration*, vol.5, no. 1, 1957, 27–41.

4248 **Mannion,** L. Characteristics of some Irish soils of limestone origin [with bibliog.] *Ir. Dept. Agric. J.*, 60, 1963, 5–37.

4249 **Mulqueen,** J. A review of drumlin soils research, 1959–1966. Dublin: An Foras Taluntais, 1967. Bibliog., pp. 54–56.

4250 **Simington,** R.C. and **Wheeler,** T.S. Sir Robert Kane's lost maps. *Ir. Dept. Agric. J.*, 44, 1947, 10–14.

4251 — and **Wheeler,** T.S. Sir Robert Kane's soil survey of Ireland: the record of a failure. *Ir. Dept. Agric.J.*, 44, 1947, 15–28. Reprinted from *Studies*, 34, 1945, 539–51.

4252 **Some Irish [Land] Surveyors.** St. Patrick's College, Maynooth, Museum. Third Tostal display souvenir catalogue, 1955, pt. 46.

Cultivation and Harvesting

4253 MURRAY, J.P. and RAFTERY, T.F. An investigation into the relative efficiency of different systems of haymaking in Ireland [with bibliog.]. *Ir. Dept. Agric. J.*, 63, 1966, 115–135.

4254 WALSH, DR. T. *and others*. The use of peatland in Irish agriculture, by Dr. T. Walsh, P.J. O'Hare and E. Quinn. *Adv. Sci.*, 14, 1957–8, 405–416.

Drainage, Reclamation

(See also nos. 4097–4102)

4255 ADAMS, R.H. Contribution to the bibliography of land drainage in Great Britain and Ireland, 1500–1947. In preparation.

4256 O'LOAN, J. Land reclamation down the years. *Ir. Dept. Agric.J.*, 55, 1959, 153–89. Includes 59 references.

4257 SCIENCE MUSEUM LIBRARY, LONDON. Some references to land reclamation and improvement in the British Isles. n.d. (*Science library bibliog.ser.*, no. 418.) Typescript; period covered 1821–1938.

Fertilisers

4258 WALSH, T., *and others*. A half century of fertiliser and lime use in Ireland, by T. Walsh, P.F. Ryan and J. Kilroy. *Stat. Social Inq. Soc.Ir. J.*, 19, 1956–7, 104–36. Period covered 1900–50, with brief assessment of previous century.

Water

4259 ROCHE, D. Rural water supply. *Administration*, vol.8, no. 4, 1960, 277–314.

Plant Pathology

4260 AINSWORTH, G.C. The plant diseases of Great Britain: a bibliography. London: 1937. Annotated.

4261 BARNER, J. *ed.* Bibliographie der Pflanzenschutz-literatur. [Bibliography of plant protection.] Berlin: 1953. 2 vols.

4262 MCKAY, ROBERT. Pioneer workers in the field of plant pathology in Ireland, and a list of papers on plant disease investigations in Ireland published prior to 1940. *Ir. Dept. Agric. J.*, 48, 1951, 5–31.

Weeds

4263 NEENAN, M. Organisation of weed research in Ireland. *Weed Research*, 4, 1964, 78.

Pests

4264 THORNBERRY, H. Warble fly eradication in Ireland. *Ir. Vet. J.*, 30, 1976, 83–88.

4265 — and KENNY, J.E. A review of investigations on the warble fly problem, 1900–1964, in Ireland. *Ir. Dept. Agric. J.*, 62, 1965, 5–16.

Field Crops

4266 FIELD CROP ABSTRACTS, compiled from world literature. Farnham, Commonwealth Agricultural Bureaux. vol. 1–, 1948–.

Cereals

4267 JESSEN, KNUD and HELBACH, HANS. Cereals in Great Britain and Ireland in prehistoric and early historic times. *Det Kongelige Danske Videnskabernes Selskab, Biologiske Skrifter*, Bd. 3, nr. 2, 1944. Bibliog., pp. 66–68.

Grasses

4268 BEDDOWS, A.R. Ryegrasses in British agriculture: a survey [with bibliog.]. University College of Wales, 1953. (*Welsh Plant Breeding Station, Bulletin ser. H. no. 17*). Perennial Ryegrass in Ireland, pp. 31–34.

4269 FARRAGHER, M.A. Grasses. *Cap. Ann.*, 1977, 116–120.

4270 O'TOOLE, M.A. Grassland research on blanket peat in Ireland [with bibliog.]. *J. Br. Grassland Soc.*, 23, 1968, 43–50.

Potatoes

4271 BOURKE, P.M. AUSTIN. A contribution to the early history of the Black leg disease of the potato. [with bibliog.]. *Ir. Dept. Agric. J.*, 63, 1966, 103–109.

4272 — Emergence of potato blight, 1843–46. *Nature*, 203, 1964, 805–808.

4273 — The use of the potato crop in pre-famine Ireland. *Stat. Soc. Inq. Soc. Ir. J.*, vol.21, pt. 6. 121st session, 1967–68, 72–96.

4274 CONNELL, K.H. The Potato in Ireland. *Clogher Rec.*, 65, 1963, 271–295. Reprinted from *Past and Present* 23, 1962, 57–71.

4275 COX A.E. and LARGE, E.C. Potato blight epidemics throughout the world. Washington: U.S. Dept of Agriculture, 1960. (*Agriculture handbook*, no. 174.) Northern Ireland and Republic of Ireland, pp. 43–59; bibliog. pp. 207–19.

4276 DAVIDSON, W.D. The history of the potato and its progress in Ireland [with bibliog.]. *Ir. Dept. Agric.J.*, 34, 1936–7, 286–307.

4277 — A review of the literature dealing with the degeneration of varieties of the potato. *R. Dublin Soc. Econ. Proc.,* 2, 1910–35, 331–89. Lists 109 papers.

4278 KENNEDY, HENRY. The importance of the potato. *Studies*, 21, 1932, 567–575.

4279 MCKAY, ROBERT. Potato diseases [with bibliogs.]. Dublin: 1955.

4280 MURPHY, PAUL A. A critical review of some recent work on the occurrence of virus complexes in the potato [with bibliog.]. *R. Dublin Soc. Sci. Proc., new ser.*, 20, 1930–3, 193–210.

4281 — and MCKAY, ROBERT. A comparison of some European and American virus diseases of the potato [with bibliog.]. *ibid.*, 20, 1930–3, 347–58.

4282 — and MCKAY, ROBERT. Methods for investigating the virus diseases of the potato, and some results obtained by their use [with bibliog.]. *ibid.*, 18, 1924–6, 169–83.

4283 SALAMAN, REDCLIFFE N. The history and social influence of the potato, with a chapter on industrial uses, by W.G. Burton. Cambridge: 1949. Bibliog., pp. 620–645.

4284 SCIENCE MUSEUM LIBRARY, LONDON. The manuring of potatoes, 1930–7. (*Science library bibliog. ser.,* no. 388.)

4285 WHITEHEAD, TATHAM *and others*. The potato in health and disease, by Tatham Whitehead, Thomas P. McIntosh, and William M. Findlay. 3rd ed. rev. Edinburgh: 1953. Bibliog., pp. 592–644.

Onions

4286 MCKAY, ROBERT. Onion diseases. Dublin: 1959.

Flax

4287 MCKAY, ROBERT. Flax diseases: an illustrated bulletin on their recognition in the field [with bibliogs.]. Dublin: 1947.

4288 NEENAN, M. and DEVEREUX, J. Some recent researches on the growing of fibre flax. [with bibliog.]. *R. Dublin Soc. Sci. Proc., Ser. B*, vol.3, no. 16, 1973, 201–220.

Tobacco

4289 EVERARD, SYLVIA. Tobacco growing in Ireland, 1584–1929. [Dublin: 1934.] 12 pp.

4290 WALKER, J.A. On the cultivation of tobacco in Ireland. *Stat. Social Inq. Soc. Ir. J.*, 8, 1885, 589–595.

Fruit

4291 CURRAN, P.L. A new apple variety: *Councillor. R. Dublin Soc. Sci. Proc., Ser. B,* vol.1, no. 14, 1965, 159–161.

4292 FINCH, T.F. and GARDINER, M.J. Pomology research centre, Ballygagin, Dungarvan, Co. Waterford. Dublin: An Foras Taluntais, 1972. (*Soil survey bulletin no. 27*)

4293 LAMB, J.G. The apple in Ireland: its history and varieties [with bibliog.]. *R. Dublin Soc. Econ. Proc.,* vol.4, no. 1, 1951, 1–63.

4294 LEISTER, INGEBORG. Orchards in County Tipperary. *Ir. Geog.*, vol.4, no. 4, 1962, 292–301. Deals mainly with cider-orchards.

Forestry

4295 ANDERSON, M.L. Items of forestry interest from the Irish statutes prior to A.D. 1800. *Ir. Forestry*, vol.1, no. 2, 1944, 6–26.

4296 BRADY, AIDAN. The history of arboriculture in Ireland. *Ir. Dept. Agric. J.*, 72, 1975, 5–11.

4297 CRAWFORD, W.H. The Woodlands of the Manor of Brownlow's – Derry, North Armagh, in the seventeenth and eighteenth centuries. *Ulster Folk.*, 10, 1964, 57–64.

4298 ELWES, HENRY JOHN and HENRY, AUGUSTINE H. The trees of Great Britain and Ireland. [1st edition reprinted]. East Ardsley: 1969–72. 7 vols. Originally published, Edinburgh: 1906–13.

4299 FITZPATRICK, H.M. Conifers: key to the genera and species, with economic notes. [with bibliog.]. 2nd. rev. ed. *R. Dublin Soc. Sci. Proc., Ser. A.* vol.2, no. 7, 1965, 67–129. Originally published *R. Dublin Soc. Sci. Proc., new ser.,* 19, 1928–30, 189–260.

4300 — The trees of Ireland, native and introduced. *ibid*., 20, 1930–3, 597–656.

4301 — The forests of Ireland: an account of the forests of Ireland from early times to the present day. Bray. [1966]. Bibliog. p. 153.

4302 FORBES, A.C. Some legendary and historical references to Irish woods and their significance. *R. Ir. Acad. Proc., Sec. B*, 41, 1932–3, 15–36.

4303 —Tree planting in Ireland during four centuries [seventeenth–twentieth]. *ibid*., *Sec. C*, 41, 1932–4, 168–99.

4304 FORESTRY ABSTRACTS, compiled from world literature; prepared by Commonwealth Forestry Bureau, Oxford. Farnham, Commonwealth Agricultural Bureau, vol. 1–, 1939–.

4305 GALLAGHER, L.U. Timber research in Ireland. [with bibliog.]. *Inst. Ind. Res. Stand. Bull*., 5, 1968, 238–243; 248.

4306 GRAY, H.J. The economics of Irish forestry. *Stat. Social Inq. Soc. Ir. J*., 117th session, 21, 1963–4, 18–44.

4307 HENRY, AUGUSTINE. Co-operation of state and citizen in Irish forestry. *Studies*, 13, 1924, 613–630.

4308 IRISH FORESTRY. Dublin, vol.1–, 1943–.

4309 JOYCE, P.N. and LORD ARDEE. Knockrath woodlands: a 20 year review. *Ir. Forestry*, vol.33, no. 2, 1976, 99–104.

4310 LEATHART, P.S. A forestry tour in the Irish Republic. *Qtr. J. Forestry*, vol.66, no. 4, 1972, 321–337.

4311 LESLIE, *Sir* SHANE. Forestry for Ireland. *Studies*, 37, 1948, 161–168.

4312 LOWE, JOHN. The Yew-trees of Great Britain and Ireland. London: 1897. Bibliog., pp. 261–4.

4313 MCCRACKEN, DONAL P. and MCCRACKEN, EILEEN. A register of trees, Co. Cork, 1790–1860. *Cork. Hist. Arch. Soc. J*., 81, 1976, 39–60.

4314 MCCRACKEN, EILEEN. The Irish woods since Tudor times: distribution and exploitation. Newton Abbot: 1971. Bibliog., pp. 171–180.

4315 — Irish woodlands, 1600 to 1800. [with bibliog.]. *Qtr. J. Forestry*., 57, 1963, 95–105.

4316 —Irish nurserymen and seedsmen, 1740–1800. *Qtr. J. Forestry*, 59, 1965, 131–139.

4317 — Notes on eighteenth-century Irish nurserymen. *Ir. Forestry*, vol. 24, no. 1, 1967, 3–22. Individuals arranged under 32 counties.

4318 — Notes on Kilkenny woods and nurserymen. *Old Kilkenny Rev.,* 22, 1970, 17–23.

4319 — A register of trees, County Kildare, 1769–1909. *Kildare Arch. Soc. J*., vol. 16, no. 1, 1977–8, 41–60.

4320 — A register of trees, Kings County, 1793–1913. *Kildare Arch. Soc. J.,* vol.15, no. 3, 1973–4, 310–318. Other registers for counties of Cavan, Cork, Kildare, Kilkenny, Limerick, Longford, Louth, Monaghan, Sligo and Tipperary are preserved in the Public Record Office, Ireland; that for Londonderry is preserved in P.R.O., N. Ireland.

4321 — Tenant planting in 19th century Ireland. *Qtr. J. Forestry*, 67, 1973, 220–226.

4322 — The woodlands of Ireland. *Ir. Hist. Stud*., 11, 1958–9, 271–296.

4323 — Woodlands of North Leinster in the 17th and 18th centuries. *Kildare Arch. Soc. J*., vol.14, no. 4, 1969, 431–442.

4324 MCEVOY, T. Forestry in Ireland. *Adv. Sci*., 14, 1957–8, 308–316.

4325 MCGOWRAN, BRIAN A. Oakwoods in Ireland. *U.C.D. Proc. Biol. Soc*., 1, 1975, 26–35.

4326 MCKAY, JOHN. Forestry in Ireland . . . Cork and Dublin: 1934. Bibliog., pp. 131–5.

4327 — Trodden gold: merchandise of silk, and paper and wood and the glory of the *Arar* tree. Dublin and Cork: 1928.

4328 MOONEY, O.V. A review of forestry in Ireland. *Inst. Ind. Res. Stand. Bull.*, vol. 5, no. 3, 1968, 71–78.

4329 NORTHERN IRELAND GOVERNMENT. Forestry in Northern Ireland. Belfast: 1970.

4330 PARKIN, K.F. Aspects of forestry in Northern Ireland. *Scot. Forestry*, 23, 1969, 293–301.

4331 PHILLIPS, J.C.L. Poplar growth in Northern Ireland. *Scot. Forestry*, 18, 1964, 261–270.

4332 SEYMOUR, WILLIAM. Notable trees at Glasnevin: Ireland's National Botanic Gardens. *Country Life*, vol.148, no. 3823, 1970, 313–4.

4333 SIMPSON, A.W. Some aspects of forestry in Northern Ireland since 1922 compared with those in Great Britain and Eire. *Qtr. J. Forestry*, 58, 1964, 287–301.

4334 SITKA SPRUCE IN IRELAND: Proceedings of symposium. *Ir. Forestry*, vol.34, no. 1, 1977, 3–54.

Glasshouses

4335 FORAS TALUNTAIS. Proceedings of the National Glasshouse Conference, 1967. Dublin: 1967.

4336 — Proceedings of the National Glasshouse Conference, 1972. Dublin: 1972.

Veterinary Medicine

4337 BARNES, T.J. The practice of veterinary public health in Ireland. *Ir. Vet. J.*, vol.31, no. 5, 1977, 61–64.

4338 GOLDEN, T.E. Eradication and control of animal diseases in Ireland. *OECD Agr. Rev.*, vol.19, no. 3, 1972, 87–91.

4339 HIRSCH, E.A. Veterinary education in Ireland: a historical review. *Ir. Vet. J.*, 23, 1969, 158–168.

4340 IRISH VETERINARY JOURNAL, vol. 1–, 1947–.

4341 O'REILLY, P.F. Mastitis control in Ireland. *Ir. Dept. Agric. J.*, 71, 1974, 105–112.

4342 SMITH, FREDERICK. The early history of veterinary literature and its British development. London: 1919–33. 4 vols.

4343 VETERINARY MEDICINE IN IRELAND – an historical review. *U.C.D. Report of the President*, 1976–77, 13–21.

4344 THE VETERINARY REGISTER OF IRELAND, 1978. Dublin: Veterinary Council, 1978. Issued annually.

Livestock

4345 AALEN, F.H.A. Transhumance in the Wicklow mountains. *Ulster Folk.*, 10, 1964, 65–72.

4346 LEE, J. Land resources as a basic factor in livestock carrying capacity. *Ir. Geog.*, 9, 1976, 63–75.

4347 —and DIAMOND, SEAN. The Potential of Irish land for livestock production. Dublin: An Foras Taluntais, 1972. (*Soil Survey Bulletin no. 26*).

4348 MASON, I.L. A world dictionary of breeds, types and varieties of livestock. Farnham, Commonwealth Agricultural Bureau, 1951.

4349 — Supplement. 1957.

4350 PRINGLE, R.O. A review of Irish agriculture chiefly with reference to the production of livestock. *R. Agr. Soc. England J., 2nd ser.*, 8, 1892, 1–76. Pringle was editor of the *Irish Farmers Gazette*.

4351 SCHARFF, R.F. The domestic animals of Ireland. *Mus. Bull.*, 4, 1919, 37–42.

Horse

(See also nos. 5967–5974)

4352 BARRETT, CYRIL. Michael Angelo Hayes. RHA, and the galloping horse. *Arts Ir.*, vol.1, no. 3, 1973, 42–47.

4353 BROWNE, NOEL PHILLIPS, *ed*. The Horse in Ireland: 1967.

4354 GAILEY, ALAN. The disappearance of the horse from the Ulster farm. *Folk Life*, 4, 1966, 51–55.

4355 HUTH, FREDERICK HENRY. Works on horses and equitation: a bibliographical record of hippology. London: 1887.

4356 THE IRISH HORSE [article]. *Ir. Dept. Agric. J.*, 34, 1936–7, 271–85.

4357 — [annual]. Dublin, Bloodstock Breeders'

and Horse Owners' Association of Ireland. vol. 1–, 1934–.

4358 IRISH HORSE YEARBOOK, 5th ed., Dublin: Bord na gCapall, 1978.

4359 McGRATH, MARY. From the Ice Age to Arkle. [the Irish Horse Museum at the National Stud, Tully, Co. Kildare]. *Pacemaker and the Horseman*, July 1977, 108–9.

4360 RIDGEWAY, WILLIAM. The origin and influence of the thoroughbred horse. Cambridge: 1905.

4361 RUEGER, MAX and MEIER, HANSPETER. Irish horses. Dublin: 1977.

4362 SCHARFF, R.F. On the Irish horse and its early history. *R.Ir. Acad. Proc., Sec. B*, 27, 1907–9, 81–6.

4363 STACK, MARY. Development of the horse. *Cap. Ann.*, 1977, 232–242.

4364 SWEENEY, TONY. The land of the horse. *Geog. Mag.*, 39, 1966–67, 764–771.

4365 WILLETT, PETER. The Thoroughbred. London: 1970.

Ass, Donkey

4366 MAHAFFY, J.P. On the introduction of the ass as a beast of burden into Ireland. *R. Ir. Acad. Proc., Sec. C*, 33, 1916–17, 530–8.

4367 SWINFEN, AVERIL. The Irish donkey. rev. ed. London: 1975. Bibliog., pp. 104–6.

4368 — Donkeys galore. Newton Abbot: 1976. Account of her donkey stud at Spanish Point, Co. Clare.

Ponies

4369 BRUNS, URSULA. Connemara: seaboard of the horses. London: 1971. Includes list of Societies of Connemara pony-breeders.

4370 EWART, J.C. The ponies of Connemara. *Ir. Dept. Agric. J.*, 1, 1900–01, 181–194, 547–566.

4371 INTERNATIONAL CONFERENCE OF CONNEMARA PONY SOCIETIES HELD ON 20th – 22nd AUGUST, 1970, in University College, Galway. Transcript of Proceedings and programme. Galway: Connemara Pony Breeders Society [1971].

4372 KELLY, SONIA. The Connemara pony. Cork: 1969.

Cattle

4373 CARLYLE, W.J. The movement of Irish cattle in Scotland. *J. Agr. Econ.*, vol.24, no. 2, 1973, 331–352.

4374 CUNNINGHAM, E.P. The genetic improvement of the Irish cattle population. *Stat. Social Inq. Soc. Ir. J.*, 21, 119th session, 1965–66, 99–130.

4375 DAY, W.R. The Hereford in Ireland. *Ir. Dept. Agric. Farm. Bull.*, August 1964, 2–9.

4376 GILLMOR, D.A. The structure and distribution of cattle breeds in the Republic of Ireland. *Ir. Dept. Agric. J.*, 66, 1969, 5–25.

4377 IRELAND, DEPARTMENT OF AGRICULTURE. Irish pedigree beef cattle: Shorthorn, Aberdeen-Angus, Hereford. Dublin: 1960.

4378 IRISH SHORTHORN BREEDERS' ASSOCIATION. Irish Shorthorns: some views by experts on the breeding and management of pedigree Shorthorn cattle. Dublin [1950].

4379 LUCAS, ANTHONY T. Cattle in ancient and medieval Irish society. *In* The O'Connell School Union Record, edited by Vincent Grogan, 1937–58, pp. 75–87.

4380 MOYLES, M.G. Dexter cattle: a historical sketch. *Ir. Dept. Agric. J.*, 56, 1960, 109–13.

4381 — Kerry cattle: a brief outline of the breed's history and development. *Ir. Dept. Agric. J.*, 53, 1956–7. Bibliog., p. 19.

4382 O'SHEA, M.J. The history of native Irish cattle. Cork: Cork University Press: 1954. (*Agricultural bulletin no. 7*). Bibliog., pp. 16–20.

4383 SCHARFF, R.F. On the origin of the Irish cattle. *Ir. Nat.*, 32, 1923, 65–76.

4384 WILSON, JAMES. The origin of the Dexter-Kerry breed of cattle. *R. Dublin Soc. Sci. Proc., new. ser.*, 12, 1909–10, 1–17.

Deer

4385 THE PHOENIX PARK DEER. *Oibre*, 3, 1966, 12.

4386 WHITEHEAD, G. KENNETH. Deer and their

management in the deer parks of Great Britain and Ireland. London: 1950.

Sheep

4387 DALY, P.J. Sheep husbandry survey in the parish of Kilmaine, Co. Mayo. Dublin: An Foras Taluntais, 1966.

4388 SCHARFF, R.F. Some notes on the Irish sheep. *Ir. Nat.,* 31, 1922, 73–6.

Pigs

4389 CODY, O.H. Piglet mortality in Ireland. *Ir. Dept. Agric. J.*, 63, 1966, 110–114.

4390 IRELAND, DEPARTMENT OF AGRICULTURE. Accredited pig herd scheme: reports. 1–, 1961–.

4391 —Pig Progeny testing reports. vol.1–, 1959–.

4392 MCCARTHY, J.C. The history of pig breeding in Ireland. [with bibliog.]. *Ir. Dept. Agric. J.*, 63, 1966, 55–63.

4393 MUSKETT, A.E. *ed*. A.A. McGuckian: a memorial volume. Belfast: 1956. Pig production in Ireland covered extensively, also section on grassland; bibliog., pp. 182–4.

Dogs

4394 BOWES, LEO. The Irish wolfhound has made a comeback. *Stream and Field*, vol.3, no. 6, 1974, 6–7.

4395 CLARKE, H. EDWARDS. A complete study of the modern greyhound. Clonmel, [1964]. Appendices. (i) Irish coursing records, 1950–1963 (ii) English coursing records, 1950–1963.

4396 GARDNER, PHYLLIS. The Irish wolfhound: a short historical sketch. Dundalk: 1931. Bibliog., pp. 242–3.

4397 HOGAN, EDMUND. The Irish wolfdog, by Edmund Hogan (1897), and The Irish wolfhound, by Capt. [George A.] Graham (1879), reprinted from the original editions for the Irish Wolfhound Club of Ireland. Dublin: 1939.

4398 JOHNS, ROWLAND. Our friend the Irish setter. London: 1932.

4399 LAMPSON, S.M. The Irish charm of the red setter. *Country Life*, 145, no. 3754, 1969, 341.

4400 LEIGHTON–BOYCE, GILBERT. Irish setters. London: 1973.

4401 MILLNER, J.K. The Irish setter; its history and training. London: 1924.

4402 REDLICH, ANNA. The dogs of Ireland. Dundalk: 1949. Includes chapter on The Irish Kennel Club.

4403 STARBUCK, ALMA J. The complete Irish wolfhound. 3rd ed. New York: 1970.

4404 SUTTON, CATHERINE G. The Irish wolfhound. Queniborough (Leics.) 1975. Bibliog., pp. 89–90.

4405 VESEY-FITZGERALD, BRIAN, *ed*. The book of the dog. London: 1948. Bibliog., pp. 1007–24.

Mink

4406 DEANE, C. DOUGLAS and O'GORMAN, FERGUS. The spread of feral mink in Ireland. *Ir. Nat. J.*, vol.16, no. 7, 1969, 198–202.

4407 FAHY, EDWARD. Bloodthirsty immigrants: the mink in Ireland. *Country Life*, vol.164, no. 4227, 1978, 110.

Dairying

4408 FOLEY, JOHN. The history of cheesemaking in Ireland. *Technol. Ir.*, vol.8, nos. 4–5, 1976, 60.

4409 — The rheological behaviour of Irish butter. *J. Soc. Dairy Technol.,* 22, 1969, 132–136.

4410 FORAS TALUNTAIS. Dairying study groups. series. no. 1– 1965–.

4411 LEWIS, COLIN A. Dairying in Ireland, with especial reference to developments in the Republic of Ireland. Tallaght (Co. Dublin): 1975.

4412 MULCAHY, M.J. Dairy research in the Republic of Ireland. *J. Soc. Dairy Technol.*, vol.19, 1966, 134–138.

4413 O'GRADA, CORMAC. The beginnings of the Irish creamery system, 1880–1914. *Econ. Hist. Rev. 2nd ser.,* vol.30, no. 2, 1977, 284–305.

Bees

4414 DIGGES, J.G. The practical bee guide: a manual of modern bee-keeping. 6th ed. London: 1928. Digges was a member of the Irish Beekeepers' Association examining board, and editor of the *Irish Bee Journal and Beekeepers' Gazette*.

4415 IRISH BEE JOURNAL. Clonmel, vol. 1–, 1947–.

FISHERIES

4416 AQUATIC SCIENCES AND FISHERIES ABSTRACTS. London, Information Retrieval Ltd., vol.1, no. 1–, 1971–. An amalgamation and continuation of 'Current Bibliography for Aquatic Sciences and Fisheries' produced by FAO and 'Aquatic Biology Abstracts' pub. by Information Retrieval Ltd.

4417 BURFIELD, S.T. [Report on the] Belmullet whaling station. *Rpt. Br. Assoc. Adv. Sci.* 1912, 145–186.

4418 CROSS, TOM. Delimiting Atlantic cod stocks through genetic studies. *Technol. Ir.*, vol.9, no. 12, 1978, 26–29.

4419 DAY, F. The fishes of Great Britain and Ireland. London and Edinburgh: 1880–4. 2 vols.

4420 DEAN, BASHFORD. A bibliography of fishes. 3 vols. *Amer. Mus. Nat. Hist.*, 1916–23. Vol. 3 includes indices, general bibliographies, periodicals relating to fishes, early works, voyages and expeditions, addenda and errata.

4421 FARRAN, G.P. Seventh report on the fishes of the Irish Atlantic slope [with bibliog.]. *R. Ir. Acad. Proc., Sec. B*, 36, 1921–4, 91–148. Previous reports were published in *Fisheries, Ireland, Scientific Investigations*, 1905, ii, [1906]; 1906, v, [1908]; 1908, iv, [1910]; 1908, v, [1910]; 1910, vi, [1911]; 1912, i, [1913].

4422 FOYLE FISHERIES COMMISSION, Dublin. Annual reports, 1952–.

4423 GIBSON, F.A. Escallops (*Pecten maximus L.*) in Irish waters. *R. Dublin Soc. Sci. Proc.*, vol. 27, no. 8, 1956, 253–271.

4424 A GUIDE TO FISH MARKS USED BY MEMBERS OF THE INTERNATIONAL COUNCIL FOR THE EXPLORATION OF THE SEA AND BY SOME NON-PARTICIPANT COUNTRIES. 3rd ed. *J. Cons. Int. Explor. Mer.*, vol.30, no. 1, 1965, 87–160. Ireland pp. 127–130.

4425 HILL, H.W. Seasonal movement of young plaice in the north-east Irish Sea. London: 1971. (*Great Britain, Ministry of Agriculture, Fisheries and Food, Fishery investigations, series II, vol. 26, no. 7*).

4426 IRELAND, DEPARTMENT OF AGRICULTURE AND FISHERIES: Fisheries Division. List of fishery leaflets numbers 1 (1938) to 58 (1973). Dublin [1974]. (*Fishery Leaflet no. 59*).

4427 — A list of scientific and engineering papers by members of the staff of the Fisheries Division of the Department of Agriculture and Fisheries, 1950–70. Dublin: Fisheries Division, 1972. (*Fishery Leaflet no. 25*).

4428 — Irish Fisheries Investigations. Ser. A. no. 1–, 1965–. Ser. B. no. 1–, 1967–.

4429 — Recommendations for the improvement of the sea fisheries of Ireland, by American Survey team (John B. Glude, Robert J. Lavell, Joseph W. Slavin and Keith A. Smith). Dublin: 1964.

4430 — Report on the project of improvement of fishing harbour facilities in Ireland, by Carl G. Bjuke. Dublin: 1960. Typescript. A list of publications of the officials of the Fisheries Branch is kept in typescript at their offices, 3 Cathal Brugha Street, Dublin, 1.

4431 IRELAND. Department of Lands, Fisheries Branch. Scientific investigations. Reports, 1902–26. None published for period 1915–19.

4432 JENKINS, JAMES TRAVIS. Bibliography of whaling. *Soc. Bibliog. Nat. Hist. J.*, vol. 2, no. 4, 1948, 71–166.

4433 — The fishes of the British Isles, both freshwater and salt. 2nd ed. London: 1936. 1st ed. 1925.

4434 JOHNSTONE, JAMES. British fisheries, their administration and their problems . . . London: 1905. Reports of the principal public inquiries held in modern times into the condition of the fisheries, official publications of British fisheries authorities, and fisheries statutes, pp. 331–40.

4435 **Meany, Tony.** The present status of fish farming and its potential in Ireland. *U.C.D. Proc. Biol. Soc.,* 1, 1975, 17–25.

4436 **Michael, N.C.** The Lower Bann fisheries. *Ulster Folk.*, 11, 1965, 1–32.

4437 **Mulcahy, Marie F.** Lymphosarcoma in the Pike, *Esox Lucius L.*, (*Pisces: Esocidae*) in Ireland. [with bibliog.] *R. Ir. Acad. Proc., Sec. B*, 63, 1963–4, 103–129.

4438 **O'Riordan, C.E.** *Nephrops Norvegicus*, the Dublin Bay Prawn, in Irish waters. [with bibliog.]. *R. Dublin Soc. Sci. Proc., Ser. B*, vol.1, no. 13, 1964, 131–157.

4439 **Scharff, R.F.** The Whale fishery in Ireland. *Ir. Nat.*, 22, 1963, 145–147.

4440 **Smith, W.C.** A short history of the Irish sea herring fisheries during the eighteenth and nineteenth centuries, 1923. (*Port Erin biological station, special publication. no. 1*)

4441 **Symposium on Fisheries.** *Administration*, vol. 7, no. 3, 1959, 203–35. Contents: Retrospective and administrative, by M.J. Gallagher; Research and international organisations, by A.E.J. Went; The role of the engineer, by Seamus O Meallain; An Bord Iascaigh Mhara, by Michael F. McNamara; Foyle Fisheries Commission, by Eamon O'Kelly; The Inland Fisheries Trust, by Edward Toner.

4442 **Twomey, Eileen,** *compiler*. Bibliography of Irish salmon. *Ir. Dept. Agric. Fish. Fishery Leaflet*, 78, 1976.

4443 **Wagstaff, Fred.** Fact and fiction about Irish pike. *Field*, vol.237, no. 6165, 1971, 62–63.

4444 **Went, Arthur E.J.** The distribution of Irish char (*Salvelinus Spp.*) [with bibliog.]. *R. Ir. Acad. Proc., Sec. B*, 50, 1944–5, 167–89.

4445 — Fishing gear in the Enniscorthy and Wexford museums. *R. Soc. Antiq. Ir. J.*, 106, 1976, 127–8.

4446 — The Galway fishery: an account of the ownership of the fishery [with bibliog.]. *ibid., Sec. C*, 48, 1942–3, 233–53.

4447 — The Galway fishery: an account of the modes of fishing together with notes on other matters connected with the fishery [with bibliog.]. *ibid., Sec. C*, 49, 1943–4, 187–219.

4448 — Historical notes on the fisheries of Lough Swilly and its tributaries. *ibid.*, 96, 1966, 121–131.

4449 — Historical notes on the fisheries of the two county Sligo rivers. [Ballisodare and Sligo]. *ibid.*, 99, 1969, 55–61.

4450 — History notes on the oyster fisheries of Ireland. *R. Ir. Acad. Proc., Sec. C*, 62, 1961–3, 195–223.

4451 — Ireland's rare sea fishes. *Ir. Nat. J.*, 13, 1959, 74–8.

4452 — The Irish pilchard fishery. *R. Ir. Acad. Proc., Sec. B*, 51, 1945–8, 81–120.

4453 — Irish salmon and salmon fisheries [with bibliog.]; being the Buckland lectures for 1953. London: 1955.

4454 —Irish salmon – a review of investigations up to 1963. [with bibliog.]. *R. Dublin Soc. Sci. Proc., Ser. A*, 1, 1959–64, 365–412.

4455 — List of Irish fishes. Dublin: 1957. Bibliog., pp. 23–7.

4456 — Notes on Irish pearls. *Ir. Nat.J.*, 9, 1947–9, 41–6.

4457 — Notes on the introduction of some freshwater fishes into Ireland. *Ir. Dept. Agric. J.*, 47, 1950, 119–24.

4458 — Oyster fisheries. *Dublin Hist. Rec.*, vol.18, no. 2, 1963, 56–63.

4459 — The pike in Ireland [with bibliog.]. *Ir. Nat. J.*, 12, 1956–8, 177–81.

4460 — The pursuit of the salmon in Ireland. *R. Ir. Acad. Proc., Sec. C*, vol.63, no. 6, 1962–4, 191–244.

4461 — Rare fishes taken in Irish waters in 1958. *Ir. Nat. J.*, 13, 1959, 31–3.

4462 — Recent records of species of fishes rare to Irish coastal waters. *Ir. Nat. J.*, 12, 1956, 68–9. List published annually.

4463 — The role of the Royal Dublin Society (established in 1731) in fisheries research and development. *R. Soc. Edinburgh Proc. Sec. B,* 73, 1972, 345–50.

4464 —Whaling from Ireland. *R. Soc. Antiq. Ir. J.*, 98, 1968, 31–6.

4465 **Westwood, T.** and **Satchell, T.** Bibliotheca piscatoria: a catalogue of books on angling, the fisheries and fish culture, with bibliographical notes on an appendix of citations touching on angling from old English authors. London: 1883. Includes parliamentary papers and statutes; new ed. in preparation.

4466 WHEELER, ALWYNE. Notes on some Irish fishes. *Ir. Nat. J.*, vol. 16, no. 3, 1968, 62–66.

4467 —Notes on inshore fishes from south-west Ireland. *ibid.*, vol. 16, no. 12, 1970, 383–7.

DOMESTIC SCIENCE

Common Practice

4468 ROCHE, D. and CHRISTOPHER, R.F. Consumer Protection: a role for local government. Dublin: 1973. (*National Prices Commission, Occasional paper no. 5.*)

Cookery

4469 BATES, MARGARET. Talking about cakes with an Irish and Scottish accent. Oxford: 1964.

4470 — The Belfast cookery book. Oxford: 1974. First published 1967.

4471 BUDIN, FRANCES MAYVILLE. Recipes from Ireland: traditional and modern. London: 1968.

4472 CRAIG, ELIZABETH. The art of Irish cooking. London: 1969.

4473 DEUTSCH, RICHARD. A plea for the revival of Irish traditional cooking. *Ir. Booklore*, vol.2, no. 1, 1972, 170–3. Includes references.

4474 FITZGIBBON, THEODORA. A taste of Ireland: Irish traditional food. London: 1968.

4475 RYAN, EILEEN. Dining in the 18th century. *Carloviana*, 1969, 28–31. Extracts from an 18th century Ms. 'Receipts' book penned in 1746 by S.P. for Miss Cicely D'Arcy which has been microfilmed by the National Library.

4476 SHERIDAN, MONICA. Monica's kitchen. Dublin: 1963.

4477 TINNE, ROSIE. Irish countryhouse cooking. Dublin: 1974.

Clothing and Personal Appearance

4478 IRISH BEAUTY. vol.1–, 1971–. Edited by June Levine and Terry Keane. Beauty, care and problems of Irish women.

Pubs

4479 BULSON, ROY. Irish pubs of character, Dublin: 1969.

4480 DAWSON, TIMOTHY. The Brazen Head revisited. *Dublin Hist. Rec.*, vol.26, no. 2, 1973, 42–51. Includes a list of taverns in old Dublin.

Hotels, Restaurants

4481 BOWEN, ELIZABETH. The Shelbourne [hotel]: a centre in Dublin life for more than a century. London: 1951.

4482 COURTENY, ASHLEY. Let's halt awhile in Great Britain and Ireland. 46th ed., London: 1979. Issues annually.

4483 DELANY, RUTH. Moyvalley Hotel. *Canaliana*, 1975, 20–25.

4484 IRISH TOURIST BOARD. Hotels and guesthouses, 1979. Dublin: [1978]. Issued annually.

4485 — Irish homes accommodation in town and country and on the farm, 1979. Dublin: [1978]. Issued annually.

4486 MACSWEENEY, EDWARD F. Public relations and publicity for hotels and restaurants. London: 1970.

4487 NORTHERN IRELAND. TOURIST BOARD. All the places to stay, 1979 [hotels, guest houses, farm and country houses and other approved accommodation]. Belfast: [1978]. Issued annually.

4488 O'CONNOR, ULICK. The Gresham Hotel, 1865–1965. [Cork, 1966]. Bibliog. p. [38].

4489 RONAY, EGON. Egon Ronay's guide, 1979: to hotels, restaurants and inns in Great Britain and Ireland . . . London, 1978. Issued annually.

Office Services

4490 O'BROIN, NOIRIN, and FARREN, GILLIAN. The working and living conditions of civil service typists. Dublin: Economic and Social Research Institute, 1978. (*Paper no.* 93)

4491 O'NUALLAIN, C. Personnel assessment and selection. Dublin: Institute of Public Administration, 1961.

Shorthand

4492 HUGHES, J.L.J. Dublin shorthand writers. *Dublin Hist. Rec.*, 13, 1952–54, 118–127.

PRINTING

General

4493 AMES, J. Typographical antiquities, or the history of printing in England, Scotland and Ireland Hildesheim: 1967. 4 vols. Reprint of the London ed. 1810–1819.

4494 ARCHBISHOP MARSH'S LIBRARY. An exhibition of early European printings. 1472–1700. Dublin: 1977. Bibliog., pp. 55–6; Ireland, pp. 41–45.

4495 BRADSHAW, HENRY. Printing in Ireland. *Brit. and Col. Print.*, 13, 1884, 259.

4496 — On printing in Ireland; a speech before the Library Association at Trinity College, Dublin, 1884, reproduced from *The Freeman's Journal*, October 3, 1884, with a note by E.R. McC. Dix and a biographical note by John S. Crone.

4497 CASAIDE, SEAMUS UA. A typographical gazetteer of Ireland, or the beginnings of printing in Ireland. Dublin: 1923.

4498 CATALOGUE OF BOOKS IN ALL LANGUAGES, ARTS AND SCIENCES, that have been printed in Ireland and published in Dublin from the year 1700 to the present time. Dublin: 1791.

4499 COTTON, HENRY. A typographical gazetteer attempted. 2nd ser. Oxford: 1866. 1st ser. published 1825; enl. ed. 1832.

4500 DIX, E.R. MCCLINTOCK. An early eighteenth century broadside on printing. *R. Ir. Acad. Proc., Sec. C*, 27, 1908–9, 401–3.

4501 — Some eighteenth century catalogues of books printed in Ireland and for sale in Dublin by booksellers. *Bibliog. Soc. Ir.*, 3, 1926–9, 81–2.

4502 — E.R. McC. Dix and the history of Irish printing. *Ir. Book Lov.*, 6, 1914–15, 124–5. From *Library World*, 17, 1915, 196–7.

4503 — History of early printing in Ireland. [1550–1800] *Belfast Nat. Hist. Phil. Soc. Proc.*, 1916–17, 5–29.

4504 DOTTIN, GEORGES. Les livres irlandais imprimés de 1571 à 1820. *Rev. Celt.*, 31, 1910, 294–99.

4505 GRAPHIC DIRECTORY 1965: a comprehensive guide to printing, publishing and advertising in Ireland. Dublin: Graphic Publications, 1965.

4506 IRISH BOOKS, printed between 1575 and 1744. Full descriptive titles, collections and notes. *c.* 1835. *National Library Mss. collection*, no. 216.

4507 LENNOX, P.J. Early printing in Ireland. Washington: 1909. Reprinted from *The Cath. Univ. Bull.*, vol. 15, nos. 3–4, 1909.

4508 LIBRARY ASSOCIATION OF IRELAND. Professional examinations, regulations and syllabus. Dublin: 1959. Reprinted from *An Leab.*, 16, 1958, 81–96. Includes bibliogs. on printing, Gaelic type, bookbinding and paper-making.

4509 MALCOLMSON, A.P.W. A catalogue of bibliographical material in the Foster/Massereene Papers, Public Record Office of Northern Ireland. *Ir. Booklore*, vol. 2, no. 1, 1972, 89–102.

4510 MOINE, HENRY LE. Typographical antiquities; being the history, origin and progress of the art of printing . . . with chronological lists of eminent printers in England, Scotland and Ireland, etc. from the best authorities. London: 1797.

4511 O'SULLEABHAIN, PADRAIG. Catholic sermon books printed in Ireland, 1700–1850. *Ir. Eccles. Rec.*, 99, 1963, 31–36.

4512 PEDDIE, ROBERT A. Bibliography of Irish printing. *Ir. Book Lov.*, 3, 1911, 51–3. List of books, pamphlets, and articles on printing, in the Typographical Library of the St. Bride Foundation, London.

4513 PLOMER, HENRY. Ireland and secret printing. *Ir. Book Lov.*, 1, 1909–10, 27–8. See also notes by Dix and others, *ibid.*, pp. 7, 116, 150, 169.

4514 — John Francton and his successors, with additional note by A.G. *Ir. Book Lov.*, 3, 1912, 109–12.

4515 POLLARD, M. Printing costs *c.* 1620. *Long-room*, no. 10, 1974, 25–29.

4516 QUINN, DAVID B. Government printing and the publications of the Irish statutes in the sixteenth century [with list of printed statutes, 1572–86]. *R. Ir. Acad.Proc., Sec. C*, 49, 1943–4, 45–129.

4517 THE RISE AND PROGRESS OF PRINTING IN IRELAND, by C.H.C. 22 pts. In *Irish Builder*, vols. 19–20, 1877–8.

4518 SIMMONS, J.S.G. Early-printed Cyrillic books in Archbishop Marsh's Library. Dublin. *Ir. Book.*, vol. 2, no. 2, 1963, 37–42.

4519 THOM, ALEX and CO. LTD. Progress in Irish printing. Dublin: 1936. Includes material on development of printing machinery, paper making, Gaelic script, photo engraving and bookbinding.

4520 WALSH, M. O'N. Irish books printed abroad, 1470–1700. *Ir. Book.*, vol. 2, no. 1, 1962–63, 1–36.

Societies

4521 HUME, A. The learned societies and printing clubs of the United Kingdom; being an account of their respective origin, history, objects, and conditions . . . their published works and transactions . . . and a general introduction with a classified index, compiled from official documents; with a supplement containing all the recently established societies and printing clubs, and their publications to the present time, by A.I. Evans. London: 1853.

4522 WILLIAMS, HAROLD. Book clubs and printing societies of Great Britain and Ireland. London: First Edition Club, 1929. Limited edition of 750 copies.

Publishers

4523 BURNHAM, RICHARD. Poor George Roberts, Dublin publisher. *Eire-Ir.*, vol.10, no. 3, 1975, 141–146. Roberts was attached to Maunsel and Company.

4524 FEEHAN, JOHN M. An Irish publisher and his world. Cork: Mercier Press. 1969. A selection of Mercier Books, pp. 138–160. The author is the founder of the Mercier Press.

Stationers

4525 DIX, E.R. MCCLINTOCK. Some notes on the Latin and Irish stocks of the Company of Stationers. *The Library*, vol. 8, 1907. For list of works of the Society of Stationers see Dix, *Books printed in Dublin in the seventeenth century*, pts. 1 and 2.

4526 POLLARD, M. James Dartas, an early Dublin stationer. *Ir. Booklore*, vol.2, no. 2, 1976, 227–229.

Printers and Booksellers

4527 BELFAST BOOKSELLERS: a bibliographical note. *Ir. Book Lov.*, 6, 1914–15, 5–7.

4528 CASAIDE, SEAMUS UA. Fictitious imprints on books in Ireland. *Bibliog. Soc. Ir.*, 3, 1926–9, 31–5.

4529 CATALOGUES OF DUBLIN BOOKSELLERS. *Ir. Book Lov.*, 6, 1914–15, 42–3.

4530 DUNTON, JOHN. *The Dublin Scuffle*, 1699, edited by J. Nichols. London: 1818. Contains notices of book auctions and booksellers of Dublin at the end of the seventeenth century.

4531 EARLY BOOK AUCTIONS IN IRELAND. *Ir. Lit. Inquirer*, edited by John Power, no. 3, 1865, 29–30.

4532 GREEVES, J.R.H. Two Irish printing families [Blow of Belfast and Grierson of Dublin]. *Belfast Nat. Hist. Phil. Soc. Proc., 2nd ser.*, 4, 1955, 38–44.

4533 GROWOLL, A. Three centuries of English book trade bibliography . . . also a list of the catalogues, &c., published for the English book trade from 1595 to 1902, by Wilberforce Eames. New York: 1903.

4534 HAMMOND, JOSEPH W. 'The King's Printers' in Ireland, 1551–1919. *Dublin Hist. Rec.*, 11, 1949–50, 29–31, 58–64, 88–96.

4535 MCKERROW, R.B. A dictionary of the printers and booksellers in England, Scotland and Ireland, and foreign printers of English books, 1557–1640. London: Bibliographical Society, 1910.

4536 MORRISON, P.J. Index of printers, publishers, and booksellers in Donald Wing's *Short-title catalogue of books* . . . Charlottesville, Bibliographical Society of the University of Virginia: 1955.

4537 PLOMER, HENRY. A dictionary of the booksellers and printers who were at work in England, Scotland and Ireland from 1641 to 1667. London: Bibliographical Society, 1907.

4538 — A dictionary of the printers and booksellers . . . from 1668 to 1725. London: Bibliographical Society, 1922.

4539 — A dictionary of the printers and booksellers . . . from 1726 to 1775. London: Bibliographical Society, 1932.

4540 POLLARD, M. John Chambers, printer and United Irishman. *Ir. Book.*, vol.3, no. 1, 1964, 1–22.

Presses

4541 DIX, E.R. MCCLINTOCK. Some private presses. *Ir. Book Lov.,* 9, 1917, 7–8.

4542 DOLMEN PRESS. Books and booklets published by the Dolmen Press, Dublin, August MCMLI – April MCMLXXI. [a checklist] Dublin: Dolmen Press, 1971.

4543 ENGLISH, N.W. The Cullean Press of Godfrey Levinge. *Ir. Booklore*, vol.3, no. 1, 1976, 1–7.

4544 FRENCH, FRANCES–JANE, The Tower Press booklists, [a bibliography]. *An Leab.*, 25, 1967, 157–171.

4545 HARTMAN, MARK. Poetry publications of the Runa Press. *Dublin Mag.*, vol.8, no. 8, 1971, 84–111. Includes a list of publications as appendix.

4546 MCCLELLAND, AIKEN. A Belfast private printing press. *Ir. Booklore*, vol.1, no. 1, 1971, 96–98.

4547 — A Co. Down private printing press. *ibid.*, vol.2, no. 2, 1976, 301–2. Ballykilbeg Press operated by William and Barclay Johnston, 1845–49.

4548 — William Johnston: a bibliography. *ibid.*, vol.3, no. 1, 1976, 57–59.

4549 MARTIN, JOHN. Bibliographical catalogue of privately printed books, 1570–1854. 2nd ed. London: 1854.

4550 MAXWELL, WILLIAM. The Dun Emer Press . . . The Cuala Press. [a bibliography] Edinburgh: 1932. Privately printed in limited edition of 30 copies.

4551 MILLER, LIAM. A brief account of the Cuala Press, formerly the Dun Emer Press founded by Elizabeth Corbet Yeats in MCMII. Dublin: Cuala Press, 1971.

4552 — Dolmen XXV: an illustrated bibliography of the Dolmen Press, 1951–1976. Dublin: Dolmen Press, 1976. Limited edition of 650 copies.

4553 — The Dun Emer Press: a lecture given at the Third Yeats International Summer School, Sligo, August 1962. *Ir. Book.*, 2, 1963, 43–52; 81–90.

4554 — The Dun Emer Press, later the Cuala Press; with a preface by Michael B. Yeats. Dublin: Dolmen Press, 1973. (*New Yeats papers VII*). Books published by the Dun Emer Press pp. 105–107; books published by the Cuala Press pp. 107–119.

4555 SMYTHE, COLIN. Rebirth of the Cuala Press. *Ir. Welcomes*, vol.21, no. 4, 1972, 31–35.

4556 TOMKINSON, G.S. Select bibliography of the principal modern presses, public and private, in Great Britain and Ireland. London: First Edition Club, 1928. Limited edition of 1,000 copies.

Typography

4557 FOLDS, G. Specimen of Irish typography, exhibiting the execution of the press in Ireland. Dublin: 1833.

4558 JENNETT, SEAN. Irish types, 1571–1958. *Brit. Print.*, 71, 1958, 50–55.

4559 LYNAM, E.W. The Irish character in print, 1571–1923. Shannon: 1969. Introduction by Alf MacLochlainn. Includes illustrations of Gaelic types introduced since 1923.

4560 MILLER, LIAM. Irish lettering and Gaelic type. *Forgnan*, vol. 1, no. 2, 1962, 22–24.

4561 POLLARD, M. An index of Irish printers' ornament of the eighteenth century. *Longroom*, 1, 1970, 41–2.

Paper Making

4562 BENSON, C. and POLLARD, M. "The Rags of Ireland are by no means the same". Irish paper used in the *Statutes at large*. *Longroom*, 2, 1970, 18–35.

4563 CLARKE, DESMOND J. Paper-making in Ireland. *An Leab.*, 12, 1954, 69–73.

4564 DIX, E.R. MCCLINTOCK. A note on paper-making in Ireland. *Dublin Pen J.*, 1, 1902–3, 231.

4565 KENNEDY, DESMOND and MACLOCHLAINN, ALF. The journals of the House of Commons: an important source of Irish paper-making history. *The Paper Maker*, vol.29, no. 1, 1960, 27–36.

4566 O'NEILL, THOMAS P. Irish papermakers and excise duty on paper, 1798–1861. *The Paper Maker*, vol. 31, 1962.

4567 POLLARD, M. White paper-making in Ireland in the 1690's. *R. Ir. Acad. Proc., Sec. C*, vol.77, no. 6, 1977, 223–234.

Printing of Shakespeare

4568 DIX, E.R. MCCLINTOCK. Earliest printing of Shakespeare's plays in Ireland. *Bibliog. Soc. Ir.*, 2, 1921–5, 18–20.

4569 — The earliest Dublin edition of Shakespeare's plays. *Athenaeum*, February 17, 1903, 77.

4570 O'HEGARTY, P.S. Some Irish eighteenth century editions of Shakespeare, not recorded by Jaggard, Stockwell, or Ford. *Ir. Book Lov.*, 32, 1952–7, 4–7.

4571 STOCKWELL, LA TOURETTE. A handlist of Shakespeare printed in Ireland during the 18th century. *Dublin Mag.*, vol.4, no. 3, 1929, 33–45.

Gaelic Printing

4572 BRADSHAW, HENRY. Printing in Irish character: letters to T.B. Reed. *Bibliog. Reg.*, 1, 1905, 6–13, 23–29.

4573 CASAIDE, SEAMUS UA. Some Irish publications in Ulster. *Ulster J. Arch.*, 16, 1910, 97–100.

4574 DIX, E.R. MCCLINTOCK. List of Irish printed books &c., from 1571 to 1820. *An Claidheamh Soluis*, January–April 1904.

4575 — *and* CASAIDE, SEAMUS UA. List of books, pamphlets, etc., printed wholly or partly in Irish from the earliest period to 1820. Dublin: 1905. Enl. ed. Dublin: 1913.

4576 LYNAM, E.W. The Irish character in print, 1571–1923. *The Library*, vol.4, 1924.

4577 MACGRATH, KEVIN. New light on the Irish printing press at Louvain. *Ir. Book Lov.*, 32, 1952–57, 36–7.

4578 MACLEAN, D. Typographia Scoto–Gadelica, or, books printed in the Gaelic of Scotland, 1567 to 1914, with bibliographical and biographical notes. Edinburgh: 1915.

4579 MADDEN, P.J. Printing in Irish. *An Leab.*, 12, 1954, 74–85.

4580 MOONEY, CANICE. Franciscan Library Ms. A. 30.4. *Ir. Book Lov.*, 27, 1940–41, 202–4. Letter dated 1638, dealing with printing of Irish works at Louvain.

4581 O'SAOTHRAI, SEAMUS. Early Gaelic printing. *Ir. Booklore*, vol. 1, no. 1, 1971, 99–101.

4582 REED, T.B. Rough preliminary list of books printed in the Irish character and language. *Celt. Mag.*, 10, 1885, 584–6. Lists 46 works for period 1571–1817.

Local Printing

4583 CASAIDE, SEAMUS UA. Bibliography of local printing: a table giving towns, periods, and references to publications where lists have appeared. *Ir. Book Lov.*, 2, 1910, 4–6.

4584 CLOUGH, E.A. *compiler*. A short-title catalogue arranged geographically of books printed and distributed by printers, publishers and booksellers in the English provincial towns and in Scotland and Ireland up to and including the year 1700. London: Library Assoc., 1969.

4585 DIX, E.R. MCCLINTOCK. Dates of earliest printing in Irish towns. *Ir. Book Lov.*, 7, 1915–16, 110–11.

4586 —Early printing in the south-east of Ireland; reprint of six articles which appeared during 1906–9. Waterford: 1910. Includes Carlow, Clonmel, Carrick-on-Suir, Cashel, Roscrea, Thurles, Wexford.

4587 — Irish provincial printing prior to 1701. *The Library, new ser.*, 2, 1901, 341–8.

4588 — A list of Irish towns and the dates of earliest printing in each. London: 1903. (*Ir. Bibliog. pamph.,* No. 6.)

4589 — Municipal records as sources of information about early printers. *Bibliog. Soc. Ir.*, 3, 1926–9, 73–4.

4590 IRISH PROVINCIAL PRESSES. Typescript, 41 p. arranged topographically, entries giving publisher or printer and date, for period 1731–1902. Copy in Trinity College Library, Dublin.

Antrim

4591 ANDERSON, JOHN. Catalogue of early Belfast printed books, 1694 to 1830, with lists of early Belfast printers, 1700–1830. Belfast: 1887. New and enl. ed. Belfast, 1890; supplements, 1894, 1902.

4592 BELFAST MUNICIPAL MUSEUM AND ART GALLERY. Quarterly notes, no. 52, 1934. Contents: List of Irish books printed abroad (lent by Dr. Samuel Simms); List of early Belfast printed books in Museum Library; Notes on old Belfast printers, by John J. Marshall.

4593 BENN, GEORGE. Early printing in Belfast. In his *History of the town of Belfast*. Belfast: 1877–80. 2 vols.

4594 CRONE, JOHN S. Ulster bibliography: Antrim. *Ulster J. Arch.*, 11, 1905, 108–112, 163–7.

4595 DIX, E.R. MCCLINTOCK. The earliest Belfast printing. *Ir. Book Lov.*, 6, 1914–15, 157–8.

4596 — Irish provincial printing [Lisburn]. *Ir. Book Lov.*, 7, 1915–16, 90–1.

4597 — Lists of books and tracts printed in Belfast in the seventeenth century. *R. Ir. Acad. Proc., Sec. C*, 33, 1916–17, 73–80.

4598 — The private press at Duncairn, Belfast. *Ir. Book Lov.*, 1, 1909–10, 7–8, 25–6.

4599 MCCANCE, STOUPPE. Bibliographical note on Greenisland printing. *Ir. Book Lov.*, 7, 1915–16, 7.

4600 MACLOCHLAINN, ALF. Belfast-printed ballad sheets. *Ir. Booklore*, vol. 1, no. 1, 1971, 21–23.

4601 YOUNG, ROBERT M. An account of some notable books printed in Belfast, 1696–1800. *The Library*, 7, 1895, 135–44.

4602 — Some notes on the early Belfast press and its productions. *Belfast Nat. Fld. Cl. Ann. Rpt. and Proc., 2nd ser.,* 3, 1888, 55–8.

Derry

4603 CRONE, JOHN S. Ulster bibliography: Derry. *Ulster J. Arch.*, 10, 1904, 151–6; 11, 1905, 27–32.

4604 DIX, E.R. MCCLINTOCK. List of books, pamphlets, newspapers, etc., printed in Londonderry prior to 1801. Dundalk: 1911. (*Ir. Bibliog. pamph.*, no. 7.)

4605 — Ulster bibliography: Derry printing, with a list, 1689–1900. *Ulster J. Arch.,* 7, 1901, 135–6, 174; 8, 1902, 24; 9, 1903, 71.

4606 — Ulster bibliography: Coleraine. *Ulster J. Arch.*, 13, 1907, 22–3.

4607 — Printing in Limavady, otherwise Newtownlimavady [1832–88]. *Ir. Book Lov.*, 12, 1920–1, 78–9.

Donegal

4608 DIX, E.R. MCCLINTOCK. Printing in Ballyshannon to 1900. *Ir. Book Lov.*, 17, 1929, 101–2.

4609 — Printing in Letterkenny [1845–53]. *Ir. Book Lov.*, 12, 1920–1, 31.

Armagh

4610 CRONE, JOHN S. Ulster bibliography: Armagh. *Ulster J. Arch.*, 14, 1908, 120–6.

4611 DIX, E.R. MCCLINTOCK. The first printing presses in Armagh and Newry. *Ulster J. Arch.*, 16, 1910, 46.

4612 — List of books and pamphlets printed at Armagh in the eighteenth century. Dublin: 1901. (*Ir. Bibliog. pamph.*, no. 2.) 2nd ed. Dundrum, 1910.

4613 — Printing in Armagh, 1801–24. *Ir. Book Lov.*, 4, 1912–13, 83–4.

4614 — Printing in Armagh since 1825. *Ir. Book Lov.*, 14, 1924, 7–10, 55–6.

4615 — Printing in Lurgan in the nineteenth century. *Ir. Book Lov.,* 13, 1921–2, 54–6.

4616 — Printing in Portadown [1851–1900]. *Ir. Book Lov.*, 7, 1915–16, 123–4, 164–5.

4617 — Ulster bibliography: Armagh. *Ulster J. Arch.*, 6, 1900, 245–6. Supplement, by Dix and others. *ibid.*, 7, 1901, 53–7.

4618 McCLELLAND, AIKEN. Provincial printing: Tandragee. [1843–1851]. *Ir. Book.*, vol.1, no. 4, 1962, 98–100.

Monaghan

4619 DIX, E.R. McCLINTOCK. List of books, pamphlets and newspapers printed in Monaghan in the eighteenth century. Dundalk: 1906. (*Ir. Bibliog. Pamph.*, no. 4.) 2nd ed. Dundalk: 1911.

4620 — Ulster bibliography: Monaghan. *Ulster J. Arch.*, 7, 1901, 102–8, 137; 8, 1902, 171; 11, 1905, 48.

4621 — Printing in Monaghan, 1801–25. *Ir. Book Lov.*, 4, 1912–13, 200–02; 5, 1913–14, 26–7.

4622 — Printing in Monaghan, 1825–30. *Ir. Book Lov.*, 10, 1918–19, 34–5, 55–6.

Down

4623 CRONE, JOHN S. Ulster bibliography: Co. Down. *Ulster J. Arch.*, 12, 1906, 35–9, 57–62; 13, 1907, 105–8.

4624 CROSSLE, FRANCIS C. Notes on the literary history of Newry, being an address delivered at the opening of the Newry Free Library on September 13, 1897. Newry: 1897.

4625 CROSSLE, PHILIP. The printers of Newry. *Newry Reporter*, March 30 – October 7, 1911. Copy in National Library of Ireland, Dublin, with manuscript notes by author. Includes list of books, pamphlets, newspapers, etc., printed in Newry from 1764 to 1909.

4626 — Printers of Newry: scrap-book of newspaper cuttings. *In* Bigger Collection, Belfast Public Reference Library.

4627 DIX, E.R. McCLINTOCK. Printing in Banbridge to 1900. *Ir. Book Lov.*, 17, 1929, 7–8.

4628 — Ulster bibliography: Downpatrick, Dungannon and Hillsborough. *Ulster J. Arch.*, 7, 1901, 172–4.

4629 — Dungannon [supplemental]. *Ulster J. Arch.*, 9, 1903, 42–3. See also nos. 4638–9.

4630 — Ulster bibliography: Newry printing. *Ulster J. Arch.*, 9, 1903, 69–71.

4631 — List of books, pamphlets, newspapers, &c., printed in Newry from 1764 to 1810. *Ulster J. Arch.*, 13, 1907, 116–19, 170–3; 14, 1908, 95–6; 15, 1909, 19, 184–5.

4632 — Printing in Newtownards in the nineteenth century. *Ir. Book Lov.*, 12, 1920, 1920–1, 101–2.

4633 LATIMER, W.T. Newry printing. *Ulster J. Arch.*, 7, 1901, 175–6.

4634 MAFFETT, R.S. Printing in Newry. *Ir. Book Lov.*, 6, 1914–15, 17–18.

Tyrone

4635 CAMPBELL, A.A. Notes on the literary history of Strabane. Omagh, 1902. Includes notes on Strabane printers.

4636 CRONE, JOHN S. Ulster bibliography: Tyrone. *Ulster J. Arch.*, 15, 1909, 95–102.

4637 DIX, E.R. McCLINTOCK. Printing in Cookstown to 1900. *Ir. Book Lov.*, 17, 1929, 137–8.

4638 — Printing in Dungannon, 1801–27. *Ir. Book Lov.*, 4, 1912–13, 188–9.

4639 — Printing in Dungannon, 1827–1900. *Ir. Book Lov.*, 8, 1916–17, 75–6. See also nos. 4628–9.

4640 — Printing in Strabane, 1801–1825. *Ir. Book Lov.*, 4, 1912–13, 114–16, 134–5.

4641 — Printing in Strabane, 1825–1900. *Ir. Book Lov.*, 7, 1915–16, 68–9, 91; 9, 1917–18, 60.

4642 — List of books and pamphlets printed in Strabane in the eighteenth century. Dublin: 1901. (*Ir. Bibliog. Pamph.*, no. 1.) 2nd ed. Dundrum: 1908.

4643 — Ulster bibliography: a list of books and pamphlets printed in Strabane in the eighteenth century, with additions by W.T. Latimer and A.A. Campbell. *Ulster J. Arch.*,

6, 1900, 1–3, 183, 246; 7, 1901, 54–6, 108, 136, 174, 176–7; 8, 1902, 83, 171.

4644 MARSHALL, JOHN J. History of Dungannon . . . and bibliography of Dungannon printing. 1929. Bibliog., pp. 129–37.

Fermanagh

4645 DIX, E.R. MCCLINTOCK. Printing in Enniskillen, 1798–1825. *Ir. Book Lov.*, 2, 1910–11, 185–6. Additional note, by J.S. Crone, *ibid.*, 5, 1913–14, 147.

4646 — Printing in Enniskillen [1826–1900]. *Ir. Book Lov.*, 7, 1915–16, 3–5, 32, 47, 92.

4647 — Ulster bibliography: Enniskillen. *Ulster J. Arch.*, 15, 1909, 172.

Cavan

4648 DIX, E.R. MCCLINTOCK. Early printing in Cavan. *Breifny Antiq. Soc. J.,* vol. 1, no. 3, 1922, 279–86.

4649 — Printing in the town of Cavan. *Ir. Book Lov.*, 1, 1909–10, 83–4.

4650 — Printing in Cavan, 1801–27. *Ir. Book Lov.*, 4, 1912–13, 165–7.

4651 — Printing in Cavan, 1828–1900. *Ir. Book Lov.*, 11, 1919–20, 6–7, 22–3, 40–1.

4652 — Ulster bibliography: Cavan. *Ulster J. Arch.*, 8, 1902, 23–4.

Leitrim

4653 DIX, E.R. MCCLINTOCK. Early printing in Leitrim. *Breifny Antiq. Soc. J.*, vol. 1, no. 3, 1922, 263–7.

Sligo

4654 DIX, E.R. MCCLINTOCK. Earliest printing in the town of Sligo [1752–1800]. *Ir. Book Lov.*, 2, 1910–11, 21–4.

4655 — Printing in Sligo during the nineteenth century. *Ir. Book Lov.*, 6, 1914–15, 52–4, 69–71, 89–90; 7, 1915–16, 47, 139; 8, 1916–17, 115.

Mayo

4656 DIX, E.R. MCCLINTOCK. Printing in Achill, 1837–66. Dublin: 1910. Also in National Library Mss. collection, no. 4260.

4657 — Printing in Ballinrobe to 1900. *Ir. Book Lov.*, 17, 1929, 9.

4658 — Printing in Castlebar during the nineteenth century. *Ir. Book Lov.*, 9, 1917–18, 47–9.

Galway

4659 DIX, E.R. MCCLINTOCK. Early Loughrea printing. *Galway Arch. Hist. Soc. J.*, 4, 1905–6, 110–12.

4660 — Earliest Loughrea printing. *Galway Arch. Hist. Soc. J.,* 5, 1907–8, 194–5.

4661 — Printing in Loughrea, 1766–1825. *Ir. Book Lov.*, 2, 1911, 151–2.

4662 — Printing in Loughrea, 1825–62. *Ir. Book Lov.*, 6, 1914–15, 175–6.

4663 — Printing in Ballinasloe, 1828–1900. *Ir. Book Lov.*, 7, 1915–16, 147–8.

4664 — Galway printing. *Galway Arch. Hist. Soc. J.*, 4, 1905–6, 62.

4665 — Printing in Galway, 1754–1820. *Ir. Book Lov.*, 2, 1910–11, 50–4.

4666 — Printing in Galway, 1801–25. *Ir. Book Lov.*, 4, 1912–13, 59–61.

4667 — Printing in Galway [1828–1900]. *Ir. Book Lov.*, 9, 1917–18, 130–131; 10, 1918–19, 9–10.

4668 — Printing in Tuam, 1774–1825. *Ir. Book Lov.*, 2, 1910–11, 101–2.

4669 — Printing in Tuam, 1825–1900. *Ir. Book Lov.*, 7, 1915–16, 40–1, 91–2.

4670 — Early Printing in Galway. *Galway Reader*. vol.1, no. 2, 1948, 13–14.

Roscommon

4671 DIX, E.R. MCCLINTOCK. Printing in Boyle [1822–97]. *Ir. Book Lov.*, 7, 1915–16, 24–6.

Longford

4672 DIX, E.R. MCCLINTOCK. Printing in Longford in the nineteenth century [1828–97]. *Ir. Book Lov.*, 12, 1920–1, 53–5.

Westmeath

4673 DIX, E.R. MCCLINTOCK. Earliest printing in Athlone. *Ir. Book Lov.*, 2, 1910–11, 84–5.

4674 — Printing in Athlone in the nineteenth century. *Ir. Book Lov.*, 6, 1914–15, 106–8, 136.

4675 — Printing in Mullingar, 1773–1825. *Ir. Book Lov.*, 2, 1910–11, 120–2.

4676 — Printing in Mullingar, 1830–1900. *Ir. Book Lov.*, 6, 1914–15, 127–8, 140–1, 160–1.

4677 TUITE, JAMES. J.C. Lyons and the Ledeston Press [Westmeath]. *Ir. Book Lov.*, 1, 1909–10, 69–71; 4, 1912–13, 98–99.

Meath

4678 DIX, E.R. MCCLINTOCK. Printing in Trim. *Ir. Book Lov.*, 1, 1909–10, 77–8.

Louth

4679 DIX, E.R. MCCLINTOCK. Another private press [Drogheda]. *Bibliog. Soc. I.,* 3, 1926–9, 75–6.

4680 — List of books, pamphlets, and newspapers printed in Drogheda, Co. Louth in the eighteenth century. Dundalk: 1904. (*Ir. Bibliog. pamph.*, no. 3). 2nd ed. Dundalk: 1911.

4681 — Printing in Dundalk, 1801–25. *Ir. Book Lov.*, 5, 1913–14, 46–7, 58–9, 78–80.

4682 — Printing in Dundalk, 1825–1900. *Ir. Book Lov.*, 8, 1916–17, 123–5; 9, 1917–18, 4.

4683 — Series of lists of provincial printing in Ireland [Drogheda]. *Ir. Book Lov.*, 4, 1912–13, 1–3.

Dublin

4684 ALDEN, JOHN. Deception in Dublin: problems in seventeenth-century Irish printing. *Stud. Bibliog.*, 6, 1954, 232–237.

4685 — Deception compounded: further problems in seventeenth-century Irish printing. *ibid.*, 11, 1958, 246–249.

4686 BENSON, C.J. A note on the printer of a Dublin edition of *The Orators*, [George Faulkner]. *Longroom*, 7, 1973, 33.

4687 CHRONOLOGICAL LIST of the printers, booksellers, engravers and printsellers of Dublin noticed by Mr. J.T. Gilbert in the three volumes of his *History of the city of Dublin*. 1859. Rotograph copy of Additional Ms. 2673, Cambridge University Library. National Library Mss. collection, no. 326.

4688 COLLINS, JAMES. Three centuries of Dublin printing. In his *Life in old Dublin*. Dublin: 1913, pp. 161–75.

4689 CONMEY, P.J. An old Dublin printing office [G. Folds, afterwards G. Drought's]. Dublin: 1898.

4690 DIX, E.R. MCCLINTOCK. Books printed in Dublin in the seventeenth century, with introduction and notes by C.W. Dugan. Dublin: 1898–1912. 5 pts.

4691 — Catalogue of early Dublin-printed books belonging to Mr. Dix. 2nd issue. Dublin: 1900.

4692 — Dublin seventeenth century printing: a new item. *Ir. Book Lov.*, 17, 1929, 12.

4693 — An early eighteenth century broadside on printing: notes upon the leaves of the first book printed in Dublin discovered in the Academy. *R. Ir. Acad. Proc., Sec. C,* 27, 1908–9, 401–6. Book of Common Prayer, 1550–1.

4694 — An early Dublin almanack by Patrick True, 1636. *R. Ir. Acad. Proc., Sec. C.*, 33, 1916, 225–9, 240.

4695 — The earliest Dublin edition of Shakespeare's plays. *Athenaeum*, February 17 1903, 177.

4696 — The earliest Dublin printer and the Company of Stationers of London. *Bibliog. Soc. Trans.*, 7, 1904, 75–85.

4697 — The earliest printing in Dublin, in the Irish, Latin, Greek, Hebrew, French, Italian, Saxon, Welsh, Syriac, Armenian, and Arabic language. *R. Ir. Acad. Proc., Sec. C*, 28, 1910, 149–56.

4698 — Early Dublin printing [1621–1700]. *Ir. Bld.*, 40, 1898, 45–46.

4699 — Early printing in Dublin: John Francton, an early Dublin printer and his work. *New. Ir. Rev.*, 9, 1898, 36–42.

4700 — The first printing of the New Testament in English at Dublin. *R. Ir. Acad. Proc., Sec. C*, 29, 1911–12, 180–85. On an edition of 1698.

4701 — French prayer book printed in Dublin, 1731. *Bibliog. Soc. Ir.,* 2, 1921–5, 96–7.

4702 — Dublin printing in the seventeenth century [new item]. *Bibliog. Soc. Ir*., 2, 1921–5, 93–5.

4703 — H. Powell, the first Dublin printer. *R. Ir. Acad.Proc., Sec. C*, 27, 1908–9, 213–16.

4704 — Humphrey Powell, Dublin's first printer: some new information. *Bibliog. Soc. Ir*., 3, 1926–9, 77–83.

4705 — Initial letters used by J. Francton, printer at Dublin. *Ir. Book Lov*., 3, 1911–12, 59, 109.

4706 — Note on the Dickson family, eighteenth century Dublin printers. *Ir. Book Lov*., 17, 1929, 45–7.

4707 — The initial letters and factotums used by John Francton, printer in Dublin. *The Library*, vol.11, 1922.

4708 — The ornaments used by John Francton, printer at Dublin. *Bibliog. Soc. Trans*., 8, 1904–6, 221–8.

4709 — The Powell family, printers in Dublin in the 18th century. *Bibliog. Soc. Ir. Pub*., vol.2, no. 5, 1923, 85–7.

4710 — Printing in Dublin prior to 1601. 2nd ed. Dublin: 1932. *Chronological list of contributions to Irish bibliography*, by E.R. McC. Dix, compiled by E. Carberry, pp. 34–41. 1st ed. appeared in 1901 as *The Earliest Dublin Printing* . . .

4711 — School books printed in Dublin from the earliest period to 1715. *Bibliog. Soc. Ir*., vol.3, no. 1, 1926.

4712 — Some English novels printed in Dublin from 1741 to 1810. Paper read before the Bibliog. Soc. Ir., October 29, 1925.

4713 — Three depositions by Dublin printers, etc., in 1712. *Ir. Book Lov*., 17, 1929, 33–5.

4714 — William Kearney, the second earliest known printer in Dublin. *R. Ir. Acad.Proc., Sec C*, 28, 1910, 157–61.

4715 DUBLIN EIGHTEENTH CENTURY PRINTERS. 30 pp. Typescript, giving name, address and date, with index, in Trinity College Library, Dublin.

4716 KIRKPATRICK, T. PERCY C. Notes on the printers in Dublin during the seventeenth century. Dublin: 1929.

4717 MACCRAITH, P. A short list of plays printed in Dublin, 1725–75, with printers' names. Paper read before Bibliog. Soc. Ir., April 29, 1925.

4718 MACPHAIL, I. A bibliography of the books printed at Trinity College, Dublin, 1734–1875. 1956. Submitted for the Academic Postgraduate Diploma in Librarianship of the University of London.

4719 — The Dublin University Press in the eighteenth century. *T.C.D. Ann. Bull*., 1956, 10–14.

4720 MARRINER, ERNEST C. Fifty years of the Cuala Press. *Colby Lib. Qtr., 3rd ser*., 11, 1953, 171–83.

4721 O'CONOR, CHARLES. George Faulkner and Jonathan Swift. *Studies*, 24, 1935, 473–486.

4722 — George Faulkner and Lord Chesterfield. *ibid*., 25, 1936, 292–304.

4723 PHILLIPS, JAMES W. A bibliographical inquiry into printing and bookselling in Dublin from 1670 to 1800. Thesis submitted to the Faculty of Language and Literature of Trinity College, University of Dublin, in fulfilment of the requirements for the degree of Doctor of Philosophy, April 15, 1952. Typescript in Trinity College, Dublin.

4724 QUINN, DAVID B. Information about Dublin printers, 1556–73, in English financial records. *Ir. Book Lov*., 28, 1941–2, 112–15.

4725 RYAN, MICHAEL J. A list of Greek and Latin classics printed in Dublin down to 1800. *Bibliog. Soc. Ir*., vol. 3, no. 2, 1926.

4726 SPEER, HAL. The Dolmen Press: the architect who builds books [Liam Miller]. *Amer. Book Coll*., vol. 9, no. 2, 1958, 21–3.

4727 STRICKLAND, W.G. Typefounding in Dublin. *Bibliog. Soc. Ir*., vol. 2, no. 2, 1922.

4728 WALL, THOMAS. The sign of Doctor Hay's Head; being some account of the hazards and fortunes of Catholic printers and publishers in Dublin from the later penal times to the present day. Dublin: 1958. Bibliog. note, pp. 149–53.

4729 WARD, CATHERINE COOGAN, and WARD, ROBERT E., *compilers*. A checklist and census of 400 imprints of the Irish printer and bookseller George Faulkner, from 1725 to 1775. Birmingham (Alabama): 1973.

4730 WARD, ROBERT E. Prince of Dublin printers: the letters of George Faulkner. Lexington: Univ. Press of Kentucky, 1972. Bibliog., pp. 137–140.

Kildare

4731 DIX, E.R. McCLINTOCK. Printing in Athy to 1900. *Ir. Book Lov.*, 17, 1929, 58–9.

Offaly

4732 DIX, E.R. McCLINTOCK. Printing in Birr, or Parsonstown, 1775–1825. *Ir. Book Lov.*, 3, 1911–12, 177–9.

Carlow

4733 DIX, E.R. McCLINTOCK. Printing in Carlow in the eighteenth century. *Ir. Book Lov.*, 11, 1919–20, 75–6, 94, 109–11, 126–7; 12, 1920–1, 11–13.

4734 MAFFETT, R.S. Bibliographical note on Carlow printing. *Ir. Book Lov.*, 7, 1915–16, 6.

Wexford

4735 DIX, E.R. McCLINTOCK. Printing in Enniscorthy. *Ir. Book Lov.*, 14, 1924, 83–4, 111.

4736 — Printing in Enniscorthy to 1900. *Ir. Book Lov.*, 17, 1929, 138–9.

4737 — Printing in Gorey. *Ir. Book Lov.*, 14, 1924, 100–1.

4738 — Printing in Wexford in the nineteenth century. *Ir. Book Lov.*, 27, 1940–1, 250–4.

Waterford

4739 BUCKLEY, JAMES. Bibliographical note on earliest Waterford printing. *Waterford S.E. Ir. Arch. Soc. J.*, 2, 1896, 209.

4740 BUTLER, MATTHEW. A Bonmahon printing house. *Ir. Book Lov.*, 32, 1952–7, 79–84.

4741 CASAIDE, SEAMUS UA. Waterford printing, 1821–1900. *Ir. Book Lov.*, 26, 1938–9, 128–33; 27, 1940–1, 149–55.

4742 COLEMAN, JAMES. Early printing in Waterford, Kilkenny, etc. *Waterford S.E. Ir. Arch. Soc. J.*, 4, 1898, 186–92, 258; 5, 1899, 60–4, 172–5; 6, 1900, 57–9, 171–3, 238–47.

4743 DIX, E.R. McCLINTOCK. The Bonmahon Press. *Ir. Book Lov.*, 1, 1909–10, 97–100. Includes list of books printed between 1852–8.

4744 — Books, newspapers and pamphlets printed in Waterford in the eighteenth century. Waterford: 1916. Reprinted from *The Waterford News*.

4745 — Printing in the city of Waterford in the seventeenth century. *R. Ir. Acad.Proc., Sec. C*, 32, 1914–16, 333–44.

4746 HURLEY, M.J. A catalogue of the collection of M.J. Hurley . . . to be disposed of, Tuesday, October 25, 1898, & following day . . . Waterford [1898]. Nos. 274–329: Books printed in or relating to Waterford, and the works of authors who were natives of, or associated with, the county or city.

4747 MACMANUS, M.J. A rare Waterford-printed book (1647) and its printer, Peter de Pienne. *Ir. Book Lov.*, 24, 1936, 75–7. Deals with *The lives of the glorious Saint David, Bishop of Menevia, patron of Wales and master of many Irish saints . . .*

Tipperary

4748 BURKE, WILLIAM P. History of Clonmel. Waterford: 1907. Clonmel printing and journalism, pp. 346–60.

4749 CASAIDE, SEAMUS UA. Clonmel printing, 1826–1900. *Ir. Book Lov.*, 25, 1937, 90–8.

4750 DIX, E.R. McCLINTOCK. Early printing in Carrick-on-Suir. *Waterford S.E. Ir. Arch. Soc. J.*, 13, 1910, 69–70.

4751 — Printing in Cashel in the nineteenth century. *Ir. Book Lov.*, 6, 1914–15, 194–7.

4752 — Printing in Clonmel, 1801–25. *Ir. Book Lov.*, 4, 1912–13, 42–6, 72.

Clare

4753 DIX, E.R. McCLINTOCK. Early printing in a Munster town: Ennis. *Cork Hist. Arch. Soc. J., 2nd ser.*, 10, 1904, 122–5.

4754 — List of books, newspapers, and pamphlets

printed at Ennis, Co. Clare in the eighteenth century. Dundrum: 1912. (*Ir. Bibliog. pamph.*, no. 8.)

4755 — Printing in Kilrush in the nineteenth century. *Ir. Book Lov.*, 9, 1917–18, 73–4.

Limerick

4756 BUCKLEY, JAMES. Some account of the earliest Limerick printing. *Cork Hist. Arch. Soc. J., 2nd ser.*, 8, 1902, 195–200.

4757 COLEMAN, JAMES. Limerick's early printed books and newspapers. *Limerick Fld. Cl. J.*, vol. 1, no. 3, 1899, 31–5; vol. 1, no 4, 1900, 45–7.

4758 DIX, E.R. MCCLINTOCK, *and others*. A further list of Limerick printed books, etc., contributed by Messrs Dix, Buckley, Coleman, and R.N. Fogarty. *Limerick Fld. Cl. J.*, vol.2, no. 6, 1902, 136–7.

4759 — List of books, pamphlets and newspapers printed in Limerick from the earliest period to 1800. Limerick: 1907. (*Ir. Bibliog. pamph.*, no. 5.) 2nd ed. Limerick, 1912.

4760 — Printing in Limerick in the nineteenth century. *Ir. Book Lov.*, 18, 1930, 39–42, 75–6, 101–2, 135–6, 163–4; 19, 1931, 117–20, 134–6, 174; 20, 1932, 84–5, 106–8, 124–6; 21, 1933, 7–9, 30–2, 56, 78–80, 109–10.

4761 HERBERT, ROBERT. Catalogue of the local collection in the city of Limerick Public Library. Pt. 1. Limerick printers and printing. Limerick: 1942. No further parts issued.

4762 — An eighteenth-century Limerick printing venture. *Ir. Book Lov.*, 28, 1941–2, 104–12.

4763 — Limerick printers and printing [5 items]. *Nth. Munster Antiq. J.*, 3, 1942–3, 124.

4764 LIMERICK PUBLIC LIBRARY. Limerick-printed books, 1725–1902. [1930.]. Typescript, 58 pp. in National Library, Dublin.

Kilkenny

4765 [CASAIDE, SEAMUS UA.] Kilkenny printing. *Ir. Book Lov.*, 17, 1927, 20.

4766 DIX, E.R. MCCLINTOCK. Kilkenny printing in the eighteenth century. *Ir. Book Lov.*, 16, 1928, 6–9, 40–1, 55–8.

4767 — Kilkenny printing in the nineteenth century. *Ir. Book Lov.*, 16, 1928, 89–109.

4768 — Printing in the city of Kilkenny in the seventeenth century. *R. Ir. Acad.Proc., Sec. C*, 32, 1914–16, 125–37.

4769 — A very rare Kilkenny-printed proclamation, and William Smith, its printer. *R. Ir. Acad.Proc., Sec. C*, 27, 1908–9, 209–12.

4770 KILKENNY PRINTING [notes]. *Ir. Book Lov.*, 19, 1931, 8–10.

Cork

4771 CORK PRINTERS. 9 pp. Typescript list with index covering period 1657–1902, in Trinity College Library, Dublin.

4772 DIX, E.R. MCCLINTOCK. Early Cork printed books, etc. *Cork Hist. Arch. Soc. J., 2nd ser.*, 29, 1923–4, 75.

4773 — Irish provincial printing prior to 1701. *The Library, new. ser.*, 2, 1901, 345.

4774 — List of all pamphlets, books, etc., printed in Cork during the seventeenth century. *R. Ir. Acad.Proc., Sec. C*, 30, 1912–13, 71–82.

4775 — List of books, etc., printed in Cork prior to 1801. *Cork Hist. Arch. Soc. J., 2nd ser.*, 25, 1919, 107–8.

4776 — List of books, pamphlets, journals, etc., printed in Cork in the seventeenth and eighteenth centuries. Cork: 1904–12. 14 pts. Reprinted from *Cork Hist. Arch. Soc. J.*, vols. 6–18, 1900–12.

4777 — Printing and printers in Fermoy. *Ir. Book Lov.*, 13, 1921–2, 76–7, 175–6.

4778 — Printing in Cork in the first quarter of the eighteenth century. *R. Ir. Acad.Proc., Sec. C*, 36, 1921–4, 10–15.

4779 — Printing in Youghal [to 1826]. *Ir. Book Lov.*, 4, 1912–13, 24–5.

4780 — Two rare seventeenth-century Cork ballads. *Cork Hist. Arch. Soc. J., 2nd ser.*, 16, 1910, 44–8.

4781 MACLOCHLAINN, ALF. Bagnells and Knights: publishers and papermakers in Cork. *Ir. Book*, vol. 1, no. 3, 1961, 70–4.

4782 MAFFETT, R.S. Cork printing: a bibliographical note. *Ir. Book Lov.*, 7, 1915, 45.

4783 POLLARD, M. 'Borrowed twelve cuts': a

Cork printer lends and borrows. *Longroom*, 8, 1973, 19–28. Henry Denmead, active from about 1805 to 1840.

Kerry

4784 DIX, E.R. MCCLINTOCK. List of newspapers, pamphlets, etc., printed in the town of Tralee from earliest date to 1820. *Kerry Arch. Mag.*, 5, 1910, 280–4.

4785 — Printing in Tralee, 1801–30. *Ir. Book Lov.*, 4, 1912–13, 149–50.

4786 — Printing in Tralee, 1828–1900. *Ir. Book Lov.*, 10, 1918–19, 79–81.

ACCOUNTANCY

4787 INSTITUTE OF CHARTERED ACCOUNTANTS IN IRELAND. Library. Catalogue. [Dublin], 1972. Supplements to date.

4788 — Library catalogue. Section R. Dublin: 1977.

4789 MORE O'FERRALL, EDWARD G. Ambrose O'Ferrall's accounts, re Miss Eliza O'Donell, 1798–1806. *Kildare Arch. Soc. J.*, vol. 15, no. 2, 1972, 161–167.

4790 ROBINSON, H.W. A history of accountants in Ireland. Dublin: 1964. Early text books on book-keeping, pp. 338–340; book-keeping text books published in Ireland, pp. 341–344.

MANAGEMENT

Bibliography

4791 IRISH MANAGEMENT INSTITUTE. Library periodical holdings. Dublin: 1971.

4792 — Manager's bookshelf: a basic library. Dublin: 1971. A classified selection of some 580 titles, sub-divided into 140 subjects and covering most aspects of management.

General Management

4793 GORMAN, LIAM, *and others*. Irish industry – how its managed, by Liam Gorman, Gerry Hynes, John McConnell, Tony Moynihan. Dublin: Irish Management Institute, 1971. Bibliog., pp. 183–5.

4794 IRISH MANAGEMENT INSTITUTE. Irish Management (*afterwards* Management). vol. 1–, 1954–. See also *The Irish Management Institute*, by M.J. Dargan, *Admin.*, vol. 5, no. 2, 1957, 63–80.

4795 MURRAY, WILLIAM. Management controls in action: a study based on action research in Coras Iompair Eireann, Radio Telefis Eireann, Roadstone Ltd. Dublin: Irish National Productivity Committee, Development Division, 1970. (*Human Sciences in industry, study no*. 6). Bibliog., pp. 188–191.

4796 TOMLIN, BREFFNI. The management of Irish industry: a research report by the Irish Management Institute. Dublin: 1966. Bibliog., pp. 419–422.

Training

4797 ANCO – THE INDUSTRIAL TRAINING AUTHORITY. Special issue of *Administration*, vol. 18, no. 1, 1970. Contents:- AnCo – the Industrial Training Authority, by Brian MacManus.– AnCo's industrial training programme for craft industries, by P.J. O'Connor.– AnCo's programme for non-craft based industries, by J.T. McCabe.– The role of the training manager, by R.D. Cruickshank.– Implementing management training and development programmes, by Dermot Egan.– Training for local authorities, by Colm O'Nualinin.– Vocational education in the services, by George C. Murphy.– Instructor/operative training – an approach and how it evolved, by Michael Foley.– Supervisory training, by John G. Sheeran.– Training in the hotel industry, by Laurence Jones.– Problems in the re-training of rural labour, by Joseph Kennedy.

Personnel Management and Administration

4798 O'MAHONY, DAVID. Economic aspects of industrial relations. Dublin: The Economic Research Institute, 1965. (*Paper no*. 24).

4799 — Industrial relations in Ireland: the background. Dublin: The Economic Research Institute, 1964. (*Paper no*. 19).

Executive Management

4800 GORMAN, LIAM, *and others*. Boards of directors in Ireland, by Liam Gorman, Anthony

Moynihan and Rod Murphy. Dublin: Irish Management Institute, 1975.

4801 — Managers in Ireland, by Liam Gorman, Ruth Handy, Tony Moynihan and Roderick Murphy. Dublin: Irish Management Institute, 1974. Bibliog. pp. 221–2.

4802 PEIRCE, M.A. and SCAIFE, W.G. Communication in industry between management and the shop floor. Dublin: Irish National Productivity Committee, 1969. (*Human sciences in industry — study* no. 2). Bibliog., pp. 101–102.

Industrial Research

4803 WALSH, THOMAS. Research institutes and public policy. *Admin*., 18, 1970, 262–284.

4804 WOODS, MICHAEL. Research in Ireland – key to economic and social development. Dublin: Institute of Public Administration. 1969. (Research ser. no. 2). Bibliog., pp. 101–3.

Time and Motion Studies

4805 IRISH NATIONAL PRODUCTIVITY COMMITTEE. Work study practices in Ireland. Dublin: 1965.

Public Relations

4806 DENNEHY, TIMOTHY. The progress of public relations in Ireland. *Admin*., 14, 1966, 135–138.

CHEMICAL AND RELATED TECHNOLOGIES

Fuels

4807 ANDREWS, C.S. Some precursors of Bord na Mona [with bibliog.]. *Stat. Social Inq. Soc. Ir. J*., 20, 1953–4, 132–55.

4808 BORD NA MONA. List of accessions to the peat section of the library, 1950–. Typescript.

4809 — A preliminary list of publications dealing exclusively with peat at the Bord na Mona experimental library, Droichead Nua, Co. Kildare. 1950. Typescript. 8 pp.

4810 — Peat abstracts, *new. ser*., no. 1–, 1952–. Typescript.

4811 COOKE, JOHN. Bog reclamation and peat development in County Kildare. *Kildare Arch. Soc. J*., vol. 14, no. 5, 1970, 576–625.

4812 DUBLIN, INTERNATIONAL PEAT SYMPOSIUM. Papers presented at the international peat symposium, Dublin, July 12–17, 1954. Held under the auspices of Bord na Mona.

4813 DWYER, D.J. The peat bogs of the Irish Republic: a problem in land use. *Geog. J*., 128, 1962, 184–193.

4814 GILLMOR, DESMOND A. The role of peat fuel in Ireland's changing energy balance. *Ir. Geog*., 9, 1976, 104–108.

4815 GREAT BRITAIN. DEPARTMENT OF SCIENTIFIC AND INDUSTRIAL RESEARCH, FUEL RESEARCH BOARD. The peat resources of Ireland; a lecture given before the Royal Dublin Society, on 5th March, 1919, by Prof. Pierce F. Purcell. London: 1920.

4816 — The winning, preparation and use of peat in Ireland – reports and other documents. London: 1921.

4817 JOHNSON, JAMES H. The commercial use of peat in Northern Ireland. *Geog. J*., 125, 1959, 398–400.

4818 LUCAS, A.T. Notes on the history of turf as fuel in Ireland to 1700 A.D. *Ulster Folk*., 15–16, 1970, 172–202.

4819 MCLOUGHLIN, A.J. and KUSTER, E. Utilisation of peat. *R. Ir. Acad.Proc., Sec. B*, vol. 72, 1972, nos. 1–3, 1–24.

4820 O'DONNELL, SEAN. Peat pays off. *Eire—Ir*., vol. 10, no. 2, 1975, 105–108.

4821 RHATIGAN, L. Peat development by Bord na Mona. *Chem. Ind*., 45, 1966, 1872–78.

4822 RYAN, HUGH. Reports upon the Irish peat industries. 2 pts. *R. Dublin Soc. Econ. Proc*., 1, 1899–1909. Bibliog., pp. 534–46.

Beverages

4823 BONNER, BRIAN. Distilling – illicit and otherwise in Inishowen. *Donegal Ann*., vol. 8, no. 1, 1969, 74–97.

COFFEY, AENEAS.

4824 DICK, WILLIAM. Aeneas Coffey (1780–1852). *Technol. Ir*., vol. 3, no. 12, 1972, 46.

4825 KERR, J.J. Aeneas Coffey and his patent still. *Dublin Hist. Rec.,* 9, 1946–8, 29–36.

4826 ROTHERY, E.J. Aeneas Coffey (1780–1852). *Ann. Sci.*, 24, 1968, 53–71. Includes Coffey's specifications and drawings for his apparatus for brewing and distilling.

4827 CONNELL, K.H. Illicit distillation: an Irish peasant industry. *Hist. Stud.*, 3, 1961, 58–91.

4828 McGUFFIN, JOHN. In praise of poteen. Belfast: Appletree Press, 1978. Bibliog., p. 119.

Food Technology

4829 FOOD, DRINK, AND TOBACCO FEDERATION. Food processing in Ireland: achievements to 1976, prospects to the early 1980's. Dublin: 1977.

4830 REILLY, V.S. *compiler*. Directory of Irish suppliers of processing/packaging machinery and storage equipment to the food industry. Dublin: An Foras Taluntais, 1978. (*Directory series, no.* 1)

Grain

4831 CULLEN, L.M. Eighteenth-century flour milling in Ireland. *Ir. Econ. Soc. Hist.*, 4, 1977, 5–25.

Textiles

4832 CRAWFORD, RONALD H. Design and the Irish linen industry. *Belfast Nat. Hist. Phil. Soc. Proc., 2nd ser.*, 7, 1961–64, 5–13.

4833 LUCAS, A.T. Cloth finishing in Ireland [with bibliog.]. *Folk Life*, 6, 1968, 18–67.

4834 — Some traditional Irish methods of cloth finishing. *Adv. Sci.*, 24, 1967, 184–192.

4835 ULSTER FOLK AND TRANSPORT MUSEUM. Illustrations of the Irish linen industry in 1783, by William Hincks. *Ulster Folk*, 23, 1977, 1–32. On a set of twelve engravings, with commentary.

Metallurgy

4836 ALLEN, I.M. Metallurgical reports on British and Irish Bronze Age implements and weapons in the Pitt Rivers Museum, by I.M. Allen, D. Britton, and H.H. Coghlan. Oxford: Pitt Rivers Museum, 1970. Bibliog., pp. 261–268.

Precision Instruments

4837 MASON, THOMAS H. Dublin opticians and instrument makers. *Dublin Hist. Rec.*, 6, 1943–4, 133–49.

4838 PRECISION INSTRUMENT MAKING IN IRELAND [including list of manufacturers, 1662–1860]. St. Patrick's College, Maynooth, Museum. Third Tostal display souvenir catalogue, 1955, pt. 44.

4839 RANDELL, B. Ludgate's analytical machine of 1909. Newcastle upon Tyne: Univ. of Newcastle upon Tyne, 1971. (*Technical report ser. no.* 15). Discusses the program-controlled mechanical calculator, designed by Percy E. Ludgate in Ireland during the years 1903 to 1909, and documents the results of a search for information about his life and work.

Horology

4840 FENNELL, GERALDINE. A list of Irish watch and clock makers. Dublin: National Museum of Ireland, 1963.

4841 FFOLLIOTT, ROSEMARY. Biographical notes on some Cork clock and watch makers. *Cork Hist. Arch. Soc. J.*, 69, 1964, 38–55.

4842 O'NEILL, BERNADINE. Marking time. *Ir. Wel.*, vol. 20, no. 4, 1971, 32–37.

Spinning Wheels

4843 BAINES, PATRICIA. Spinning wheels, spinners and spinning. London: 1977. Bibliog., pp. 240–6.

4844 THOMPSON, G.B. *compiler*. Spinning wheels. Belfast: Ulster Museum, 1966. (*Publication no.* 168).

Coachbuilding

4845 HUTTON, A.W. Technical education as applied to coachbuilders, and the history of coachbuilding in Ireland: a lecture delivered before the Operative Coachbuilders of Belfast. Belfast: 1902.

Building

4846 BUILD. Dublin. vol. 1–, 1965–.

4847 BUILDING CONSTRUCTION AND ENGINEERING SURVEY. Dublin: 1954–.

4848 FLEMING, M.C. Economic aspects of new methods of building with particular reference to the British Isles, the Continent and America. *Stat. Social Inq. Soc. Ir. J.*, vol. 21, pt. 3, 1964–5, 120–142.

4849 IRISH BUILDER. Dublin. (Entitled *Dublin Builder* for period 1859–66). vol. 1–, 1859–.

4850 MANNING, P.I. Belfast's building stones. *Ir. Nat. J.*, vol. 15, no. 1, 1965, 5–8.

FINE ARTS

Bibliography

4851 ART INDEX. New York, vol. 1–, 1929–.

4852 COURTAULD INSTITUTE OF ART. Annual bibliography of the history of British art. vol. 1–, 1934–. Cambridge: 1936–.

4853 GREAT BRITAIN. Privy Council, Committee on Education. The first proofs of the universal catalogue of books on art, compiled for the use of the National Art Library and the Schools of Art in the United Kingdom. London: 1870. 2 vols.

4854 — Supplement. London: 1877.

4855 IRISH ART: a volume of articles and illustrations. Dublin: 1944. Supplement: the literature of art, pp. 117–55, gives selections of books (not confined to Irish material) in the following Dublin libraries: National Library, Central Catholic Library, City of Dublin Public Libraries, Trinity College, University College and the Royal Dublin Society.

4856 LEWINE, J. Bibliography of eighteenth century art and illustrated books; being a guide to collectors of illustrated works in English and French of the period. London: 1898. Limited edition of 1,000 copies.

4857 NATIONAL LIBRARY OF IRELAND. Books on Ireland. Dublin, Cultural Relations Committee, 1953. Art and music, pp. 42–5.

4858 — Books useful to art students in the National Library. Dublin: 1906.

Aesthetics

4859 TEMPLEMAN, WILLIAM D. Contributions to the bibliography of eighteenth century aesthetics. *Mod. Phil.*, 30, 1932–3, 309–16.

Dictionaries

4860 BENEZIT, E. Dictionnaire critique et documentaire des peintres, sculpteurs, dessinateurs et graveurs de tous les temps et de tous les pays par un groupe d'écrivains spécialistes français et étrangers. Nouvelle édition . . . France, Librairie Grund, 1948–55. 8 vols.

4861 STRICKLAND, W.G. Dictionary of Irish artists [facsimile reprint]. Shannon: Irish Univ. Press, 1969, 2 vols. Includes as an appendix *A historical account of art institutions in Ireland.*

4862 WATERS, GRANT M. Dictionary of British artists working 1900–1950. Eastbourne: 1975.

Art Galleries

4863 ABSE, JOAN. The art galleries of Britain and Ireland: a guide to their collections. London: 1975.

4864 BARROW, VIOLA. Enjoying the National Gallery. *Dublin Hist. Rec.*, vol. 25, no. 3, 1972, 81–92.

4865 — Hugh Lane Municipal Gallery of Modern Art. *Dublin Hist. Rec.*, vol. 30, no. 4, 1977, 143–4.

4866 NATIONAL GALLERY OF IRELAND. Catalogue of pictures and other works of art in the National Gallery of Ireland and the National Portrait Gallery. Dublin: 1928.

4867 WHITE, JAMES. National Gallery of Ireland. London: 1968. Catalogue of painters and sculptors, pp. 209–224.

4868 — National Gallery of Ireland: recent acquisitions. *Apollo*, vol. 85, no. 60, 1967, 122–125.

Exhibitions — Catalogues

4869 DAY, ROBERT. Art catalogue of the first Munster exhibition, with notes by R. Day.

Cork Hist. Arch. Soc. J., 2nd ser., 4, 1898, 308–17.

4870 KELLY, JOHN C. Rosc '67. *Studies*, 56, 1967, 369–375.

4871 ROSC. Irish art in the 19th century: an exhibition of Irish Victorian art at Crawford Municipal School of Art . . . 1971. Dublin: 1971.

4872 — Irish art, 1900–1950: an exhibition in association with Rosc Teoranta, at the Crawford Municipal Art Gallery, Cork, December 1, 1975 – January 31, 1976. [Dublin, 1975].

4873 — ROSC '77; the poetry of vision: an international exhibition of modern art and early animal art. [Dublin, 1977].

4874 — WILSON, DAVID M. Art of the Viking age: the Rosc exhibition in Dublin [1971]. *Apollo*, 94, 1971, 254–261.

4875 STRICKLAND, W.G. A descriptive catalogue of the pictures, busts and statues in Trinity College, Dublin, and in the Provost's house. Dublin: 1916.

History

4876 ALLEN, J. ROMILLY. Celtic art in pagan and Christian times. London: 1904. Bibliog. footnotes.

4877 ARMSTRONG, WALTER. Art in Great Britain and Ireland. London: 1909. Bibliogs. appended to each chapter.

4878 ARNOLD, BRUCE. A concise history of Irish art. London: 1969. Bibliog., pp. 206–7.

4879 ART IN ULSTER. Belfast: 1977. vol. 1. Paintings, drawings, prints and sculpture for the last 400 years to 1957, by John Hewitt, with biographies of the artists by Theo Snoddy. vol. 2. A history of painting, sculpture and printmaking, 1957–1977, by Mike Catto, with selected biographical notes by Theo Snoddy.

4880 THE ARTS IN IRELAND. *Apollo*, vol. 84, no. 56, 1966, 256–329.

4881 BARRETT, CYRIL. Irish art in the nineteenth century. *Connoisseur*, vol. 178, no. 718, 1971, 230–237.

4882 — Irish nationalism and art, 1800–1921. *Studies*, 64, 1975, 393–409.

4883 BELL, SAM HANNA, *and others*. The arts in Ulster: a symposium, edited by Sam Hanna Bell, Nesca A. Robb, and John Hewitt. London: 1951. Bibliog., pp. 171–3.

4884 BODKIN, THOMAS. Report on the arts in Ireland. Dublin: 1949.

4885 DENSON, ALAN, *compiler*. Thomas Bodkin: a bio-bibliographical survey with a bibliographical survey of his family. Dublin: 1966.

4886 FITZ–SIMON, CHRISTOPHER. The arts in Ireland: a chronology. In preparation; to be published in 1980.

4887 HARBISON, PETER, *and others*. Irish art and architecture from prehistory to the present, by Peter Harbison, Homan Potterton, and Jeanne Sheehy. London: 1978. Bibliog., pp. 265–268.

4888 HENRY, FRANÇOISE. Irish art during the Viking invasions. London: 1967. Bibliog., pp. 206–213.

4889 — Irish art in the early Christian period (to 800 A.D.). rev. ed., London: 1965. First pub. 1940. Bibliog., pp. 225–232.

4890 — Irish art in the Romanesque period (1020–1170 A.D.). London: 1970. Bibliog., pp. 211–216.

4891 — L'Art Irlandais. Paris, 1963–64. 3 vols. (*La nuits des temps*, 18–20)

4892 — RICHARDSON, HILARY. Bibliography of Dr. Françoise Henry. *Studies*, 64, 1975, 313–325.

4893 — WHITE, JAMES. Françoise Henry. *Studies*, 64, 1975, 307–312.

4894 LONGLEY, MICHAEL, *ed*. Causeway: the arts in Ulster. Belfast and Dublin: 1971. Bibliog., pp. 173–176.

4895 LUCAS, A.T. Treasures of Ireland: Irish pagan and early Christian art: a commentary. Dublin and London: 1973. Bibliog., pp. 187–9.

4896 MOORE, DESMOND F. The Royal Hibernian Academy. *Dublin Hist. Rec.*, vol. 21, no. 1, 1966, 28–37.

4897 PASQUIN, ANTHONY (i.e. John Williams). An authentic history of the professors of painting, sculpture and architecture who have practised in Ireland . . . London: 1796.

4898 RAFTERY, JOSEPH. *ed.* Christian art in ancient Ireland. 2 vols., Dublin: 1941. Bibliog., pp. 169–76; vol. 1, edited by Adolf Mahr. Dublin: 1932.

4899 RICHARDS, J.M. Provision for the arts: report of an inquiry carried out during 1974–5 throughout the twenty-six counties of the Republic of Ireland. Dublin: The Arts Council and the Calouste Gulbenkian Foundation, 1976. Appendix III. Cultural activities, societies and buildings in the 26 counties, pp. 120–154.

4900 ROE, HELEN M. Some aspects of medieval culture in Ireland. *R. Soc. Antiq. Ir. J.*, 96, 1966, 105–109.

4901 SANDARS, N.K. Orient and orientalizing in early Christian art. *Antiquity,* 45, 1971, 103–112.

4902 STOKES, MARGARET. Early Christian art in Ireland. London: 1894. First published 1887.

4903 TREASURES OF EARLY IRISH ART, 1500 B.C. to A.D. 1500. from the collections of the National Museum of Ireland, Royal Irish Academy, [and] Trinity College, Dublin. Exhibited at the Metropolitan Museum of Art, The Fine Arts Museum of San Francisco, M.H. de Young Memorial Museum, Museum of Art, Carnegie Institute, Pittsburgh, Museum of Fine Arts, Boston, [and] Philadelphia Museum of Art. New York: 1977. Photography by Lee Boltin.

CIVIC AND LANDSCAPE ART

Area Planning

4904 AN FORAS FORBARTHA TEORANTA/THE NATIONAL INSTITUTE FOR PHYSICAL PLANNING AND CONSTRUCTION RESEARCH. The following bibliographies were prepared by the library staff.

4905 O'BEIRNE T. and HUGHES, N. The Social, economic and technical problems of housing. Dublin: 1973, pp. 22. (*Lib/1*).

4906 CONROY, M. Landscaping for housing. Dublin: 1974, pp. 10. (*Lib/2*).

4907 HUGHES, N. Bridge bearings. Dublin: 1972, pp. 3. (*Lib/3*).

4908 NORRIE, A. Military barracks. Dublin: 1973, pp. 6. (*Lib/4*).

4909 NORRIE, A. Asbestos-cement for cladding and roofing. Dublin: 1973, pp. 2. (*Lib/5*).

4910 HUGHES, N. The Economic consequences of the closure of city centres to traffic: pedestrian shopping centres. Dublin: 1973, pp. 8. (*Lib/6*).

4911 CONROY, M. Evaluation techniques in planning. Dublin: 1974, pp. 8. (*Lib/7*).

4912 CONROY, M. Landscape evaluation. Dublin: 1974, pp. 4. (*Lib/8*).

4913 HUGHES, N. Sewage treatment: activated sludge process, aeration. Dublin: 1974, pp. 6. (*Lib/9*).

4914 HUGHES, N. Joinery workshops. Dublin: 1973, pp. 4. (*Lib/10*).

4915 NORRIE, A. Quality control in building. Dublin: 1973, pp. 5. (*Lib/11*).

4916 HUGHES N. Food manufacture: surfacing of walls for hygienic purposes. Dublin: 1973, pp. 2. (*Lib/12*).

4917 HUGHES, N. Dublin development. Dublin: 1973, pp. 5. (*Lib/13*).

4918 HUGHES, N. Building cost control. Dublin: 1973, pp. 9. (*Lib/14*).

4919 HUGHES, N. Parking: design and construction of multi-storey car parks. Dublin: 1973, pp. 6. (*Lib/15*).

4920 NORRIE, A. The role of the resident engineer in road construction. Dublin: 1973, pp. 3 (*Lib/16*).

4921 NORRIE, A. Market design. Dublin: 1973, pp. 3. (*Lib/17*).

4922 HUGHES, N. Northern Ireland: planning and development. Dublin: 1973, pp. 10. (*Lib/18*)

4923 NORRIE, A. Organisation of building sites. Dublin: 1973, pp. 10. (*Lib/19*).

4924 NORRIE, A. Planning in Ireland. Dublin: 1972, pp. 10. (*Lib/20*).

4925 EARLY, B. and HUGHES, N. Housing in the Republic of Ireland. Dublin: 1973, pp. 10. (*Lib/21*).

4926 NORRIE, A. Building industry – contractor – consultant relationships. Dublin: 1973, pp. 3. (*Lib/22*).

4927 HUGHES, N. Location of industry. Dublin: 1973, pp. 7. (*Lib/23*).

4928 CUMMINS, C. Stone in building. Dublin: 1974, pp. 3. (*Lib/24*).

4929 HUGHES, N. Roads and transportation: recommended literature for local authority libraries. Dublin: 1973 pp. 8. (*Lib/25*).

4930 CONROY, M. and HUGHES, N. The environmental effects of petro–chemical industries. Dublin: 1973, pp. 10. (*Lib/26*).

4931 HUGHES, N. Tunnelling: effects of deep tunnelling and excavations on boulder clay. Dublin: 1973, pp. 4. (*Lib/27*).

4932 CONROY, M. Shopping, retail structure, characteristics, trends and forecasts. Dublin: 1973, pp. 6. (*Lib/28*).

4933 CONROY, M. Children's play in residential areas. Dublin: 1973, pp. 4. (*Lib/29*).

4934 HUGHES, N. Design and layout of road intersections. Dublin: 1973, pp. 12. (*Lib/30*).

4935 CONROY, M. Use of gardens in residential areas. Dublin: 1973, pp. 4. (*Lib/31*).

4936 CONROY, M. Social facilities in residential areas. Dublin: 1973, pp. 4. (*Lib/32*).

4937 HUGHES, N. The role of the private developer and local authorities in urban renewal. Dublin: 1973, pp. 12. (*Lib/33*).

4938 CONROY, M. Processing of refuse. Dublin: 1973, pp. 10. (*Lib/34*)

4939 HUGHES, N. Ready-mixed concrete. Dublin: 1973, pp. 14. (*Lib/35*)

4940 CONROY, M. and HUGHES, N. Social aspects of regional development in Ireland. Dublin: 1973, pp. 5. (*Lib/36*).

4941 CONROY, M. Open space – standards and requirements. Dublin: 1973, pp. 8. (*Lib/37*)

4942 HUGHES, N. Construction safety. Dublin: 1973, pp. 7. (*Lib/38*).

4943 HUGHES, N. and NORRIE, A. Precast concrete cladding. Dublin: 1973, pp. 4. (*Lib/39*).

4944 HUGHES, N. Sports grounds and sports centres. Dublin: 1973, pp. 7. (*Lib/40*).

4945 HUGHES, N. Rumble strips. Dublin: 1973, pp. 6. (*Lib/41*).

4946 HUGHES, N. Construction underpinning. Dublin: 1973, pp. 3. (*Lib/42*).

4947 HUGHES, N. Culverts, design and construction. Dublin: 1973, pp. 4. (*Lib/43*).

4948 CONROY, M. Planned programming budgeting systems. Dublin: 1973, pp. 12. (*Lib/44*)

4949 HUGHES, N. Office management, with particular reference to insurance organisations. Dublin: 1973, pp. 6. (*Lib/45*)

4950 CONROY, M. Education for planners. Dublin: 1973, pp. 6. (*Lib/46*)

4951 CONROY, M. Recreational day trips. Dublin: 1973, pp. 5. (*Lib/47*)

4952 NORRIE, A. Planning and design of library buildings – with particular reference to University Libraries. Dublin: 1973, pp. 8. (*Lib/48*)

4953 CONROY, M. Public participation in planning. Dublin: 1973, pp. 5. (*Lib/49*)

4954 HUGHES, N. Post primary schools – design and construction. Dublin: 1974, pp. 11. (*Lib/50*)

4955 CUMMINS, C. Building regulations in Europe. Dublin: 1974, pp. 10. (*Lib/51*)

4956 HUGHES, N. Training of firemen. Dublin: 1974, pp. 3. (*Lib/52*)

4957 CONROY, M. Second homes. Dublin: 1973, pp. 5. (*Lib/53*).

4958 CUMMINS, C. and HUGHES, N. Thermal insulation of buildings. Dublin: 1974, pp. 28. (*Lib/54*).

4959 CUMMINS, C. Thermal environment in housing: human comfort requirements. Dublin: 1974, pp. 10. (*Lib/55*).

4960 HUGHES, N. Shore projection: coastal works. Dublin: 1974, pp. 6. (*Lib/56*)

4961 HUGHES, N. Water evaporation. Dublin: 1974, pp. 3. (*Lib/57*).

4962 HUGHES, N. Rainfall and rainfall measurement. Dublin: 1974, pp. 3. (*Lib/58*)

4963 HUGHES, N. Hospitals: planning design and construction. Dublin: 1974, pp. 18. (*Lib/59*).

4964 O'GRADY, M. Housing estate layout. Dublin: 1974, pp. 9. (*Lib/60*).

4965 CUMMINS, C. Planning for remote rural communities. Dublin: 1974, pp. 3. (*Lib/61*).

4966 CONROY, M. Some alternatives to timber in the building industry. Dublin: 1973, pp. 8. (*Lib/62*).

4967 HUGHES, N.J. Mining industry finance. Dublin: 1975, pp. 9. (*Lib/63*).

4968 CORR, D. and HUGHES, N. Precast concrete use in Ireland 1965–1975. Dublin: 1975, pp. 8. (*Lib/64*).

4969 HUGHES, N. Prestressed concrete use in Ireland 1965–1975. Dublin: 1975, pp. 6. (*Lib/65*).

4970 CORR, D. House purchase finance. Dublin: 1975, pp. 20. (*Lib/66*).

4971 EARLY, B. and HUGHES, N. Housing in the Republic of Ireland. Dublin: 1975, pp. 6. (*Lib/67*).

4972 HUGHES, N. Planning in Ireland 1972–1975. Dublin: 1975, pp. 11. (*Lib/68*).

4973 HUGHES, N.J. Role of research institutes in Ireland. Dublin: 1975, pp. 9. (*Lib/69*).

4974 CORR, D. Bills of quantities. Dublin: 1975, pp. 12. (*Lib/70*).

4975 CORR, D. Floors: concrete ground floors. Dublin: 1975, pp. 8. (*Lib/71*).

4976 CORR, D. Floors: suspended slabs. Dublin: 1975, pp. 14. (*Lib/72*).

4977 CORR, D. Floors: finishes to concrete slabs. Dublin: 1975, pp. 10. (*Lib/73*).

4978 HUGHES, N.J. Management of research. Dublin: 1975, pp. 10. (*Lib/74*).

4979 CORR, D. Quantity surveyors in the public sector. Dublin: 1975, pp. 4. (*Lib/75*).

4980 HUGHES, N.J. Village conservation in Ireland: Laois, Offaly with particular reference to Cadamstown, Camross, Clonslee, Kinnity, Mountrath and Rossenalis. Dublin: 1975, pp. 5. (*Lib/76*).

4981 HUGHES, N.J. Commercial vehicles: anti-skid and anti-jack knifing braking systems. Dublin: 1975, pp. 8. (*Lib/77*).

4982 HUGHES, N.J. Village conservation. Dublin: 1975, pp. 10. (*Lib/78*).

4983 CORR, D. Tolerances. Dublin: 1975, pp. 16. (*Lib/79*).

4984 CONROY, M. EAHY–75. Dublin: 1975, pp. 25. (*Lib/80*). (EAHY: European Architectual Heritage Year.)

4985 GOOTING, ROHINI. Oil and gas related activities onshore – infrastructural and social impacts. Dublin: 1975, pp. 9. (*Lib/81*).

4986 CORR, D. Value analysis/engineering. Dublin: 1975, pp. 13. (*Lib/82*).

4987 O'PHILBIN, M. and MADDOCK, M. Condensation in dwellings. Dublin: 1975, pp. 12. (*Lib/83*). See also no. 5013.

4988 CORR, D. Use of space in dwellings. Dublin: 1975, pp. 8. (*Lib/84*).

4989 CORR, D. Timber. Dublin: 1976, pp. 92. (*Lib/85*).

4990 HUGHES, N. Roads and transportation: Recommended literature for local authority libraries. Dublin: 1976, pp. 45. (*Lib/86*).

4991 HUGHES, N. Phosphorous removal from sewage by chemical precipitation. Dublin: 1976, pp. 7. (*Lib/87*).

4992 CORR, D. Building client/building team. Dublin: 1976, pp. 4. (*Lib/88*).

4993 CORR, D. Concrete specification. Dublin: 1976, pp. 7. (*Lib/89*).

4994 HUGHES, N. Estuarine pollution: mathematical and hydraulic models. Dublin: 1976, pp. 5. (*Lib/90*).

4995 HUGHES, N. Coastal zone management. Dublin: 1976, pp. 4. (*Lib/91*).

4996 CORR, D. Private/public housing. Dublin: 1976, pp. 7. (*Lib/92*).

4997 CONROY, M. Office location. Dublin: 1976, pp. 10. (*Lib/93*).

4998 HUGHES, N. Professional ethics and the engineer. Dublin: 1976, pp. 6. (*Lib/94*).

4999 CORR, D. Computer aided building design. Dublin: 1976, pp. 23. (*Lib/95*).

5000 HUGHES, N. Improving environmental working conditions. Dublin: 1976, pp. 7. (*Lib/96*).

5001 CORR, D. Surveying instruments. Dublin: 1976, pp. 27. (*Lib/97*).

5002 HUGHES, N. Structural steelwork design. Dublin: 1976, pp. 5. (*Lib/98*).

5003 HUGHES, N. Microforms. Dublin: 1976, pp. 11. (*Lib/99*).

5004 CORR, D. Building performance. Dublin: 1977, pp. 47. (*Lib/100*).

5005 CONROY, M. Inner city areas – decline, deprivation, obsolescence. Dublin: 1977, pp. 12. (*Lib/101*).

5006 HUGHES, N. Hospitals: planning, design and construction. Dublin: 1977, pp. 10. (*Lib/102*).

5007 CONROY, M. Environmental effects of zinc smelters. Dublin: 1977, pp. 6. (*Lib/103*).

5008 HUGHES, N. Reorganization and decentralization of planning boundaries. Dublin: 1977, pp. 6. (*Lib/104*).

5009 CORR, D. Free standing walls. Dublin: 1977, pp. 8. (*Lib/105*).

5010 HUGHES, N. Land use/transportation studies. Dublin: 1977, pp. 5. (*Lib/106*).

5011 CONROY, M. Ireland and offshore oil. Dublin: 1977, pp. 11. (*Lib/107*).

5012 CONROY, M. The role of local authorities in the provision of facilities for outdoor recreation. Dublin: 1978, pp. 5. (*Lib/108*).

5013 CORR, D. Condensation 1974 – (Revision of *Lib*/83). Dublin: 1978, pp. 6. (*Lib/109*).

5014 CORR, D. Glass reinforced plastics. Dublin: 1978, pp. 16. (*Lib/110*).

5015 HUGHES, N. Desalination. Dublin: 1978, pp. 7. (*Lib/111*).

5016 CONROY, M. Planning and shopping provision. Dublin: 1978, pp. 10. (*Lib/112*).

5017 CONROY, M. Office decentralization – human attitudes. Dublin: 1978, pp. 3. (*Lib/113*).

5018 CONROY, M. Planning and nuclear power stations. Dublin: 1978, pp. 11. (*Lib/114*).

5019 CORR, D. Housing costs. Dublin: 1978, pp. 7. (*Lib/115*).

5020 CONROY, M. Urban and regional data systems. Dublin: 1978, pp. 16. (*Lib/116*)

5021 ADAM, A.A. and HUGHES, N.J. Dublin development, 1973–1977. Dublin: 1978, pp. 12. (*Lib/117*).

5022 HUGHES, N.J. Water pollution and sanitary services: recommended literature for local authority libraries. Dublin: 1978, pp. 17. (*Lib/118*).

5023 ARCHER, K. and CONROY, M. Concrete platforms for the oil industry. Dublin: 1978, pp. 5. (*Lib/119*).

5024 CORR, D. Solar energy. Dublin: 1978, pp. 37. (*Lib/120*).

5025 CORR, D. Open-drained joints. Dublin: 1978, pp. 4. (*Lib/121*).

Regional Planning

5026 BRADY, SHIPMAN, and MARTIN, *firm*. National coastline study. Dublin: An Foras Forbartha, 1972–3. 3 vols.

5027 BUCHANAN, COLIN, *and partners*. Regional studies in Ireland. Dublin: An Foras Forbartha, 1969.

5028 CAMBLIN, GILBERT. Regional planning in Northern Ireland. *Chart. Surv*., 96, 1963–4, 385–390.

5029 CROTTY, RAYMOND. Regional planning for Ireland: the Buchanan report. *Studies*, 58, 1969, 225–239.

5030 DUBLIN COUNTY COUNCIL. Dublin county development plan; 1970 draft as revised and adopted by Dublin County Council on 11th February, 1971. Dublin: 1971.

5031 AN FORAS FORBARTHA TEORANTA/THE NATIONAL INSTITUTE FOR PHYSICAL PLANNING AND CONSTRUCTION RESEARCH. Urban and regional research projects in Ireland, 1975: an annotated list prepared by An Foras Forbartha for the United Nations Economic Commission for Europe . . . Dublin: 1976.

5032 — Brittas Bay: a planning and conservation study. Dublin: 1973.

5033 NEWMAN, JEREMIAH. New dimensions in regional planning: a case study of Ireland. Dublin: 1967.

5034 NORTHERN IRELAND. MINISTRY OF HEALTH AND LOCAL GOVERNMENT. Belfast regional survey and plan, 1962: a report prepared for the Government of Northern Ireland, by Sir. Robert H. Matthew. Belfast: 1964. 2 vols.

5035 O'FARRELL, PATRICK N. Regional development in Ireland: problems of goal formulation and objective specification. *Econ. Soc. Rev.*, vol. 2, no. 1, 1970, 71–92.

5036 VINEY, MICHAEL, *ed.* Seven seminars: an appraisal of regional planning in Ireland. Report on the 'Regional Planning Conference Ireland, 1969' held in Belfast, March 1969. Dublin: An Foras Forbartha, 1970.

5037 WALKER, ROBIN. A regional plan for Ireland. *R. Inst. Br. Arch. J.*, 73, 1966, 519–521.

Town Planning — Housing

5038 CAMBLIN, GILBERT. New towns and national parks in Northern Ireland. *Chart. Surv.*, 98, 1965, 97–101.

5039 — The town in Ulster: an account of the origin and building of the towns of the province, and the development of their rural setting . . . Belfast: 1951. Bibliog., pp. 111–16.

5040 COLIVET, M.P. The Housing Board, 1932–44. *Administration*, vol. 2, no. 3, 1954, 83–6.

5041 FORGNAN: journal of the Building Centre, Dublin. vol. 1, nos. 1–7, 1962.

5042 HOUSING. 1: The social background, by Philip Monaghan; 2: Layout and design, by D.P. Smyth; 3: Finance, by G.A. Meagher. *Administration*, vol. 7, no. 2, 1959, 166–202.

5043 HUNTER, R.J. Towns in the Ulster Plantation. *Stud. Hib.*, 11, 1971, 40–79.

5044 KELLY, DEIRDRE. Hands off Dublin. Dublin: 1976.

5045 LICHFIELD, NATHANIEL. Limerick Regional Plan. Interim report on the economic, social and technical problems of the planning of the Limerick city/South Clare/ Shannon industrial estate complex, July 1963. Dublin: 1963.

5046 — vol. 2. Advisory outline plan (with additional material from vol. 1.). Report. Dublin: 1967.

5047 — Urban renewal in Dublin: the north central redevelopment area. *R. Inst. Arch. Ir. Yearbook*, 1967, 34–43.

5048 MCCONNELL, R. SHEAN. Planning for urban exposure. *Chart. Surv.*, 100, 1967, 121–131. Deals with Belfast region.

5049 NEILL, DESMOND G. Housing and the social aspects of town and country planning in Northern Ireland. *Administration*, vol. 2, no. 3, 1954, 49–60.

5050 SHAFFREY, PATRICK. The Irish town: an approach to survival. Dublin: 1975. Bibliog., p. 187.

5051 WRIGHT, MYLES. The planning and future development of the Dublin region; preliminary report . . . Dublin: 1965.

5052 — The Dublin region: advisory regional plan and final report. Dublin: 1967.

Landscape Gardening

5053 BUTLER, SUSAN. A Zen garden in Kildare. *Ir. Wel.*, vol. 27, no. 2, 1978, 22–27. Japanese gardens at Tully.

5054 FITZ–GERALD, DESMOND. Irish gardens of the eighteenth century. *Apollo*, vol. 88, 1968, 185–197, 204–209.

5055 GREHAN, IDA. The gardens of Powerscourt are as beautiful as ever. *Ir. Wel.*, vol. 35, no. 2, 1976, 34–36.

5056 HELLYER, ARTHUR. Pilgrimage to eternity: the Japanese garden at Tully House, Kildare. *Country Life*, vol. 164, no. 4227, 1978, 86–7.

5057 HYAMS, EDWARD. Irish gardens. London: 1967.

5058 MALINS, EDWARD, and GLIN, KNIGHT OF. Lost demesnes: Irish landscape gardening, 1660–1845. London: 1976. Bibliog., pp. 198–200.

5059 — MRS. DELANY [Mary Granville] and landscaping in Ireland. *Ir. Georg. Soc. Qtr. Bull.*, vol. 11, nos. 2–3, 1968, 1–16.

5060 ROPER, LANNING. A cosmopolitan garden: Glenveagh Castle, Co. Donegal. *Country Life*, vol. 153, no. 3961, 1973, 1468–70.

5061 — Garden of a collector and plantsman: Malahide Castle, Co. Dublin. *Country Life*, vol. 159, no. 4114, 1976, 1172–3.

5062 — A great Irish river garden: Mount Usher, Ashford, Co. Wicklow. *Country Life*, vol. 155, no. 4012, 1974, 1282–5.

Parks

5063 FALKINER, C. LITTON. The Phoenix Park, its origin and early history, with some notices of its royal and viceregal residences . *R. Ir. Acad. Proc., 3rd ser.*, vol. 6, 1900–2, 465–488.

5064 GORHAM, MAURICE. The Phoenix Park. *Ir. Wel.*, vol. 12, no. 6, 1963–64, 17–19.

5065 HORNER, ARNOLD. Carton, Co. Kildare: a case study of the making of an Irish demesne. *Ir. Georg. Soc. Qtr. Bull.*, vol. 18, nos. 2–3, 1975, 45–103. Appendix: The maps of Carton, pp. 90–100.

5066 MACGOWAN, KENNETH. The Phoenix Park. Dublin: 1967.

Structures in Landscaping

5067 GUINNESS, DESMOND, and GLIN, KNIGHT OF. The Conolly Folly: a case for Richard Castle. *Ir. Georg. Soc. Qtr. Bull.*, vol. 6, no. 4, 1963, 61–74. Obelisk at Castletown, Co. Kildare.

5068 — Follies in Ireland. *Ir. Georg. Soc. Qtr. Bull.*, vol. 14, nos. 1–2, 1971, 21–28.

5069 — JONES, BARBARA. Follies and grottoes. 2nd ed. heavily revised and enlarged. London: 1974. Bibliog., pp. 445–6; Ireland (arranged by county) pp. 426–440.

Landscape Conservation

5070 AN TAISCE/NATIONAL TRUST FOR IRELAND. The Hill of Howth: a conservation study for An Taisce, by Anthony O'Neill. Dublin: 1971.

5071 — Study of amenity planning issues in Dublin and Dun Laoghaire. Dublin: 1967.

ARCHITECTURE

Bibliography

5072 CRAIG, MAURICE J. Towards a bibliography of Irish architecture. Paper read before the Bibliographical Society of Ireland, February 27, 1950; not published, but Dr. Craig hopes to extend same for publication in the near future.

5073 ROYAL INSTITUTE OF BRITISH ARCHITECTS. Catalogue . . . of the library. London, 1937–8. 2 vols. vol. 1. Author catalogue of books and manuscripts. vol. 2. Classified index and alphabetical subject index of books and manuscripts.

Periodicals

5074 IRISH GEORGIAN SOCIETY QUARTERLY BULLETIN. Dublin, vol. 1–, 1958–.

Architectural Drawings

5075 IRISH ARCHITECTURAL RECORDS ASSOCIATION. Irish architectural drawings: an exhibition to commemorate the 25th anniversary of the Irish Architectural Records Association. Dublin: The Municipal Gallery of Art; Belfast: The Ulster Museum; The Armagh Museum. London: The Royal Institute of British Architects. 1965.

5076 MEAGHER, NIALL. A Gandon drawing of the portico at Emo [Park House]. *Co. Kildare Arch. Soc. J.*, vol.14, no. 4, 1969, 377–381.

5077 NATIONAL GALLERY OF IRELAND. The architecture of Ireland in drawings and paintings. Dublin: 1975. Exhibition catalogue of 191 items assembled for European Architectural Heritage Year, 1975.

History

5078 BLIGH, *Mrs.* ADRIAN. Some Georgian architecture in town and country. *Old Kilkenny Rev.*, 15, 1963, 43–48.

5079 BRETT, C.E.B. Conservation amid destruction. *Country Life*, vol. 156, no. 4032, 1974, 1016–18. Destruction of buildings in Northern Ireland by bombing.

5080 CRAIG, MAURICE J. Dublin: 1660–1860. London: 1952. Bibliog., pp. 342–52.

5081 — and GLIN, KNIGHT OF. Ireland observed: a handbook to the buildings and antiquities. Cork: 1970. Bibliog., pp. 110–111.

5082 DANAHER, KEVIN. Ireland's vernacular architecture. Cork: 1975. (*Cultural Relations Committee of Ireland. Irish life and culture series*).

5083 DUNRAVEN, EDWIN RICHARD WINDHAM

WYNDHAM–QUIN, *3rd Earl of.* Notes on Irish architecture, edited by Margaret Stokes. London: 1875–77.

5084 GUINNESS, DESMOND and SADLER, JULIUS TROUSDALE, *Jr.* The Palladian style in England, Ireland and America. London: 1976. Bibliog., pp. 179–180.

5085 HARBISON, PETER and FOX, KEVIN. Some aspects of Irish architecture [and chronological table.] *Ir. Wel.*, vol. 24, no. 1, 1975, 20–27.

5086 LECLERC, [WILLIAM] PERCY. Architecture in Ireland [a general survey]. *Forgnan*, vol.1, no. 3, 1962, 13–18.

5087 LUCAS, A.T. Harold G. Leask, M.Arch., Litt.D., Past President [obituary, with a list of published works]. *R. Soc. Antiq. Ir. J.*, vol. 96, 1966 1–6. 81 items mainly on architecture.

5088 MCNAMARA, T.F. The architecture of Cork, 1700–1900. *R. Inst. Arch. Ir. yearbook*, 1960, 15–39.

5089 MCPARLAND, EDWARD. The Wide Street Commissioners: their importance for Dublin architecture in the late 18th – early 19th century. *Ir. Georg. Soc. Qtr. Bull.*, vol.15, no. 1, 1972, 1–32.

5090 RANKIN, PETER. Irish building ventures of the earl bishop of Derry, 1730–1803. Belfast, Ulster Architectural Heritage Society, 1972. (Frederick Hervey, 4th Earl of Bristol and Bishop of Derry)

5091 SHEEHY, JEANNE. J.J. McCarthy and the Gothic revival in Ireland. Belfast: Ulster Arch. Her. Soc., 1977. Bibliog., p. 70.

5092 STALLEY, R.A. Architecture and sculpture in Ireland, 1150–1350. Dublin: 1971.

5093 STOLL, ROBERT. Architecture and sculpture in early Britain: Celtic, Saxon, Norman. London: 1967.

5094 SUMMERSON, SIR JOHN. Architecture in Britain, 1530 to 1830. 5th ed., London: 1969. (*Pelican History of Art*). Bibliog., pp. 363–370.

Architects

5095 COLVIN, HOWARD MONTAGU. A biographical dictionary of British architects, 1600–1840 [New ed.]. London: 1978. Previous ed. published as 'A biographical dictionary . . . 1660–1840', London: 1954.

5096 CRONIN, DAVID, W. Architects in the new Ireland and a changing Europe. *Green Book*, 1964, 5–15. Inaugural address by the President of the Architectural Association of Ireland.

5097 IRISH GEORGIAN SOCIETY: Biographical Dictionary of Irish Architects. Sample entries: Sir William Robinson, by Rolf Loeber. Sir Edward L. Pearce, by Maurice Craig. Thomas Ivory, by Edward McParland. Roger Mulholland, by C.E.B. Brett. Sir John MacNeill, by Jeanne Sheehy. William H. Lynn, by Hugh Dixon. *Ir. Georg. Soc. Qtr. Bull.*, vol.17, nos. 1–2, 1974.

5098 ROYAL INSTITUTE OF BRITISH ARCHITECTS. Index of architects of several countries and many periods (except English mediaeval) in nearly sixty old and new selected indexes, and indexed specialist works incorporating some earlier indexes with references to volumes and pages containing nearly 4,000 names and 10,000 references. 1956. Typescript; copy in Royal Dublin Society Library.

5099 ROYAL INSTITUTE OF THE ARCHITECTS OF IRELAND. Yearbook, 1961. Includes list of town planning authorities, also organisations in the building trade.

5100 — A biographical dictionary of Irish architects. In preparation.

5101 WARE, DOROTHY. A short dictionary of British architects. London: Allen and Unwin, 1967. Includes indexes of persons and places.

Individual Architects

BINDON, FRANCIS.

5102 GLIN, KNIGHT OF. Francis Bindon: his life and works. *Ir. Georg. Soc. Qtr. Bull.*, vol. 10, nos. 2–3, 1967, 3–36.

BYRNE, PATRICK.

5103 CURRAN, C.P. Patrick Byrne: architect. *Studies*, 33, 1944, 193–203.

5104 RAFTERY, PATRICK. The last of the traditionalists: Patrick Byrne, 1783–1864. *Ir. Georg. Soc. Qtr. Bull.*, 7, 1964, 48–67.

CASTLE, RICHARD.
5105 GLIN, KNIGHT OF. Richard Castle, architect: his biography and works; a synopsis. [with bibliog.]. *Ir. Georg. Soc. Qtr. Bull.*, vol. 7, no. 1, 1964, 31–38.

CHAMBERS, SIR WILLIAM.
5106 HARRIS, JOHN. Sir William Chambers, friend of Charlemont. *Ir. Georg. Soc. Qtr. Bull.*, 8, 1965, 67–100. Includes *Catalogue of projects* with bibliographical references.

DUCKART, DAVIS.
5107 GLIN, KNIGHT OF. A Baroque Palladian in Ireland: the Architecture of Davis Duckart. *Country Life*, 142, 1967, 735–739, 798–801.

GANDON, JAMES.
5108 MCPARLAND, E. James Gandon and the Royal Exchange Competition, 1768–69. *R. Soc. Antiq. Ir. J.*, 102, 1972, 58–72.

5109 MULVANEY, THOMAS J. *ed.* The life of James Gandon. London: Cornmarket Press, 1969. Facsimile reprint with new introduction, notes, appendices and index, by Maurice Craig.

IVORY, THOMAS.
5110 MCPARLAND, E. Thomas Ivory, architect. Ballycotton (Co. Cork). Gifford and Craven, 1973. (*Gatherum series no. 4.*)

JOHNSTON, FRANCIS.
5111 A letter [29/2/1820] from Francis Johnston [architect, to the author of Brewer's *Beauties of Ireland* (1826)]. *Ir. Georg. Soc. Qtr. Bull.*, vol. 6, no. 1, 1963, 1–5. An account of the buildings erected or planned by Johnston.

5112 — HENCHY, PATRICK. Francis Johnston, architect, 1760–1829. *Dublin Hist. Rec.*, 11, 1949–50, 1–16.

5113 — MCPARLAND, E. Francis Johnston, architect, 1760–1829. [with bibliog.] *Ir. Georg. Soc. Qtr. Bull.*, vol. 12, nos. 3–4, 1969, 62–139.

MULHOLLAND, ROGER.
5114 BRETT, C.E.B. Roger Mulholland, architect, of Belfast, 1740–1818. Belfast: Ulster Arch. Her. Soc., 1976.

PAIN, JAMES.
5115 GREEN, J.F. James and George Richard Pain. *Green Book*, 1965, 4–10.

PEARCE, SIR EDWARD LOVETT.
5116 SADLEIR, THOMAS U. Sir Edward Lovett Pearce. *Kildare Arch. Soc. J.*, 10, 1924–9, 231–244.

TURNER, THOMAS.
5117 DIXON, HUGH and ROWAN, ALISTAIR. The architecture of Thomas Turner. *Country Life*, vol.153, no. 3961, 1973, 1495–6.

WEST, ROBERT.
5118 GUINNESS, DESMOND. Robert West, architect and stuccodore. *Ir. Wel.*, vol.12, no. 6, 1963–4, 21–24.

WOODWARD, BENJAMIN.
5119 CURRAN, C.P. Benjamin Woodward, Ruskin and the O'Sheas. *Studies*, 29, 1940, 255–268.

Ulster

5120 DIXON, HUGH. An introduction to Ulster architecture. Belfast: Ulster Arch. Her. Soc., 1975. Bibliog., p. 91.

5121 — Ulster architecture, 1800–1900: an exhibition of architectural drawings, with photographs and portraits . . . The Ulster Museum, 27th October 1972–2nd January 1973. Belfast: Ulster Arch. Her. Soc., 1972.

5122 EVANS, DAVID. An introduction to modern Ulster architecture. Belfast: Ulster Arch. Her. Soc., 1977. Bibliog., p. 91.

5123 ROWAN, ALISTAIR. Ulster's architectural identity. *Country Life*, vol.149, no. 3859, 1971, 1304–6.

Antrim

5124 BRETT, C.E.B. Buildings of Belfast, 1700–1914. London: 1967.

5125 — Historic buildings, groups of buildings, areas of architectural importance in the Glens of Antrim.Belfast: Ulster Arch. Her. Soc., 1972.

5126 — Historic buildings, groups of buildings, areas of architectural importance in the island of Rathlin. Belfast: Ulster Arch. Her. Soc., 1974.

5127 — and DUNLEATH, *Lady*. List of historic buildings, groups of buildings, areas of architectural importance in the borough of Lisburn. Belfast: Ulster Arch. Her. Soc., [1969].

5128 — and McKINSTRY, R. Survey and recommendations for the Joy Street and Hamilton Street district of Belfast: Ulster Arch. Her. Soc., 1978.

5129 CAMPBELL, GORDON and CROWTHER, SUSAN. Historic buildings, groups of buildings, areas of architectural importance in the town of Carrickfergus. Belfast: Ulster Arch. Her. Soc., 1978.

5130 DIXON, HUGH and EVANS, DAVID. Historic buildings etc. in vicinity of Queen's University. rev. ed., Belfast: Ulster Arch. Her. Soc., 1975. Original edition compiled by A.J. Rowan and C.E.B. Brett, 1968.

5131 GIRVAN, W.D. List of historic buildings, groups of buildings, areas of architectural importance in Coleraine and Portstewart. Belfast: Ulster Arch. Her. Soc., 1972.

5132 — List of historic buildings, groups of buildings, areas of architectural importance in North Antrim, including the towns of Portrush, Ballymoney and Bushmills. Belfast: Ulster Arch. Her. Soc., 1972.

5133 — and ROWAN, A.J. Second list of historic buildings, groups of buildings, areas of architectural importance in West Antrim, within the designated area of Antrim and Ballymena development commission: including the villages of Crumlin, Glenavy, Templepatrick, Toome, Portglenone, Doagh, Ballyeaston, Clough, Cloughmills and Newtown Crommelin. Belfast: Ulster Arch. Her. Soc., 1970.

5134 — *and others*. List of historic buildings, groups of buildings, areas of architectural importance in Antrim and Ballymena, Muckamore, Galgorm, Randalstown, Gracehill, Ahoghill, Broughshane, Kells, Connor and Mossley. Prepared by D. Girvan, R. Oram and A. Rowan. Belfast: Ulster Arch. Her. Soc., [1970].

Armagh

5135 BRETT, C.E.B. *and others*. List of historic buildings, groups of buildings, areas of architectural importance in the vicinity of Lurgan and Portadown, prepared by C.E.B. Brett, Lady Dunleath, R. Oram and A.J. Rowan. Belfast: Ulster Arch. Her. Soc., [1969].

5136 ORAM, R.W. List of historic buildings, groups of buildings, areas of architectural importance in the area of Craigavon falling within Craigavon urban district. Belfast: Ulster Arch. Her. Soc., [1969].

5137 ULSTER ARCHITECTURAL HERITAGE SOCIETY. List of historic buildings, groups of buildings, buildings of architectural importance in the area of Craigavon falling within the Moira district. Belfast: [1969].

Down

5138 BELL, G. PHILIP *and others*. Survey, with lists of buildings, groups of buildings, and buildings of architectural importance in and near Portaferry and Strangford, prepared by G. Philip Bell, C.E.B. Brett and Sir Robert Matthew. Belfast: Ulster Arch. Her. Soc., [1969].

5139 BRETT, C.E.B. *compiler*. Historic buildings, groups of buildings, areas of architectural importance in the towns and villages of East Down, including Ardglass, Killough, Dundrum, Clough, Seaforde, Loughinisland, Killyleagh, Killinchy and Crossgar. Belfast: Ulster Arch. Her. Soc., 1973.

5140 — Historic buildings, groups of buildings, areas of architectural importance in the towns and villages of Mid Down: Hillsborough, Dromore, Dromara, Ballynahinch, The Spa, Drumaness and Saintfield. Belfast: Ulster Arch. Her. Soc., 1974.

5141 — and DUNLEATH, *Lady*. List of historic buildings, areas of architectural importance in the borough of Banbridge. Belfast: Ulster Arch. Her. Soc., [1969].

5142 DIXON, HUGH *and others*. Historic buildings, groups of buildings, buildings of architectural importance in Donaghadee and Portpatrick, by Hugh Dixon, Kenneth Kenmuir and Jill Kennett. Belfast: Ulster Arch. Her. Soc., 1977.

5143 DUNLEATH, *Lady, and others*. List of historic buildings, groups of buildings, areas of architectural importance in the town of Downpatrick, prepared by Lady Dunleath, P.J. Rankin and A.J. Rowan. Belfast: Ulster Arch. Her. Soc., 1970.

5144 RANKIN, P.J. Historic buildings, groups of buildings, areas of architectural importance in the Mourne area of South Down, including Annalong, Annsborough, Attical, Bryansford, Castlewellan, Clonvaraghan, Drumarod, Greencastle, Kilkeel, Kilmegan, Maghera and Newcastle. Belfast: Ulster Arch. Her. Soc., 1975.

5145 ULSTER ARCHITECTURAL HERITAGE SOCIETY. List of historic buildings, groups of buildings, areas of architectural importance in the designated area of the Craigavon development commission. Belfast: 1970. This composite volume reprints, within a single cover, the three lists of buildings published separately during 1969 for the towns of Lurgan and Portadown, Moira rural district and Craigavon urban district.

Fermanagh

5146 DIXON, HUGH. *compiler*. List of historic buildings, groups of buildings, areas of architectural importance in the town of Enniskillen. Belfast: Ulster Arch. Her. Soc., 1973.

Monaghan

5147 BRETT, C.E.B. List of historic buildings, groups of buildings ... in the area of Monaghan. Belfast: Ulster Arch. Her. Soc., and An Taisce, Co. Monaghan Branch, 1970.

Derry

5148 FERGUSON, W.S. *and others*. List of historic buildings, groups of buildings, areas of architectural importance in and near the city of Derry. Prepared by W.S. Ferguson, A.J. Rowan and J.J. Tracey. Belfast: Ulster Arch Her. Soc., 1970.

5149 GIRVAN, W.D. Historic buildings, groups of buildings, areas of architectural importance in North Derry including Limavady, Ballykelly, Castlerock, Downhill and Magilligan. Belfast: Ulster Arch. Her. Soc., 1975.

Tyrone

5150 ULSTER ARCHITECTURAL HERITAGE SOCIETY. Historic buildings, groups of buildings, areas of architectural importance in and near Dungannon and Cookstown; Coalisland, Stewartstown, Tullyhogue, Newmills, Donaghmore, Castlecaulfield and Pomeroy. Belfast: Ulster Arch. Her. Soc., 1971.

Dublin

5151 CORNFORTH, JOHN. The fate of Georgian Dublin. *Country Life*, vol. 146, no. 3790, 1969, 1030–1032.

5152 MEENAN, F.O.C. The Georgian squares of Dublin and the professions. *Studies*, 58, 1969, 405–414.

5153 MITCHELL, FLORA H. Vanishing Dublin. Dublin: 1966.

5154 O'BEIRNE, TOMAS, *ed*. A guide to modern architecture in Dublin. Dublin: Architecture in Ireland, 1978. 109 illustrations of buildings giving details of functions, architect, client and date of completion.

5155 POOL, ROBERT and CASH, JOHN. Views of the most remarkable public buildings, monuments and other edificies in the city of Dublin. 1st ed. reprinted. Introduction by Maurice Craig. Shannon: Irish Univ. Press, 1970. Facsimile reprint of 1st ed. Dublin: 1870.

5156 ROYAL INSTITUTE OF ARCHITECTS OF IRELAND. Dublin: a city in crisis, edited by Patrick Delany. Dublin: 1975.

Offaly

5157 SHEEHY, MARGARET. Architecture in Offaly. *Kildare Arch. Soc. J.*, vol. 14, no 1, 1964–65, 1–28.

Leix

5158 SEVEN HOUSES IN COUNTY LEIX. *Ir. Georg. Soc. Qtr. Bull.*, vol.16, no. 4, 1973, 95–120. Contents: Summer Grove (The property of Mr and Mrs Barry Whelan), by Maurice Craig. James Gandon at Emo Court (The property of Mr and Mrs. Cholmeley Harrison), by Edward McParland. The buildings of Castle Durrow (The property of the Presentation Sisters) by Rolf Loeber. Wilton House, Portarlington (The property of Mr. and Mrs. Cecil Mathews). A case for Richard Castle, by David J. Griffin. Roundwood House (The property of the Irish Georgian Society) by John O'Connell. Coffsborough, Co. Leix (The property of the Irish Land

Commission) by David J. Griffin. Abbey Leix, Abbeyleix, Co. Leix (The property of Viscount and Viscountess de Vesci) by Desmond Guinness.

Kilkenny

5159 LANIGAN, KATHERINE M. and TYLER, GERALD, *ed*. Kilkenny: its architecture and history. Kilkenny: An Taisce, 1977. Bib. ref., pp. 110–112.

5160 SMITHWICK, PETER. Georgian Kilkenny. *Ir. Georg. Soc. Qtr. Bull.*, vol. 5, no. 4, 1963, 75–96.

Masonry, Plaster and Stucco Work

5161 AYSCOUGH, ANTHONY. Country house baroque: photographs of eighteenth century ornament, mostly stucco work in English and Irish country houses and in some Dublin houses. With a foreword by Sacheverell Sitwell and a descriptive text by M. Jourdain. London: Heywood Hill Ltd., 1940. Contains 45 plates.

5162 CURRAN, C.P. Cesare Ripa and the Dublin stuccodores. *Studies*, 28, 1939, 237–248.

5163 — Dublin plaster work. *R. Soc. Antiq. Ir. J.*, 70, 1940, 1–56.

5164 — Dublin decorative plasterwork of the seventeenth and eighteenth centuries. London: 1967. Bibliog., pp. 113–115; includes 177 illustrations.

5165 — Michael Stapleton: Dublin stuccodore. *Studies*, 28, 1939, 439–449.

5166 GUINNESS, DESMOND. Irish rococo plasterwork. *Creation*, vol. 9, no. 9, 1965, 69–71.

5167 RUCH, JOHN. Coade stone in Ireland. *Ir. Georg. Soc. Qtr. Bull.*, vol. 13, no. 4, 1970, 1–12. Coade Ornamental Stone Manufactory of Lambeth make all types of architectural and sculptural ornaments.

5168 WATERMAN, D.M. Somersetshire and other foreign building stone in medieval Ireland, *c.* 1175–1400. *Ulster J. Arch.*, 33, 1970, 63–75.

Structural Elements – Walls

5169 FLEMING, J.S. The Town-Wall fortifications of Ireland. Paisley, 1914.

Public Buildings

5170 ATKINSON, FELLO. Discipline at Dundalk (Carroll Tobacco Factory Offices). *Arch. Rev.*, 149, 1971, 45–54.

5171 BRETT, C.E.B. Court houses and market houses of the province of Ulster. Belfast: Ulster Arch. Her. Soc., 1973. Bibliog., p. 25.

5172 COUNTY HALL at Galgam Road, Ballymena, Co. Antrim. *Arch. J.*, vol. 154, no. 47, 1971, 1169–1180.

5173 CRAIG, MAURICE. A parliament and its extensions (Parliament House, Dublin and afterwards Bank of Ireland). *Country Life*, 138, 1965, 552–3.

5174 CULLITON, JAMES A. The City Hall, Dublin. *Dublin Hist. Rec.*, 16, 1960–61, 96–105.

5175 — The Four Courts, Dublin. *Dublin Hist. Rec.*, 21, 1966–67, 116–126.

5176 CURRAN, C.P. The Rotunda hospital: its architects and craftsmen. 2nd ed. (abridged). Dublin: 1946. 1st ed. 1945.

5177 JORDAN, R. FURNEAUX. United States Embassy, Dublin (Architect, John M. Johansen). *Arch. Rev.*, 136, 1964, 421–425.

5178 MACMAHON, BRYAN. Shop Fronts. *Ir. Wel.*, vol.20, no. 3, 1971, 32–36.

5179 O'KELLY, DESMOND REA and MULCAHY, SEAN. Liberty Hall (with discussion). *Inst. Civ. Eng. Ir. Trans.*, 92, 1965–66, 70–110.

5180 QUINN, MICHAEL. Drawings intended to mislead?: the strange saga of the Central Bank. *Plan*, vol.4, no. 14, 1974, 14–15.

5181 SCOTT TALLON WALKER, (architects). Goffs Bloodstock Sales Centre, Kildare. *R. Inst. Brit. Arch. J.*, 83, 1976, 10–15.

5182 TOBIN, JOHN R. Leinster House, seat of Dail Eireann/Seanad Eireann. Dublin: 1975.

5183 WRIGHT, LANCE. Airport Hotel at Dublin Airport, Ireland, for Trust Houses (Ireland) Ltd., by Stephenson,Gibney and Associates. *Arch. J.*, vol.155,no. 18, 1972, 959–977.

5184 — Management Institute, Sandyford, Co. Dublin. *Arch. Rev.*, vol. 161, no. 961, 1977, 166–171. Architects: Stephenson, Gibney and Associates.

Railway Stations

5185 SHEEHY, JEANNE. Kingsbridge Station. Ballycotton (Co. Cork). Gifford and Craven, 1973. (*Gatherum ser.* no. 1).

Arches, Gateways, Walls

5186 FFOLLIOTT, ROSEMARY. Entrance gates. (With 15 illustrations). *Ir. Ancest.*, 2, 1970, 128–131.

5187 TYLER, GERALD. The Iron gate: relic of a forgotten craft. *Ir. Wel.*, vol.23, no. 6, 1974, 40–43.

Ecclesiastical Architecture

5188 ANDERSON, WILLIAM and HICKS, CLIVE. Cathedrals in Britain and Ireland from early times to the reign of Henry VIII. London: 1978.

5189 BARROW, LENNOX. Killashee Church Tower. *Kildare Arch. Soc. J.*, vol.15, no. 2, 1972, 186–194.

5190 BARROW, VIOLET B.M. Mr. Street's Christ Church. *Dublin Hist. Rec.*, vol. 26, no. 4, 1973, 120–131. The restoration of Christ Church Cathedral, by George Edmund Street, architect.

5191 BRASH, R.R. The ecclesiastical architecture of Ireland to the close of the twelfth century. Dublin: 1875.

5192 CHAMPNEYS, ARTHUR C. Irish ecclesiastical architecture with some notice of similar related work in England, Scotland and elsewhere. London and Dublin: 1910. Bibliog., pp. xxiii–xxix.

5193 CONLON, PATRICK. Notes on St. Francis Abbey, Kilkenny. *Old Kilk. Rev., new ser.*, vol.1, no. 2, 1975, 80–84.

5194 COOMBES, REV. JAMES. Catholic churches of the nineteenth century: some newspaper sources. *Cork. Hist. Arch. Soc. J.*, 81, 1975, 1–12.

5195 CROOKSHANK, ANNE. Eighteenth century alterations, improvements and furnishings in St. Michan's Church, Dublin. *Studies*, 64, 1975, 386–392.

5196 DAY, J. GODFREY. and PATTON, HENRY E. The cathedrals of the Church of Ireland. London and Dublin: 1932. Bibliog., p. 170.

5197 DE BREFFNY, BRIAN and MOTT, GEORGE. The churches and abbeys of Ireland. London: 1976.

5198 EGAN, REV. THOMAS A. Ireland's unique abbey: the abbey that refused to die. (St. Patrick's Abbey, Ballintubber, Mayo). *Cap. Ann.*, 1963, 215–234.

5199 FALLOW, T.M. The cathedral churches of Ireland, being notes, more especially on the smaller and less known of those churches. London [1894].

5200 FITZGERALD, M.J. Holycross Abbey (Co. Tipperary). *Ir. Wel.*, vol.20, no. 3, 1971, 6–9.

5201 HANDLEY–READ, CHARLES. St. Fin Barre's cathedral. *Country Life*, 141, 1967, 423–430. Mr. Handley-Read is at present working on a life of William Burges (1827–1881) architect of the cathedral.

5202 HAYES, WILLIAM J. Holy Cross Abbey (Co. Tipperary): restoration in progress. *Cap. Ann.*, 1972, 286–301.

5203 HEGARTY, MAUREEN. Jerpoint. *Old Kilk. Rev.*, 23, 1971, 4–14.

5204 JACKSON, ROBERT WYSE. Cathedrals of the Church of Ireland. Dublin: APCK, 1971.

5205 KANE, EILEEN. John Henry Newman's Catholic University Church in Dublin. *Studies*, 66, 1977, 105–120.

5206 LEASK, HAROLD G. Irish churches and monastic buildings. Dundalk, 1955–60. 3 vols. vol. 1: The first phases and the Romanesque. vol. 2: Gothic architecture to A.D. 1400. vol. 3: Medieval Gothic: the last phases.

5207 MCCARTHY, MICHAEL. Eighteenth-century cathedral restoration (correspondence relating to St. Canice's Cathedral, Kilkenny). *Studies*, 65, 1976, 330–343; *ibid.*, 66, 1977, 60–76.

5208 NOLAN, KEVIN. The Ancient Church and parish of Kilternan, Co. Dublin. *Dublin Hist. Rec.*, 2, 1939–40, 38–40.

5209 PETRIE, GEORGE. The Ecclesiastical architecture of Ireland: an essay on the origin and uses of the Round Towers of Ireland.

Photographic facsimile of the second edition [with an] introduction by Liam de Paor. Shannon: 1970. 1st ed. Dublin, 1845.

5210 PHELAN, MARGARET M. St. Mary's Cathedral (Kilkenny): a personal approach. *Old Kilk. Rev*., 24, 1972, 4–17.

5211 SMITH, J.T. Ardmore Cathedral. *R. Soc. Antiq. Ir. J*., 102, 1972, 1–13.

5212 STALLEY, ROGER. Christ Church, Dublin: the late Romanesque building campaign. Ballycotton (Co. Cork): 1973. (*Gatherum series no. 2*)

5213 — Corcomroe Abbey: some observations on its architectural history. *R. Soc. Antiq. Ir. J*., 105, 1975, 25–46.

5214 — Mellifont Abbey: some observations on its architectural history. *Studies*, 64, 1975, 347–367.

5215 STOKES, MARGARET. Early Christian architecture in Ireland. London: 1878.

5216 SYNNOTT, PIERCE. Furness Church. *Kildare Arch. Soc. J*., vol.14, no. 4, 1969, 457–472.

5217 WEBSTER, CHARLES A. The diocese of Ross and its ancient churches [with bibliog.]. *R.Ir.Acad.Proc.,Sec. C*, 40, 1929–31, 255–95.

5218 WHEELER, H.A. and CRAIG, MAURICE J. The Dublin city churches of the Church of Ireland. Dublin: 1948. Bibliog., pp. 47.

5219 WYNNE, MICHAEL. The Church of the Redeemer, Dundalk. *Furrow*, 20, 1969, 411–414.

Towers

5220 BARROW, LENNOX. The Round Tower of Kildare. *Kildare Arch. Soc. J*., vol.15, no. 4, 1974–5, 406–418.

5221 — The Round Towers of County Dublin. *Dublin Hist. Rec*., vol.28, no. 2, 1975, 57–69.

5222 COLEMAN, JAMES. Chronological list of works on the round towers of Ireland. Ms. of 6 pp. in National Library, Dublin.

5223 ENOCH, VICTOR J. The Martello Towers. *Ir. Wel*., vol.25, no. 3, 1976, 26–29.

5224 MARTELLO TOWERS IN IRELAND. *Oibre*, 9, 1972, 21–22.

5225 PETRIE, GEORGE. The ecclesiastical architecture of Ireland anterior to the Anglo-Norman invasion: an essay on the round towers of Ireland. 2nd ed. Dublin: 1845. 1st ed. formed vol. 20 of the *Royal Irish Academy Transactions*, 1845.

5226 PHIPPS, CHARLES BENJAMIN. The monastic round towers of Ireland. 249 pp. of typescript including bibliography of 9 pp.; copy in Royal Dublin Society Library.

5227 SUTCLIFFE, SHEILA. Martello Towers. Newton Abbot: 1972. Bibliog., pp. 168–170.

5228 WESTROPP, THOMAS J. A list of the round towers of Ireland, with notes on those which have been demolished, and on four in the County of Mayo. *R. Ir. Acad. Proc. 3rd Ser*., vol.5, 1898–1900, 294–311.

Tombs

5229 CRAIG, MAURICE. Mausoleums in Ireland. *Studies*, 64, 1975, 410–423.

5230 MOORE, DR. BERYL F.E. Tombs in St. Mary's ruined church, Killeen. *Riocht na Midhe*, vol.4, no. 4, 1970, 24–29.

Educational and Research Buildings

5231 BYRNE, GERRY. New University complex at Belfield. *Build*, vol.9, no. 8, 1972, 33–40.

5232 DIXON, HUGH. [Sir John] Soane and the Belfast Academical Institute. Ballycotton (Co. Cork): 1976. (*Gatherum series* no. 8).

Libraries

TRINITY COLLEGE DUBLIN.

5233 Library at Trinity College Dublin. *Arch J*., 146, 1967, 903–922.

5234 COLQUHOUN, ALAN. Library, Trinity College, Dublin. *Arch. Rev*., 142, 1967, 265–277.

5235 CROOKSHANK, ANNE. The Long Room. Ballycotton (Co. Cork): 1976. (*Gatherum series* no. 6).

5236 MCPARLAND, EDWARD. Trinity College, Dublin. *Country Life*, vol.159, no. 4114, 1976, 1166–9.

5237 WRIGHT, LANCE. Library at Trinity College,

Dublin [reappraisal]. *Arch. J.*, vol.156, no. 30, 1972, 205–216.

5238 UNIVERSITY COLLEGE, DUBLIN. Wright, Lance. University College, Dublin. *Arch. J.*, vol.157, no. 15, 1973, 857–878.

Residential Buildings

5239 AALEN, F.H.A. The Evaluation of the traditional house in western Ireland. *R. Soc. Antiq. Ir. J.*, 96, 1966, 47–58.

5240 — The house types of Gola Island, Co. Donegal. *Folklife*, 8, 1970, 32–44.

5241 BENCE-JONES, MARK. Burke's Guide to country houses. London: Burke's Peerage Ltd., vol.1. Ireland, 1978. Select Bibliog., x–xiii.

5242 — Lost Irish country houses. *Country Life*, vol.155, no. 4012, 1974, 1262–4; *ibid.*, no. 4013, 1974, 1356–8. Killarney House, Castle Bernard, Dunboy Castle, Rostellan Castle, Co. Cork, Woodstock, Co. Kilkenny, Castleboro, Co. Wexford, Ardfert House, Co. Kerry, Rockingham, Co. Roscommon, Shanbally Castle, Co. Tipperary, Convamore, Co. Cork.

5243 CASTLES, HOUSES AND GARDENS OF IRELAND, open to the public: official guide to the Historic Irish Tourist Houses and Gardens Association. [Dublin, 1970].

5244 COLVIN, HOWARD and HARRIS, JOHN, The Country seat: studies in the history of the British country house; presented to Sir John Summerson on his sixty-fifth birthday together with a select bibliography of his published writings. London: 1970. Contents include Portumna Castle, Co. Galway, by Maurice Craig, Summerhill, Co. Meath, by the Knight of Glin and James Gandon's work at Carriglas, Co. Longford, by the Knight of Glin.

5245 CRAIG, MAURICE. Classic Irish houses of the middle size. London and New York: 1976. Bibliog., p. 167.

5246 — New light at Jigginstown. *Ulster J. Arch.*, 33, 1970, 107–110.

5247 DANAHER, KEVIN. The gabled house – a basic architecture. *Forgnan*, vol. 1, no. 7, 1962, 17–21.

5248 — Some notes on traditional house types in County Kildare. *Kildare Arch. Soc. J.*, vol.14, no. 2, 1966–67, 234–246.

5249 — Traditional forms of the dwellinghouse in Ireland. *R. Soc. Antiq. Ir. J.*, 102, 1972, 77–96.

5250 DE BREFFNY, BRIAN and FFOLLIOTT, ROSEMARY. The houses of Ireland: domestic architecture from the medieval castle to the Edwardian villa. London: 1975.

5251 ENGLISH, N.W. Some country houses near Athlone. *Ir. Ancest.*, vol. 5, no. 1, 1973, 17–24.

5252 — Some Irish country houses near Athlone. *Ir. Ancest.*, vol.6, no. 3, 1974, 79–85.

5253 EVANS, E. ESTYN. Traditional houses of Rathlin Island. *Ulster Folk.*, 19, 1973, 13–19.

5254 FFOLLIOTT, ROSEMARY. Houses in provincial towns. *Ir. Ancest.*, vol.7, no. 2, 1975, 97–99.

5255 — Some lesser known country houses in Munster and Leinster. *ibid.*, vol.3, no. 1, 1970, 49–51.

5256 [FITZGERALD, DESMOND JOHN VILLIERS]. Architectural books and 'Palladianism' in Ireland: a study of three eighteenth-century houses. [i.e. Newberry Hall and Lodge Park, Co. Kildare, and Colganstown House, Co. Dublin], by the Knight of Glin. *Ir. Georg. Soc. Qtr. Bull.*, vol.5, nos. 2–3, 1962, 11–35.

5257 GAILEY, ALAN. Some developments and adaptations of traditional house types. *In* Folk and Farm, edited by C.O'Danachair, 1976, pp. 54–71.

5258 GEOGHEGAN, JOSEPH A. Notes on 18th century houses. *Dublin Hist. Rec.*, 7, 1944–5, 41–54.

5259 GUINNESS, DESMOND and RYAN, WILLIAM. Irish Houses and Castles. London: 1971.

5260 HARRISSON, WILMOT. Memorable Dublin houses, with illustrative anecdotes, [facsimile reprint] with a new introduction by Maurice Craig. East Ardsley (Yorks.): 1971. First published Dublin 1890.

5261 HENDRY, JOHN. House plans in four villages in County Down. *Ulster Folk.*, 20, 1974, 49–60.

5262 HISTORIC HOUSES, CASTLES AND GARDENS IN GREAT BRITAIN AND IRELAND. London: 1977.

5263 IDE, JOHN J. Irish country houses of the Georgian period. New York: 1959.

5264 IRISH GEORGIAN SOCIETY. The Georgian Society records of eighteenth century domestic architecture and decoration in Dublin; introduction by Desmond Guinness. Shannon: 1969. 5 vols. Originally published Dublin: 1909–13.

5265 JOPE, EDWARD M. *ed*. Studies in building history: essays in recognition of the work of B.H. St. J. O'Neil. London: 1961. Early seventeenth century houses in Ireland, by H.G. Leask, pp. 243–250.

5266 LOEBER, ROLF. Irish country houses and castles of the late Caroline period: an unremembered past recaptured, I. Introduction. *Ir. Georg. Soc. Qtr. Bull.*, vol.16, nos. 1–2, 1973, 1–70.

5267 LUCAS, A.T. Contributions to the history of the Irish house: a possible ancestry of the bed-outshot [Cuilteach]. *Folklife*, 8, 1970, 81–98.

5268 MILTON, THOMAS, *engraver*. The seats and demesnes of the nobility and gentry of Ireland . . . engraved by Thomas Milton, from drawings by the most eminent artists, with descriptions of each view. Dublin: Dublin Press for the Irish Georgian Society. vol. 1, 1963. 1st published 1783.

5269 MORRIS, F.O. A series of picturesque views of seats of the noblemen and gentlemen of Great Britain and Ireland with descriptive and historical letterpress. London: [1866–80]. 6 vols.

5270 POOL, ROBERT and CASH, JOHN. View of the most remarkable public buildings, monuments and other edifices in . . . Dublin, delineated by R.P. and J.C., with historical descriptions of each building. Dublin: 1780.

5271 SADLEIR, THOMAS U., and DICKINSON, PAGE L. Georgian mansions in Ireland, with some account of Georgian architecture and decoration. Dublin: 1915. Supplements the five volumes of the Georgian Society.

Large Private Dwellings

5272 BEIT, *Sir* ALFRED. Russborough, Blessington, County Wicklow. Dublin: 1978. (*The Irish Heritage series: 13*).

5273 BENCE-JONES, MARK. Lissadell. (Co. Sligo). *Ir. Wel.*, vol.19, no. 4, 1970, 33–37.

5274 BOYLAN, LENA. Castletown and its owners. [Leixlip, Irish Georgian Society, 1972].— Pt. 2. The Conollys of Castletown, 1973.

5275 — Kildare Lodge: Lord Edward Fitzgerald's house. *Kildare Arch. Soc. J.*, vol.16, no. 1, 1977–8, 26–35.

5276 — Robert Emmet's house at Rathfarnham. *Dublin Hist. Rec.*, vol.31, no. 2, 1978, 55–58.

5277 CAMPBELL, *The Rev.* JOHN P. Two memorable Dublin houses (Belvedere House and Drumcondra House). *Dublin Hist. Rec.*, 2, 1939–40, 141–155.

5278 CORNFORTH, JOHN. Adare Manor, Co. Limerick. *Country Life*, 145, 1969, 1230–1234, 1302–1306, 1366–1369. The seat of the Earls of Dunraven.

5279 — Mount Kennedy, Co. Wicklow: The home of Mr. and Mrs. Ernest Hull. *Country Life*, 138, 1965, 1128–31, 1256–59.

5280 — Rathbeale Hall, Co. Dublin. *Country Life*, 152, 1972, 450–454.

5281 — Russborough, Co. Wicklow: the home of Sir Alfred and Lady Beit. *Country Life*, 134, 1963, 1464–7, 1623–7, 1686–90.

5282 COX, LIAM. Historic Moyelly: home of Colonel Richard Grace. *Old Athlone Soc. J.*, vol.1, no. 4, 1974–5, 238–241.

5283 CRAIG, MAURICE. Bellamont Forest, Co. Cavan. The house of Major-General and Mrs. E. Dorman O'Gorman. *Country Life*, 135, 1964, 1258–61, 1330–33.

5284 — and GLIN, KNIGHT OF. Castletown, Co. Kildare. *Country Life*, 145, 1969, 722–726, 798–802, 882–885. The property of the Hon. Desmond Guinness and the headquarters of the Irish Georgian Society.

5285 GIROUARD, MARK. Whitfield Court, Co. Waterford: the home of Major-General and Lady Katherine Dawney. *Country Life*, 142, 1967, 522–526.

5286 — Westport House, Co. Mayo, Ireland. *Country Life*, 137, 1965, 1010–1013, 1074–1077. The seat of the Marquess of Sligo.

5287 GLIN, KNIGHT OF. New light on Castletown, Co. Kildare. *Ir. Georg. Soc. Qtr. Bull.*, 8, 1965, 3–9.

5288 — The Temple of the Winds: an antique banqueting house. [Mount Stewart, Co. Down]. *Connoisseur*, vol.167, no. 674, 1968, 206–209.

5289 GUINNESS, DESMOND. Castletown House [Celbridge, Co. Kildare]. *Ir. Wel.*, vol.17, no. 1, 1968, 31–36.

5290 HUNT, JOHN. An Irish 'villa' for an Italian ambassador. [Lucan House, Co. Dublin]. *Connoisseur*, vol.160, no. 643, 1965, 2–6.

5291 MCPARLAND, EDWARD. Ballyfin, Co. Leix: the property of the Patrican College. *Country Life*, 154, 1973, 702–705, 774–777.

5292 — Emo House, Co. Leix: the house of Mr. and Mrs. Cholmeley Harrison. *Country Life*, 155, 1974, 1274–1277, 1346–49.

5293 — Sir Richard Morrisson's country houses: the smaller villas. *Country Life*, 153, 1973, 1462–6, 1538–41.

5294 MALINS, EDWARD. Coole Park, [Galway]. *Ir. Georg. Soc. Qtr. Bull.*, vol.13, no. 1, 1970, 20–29. Home of Lady Gregory.

5295 O'CONNELL, JOHN J. Castletown House, Piltown, Co. Kilkenny: the home of Mr. and Mrs. Charles Blaque. *Old Kilk. Rev.*, 25, 1973, 29–33.

5296 O'DEA, L. Rathfarnham House. *Dublin Hist. Rec.*, 15, 1958–60, 116–121, 128.

5297 O'MAHONY, EOIN. Castletown Cox [Co. Kilkenny]. *Forgnan*, vol.1, no. 7, 1962, 6–8. House built in 1760s for Michael Cox, Archbishop of Cashel and former Bishop of Ossory.

5298 O'SULLIVAN, T.F. The big house [Borris House, home of the Kavanaghs, Co. Cavan]. *Cap. Ann.*, 1977, 220–231.

5299 PECK, CAROLA. Rathbeale Hall, Swords, Co. Dublin. *Dublin Hist. Rec.*, vol.26, no. 4, 1973, 132–136.

5300 RANKIN, PETER. Downhill, Co. Derry. *Country Life*, 150, 1971, 94–97, 154–157.

5301 ROBERTSHAW, URSULA. Westport House. [Co. Mayo]. *Illus. London News*, vol.251, no. 6653, 1967, 18–21.

5302 — Bantry House: defender of the bay. *ibid.*, vol.260, no. 6892, 1972, 65–69.

5303 ROTHE HOUSE, Kilkenny. *Oibre*, no. 3, 1966, 13–14.

5304 ROWAN, ALISTAIR. Ballywater Park, Co. Down. The home of Lord and Lady Dunleath. *Country Life*, 141, 1967, 456–460, 516–520. 2nd part deals with the Mulhollands, a family of linen manufacturers and with their relations with Sir Charles Lanyon, architect of the house.

5305 — Killyleagh Castle, Co. Down: the home of Lt. Col. and Mrs. D.A. Rowan Hamilton. *Country Life*, 147, 1970, 690–693, 774–777.

5306 RYAN, EILEEN. Monasterevan House [Co. Kildare]. *Kildare Arch. Soc. J.*, vol.14, no. 1, 1964–5, 47–49.

5307 SCANTLEBURY, *The Rev.* C. Belvedere House. [Dublin]. *Dublin Hist. Rec.*, 13, 1952–54, 128–132.

Suburban and Rural Types

5308 FFOLLIOTT, ROSEMARY. Cottages and farmhouses. *Ir. Ancest.*, vol.4, no. 1, 1972, 30–35.

5309 FITZSIMONS, JACK. Bungalow bliss. 5th ed. Kells: Kells Art Studio. 1975. On cover: 1976 edition. Eighty house designs approved for all grants.

Castles

5310 ADAMS, C.L. Castles of Ireland: some fortress histories and legends [with bibliogs.]. London: 1904.

5311 BRUCE-JONES, MARK. An aesthete's Irish castle: Dromore Castle, Co. Limerick. *Country Life*, 136, 1964, 1274–1277.

5312 — Thomastown Castle, Co. Tipperary: the property of Archbishop Mathew. *Country Life*, vol. 146, no. 3787, 1969, 818–824.

5313 CAHER CASTLE [Co. Tipperary]. *Oibre*. no. 9, 1972, 9–10.

5314 CLAFFEY, JOHN A. Ballintubber Castle, Co. Roscommon. *Old Athlone Soc. J.*, vol. 1, 1969–75, 143–146, 218–221.

5315 — The Medieval castle of Athlone. *Old Athlone Soc. J.*, vol. 1, no. 2, 1970–71, 55–60.

5316 CORNFORTH, JOHN. Ballinlough Castle, Co. Westmeath: the seat of Sir Hugh Nugent. *Country Life*, vol.164, no. 4227, 1978, 90–93.

5317 — Dublin Castle. *Country Life*, vol.148, no. 3823, 1970, 284–287; *ibid*., no. 3824, 342–345.

5318 — Dunsany Castle, Co. Meath: the seat of Lord Dunsany. *Country Life*, vol.149, no. 3859, 1971, 1296–1300; *ibid*., no. 3860, 1364–67.

5319 — Malahide and after: an opening of special significance. *Country Life*, vol.162, no. 4176, 1977, 66–68. On the future of Malahide Castle.

5320 CRAIG, MAURICE. Portumna Castle [Co. Galway]. Ballycotton (Co. Cork): 1976. (*Gatherum series* no. 7).

5321 DE BREFFNY, BRIAN. Castles of Ireland. London: 1977.

5322 GIROUARD, MARK. Birr Castle, Co. Offaly. *Country Life*, 137, 1965, 410–414, 468–471, 526–529.

5323 — Humewood Castle, Co. Wicklow. *Country Life*, vol.143, 1968, 1212–1215, 1282–1285.

5324 — Modernising an Irish country house: Tullynally Castle, Co. Westmeath. *Country Life*, 150, 1971, 1780–83, 1834–37.

5325 HUGHES, JAMES L.J. Dublin Castle in the seventeenth century: a topographical reconstruction [with bibliog.]. *Dublin Hist. Rec*., 2, 1939–40, 81–97, 111.

5326 JOPE, E.M. Moyry, Charlemont, Castleraw and Richhill: fortification to architecture in the north of Ireland. *Ulster J. Arch., 3rd ser*., 23, 1960, 97–123.

5327 KELLY, MARTIN J. The owners and tenants of Barberstown Castle. *Kildare Arch. Soc. J*., vol. 16, no. 1, 1977–8, 61–67. Penkinson, Sutton, Gaydon, Von Homreigh, Henty and Camcross families.

5328 LANIGAN, KATHERINE. M. Kilkenny Castle. Kilkenny: 1967.

5329 LEASK, HAROLD G. Irish castles, 1180 to 1310. Reprinted from *Archaeol.J.*, 93, 1937, 143–99.

5330 — Castles and their place in history. *Ir. Sword*, vol.10, no. 41, 1972, 235–243.

5331 — Irish castles and castellated houses. Dundalk: Dundalgan Press, 1973. Reprint of 2nd ed. 1944.

5332 MAHER, JAMES. *ed*. Ormonde Castle, Carrick-on-Suir, Co. Tipperary. Clonmel: 1970.

5333 ROWAN, A.J. Georgian Castles in Ireland: *Ir. Georg. Soc. Qtr. Bull*., vol.7, no. 1, 1964, 3–30.

5334 SCANTLEBURY, *The Rev*. C. Rathfarnham Castle. *Dublin Hist. Rec*., 12, 1951, 20–30.

5335 TIERNEY, MARK and CORNFORTH, JOHN. Glenstal Castle, Co. Limerick. *Country Life*, vol.156, no. 4031, 1974, 934–937.

5336 TUTTY, MICHAEL J. Malahide Castle. *Dublin Hist. Rec*., vol.31, no. 3, 1978, 93–96.

5337 WATERMAN, D.M. Sir John Davies and his Ulster buildings: Castlederg and Castle Curlews, Co. Tyrone. *Ulster J. Arch., 3rd ser*., 23, 1960, 89–96.

5338 — Castle Balfour, Lisnaskea. Co. Fermanagh. *Ulster J. Arch*., 31, 1968, 71–76.

5339 WESTROPP, THOMAS JOHNSON. The ancient castles of the county of Limerick. *R. Ir. Acad. Proc. Sec. C*., vol.26, 1906–7, 55–108, 143–264.

Accessories, Domestic Structures

5340 FFOLLIOTT, ROSEMARY. The charm of Irish gate lodges. *Ir. Ancest*., vol.3, no. 2, 1971, 102–104.

Doors and Doorways

5341 CRAIG, MAURICE. Dublin doorways. *Ir. Wel*., vol. 21, no. 4, 1972, 19–26.

5342 GOODISON, NICHOLAS. The door furniture at Ely House [Dublin]. *Ir. Georg. Soc. Qtr. Bull*., vol.12, nos. 2–3, 1970, 45–48.

Sacramental Furniture

5343 ROE, HELEN MAYBURY. Medieval fonts of Meath Navan: Meath Archaeological and Historical Society, 1968.

SCULPTURE

5344 BARROW, VIOLA. Dublin Custom House – the river heads. *Dublin Hist. Rec.*, vol.29, no. 1, 1975, 24–27.

5345 FFOLLIOTT, ROSEMARY. Heraldic or ornamental animal figures in Ireland. *Ir. Ancest.*, vol.5, no. 2, 1973, 84–86.

5346 FRIIS, HJALMAR. Rytterstatuens historie i Europa fra oldtiden indtil thorvaldsen. Copenhagen: 1933. Barokken i England og Irland, pp. 313–33. Account of equestrian statues.

5347 GRANT, MAURICE HAROLD. A dictionary of British sculptors from the thirteenth century to the twentieth century. London: 1953.

5348 GUNNIS, RUPERT. Dictionary of British sculptors, 1660–1851. New rev. ed. London: 1968.

5349 HARBISON, PETER. The Castledillon stone: *Kildare Arch Soc. J.*, vol.15, no. 2, 1972, 136–140.

5350 — Some medieval sculpture in Kerry. *Kerry Arch. Hist. Soc. J.*, 6, 1973, 9–25.

5251 — The vanished faces of Ireland. *Studies*, 65, 1976, 53–62. Lists Irish sculpture which has been lost or stolen.

5352 HENRY, FRANÇOISE. La sculpture irlandaise pendant les douze premiers siècles de l'ère Chrétienne. Paris: 1933. 2 vols. Bibliog., vol.1, pp. 199–213; 223–9.

5353 HICKEY, HELEN. Images of stone. Belfast: 1976. Figure sculptures of the Lough Erne Basin.

5354 HUNT, JOHN. The influence of alabaster carvings on medieval sculpture in Ennis friary. *Nth. Munster Antiq. J.*, 17, 1975, 35–41.

5355 — and HARBISON, PETER. Medieval English alabasters in Ireland. *Studies*, 65, 1976, 310–321.

5356 LEASK, HAROLD G. Dublin Custom House: the Riverine sculptures. *R. Soc. Antiq. Ir. J.*, 75, 1945, 187–194.

5357 MACLEOD, CATRIONA. Mediaeval wooden figure sculptures in Ireland. *R. Soc. Antiq. Ir. J.*, 75, 1945, 167–182, 195–203.

5358 NATIONAL GALLERY OF IRELAND. Catalogue of the sculptures, 1975. Dublin: 1975.

5359 O MURCHADHA, DOMHNALL. Stone sculpture in pre-Norman Ireland. *Cap. Ann.*, 1969, 172–200.

5360 STALLEY, ROGER. A[n anonymous] Romanesque sculptor in Connaught. *Country Life*, vol. 153, no. 3965, 1973, 1826–1830. On the monasteries at Boyle and Ballintober, Boyle Abbey, Co. Roscommon.

Sculptors

CAREW, JOHN EDWARD.

5361 FINCH, R.H.C. The life and work of J.E. Carew. *Ir. Georg. Soc. Qtr. Bull.*, 9, 1966, 85–95.

CONNOR, JEROME.

5362 ALLEN, MAIRIN. Jerome Connor. *Cap. Ann.*, 1963, 347–368; 1964, 353–369.

HUGHES, JOHN.

5363 DENSON, ALAN. John Hughes, sculptor, 1865–1941: a documentary biography. Kendal: The author, 1969. Edition limited to 150 copies.

5364 — John Hughes, R.H.A., 1865–1941: a neglected Irish sculptor. *Cap. Ann.*, 1975, 126–137.

KIDWELL, WILLIAM.

5365 POTTERTON, HOMAN. William Kidwell, sculptor, *c.* 1664–1736, and some contemporary mason-sculptors in Ireland. *Ir. Georg. Soc. Qtr. Bull.*, 15, 1972, 80–124.

MORRIS, FRANK.

5366 WARREN, MICHAEL. Frank Morris, sculptor. *Introspect*, no. 3, 1977, 13–14.

O'CONNOR, ANDREW.

5367 GIBBON, MONK. Andrew O'Connor, sculptor. *Ir. Wel.*, vol. 24, no. 2, 1975, 7–10.

5368 POTTERTON, HOMAN. Andrew O'Connor, 1874–1941: a complementary catalogue to the exhibition marking the centenary of the sculptor's birth, Trinity College, Dublin, September 1974. Dublin: 1974.

O'SHEA, JOHN, and O'SHEA, JAMES.

5369 MCGRATH, RAYMOND. [Benjamin] Woodward and the O'Sheas. *Ir. Wel.*, vol. 31, no. 5, 1973, 27–30. The O'Sheas were stone carvers for Woodward's firm, and were responsible for the carvings on the Kildare Street Club.

SAINT–GAUDENS, AUGUSTUS.

5370 SNODDY, OLIVER. Augustus Saint-Gaudens. *Cap. Ann.*, 1971, 197–208. Sculptor of Parnell monument.

STUART, IAN.

5371 WHITE, JAMES. Ian Stuart, sculptor of our time. *Forgnan*, vol. 1, no. 4, 1962, 10–12.

Monuments

5372 BARRETT, CYRIL. The Crozier memorial. Ballycotton (Co. Cork): Gifford and Craven, 1976. (*Gatherum series no*. 5). Memorial to Capt. F.R.M. Crozier, who lost his life in search of the North West Passage, stands in Church Square, Banbridge, Co. Down.

5373 BOLGER, WILLIAM, and SHARE, BERNARD. And Nelson on his pillar, 1808/1966: a retrospective record. Dublin: Nonpareil, 1976. Account of Nelson's Pillar, blown up on 8th March 1966.

5374 BORD FAILTE EIREANN. National monuments of Ireland in the charge of the Commissioners of Public Works in Ireland. Dublin: 1964. Includes map showing sites of monuments.

5375 CREERY, OLIVE. Index to the references to national and ancient monuments in Co. Galway, contained in the annual reports of the Office of Public Works, Ireland, between the years 1875 and 1909. *Galway Arch. Hist. Soc. J.*, 7, 1911–12, 120–4.

5376 CROOKSHANK, ANNE. Lord Cork and his monuments. *Country Life*, vol. 149, no. 3859, 1971, 1288–1290. 1st Earl of Cork (1566–1643), patron of monumental sculptors.

5377 DIXON, F.E. Dublin portrait statues [list of 67 statues and sculptors]. *Dublin Hist. Rec.*, vol. 31, no. 2, 1978, 60–69.

5378 GARNETT, P.F. The Wellington testimonial [Wellington monument, Phoenix Park, Dublin]. *Dublin Hist. Rec.*, 13, 1952–54, 48–61.

5379 HARBISON, PETER. Guide to the national monuments in the republic of Ireland, including a selection of other monuments not in state care. New ed. Dublin: 1975. Bibliog., p. 269.

5380 HENCHY, PATRICK. Nelson's Pillar. *Dublin Hist. Rec.*, 10, 1948–9, 53–63.

5381 HUNT, JOHN. Irish medieval figure sculptor, 1200–1600: a study of Irish tombs with notes on costume and armour, by John Hunt with assistance and contributions from Peter Harbison. Dublin and London: 1974. 2 vols.

5382 MOTT, GEORGE. Monuments of Irish interest in St. Isidore's, Rome, transcribed and photographed by George Mott. *Ir. Ancest.*, 10, 1978, 15–17.

5383 NORTHERN IRELAND, Ancient Monuments Advisory Council. A preliminary survey of the ancient monuments of Northern Ireland. General editor, D.A. Chart. Belfast: 1940. Bibliog., pp. 263–4.

5384 NORTHERN IRELAND. MINISTRY OF FINANCE. Ancient monuments of Northern Ireland. Belfast. Vol. 1. In state care. 5th ed., 1966. Vol. 2. Not in state care. 3rd ed., 1969.

5385 POTTERTON, HOMAN. Dublin's vanishing monuments. *Country Life*, vol. 155, no. 4012, 1974, 1304–5.

5386 — Irish church monuments, 1570–1880 [a catalogue]. Belfast: Ulster Architectural Heritage Society, 1975.

5387 — The O'Connell monument. Ballycotton (Co. Cork): Gifford and Craven, 1973. (*Gatherum series no*. 3). Daniel O'Connell monument, O'Connell St., Dublin.

5388 RAE, E.C. The [James] Rice monument in Waterford cathedral. *R. Ir. Acad. Proc., Sec. C*, vol. 69, no. 1, 1970, 1–14.

Crosses

5389 DE VAL, SEAMAS S. The high crosses of Ireland. *Old Wexford Soc. J.*, vol. 3, no. 1, 1970, 21–25.

5390 HENRY, FRANÇOISE. Irish high crosses. Dublin: 1964. (*Cultural Relations Committee of Ireland, Irish life and culture ser.*) Bibliog., pp. 61–2.

5391 PORTER, ARTHUR KINGSLEY. The crosses and culture of Ireland. New Haven: Metropolitan Museum of Art, 1931.

5392 ROE, HELEN M. The high crosses of Kells. Meath: 1959. Bibliog., p. 65.

5393 — The Irish high cross: morphology and iconography. *R. Soc. Antiq. Ir. J.*, 95, 1965, 213–226.

5394 SEXTON, ERIC H.L. A descriptive and bibliographical list of Irish figure sculptors of the early Christian period, with a critical assessment of their significance. Portland, Maine: 1946. Limited ed. of 450 copies; deals mainly with crosses.

NUMISMATICS, COINS

5395 BRENNAN, JOHN. The new coinage. *Eire-Ir.*, vol. 5, no. 2, 1970, 140–1.

5396 — Ireland's Viking coinage. *ibid.*, vol. 5, no. 4, 1970, 92–96.

5397 BROWN, I.D. and DOLLEY, MICHAEL. A bibliography of coin hoards of Great Britain and Ireland, 1500–1967. London: 1971. (*Royal Numismatic Society special pub*. no. 6).

5398 CARSON, R.A.G. and O'KELLY, CLARE. A catalogue of the Roman coins from Newgrange, Co. Meath, and notes on the coins and related finds. *R. Ir. Acad. Proc., Sec. C*, vol. 77, no. 2, 1977, 35–55.

5399 CLEEVE, BRIAN, *ed*. W.B. Yeats and the designing of Ireland's coinage: texts by W.B. Yeats and others. Dublin: Dolmen Press, 1972. (*New Yeats papers* III).

5400 DOLLEY, MICHAEL. The Irish mints of Edward I in the light of the coin-hoards from Ireland and Great Britain. *R. Ir. Acad. Proc., Sec. C*, vol. 66, no. 3, 1968, 235–297.

5401 — Medieval Anglo-Irish coins. London: 1972. Bibliog., pp. 75–80.

5402 — The medieval coin-hoards of Thomond. *Nth. Munster Antiq. J.*, 12, 1969, 23–34.

5403 — The pattern of Elizabethan coin-hoards from Ireland. *Ulster J. Arch.*, 33, 1970, 77–88.

5404 — Two unpublished letters of a distinguished Cork antiquary. *Cork Hist. Arch. Soc. J.*, 68, 1963, 55–65. Richard Sainthill (1787–1869), addressed to Jonathan Rashleigh, numismatist.

5405 — Four unpublished letters from Aquilla Smith to the Cork numismatist Richard Sainthill. *ibid.*, 77, 1972, 28–38.

5406 DOWLE, ANTHONY, and FINN, PATRICK. The guide book to the coinage of Ireland from 995 A.D. to the present day. London: 1969. Bibliog., pp. 119–124; includes valuations.

5407 DUBLIN SCIENCE AND ART MUSEUM. Catalogue of Irish coins. Dublin: 1895.

5408 DYKES, DAVID WILMER. The Anglo-Irish coinage and the ancient arms of Ireland. *R. Soc. Antiq. Ir. J.*, 96, 1966, 111–120.

5409 [FORRER, L.]. Bibliographie numismatique du royaume-uni de Grande-Bretagne et Irlande comprenant les colonies. Genève: 1889.

5410 GHALL, SEAN, *pseud.* (*i.e.* H.E. Kenny). A bibliography of Irish numismatics. Paper read before the Library Association of Ireland, January 29, 1908.

5411 GRUEBER, H.A. Handbook of the coins of Great Britain and Ireland in the British Museum. London: 1899.

5412 HILL, G.F. Coins and medals. London: 1920. (*Helps for students of history*, No. 36.) Bibliog., pp. 54–5.

5413 IRISH NUMISMATICS. Dublin, vol. 1–, 1968–.

5414 NATIONAL MUSEUM OF IRELAND. The earliest Anglo-Irish coinage, by William O'Sullivan. Dublin: 1964.

5415 O'HEGARTY, P.S. The Cork numismatist [John Lindsay]. *Ir. Book Lov.*, 28, 1941–2, 134. Lindsay was author of *A view of the coinage of Ireland* . . . 1839.

5416 O'SULLIVAN, WILLIAM. The earliest Irish coinage. Dublin: National Museum of Ireland, 1961. Reprinted from *R. Soc. Antiq. Ir. J.*, vol. 79, 1949.

5417 SEABY, PETER, *compiler*. Coins and tokens of Ireland. London: 1974. (*Seaby's standard catalogue, pt.* 3).

5418 WENT, ARTHUR E.J. The coinage of Ireland: 1000 A.D. to the present day. *Ir. Wel.*, vol. 12, no. 4, 1963, 21–24.

5419 YEATS, W.B. The designing of Ireland's coinage. *Ir. Wel.*, vol. 15, no. 2, 1966, 14–18.

5420 YOUNG, DEREK. Coin catalogue of Ireland, 1692–1969. 4th ed., Dublin: 1974.

Medals and Medallists

5421 BRITISH MUSEUM. Medallic illustrations of the history of Great Britain and Ireland. London: 1904–11. 19 pts.

5422 CRESSWELL, O.D. Irish medals. Belfast: the author, 54 Rosscoole Park, 1961. Typescript.

5423 DAWSON, H.R. A memoir of the medals and medallists connected with Ireland. Dublin: 1839.

5424 FRAZER, WILLIAM. The medallists of Ireland and their work. *R. Soc. Antiq. Ir. J., 4th ser.*, 7, 1885–6, 443–466, 608–619; 8, 1887–8, 189–208. On the Mossops and Woodhouses.

5425 HAWKINS, EDWARD, *and others*. Medallic illustrations of the history of Great Britain and Ireland to the death of George II, compiled by Edward Hawkins, and edited by Augustus W. Franks and Herbert A. Grueber. London: British Museum, 1885. 2 vols.

5426 SNODDY, OLIVER. Two military medals by William Mossop (1751–1805). *Ir. Sword*, 6, 1963–4, 252–256.

5427 WENT, ARTHUR E.J. The Cunningham medal of the Royal Irish Academy. *R. Ir. Acad. Proc., Sec. C*, 73, 1973, 99–105.

5428 — Medallic illustrations of Dublin history. *Dublin Hist. Rec.*, vol. 31, no. 3, 1978, 97–104.

5429 — The medals of the Royal Dublin Society. Dublin: 1973. Reprinted from *R. Dublin Soc. Sci. Proc., Sec. B*, vol. 3, no. 13, 1973.

5430 — William Mossop, eighteenth century Irish medallist. *Dublin Hist. Rec.*, vol. 28, no. 3, 1975, 93–99.

5431 WYNNE, MICHAEL. The portrait medallions of John van Nost the Younger. *Ir. Georg. Soc. Qtr. Bull.*, vol. 18, no. 1, 1975, 37–40.

Seals

5432 ARMSTRONG, E.C.R. Irish seal-matrices and seals. Dublin: 1913.

Tokens

5433 BOYNE, W. Trade tokens issued in the seventeenth century in England, Wales and Ireland. New and rev. ed. by G.C. Williamson. London: 1889–91. 2 vols.

5434 DAVIS, WILLIAM JOHN. The nineteenth century token coinage of Great Britain, Ireland, the Channel Islands and the Isle of Man, to which are added tokens of over one penny value of any period. [1st ed.] reprinted, London: 1969. First published London: 1904.

5435 DE BREFFNY, BRIAN. Businessmen who issued tokens in Ireland, 1653–1679. *Ir. Ancest.*, 10, 1978, 51–60.

5436 SEABY, W.A. Catalogue of Ulster tokens, tickets, vouchers, checks, passes, etc. (mostly dating from the mid- to late-nineteenth century and the early part of the twentieth century). *Ulster J. Arch.*, 34, 1971, 96–106.

CERAMICS, POTTERY

5437 CUSHION, J.P. and HONEY, W.B. *compilers*. Handbook of pottery and porcelain marks. London: 1956. Ireland (Belfast, Belleek, and Dublin), pp. 282–3.

5438 FRASER, *Mrs.* A.M. Some early Dublin potters. *Dublin Hist. Rec.*, 12, 1951, 47–58.

5439 JENKS, MARGARET. Notes on the history of Belleek pottery. *Donegal Ann.*, vol. 10, no. 3, 1973, 316–321.

5440 JOHNSTON, A.W. A catalogue of Greek vases in public collections in Ireland. *R. Ir. Acad. Proc., Sec. C*, vol. 73, no. 9, 1973, 339–506.

5441 LONGFIELD, ADA K. Irish delft. *Ir. Georg. Soc. Qtr. Bull.*, 14, 1971, 36–55.

5442 MCCRUM, S. The Belleek pottery. Belfast: 1972. (*Ulster Museum pub. no.* 188).

5443 MCDONAGH, D. Arklow pottery. *Technol. Ir.*, vol. 2, nos. 4–5, 1970, 28–31.

5444 MURRAY, SHEILA. Potters in Ireland. Edinburgh and London: Johnston and Bacon; Dublin: Zircon Publishing Ltd., 1973.

5445 ROSC. Irish delftware: [catalogue of] an exhibition of 18th century Irish delftware at Castletown House, Celbridge, Co. Kildare. Dublin: 1971.

5446 **Ryan, Michael.** Native pottery in early historic Ireland. *R. Ir. Acad. Proc., Sec. C*, vol. 73, no. 11, 1973, 619–645.

5447 **Shinn, Charles** and **Shinn, Dorrie.** The illustrated guide to Victorian Parian china. London: 1971. Bibliog., pp. 119–120; gives an account of the Belleek factory, Co. Fermanagh.

5448 **Westropp, M.S. Dudley.** Notes on the pottery manufacture in Ireland. *R. Ir. Acad. Proc., Sec. C*, 32, 1914–16, 1–27.

METALWORK

5449 **Buckley, J.J.** Some Irish altar plate: a descriptive list of chalices and patens, dating from the fourteenth to the end of the seventeenth century, now preserved in the National Museum and in certain churches. Dublin: Royal Society of Antiquaries of Ireland, 1943.

5450 **Pryor, Francis.** A descriptive catalogue of some ancient Irish metalwork in the collections of the Royal Ontario Museum, Toronto. *R. Soc. Antiq. Ir. J.*, 106, 1976, 73–91.

5451 **Raftery, Joseph.** Metalwork in early Christian Ireland. *Ir. Wel.*, vol. 14, no. 2, 1965, 18–23.

5452 **Westropp, M.S.D.** Metalwork: bronze and brass. Dublin: National Museum of Science and Art, 1911.

5453 **Whitfield, Niamh.** The original appearance of the Tara brooch. *R. Soc. Antiq. Ir. J.*, 106, 1976, 5–30.

GOLD AND SILVER

5454 **Bennett, Douglas.** Irish Georgian silver. London: 1972. Bibliog., p. 357. Pt. 1. The Company of Goldsmiths. Pt. 2. The work of the goldsmiths of Dublin. Pt. 3. Other Irish goldsmiths. Pt. 4. Fakes, forgeries and substandard goods. Pt. 5. A guide to hall-marks. Appendix A. Dublin makers and their marks frim 1714 to 1830. Appendix B. Names of Cork goldsmiths registered in the books of the Dublin Goldsmiths Company in 1784 and following years. Appendix C. Names of Limerick goldsmiths. Appendix D. Alphabetical list of persons in the provincial towns (not including Cork or Limerick).

5455 — Nineteenth century silver, and an interesting recent acquisition by the Old Dublin Society. *Dublin Hist. Rec.*, vol. 28, no. 1, 1974, 17–20.

5456 — Silver in Dublin. *Ir. Ancest.*, 8, 1976, 13–16.

5457 **Bradbury, Frederick,** *compiler*. British and Irish silver Assay Office marks, 1864–1963; with notes on gold markings, and marks on foreign imported silver and gold plate . . . 11th ed., Sheffield: 1964.

5458 **Davis, Frank.** Irish silver, Chinese ceramics. *Country Life*, 136, 1964, 1752–3.

5459 **Chaffers, W.** Hall marks on gold and silver plate, illustrated with revised tables of annual date letters employed in the Assay Offices of England, Scotland and Ireland. 10th ed., extended and enlarged, and with the addition of new date letters and marks, and a bibliography, by C.A. Markham. London: 1922. Bibliog., pp. 374–83.

5460 **Gorman, M.J.** An internationally-known hotelier and his private collection of silver. *Connoisseur*, 165, 1967, 94–99.

5461 **Jackson, Charles James.** English goldsmiths and their marks: a history of the goldsmiths and plateworkers of England, Scotland and Ireland. 2nd ed. London: 1949. 1st ed. 1905.

5462 **Jackson, Robert Wyse.** An introduction to Irish silver. *Nth. Munster Antiq. J.*, 9, 1962–3, 1–24.

5463 — Irish silver. Cork and Dublin: 1972. Bibliog., pp. 76 and 85.

5464 **Maryon, Herbert.** The technical methods of the Irish [gold]-smiths in the bronze and early iron ages. *R. Ir. Acad. Proc., Sec. C*, 44, 1937–8, 181–228.

5465 **Naylor, Henry.** Eighteenth-century Dublin silver. *Dublin Hist. Rec.*, 12, 1951, 14–19, 59–63.

5466 **Rosc.** Irish silver: [catalogue of] an exhibition of Irish silver from 1630–1820 at Trinity College, Dublin. Dublin: 1971.

5467 **Ticher, Kurt.** Irish silver in the Rococo period. Shannon: 1972.

5468 — Three Huguenot goldsmiths in Dublin in the early 1700s. *Ir. Georg. Soc. Qtr. Bull.*,

15, 1972, 73–79. David Rummieu, Francis Girard and Peter Gervais.

5469 TOWNSHEND, FRANCIS. Irish documents on silver and gold. *Country Life*, vol. 139, no. 3614, 1966, 1491–1494.

5470 — Irish silver: decoration and re-decoration. *Ir. Georg. Soc. Qtr. Bull.*, 8, 1965, 10–38.

5471 WENHAM, E. Domestic silver of Great Britain and Ireland. London: 1940.

5472 WESTROPP, M.S.D. Metal work: gold and silver. 5th ed., Dublin: National Museum of Ireland: 1934.

Pewter, Brass-ware

5473 COTTERELL, HOWARD HERSHEL, and WESTROPP, M.S. DUDLEY. Irish pewterers. *R. Soc. Antiq. Ir. J.*, 47, 1917, 47–66.

5474 — Old pewter: its makers and marks in England, Scotland and Ireland. An account of the old pewterer and his craft, illustrating all known marks and secondary marks of the old pewterers, with a series of plates showing the chief types of their wares. London: 1929. Bibliog., p. 423. reprinted 1963.

5475 PAGE–PHILLIPS, JOHN. Macklin's monumental brasses; including a bibliography and a list of figure brasses remaining in churches in the United Kingdom, re-written by John Page-Phillips. New ed. with maps. London: 1972. Bibliog., pp. 117–124.

5476 STEPHENSON, M. A list of monumental brasses in the British Isles. London: 1926.

5477 — Appendix to *A list of monumental brasses in the British Isles*. London: 1938.

DRAWING

5478 BRITISH MUSEUM. Catalogue of drawings by British artists and artists of foreign origin working in Great Britain . . . in the British Museum, by L. Binyon. London: 1898–1907. 4 vols.

5479 GABRIEL BERANGER'S DUBLIN DRAWINGS. *Dublin Hist. Rec.*, 8, 1945–6, 159–60.

5480 INDEX TO THE DRAWINGS OF IRISH ANTIQUITIES in the sketch books [12 vols., large, oblong folio] of the late George Victor du Noyer, belonging to the Royal Society of Antiquaries of Ireland. *R. Soc. Antiq. Ir. J.*, 20, 1902, 261–8. Arranged under counties.

MCCORMICK, ARTHUR D.

5481 DALE, W.S. Arthur David McCormick, R.I., book illustrator and artist. *Ir. Booklore*, vol. 1, no. 2, 1971, 243–8.

PURSER, SARAH.

5482 O'GRADY, JOHN M. Sarah Purser, 1848–1943. *Cap. Ann.*, 1977, 89–104.

SCOTT, WILLIAM.

5483 FLANAGAN, TERENCE P. Drawings of William Scott: William Scott talks about drawing. *Arts. Ir.*, vol. 1, no. 3, 1973, 25–32.

5484 SEYMOUR, ST. JOHN. Old Dublin caricatures [a catalogue]. *R. Soc. Antiq. Ir. J.*, 37, 1907, 69–73.

Decorative Arts, Design

5485 ARTS AND CRAFTS SOCIETY OF IRELAND. Journal and proceedings, 1896–1901. Contents include: The modern Irish lace industry, by James Brennan. On maces and insignia of Irish corporations, &c., by John Ribton Garstin. Art and industry in Ireland, by T.W. Rolleston. An Irish sculptor – John Hughes, R.H.A., by A.E.

5486 CORAS TRACHTALA. [Irish Export Board]. Design in Ireland: report of the Scandinavian Design Group in Ireland, 1961; by Kaj Franck, Erik Herlow, Ake Huldt, Gunnar Biilman Petersen, Erik Chr. Sorensen. Dublin [1962].

5487 CRAWFORD, HENRY S. Handbook of carved ornament from Irish monuments of the Christian period. Dublin: Royal Society of Antiquaries of Ireland, 1926.

5488 HICKEY, TONY. The Kilkenny Design Workshops. *Arts Ir.*, vol. 1, no. 3, 1973, 33–41.

5489 LEEDS, E.T. Celtic ornament in the British Isles down to A.D. 700. Oxford: 1933.

5490 MAHR, ADOLF. Ancient Irish handicraft. *Thomond Arch. Soc. Fld. Cl.*, 1939. Bibliog., pp. 21–2.

5491 MERNE, JOHN G. A handbook of Celtic ornament: a complete course in the construction and development of Celtic ornament for art and craft students, with over 700 illustrations. Cork and Dublin: 1974.

5492 NICASSIO, SUSAN. Handcrafts of Slieve Bawn. *Ir. Wel.*, vol. 24, no. 3, 1975, 31–34. The Co-operative Handcraft Market, Strokestown, Co. Roscommon.

5493 ROSC. Modern graphics and multiples: [catalogue of exhibition held at] Bishop's Palace, Waterford . . . 1971. Dublin: 1971.

5494 RUSHE, DESMOND. Dublin's Project Arts Centre: painting, sculpture, theatre, music, film – a co-operative of all the arts. *Ir. Wel.*, vol. 25, no. 3, 1976, 16–19.

5495 SCHULTHEISS, LUDWIG J. Irish craftmanship and design – then and now. *Development*, 69, 1965, 30–48.

5496 WORLD CRAFTS COUNCIL. IRISH SECTION. Irish craftsmanship. Dublin: 1970.

Antiques

5497 THE ANTIQUES YEARBOOK, ENCYCLOPAEDIA AND DIRECTORY. London: 1949–. From 1956–7 includes section on Irish antique dealers.

5498 STACPOOLE, GEORGE, *ed.* A guide to Irish antiques and antique dealers. Dublin: 1968.

Wallpaper

5499 ENTWISTLE, E.A. A literary history of wallpaper. London: 1960.

5500 LONGFIELD, A.K. An Irish discovery of pilaster panels and decorative strips. *Arts. Ir.*, vol. 1, no. 3, 1973, 12–13.

5501 — Old wallpapers in Ireland. *Ir. Georg. Soc. Qtr. Bull.*, vol. 10, no. 1, 1967, 1–25.

Illumination of Manuscripts and Books

5502 NORDENFALK, CARL. Celtic and Anglo-Saxon painting: book illumination in the British Isles, 600–800. London: 1977. Bibliog., pp. 27–8.

TEXTILE ARTS

Tapestry

5503 BUCKLEY, J.J. Irish tapestry. *Museum Bull.*, 4, 1914, 2–10.

5504 LONGFIELD, ADA KATHLEEN. History of tapestry-making in Ireland in the 17th and 18th centuries. *R. Soc. Antiq. Ir. J.*, 68, 1938, 91–105.

Needle and Handwork

5505 BOYLE, ELIZABETH. Embroidery and lacemaking in Ulster [with bibliog.]. *Ulster Folk.*, 10, 1964, 5–22.

5506 Irish embroidery and lacemaking: 1600–1800 [with bibliog.]. *Ulster Folk.*, 1, 12, 1966, 52–65.

5507 BUCKLEY, J.J. Irish lace. *Museum Bull.*, 3, 1913, 1–6.

5508 COATS, J. and P. LTD., Irish crochet [12 designs in Coats-Mercer-crochet]. Glasgow: [1965].

5509 HEFFERNAN, LOLA M. Needlework and dressmaking: a course in dressmaking. Dublin: [1964].

5510 JONES, LAURA. Quilting. *Ulster Folk.*, 21, 1975, 1–9.

5511 MITCHELL, LILLIAS. Handspinning and weaving in Ireland. *Ir. Geog.*, vol. 1, no. 5, 1948, 129–133.

5512 — The wonderful work of the weaver. Dublin: 1972.

5513 O'SULLIVAN, JOHN C. An eighteenth century sampler. *Kildare Arch. Soc. J.*, vol. 15, no. 4, 1974–5, 434–6.

5514 PALLISER, *Mrs.* BURY. History of lace; new ed., rev., rewritten and enl., edited by M. Jourdain and Alice Dryden. London: 1902. Ireland, pp. 435–446.

5515 PETHEBRIDGE, JEANETTE E. A manual of lace. London: 1947. Includes Carrickmacross, Limerick, and Youghal Point.

5516 WARDLE, PATRICIA. Victorian lace. London: 1968. Bibliog., pp. 267–270; Ireland, pp. 173–200.

5517 WILLIAMS, GABRIELLE. Irish handwoven silk poplin. *Ir. Wel.*, vol. 24, no. 2, 1975, 15–19.

Printing, Painting, Dyeing

5518 LONGFIELD, ADA KATHLEEN. Archibald Hamilton Rowan, calico printer in America,

1797–1799. *Kildare Arch. Soc. J.*, vol. 15, no. 2, 1972, 178–185.

5519 — Early Irish printed fabric. *Country Life*, vol. 152, no. 3937, 1972, 1578–9.

5520 — Irish conceits of birds and blooms: the embossed pictures of Samuel Dixon. *Country Life*, vol. 144, no. 3744, 1968, 1457–60.

5521 — Samuel Dixon's embossed pictures. *R. Soc. Antiq. Ir. J.*, 96, 1966, 133–140.

Glass

5522 BOYDELL, MARY. Made for convivial clinking: 19th-century Anglo-Irish glass. *Country Life*, vol. 156, no. 4030, 1974, 852–854.

5523 — Some Dublin glass-makers. *Dublin Hist. Rec.*, vol. 27, no. 2, 1974, 42–48.

5524 — A versatile national emblem: the shamrock on Irish glass. *Country Life*, vol. 155, no. 4012, 1974, 1280–1.

5525 — Waterford glass. *Arts Ir.*, vol. 1, no. 4, 1973, 9–15.

5526 DAVIS, DEREK C. English and Irish antique glass. London: 1964. Bibliog., pp. 145–6.

5527 DOWNEY, ALAN. The story of Waterford glass. Waterford: 1952.

5528 DUNCAN, GEORGE SANG. Bibliography of glass: from the earliest records to 1940 . . . edited by Violet Dimbleby, subject index prepared by Frank Newby. London: Society of Glass Technology, 1960.

5529 ELVILLE, E.M. English and Irish cut glass, 1750–1950. London: 1953.

5530 HUGHES, G. BERNARD. English, Scottish and Irish table glass.London: 1956. Bibliog., pp. 391–3.

5531 — The heyday of Irish decanters. *Country Life*, 136, 1964, 510–1.

5532 MACLEOD, CATRIONA. The Corporation of Ardfert glass loving cup. *Kerry Arch. Hist. Soc. J.*, 7, 1974, 134–8.

5533 — The earliest dated Irish drinking glass, Dublin: 1715. *R. Soc. Antiq. Ir. J.,* 103, 1973, 47–50.

5534 — Late eighteenth-century Dublin finger bowls in the National Museum of Ireland. *ibid.*, 96, 1966, 141–6.

5535 — A short history of Irish cut glass. *Technol. Ir.*, vol. 6, no. 6, 1974, 15–19.

5536 — The Ouzel Galley Society glass loving cup (Dublin *c.* 1800–1805). *Ir. Georg. Soc. Qtr. Bull.*, vol. 15, no. 2, 1972, 65–71.

5537 — 'The land we live in': a toast on Cork decanters. *Cork Hist. Arch. Soc. J.*, 83, 1978, 59–65.

5538 MORTIMER, MARTIN. The Irish mirror chandelier. *Country Life*, 150, 1971, 1741–2.

5539 MURRAY, SHEILA and BEASLEY, ALAN. Irish glass. Edinburgh and London: Johnston and Bacon. Dublin: Zircon Publishing Ltd., 1973.

5540 ROSC. Irish glass from the eighteenth century to the present day. [Catalogue of exhibition held at] City Art Gallery, Limerick . . . Dublin: 1971.

5541 SEABY, WILFRED A. Finest Irish Williamite glass. *Country Life*, 138, 1965, 1635–6.

5542 THORPE, WILLIAM ARNOLD. A history of English and Irish glass. London: 1929. 2 vols. Bibliog., vol. 1, pp. 341–9.

5543 WARREN, PHELPS. Irish glass: the age of exuberance. London: 1970. Bibliog., pp. 150–1.

5544 WESTROPP, M.S. DUDLEY. Irish glass. *Belfast Nat. Hist. Phil. Soc. Proc.,* session 1914–15, 12–56.

5545 — Glass: Irish glass. 3rd ed., Dublin: National Museum of Science and Art, 1920.

5546 — Irish glass: a history of glass-making in Ireland from the sixteenth century; revised edition with additional text and illustrations, edited by Mary Boydell. Dublin: 1978. 1st ed., London: 1920.

Stained Glass

CLARKE, HARRY.

5547 BOWE, NICOLA GORDON. Harry Clarke. *Ir. Today*, 923, 1978, 4–8.

5548 — DOWLING, WILLIAM J. Harry Clarke: Dublin stained glass artist. *Dublin Hist. Rec.*, vol. 17, no. 2, 1962, 55–61.

HEALY, MICHAEL.

5549 CURRAN, C.P. Michael Healy: stained glass worker, 1873–1941. *Studies,* 31, 1942, 65–81.

HONE, EVIE,

5550 CURRAN, C.P. Evie Hone: stained glass worker, 1894–1955. *Studies*, 44, 1955, 129–42. Includes list of her stained glass windows.

5551 — FROST, STELLA, *ed*. A tribute to Evie Hone and Mainie Jellett. Dublin: 1957.

5552 — WHITE, JAMES. *compiler*. E. Hone, 1894–1955; [catalogue of an exhibition of her work sponsored by] the Arts Council Gallery and the Tate Gallery, London: January 2–February 15, 1959. [London], 1959.

M'ALLISTER, GEORGE.

5553 FRASER, *Mrs*. A.M. George M'Allister, glass-painter. *Dublin Hist. Rec*., 9, 1946–8, 128–136.

Furniture

5554 AALEN, F.H.A. Furnishings of traditional houses in the Wicklow hills. *Ulster Folk*., 13, 1967, 61–67.

5555 FFOLLIOTT, ROSEMARY and DE BREFFNY, BRIAN. The contents of Burton Hall, Co. Cork, in 1686. *Ir. Ancest*., vol. 5, no. 2, 1973, 104–113.

5556 GAILEY, ALAN. Kitchen furniture [with glossary of household terms, compiled by G.B. Adams.]. *Ulster Folk*., 12, 1966, 18–34.

5557 HINCKLEY, F. LEWIS. A directory of antique furniture: the authentic classification of European and American designs for professionals and connoisseurs. New York: 1952. Irish furniture, based on English and continental designs (plates 677–878) pp. 221–281.

5558 HUGHES, G. BERNARD. Irish bog-wood furniture. *Country Life*, vol. 149, no. 3859, 1971, 1318–21.

5559 PAMPLIN, ALEC S. Furniture design in Ireland. *Technol Ir*., vol. 2, nos. 4–5, 1970, 14–18.

PAINTING

5560 ANTIQUE COLLECTORS' CLUB. The dictionary of British artists, 1880–1940: an Antique Collectors' Club research project listing 41,000 artists, compiled by J. Johnson and A. Greutzner. Woodbridge (Suffolk): 1976.

5561 — The dictionary of British watercolour artists up to 1920, compiled by H.L. Mallalieu. Woodbridge (Suffolk): 1976.

5562 BODKIN, THOMAS. Four Irish landscape painters: George Barret, R.A., James A. O'Connor, Walter F. Osborne, R.H.A., Nathaniel Hone, R.H.A. Dublin and London: 1920. Appendices include bibliography and various lists of works of the artists including prices realised at auction.

5563 BRYAN, MICHAEL. Bryan's Dictionary of painters and engravers. New rev. and enl. ed. by George C. Williamson. London, 1930–4. 5 vols.

5564 CROOKSHANK, ANNE. Early landscape painters in Ireland. *Country Life*, vol. 152, no. 3923, 1972, 468–472.

5565 — and GLIN, KNIGHT OF. Painters of Ireland, *c*.1660–1920. London: 1978. Bibliog., pp. 293–295.

5566 FALLON, BRIAN. Irish painting in the fifties. *Arts Ir*., vol. 3, no. 1, 1975, 24–36.

5567 FLANAGAN, T.P. The artists in Northern Ireland. *Arts Ir*., vol. 1, no. 1, 1972, 36–45.

5568 FOSKETT, DAPHNE. British portrait miniatures: a history. London: 1963. Bibliog., pp. 185–188.

5569 — A dictionary of British miniature painters. London: 1972. 2 vols.

5570 FOSTER, J.J. A dictionary of painters of miniatures (1525–1850), with some account of exhibitions, collections, sales, etc., pertaining to them. London: 1926.

5571 GRANT, MAURICE HAROLD. A dictionary of British landscape painters from the sixteenth century to the early twentieth century. Leigh-on-Sea: 1952.

5572 GRAVES, ALGERNON, *compiler*. A dictionary of artists who have exhibited works in the principal London exhibitions from 1760 to 1893. Facsimile reprint of 3rd ed. with additions and corrections. Bath: 1969.

5573 HARDIE, MARTIN. Water-colour painting in Britain. London. vol. 1. The Eighteenth century. 1966. Vol. 2. The Romantic period. 1967. Vol. 3. The Victorian period. 1968.

5574 JELLETT, MAINIE. The artist's vision: lectures and essays on art, with an introduction by Albert Gleizes; edited by Eileen MacCarvill. Dundalk: 1958. Treats mainly of modern painting.

5575 LANE, HUGH. Catalogue of the exhibition of pictures by old masters given and bequeathed . . . by the late Sir Hugh Lane. Dublin: 1918. Includes short biographical note, also the will of the late Sir Hugh Lane.

5576 — TRIBUTE TO SIR HUGH LANE. Cork: Cork University Press, 1961.

5577 — BARROW, VIOLA. Hugh Lane. *Dublin Hist. Rec.*, vol. 28, no. 4, 1975, 122–137.

5578 — BODKIN, THOMAS. Hugh Lane and his pictures. Paris: 1932. Limited ed. of 400 copies, privately printed. 2nd ed. Dublin [1934]; 3rd ed. Dublin, The Arts Council, 1956.

5579 LISTER, RAYMOND. A title-list of books on miniature painting compiled for the use of artists, collectors and connoisseurs. Cambridge: 1952. Limited ed. of sixty copies of which fifty were for sale.

5580 MACGONIGAL, CIARAN. Dictionary of women artists in Ireland, 1870–1970. In preparation.

5581 MACGREEVY, THOMAS. Fifty years of Irish painting, 1900–1950. *Cap. Ann.*, 1949, 497–512.

5582 NATIONAL GALLERY OF IRELAND. Catalogue of the paintings. Dublin: 1971. The first catalogue to be published this century with a complete list of all paintings in tempera, fresco or oil.

5583 — Concise catalogue of the oil paintings. Dublin: 1964.

5584 RIVERS, ELIZABETH. Modern painting in Ireland. *Studies*, 50, 1961, 175–83.

5585 PYLE, HILARY. Modern art in Ireland: an introduction. *Eire-Ir.*, vol. 4, no. 4, 1969, 35–41.

5586 ROSC. The Irish imagination, 1959–1971. [Catalogue of exhibition held at] Municipal Gallery of Modern Art . . . 1971. Dublin: 1971.

5587 SNODDY, THEO. A dictionary of twentieth century Irish artists. In preparation.

5588 STRICKLAND, W.G. Dictionary of Irish artists [facsimile reprint]. Shannon: Irish Univ. Press, 1969. 2 vols. Includes as an appendix *A historical account of art institutions in Ireland*.

5589 WHITE, JAMES. *compiler*. Paintings from Irish collections [catalogue of an exhibition], May to August 1957. Dublin: Municipal Gallery of Modern Art, 1957.

5590 — Early American painters in Ireland. *Arts Ir.*, vol. 1, no. 4, 1973, 33–37. Includes a note of Irish artists in the United States.

5591 — John Butler Yeats and the Irish renaissance; with pictures from the collection of Michael Butler Yeats and from the National Gallery of Ireland. Dublin: Dolmen Press, 1972.

Portraits

5592 A.L.A. PORTRAIT INDEX: index to portraits contained in printed books and periodicals, edited by Wilson Coolidge Lane and Nian E. Browne. Washington, Library of Congress, 1906.

5593 CORNFORTH, JOHN and GLIN, KNIGHT OF. Irish portraits and the British school. *Country Life*, vol. 146, no. 3791, 1969, 1096–7.

5594 CROOKSHANK, ANNE. Irish artists and their portraiture. *Connoisseur*, vol. 172, no. 694, 1969, 235–243.

5595 — and GLIN, KNIGHT OF. Irish portraits, 1660–1860: catalogue [of exhibition] National Gallery of Ireland . . . National Portrait Gallery, London . . . Ulster Museum . . . Dublin: 1969.

5596 HUSSEY, MARY OLIVE. A century of Dublin portrait-painters, 1750–1850. *Dublin Hist. Rec.*, 18, 1963, 101–121.

5597 MADDISON, R.E.W. The portraiture of the Honourable Robert Boyle [with 55 plates]. *Ann. Sci.*, 15, 1959, 141–214.

5598 NATIONAL GALLERY OF IRELAND. The Irish, 1870–1970: a portrait exhibition for the Dublin Arts Festival . . . 1974. Dublin: 1974.

5599 NATIONAL LIBRARY OF IRELAND. Catalogue of engraved Irish portraits mainly in the Joly collection and of original drawings, by Rosalind M. Elmes. Dublin [1936].

5600 — Catalogue of Irish portraits. 3 vols. Manuscript catalogue maintained in Reading Room.

5601 PYLE, HILARY. The portraits of Estella Solomons, A.R.H.A. *Dubliner*, vol. 3, no. 3, 1964, 16–20. Includes four portraits of George Russell (AE), Joseph Campbell, Jack B. Yeats, Thomas Bodkin.

5602 ULSTER MUSEUM. An exhibition of portraits of great Irish men and women. Belfast, 1965. (*Publication no*. 173). Exhibition organised by Anne Crookshank.

5603 WATSON, ROSS. Irish portraits in American collections. *Ir. Georg. Soc. Qtr. Bull*., vol. 12, no. 2, 1969, 31–60.

5604 WHITE, JAMES. A questioning look at Irish portraits. *Country Life*, vol. 165, no. 3767, 1969, 1255–58.

5605 WILSON, T.G. Pooley's portrait of Swift. *Dublin Mag*., vol. 8, nos. 1–2, 1969, 47–50. Thomas Pooley (1646–1723), one of the earliest known Irish portrait painters.

5606 WYNNE, MICHAEL. Portraits by Hugh Howard (1675–1738) in the college collection. *Hermathena*, 111, 1971, 58–60.

Individual Painters

ASHFORD, WILLIAM.

5607 WYNNE, MICHAEL. William Ashford and the Royal Charter School, Clontarf, County Dublin. *Ir. Georg. Soc. Qtr. Bull*., vol. 10, no. 4, 1967, 20–24.

BARRY, JAMES.

5608 ALLAN, DAVID. The progress of human culture and knowledge. *Connoisseur*, vol. 186, no. 748, 1974, 100–109. Paintings of James Barry.

5609 — BODKIN, THOMAS. James Barry. *Studies*, 11, 1922, 83–96.

BROWN, DEBORAH.

5610 CROOKSHANK, ANNE. Deborah Brown. *Arts Ir*., vol. 1, no. 4, 1973, 38–49.

BUCK, FREDERICK.

5611 FFOLLIOTT, ROSEMARY. The swift rise and slow decline of Frederick Buck [miniaturist]. *Ir. Ancest*., 7, 1975, 15–24.

BURKE, P.

5612 HARBISON, PETER. P. Burk(e)'s painting of Youghal: the earliest known signed townscape by an Irish artist; with a note by Michael Wynne on P. Burk(e) and early landscape painting. *Cork Hist. Arch. Soc. J*., 78, 1973, 66–79.

CHINNERY, GEORGE.

5613 BERRY-HILL, HENRY, *and* BERRY-HILL, SIDNEY. George Chinnery, 1774–1852: artist of the China coast. Leigh-on-Sea: 1963.

5614 —ORMOND, RICHARD. George Chinnery and the Keswick family. *Connoisseur*, 175, 1970, 245–255.

COLLINS, PATRICK.

5615 WHITE, JAMES. Patrick Collins, painter. *Forgnan*, vol. 1, no. 2, 1962, 20–1.

COOKE, BARRIE.

5616 MONTAGUE, JOHN. The painting of Barrie Cooke. *Dubliner*, vol. 3, no. 1, 1964, 38–41.

FAGAN, ROBERT.

5617 DE BREFFNY, BRIAN. Robert Fagan, artist. *Ir. Ancest*., vol. 3, no. 2, 1971, 71–78.

5618 — TREVELYAN, RALEIGH. Robert Fagan: an Irish Bohemian in Italy. *Apollo*, vol. 96, no. 128, 1972, 298–311.

FRYE, THOMAS.

5619 WYNNE, MICHAEL. A note on Thomas Frye (1710–1762). *Ir. Georg. Soc. Qtr. Bull*., vol. 13, nos. 2–3, 1970, 38–44.

HEALY, ROBERT.

5620 GUINNESS, DESMOND. Robert Healy, Irish sporting artist. *Ir. Wel*., vol. 21, no. 4, 1972, 10–14.

5621 — Robert Healy, Irish sporting artist. *Stream and Field*, vol. 3, no. 6, 1974, 16–17.

HENRY, PAUL.

5622 DAWSON, GEORGE. Paul Henry, 1876–1958. *Ir. Wel*., vol. 25, no. 2, 1976, 18–25.

HILL, DEREK.

5623 GIBBON, MONK. Paintings of Derek Hill. *Dubliner*, 6, 1963, 40–43.

HONE, EVIE.

5624 WYNNE, MICHAEL. The Irish archaeological

inspiration of Evie Hone: a preliminary study. *Kildare Arch. Soc. J.*, vol. 14, no. 2, 1966–67, 247–253. Includes list of works.

HONE, NATHANIEL.

5625 BUTLIN, MARTIN. An eighteenth-century art scandal: Nathaniel Hone's 'The Conjuror.' *Connoisseur*, vol. 174, no. 699, 1970, 1–9.

5626 —PYLE, HILARY. Nathaniel Hone, 1718–1784: an eighteenth-century Irish artist. *Arts. Ir.*, vol. 1, no. 3, 1973, 54–63.

HORE, JAMES.

5627 WYNNE, MICHAEL. James Hore, active 1829–1837. *Studies*, 65, 1976, 46–51.

JELLETT, MAINIE.

5628 ARNOLD, BRUCE. Mainie Jellett, 1897–1944 [a catalogue]. Dublin: The Neptune Gallery, 1974.

5629 — MACCARVILL, EILEEN, *ed.* The artist's vision: lectures and essays on art. Dundalk: Dundalgan Press, 1958.

5630 — MUNICIPAL GALLERY OF MODERN ART. Mainie Jellett, 1897–1944 [exhibition of paintings and drawings]. Dublin: 1962.

KING, RICHARD.

5631 — In tribute to Richard King. *Cap. Ann.*, 1975, 169–215. Artist and stained glass worker; includes a list of his principal works.

KINGSTON, RICHARD.

5632 BURLEIGH, MARIAN. The future and Richard Kingston. *Forgnan*, vol. 1, no. 6, 1962, 5–9.

LAVERY, JOHN.

5633 — The life of a painter [autobiography]. Dublin: 1940. Appendix: Pictures in public galleries, 1888–1939.

5634 — SHAW–SPARROW, WALTER. John Lavery and his work. London [1911]. Appendices: Pictures and sketches from 1880–1900: a selected list, pp. 171–181; pictures and sketches from 1901–1911: a selected list, pp. 182–194; pictures in public galleries: British and foreign, pp. 195–199.

LE BROCQUY, LOUIS.

5635 — A retrospective selection of oil paintings, 1939–1966 . . . Dublin: 1966.

5636 — MONTAGUE, JOHN. Primal scream: the later Le Brocquy. *Arts Ir.*, vol. 2, no. 1, 1973, 4–14.

LE BROCQUY, SYBIL.

5637 SYBIL LE BROCQUY Memorial Committee. Sybil Le Brocquy, 1892–1973. Dublin: 1976. Edition of 400 copies.

LEECH, WILLIAM JOHN.

5638 DENSON, ALAN. An Irish artist: W.J. Leech, R.H.A., (1881–1968). Kendal: The author. Vol. 1. An introductory guide to his artistic career. 1968. Vol. 2-3. His life work: a catalogue. Pts. 1–2. 1969–70. Vol. 4. A memoir. *In preparation.*

5639 — W.J. Leech, R.H.A.: a great Irish artist, (1881–1968). *Cap. Ann.*, 1974, 119–127.

LEWIS, JOHN.

5640 O'CONNOR, ANDREW. John Lewis: a Smock Alley scene painter. *Studies,* 66, 1977, 51–59.

MACLISE, DANIEL.

5641 FALLON, BRIAN. Daniel Maclise, 1806–1870. *Dublin Mag.*, vol. 9, no. 2, 1971–2, 81–87.

5642 — ORMOND, RICHARD. Daniel Maclise. *Burlington Mag.*, 110, 1968, 685–693. Includes selected list of Maclise's more important oil and fresco paintings.

5643 — TURPIN, JOHN. Daniel Maclise and his place in Victorian art. *Anglo-Ir. Stud.*, 1, 1975, 51–69.

5644 — German influence on Daniel Maclise. *Apollo*, vol. 97, no. 132, 1973, 169–175.

5645 — The Irish background of Daniel Maclise, 1806–1870. *Cap. Ann.*, 1970, 177–194.

MACWEENEY, LESLIE.

5656 KINSELLA, THOMAS. The art of Leslie MacWeeney. *Forgnan*, vol. 1, no. 3, 1962, 19–22.

MAGUIRE, EDWARD.

5647 MURPHY, HAYDEN. Edward Maguire: a profile. *Arts Ir.*, vol. 2, no. 4, 1974, 38–48.

MIDDLETON, COLIN.

5648 LONGLEY, MICHAEL. Colin Middleton. *Dublin Mag.*, vol. 6, nos. 3–4, 1967, 40–43.

NOLAN, SYDNEY.

5649 WALKER, DOROTHY. Sidney Nolan. *Arts Ir.*, vol. 2, no. 1, 1973, 34–42. Australian artist; exhibition in Royal Dublin Society, June 1973.

O'CONNOR, JAMES ARTHUR.

5650 WHITE, JAMES. O'Connor at Westport House: an Irish landscape painter. *Apollo*, vol. 80, no. 29, 1964, 42–43.

O'DOHERTY, BRIAN.

5651 WALKER, DOROTHY. Brian O'Doherty [and] Patrick Ireland. *Arts Ir.*, vol. 2, no. 4, 1974, 4–15.

ORPEN, SIR WILLIAM.

5652 DAVIS, FRANK. Orpen in the ascendant. *Country Life*, vol. 154, no. 3989, 1973, 1902–3.

5653 — KONODY, P.G. and DARK, SIDNEY. Sir William Orpen, artist and man. London: 1932. Chronological list of paintings, pp. 265–283.

5654 — MACGONIGAL, CIARAN. Irish art and artists. Pt. 1, Sir William Orpen, RA, RHA, KBE, 1878–1931. *Ir. Today*, no. 925, 1978, 4–6.

5655 — RYAN, THOMAS. William Orpen. *Dubliner*, vol. 3, no. 4, 1964, 22–32.

OSBORNE, WALTER.

5656 GWYNN, STEPHEN. Walter Osborne and Ireland, 1859–1903. *Studies*, 32, 1943, 463–466.

5657 — HUSSEY, MARY OLIVE. Tribute to Walter Osborne, R.H.A., R.A. *Dublin Hist. Rec.*, vol. 22, no. 2, 1968, 201–213.

5658 — SHEEHY, JEANNE. Walter Osborne. Ballycotton (Co. Cork): Gifford and Craven, 1974. Bibliog., pp. 159–164.

PYE, PATRICK.

5659 WEBER, RICHARD. Patrick Pye. *Forgnan*, vol. 1, no. 5, 1962, 13–15.

ROBERTS, THOMAS.

5660 NATIONAL GALLERY OF IRELAND. Thomas Roberts, 1748–1778: Irish landscape artist. A bi-centenary exhibition. Dublin: 1978.

5661 — WYNNE, MICHAEL. Thomas Roberts, 1748–1778: some reflections on the bicentenary of his death. *Studies*, 66, 1977, 299–308.

SCOTT, PAT.

5662 WALKER, DOROTHY. Pat Scott. *Arts Ir.*, vol. 1, no. 1, 1972, 24–33.

STUART, GILBERT.

5663 MOUNT, CHARLES MERRILL. The Irish career of Gilbert Stuart. *Ir. Georg. Soc. Qtr. Bull.*, vol. 6, no. 1, 1963, 6–28.

TUDOR, JOSEPH.

5664 CROOKSHANK, ANNE, and GLIN, KNIGHT OF. Note on a newly discovered landscape by Joseph Tudor. *Studies*, 65, 1976, 235–8. Panoramic view of Boyne Valley.

WADE, JONATHAN.

5665 SHARPE, HENRY. Jonathan Wade: his life and art – a brief study. Clondalkin (Co. Dublin): 1977.

WALDRE, VINCENT.

5666 GILMARTIN, JOHN. Vincent Waldre's ceiling paintings in Dublin Castle. *Apollo*, vol. 95, no. 119, 1972, 42–47.

WHEATLEY, FRANCIS.

5667 WATSON, ROSS. Francis Wheatley in Ireland. *Ir. Georg. Soc. Qtr. Bull.*, 9, 1966, 35–49. An expanded version of a short notice which appeared in *Apollo*, vol. 82, 1965.

WILLIAMS, ALEXANDER.

5668 LEDBETTER, GORDON T. Alexander Williams (1846–1930): sidelights on a Victorian painter. *Ir. Ancest.*, vol. 7, no. 2, 1975, 83–86.

YEATS, JACK B.

5669 — Jack B. Yeats (1871–1957): early watercolours [an exhibition], April 6–29, 1961. London: The Waddington Galleries [1961].

5670 — Jack B. Yeats, 1871–1957: [catalogue of exhibition of] paintings, . . . 1971. London: Victor Waddington, 1971.

5671 — CURRAN, C.P. Jack B. Yeats, R.H.A. *Studies*, 30, 1941, 75–89.

5672 — MCHUGH, ROGER. Jack B. Yeats, 1871–1957. *Ir. Wel.*, vol. 20, no. 2, 1971, 16–34.

5673 — NEVE, CHRISTOPHER. Jack Yeats: rider to the sea. *Country Life*, vol. 148, no. 3823, 1970, 279–282.

5674 — PYLE, HILARY. Jack B. Yeats: a biography. London: 1970. Bibliog., pp. 175–201; exhibitions of the work of Jack B. Yeats, pp. 203–219.

5675 — ROSC. Jack B. Yeats and his family: [catalogue of] an exhibition of the works of Jack B. Yeats and his family at Sligo County Library and Museum . . . December, 1971. Dublin: 1971.

5676 — ROSE, MARILYN GADDIS. Jack B. Yeats: Irish rebel in modern art. *Eire-Ir.*, vol. 7, no. 2, 1972, 95–105.

5677 — WHITE, JAMES. Jack B. Yeats: drawings and paintings. London: 1971.

ENGRAVING

5678 ABBEY, JOHN ROLAND, *compiler*. Scenery of Great Britain and Ireland in aquatint and lithography, 1770–1860, from the library of J.R. Abbey: a bibliographical catalogue. [Facsimile reprint]. Folkestone: Dawsons: 1972. Ireland, pp. 302–21.

5679 ALEXANDER, DAVID. The Dublin group: Irish mezzotint engravers in London, 1750–1775. *Ir. Georg. Soc. Qtr. Bull.*, vol. 16, no. 3, 1973, 73–93.

5680 BRYAN, MICHAEL. Bryan's Dictionary of painters and engravers. New rev. and enl. ed. by George C. Williamson. London: 1930–4. 5 vols.

5681 CORNFORTH, JOHN. A happy marriage of art and craft: Irish mezzotints after English portraits. *Country Life*, vol. 154, no. 3973, 1973, 454–5.

5682 COSGRAVE, E. MACDOWEL. A contribution towards a catalogue of engravings of Dublin up to 1800. *R.Soc. Antiq.Ir. J.*, 35, 1905, 95–109, 363–76.

5683 — A contribution towards a catalogue of nineteenth-century engravings of Dublin. *ibid.*, 36, 1906, 400–19; 37, 1907, 41–60.

5684 DAY, ROBERT. Notice of bookplates engraved by Cork artists. *R. Hist. Arch. Soc. Ir. J., 4th ser.*, 7, 1885–6, 10.

5685 GRANT, MAURICE HAROLD. A dictionary of British etchers. London: 1952.

5686 LONGFIELD, A.K. Print-rooms. *Kildare Arch. Soc. J.*, vol. 14, no. 5, 1970, 568–575.

5687 LYNCH, F. A catalogue of engravings in *Walker's Hibernian Magazine*, 1772–1812. Completed for Fellowship of the Library Association of Ireland.

5688 NATIONAL LIBRARY OF IRELAND. Catalogue of Irish topographical prints and original drawings, by Rosalind M. Elmes; new rev. and enl. ed. by Michael Hewson. Dublin: 1975. 1st ed., Dublin: 1943.

5689 NOBLE, GEORGE, *Count Plunkett*. Some Irish engravers (in exile). *Cap. Ann.*, 1968, 271–276.

5690 RAFTERY, P.J. The Brocas family, notable Dublin artists. *Univ. Rev.*, vol. 2, no. 6, 1959, 17–25. Also appears in *Dublin Hist. Rec.*, vol. 17, no. 1, 1961, 25–34.

5691 — Who was Malton? *Univ. Rev.*, vol. 1, no. 7, 1955, 63–74. Includes annotated list of James Malton's Views of Dublin.

5692 SIBLEY, W. Old Dublin engravings. *Dublin Hist. Rec.*, 20, 1964–5, 29–40.

Banknotes

5693 YOUNG, DEREK. Legal tender notes, 1928–1972. Dublin: 1974.

PHOTOGRAPHY

5694 DOYLE, COLMAN. The people of Ireland. Cork: 1971.

5695 FERGUS BOURKE [photographer]. *Arts Ir.*, vol. 1, no. 1, 1972, 46–51.

5696 FRENCH, ROBERT. The light of other days: Irish life at the turn of the century in the photographs of Robert French. Edited and with an introduction by Kieran Hickey. London: 1973.

5697 GORHAM, MAURICE, *ed.* Dublin from old photographs. London: 1972.

5698 — Ireland from old photographs. London: 1971.

5699 HICKEY, KIERAN. Robert French and the Lawrence collection [of Victorian photographs consisting of 50,000 glass negatives which is housed in the National Library of Ireland]. *Ir. Wel.*, vol. 19, no. 5, 1971, 36–40.

5700 MERNE, OSCAR S. The story of the Photographic Society of Ireland, 1854–1954. Dublin: 1954.

5701 NUNN, G.W.A., *ed.* British sources of photographs and pictures. London: 1952.

5702 SYNGE, J.M. My wallet of photographs: the collected photographs of J.M. Synge, arranged and introduced by Lilo Stephens. Dublin: 1971.

5703 WALL, JOHN. *compiler*. Directory of British photographic collections. London: 1977. (*Royal Photographic Society publication*).

Cinematography

5704 GRIERSON, JOHN. A film policy for Ireland. *Studies*, 37, 1948, 283–291.

5705 MORRISON, GEORGE. An Irish national film archive. *Eire-Ir.*, vol. 1, no. 4, 1966, 39–62.

5706 O'CONNOR, SEAMUS. A national need: an Irish film archive. *Studies*, 54, 1965, 83-90.

5707 O'LAOGHAIRE, COLM. The mystique of Robert Flaherty. *Dubliner*, vol. 3, no. 2, 1964, 26–34.

MUSIC

Bibliography

5708 BIBLIOTHECA MUSICO–LITURGIA: a descriptive handlist of the musical and Latin-liturgical Mss. of the Middle Ages preserved in the libraries of Great Britain and Ireland: drawn up by Walter H. Frere . . . and printed for the members of the Plainsong and Mediaeval Music Society. Burnham, Bucks: [1901–32]. 2 vols.

5709 BRITISH CATALOGUE OF MUSIC: a record of music and books about music recently published in Great Britain, based upon the material deposited at the Copyright Receipt Office of the British Museum, arranged according to a system of classification with an alphabetical index under composers, titles, arrangers, instruments, etc., and a list of music publishers. vol. 1–, 1957–. London: 1958–.

5710 BRITISH UNION CATALOGUE OF EARLY MUSIC, printed before the year 1801: a record of the holdings of over one hundred libraries throughout the British Isles; edited by Edith B. Schnapper. London: 1957. 2 vols.

5711 DARRELL, R.D. *compiler*. Schirmer's Guide to books on music and musicians: a practical bibliography. New York: 1951.

5712 DEAKIN, ANDREW. Musical bibliography: a catalogue of the musical works (historical, theoretical, polemical, etc.), published in England during the fifteenth, sixteenth, seventeenth and eighteenth centuries, chronologically arranged with notes and observations on the principal works. Birmingham: 1892.

5713 — Outlines of music bibliography: a catalogue of early music and musical works printed or otherwise produced in the British Isles . . . Birmingham: 1899. Pt. 1. (Extends to 1650 only.) No further parts published.

5714 FLOOD, W.H. GRATTAN. Irish musical bibliography. *Sonderabdruck aus Sammelbande der Internationalen Musikgesellschaft, Jahrg.* 13, *Heft* 3, 1912.

5715 FRAZER, WILLIAM. List of works on Irish music. *N. and Q., ser.* 7, vol. 4, 1887, 510.

5716 SCHOLES, PERCY A., *ed*. Oxford companion to music . . . 10th ed. rev. and reset, edited by John O. Ward. London: 1970.

General

5717 ACTON, CHARLES. The schools and music: reflections on promise. *Eire-Ir.*, vol. 5, no. 1, 1970, 98–110.

5718 BRODY, ELAINE and BROOK, CLIVE. The music guide to Great Britain: England, Scotland, Wales, Ireland. London: 1976.

5719 DAWSON, TIMOTHY. The city music and city bands. *Dublin Hist. Rec.*, vol. 25, no. 3, 1972, 102–116.

5720 KEOGH, HENRY J. Musical perspectives at St. Fin Barre's. *Cork Hist. Arch. Soc. J.*, 71, 1966, 129–137.

5721 MOLLOY, DINAH, *compiler*. Find your music in Dublin and district. Dublin: 1974.

5722 O'LOCHLAINN, COLM. Authority in Irish music. *Ceol*, vol. 1, no. 2, 1963, 18–22.

5723 TRAVIS, JAMES. Beethoven's Irish symphony. *Eire-Ir.*, vol. 7, no. 4, 1972, 103–107.

5724 — Miscellanea musica Celtica. New York: Institute of Mediaeval Music, 1968.

Catalogues

5725 AN GUM. Catalogue of music. Baile Atha Cliath. [1944.]

5726 MUSIC ASSOCIATION OF IRELAND. George Frideric Handel, 1685–1759 [catalogue of the Handel exhibition at the Civic Museum, Dublin]. Dublin: 1959. Includes note of works printed in Dublin.

5727 SQUIRE, W. BARCLAY. Catalogue of printed music published between 1487 and 1800 now in the British Museum. London: 1912.

5728 — Second supplement . . . by W.C. Smith. London: 1940. First supplement forms part of the main work.

Collections

5729 BUNTING, EDWARD. The ancient music of Ireland: an edition comprising the three collections by Edward Bunting, originally published in 1796, 1809, and 1840. Dublin: 1969.

5730 CASAIDE, SEAMUS UA. The Farmer and O'Reilly collection of Irish music. *Ir. Book Lov.*, 28, 1941–2, 62–6.

5731 FLOOD, W.H. GRATTAN. *Aria di Camera*: oldest printed collection of Irish music, 1727. *Bibliog. Soc. Ir.*,2, 1921–5, 97–101.

5732 O'DONOGHUE, DAVID JAMES. Feis Ceoil, 1899: catalogue of the musical loan exhibition held in the National Library and National Museum, Dublin, May 1899. Dublin: 1899. A nearly complete bibliography of collections of Irish music.

5733 O'SULLIVAN, DONAL J. *ed.* The Bunting collection of Irish folk music and songs. Pts. 1–5. *Ir. Folk Song Soc. J.*, vol. 22–7, 1927–36. Vol. 22. General list of works referred to in the notes to the songs, pp. xxix–xxxiii; bibliography of Bunting's printed collections, by Seamus O'Casaide, pp. xxxv–xxxvii.

5734 PETRIE, G. *ed.* The Petrie collection of the ancient music of Ireland. Dublin: 1855. Words and melodies of some 300 Irish traditional airs, arranged for the piano and fully annotated with background material.

History

5735 BOYDELL, BRIAN. Venues for music in 18th century Dublin. *Dublin Hist. Rec.*, vol. 29, no. 1, 1975, 28–34.

5736 CALDER, GRACE J. George Petrie and the ancient music of Ireland. Dublin: Dolmen Press: 1968.

5737 FLEISCHMANN, ALOYS, *ed.* Music in Ireland: a symposium. Cork and Oxford: 1952. Contents include: Musical instrument collections in the National Museum of Ireland, by L.S. Gogan, pp. 299–307; Musical collection of the Irish Folklore Commission, by Sean O'Suilleabhain, pp. 308–9; Musical collection in the library of Trinity College, by G.H.P. Hewson, pp. 310–11; Music in the National Library of Ireland, by Donal O'Sullivan, pp. 312–15; The Plunkett collection of music in the National Library of Ireland, by Eimear O'Broin, pp. 316–18; Manuscript and printed music in Marsh's Library, by Newport B. White, pp. 319–21; manuscript Irish music in the library of the Royal Irish Academy, by Caitlin Bonfield, pp. 322–32; The Music books of the Cashel Diocesan Library, by R. Wyse Jackson, pp. 333–5; The Music libraries of University College. Dublin, University College, Cork, St. Patrick's College, Maynooth, Queen's University Belfast, and the Linen Hall Library, pp. 336–8.

5738 — and GLEESON, RYTA. Music in ancient Munster and monastic Cork. *Cork Hist. Arch. Soc. J.*, 70, 1965, 79–98.

5739 FLOOD, WILLIAM HENRY GRATTAN. A history of Irish music [3rd ed. reprinted]; introduction by Seoirse Bodley. Shannon: 1970. Bibliog., pp. 337–340.

5740 GROOCOCK, JOSEPH. A general survey of music in the Republic of Ireland. Dublin: 1961.

5741 HOGAN, ITA MARGARET. Anglo-Irish music, 1780–1830. Cork: 1966. Biographies (principal Anglo-Irish composers, foreign composers resident in Ireland, lesser known Anglo-Irish and foreign musicians, and visiting musicians), pp. 165–235; bibliog., pp. 236–242.

5742 JONES, PERCY. A survey of the music of Ireland. *Ir. Eccles. Rec.*, 87, 1957, 170–178, 252–259, 355–360.

5743 MURRAY, CELINE, and FINNERTY, BERNADETTE. Traditional Irish music in County Westmeath. [Mullingar: 1963]. Reprinted from the *Westmeath Examiner*, May–June, 1963.

Biography

General

5744 ACTON, CHARLES. Modern Irish musicians. *Ir. Today*, 888, 1976, 4–6.

5745 BROWN, JAMES D. Biographical dictionary of musicians, with a bibliography of English writings on music. Paisley and London: 1886.

5746 CONLON, J.F. Some Irish poets and musicians. Cork: 1974.

5747 DEALE, EDGAR M. *ed*. A catalogue of contemporary Irish composers. 2nd ed., Dublin: Musical Association of Ireland, 1975.

5748 FEEHAN, FANNY. Living Irish composers. *Ir. Today*, 886, 1976, 6–8.

5749 O'LOCHLAINN, COLM. Anglo-Irish songwriters since Moore. *Bibliog. Soc. Ir.,* vol.6, no. 1, 1960.

5750 O'NEILL, THOMAS. Irish minstrels and musicians, with numerous dissertations on related subjects. [1st ed. reprinted], Wakefield: 1973. 1st pub. Chicago: 1913.

Individual

BALFE, MICHAEL WILLIAM.

5751 BRUNSKILL, H.O. Michael William Balfe. *Dublin Hist. Rec*., 16, 1960–61, 58–64.

BODLEY, SEOIRSE.

5752 ACTON, CHARLES. Interview with Seoirse Bodley. *Eire-Ir*., vol. 5, no. 3, 1970, 117–133.

BOYDELL, BRIAN.

5753 ACTON, CHARLES. Interview with Brian Boydell. *Eire-Ir*., vol. 5, no. 4,1970, 97–111.

BOYLE, INA.

5754 MACONCHY, ELIZABETH. Ina Boyle: an appreciation with a select list of her music. Dublin: Dolmen Press, 1974. Edition limited to 300 copies.

CAROLAN, TURLOUGH.

5755 O'SULLIVAN, DONAL J. Carolan: the life, times and music of an Irish harper. London: 1958. 2 vols. Vol. 1, pp. 125–35, The sources of the tunes; pp. 141–2, The sources of the poems. Vol. 2, pp. 3–4, Conspectus of authorities.

5756 YEATS, GRAINNE. Turlough Carolan, Ireland's national composer. *Arts Ir*., vol. 1, no. 4, 1973, 54–58.

COGAN, PHILIP.

5757 GUNN, DOUGLAS. Philip Cogan (1748–1833). *Counterpoint, Feb*. 1971, 7–8, 14. Cork composer.

FIELD, JOHN.

5758 BOWLES, MICHAEL. John Field, 1782–1837. *Cap. Ann*., 1971, 149–154.

5759 BRANSON, DAVID. John Field and Chopin. London: 1972. List of Field's works, pp. 199–202; bibliog., p.203.

5760 HOPKINSON, CECIL. A bibliographical thematic catalogue of the works of John Field, 1782–1837. London: 1961.

5761 KELLY, MAIRE. John Field. *Studies*, 33, 1944, 516–526.

5762 PIGGOTT, PATRICK. The life and music of John Field, 1782–1837: creator of the nocturne. London: 1973. Bibliog., pp. 271–275.

5763 TEMPERLEY, NICHOLAS. John Field and the first nocturne. *Mus. Lett*., vol. 56, nos. 3–4, 1975, 335–340.

5764 TYSON, ALAN. John Field's earliest compositions. *Mus. Lett*., vol. 47, 1966, 239–48.

FLOOD, WILLIAM HENRY GRATTAN.

5765 FLOOD, WILLIAM GRATTAN. Renowned Irish musicologist. *Cap. Ann*., 1974, 56–62.

FRENCH, PERCY.

5766 HEALY, JAMES N. Percy French and his songs. Cork and London: 1966.

GILMORE, PATRICK SARSFIELD.

5767 FAHY, JAMES. Patrick Sarsfield Gilmore. *Cap. Ann*., 1974, 265–9.

HADLEY, PATRICK.

5768 PALMER, CHRISTOPHER. Patrick Hadley – the man and his music. *Mus. Lett*., 55, 1974, 151–66.

HANDEL, GEORGE FRIDERIC.

5769 FRASER, *Mrs.* A.M. Handel in Dublin. *Dublin Hist. Rec*., 13, 1952–54, 72–8.

5770 TOBIN, JOHN. Handel at work. London: 1964. An examination of the manuscripts of Handel's *Messiah* including the Dublin score.

MCCORMACK, JOHN.

5771 FOXALL, RAYMOND. John McCormack. London: 1963.

MAY, FREDERICK.

5772 S., T.O. Spring nocturne: a profile of Frederick May. *Counterpoint*, Nov. 1970, 14–18.

O'MARA, JOSEPH.

5773 POTTERTON, ROBERT. Joseph O'Mara – famous tenor and actor. *Counterpoint,* Sept., 1972, 10–12.

O'RIADA, SEAN.

5774 ACTON, CHARLES. Interview with Sean O'Riada. *Eire-Ir.*, vol. 6, no. 1, 1971, 106–15.

5775 — Sean O'Riada – an introduction. *Atlantis*, 3, 1971, 10–17.

5776 BODLEY, SEOIRSE. Remembering Sean Ó Riada. *Cap. Ann.*, 1972, 302–304.

PIERSE, NICHOLAS DALL.

5777 PIERSE, JOHN H. Nicholas Dall Pierse of Co. Kerry, harper. *Kerry Arch. Hist. Soc. J.*, 6, 1973, 40–75.

POTTER, A.J.

5778 ACTON, CHARLES. Interview with A.J. Potter. *Eire-Ir.*, vol. 5, no. 2, 1970, 115–40.

STANFORD, CHARLES VILLIERS.

5779 HUDSON, FREDERICK. C.V. Stanford: nova bibliographica. *Mus. Times*, 104, 1963, 728–31; 105, 1964, 734–38; 108, 1967, 326.

STEWART, *Sir* ROBERT.

5780 CULWICK, J.C. The works of Sir Robert Stewart ... catalogue of his musical compositions, such as have been performed, printed, or are still in manuscript; together with a list of his principal literary works. Dublin: 1902.

TROY, DERMOT.

5781 DALBERG, FREDERICK, *and others*. In tribute to Dermot Troy, 1927–1962, by Frederick Dalberg, Mattiwilda Dobbs, Gerald J. Duffy, Veronica Dunne, Heinz Hoppe, Prof. Anthony G. Hughes, James Johnston, Prof. John F. Larchet, Prof. Michael O'Higgins, Ernest Poettgen and Thomas Tipton. *Cap. Ann.*, 1964, 171–202.

WOODWARD, RICHARD.

5782 GUNN, DOUGLAS. Richard Woodward, 1743–1777. *Counterpoint*, May 1970, 14–17.

Music and Publishing

5783 DIX, E.R. MCCLINTOCK. Some Dublin music printers and sellers of the eighteenth century. *Ir. Book Lov.*, 18, 1930, 26–28.

5784 DUIGNAN, LASAIRIONA. A checklist of the publications of John and William Neale. *Ir. Booklore*, vol. 2, no. 2, 1976, 231–237.

5785 FLOOD, W.H. GRATTAN. Dublin music printing from 1685 to 1750. *Bibliog. Soc. Ir.*, vol. 2, no. 1, 1921, 7–12.

5786 — Dublin music printing from 1750 to 1790. *ibid.*, vol. 2, no. 5, 1923, 101–6.

5787 — John and William Neale, music printers, 1721–41. *ibid.*, vol. 3, 1926–9, 85–9.

5788 — Music printing in Dublin from 1700 to 1750. *R. Soc. Antiq. Ir. J.*, 38, 1908, 236–40.

5789 HUMPHRIES, CHARLES and SMITH, WILLIAM C. Music publishing in the British Isles from the earliest times to the middle of the nineteenth century: a dictionary of engravers, printers, publishers and music sellers, with a historical introduction. London: 1954.

5790 KIDSON, FRANK. British music publishers, printers and engravers, with bibliographical lists of musical works published. London: 1900. Includes list of Dublin musical publications for period 1736–1836.

Kinds of Music

5791 ENGEL, CARL. The literature of national music. London: 1879. Reprinted from *The Musical Times*, July 1878 – March 1879.

Opera

5792 LOEWENBERG, ALFRED. Annals of opera 1597–1940. 3rd ed. rev. and corrected. London: 1978. 1st ed. Cambridge: 1943. Under each opera gives details and dates of first performances, etc.

5793 MCASEY, CARMEL C. Dubliners and opera. *Dublin Hist. Rec.*, vol. 23, nos. 2–3, 1969, 45–55.

5794 WALSH, T.J. Opera in Dublin, 1705–1797: the social scene. Dublin: 1973. Bibliog., pp. 365–369. Appendix C. A list of first performances of the more important operas, masques and stage oratorios produced in Dublin between 1705 and 1797. Appendix D. Classified list of performances of Italian and French opera given in Dublin between 1761 and 1789.

Church Music

5795 BUMPUS, JOHN S. Irish church composers and the Irish cathedrals. *Mus. Assoc. Proc., 26th session*, 1899–1900, 79–113, 115–59.

Vocal Music, Folk Song

5796 COLUM, PADRAIC. Broadsheet ballads, being a collection of popular songs. Dublin: 1913.

5797 DIX, E.R. MCCLINTOCK. Galway song books. *Galway Arch. Hist. Soc. J.*, 4, 1905–6, 178–9.

5798 — Irish chap books, song books and ballads. *Ir. Book Lov.*, 2, 1910–11, 33–5.

5799 — Irish song books in the Royal Irish Academy. *Ir. Book Lov.*, 2, 1910–11, 81–3.

5800 FRENCH, [WILLIAM] PERCY. Prose, poems and parodies, edited by Mrs. de Burgh Daly. Dublin: 1925.

5801 — Chronicles and poems of Percy French; edited by his sister, Mrs. de Burgh Daly. Dublin: 1922.

5802 IRISH FOLK MUSIC STUDIES. Dublin: Folk Music Society of Ireland. vol. 1–, 1972–73–.

5803 KENNEDY, PETER, *ed.* Folksong of Britain and Ireland. London: 1975. Bibliog., pp. 804–8.

5804 MCCANCE, STOUPPE. Some Ulster song books. *Ir. Book Lov.*, 7, 1915–16, 108–10.

5805 MOORE, THOMAS. The sources of Moore's melodies; by Veronica ni Chinneide. *R. Soc. Antiq. Ir.J.*, 89, 1959, 109–34.

5806 O'DUIBHGINN, SEOSAMH. Donall Og: taighde ar an amhran. Baile Atha Cliath: 1960. Bibliog., pp. 132–4.

5807 O'LOCHLAINN, COLM. Irish street ballads, collected and annotated by Colm O'Lochlainn, and adorned with woodcuts from the original broadsheets. Dublin: 1939. Other editions, Dublin, 1946; New York, Citadel Press, 1960.

5808 — More Irish street ballads. Dublin: 1965.

5809 — Songwriters of Ireland in the English tongue. Dublin: 1967.

5810 O'NEILL, FRANCIS. Irish folk music: a fascinating hobby, with some account of allied subjects including O'Farrell's Treatise on the Irish or Union pipes, and Touhey's Hints to amateur pipers. [1st ed. reprinted], with a new introduction by Barry O'Neill. Wakefield: 1973. Facsimile reprint of 1st ed., Chicago: 1910. List of O'Neill's works on Irish music in Introduction.

5811 — Irish minstrels and musicians with numerous dissertations on related subjects. [1st ed. reprinted], with a new introduction by Barry O'Neill. Wakefield: 1973. Facsimile reprint of 1st ed., Chicago: 1913.

5812 O'SULLIVAN, DONAL J. Dublin slang songs, with music. *Dublin Hist. Rec.*, 1, 1938–39, 75–93.

5813 — Irish folk music and song. Dublin: 1952. (*Irish life and culture series*.) Bibliog., pp. 61–2.

5814 — Songs of the Irish: an anthology of Irish folk music and poetry with English verse translation. Dublin: 1960.

5815 ZIMMERMAN, GEORGES-DENIS. Songs of the Irish rebellion: political street ballads and rebel songs, 1780–1900. Dublin: 1967. Bibliog., pp. 321–334.

Dance Music

5816 BREATHNACH, BREANDAN. An Italian origin for the Irish jig. *Bealoideas*, vols. 39–41, 1971–73, 69–78.

5817 TOWNSEND, DECLAN F. The origins and early history of the Irish jig. *Eire-Ir.*, vol. 6, no. 2, 1971, 59–65.

Musical Instruments

5818 ACTON, CHARLES. Rediscovery of the harp tradition. *Eire-Ir.*, vol. 7, no. 4, 1972, 114–132.

5819 ARMSTRONG, ROBERT BRUCE. The Irish and the Highland harps. Introduction by Seoirse Bodley. Shannon: 1969. Facsimile reprint of vol. 1 of 'Musical instruments.'

5820 — Musical instruments. Edinburgh: 1904–8. 2 vols. Vol. 1. The Irish and the Highland harps. Vol. 2. English and Irish instruments. Edition limited to 180 copies.

5821 ASKEW, GILBERT. *compiler*. A bibliography of the bag-pipe. Newcastle-upon-Tyne: Northumbrian Pipers' Society, 1932.

5822 BARTON, E.G. A list of interesting old house organs in the Dublin district with some pertinent details on each. *Dublin Hist. Rec*., vol. 17, no. 2, 1962, 74–76.

5823 BODLEY, SEOIRSE. The Uileann pipes. *Ir. Wel*., vol. 14, no. 1, 1965, 6–9.

5824 CHRIST CHURCH CATHEDRAL, DUBLIN. [Specification of organ]. *Organ*, 5, 1925–26, 183.

5825 CLUTTON, CECIL. Two organs in Ulster [Down Cathedral and the Ulster Hall, Belfast]. *Organ*, 37, 1957–58, 15–23.

5826 DUNLEATH, LORD, and CLUTTON, CECIL. The rebuilt organ at Down Cathedral. *Organ*, 46, 1966–67, 165–172.

5827 GALLAGHER, E.W. The organ at Galway Cathedral. *Organ*, 46, 1966–67, 147–154.

5828 HOLMES, JOHN. The Trinity College organs in the seventeenth and eighteenth centuries, with particular reference to the legend of the 'Spanish' organ. *Hermathena*, 113, 1972, 40–48.

5829 MCCLELLAND, AIKEN. The Irish Harp Society [1808–1840]. *Ulster Folk*., 21, 1975, 15–24.

5830 MCGOOGAN, A. Thomas Perry: an eighteenth century Irish musical instrument maker. *Mus. Bull*., vol. 1, no. 3, 1911, 11–14.

5831 O'KELLY, FACHTNA. The harpsichord-maker [Cathal Gannon]. *Ir. Wel*., vol., 21, no. 6, 1973, 21–22.

5832 OXFORD UNIVERSITY, Pitt Rivers Museum. Bagpipes; by Anthony Baines. Oxford: 1960. (*Occasional papers on technology,* no. 9.) Bibliog., pp. 132–3.

5833 POPE, R.A.D. Organs of St. Patrick's Cathedral, Dublin. *Organ*, 15, 1935–36, 201–208. Includes list of organists for period 1509–1920.

5834 RIMMER, JOAN. The Irish harp. Cork: 1969. (*Irish life and culture ser. no*. 16) Index of extant Irish harps, pp. 75–78.

5835 STANTON, G.R. The Armstrong Collection of Musical Instruments. *Mus. Bull*., 4, 1914, 43–46.

5836 TIGHE, JOAN. Thomas Perry [musical instrument maker] of Anglesea Street, Dublin. *Dublin Hist. Rec*., vol. 18, no. 1, 1962, 24–31.

Recordings

5837 ACTON, CHARLES. A review of phonograph records of Irish interest. *Eire-Ir*., vol. 3, no. 3, 1968, 113–156.

5838 ROE, L.F. MACDERMOTT. The John McCormack discography. Lingfield: 1972.

5839 SHIELDS, HUGH, and SHIELDS, LISA. Irish folk-song recordings, 1966–1972: an index of tapes in the Ulster Folk and Transport Museum. *Ulster Folk*., 21, 1975, 25–54.

RECREATIONAL AND PERFORMING ARTS

Broadcasting, Television

5840 ADMINISTRATION, vol. 15, no. 3, 1967. Radio Telefis Eireann.

5841 BYRNE, GAY. To whom it concerns: ten years of the Late Late Show. Dublin: 1972.

5842 DOWLING, JACK, *and others*. Sit down and be counted: the cultural evolution of a television station, by Jack Dowling, Lelia Doolan and Bob Quinn. Dublin: 1969.

5843 FISHER, DESMOND. Broadcasting in Ireland. London: 1978. Bibliog., pp. 119–120.

5844 FORECAST, K.G. Radio Eireann listeners research inquiries, 1953–5. *Stat. Social Inq. Soc. Ir. J*., 19, 1955–6, 1–28.

5845 GORHAM, MAURICE. Forty years of Irish broadcasting. Dublin: 1967.

5846 IRISH BROADCASTING REVIEW. Dublin: Radio Telefis Eireann. no. 1–, 1978–.

5847 McREDMOND, LOUIS, *ed*. Written on the wind: personal memories of Irish radio, 1926–76. Dublin: 1976.

5848 RADIO TELEFIS EIREANN. RTE handbook, 1978, and Annual report for 1977. Dublin: 1978. Published annually.

Cinema

5849 IRISH CINEMA HANDBOOK. Dublin: 1943.

5850 O CONLUAIN, PROINSIAS. Sceal na scannan. Baile Atha Cliath: 1953. Bibliog., pp. 223–8; books on the films available in Dublin public libraries, pp. 229–34; 35-mm. sound films made in Ireland, pp. 234–44; documentaries made in Ireland, pp. 245–54; historical films in the National Library, Dublin, pp. 255–60.

Theatre

(See also Drama, nos. 6183–6271)

5851 BAKER, D.E. The Companion to the playhouse; or, an historical account of all the dramatic writers (and their works) that have appeared in Great Britain and Ireland from the commencement of our theatrical exhibitions to the present year 1764. London: 1764. 2 vols.

5852 — [Another edition]; edited by Isaac Reed [as *Biographia Dramatica*]. London: 1782. 2 vols.

5853 — [Another edition], edited by Stephen Jones [as *Biographica Dramatica*]. London: 1812–13. 3 vols. in 4.

5854 BELL, SAM HANNA. The theatre in Ulster: a survey of the dramatic movement in Ulster from 1902 until the present day. Dublin, 1972. Appendix 1. First productions of the Ulster Literary Theatre. Appendix 2. First productions of the Ulster Group Theatre. Appendix 3. Lyric Players Theatre productions.

5855 BOURGEOIS, MAURICE. John Millington Synge and the Irish theatre [1st ed. reprinted], New York: 1965. Originally published London: 1913; bibliog., pp. 251–304.

5856 BRITISH DRAMA LEAGUE. The Players library and bibliography of the theatre, compiled by Violet Kent. London: 1930.

5857 — The Players library: the catalogue of the British Drama League. London: 1950. Supplements: no. 1, 1951; no. 2, 1954; no. 3, 1956.

5858 CHETWOOD, WILLIAM RUFUS. A general history of the stage; (more particularly the Irish theatre) . . . with the memoirs of most of the principal performers, that have appeared on the Dublin stage for the past fifty years. Dublin: 1749.

5859 CLARENCE, REGINALD, *compiler*. The Stage cyclopaedia: a bibliography of plays. An alphabetical list of plays and other stage pieces of which any record can be found since the commencement of the English stage, together with descriptions, authors' names, dates and places of production, and other useful information, comprising in all nearly 50,000 plays and extending over a period of upwards of 500 years. London: 1909.

5860 CLARK, WILLIAM SMITH. The early Irish stage: the beginnings to 1720. Oxford: 1955. Bibliog., pp. 210–17.

5861 — The Irish stage in the county towns, 1720 to 1800. Oxford: 1965. Bibliog., pp. 379–388. Appendix A. Plays acted in Ireland outside Dublin, 1720–1800. Appendix B. Actors and actresses in Ireland outside Dublin: 1720–1800.

5862 COURTNEY, MARIE-THERESE. Edward Martyn and the Irish theatre. New York: 1956. Bibliog., pp. 172–88.

5863 CRONIN, JOHN. Macready, Griffin and the tragedy *Gisippus*. *Eire-Ir*., vol. 11, no. 1, 1976, 34–44. William Charles Macready, actor-manager, and Gerald Griffin, author of *Gisippus*.

5864 DE BURCA, SEAMUS. The Queen's Royal Theatre, 1829–1966. *Dublin Hist. Rec*., vol. 27, no. 1, 1973, 10–26.

5865 FALLON, GABRIEL. Some aspects of Irish theatre. *Studies*, 36, 1947, 296–306.

5866 FAUGHNAN, LESLIE. The future of the Abbey Theatre: towards a new dynamic. *Studies*, 55, 1966, 236–246.

5867 FAY, FRANK J. Towards a national theatre: the dramatic criticism of Frank J. Fay, edited and with an introduction by Robert Hogan. Dublin: 1970. (*Irish theatre series, no*. 1)

5868 FAY, GERARD. The Abbey Theatre: cradle of genius. Dublin: 1958. Bibliog., p. 153; list of plays [1899–1958], pp. 161–86.

5869 FERRAR, HAROLD. Robert Emmet in Irish drama. *Eire-Ir.*, vol. 1, no. 2, 1966, 19–28.

5870 FLANNERY, JAMES W. Miss Annie F. Horniman and the Abbey Theatre. Dublin: 1970. (*Irish theatre series, no.* 3)

5871 — W.B. Yeats and the idea of a theatre: the early Abbey Theatre in theory and practice. New Haven and London: 1976. Bibliog., pp. 378–398.

5872 FRENCH, FRANCES-JANE. The Abbey Theatre series of plays: a bibliography. Dublin: 1969.

5873 GAILEY, ALAN. The folk-play in Ireland. *Stud. Hib.*, 6, 1966, 113–154.

5874 GATE THEATRE, DUBLIN. List of productions, 1928–58. In *Mantle of Harlequin*, by Hilton Edwards. Dublin: 1958, pp. ix–xii.

5875 GREGORY, *Lady*. Our Irish theatre: a chapter of autobiography. With a foreword by Roger McHugh. 3rd ed. rev. and enl. Gerrards Cross: 1972. 1st published New York and London: 1913.

5876 HOBSON, BULMER, *ed.* The Gate Theatre, Dublin. Dublin: 1934. Limited edition of 650 copies.

5877 HOGAN, ROBERT, and KILROY, JAMES. The modern Irish drama: a documentary history. Dublin: Dolmen Press. Vol. 1. The Irish literary theatre, 1899–1901. 1975. Vol. 2. Laying the foundations, 1902–04. 1976. Vol. 3. The Abbey Theatre: the years of Synge. 1978.

5878 — and O'NEILL, MICHAEL J. An introduction to Joseph Holloway. *Dubliner*, vol. 3, no. 4, 1964, 6–16. Description of Holloway's manuscript *Impressions of a Dublin Playgoer*, which comprises 221 volumes and is in the National Library.

5879 — and O'NEILL, MICHAEL J. *ed.* Joseph Holloway's Abbey Theatre: a selection from his unpublished journal *Impressions of a Dublin Playgoer*. London: 1967.

5880 KAVANAGH, PETER. The Irish theatre; being a history of the drama in Ireland from the earliest period up to the present day. Tralee: 1946. Bibliog., pp. 443–65.

5881 — The story of the Abbey Theatre from its origins in 1899 to the present. New York: 1950. Bibliog., pp. 225–8.

5882 LOEWENBERG, ALFRED. The theatre of the British Isles, excluding London: a bibliography. London, Society for Theatrical Research: 1950.

5883 LOWE, ROBERT W. A bibliographical account of English theatrical literature from the earliest times to the present day. London: 1888. Limited edition of 500 copies.

5884 MACANNA, TOMAS. Ernest Blythe and the Abbey. *Threshold*, 26, 1975, 100–105.

5885 MACLIAMMOIR, MICHAEL. Dramatic accidents: the Irish theatre in the twentieth century. *In* Theatre 72, edited by Sheridan Morley. London: 1972, pp. 37–49.

5886 — Theatre in Ireland. 2nd ed., Dublin: 1964.

5887 MACNAMARA, BRINSLEY. Abbey plays, 1899–1948, including the productions of the Irish Literary Theatre, with a commentary . . . and an index of playwrights. Dublin: 1949.

5888 MALONE, ANDREW E. The plays of Lady Gregory. *Studies*, 13, 1924, 247–258.

5889 MANDER, RAYMOND, and MITCHENSON, JOE. Theatrical companion to Shaw: a pictorial record of the first performances of the plays of George Bernard Shaw. London: 1954. Includes lists of characters and casts.

5890 MEISEL, MARTIN. Shaw and the nineteenth-century theater. Princeton and London: 1963. Bibliog., pp. 451–460.

5891 MILLER, LIAM. Eden and after: the Irish theatre, 1945–1966. *Studies*, 55, 1966, 231–235.

5892 O'BRIEN, BRENDAN. Early days of garrison theatre in Athlone. *Old Athlone Soc. J.*, vol. 1, no. 4, 1974–5, 275–280.

5893 O'DRISCOLL, ROBERT, *ed.* Theatre and nationalism in twentieth-century Ireland. London: 1971.

5894 O'HEGARTY, P.S. The Abbey Theatre (Wolfhound) series of plays. *Dublin Mag.*, *new series.*, vol. 22, no. 2, 1947, 41–2.

5895 O'MAHONEY, MATHEW. Play guide for Irish amateurs. Dublin: 1946.

5896 — Progress guide to Anglo-Irish plays. Dublin: 1960.

5897 O'NEILL, J.J. A bibliographical account of Irish theatrical literature: Pt. 1. General history, players and theatrical periodicals. *Bibliog. Soc. Ir.*, vol. 1, no. 6, 1920. No further parts published.

5898 — Irish theatrical history: a bibliographical essay. *An Leab.*, vol. 2, no. 2, 1907, 115–22.

5899 PAGE, SEAN. The Abbey Theatre. *Dublin Mag.*, vol. 5, nos. 3–4, 1966, 6–14.

5900 PINTER, HAROLD. Mac [Anew McMaster]. London: 1968.

5901 ROBINSON, LENNOX, *ed*. The Irish theatre: lectures delivered during the Abbey Theatre Festival held in Dublin in August 1938. London: 1939. Bibliog., pp. xi–xiii.

5902 ROWELL, GEORGE. The Victorian theatre: a survey. London: 1956. A bibliography of the English theatre, 1792–1914, pp. 159–89.

5903 SCHULL, REBECCA. Dublin Focus Theatre. *Arts Ir.*, vol. 3, no. 1, 1975, 50–56.

5904 SETTERQUIST, JAN. Ibsen and the beginnings of Anglo-Irish drama: no. 2. Edward Martyn. Upsala, 1960. (*Upsala Irish studies*, no. 5.) Bibliog., pp. 102–9.

5905 SHELDON, ESTHER K. Thomas Sheridan of Smock-Alley, recording his life as actor and theater manager in both Dublin and London; and including a Smock-Alley calendar for the years of his management. Princeton: 1967. Bibliog., pp. 479–491.

5906 STOCKWELL, LA TOURETTE. Dublin theatres and theatre customs (1637–1820). [1st ed. reprinted]. New York and London: 1968. First published Kingsport, Tennessee, 1938; bibliog., pp. 379–397.

5907 TOWNLEY, C. Galway's early association with the theatre. *Galway Reader*, vol. 4, no. 1, 1953, 62–70.

5908 WATTERS, EUGENE and MURTAGH, MATTHEW. Infinite variety: Dan Lowrey's Music Hall, 1879–97. Dublin: 1975.

5909 YOUNG, DEREK. Stagecast: Irish stage and screen directory, 1970. 8th ed., Dublin: 1971.

Mumming

5910 GLASSIE, HENRY. All silver and no brass: an Irish Christmas mumming. Dublin: 1976. Bibliog., pp. 162–169.

Dancing

5911 O'RAFFERTY, PEADAR and O'RAFFERTY, GERALD. Dances of Ireland. London: 1953. (*Handbooks of European national dances series*.) Bibliog., p. 40.

OUTDOOR SPORTS AND GAMES

5912 ARMITAGE, THOMAS. A bibliography of the national games: hurling, football, handball and camoguidheacht. [1956] Typescript. Presented as a thesis for Fellowship of the Library Association of Ireland.

5913 NATIONAL LIBRARY OF IRELAND. Books on Ireland. Dublin: 1953. Description (including topography), travel and sport, pp. 9–13.

Handball

5914 McELLIGOTT, T.J. Handball – a game for idle hands? *Ir. Wel.*, vol. 20, no. 2, 1971, 6–10.

Rugby

5915 COGLEY, FRED. Yearbook of Irish rugby. Dublin: 1970.

5916 DUBLIN UNIVERSITY. Dublin University Football Club, 1866–1972. Dublin: 1973. A photographic record.

5917 NOLAN, BARRY S. *compiler*. Ireland's golden rugby years. Dublin: [1953].

5918 REDMOND, GARRY, *ed*. Lansdowne Football Club centenary, 1872–1972: a club history. Dublin: 1972.

5919 THOMAS, J.B.G. Great rugger clubs. London: 1962. Ireland, pp. 124–56.

5920 VAN ESBECK, EDMUND. One hundred years of Irish rugby: the official history of the Irish Rugby Football Union. Dublin: 1974.

Soccer

5921 BRODIE, MALCOLM, and ROSSER, RONALD.

Northern Ireland soccer year book, 1969/70. Belfast [1970].

5922 DUNNE, NOEL, and RYAN, SEAN. The Bass book of Irish soccer. Dublin and Cork: 1975.

Gaelic

5923 BOURKE, MARCUS. The early G.A.A. in south Ulster. *Clogher Rec.*, vol. 7, no. 1, 1969, 5–26.

5924 BLYTHE, EARNAN P. The first decade of the G.A.A. in Dublin. *Dublin Hist. Rec.*, vol. 19, no. 1, 1963, 16–26.

5925 — Cold war in the Dublin G.A.A., 1887. *Dublin Hist. Rec.*, vol. 22, no. 3, 1968, 252–262.

5926 GAELIC ATHLETIC ASSOCIATION. Sixty glorious years of the G.A.A. Dublin: 1947.

5927 GUINEY, DAVID. Book of Gaelic football. Dublin: 1976.

5928 MACLUA, BRENDAN. The steadfast rule: a history of the G.A.A. ban. Dublin: 1967.

5929 O'HEHIR, MICHAEL. World of Gaelic games. Dublin: 1974.

5930 O'SUILLEABHAIN, EAMON N.M. The art and science of Gaelic football. Tralee: 1958.

Tennis

5931 O'CONNOR, ULICK. The Fitzwilliam story, 1877–1977. [Dublin, 1977]. Includes results of lawn tennis championships of Ireland, 1879 to date, also chapter on squash rackets.

5932 SHERIDAN, PETER, *ed*. Irish tennis yearbook '76. Dublin: Irish Lawn Tennis Association: 1976.

Golf

5933 GUINEY, DAVID. The Dunlop book of golf. Dublin: 1973.

5934 HOUGHTON, GEORGE. Golf addict among the Irish. London: 1965.

5935 IRISH GOLF. Dublin, vol. 1–, 1923–.

5936 MURRAY, J.P. *ed*. Golfing in Ireland, 1952. Dublin: 1953. vol. 2, 1953.

5937 — and GIBB, EILEEN. A challenge from Ireland. *Golf Monthly*, vol. 60, no. 1, 1970, 43–50. A guide to Irish golf courses.

5938 RUDDY, PAT. *ed*. Golf 77: the encyclopaedia for Irish golfers. Dublin: 1976.

Hockey

5939 DAGG, T.S.C. Hockey in Ireland. Tralee: 1944. Includes chapter on hurling and hurley.

5940 IRISH HOCKEY RECORDS to 1933–4: facts and figures of the game in Ireland. Skibbereen [1934].

Hurling

5941 O'MAOLFABHAIL, ART. Caman: two thousand years of hurling in Ireland; an attempt to trace the history and development of the stick-and-ball game in Ireland . . . Dundalk: 1973.

5942 SMITH, RAYMOND. Decades of glory: a comprehensive history of the national game. Dublin: 1966.

5943 — Players No. 6 book of Hurling: a popular history of the national game (1884–1974). Dublin: 1974.

Cricket

5944 HONE, W.P. Cricket in Ireland. Tralee [1955]. Statistics, pp. 182–7.

Athletics

5945 POZZOLI, PETER R. Irish women's athletics. Enfield (London): Women's Track and Field World: 1977. A verbal, pictorial and statistical record.

Mountaineering

5946 COLEMAN, J.C. The mountains of Killarney. Dundalk: 1948. Reprinted 1975.

5947 DOCHARTY, WILLIAM MCKNIGHT. Supplement to A selection of some 900 British and Irish mountain tops and A selection of 100 tops under 2500 feet. Edinburgh: The Darien Press, 1962. 2 vols. Original vol. published in 1954.

5948 IRISH MOUNTAINEERING: journal of the

Irish Mountaineering Club. Dublin: vol.1–, 1950–.

5949 MALONE, J.B. Walking in Wicklow: a guide for travellers (afoot and awheel) through the Wicklow mountains. Dublin: 1964.

5950 PYATT, EDWARD C. Where to climb in the British Isles. London: 1960. Ireland [with bibliog.], pp. 265–87.

5951 WALL, C.W. Mountaineering in Ireland, with an introduction by R. Lloyd Praeger. Revised by Joss Lynam, and including a list of the mountains attaining an altitude of 2,000 feet or over. Dublin: 1976. First published 1939. Bibliog., pp. 83–4.

Motoring

5952 IRISH MOTORIST HANDBOOK; 4th ed. compiled, edited and revised by R. Johnston. Dublin [1960].

5953 LARGE, W.H. British kings of speed in Ireland: a 70th anniversary remembered. *Country Life*, vol. 154, no. 3982, 1973, 1148–9. On the Gordon Bennett Trophy Race run in 1903.

5954 LUCEY, DAVID. The Silver Stream [first motor car assembled in Ireland]. *Kildare Arch. Soc. J.*, vol.15, no. 5, 1975–6, 472, 504.

5955 TRENT, CHRISTOPHER. Motoring on Irish byways: a practical guide for wayfarers. London: 1965.

Boxing

5956 MYLER, PATRICK. Regency rogue: Dan Donnelly, his life and legends. Dublin: 1976. Bibliog., pp. 160–1.

Sailing, Yachting

5957 BORD FAILTE EIREANN. Pilot book of the River Shannon. Dublin: 1955.

5958 CLARK, WALLACE. Sailing round Ireland. London: 1976. Bibliog., p. 176.

5959 IRISH CRUISING CLUB. Sailing directions for the East and North coasts of Ireland. 4th ed., Dublin: 1965.

5960 — Sailing directions for the south and west coasts of Ireland. 3rd ed. Dublin: 1962.

5961 KEMP, ROBERT. Irish sea cruising guide. London: 1976.

5962 MCKNIGHT, HUGH. Europe's most underrated river. *Yacht Boat. Week.*, vol. 46, no. 8, 1972, 8–9. Short account of cruising on the Shannon.

5963 MACNALLY, ERROL F., *ed.* Irish yachting, 1720–1946. Dublin [1946].

5964 RANSOM, P.J.G. Holiday cruising in Ireland: a guide to Irish inland waterways. Newton Abbot: 1971. Bibliog., pp. 145–6.

5965 RICE, HARRY J. Charts of the River Shannon, with navigational details. Athlone: 1955. Reprinted from *Thanks for the memory*.

Greyhound Racing

5966 COMYN, JOHN, *ed.* Trap to line: 50 years of greyhound racing in Ireland, 1927–77. Dublin: 1977.

Horsemanship, Racing

(See also nos. 4352–4365)

5967 GRAHAM, SEAN P. Racing annual. Dublin: 1976/77–. 1976–.

5968 HERBERT, IVOR. Arkle: the story of a champion. London: 1966.

5969 IRISH HORSEMAN'S MAGAZINE. Dublin. vol. 1–, 1965–.

5970 MURDOCH, JOHN. Arkle. *Ir. Wel.*, vol. 15, no. 1, 1966, 7–12.

5971 O'FARRELL, MICHAEL. Horse racing and the Irish horse. *Cap. Ann.*, 1971, 117–127.

5972 RINGROSE, W.A. The [Army] equitation school. *Ir. Def. J.*, 32, 1972, 123–126.

5973 TOWERS-CLARK, PETER, and ROSS, MICHAEL, *eds*. Directory of the turf. [rev. ed.]. Ascot: 1976. Includes details of racing authorities, owners, trainers, jockeys, studs, bloodstock agencies, and racecourses.

5974 WATSON, S.J. Between the flags: a history of Irish steeplechasing. Dublin: 1969. Bibliog., pp. 354–357; appendices include list of stewards of the Irish National Hunt Steeplechase Committee, 1872–1969, winners of the Irish Grand National, 1870–1969, Conyngham Cup, 1865–1964, and Galway Plate, 1869–1969.

Show Jumping

5975 WILLIAMS, DORIAN. Show jumping: the great ones. London: 1970. Seamus Hayes, pp. 75–83; Iris Kellett, pp. 114–5.

5976 WYLIE, W.E. The development of horse jumping at the Royal Dublin Society's shows. 2nd ed. Dublin: 1952. 1st ed., Dublin: 1939.

Fishing

5977 BORD FAILTE EIREANN. The angler's guide to Ireland. 5th ed. Dublin: 1957.

5978 — Brown trout fishing in Ireland. Dublin: 1964.

5979 — Ireland: sea angling guide. Dublin: 1960.

5980 — Salmon and sea trout fishing in Ireland. Dublin: 1960.

5981 COLEMAN, JAMES. A chronological list of books on angling, sport, &c., in Ireland. Paper read before the Bibliographical Society of Ireland, October 27, 1924. Ms. 5 p. in National Library.

5982 GAFFEY, LAURIE. Fresh water fishing in Ireland. Dublin: 1950.

5983 GRIMBLE, AUGUSTUS. The salmon rivers of Ireland. London: Kegan Paul, 1903. Edition limited to 250 copies.

5984 HANNA, THOMAS J. Fly-fishing in Ireland. London: 1933.

5985 MAXTONE–GRAHAM, J.A. Michael Rogan – lord of the flies. *Ir. Wel.*, vol. 20, no. 4, 1971, 20–25.

5986 SINCLAIR, C.E.R. Coarse fishing in Ireland. London: 1949.

Hunting

5987 BOWEN, MURIEL. Irish hunting. Tralee [1955]. List of Masters. pp. 213–22.

5988 FITZPATRICK, B.M. Irish sport and sportsmen. Dublin: 1878. Deals mainly with hunting and gives short account of the various packs.

5989 HIGGINSON, A. HENRY. British and American sporting authors: their writings and biographies. With a bibliography by Sydney R. Smith. Berryville, Virginia: 1949.

5990 IRISH HUNTING YEARBOOK AND WHO'S WHO. 1953/54–. Dublin: 1954–.

5991 LEWIS, COLIN A. Hunting in Ireland: an historical and geographical analysis. London: 1975.

5992 LONGRIGG, ROGER. The history of foxhunting. London: 1975. Chapters 11 and 15 devoted to Ireland.

5993 VESEY-FITZGERALD, BRIAN *ed*. The book of the horse. London: 1946. Bibliography of books on hunting, compiled by A.H. Higginson, pp. 807–49.

5994 WATSON, J.N.P. Ireland's first county hunt: the Kilkenny. *Country Life*, vol. 159, no. 4098, 1976, 130–1.

5995 — The spirit of the Kildare. *ibid*., vol. 152, no. 3937, 1972, 1568–69.

5996 — From Gascony to Limerick: the Scarteen Black and Tans. *ibid*., vol. 154, no. 3991, 1973, 2104–5.

5997 WHITEHEAD, GEORGE KENNETH, *compiler*. The deer stalking grounds of Great Britain and Ireland. London: 1960. Bibliog., pp. 502–7.

Falconry

5998 JOCHER, ERNST C.F. Falcons fly in Ireland. Cork: 1967. Author has set up the Falconry of Ireland, at Clonmel, Co. Tipperary, to provide an opportunity of seeing the birds, and also to revive the art and sport in Ireland.

LITERATURE

Bibliography

5999 ANGLO–IRISH LITERATURE [bibliog]. *New Camb. Bibliog. Eng. Lit.*, 3, 1969, 1885–1948.

6000 ANNUAL BIBLIOGRAPHY OF ENGLISH LANGUAGE AND LITERATURE. Edited for the Modern Humanities Research Association. Cambridge, vol. 1–, 1920–.

6001 BELL, INGLIS F. and BAIRD, DONALD. The

English novel, 1578–1956: a checklist of twentieth-century criticism. London: 1974. Reprint of 1958 edition.

6002 BOYD, ERNEST. Ireland's literary renaissance. New rev. ed. Dublin [reprinted]: 1968. Bibliog., pp. 429–445.

6003 BROWN, STEPHEN J.M. *ed*., A guide to books on Ireland. Pt. I. Prose literature, poetry, music and plays. (Facsimile reprint of 1st ed.) New York: 1970. 1st edition published Dublin 1912.

6004 — Ireland in books, 1945. *Ir. Mon*., April 1946, 137–47.

6005 FARRAR, CLARISSA P., and EVANS, AUSTIN P. Bibliography of English translations from medieval sources. New York and London: 1946.

6006 FISHER, JOHN H. The medieval literature of Western Europe: a review of research, mainly 1930–1960. New York and London: 1966. Medieval Celtic literature, pp. 382–409.

6007 FINNERAN, RICHARD J., *ed*. Anglo-Irish literature: a review of research. New York: 1976. An important work; includes survey of general works, Maria Edgeworth, Lady Morgan, Charles Lever, Gerald Griffin, William Carleton, Standish O'Grady, Maturin, Le Fanu, Somerville and Ross, Thomas Moore, James C. Mangan, Thomas Davis, Francis Mahony (Father Prout), William Allingham, Sir Samuel Ferguson, Dion Boucicault, Oscar Wilde, George Moore, Bernard Shaw, W.B. Yeats, J.M. Synge, James Joyce, Lady Gregory, A.E., Gogarty, James Stephens, O'Casey, and The modern drama.

6008 HARMON, MAURICE. Modern Irish literature, 1800–1967: a reader's guide. Dublin: The Dolmen Press, 1967.

6009 — Select bibliography for the study of Anglo-Irish literature and its backgrounds. Portmarnock: Wolfhound Press, 1977.

6010 HAZLITT, W.C. Handbook to the popular, poetical and dramatic literature of Great Britain, from the invention of printing to the Restoration. London: 1867.

6011 — Collections and notes. 1876.

6012 — Second series of bibliographical collections and notes, 1474–1700. 1882.

6013 —Third series . . . 1887.

6014 — Supplements to the 3rd series. 1889, 1892.

6015 — Bibliographical collections and notes made during the years 1893–1903. 1903.

6016 — A general index to Hazlitt's *Handbook* and to his *Bibliographical collections*, 1867–89, by G.J. Gray. London: 1893.

6017 HUNGARIAN P.E.N. CLUB. Irish literature in Hungarian translation: a bibliography compiled and published for the Golden Jubilee Congress of International P.E.N. held in Dublin in September 1971. Budapest: 1971. Translations from English to Hungarian.

6018 INTERNATIONAL ASSOCIATION FOR THE STUDY OF ANGLO–IRISH LITERATURE. Bibliography Bulletin. *Ir. Univ. Rev*., vol.2, no. 1, 1972, 79–110. This is the first report of the Bibliography Subcommittee of IASAIL which was set up in 1970 and includes literature in Japanese and Arabic and also a comprehensive author index. Is published annually.

6019 KERSNOWSKI, FRANK L. *and others*. A bibliography of modern Irish and Anglo-Irish literature, by F.L. Kersnowski, C.W. Spinks and Laird Loomis. San Antonio (Texas): Texas U.P., 1977. Contains bibliographies of the following: Samuel Beckett, Brendan Behan, Elizabeth Bowen, Shan F. Bullock, Joseph Campbell, Joyce Cary, Austin Clarke, Padraic Colum, Daniel Corkery, Cecil Day Lewis, Denis Devlin, Lord Dunsany, Laurence Durrell, John St. John Greer Ervine, George Fitzmaurice, Oliver St. John Gogarty, Robert Graves, Lady Gregory, F.R. Higgins, Douglas Hyde, Denis Johnston, James Joyce, Patrick Kavanagh, Benedict Kiely, Thomas Kinsella, Mary Lavin, Donagh MacDonagh, Thomas MacDonagh, Michael McLaverty, Louis MacNeice, Ethel Mannin, Edward Martyn, Rutherford Mayne, Ewart Milne, John Montague, Brian Moore, George Moore, Richard Murphy, T.C. Murray, Sean O'Casey, Frank O'Connor, Eimar O'Duffy, Sean O'Faolain, Roibeard O'Farachain, Liam O'Flaherty, Standish James O'Grady, Seamus O'Kelly, Brian O'Nolan, Conal Holmes O'Connell, C. O'Riordan, Patrick Henry Pearse, Lennox

Robinson, W.R. Rodgers, George William Russell, George Bernard Shaw, Somerville and Ross, James Stephens, Francis Stuart, John Millington Synge, Honor Tracy, Katherine Tynan (Hinkson), William Butler Yeats.

6020 LOWNDES, WILLIAM THOMAS. The Bibliographer's manual of English literature, containing an account of rare, curious, and useful books, published in or relating to Great Britain and Ireland, from the invention of printing; with bibliographical and critical notices, collections of rarer articles, and the prices at which they have been sold. New ed., rev., corr., and enl. with an appendix relating to the books of literary and scientific societies, by Henry G. Bohn. With an essay on William T. Lowndes, by Francesco Cordasco and an appreciation by Lowell Kerr. [Facsimile reprint]. Detroit: Gale Research Co., 1967. 8 vols.

6021 NATIONAL BOOK COUNCIL, LONDON. Irish literature in English, 1900–29. 2nd ed. London: 1929. (*Book list*, no.96.)

6022 NEW CAMBRIDGE BIBLIOGRAPHY OF ENGLISH LITERATURE. Vol.1. 600–1600. Edited by George Watson. 1974. Vol.2. 1600–1800. Edited by George Watson. 1971. Vol.3. 1800–1900. Edited by George Watson. 1969. Vol.4. 1900–1950. Edited by I.R. Willison. 1972. Vol.5. Index. Compiled by J.D. Pickles. 1977.

6023 NORTHUP, CLARK SUTHERLAND. A register of the English language and literature. New Haven, Conn.: 1925.

6024 PHILOLOGICAL QUARTERLY. English literature, 1600–1800: a bibliography of modern studies. Vol.1, 1926–38, 1950; Vol.2. 1939–50, 1952; Vol.3. 1951–1956, 1962. In progress.

6025 POWER, JOHN. Bibliotheca Hibernica: a manual of Irish literatori, being a list of all writings by Irishmen, and persons enjoying preferment of office in Ireland, and also of works relating to Ireland, printed in other parts, from the invention of printing to the present time, with biographical notices, bibliographical remarks, critical notes, collations of the rarer articles, to which is prefixed a dissertation on early printing in Ireland. Dublin: 1865.

6026 RAFROIDI, PATRICK. The year's work in Anglo-Irish literature. *Etudes Irlandaises*, no. 4, 1975, 157–211.

6027 ROYAL IRISH ACADEMY: Committee for the study of Anglo-Irish language and literature. Handlist of work in progress. Dublin; no. 1–, 1969–.

6028 SAUL, G.B. Ancient and medieval Irish literature: an introductory bibliography. *New York P.L. Bull.*, 58, 1954, 392–6.

6029 — Introductory bibliography in Anglo-Irish literature. *ibid.*, pp. 429–35.

6030 TANNER, THOMAS. Bibliotheca Britannico-Hibernica; sive de scriptoribus qui in Anglia, Scotia et Hiberniae . . . London: 1748. Valuable work giving account of early English, Irish and Scottish writers with a list of their manuscripts and printed works.

6031 TEMPLEMAN, WILLIAM D., *ed.* Bibliographies of studies in Victorian literature for the thirteen years, 1932–44. Urbana, Illinois: 1945.

6032 TOBIN, JAMES E. Eighteenth century English literature and its cultural background: a bibliography, New York: 1939.

6033 VAN PATTEN, NATHAN. An index to bibliographies and bibliographical contributions relating to the work of American and British authors, 1923–1932. [Facsimile reprint of 1934 ed.]. New York: 1969.

6034 WRIGHT, AUSTIN, *ed.* Bibliographies of studies in Victorian literature for the ten years 1945–1954. Urbana: 1956.

6035 YEAR'S WORK IN ENGLISH STUDIES. London: The English Association, vol. 1–, 1919–.

Biographical Dictionaries

6036 ALLIBONE, S.A. A critical dictionary of English literature and British and American authors, living and deceased, from the earliest accounts to the latter half of the nineteenth century. Containing over forty-six thousand articles with forty indexes of subjects. Philadelphia and London: 1859–71. 3 vols.

6037 — Supplement, containing over thirty-seven thousand articles and enumerating over ninety-three thousand titles; by J.F. Kirk. Philadelphia and London: 1891. 2 vols. Reprinted 1899.

6038 CLEEVE, BRIAN. Dictionary of Irish writers. Cork: 1966. 1st series. Fiction, novelists, playwrights, poets, short story writers in English.

6039 EVERYMAN'S DICTIONARY OF LITERARY BIOGRAPHY, English and American; compiled after John W. Cousin, by D.C. Browning. 2nd ed. London: 1960. 1st ed. 1958.

6040 KUNITZ, STANLEY J., and HAYCRAFT, H. Twentieth century authors: a biographical dictionary of modern literature; complete in one volume with 1,850 biographies and 1,700 portraits. New York: 1942.

6041 — First supplement. New York: 1955.

6042 — and HAYCRAFT, H. British authors before 1800: a biographical dictionary, complete in one volume, with 650 biographies and 200 portraits. New York: 1952.

6043 — British authors of the nineteenth century, complete in one volume, with 1,000 biographies and 350 portraits. New York: 1936.

Periodicals

6044 HOLZAPFEL, R.P. A survey of Irish literary periodicals from 1900 to the present day. Thesis accepted for degree of M. Litt., 1963–64; available in T.C.D. library.

6045 POWER, JOHN. List of Irish periodical publications (chiefly literary) from 1729 to the present time. London: 1866. 250 copies printed: appeared originally in part in *N. & Q.*, March-April 1866, and *Ir. Lit. Inquirer*, no. 4, 1866, with additions and corrections.

Societies

6046 BELFAST LITERARY SOCIETY, 1801–1901: historical sketch with memoirs of some distinguished members. Belfast: 1902. Appendix 2, pp. 155–90: Alphabetical list of members, with titles of their papers, 1801–1901. Limited ed. of 300 copies.

6047 HANDLEY-TAYLOR, GEOFFREY, *compiler*. Literary, debating and dialect societies of Great Britain, Ireland and France. Hull and London: 1951–4. 5 pts.

6048 MAHONY, TINA HUNT. The Dublin Verse-Speaking Society and the Lyric Theatre Company. *Ir. Univ. Rev.*, vol.4, no. 1, 1974, 65–73.

6049 NATIONAL LITERARY SOCIETY. A list of books and pamphlets written by the members of the National Literary Society, Dublin. *Nat. Lit. Soc. J.*, 1, 1900, 112–32.

Biography

6050 BERKENHOUT, JOHN. Biographica literaria, containing the lives of English, Scottish and Irish authors. London: 1777.

6051 CONTEMPORARY AUTHORS. Detroit: Gale Research Company, vol.1–, 1962–.

6052 DAICHES, DAVID. The present age after 1920. London: 1958. (*Introduction to English literature*, vol. 5.) Bibliographies of the following are included: Elizabeth Bowen, Joyce Cary, St. John Ervine, James Hanley, William Denis Johnston, C.D. Lewis, Louis MacNeice, Olivia Manning, Ethel Colburn Mayne, C.K. Munro, Kate O'Brien, Sean O'Casey, Liam O'Flaherty, Forrest Reid, William Robert Rodgers, George William Russell, James Stephens, L.A.G. Strong, Dorothy Violet Wellesley, Rebecca West, William Butler Yeats.

6053 ENKVIST, NILS ERIK. British and American literary letters in Scandinavian public collections. *Acta Academiae Aboensis, Humaniora*, vol.27, no. 3, 1964. Includes references for William Allingham, Sir Robert S. Bell, George Berkeley, Marguerite, Countess of Blessington, Robert Boyle, James Bryce Bryce, William Congreve, Aubrey Thomas de Vere, Alfred Denis Godley, James Hanley, Charles James Lever, Justin Huntly McCarthy, Thomas Moore, Lady Sydney Morgan, George Bernard Shaw and Richard Brinsley Sheridan.

6054 MAGUIRE, W.J. Irish literary figures: biographies in miniature. Dublin: 1945. Vol.1. No more published.

6055 MILLET, FRED. B. Contemporary British literature: a critical survey and 232 author-bibliographies. 3rd rev. and enl. ed. based on the 2nd rev. and enl. ed. by John M. Manly and Edith Rickert. London: 1935. Each entry contains short biography, bibliography, studies and reviews, and includes the-following: Elizabeth Bowen, Padraic Colum, Daniel Corkery, C. Day Lewis, Lord Dunsany, St. John Ervine, Lady Gregory, James Hanley, Katharine Tynan (Hinkson), Norah Hoult, Douglas Hyde, James Joyce, Shane Leslie, Robert Lynd, Ethel Colburn Mayne, George Moore, C.K. Munro, Charles W.K. MacMullan, T.C. Murray, Sean O'Casey, Sean O'Faolain, Liam O'Flaherty, Conal O'Riordan, Lennox Robinson, George W. Russell (AE), George Bernard Shaw, James Stephens, L.A.G. Strong, Francis Stuart, Rebecca West (Cicily Isabel Fairfield), W.B. Yeats.

6056 MILLS, ABRAHAM. The literature and the literary men of Great Britain and Ireland. 2nd ed. New York: 1854. 2 vols. 1st ed. 1851. 2 vols.

6057 STEWART, J.I.M. Eight modern writers. Oxford: 1963. (*Oxford History of English literature*, vol. 12). Bibliog., Bernard Shaw, 1856–1950, pp. 649–656; William Butler Yeats, 1856–1939, pp. 671–679; James Joyce, 1882–1941, pp. 680–686.

6058 TEMPLE, RUTH Z. Twentieth century British literature; a reference guide and bibliography. New York: 1968. Bibliog., of following included: Samuel Beckett, Brendan Behan, Elizabeth Bowen, Paul Vincent Carroll, Joyce Cary, Austin Clarke, Padraic Colum, Lord Dunsany, John Eglinton, St. John Ervine, Oliver St. John Gogarty, Lady Gregory, Stephen Gwynn, James Hanley, Denis Johnston, James Joyce, Shane Leslie, C. Day Lewis, Robert Lynd, Louis MacNeice, George Moore, Iris Murdoch, Sean O'Casey, Frank O'Connor, Sean O'Faolain, Liam O'Flaherty, Forest Reid, W.R. Rodgers, George William Russell (AE), George Bernard Shaw, James Stephens, L.A.G. Strong, Francis Stuart, John Millington Synge, Kathleen Tynan, Dorothy Wellesley, Rebecca West, William Butler Yeats.

6059 WALPOLE, HORATIO, *Earl of Orford.* A catalogue of the royal and noble authors of England, Scotland, and Ireland; with lists of their works. Enlarged . . . by Thomas Park. London: 1806. 1st ed. 1758.

6060 WARE, JAMES. The history of the writers of Ireland, in two books, viz. 1:Such writers who were born in that kingdom, and 2:Such who, though foreigners, enjoyed preferments or offices there, or had their education in it; with an account of all the works they published. Written in Latin . . . translated . . . revised and improved . . . and continued down to the beginning of the present century, by Walter Harris. Dublin: 1764. 2 vols.

6061 WRIGHT, THOMAS. Biographia Britannica Literaria; or biography of literary characters of Great Britain and Ireland. London: 1842–6, 2 vols. Reprinted Detroit, Gale Research Co., 1968.

6062 WAKEMAN, JOHN, *ed.* World authors, 1950–1970, New York: 1975.

Literary History

6063 BOYD, ERNEST A. Ireland's literary renaissance. Dublin: London and New York: 1916. Bibliog., pp. 401–15.

6064 CAHILL, SUSAN and CAHILL, THOMAS. A literary guide to Ireland. New York: 1973.

6065 CARPENTER, ANDREW. *ed.* Place, personality and the Irish writer. Gerrards Cross: 1977. (*Irish Literary studies*, I).

6066 CHRISTIANSEN, REIDAR TH. The Vikings and the Viking wars in Irish and Gaelic tradition. Oslo: 1931.

6067 COSTELLO, PETER. The heart grown brutal: the Irish revolution in literature, from Parnell to the death of Yeats, 1891–1939. London and Totowa (N.J.): 1977. Bibliog., pp. 308–318.

6068 CRONE, J.S. The R[oyal] I[rish] C[onstabulary] in literature. *Ir. Book Lov.*, 12, 1920, 7–9, 29–31.

6069 DUNN, DOUGLAS. Two decades of Irish writing – a critical survey. Cheadle (Cheshire): 1975.

6070 FALLIS, RICHARD. The Irish Renaissance. New York: 1977. Bibliog., pp. 289–302.

6071 FREEMAN, JOHN. Literature and locality: the literary topography of Britain and Ireland. London: 1963. Ireland, pp. 305–327.

6072 HARMON, MAURICE. Aspects of the peasantry in Anglo-Irish literature from 1800 to 1916. *Stud. Hib.*, 15, 1975, 105–27.

6073 — By memory inspired: themes and forces in

recent Irish writing. *Eire-Ir.*, vol.8, no. 2, 1973, 3–19.

6074 HOWARTH, HERBERT. The Irish writers, 1880–1940: literature under Parnell's star. London: 1958.

6075 HULL, ELEANOR. A textbook of Irish literature. Dublin: 1906–8. 2 vols. Bibliog., vol. 2, pp. 237–46.

6076 HYDE, DOUGLAS. A literary history of Ireland from earliest times to the present day. New edition with introduction by Brian O'Cuiv. London and New York: 1967. 1st published London:1899.

6077 IRELAND, DENIS. Books and writers in North-East Ulster. *Bell*, vol. 4, no. 5, 1942, 317–322.

6078 KELLY, JOHN S. The fall of Parnell and the rise of Irish literature: an investigation. *Anglo–Ir. Stud.*, 2, 1976, 1–23.

6079 KENNY, HERBERT A. Literary Dublin: a history. New York and Dublin: 1974. Bibliog., pp. 325–8.

6080 KIDD, WALTER E. British winners of the Nobel literary prize. Norman: Univ. of Oklahoma press: 1973. William Butler Yeats, by James V. Baker, pp. 44–82; George Bernard Shaw, by Edwin E. Pettet, pp. 83–129; Samuel Beckett, by Sandford Sternlicht, pp. 237–265.

6081 KIELY, BENEDICT. The Great gazebo. *Eire–Ir.*, vol.2, no. 4, 1967, 72–86. Preliminary sketch of the relations between Irish literature and some of the great houses of the landed classes.

6082 KING, BRUCE, *ed*. Literatures of the world in English. London and Boston: 1974. Ireland, by A. Norman Jeffares, pp. 98–115.

6083 MCCARTHY, JUSTIN, *ed*. Irish literature. Philadelphia [1904]. 10 vols in 5.

6084 M'GEE, THOMAS D'ARCY. The Irish writers of the seventeenth century. Dublin: 1846.

6085 MACLEAN, MAGNUS. The literature of the Celts: its history and romance. London: 1902.

6086 MCMAHON, SEAN. The new Irish writers. *Eire–Ir.*, vol. 9, no. 1, 1974, 136–143.

6087 MARCUS, PHILLIP L. Old Irish myth and modern Irish literature. *Ir. Univ. Rev.*, vol.1, no. 1, 1970, 67–85.

6088 MAXWELL, D.E.S. Imagining the North: violence and the writers. *Eire–Ir.*, vol.8, no. 2, 1973, 91–106.

6089 MORRIS, LLOYD R. The Celtic dawn: a survey of the renascence in Ireland, 1889–1916 [reprint of 1st ed.] New York: 1970. Movements concerned with literature, the drama, the revival of the Gaelic language, economic and social reform, and poetical thought.

6090 O'CONNOR, FRANK. The backward look: a survey of Irish literature. London: 1967. Bibliog., pp. 257–259.

6091 O'DRISCOLL, ROBERT. Ferguson and the idea of an Irish national literature. *Eire–Ir.*, vol.6, no. 1, 1971, 82–95.

6092 O'FAOLAIN, SEAN. Fifty years of Irish writing [1910–1960]. *Studies*, 51, 1962, 93–105.

6093 O'GRADY, STANDISH JAMES. Early bardic literature, Ireland. [Facsimile ed.]. New York: Lemma Publishing Corp., 1970. 1st ed. London.

6094 THE OXFORD LITERARY GUIDE TO THE BRITISH ISLES, compiled by Dorothy Eagle and Hilary Carnell. Oxford: 1977.

6095 PORTER, RAYMOND J. and BROPHY, JAMES D. Modern Irish literature: essays in honour of William York Tindall. New York: 1972. (*The Library of Irish Studies*, vol. 1)

6096 POWER, PATRICK C. A literary history of Ireland. Cork: 1969.

6097 RAFROIDI, PATRICK. The uses of Irish myth in the nineteenth century. *Studies*, 62, 1973, 251–261.

6098 — *and others*. France-Ireland: literary relations, edited by P. Rafroidi, Guy Fehlmann and Maitu Mac Conmara. Lille: Université de Lille III, Paris: Editions Universitaire, 1974. Includes material on Maria Edgeworth, Wolfe Tone, Charles R. Maturin, John Banim, Somerville and Ross, Yeats, Synge, Joyce, Ernest Boyd, Sean O'Casey and Samuel Beckett.

6099 RIVOALLAN, A. Littérature irlandaise contemporaine. Paris: [1939].

6100 RONSLEY, JOSEPH, *ed*. Myth and reality in Irish literature. Waterloo (Ontario): 1977.

6101 RYAN, WILLIAM PATRICK. The Irish literary revival: its history, pioneers and possibilities. [Facsimile ed.] New York: Lemma Pub. Corp.: 1970. 1st ed. London: 1894.

6102 SEYMOUR-SMITH, MARTIN. Guide to modern world literature. London: 1973. British literature, pp. 191–323.

6103 TAYLOR, ESTELLA RUTH. The modern Irish writers: cross currents of criticism. Lawrence, Kansas: 1954. Bibliog., pp. 166–70.

POETRY

6104 ALSPACH, RUSSELL K. Irish poetry from the English invasion to 1798. 2nd ed. Philadelphia: 1959. Bibliog., pp. 133–40.

6105 ARMITAGE, EVELYN NOBLE. The Quaker poets of Great Britain and Ireland. London: 1896.

6106 BROWN, M.J. Historical ballad poetry of Ireland; with an introduction by Stephen J. Brown. London: 1912.

6107 BROWN, TERENCE. Northern voices: poets from Ulster. Dublin: 1975. Bibliog., pp. 241–244.

6108 CLARKE, AUSTIN. Poetry in modern Ireland. Dublin: 1951. (*Cultural relations ser*., no. 2.) Bibliog., pp. 70–1.

6109 CONTEMPORARY POETS; with a preface by C. Day Lewis. Edited by James Vinson. 2nd ed. London and New York: 1975. (*Contemporary writers of the English language vol. I*)

6110 FARREN, ROBERT. The course of Irish verse in English. London: 1948. Bibliog., pp. 169–171.

6111 FOSTER, JOHN WILSON. The topographical tradition in Anglo-Irish poetry. *Ir. Univ. Rev*., 4, 1974, 169–187.

6112 HOAGLAND, KATHLEEN, *ed*. One thousand years of Irish poetry: the Gaelic and Anglo-Irish poets from pagan times to the present. New York: 1949.

6113 JACKSON, KENNETH. Studies in early Celtic nature poetry. Cambridge: 1935. Bibliog., pp. 199–200.

6114 KERSNOWSKI, FRANK. The outsiders: poets of contemporary Ireland. Fort Worth (Texas): 1975. Bibliog., pp. 191–3.

6115 LOFTUS, RICHARD J. Nationalism in modern Anglo-Irish poetry. Madison and Milwaukee: 1964. Bibliog., pp. 334–346.

6116 MURPHY, GERARD. The origin of Irish nature poetry. *Studies*, 20, 1931, 87–102.

6117 O'DONOGHUE, D.J. The Poets of Ireland: a biographical and bibliographical dictionary of Irish writers of English verse [Facsimile reprint]. New York: 1970.

6118 POWER, PATRICK C. The story of Anglo-Irish poetry (1800–1922). Cork: 1967. Bibliog., pp. 181–2.

6119 REDSHAW, THOMAS DILLON. *Ri* as in regional: three Ulster poets. *Eire–Ir*., vol. 9, no. 2, 1974, 41–64. Seamus Heaney, Seamus Deane and John Montague.

6120 [SHIELS, ROBERT.] The lives of the poets of Great Britain and Ireland, to the time of Dean Swift; compiled from ample material scattered in a variety of books, and especially from the MS. notes of the late ingenious Mr. Coxeter and others, collected for this design by Mr. [Theophilus] Cibber. In four [*sic*, five] volumes. London: 1753.

6121 SINNOTT, T.D. Anglo-Irish poets and poetry of Wexford. *An Leab*., 6, 1937–9, 79–83, 132–6.

6122 SKELTON, ROBIN. *ed*. Six Irish poets: Austin Clarke, Richard Kell, Thomas Kinsella, John Montague, Richard Murphy, Richard Weber, London: 1962. Bibliog., p. 134.

Individual Poets

BECKETT, SAMUEL.

6123 HARVEY, LAWRENCE E. Samuel Beckett: poet and critic. Princeton (N.J.), 1970.

CLARKE, AUSTIN.

6124 DODSWORTH, MARTIN. 'Jingle-go-Jangle': feeling and expression in Austin Clarke's poetry. *Ir. Univ. Rev*., vol. 4, no. 1, 1974, 117–127.

6125 KENNELLY, BRENDAN. Austin Clarke and the epic poem. *Ir. Univ. Rev*., vol.4, no. 1, 1974, 26–40.

6126 KINSELLA, THOMAS. The poetic career of Austin Clarke. *Ir. Univ. Rev*., vol. 4, no. 1, 1974, 128–136.

6127 MARTIN, AUGUSTINE. The rediscovery of Austin Clarke. *Studies*, 54, 1965, 408–434.

6128 MERCIER, VIVIAN. Mortal anguish, moral pride: Austin Clarke's religious lyrics. *Ir. Univ. Rev.*, vol.4, no. 1, 1974, 91–99.

6129 MURPHY, DANIEL J. The religious lyrics and satires of Austin Clarke. *Hermathena*, 122, 1977, 46–64.

6130 SEALY, DOUGLAS. Austin Clarke: a survey of his work. *Dubliner*, 6, 1963, 7–34.

6131 WELCH, ROBERT. Austin Clarke and Gaelic poetic tradition. *Ir. Univ. Rev.*, vol.4, no. 1, 1974, 41–51.

DEVLIN, DENIS.

6132 COFFEY, BRIAN. Of Denis Devlin: vestiges, sentences, presages [with bibliog]. *Univ. Rev.*, vol. 2, no. 11, 1961, 3–18.

6133 SMITH, STAN. Precarious quest: the poetry of Denis Devlin. *Ir. Univ. Rev.*, 8, 1978, 51–67.

DONAGHY, JOHN LYLE.

6134 COULTER, GEOFFREY. John Lyle Donaghy: an Ulster poet. *Cap. Ann.*, 1973, 86–92.

FALLON, PADRAIC.

6135 HARMON, MAURICE. The poetry of Padraic Fallon. *Studies*, 64, 1975, 269–281.

GOLDSMITH, OLIVER.

6136 TODD, WILLIAM B. The 'Private Issues' of *The Deserted Village*. *Stud. Bibliog.*, 6, 1954, 25–44.

HEANEY, SEAMUS.

6137 BIDWELL, BRUCE. A soft grip on the sick place: the bogland poetry of Seamus Heaney. *Dublin Mag.*, vol.10, no. 3, 1973–4, 86–90.

6138 MCCORMACK, W.J. Straight lines becoming circles: the poetry of Seamus Heaney and Derek Mahon. *Acorn*, 17, 1972, 29–33, 39–43.

HEWITT, JOHN.

6139 SEALY, DOUGLAS. An individual flavour: the collected poems of John Hewitt. *Dublin Mag.*, vol.8, nos. 1–2, 1969, 19–25.

KAVANAGH, PATRICK.

6140 WARNER, ALAN. The poetry of Patrick Kavanagh (1904–1967). *English*, vol.18, no. 102, 1969, 98–103.

KINSELLA, THOMAS.

6141 BEDIENT, CALVIN. Eight contemporary poets . . . London: 1974. Thomas Kinsella, pp. 119–138. Bibliog., pp. 183–4.

6142 FREYER, MICHAEL G., *compiler*. The books of Thomas Kinsella: a checklist. *Dublin Mag.*, vol. 5, no. 2, 1966, 79–81.

6143 HARMON, MAURICE. The poetry of Thomas Kinsella: 'with darkness for a nest?' Dublin: 1974. Bibliog., pp. 123–124.

6144 LONGLEY, EDNA. The heroic agenda: poetry of Thomas Kinsella. *Dublin Mag.*, vol. 5, no. 2, 1966, 61–78.

6145 REDSHAW, THOMAS DILLON. Note to Kinsella's 'Butcher's Dozen'. *Eire–Ir.*, vol.7, no. 3, 1972, 100–7.

6146 SKELTON, ROBIN. The poetry of Thomas Kinsella. *Eire–Ir.*, vol. 4, no. 1, 1969, 86–108.

6147 WOODBRIDGE, HENSLEY C. Thomas Kinsella: a bibliography. *Eire–Ir.*, vol.2, no. 2, 1967, 122–133.

LEDWIDGE, FRANCIS.

6148 COLUM, PADRAIC. Francis Ledwidge. *Dubliner*, vol. 3, no. 2, 1964, 21–24.

LONGLEY, MICHAEL.

6149 ALLEN, MICHAEL. Options: the poetry of Michael Longley. *Eire–Ir.*, vol.10, no. 4, 1975, 129–136.

MACNEICE, LOUIS.

6150 BROWN, TERENCE. Louis MacNeice, 1907–1963: his poetry. *Studies*, 59, 1970, 253–266.

6151 — Louis MacNeice: sceptical vision. Dublin and New York: 1975. Bibliog., pp. 196–9.

6152 DAVIN, DAN. In a green grave: recollections of Louis MacNeice. *Encounter*, vol.39, no. 2, 1972, 42–49.

6153 MCKINNON, WILLIAM T. Apollo's blended dream: a study of the poetry of Louis MacNeice. London: 1971. Bibliog., pp. 219–228.

6154 MOORE, D.B. The poetry of Louis MacNeice; with an introduction by G.S. Fraser. Leicester: 1972. Bibliog., pp. 251–6.

6155 SEALY, DOUGLAS. Louis MacNeice. *Dubliner*, vol.3, no. 1, 1964, 4–13.

MANGAN, JAMES CLARENCE.

6156 HOLZAPFEL, R.P. Mangan's poetry in the *Dublin University Magazine*: a bibliography. *Hermathena*, 105, 1967, 40–54.

MONTAGUE, JOHN.

6157 LUCY, SEAN. John Montague's *The Rough Field*: an introductory note. *Studies*, 63, 1974, 29–30.

6158 REDSHAW, THOMAS D. John Montague's *The Rough Field: Topos and Texne. ibid.*, 63, 1974, 31–46.

O'DONNELLY, PATRICK.

6159 MCRORY, *Very Rev.* MICHAEL. Life and times of Doctor Patrick O'Donnelly, 1649–1716: 'The Bard of Armagh'. *Sean Ard.*, vol. 5, no. 1, 1969, 3–33.

O'SULLIVAN, TIMOTHY.

6160 CASAIDE, SEAMUS UA. The bibliography of Timothy O'Sullivan's (Tadhg Gaidhlach) *Pious Miscellany*, by James Cassedy. *Gael. J.*, 15, 1905, 49–51.

6161 — Some editions of O'Sullivan's *Miscellany. Waterford S.E. Ir. Arch. Soc. J.*, 14, 1911, 113–22.

RODGERS, W.R.

6162 ORMSBY, FRANK. Host of relations: the poetry of W.R. Rodgers. *Honest Ulsterman*, 24, 1970, 24–28.

ROWLEY, RICHARD.

6163 Apollo in Mourne: poems, plays and stories, edited by Victor Price. Belfast: 1978. Sel. bibliog., pp. 133–134.

STEPHENS, JAMES.

6164 O'RIORDAN, JOHN. James Stephens, the leprechaun poet. *Lib. Rev.*, 24, 1974–5, 343–6.

SWIFT, JONATHAN.

6165 SHINAGEL, MICHAEL., *ed*. A concordance to the poems of Jonathan Swift. Ithaca and London: 1972. (*The Cornell Concordances*).

6166 UPHAUS, ROBERT W. Swift's Stella poems and fidelity to experience. *Eire–Ir.*, vol.5, no. 3, 1970, 40–52.

6167 WILLIAMS, H., *ed*. The poems of Jonathan Swift. Oxford: 1937. 3 vols. Bibliog., vol. 1, pp. xlviii–lxii.

WILDE, OSCAR.

6168 HORODISCH, ABRAHAM. Oscar Wilde's *Ballad of Reading Gaol:* bibliographical study. New York: 1954. Limited edition of 326 numbered copies.

YEATS, WILLIAM BUTLER.

6169 BOLAND, EAVAN. Precepts of art in Yeats's poetry. *Dublin Mag.*, 4, 1965, 8–13.

6170 DYSON, A.E., *ed*. English poetry: select bibliographical guides. London: 1971. Yeats, 1865–1939, by Jon Stallworthy, pp. 345–59.

6171 FRIEDMAN, BARTON R. Yeats, [Lionel] Johnson, and Ireland's heroic dead: toward a poetry of politics. *Eire–Ir.*, vol.7, no. 4, 1972, 32–47.

6172 GREER, SAMMYE CRAWFORD. The Poet's role in an age of emptiness and chaos: a reading of Yeats's *Meditation in time of civil war. Eire–Ir.*, vol. 7, no. 3, 1972, 82–92.

6173 HARRIS, DANIEL A. Yeats, Coole Park and Ballylee. Baltimore and London: 1974. Examines his poetry about Lady Gregory's estate and his own tower.

6174 HIRSCHBERG, STUART. Yeats and the meditative poem. *Eire–Ir.*, vol. 9, no. 4, 1974, 94–101.

6175 JEFFARES, A. NORMAN. The poetry of W.B. Yeats. London: 1961. (*Studies in English Literature no. 4*.)

6176 — A commentary on the *Collected poems of W.B. Yeats*. London: 1968.

6177 MEIR, COLIN. The Ballads and songs of W.B. Yeats: the Anglo-Irish heritage in subject and style. London: 1974. Bibliog., pp. 132–136.

6178 PARKIN, ANDREW. Dramatic elements in the poetry of W.B. Yeats. *Anglo–Ir. Stud.*, 2, 1976, 109–127.

6179 PARRISH, STEPHEN MAXFIELD, *ed*. A concordance to the poems of W.B. Yeats, programmed by James Allan Painter. Ithaca: 1963.

6180 SNUKAL, ROBERT. High talk: the philosophical poetry of W.B. Yeats. Cambridge: 1973.

6181 STALLWORTHY, JON. Vision and revision in Yeats's *Last Poems*. Oxford: 1969.

6182 YOUNG, DUDLEY. Out of Ireland: a reading of Yeats's poetry. Cheadle Hulme: 1975.

DRAMA

6183 BARTLEY, J.O. Teague, Shenkin and Sawney; being an historical study of the earliest Irish, Welsh and Scottish characters in English plays. Cork: 1954. Bibliog., pp. 317–25; list of plays, pp. 255–71.

6184 BOOK ASSOCIATION OF IRELAND. Bibliography and miscellaneous literature: plays and poetry. *Ir. Lib. Bull.*, 7, 1946, 36–7.

6185 BOYD, ERNEST A. The contemporary drama of Ireland. Boston: 1917. Bibliog., pp. 201–10.

6186 CLARK, WILLIAM SMITH. The Early Irish stage: the beginnings to 1720. Oxford: 1955. Bibliog., pp. 210–217; Appendix A. Documents relating to the Office of Master of the Revels in Ireland, 1660–1684: Appendix B. Documents relating to the case of John Thurmond vs. the Patentee and Sharers of the Theatre Royal, Dublin, 1713. Appendix C. Plays acted at the Dublin Theatres, 1637–1720; Appendix D. Actors and actresses at the Dublin Theatres, 1637–1720.

6187 CONTEMPORARY DRAMATISTS; *editor* James Vinson; *associate editor*, D.L. Kirkpatrick. 2nd ed. London and New York: 1977. (*Contemporary writers of the English language*).

6188 DIX, E.R. MCCLINTOCK. Plays printed in Ireland before 1701. *Ir Book Lov.*, 17, 1929, 36–7.

6189 DRAMA IN IRELAND [collection of essays on contemporary scene]. *Ir. Hib.*, vol. 4, no. 3, 1960.

6190 ELLIS–FERMOR, UNA. The Irish dramatic movement. London: 1939. Bibliog., pp. 223–7. 2nd ed. 1954. The 1st ed. contains the better bibliography.

6191 GAILEY, ALAN. Irish folk drama. Cork: 1969.

6192 HARBAGE, ALFRED. Annals of English drama, 975–1700: an analytical record of all plays, extant or lost, chronologically arranged and indexed by authors, titles, dramatic companies, etc. Revised by S. Schoenbaum. London: 1964.

6193 — Annals of English drama, 975–1700: a supplement to the revised edition, by S. Schoenbaum. Evanston (Illinois): 1966.

6194 HOGAN, ROBERT. After the renaissance: a critical history of the Irish drama since *The Plough and the Stars*. London: 1968. Bibliog., pp. 259–274.

6195 HUGHES, S.C. The pre-Victorian drama in Dublin. Dublin: 1904.

6196 MIKHAIL, E.H. A bibliography of modern Irish drama, 1899–1970. London: 1972.

6197 — Dissertations on Anglo-Irish drama: a bibliography of studies, 1870–1970. London: 1973.

6198 NICOLL, ALLARDYCE. A history of English drama, 1660–1900. Cambridge: 1952–9. 6 vols. Handlist of Restoration plays, vol. 1, pp. 386–447. Handlist of plays, 1700–50. vol. 2, pp. 293–387. Handlist of plays, 1750–1800. vol. 3, pp. 232–348. Handlist of plays produced between 1800 and 1850 with supplementary notes. vol. 4, pp. 245–643. Handlist of plays, 1850–1900, with supplementary notes. vol. 5, pp. 220–850. A short title alphabetical catalogue of plays produced or printed in England from 1660 to 1900. vol. 6, pp. 1–565.

6199 — English drama, 1900–1930: the beginning of the modern period. Cambridge: 1973. Handlist of plays, 1900–1930, pp. 451–1053.

6200 O HAODHA, MICHAEL, *compiler*. A list of plays about Robert Emmet. *Ir. Book.*, 2, 1963, 53–57.

6201 PRICE, ALAN. Synge and Anglo-Irish drama. London: 1961. Bibliog., pp. 229–231.

6202 SAHAL, N. Sixty years of realistic Irish drama (1900–1960). Bombay, Calcutta, Madras, Macmillan and Co. Ltd.: 1971. Bibliog., pp. 217–220.

6203 UNITED STATES. National Service Bureau publication, no. 47-L. Irish plays: a bibliography compiled by the Play Department, National Service Bureau, Federal Theatre project. New York: 1938. Typescript; foreword by Maurice N. O'Brien.

6204 WEYGANDT, C. Irish plays and playwrights. London: 1913.

Individual Dramatists

BECKETT, SAMUEL.

6205 DUCKWORTH, COLIN. Angels of darkness: dramatic effect in Samuel Beckett with special reference to Eugene Ionesco. London: 1972. Bibliog., pp. 146–147.

6206 FLETCHER, JOHN and SPURLING, JOHN. Beckett: a study of his plays. London: 1972. Bibliog., pp. 147–149.

6207 HAYMAN, RONALD. Samuel Beckett. London: 1970. (*Contemporary Playwrights*) Bibliog., p. vii; first published 1968.

6208 KNOWLSON, JAMES. Light and darkness in the theatre of Samuel Beckett. London: 1972.

6209 PARKIN, ANDREW. Monologue into monodrama: aspects of Samuel Beckett's plays. *Eire–Ir.*, vol. 9, no. 4, 1974, 32–41.

6210 WATSON, GEORGE. Beckett's *Waiting for Godot*: a reappraisal. *May. Rev.*, vol. 4, no. 1, 1975, 17–35.

6211 WEBB, EUGENE. The Plays of Samuel Beckett. London: 1972. Bibliog., pp. 151–155.

6212 ZILLIACUS, CLAS. Beckett and broadcasting: a study of the works of Samuel Beckett for and in radio and television. *Acta Academiae Aboensis, Ser. A. Humaniora*, vol.51, no. 2, 1976, 1–223. Bibliog., pp. 211–223.

BEHAN, BRENDAN.

6213 HENDRICK, JOHAN. The 'Theatre of Fun': in defence of Brendan Behan's *The Hostage*. *Anglo–Ir. Stud.*, 3, 1977, 85–95.

6214 KLEINSTUCK, JOHANNES. Brendan Behan's 'The Hostage'. *Essays and Studies*, 24, 1971, 69–82.

BOUCICAULT, DION.

6215 The Dolmen Boucicault; edited by David Krause, with an essay by the editor on The Theatre of Dion Boucicault, and the complete authentic texts of Boucicault's three Irish plays *The Colleen Bawn, or The Brides of Garryowen, Arrah na Pogue, or The Wicklow Wedding, The Shaughraun.* Dublin: 1964. Bibliog., pp. 246–253.

6216 Kerry, or Night and morning. With an introduction by Hilary Berrow. *Ir. Univ. Rev.*, vol. 3, no. 1, 1973, 31–50.

6217 McMAHON, SEAN. The Wearing of the green: the Irish plays of Dion Boucicault. *Eire–Ir.*, vol.2, no. 2, 1967, 98–111.

CARROLL, PAUL VINCENT.

6218 CONWAY, JOHN D. The satires of Paul Vincent Carroll. *Eire–Ir.*, vol. 7, no. 3, 1972, 13–23.

6219 McMAHON, SEAN. Oisin's return: the protest plays of Paul Vincent Carroll. *Eire–Ir.*, vol. 2, no. 3, 1967, 46–65.

CLARKE, AUSTIN.

6220 McHUGH, ROGER. The Plays of Austin Clarke. *Ir. Univ. Rev.*, vol. 4, no. 1, 1974, 52–64.

COLUM, PADRAIC.

6221 BOWEN, ZACK. Padraic Colum and Irish drama. *Eire–Ir.*, vol. 5, no. 4, 1970, 71–82.

CONGREVE, WILLIAM.

6222 VAN VORIS, W.H. The cultivated stance: the designs of Congreve's plays. Dublin: 1965.

CORKERY, DANIEL.

6223 SAUL, GEORGE BRANDON, Daniel Corkery's *Fohnan the sculptor. J. Ir. Lit.*, vol. 2, nos. 2–3, 98–138. Includes bibliographical and biographical data.

FITZMAURICE, GEORGE.

6224 COGHLIN, MATTHEW N. Audience and character in George Fitzmaurice's *The magic glasses. Dublin Mag.*, vol. 10, no. 3, 1973–4, 94–115.

6225 — Farce transcended: George Fitzmaurice's *The toothache. Eire-Ir.*, vol. 10, no. 4, 1975, 85–100.

6226 CONBERE, JOHN P. The obscurity of George Fitzmaurice. *Eire–Ir.*, vol. 6, no. 1, 1971, 17–26.

6227 SLAUGHTER, HOWARD K. George Fitzmaurice and his *Enchanted land*. Dublin: 1972. (*Irish Theatre series 2*). A checklist of his published work by Liam Miller, pp. 57–59.

GOLDSMITH, OLIVER.

6228 HASSERT, MARGARET. Appraisals: the plays of Oliver Goldsmith. *J. Ir. Lit.*, vol. 3, no. 3, 1974, 39–48.

6229 TODD, WILLIAM B. The first editions of *The Good Natur'd Man and She Stoops to Conquer. Stud. Bibliog.*, 11, 1958, 133–142.

GREGORY, *Lady*.

6230 SADDLEMYER, ANN. In defence of Lady Gregory, playwright. Dublin: 1966. A chronological chart of Lady Gregory's major works, pp. 107–115.

HYDE, DOUGLAS.

6231 DUNLEAVY, GARETH and DUNLEAVY, JANET EGLESON. Editor [George] Moore to playwright Hyde: on the making of *The Tinker and the Fairy*. *Ir. Univ. Rev*., vol. 3, no. 1, 1973, 17–30.

JOHNSTON, DENIS.

6232 FERRAR, HAROLD. Denis Johnston's Irish theatre. Dublin: 1978. (*Irish Theatre series* 5). Bibliog., pp. 143–4.

MACKLIN, CHARLES.

6233 Four comedies, by Charles Macklin:- Love à la mode, The true born Irishman, The School for Hundreds [and] The man of the world, edited, and with a biographical and critical sketch of Macklin, by J.O. Bartley. London: 1968.

MOORE, GEORGE.

6234 NEWLIN, PAUL A. The Artful failure of George Moore's plays. *Eire–Ir*., vol. 8, no. 1, 1973, 62–84.

MURRAY, T.C.

6235 FITZGIBBON, T. GERALD. The Elements of conflict in the plays of T.C. Murray. *Studies*, 64, 1975, 59–65.

O'CASEY, SEAN.

6236 A bunch of blue ribbons: a conversation with Mrs. Sean O'Casey and Brenna Katz on the women in O'Casey's plays. *Arts Ir*., vol. 1, no. 1, 1972, 13–23.

6237 AYLING, RONALD. 'To bring harmony': recurrent patterns in O'Casey's drama. *Eire–Ir*., vol.10, no. 3, 1975, 62–78.

6238 BENSTOCK, BERNARD. Paycock and others: Sean O'Casey's world. Dublin and New York: 1976. Bibliog., pp. 306–9.

6239 KILROY, THOMAS, *ed*. Sean O'Casey: a collection of critical essays. Englewood Cliffs, N.J.: 1975. (*Twentieth Century Views*).

6240 ROLLINS, RONALD G. Pervasive patterns in *The Silver Tassie*. *Eire–Ir*., vol. 6, no. 4, 1971, 29–37.

6241 SCHRANK, BERNICE. 'You needn't say no more,': language and the problems of communication in Sean O'Casey's *The Shadow of a Gunman*. *Ir. Univ. Rev*., vol. 8, no. 1, 1978, 23–37.

6242 SNOWDEN, J.A. Sean O'Casey and naturalism. *Essays and Studies*, 24, 1971, 56–68.

6243 SEAN O'CASEY REVIEW. vol. 2, no. 2, Spring 1976. Special Commemorative number [of the] fiftieth anniversary [of] *The Plough and the Stars*. Includes the Genesis of *The Plough and the Stars*: a bibliographical note, by Ronald Ayling and Michael J. Durkan, pp. 87–91.

6244 SEAN O'CASEY REVIEW. vol. 4, no. 2, 1978. Commemorative number – *The Silver Tassie*, 1928–1978.

SHAW, GEORGE BERNARD.

6245 CROMPTON, LOUIS. Shaw the dramatist: a study of the intellectual background of the major plays. London: 1971.

6246 EISENBUD, JULE. Possible sources of Shaw's 'Pygmalion'. *N. & Q., new ser*., 24, 1977, 442–8.

6247 EVANS, T.F. Shaw: the critical heritage. London: 1976. Bibliog., pp. 408–410.

6248 HARDWICK, MICHAEL and HARDWICK, MOLLIE. The Bernard Shaw companion. London: 1973. Includes summaries of plots of plays, chronology of his novels and other writings and an extensive Who's Who of his characters.

6249 JENCKES, NORMA. The rejection of Shaw's Irish play: *John Bull's Other Island*. *Eire–Ir*., vol.10. no. 1, 1975, 38–53.

6250 MORGAN, MARGERY M. The Shavian playground: an exploration of the art of George Bernard Shaw. London: 1972. Bibliog. note, pp. 345–349.

6251 WEINTRAUB, STANLEY. Shaw's 'Lear'. *Ariel*, vol. 1, no. 3, 1970, 59–68.

6252 WISENTHAL, J.L. The marriage of contraries: Bernard Shaw's middle plays. Cambridge (Mass.): 1974.

SHERIDAN, RICHARD BRINSLEY.

6253 LOFTIS, JOHN. Sheridan and the drama of Georgian England. Oxford: 1976. Bibliog., pp. 161–4.

SHIELS, GEORGE.

6254 KENNEDY, DAVID. George Shiels: a playwright at work. *Threshold*, 25, 1974, 50–58.

SYNGE, JOHN M.

6255 FLOOD, JEANNE A. Thematic variation in Synge's early peasant plays. *Eire–Ir.*, vol.7, no. 3, 1972, 72–81.

6256 FOSTER, LESLIE D. Heroic strivings in *The Playboy of the Western World. Eire–Ir.*, vol. 8, no. 1, 1973, 85–94.

6257 GRENE, NICHOLAS. Synge's creative development in the *Aran Islands. Long-room*, 10, 1974, 30–36.

6258 HULL, KEITH N. Nature's storms and stormy natures in Synge's *Aran Islands. Eire–Ir.*, vol. 7, no. 3, 1972, 63–71.

6259 LEVITT, PAUL M. The structural craftsmanship of J.M. Synge's *Riders to the Sea. Eire–Ir.*, vol.4, no. 1, 1969, 53–61.

6260 O'RIORDAN, JOHN. Playwright of the Western World. *Lib. Rev.*, 23, 1971, 140–145.

6261 SKELTON, ROBIN. J.M. Synge and *The Shadow of the Glen. English*, vol. 18, no. 102, 1969, 91–97.

WILDE, OSCAR.

6262 JORDAN, ROBERT J. Satire and fantasy in Wilde's *The Importance of Being Earnest. Ariel*, vol. 1, no. 3, 1970, 101–109.

6263 MATLOCK, KATE. Appraisals: the plays of Oscar Wilde. *J. Ir. Lit.*, vol. 4, no. 2, 1975, 95–106.

YEATS, WILLIAM BUTLER.

6264 DOMVILLE, ERIC, *ed.* A Concordance to the plays of W.B. Yeats. Ithaca and London, 1972. 2 vols. Based on *The variorum edition of the plays of W.B. Yeats*, edited by Russell K. Alspach.

6265 JEFFARES, A. NORMAN, and KNOWLAND, A.S. A commentary on the collected plays of W.B. Yeats. London: 1975.

6266 KNOX, DAVID BLAKE. Ideological factors in Yeats's early drama. *Anglo–Ir. Stud.*, 1, 1975, 83–96.

6267 MILLER, LIAM. The noble drama of W.B. Yeats. Dublin: 1977.

6268 MOORE, JOHN REES. Marks of love and death: Yeats as dramatist. Ithaca and London: 1971.

6269 NATHAN, LEONARD E. The tragic drama of William Butler Yeats: figures in a dance. New York and London: 1965.

6270 PARKIN, ANDREW. Similarities in the plays of Yeats and Beckett. *Ariel*, vol. 1, no. 3, 1970, 49–58.

6271 SKENE, REG. The Cuchulain plays of W.B. Yeats: a study. London: 1974. Bibliog., pp. 265–271.

FICTION

6272 BAKER, ERNEST A. A guide to historical fiction. London: 1914.

6273 — and PACKMAN, JAMES. A guide to the best fiction, English and American, including translations from foreign languages. New enl. ed. London: 1932.

6274 BELFAST LIBRARY AND SOCIETY FOR PROMOTING KNOWLEDGE (Linen Hall Library). Catalogue of prose fiction. Belfast: 1894.

6275 BLOCK, ANDREW. The English novel, 1740–1850: a catalogue including prose romances, short stories, and translations of foreign fiction. New rev. ed. London: 1961. 1st ed. 1939.

6276 BROWN, STEPHEN J. Ireland in fiction: a guide to Irish novels, tales, romances and folklore. 2nd ed. Dublin: 1919. 1st ed., 1916, was an expansion of *A reader's guide to Irish fiction*, 1910. A sequel to above is being prepared with the assistance of the Library Association of Ireland.

6277 — Irish fiction for boys. *Studies*, 7, 1918, 665–70; *ibid.*, 8, 1919, 469–72, 658–63.

6278 — Irish story-books for boys and girls: a descriptive catalogue for the use of parochial, children of Mary, private and other libraries, etc. Dublin: 1922.

6279 — Novels and tales by Catholic writers: a catalogue. 8th ed. rev. Dublin: 1946.

6280 — Irish historical fiction. *Studies*, 4, 1915, 441–53.

6281 BUCKLEY, J.A. and WILLIAMS, W.T. A guide to British historical fiction. London: 1912.

6282 BUCKLEY, MARY. Attitudes to nationality in four nineteenth-century novelists. *Cork Hist. Arch. Soc. J.*, 78, 1973, 27–34, 109–116; 79, 1974, 129–136; 80, 1975, 91–94. Maria Edgeworth, William Carleton, Charles Lever and Mrs. S.C. Hall.

6283 CONNOLLY, PETER R. The priest in Irish fiction. *Furrow*, 9, 1958, 782–97.

6284 CONTEMPORARY NOVELISTS; editor, James Vinson; associate editor, D.L. Kirkpatrick. 2nd ed., London and New York: 1976. (*Contemporary writers of the English language*)

6285 DONNELLY, BRIAN. The Big House in the recent novel. *Studies*, 64, 1975, 133–142.

6286 DYSON, A.E., *ed*. The English novel: select bibliographical guides. London: 1974. Swift, by Louis A. Landa, pp. 30–55; Sterne, by Duncan Isles, pp. 90–111.

6287 FICTION INDEX: a guide to over 10,000 works of fiction . . . compiled by G.B. Cotton and Alan Glencross. London, Association of Assistant Librarians: 1953.

6288 — Fiction index, vol.2. London: 1957.

6289 FLANAGAN, THOMAS. The Irish novelists, 1800–50. New York: 1959. Bibliog., pp. 343–51. Includes Maria Edgeworth, Lady Morgan, John Banim, Gerald Griffin, and William Carleton.

6290 GARLAND PUBLISHING INC. Ireland from the Act of Union, 1800, to the death of Parnell, 1891: seventy-seven novels and collections of shorter stories by twenty-two Irish and Anglo-Irish novelists, selected by Prof. Robert Lee Wolf, with a special introductory essay by him on each author. New York [1978]. (*Nineteenth Century Fiction, ser. 2.*)

6291 HARMON, MAURICE. Contemporary Irish fiction. *Ir. Today*, 883, 1976, 2–3.

6292 KIELY, BENEDICT. Modern Irish fiction: a critique. Dublin: 1950. Bibliog., pp. 163–70.

6293 KRANS, HORATIO SHEAFE. Irish life in Irish fiction. New York: 1903. Bibliog., pp. 327–34; lists important stories and novelists whose literary activity began before 1850.

6294 LECLAIRE, LUCIEN. A general analytical bibliography of the regional novelists of the British Isles, 1800–1950. Paris: 1954. Index to Irish counties, pp. 384–7.

6295 MCBURNEY, WILLIAM HARLIN, *compiler*. A check list of English prose fiction, 1700–39. Cambridge, Mass.: 1960. Bibliog., pp. 125–8.

6296 MACCARTHY, B.G. Irish regional novelists of the early nineteenth century. *Dublin Mag.*, n.s., vol. 21, no. 1, 1946, 26–32; *ibid.*, no. 3, 38–37.

6297 — Women writers: their contribution to the English novel, 1621–1744. Cork: 1944.

6298 — The later women novelists, 1744–1818. Cork: 1947. Bibliog., pp. 283–90.

6299 MACDONAGH, OLIVER. The nineteenth century novel and Irish social history: some aspects. Dublin: National Univ. of Ireland, 1970. O'Donnell lecture delivered at Univ. College, Cork on April 21st 1970. Discusses Edgeworth's *Castle Rackrent,* Carleton's *Valentine M'Clutchy,* Trollope's *The Kellys and the O'Kellys*, Sheehan's *Luke Delmege* and *The Real Charlotte* by Somerville and Ross.

6300 MACMAHON, SEAN. The priest in recent Irish fiction. *Eire-Ir.*, vol. 3, no. 2, 1968, 105–114.

6301 MARTIN, AUGUSTINE. Inherited dissent: the dilemma of the Irish writer. *Studies,* 54, 1965, 1–20.

6302 MERCIER, VIVIAN, and GREENE, DAVID H., *eds*. One thousand years of Irish prose. Pt. 1.: The literary revival. New York: 1952. Biographical notes, pp. 595–607. Pt. 2: *Gael and Saxon* in preparation.

6303 NIELD, JONATHAN. A guide to the best historical novels and tales, 5th ed. London: 1929.

6304 O'BRIEN, GEORGE. The fictional Irishman, 1665–1850. *Studies*, 66, 1977, 319–329.

6305 O'HEGARTY, P.S. About Ulster novelists. *Bell*, 4, 1942, 289–97.

6306 SADLEIR, MICHAEL. Nineteenth century fiction: a bibliographical record based on his own collection. London: 1951. 2 vols.

6307 SUMMERS, MONTAGUE. A Gothic bibliography. London [1969]. Originally published 1940.

Novelists

BECKETT, SAMUEL.

6308 FINNEY, BRIAN, 'Since how it is': a study of Samuel Beckett's later fiction. London: 1972.

6309 FLETCHER, JOHN. The novels of Samuel Beckett. 2nd ed., London: 1970. Bibliog., pp. 240–5.

6310 KENNEDY, SIGHLE. Murphy's bed: a study of real sources and sur-real associations in Samuel Beckett's first novel. Lewisburg: 1971. Bibliog., pp. 309–316.

6311 KENNER, HUGH. A reader's guide to Samuel Beckett. London: 1973. Bibliog., pp. 201–202.

BRODERICK, JOHN.

6312 MCMAHON, SEAN. Town and country [study of John Broderick's novels]. *Eire-Ir.*, vol. 6, no. 1, 1971, 120–131.

CARLETON, WILLIAM.

6313 CHESTNUTT, MARGARET. Studies in the short stories of William Carleton. *Acta Universitatis Gothoburgensis: Gothenburg Studies in English*, no. 34, 1976.

6314 IBARRA, EILEEN. William Carleton: an introduction. *Eire-Ir.*, vol. 5, no. 1, 1970, 81–86.

6315 O'BRIEN, H.J. The poor scholar: the oral style of William Carleton. *Aquarius*, 4, 1971, 74–82.

CARROLL, PAUL VINCENT.

6316 ROMAN, DIANE, and HAMILTON, MARY. Paul Vincent Carroll's first fiction, with a checklist of early stories. *J. Ir. Lit.*, vol. 1, no. 3, 1972, 72–84.

CARY, JOYCE.

6317 FISHER, BARBARA. Joyce Cary's published writings. *Bod. Lib. Rec.*, 8, 1970, 213–28.

6318 GARDNER, HELEN. The novels of Joyce Cary. *Essays and Studies*, 1975, 76–93.

6319 MAHOOD, M.M. Joyce Cary's Africa. London: 1964. The background to his African novels.

6320 SODERSKOG, INGVAR. Joyce Cary's 'Hard conceptual labour': a structural analysis of *To be a pilgrim*. *Acta Universitatis Gothoburgensis; Gothenburg Studies in English*, no. 36, 1977.

6321 WOLKENFELD, JACK. Joyce Cary: the developing style. New York and London: 1968. Bibliog., pp. 193–6.

EDGEWORTH, MARIA.

6322 Castle Rackrent; edited with an introduction by George Watson. London: 1964. Select bibliog., pp. xxix–xxx.

6323 HAWTHORNE, MARK. Doubt and dogma in Maria Edgeworth. Gainesville: Univ. of Florida Press, 1967. *(Univ. of Florida monographs. Humanities, no. 25)*

6324 JEFFARES, A. NORMAN. Maria Edgeworth's *Ormond*. *English*, vol. 18, no. 102, 1969, 85–90.

6325 MCCORMACK, W.J. *The Absentee* and Maria Edgeworth's notion of didactic fiction. *Atlantis*, 5, 1973, 123–135.

6326 MCHUGH, ROGER. Maria Edgeworth's Irish novels. *Studies*, 27, 1938, 556–570.

6327 MURRAY, PATRICK. The Irish novels of Maria Edgeworth. *Studies,* 59, 1970, 267–278.

GRIFFIN, GERALD.

6328 CRONIN, JOHN. Gerald Griffin and 'The Collegians': reconstruction. *Univ. Rev.*, vol. 5, no. 1, 1968, 51–63.

6329 — GERALD GRIFFIN: a forgotten novel [*Adventures of an Irish giant*]. *Eire-Ir.*, vol. 5, no. 3, 1970, 32–39.

HANLEY, JAMES.

6330 STOKES, EDWARD. The novels of James Hanley. Melbourne: 1964. Bibliog., pp. 203–4.

HIGGINS, AIDAN.

6331 BEJA, MORRIS: Felons of our selves: the fiction of Aidan Higgins. *Ir. Univ. Rev.*, vol. 3, no. 2, 1973, 163–178.

JOHNSTON, JENNIFER.

6332 MCMAHON, SEAN. Anglo-Irish attitudes: the novels of Jennifer Johnston. *Eire-Ir.*, vol. 10, no. 3, 1975, 137–141.

JOYCE, JAMES.

6333 ADAMS, ROBERT MARTIN. Surface and symbol: the consistency of James Joyce's *Ulysses*. New York and London: 1962.

6334 ARNOLD, ARMIN. James Joyce. New York: 1969.

6335 BEECHHOLD, HENRY F. Joyce's otherworld. *Eire-Ir.*, vol. 7, no. 1, 1972, 103–115.

6336 BEGNAL, MICHAEL H. and ECKLEY, GRACE. Narrator and character in *Finnegans Wake*. Lewisburg and London: 1977.

6337 — and SENN, FRITZ. A conceptual guide to *Finnegans Wake*. London: 1974.

6338 BENSTOCK, BERNARD. Joyce — again's wake: an analysis of *Finnegans Wake*. Seattle and London: 1966. Bibliog., pp. 305–309.

6339 BLAMIRES, HARRY. The Bloomsday book: a guide through Joyce's *Ulysses*. London: 1966.

6340 BOWEN, ZACK. Musical allusions in the works of James Joyce: early poetry through *Ulysses*. Albany and Dublin: 1975. Bibliog., pp. 358–361.

6341 BROWN, HOMER OBED. James Joyce's early fiction: the biography of a form. Cleveland and London: 1972.

6342 BUGDEN, FRANK. James Joyce and the making of *Ulysses* and other writings, with an introduction by Clive Hart. London: 1972. Photolitho facsimile of 1934 British ed.

6343 BURGESS, ANTHONY. Joysprick: an introduction to the language of James Joyce. London: 1973. *(The Language Library)*. Bibliog., pp. 179–181.

6344 CONNOLLY, THOMAS. Joyce's *Portrait,* criticisms and critiques. London: 1964. Bibliog., pp. 329–335.

6345 CROSS, RICHARD. Flaubert and Joyce: the rite of fiction. Princeton: 1971.

6346 DALTON, JACK P. The text of *Ulysses. Eire—Ir.*, vol. 7, no. 2, 1972, 67–83.

6347 — and HART, CLIVE, *ed*. Twelve and a tilly: essays on the occasion of the 25th anniversary of *Finnegans Wake*. London: 1966.

6348 DEANE, SEAMUS. The Joycean triumph: *Ulysses* fifty years after. *Encounter,* vol. 39, no. 3, 1972, 42–51.

6349 DENNING, ROBERT H. *ed.* James Joyce: the critical heritage. London: 1970. 2 vol. Vol. 1. 1902–1927. Vol. 2. 1928–1941. Vol. 2. contains 4 appendices – (A) Early editions of the writings of James Joyce. (B) Selective Bibliography. (C) Book-length studies published during Joyce's lifetime and critical studies which have been collected or reprinted and are readily accessible. (D) Reviews and early critical studies excluded from this volume.

6350 ECKLEY, GRACE. Ohio's Irish Militia and Joyce's *Ulysses. Eire—Ir.*, vol. 9, no. 4, 1974, 102–116.

6351 FLYNN, BRIAN. Form and technique in *Ulysses*. *Zenith*, 2, 1972, 25–30.

6352 GARVIN, JOHN: James Joyce's disunited kingdom and the Irish dimension. Dublin and New York: 1976. Bibliog., pp. 243–7.

6353 GOLDMAN, ARNOLD. The Joyce paradox: form and freedom in his fiction. London: 1966.

6354 HARMON, MAURICE, *ed.* The Celtic master: contributions to the first James Joyce Symposium held in Dublin, 1967. Essays by Donagh MacDonagh, Niall Montgomery, Norman Silverstein, Margaret C. Solomon and Stanley Sultan. Dublin: 1969.

6355 HART, CLIVE, and HAYMAN, DAVID. James Joyce's *Ulysses*: critical essays. Berkeley, Los Angeles and London: 1974.

6356 — and KNUTT, LEO. A topographical guide to James Joyce's *Ulysses*. Colchester: 1975. 2 vols. Vol. 1. Text. Vol. 2. Maps.

6357 — and SENN, FRITZ, *ed.* A Wake digest. Sydney: 1968.

6358 JAMES JOYCE QUARTERLY. Vol. 10, no. 1, 1972. Special issue devoted to *Ulysses*.

6359 — *Finnegans Wake* Issue. *ibid*., vol. 11, no. 4, 1974.

6360 KELL, RICHARD. The Goddess theme in *A Portrait of the Artist*. *Dublin Mag.,* vol. 9, no. 3, 1972, 100–108.

6361 KELLEHER, JOHN V. Identifying the Irish printed sources for *Finnegans Wake*. *Ir. Univ. Rev.*, vol. 1, no. 2, 1971, 161–177.

6362 KIELY, ROBERT. Joyce and Lawrence by the Beautiful Sea. *Anglo-Ir. Stud*., vol. 3, 1977, 1–18.

6363 KLUG, MICHAEL A. The comic structure of Joyce's *Ulysses. Eire-Ir.*, vol. 11, no. 1, 1976, 63–84.

6364 LITZ, A. WALTON. The art of James Joyce: method and design in *Ulysses* and *Finnegans Wake*. New York: 1964

6365 — James Joyce. rev. ed., Boston: 1972. Sel. bibliog., pp. 129–138.

6366 MCHUGH, ROLAND. The Sigla of *Finnegans Wake.* London: 1976. Bibliog., 139–145.

6367 MADDOX, JAMES H., *Jr*. Joyce's *Ulysses* and the assault upon character. London and New Jersey: 1978.

6368 MARTIN, AUGUSTINE. Priest and artist in Joyce's early fiction. *Anglo-Ir. Stud.*, 2, 1976, 69–81.

6369 MASON, MICHAEL. James Joyce: *Ulysses.* London: 1972. *(Studies in English Literature no. 50)*

6370 O'HEHIR, BRENDAN. A Gaelic lexicon for *Finnegans Wake* and glossary for Joyce's other works. Berkeley, Los Angeles and London: 1967.

6371 PEAKE, C.H. James Joyce: the citizen and the artist. London: 1977. Deals with Joyce's narrative fiction.

6372 POWER, ARTHUR. On the presentation of *Ulysses* to Nora. *Dublin Mag.*, vol. 9, no. 3, 1972, 11–13.

6373 RYF, ROBERT S. A new approach to Joyce: the *Portrait of the Artist* as a guidebook. Berkeley and Los Angeles: 1964.

6374 SCHOLES, ROBERT, and KAIN, RICHARD M. The workshop of Daedalus: James Joyce and the raw materials for *A Portrait of the artist as a young man.* Evanston, Ill: 1965.

6375 SEIDEL, MICHAEL. Epic geography: James Joyce's *Ulysses*. Princeton: 1976.

6376 SENN, FRITZ. New light on Joyce from the Dublin Symposium. Bloomington and London: 1972.

6377 SLOMCZYNSKI, MACIEJ. Upon first decoding *Finnegans Wake. Polish Perspectives*, vol. 16, no. 11, 1973, 21–37.

6378 STALEY, THOMAS F. *ed*. Fifty years of *Ulysses*. Bloomington and London: 1974.

6379 — James Joyce today: essays on the major works. Bloomington: 1966.

6380 THORNTON, WELDON. Allusions in *Ulysses:* an annotated list. Chapel Hill: 1968. Bibliog., pp. 507–522.

6381 TINDALL, WILLIAM YORK. A reader's guide to *Finnegans Wake*. London: 1969. Bibliog., pp. 333–334.

6382 TORCHIANA, DONALD T. The opening of *Dubliners*: a recommendation. *Ir. Univ. Rev.*, vol. 1, no. 2, 1971, 149–160.

6383 A WAKE NEWSLETTER. New South Wales: Newcastle University College. vol. 1-, 1964-.

6384 WEIR, LORRAINE. Phoenix Park in *Finnegans Wake. Ir. Univ. Rev.*, vol. 5, no. 2, 1975, 230–249.

6385 WROBLEWSKI, ANDRZEJ. The trials of Leopold Bloom. *Polish Perspectives*, vol. 13, no. 6, 1969, 69–75. A review of Polish production of *Ulysses.*

KAVANAGH, PATRICK.

6386 MCMAHON, SEAN. The parish and the universe: a consideration of *Tarry Flynn. Eire-Ir.*, vol. 3, no. 3, 1968, 157–169.

KIELY, BENEDICT.

6387 FOSTER, JOHN WILSON. Dog among the moles: the fictional world of Benedict Kiely. *Dublin Mag.*, vol. 8, no. 6, 1970–71, 24–31.

LAVIN, MARY.

6388 DUNLEAVY, JANET EGLESON. The fiction of Mary Lavin: universal sensibility in a particular milieu. *Ir. Univ. Rev.*, vol. 7, no. 2, 1977, 222–236.

6389 MARTIN, AUGUSTINE. A skeleton key to the stories of Mary Lavin. *Studies,* 52, 1963, 393–406.

6390 MURRAY, THOMAS J. Mary Lavin's world: lovers and strangers. *Eire-Ir.*, vol. 7, no. 2, 1972, 122–131.

LE FANU, JOSEPH SHERIDAN.

6391 MCCORMACK, W.J. Sheridan Le Fanu and the authorship of anonymous fiction in the *Dublin University Magazine. Longroom,* nos. 14–15, 1976–77, 32–36.

6392 — Sheridan Le Fanu's *Uncle Silas*, *ibid.*, 2, 1970, 19–24.

6393 — Swedenborgianism as structure in Le Fanu's *Uncle Silas. ibid.*, 6, 1972, 23–29.

MCGAHERN, JOHN.

6394 CRONIN, JOHN. 'The Dark' is not light enough: the fiction of John MacGahern. *Studies*, 58, 1969, 427–432.

6395 KEHOE, KIERAN. Never nowhere without no: John McGahern's fiction. *St. Stephens*, vol. 3, no. 2, 1975, 48–52.

MACINTYRE, TOM.

6396 DENMAN, PETER. Form and fiction in the stories of Tom MacIntyre. *Etudes Irlandaises*, 4, 1975, 87–94.

MCLAVERTY, MICHAEL.

6397 FOSTER, JOHN WILSON. McLaverty's people. *Eire-Ir.*, vol. 6, no. 3, 1971, 92–105.

MACMANUS, FRANCIS

6398 MCMAHON, SEAN. Francis MacManus's novels of modern Ireland. *Eire-Ir.*, vol. 5, no. 1, 1970, 116–130.

MCNEILL, JANET.

6399 FOSTER, JOHN WILSON. Zoo stories: the novels of Janet McNeill. *Eire-Ir.*, vol. 9, no. 1, 1974, 104–114.

MATURIN, CHARLES ROBERT.

6400 Melmoth the wanderer: a tale. Edited with an introduction by Douglas Grant. London: 1968. Select bibliog., p. xviii.

MOORE, BRIAN.

6401 FOSTER, JOHN WILSON. Crisis and ritual in Brian Moore's Belfast novels. *Eire-Ir.*, vol. 3, no. 3, 1968, 66–74.

6402 GALLAGHER, MICHAEL PAUL. The novels of Brian Moore. *Studies,* 60, 1971, 180–194.

6403 PORTER, RAYMOND J. Mystery, miracle and faith in Brian Moore's *Catholics*. *Eire-Ir.*, vol. 10, no. 3, 1975, 79–88.

6404 PROSKY, MURRAY. The crisis of identity in the novels of Brian Moore. *Eire-Ir.*, vol. 6, no. 3, 1971, 106–118.

MOORE, GEORGE.

6405 BENNETT, LINDA. George Moore and James Joyce: story teller versus stylist. *Studies*, 66, 1977, 275–291.

6406 CARY, MEREDITH. George Moore's *Roman Experimental (Hail and Farewell)*. *Eire-Ir.*, vol. 9, no. 4, 1974, 142–150.

6407 CRONIN, JOHN. George Moore's *The Lake*: a possible source. *Eire-Ir.*, vol. 6, no. 3, 1971, 12–15.

6408 CUSACK, SORCHA. George Moore — the French Irishman. *Dublin Mag.*, vol. 8, no. 7, 1971, 36–45.

6409 KENNEDY, *Sister* EILEEN. Moore's *Untilled Field* and Joyce's *Dubliners*. *Eire-Ir.*, vol. 5, no. 3, 1970, 81–89.

6410 NEWELL, KENNETH B. The 'Wedding Gown' group in George Moore's *The Untilled Field*. *Eire-Ir.*, vol. 8, no. 4, 1973, 70–83.

MORGAN, *Lady*.

6411 NEWCOMER, JAMES. *Manor Sackville:* Lady Morgan's study of Ireland's perilous case. *Eire-Ir.*, vol. 10, no. 3, 1975, 11–17.

MURDOCH, IRIS.

6412 BYATT, A.S. Degrees of freedom: the novels of Iris Murdoch. London: 1965. Bibliog., pp. 217–218.

6413 EMERSON, DONALD. Violence and survival in the novels of Iris Murdoch. *Trans. Wisconsin Acad.*, 57, 1969, 21–28.

6414 STUBBS, PATRICIA. Two contemporary views on fiction: Iris Murdoch and Muriel Spark. *English*, vol. 23, no. 117, 1974, 102–110.

O'BRIEN, FLANN.

6415 APROBERTS, RUTH. *At Swim Two-Birds* and the novel as self-evident sham. *Eire-Ir.*, vol. 6, no. 2, 1971, 76–97.

6416 BENSTOCK, BERNARD. The three faces of Brian Nolan. *Eire-Ir.*, vol. 3, no. 3, 1968, 51–65. (Brian Nolan (or O'Nolan), Flann O'Brien and Myles na Gopaleen)

6417 CLISSMAN, ANNE. Flann O'Brien: a critical introduction to his writings: the story teller's book-web. Dublin and New York: 1975. Bibliog., pp. 359–365.

6418 JANIK, DEL IVAN. Flann O'Brien: the novelist as critic. *Eire-Ir.*, vol. 4, no. 4, 1969, 64–72.

6419 REDSHAW, THOMAS DILLON. O'Nolan's first Limbo: on the imaginative structure of *At Swim Two-Birds*. *Dublin Mag.*, vol. 9, no. 2, 1971–2, 89–99.

6420 WAIN, JOHN. To write for my own race: the fiction of Flann O'Brien. *Encounter,* vol. 29, no. 1, 1967, 71–85.

O'CONNOR, FRANK.

6421 CASEY, DANIEL J. The Seanachie's voice in three stories by Frank O'Connor. *Anglo-Ir. Stud.*, 3, 1977, 96–107.

6422 COOKE, MICHAEL G. Frank O'Connor and the fiction of artlessness. *Univ. Rev.*, vol. 5, no. 1, 1968, 87–102.

6423 DAVENPORT, GARY T. Frank O'Connor and the comedy of revolution. *Eire-Ir.*, vol. 8, no. 2, 1973, 108–116.

6424 KRAMER, C.R. Experimentation in technique: Frank O'Connor's 'Judas'. *Dublin Mag.*, vol. 8, nos. 1–2, 1969, 31–38.

6425 SHEEHY, MAURICE, *ed.* Michael/Frank: studies on Frank O'Connor with a bibliography of his writings. Dublin and London: 1969.

O'DONNELL, PEADAR.

6426 FREYER, GRATTAN. 'Big windows': the writings of Peadar O'Donnell. *Eire-Ir.*, vol. 11, no. 1, 1976, 106–114.

O'DUFFY, EIMAR.

6427 HOGAN, ROBERT. Eimar O'Duffy. Lewisburg; 1972. *(Irish Writers Series)*. Bibliog., pp. 82–4.

O'FAOLAIN, SEAN.

6428 HANLEY, KATHERINE. The short stories of Sean O'Faolain: theory and practice. *Eire-Ir.*, vol. 6, no. 3, 1971, 3–11.

6429 HARMON, MAURICE. Sean O'Faolain: a critical introduction. Notre Dame: 1966. Bibliog., pp. 203–217.

6430 MCMAHON, SEAN. O my youth, O my Country. *Eire-Ir.*, vol. 6, no. 3, 1971, 145–155. A study of Sean O'Faolain's *A nest of single folk* (1933).

6431 RIPPIER, JOSEPH STACEY. The short stories of Sean O'Faolain. Gerrards Cross: 1976.

O'FLAHERTY, LIAM.

6432 BOYLE, PATRICK. The short stories of Liam O'Flaherty. *Dublin Mag.*, vol. 9, no. 2, 1971–2, 21–30.

6433 DONNELLY, BRIAN. A nation gone wrong: Liam O'Flaherty's vision of modern Ireland. *Studies*, 63, 1974, 71–81.

6434 MURPHY, MAUREEN O'ROURKE. The double vision of Liam O'Flaherty. *Eire-Ir.*, vol. 8, no. 3, 1973, 20–25.

6435 O'BRIEN, H.J. Liam O'Flaherty's *The Informer*. *Dublin Mag.*, vol. 9, no. 4, 1972, 56–58.

6436 O'CONNOR, HELENE. Liam O'Flaherty: Literary ecologist. *Eire-Ir.*, vol. 7, no. 2, 1972, 47–54.

6437 SAUL, GEORGE BRANDON. A wild swing: the short stories of Liam O'Flaherty. *Rev. Eng. Lit.*, vol. 4, no. 3, 1963, 108–113.

6438 SHEERAN, PATRICK F. The novels of Liam O'Flaherty: a study in romantic realism. Dublin: 1976. Bibliog., pp. 313–5.

6439 ZNEIMER, JOHN. The literary vision of Liam O'Flaherty. Syracuse (N.Y.): 1970. Bibliog., pp. 199–203.

O'KELLY, SEUMAS.

6440 GRENNAN, EAMON. Figures in a landscape: the short stories of Seumas O'Kelly. *Studies*, 56, 1967, 283–296.

PLUNKETT, JAMES.

6441 ORMSBY, FRANK. The short stories of James Plunkett. *Hon. Ulst.,* 20, 1969, 10–16.

REID, FORREST.

6442 FRASER, MAURICE. The death of Narcussus. London: 1976. Bibliog., pp. 237–240. Study of paedophilia by analysis of works of novelists and dramatists including Forrest Reid.

6443 TAYLOR, BRIAN. Forrest Reid and the literature of nostalgia. *Studies*, 65, 1976, 291–6.

6444 — A strangely familiar scene: a note on landscape and locality in Forrest Reid. *Ir. Univ. Rev.*, vol. 7, no. 2, 1977, 213–218.

6445 WILSON, ROBERT BRYAN. Forrest Reid, novelist and critic. *Ir. Booklore,* vol. 2, no. 1, 1972, 112–115.

SHEEHAN, *Canon* PATRICK AUGUSTINE.

6446 COLEMAN, ANTHONY. Priest as artist: the dilemma of Canon Sheehan. *Studies*, 58, 1969, 30–41.

SOMERVILLE, EDITH and ROSS, MARTIN.

6447 LYONS, F.S.L. The twilight of the Big House. *Ariel,* vol. 1, no. 3, 1970, 110–122.

6448 POWELL, VIOLET. The Irish cousins; the books and background of Somerville and Ross. London: 1970.

6449 POWER, ANN. The big house of Somerville and Ross. *Dubliner*, vol. 3, no. 1, 1964, 43–53. On the novels of Somerville and Ross, particularly the *Irish R.M.* books.

STEPHENS, JAMES.

6450 MCFATE, PATRICIA ANNE. James Stephens's *Deirdre* and its legendary sources. *Eire-Ir.*, vol. 4, no. 3, 1969, 87–93.

6451 MARTIN, AUGUSTINE. James Stephens: a critical study. Dublin: 1977. Bibliog., pp. 170–3.

6452 — Stephens's *Deirdre*. *Univ. Rev.*, vol. 3, no. 7, 1965, 25–38.

STERNE, LAURENCE.

6453 CASH, ARTHUR H. and STEDMOND, JOHN M. The winged skull: papers from the Laurence Sterne Bicentenary Conference. London: 1971. Towards a Sterne bibliography:

Books and other material displayed at the Sterne conference, by Kenneth Monkman and J.C. Oates, 279–310; American editions of Laurence Sterne to 1800: a checklist, by Lodwick Hartley, 311–312.

6454 HARTLEY, LODWICK. Laurence Sterne in the twentieth century: an essay and a bibliography of Sternean Studies. Univ. of North Carolina Press: 1966.

6455 THOMSON, DAVID. Wild excursions: the life and fiction of Laurence Sterne. London: 1972. Bibliog., pp. 293–296.

STOKER, BRAM.

6456 The annotated Dracula: Dracula. Introduction, notes, and bibliography by Leonard Wolf. London and New York: 1976.

6457 AYLES, DAPHNE. The two worlds of Bram Stoker. *Dublin Mag.*, vol. 9, no. 2, 1971–2, 62–66.

6458 BIERMAN, JOSEPH S. The genesis and dating of Dracula from Bram Stoker's working notes. *N. and Q., new ser.*, 24, 1977, 39–41.

STUART, FRANCIS

6459 NATTERSTAD, J.H. Francis Stuart: at the edge of recognition. *Eire–Ir.*, vol. 9, no. 3, 1974, 69–85.

6460 O'BRIEN, H.J. St. Catherine of Siena in Ireland. *Eire-Ir.*, vol. 6, no. 2, 1971, 98–110. A study of Francis Stuart's *Pigeon Irish* (1932).

6461 — Francis Stuart's *Cathleen Ni Houlahan. Dublin Mag.*, vol. 8, no. 8, 1971, 48–54.

6462 WILKINS, PAUL. Francis Stuart's *Black List, Section II. Dublin Mag.*, vol. 10, no. 3, 1973–4, 38–45.

TROLLOPE, ANTHONY.

6463 STEWART, IAN. Go west, young man: Anthony Trollope's early days in Ireland. *Country Life*, vol. 149, no. 3859, 1971, 1325–28.

6464 WITTIG, E.W. Trollope's Irish fiction. *Eire-Ir.*, vol. 9, no. 3, 1974, 87–118.

Oratory

6465 DOLAN, T.P. Irish oratory from Emmet to Casement. *Ir. Univ. Rev.,* vol. 6, no. 2, 1976, 151–163.

6466 GRIFFITH, FRANCIS. Contemporary opinion of O'Connell's oratory. *Eire-Ir.*, vol. 7, no. 3, 1972, 24–28.

GAELIC LITERATURE

6467 ARBOIS DE JUBAINVILLE, HENRY D'. Essai d'un catalogue de la littérature épique de l'Irlande, précédé d'une étude sur les manuscrits en langue Irlandaise conservés dans Iles Britanniques et sur le continent. Paris: 1883.

6468 — Supplement . . . By Georges Dottin. *Rev. Celt.,* 33, 1912, 1–40. For bibliography of Arbois de Jubainville see *Rev. Celt.*, 32, 1911, 456–74.

6469 BREATHNACH, R.A. The end of a tradition: a survey of eithteenth century Irish literature. *Stud. Hib.*, 1, 1961, 128–50.

6470 — Two eighteenth century Irish scholars: J.C. Walker and Charlotte Brooke. *Stud. Hib.*, 5, 1965, 88–97.

6471 BROMWICH, RACHAEL. Medieval Celtic Literature: a select bibliography. Toronto: 1974. (*Medieval bibliographies no. 5*). Aim of the series is to further the interdisciplinary approach to the study of the Middle Ages . . . and is primarily to assist newcomers to the subject.

6472 CARNEY, JAMES. The deeper level of early Irish literature. *Cap. Ann.*, 1969, 160–171.

6473 — Early Irish poetry. Cork: 1965.

6474 CHICAGO PUBLIC LIBRARY. Leabhair gaedhilge: Irish books in the library. Chicago: 1942.

6475 CLEEVE, BRIAN. Dictionary of Irish writers. Cork: 1971. Vol. 3. Writers in the Irish language.

6476 CULLEN, L.M. *The Hidden Ireland*: reassessment of a concept. *Stud. Hib.*, 9, 1969, 7–47. *The Hidden Ireland*, by Daniel Corkery, first pub. in 1925.

6477 DE BLACAM, AODH. Gaelic literature surveyed [new ed.]; with an additional chapter by Eoghan O'Hanluain. Dublin: 1973. 1st ed. 1929.

6478 DILLON, MYLES. Early Irish Literature. Chicago: 1948.

6479 DOTTIN, GEORGES. La littérature gaelique de l'Irlande. *Revue de synthèse historique,* 3, 1901, 60–97.

6480 — The Gaelic literature of Ireland; translated by Joseph Dunn. Washington: 1906.

Privately printed. For bibliography of Georges Dottin, by himself, for period 1896–1910, see *Annales de Bretagne*, 38, 1929, 505–25.

6481 GREENE, DAVID. Fifty years of writing in Irish. *Studies*, 55, 1966, 51–59.

6482 — Writing in Irish today. Cork: 1972.

6483 HAE, R. DE, and DHONNCHADHA, BRIGHID NI. Clar litrihdeachta na nua-ghaedhilge, 1850–1936. Dublin: 1938–40. 3 vols.

6484 IRISH TEXTS SOCIETY. London and (afterwards) Dublin. Publications. vol. 1–, 1899–.

6485 KINSELLA, THOMAS. The Tain [Bo Cuailgne]: a guide. *Ir. Wel.*, vol. 24, no. 6, 1975, 19–30.

6486 KNOTT, ELEANOR, and MURPHY, GERARD. Early Irish literature; introduction by James Carney. London: 1966.

6487 KRAUSE, DAVID. The Hidden Oisin. *Stud. Hib.*, 6, 1966, 7–24. On Ossianic poetry.

6488 MACDONAGH, THOMAS. Literature in Ireland: studies Irish and Anglo-Irish. Dublin [1916]. Bibliog., pp. 239–41.

6489 MEYER, KUNO. Rawlinson B 502: a collection of pieces in prose and verse in the Irish language compiled during the eleventh and twelfth centuries, now published in facsimile from the original manuscript in the Bodleian Library. Oxford: 1909.

6490 O'DROIGHNEAIN, MUIRIS. Taighde i gcomhair stair litridheachta na nua-ghaedhilge o 1882 anuas. Baile Atha Cliath: 1936.

6491 AN TOIREACHTAS, 1947. Taisbeantas leabhar ghaedhilge. Irish book exhibition. Dublin: 1947.

6492 O'LAOGHAIRE, DIARMUID. Nature poetry in Irish. *Cap. Ann.*, 1974, 242–252.

6493 O'LOCHLAINN, COLM. The Gaelic Society of London, 1840, and its library. *Ir. Book Lov.*, 30, 1946–8, 80–4. A description of *Catalogue of books, tracts and papers belonging to the . . . Society*. London: 1840.

6494 O'LOONEY, BRIAN. On ancient historic tales in the Irish language. *R. Ir. Acad. Proc., ser. 2*, 1, 1870–9, 215–50.

6495 O'NEILL, SEAMUS. The Hidden Ulster: Gaelic pioneers of the North. *Studies*, 55, 1966, 60–66.

6496 O'SULLIVAN, DONAL. Thaddaeus Connellan and his books of Irish poetry. *Eigse,* 3, 1941–2, 278–304.

6497 POLLARD, M. The Sairseal agus Dill collection. *Longroom*, 1, 1970, 43. Donation to Trinity College, Dublin of 218 vols.

6498 ROBINSON, FRED NORRIS. Satirists and enchanters in early Irish literature. [Chicago]. American Committee for Irish Studies, (*Reports in Irish Studies no. 1*). [1967].

6499 RYAN, DESMOND. The sword of light: from the Four Masters to Douglas Hyde, 1636–1938. London: 1939. Bibliog., pp. 247–50.

6500 SAUL, GEORGE BRANDON. Traditional Irish literature and its backgrounds. Lewisburg: 1970. A revision of *The Shadow of the Three Queens*, first pub. 1953.

6501 SHAW, FRANCIS. Medieval medico-philosophical treatises in the Irish language. In *Feil-sgribhinn Eoin mic Neill*, edited by Rev. John Ryan. Dublin: 1940, pp. 144–57.

6502 THOMSON, DERICK S. The Gaelic sources of MacPherson's Ossian. Edinburgh and London [1952]. *(Aberdeen University study ser.*, no. 130.)

6503 THURNEYSEN, RUDOLF. Die Irische Helden-und Konigsage bis zum Siebzehnten Jahrhundert. Teil 1 und 2 Halle (Saale), 1921.

6504 — Zu Irischen Handschriften und Litteraturdenk Malern. *Abhandlungen der Königlichen Gesellschaft der Wissenschaften zu Gottingen, Philologisch-historische Klasse, Neue Folge, Bd.* 14, 2–3, 1912–13.

6505 TORNA, *pseud.* (*i.e.*, Tadg O'Donoghue). Clar Scribhinni Thorna o 1896 anuas go 1945 A.D. Diarmuid o h-Ealuighthe do thiom-suigh. In *Feilscribhinn Torna*, edited by Seamus Pender. Cork: 1947, pp. 225–58.

6506 — List of the literary works in Irish of Tadg O'Donoghue. Cork: 1916.

6507 TRAVIS, JAMES. Early Celtic versecraft: origin, development, diffusion. Shannon: 1973.

6508 WALSH, PAUL. Gleanings from Irish manuscripts. Dublin: 1918. 2nd ed. 1933.

6509 — Irish men of learning: studies. Dublin: 1947.

6510 WELCH, ROBERT. Douglas Hyde and his translations of Gaelic verse. *Studies*, 64, 1975, 243–257.

6511 WILLIAM, J.E. CAERWYN. The Court poet in medieval Ireland. London: 1971.

6512 WILLIAMS, N.J.A. Irish satire and its sources. *Stud. Celt.*, vols. 12–13, 1977–8, 217–246.

Humour, Satire

6513 EID, LEROY V. *Puck* and the Irish: 'the one American idea'. The satirical magazine. *Eire-Ir.*, vol. 11, no. 2, 1976, 18–35.

6514 MERCIER, VIVIAN. The Irish comic tradition. Oxford: 1962.

6515 MESSENGER, JOHN C. Humour in an Irish folk community. *Ir. Univ. Rev.*, vol. 6, no. 2, 1976, 214–222.

6516 MORROW, H.L. Taking the Irish bull by the horns. *Ir. Wel.*, vol. 20, no. 5, 1972, 10–13.

6517 O'DONOGHUE, DAVID JAMES (ed.). The humour of Ireland ... with biographical index and notes. London: 1898.

SWIFT, JONATHAN.

6518 BROWN, DANIEL R. Swift and the limitations of satire. *Dublin Mag.*, vol. 9, no. 4, 1972, 68–78.

6519 COUGHLIN, MATTHEW N. 'This deluge of brass': rhetoric in the first and fourth Drapier Letters. *Eire-Ir.*, vol. 11, no. 2, 1976, 77–91.

6520 DONOGHUE, DENIS. Jonathan Swift: a critical introduction. Cambridge: 1969.

6521 GRAVIL, RICHARD. Swift: *Gulliver's travels*, a casebook. London: 1976. Bibliog., pp. 248–250.

6522 MURRAY, PATRICK. Some notes on the interpretation of Swift's satires. *Ir. Eccles. Rec.*, 110, 1968, 158–172.

6523 — Further notes on the interpretation of Swift's satires. *ibid.*, 110, 1968, 265–276.

6524 PIPER, WILLIAM BOWMAN. The sense of *Gulliver's travels. Rice Univ. Stud.*, vol. 61, no. 1, 1975, 75–106.

6525 PROBYN, CLIVE T. *ed.* The art of Jonathan Swift. London: 1978.

6526 QUINTANA, RICARDO. The mind and art of Jonathan Swift. 2nd ed. London: 1953. Bibliog., pp. 367–77. 1st ed. 1936.

6527 RAWSON, C.J. Gulliver and the gentle reader: studies in Swift and our time. London and Boston: 1973.

6528 WARD, DAVID. Jonathan Swift: an introductory essay. London: 1973. Bibliog., pp. 205–211.

6529 WILLIAMS, KATHLEEN. Jonathan Swift. London and New York: 1968. Bibliog., pp. 107–111.

German Literature

6530 O'NEILL, PATRICK. German literature and the *Dublin University Magazine,* 1833–50: a checklist and commentary. *Longroom*, 14–15, 1976–77, 20–31.

6531 — The reception of German literature in Ireland, 1750–1850. *Stud. Hib.*, 16, 1976, 122–139.

Latin Writers, Orientalists

6532 BAXTER, JAMES HOUSTON, *and others.* An index of British and Irish Latin writers, A.D. 400–1520, by J.H. Baxter, Charles Johnson and James Field Willard. *Archivium Latinitatis medii aevi (Bull. du Cange),* 7, 1932, 7–219.

6533 ESPOSITO, MARIO. The Latin writers of mediaeval Ireland. *Hermathena*, 14, 1906–7, 519–29.

6534 — Supplement. *ibid.*, 15, 1908–9, 353–64.

6535 — Notes on the Latin writers of mediaeval Ireland, by L. Gougaud. *Ir. Theol. Qtr.,* 4, 1909, 57–65. A criticism of Esposito's list with additions.

6536 — The Latin writers of mediaeval Ireland. *ibid.*, 4, 1909, 181–5. A reply to Gougaud's article.

6537 — Hiberno-Latin manuscripts in the libraries of Switzerland. *R. Ir. Acad. Proc., Sec. C,* 28, 1910, 62–95; 30, 1912–13, 1–14.

6538 — Notes on mediaeval Hiberno-Latin and Hiberno-French literature. *Hermathena,* 16, 1910–11, 58–72, 325–33.

6539 — A bibliography of the Latin writers of mediaeval Ireland. *Studies*, 2, 1913, 495–521.

6540 MANSOOR, M. The story of Irish Orientalism. Dublin: 1944. Bibliog., pp. 63–4.

6541 PATTON, ELSIE. Turner Macon: distinguished soldier and Persian scholar (1792–1836). *Ir. Book.*, vol. 1, no. 1, 1971, 24–29.

6542 STANFORD, W.B. Towards a history of classical influences in Ireland. [with bibliog.] *R. Ir. Acad. Proc., Sec. C.*, 70, 1970, 13–91.

6543 TOTOLOS, ALICIA, *compiler*. Research in classical studies for university degrees in Great Britain and Ireland. Univ. of London, *Institute of Classical Studies, Bulletin no. 16,* 1969.

GEOGRAPHY, TRAVEL

Bibliography

6544 ANDERSON, JOHN P. The Book of British Topography. [1st ed. reprinted] with a new introduction by Jack Simmons. Wakefield: 1976. Facsimile reprint of 1st ed. London: 1881. Ireland, pp. 414–43.

6545 BANDINEL, B. A catalogue of the books relating to British topography, and Saxon and Northern literature, bequeathed to the Bodleian Library in the year 1799, by Richard Gough. Oxford: 1814. Ireland, pp. 368–84.

6546 BATES, E.S. Touring in 1600: a study in the development of travel as a means of education. London: 1911. Bibliog., pp. 389–406.

6547 BOOK ASSOCIATION OF IRELAND. General description and local history. *Ir. Lib. Bull.*, vol. 6, no. 4, 1945, 85–8.

6548 BREATHNACH, MICHAEL S. and FAHY, GERARD, *compilers*. Readings in geography: a bibliography. *Oideas*, 7, 1971, 29–36.

6549 COX, EDWARD GODFREY. A reference guide to the literature of travel, including voyages, geographical descriptions, adventures, shipwrecks and expeditions. Seattle: 1935–49. 3 vols. (*Washington Univ. pub. in language and literature,* vols. 9, 10 and 12.)

6550 DANIELL, WALTER V. and NIELD, FREDERICK J. Manual of British topography: a catalogue of county and local histories, pamphlets, views, drawings, maps, etc., connected with and illustrating the principal localities in the United Kingdom. London: 1909.

6551 DAVIES, GORDON L. Dr. Anthony Farrington and the Geographical Society of Ireland [and] A bibliography of the scientific writings of A. Farrington. *Ir. Geog.*, vol. 4, no. 5, 1963, 311–320.

6552 DAVIES, K. MARY. A bibliography of Mr. T.W. Freeman's contributions to the geography of Ireland. *Ir. Geog.*, vol. 6, no. 5, 1973, 529–531.

6553 FORDHAM, HERBERT GEORGE. The road-books and itineraries of Ireland, 1647 to 1850: a catalogue. *Bibliog. Soc. Ir.*, vol. 2, no. 4, 1923, 63–76.

6554 GOUGH, RICHARD. British topography; or, an historical account of what has been done for illustrating the topographical antiquities of Great Britain and Ireland. London: 1780. 2 vols.

6555 HUMPHREYS, ARTHUR LEE. A handbook to county bibliography; being a bibliography of bibliographies relating to the counties and towns of Great Britain and Ireland. London: 1917. Includes all systematic bibliographies, also source books, indexes, etc., of local history or topographical material.

6556 LECTOR, *pseud.* Bibliography of Irish [county] surveys. *Dublin Pen. J.,* January 31, 1903, 598.

6557 LIBRARY ASSOCIATION, County Libraries Group. Face of Ireland. 2nd ed. Durham: 1968. (*Reader's guide no. 105).*

6558 MICKS, WILLIAM L. A catalogue of the library of the late W.L. Micks . . . comprising a unique collection of Irish tours, also Irish topography, genealogy, history, biographies and antiquities. 1929. Typescript in National Library, Dublin.

6559 ROYAL GEOGRAPHICAL SOCIETY. Review of British geographical work during the hundred years, 1789–1889: bibliography. London: 1893.

6560 UNITED STATES. Library of Congress, European affairs division. Introduction to Europe: a selective guide to background reading. Washington: 1950. Ireland, pp. 11–17.

6561 — Supplement, 1950–5. Washington: 1955. Ireland, pp. 20–5.

6562 UPCOTT, W. and SMITH, JOHN RUSSELL. A catalogue of ten thousand tracts and pamphlets and fifty thousand prints and drawings, illustrating the topography and antiquities of England, Wales, Scotland and Ireland . . . offered for sale by Alfred Russell Smith. London: 1878.

6563 WRIGHT, JOHN KIRTLAND and PLATT, ELIZABETH T. Aids to geographical research: bibliographies, periodicals, atlases, gazetteers, and other reference books. 2nd ed. rev. New York, American Geographical Society: 1948.

Gazetteers

6564 AUTOMOBILE ASSOCIATION. Illustrated road book of Ireland, with gazetteer, itineraries, maps and town plans. 2nd illus. ed. Dublin: 1970.

6565 INGLIS, HARRY R.G. The Contour road book of Ireland: a series of elevation plans of the roads, with measurements and descriptive letterpress. 2nd ed. extensively rev. and extended by Robert M.G. Inglis. Edinburgh and London: 1962.

6566 KILLANIN, MICHAEL MORRIS, *3rd baron*, and DUIGNAN, MICHAEL. The Shell guide to Ireland. 2nd ed. London: 1967. Bibliog., pp. 481–3.

6567 LEHANE, BRENDAN. Companion guide to Ireland. London: 1973. Bibliog., pp. 460–462.

Tours

6568 FACKLER, HERBERT V. Wordsworth in Ireland, 1829: a survey of his tour. *Eire-Ir.*, vol. 6, no. 1, 1971, 53–64.

6569 GLIN, KNIGHT OF, *ed*. The Irish tour of an eighteenth-century antiquary and his notions about Irish round towers. *Ir. Wel.*, vol. 19, no. 3, 1970, 6–12. Owen Salusbury Brereton, travelled in Ireland 1634–5 (published by the Chetham Society in 1844).

6570 HEANEY, HENRY. Tourists in Ireland, 1800–1850: evaluative bibliography. Typescript; submitted to Library Association for Fellowship, 1968.

6571 O'DONOGHUE, D.J. Sir Walter Scott's tour in Ireland in 1825 [facsimile reprint] Folcroft, Pa.: 1976. Limited ed. of 100 copies.

6572 PANTER, G.W. Bibliography of Irish tours, with remarks on those before 1700. Paper read before the Bibliographical Society of Ireland, January 29, 1923.

6573 YOUNG, ARTHUR. A tour in Ireland, 1776–1779, edited by A.W. Hutton; [reprinted with a] new introduction by J.B. Ruane. Shannon: 1970. 2 vols. Bibliography of Arthur Young, by J.P. Anderson, vol. 2, pp. 349–74.

Post Cards

6574 KING, JEREMIAH. Bibliography of Irish pictorial post cards. London: 1903.

Periodicals

6575 DAVIS, E. JEFFRIES, and TAYLOR, E.G.R., *compilers*. Guide to periodicals and bibliographies dealing with geography, archaeology and history. London: 1938. *(Historical Association pamphlets,* no. 110.)

6576 IRISH GEOGRAPHY: bulletin of the Geographical Society of Ireland. Dublin: vol. 1–, 1944–. From vol. 5 includes annual list 'Geographical literature relating to Ireland'.

General

6577 ANDREWS, J.H. William Petty (*The Making of Irish Geography, I*). *Ir. Geog.*, 9, 1976, 100–103.

6578 ASHE, GEOFFREY. Land to the west: St. Brendan's voyage to America. London: 1962. Bibliog., pp. 333–40.

6579 BRITISH ASSOCIATION FOR THE ADVANCEMENT OF SCIENCE. A view of Ireland: twelve essays on different aspects of Irish life and the Irish countryside, edited by James Meenan and David A. Webb. Dublin: 1957. Includes bibliogs., and covers the following aspects – physiography and climate, geology, botany, zoology, inland fisheries, economic structure, peat, archaeology, folklore, language, and the city of Dublin.

6580 COLMAN, HENRY, *ed.* Eire today. Dublin, 1947. Bibliog., pp. 144–7.

6581 CONNELLAN, OWEN. On the rivers of Ireland, with the derivations of their names. *R. Ir. Acad. Proc.*, 10, 1866–69, 443–458.

6582 CROSSLEY-HOLLAND, KEVIN. Pieces of land: journeys to eight islands. London: 1972. Bibliog., pp. 283–290. Includes Tory and Inishmore islands.

6583 DAVIES, GORDON L. Thomas Walter Freeman and the geography of Ireland – a tribute. *Ir. Geog.*, vol. 6, no. 5, 1973, 521–528.

6584 GARDNER, RAYMOND. Land of time enough. London: 1977. Bibliog., pp. 223–4. Journey through the waterways of Ireland.

6585 JOHNSON, JAMES H. *The Irish Tithe Composition Applotment Books* as a geographical source [with bibliogs.]. *Ir. Geog.*, vol. 3, no. 5, 1958, 254–62.

6586 MOULD, DAPHNE D.C. POCHIN. Ireland from the air. Newton Abbot: 1972.

6587 PRAEGER, ROBERT LLOYD. The way that I went: an Irishman in Ireland. Dublin and London: 1937.

6588 RICE, H.J. Thanks for the memory; being personal reminiscences, traditions, history and navigational details about the River Shannon. [Reprint of 1st ed.]. Athlone: 1974. Limited ed. of 500 copies.

6589 SAORSTAT EIREANN. Irish Free State official handbook. Dublin: 1932. Includes valuable bibliogs.

6590 TAYLOR, E.G.R. Tudor geography, 1485–1583. London: 1930. Bibliog., pp. 162–243.

6591 — Later Tudor and early Stuart geography, 1583–1650. London: 1934. Bibliog., pp. 177–298.

Historical Geography

6592 AALEN, F.H.A. Man and the landscape in Ireland. London and New York: 1978. Consolidated bibliography pp. 313–334.

6593 FREEMAN, T.W. Ireland: a general and regional geography. 4th ed. rev., London: 1972. Bibliog., pp. 507–541.

6594 MCCOURT, DESMOND. The use of oral tradition in Irish historical geography. *Ir. Geog.*, vol. 6, no. 4, 1972, 394–410.

6595 MITCHELL, FRANK. The Irish landscape. London: 1976.

Place Names

6596 ANDERSON, THORSTEN and SANDRED, KARL INGE, *eds.* The Vikings: proceedings of the symposium of the Faculty of Arts of Upsala University, June 6–9, 1977. *(Acta Universitatis Upsaliensis: Symposia Universitatis Upsaliensis Annum Quingentesimum, 8)*. The evidence of language and placenames of Ireland, by David Greene. pp. 119–123.

6597 ASSOCIATION FOR THE PRESERVATION OF THE MEMORIALS OF THE DEAD, Ireland. Consolidated index of surnames and placenames in the Journal, vols. 1–7, 1888–1909. Compiled by Miss Vigors and Mrs. Peirce G. Mahony. Dublin: 1914.

6598 DINNSEANCHAS: An Cumann Logainmneacha. Baile Atha Cliath. Iml. 1–, 1964–.

6599 GOBLET, YANN MORVAN. Topographical index of the parishes and townlands of Ireland in Sir William Petty's Ms. barony maps (*c*.1655–9). Dublin: Irish Manuscripts Commission: 1932.

6600 HOGAN, EDMUND. Onomasticon Goedelicum locorum et tribuum Hiberniae et Scotiae: an index, with identifications, to the Gaelic names of places and tribes. Dublin: 1910. Bibliog., pp. xi–xiv.

6601 JOYCE, P.W. The origin and history of Irish names of places [Facsimile reprint]. Wakefield: 1972–3. 2 vols.

6602 LIST OF BOOKS ON PLACE NAMES. In Best's *Bibliography of Irish philology, etc.,* 1913, pp. 19–21. 1942 ed., pp. 9–17.

6603 MACAODHA, BREANDAN S. Placename research in Ireland. *Anglo. Ir. Stud.*, 1, 1975, 97–104.

6604 O'CIOBHAIN, BREANDAN. Toponomia Hiberniae, I: baruntacht. Dhun Ciarain Thuaidh/ Barony of Dunkerron North. Dublin: 1978.

6605 O'SIOCHFHRADHA, PADRAIG (*i.e.,* An Seabhac). Triocha-cead Chorca Dhuibne. Tiomargadh ar a log-ainmneacha agus ar sheanchas a ghabhann leo san mar aon le sloinnte agus ainmneacha daoine. Baile Atha Cliath: 1939. Bibliog., pp. xxi–xxiii.

6606 PRICE, LIAM. The place names of Co. Wicklow [with bibliogs.]. Dublin: 1945–67. 7 pts.

6607 — The antiquities and place names of South County Dublin. *Dublin Hist. Rec.*, 2, 1939–40, 121–133.

6608 — The place names of the barony of Arklow, county of Wicklow: their early forms collected. *R. Ir. Acad. Proc., Sec. C,* 46, 1940–1, 237–86.

6609 — The place names of the barony of Newcastle, Co. Wicklow. *R. Ir. Acad. Proc., Sec. C,* 44, 1937–8, 139–79.

6610 TAYLOR, A.B. British and Irish place-names in old Norse literature. *Universitet i Bergin arbok, historisk-antikvarisk rekke, nr.* 1, 1955, 113–22.

6611 ULSTER PLACE NAME SOCIETY. Bulletin. vol. 1–, 1952–.

6612 WALSH, *The Rev.* PAUL. The placenames of Westmeath. Dublin: 1957.

6613 WARD, MICHAEL. Townland names in the barony of Dunboyne. *Riocht na Midhe,* vol. 5, no. 4, 1974, 20–32.

ARCHAEOLOGY, ANTIQUITIES

Bibliography

6614 Bibliography of periodical literature relating to the archaeology of Ulster: a short review for the year 1937, by Basil Megaw. *Ulster J. Arch., 3rd ser.*, 1, 1938, 231–4.

6615 — 1938. *ibid.*, 2, 1939, 287–91.

6616 — 1939. By B. Megaw and E.E. Evans. *ibid.*, 3, 1940, 170–1.

6617 — 1940. By O. Davies. *ibid.*, 4, 1941, 151–2.

6618 — 1941–2. By J.M. Mogey. *ibid.*, 6, 1943, 142–3.

6619 — 1943–5. By E.R.R. Green and J.M. Mogey. *ibid.*, 9, 1946, 128–9.

6620 — 1946–7. By J.M. Sidebotham. *ibid.*, 11, 1948, 134–5.

6621 — 1948–50. By E.M. Jope. *ibid.*, 13, 1950, 108–11.

6622 COUNCIL FOR BRITISH ARCHAEOLOGY. Archaeological bibliography for Great Britain and Ireland, 1950–1–. London: 1954–. Preceded by *Archaeological Bulletin for the British Isles,* 1940–9.

6623 GOMME, GEORGE LAURENCE, and GOMME, BERNARD, *eds.* Index of archaeological papers, 1665–1890. London: 1907. Continued annually as *Index of archaeological papers,* from 1891 to 1910.

6624 LIST OF PAPERS AND ILLUSTRATIONS on the antiquities of Youghal, which have appeared in *The Journal of the Royal Society of Antiquaries of Ireland. ibid.*, 33, 1903, 344.

6625 MCNEILL, CHARLES. A short bibliography of Irish archaeology. *Bibliog. Soc. Ir.*, vol. 3, no. 10, 1927. Includes county histories.

6626 YEAR'S WORK IN ARCHAEOLOGY. London: 1921–38.

Catalogues

6627 BELFAST MUSEUM. Descriptive catalogue of the collection of antiquities, etc., illustrative of Irish history, exhibited . . . at the 22nd meeting of the British Association, 1852. Belfast: 1852.

6628 CROKER, THOMAS CROFTON. Catalogue of a collection of antiquities formed by T.C. Croker. London: 1854.

6629 ROYAL IRISH ACADEMY. A descriptive catalogue of the antiquities, etc., in the Museum of the Royal Irish Academy, by Sir W.R.W. Wilde. Dublin: 1857–61. 2 vols.

Collecting, Preservation

6630 KILKENNY AND SOUTH EAST OF IRELAND ARCHAEOLOGICAL SOCIETY. Hints and queries, intended to promote the preservation of antiquities, and the collecting and arrangement of information on the subject of local history and tradition. Dublin: 1858.

Societies

6631 GILBERT, JOHN THOMAS. The historic literature of Ireland: an essay on the publications of the Irish Archaeological Society. Dublin: 1851. Reprinted from *The Ir. Qtr. Rev.*

6632 IRISH ARCHAEOLOGICAL AND LITERARY SOCIETIES, etc., past and present. By M.R.S.A.I. *Dublin Pen. J., new ser.,* 1, 1902–3, 123.

6633 LOVE, WALTER D. The Hibernian Antiquarian Society: a forgotten predecessor to the Royal Irish Academy. *Studies*, 50, 1962, 419–431.

6634 ROYAL ARCHAEOLOGICAL INSTITUTE OF GREAT BRITAIN AND IRELAND. Archaeological Journal. vol. 1–, 1844–. Index to vols. 1–25, 1878.

6635 — Catalogue of the library. London: 1890. Author catalogue with topographical index.

6636 ROYAL SOCIETY OF ANTIQUARIES OF IRELAND. Journal, vol. 1–, 1849–. Index, vols. 1–19, 1849–89, vol. 20, Dublin, 1902: vols. 21–40, 1891–1910, Dublin, 1915; vols. 41–60, 1911–30, Dublin, 1933. Formerly The Royal Historical and Archaeological Association of Ireland, founded in 1849 as The Kilkenny Archaeological Association, and from 1854–67 The Kilkenny and South East of Ireland Archaeological Society.

General

6637 APSIMON, A.M. The earlier Bronze Age in the North of Ireland [with bibliog.]. *Ulster J. Arch., 3rd ser.*, 32, 1969, 28–72. Appendix: Earlier Bronze Age pottery from the North of Ireland.

6638 — Ballynagilly [Co. Tyrone]. *Current Archaeology*, 24, 1971, 11–13.

6639 BATESON, J.D. Roman material from Ireland: a re-consideration [with bibliog.]. *R. Ir. Acad. Proc., Sec. C.*, 73, 1973, 21–97. Includes 90 numismatic finds and over 50 non-numismatic discoveries.

6640 BRIGGS, C. STEPHEN. Dealing with antiquities in 19th century Dublin. *Dublin Hist. Rec.*, vol. 31, no. 4, 1978, 146–148.

6641 BURL, AUBREY. The Stone Circles of the British Isles. New Haven and London: 1976. Bibliog., pp. 376–395; The Stone Circles of Ireland, pp. 213–253.

6642 CLARKE, D.L. Beaker pottery of Great Britain and Ireland. London: 1970. *(Gulbenkian archaeological series*).

6643 COFFEY, GEORGE. The Bronze age in Ireland. Dublin: 1913.

6644 — New Grange and other incised tumuli in Ireland [2nd ed.] Poole: 1977. First pub. 1912.

6645 COUNCIL FOR BRITISH ARCHAEOLOGY. Archaeological site index to radiocarbon dates for Great Britain and Ireland, covering dates published in the period up to December 1970, with acknowledgement to the publishers of *Radiocarbon* (American Journal of Science) [and first list of addenda to . . . 31st December 1971] London: 1971–2. *(British Archaeological Abstracts Supplement)*.

6646 CURRENT ARCHAEOLOGY 22, 1970. Issue devoted to current archaeology in Ireland. Reports on Knowth, New Grange, Court Cairns, Navan Fort, Dun Ailinne. Dublin.

6647 DE BRUN, PADRAIG. John Windele and Father John Casey: Windele's visit to Inis Tuaisceart in 1838. *J. Kerry Arch. Hist. Soc.*, 7, 1974, 71–106.

6648 DELANEY, T.G. *ed.* Excavations, 1973: summary account of archaeological work in Ireland. Belfast: Ulster Museum: 1974. Summary for 1974 issued in 1975.

6649 DE PAOR, LIAM. Excavations at Mellifont Abbey, Co. Louth. *R. Ir. Acad. Proc., Sec. C.*, vol. 68, no. 2, 1969, 109–164.

6650 DE VALERA, RUAIDHRI, and O'NUALLAIN, SEAN. Survey of the megalithic tombs of Ireland. Dublin. Vol. 1. Co. Clare, 1961. Vol. 2. Co. Mayo, 1964. Vol. 3. Counties Galway-Roscommon- Leitrim- Longford-Westmeath- Laoighis- Offaly- Kildare-Cavan, 1972.

6651 DUNBOY CASTLE, CO. CORK. Excavated by the late Dr. E.M. Fahy; report compiled by Margaret Gowen. *Cork Hist. Arch. Soc. J.*, 83, 1978, 1–49.

6652 EOGAN, GEORGE. Catalogue of Irish bronze swords. Dublin: 1965. Bibliog., pp. 184–188.

6653 — A decade of excavations at Knowth, Co. Meath. *Ir. Univ. Rev.*, vol. 3, no. 1, 1973, 66–79.

6654 — Excavations at Knowth, Co. Meath, 1962–1965 [with bibliog.]. *R. Ir. Acad. Proc., Sec. C.,* 66, 1968, 299–400.

6655 — Excavations at Knowth, Co. Meath, 1968. *Antiquity*, vol. 43, 1969, 8–14.

6656 — The Later Bronze age in Ireland in the light of recent research. *Prehist. Soc. Proc.*, 30, 1964, 268–351.

6657 EVANS, E. ESTYN. Archaeology in Ulster since 1920 [with bibliog.]. *Ulster J. Arch.*, 31, 1968, 3–8.

6658 — Prehistoric and early Christian Ireland: a guide. London: 1966. Bibliog., pp. 223–230.

6659 FORDE-JOHNSTON, J. Prehistoric Britain and Ireland. London: 1966. Bibliog., pp. 201–4.

6660 HARBISON, PETER. The Archaeology of Ireland. London: 1976.

6661 — The Axes of the early bronze age in Ireland. Munchen: 1969. *(Praehistorische Bronzefunde, Abteilung IX, Band I)*.

6662 — Catalogue of Irish early bronze age associated finds containing copper or bronze. *R. Ir. Acad. Proc., Sec. C.*, 67, 1968, 35–91.

6663 — The Daggers and the halberds of the early bronze age in Ireland. Munchen: 1969. *(Praehistorische Bronzefunde, Abteilung VI, Band I)*.

6664 — The Earlier Bronze Age in Ireland, late 3rd millennium – *c.* 1200 B.C. *R. Soc. Antiq. Ir. J.*, 103, 1973, 93–152.

6665 — Guide to the national monuments in the Republic of Ireland, including a selection of other monuments not in state care. Dublin: 1970. Select Bibliog., p. 269.

6666 — The Old Irish 'chariot' [with bibliog.]. *Antiquity*, 45, 1971, 171–177.

6667 — The relative chronology of Irish Early Bronze Age pottery. *R. Soc. Antiq. Ir. J.*, 99, 1969, 63–82.

6668 HARDING, D.W., *ed.* Hillforts: later prehistoric earthworks in Britain and Ireland. London: 1976.

6669 HAWORTH, RICHARD. The Horse harness of the Irish early iron age. *Ulster J. Arch.*, 34, 1971, 26–49.

6670 HENCKEN, H. O'NEILL. Cahercommaun: a stone fort in County Clare. Dublin: 1938. *(R. Soc. Antiq. Ir., extra vol.*, 1938).

6671 HERITY, MICHAEL. From Lhuyd to Coffey: new information from unpublished descriptions of the Boyne Valley tombs. *Stud. Hib.*, 7, 1967, 127–145.

6672 — Irish passage graves: Neolithic tomb-builders in Ireland and Britain, 2500 B.C. Dublin: 1974. Bibliog., pp. 295–304.

6673 — and EOGAN, GEORGE. Ireland in prehistory. London: 1977. Bibliog., pp. 256–282.

6674 — *and others*. The 'Larne' material in Lord Antrim's collection at the Ashmolean museum, Oxford, by M. Herity, E.E. Evans and B.R.S. Megaw. *R. Ir. Acad. Proc., Ser. C.*, vol. 67, no. 2, 1968, 9–34.

6675 KANE, WILLIAM FRANCIS DE VISMES. The black Pig's Dyke: the ancient boundary fortifications of Uladh. *R. Ir. Acad. Proc., Sec. C.*, 27, 1908–9, 301–328.

6676 KAVANAGH, RHODA M. The encrusted urn in Ireland [with bibliog]. *R. Ir. Acad. Proc., Sec. C.*, vol. 73, no. 10, 1974, 507–617.

6677 — Collared and Cordoned cinerary urns in Ireland. *ibid.*, *Sec. C.*, vol. 76, no. 16, 1976, 293–403.

6678 LAING, LLOYD. The Archaeology of late Celtic Britain and Ireland, *c.* 400 – 1200 A.D. London: 1975. Bibliog., [Ireland], pp. 409–11.

6679 LAWLOR, HENRY CAIRNES. Ulster: its archaeology and antiquities [with bibliogs]. Belfast: 1928.

6680 LUCAS, A.T. Souterrains: the literary evidence. *Bealoideas*, 39–41, 1971–3, 165–191.

6681 MACALISTER, R.A.S. Ancient Ireland: a study in the lessons of archaeology and history. London: 1935. Notes and references, pp. 283–99.

6682 — The Archaeology of Ireland. 2nd ed. rev. London: 1949. Bibliog. pp. 383–6.

6683 — Tara: a pagan sanctuary of ancient Ireland. London: 1931. Bibliog. notes, pp. 193–201.

6684 MAHR, ADOLF. Ancient Irish handicraft. *Thomond Arch. Soc. Fld. Cl.*, 1939. Bibliog., pp. 21–2.

6685 — New aspects and problems in Irish history. Reprinted from the *Proceedings of the Prehistoric Society of East Anglia, new ser.*, vol. 3, 1937. Bibliog., pp. 428–36.

6686 MARTIN, CECIL P. Prehistoric man in Ireland. London: 1935. Bibliog., pp. 169–78.

6687 MITCHELL, G.F. The relative ages of archaeological objects recently found in bogs in Ireland [with bibliog.]. *R. Ir. Acad. Proc., Sec. C*, 50, 1944–5, 1–19.

6688 — Some chronological implications of the Irish mesolithic [with bibliog]. *Ulster J. Arch.*, 33, 1970, 3–14.

6689 MOORE, DONALD, *ed.* The Irish sea province in archaeology and history. Cardiff: 1970. Contents include: The early prehistoric period around the Irish Sea, by Michael Herity. The later prehistoric migrations across the Irish Sea, by H.N. Savory. Problems of Irish ring-forts, by Michael J. O'Kelly. Was there an Irish Sea culture – province in the dark ages?, by Leslie Alcock. Early literary contacts between Wales and Ireland, by Nora K. Chadwick. Irish Sea influence on the English church, by the Rev. R.W.D. Fenn. The Vikings and the Irish Sea, by P.H. Sawyer. Irish vernacular architecture in relation to the Irish Sea, by Caoimhin O'Danachair.

6690 MOVIUS, HALLAM L. Irish Stone Age: its chronology, development and relationships. Cambridge: 1942. Bibliog. pp. 295–319.

6691 NORMAN, E.R., and ST. JOSEPH, J.K.S. The early development of Irish society: the evidence of aerial photography. Cambridge: 1969. Bibliog., pp. 122–124.

6692 NORTHERN IRELAND, Ministry of Finance: Archaeological survey of Northern Ireland. An archaeological survey of County Down. Belfast: 1966. Bibliog., p. 458.

6693 O'BRIEN, D. MADDISON. A list of some archaeological sites on the Berehaven Peninsula. *Cork Hist. Arch. Soc. J.*, 75, 1970, 12–24.

6694 O'KELLY, CLARE. Illustrated guide to Newgrange and the other Boyne monuments. 3rd ed. rev. and enlarged. Blackrock (Cork): 1978. 1st ed. Wexford, 1967. Bibliog., pp. 133–5.

6695 O'KELLY, M.J., and O'KELLY, C. Illustrated guide to Lough Gur, Co. Limerick. Blackrock (Cork): 1978.

6696 O'NUALLAIN, SEAN. A ruined megalithic cemetery in Co. Donegal and its context in the Irish passage grave series. *R. Soc. Antiq. Ir. J.*, 98, 1968, 1–29. Includes distribution map of Irish passage graves with bibliog. references.

6697 — The stone circle complex of Cork and Kerry. [with bibliog.]. *R. Soc. Antiq. Ir. J.*, 105, 1975, 83–131.

6698 O'RIORDAIN, SEAN. Antiquities of the Irish countryside. 5th ed. rev. by Ruaidhri de Valera. London and New York: 1974. Bibliog., pp. 161–9.

6699 — and DANIEL, GLYN. New Grange and the Bend of the Boyne. London: 1964. *(Ancient peoples and places, vol. 40)*. Bibliog., pp. 154–157.

6700 PIGGOTT, STUART. The Neolithic cultures of the British Isles. Cambridge: 1954. Bibliog., pp. 387–410.

6701 — Ireland and Britain in prehistory: changing viewpoints and perspectives. *Cork Hist. Arch. Soc. J.*, 71, 1966, 5–18.

6702 PROUDFOOT, BRUCE. Irish raths and cashels: some notes on chronology, origins and survival [with bibliog. of excavated raths and cashels]. *Ulster J. Arch.*, 33, 1970, 37–48.

6703 RADFORD, C.A. RALEGH. Devenish [island, in Lough Erne, Co. Fermanagh]. *Ulster J. Arch.*, 33, 1970, 55–62.

6704 RAFTERY, BARRY. Freestone Hill, Co. Kilkenny: an iron age hillfort and bronze age cairn. *R. Ir. Acad. Proc., Sec. C.*, vol. 68, no. 1, 1969, 1–108.

6705 — The Rathgall hillfort, County Wicklow. *Antiquity*, 44, 1970, 51–54.

6706 — Rathgall : a Late Bronze Age burial in Ireland. *Antiquity*, 47, 1973, 293–295.

6707 RAFTERY, JOSEPH. Irish prehistoric gold objects: new light on the source of the metal. *R. Soc. Antiq. Ir. J.*, 101, 1971, 101–105.

ROYAL SOCIETY OF ANTIQUARIES OF IRELAND. Antiquarian handbook series.

6708 1. Dunsany, Tara, and Glendalough illustrated. 1895.

6709 2. The western islands, and the antiquities of Galway, Athenry, Roscommon, &c., illustrated. 1897.

6710 3. The western islands (continued), including the coasts of Clare, Kerry, Cork and Waterford, the islands of Scattery and Skellig Michael, with notices of Cloyne and Lismore. 1898. Includes Cork Harbour, by James Coleman.

6711 4. (The western islands of Scotland).

6712 5. The antiquities of northern Clare, including Ennis, Clare and Quin abbeys. 1900.

6713 6. Illustrated guide to the northern, western and southern islands, and coast of Ireland. 1905.

6714 7. The antiquities of Limerick and its neighbourhood, by T.J. Westropp, R.A.S. Macalister and G.U. MacNamara. 1916.

6715 SCOTT, B.G. Metallographic study of some early iron tools and weapons from Ireland. *R. Ir. Acad. Proc., Sec. C,*, vol. 77, no. 12, 1977, 301–317.

6716 SHETELIG, HAAKON, *ed.* Viking antiquities in Great Britain and Ireland [with bibliogs.]. Oslo: 1940. 5 pts.

6717 SWEETMAN, R. DAVID. Trim Castle archaeological excavations (preliminary report). *Riocht na Midhe*, vol. 5, no. 4, 1974, 69–77.

6718 THOMAS, CHARLES, *ed*. The Iron Age in the Irish sea province. London: 1972. *(C.B.A. Research Report, 9)*

6719 TWOHIG, DERMOT C. Recent souterrain research in Co. Cork. *Cork Hist. Arch. Soc. J.*, 81, 1976, 19–38.

6720 WADDELL, JOHN. Irish bronze age cists: a survey. *R. Soc. Antiq. Ir. J.*, 100, 1970, 91–139.

6721 WAKEMAN, WILLIAM FREDERICK. A handbook of Irish antiquities, pagan and Christian. [Facsimile reprint of 2nd ed.]. London, 1970. 1st edition published as *Archaeologia Hiberniae*, Dublin: 1848; 2nd ed. Dublin: 1891.

6722 WESTROPP, THOMAS JOHNSON. The progress of Irish archaeology [with bibliog. ref.] *R. Soc. Antiq. Ir. J.,* 46, 1916, 2–26.

6723 — The Cahers of Co. Clare: their names, features and bibliography. *R. Ir. Acad. Proc., 3rd ser.*, 6, 1900–2, 415–49.

6724 WIJNGAARDEN-BAKKER, LOUISE H. VAN. The animal remains from the Beaker settlement at Newgrange, Co. Meath: first report – [with bibliog.]. *R. Ir. Acad. Proc., Sec. C.*, vol. 74, no. 11, 1974, 313–383.

6725 WOOD-MARTIN, WILLIAM GREGORY. Pagan Ireland, an archaeological sketch: a handbook of Irish Pre-Christian antiquities. London: 1895. Bibliography of papers and works on Irish Pre-Christian archaeology (arranged by subjects and authors), pp. 595–655.

6726 — Traces of the elder faiths of Ireland: a folklore sketch. A handbook of Irish Pre-Christian traditions. London, 1902: 2 vols. Bibliog., vol. 2, pp. 327–422, which includes the following: amber, amulets, antiquities, architecture, bog butter, bronze, bullans, caves, clothing, fictilia, flint and stone implements, folklore, forgeries, fossil mammalia, geology, glass, gold, human crania, osseous remains and ethnography, jade, jet, middens, lake dwellings, ogham, querns, raths, religion, rock sculptures and ornamentations, Roman coins, rude stone monuments, runes, settlements, silver, souterrains, urns of stone, vivianite, and wooden objects.

Archaeologists

6727 MACALISTER, R.A.S. Ireland in pre-Celtic times. Dublin and London: 1921. Chapter 1 includes valuable biographical notes on Irish archaeological writers.

6728 — Robert Alexander Steward MacAlister, 1871–1950: a bibliography of his published works, by Mary Lou Brennan. *R. Soc. Antiq. Ir. J.*, 103, 1973, 167–176.

6729 SOME MEMORABLE CORK ARCHAEOLOGISTS [John Windele, Richard Rolt Brash, and Richard Caulfield.]. *Cork Hist. Arch. Soc. J., 2nd ser.*, 6, 1900, 32–47.

6730 WAKEMAN, W.F. Statement of services to Irish archaeology, with lists of articles contributed to various publications. *R. Hist. Arch. Soc. Ir. J.*, 18, 1888, 486–90.

Lake Dwellings

6731 MUNRO, ROBERT. The lake-dwellings of Europe; being the Rhind lectures in archaeology for 1888. London: 1890. Bibliog., pp. 555–83; Irish crannogs, pp. 349–95.

Palaeography

6732 LOWE, E.A. Codices Latini antiquiores: a palaeographical guide to Latin manuscripts prior to the ninth century. Oxford: Union Academique Internationale, 1934–50. 5 pts. Pt. 2. Great Britain and Ireland.

6733 STOKES, WHITLEY, and STRACHAN, JOHN, *eds.* Thesaurus Palaeohibernicus: a collection of old-Irish glosses, scholia prose and verse. Cambridge: 1901–3. 2 vols.

Epigraphy

6734 MACALISTER, R.A.S. Studies in Irish epigraphy: a collection of revised writings of the ancient inscriptions of Ireland, with introduction and notes. London: 1897–1907. 3 pts.

6735 — Corpus inscriptionum insularum Celticarum. Dublin: Irish Manuscripts Commission, 1945–9. 2 vols.

6736 PETRIE, GEORGE. Christian inscriptions in the Irish language, edited by M. Stokes, with bibliography and historical notes. Dublin: 1872–8. 2 vols.

CELTS

6737 BIBLIOTHECA CELTICA: a register of publications relating to Wales and the Celtish people and language. Aberystwyth, National Library of Wales. vol. 1–, 1909–.

6738 CHADWICK, NORA. The Celts. London: 1970. Celtic literature, pp. 255–291.

6739 DOTTIN, GEORGES. Manuel pour servir a l'étude de l'antiquité celtique. Paris: 1906. (*La Bretagne et les pays celtique IV.*) 2nd ed. 1915.

6740 ETUDES CELTIQUES. Paris, vol. 1–, 1936–.

6741 HARVARD UNIVERSITY LIBRARY. Celtic literature: classification schedule, classified listing by call number, chronological listing, author and title listing. Cambridge (Mass.): 1970. *(Widener Library Shelf-list no. 25).*

6742 HUBERT, HENRI. The greatness and decline of the Celts . . . London: 1934. Bibliog., pp. 281–99.

6743 —The Rise of the Celts . . . London: 1934. Bibliog., pp. 303–21.

6744 POWELL, T.G.E. The Celts. London: 1958. (*Ancient peoples and places ser.,* vol. 6.) Bibliog., pp. 189–200.

6745 RAFTERY, *Dr.* JOSEPH, *ed.* The Celts. Cork: 1964. *(Thomas Davis Lectures series).*

6746 RIVOALLAN, A. Présence des Celtes. Paris: 1957. (*Nouvelle librarie Celtique.*) Bibliog., pp. 425–9.

BIOGRAPHY

6747 ARNIM, MAX. Internationale Personalbibliographie, 1850–1935. Leipzig, Stuttgart: 1944–52. 2 vols. First published 1936.

6748 BIOGRAPHY INDEX: a cumulative index to biographical material in books and magazines. New York, vol. 1–, 1846–.

6749 BOOK ASSOCIATION OF IRELAND. Biographical works published, 1934–44, about Irishmen or persons connected with Ireland. *Ir. Lib. Bull.,* 5, 1944, 92–6.

6750 COXHEAD, ELIZABETH. Daughters of Erin: five women of the Irish Renascence. London: 1965. Maud Gonne, Constance Markievicz, Sarah Purser, Sara Allgood and Maire O'Neill.

6751 CURLEY, WALTER J.P. Monarchs-in-waiting. New York: 1973. Ireland (1) The O'Conor Don – Rev. Charles Denis Mary Joseph Anthony O'Conor. (2) The Right Honorable Lord Inchiquin, 17th baron of Inchiquin, Sir Phaedrig Lucius Ambrose O'Brien, 9th baronet of Lemeneagh. (3) Fourth Baron O'Neill, Lord Raymond Arthur Clanaboy O'Neill.

6752 FFOLLIOTT, ROSEMARY. An index to Co. Cork biographical material in Irish newspapers. *An Leab.*, 20, 1962, 19–22.

6753 HICKEY, DES, and SMITH, GUS. A paler shade of green. London: 1972. A study of the expatriates of the world Irish arts scene.

6754 KEANEY, MARIAN. Westmeath authors: a bibliographical and biographical study. Mullingar: 1969.

6755 LIST OF NAMES OF IRISH BIOGRAPHIES in the 'D.N.B.' 2nd supplement, vols. 1–3. *Ir. Book Lov.,* 3, 1912, 205–7; 4, 1913, 80–2, 116–17.

6756 McTERNAN, JOHN C. Here's to their memory: profiles of distinguished Sligonians of bygone days. Dublin and Cork: 1977.

6757 MAHER, HELEN. Galway authors: a contribution towards a biographical and bibliographical index, with an essay on the history and literature in Galway. Galway: 1976.

6758 MATTHEWS, WILLIAM, *compiler*. British autobiographies: an annotated bibliography of British autobiographies published or written before 1951. Berkeley and Los Angeles: 1955. Includes subject index.

6759 — British diaries: an annotated bibliography of British diaries written between 1442 and 1942. Berkeley and Los Angeles: 1950.

6760 O'DONOGHUE, D.J. The geographical distribution of Irish ability. Dublin: 1906. *See also* Irish intellect: its geographical distribution, by D. Edgar Flinn. *Stat. Social Inq. Soc. Ir. J.*, 98, 1919–20, 76–89.

6761 O'KELLY, SEAMUS G. Sweethearts of the Irish rebels. Dublin: 1968. Eighteenth and nineteenth centuries.

6762 O'RAHILLY, THOMAS F. Irish poets, historians and judges in English documents, 1538–1615. *R. Ir. Acad. Proc., Sec. C,* 36, 1921–4, 86–120. Includes index of persons and places.

6763 O'REILLY, EDWARD. A chronological account of nearly four hundred Irish writers commencing with the earliest account of Irish history, and carried down to the year of our Lord 1750: with a descriptive catalogue of such of their works as are still extant in verse or prose, consisting of upwards of one thousand separate tracts. *Iberno-Celtic Soc. Trans.*, vol. 1, pt. 1, 1820.

6764 O SUILLEABHAIN, SEAN. Longford authors: a biographical and bibliographical dictionary. Mullingar: 1978.

6765 POGGENDORFF, JOHAN CHRISTIAN. Biographisch-literarisches Handworterbuch zur Geschichte der Exacten Wissenschaften. Leipzig: 1863–1940. 6 vols. Facsimile reprint in 10 volumes. Ann Arbor: 1945.

6766 RICHES, PHYLLIS M. An analytical bibliography of universal collected biography, comprising books published in the English tongue in Great Britain and Ireland, America and the British dominions. London: 1934.

6767 SHARE, BERNARD. Irish lives: biographies of fifty famous Irish men and women. Dublin: 1971. Not paginated.

6768 SOMERVILLE–LARGE, PETER. Irish eccentrics. London: 1975.

6769 WHITE, NEWPORT J.D. Four good men: Luke Challoner, Fellow of Trinity College, Dublin, 1592. Jeremy Taylor, Vice-Chancellor of the University of Dublin, 1660–1667. Narcissus Marsh, Provost of Trinity College, Dublin, 1678–1683. Elias Bouhereau, first public librarian in Ireland, 1701–19. Dublin: 1917. The Bouhereau Mss. in Marsh's library, pp. 93–97.

6770 WHO'S WHO, WHAT'S WHAT AND WHERE IN IRELAND compiled by Zircon Publishing Ltd in association with the *Irish Times.* London and Dublin: 1973.

6771 WILLIS, J. Lives of illustrious and distinguished Irishmen. Dublin: 1840–7. 6 vols.

Biographical Dictionaries

6772 BOYLAN, HENRY. A dictionary of Irish biography. Dublin: 1978. Bibliog., pp. 379–385.

6773 CLEEVE, BRIAN. Dictionary of Irish writers. Cork: 1969. 2nd series. Non-fiction.

6774 CRONE, J.S. Concise dictionary of Irish biography; rev. ed. Dublin: 1937. First published 1928.

6775 ECCLES, MARK. A biographical dictionary of Elizabethan authors. In preparation; is intended to give concise accounts of the lives and works of all English, Scottish, Irish and Welsh authors who wrote books of any kind during the reign of Elizabeth (1558–1603). See *Huntingdon Library Quarterly*, vol. 5, 1941–2, 281–302.

6776 HYAMSON, ALBERT M. A dictionary of universal biography of all ages and of all peoples. [Reprint of 2nd ed.]. London: 1976. First published, London: 1916; 2nd ed., 1951.

6777 IRISH ACADEMY OF LETTERS. Selections from *A Dictionary of Irish writers,* edited by Joseph Hone. Dublin: 1944.

6778 O'DONOGHUE, D.J., *compiler*. A summary dictionary of Irish biography [c. 1900]. Ms. 756 in National Library.

6779 RYAN, RICHARD. Biographia Hibernica: a biographical dictionary of the worthies of Ireland. London: 1821. 2 vols.

6780 STEPHEN, LESLIE and LEE, SIDNEY, *eds*. Dictionary of national biography. London: 1885–1900. 63 vols. Supplements to date. Invaluable source of bibliographical material.

6781 THOM'S IRISH WHO'S WHO: a biographical book of reference of prominent men and women in Irish life at home and abroad. Dublin: 1923.

6782 [WATKINS, JOHN, and SHOBERT, FREDERIC.] A biographical dictionary of the living authors of Great Britain and Ireland: comprising literary memoirs and anecdotes of their lives, and a chronological register of their publications, with the number of editions printed, including notices of some foreign writers whose works have been occasionally published in England. London: 1816.

6783 WEBB, ALFRED. A compendium of Irish biography, comprising sketches of distinguished Irishmen. Dublin: 1878. An invaluable work which has never been wholly superseded.

6784 WHO'S WHO: an annual biographical dictionary. London: 1849–.

Religious Biography

(See also Individual biography)

6785 BROWN, STEPHEN J. An index to Catholic biographies. 2nd ed. London: 1935. 1st ed. Dublin: 1930.

6786 COLEMAN, JAMES. Seven Cork clerical writers. [The Rev. Charles Bernard Gibson, Dr. William Maziere Brady, Very Rev. Dominick Murphy, The Rev. Thomas England, The Rev. Matthew Horgan, The Rev. Richard Smiddy, The Rev. James Goodman]. *Cork Hist. Arch. Soc. J., 2nd ser.*, 9, 1903, 141–55.

Legal Biography

6787 BALL, F. ELRINGTON. The judges in Ireland, 1221–1921. London: 1926. 2 vols. Bibliog. footnotes.

Trinity College

6788 BURTCHAELL, G.D., and SADLEIR, T.U. Alumni Dublinenses: a register of students, graduates and provosts of Trinity College in the University of Dublin. 2nd ed. Dublin: 1935. 1st ed. 1924.

6789 CRUICKSHANK, JOHN. E.J. Arnould, Professor of French (Trinity College, Dublin), 1946–70. [with bibliog.] *Hermathena*, 121, 1976, 18–24.

6790 SADLEIR, T.U., and WATSON, HELEN M. A record of seventeenth century alumni. *Hermathena,* no. 89, 1957, 54–8. Supplements material in *Alumni Dublinenses*.

6791 WEBB, D.A. *ed.* Of one company: biographical studies of famous Trinity [College] men. Dublin: 1951.

6792 WINNETT, ARTHUR ROBERT. Peter Browne: provost [of T.C.D.], bishop, metaphysician. London: S.P.C.K., 1974. *(Church historical series* no. 95) Sources and bibliog., pp. 247–256.

INDIVIDUAL BIOGRAPHY

A

ADENEY, WALTER ERNEST.

6793 Award of the Boyle medal . . .[with bibliog.]. *R. Dublin Soc. Sci. Proc., new series,* 19, 1928–30, 11–15.

ALCOCK, DEBORAH.

6794 BYARD, E.J. Deborah Alcock: a bibliography. *Ir. Book Lov.,* 4, 1913, 150–1; obituary notice, *ibid*., p. 143.

ALEXANDER, CECIL FRANCES.

6795 LOVELL, E.W. A green hill far away: a life of Mrs. C.F. Alexander. Dublin and London: 1970.

ALEXANDER, WILLIAM, *archbishop,* 1824–1911.

6796 Biography and bibliographical note. *Ir. Book Lov.*, 3, 1911–12, 35–6.

ALLINGHAM, WILLIAM.

6797 Bibliography. *New Camb. Bibliog. Eng. Lit.*, 3, 1969, 502–3.

6798 ALLINGHAM, H. and RADFORD D. *eds*. William Allingham: a diary. London: 1907. List of works, pp. 390–1.

6799 McMAHON, SEAN. The boy from his bedroom window. *Eire-Ir.*, vol. 5, no. 2, 1970, 142–153.

6800 O'HEGARTY, P.S. A bibliography of William Allingham. *Dublin Mag., new series*, vol. 20, no. 1, 1945, 42–52; *ibid.*, no. 3, 1945, 62. See also article, *ibid.*, no. 2, 34–8.

6801 SHIELDS, HUGH. Allingham and folk song. *Hermathena*, 117, 1974, 23–36.

6802 WARNER, ALAN. Patricius Walker: a Victorian Irishman on foot. *Eire-Ir.*, vol. 8, no. 3, 1973, 70–80. Patricius Walker was the pseudonym used by Allingham when he wrote of his rambles through England, Scotland and France.

6803 — William Allingham: an introduction. Dublin: 1971.

6804 — William Allingham: bibliographical survey. *Ir. Booklore*, vol. 2, no. 2, 1976, 303–7.

ANDERSON, JOHN.

6805 Irish bibliographers, no. 2. John Anderson. *Ir. Book Lov.*, 14, 1924, 19–20.

ARBOIS DE JUBAINVILLE, H. D'.

6806 Bibliographie des oeuvres de Henry d'Arbois de Jubainville. *Rev. Celt.,* 32, 1911, 456–74.

ATKINS, WILLIAM RINGROSE GELSTON.

6807 Award of the Boyle medal . . . [with bibliog.]. *R. Dublin Soc. Sci. Proc., new series,* 19, 1928–30, 1–9.

6808 POOLE, H.H. William Ringrose Gelston Atkins, 1884–1959 [with bibliog.]. *Biog. Mem. R. Soc.*, 5, 1959, 1–22.

ATKINSON, SARAH.

6809 WOODNUTT, K. Sarah Atkinson as a social worker. *Dublin Hist. Rec.*, 21, 1966–67, 132–138.

AYLWARD, *Canon* RICHARD.

6810 WALTON, JULIAN C. Richard Canon Aylward, (Antiquarian), 1872–1954. *Old, Kilk. Rev. new ser.*, vol. 1, no. 5, 1978, 349–351.

B

BAILEY, WILLIAM FREDERIC.

6811 Bibliography. *Ir. Book. Lov.*, 8, 1916–17, 141.

BALL, FRANCES MARY TERESA.

6812 'Loreto Sister, A.' *pseud*. Joyful mother of children: Mother Frances Mary Teresa Ball. Dublin: 1961. Bibliog., pp. 327–8. Foundress of Loreto, the Irish branch of the Institute of the Blessed Virgin Mary.

BANIM, JOHN, and BANIM, MICHAEL.

6813 Bibliography. *New Camb. Bibliog. Eng. Lit.*, 3, 1969, 707–709.

6814 LANIGAN, KATHERINE M. The Banim brothers: a re-assessment. *Old. Kilk. Rev.*, 25, 1973, 2–12.

6815 McCORMACK, W.J. A manuscript letter from Michael Banim (1874). *Eire-Ir.*, vol. 8, no. 1, 1973, 95–96.

BARLOW, JANE.

6816 Bibliography. *Ir. Book Lov.*, 8, 1916–17, 141–2.

6817 Bibliography, *New Camb. Bibliog. Eng. Lit.*, 3, 1969, 1908.

BARRY, MICHAEL JOSEPH.

6818 Bibliography. *Ir. Book Lov.*, 9, 1917–18, 27.

BARRY, VINCENT.

6819 Award of the Boyle Medal . . ., *R. Dublin Soc. Sci. Proc., Ser. A,* 3, 1967–70, 149–151.

6820 Obituary. *R. Ir. Acad. Ann. Rpt.*, 1975–6, 2–3.

BEAUFORT, *Dr.* DANIEL AUGUSTUS.

6821 ELLISON, C.C. Remembering Dr. Beaufort. *Ir. Georg. Soc. Qtr. Bull.*, vol. 18, no. 1, 1975, 1–36. Topographer and architect.

BEAUFORT, *Sir* FRANCIS.

6822 FRIENDLY, ALFRED. Beaufort of the Admiralty: the life of Sir Francis Beaufort, 1774–1857. London: 1977. Bibliog., pp. 347–352.

BECKETT, SAMUEL.

6823 Bibliography. *New Camb. Bibliog. Eng. Lit.*, 4, 1972, 885–906.

6824 Beckettiana. *Longroom*, 7, 1973, 34.

6825 ARNOLD, BRUCE. Samuel Beckett. *Dubliner*, vol. 3, no. 2, 1964, 6–16.

6826 BLAIR, DEIRDRE. Samuel Beckett: a biography. London: 1978.

6827 COHN, RUBY. Samuel Beckett: a collection of criticism. London and New York: 1975. Bibliog., pp. 137–8.

6828 DOHERTY, FRANCIS. Samuel Beckett. London: 1971. Bibliog., pp. 153–4.

6829 FEDERMAN, RAYMOND and FLETCHER, JOHN. Samuel Beckett, his works and his critics: an essay in bibliography. Berkeley: 1970.

6830 JAMES JOYCE QUARTERLY, vol. 8, no. 4, 1971. Special Beckett issue.

6831 JOURNAL OF BECKETT STUDIES. London, no. 1–. 1977–.

6832 MAYS, JAMES. Samuel Beckett Bibliography: comments and corrections. *Ir. Univ. Rev.*, vol. 2, no. 2, 1972, 189–207. On *Samuel Beckett: his works and his critics,* by Federman and Fletcher.

6833 PILLING, JOHN. Samuel Beckett. London: 1976. Bibliog., pp. 227–235.

6834 Reading University Library. Samuel Beckett: an exhibition held at Reading University Library, May to July 1971. Catalogue by James Knowlson, foreword by A.J. Leventhal. London: 1971.

6835 ROBINSON, MICHAEL. The long sonata of the dead: a study of Samuel Beckett. London: 1969. Bibliog., pp. 303–8.

6836 SCOTT, NATHAN A. Samuel Beckett. London: 1865. *(Studies in modern European literature).* Bibliog., pp. 135–141.

6837 TINDALL, WILLIAM YORK. Samuel Beckett. New York and London: 1964, Bibliog., pp. 46–48.

BEDELL, WILLIAM, *Bishop of Kilmore*.

6838 GAMBLE, W. William Bedell, his life and times. [Dublin, 1951]

6839 SHUCKBURGH, E.S., *ed*. Two biographies of William Bedell, Bishop of Kilmore [by his son, William Bedell, and the Rev. Alexander Clogie], with a selection of his letters and an unpublished treatise. Cambridge: 1902. Translator of the Bible and Prayer Book into Irish.

BEERE, THEKLA.

6840 O'ROURKE, FRANCES. Dr. Thekla Beere: a profile. *Admin*., vol. 23, no. 1, 1975, 19–30.

BEHAN, BRENDAN.

6841 BEHAN, BEATRICE. My life with Brendan. London: 1973.

6842 BOYLE, TED E. Brendan Behan. New York: 1969. *(Twayne's English Authors series)* Selected Bibliog., pp. 143–145.

6843 JEFFS, RAE. Brendan Behan, man and showman. London: 1966.

6844 KEARNEY, COLBERT: The writings of Brendan Behan. Dublin and London: 1977.

6845 O'CONNOR, ULICK. Brendan Behan. London: 1970. Bibliog., pp. 9–12.

BERNARD, JOHN HENRY

6846 MURRAY, ROBERT H. Archbishop Bernard, professor, prelate and provost. London: 1931. Bibliog., pp. 378–9.

BIANCONI, CHARLES.

6847 BIANCONI, M. O'C., *and* WATSON, S.J. Bianconi, king of the Irish roads. Dublin: 1962.

6848 MAGUIRE, MAIRIN. Charles Bianconi (1786–1875): his historical association with the Monaghan Brewery. *Clogher Rec.*, vol. 9, no. 1, 1976, 113–4.

BICKERSTAFFE, ISAAC.

6849 Bibliography. *New Camb. Bibliog. Eng. Lit.*, 2, 1971, 825–6.

BIGGER, FRANCIS JOSEPH

6850 In remembrance: articles and sketches, biographical, historical and topographical. Edited by John S. Crone and F.C. Bigger. Dublin: 1927. Bibliog., pp. 185–8; Chronological list of articles and sketches and writings, pp. 189–201.

BIRMINGHAM, GEORGE A., *pseud.* (i.e. James Owen Hannay).

6851 Bibliography, *New Camb. Bibliog. Eng. Lit.*, 4, 1972, 529–530.

6852 MACKEY, W.E. The novels of 'George A. Birmingham': a list of first editions. *T.C.D. Ann. Bull.,* 1955, 14–16.

6853 O'DONNELL, H.A. A literary survey of the novels of Canon J.O. Hannay. Thesis accepted for M.A., Queen's University, Belfast, 1958–9.

BLACKER, BEAVER H.

6854 Irish bibliographers, no. 1: The Rev. Beaver H. Blacker. *Ir. Book Lov.,* 14, 1924, 3–5.

BLACKWOOD, FREDERICK TEMPLE HAMILTON.

6855 BLACK, CHARLES E. DRUMMOND. The Marquess of Dufferin and Ava, diplomatist, viceroy, statesman. London: 1903. Appendix: List of works in the catalogue of the British Museum Library, under the name of Blackwood (Frederick Temple Hamilton), Marquess of Dufferin and Ava, G.C.B., etc., pp. 394–6.

BLAKE, *Sir* HENRY.

6856 Bibliography. *Ir. Book Lov.*, 9, 1918, 111.

BLAQUIERE, *Sir* JOHN.

6857 TIGHE, JOAN. Sir John Blaquiere in Dublin. *Dublin Hist. Rec.,* vol. 24, no. 2, 1971, 3–14.

BLESSINGTON, MARGUERITE GARDINER, *Countess of.*

6858 Bibliography. *New Camb. Bibliog. Eng. Lit.*, 3, 1969, 710–711.

6859 MORRISON, ALFRED. The collection of autograph letters and historical documents formed by Alfred Morrison . . . the Blessington papers. 1895. Privately printed.

6860 SADLEIR, MICHAEL. Blessington-D'Orsay: a masquerade. London: 1933. Bibliog., pp. 391–3.

BLYTHE, ERNEST.

6861 O'GADHRA, NOLLAIG. Earnan de Blaghd, 1880–1975. *Eire-Ir.*, vol. 11, no. 3, 1976, 93–105.

BODKIN, THOMAS.

6862 DENSON, ALAN, *compiler*. Thomas Bodkin: a bio-bibliographical survey with a bibliographical survey of his family. Dublin: 1966.

BOLGER, BRYAN.

6863 DIXON, F.E. The papers of Bryan Bolger. *Dublin Hist. Rec.*, vol. 26, no. 2, 1973, 62–64.

6864 KELLY, THOMAS. Papers of Bryan Bolger [quantity surveyor], 1792–1834. *Dublin Hist. Rec.*, 3, 1940–41, 8–18.

6865 MCPARLAND, EDWARD. The papers of Bryan Bolger, measurer. *Dublin Hist. Rec.*, 25, 1971–2, 120–131. Bolger was a measurer of buildings in Dublin in the late 18th and early 19th centuries.

BOND, OLIVER.

6866 MAHER, *Miss* MAURA. Oliver Bond. *Dublin Hist. Rec.,* 11, 1949–50, 90–115. Bond was a member of the Society of the United Irishmen.

BOUCICAULT, DION.

6867 ROMAN, DIANE P., *and* HAMILTON, MARY T. Boucicault and the Anne Jordan affair. *J. Ir. Lit.*, vol. 1, no. 2, 1972, 120–127.

BOWEN, ELIZABETH.

6868 Bibliography. *New Camb. Bibliog. Eng. Lit.*, 4, 1972, 534–5.

6869 GLENDINNING, VICTORIA. Elizabeth Bowen: portrait of a writer. London: 1977. Bibliog., pp. 247–249.

6870 HEATH, WILLIAM. Elizabeth Bowen: an introduction to her novels. Madison, Univ. of Wisconsin Press: 1961. Bibliog., pp. 170–6.

BOYLE, ROBERT.

6871 Catalogus librorum tractatuumq: philosophicorum, a dom. Roberto Boyle . . . scriptorum . . . cui accessit librorum etiam theologicorum, qui ab eodem authore exarati sunt nomenclatura. Londini: 1688.

6872 [Another edition] Catalogue of the philosophical books and tracts written by the honourable Robert Boyle . . . to which is added a catalogue of the theological books, written by the same author. London: 1689. Further editions appeared in 1690 and 1692.

6873 BROWN, T.J. English scientific autographs II: Robert Boyle, 1627–1691. *Book Coll.*, 13, 1964, 487.

6874 FULTON, T.F. A bibliography of . . . Robert Boyle. 2nd ed, Oxford: 1961. First appeared in *The Oxford Bibliog. Soc. Proc.*, vol. 3, pt. 1, 1931; also separate edition, Oxford, 1932, with Addenda. Oxford: 1934. Further Addenda published in *The Oxford Bibliog. Soc. Pub., new ser.*, 1, 1948, 33–8.

6875 LYNCH, KATHLEEN M. Robert Boyle, First Earl of Orrery. Knoxville: 1965. Bibliog., pp. 283–291.

6876 MADDISON, R.E.W. A tentative index of the correspondence of the Honourable Robert Boyle. Reprinted from *R. Soc. N. and R.*, vol. 12, no. 2, 1958, 128–201.

6877 — The earliest published writing of Robert Boyle. *Ann. Sci.*, vol. 17, no. 3, 1961, 165–173.

6878 — The life of the Honourable Robert Boyle. London: 1969.

BOYLE, WILLIAM.

6879 Bibliography. *New Camb. Bibliog. Eng. Lit.*, 3, 1969, 1939.

BRADSHAW, HENRY.

6880 CRONE, JOHN S. Henry Bradshaw, his life and work. *Ir. Book Lov.,* 19, 1931, 41–54.

BRENDAN, *Saint*.

6881 SELMER, CARL, *ed.* Navigatio sancti Brendani Abbatis from early Latin manuscripts. Notre Dame: 1959. (*Univ. of Notre Dame pub. in mediaeval stud.,* vol. 16.)

BRENNAN, EDWARD JOHN.

6882 Bibliography. *Ir. Book Lov.*, 8, 1916–17, 142.

BROOK, *The Rev*., JAMES MARK S.B.

6883 Bibliography. *Ir. Book Lov.*, 9, 1918, 111.

BROOKE, HENRY.

6884 Bibliography. *New Camb. Bibliog. Eng. Lit.*, 2, 1971, 785–6.

6885 BAKER, E.A. *ed.* Fool of quality. London: 1906. Bibliog. pp. xxxiii–xxxiv.

BROWN, FRANCES.

6886 Bibliography. *Ir. Book Lov.*, 8, 1916–17, 51. The blind girl of Donegal.

BROWN, STEPHEN J.

6887 Publications by The Rev. Stephen J. Brown, S.J. [brochure]. Dublin: Sign of the Three Candles [1955]. See also *An Leab.*, vol. 8, no. 4, 1945, 141–3.

BROWN, WILLIAM.

6888 WALSH, MICHELINE. Unpublished Admiral Brown documents in Madrid. *Ir. Sword,* vol. 3, no. 10, 1957, 17–19. Founder of Argentine navy.

BRYANT, SOPHIE.

6889 Sophie Bryant, D.Sc., Litt. D., 1850–1922. [London: North London Collegiate School, 1922] For private circulation. Bibliog., pp. 70–71.

BURKE, EDMUND.

6890 Bibliography. *New Camb. Bibliog. Eng. Lit.*, 2, 1971, 1184–91.

6891 BOULTON, J.T., *ed*. A philosophical enquiry into the origin of our ideas of the sublime and beautiful. London: 1958. A list of editions of the *Enquiry* published during Burke's lifetime, pp. 179–82.

6892 CHAPMAN, GERALD W. Edmund Burke: the practical imagination. Cambridge, Mass.: 1967. Bibliog., pp. 287–293.

6893 COPELAND, T.W., and SMITH, M.S. A check-list of the correspondence of Burke. Cambridge: Index Society. 1955.

6894 CORDASCO, FRANCESCO. Edmund Burke: a hand-list of critical notices and studies. New York: 1950. (*Eighteenth-century bibliog. pamphlets,* no. 12.)

6895 DIX, E.R. McC. Dublin editions of Burke's writings prior to 1801. *Ir. Book Lov.*, 20, 1932, 32–3.

6896 MAGNUS, PHILIP. Edmund Burke: a life. London: 1939. Bibliog., pp. 351–5.

6897 TODD, WILLIAM B. A bibliography of Edmund Burke. London: 1964. *(The Soho Bibliographies no.* XVII).

6898 UTLEY, T.E. Edmund Burke. London: 1957. (*Writers and their works ser.,* no. 87.) Bibliog., pp. 33–6.

BURKE, OLIVER JOSEPH.

6899 COLEMAN, JAMES. Bibliography of Thomas O'Neill Russell and Oliver Joseph Burke. *Bibliog. Soc. Ir.*, Vol. 1, no. 4, 1919, 33–6.

BURKE, ULICK J.

6900 COLEMAN, JAMES. Bibliography of The Very Rev. Canon Ulick J. Burke, M.R.I.A., one time president of St. Jarleth's College, Tuam, Co. Galway. Ms. of 6 p. in National Library.

BURROWES, ROBERT.

6901 BLACKER, BEAVER H. The writings of Robert Burrowes, D.D., Dean of Cork, and Rector of Drumragh, diocese of Derry. *Ir. Eccles. Gaz.*, 1879, 423.

BURY, JOHN BAGNELL.

6902 Bibliography. *New Camb. Bibliog. Eng. Lit.*, 4, 1972, 1143–5.

6903 BAYNES, NORMAN H., *compiler*. A bibliography of the works of J.B. Bury, with a memoir. Cambridge: 1929.

BUSHE, CHARLES KENDAL.

6904 SOMERVILLE, E. Œ., and ROSS, MARTIN. An incorruptible Irishman; being an account of Chief Justice Charles Kendal Bushe, and of his wife, Nancy Crampton, and their times. 1767–1843. London: 1932. Bibliog., p. 260.

BUTCHER, SAMUEL.
6905 BLACKER, BEAVER H. The writings of Samuel Butcher, D.D. Lord Bishop of Meath. *Ir. Eccles. Gaz.*, 1878, 230.

BUTLER, JAMES.
6906 BURGHCLERE, LADY. The life of James, first duke of Ormonde, 1610–1688. London: 1912. 2 vols. Bibliog., vol. 2, pp. 427–32.

BUTLER, *Sir* TONY.
6907 BUTLER, GEORGE. Sir Tony Butler, solicitor-general in Ireland, 1689–90. *Dublin Hist. Rec.*, vol. 23, no. 4, 1970, 113–126.

BUTLER, *Sir* WILLIAM.
6908 MCCOURT, EDWARD. Remember Butler: the story of Sir William Butler. London: 1967. Bibliog., pp. 267–269. Author of *The Great Lone Land*, and other works.

BUTT, ISAAC.
6909 MACD[ONAGH], F[RANK]. Bibliography of Isaac Butt. *Ir. Book Lov.*, 5, 1914, 54–6.

6910 WHITE, TERENCE DE VERE. Road of excess. Dublin: 1946. Bibliog., pp. 383–4.

BYRNE, DONN.
6911 MACAULEY, THURSTON. Donn Byrne, bard of Armagh. London: [1930]. Bibliog., pp. 175–9.

6912 WINTHROP, WETHERBEE. (Brian Oswald): Donn Byrne, a bibliography. Boston: 1938.

6913 — Donn Byrne: a bibliography. New York: 1949.

C

CAMPBELL, GEORGE.
6914 MCDONALD, ROBERT. On George Campbell. *Dublin Mag.*, vol. 5, nos. 3–4, 1966, 39–43.

CAMPBELL, JOSEPH.
6915 O'HEGARTY, P.S. Bibliographical notes [Bibliography of Joseph Campbell]. *Dublin Mag., new series,* vol. 15, no. 4, 1940, 58–61.

CARLETON, WILLIAM.
6916 Bibliography. *New Camb. Bibliog. Eng. Lit.*, 3, 1969, 713–5.

6917 BROWN, TERENCE. The death of William Carleton, 1869. *Hermathena*, 110, 1970, 81–85.

6918 CARLETON NEWSLETTER. Gainesville, Florida. vol. 1-, 1970-. A feature of the Newsletter is the listing of Carleton's works held in Irish and American libraries.

6919 CASEY, DANIEL J. Carleton in Louth. *Louth Arch. J.*, vol. 17, no. 2, 1970, 97–106.

6920 KIELY, BENEDICT. Poor scholar: a study of the works and days of William Carleton (1794–1869) [Reprint of 1st ed.] Dublin: 1972. 1st ed. 1947.

6921 O'DONOGHUE, DAVID J. The life of William Carleton; being his autobiography and letters, and an account of his life and writings from the point at which the autobiography breaks off. London: 1896. 2 vols. Bibliog. of Carleton's writings, vol. 1, pp. lvii–lxiv.

CARRIGAN, *Canon* WILLIAM
6922 PHELAN, MARGARET M. William Canon Carrigan, 1860–1924. *Old Kilk. Rev., new ser.*, vol. 1, no. 3, 1976, 148–157. Author of 'The History and Antiquities of the Diocese of Ossory.'

CARROLL, PAUL VINCENT.
6923 Bibliography. *New Camb. Bibliog. Eng. Lit.*, 4, 1972, 921–2.

6924 DOYLE, PAUL A. Paul Vincent Carroll. Lewisburg: 1971. *(Irish Writers Series)* Bibliog., pp. 111–115.

6925 O'DONOVAN, JOHN. An interview with Paul Vincent Carroll. *J. Ir. Lit.*, vol. 1, no. 1, 1972, 7–14. This issue is devoted to Paul Vincent Carroll and includes a selection of letters to Robert Hogan.

CARSON, EDWARD.
6926 HYDE, H. MONTGOMERY. Carson: the life of Sir Edward Carson, Lord Carson of Duncairn. [1st ed. reprinted] with a new introduction by the author. London: 1974. Bibliog., pp. 498–501.

CARY, JOYCE.
6927 Bibliography. *New Camb. Bibliog. Eng. Lit.*, 4, 1972, 548–9.

6928 FOSTER, MALCOLM. Joyce Cary: a biography. London: 1968. Bibliog., pp. 541–2.

6929 NOBLE, R.W. Joyce Cary. Edinburgh: 1973. *(Writers and critics series)* Bibliog., pp. 115–118.

6930 WRIGHT, ANDREW. Joyce Cary: a preface to his novels. London: 1958. Bibliog., pp. 174–81.

CASEMENT, ROGER.

6931 BEGNAL, MICHAEL. Eva Gore-Booth on behalf of Roger Casement: an unpublished appeal. *Eire-Ir.*, vol. 6, no. 1, 1971, 11–16.

6932 CURRY, CHARLES E., *ed.* Sir Roger Casement's diaries: his mission to Germany and the Findlay affair. Munich, Arche Pub. Co., 1922.

6933 GWYNN, DENIS. Roger Casement's last weeks. *Studies*, 54, 1965, 63–73.

6934 MCHUGH, ROGER. Casement: the Public Record Office manuscripts. *Threshold,* vol. 4, no. 1, 1960, 28–57.

6935 MACKEY, HERBERT O. The life and times of Roger Casement. Dublin: 1954. Bibliog. p. 144.

6936 — Roger Casement: the forged diaries. Dublin: 1966. Bibliog., pp. 94–5.

6937 MALONEY, WILLIAM J. The forged Casement diaries. Dublin and Cork: 1936. Notes and ref., pp. 219–69.

6938 O'HEGARTY, P.S. A bibliography of Roger Casement. *Dublin Mag., new series,* vol. 24, no. 2, 1949, 31–4.

6939 PARMITER, GEOFFREY DE C. Roger Casement. London: 1936. Bibliog., pp. 363–5.

6940 REID, B.L. The lives of Roger Casement. New Haven and London: 1976. Bibliog., pp. 517–520.

6941 SINGLETON-GATES, PETER, and GIRODIAS, MAURICE. The Black diaries: an account of Roger Casement's life and times with a collection of his diaries and public writings. Paris, Olympia Press: 1959. Special edition limited to 1,500 numbered copies.

6942 — [Another edition]. London: 1959.

CASEY, JUANITA.

6943 JOURNAL OF IRISH LITERATURE, vol. 1, no. 3, 1972. Special issue on Juanita Casey.

CASTLEREAGH, ROBERT STEWART, *Viscount.*

6944 DERRY, JOHN W. Castlereagh. London: 1976. Bibliog., pp. 239–241.

CAULFEILD, JAMES.

6945 CRAIG, MAURICE JAMES. The volunteer earl; being the life and times of James Caulfeild, first Earl of Charlemont. London: 1948. Bibliog., note, pp. ix-x.

6946 GILBERT, JOHN T. The manuscripts and correspondence of James, first Earl of Charlemont. London, Royal Commission on Historical Manuscripts, 1891–4. 2 vols. These volumes form Appendix 10 to the 12th Report, and Appendix 8 to the 13th Report of the Royal Commission.

CAULFIELD, RICHARD.

6947 C[OLEMAN], J[AMES]. Dr. Caulfield's contributions to the *Gentleman's Magazine. Cork Hist. Arch. Soc. J., 2nd series.*, 9, 1903, 189–98, 268–74; *ibid.*, 10, 1904, 48–56.

6948 LUNHAM, T.A. Memoir of the late Richard Caulfield [with bibliog.]. *R. Hist. Arch. Soc. Ir. J., 4th ser.,* 8, 1887–8, 171–5.

CHILDERS, ERSKINE.

6949 Bibliography. *New Camb. Bibliog. Eng. Lit.*, 4, 1972, 551.

6950 COX, TOM. Damned Englishman: a study of Erskine Childers (1870–1922). Hicksville (N.Y.): 1975. Bibliog., pp. 357–364.

6951 WILKINSON, BURKE. Erskine Childers: Boston connection. *Cap. Ann.*, 1977, 265–273.

CLAPHAM, ALFRED.

6952 Papers by Sir Alfred Clapham, with a memoir and bibliography. *R. Arch. Inst. supp.,* 1952. Reprinted from the memorial volume of *The Archaeol. J.,* vol. 106.

CLARE, *Sister* MARY FRANCEIS.

6953 EAGAR, IRENE FFRENCH. The nun of Kenmare. Cork: 1970. List of books by Margaret Anna Cusack, pp. 219–220. Sister Clare, born Margaret Anna Cusack. See also *Ir. Book Lov.*, 6, 1914–15, 133–4.

CLARE, WALLACE.

6954 George Clare Wallace, 1895–1963 [obituary notice]. *Ir. Geneal.*, vol. 3., no. 8, 1963, 282–286.

CLARKE, AUSTIN.

6955 Bibliography. *New Camb. Bibliog. Eng. Lit.*, 4, 1972, 248–9.

6956 HALPERN, SUSAN. Austin Clarke, his life and works. Dublin: 1974. Bibliog., pp. 188–195.

6957 HARMON, MAURICE. Notes towards a biography. *Ir. Univ. Rev.*, vol. 4, no. 1, 1974, 13–25.

6958 IRISH UNIVERSITY REVIEW, vol. 4, no. 1, 1974. Austin Clarke special issue. Includes

Austin Clarke: a bibliography, by Gerard Lyre., pp. 137–155.

6959 MacManus, M.J. Bibliographies of Irish writers, no. 8: Austin Clarke. *Dublin Mag., new series.*, vol. 10, no. 2, 1935, 41–3.

6960 Montague, John, and Miller, Liam. *compilers*. A tribute to Austin Clarke on his seventieth birthday, 9 May, 1966. Dolmen Press: 1966. *(Dolmen editions iv)*. The books of Austin Clarke: a checklist, by Liam Miller, pp. 23–27. A revised and extended list which originally appeared in *The Dubliner*, no. 6, 1963, 35–39.

6961 Redshaw, Thomas Dillon. His works: a memorial: Austin Clarke, (1896–1974). *Eire-Ir.*, vol. 9, no. 2, 1974, 107–115.

Clinch, Phyllis E.M.

6962 Award of the Boyle Medal . . . [with bibliog.] *R. Dublin Soc. Sci. Proc. Ser. A*, 1, 1959–64, 211–4.

Cockran, Bourke.

6963 McGurrin, James. Bourke Cockran: a freelance in American politics. New York: 1948. Bibliog., pp. 337–9.

Coffey, Charles.

6964 Bibliography. *New Camb. Bibliog. Eng. Lit.*, 2, 1971, 787.

Colgan, John (1592–1658).

6965 O'Donnell, Terence. Father John Colgan, O.F.M.: essays in commemoration of the third centenary of his death. Dublin: 1959. Bibliog. footnotes.

6966 Reeves, William. Irish library, no. 1: [John] Colgan's works. *Ulster J. Arch.* 1, 1853, 295–302.

Collins, Michael.

6967 O'Hegarty, P.S. A bibliography of the books of Arthur Griffith, Michael Collins, and Kevin O'Higgins. *Dublin Mag., new series.*, vol. 12, no. 1, 1937, 61–67.

6968 Taylor, Rex. Michael Collins. London: 1958. Bibliog., pp. 335–7.

Collis, Maurice Stewart.

6969 Bibliography. *New Camb. Bibliog. Eng. Lit.*, 4, 1972, 1314.

Colum, Padraic.

6970 Bibliography. *New Camb. Bibliog. Eng. Lit.*, 3, 1969, 1942–3.

6971 Bowen, Zack. Padraic Colum: a biographical-critical introduction; with a preface by Harry T. Moore. Carbondale and Edwardsville; Southern Illinois U.P.: London and Amsterdam, Feffer and Simons Inc., 1970. Bibliog., pp. 155–7.

6972 Denson, Alan. Padraic Colum: an appreciation with a checklist of his publications. *Dublin Mag.*, 6, 1967, 50–67, 83–85.

6973 — Padraic Colum, 1881–1972. *Cap. Ann.*, 1973, 45–54.

6974 Journal of Irish Literature, vol. 2, no. 1, 1973. Special Padraic Colum number.

6975 MacLiammoir, Michael. Padraic Colum. *Ir. Wel.*, vol. 21, no. 5, 1973, 8–9.

6976 Murphy, Ann. Padraic Colum remembered. *Dublin Mag.*, vol. 10, no. 4, 1974, 24–30.

6977 Weaver, Jack W. The Padraic Colum I knew. *J. Ir. Lit.*, vol. 3, no. 3, 1974, 49–50.

Connell, Kenneth H.

6978 Kenneth H. Connell, 1917–1973. *Econ. Soc. Rev.*, vol. 6, no. 1, 1974, 1–4. Author of *The Population of Ireland.*

6979 Drake, Michael. Prof. K.H. Connell [obituary]. *Ir. Hist. Stud.*, vol. 19, no. 73, 1974, 83–5.

6980 Hartwell, R.M. Kenneth H. Connell: an appreciation. [with bibliog of his writings, compiled by M. Daly]. *Ir. Econ. Soc. Hist.*, vol. 1, 1974, 7–14.

Connolly, James.

6981 Fox, R.M. James Connolly, the forerunner. Tralee: 1946. Bibliog., pp. 251–2.

6982 Greaves, C. Desmond. The life and times of James Connolly. London: 1961. Bibliog., pp. 348–53.

6983 Levenson, Samuel. James Connolly: a biography. London: 1973. Bibliog., pp. 337–339.

6984 O'Hegarty, P.S. A bibliography of the books of James Connolly. *Dublin Mag., new series,* vol. 11, no. 2, 1936, 62–4.

6985 Ryan, Desmond. James Connolly, his life and writings . . . Dublin: 1924. Bibliog., pp. 133–4.

Conolly, *Lady* Louisa.

6986 Fitzgerald, Brian. Lady Louisa Conolly,

1743–1821: an Anglo-Irish biography. London: 1959. Bibliog., pp. 189–90.

CONWAY, *Prof.* EDWARD J.

6987 Award of the Boyle medal . . ., *R. Dublin Soc. Sci. Proc., Ser. A,* 3, 1967–70, 137–139.

CONWELL, EUGENE.

6988 LUKE, *The Rev. Bro., ed.* Letters from Maynooth: calendar of letters of Rev. Eugene Conwell, 1798–1805. 2nd ed. rev. enl. Dundalk: 1942. First published in *Louth Arch. J.*, vol. 9, no. 4, 1940.

CORKERY, DANIEL.

6989 Bibliography. *New Camb. Bibliog. Eng. Lit.*, 4, 1972, 923–4.

COSTELLO, JOHN A.

6990 Obituary. *R. Ir. Acad. Ann. Rpt.*, 1975–6, 4.

COTTER, JAMES

6991 HOGAN, WILLIAM, and O'BUACHALLA, LIAM. The letters and papers of James Cotter, junior, 1689–1720. *Cork Hist. Arch. Soc. J.*, 68, 1963, 66–95. *ibid.*, 69, 1964, 136–138.

COX, WATTY.

6992 CASAIDE, SEAMUS UA. Watty Cox and his publications. *Bibliog. Soc. Ir.,* 5, 1933–8, 19–38.

CRAIG, JOHN DUNCAN.

6993 BYARD, E.J. John Duncan Craig, M.A., D.D. [obituary and bibliog.]. *Ir. Book Lov.,* 1, 1909–10, 165–6.

CROSSLE, FRANCIS CLEMENTS.

6994 McCLELLAND, AIKEN. Francis Clements Crossle. [with bibliog.]. *Ir. Booklore*, vol. 1, no. 2, 1971, 177–8.

CROSTHWAITE, J.C.

6995 BLACKER, BEAVER H. The writings of the Rev. J.C. Crosthwaite, M.A., vicar choral of Christ Church, Dublin, 1834–44. *Ir. Eccles. Gaz.*, 1875, 269.

CRUISE O'BRIEN, CONOR.

6996 An interview with Conor Cruise O'Brien. *J.J. Qtr.*, vol. 11, no. 3, 1974, 201–209.

6997 HENDERSON, JOANNE L., *compiler*. A Conor Cruise O'Brien checklist. *J. Ir. Lit.*, vol. 3, no. 2, 1974, 49–64.

6998 O'BRIEN, DARCY. Conor Cruise O'Brien. *J.J. Qtr.*, vol. 11, no. 3, 1974, 210–220.

6999 YOUNG-BRUEHL, ELISABETH and HOGAN, ROBERT. Conor Cruise O'Brien: an appraisal. *J. Ir. Lit.*, vol. 3, no. 2, 1974, 3–48. Most of Conor Cruise O'Brien's early books and articles were published under the pen name of Donat O'Donnell.

CURRAN, CONSTANTINE P.

7000 BODKIN, MATHIAS. Constantine P. Curran, 1886–1972. *Studies*, 61, 1972, 171–174. Includes list of articles by C.P. Curran appearing in *Studies*.

7001 KAIN, RICHARD M. Constantine P. Curran, (1883–1972) (*sic*). *Eire-Ir.*, vol. 7, no. 4, 1972, 101–3.

CURRAN, JOHN PHILPOT.

7002 MOORE, DESMOND F. An epilogue of the nineteenth century: John Philpot Curran and his family. *Dublin Hist. Rec.*, 15, 1958–60, 50–61.

7003 STEPHENSON, P.J. Burial of John Philpot Curran. *Dublin Hist. Rec.,* vol. 13, 1952–54, 151–154.

CURTIS, EDMUND.

7004 MOODY, T.W. The writings of Edmund Curtis [a bibliography]. *Ir. Hist. Stud.* 3, 1942–3, 393–400.

D

DARLEY, GEORGE.

7005 Memoir and bibliography. *Ir. Book Lov.*, 3, 1911–12, 17–19.

7006 WOOLF, CECIL. Some uncollected authors XXVIII: George Darley, 1795–1846 [with check-list of first editions]. *Book Coll.,* 10, 1961, 186–92.

DAUNT, W.J. O'NEILL

7007 COLEMAN, JAMES. Bibliography of W.J. O'Neill Daunt. Paper read before the *Bibliog. Soc. Ir.*, March 26, 1925.

DAVIES, JOHN HENRY.

7008 L[ETT], H.W. Obituary and bibliography. *Ir. Nat.,* 18, 1909, 235–6.

DAVIES, ROWLAND.

7009 BLACKER, BEAVER H. The writings of Rowland Davies, LL.D., Dean of Cork. *Ir. Eccles. Gaz.*, 1876, 49.

DAVIS, THOMAS.

7010 COLEMAN, JAMES. Bibliography of Thomas Davis (1814–45). Ms. of 6 p. in National Library, Dublin.

7011 DOUGLAS, J.M., and ROLLESTON, T.W. Biographical note and bibliography. *Ir. Book Lov.,* 6, 1914–15, 65–9.

7012 MOODY, T.W. Thomas Davis, 1814–45: a centenary address delivered in Trinity College, Dublin, on June 12, 1945, at a public meeting of the College Historical Society. Dublin: 1945. Bibliog., pp. 61–3.

7013 — Thomas Davis and the Irish nation [with bibliog.]. *Hermathena*, 103, 1966, 5–31.

DAVITT, MICHAEL.

7014 CAHALAN, JAMES M. Michael Davitt: the 'preacher of ideas', 1881–1906. *Eire-Ir.*, vol. 11, no. 1, 1976, 13–33.

7015 COLEMAN, JAMES. Bibliography of Michael Davitt. Ms. of 6 p. in National Library, Dublin.

DAY, ROBERT.

7016 LEE, P.G. Our late President [obituary notice and bibliog.] *Cork Hist. Arch. Soc. J., 2nd ser.,* 20, 1914, 109–13.

DAY-LEWIS, CECIL.

7017 Bibliography. *New Camb. Bibliog. Eng. Lit.*, 4, 1972, 253–5.

7018 HANDLEY-TAYLOR, GEOFFREY, and SMITH, TIMOTHY D'ARCH., *compilers*. C. Day-Lewis, the poet laureate: a bibliography. Chicago and London: 1968.

DE BURGH, WILLIAM.

7019 BLACKER, BEAVER H. The writings of William de Burgh, D.D., Rector of Ardboe, in the diocese of Armagh. *Ir. Eccles. Gaz.*, 1876, 315–16.

DEEVY, TERESA.

7020 Bibliography. *New Camb. Bibliog. Eng. Lit.*, 4, 1972, 931–2.

DENN, PATRICK

7021 MACLOCHLAINN, A. Patrick Denn [biographical note and bibliog.]. *Ir. Book Lov.* 32, 1952–7, 142–3.

DENNY, *Lady* ARBELLA;

7022 BUTLER, *Miss* Beatrice Bayley. Lady Arbella Denny, 1707–1792. *Dublin Hist. Rec.*, 9, 1946–8, 1–20.

DE VALERA, EAMON.

7023 Obituary. *R. Ir. Acad. Ann. Rpt.*, 1975–6, 5–6.

7024 BROMAGE, MARY C. De Valera and the march of a nation. London: 1956. Bibliog., pp. 303–12.

7025 FITZGERALD, ALEXIS. Eamon de Valera. *Studies*, 64, 1975, 207–214.

7026 FITZGIBBON, CONSTANTINE. The life and times of Eamon de Valera; illustrative material by George Morrison. Dublin: 1973.

7027 PAKENHAM, FRANK. Eamon de Valera, by the Earl of Longford and Thomas P. O'Neill. London: 1970.

7028 RYAN, DESMOND. Unique dictator: a study of Eamon de Valera. London: 1936. Bibliog., pp. 300–1.

7029 SEVERN, BILL. Irish statesman and rebel: the two lives of Eamon de Valera. Folkestone: 1971.

DE VERE, AUBREY.

7030 Bibliography. *New Camb. Bibliog. Eng. Lit.*, 3, 1969, 1903–4.

7031 REILLY, S.M. PARACLITA. Aubrey de Vere, Victorian observer. Dublin: 1956. Bibliog., pp. 167–74.

7032 WINCKLER, P., and STONE, W. De Vere: a bibliography. *Victorian Newsletter no. 10,* 1956.

DEVLIN, BERNADETTE.

7033 DAVIDSON, SARA. Bernadette Devlin: an Irish revolutionary in Irish America. *Harper's Mag.*, vol. 240, no. 1436, 1970, 78–87.

DICKINSON, CHARLES.

7034 BLACKER, BEAVER H. The writings of Charles Dickinson, D.D., Bishop of Meath. *Ir. Eccles. Gaz.,* 1876, 115–16.

DICKSON, WILLIAM STEEL.

7035 BAILIE, W.D. William Steel Dickson, D.D., (1744–1824). *Ir. Booklore*, vol. 2, no. 2, 1976, 239–267.

DILLON, JOHN.

7036 LYONS, F.S.L. John Dillon: a biography. London: 1968. Bibliog., pp. 487–495.

DILLON, MYLES.

7037 Obituary. *R. Ir. Acad. Ann. Rpt.*, 1972–73, 2–3.

DIXON, HENRY HORATIO.

7038 Award of the Boyle medal [with bibliog.]. *R. Dublin Soc. Sci. Proc., new series,* 15, 1916–20, 179–84.

BOBBS, ARTHUR.

7039 CLARKE, DESMOND. Arthur Dobbs, Esquire, 1689–1765; surveyor-general of Ireland, prospector and governor of North Carolina. London and Philadelphia: 1958. Bibliog., pp. 222–3.

DONAGHY, JOHN LYLE.

7040 John Lyle Donaghy, 1902–49, memorial number [with bibliog.]. *Rann*, no. 6, 1949.

DOWDEN, EDWARD.

7041 BYARD, E.J. Bibliography of Edward Dowden. *Ir. Book Lov.*, 4, 1912–13, 185–7.

DOYLE, RICHARD.

7042 HAMBOURG, DARIA. Richard Doyle, his life and work. London: 1948. *(English masters of black-and-white series)*. Bibliog., pp. 31–2.

DOYLE, WILLIAM

7043 O'RAHILLY, ALFRED. Father William Doyle, S.J.: a spiritual study. 3rd ed. rev. and enl. London: 1925. Bibliog., pp. 562–3.

DUFFY, CHARLES GAVAN.

7044 DOUGLAS, JOHN M. Sir Charles Gavan Duffy: a bibliography. *Ir. Book Lov.*, 7, 1915–16, 177–80; 8, 1916–17, 7.

7045 O'BROIN, LEON. Charles Gavan Duffy, patriot and statesman: the story of Charles Gavan Duffy (1816–1903). Dublin: 1967. Bibliog., pp. 158–160. Founder of *The Nation* with Thomas Davis and John Blake Dillon.

DUNSANY, *Lord*.

7046 Bibliography. *New Camb. Bibliog. Eng. Lit.*, 3, 1969, 1945–8.

7047 AMORY, MARK. Biography of Lord Dunsany. London: 1972. The works of Lord Dunsany, pp. 283–285.

7048 BLACK, H.M. A check list of first editions of works of Lord Dunsany. *T.C.D. Ann. Bull.*, 1957, 4–8.

7049 DANIELSON, H. Bibliographies of modern authors. London: 1921. Bibliog. of Lord Dunsany, pp. 65–75. Material appeared originally in *The Bookman's Journal*, 1919–20.

7050 STODDARD, F.G. A bibliography of Lord Dunsany and an analytical catalogue of the Dunsany collection at the University of Texas. In preparation.

DWYER, MICHAEL.

7051 DICKSON, CHARLES. Life of Michael Dwyer, with some account of his companions. Dublin: 1944. Bibliog., pp. 411–14.

E

EDGEWORTH, *The Abbé*.

7052 WOODGATE, M.V. The Abbé Edgeworth (1745–1807). Dublin: [1945]. Bibliog., p. [237].

EDGEWORTH, MARIA.

7053 Bibliography. *New Camb. Bibliog. Eng. Lit.*, 3, 1969, 665–70, 1087.

7054 BUTLER, MARILYN. Maria Edgeworth: a literary biography. Oxford: 1972. Bibliog., pp. 501–509.

7055 COLVIN, CHRISTINE EDGEWORTH. Two unpublished Mss by Maria Edgeworth. *Rev. Eng. Lit.*, vol. 8, no. 4, 1967, 53–61.

7056 A Dictionary of the characters of Maria Edgeworth's novels; thesis submitted for M.A., 1914, to University of Kansas graduate school. *(Univ. of Kansas pub. library series,* no. 2, 1949.)

7057 HAWTHORNE, MARK D. Maria Edgeworth's unpleasant lesson: the shaping of character. *Studies*, 64, 1975, 167–177.

7058 HURST, MICHAEL. Maria Edgeworth and the public scene: intellect, fine feeling and landlordism in the Age of Reform. London: 1969. Bibliog., pp. 192–199.

7059 MURRAY, PATRICK. Maria Edgeworth and her father: the literary partnership. *Eire-Ir.*, vol. 6, no. 3, 1971, 39–50.

7060 NEWBY, P.H. Maria Edgeworth. London: 1950. (*English novelists ser.)* Bibliog., pp. [95–6].

7061 NEWCOMER, JAMES. Maria Edgeworth, the novelist, 1767–1849: a bicentennial study. Fort Worth: 1967.

7062 POLLARD, M. The first Irish edition of Maria Edgeworth's *Parent's Assistant. Ir. Book*, vol. 1, no 4, 1962, 85–88. See also *Book Coll.*, 20, 1971, 347–351; 21, 1972, 127–8: 23, 1974, 258–9.

7063 SLADE, BERTHA COOLIDGE. Maria Edgeworth, 1767–1849: a bibliographical tribute. London: 1937. Limited ed. of 250 copies.

EDGEWORTH, RICHARD LOVELL.

7064 CLARKE, DESMOND. The ingenious Mr.

Edgeworth. London: 1965. Bibliog., pp. 246–7.

7065 SCHOFIELD, ROBERT E. The Lunar Society of Birmingham: a solid history of provincial science and industry in eighteenth-century England. Oxford: 1963. Bibliography of Richard Lovell Edgeworth, pp. 447–8.

EDWARDS, HILTON.

7066 An interview with Hilton Edwards and Michael MacLiammoir, conducted by Gordon Henderson. *J. Ir. Lit.*, vol. 2, nos. 2–3, 1973, 79–97.

EGLINTON, JOHN.

7067 BRYSON, MARY E. 'Our one philosophical critic': John Eglinton. *Eire-Ir.*, vol. 10, no. 2, 1975, 81–88.

EMMET, ROBERT.

7068 CHICAGO PUBLIC LIBRARY. List of books and magazine articles in the Chicago Public Library. Chicago: 1910.

7069 MCCABE, A.M.E. The medical connections of Robert Emmet. *Ir. J. Med. Sci., 6th ser.*, no. 448, 1963, 171–184.

7070 MACLEOD, CATRIONA. Robert Emmet. Dublin: 1935. Bibliog., pp. 140–2.

7071 O'BROIN, LEON. The unfortunate Mr. Robert Emmet. Dublin: 1958. Bibliog., pp. 193–4.

7072 POSTGATE, RAYMOND W. Robert Emmet. London: 1931. Bibliog., pp. 327–36.

ERVINE, ST. JOHN.

7073 Bibliography. *New Camb. Bibliog. Eng. Lit.*, 3, 1969, 1945.

7074 BOYD, JOHN. St. John Ervine: a bibliographical note. *Threshold,* 25, 1974, 101–115.

7075 HOWARD, PAULA. St. John Ervine: a bibliography of his published works. *Ir. Booklore*, vol. 1, no. 2, 1971, 203–209; vol. 2, no. 1, 1972, 164.

EVANS, EDWARD.

7076 O'DONOGHUE, D.J. Biographical note and bibliog. *Ir. Book Lov.,* 10, 1918–19, 57–8.

F

FAHY, EDWARD M.

7077 O'CONNELL, C.S. Edward M. Fahy, Ph.D. [obituary]. *Ir. Geog.*, 8, 1975, 132–3.

FALKINER, CAESAR LITTON.

7078 Bibliography. *Camb. Bibliog. Eng. Lit.*, 3, 1949, 930.

FARRINGTON, ANTHONY.

7079 Obituary. *R. Ir. Acad. Ann. Rpt.*, 1972–73, 3–4.

FERGUSON, HARRY.

7080 FRASER, COLIN. Harry Ferguson, inventor and pioneer. London: 1972. Inventor of the farm tractor.

FERGUSON. *Sir* SAMUEL.

7081 Bibliography. *New Camb. Bibliog. Eng. Lit.*, 3, 1969, 1901–2.

7082 Belfast Museum and Art Gallery. Centenary anniversary, 1810–1910, of Sir Samuel Ferguson, of Belfast: catalogue of a loan exhibition of pictures and books and manuscripts of Ferguson and his friends. Belfast: 1910.

7083 FERGUSON, *Lady*. Sir Samuel Ferguson in the Ireland of his day. Edinburgh and London,1896. 2 vols .Bibliog.,vol. 2, pp.369–74.

FIELDING-HALL, HAROLD PATRICK.

7084 Bibliography. *Ir. Book Lov.*, 8, 1916–17, 143.

FITZGERALD, EDWARD.

7085 TAYLOR, IDA A. The life of Lord Edward Fitzgerald, 1763–98. London: 1903. Bibliog., pp. 339–40.

FITZGERALD, GERALD.

7086 DONOUGH, BRYAN. Gerald Fitzgerald, the Great Earl of Kildare (1456–1513). Dublin: 1933. Bibliog., pp. xiv–xxiii.

FITZGERALD, *Lord* WALTER.

7087 HARBISON, PETER. Commemorating Lord Walter Fitzgerald. *Kildare Arch. Soc. J.*, vol. 15, no. 3, 1973–4, 230–1.

FITZMAURICE, GEORGE.

7088 Bibliography. *New Camb. Bibliog. Eng. Lit.*, 3, 1969, 1941–2.

7089 GELDERMAN, CAROL. Austin Clarke and Yeats's alleged jealousy of George Fitzmaurice. *Eire-Ir.*, vol. 8, no. 2, 1973, 62–70.

7090 HENDERSON, JOANNE L. Checklist of four Kerry writers: George Fitzmaurice, Maurice Walsh, Bryan MacMahon and John B. Keane. *J. Ir. Lit.*, vol. 1, no. 2, 1972, 101–119.

7091 MILLER, LIAM. George Fitzmaurice: a bibliographical note. *Ir. Writ.*, no. 15, 1951, 47–8.

FITZPATRICK, WILLIAM JOHN.

7092 A busy biographer [with bibliog]. *Ir. Book Lov.*, 10, 1918–19, 27–30.

FLEMING, PATRICK.

7093 REEVES, WILLIAM. Irish library, no. 2: Fleming's *Collectanea Sacra. Ulster J. Arch.*, 2, 1854, 253–261.

FLOOD, W.H. GRATTAN.

7094 Bibliography. *Ir. Book Lov.,* 9, 1917, 32.

7095 DIX, E.R. McC. W.H. Grattan Flood. *ibid.*, 17, 1929, 12.

FOSTER, JEANNE ROBERT.

7096 LONDREVILLE, RICHARD. Jeanne Robert Foster. *Eire-Ir.*, vol. 5, no. 1, 1970, 38–44.

FOSTER, VERE.

7097 MCNEILL, MARY. Vere Foster, 1819–1900: an Irish benefactor. Newton Abbot: 1971. Bibliog., pp. 247–249.

FRIEL, BRIAN.

7098 MAXWELL, D.E.S. Brian Friel. Lewisburg: 1973. *(Irish writers series)*. Bibliog., pp. 111–112.

7099 WARNER, ALAN. Introducing Brian Friel. *Acorn*, 14, 1970, 25–28.

G

GALLAGHER, JAMES, *Bishop of Raphoe.*

7100 Seanmoiri muighe nuadhad . . . an ceathramhadh imleabhar. Baile Atha Cliath: 1911. Bibliog., by Seamus ua Casaide, pp. xiii–xiv.

GALLAGHER, *The Rev.*, PATRICK.

7101 Published works by the Rev. P. O'Gallachair. *Donegal Ann.*, vol. 5, no. 2, 1962, iv–vi.

GAMBLE, *Dr.* JOHN.

7102 CAMPBELL, A. ALBERT. Biographical note and bibliography. *Ir. Book Lov.*, 1, 1909–10, 20–21.

GANLY, PATRICK.

7103 SIMINGTON, R.C. and FARRINGTON, A. A forgotten pioneer: Patrick Ganly, geologist, surveyor and civil engineer. *Ir. Dept. Agric. J.*, 46, 1949, 36–50.

GIBBINGS, ROBERT.

7104 Bibliography. *New Camb. Bibliog. Eng. Lit.*, 4, 1972, 1317.

7105 EMPSON, PATRICIA, *ed*. The wood engravings of Robert Gibbings. London: 1959. Books illustrated with engraving by R. Gibbings, pp. 353–5.

7106 KIRKUS, A. MARY. Robert Gibbings: a bibliography. London: 1962. Includes check list and notes on the Golden Cockerel Press.

GIBBON, MONK.

7107 DENSON, ALAN. Monk Gibbon: an appreciation [with checklist of his publications]. *Dublin Mag.*, vol. 5, nos. 3–4, 1966, 15–22.

7108 WRIGHT, BARBARA. The prose work of Monk Gibbon. *Dublin Mag.*, vol. 7, nos. 2–4, 1968, 51–62

GIBBON, SKEFFINGTON.

7109 CASAIDE, SEAMUS UA. Skeffington Gibbon in the Goldsmith country. *Ir. Book Lov.*, 22, 1934, 58–62.

GILBERT, *Lady*. (ROSA MULHOLLAND.).

7110 Bibliography. *Ir. Book Lov.*, 13, 1921–2, 21–2.

GILBERT, *Sir* JOHN THOMAS.

7111 Bibliography. *New Camb. Bibliog. Eng. Lit.*, 3, 1969, 1891.

7112 DIXON F.E. Sir John T. Gilbert, 1829–1898. *Dublin Hist. Rec.*, 22, 1968, 272–287. Includes an index of the illustrations in the *Calendar of Ancient Records of Dublin*, vols. 1–18.

7113 GILBERT, *Lady*. Life of Sir John T. Gilbert. London: 1905. Bibliog., pp. 445–8.

GIRALDUS CAMBRENSIS.

7114 JONES, W.R. *Giraldus redivivus* – English historians, Irish apologists, and the work of Gerald of Wales. *Eire-Ir.*, vol. 9, no. 3, 1974, 3–20.

7115 MARTIN, F.X. Gerald of Wales: Norman reporter on Ireland. *Studies*, 58, 1969, 279–292.

GODKIN, JAMES.

7116 CAMPBELL, A.A. Memoir and bibliography. *Ir. Book Lov.*, 2, 1910–11, 117–19.

GOGARTY, OLIVER ST. JOHN.

7117 Bibliography. *New Camb. Bibliog. Eng. Lit.*, 4, 1972, 283–4.

7118 LYONS, J.B. Oliver St. John Gogarty: early phase. *J. Ir. Coll. Phys. Surg.*, vol. 5, no. 2, 1975, 67–72.

7119 — Oliver St. John Gogarty: the productive years. *Studies*, 66, 1977, 145–163.

GOLDSMITH, OLIVER.

7120 BALDERSTON, KATHERINE CANBY. A census of the manuscripts of Oliver Goldsmith. London and New York: 1927.

7121 Bibliography. *New Camb. Bibliog. Eng. Lit.*, 2, 1971, 1191–1210.

7122 COLE, RICHARD C. Oliver Goldsmith's reputation in Ireland, 1762–74. *Mod. Phil.*, vol. 68, no. 1, 1970, 65–70.

7123 DIX, E.R. McC. The works of Oliver Goldsmith: hand-list of Dublin editions before 1801. *Bibliog. Soc. Ir.*, 3, 1926–9, 93–101.

7124 DOBSON, AUSTIN. The Life of Oliver Goldsmith: London: 1888. Bibliography by J.P. Anderson, pp. i–xxiii, at end of volume.

7125 — The Vicar Of Wakefield; being a facsimile reproduction of the 1st edition in 1766; with an introduction by A. Dobson, and a bibliographical list of editions of 'The Vicar of Wakefield', published in England and abroad. London: 1885. See also *Camb. Hist. Eng. Lit.*, vol. 10, 1913.

7126 GINGER, JOHN. The notable man: the life and times of Oliver Goldsmith. London: 1977. Bibliog., pp. 395–400.

7127 JEFFARES, A. NORMAN. Goldsmith, the good natured man. *Hermathena*, no. 119, 1975, 5-19.

7128 KIRK, CLARA M. Oliver Goldsmith. Boston: 1967. *(Twayne's English authors ser.)*. Bibliog., pp. 195–7.

7129 LEE, GERALD. Oliver Goldsmith. *Dublin Hist. Rec.*, vol. 26, no. 1, 1972, 2–17.

7130 MURRAY, PATRICK. The riddle of Goldsmith's ancestry. *Studies*, 63, 1974, 177–190.

7131 QUINTANA, RICARDO. Oliver Goldsmith: a Georgian study. London: 1969.

7132 SCOTT, TEMPLE. Oliver Goldsmith, bibliographically and biographically considered. New York: 1928. Based on the collection of W.M. Elkins of Philadelphia.

7133 SELLS, ARTHUR LYTTON. Les sources françaises de Goldsmith. Paris: 1924.

7134 — Oliver Goldsmith: his life and works. London: 1974. Bibliog., pp. 411–412.

7135 SOTHEBY and Co. Catalogue of the very extensive collection of the writings of Oliver Goldsmith, the property of W. Swanston. London: 1926.

7136 WARDLE, RALPH M. Oliver Goldsmith. Lawrence (Kansas) and London: 1957. Bibliog. notes, pp. 298–319.

GRATTAN, HENRY.

7137 MCHUGH, ROGER J. Henry Grattan. Dublin: 1936. Bibliog., pp. 187–9.

GRAVES, ALFRED PERCEVAL.

7138 Bibliography. *New Camb. Bibliog. Eng. Lit.*, 3, 1969, 1907–8.

7139 To return to all that: an autobiography. Dublin and London: 1930. Bibliog. pp. 347–50.

GREEN, ALICE STOPFORD.

7140 MCDOWELL, R.B. Alice Stopford Green: a passionate historian. Dublin: 1967. Bibliog., pp. 113–4.

GREGORY, ANNE.

7141 Me and Nu: childhood at Coole. Gerrards Cross (Bucks.): Colin Smythe. 1970. Grandchild of Lady Gregory.

GREGORY, ISABELLA AUGUSTA, Lady.

7142 Bibliography. *New Camb. Bibliog. Eng. Lit.*, 3, 1969, 1939–41.

7143 ADAMS, HAZARD. Lady Gregory. Lewisburg: 1973. Bibliog., pp. 104–106.

7144 COXHEAD, ELIZABETH. Lady Gregory: a literary portrait. 2nd ed. rev. and enlarged. London: 1966. Bibliog., pp. 219–221.

7145 HENN, T.R. and SMYTHE, COLIN. *gen. eds.* The collected works of Lady Gregory. Gerrards Cross. vol. 18. General index, bibliography and catalogue of the libraries at Coole. In preparation.

7146 MIKHAIL, E.H. *ed.* Lady Gregory: interviews and recollections. London: 1977.

GRIFFIN, GERALD.

7147 Bibliography. *New Camb. Bibliog. Eng. Lit.*, 3, 1969, 931–2. See also *Catalogue of the Gerald Griffin Memoriam Library*. Enniskerry: 1901.

7148 CRONIN, JOHN. Gerald Griffin (1803–1840): a critical biography. Cambridge: 1978. Bibliog., pp. 152–160.

7149 — Gerald Griffin in London, 1823–1827. *Ir. Booklore*, vol. 2, no. 1, 1972, 116–41.

7150 — Gerald Griffin's Common-Place Book A. *Eire-Ir.*, vol. 4, no. 3, 1969, 22–37.

7151 — A select list of works concerning Gerald Griffin (arranged in chronological order). *Ir. Booklore*, vol. 1, no. 2, 1971, 150–156.

7152 — Some unpublished letters of Gerald Griffin. *Eire-Ir.*, vol. 9, no. 4, 1974, 42–68.

7153 KIELY, BENEDICT. The two masks of Gerald Griffin. *Studies,* 61, 1972, 241–251.

GRIFFITH, AMYAS.

7154 MCCLELLAND, AIKEN. Amyas Griffith, [1746–1801]. *Ir. Booklore*, vol. 2, no. 1, 1972, 7–21.

GRIFFITH, ARTHUR.

7155 O'HEGARTY, P.S. A bibliography of the books of Arthur Griffith . . . *Dublin Mag., new series*, vol. 12, no. 1, 1937, 61–7.

7156 O'LUING, SEAN. Art O Griofa. Baile Atha Cliath: 1953. Bibliog., pp. 415–20.

7157 — Arthur Griffith, 1871–1922: thoughts on a centenary. *Studies*, 60, 1971, 127–138.

GRIFFITH, *Sir* JOHN PURSER.

7158 Award of the Boyle medal [with bibliog.]. *R. Dublin Soc. Sci. Proc., new series,* 20, 1930–3, 85–7.

GRIFFITH, *Sir* RICHARD.

7159 HUSSEY, MARY OLIVE. Sir Richard Griffith – the man and his work. *Dublin Hist. Rec.,* 20, 1964–65, 57–75.

7160 — Sir Richard Griffith – the man and his work. *Admin.*, 14, 1966, 314–326.

GRUBB, *Sir* HOWARD.

7161 Award of the Boyle medal [with bibliog.]. *R. Dublin Soc. Sci. Proc., new series,* 13, 1912, 288–92.

GUINAN, JOHN.

7162 Obituary and bibliography. *Ir. Book Lov.*, 30, 1946–8, 11–12.

GWYNN, AUBREY.

7163 Medieval studies presented to Aubrey Gwynn, S.J.: edited by J.A. Watt, J.B. Morrall and F.X. Martin. Dublin: 1961. The historical writings of Reverend Professor Aubrey Gwynn, by F.X. Martin, pp. 502–9.

H

HACKETT, FLORENCE MARY.

7164 DELAHUNTY, JAMES. The cruellest month: in memoriam Florence Hackett (1884–1963). *Kilkenny Mag.*, 10, 1963, 35–53.

HALL, ANNA MARIA, *née* FIELDING.

7165 Bibliography. *New Camb. Bibliog. Eng. Lit.*, 3, 1969, 932–3, 1090.

HAMILTON, ANTHONY.

7166 CLARKE, RUTH. Anthony Hamilton (author of *Memoirs of Count Grammont*), his life and works and his family. London: 1921. Bibliog., pp. 313–36.

HAMILTON, EDWIN.

7167 Bibliography. *Ir. Book Lov.*, 11, 1919–20, 15.

HAMILTON, GEORGE.

7168 BLACKER, BEAVER H. The writings of Rev. George Hamilton, M.A., rector of Killermagh in the diocese of Ossory. *Ir. Eccles. Gaz.*, 1876, 153.

HAMILTON, JOHN.

7169 Sixty years experience as an Irish landlord: memoirs of John Hamilton, D.L., of St. Ernan's, Donegal; edited with an introduction by Rev. H.C. White. London [1894]. Bibliog., pp. xxxviii–liii; 310–21.

HANLEY, JAMES.

7170 Bibliography. *New Camb. Bibliog. Eng. Lit.*, 4, 1972, 596–7.

HAUGHTON, SAMUEL.

7171 JESSOP, W.J.E. Samuel Haughton: a Victorian polymath. *Hermathena*, 116, 1973, 5–26.

HAYES, RICHARD JAMES.

7172 Obituary. *R. Ir. Acad. Ann. Rpt.*, 1975–6, 6–7.

HAYES-MCCOY, G.A.

7173 Obituary. *R. Ir. Acad. Ann. Rpt.*, 1975–6, 7–8.

7174 HARMAN, MURTAGH. The historical writings of G.A. Hayes-McCoy. *Ir. Sword*, vol. 12, no. 47, 1975, 83–89.

7175 SIMMS, J.G. G.A. Hayes-McCoy (1911–75). *Ir. Hist. Stud.*, 20, 1976, 51–2.

HAYMAN, *Canon* SAMUEL.

7176 LUNHAM, T.A. Memoir of the late Canon Hayman [with bibliog.]. *R. Hist. Arch. Soc. Ir. J., 4th ser.*, 3, 1887–8, 165–70.

HAYWARD, RICHARD.

7177 ADAMS, G.B. Richard Hayward: a bibliography of his published works. *Ir. Booklore*, vol. 3, no. 1, 1976, 51–56.

HEALEY, *Rev.* JOHN, *Archbishop of Tuam.*

7178 Bibliography. *Ir. Book Lov.*, 9, 1918, 112.

HEALY, JOHN.

7179 CONNAUGHTON, PADRAIG. John Healy [Backbencher]. *Zenith*, 2, 1972, 54–57.

HEALEY, T.M.

7180 C[RONE], J.S. Bibliography of the late T.M. Healy. *Ir. Book Lov.,* 19, 1931, 36.

HENN, *Dr.* THOMAS RICE.

7181 D[RUDY], P.J. Dr. Thomas Rice Henn: Anglo-Irish scholar [obituary]. *Anglo-Irish Stud.*, 1, 1975, 117.

HERVEY, FREDERICK, *4th Earl of Bristol and Bishop of Derry.*

7182 FORD, BRINSLEY. The Earl-bishop: an eccentric and capricious patron of the arts. *Apollo*, vol. 99, no. 148, 1974, 426–434.

7183 FOTHERGILL, BRIAN. The mitred earl: an eighteenth century eccentric. London: 1974. Bibliog., pp. 246–7.

7184 PATERSON, T.G.F. The edifying Bishop: 'Bishop's Folly'. *Ir. Georg. Soc. Qtr. Bull.*, 9, 1966, 67–83.

7185 WALSH, JOHN R. Frederick Augustus Hervey, 1730–1803: fourth Earl of Bristol, Bishop of Derry. 'Le bienfaiteur des catholiques.' Maynooth: 1972. *(Maynooth historical series* no. 1). Bibliog., pp. 49–52.

HIFFERNAN, PAUL.

7186 KIRKPATRICK, T. PERCY C. A note on the life and writings of Paul Hiffernan, M.D. [with bibliog.]. *Ir. Book Lov.*, 19, 1931, 11–21.

HIGGINS, FRANCIS.

7187 LYSAGHT, MOIRA. The Sham Squire. *Dublin Hist. Rec.* vol. 25, no. 2, 1972, 64–74.

HIGGINS, FREDERICK ROBERT.

7188 Bibliography. *New Camb. Bibliog. Eng. Lit.*, 4, 1972, 290–1.

189 MACMANUS, M.J. Bibliography of F.R. Higgins (1896–1941). *Dublin Mag., new series*, vol. 21, no. 3, 1946, 43–5.

HOEY, WILLIAM.

7190 Bibliography. *Ir. Book Lov.*, 9, 1917–18, 139.

HOGAN, EDMUND.

7191 Bibliography. *Ir. Book. Lov.*, 9, 1917–18, 64–5.

7192 MACERLEAN, JOHN. Bibliography of Dr. Hogan, arranged in chronological order. *Studies*, 6, 1917, 668–71.

HOGAN, JAMES.

7193 O'FLAHERTY, KATHLEEN. James Hogan: 1898–1963 [Professor of History, University College, Cork]. *Studies,* 53, 1964, 57–60.

HOGAN, MICHAEL.

7194 HERBERT, ROBERT. A bibliography of Michael Hogan, bard of Thomond. *Ir. Book Lov.*, 27, 1940–1, 276–9.

HOLLAND, JOHN P.

7195 MORRIS, RICHARD KNOWLES. John P. Holland, 1841–1914: inventor of the modern submarine. Annapolis (Maryland): United States Naval Institute: 1966. Bibliog., pp. 197–202.

HOLMES, WILLIAM A.

7196 BLACKER, BEAVER H. The writings of William Anthony Holmes, D.D., Chancellor of Cashel and Rector of Templemore. *Ir. Eccles. Gaz.*, 1876, 77.

HOOKE, LUKE JOSEPH.

7197 GWYNN, AUBREY. A forgotten Irish theologian. *Studies*, 63, 1974, 259–268.

HOPPER, NORA (*later* Chesson).

7198 Bibliography. *New Camb. Bibliog. Eng. Lit.*, 3, 1969, 1916.

HOULT, NORAH.

7199 Bibliography. *New Camb. Bibliog. Eng. Lit.*, 4, 1972, 605–6.

HUME, ABRAHAM.

7200 MORLEY, JOHN COOPER. A brief memoir of the Rev. Abraham Hume . . . with a chronological list of his published writings, 1845–85. Liverpool: 1887. Born in Greenogue, Co. Down, February 9, 1814.

HUNT, JOHN.

7201 HARBISON, PETER. Obituary of John Hunt. (1900–1976) [with bibliog.] *Studies*, 65, 1976, 322–329.

HYDE, DOUGLAS.
7202 Bibliography. *New Camb. Bibliog. Eng. Lit.*, 3, 1969, 1909–10.

7203 DALY, DOMINIC. The young Douglas Hyde: the dawn of the Irish revolution and renaissance, 1874–1893. Dublin: 1974. Bibliog., pp. 223–226.

7204 DE BHALDRAITHE, TOMAS. Aguisin le clar saothair An Chraoibhin. *Galvia*, 4, 1957, 18–24. Supplements O'Hegarty's bibliography.

7205 DUNLEAVY, GARETH W. The birthplace of Douglas Hyde. *Eire-Ir.*, vol. 9, no. 4, 1974, 28–31.

7206 — Douglas Hyde. Lewisburg and London: 1974. Bibliog., pp. 91-92.

7207 O'DALAIGH, DOIMINIC. The young Douglas Hyde. *Stud. Hib.*, 10, 1970, 108–135.

7208 O'HEGARTY, P.S. A bibliography of Dr. Douglas Hyde. *Dublin Mag., new series,* vol. 14, no. 1, 1939, 57–66; *ibid.*, no. 2, 72–8.

I

INGRAM, JOHN KELLS.
7209 [LYSTER, T.W.]. Bibliography of the writings of John Kells Ingram, 1823–1907, with a brief chronology. *An Leab.*, vol. 3, no. 1, 1909, 1–46.

J

JEBB, JOHN.
7210 BLACKER, BEAVER H. The writings of John Jebb, D.D., Bishop of Limerick, Ardfert and Aghadoe. *Ir. Eccles. Gaz.*, 1876, 76–7.

JEPHSON, ROBERT.
7211 Bibliography. *New Camb. Bibliog. Eng. Lit.*, 2, 1971, 844.

JOHNSTON, DENIS.
7212 An interview with Denis Johnston, conducted by Gordon Henderson. *J. Ir. Lit.*, vol. 2, nos. 2–3, 1973, 30–44.

7213 Bibliography. *New Camb. Bibliog. Eng. Lit.*, 4, 1972, 957–8.

JOHNSTON, JOSEPH.
7214 Joseph Johnston, 1890–1972 [obituary]. *Econ. Soc. Rev.*, vol. 4, no. 2, 1972, 197–199.

JOLY, JOHN.
7215 Award of the Boyle medal [with bibliog.]. *R. Dublin Soc. Sci. Proc., new ser.,* 13, 1911, 142–7.

7216 John Joly, 1857–1933 [with bibliog.] *R. Soc. Obit. N.*, 3, 1934, 259–286.

JONES, HENRY.
7217 Bibliography. *New Camb. Bibliog. Eng. Lit.*, 2, 1971, 662–3.

JONES, MICHAEL.
7218 KERR, ARCHIBALD W.M. An Ironside of Ireland: the remarkable career of Lieut. General Michael Jones, Governor of Dublin and commander of the parliamentary forces in Leinster, 1647–9. London [1923]. Bibliog., pp. 145–6.

JOYCE, JAMES.
7219 Bibliography. *New Camb. Bibliog. Eng. Lit.*, 4, 1972, 444–471.

7220 ATHERTON, JAMES S. The books of the Wake: a study of literary allusions in . . . *Finnegans Wake*. London: 1959. Bibliog., pp. 291–6.

7221 BERRONE, LOUIS, *ed.* James Joyce in Padua. New York: 1977. Bibliog., pp. 141–6.

7222 CONNOLLY, THOMAS EDMUND. The personal library of James Joyce: a descriptive bibliography. [2nd ed. Buffalo, 1957.] This collection is in the Lockwood Memorial Library in the University of Buffalo; first ed. was published in *The University of Buffalo Studies*, vol. 22, no. 1, 1955, and records some marginalia.

7223 DALY, LEO. James Joyce and the Mullingar connection. Dublin: 1975. *(Dolmen editions xx)*.

7224 DENNING, ROBERT H. A bibliography of James Joyce studies. Lawrence: 1964. *(University of Kansas publications, Library series 18).* Addenda to Denning bibliography, by Richard M. Kain. *J.J. Qtr.*, vol. 3, no. 2, 1966, 154–159.

7225 THE DUBLIN MAGAZINE vol. 10, no. 2, 1973. Special issue on Joyce.

7225A ELLMANN, RICHARD. James Joyce. London and New York: 1959. Bibliog. notes, pp. 757–817.

7226 **Finneran, Richard J.** James Joyce and James Stephens: the record of a friendship with unpublished letters from Joyce to Stephens. *J.J. Qtr.*, vol. 11, no. 3, 1974, 279–292.

7227 **Goldberg, S.L.** The classical temper: a study of James Joyce's *Ulysses*. London: 1961. Bibliog. notes, pp. 316–40.

7228 **Igoe, Vivian.** Some references to canals in the works of James Joyce. *Canaliana*, 1975, 33–36.

7229 **Illinois, Southern Illinois University Library.** James Joyce: an exhibition from the collection of Dr. H.K. Croessman, February 1957; [catalogue prepared by Alan M. Cohn]. Illinois: 1957.

7230 **James Joyce Quarterly.** Oklahoma. vol. 1–, 1963–, Five-year cumulative bibliography, vols. 1–5, 1963–1968. Cumulative Index, vols. 1–10, 1963–72, compiled by John Van Coorhis and John Metzner, 1973.

7231 **James Joyce Review.** New York: vols. 1–3, 1957–59.

7232 **Kain, Richard M.** Portraits of James Joyce: a preliminary check list. *In* A James Joyce miscellany, 2nd ser., edited by M. Magalaner. Carbondale: 1959, pp. 111–117.

7233 — and **Cohn, Alan M.** Portraits of James Joyce: a revised list. *J.J. Qtr.*, 3, 1965–66, 205–212.

7234 **Litz, A. Walton.** The art of James Joyce: method and design in *Ulysses* and *Finnegans Wake*. London: 1961. Bibliog. notes, pp. 129–49.

7235 **Lyons, J.B.** James Joyce's miltonic affliction. *Ir. J. Med. Sci., 7th ser.* vol. 1, 1968, 157–165, 203–210.

7236 — James Joyce and medicine. Dublin: 1973. Bibliog., pp. 240–243.

7237 **MacCarvill, Eileen.** Joyce at the University. *St. Stephen's*, Michaelmas no., 1960, 14–17; *ibid.*, Trinity no., 1961, 19–24. Undergraduate life at University College, Dublin.

7238 **Mason, Ellsworth** and **Ellman, Richard,** *eds*. The critical writings of James Joyce. London: 1959.

7239 **Mizener, Arthur.** The Cornell Joyce collection. Cornell Univ., 1958. A prolegomena to the collection made by Joyce's brother, Stanislaus.

7240 **O'Hegarty, P.S.** A bibliography of James Joyce. *Dublin Mag., new ser.*, vol. 21, no. 1, 1946, 38–47.

7241 **Parker, Alan Dean.** James Joyce: a bibliography of his writings, critical material and miscellanea. Boston, Mass: 1948. *(Useful reference ser.*, no. 76.)

7242 — James Joyce: addenda to Alan Parker's bibliography, by William White. *Bibliog. Soc. Amer. Papers,* 43, 1949, 401–11.

7243 — Addenda to James Joyce bibliography, 1950–3. *James Joyce Review*, vol. 1, no. 2, 1957, 9–25.

7244 — Addenda to James Joyce bibliography, 1954–7. *ibid.*, vol. 1, no. 3, 1957, 3–24.

7245 — Supplement to James Joyce bibliography, 1954–7; by Richard M. Kain. *ibid.*, vol. 1, no. 4, 1957, 38–40.

7246 — Further supplement to James Joyce bibliography, 1950–7, by Alan M. Cohn. *ibid.*, vol. 2, nos. 1–2, 1958, 40–54.

7247 — Additional supplement to James Joyce bibliography, 1950–9; by Alan M. Cohn and H.K. Croessman. *ibid.*, vol. 3, nos. 1–2, 1959, 16–39.

7248 — Supplementary JJ checklist, 1959, compiled by Alan M. Cohn. *J.J. Qtr.*, vol. 3, no. 3, 1966, 196–204.

7249 — Supplemental JJ checklist, 1960–1, compiled by Alan M. Cohn. *ibid.*, vol. 3, no. 2, 1966, 141–153.

7250 — Supplemental JJ checklist, 1962, compiled by Alan M. Cohn and Richard M. Kain. *ibid.*, vol. 1, no. 2, 1964, 15–22.

7251 — Supplemental JJ checklist, 1963, compiled by Alan M. Cohn. *ibid.*, vol. 2, no. 1, 1964, 50–60. Further checklists appear annually in *J.J. Qtr*.

7252 **Shechner, Mark.** James Joyce and psychoanalysis: a selected checklist. *James Joyce Quarterly.*, vol. 13, no. 3, 1976, 383–4.

7253 **Scholes, Robert E.** *compiler*. The Cornell Joyce collection: a catalogue. Ithaca (N.Y.), Cornell University: 1961.

7254 **Slocum, John J.** and **Cahoon, Herbert.** A bibliography of James Joyce, 1882–1941. London and New Haven: 1953. Reprinted Westport (Conn.): 1972. Based on the Joyce Library, formed . . . by John J. Slocum . . . which is now in Yale University Library. *See also* Song in the works of James Joyce, by Matthew J.C. Hodgart and Mabel P. Worthington. Philadelphia: 1959. Musical settings of texts by James Joyce: a supplement to section F of Slocum and Cahoon's *Bibliography* . . .by S. Hill. *Longroom*, 2, 1970, 12–17. Musical settings of texts by James Joyce: a further supplement, by Alan M. Cohn. *Longroom*, 6, 1972, 17–21.

7255 **Spielberg, Peter M.** James Joyce's manuscripts and letters at the University of Buffalo: a catalogue. New York: 1962.

7256 **Spoerri, James Fuller.** Catalog of a collection of the works of James Joyce, exhibited at the Newberry Library, March 1 to March 26, 1948. Chicago: 1948. Sixty copies . . . distinctively bound.

7257 — *Finnegans Wake*, by James Joyce: a check-list including publications of portions under the title *Work in progress*. Evanston, Ill., Northwestern University Library: 1953. Issued on the occasion of a James Joyce exhibit drawn from the James F. Spoerri collection of Joyceana and held in the Charles Deering Library, Northwestern Univ., Evanston, Illinois, December 1952–January 1953.

7258 **Stewart, J.I.M.** James Joyce. London: British Council, 1957. *(Writers and their work ser.)* Select bibliog., pp. 39–43.

7259 **Tindall, William York.** A reader's guide to James Joyce. London [1960]. Bibliog., pp. 297–9.

7260 **Walker, B.M.** James Joyce: a bibliography. *Manchester Rev.*, 8, *Spring*, 1958, 151–60. Supplements *Bibliography of James Joyce*, 1882–1941, by J.J. Slocum and H. Cahoon.

7261 **Weir, Lorraine.** Joyce, myth and memory: on his blindness. *Ir. Univ. Rev.*, vol. 2, no. 2, 1972, 172–188.

Joyce, Patrick Weston and **Joyce, Robert Dwyer.**

7262 **Joyce, Mannix.** The Joyce brothers of Glenosheen. *Cap. Ann.*, 1969, 257–287.

Joyce, Stanislaus.

7263 **Healey, George H.**, *ed.* The complete Dublin diary of Stanislaus Joyce. Ithaca and London: 1971.

K

Kavanagh, Arthur McMorrough.

7264 **McCormick, Donald.** The Incredible Mr. Kavanagh. London: 1960. Bibliog., p. 199.

Kavanagh, Patrick.

7265 Bibliography. *New Camb. Bibliog. Eng. Lit.*, 4, 1972, 292–3.

7266 **Boylan, Francis.** Patrick Kavanagh. *Ishmael*, vol. 1, no. 3, 1972–3, 26–62.

7267 **Green, Martin.** Patrick Kavanagh. Monaghan poet. *Ir. Wel.*, vol. 20, no. 5, 1972, 34–36.

7268 **Journal of Irish Literature**, vol. 6, no. 1, 1977. Special Patrick Kavanagh Number.

7269 **Kavanagh, Peter**, *ed.* Lapped furrows: correspondence, 1933–1967, between Patrick and Peter Kavanagh: with other documents. New York: The Peter Kavanagh Hand Press: 1969.

7270 **Kennelly, Brendan.** Patrick Kavanagh. *Ariel*, vol. 1, no. 3, 1970, 7–28.

7271 **Nemo, John.** A bibliography of writings by and about Patrick Kavanagh. *Ir. Univ. Rev.*, vol. 3, no. 1, 1973, 80–106.

7272 — A joust with the Philistines: Patrick Kavanagh's cultural criticism. *J. Ir. Lit.*, vol. 4, no. 2, 1975, 65–75.

7273 — The Green Knight: Patrick Kavanagh's venture into criticism. *Studies*, 63, 1974, 282–294.

7274 **O'Brien, Darcy.** Patrick Kavanagh. Lewisburg and London: 1975. Bibliog., pp. 71–72.

7275 **Potts, Paul.** Patrick Kavanagh. *Twentieth Century*, vol. 177, no. 1038, 1968, 48–51.

7276 **Sealy, Douglas.** The writings of Patrick Kavanagh [with bibliog]. *Dublin Mag.*, vol. 4, nos. 3–4, 1965, 5–23.

7277 **Warner, Alan.** Clay is the work: Patrick Kavanagh, 1904–1967. Dublin: 1973. Patrick Kavanagh: a checklist, pp. 122–128.

KEANE, JOHN B.

7278 The Hidden Ireland of John B. Keane. *Eire-Ir.*, vol. 3, no. 2, 1968, 14–26.

KEARNEY, PEADAR.

7279 DE BURCA, SEAMUS. Peadar Kearney (1883–1942): soldier, poet, singer. *Dublin Hist. Rec.*, vol. 28, no. 2, 1975, 42–56. Author of the *Soldier's Song*.

KELLY, DENIS.

7280 BLACKER, BEAVER H. The writings of the Rev. Denis Kelly, M.A., sometime vicar of Killyon, in the diocese of Elphin. *Ir. Eccles. Gaz.*, 1875, 269–70.

KELLY, HUGH.

7281 Bibliography. *New Camb. Bibliog. Eng. Lit.*, 2, 1971, 845.

KELLY, THOMAS.

7282 Memorial portrait of the late Alderman Thomas Kelly, T.D. *Dublin Hist. Rec.*, 9, 1946–8, 96–104.

KENEALY, EDWARD VAUGHAN.

7283 Bibliography. *Ir. Book Lov.*, 11, 1919–20, 5–6.

KENNEDY, DAVID.

7284 BECKETT, J.C. David Kennedy (1904–74) [obituary]. *Ir. Hist. Stud.*, 20, 1976, 49–50.

KETTLE, THOMAS.

7285 The Day's burden and other essays. Dublin: 1968. Includes Memoir, by Mary S. Kettle, which was originally published in *The Ways of War*, 1917.

7286 CLERY, ARTHUR E. Thomas Kettle. *Studies*, 5, 1916, 503–505.

7287 HERBERT, BEDA. Tom Kettle, 1880–1916. *Cap. Ann.*, 1967, 420–427.

7288 SCOTT, BONNIE K. Thomas Kettle, 1880–1916. *J. Ir. Lit.*, vol. 3, no. 2, 1974, 75–91. Includes a selected Kettle bibliography.

KIELY, BENEDICT.

7289 An interview with Benedict Kiely. *J.J. Qtr.*, vol. 11, no. 3, 1974, 189–200.

7290 CASEY, DANIEL J. Benedict Kiely. Lewisburg and London: 1974. *(Irish Writers series)*. Bibliog., pp. 105–7.

KILLANIN, *Lord*.

7291 LIVIA, ANNE. Lord Killanin. *Ir. Wel.*, vol. 23, no. 1, 1974, 33–34.

KILMER, JOYCE.

7292 GAVIN, TADHG. Joyce Kilmer, 1886–1918. *Cap. Ann.*, 1977, 294–308.

KING, WILLIAM.

7293 KING, CHARLES S., *ed.* A great archbishop of Dublin, William King, D.D., 1650–1729: his autobiography, family, and a selection from his correspondence. London: 1906. Bibliog. pp. 307–8. King's collection of Mss. is now preserved in the National Library, Dublin.

KIRWAN, RICHARD.

7294 DIXON, F.E. Richard Kirwan: the Dublin philosopher. *Dublin Hist. Rec.*, vol. 24, no. 3, 1971, 53–64.

7295 DONOVAN, MICHAEL. Bibliographical account of the late Richard Kirwan, President of the Royal Irish Academy. *R. Ir. Acad. Proc.*, 4, 1847–50, appendix 8. Bibliog., pp. xcv–xcviii.

7296 MCLOUGHLIN, P.J. Richard Kirwan, 1733–1812. *Studies*, 28, 1939, 461–474, 593–605; 29, 1940, 71–83, 281–300.

L

LALOR, JAMES FINTAN.

7297 MCALISTER, T.G. James Fintan Lalor. *Zenith*, vol. 1, 1971, 23–31.

7298 O'NEILL, THOMAS P. The papers of James Fintan Lalor in the National Library. *Ir. Book Lov.*, 30, 1946, 84–6.

LANE, HUGH.

7299 GREGORY, *Lady*. Sir Hugh Lane: his life and legacy. Gerrards Cross (Bucks), 1973. *(The Coole edition),* This volume contains Hugh Lane's Life and achievement, 'Case for the return of Hugh Lane's Pictures', and other pamphlets, articles and letters, including those by W.B. Yeats.

LARKIN, JAMES.

7300 LARKIN, EMMET. James Larkin, Irish labour leader, 1876–1947. [1st ed. reprinted] London: 1977. 1st ed., 1965.

LARMINIE, WILLIAM.

7301 Bibliography. *New Camb. Bibliog. Eng. Lit.*, 3, 1969, 1908.

7302 O'MEARA, JOHN J. William Larminie, 1849–1900. *Studies*, 36, 1947, 90–96.

LAVIN, MARY.

7303 BOWEN, ZACK. Mary Lavin. Lewisburg and London: 1975. Bibliog., pp. 73–77.

7304 CASWELL, ROBERT W. Mary Lavin: breaking a pathway. *Dublin Mag.*, vol. 6, no. 2, 1967, 32–44.

7305 DOYLE, PAUL A. Mary Lavin: a checklist. *Bibliog. Soc. Amer. Papers*, 63, 1969, 317–21.

7306 O'CONNOR, FRANK. The girl at the gaol gate. *Rev. Eng. Lit.*, vol. 1, no. 2, 1960, 25–33.

7307 PETERSON, RICHARD. Mary Lavin. Boston: 1978. *(Twayne's English authors ser.)*.

LAWLESS, EMILY.

7308 Bibliography. *New Camb. Bibliog. Eng. Lit.*, 3, 1969, 1907.

LEASK, HAROLD.

7309 LUCAS, A.T. Harold G. Leask, M. Arch., Litt. D., Past President. [obituary notice, and list of published works, compiled by Mrs. Ada K. Leask]. *R. Soc. Antiq. Ir. J.*, 96, 1966, 1–6.

LECKY, WILLIAM E.H.

7310 AUCHMUTY, JAMES JOHNSTON. Lecky: a biographical and critical essay. Dublin: 1945. Bibliog. p. 130.

7311 — The Lecky-Lea correspondence in the Henry Charles Lea Library of the University of Pennsylvania, Philadelphia, U.S.A. *Hermathena*, 92, 1958, 45–61.

7312 HYDE, H. MONTGOMERY, *ed.* A Victorian historian: private letters of W.E.H. Lecky, 1859–78. London: 1947. Bibliog., p. 91.

LEDWIDGE, FRANCIS.

7313 Bibliography. *New Camb. Bibliog. Eng. Lit.*, 4, 1972, 295–6.

7314 CURTAYNE, ALICE. Francis Ledwidge: a life of the poet (1887–1917). London: 1972. Bibliog., pp. 198–201.

7315 DANIELSON, H. Bibliographies of modern authors. London: 1921.

LE FANU, JOSEPH SHERIDAN.

7316 Bibliography. *New Camb. Bibliog. Eng. Lit.*, 3, 1969, 942–3.

7317 BEGNAL, MICHAEL H. Joseph Sheridan Le Fanu. Lewisburg: 1971. Bibliog., pp. 85–87.

7318 BROWNE, NELSON. Sheridan Le Fanu. London: 1951. Bibliog., pp. 128–31.

7319 BYRNE, PATRICK F. Joseph Sheridan Le Fanu: a centenary memoir. *Dublin Hist. Rec.*, vol. 26, no. 3, 1973, 80–92.

7320 DENMAN, PETER. LeFanu and [Bram] Stoker: a probable connection. *Eire-Ir.*, vol. 9, no. 1, 1974, 152–158.

7321 ELLIS, S.M. Bibliography of Joseph Sheridan Le Fanu. *Ir. Book Lov.*, 8, 1916, 30–33.

7322 — Wilkie Collins, Le Fanu *and others*. London: 1951. List of works by J.S. Le Fanu, pp. 179–91. First published 1931.

7323 LE FANU, WILLIAM. Notebooks of Sheridan Le Fanu. *Longroom*, 14–15, 1976, 77, 37–40.

7324 LOUGHEED, W.C. An addition to the Le Fanu Bibliography. *N. and Q., new series*, vol. 11, 1964, 224.

7325 MCCORMACK, W.J. J. Sheridan Le Fanu: letters to William Blackwood and John Forster. *Longroom*, 8, 1973, 29–36.

7326 MACMANUS, M.J. Some points in the bibliography of Joseph Sheridan Le Fanu. *Dublin Mag., new ser.,* vol. 9, no. 3, 1934, 55–7.

7327 MADOC-JONES, ENID. Sheridan Le Fanu and Anglesey [Wales]. *Anglesey Hist. Soc. Trans.*, 1961, 69–76.

7328 SULLIVAN, KEVIN. Sheridan Le Fanu: the Purcell Papers, 1838–40. *Ir. Univ. Rev.*, vol. 2, no. 1, 1972, 5–19. Le Fanu used the pseudonym 'The Reverend Francis Purcell' in the Dublin University Magazine; his introductions were collected, edited, and published under the title The Purcell Papers by Alfred Perceval Graves in 1880.

LESLIE, SHANE.

7329 Bibliography. *New Camb. Bibliog. Eng. Lit.*, 4, 1972, 1186–7.

7330 HALL, DAVID J. Shane Leslie. *(Some Uncollected authors* XLVII). *Book Coll.*, 24, 1975, 565–585.

L'ESTRANGE, THOMAS.

7331 Biographical note and bibliography. *Ir. Book Lov.*, 7, 1915, 43–5.

LEVER, CHARLES.

7332 Bibliography. *New Camb. Bibliog. Eng. Lit.*, 3, 1969, 943–4.

7333 McHugh, Roger J. Charles Lever. *Studies*, 27, 1938, 247–260.

7334 Stevenson, Lionel. Dr. Quicksilver: the life of Charles Lever. London: 1939. Bibliog., pp. 297–301.

Lewis, Clive Staples.

7335 Gilbert, Douglas, and Kilby, Clyde S. C.S. Lewis: images of his world. London: 1973.

7336 Green, Roger, and Hooper, Walter. C.S. Lewis: a biography. London: 1974.

Little, *Canon* William J.K.

7337 Bibliography. *Ir. Book Lov.*, 9, 1918, 112.

Lover, Samuel.

7338 Bibliography. *New Camb. Bibliog. Eng. Lit.*, 3, 1969, 744–6.

Low, Charles Rathbone.

7339 Bibliography. *Ir. Book Lov.*, 9, 1917–18, 139.

Lucas, A.T.

7340 O'Danachair, Caoimhin. Folk and Farm: essays in honour of A.T. Lucas. Dublin: Royal Society of Antiquarians of Ireland, 1976. The published work of A.T. Lucas, compiled by Etienne Rynne, pp. 9–14.

Luce, Arthur Aston.

7341 Arthur Aston Luce, Fellow of Trinity College, Dublin, 1912–1977. [Special issue] *Hermathena*, 123, 1977. A bibliography of the published writings of Dr. A.A. Luce, by David Berman, 11–18.

Lynch, Patricia.

7342 Bibliography. *New Camb. Bibliog. Eng. Lit.*, 4, 1972, 804–5.

Lynd, Robert.

7343 Bibliography. *New Camb. Bibliog. Eng. Lit.*, 4, 1972, 1083–4.

Lysaght, Sydney Roche.

7344 MacLysaght, Edward. Sidney Roche Lysaght: the author and the man. *Cap. Ann.*, 1975, 225–229.

M

MacBride, Maud Gonne.

7345 Ni Eireamhoin, Eibhlin. Two great Irishwomen: Maud Gonne MacBride and Constance Markievicz. Dublin: 1971. Bibliog., p. 79.

MacBride, Sean.

7346 O'Grady, Desmond. Sean MacBride. *Month*, 3, 1971, 73–76.

McCahan, Robert.

7347 McClelland, Aiken. Robert McCahan of Ballycastle, Co. Antrim. *Ir. Booklore*, vol. 1, no. 1, 1971, 90–91. A list of 23 pamphlets.

McCall, John.

7348 Bowen, B.P. A scribe of the Liberties: John McCall. *Dublin Hist. Rec.*, 5, 1942–3, 81–91.

MacCarthy, Callaghan, *3rd Earl of Clancarthy.*

7349 MacCarthy, William P. The litigious earl. *Cork Hist. Arch. Soc. J.*, 70, 1965, 7–13.

McCarthy, Denis Florence.

7350 Bibliography. *Ir. Book Lov.*, 8, 1916–17, 123.

7351 Bibliography. *New Camb. Bibliog. Eng. Lit.*, 3, 1969, 1904.

7352 Coleman, James. Bibliography of Denis Florence McCarthy. Paper read before the Bibliographical Society of Ireland, February 23, 1925.

MacCarthy, Justin, *Viscount Mountcashel (d. 1694).*

7353 Murphy, John H. Justin MacCarthy, Lord Mountcashel, commander of the first Irish brigade in France. Cork: 1959. Bibliog., pp. 59–62.

McCarthy, Justin (1830–1912).

7354 Byard, Edwin J. Biographical note and bibliography. *Ir. Book Lov.*, 3, 1911–12, 181–4.

McClelland, John A.

7355 Award of the Boyle medal . . . [with bibliog.]. *R. Dublin Soc. Sci. Proc., new series,* 15, 1916–20, 677–9.

MacConmara, Donnchadh Ruadh.

7356 Casaide, Seamus ua. Bibliographical and genealogical notes on Donnchadh Ruadh MacConmara. *Waterford S.E. Ir. Arch. Soc. J.*, 13, 1910, 131–9.

McCormack, John.

7357 McCormack, Lily. I hear you calling me. London [1950]. A McCormack discography, by Philip F. Rodern, pp. 222–32; reprinted from *The Gramophone*.

7358 Strong, L.A.G. John McCormack: the story of a singer. London: 1941. Includes list of records by singers mentioned and recordings by McCormack, pp. 271–92.

MCCORMICK, F.J.
7359 FALLON, GABRIEL. F.J. McCormick: an appreciation. *Studies,* 36, 1947, 181–186.

MCCRACKEN, MARY ANN.
7360 MCNEILL, MARY. The life and times of Mary Anne McCracken: a Belfast panorama. Dublin: 1960. Bibliog., pp. 309–10.

MACDONAGH, DONAGH.
7361 Bibliography. *New Camb. Bibliog. Eng. Lit.*, 4, 1972, 963.

MACDONAGH, MICHAEL.
7362 FENNING, *The Rev.* HUGH. Michael MacDonagh, O.P., Bishop of Kilmore, 1728–46. *Ir. Eccles. Rec.,* 106, 1966, 138–153.

MACDONAGH, TERENCE.
7363 Bibliography. *Donegal Ann.*, vol. 4, no. 1, 1958 [ii–iv].

MACDONAGH, THOMAS.
7364 Bibliography. *New Camb. Bibliog. Eng. Lit.*, 4, 1972, 302–3.

7365 PARKS, EDEL WINFIELD, and WELLS, AILEEN. Thomas MacDonagh: the man, the patriot, the writer. Athens: Univ. of Georgia, 1967.

MACFADDEN, *The Rev.* JAMES.
7366 Bibliography. *Ir. Book Lov.*, 8, 1916–17, 143.

MCGEE, THOMAS D'ARCY.
7367 COLEMAN, JAMES. Bibliography of Thomas D'Arcy Magee. *Bibliog. Soc. Ir.*, vol. 2, no. 7, 1925.

7368 PHELAN, JOSEPHINE. The ardent exile: the life and times of Thomas D'Arcy McGee. Toronto: 1951. Bibliog., pp. 307–10.

MCGHEE, ROBERT J.
7369 BLACKER, BEAVER H. The writings of the Rev. Robert J. McGhee, M.A., sometime minister of Harold's Cross Church, Dublin. *Ir. Eccles. Gaz.*, 1876, 255–7.

MCGRATH, MILER.
7370 MARRON, LAWRENCE, *ed.* Documents from the state papers concerning Miler McGrath. *Arch. Hib.,* 21, 1958, 75–189.

MACGREEVY, THOMAS.
7371 In tribute to Thomas MacGreevy, poet and connoisseur of the arts. *Cap. Ann.*, 1965, 277–302.

MACHALE, JOHN.
7372 COSTELLO, NUALA. John MacHale, Archbishop of Tuam. Dublin: 1939. Bibliog. of Irish works, pp. 145–6.

7373 O'REILLY, *The Rev.* BERNARD. Dr. John McHale, Archbishop of Tuam: his life, times and correspondence. New York: 1890. 2 vols.

MCKAY, ROBERT.
7374 Award of the Boyle Medal . . . [with bibliog.]. *R. Dublin Soc. Sci. Proc., new ser.,* 27, 1957, 325–30.

MACKLIN, CHARLES.
7375 Bibliography. *New Camb. Bibliog. Eng. Lit.*, 2, 1971, 849–50.

MCLAUGHLIN, *The Rt. Rev.* PATRICK J.
7376 Obituary. *R. Ir. Acad. Ann. Rpt.*, 1973–4, 5–6.

MACLIAMMOIR, MICHAEL.
7377 Bibliography. *New Camb. Bibliog. Eng. Lit.*, 4, 1972, 964–5.

MACLYSAGHT, EDWARD A.
7378 RYNNE, ETIENNE, *compiler*. Published work of E. Lysaght, E.A. MacLysaght, Eamonn MacGiolla Iasachta. *Nth. Munster Antiq. J.*, 17, 1975, 7–11.

MACMAHON, BRYAN.
7379 HENDERSON, GORDON. An interview with Bryan MacMahon. *J. Ir. Lit.*, vol. 3, no. 3, 1974, 3–23.

MACMANUS, FRANCIS.
7380 KIELY, BENEDICT. In memoriam: Francis MacManus, 1909–1966 (with bibliog.). *Kilk. Mag.*, 14, 1966, 121–136.

7381 SHERIDAN, JOHN D. Francis MacManus, 1909–1966. *Studies*, 55, 1966, 269–276.

MCMANUS, L. (*i.e.*, Charlotte Elizabeth McManus).
7382 O'HEGARTY, P.S. L. McManus. *Dublin Mag.*, *new ser.*, vol. 20, no. 1, 1945, 68.

MACMANUS, M.J.
7383 MACCARTHY, VERONICA. M.J. MacManus, journalist and bibliophile. *Cap. Ann.*, 1971, 164–171.

7384 O'HEGARTY, P.S. Obituary and bibliography. *Dublin Mag., new ser.*, vol. 27, no. 1, 1952, 45.

MACMANUS, TERENCE BELLEW.

7385 MCALLISTER, THOMAS G. Terence Bellew McManus, 1811(?)–1861: a short biography. Maynooth: 1972.

MACNALLY, LEONARD.

7386 Bibliography. *New Camb. Bibliog. Eng. Lit.*, 2, 1971, 850.

MACNAMARA, BRINSLEY (*i.e.*, John Weldon).

7387 Bibliography. *New Camb. Bibliog. Eng. Lit.*, 4, 1972, 965.

7388 MCDONNELL, MICHAEL, *compiler*. Brinsley MacNamara (1890–1963): a checklist. *J. Ir. Lit.*, vol. 4, no. 2, 1975, 79–88.

7389 O'SAOTHRAI, SEAMUS. Brinsley MacNamara (1890–1963). *Ir. Booklore*, vol. 2, no. 1, 1972, 75–81.

MCNAMARA, JOHN.

7390 CASAIDE, SEAMUS UA. John McNamara: a collector of Irish Mss. [with list]. *Ir. Book Lov.*, 21, 1933, 57–64.

MACNAMARA, *The Rev.* THOMAS.

7391 KELLY, JOSEPH P. *The Rev.* THOMAS MACNAMARA, C.M., 1808–1892. *Riocht na Midhe*, vol. 5, no. 4, 1974, 60–67.

MACNEICE, LOUIS.

7392 Bibliography. *New Camb. Bibliog. Eng. Lit.*, 4, 1972, 303–5.

7393 ARMITAGE, C.M. and CLARK, NEIL. A bibliography of the works of Louis MacNeice. London: 1973.

7394 BROWN, TERENCE. Walter Pater, Louis MacNeice and the privileged moment. *Hermathena*, 114, 1972, 31–42.

7395 — and REID, ALEC, *eds*. Time was away: the world of Louis MacNeice. Dublin: 1974. Books written by Louis MacNeice, a checklist, by Christopher M. Armitage, pp. 131–139; Radio scripts, 1941–1963, by R.D. Smith, pp. 141–148.

7396 SMITH, ELTON EDWARD. Louis MacNeice. New York: 1970. Bibliog., pp. 215–224.

7397 STODDARD, F.G. A bibliography of Louis MacNeice. In preparation.

MACNEILL, EOIN.

7398 MANSERGH, NICHOLAS. Eoin MacNeill – a re-appraisal. *Studies*, 63, 1974, 133–140. Review article of *The Scholar Revolutionary*, ed. by F.X. Martin and F.J. Bryne.

7399 MARTIN, F.X. The writings of Eoin MacNeill. *Ir. Hist. Stud.*, 6, 1948–9, 44–62.

7400 O'SULLIVAN, SILE. A case for research: some notes on letters received by Eoin (John) MacNeill. *Ir. Arch. Bull.*, vol. 3, no. 2, 1973, 2–4. Letters from Father Peter O'Leary, author of *Seadna*.

7401 RYAN, JOHN, *ed.* Essays and studies presented to Prof. Eoin MacNeill on the occasion of his seventieth birthday, May 15, 1938. Dublin: 1940. Bibliog. pp. 581–3.

MACNEVEN, *Dr.* WILLIAM.

7402 MACCRAIMHIN, SEAMUS. MacNeven of ninety-eight: doctor, scientist. *Dublin Hist. Rec.*, vol. 27, no. 2, 1974, 65–69.

MACSWINEY, TERENCE.

7403 CHAVASSE, MOIRIN, Terence MacSwiney. Dublin and London: 1961. Lord Mayor of Cork.

MADDEN, PATRICK GERARD.

7404 ANDREWS, J.H. Patrick Gerard Madden (obituary). *Ir. Geog.*, 7, 1974, 127–8.

MADDEN, RICHARD ROBERT.

7405 MURRAY, DAVID R. Richard Robert Madden: his career as a slavery abolitionist. *Studies*, 61, 1972, 41–53.

7406 O'BROIN, LEON. R.R. Madden: historian of the United Irishman. *Ir. Univ. Rev.*, vol. 2, no. 1, 1972, 20–33.

MAHAFFY, *The Rev. Sir* JOHN PENTLAND.

7407 Obituary and bibliography. *Ir. Book Lov.*, 10, 1918–19, 112.

7408 STANFORD, W.B. and MCDOWELL, R.B. Mahaffy; a biography of an Anglo-Irishman. London: 1971. Bibliog., pp. 255–272.

MAHER, *Fr.* JAMES.

7409 BURNS, ALEC. *Fr.* James Maher, 1793–1874. *Carloviana*, vol. 2, no. 24, 1975, 23–25.

MAHONY, FRANCIS SYLVESTER.

7410 Bibliography. *New Camb. Bibliog. Eng. Lit.*, 3, 1969, 1390–1.

MALLET, JOHN.

7411 TUTTY, MICHAEL J. John and Robert Mallet, 1780–1881. *Dublin Hist. Rec.*, vol. 29, no. 2, 1976, 42–58.

MANGAN, JAMES CLARENCE.

7412 Autobiography of James Clarence Mangan,

edited from the manuscript by James Kilroy. Dublin: 1968.

7413 CHUTO, JACQUES. Mangan and the Irys Herfner articles in the *Dublin University Magazine. Hermathena*. 111, 1971, 55–57.

7414 — Mangan's 'Antique Deposit' in TCD Library. *Longroom*, 2, 1970, 38–39. Mangan worked in the library as a cataloguer for some years.

7415 — A further glance at Mangan and the library. *Longroom*, 5, 1972, 9–10.

7416 HOLZAPFEL, RUDOLPH PATRICK. James Clarence Mangan: a checklist of printed and other sources. Dublin: 1969. Limited edition of 200 copies.

7417 KILROY, JAMES. James Clarence Mangan. Lewisburg: 1970. *(Irish writers series)*. Bibliog., pp. 73–4.

7418 MACCARVILL, E. Mangan's contributions to the *Dublin University Magazine:* bibliography and notes. Paper read before the Bibliographical Society of Ireland, April 24, 1944.

7419 O'DONOGHUE, D.J. The life and writings of James Clarence Mangan. Edinburgh and Dublin: 1897.

7420 O'HEGARTY, P.S. A bibliography of James Clarence Mangan. *Dublin. Mag., new series,* vol. 16, no. 1, 1941, 56–61.

7421 O'NEILL, GEORGE, *ed.* Some unpublished Mangan Mss. *Studies*, 9, 1920, 118–28.

7422 THOMPSON, FRANCIS J. Mangan in America, 1850–60: Mitchel, Maryland and Melville. *Dublin Mag. new series,* vol. 27, no. 3, 1952, 30–41.

7423 WELCH, ROBERT. 'In wreathed swell': James Clarence Mangan, translator from the Irish. *Eire-Ir.*, vol. 11, no. 2, 1976, 36–55.

MARKIEVICZ, CONSTANCE.

7424 MARRECO, ANNE. The rebel countess: the life and times of Constance Markievicz. London: 1967. Bibliog., pp. 307–309.

MARSHALL, JOHN J.

7425 John J. Marshall – a bibliography. *Ir. Booklore*, vol. 1, no. 1, 1971, 30–39.

MATURIN, CHARLES ROBERT.

7426 Melmoth the wanderer; a new ed. from the original text. With a memoir and bibliography of Maturin's works. London: 1892, 3 vols.

7427 Melmoth the wanderer; introduction by William F. Axton. Lincoln, University of Nebraska: 1961. Bibliog., p. xix.

MAXWELL, WILLIAM HAMILTON.

7428 Bibliography. *New Camb. Bibliog. Eng. Lit.*, 3, 1969, 747–8.

7429 MCKELVIE, COLIN. Notes towards a bibliography of William Hamilton Maxwell. (1792–1850), *Ir. Booklore*, vol. 3, no. 1, 1976, 33–42.

MAYNE, ETHEL COLBURN.

7430 Bibliography. *New Camb. Bibliog. Eng. Lit.*, 4, 1972, 669.

MAYNE, RUTHERFORD (*i.e.* Samuel Waddell).

7431 Bibliography. *New Camb. Bibliog. Eng. Lit.,* 3, 1969, 1941.

MEAGHER, THOMAS FRANCIS.

7432 ATHEARN, ROBERT G. Thomas Francis Meagher: an Irish revolutionary in America. Boulder, University of Colorado: 1949. *(Studies in Hist. ser.*, no. 1.) Bibliog., pp. 172–8.

MEEHAN, CHARELS PATRICK.

7433 Centenary of Father Meehan [with bibliog.]. *Ir. Book Lov.*, 4, 1912–13, 25–7.

MEYLER, WALTER THOMAS.

7434 DAWSON, T. Some echoes of St. Catherine's Bells. *Dublin Hist. Rec.*, vol. 31, no. 3, 1978, 82–93. Meyler's autobiography 'St. Catherine's Bells' was published in 2 vols., 1868–70.

MILLER, GEORGE.

7435 BLACKER, BEAVER H. The writings of George Miller, D.D., Vicar-General of Armagh. *Ir. Eccles. Gaz.*, 1875, 180–1.

MILLIGAN, ALICE.

7436 Obituary and bibliography. *Ir. Book Lov.*, 32, 1952–7, 63–4.

MITCHEL, JOHN.

7437 DOUGLAS, JOHN M. Bibliography of John Mitchel. *Ir. Book Lov.* 7, 1915, 86–8.

7438 MACMANUS, M.J. Bibliography of the writings of John Mitchel. *Dublin Mag.*, *new ser.* vol. 16, no. 2, 1941, 42–50.

MITCHELL, SUSAN L.

7439 KAIN, RICHARD M. Susan L. Mitchell.

Lewisburg: 1972. *(Irish writers series)*. Bibliog., pp. 97–163.

MOLYNEUX, WILLIAM.

7440 HOPPEN, K. THEODORE. The Royal Society and Ireland: William Molyneux, F.R.S. (1656–1698). *R. Soc. N. and R.*, 18, 1963, 125–135.

MONTGOMERY, H.R.

7441 CAMPBELL, A.A. Bibliography. *Ir. Book Lov.*, 9, 1918, 72.

MOORE, BRIAN.

7442 FLOOD, JEANNE. Brian Moore. Lewisburg: 1974. *(Irish Writers series)*. Bibliog., pp. 97–8.

7443 STUDING, RICHARD. A Brian Moore bibliography. *Eire-Ir.*, vol. 10, no. 3, 1975, 89–105.

MOORE, GEORGE.

7444 Bibliography. *New Camb. Bibliog. Eng. Lit.*, 4, 1969, 1014–1019.

7445 BLACK, H.M. A checklist of the first editions of works by James Stephens and George Moore. *T.C.D. Ann. Bull.*, 1955, 4–11.

7446 COLLET, GEORGES-PAUL. George Moore et France. Genève and Paris: 1957. Bibliog., pp. 215–25.

7447 DANIELSON, HENRY. A bibliography of the works of George Moore, 1878–1921. In *A Portrait of George Moore,* by John Freeman. London: 1922.

7448 DUNLEAVY, JANET EGLESON, George Moore: the artist's vision, the storyteller's art. Lewisburg: 1973. Bibliog., pp. 145–150.

7449 GILCHER, EDWIN. A bibliography of George Moore. DeKalb, Illinois: 1970.

7450 GLENAVY, BEATRICE *Lady*. Memoirs of George Moore. *Dublin Mag.,* vol. 5, nos. 3–4, 1966, 57–61.

7451 HONE, JOSEPH. The life of George Moore. London: 1936. The works of George Moore: a short bibliography, pp. 498–502.

7452 LYONS, F.S.L. George Moore and Edward Martyn. *Hermathena,* 98, 1964, 9–32.

7453 NEJDEFORS-FRISK, SORIJA. George Moore's naturalistic prose. Upsala and Dublin: 1952. (*Upsala Irish studies*, no. 4.) Bibliog., pp. 132–5.

7454 OWENS, GRAHAM, *ed*. George Moore's mind and art: essays. Edinburgh: 1968.

7455 SEYMOUR-SMITH, MARTIN. Rediscovering George Moore. *Encounter*, vol. 35, no. 6, 1970, 58–67.

7456 WOLFE, HUMBERT. George Moore. London: 1931. *(Modern Writers series)*. Bibliog. of George Moore's writings (1878–1930), pp. 153–6.

MOORE, THOMAS.

7457 Bibliography. *New Camb. Bibliog. Eng. Lit.*, 3, 1969, 263–7, 1889.

7458 BENNETT, BETTY T. An unpublished letter from Thomas Moore to Mary Shelley. *N. and Q., new ser.*, 23, 1976, 114.

7459 Catalogue of vocal music by Thomas Moore and Sir John Stevenson. London: 1814.

7460 DE VERE WHITE, TERENCE. Tom Moore: the Irish poet. London: 1977. Bibliog., pp. 271–3.

7461 DOWDEN, WILFRED S. 'Let Erin remember': a re-examination of the journal of Thomas Moore. *Rice Univ. Stud*, vol. 61, no. 1, 1975, 39–50.

7462 GIBSON, ANDREW. Thomas Moore and his first editions. Belfast: 1904.

7463 HELLMAN, FLORENCE S. List of references in the Library of Congress relating to Thomas Moore, 1779–1852 (exclusive of music). [Washington]: 1932. Typescript.

7464 MACCALL, SEAMUS. Thomas Moore. London and Dublin: 1935. Chronological list of Moore's works, pp. 125–32.

7465 MACMANUS, M.J. A bibliography of Thomas Moore. *Dublin Mag., new series*. vol. 8, no. 2, 1933, 55–61; no. 3, 60–5; no. 4, 56–63; vol. 9, no. 2, 1934, 54–5.

7466 — A bibliographical hand-list of the first editions of Thomas Moore. Dublin: 1934. First appeared serially in the *Dublin Magazine.*

7467 MACWHITE, EOIN. Thomas Moore and Poland. *R. Ir. Acad. Proc., Sec. C.*, 72, 1972, 49–62.

7468 MUIR, P.H. Moore's Irish melodies. *Colophon*, no. 15, 1933.

7469 STRONG, L.A.G. The minstrel boy: a portrait of Tom Moore. London: 1937. Bibliog., pp. 307–9.

MORAN, *Cardinal* PATRICK FRANCIS.

7470 Biographical note and bibliography. *Ir. Book Lov.*, 3, 1911–12, 36–7.

MOSSOM, ROBERT.

7471 REDGE, J. INGLE. Dr. Robert Mossom, Bishop of Derry, with a bibliography of his works, reprinted with additions from *The Palatine Note Book*, 1881–2. Manchester: 1882.

MULALLY, MARIA THERESA.

7472 SAVAGE, ROLAND BURKE. A valiant Dublin woman: the story of George's Hill (1766–1940). Dublin: 1940. Bibliog., pp. 308–12.

MULCAHY, RICHARD.

7473 HOLLAND, AILSA C. A note on the papers of Richard Mulcahy, [1919–1970]. *Ir. Arch. Bull.*, vol. 3, no. 2, 1973, 14–17.

MULVANY, ETHEL.

7474 GRAHAME, J.A.K. Miss Ethel Mulvany, F.R. Econ. S. (obituary). *Ir. Geog.*, 8, 1975, 132.

MURDOCH, IRIS.

7475 BALDANZA, FRANK. Iris Murdoch. New York: 1974. Bibliog., pp. 179–184.

7476 TOMINAGA, THOMAS T. and SCHNEIDERMEYER, WILMA. Iris Murdoch and Muriel Spark. New Jersey: 1976. *(Author bibliographies, no.* 27).

MURPHY, *Canon* (P.P., Macroom)

7477 Biography and bibliography. *Ir. Book Lov.*, 7, 1916, 148–50.

MURPHY, ARTHUR.

7478 Bibliography. *New Camb. Bibliog. Eng. Lit.*, 2, 1971, 851–3.

MURPHY, GERARD.

7479 O'LOCHLAINN, COLM. Gerard Murphy, 1901–59 [with bibliog.]. *Studies*, 48, 1959, 332–5.

MURPHY, PAUL A.

7480 Award of the Boyle Medal . . . [with bibliog.]. *R. Dublin Soc. Sci. Proc., new ser.,* 20, 1930–3, 547–9.

MURPHY, RICHARD.

7481 HARMON, MAURICE. *ed.* Richard Murphy: poet of two traditions; interdisciplinary studies. Portmarnock (Co. Dublin), 1978. A Richard Murphy Bibliography, by Mary Fitzgerald, pp. 104–117.

7482 IRISH UNIVERSITY REVIEW. Vol. 7, no. 1, 1977. Special Issue: Richard Murphy. Includes a Richard Murphy bibliography, compiled by Mary Fitzgerald.

MURRAY, T.C.

7483 Bibliography. *New Camb. Bibliog. Eng. Lit.*, 3, 1969, 1944–5.

N

NEWMAN, JOHN HENRY, *Cardinal.*

7484 Bibliography. *New Camb. Bibliog. Eng. Lit.*, 3, 1969, 1311–40, 1577.

7485 BRITISH LIBRARY. John Henry Newman: an excerpt from the General Catalogue of Printed Books. London: British Museum for the British Library Board, 1974.

7486 CAMERON, J.M. John Henry Newman. London: British Council: 1956. *(Writers and their work series.)* Bibliog., pp. 39–44.

7487 DELATTRE, F. La Pensée de J.H. Newman. Paris: 1914. Bibliog., pp. 297–302.

7488 DENNIGAN, MAIREAD. Works of J.H. Newman: a checklist compiled from printed sources in the Library at University College, Dublin. Dublin: Library, University College, 1974.

7489 DESSAIN, CHARLES STEPHEN. Cardinal Newman's papers: a complete edition of his letters. *Dublin Rev.*, 486, 1960–1, 291–6.

7490 GUIBERT, J. Le réveil du Catholicisme en Angleterre au XIXe siècle. Paris: 1907. Bibliog., pp. 311–35.

7491 GUITTON, J. La philosophie de Newman. Paris: 1933. Bibliog., pp. 195–230.

7492 LAPALI, AMERICO D. John Henry Newman. New York: 1973. Bibliog., pp. 149–155.

7493 List of references on John Henry Newman. Washington: Library of Congress, 1921. Typescript.

7494 List of works written and edited by . . . Cardinal Newman, in the library of Sir William H. Cope, Bart., at Bramshill, Portsmouth [1888]. Privately printed.

7495 Newman commemoration, 1852–1952: catalogue of an exhibition of books, documents and manuscripts relating to Cardinal Newman, Newman House [Dublin], October 20–26, 1952. Dublin: 1952.

7496 **Rickaby, Joseph.** Index to all the works of John Henry, Cardinal Newman. London: 1914.

7497 **Sloane, Clarence E.** John Henry Newman: an illustrated brochure of his first editions. Holy Cross College [Worcester, Mass., 1953].

7498 **Whyte, J.H.** Newman in Dublin: fresh light from *The Archives of Propaganda. Dublin Rev.*, 483, 1960, 31–9. See also *Times Lit. Supp.*, April 22, 1960, 257.

Nightingale, Florence.

7499 **Lysaght, Moira.** Florence Nightingale and her Irish connections. *Cap. Ann.*, 1977, 121–129.

Nolan, Patrick J.

7500 Award of the Boyle medal. . . . *R. Dublin Soc. Sci. Proc., Ser. A.* 4, 1970–73, 159–60.

Nugent, William.

7501 **Iske, Basil.** The green cockatrice. Dublin: Meath Archaeological and Historical Society, 1978. Bibliog., pp. 199–201.

O

O'Brien, Bronterre.

7502 **Plummer, Alfred.** Bronterre: a political biography of Bronterre O'Brien, 1804–1864. London: 1971. Bibliog., pp. 277–281.

O'Brien, Charlotte Grace.

7503 **Joyce, Mannix.** Charlotte Grace O'Brien. *Cap. Ann.*, 1974, 324–340.

O'Brien, Edna.

7504 **Eckley, Grace.** Edna O'Brien. Lewisburg: 1974. *(Irish Writers Series)* Bibliog., pp. 85–88.

7505 **Merrill, Charles.** Edna O'Brien, superstar. *Arts. Ir.*, vol. 3, no. 2, 1975, 14–17.

O'Brien, Fitz-James.

7506 **Wolle, Francis.** Fitz-James O'Brien: a literary Bohemian of the 1850s. Boulder: 1944. *(Colorado Univ. studies, ser. B,* vol. 2, no. 2.) Bibliog., pp. 252–93.

O'Brien, Flann. (*i.e.* Brian O'Nolan).

7507 Bibliography. *New Camb. Bibliog. Eng. Lit.*, 4, 1972, 683.

7508 **Journal of Irish Literature.** Vol. 3, no. 1, 1974. A Flann O'Brien-Myles na Gopaleen number. Contents include: Brian O'Nolan, scholar, satirist and wit, by Seamus Kelly – Who was Myles, and what was he, by David Powell. – Extremely fictitious: the fiction of Flann O'Brien, by Miles Orvell. – A checklist of Brian O'Nolan, by David Powell.

7509 **Mays, J.C.C.** Brian O'Nolan and Joyce on art and life. *J.J. Qtr.*, vol. 11, no. 3, 1974, 238–256.

7510 **O'Keefe, Timothy,** *ed.* Myles: portraits of Brian O'Nolan. London: 1973.

7511 **Orvell, Miles** and **Powell, David.** Myles na Gopaleen: mystic, horse-doctor, hackney journalist and ideological catalyst. *Eire-Ir.*, vol. 10, no. 2, 1975, 44–72.

7512 **Phelan, Michael.** Watcher in the wings: a lingering look at Myles na Gopaleen. *Admin.*, vol. 24, no. 1, 1976, 96–106.

7513 **Power, Mary Jane.** Early na Gopaleeana. *Dublin Mag.*, vol. 8, no. 7, 1971, 63–65.

O'Brien, George.

7514 Obituary. *R. Ir. Acad. Ann. Rpt.*, 1973–74, 2–4.

7515 **Meenan, James F.** George O'Brien, 1892–1973. *Studies*, 63, 1974, 17–28.

O'Brien, James Thomas.

7516 **Blacker, Beaver H.** The writings of James Thomas O'Brien, D.D., Bishop of Ossory, Ferns and Leighlin. *Ir. Eccles. Gaz.*, 1875, 210–11.

O'Brien, Richard Barry.

7517 Bibliography. *Ir. Book Lov.*, 9, 1918, 113.

O'Brien, William.

7518 **Coombes,** *The Rev.* **James.** Doctor William O'Brien of Glenaar. *Cork Hist. Arch. Soc. J.*, vol. 82, pt. 2, 1977, 115–126.

O'Brien, William.

7519 **MacDonagh, Michael.** The life of William O'Brien, the Irish nationalist: a biographical study of Irish nationalism, constitutional and revolutionary. London: 1928. O'Brien as a man of letters, pp. 262–74.

O'Brien, William Smith.

7520 **Coleman, James.** Bibliography of William Smith O'Brien. Ms. 3 p. in National Library, Dublin.

O'Cadhain, Mairtin.

7521 **McCormack, W.J.** A preliminary checklist

of the separate publications of Mairtin O'Cadhain. *Longroom*, 2, 1970, 7–9.

O'CALLAGHAN, EDMUND BAILEY.

7522 An Irish American writer [with bibliog.]. *Ir. Book Lov.*, 4, 1912–13, 102.

O'CASEY, SEAN.

7523 Bibliography. *New Camb. Bibliog. Eng. Lit.*, 4, 1972, 879–885.

7524 ARMSTRONG, WILLIAM A. Sean O'Casey. London: British Council of the National Book League, 1967. *(Writers and their works, no. 198)*

7525 AYLING, RONALD. Detailed catalogue of Sean O'Casey's papers at the time of his death. *S.O'C. Rev.*, vol. 1, no. 2, 1975, 48–65; vol. 2. no. 1, 1975, 64–77; vol. 3, no. 1, 1976, 58–70.

7526 — Sean O'Casey and the Abbey Theatre Company. *Ir. Univ. Rev.*, vol. 3, no. 1, 1973, 5–16.

7527 — and DURKAN, MICHAEL J. Sean O'Casey: a bibliography. London: 1978.

7528 — Works by Sean O'Casey in translation. *S. O'C. Rev.,* vol. 1, no. 2, 1975, 4–18; vol. 2, no. 1, 1975, 5–11.

7529 BEANSTOCK, BERNARD. Sean O'Casey. Lewisburg: 1970. *(Irish writers series)*. Bibliog., pp. 121–3.

7530 BLACK, H.M. A checklist of 1st editions of works by Lord Dunsany and Sean O'Casey. *T.C.D. Ann. Bull.*, 1957, 4–9.

7531 FALLON, GABRIEL. Sean O'Casey: the man I knew. London: 1965.

7532 HOGAN, ROBERT GOODE. Sean O'Casey's experiments in dramatic form. Ann Arbor, University Microfilms [1956]· *(Publication no. 18, 581.)* Microfilm copy (positive) of typescript.

7533 — *ed.*, Feathers from the Green Crow. Sean O'Casey, 1905–1925. London: 1963.

7534 JAMES JOYCE QUARTERLY, vol. 8, no. 1, 1970. O'Casey issue.

7535 KRAUSE, DAVID. Sean O'Casey: the man and his work. London: 1967. Originally published 1960.

7536 MIKHAIL, E.H. Dissertations on Sean O'Casey. *S.O'C. Rev.*, vol. 2, no. 1, 1975, 47–51.

7537 — Sean O'Casey: a bibliography of criticism. London: 1972.

7538 — Sean O'Casey's studies: an annual bibliography. *S.O'C. Rev.*, vol. 3, no. 1, 1976, 71–88.

7539 O'CASEY, BREON. Sean O'Casey: a portrait. *Threshold*, 26, 1975, 95–99.

7540 O'CASEY, EILEEN. Sean. Edited with an introduction by J.C. Trewin. London: 1971.

7541 SEAN O'CASEY REVIEW. Holbrook, (N.Y.): 1–, 1974–.

O'CLEIRIGH, MICHAEL.

7542 JENNINGS, BRENDAN. Michael O'Cleirigh, chief of the Four Masters. Dublin: 1936. Bibliogs., pp. 184–210, 219–20.

7543 O'BRIEN, SYLVESTER, *ed.* Measgra i gcuimhne Mhichil ui Chleirigh: miscellany of historical and linguistic studies in honour of Brother Michael O'Cleirigh, O.F.M., chief of the Four Masters, 1643–1943. Dublin: 1944. Bibliog., p. xviii.

O'CONNELL, DANIEL.

7544 COLEMAN, JAMES. Bibliography of Daniel O'Connell, the liberator of Ireland. Ms., 3 p. in National Library, Dublin.

7545 Daniel O'Connell, 1775–1847: [Catalogue of] exhibition of O'Connell family papers to mark the bicentenary of his birth. Dublin: Univ. College, 1975. Bibliog., p. 50.

7546 EDWARDS, R. DUDLEY. Daniel O'Connell and his world. London: 1975. Bibliog., pp. 104–5.

7547 GWYNN, DENIS. Daniel O'Connell. Rev. centenary ed. Cork: 1947. Bibliog., p. 262.

7548 O'BROIN, LEON. The trial and imprisonment of O'Connell, 1843. *Eire-Ir.*, vol. 8, no. 4, 1973, 39–54.

7549 O'CONNELL, MAURICE R. O'Connell reconsidered. *Studies*, 64, 1975, 107–119.

7550 O'SULLIVAN, HANNA. A bibliography of Daniel O'Connell (The Liberator), 1775–1847. Presented as thesis for Fellowship of the Library Association of Ireland, 1976.

7551 PETUCHOUSKI, ELIZABETH. Mr. Punch and Daniel O'Connell. *Eire-Ir.*, vol. 7, no. 4, 1972, 12–31.

O'CONNOR, FEARGUS.

7552 READ, DONALD, and GLASGOW, ERIC. Feargus O'Connor, Irishman and Chartist. London: 1961. Bibliog., pp. 152–6.

O'CONNOR, FRANK. (*i.e.* Michael Francis O'Donovan).

7553 Bibliography. *New Camb. Bibliog. Eng. Lit.*, 4, 1972, 684–5.

7554 BRENNER, GERRY. Frank O'Connor: a bibliography. *West Coast Review,* 2 (Fall), 1967, 55–64.

7555 FLANAGAN, THOMAS. Frank O'Connor, 1903–1966. *Kilk. Mag.*, 15, 1967, 62–76. Reprinted from *The Kenyon Review.*

7556 JOURNAL OF IRISH LITERATURE. vol. 4, no. 1, 1975. A Frank O'Connor number.

7557 MATTHEWS, JAMES H. Frank O'Connor. Lewisburg and London: 1976. *(The Irish Writers series)* Bibliog., pp. 91–4.

7558 WOHLGELERNTER, MAURICE. Frank O'Connor, an introduction. New York: 1977. Bibliog., pp. 207–213.

O'CURRY, EUGENE.

7559 Eugene O'Curry's early life: details from an unpublished letter. *Nth. Munster Antiq. J.*, 10, 1966–67, 143–147.

7560 O'HAODHA, MICHALL. Eugene O'Curry and Thomond. *Eire-Ir.*, vol. 1, no. 1, 1965–6, 69–76.

O'DALY, DOMINIC.

7561 CURTIN, BENVENUTA. Dominic O'Daly: an Irish diplomat. *Stud. Hib.*, 5, 1965, 98–112.

O'DOMHNAILL, SEAN.

7562 Obituary and bibliography. *Donegal Ann.*, vol. 4, no. 3, 1960, 287–8. Bibliographer of Co. Donegal.

O'DONNELL, FRANK HUGH.

7563 Bibliography. *Ir. Book Lov.*, 8, 1916–17, 70.

O'DONNELL, PEADAR.

7564 DOYLE, PAUL A. Peadar O'Donnell: a checklist. *Bull. Bibliog.,* vol. 28, no. 1, 1971, 3–4.

7565 FREYER, GRATTAN. Peadar O'Donnell. Lewisburg: 1973. *(Irish writers series)*. Bibliog., pp. 125–128.

7566 MCINERNEY, MICHAEL. Peadar O'Donnell, Irish social rebel. Dublin: The O'Brien Press, 1974. Bibliog. note, pp. 246–7.

O'DONNELL, TERENCE.

7567 Father Terence O'Donnell, O.F.M. (obituary notice and bibliog.) *Donegal Ann.*, vol. 6, no. 1, 1964, 93–95.

O'DONNELL, *Father* WILLIAM.

7568 'The Waterloo Priest'. *Donegal Ann.*, vol. 12, no. 1, 1977, 62–67.

O'DONOGHUE, DAVID JAMES.

7569 David James O'Donoghue (obituary and bibliog. note). *Ir. Book L.*, vol. 9, 1917–18, 5–7.

O'DONOVAN, EDMOND.

7570 DELOUGHRY, RICHARD J. Edmond O'Donovan. *Old Kilkenny Rev.*, 24, 1972, 18–28. Foreign correspondent and author of *The Merv Oasis*, 1882.

7571 HAYES, *Dr.* RICHARD. A famous war correspondent. *Studies,* 36, 1947, 40–48.

O'DONOVAN, JOHN.

7572 DIXON, HENRY. Bibliography of works written, translated or edited by John O'Donovan. *An Leab.*, vol. 2, no. 1, 1906, 23–29.

O'DUFFY, EIMAR.

7573 MACKOCHLAINN, ALF. Eimar O'Duffy: a bibliographical biography. *Ir. Book,* vol. 1, no. 2, 1959–60, 37–46.

O'FAOLAIN, SEAN.

7574 Bibliography. *New Camb. Bibliog. Eng. Lit.* 4, 1972, 685–6.

7575 DOYLE, PAUL A. Sean O'Faolain. New York: 1968. *(Twayne English authors series)*. Bibliog., pp. 143–152.

7576 — Sean O'Faolain and *The Bell*. *Eire-Ir.*, vol. 1, no. 3, 1966, 56–62.

7577 IRISH UNIVERSITY REVIEW. vol. 6, no. 1, 1976. Sean O'Faolain special issue.

O'FLAHERTY, LIAM.

7578 Bibliography. *New Camb. Bibliog. Eng. Lit.*, 4, 1972, 686–7.

7579 DOYLE, PAUL A. Liam O'Flaherty. New York: 1971. *(Twayne English authors series).* Bibliog., pp. 137–149.

7580 — O'Flaherty: an annotated bibliography. Troy (N.Y.), 1972.

7581 GAWSWORTH, JOHN. Ten contemporaries: notes towards their definitive bibliographies. 2nd ser. London: 1933. Bibliog., pp. 144–60.

7582 HAMPTON, ANGELINE A. Liam O'Flaherty: additions to the checklist. *Eire-Ir.*, vol. 6, no. 4, 1971, 87–94.

7583 O'BRIEN, JAMES H. Liam O'Flaherty. Lewisburg: 1973. *(Irish writers series)*. Bibliog., pp. 118–124.

O'FLYNN, JAMES CHRISTOPHER.

7584 O'DONOGHUE, RICHARD. '. . . Like a tree planted . . .'. Dublin and Sydney: 1967. 'Father O'Flynn of the Loft'.

O'GRADY, STANDISH.

7585 GWYNN, DENIS. Standish O'Grady. *Old Kilk. Rev.*, 22, 1970, 11–14.

7586 MCKENNA, JOHN R. The Standish O'Grady collection at Colby College: a checklist. *Colby Lib. Qtr., ser.* 4, no. 16, 1958, 291–9.

7587 MARCUS, PHILIP L. Standish O'Grady. Lewisburg: 1970. *(Irish writers series)*. Bibliog., pp. 90–92.

7588 O'HEGARTY, P.S. Bibliographies of Irish authors, no. 2: Standish O'Grady. *Dublin Mag., new series,* vol. [5], no. 2, 1930, 49–56.

O'HALLORAN, SYLVESTER.

7589 COLEMAN, JAMES. Bibliography of Dr. Sylvester O'Halloran. Paper read before the Bibliographical Society of Ireland, October 29, 1925.

O'HANLON, REDMOND.

7590 MOODY, T.W. Redmond O'Hanlon. *Belfast Nat. Hist. Phil. Soc. Proc., new ser.,* vol. 1, pt.1, 1935–6, 17–33.

O'HARA, KANE.

7591 Bibliography. *New Camb. Bibliog. Eng. Lit.*, 2, 1971, 854.

O'HIGGINS, AMBROSE.

7592 DE BREFFNY, BRIAN. Ambrose O'Higgins: an enquiry into his origins and ancestry. *Ir. Ancest.*, 2, 1970, 81–89.

O'HIGGINS, KEVIN.

7593 WHITE, TERENCE DE VERE. Kevin O'Higgins. London: 1948. Bibliog., pp. 243–50.

O'KEEFE, J.G.

7594 MACCOLUIM, F., and O'CUIV, S. The late J.G. O'Keefe: bibliography by Colm O'Lochlainn. *Ir. Book Lov.*, 26, 1938–9, 26–9.

7595 O'KEEFE, JOHN. Bibliography. *New Camb. Bibliog. Eng. Lit.*, 2, 1971, 854.

O'KELLY, PATRICK.

7596 BOURKE, F.S. An itinerant poet: Patrick O'Kelly [with bibliog.]. *Ir. Book Lov.*, 23, 1935, 42–45.

O'KELLY, PATRICK.

7597 Patrick O'Kelly, an historian of the rebellion of 1798 [with bibliog.]. *Ir. Book Lov.*, 28, 1941–2, 37–42.

O'KELLY, SEAMUS.

7598 Bibliography. *New Camb. Bibliog. Eng. Lit.*, 4, 1972, 687–8.

7599 SAUL, GEORGE BRANDON. Seamus O'Kelly. Lewisburg: 1971. (*Irish writers series*). Annotated bibliography of O'Kelly, pp. 181–98; selective bibliography of secondary works, pp. 99–101.

O'LAVERTY, JAMES.

7600 BIGGER, FRANCIS JOSEPH. The Right Rev. Monsignor O'Laverty [with bibliog.]. *An Leab.*, vol. 2, no. 2, 1907, 109–14.

O'LEARY, *The Rev.* PETER CANON.

7601 O'CUIV, SHAN. Materials for a bibliography of the Very Rev. Peter Canon O'Leary, 1839–1920. Supplement to *Celtica*, vol. 2, pt. 2, 1954. See also review with notes and corrections, by Seamus Lankford, *An Leab.*, 12, 1954, 50–1, 54.

O'LOUGHLIN, THOMAS J.

7602 MCADAMS, J. LEO. Count Thomas J. O'Loughlin. *Old Kilk. Rev., new ser.*, vol. 1, no. 2, 1975, 105–117.

O'MAHONY, EOIN.

7603 CURTAYNE, ALICE: Remembering Eoin O'Mahony. *Canaliana,* 1970, 25–28.

7604 RYAN, JOHN. The Lost – umbilical chord. (Eoin O'Mahony, 1905–1970). *Dublin Mag.*, 9, 1971, 96–101.

O'MAHONY, *The Rev.* TIMOTHY J.

7605 Bibliography. *Ir. Book Lov.*, 8, 1916–17, 143.

O'MALLEY, GRACE.

7606 MAGUIRE, CONOR. Grace O'Malley: the Queen of the west. *Studies*, 32, 1943, 225–230. Granuaile, daughter of Dubhdhara O'Maille.

7607 POWER, ARTHUR. Some facts about Grian-nua Uaile (Grace O'Malley). *Galway Reader,* vol. 3, no. 3, 1951, 99–109.

O'MOLLOY, FRANCIS.
7608 Bibliography and biographical note. *Ir. Book Lov.*, 18, 1930, 8–10.

O'NEILL, HUGH.
7609 O'FAOLAIN, SEAN. The great O'Neill: a biography of Hugh O'Neill, Earl of Tyrone, 1550–1616. London: 1942. Bibliog., p. 284.

O'NEILL, MOIRA. (Nesta Higginson, *later* Skrine).
7610 Bibliography. *New Camb. Bibliog. Eng. Lit.*, 3, 1969, 1910.

O'NEILL, OWEN ROE.
7611 O'NEILL, ELIZABETH. Owen Roe O'Neill. Dublin: 1937. Bibliog., p. 112.

O'RAHILLY, ALFRED.
7612 GWYNN, DENIS. Monsignor Alfred O'Rahilly (1884–1969). *Studies*, 58, 1969, 368–375.

7613 O'FLAHERTY, KATHLEEN. Professor Alfred O'Rahilly: an appreciation. *Univ. Rev.*, vol. 1, no. 4, 1955, 13–20.

O'SULLIVAN, MARY J. DONOVAN.
7614 HAYES-MCCOY, G.A. Mary J. Donovan O'Sullivan (obituary). *Ann. Hib.*, 26, 1970, xii, xiv. Her writings are extensive, and she was the author of *Old Galway* and *Italian merchant bankers in Ireland in the twentieth century*.

O'SULLIVAN, SEUMAS. (*i.e.* James Sullivan Starkey).
7615 Bibliography. *New Camb. Bibliog. Eng. Lit.*, 4, 1972, 323–4.

7616 DENSON, ALAN. Seumas O'Sullivan (James Sullivan Starkey) 1879–1958: a checklist of his publications, foreword by Padraic Colum. Kendal (Westmorland): the author, 1969.

7617 MACMANUS, M.J. Bibliographies of Irish authors, no. 3: Seumas O'Sullivan. *Dublin Mag.*, vol. [5], no. 3, 1930, 47–50.

7618 MILLER, LIAM, *ed.* Retrospect: the work of Seumas O'Sullivan, 1897–1908, and Estella F. Solomons, 1882–1968. Dublin: 1973. The books of Seumas O'Sullivan (James Sullivan Starkey, 1879–1958), a bibliographical checklist, compiled by Alan Denson, pp. 99–103; an earlier version appeared in the *Dublin Magazine*, vol. 7, nos. 2–4, 1969.

O'SULLIVAN BEARE, PHILIP.
7619 BYRNE, MATTHEW J., *ed.* O'Sullivan Beare's Ireland under Elizabeth . . . Dublin 1903. Bibliog. pp. xvi–xviii.

7620 GWYNN, *The Rev.* AUBREY. An unpublished work of Philip O'Sullivan Beare. *Anal. Hib.*, 6, 1934, 1–11.

OULTON, *The Rev.* J.E.L.
7621 HARRISS, H.M. *ed.* Fundamentals of the faith: papers, addresses and sermons. . . . with a memoir. London: 1958. Principal works of J.E.L. Oulton, p. 20.

OWENSON, SYDNEY, *afterwards* Lady Morgan.
7622 Bibliography. *New Camb. Bibliog. Eng. Lit.*, 3, 1969, 754–5.

7623 STEVENSON, LIONEL. The wild Irish girl: the life of Sydney Owenson, Lady Morgan (1776–1859). London: 1936. Bibliog., pp. 317–24.

P

PALLES, CHRISTOPHER.
7624 DELANEY, V.T.H. Christopher Palles, Lord Chief Baron of Her Majesty's Court of Exchequer in Ireland, 1874–1916: his life and times. Dublin: 1960. Bibliog., pp. 188–92.

PARKE, HERBERT WILLIAM.
7625 Bibliography of writings by H.W. Parke. *Hermathena*, 118, 1974, 156–158.

PARNELL, CHARLES STEWART.
7626 ABELS, JULES. The Parnell tragedy. London: 1966. Bibliog., pp. 393–396.

7627 FOSTER, R.F. Charles Stewart Parnell: the man and his family. Hassocks (Sussex), 1976. Bibliog., pp. 329–338.

7628 HASLIP, JOAN. Parnell: a biography. London: 1936. Bibliog., pp. 395–7.

7629 HAYES, MICHAEL VICTORY. The Young Charles Stewart Parnell. 1874–1876. *Eire-Ir.*, vol. 8, no. 2, 1973, 42–61.

7630 HUGHES, MARIE. The Parnell sisters (Delia, Emily, Sophia, Anna, Fanny and Theodosia). *Dublin Hist. Rec.*, vol. 21, no. 1, 1966, 14–27.

7631 LYONS, F.S.L. The fall of Parnell, 1890–91. London: 1960. Bibliog., pp. 333–45.

7632 — Parnell. Dundalk: 1963. *(Dublin Histori-*

cal Association: Irish History Series, no. 3) Bibliog., pp. 37–39.

7633 — Charles Stewart Parnell. London: 1977.

7634 MARTIN, GED. Parnell at Cambridge: the education of an Irish nationalist. *Ir. Hist. Stud.*, vol. 19, no. 73, 1974, 72–82.

7635 MOODY, T.W. *The Times* versus Parnell and Co., 1887–90. *Hist. Stud.*, 6, 1968, 147–182.

7636 O'BROIN, LEON. Parnell: beathaisnes. Baile Atha Cliath, 1937. Bibliog., pp. 556–7.

7637 O'SHEA, KATHERINE. Charles Stewart Parnell: his love story and political life. [1st ed. reprinted]. London: 1973. First published 1914.

PARNELL, JOHN HOWARD.

7638 STERN, FREDERICK C. The other Parnell. *Eire-Ir.*, vol. 7, no. 3, 1972, 3–12. Brother of Charles Stewart Parnell.

PATERSON, THOMAS GEORGE FARQUHAR.

7639 EVANS, E.E. Thomas George Farquhar Paterson, O.B.E., M.A., M.R.I.A. *Ulster J. Arch., 3rd ser.*, 34, 1971, 1–2.

PEARSE, MARGARET MARY.

7640 DE BARRA, EAMONN. A valiant woman. *Cap. Ann.*, 1969, 53–56.

PEARSE, PATRICK.

7641 CARTHY, XAVIER. In bloody protest: the tragedy of Patrick Pearse. Dublin: 1978. Bibliog., pp. 141–147.

7642 EDWARDS, RUTH DUDLEY. Patrick Pearse: the triumph of failure. London: 1977. Bibliog., pp. 362–372.

7643 LE ROUX, LOUIS N. La vie de Patrice Pearse . . . [Paris]: 1932. Bibliog., pp. 331–5.

PECHERIN, VLADIMIR.

7644 MACWHITE, EOIN. Vladimir Pecherin, 1807–1885: the first chaplain of the Mater Hospital, Dublin, and the first Russian political emigré. *Studies*, 60, 1971, 295–310: 61, 1972, 23–40.

PERY, EDMOND SEXTEN.

7645 MALCOLMSON, A.P.W. Speaker Pery and the Pery Papers. *Nth. Munster Antiq. J.*, 16, 1973–4, 33–60.

PETHYBRIDGE, GEORGE H.

7646 Award of the Boyle medal . . . [with bibliog.]. *R. Dublin Soc. Sci. Proc., new ser.*, 16, 1920–2, 226–32.

PETRIE, GEORGE.

7647 Aspects of George Petrie. *R. Ir. Acad. Proc., Sec. C.,* 72, 1972, 153–269.

1. George Petrie, 1789–1866: a reassessment, by Joseph Raftery.
2. George Petrie and the collecting of Irish manuscripts, by David Greene.
3. George Petrie and a century of Irish numismatics, by M. Dolley.
4. Petrie's contribution to Irish music, by A. Fleischmann.
5. An essay on military architecture in Ireland previous to the English invasion, by George Petrie [with] notes and explanatory appendix by D.J.S. O'Malley.

7648 DILLON, MYLES. George Petrie (1789–1866). *Studies,* 56, 1967, 266–276.

7649 O'SULLIVAN, CATHERINE. George Petrie, LL.D., M.R.I.A., 1789–1866. *Dublin Hist. Rec.*, vol. 25, no. 1, 1971, 3–10.

PILKINGTON, LETITIA.

7650 Memoirs of Mrs. Letitia Pilkington, 1712–50, written by herself; with an introduction by I. Barry. London: 1928. Bibliographical note, by J. Isaacs, pp. 467–72.

PIRRIE, WILLIAM JAMES.

7651 JEFFERSON, HERBERT. Viscount Pirrie of Belfast . . . Belfast [1948]. Bibliog., pp. v–vi.

PLUNKET, MARGARET.

7652 LEESON, FRANCIS. Peg Plunket, lady of pleasure. *Ir. Ancest.*, vol. 3, no. 1, 1971, 1–4.

PLUNKETT, HORACE.

7653 DIGBY, MARGARET. Horace Plunkett: an Anglo-American Irishman. Oxford: 1949.

7654 MEGHEN, P.J. Sir Horace Plunkett as an administrator. *Admin.*, 14, 1966, 227–245.

PLUNKETT, OLIVER.

7655 CURTAYNE, ALICE. The trial of Oliver Plunkett. London and New York: 1953. Bibliog. notes pp. 237–239.

7656 CURTIS, EMMANUEL. Blessed Oliver Plunkett. Dublin: 1963. Bibliog., pp. 220–232.

POEKRICH, RICHARD.

7657 DIXON, F.E. Richard Poekrich (with bibliog.) *Dublin Hist. Rec.*, 10, 1948–9, 17–32.

7658 FLEETWOOD, JOHN. Richard Poekrich (1695–1759): an Irish Leonardo da Vinci manqué? *In* Essays in honour of J.D.H. Widdess, edited by Eoin O'Brien. Dublin: 1978.

POOLE, H.H.
7659 Award of the Boyle medal . . .[with bibliog.]. *R. Dublin Soc. Sci. Proc., new ser.,* 21, 1933–8, 453–6.

PORTER, JAMES.
7660 BIGGER, FRANCIS JOSEPH. James Porter (1753–98), with some notes on *Billy Bluff* and *Paddy's resource. Ir. Book Lov.,* 13, 1921–2, 126–31.

7661 MACLOINSIGH, SEAN. Reverend James Porter (1753–1798). *Donegal Ann.*, vol. 8, no. 1, 1969, 7–15.

POTAMIAN, BROTHER, (*i.e.*, Michael Francis O'Reilly).
7662 BATTERSBY, W.J. Brother Potamian, educator and scientist. London: 1953. Bibliog., pp. 179–80.

POTTER, MAUREEN.
7663 NICASSIO, SUSAN. Maureen Potter – just make them laugh, that's all. *Ir. Wel.*, vol. 23, no. 6, 1974, 36–39.

PRENDERGAST, JOHN PATRICK.
7664 Bibliography. *Camb. Bibliog. Eng. Lit.*, 3, 1940, 928–9.

7665 FINEGAN, FRANCIS. John Patrick Prendergast. *Studies*, 38, 1939, 218–229.

PRESTON, THOMAS.
7666 Award of the Boyle medal . . .[with bibliog.]. *R. Dublin Soc. Sci. Proc., new ser.,* 9, 1899–1902, 543–6.

PRESTON, WILLIAM.
7667 PRESTON, CHRISTOPHER. Life and writings of William Preston, 1753–1807. *Studies*, 31, 1942, 377–86.

PRIM, JOHN GEORGE AUGUSTUS.
7668 MCEVOY, FRANK. John George Augustus Prim, 1821–1875. *Old Kilk. Rev., new ser.*, vol. 1, no. 3, 1976, 158–168.

7669 PHELAN, MARGARET. John George Augustus Prim, 1821–1875. *R. Soc. Antiq. Ir. J.*, 105, 1975, 159–161. Prim was Hon. Secretary of Kilkenny Archaeological Society.

PRIOR, THOMAS.
7670 CLARKE, DESMOND. Thomas Prior, 1681–1751, founder of the Royal Dublin Society. Dublin: 1951. Bibliog., pp. 58–60.

Q

QUIN, HENRY GEORGE.
7671 RAU, ARTHUR. Henry George Quin, 1760–1805. *Book Coll.*, 13, 1964, 449–462.

QUIRKE, HENRY.
7672 Bibliography. *Ir. Book Lov.*, 8, 1916–17, 143–4.

R

REDMOND, JOHN EDWARD, *M.P.*
7673 Bibliography. *Ir. Book Lov.*, 9, 1917–18, 113.

REEVES, WILLIAM.
7674 FERGUSON, *Lady*. Life of the Rt. Rev. William Reeves, D.D., Lord Bishop of Down, Connor and Dromore. Dublin: 1893. Bibliography, by John Ribton Garstin, pp. 187–210.

REID, FORREST.
7675 BELFAST MUSEUM AND ART GALLERY. Forrest Reid: an exhibition of books and manuscripts held . . . September 2–23, 1953. Belfast: 1954.

7676 Bibliography. *New Camb. Bibliog. Eng. Lit.*, 4, 1972, 719–20.

7677 BURLINGHAM, RUSSELL. Forrest Reid, a portrait and a study. London: 1953. Bibliography of the writings of Forrest Reid, pp. 227–50.

7678 THRESHOLD. 28, Spring 1977. Special issue devoted to Reid.

RIDDELL, MRS. J.H.
7679 A bibliography of Mrs. J.H. Riddell, by E.F. Bleiler. *In* The Collected Ghost Stories of Mrs. J.H. Riddell, selected and introduced by E.F. Bleiler. New York: Dover Pub., 1977.

7680 ELLIS, S.M. Wilkie Collins, Le Fanu and others. London: 1951. List of works by Mrs. Riddell, pp. 323–35.

ROBINSON, LENNOX.
7681 Bibliography. *New Camb. Bibliog. Eng. Lit.*, 3, 1969, 1943–4.

7682 Obituary and bibliography. *Ir Times*, October 15, 1958.

7683 O'NEILL, MICHAEL J. Lennox Robinson. New York: 1964. *(Twayne's English Authors series: 9)* Bibliog., pp. 181–184.

RODGERS, WILLIAM ROBERT.

7684 Bibliography. *New Camb. Bibliog. Eng. Lit.*, 4, 1972, 333.

7685 O'BRIEN, DARCY. W.R. Rodgers (1909–1969). Lewisburg: 1970. *(Irish writers series).*

ROLLESTON, THOMAS WILLIAM HOGAN.

7686 Bibliography. *New Camb. Bibliog. Eng. Lit.*, 3, 1909, 1969.

RONAN, *The Rev.* MYLES V.

7687 MACGIOLLA PHADRAIG, BRIAN. An tAthair Maolmhuire O Ronain, S.P., D. Litt., M.R.I.A. [with bibliog.]. *Rep. Nov., 2*, 1957–60, 223–7.

ROS, AMANDA MCKITTRICK.

7688 LOUDAN, JACK. O rare Amanda: the life of Amanda McKittrick Ros. 2nd ed., London: 1969. First published London: 1954. A bibliography, by T. Stanley Mercer, pp. 195–200.

RUSSELL, GEORGE WILLIAM. (*i.e.*, AE.)

7689 Bibliographies of Irish authors, no. 1: 'AE' (George W. Russell). *Dublin Mag., new ser.*, vol. 5, 1930, no. 1, 44–52.

7690 Bibliography. *New Camb. Bibliog. Eng. Lit.*, 3, 1969, 1912–1915.

7691 A checklist of first editions of works by John Millington Synge and George William Russell. *T.C.D. Ann. Bull.*, 1956, 4–9.

7692 CHRISTENSEN, LIS. George Moore's portrait of AE in *Hail and Farewell*. *Ir. Univ. Rev.*, vol. 4, no. 2, 1974, 248–267.

7693 DAVIS, ROBERT BERNARD: George William Russell ('AE'). London and Boston (Mass.): 1977. Bibliog., pp. 155–8.

7694 DENSON, ALAN. Printed writings by George W. Russell (AE): a bibliography with some notes on his pictures and portraits, compiled by Alan Denson. Foreword by Padraic Colum, reminiscences of AE by M.J. Bonn, a note on AE and painting by Thomas Bodkin. London: 1961.

7695 EGLINTON, JOHN. A memoir of AE: George William Russell. London: 1937. Bibliog., pp. 287–9.

7696 KINDILIEN, CARLIN T. George William Russell (AE) and the Colby collection. *Colby Lib. Qtr., ser. 4*, no. 2, 1955, 31–55.

7697 MACMANUS, M.J. Additions to the bibliography of AE. *Dublin Mag., new ser.,* 10, 1935, 74–6.

7698 Salutation: a poem on the Irish rebellion of 1916. By AE. London: 1917. Bibliog., pp. 5–6. Twenty-five copies privately printed.

7699 SUMMERFIELD, HENRY. That myriad-minded man: a biography of George William Russell, 'AE', 1867–1935. Gerrards Cross (Bucks.): 1975.

RUSSELL, MATTHEW.

7700 BYARD, EDWIN J. Father Matthew Russell: a bibliography. *Ir. Book Lov.*, 4, 1912–13, 62–3.

RUSSELL, THOMAS.

7701 MACGIOLLA EASPAIG, SEAMUS N. Tomas Ruiseil. Baile Atha Cliath: 1957. Bibliog., pp. 251–5.

RUSSELL, THOMAS O'NEILL.

7702 COLEMAN, JAMES. Bibliography of Thomas O'Neill Russell. *Bibliog. Soc. Ir.*, vol. 1, no. 4, 1919, 33–6.

RUTHERFORD, JOHN.

7703 Bibliography. *Ir. Book Lov.*, 1, 1909–10, 141–4.

7704 RYAN, *The Rev. Professor* JOHN, S.J., M.A., D.Litt., M.R.I.A.
Obituary. *Nth. Munster Antiq. J.*, 16, 1973–4, 105–6.

7705 Obituary. *R. Ir. Acad. Ann. Rpt.*, 1973–4, 6.

S

SAUNDERS, GEORGE.

7706 Obituary and bibliography. *Ir. Book Lov.*, 4, 1912–13, 175–6.

SAYERS, PEIG.

7707 Peig: the autobiography of Peig Sayers of the Great Blasket Island, translated into English by Bryan MacMahon. Dublin: 1973.

7708 O'SULLEABBAIN, SEAN. Peig Sayers. *Eire-Ir.*, vol. 5, no. 1, 1970, 86–91.

SHACKLETON, MARY.

7709 GOODBODY, OLIVE C. Letters of Mary and Sarah Shackleton, 1767 to 1775. *Kildare Arch. Soc. J.*, vol. 14, no. 4, 1969, 415–430; 15, no. 1, 1971, 59–70. Mary Shackleton (*later* Leadbeater) is best known as the author of *The Annals of Ballitore.*

SHAW, GEORGE BERNARD.

7710 Bibliography. *New Camb. Bibliog. Eng. Lit.*, 3, 1969, 1169–82.

7711 AMERICAN ART ASSOCIATION. First editions and autograph letters of George Bernard Shaw. New York: 1933.

7712 BROAD, C. LEWIS and BROAD, VIOLET M. Dictionary to the plays and novels of Bernard Shaw, with bibliography of his works and of literature concerning him, with a record of the principal Shavian play productions. London: 1929.

7713 BROWN, T.J. George Bernard Shaw, 1856–1950. *Book Coll.*, 13, 1964, 195.

7714 DU CANN, C.G.L. The loves of George Bernard Shaw. London: 1963.

7715 HEYDET, X. Shaw-kompendium: Verzeichnis und Analyse seiner Werke, Shaw-bibliographie, Verzeichnis der Literatur über Shaw, Verzeichnis der Auffuhrungen seiner Werke in England und Deutschland. Paris: 1936.

7716 HOLMES, M. Some bibliographical notes on the novels of George Bernard Shaw; with some comments by Shaw. London [1929].

7717 LOEWENSTEIN, F.E. The rehearsal copies of Bernard Shaw's plays: a bibliographical study. London: 1950.

7718 NATIONAL BOOK LEAGUE, London. Bernard Shaw: catalogue of an exhibition . . . London: 1946.

7719 — Selected books on Bernard Shaw. London: 1956.

7720 NORTH CAROLINA University. An exhibition of selections from the Archibald Henderson collection of Bernard Shaw, November–December 1956. Typescript.

7721 ROSSET, B.C. Shaw of Dublin: the formative years. Pennsylvania: 1964. Bibliog., pp. 359–364.

7722 TERRY, ALTHA ELIZABETH. Jeanne d'Arc in periodical literature, 1894–1929, with special reference to Bernard Shaw's *Saint Joan*. New York, Institute of French studies: 1930.

7723 WAGENKNECHT, EDWARD. A guide to Bernard Shaw. New York and London: 1929.

7724 WARD, A.C. Bernard Shaw [New ed.] reprinted with minor amendments and additions to bibliography. London: British Council: 1970. *(Writers and their work, no. 1)*.

7725 WEINTRAUB, STANLEY, *ed.* Shaw: an autobiography, 1856–1898; selected from his writings by S. Weintraub. London: 1970.

7726 WELLS, G.H. A bibliography of the books and pamphlets of George Bernard Shaw. Supplement to *Bookman's Journal,* 1929.

7727 WILSON, COLIN. Bernard Shaw: a reassessment. London: 1969.

SHEEHY, EDMUND J.

7728 Award of the Boyle medal to Professor E.J. Sheehy, D. Sc., F.R.C.Sc.I. *R. Dublin Soc. Sci. Proc.*, 25, 1949–51, 200.

SHEIL, RICHARD LALOR.

7729 Bibliography. *New Camb. Bibliog. Eng. Lit.*, 3, 1969, 1138–9.

SHERIDAN, FRANCES.

7730 RUSSELL, NORMA H. Frances Sheridan, 1724–1766. *Book Coll*, 13, 1964, 196–205. Mother of Richard Brinsley Sheridan.

SHERIDAN, RICHARD BRINSLEY.

7731 Bibliography. *New Camb. Bibliog. Eng. Lit.*, 2, 1971, 816–24.

7732 BINGHAM, MADELINE. Sheridan: the track of a comet. London: 1972. Bibliog., pp. 372–5.

7733 DARLINGTON, W.A. Sheridan, 1751–1816. London: British Council, 1951. *(Writers and their work series)*. Bibliog., pp. 27–9.

7734 GIBBS, LEWIS. Sheridan. London: 1947. Bibliog., pp. 273–4.

7735 HALL, ELIZABETH. Sheridan and the Rev. William Lisle Bowles: an uncollected Bowles poem and the dating of two Sheridan letters. *N. and Q., new ser.*, 23, 1976, 106–7.

7736 Hand-list of plays by Richard Brinsley Sheridan, printed in Dublin, Cork, and Belfast. In Ms in National Library, Dublin.

7737 NETTLETON, G.H. Sheridan's major dramas. Boston: 1906. Bibliog., pp. cxi-cxvii.

7738 PANTER, GEORGE W. Early editions of Sheridan. *Times Lit. Supp.*, April 15, 1926, 283.

7739 **Rhodes, R. Crompton.** *ed.* The plays and poems of Richard Brinsley Sheridan . . . with introduction, appendices and bibliographies. Oxford: 1928. 3 vols. The bibliographies record every discoverable edition of the plays and poems.

7740 — Sheridan: a study in theatrical bibliography. *London Mercury*, 15, 1927, 381–90.

7741 — Sheridan bibliography. *Times Lit. Supp.,* June 17, 1926, 414.

7742 — Some aspects of Sheridan bibliography. *The Library, 4th ser.,* 9, 1929, 233–59.

7743 — Harlequin Sheridan; the man and the legends; with a bibliography and appendices. Oxford: 1933.

7744 **Sanders, Lloyd C.** Life of Richard Brinsley Sheridan. London: 1890. *(Great writers series).* Bibliography, by John P. Anderson, appended, pp. i-xi.

7745 **Sichel, W.** Sheridan. London: 1909. 2 vols. Bibliog., vol. 2, pp. 445–59.

7746 **Williams, I.A.** Seven eighteenth-century bibliographies. London: 1924.

Shiels, George.

7747 Bibliography. *New Camb. Bibliog. Eng. Lit.*, 4, 1972, 979–80.

Shirley, James.

7748 **Tannenbaum, Samuel A., and Tannenbaum, Dorothy R.** James Shirley: a concise bibliography. New York: 1946. *(Elizabethan bibliographies,* no. 34.)

Shorter, Dora Sigerson.

7749 Bibliography. *Ir. Book Lov.*, 9, 1917–18, 86–7.

7750 — S., E.O. Bibliography of Dora Sigerson Shorter. *Studies*, 7, 1918, 144–145.

7751 [**Wise, Thomas James.**] The books of Dora Sigerson Shorter. Edinburgh: 1924. Thirty copies privately printed.

Sigerson, George

7752 Bibliography. *New Camb. Bibliog. Eng. Lit.* 3, 1969, 1905–6.

7753 **Hyde, Douglas.** George Sigerson (1836–1925). *Studies*, 14, 1925, 1–18.

Sirr, Joseph D'Arcy, *D.D.*

7754 **Sirr, Henry.** A memoir and bibliography. *Ir. Book Lov.*, 2, 1910–11, 36–9.

Smithson, Harriet.

7755 **Rynne, Etienne.** Harriet Smithson, the Ennis-born wife of Hector Berlioz. *Nth. Munster Antiq. J.*, vol. 12, 1969, 81–84.

Somerville, Edith Œnone and **'Martin Ross'**, (*i.e.* Violet Florence Martin).

7756 Bibliography. *New Camb. Bibliog. Eng. Lit.*, 4, 1972, 739–40.

7757 **Collis, Maurice.** Somerville and Ross: a biography. London: 1968. Note on manuscript sources, pp. 279–80.

7758 **Cronin, John.** Somerville and Ross. Lewisburg: 1972. Bibliog., pp. 108–111.

7759 **Cummins, Geraldine.** Dr. E. Œ. Somerville. London: 1952. The first editions of Edith Œnone Somerville and Violet Florence Martin: a bibliography, compiled by Robert Vaughan, pp. 243–71.

7760 **Hudson, Elizabeth,** A bibliography of the first editions of the works of E. Œ. Somerville and Martin Ross [pseudonym of Violet Florence Martin] . . . with explanatory notes by E. Œ. Somerville. New York: 1942. 300 copies printed.

7761 Somerville and Ross: a symposium. Belfast: Queen's University, [1969]. Includes catalogue of exhibition of paintings by Edith Œnone Somerville.

Spenser, Edmund.

7762 **Henley, Pauline.** Spenser in Ireland. Cork and Dublin: 1928. Bibliog., pp. 212–14.

Stanford, Charles Villiers.

7763 **Greene, Harry Plunket.** Charles Villiers Stanford. London: 1935. Compositions and writings, pp. 183–235.

Starkie, Walter.

7764 Bibliography. *New Camb. Bibliog. Eng. Lit.*, 4, 1972, 1325.

Steele, Richard.

7765 Bibliography. *Camb. Bibliog. Eng. Lit.*, 2, 1940, 608–12.

7766 **Aitken, G.A.** Richard Steele. London: 1889. 2 vols. Full bibliography in vol. 2, appendix 5.

7767 **Blanchard, R.** The Christian hero: a bibliography. *The Library,* vol. 10, 1929.

7768 CARPENTER, G.R. Selections from the works of Steele. Boston: 1897. Includes a useful hand-list.

7769 CONNELY, WILLARD. Sir Richard Steele. London: 1937. Bibliog. notes, pp. 421–40. First published 1934.

STEPHENS, JAMES.

7770 Bibliography. *New Camb. Bibliog. Eng. Lit.*, 4, 1972, 360–2.

7771 BLUM, GEOFFREY. Some notes for Stephens bibliophiles. *J. Ir. Lit.*, vol. 4, no. 3, 1975, 193–198. Intended as supplement to bibliographies of Birgit Bramsback and Richard J. Finneran.

7772 BRAMSBACK, BIRGIT. James Stephens: a literary and bibliographical study. Upsala and Dublin: 1959. *(Upsala Irish studies*, no. 4.)

7773 FINNERAN, RICHARD J. *ed.* Letters of James Stephens, with an appendix listing Stephens's published writings. London: 1974. Bibliog., pp. 420–458.

7774 — Corrections to the letters of James Stephens. *J. Ir. Lit.*, vol. 4, no. 3, 1975, 198–200.

7775 JOURNAL OF IRISH LITERATURE. Vol. 4, no. 3, 1975. A James Stephens number.

7776 PYLE, HILARY. James Stephens: his work and an account of his life. London: 1965. Bibliog., pp. 183–191.

7777 A Tribute to James Stephens, 1882–1950. *Colby Lib. Qtr., ser.* 5, no. 9, 1961. Bibliography, pp. 224–52; includes essays by Oliver St. John Gogarty, Birgit Bramsback and Richard Cary.

7778 WILLIAMS, I.A. John Collings Squire and James Stephens. London, 1922. (*Bibliographies of modern authors,* no. 4.) Based upon lists originally appearing in *The London Mercury*, vol. 4, 1921.

STERNE, LAURENCE.

7779 BAKER, VAN R. Laurence Sterne's family in France. *N. and Q. new series.*, vol. 22, 1975, 497–501.

7780 Bibliography. *New Camb. Bibliog. Eng. Lit.*, 2, 1971, 948–62.

7781 BRITISH LIBRARY. Laurence Sterne: an excerpt from the General Catalogue of Printed Books. London: British Museum for the Board, 1974.

7782 CASH, ARTHUR H. Laurence Sterne: the early and middle years. London: 1975. Bibliog., pp. xix-xxiv, Appendix: Portraits of Sterne, pp. 299–316.

7783 CORDASCO, FRANCESCO. Laurence Sterne: a list of critical studies published from 1896 to 1946. Brooklyn: 1948. (*Eighteenth-century bibliographical pamphlets*, no. 4).

7784 CROSS, WILBUR L. The life and times of Laurence Sterne. 3rd ed. with alterations and additions. New Haven and London: 1929. Bibliography of published works and Mss., pp. 596–632.

STOKER, BRAM.

7785 FARSON, DANIEL: The man who wrote *Dracula*: a biography of Bram Stoker. London: 1975.

7786 LUDLAM, HARRY. A biography of Dracula: the life story of Bram Stoker. London: 1962.

STOKES, *The Rev.* GEORGE THOMAS.

7787 Bibliography. *R. Soc. Antiq. Ir. J.*, 28, 1898, viii.

STOKES, MARGARET.

7788 COLEMAN, JAMES. Bibliography of Margaret Stokes. Ms. of 2 p. in National Library, Dublin.

7789 FITZG.[ERALD], W. Bibliography. *Kildare Arch. Soc. J.*, 3, 1899–1902, 201–5.

STOKES, WILLIAM

7790 STOKES, WILLIAM. William Stokes, his life and work, by his son. London: 1898. Bibliog., pp. 243–7.

STONEY, G.J.

7791 Award of the Boyle medal . . . [with bibliog.]. *R. Dublin Soc. Sci. Proc., new ser.* 9, 1899–1902, 97–106.

STOPFORD, EDWARD A.

7792 BLACKER, BEAVER H. The writings of Edward Adderley Stopford, LL.D., Archdeacon and Vicar-General of Meath. *Ir. Eccles. Gaz.*, 1876, 354–5.

STRONG, LEONARD ALFRED GEORGE.

7793 Bibliography. *New Camb. Bibliog. Eng. Lit.*, 4, 1972, 744–6.

7794 GAWSWORTH, JOHN. Ten contemporaries: notes towards their definitive bibliographies. 2nd ser. London: 1933. Bibliog., pp. 219–34.

STUART, FRANCIS.

7795 A Festschrift for Francis Stuart on his seventieth birthday, 28th April, 1972. Dublin, 1972. *(Dolmen editions, 15)*. Limited to 1,000 copies. Includes An introduction to Francis Stuart's novels, by W.J. McCormack, and The Books of Francis Stuart, by W.J. McCormack.

7796 THE JOURNAL OF IRISH LITERATURE, vol. 5, no. 1, 1976. A Francis Stuart Number. Francis Stuart: a checklist by J.H. Natterstad, pp. 39–45.

7797 McCORMACK, W.J. Francis Stuart: a checklist and commentary. *Longroom*, 2, 1970, 38–49.

7798 NATTERSTAD, J.H. Francis Stuart. Lewisburg and London: 1974. *(Irish Writers Series)*. Bibliog., pp. 86–88.

SULLIVAN BROTHERS.

7799 COLEMAN, JAMES. Bibliography of the brothers Sullivan [*i.e.*, Richard, Denis Baylor, Alexander Martin, and Timothy Daniel, of Bantry, Co. Cork]. *Bibliog. Soc. Ir.*, vol. 3, no. 3, 1926–9.

SWIFT, JONATHAN, *Dean of St. Patrick's.*

7800 ACWORTH, BERNARD. Swift. London: 1947. Swift's Biographers, pp. 195–205.

7801 Bibliography. *New Camb. Bibliog. Eng. Lit.*, 2, 1971, 1054–1091.

7802 CARPENTER, ANDREW. Archbishop King and Swift's appointment as Dean of St. Patrick's. *Longroom*, 10, 1974, 11–13.

7803 DAVIS, H. Recent studies of Swift: a survey. *Toronto Univ. Qtr.,* vol. 7, 1938.

7804 DOBELL, PERCY J. A catalogue of works by Dr. Jonathan Swift, together with contemporary works relating to or illustrative of the life and works of the Dean of St. Patrick's, Dublin. London: 1933. *(Catalogue,* no. 105).

7805 EHRENPREIS, IRVIN. Swift: the man, his works and the age. London. Vol. 1. Mr. Swift and his contemporaries. 1962. Vol. 2. Dr. Swift. 1967.

7806 EWALD, WILLIAM BRAGG. The masks of Jonathan Swift. Oxford: 1954. Bibliog., pp. 191–7.

7807 FERGUSON, OLIVER W. Jonathan Swift and Ireland. Urbana: 1962. Bibliog., pp. 198–203.

7808 GILBERT, JACK G. Jonathan Swift: romantic and cynic moralist. Austin: 1966.

7809 GOLDBERG, GERALD Y. Jonathan Swift and contemporary Cork. Cork: 1967.

7810 HARDY, EVELYN. The conjured spirit, Swift: a study in the relationship of Swift, Stella, and Vanessa. London: 1949. Bibliog., pp 255–9.

7811 [HAYWARD, JOHN D.]. A catalogue of printed books and manuscripts by Jonathan Swift, D.D., exhibited in the Old Schools in the University of Cambridge. Cambridge: 1945.

7812 HUBBARD, L.L. Contributions towards a bibliography of *Gulliver's Travels* to establish the number and order of issue of the Motte editions of 1726 and 1727. Chicago: 1922.

7813 IRELAND. NATIONAL GALLERY. Swift and his age: a tercentenary exhibition, 1967.

7814 JACKSON, W. SPENCER: Bibliography of Swift's works. *In* The Prose works of Jonathan Swift, edited by Temple Scott, vol. 12, pp. 113–241.

7815 JEFFARES, A. NORMAN. *ed.* Fair liberty was all his cry: a tercentenary tribute to Jonathan Swift, 1667–1745. London and New York: 1967. A checklist of critical and biographical writings on Jonathan Swift, 1945–65, by Claire Lamont, pp. 356–391.

7816 — Swift. London: 1968. Bibliog., pp. 267–269.

7817 — Swift and the Ireland of his day. *Ir. Univ. Rev.*, vol. 2, no. 2, 1972, 115–132.

7818 JOHNSTON, DENIS. The mysterious origin of Dean Swift. *Dublin Hist. Rec.*, 3, 1940–41, 81–97.

7819 — In search of Swift. Dublin: 1959. Bibliog., pp. 225–31.

7820 — Swift of Dublin. *Eire-Ir.*, vol. 3, no. 3, 1968, 38–50.

7821 LANDA, LOUIS A. and TOBIN, JAMES EDWARD. Jonathan Swift: a list of critical studies published from 1895 to 1945, to which is added remarks on some Swift manuscripts in the United States by Herbert Davis. New York: 1945.

7822 **Lane-Poole**, S. Notes for a bibliography of Swift. *Bibliographer*, November 1884. Reprinted separately: 1884.

7823 **Le Fanu**, T.P. Catalogue of Dean Swift's Library in 1715, with an inventory of his personal property in 1742. *R. Ir. Acad. Proc., Sec. C,* 37, 1924–7, 263–75.

7824 **Longfield**, A.K. Longfields of Kilbride and a link with Swift. *Kildare Arch. Soc. J.*, vol. 15, no. 1, 1971, 29–37.

7825 **MacCarvill, Eileen**. Swift and the Vanhomrighs. *Kildare Arch. Soc. J.*, vol. 14, no. 2, 1966–67, 95–126.

7826 **McElrath, Joseph** R., *Jr.* Swift's friend: Dr. Patrick Delany. *Eire-Ir.*, vol. 5, no. 3, 1970, 53–62.

7827 **MacManus**, M.J. An unrecorded Swift item. *Ir. Book Lov.*, 30, 1946–8, 52–4.

7828 **Moore**, *Prof.* J.N.P. The Personality of Jonathan Swift. *Ir. Coll. Phys. Surg. J.*, vol. 6, no. 3, 1977, 92–98.

7829 **Murray, Patrick**. Swift: the sceptical conformist. *Studies*, 58, 1969, 357–367.

7830 **Murry, J. Middleton**. Swift. London: British Council, 1955. A Select bibliog., pp. 35–44.

7831 **O'Hegarty**, P.S. Some bibliographical notes on Dublin editions of Swift. *Dublin Mag., new series*., vol. 14, no. 1, 1939, 67–70.

7832 **Osborn, James** M. Swiftiana in the Osborn collection at Yale. *Univ. Rev.*, vol. 4, no. 1, 1967, 72–83.

7833 **Reynolds, James**. Jonathan Swift – vicar of Laracor. *Riocht na Midhe*, vol. 4, no. 1, 1967, 41–54.

7834 **Rothschild Library**. A catalogue of eighteenth century printed books and manuscripts. Cambridge: 1954. 2 vols. Bibliography of Swift, vol. 2, pp. 543–643. Privately printed.

7835 **Simms**, J.G. Dean Swift and County Armagh. *Sean Ard.*, vol. 6, no. 1, 1971, 131–140.

7836 **Stathis**, J.J. A bibliography of Swift studies, 1945–65. Nashville, 1967.

7837 **Teerink**, H. A bibliography of the writings of Jonathan Swift; 2nd ed. revised and corrected by Dr. H. Teerink. Edited by Arthur H. Scouten. Philadelphia: 1963.

7838 **Trinity College, Dublin**. Catalogue of the exhibition held in the library of Trinity College, Dublin, from October 19 to November 23, 1945, to commemorate the bicentenary of the death of Jonathan Swift. Dublin: 1945.

7839 **Voigt, Milton**. Swift and the twentieth century. Detroit: 1964.

7840 **White, Newport** B. Bibliography of Dean Swift. *Times Lit. Supp*. June 9, 1927, 408. Addenda to W. Spencer Jackson's Bibliography.

7841 — Swiftiana in Marsh's Library. *Hermathena*, 11, 1901, 369–81. Reprinted in *An account of Archbishop Marsh's Library.* Dublin, 1926.

7842 **Wiley**, A.N. Jonathan Swift, 1667–1745: an exhibition of printed books at the University of Texas, October 19 to December 31, 1945. Austin: 1945.

7843 **Williams, Harold**. Dean Swift's Library, with a facsimile of the original sale catalogue, and some account of two manuscript lists of his books. Cambridge: 1932. Edition limited to 350 copies.

7844 — The Motte editions of *Gulliver's Travels*. London, 1925. Appeared originally in *The Library*, vol. 6, 1925; see also the authoritative bibliography of the early editions in his edition of *Gulliver's Travels*, First Edition Club: 1926.

7845 — The poems of Jonathan Swift, edited by H. Williams. Oxford: 1937. 3 vols. Bibliog., vol. 1, pp. xlviii-lxii.

7846 — Jonathan Swift and the Four Last Years of the Queen. *The Library, 4th ser.*, 16, 1936, 61–90.

7847 **Wilson**, T.G. Swift: the prince of journalists. *Dublin Mag.*, vol. 6, nos. 3–4, 1967, 46–73.

7848 — Swift in Trinity. *Dublin Mag.*, vol. 5, no. 2, 1966, 10–22.

Synge, John Lighton.

7849 Award of the Boyle medal . . . *R. Dublin Soc. Sci. Proc., Ser. A,* 4, 1970–73, 251–2.

SYNGE, JOHN MILLINGTON.

7850 The autobiography of J.M. Synge, constructed from the manuscripts, by Alan Price, with fourteen photographs by J.M. Synge, and an essay on Synge and the photography of his time, by P.J. Pocock. Dublin and London: 1965.

7851 Bibliography. *New Camb. Bibliog. Eng. Lit.*, 3, 1969, 1934–8.

7852 BOURGEOIS, MAURICE. John Millington Synge and the Irish theatre. London: 1913. Bibliog., pp. 251–313.

7853 BUSHRUI, S.B. *ed.* Sunshine and the moon's delight: a centenary tribute to John Millington Synge, 1871–1909. Gerrards Cross: 1972. Select bibliog., pp. 317–338.

7854 CARPENTER, ANDREW. Two passages from Synge's notebooks. *Hermathena*, 120, 1976, 35–38.

7855 CORKERY, DANIEL. Synge and Anglo-Irish literature: a study. Cork, Dublin and London: 1931. Bibliog., pp. 245–7.

7856 COXHEAD, ELIZABETH. J.M. Synge and Lady Gregory. London: 1962. *(Writers and their work series no. 149)*.

7857 DYSINGER, ROBERT E. Bibliography and supplement. *Colby Lib. Qtr. ser. 4,* nos. 9 and 11, 1957. Includes biographical and critical material.

7858 FLOOD, JEANNE. The pre-Aran writing of J.M. Synge. *Eire-Ir.*, vol. 5, no. 3, 1970, 63–80.

7859 FRENCH, FRANCES-JANE. Bibliography of Synge. In preparation as final volume of Oxford University Press's definitive edition of Synge.

7860 GERSTENBERGER, DONNA: John Millington Synge. New York: 1964. *(Twayne's English authors series)*. Bibliog., pp. 142–152.

7861 GREENE, DAVID H. J.M. Synge – a centenary appraisal. *Eire-Ir.*, vol. 6, no. 4, 1971, 71–86.

7862 — and STEPHENS, EDWARD M. J.M. Synge, 1871–1909. New York: 1959. Bibliog., pp. 308–10.

7863 HENN, T.R. John Millington Synge: a reconsideration. *Hermathena*, 112, 1971, 5–21.

7864 JOCHUM, K.P.S. Maud Gonne on Synge. *Eire-Ir.*, vol. 6, no. 4, 1971, 65–70.

7865 KELSALL, MALCOLM. Synge in Aran. *Ir. Univ. Rev.*, vol. 5, no. 2, 1975, 254–270.

7866 KILROY, JAMES. The 'Playboy' riots. Dublin: Dolmen Press: 1971. *(Irish writers series, no. 4)*.

7867 KRIEGER, HANS. J.M. Synge, ein Dichter der . . . Keltischen Renaissance. Marburg: 1916. Includes full bibliography.

7868 LEVITT, PAUL M. J.M. Synge: a bibliography of published criticism. Dublin: Irish University Press, 1974. For review by Weldon Thornton see *J. Ir. Lit.*, vol. 3, no. 3, 1974, 51–55.

7869 MACMANUS, M.J. John Millington Synge. (*Bibliographies of Irish authors*, no. 4.) *Dublin Mag.*, vol. 5, no. 4, 1930, 47–51.

7870 MIKHAIL, E.H. J.M. Synge: a bibliography of criticism. London: 1975.

7871 — *ed.* J.M. Synge: interviews and recollections. London: 1977.

7872 O'HEGARTY, P.S. Some notes on the bibliography of J.M. Synge, supplemental to Bourgeois and MacManus. *Dublin Mag., new series.,* vol. 17, no. 1, 1942, 56–8.

7873 SADDLEMYER, ANN. Infinite riches in a little room – the manuscripts of John Millington Synge. *Longroom*, 2, 1970, 23–31.

7874 — *ed.*, Letters to Molly: John Millington Synge to Maire O'Neill, 1906–1909. Cambridge (Mass.): 1971.

7875 — *ed.*, Some letters of John M. Synge to Lady Gregory and W.B. Yeats. Dublin: Cuala Press, 1971. Limited edition of 500 copies.

7876 SETTERQUIST, JAN. Ibsen and the beginnings of Anglo-Irish drama. Pt. 1. John Millington Synge. Upsala and Dublin, 1951. *(Upsala Irish studies,* no. 2.) Bibliog., pp. 92–4.

7877 SKELTON, ROBIN. J.M. Synge and his world. London: 1971.

7878 — J.M. Synge. Lewisburg: 1972. *(Irish writers series)* Select bibliog., pp. 86–89.

7879 — The writings of J.M. Synge. London: 1971.

7880 TRINITY COLLEGE, DUBLIN. A check-list of first editions of works by John Millington Synge and George William Russell. *T.C.D. Ann. Bull.*, 1956, 4–9.

7881 — John Millington Synge, 1871–1909: a catalogue of an exhibition held at Trinity College Library, Dublin, on the occasion of the fiftieth anniversary of his death [compiled by Ian MacPhail and M. Pollard]. Dublin: 1959.

7882 — The Synge manuscripts in the library of Trinity College, Dublin: a catalogue prepared on the occasion of the Synge centenary exhibition, 1971. Dublin: Dolmen Press, 1971.

T

TALBOT, GEORGE.

7883 HEYDT, ODO VAN DER. Monsignor Talbot de Malahide. *Wisc. Rev.*, 502, 1964–65, 290–380.

TALBOT, MATT.

7884 PURCELL, MARY. Matt Talbot and his times. [rev. ed.] Alcester and Dublin: [1976]. Bibliog., pp. 235–238.

THOMPSON, ROBERT HELY.

7885 Bibliography. *Ir. Book Lov.*, 8, 1916–17, 144.

TIERNEY, MICHAEL.

7886 Obituary. *R. Ir. Acad. Ann. Rpt.*, 1975–6, 10–11.

7887 HOGAN, JEREMIAH J. Michael Tierney, 1894–1975. *Studies*, 65, 1976, 177–191.

TIGHE, MARY.

7888 HENCHY, PATRICK. The works of Mary Tighe, published and unpublished. *Bibliog. Soc. Ir.*, vol. 6, no. 6, 1957.

TODD, JAMES HENTHORN.

7889 BLACKER, BEAVER H. The writings of James Henthorn Todd, D.D.,Senior Fellow of T.C.D., Regius Professor of Hebrew in the University and Precentor of St. Patrick's Cathedral, Dublin. *Ir. Eccles. Gaz.*, 1876, 224–5.

7890 SIMMS, G.O. James Henthorn Todd. *Hermathena*, 109, 1969, 5–23.

TODHUNTER, JOHN.

7891 Bibliography. *Ir. Book Lov.*, 8, 1916–17, 71–2.

7892 Bibliography. *New Camb. Bibliog. Eng. Lit.*, 3, 1969, 1906.

TOLAND, JOHN.

7893 HEINEMANN, F.H. Prolegomena to a Toland bibliography. *N. and Q.*, 185, 1943, 182–186.

7894 NICHOLL, H.F. John Toland: religion without mystery. *Hermathena,* 100, 1965, 54–65.

7895 SIMMS, J.G. John Toland (1670–1722), a Donegal heretic. *Ir. Hist. Stud.*, 16, 1968–69, 304–320.

TOMELTY, JOSEPH.

7896 GRACEY, J.W. Joseph Tomelty, an introductory bibliography. *Ir. Book.*, vol. 1, no. 2, 1971, 226–234.

TORRENS, WILLIAM McC.

7897 COLEMAN, JAMES. Bibliography of Wm. McC. Torrens. Paper read before the Bibliographical Society of Ireland, October 29, 1925.

TRENCH, FREDERIC HERBERT.

7898 Bibliography. *New Camb. Bibliog. Eng. Lit.*, 3, 1969, 1911.

TRENCH, RICHARD CHENEVIX, *Archbishop of Dublin.*

7899 BROMLEY, J. The man of ten talents: a portrait of C. Trench, 1807–86, philologist, poet, theologian, archbishop. London: 1959. Bibliog., pp. 246–7.

TREVOR, WILLIAM.

7900 MORTIMER, MARK. William Trevor in Dublin. *Etudes Irlandaises*, 4, 1975, 77–85.

TROTTER, JOHN BERNARD.

7901 BIGGER, FRANCIS JOSEPH. Biographical notice and bibliography. *Ir. Book Lov.*, 1, 1909–10, 41–2; 59–60; 85–6.

TWEEDY, OWEN.

7902 CROWE, THOMAS, *ed.* Gathering moss: a memoir of Owen Tweedy. London: 1967.

TYNAN, KATHARINE. (*later* Hinkson).

7903 Bibliography. *New Camb. Bibliog. Eng. Lit.*, 3, 1969, 1910.

7904 ATKINSON, F.G. Katharine Tynan Hinkson: three unpublished letters. *N. and Q., new series,* 24, 1977, 439–441.

7905 DE LAURA, DAVID J. Such good friends: four letters of Gerard Manley Hopkins to Katharine Tynan. *Studies*, 63, 1974, 389–396.

7906 ROSE, MARILYN GADDIS. Katharine Tynan. Lewisburg and London: 1974. Bibliog., pp. 94–97.

U

URWICK, WILLIAM.

7907 The life and letters of William Urwick, D.D., by his son [William Urwick]. London: 1870. Bibliog., p. 432.

W

WADDELL, HELEN JANE.

7908 Bibliography. *New Camb. Bibliog. Eng. Lit.*, 4, 1972, 1127–8.

7909 BLACKETT, MONICA. The mark of the maker: a portrait of Helen Waddell. London: 1973.

WALL, MERVYN.

7910 HOGAN, ROBERT. Mervyn Wall. Lewisburg: 1972. Bibliog., pp. 74–75.

WALSH, PAUL.

7911 BRADY, JOHN. The writings of Paul Walsh [a bibliography]. *Ir. Hist. Stud.*, 3, 1942–3, 193–208.

WARD, EDWARD.

7912 Bibliography. *New Camb. Bibliog. Eng. Lit.*, 2, 1971, 1091–5.

WELLESLEY, DOROTHY VIOLET.

7913 Bibliography. *New Camb. Bibliog Eng. Lit.*, 4, 1972, 375–6.

WESLEY, JOHN and WESLEY, CHARLES.

7914 GREEN, RICHARD. The works of John and Charles Wesley: a bibliography containing an exact account of all the publications issued by the brothers Wesley, arranged in chronological order, with a list of the early editions, and descriptive and illustrative notes. London: 1896.

WEST, REBECCA. (*i.e.* Cicily Isabel Fairfield)

7915 Bibliography. *New Camb. Bibliog. Eng. Lit.*, 4, 1972, 770–1.

7916 HUTCHINSON, EVELYN. A preliminary list of the writings of Rebecca West, 1912–51. [Facsimile reprint]. Folcraft, Pa., Folcraft Library editions, 1973. 1st published New Haven: Yale University Library, 1957.

WESTROPP, HODDER MICHAEL.

7917 COLEMAN, JAMES. Bibliography of Hodder M. Westropp. Paper read before the Bibliographical Society of Ireland, April 29, 1925. Ms. of 2 p. in National Library, Dublin.

WHATELY, RICHARD, *Archbishop of Dublin.*

7918 Bibliography. *New Camb. Bibliog. Eng. Lit.*, 3, 1969, 1307–8, 1599, 1604.

7919 Catalogue of the collection of the works . . . 23 vols. In *Catalogue of the Library of the Royal Dublin Society,* supplement, 1850, pp. 140–4: supplemental catalogue . . . 1849 to 1858, *ibid.,* pp. 298–301.

WHITE, T.H.

7920 MOTIN, SVEN ERIC. Appraisals: T.H. White, 1906–1964. *J. Ir. Lit.* vol. 2, nos. 2–3, 1973, 142–150. An account of the 6 years he spent in Ireland.

7921 WARNER, SYLVIA TOWNSEND. T.H. White: a biography. London: 1967. Bibliog., pp. 346–8.

WILDE, *Lady*. (*née* Jane Francesca Elgee)

7922 Bibliography. *New Camb. Bibliog. Eng. Lit.*, 3, 1969, 1905.

7923 COLEMAN, JAMES. Bibliography of Lady Wilde. *Ir. Book Lov.*, 20, 1932, 60, 74.

7924 WYNDHAM, HORACE. Speranza: a biography of Lady Wilde. London: 1951. Bibliog., p. [196].

WILDE, OSCAR FINGALL O'FLAHERTIE WILLS.

7925 Bibliography. *New Camb. Bibliog. Eng. Lit.*, 3, 1969, 1097, 1182–8.

7926 CALIFORNIA UNIVERSITY. Oscar Wilde and his literary circle: a catalogue of manuscripts and letters in the William Andrews Clark Memorial Library, compiled by John Charles Finzi. Berkeley and London: 1957.

7927 COWAN, R.E., and CLARK, W.A. The library of W.A. Clark: Wilde and Wildeana. San Francisco, 1922.

7928 DE BREFFNY, BRIAN. The paternal ancestry of Oscar Wilde. *Ir. Ancest.*, vol. 5, no. 2, 1973, 96–99.

7929 LAVER, JAMES. Oscar Wilde. Reprinted with additions to bibliography. London: British Council and the National Book League, 1968.

7930 MASON, STUART. (*i.e.* Christopher Millard).

Bibliography of Oscar Wilde. new ed., introduced by Timothy d'Arch Smith. London: 1967. Reviewed in *Book Coll.*, 16, 1967, 530–534.

7931 MIKHAIL, E.H. Oscar Wilde: an annotated bibliography of criticism. London: 1978.

7932 NELSON, WALTER W. Oscar Wilde in Sweden and other essays. Dublin: 1965.

7933 PINE, RICHARD. The personality of Wilde. *Dublin Mag.*, vol. 9, no. 2, 1971–2, 52–59.

7934 TRINITY COLLEGE DUBLIN. Catalogue of an exhibition of books and manuscripts in commemoration of the centenary of the birth of Oscar Wilde, 1954. Dublin: 1954.

WILDE, *Sir* WILLIAM.

7935 WILSON. T.G. Victorian doctor; being the life of Sir William Wilde. Wakefield: 1974. Originally published London: 1942. Bibliog., pp. 327–330.

WINGFIELD, SHEILA.

7936 Bibliography. *New Camb. Bibliog. Eng. Lit.*, 4, 1972, 377.

WOFFINGTON, MARGARET.

7937 DUNBAR, JANET. Peg Woffington and her world. London: 1968. Bibliog., pp. 239–241.

7938 LUCEY, JANET CAMDEN. Lovely Peggy: the life and times of Margaret Woffington. London: 1952. Bibliog., pp. 258–61.

7939 MCASEY, C. C. Peg Woffington. *Dublin Hist. Rec.*, vol. 23, no. 1, 1969, 23–35.

7940 STEWART, IAN. A belle among the beaux: Peg Woffington's return to Dublin. *Country Life*, vol. 148, no. 3832, 1970, 804–806.

WOGAN, EDWARD.

7941 MAURICE, FREDERICK. The adventures of Edward Wogan. London: 1945. Bibliog., pp. 163–4.

WOOD-MARTIN, WILLIAM GREGORY.

7942 COLEMAN, JAMES. Obituary and bibliography. *Ir. Book Lov.*, 9, 1917–18, 87.

WRIGHT, G.N.

7943 COLEMAN, JAMES. Bibliography of Rev. G.N. Wright. Paper read before the Bibliographical Society of Ireland, October 29, 1925.

WYSE, THOMAS.

7944 AUCHMUTY, JAMES JOHNSTON. Sir Thomas Wyse, 1791–1862: the life and career of an educator and diplomat. London: 1939. Bibliog., pp. 304–11.

Y

YEATS, JACK B.

7945 MACC[ARVILL], E. Jack B. Yeats – his books. *Dublin Mag., new ser.*, vol. 20, no. 3, 1945, 47–52. See also article, *ibid.*, pp. 38–41.

7946 MCHUGH, ROGER, (*ed*). Jack B. Yeats: a centenary gathering, by Samuel Beckett, Martha Caldwell, Brian O'Doherty, Ernie O'Malley, Shotaro Oshima, Marilyn Gaddis Rose and Terence de Vere White. Dublin: Dolmen Press, 1971. *(The Tower series of Anglo-Irish studies, no. 3)* A bibliography of the published writings of Jack B. Yeats, by Martha Caldwell, pp. 110–114.

7947 MAYS, JAMES. Jack B. Yeats: some comments on his books. *Ir. Univ. Rev.*, vol. 2, no. 1, 1972, 34–54.

7948 PYLE, HILARY. 'Men of destiny' – Jack B. and W.B. Yeats: the background and the symbols. *Studies*, 66, 1977, 188–213.

7949 RYNNE, STEPHEN. Tea with Jack B. Yeats, 1940. *Eire-Ir.*, vol. 7, no. 2, 1972, 106–109.

YEATS, JOHN BUTLER.

7950 ARCHIBALD, DOUGLAS N. John Butler Yeats. Lewisburg and London: 1974. *(Irish writers series)*.

7951 Letters from Bedford Park: a selection from the correspondence (1890–1901) of John Butler Yeats. Edited with introduction by William M. Murphy. Dublin: Cuala Press, 1972. Edition of 500 copies.

7952 MURPHY, WILLIAM M. Prodigal father: the life of John Butler Yeats, (1839–1922). Ithaca and London: 1978. Bibliog., pp. 543–547.

7953 WHITE, JAMES. John Butler Yeats and the Irish Renaissance, with pictures from the collection of Michael Butler Yeats and from the National Gallery of Ireland. Dublin: The Dolmen Press, 1972.

YEATS, WILLIAM BUTLER.

7954 Bibliography. *New Camb. Bibliog. Eng. Lit.*, 3, 1969, 1110, 1915–34.

7955 ADLARD, JOHN. An unnoticed Yeats item. *N. and Q., new ser.*, 16, 1969, 255.

7956 ALSPACH, RUSSELL K. Additions to Allan Wade's *Bibliography of W.B. Yeats. Ir. Book*, 2, 1963, 91–114.

7957 BJERSBY, BIRGIT. The interpretation of the Cuchulain legend in the works of W.B. Yeats. Upsala and Dublin: 1950. *(Upsala Irish studies,* no. 1). Bibliog., pp. 175–83.

7958 BLACK, HESTER M. William Butler Yeats: a catalog of an exhibition from the P.S. O'Hegarty collection in the University of Kansas Library. Lawrence: 1958.

7959 BRAMSBACK, BIRGIT. William Butler Yeats and folklore material. *Bealoideas*, 39–41, 1971–73, 56–68.

7960 BROWN, T.J. English literary autographs XLIX: William Butler Yeats, 1865–1939. *Book Coll.*, 13, 1964, 53.

7961 CARDEN, MARY. The few and the many: an examination of W.B. Yeats's politics. *Studies*, 58, 1969, 51–62.

7962 CROSS, K.G.W. and DUNLOP, R.T. A bibliography of Yeats's criticism, 1887–1965. London: 1971.

7963 DOLMEN PRESS YEATS CENTENARY PAPERS MCMLXV. Dublin, 1–12, 1965–68.

7964 DOUGAN R.O., *compiler*. W.B. Yeats: manuscripts and printed books exhibited in the Library of Trinity College, Dublin, 1956. Dublin: 1956.

7965 EASTON, MALCOLM. T. Sturge Moore and W.B. Yeats. *Apollo*, vol. 92, no. 104, 1970, 298–300.

7966 Exhibition catalogue: W.B. Yeats: images of a poet. May 3 to June 3, 1961, Whitworth Art Gallery, University of Manchester. June 17 to July 1, 1961. An Chomhairle Earlion, The Building Centre, Dublin, 1961, Books and Mss. catalogue, pp. 131–50.

7967 FINNERAN, RICHARD J. W.B. Yeats and Wilfrid Scawen Blunt: a misattribution. *Ir. Univ. Rev.*, vol. 8, no. 2, 1978, 203–207.

7968 — Letters to W.B. Yeats, edited by Richard J. Finneran, George Mills Harper, William M. Murphy, with the assistance of Alan B. Himber. London: 1977. 2 vols.

7969 FITZPATRICK, DAVID. Yeats in the Senate. *Stud. Hib.*, 12, 1972, 7–26.

7970 FRAYNE, JOHN P. *ed.* Uncollected prose of W.B. Yeats. London. vol. 1. First reviews and articles, 1886–1896, 1970. vol. 2, Reviews, articles and other miscellaneous prose, 1897–1939, 1975.

7971 HALL, JAMES and STEINMANN, MARTIN *eds.* The permanence of Yeats. New York: 1961. A select bibliography of articles and books, in whole or in part, on Yeats, pp. 349–71.

7972 HANLEY, MARY. Thoor Ballylee – home of William Butler Yeats, edited by Liam Miller from a paper given by Mary Hanley to the Kiltartan Society in 1961. With a foreword by T.R. Henn. Dublin: 1965.

7973 HARPER, GEORGE MILLS. Yeats's Golden Dawn. London: 1974.

7974 HONE, JOSEPH. W.B. Yeats, a bio-bibliography. *Ir. Lib. Bull., new ser.*, 9, 1948, 167–72.

7975 — W.B. Yeats, 1865–1939. 2nd ed. London: 1962. Prev. ed. 1943.

7976 THE IRISH BOOK. vol. 2, nos. 3–4, 1963. Special Yeats Issue. Contents; Two letters to John O'Leary, by W.B. Yeats. – W.B. Yeats and Edward Calvert, by Raymond Lister – The Dun Emer Press, by Liam Miller. – Additions to Allan Wade's Bibliography of W.B. Yeats, by Russell K. Alspach. – Yeats as reviewer: The Bookman, 1892–1899, by Peter Faulkner.– The Yeats Memorial Museum, Sligo, by Nora Niland.

7977 JEFFARES, A. NORMAN. An account of recent Yeatsiana. *Hermathena*, 72, 1948, 21–43.

7978 — W.B. Yeats: man and poet. London: 1949. Bibliog., pp. 339–50.

7979 — The circus animals: essays on W.B. Yeats. London: 1970.

7980 — W.B. Yeats. London: 1971. Appendix: Some biographical details, pp. 107–112; bibliog., pp. 113–118.

7981 — and CROSS, K.G.W., *eds*. In excited reverie: a centenary tribute to William Butler Yeats, 1865–1939. London and New York: 1965.

7982 JOCHUM, K.P.S. W.B. Yeats: a classified bibliography of criticism: including additions to Allan Wade's *Bibliography of the writings of W.B. Yeats* and a section on the Irish literary and dramatic revival. London and Urbana: 1978.

7983 JOHNSON, COLTON. Some unnoticed contributions to periodicals by W.B. Yeats. *N. and Q.*, 217, 1972, 48–52.

7984 JOHNSTON, DILLON. The perpetual self of Yeats's autobiographies. *Eire-Ir.*, vol. 9, no. 4, 1974, 69–85.

7985 JOURNAL OF IRISH LITERATURE. vol. 5, no. 2, 1976. Special issue on W.B. Yeats and his critics.

7986 KAIN, RICHARD M. The status of Yeats's scholarship. *Eire-Ir.*, vol. 2, no. 3, 1967, 102–110.

7987 KIRBY, SHEELAH. The Yeats country; a guide to places in the west of Ireland associated with the life and writings of William Butler Yeats. 2nd ed. rev. Dublin: 1963.

7988 LISTER, RAYMOND. W.B. Yeats and Edward Calvert. *Ir. Book*, 2, 1963, 72–80.

7989 MCGARRY, JAMES P. *ed.* Place names in the writings of William Butler Yeats, by James P. McGarry, edited and with additional material by Edward Malins, and a preface by Kathleen Raine. Gerrards Cross: 1976. Bibliog., pp. 92–3.

7990 MCHUGH, ROGER, *ed.* W.B. Yeats's letters to Katharine Tynan. Dublin: 1953. Bibliog., pp. 185–6.

7991 — *ed.*, Ah! sweet dancer: W.B. Yeats, Margot Ruddock: a correspondence. London: 1970. Bibliog., pp. 135–6.

7992 MACLIAMMOIR, MICHAEL and BOLAND, EAVAN. W.B. Yeats and his world. London: 1971.

7993 MARCUS, PHILLIP L. Yeats and the beginning of the Irish Renaissance. Ithaca and London: 1970.

7994 MIKHAIL, E.H. *ed.* W.B. Yeats: interviews and recollections. London: 1977. 2 vols.

7995 MURPHY, WILLIAM M. Father and son: the early education of William Butler Yeats. *Rev. Eng. Lit.*, vol. 8, no. 4, 1967, 75–96.

7996 NATIONAL GALLERY OF IRELAND. W.B. Yeats: a centenary exhibition. Dublin: 1965. Bibliog., pp. 7–9.

7997 NEW YEATS PAPERS. Dublin. 1–, 1971–.

7998 NILAND, NORA. The Yeats Memorial Museum, Sligo. *Ir. Book*, 2, 1963, 122–126.

7999 O'HAODHA, MICHAEL. When was Yeats first published? *Eire-Ir.*, vol. 2, no. 2, 1967, 67–71.

8000 O'HEGARTY, P.S. Notes on the bibliography of W.B. Yeats. No. 1: Notes on, and supplemental to, the existing bibliographies by Mr. Allan Wade and Mr. A.J.A. Symons, 1886–1922. *Dublin Mag., new ser.*, vol. 14, no. 4, 1939, 61–5. No. 2: A hand-list, 1922–39, to complete Symons. *ibid.*, vol. 15, no. 1, 1940, 37–42.

8001 REID, FORREST. W.B. Yeats: a critical study. London: 1915. Bibliog., pp. 253–8.

8002 ROSE, SHIRLEY. Dorothy Richardson recalls Yeats. *Eire-Ir.*, vol. 7, no. 1, 1972, 96–102.

8003 ROTH, WILLIAM M. A catalogue of English and American first editions of William Butler Yeats; prepared for an exhibition of his works held in the Yale University Library, beginning May 15, 1939. New Haven [Portland, Maine], 1939. A partial list of essays and poems in periodicals, pp. 81–104.

8004 SAUL, GEORGE BRANDON. Prolegomena to the study of Yeats's poems. Philadelphia and London: 1957.

8005 — Prolegomena to the study of Yeats's plays. Philadelphia and London: 1958.

8006 SKELTON, ROBIN, and SADDLEMYER, ANN. *ed.* The world of W.B. Yeats: a symposium and catalogue. Dublin: 1965.

8007 STOLL, JOHN E. The great deluge: a Yeats bibliography. Troy (N.Y.): 1971.

8008 SYMONS, A.J.A. A bibliography of the first editions of books by William Butler Yeats. London: First Edition Club, 1924.

8009 WADE, ALLAN. A bibliography of the writings of W.B. Yeats. 3rd ed. rev. and edited by Russell K. Alspach. London: 1968. *(Soho bibliographies, no. 1)* For *errata* and *addenda*, see *Longroom*, 8, 1973, 41–2.

8010 WEBSTER, BRENDA S. Yeats: a psychoanalytic study. London: 1974.

8011 YEATS STUDIES: an international journal, edited by Robert O'Driscoll. Shannon: 1971. Nos. 1–2, 1971–2.

YOUNG, ELLA.

8012 LYNAM, W.W. Ella Young: a memoir. *Eire-Ir.*, vol. 8, no. 3, 1975, 65–69.

YOUNG, MATTHEW.

8013 BLACKER, BEAVER H. The writings of Matthew Young, D.D., Bishop of Clonfert. *Ir. Eccles. Gaz.,* 1876, 180–1.

YOUNGE, MARIANNE. (*i.e.*, M.A. Rathkyle.)

8014 Bibliography. *Ir. Book Lov.*, 8, 1916–17, 144.

Z

ZOZIMUS. (*i.e.* Michael Moran).

8015 Memoir of the great original Zozimus (Michael Moran), the celebrated Dublin street rhymer and reciter, with his songs, sayings and recitations, by Gulielmus Dubliniensis Humoriensis; a facsimile edition with an introduction by Dr. Thomas Wall. Blackrock: 1976. *(Carraig chapbooks, 6*). First published 1871.

8016 MCCALL, P.J. Zozimus. *Dublin Hist. Rec.*, 7, 1944–45, 134–149.

GENEALOGY, HERALDRY

8017 BARRY J. Guide to records of the Genealogical office, Dublin: with a commentary on heraldry in Ireland and on the history of the Office. *Anal. Hib.*, 26, 1970, 1–43.

8018 BLACK, J. ANDERSON. Your Irish ancestors. London and New York: 1974. Bibliog., pp. 250–1.

8019 BURKE, *Sir* JOHN BERNARD. A genealogical and heraldic history of the commoners of Great Britain and Ireland, enjoying territorial possessions on high official rank; but uninvested with heritable honours. London: 1835–38. 4 vols.

8020 — A genealogical and heraldic history of the landed gentry of Ireland: new rev. ed. by A.C. Fox-Davies. London: 1912.

8021 CLARE, *The Rev*. WALLACE. Irish genealogy. *Geneal. Mag.,* June, 1932, pp. 43–9. Gives an account of the more important records in existence which are of value.

8022 — A simple guide to Irish genealogy. 3rd rev. ed. by Rosemary Ffolliott. London: 1966. Bibliog., pp. 31–43.

8023 DE BREFFNY, BRIAN, *compiler*. Bibliography of Irish family history and genealogy. Cork and Dublin: 1974.

8024 DENNY, H.L.L. Anglo-Irish genealogy; a paper read before the Society of Genealogists of London, May 1916.

8025 FALLEY, MARGARET DICKSON. Genealogical research in Ireland: a survey made in 1951. [Evanston, Ill.] 1952. Copy in National Library, Ireland.

8026 — Irish and Scotch-Irish ancestral research: a guide to the genealogical records, methods and sources in Ireland. Evanston, Ill. [1962]. 2 vols.

8027 FILBY, P. WILLIAM, *compiler*. American and British genealogy and heraldry: a selected list of books. 2nd ed. Chicago: 1975. Ireland., pp. 310–20.

8028 GATFIELD, GEORGE. Guide to printed books and manuscripts relating to English and foreign heraldry and genealogy, being a classified catalogue of works of those branches of literature. London: 1892. 300 copies printed.

8029 HARRISON, H.G. A select bibliography of English genealogy, with brief lists for Wales, Scotland and Ireland: a manual for students. London: 1937. Ireland, pp. 151–9.

8030 HERALDIC ARTISTS LTD. Handbook on Irish genealogy: how to trace your ancestors and relatives in Ireland. Enl. ed., Dublin: 1976.

8031 THE IRISH ANCESTOR, edited by Rosemary Ffolliott. Dublin. vol. 1–, 1969–.

8032 JOURNAL OF THE BUTLER SOCIETY. Kilkenny, vol. 1–, 1968–.

8033 'LIBRARIAN, THE'. Subject guide to books. Vol. 2, Biography, family history, heraldry, genealogy, etc. London: 1960.

8034 MARSHALL, GEORGE W. The Genealogist's guide. 4th ed. Guildford: 1903. Privately printed. For continuation see *A genealogical guide,* by J.B. Whitmore.

8035 MORAN, T. WHITLEY. The Fermanagh genealogies: a provisional English index to the pedigrees. *Ir. Geneal.*, vol. 5, no. 3, 1976, 290–7.

8036 — The mediaeval Gaelic genealogies. *Ir. Geneal.*, vol. 4, no. 4, 1971, 267–274; vol. 4, no. 5, 1972, 417–428; vol. 5, no. 1, 1974, 5–20.

8037 MOULE, THOMAS. Bibliotheca heraldica Magnae Britanniae: an analytical catalogue of books on genealogy, heraldry, etc. London: 1822.

8038 NICHOLLS, K.W. The Irish genealogies: their value and defects. *Ir. Geneal.*, vol. 5, no. 2, 1975, 256–261.

8039 O'BRIEN, M.A., *ed.* Corpus genealogiarum Hiberniae. Dublin, vol. 1, 1962.

8040 PENDER. S. A guide to Irish genealogical collections. *Anal. Hib.*, no. 7, 1935.

8041 PINE, L.G. Your family tree: a guide to genealogical sources. London: 1962. Ireland, pp. 97–146.

8042 SURVEY OF DOCUMENTS IN PRIVATE KEEPING: 1st series, by Edward MacLysaght. *Anal. Hib.*, no. 15, 1944.

8043 — 2nd series, by John F. Ainsworth and Edward MacLysaght. *ibid.*, no. 20, 1958.

8044 — 3rd series, by John F. Ainsworth. *ibid.*, no. 25, 1967.

8045 WHITMORE, J.B., *compiler*. A genealogical guide: an index to British pedigrees, in continuation of Marshall's *Genealogist's guide*. London: 1953.

Family History

8046 BURKE'S FAMILY INDEX. London: 1976.

8047 BURKE'S IRISH FAMILY RECORDS. London: 1976.

8048 CASEY, ALBERT EUGENE, and DOWLING, THOMAS EUGENE P., *compilers*. Okief, Coshe Mang, Slieve Lougher and Upper Blackwater in Ireland. Published and bound privately for the Knocknagree Historical Fund, Birmingham, Alabama. 1952–71. 15 vols.

Vol. 2: Baptisms, marriages and deaths, baronry of Duhallow.

Vol. 3: Baptisms, marriages and deaths, barony of Duhallow and Magunihy, and distribution of surnames.

Vol. 4: North Cork and East Kerry, 1900 B.C. to A.D. 1900: births, marriages, deaths, wills, administrations, census, history, prehistory, and physical anthropometry. (Additional notes on O'Casey of Cianachta-Breagh and Lune.) Bibliog., pp. 446–52.

Vol. 5–8: Historical and genealogical items relating to North Cork and East Kerry.

Vol. 9: Annals of the Kingdom of Ireland, by the Four Masters . . . trans . . . by John O'Donovan, 1856. Vols. 1–2, and index, photocopied by A.E. Casey.

Vol. 10: The ancient and present state of the county and City of Cork [and] The ancient and present state of the county of Kerry, by Charles Smith, [and two studies on blood groups].

Vol. 11: Historical and genealogical items relating to all of Ireland, 3100 B.C. – 1499 A.D.; Counties Cork and Kerry, 1500–1799 A.D.; North Cork and East Kerry, 1800–1922.

Vol. 12: Historical and genealogical items relating to North Cork and East Kerry. Annals of the Kingdom of Ireland, by the Four Masters . . . vol. 3–5, photocopied by A.E. Casey and Nell Frances Lowery.

Vol. 13: Annals of the Kingdom of Ireland . . . vol. 6; The Irish version of the Historia Britonum of Nennius, ed. with translation by James Henthorn Todd . . . Dublin, 1848; The History of Ireland, by Geoffrey Keating, vol. 4; Annales Cambriae and old Welsh genealogies from Harleian Ms. 3859; Princes of Gwynedd, by Egerton Phillimore.

Vol. 14: Historical and genealogical items relating to North Cork and East Kerry.
Extracts from over 40 sources on baptisms, marriages, burials, abstracts of wills; and sections from Richard Griffith's General Valuation of rateable property in Ireland.

Vol 15: Historical, biographical and genealogical items relating to counties Cork and Kerry.

8049 COLLINS, JOHN T. Co. Cork families, 1630–5. *Cork Hist. Arch. Soc. J.* vol. 66, no. 204, 1961, 126–9.

8050 CRONE, J.S. Bibliography of Irish family history. *Ir. Book Lov.,* 5, 1913–14, 91–2, 110–12, 151–2, 168, 204, 223–4; 6, 1914–15, 83–4, 116.

8051 DE BREFFNY, BRIAN, *compiler*. Bibliography of Irish family history and genealogy. Cork and Dublin: 1974.

8052 DUNLEAVY, GARETH W. and DUNLEAVY, JANET EGLESON. The O'Conor papers: a descriptive catalogue and surname register of the materials at Clonalis House. Madison (Wisconsin): 1977. Clonalis, home of O'Conor Don, is situated in Castlerea, Co. Roscommon.

8053 — The catalogue of the O'Conor Papers [1575–1925]. *Studies*, 62, 1973, 205–219.

8054 — The O'Conor Papers: their significance to genealogists. *Eire-Ir.*, vol. 11, no. 2, 1976, 104–118.

8055 EDWARDS, R. DUDLEY. Irish families: the archival aspect. Dublin: 1974.

8056 GREEVES, J.R.H. The study of family history. *Ir. Comm. Hist. Sci. Bull., new ser.,* vol. 5, no. 65, 1954, 6–8.

8057 GREHAN, IDA. Irish family names: highlights of 50 family histories. London: 1973.

8058 HALLIDAY, BERNARD. Ireland and Irish families: catalogue of a special collection of books on Ireland, and a remarkable collection of original manuscripts and deeds from 1500 to 1850, relating to the principal families of Ireland . . . mostly from the collection of Rev. J. Graves . . . Leicester: 1904.

8059 HOWARD, J.J. and CRISP, F.A. *eds*. Visitation of Ireland. 1897–1917. 6 vols. Privately printed.

8060 JACKSON, DONALD. Intermarriage in Ireland, 1550–1650. Montreal: 1970. Bibliog., pp. 83–4.

8061 LECTOR, *pseud*. Irish county and family histories. *Dublin Pen. J.*, 1, 1902–3, 598–9, 628; 2, 1903–4, 24.

8062 MACLYSAGHT, EDWARD. Irish families, their names, arms and origins. 3rd ed. rev., Dublin: 1972. 1st pub. 1957. Bibliog., pp. 316–336.

8063 — More Irish families. Galway and Dublin: 1960. Bibliog. – family histories. pp. 285–8; the Irish abroad, pp. 289–90.

8064 — Supplement to Irish families. Dublin: 1964.

8065 MONTGOMERY-MASSINGBERD, HUGH. Burke's introduction to Irish ancestry. London: 1976.

8066 MULLIN, T.H. Families of Ballyrashane: a district in Northern Ireland. Belfast: 1969.

8067 O'FARRELL, JOHN. Irish families in ancient Quebec records. *Eire-Ir.*, vol. 2, no. 4, 1967, 19–35.

8068 THOMSON, T.R. *compiler*. A catalogue of British family histories. 3rd ed., London: 1976.

Surnames, Christian Names

8069 DE BREFFNY, BRIAN. Christian names in Ireland. *Ir. Ancest.*, 1, 1969, 34–40.

8070 FOX, J.R. Structure of personal names on Tory Island. *Man*, 63, 1963, 153–155.

8071 KELLY, P. *ed*. Irish family names: with origins, meanings, clans, arms, crests and mottoes, collected from the living Gaelic and from authoritative books, manuscripts and public documents: edited with introduction, notes and Gaelic script. Chicago: 1939.

8072 LIST OF BOOKS ON PERSONAL NAMES. In Best's *Bibliography of Irish Philology* . . . 1913, 17–19; 1942, 7–9.

8073 MACLYSAGHT, EDWARD. Christian names in Ireland. *Nth. Munster Antiq. J.*, 13, 1970, 53–56.

8074 — The surnames of Ireland. 3rd ed. rev. and corrected. Dublin: 1978. Bibliog. of Irish family history, pp. 305–368.

8075 MATHESON, ROBERT EDWIN. Special report on surnames in Ireland [together with] varieties and synonyms of surnames and Christian names in Ireland. Baltimore: 1968. 2 vols. in 1. Originally published 1890, 1909.

8076 REANEY, P.H. A Dictionary of British surnames; 2nd ed. with corrections and additions by R.M. Wilson. London and Boston: 1976.

8077 WOULFE, P. Sloinnte Gaedheal is gall: Irish names and surnames; collected and edited with explanatory and historical notes. Dublin: 1923. See also *Ir. Eccles. Rec., 5th ser.,* 23, 1924, 337–53.

8078 — Irish names for children. Revised by Gerard Slevin. Dublin: 1974. Orig. pub. 1923.

Registers of Wills etc. - General

8079 CARY, GEORGE S. Parish registers of St. Nicholas within, Dublin, 1671–1865. Weybread: 1939.

8080 COLEBORN, C.F. Naas Church records, 1679–1877. *Kildare Arch. Soc. J.*, vol. 14, no. 2, 1966–67, 267–268.

8081 INDEX TO BIRTHS, MARRIAGES AND DEATHS in a file of *The Hibernian Chronicle*, October 1769 to April 1802. London, Society of Genealogists, 1936.

8082 LEADER, MICHAEL. Transcripts of Co. Cork parish registers. *Ir. Geneal.*, vol. 3, no. 5, 1960, 170–172.

8083 MCAULIFFE, E.J. *compiler*. Dublin city registers of the Church of Ireland [a list]. *Ir. Geneal.*, vol. 5, no. 2, 1975, 267–9.

8084 MACCAFFREY, JAMES. [A calendar of the Catholic] parochial registers. *Arch. Hib.*, 3, 1914, 366–406.

8085 MCCLELLAND, AIKEN. Irish Presbyterian registers. *Ir. Geneal.*, vol. 3, no. 4, 1959, 144–7.

8086 — Marriage and obituary notices of literary and bibliographic interest in the Belfast press, 1801–1814. *Ir. Booklore*, vol. 3, no. 1, 1976, 15–27.

8087 MOORHOUSE, B-ANN. Notices of Irish-born persons in New York city newspapers. *Ir. Ancest.*, vol. 5, no. 1, 1973, 24–27.

8088 PARISH REGISTERS AND RELATED MATERIAL in the Public Record Office. *Rep. D.K. Pub. Rec. Ir.*, no. 58, 1951, 116–19.

8089 REPORT ON THE TRANSCRIPTION AND PUBLICATION OF PARISH REGISTERS, etc. *R. Soc. Antiq. Ir. J.,* 22, 1892, supplement to appendix, pp. 1–16.

8090 SOCIETY OF GENEALOGISTS. Catalogue of the parish registers in the possession of the Society of Genealogists. 3rd ed. London: 1970.

Wills

8091 BERRY, HENRY F. Register of wills and inventories of the diocese of Dublin in the time of Archbishops Tregury and Walton, 1457–83 . . . Dublin, 1898. *(R. Soc. Antiq. Ir.,* extra volume for 1896–7.). Bibliog., pp. 241–4.

8092 CARY, GEORGE S. Index to the wills of the diocese of Kildare in the Public Record Office of Ireland. *Kildare Arch. Soc. J.,* 4, 1903–5, 473–91.

8093 CLARE, WALLACE, *ed*. A guide to copies and abstracts of Irish wills, 1st ser. March, Cambridgeshire: 1930. (*Ir. geneal. guides,* no. 1).

8094 EUSTACE, P. BERYL. Registry of Deeds, Dublin: abstracts of wills. Dublin, Irish Manuscripts Commission, 1954–6. 2 vols.. Vol. 1. 1708–45; Vol. 2, 1746–85.

8095 — Index of will abstracts in the Genealogical Office, Dublin. *Anal. Hib.*, 17, 1949, 147–348.

8096 INDEX TO ARDAGH WILLS. Supplement to the *Irish Ancestor*, 1971.

8097 INDEXES TO IRISH WILLS.
Vol. 1: Ossory, Leighlin, Ferns, Kildare; by W.P. Phillimore. 1909.
Vol. 2: Cork and Ross, Cloyne; by W.P.W. Phillimore. 1910.
Vol. 3: Cashel and Emly, Waterford and Lismore, Killaloe and Kilfenora, Limerick, Ardfert, and Aghadoe; by Gertrude Thrift. 1913.
Vol. 4: Dromore, Newry and Mourne; by Gertrude Thrift. 1918.
Vol. 5: Derry and Raphoe; by Gertrude Thrift. 1920.
Reprinted, 5 vols. in one, Genealogical Pub. Co., Baltimore: 1970.

8098 KILDARE DIOCESAN WILLS. *Kildare Arch. Soc. J.*, 12, 1935–45, 115–23, 188–9, 222–5, 269–72, 330–1, 425–7.

8099 LIST OF ORIGINAL PROBATES, etc. and official copies of wills, grants, etc., presented, 1928; wills in salved prerogative will books, and wills and grants of administration in salved Down and Connor will and grant books. *Rep. D. K. Pub. Rec. Ir.*, no. 56, 1931, 79–202.

8100 SMYTHE-WOOD, PATRICK. Index to Kilmore diocesan wills. Stroud: 1975. Privately printed.

8101 TESTAMENTARY, MATRIMONIAL AND ECCLESIASTICAL DOCUMENTS.
A. List of original probates, etc., and official copies of wills, grants, etc.
B. List of original unproved wills (never lodged for probate), duplicates of wills and plain copies of wills, grants, etc.
Rep. D.K. Pub. Rec. Ir., no. 57, 1936, 62–467.

8102 VICARS, ARTHUR. Index to the prerogative wills of Ireland, 1536–1810. Dublin: 1897.

Births

8103 LIST OF PARISHES, for which parochial returns of baptisms, etc., made annually to the Bishops' visitations, are preserved in the Public Record Office, which to some extent supply defects of the parish registers. *Rep. D.K. Pub. Rec. Ir.,* no. 41, 1909, 26–33.

8104 LIST OF PARISHES OF THE FORMER ESTABLISHED CHURCH OF IRELAND, the registers of baptisms of which are preserved in the Public Record Office of Ireland. *Rep. D.K. Pub. Rec. Ir.,* no. 41, 1909, 16–25.

8105 TURNER, BRIAN S. The Methodist baptismal registers of County Louth, 1829–1865. *Louth Arch. J.*, vol. 18, no. 2, 1974, 132–139.

8106 FARRAR, HENRY. Irish marriages, being an index to the marriages in *Walker's Hibernian Magazine,* 1771 to 1812; with an appendix from the notes of Sir Arthur Vicars . . . of the births, marriages, and deaths in *The Anthologia Hibernica*, 1793 and 1794. Phillimore, 1897. 2 vols. Seventy-five copies privately printed.

8107 FFOLLIOTT, ROSEMARY. Index to Raphoe marriage licence bonds, 1710–1755 and 1817–1830. Supplement to the *Irish Ancestor*, 1969.

8108 — Indexes to Clonfert marriage licence bonds, wills and administration bonds. Supplement to the *Irish Ancestor*, 1970.

8109 GILLMAN, HERBERT WEBB. Index to the marriage licence bonds of the diocese of Cork and Ross, Ireland, for the years from 1623 to 1750. Appendix to *Cork Hist. Arch. Soc. J., 2nd ser.* vol. 2, 1896. Also published separately.

8110 LINN, RICHARD, *ed*. Marriage register of the Presbyterian congregation of Banbridge, Co. Down, 1756–94. *R. Soc. Antiq. Ir. J.,* 39, 1909, 75–84.

8111 O'GRADY, GUILLAMORE. Index to Kildare marriage licence bonds. *Kildare Arch. Soc. J.*, 11, 1930–5, 43–58, 114–33; 12, 1935–45, 12–29, 74–98.

8112 STANLEY-TORNEY, HENRY C. Ferns marriage licences. *Kildare Arch. Soc. J.*, 9, 1918–21, 34–59, 178–90, 227–45, 292–300, 366–75, 454–6; 10, 1922–8, 29–31, 61–99, 125–49, 174–94.

8113 WOOD, HERBERT. Report on certain registers of irregular marriages celebrated by unlicensed clergymen, known as couple-beggars. *Rep. D.K. Pub. Rec. Ir.*, no. 34, 1902, 22–9.

Deaths

8114 ASSOCIATION FOR THE PRESERVATION OF THE MEMORIALS OF THE DEAD IN IRELAND. Journal, 1888–1920. *Afterwards* Journal of the Irish Memorials Association, 1921–1937.

8115 CANTWELL, BRIAN, *compiler*. Memorials of the dead in North-East Wicklow. *Ir. Geneal.*, vol. 5, no. 1, 1974, 140. Bound volume containing 2027 inscriptions is in the library of the Irish Genealogical Research Society.

8116 CLARKE, R.S.J., *compiler*. Gravestone inscriptions. Belfast: Ulster-Scot Historical Foundation. Vol. 1–, 1966–.

8117 HENCHION, R. The gravestone inscriptions of Co. Cork. *Cork Arch. Hist. Soc. J.*, 72–, 1967–.

8118 AN INDEX TO THE BIOGRAPHICAL AND OBITUARY NOTICES in *The Gentleman's Magazine,* 1731–80. London: 1891. *(Index Soc.,* vol. 15.)

8119 INDEX OF THE CHURCHYARDS AND BUILDINGS, from which inscriptions on tombs and mural slabs have appeared in the *Journal of the Association for the Preservation of the Memorials of the Dead in Ireland,* 1888 to 1908 inclusive. Dublin: 1909.

8120 **Musgrave, William.** A general nomenclator and obituary prior to 1800 so far as the same relates to England, Scotland and Ireland. London: 1899–1901. 6 vols. (*Harleian Soc. pub.*, nos. 44–9.)

8121 **Walker's Hibernian Magazine.** Index to deaths in Walker's Hibernian Magazine, vols. 1–35. Compiled by M. Burke, P. Hanlon, J. McKenna, L. Cully and E. Clossick for Fellowship of the Library Association of Ireland.

Heraldry

8122 **Cope, S. Trehearne.** Heraldry, flags and seals: a select bibliography, with annotations, covering the period 1920 to 1945. *J. Document.,* vol. 4, no. 2, 1948, 92–146.

8123 **Skey, William A.** The Heraldic Calendar: a list of the nobility and gentry whose arms are registered and pedigrees recorded in the Heralds' Office in Ireland. Dublin: 1846.

Crests, Bearings

8124 **Burke, Bernard.** The general armory of England, Scotland, Ireland and Wales; comprising a registry of armorial bearings from the earliest times to the present time, with a supplement. [1884 ed. reprinted.] London: 1961. 1st ed. 1842.

8125 **Fairbairn, J.** Fairbairn's Book of Crests of the families of Great Britain and Ireland. 4th ed. rev. and enl. by A.C. Fox-Davies. Edinburgh: 1905. 2 vols. 1st ed. 1859.

8126 **Fox-Davies, A.C.** The book of public arms: a complete encyclopaedia of all royal, territorial, municipal, corporate, official and impersonal arms. London: 1915. 1st ed. 1894.

8127 **Papworth, J.W. and Morant, A.W.W.** An alphabetical dictionary of coats of arms belonging to families in Great Britain and Ireland; forming an extensive ordinary of British armorials . . . London: 1874.

Flags

8128 **Hayes-McCoy, Gerald A.** A history of Irish flags from earliest times. Dublin: 1979.

8129 **Snoddy, Oliver.** Fenian flags. *Ir. Sword*, vol. 8, no. 30, 1967, 1–9.

Nobility

8130 **Beatson, Robert.** A political index to the histories of Great Britain and Ireland; or, a complete register of the hereditary honours, public offices, and persons in office from the earliest periods to the present time. 3rd ed. London: 1806. 3 vols.

8131 **Burke, Bernard.** A genealogical history of the dormant, abeyant, forfeited and extinct peerages of the British Empire. [1st ed. reprinted] London: 1969.

8132 — and **Burke, J.** A genealogical and heraldic history of the extinct and dormant baronetcies of England, Ireland and Scotland. 2nd ed. London: 1844.

8133 — Burke's Genealogical and heraldic history of the landed gentry of Ireland. New ed., edited by L.G. Pine. London: 1958.

8134 **Cokayne, G.E.** The complete peerage; or, A history of the House of Lords and all its members from the earliest times. Rev. ed. London, vol. 1–, 1910–.

8135 **O'Hart, John.** Irish pedigrees; or, the origin and stem of the Irish nation. 5th ed. Dublin: 1892. 2 vols. Reprinted Baltimore: 1976.

8136 — The Irish and Anglo-Irish landed gentry when Cromwell came to Ireland; or, supplement to *Irish pedigrees*. Dublin: 1892. Bibliogs., pp. xviii, 1–3.

8137 **Pine, L.G.** The new extinct peerage, 1884–1971. London: 1972.

8138 **Solly, Edward,** *compiler*. An index of hereditary English, Scottish and Irish titles of honour. London: 1880. (*Index Soc.,* vol. 5.)

8139 **Young, Charles George.** Catalogue of works on the peerage of England, Scotland, and Ireland, in the library of C.G. Young. 2nd ed. London: 1828. 1st ed. 1826. Privately printed.

Templars

8140 **MacNiocaill, G.** Documents relating to the suppression of the Templars in Ireland. *Anal. Hib.*, 24, 1967, 183–226.

8141 **Wood, Herbert.** The Templars in Ireland. *R. Ir. Acad. Proc. Sec. C.*, 26, 1906–7, 327–377. Appendix A lists Possessions of Templars in Ireland.

HISTORY

Bibliography

8142 AMERICAN HISTORICAL ASSOCIATION. Guide to historical literature. New York: 1961. Ireland, pp. 437–9.

8143 ANNUAL BIBLIOGRAPHY OF BRITISH AND IRISH HISTORY. Hassocks, 1975–.

8144 [BIBLIOGRAPHY for] those who intend writing a historical paper, whether on a locality, a family, or antiquities . . . *Louth Arch. J.*, vol. 1, no. 3, 1906, 91–2.

8145 BOOK ASSOCIATION OF IRELAND. Catalogue of Irish historical books published during the period 1934–44. *Ir. Lib. Bull.*, vol. 5, no. 3, 1944, pp. xxxi–xxxiv.

8146 BRADY, JOHN. Some of the sources of local history. *Irisleabhair Muighe Nuadhat*, 1946, 15–18.

8147 BUCKLEY, K. The records of the Irish Land Commission as a source of historical reference. *Ir. Hist. Stud.*, 8, 1952–3, 28–36.

8148 CLARK, G. KITSON, and ELTON, G.R. Guide to research facilities in history in the universities of Great Britain and Ireland. 2nd ed. Cambridge: 1965.

8149 COLLECTANEA HIBERNICA: sources for Irish history. Dublin: no. 1-, 1958-.

8150 CONDON, JOHN. A short bibliography of Irish history. *An Leab.,* vol. 1, no. 1, 1905, 40–52; no. 2, 1905, 85–95; vol 2, no. 1, 1906, 48–63; no. 2, 1907, 148–59; vol. 3, no. 1, 1909, 47–69.

8151 COULTER, EDITH M., and GERSTENFELD, MELANIE. Historical bibliographies: a systematic and annotated guide. Berkeley: 1935.

8152 CURTIS, EDMUND, and MCDOWELL, R.B., *eds*. Irish historical documents, 1172–1922. London: 1943.

8153 D'ALTON, JOHN. Brief essay on the native annals and other sources for illustrating the history and topography of Ireland. [Dublin, 1845].

8154 – Catalogue of the manuscript indexes and compilations of John D'Alton. Dublin, n.d. Copy in National Library, Dublin.

8155 DARWIN, KENNETH. Sources for townland history. *Ulster Folklife*, 3, 1957, 55–63.

8156 FREWER, LOUIS B. Bibliography of historical writings published in Great Britain and the Empire, 1940–5. Oxford: 1947. See also no. 8171.

8157 GHALL, SEAN, *pseud.* Bibliography of Irish history. *Ir. Book Lov.*, 13, 1921–2, 73–4.

8158 GLEESON, DERMOT F. Sources for local history in the period 1200–1700. *Cork Hist. Arch. Soc. J., 2nd ser.,* 46, 1941, 123–9.

8159 — Your parish and its history, including how to write a parish history. *Ir. Eccles Rec.,* 93, 1960, 1–18.

8160 GRAVES, EDGAR B. A Bibliography of English history to 1485, based on *The Sources and literature of English history from the earliest times to about 1485,* by Charles Gross. Oxford: 1975.

8161 GREAT BRITAIN. H.M. Stationery Office. Catalogue of English, Scottish and Irish Record publications, etc. London: 1911.

8162 HALL, HUBERT. List and index of the publications of the Royal Historical Society, 1871–1924, and of the Camden Society, 1840–97. London: 1925.

8163 HARDY, THOMAS DUFFUS. Descriptive catalogue of materials relating to the history of Great Britain and Ireland to the end of the reign of Henry VII. London: Rolls series, 1862–71. 3 vols. in 4.

8164 HAYES, R.J. Irish historical sources in foreign archives. *Archivalische Zeitschrift*, vols. 50–1, 1955, 235–6.

8165 HELPS FOR STUDENTS OF HISTORY, vol. 7, (nos. 7, 32–35). Irish records and history. London: 1918–1924. Reprinted: London 1969.
No. 7. A short guide to the principal classes of documents preserved in the Public Record Office, Dublin, by the Rev. Robert H. Murray.
No. 32. A short guide to some manuscripts in the library of Trinity College, Dublin, by the Rev. Robert H. Murray.
No. 33. Ireland, 1494–1603, by the Rev. Robert H. Murray.
No. 34. Ireland, 1603–1714, by the Rev. Robert H. Murray.

No. 35. Ireland, 1714–1829, by the Rev. Robert H. Murray.

8166 HISTORICAL ABSTRACTS, 1775–1945: a quarterly of abstracts of historical articles appearing currently in periodicals the world over. New York, vol. 1-, 1955-.

8167 HOARE, RICHARD C. A catalogue of books relating to the history and topography of England, Wales, Scotland and Ireland, compiled from his library at Stourhead in Wiltshire. London: 1815.

8168 — Catalogue of the Hoare Library at Stourhead, Co. Wilts . . . [compiled by J.B. Nichols]. London: 1840. This includes the greater part of the catalogue printed in 1815 which was limited to 25 copies.

8169 INTERNATIONAL COMMITTEE OF HISTORICAL SCIENCES. International bibliography of historical sciences. vol. 1-, 1926-, Washington, 1930-.

8170 JOHNSTON, EDITH M. Irish history: a select bibliography. London: 1969. *(Helps for students of History no. 73)*

8171 LANCASTER, JOAN C. *compiler*. Bibliography of historical works issued in the United Kingdom, 1946–56. London: Institute of Historical Research: 1957. See also no. 8156.

8172 LEE, GUY CARLETON. Leading documents of English history, together with illustrative material from contemporary writers and a bibliography of sources. London: 1900.

8173 LIBRARIAN, THE. Subject guide to books. Vol. 1. History, travel and description, edited by Lionel R. McColvin. London: 1959.

8174 LOUGH, THOMAS. The Irish library of the Rt. Hon. T. Lough, presented to the Breifnian Antiquarian Society, by his wife. *Breifny Antiq. Soc. J.*, 1, 1922, 342–3. Lists 140 items.

8175 MACARTHUR, WILLIAM. Bibliography of histories of Irish counties and towns. *N. and Q., 11th ser.,* 11, 1915, 103–4, 183–4, 315–16; 12, 1915, 24–5, 210, 276–7, 375–6; *12th ser.*, 1, 1916, 422–4; 2, 1916, 22–4, 141–2, 246–7, 286–7, 406–7, 445–6, 522–4.

8176 [MACRAY, WILLIAM DUNN.] A manual of British historians to A.D. 1600; containing a chronological account of the early chroniclers and monkish writers, their printed works and unpublished Mss. London: 1845. Bibliog., pp. xi–xv.

8177 MARSH'S LIBRARY, DUBLIN. Ms. catalogue of the Irish historical Mss. in Marsh's Library, Dublin: 1864. See sale catalogue of D.H. Kelly, 1875.

8178 MAXWELL, CONSTANTIA. A brief bibliography of Irish history. Dublin: 1911.

8179 — A short bibliography of Irish history. London: Historical Association, 1921.

8180 — A short book list on Irish, Scottish and Welsh history. Compiled by C. Maxwell, W. Croft Dickinson and David Williams. London: 1952. *(Historical Association teaching of history leaflet*, no. 11.)

8181 MOODY, T.W., *ed*. Irish historiography, 1936–70. Dublin: 1971. Chapters I–VII were first published in *Irish Historical Studies* in 1967–8 and 1970 as a series entitled 'Thirty years work in Irish history'.

8182 MULVEY, HELEN FRANCES. Modern Irish history since 1940: a bibliographical survey, 1600–1922. *Historian*, 17, 1964–5, 516–59.

8183 NICOLSON, WILLIAM, *Archbishop of Cashel*. The Irish historical library, pointing at most of the authors and records in print or manuscript, which may be serviceable to the compilers of a general history of Ireland. Dublin: 1724. Also published with English and Scotch libraries in 1736, 1776, 1796.

8184 NOLAN, WILLIAM. Sources for local studies. [Dublin, 1977].

8185 O'CURRY, EUGENE. Lectures on the manuscript materials of ancient Irish history; delivered at the Catholic University of Ireland during the sessions of 1855 and 1856. Dublin: 1861. Reprinted 1873.

8186 O'NEILL, THOMAS P. Sources of Irish Local history. 1st series. Dublin: 1958. First appeared in *An Leab.*; covers early historical sources, ecclesiastical records, legal records, maps and surveys, newspapers, pictures [engravings, drawings, photographs], descriptive works, British parliamentary papers.

8187 PAETOW, LOUIS JOHN. A guide to the study of medieval history. Rev. ed. prepared under the auspices of the Mediaeval Academy of America. London: 1931. 1st ed. 1917.

8188 PENDER, SEAMUS. How to study local history. *Cork Hist. Arch. Soc. J., 2nd ser.,* 46, 1941, 110–22.

8189 REPORT OF SEARCHES for originals, records, and manuscript copies of charters and statutes in England and Ireland. London, Commissioner upon the Public Records of the Kingdom, 1806. Period covered, 1200–1702.

8190 ROYAL HISTORY SOCIETY. Writings on British history: a bibliography of books and articles on the history of Great Britain from about A.D. 450 to 1914, published during the year . . . with an appendix containing a select list of publications . . . on British history since 1914, compiled by Alexander Taylor Milne. vol. 1-, 1934-. London: 1937-.

8191 STOKES, GEORGE THOMAS. Some worthies of the Irish Church . . . London: 1900. The sources of local history, pp. 337–47.

8192 WARE, JAMES. The history of the writers of Ireland . . . translated, revised and improved . . . and continued down to the beginnings of the present century, by Walter Harris. Dublin: 1764. 2 vols. *See also* Sir James Ware, historian and antiquary (1594–1666): an address delivered in Trinity College, Dublin, June 1932. Dublin: 1933.

8193 WILLIAMS, T. DESMOND, *ed.* Historical studies: papers read before the second Irish conference of historians. London: 1958. Contains *The Sources for medieval Anglo-Irish history,* by E. St. John Brooks, pp. 86–92; *Bibliographical note on medieval Anglo-Irish history*, by Aubrey Gwynn, pp. 93–9.

Periodicals

8194 AMERICAN IRISH HISTORICAL SOCIETY. Journal. New York, vol. 1-, 1898-.

8195 ANGLO-IRISH STUDIES. Chalfont St. Giles (Bucks.) vol. 1-, 1975-. Pub. annually.

8196 CARON, P. and JARYC, M., *ed.* World list of historical periodicals and bibliographies. Oxford: International Committee of Historical Sciences, 1939.

8197 IRISH COMMITTEE OF HISTORICAL SCIENCES. Bulletin. Dublin: 1st ser., no. 1-, 1939-. Indexes, nos. 1–33, 1939–44; nos. 34–59, 1944–8. Typescript.

8198 IRISH HISTORICAL STUDIES. Dublin, vol. 1-, 1938-. Contains annual list of current writings in Irish history from 1936 to date. *See also* The first forty years, by T.W. Moody, vol. 20, no. 80, 1977, 377–383. Supplement I, 1968. Contents: Index to *Irish Historical Studies* vols. i-xv: contributors and subjects, works reviewed or noticed, by Esther Semple. – Rules for contributors to *Irish Historical Studies*, revised edition. Appendix: list of bibliographical abbreviations and short titles, by T.W. Moody. – Corrigenda in *Irish Historical Studies*, vols. i-xv.

8199 O'DUFAIGH, SEOSAMH. Irish local historical and archaeological journals. *Eire-Ir.*, vol. 5, no. 3, 1970, 90–99. Details of 22 journals (with locations) which have been in publication subsequent to 1960.

Public Records

8200 AN ACCOUNT OF THE PROCEEDINGS taken for the recovery, arrangement, and preservation of the public records of Ireland. *Monthly Museum*, 1, 1814, 397–9; 2, 1814, 140–2.

8201 BELL, J. BOWYER. Contemporary Irish archival resources. *Admin.*, 18, 1970, 174–178. Discusses the availability of contemporary archives.

8202 BURKE, BERNARD. Returns relating to Record publications, Ireland . . . published up to the end of the year 1866. Returned by Sir Bernard J. Burke, Ulster King of Arms. Ordered by House of Commons to be printed, December 2, 1867.

8203 CHART, D.A. The Public Record Office of Northern Ireland, 1924–36. *Ir. Hist. Stud.*, 1, 1938–39, 42–57.

8204 DARWIN, KENNETH. The Public Record Office of Northern Ireland. *Archives*, 6, 1963–64, 108–116.

8205 — The Public Record Office of Northern Ireland. *Ir. Ancest.*, 1, 1969, 11–16.

8206 GARSTIN, JOHN RIBTON. List of documents transferred from Armagh Diocesan Registry to the Public Record Office, Dublin. *Louth Arch. J.*, 3, 1915, 347–56.

8207 [GILBERT, JOHN T.] English commissioners and Irish records: a letter in reference to the publication of *The Calendars of the Patent and Close Rolls of Ireland. By An Irish Archivist.* London: 1865.

8208 — On the history, position and treatment of the public records in Ireland. 2nd ed. London: 1864. This is the second edition of *Record Revelations, etc.*, London: 1863, which was largely devoted to an attack upon Morrin's *Calendars of the Patent and Close Rolls, 1861-2*. In the preface to vol. 1 of these calendars there is a useful account of the history of Irish records and the Irish Records Commission.

8209 GRIFFITH, MARGARET. A short guide to the Public Record Office of Ireland. *Ir. Hist. Stud.*, 8, 1952–3, 45–58.

8210 — The Irish Record Commission, 1810–30. *Ir. Hist. Stud.*, 7, 1950–1, 17–38.

8211 IRELAND. PUBLIC RECORD OFFICE. Report of the Deputy Keeper. Dublin: nos. 1–59, 1869–1964.

8212 IRISH ARCHIVES BULLETIN: Journal of the Irish Society for Archives, edited by P.J. White. Dublin, vol. 1–, 1971–.

8213 LIST OF DUBLIN CORPORATION RECORDS exhibited at meeting of the Royal Society of Antiquaries of Ireland, March 11, 1891. *R. Soc. Antiq. Ir. J.*, 21, 1891, 421–5.

8214 MACFARLANE, L.J. The Vatican archives, with special reference to sources for British [and Irish] medieval history. *Archives*, vol. 4, no. 21, 1959, 29–44; vol. 4, no. 22, 1959, 84–101.

8215 MALCOLMSON, A.P.W. The publications programme of the Public Record Office of Northern Ireland. *Ir. Booklore*, vol. 1, no. 2, 1971, 210–216.

8216 MURRAY, ROBERT HENRY. A short guide to the principal classes of documents preserved in the Public Record Office, Dublin. London, 1919. *(Helps for students of History,* no. 7).

8217 NATIONAL LIBRARY OF IRELAND. Report of the Council of Trustees. Dublin: 1901–.

8218 NORTHERN IRELAND. Ministry of Finance. Report of the Deputy Keeper of the Records. Belfast: 1924–68. Each report includes index to documents (other than normal increments) deposited during the year.

8219 O'DUILL, GREAGOIR. Sir John Gilbert and archival reform. *Dublin Hist. Rec.*, vol. 30, no. 4, 1977, 136–142.

8220 PHAIR, P.B. Guide to the Registry of Deeds. *Anal. Hib.*, 23, 1966, 259–276.

8221 QUINN, DAVID BEERS. Irish records, 1929–33: a survey. *Bull. Inst. Hist. Res.*, 11, 1933–4, 99–104.

8222 REPORTS FROM THE COMMITTEE appointed by his Majesty to execute the measures recommended in an address to the House of Commons respecting the public records of Ireland. Dublin: 1813–25. 3 vols. Contains fifteen reports of basic importance to the student pursuing research in the public records; 16th and 17th reports are in *Parliamentary Papers*, vol. 12, 1828; 18th and 19th, *ibid.*, vol. 16, 1830. The supplement to the 8th report, 1819, contains valuable inventories of plea, pipe, memoranda rolls, etc. The Irish Record Commission was created in 1810 and expired in 1830. Since 1869 the Deputy Keeper of Public Records in Ireland has issued annual reports.

8223 ROEBUCK, PETER. The Irish Registry of Deeds: a comparative study. *Ir. Hist. Stud.*, vol. 18, no. 69, 1972, 61–73.

8224 SCARGILL-BIRD, S.R. A guide to the various classes of documents preserved in the Public Record Office [London]. 3rd ed. London: 1908. 1st ed. 1891.

8225 SMYTH, PETER. Thirty years on. *Ir. Arch Bull.*, 5, 1975, 31–40. 2129 files which the Public Record Office, Northern Ireland, holds from Government departments which have been opened under the public access rule.

8226 UNIVERSITY COLLEGE, DUBLIN. Preliminary guide to the collections of the Archives Department, University College, Dublin, 1976.

8227 WOOD, HERBERT. A guide to the records deposited in the Public Record Office of Ireland. Dublin: 1919. Lists Irish Record and Rolls publications, pp. 329–30, also *Annual Reports of the Deputy Keeper of the Public Records,* nos. 1–50, 1869–1918, pp. 331–4.

8228 — The destruction of the public records: the loss to Irish history. *Studies*, 11, 1922, 363–378.

8229 — The public records of Ireland before and after 1922. *R. Hist. Soc. Trans., 4th ser.,* 13, 1930, 17–49.

Proclamations, Broadsides.

8230 BIBLIOTHECA LINDESIANA. Hand list of a collection of broadside proclamations issued by authority of the Kings and Queens of Great Britain and Ireland. 1886.

8231 — [Another ed.]. Hand list of proclamations. First revision [by James Ludovic Lindsay, Earl of Crawford and Balcarres]. Aberdeen, 1892–1901.

8232 — Supplement, 1521–1765. 1901.

8233 — Bibliotheca Lindesiana, vols. 5–6. A bibliography of Royal proclamations of the Tudor and Stuart sovereigns and of others published under authority, 1485–1714, with an historical essay on their origin and use, by Robert Steele. Oxford: 1910. vol. 1: England and Wales; vol. 2, pt. 1: Ireland; pt. 2: Scotland. E.R. McC. Dix abstracted Dublin printers of proclamations for period 1623–90 from these volumes, which is in manuscript in the National Library, Dublin.

8234 — Bibliotheca Lindesiana, vol. 8. Hand list of proclamations issued by Royal and other constitutional authorities. 1714–1910, George I to Edward VII. Together with an index of names and places. Wigan: 1913.

8235 THE CATALOGUE OF 'PROCLAMATIONS' FROM 1618 to 1660. *Rep. D.K. Pub. Rec. Ir.*, 22, 1890, 35–41.

8236 LEMON, ROBERT, *compiler*. Catalogue of a collection of printed broadsides in the possession of the Society of Antiquaries of London. London: 1866. Covers period 1513–1815.

8237 LONDON UNIVERSITY. Catalogue of the collection of English, Scottish and Irish proclamations in the University Library (Goldsmith's Library of Economic Literature), at the central building of the University of London. London: 1928. With a few exceptions covers the last sixty years of the seventeenth century.

8238 MACGIOLLA CHOILLE, BREANDAN. Forograi Philadelphia [agus liosta de na forograi]. *Galvia*, 2, 1955, 20–38. Covers period 1652–91.

8239 THE PROCLAMATIONS ISSUED BY THE LORD LIEUTENANT AND COUNCIL OF IRELAND, 1618 to 1875, as well as some issued by the King. *Rep. D.K. Pub. Rec. Ir.*, 23, 1891, 25–74; 24, 1892, 33–93.

General

8240 ANDREWS, J.H. History in the ordnance map: an introduction for Irish readers. Dublin: 1974.

8241 BECKETT, J.C. The Anglo-Irish tradition. London: 1976.

8242 — Confrontations: studies in Irish history. London: 1972.

8243 — A short history of Ireland. 4th ed., London: 1971. First pub. 1952. Bibliog., pp. 185–190.

8244 BUTLER, WILLIAM F.T. Gleanings from Irish history. London: 1925. Bibliog., pp. 297–302.

8245 BYRNE, FRANCIS JOHN. Irish kings and high-kings. London: 1973.

8246 CHAUVIRE, ROGER. History of Ireland. Dublin: 1952. Bibliog., pp. 123–7.

8247 COOGAN, TIM PAT. The Irish: a personal view. London: 1975.

8248 CURTIS, EDMUND. A history of Ireland. 6th ed. rev. London: 1950. Bibliog., pp 413–16.

8249 — A history of medieval Ireland from 1086 to 1513. Enl. ed. London: 1938. Bibliog., pp. xi–xiii.

8250 D'ALTON, EDWARD A. History of Ireland, from the earliest times to the present day. Dublin: 1903–10. 3 vols. Bibliog., vol. 2, pp. 571–6.

8251 EDWARDS, ROBERT DUDLEY. A new history of Ireland. Dublin: 1972.

8252 EDWARDS, RUTH DUDLEY. An atlas of Irish history. London: 1973.

8253 EMMET, THOMAS ADDIS. Ireland under English rule, or a plea for the plaintiff. 2nd ed. New York and London: 1909. 2 vols. Bibliog., vol. 1, pp. xxvii–xxxv.

8254 GOBLET, Y.M. La transformation de la géographie politique de l'Irlande au XVIIe siècle dans les cartes et essais anthropogéographiques de Sir William Petty. Paris: 1930. 2 vols. Bibliog., vol. 1, pp. ix–xlix.

8255 GORMAN, MICHAEL, *ed*. Ireland by the Irish. London: 1963. Bibliog., pp. 159–162.

8256 GRAVES, JAMES. Register of historical portraits. *Kilkenny S.E. Ir. Arch. Soc. J., new ser.,* 2, 1858–9, 232–8; 4, 1862–3, 138–40.

8257 GUTCH, JOHN. Collectanea curiosa; or miscellaneous tracts relating to the history and antiquities of England and Ireland, the Universities of Oxford and Cambridge, etc., chiefly collected from the manuscripts of Archbishop Sancroft. Oxford: 1781. 2 vols.

8258 HARDIMAN, JAMES. Ancient Irish deeds and writings from the twelfth to the seventeenth century. Dublin: 1826.

8259 HAYDEN, MARY and MOONAN, GEORGE A. A short history of the Irish people from the earliest times to 1920. Dublin: 1921.

8260 HUGHES, J.L.J. The Chief Secretaries in Ireland, 1566–1921. *Ir. Hist. Stud.,* 8, 1952–3, 59–72.

8261 — Patentee officers in Ireland, 1173–1826, including high sheriffs, 1661–84 and 1761–1816. Dublin: 1960.

8262 INGLIS, BRIAN. The story of Ireland. London: 1956. Bibliog., pp. 259–62.

8263 IRELAND, DEPARTMENT OF FOREIGN AFFAIRS. Facts about Ireland. [3rd ed.]. Dublin: 1978. Bibliog. pp. 245–55.

8264 JOYCE, PATRICK WESTON. A social history of ancient Ireland. 2nd ed. London and Dublin: 1913.

8265 KELLEHER, JOHN V. The Tain [Bo Cuailgne] and the Annals. *Eriu*, 22, 1971, 107–127.

8266 LAWLESS, EMILY. Ireland: with chapters on the Irish Free State, by Michael MacDonagh. 3rd ed. London: 1923. Bibliog., pp. 481–3.

8267 LECTOR, *pseud*. Irish county and family histories. *Dublin Pen. J.*, 31 January, 1903, 598–599, 628.

8268 LYDON, J.F. The Lordship of Ireland in the Middle Ages. Dublin and London: 1972.

8269 MARTIN, F.X. The Thomas Davis Lectures, 1953–67. [including list]. *Ir. Hist. Stud.*, vol. 15, no. 59, 1967, 276–302.

8270 MAXWELL, CONSTANTIA. The stranger in Ireland, from the reign of Elizabeth to the Great Famine. London: 1954. Bibliog., pp. 332–334.

8271 MOODY, T.W. A new history of Ireland. *Ir. Hist. Stud.*, 16, 1968–69, 241–257.

8272 — and MARTIN, F.X., *eds*. The Course of Irish history. Cork: 1967. Bibliog., pp. 350–367.

8273 MORRIS, WILLIAM O'CONNOR. Ireland, 1494–1905. Revised, with an additional chapter (1868–1905), notes, etc., by Robert Dunlop. London: 1909. Bibliog., pp. 389–402.

8274 MURRAY, ROBERT H. and LAW, HUGH. Ireland. London: 1924. *(Nations of today ser.)* Bibliog., pp. 279–81.

8275 — Revolutionary Ireland and its settlement. London: 1911. Bibliog., pp. 421–38.

8276 O'BRIEN, MAIRE, and O'BRIEN, CONOR CRUISE. A concise history of Ireland. London: 1972. Bibliog., pp. 175–177.

8277 O'CORRAIN, DONNCHA. Ireland before the Normans. Dublin: 1972. Bibliog., pp. 193–202.

8278 O'DANACHAIR, CAOIMHIN. The Shannon in military history. *Nth. Munster Antiq. J.*, 14, 1971, 53–64.

8279 O'FARRELL, PATRICK. Millenialism, Messianism and Utopianism in Irish history. *Anglo-Ir. Stud.*, 2, 1976, 45–68.

8280 O'HANLON, THOMAS J. The Irish: portrait of a people. London: 1976.

8281 POWICKE, F. MAURICE, and FRYDE, E.B. *compilers*. Handbook of British chronology. 2nd ed. London, Royal Historical Society, 1961. Irish material includes lists of Chief Governors, 1172–1952, pp. 147–68; Chief Secretaries, 1566–1922, pp. 169–71; Archbishops and Bishops (Church of Ireland and

Roman Catholic), pp. 302–412; Dukes, Marquesses and Earls, pp. 457–65.

8282 SMITH, R.J. Ireland's renaissance. Dublin: 1903. Bibliog., pp. 350–2.

8283 STANFORD, W.B. Ireland and the classical tradition. Dublin: 1976. Bibliog., pp. 251–4.

8284 VALLANCEY, CHARLES. Collectanea de rebus Hibernicis; or, tracts relative to the history and antiquities of Ireland. Published from the original manuscripts . . . Dublin: 1770–1804. 6 vols.

8285 WALLACE, MARTIN. The Irish: how they live and work. Newton Abbot: 1972.

8286 WARREN, RAOUL DE. L'Irlande et ses institutions politiques, leur évolution – leur état actuel. Paris: 1928. Bibliog., pp. 483–8.

8287 WHITE, TERENCE DE VERE. Ireland. London: 1968. Bibliog., pp. 171–5.

8288 WOOD, HERBERT. The office of Chief Governor of Ireland, 1172–1509 [with a list of Chief Governors]. *R. Ir. Acad. Proc., Sec. C.*, 36, 1921–4, 206–38.

8289 — The offices of Secretary of State for Ireland and Keeper of the Signet or Privy Seal [with a list of Secretaries for 1500–1829]. *ibid.*, 38, 1928–9, 51–68.

HISTORY BY PERIOD

Earliest Times to the Anglo-Norman Invasion, 1172

8290 BONSER, WILFRID. An Anglo-Saxon and Celtic bibliography (450–1087). Oxford: 1957. 2 vols.

8291 BRUYSSEL, ERNEST VAN. Etude bibliographique sur les chroniquers anglais, écossais, et irlandais. *Commission royale d'histoire de Belgique, Compte rendu, 3rd ser.*, 3, 1862, 79–118.

8292 BUGGE, ALEXANDER, Contributions to the history of the Norsemen in Ireland.
1. The Royal race of Dublin.
2. Norse elements in Gaelic tradition of modern times.
3. Norse settlements round the Bristol Channel.
Videnskabsselskabets Skrifter, Historisk-filosofisk Klasse, 4–6, 1900.

8293 BYRNE, FRANCIS JOHN. The Rise of Ui Neill and the high-kingship of Ireland. Dublin [1970]. *(O'Donnell lecture no. 13)*.

8294 — Tribes and tribalism in early Ireland. *Eriu*, 22, 1971, 128–166.

8295 DALTON, G.F. The alternating dynasties, 734–1022. *Stud. Hib.,* 16, 1976, 46–53. On the kingship of Ireland.

8296 DE PAOR, MAIRE and DE PAOR, LIAM. Early Christian Ireland. London: 1958. *(Ancient peoples and places ser.)*

8297 FITZPATRICK, BENEDICT. Ireland and the foundations of Europe. New York and London: 1927. Bibliog., pp. 400–411.

8298 — Ireland and the making of Britain. New York and London: 1922. Bibliog., pp 337–8.

8299 FURLONG, NICHOLAS. Dermot [MacMurrough] king of Leinster and the foreigners. Tralee: 1973. Bibliog., pp. 175–179.

8300 GOGAN, LIAM S. Ptolemaic Ireland. *Cap. Ann.*, 1974, 128–142.

8301 GRAVES, EDGAR B. A bibliography of English history to 1485. Oxford: 1975. Based on *The sources and literature of English history from the earliest times to about 1485,* by Charles Gross. 2nd ed. London: 1915.

8302 HUGHES, KATHLEEN. Early Christian Ireland: introduction to the sources. London: 1972. Bibliog., pp. 302–315.

8303 INTERNATIONAL CONGRESS OF CELTIC STUDIES. Proceedings of the International Congress of Celtic Studies, held in Dublin, 6–10 July, 1959. Dublin: 1962. Central theme of the contributions is The Impact of the Scandinavian Invasions on the Celtic-speaking peoples, *c*. 800–1100 A.D.

8304 LUCAS, A.T. Irish-Norse relations: time for a reappraisal. *Cork Hist. Arch. Soc. J.*, 71, 1966, 62–75.

8305 MACCALL, SEAMUS. And so began the Irish nation. Dublin: 1931. Bibliog., pp. 455–60.

8306 MACCARTHAIGH, PADRAIG. Ireland versus England: the first battle – Clais an Chro [the Hollow of the Slaughter]. *Old Kilk. Rev.*, 24, 1972, 37–41.

8307 MACNALLY, ROBERT, *S.J.* Old Ireland. Dublin: 1965.

8308 MacNeill, Eoin. The authorship and structure of *The Annals of Tigernach* including the writings ascribed to Tigernach. *Eriu,* 7, 1914, 30–113.

8309 MacNeill, John. An Irish historical tract dated A.D. 721. *R. Ir. Acad. Proc., Sec. C,* 28, 1910, 123–48.

8310 MacNiocaill, Gearoid. The medieval Irish annals. Dublin: 1975. *(Medieval Irish History series no. 3*). Bibliog., pp. 42–49.

8311 Morris, John. The Chronicles of Eusebius: Irish fragments. *(Univ. of London, Institute of Classical Studies, Bulletin no. 19,* 1972, 80–93). Eusebius's Chronicle was a major source for later chronicles including the Irish Annals. A bibliog. note gives details of the Irish Annals.

8312 O'Brien, Barry M. The Generalship of Brian Boru. *Ir. Def. J.*, 30, 1970, 381–386.

8313 O'Buachalla, Liam. The construction of the Irish annals, 429–66. *Cork Hist. Arch. Soc. J.*, 63, 1958, 103–115.

8314 — Notes on the early Irish annals, 467–550. *ibid.*, 64, 1959, 73–81.

8315 O'Conor, Charles. Rerum Hibernicarum scriptores veteres. Buckingham, 1814–26. 4 vols. Annals of Boyle, Annals of Innisfallen, Annals of the Four Masters, Annals of Ulster, Tigernach's Annals.

8316 O'Corrain, Donncha. The Career of Diarmait Mac Mael na mBo. *Old Wexford Soc. J.*, vol. 3, no. 1, 1970, 27–35.

8317 — Irish regnal succession: a reappraisal. *Stud. Hib.*, 11, 1971, 7–39.

8318 O'Curry, Eugene. Lectures on the manuscript materials of ancient Irish history; delivered at the Catholic University of Ireland during the sessions of 1855 and 1856. Dublin: 1861. Reprinted 1873.

8319 O'Donovan, John. *ed*. Annals of the Kingdom of Ireland, by the Four Masters. London: 1966. 7 vols. A reprint of the 2nd (1856) ed. of this great source book for early Irish history.

8320 O'Dwyer, B.W. The Annals of Connacht and Loch Ce and the monasteries of Boyle and Holy Trinity. *R. Ir. Acad. Proc., Sec. B.*, vol. 72, no. 4, 1972, 83–101.

8321 O'Rahilly, Thomas F. Early Irish history and mythology. Dublin: 1946. Bibliog., pp. 562–4.

8322 Ryan, John. Early Irish-German associations. *Cap. Ann.*, 1969, 148–159.

8323 Sheehy, Maurice P. *ed*. Pontificia Hibernica: medieval Papal chancery documents concerning Ireland, 640–1261. Dublin: vol. 1, 1962. Bibliog., pp. xliii – liii.

8324 Smyth, A.P. The earliest Irish Annals: their first contemporary entries, and the earliest centres of recording. *R. Ir. Acad. Proc., Sec. C.*, 72, 1972, 1–48.

8325 — Scandinavian kings in the British Isles. London: 1977. *(Oxford historical monographs)*. Bibliog., pp. 281–292.

8326 Stacpoole, *Miss* G.C. Gormflaith and the Northmen of Dublin. *Dublin Hist. Rec.*, 20, 1964–5, 4–18.

8327 Thomas, Charles. Britain and Ireland in early Christian times, A.D. 400–800. London: 1971. Bibliog., pp. 136–139.

8328 Villanueva, Joachimo Laurentio. Phoenician Ireland; translated and illustrated with notes, an additional plate and Ptolemy's map [of Ireland] made modern by. Henry O'Brien. 2nd ed. with a biographical introduction by his brother. London: 1837.

8329 Warren, W.L. The Interpretation of twelfth-century Irish history. *Hist. Stud.*, 7, 1969, 1–19.

Anglo-Norman Invasion to Tudor Period, 1172–1485

8330 Armstrong, Olive. Edward Bruce's invasion of Ireland. London: 1923. Bibliog., pp. ix–xiii.

8331 Asplin, P.W.A. Medieval Ireland, *c*. 1170–1495: a bibliography of secondary works. Dublin: 1971.

8332 Barry, John G. The Norman invasion of Ireland: a new approach. *Cork Hist. Arch. Soc. J.*, 75, 1970, 105–124.

8333 Bernardis, Vincenzo. Italy and Ireland in the Middle Ages. Dublin: 1950. Bibliog., pp. 218–21.

8334 Campbell, William, *ed.* Chronicles and memorials of Great Britain and Ireland during the Middle Ages. Materials for a history of the reign of Henry VII from original documents preserved in the Public Record Office, London: 1873–7. 2 vols. (*Rolls series.*).

8335 COSGROVE, ART. The Execution of the Earl of Desmond, 1468. *Kerry Arch. Hist. Soc. J.*, 8, 1975, 11–27.

8336 CURTIS, EDMUND. Calendar of Ormond deeds, 1172–1603. Dublin, Irish Manuscripts Commission, 1932–43. 6 vols.

8337 DE COURCY IRELAND, JOHN. Norman townsmen and sea traders. *Canaliana,* 1969, 6–13.

8338 DOLLEY, MICHAEL. Anglo-Norman Ireland, *c.*1100–1318. Dublin: 1972. *(The Gill History of Ireland).* Bibliog., pp. 190–196.

8339 FRAME, ROBIN. The Bruces in Ireland, 1315–18. *Ir. Hist. Stud.*, vol. 19, no. 73, 1974, 3–37.

8340 — The Justiciarship of Ralph Ufford: warfare and politics in fourteenth-century Ireland. *Stud. Hib.*, 13, 1973, 7–47.

8341 GILBERT, *Sir* JOHN THOMAS. *ed.* Historic and municipal documents, Ireland, A.D. 1172–1320. London: 1870.

8342 HAND, GEOFFREY J. Material used in 'Calendar of documents relating to Ireland' [1171–1307]. *Ir. Hist. Stud.*, vol. 12, no. 46, 1960, 99–104.

8343 JACOB, E.F. The fifteenth century, 1399–1485. London: 1961. *(Oxford history of England*, vol. 6). Ireland, bibliog., p. 721.

8344 LYDON, J.F. The Bruce invasion of Ireland. *Hist. Stud.*, 4, 1963, 111–125.

8345 — Richard II's expeditions to Ireland. *R. Soc. Antiq. Ir. J.*, 93, 1963, 135–149.

8346 — Three Exchequer documents from the reign of Henry the third. *R. Ir. Acad. Proc., Sec. C.*, vol. 65, no. 1, 1966, 1–27.

8347 MCGURK, J.J.N. Gerald of Wales. *Hist. Today*, 25, 1975, 255–261, 340–347. Author of *The Topography of Ireland,* and *The Conquest of Ireland*.

8348 MACIOMHAIR, *The Rev.* DIARMUID. Bruce's invasion of Ireland and first campaign in County Louth. *Ir. Sword,* vol. 10, no. 40, 1972, 188–212.

8349 MCKISACK, MAY. The fourteenth century, 1307–99. London: 1959. *(Oxford history of England,* vol. 5.) Ireland, bibliog., pp. 563–4.

8350 MARTIN, F.X. The First Normans in Munster. *Cork Hist. Arch. Soc. J.*, 76, 1971, 48–71.

8351 — No hero in the house: Diarmait Mac Murchada and the coming of the Normans to Ireland. Dublin: 1975. *(O'Donnell Lecture)*.

8352 ORPEN, GODDARD HENRY. Ireland under the Normans, 1169–1333. Oxford, 1911–20. 4 vols.

8353 OTWAY-RUTHVEN, A.J. The Chief Governors of medieval Ireland. *R. Soc. Antiq. Ir. J.*, 95, 1965, 227–236.

8354 — A History of medieval Ireland.London and New York: 1968. Bibliog., pp. 409–422.

8355 OTWAY-RUTHVEN, JOCELYN. The character of Norman settlement in Ireland. *Hist. Stud.*, 5, 1965, 75–84.

8356 — Ireland in the 1350's: Sir Thomas de Rokeby and his successors. *R. Soc. Antiq. Ir. J.*, 97, 1967, 47–59.

8357 — Royal service in Ireland. *R. Soc. Antiq. Ir. J.*, 98, 1968, 37–46. Includes list of Proclamations of Royal Service for period 1212–1480.

8358 POWICKE, F. MAURICE. The thirteenth century. 1216–1307. London: 1953. *(Oxford history of England,* vol. 4.) Ireland, bibliog., pp. 755–6.

8359 RERUM BRITANNICARUM MEDII AEVI SCRIPTORES: or, chronicles and memorials of Great Britain and Ireland during the Middle Ages. London: 1858–1911. *(Rolls series.)*

8360 ROCHE, RICHARD. The Norman invasion of Ireland. Tralee: 1970.

8361 ST. JOHN BROOKS, ERIC. Knights' fees in counties Wexford, Carlow and Kilkenny (thirteenth to fifteenth century) with commentary by E. St. John Brooks. Dublin, Irish Manuscripts Commission, 1950. Bibliog., pp. xi–xiv.

8362 — Unpublished charters relating to Ireland, 1172–82, from the archives of the city of Exeter. *R. Ir. Acad. Proc., Sec. C,* 43, 1935–7, 313–66.

8363 — The sources for medieval Anglo-Irish history. *Hist. Stud.*, 1, 1958, 86–92.

8364 SIMS, KATHERINE. The Archbishops of Armagh and the O'Neills, 1347–1471. *Ir.*

Hist. Stud., vol. 19, no. 73, 1974, 38–55.

8365 SMYLY, J. GILBERT. Old Latin deeds in the library of Trinity College.
1: 1246–1317. *Hermathena,* no. 66, 1945, 25–39.
2: 1318–1359. *ibid.*, 67, 1946, 1–30.
3: 1348–1403. *ibid.*, 69, 1947, 31–48.
4: 1404–1453. *ibid.*, 70, 1947, 1–21.
5: 1453–1508. *ibid.*, 71, 1948, 36–51.
6: 1509–1522. *ibid.*, 72, 1948, 115–20.
7: 1523–1538. *ibid.*, 74, 1949, 60–7.

8366 SWEETMAN, H.S. and HANDCOCK, G.F. *eds*. Calendar of documents relating to Ireland, 1171–1307, preserved in the Public Record Office, London. London: 1875–86. 5 vols. *(Rolls series)*.

8367 TUCK, ANTHONY. Anglo-Irish relations, 1382–1393. *R. Ir. Acad. Proc., Sec. C.*, vol. 69, no. 2, 1970, 15–31.

8368 WARREN, W.L. The Historian as 'Private Eye'. *Hist. Stud.*, 9, 1974, 1–18. King John and the Irish barons.

Tudor Period, 1485–1603

8369 BAGWELL, RICHARD. Ireland under the Tudors, with a succinct account of the earlier history. London: 1885–90. 3 vols. Reprinted, London: 1963.

8370 BENVENUTA, *Sister* M. The Geraldine war – rebellion or crusade? *Ir. Eccles Rec.*, 103, 1965, 148–157.

8371 BOYLE, ALEXANDER. Once more Kinsale. *Ir. Eccles Rec.*, 103, 1965, 292–298. On the siege and battle of Kinsale, 1601.

8372 CANNY, NICHOLAS P. The Elizabethan conquest of Ireland: a pattern established, 1565–76. Hassocks (Sussex): 1976. Bibliog., pp. 186–198.

8373 — Hugh O'Neill, Earl of Tyrone, and the changing face of Gaelic Ulster. *Stud. Hib.*, 10, 1970, 7–35.

8374 DAVIES, JOHN. Discovery of the true causes why Ireland was never entirely subdued. [new ed. rev.] Introduction by Prof. John Barry: 1969. First ed. London: 1612.

8375 DUNLOP, ROBERT. Ireland to the Settlement of Ulster; from the beginning of the sixteenth century to 1611. *Camb. Mod. Hist.*, vol. 3, 1904. Bibliog., pp. 852–9.

8376 EDWARDS, ROBERT DUDLEY. Church and state in Tudor Ireland: a history of penal laws against Irish Catholics, 1534–1603. London: 1935. Bibliog., pp. 313–32.

8377 — Ireland in the age of the Tudors: the distruction of Hiberno-Norman civilization. London and New York: 1977. Appendix: Historians and sixteenth century Ireland, pp. 185–196. Bibliog., pp. 202–215.

8378 ELLIS, STEVEN G. The Kildare rebellion and the early Henrician reformation. *Hist. J.*, vol. 19, no. 4, 1976, 807–830.

8379 — Tudor policy and the Kildare ascendancy in the lordship of Ireland, 1496–1534. *Ir. Hist. Stud.*, vol. 20, no. 79, 1977, 235–271.

8380 FALLON, NIALL. The Armada in Ireland. London: 1978. Bibliog., pp. 225–7.

8381 HAMILTON, H.C. *and others, eds*. Calendar of state papers relating to Ireland. London: 1860–1912. 11 vols. Covers period 1509–1603.

8382 HASSENCAMP, R. Geschichte Irlands von der Reformation bis zu seiner union mit England. Leipzig: 1886. Bibliog., pp. 314–24.

8383 — The history of Ireland from the Reformation to the Union; translated from the German by E.A. Robinson. London: 1888. English edition contains bibliog. notes only.

8384 HAYES-MCCOY, GERALD A. Scots mercenary forces in Ireland (1565–1603): an account of their services during that period, of the reaction of their activities on Scottish affairs, and of the effect of their presence in Ireland . . . Dublin and London: 1937. Bibliog., pp. 361–72.

8385 — Gaelic society in Ireland in the late sixteenth century. *Hist. Stud.*, 4, 1963, 45–61.

8386 HENRY, L.W. Contemporary sources for Essex's lieutenancy in Ireland, 1599. *Ir. Hist. Stud.*, 11, 1958, 8–17.

8387 HINTON, EDWARD M. Ireland through Tudor eyes. Philadelphia, Univ. of Philadelphia, 1935. Bibliog., pp. 104–7.

8388 HISTORICAL MANUSCRIPTS COMMISSION. The manuscripts of Charles Haliday, Esq., of Dublin. Acts of the Privy Council in Ireland, 1556–71. London. (*15th Report, Appendix, pt. 3, 1897.*)

8389 **Irish Manuscripts Commission.** The Tanner letters: original documents and notices of Irish affairs in the sixteenth and seventeenth centuries, extracted from the collection in the Bodleian Library, Oxford, by Charles McNeill. Dublin: 1943.

8390 **Jones, Frederick M.** Mountjoy, 1563–1606: the last Elizabethan deputy. Dublin: 1958. Bibliog., pp. 193–200.

8391 **List of Spanish State Papers Relating to Ireland** preserved in the Castle of Simancas. *Ir. Book Lov.,* 20, 1932, 100–3.

8392 **MacCurtain, Margaret.** The fall of the House of Desmond. *Kerry Arch. Hist. Soc. J.*, 8, 1975, 28–44.

8393 **Mathew, David.** The Celtic peoples and Renaissance Europe: a study of the Celtic and Spanish influences on Elizabethan history. London and New York: 1933. Documents relating to Ireland, pp. 476–481.

8394 **Maxwell, Constantia.** Irish history from contemporary sources (1509–1610). London: 1923.

8395 **Morrin, James.** Calendar of the Patent and Close Rolls of Chancery in Ireland. Dublin: 1861–3. 2 vols. Covers periods 1514–1602 and 1625–33.

8396 **Morton, Grenfell.** Elizabethan Ireland. London: 1971. Bibliog., pp. 147–155.

8397 **Morton, R.C.** The enterprise of Ulster. *Hist. Today*, 17, 1967, 114–121. Deals with plantation and settlement.

8398 **Murray, Robert H.** Ireland, 1494–1603. London: 1920. *(Helps for students of history,* no. 33)

8399 **O'Brien, Barry M.** Red Hugh O'Donnell, the soldier. *Ir. Def. J.*, 31, 1971, 73–78.

8400 **O'Sullivan Bear, Philip.** Ireland under Elizabeth: chapters towards a history of Ireland in the reign of Elizabeth, being a portion of the history of Catholic Ireland, translated from the original Latin by Matthew J. Byrne. London: 1970. Facsimile reprint of 1st ed. of translation, Dublin: 1903.

8401 **Piveronus, Peter J.** The Desmond Imperial alliance of 1529: its effect on Henry VIII's policy toward Ireland. *Eire-Ir.*, vol. 10, no. 2, 1975, 19–31.

8402 **Povey, Kenneth.** The sources for a bibliography of Irish history, 1500–1700. *Ir. Hist. Stud.*, 1, 1939, 393–403.

8403 **Quinn, David B.** Guide to English financial records for Irish history, 1461–1558, with illustrative extracts, 1461–1509. *Anal. Hib.*, 10, 1941, 1–69.

8404 — The Elizabethans and the Irish. Ithaca (N.Y.): 1966. Bibliog., pp. 188–190.

8405 — The Munster Plantation: problems and opportunities. *Cork Hist. Arch. Soc. J.*, 71, 1966, 19–40.

8406 **Read, Conyers,** *ed*. Bibliography of British history: Tudor period, 1485–1603. 2nd ed. Oxford: 1959. First published 1933; for 'Addenda and Corrigenda' to 2nd ed. see *Ir. Hist. Stud.*, 12, 1961, 283–8.

8407 **Roberts, Richard Arthur.** List of volumes of state papers relating to Great Britain and Ireland . . . Pt. 1. London, Public Record Office, 1894. (Lists and indexes, no. iii). Period covered 1547–1760; no further parts issued.

8408 **Silke, J.** Red Hugh O'Donnell, 1572–1601: a biographical survey. *Donegal Ann.*, vol. 5, no. 1, 1961, 1–19.

8409 — Ireland and Europe, 1559–1607. Dundalk: 1966. Bibliog., pp. 29–30.

8410 — Kinsale: the Spanish intervention in Ireland at the end of the Elizabethan wars. Liverpool: 1970. Bibliog., pp. 182–191.

8411 — Spanish intervention in Ireland, 1601–2: Spanish bibliography. *Stud. Hib.*, 3, 1963, 179–190.

8412 **Somerville,** *Vice Admiral* **Boyle.** The Spanish expedition to Ireland, 1601, [with bibliog.]. *Ir. Sword*, vol. 7, no. 26, 1965, 37–57.

8413 **Somerville-Large, Peter.** From Bantry Bay to Leitrim: a journey in search of O'Sullivan Beare. London: 1974. Bibliog., pp. 259–261.

Stuart Period to Eighteenth Century, 1603–1714

8414 **Abbott, Wilbur Cortez.** A bibliography of Oliver Cromwell: a list of printed materials relating to Oliver Cromwell, together with a list of portraits and caricatures. Cambridge (Mass.): 1929. Rich in Irish material; see also *Writings on Oliver Cromwell since 1929,* by P.H. Hardacre, *J. Mod. Hist.*, 33, 1961.

8415 ACCOUNT OF THE PROTESTANT WRITERS ON THE REBELLION OF 1641. London: 1747.

8416 BAGWELL, R. Ireland under the Stuarts. London: 1909–16. 3 vols. Reprinted, London: 1963.

8417 BARNARD, T.C. Cromwellian Ireland: English government and reform in Ireland, 1649–1660. London: 1975. Bibliog., pp. 306–329.

8418 BECKETT, J.C. The Confederation of Kilkenny reviewed [with bibliog.]. *Hist. Stud.*, 2, 1959, 29–41.

8419 BERMAN, DAVID. David Hume on the 1641 rebellion in Ireland. *Studies*, 65, 1976, 101–112.

8420 BRITISH MUSEUM. Catalogue of the pamphlets, books, newspapers and manuscripts relating to the Civil War, the Commonwealth and Restoration, collected by George Thomason, 1640–61. London: 1908. 2 vols.

8421 CANNY, NICHOLAS P. The Flight of the Earls, 1607. *Ir. Hist. Stud.,* 17, 1970–1, 380–399.

8422 CARTY, JAMES, *compiler*. Ireland from the Flight of the Earls to Grattan's parliament, (1607–1782): a documentary record. Dublin: 1949.

8423 CASWAY, JERROLD. George Monck and the controversial Catholic truce of 1649. *Stud. Hib.*, 16, 1976, 54–72.

8424 — Owen Roe O'Neill's return to Ireland in 1642: the diplomatic background. *ibid.*, 9, 1969, 48–64.

8425 CLARKE, AIDAN. The Army and politics in Ireland, 1625–30. *Stud. Hib.*, 4, 1964, 28–53.

8426 CONWAY, DOMINIC. Guide to documents of Irish and British interest in Fondo Borghese, ser. 1, *c.* 1592–1621. *Arch. Hib.,* 23, 1960, 1–147. Available on microfilm in National Library, Dublin.

8427 COOMBES, *The Rev.* J. A Castlehaven episode in the Nine Years War. *Cork Hist. Arch. Soc. J.*, 77, 1972, 40–44.

8428 COONAN, THOMAS L. The Irish Catholic confederacy and the Puritan revolution. Dublin: 1954. Bibliog., pp. 344–59.

8429 COOPER, J.P. Strafford and the Byrnes' Country. *Ir. Hist. Stud.*, 15, 1966, 1–20. Byrnes' country was defined in 1626 as fourteen parishes running along the coast of Wicklow from Delgany to Ennereilly about 4 miles north of Arklow.

8430 COX, LIAM. The Williamite war in Westmeath and Ginkle's march to Athlone. *Ir. Sword,* 9, 1969–70, 308–317.

8431 CREGAN, DONAL F. An Irish cavalier: Daniel O'Neill in the Civil wars, 1642–51. *Stud. Hib.*, 4, 1964, 104–133.

8432 — An Irish cavalier: Daniel O'Neill in exile and restoration, 1651–64. *ibid.*, 5, 1965, 42–77.

8433 DALRYMPLE, JOHN. Memoirs of Great Britain and Ireland . . . London: 1771–3. New ed., 3 vols., 1790. Vol. 2 is a valuable collection of documents.

8434 DALTON, NOEL. Cromwell: a paradox. *Zenith*, 2, 1972, 17–23.

8435 DANAHER, K. and SIMMS, J.G., *eds*. The Danish force in Ireland, 1690–1691. Dublin: 1962.

8436 DAVIES, GODFREY. Bibliography of British history, Stuart period, 1603–1714. 2nd ed. [edited by Mary Frear Keeler]. Oxford: 1970. Ireland, pp. 564–610.

8437 — A Student's guide to the manuscripts relating to English history in the seventeenth century in the Bodleian Library. London: 1922. *(Helps for students of history*, no. 47).

8438 DUNLOP, ROBERT. Ireland from the Plantation of Ulster to the Cromwellian settlement (1611–59). *Camb. Mod. Hist.*, vol. 4, 1906. Bibliog., pp. 913–18.

8439 — Ireland from the Restoration to the Act of Resumption (1660–1700). *Camb. Mod. Hist.,* vol. 5, 1908. Bibliog., pp. 829–37.

8440 ELLIS, PETER BERESFORD. The Boyne water: the battle of the Boyne, 1690. London: 1976. Bibliog., pp. 154–6.

8441 — Hell or Connaught! the Cromwellian colonisation of Ireland, 1652–1660. London: 1975. Bibliog., pp. 253–8.

8442 ESSON, D.M.R. The curse of Cromwell: a history of the Ironside conquest of Ireland, 1649–53. London: 1971.

8443 FALKINER, C. LITTON. Barnaby Rich's *Rembrances of the state of Ireland, 1612:* with notes of other manuscript reports by the same writer, on Ireland under James the First. *R. Ir. Acad. Proc., Sec. C.,* 26, 1906–7, 125–42.

8444 — Illustrations of Irish history and topography mainly of the seventeenth century. London: 1904.

8445 FENLON, DERMOT B. Wentworth and the Parliament of 1634: an essay in chronology. *R. Soc. Antiq. Ir. J.*, 94, 1964, 159–175.

8446 FITZGERALD, BRIAN. The Anglo-Irish: three representative types – Cork, Ormonde, Swift, 1602–1745. London: 1952. Bibliog., pp. 361–3.

8447 FRASER, ANTONIA. Cromwell, our chief of men. London: 1973. Bibliog., pp. 728–44.

8448 GEROULD, JAMES THAYER, *compiler*. Sources of English history of the seventeenth century, 1603–89, in the University of Minnesota Library, with a selection of secondary material. Minneapolis, 1921. *(Research pub. of the Univ. of Minnesota, bibliog. ser.,* no. 1.)

8449 GILBERT, JOHN T. A Jacobite narrative of the war in Ireland, 1688–1691. [reprint of 1st ed.] introduction by J.G. Simms. Shannon: 1971. 1st ed. Dublin: 1892.

8450 GRAY, TONY. No surrender! The siege of Londonderry, 1689. London: 1975. Bibliog., pp. 207–210.

8451 GROSE, CLYDE LECLARE. A select bibliography of British history, 1660–1760. Chicago: 1939.

8452 — Studies of 1931–40 on British history, 1660–1760. *J. Mod. Hist.*, 12, 1940, 515–34. See also 1930 volume of journal for publications appearing from 1900 to 1930.

8453 GUTHRIE, DOROTHY A., and GROSE, CLYDE LECLARE. Forty years of Jacobite bibliography. *J. Mod. Hist.*, 11, 1939, 49–60.

8454 HEWSON, MICHAEL. Robert Stearne's Diary of the Williamite campaign. *Ir. Def. J.*, 37, 1977, 49–53.

8455 HILL, GEORGE. An historical account of the Plantation in Ulster at the commencement of the seventeenth century, 1608–20. Belfast: 1877. Reprinted, with introduction by John G. Barry, Shannon: 1970.

8456 HYNES, MICHAEL J. The Mission of Rinuccini, nuncio extraordinary to Ireland, 1645–9. Dublin: 1932. Bibliog., pp. xiii–xviii.

8457 IRISH MANUSCRIPTS COMMISSION. Calendar of the Orrery papers; compiled by Edward MacLysaght. Dublin: 1941.

8458 — Letters and papers relating to the Irish rebellion between 1642–6; edited by James Hogan. Dublin: 1936.

8459 JORDAN, JOHN. The Jacobite wars: some Danish sources. *Studies,* 43, 1954, 431–40.

8460 KEARNEY, HUGH, F. Strafford in Ireland, 1633–41: a study in absolutism. Manchester: 1959. Bibliog., pp. 277–85.

8461 LOEBER, ROLF. An introduction to the Dutch influence in 17th and 18th century Ireland: an unexplored field. *Ir. Georg. Soc. Qtr. Bull.*, vol. 13, nos. 2–3, 1970, 1–29. Covers history, agriculture, manufactures, architecture, gardens and sculptors.

8462 LOWE, JOHN. Charles I and the confederation of Kilkenny. *Ir. Hist. Stud.*, 14, 1964–65, 1–19.

8463 — The Glamorgan mission to Ireland, 1645–6. *Stud. Hib.*, 4, 1964, 155–196.

8464 MACCURTAIN, MARGARET. Tudor and Stuart Ireland. Dublin and London: 1972. *(Gill History of Ireland 7.)* Bibliog., pp. 197–200.

8465 MACGILLIVRAY, ROYCE. Edmund Borlase, historian of the Irish Rebellion. *Stud. Hib.*, 9, 1969, 86–92.

8466 MCGUIRE, JAMES I. Why was Ormonde dismissed in 1669? *Ir. Hist. Stud.*, vol. 18, no. 71, 1973, 295–312.

8467 MACLYSAGHT, EDWARD. Irish life in the seventeenth century. 3rd ed. Shannon: 1969. Bibliog., pp. 452–466.

8468 MAHAFFY, ROBERT P. *and others*. Calendar of the State papers relating to Ireland, 1603–70. London: 1872–1911. 13 vols. After 1670 are included in *The Calendar of Irish State Papers Domestic*.

8469 MELVIN, PATRICK. The Irish army and the revolution of 1688. *Ir. Sword,* 9, 1969–70, 288–307.

8470 — Irish troop movements and James II's army in 1688. *ibid.*, 10, 1971–2, 87–105.

8471 — Sir Paul Rycaut's memoranda and letters from Ireland, 1686–1687. *Anal. Hib.*, 27, 1972, 125–182.

8472 MILLER, AMOS. Sir Richard Grenville, governor of Trim: the career and character of an English soldier in Ireland, 1642–3. *Riocht na Midhe*, vol. 5, no. 3, 1973, 63–84.

8473 MILLER, JOHN. Thomas Sheridan (1646–1712) and his 'Narrative'. *Ir.. Hist. Stud.,* vol. 20, no. 78, 1976, 105–128.

8474 MURRAY, ROBERT H. Ireland, 1603–1714. London: 1920. (*Helps for students of history,* no. 34.)

8475 — The journal of John Stevens, containing a brief account of the war in Ireland, 1689–91. Oxford: 1912. Bibliog., pp. 220–230.

8476 — Revolutionary Ireland and its settlement. London: 1911. Bibliog., pp. 421–38.

8477 O'BRIEN, GEORGE, *ed*. Advertisements for Ireland, being a description of the state of Ireland in the reign of James I, contained in a manuscript in the Library of Trinity College, Dublin. *(Extra volume of the Royal Society of Antiquaries of Ireland, 1923.)*

8478 O'CAHAN, T.S. Owen Roe O'Neill. London: 1968.

8479 O'CONNOR, G.B. Stuart Ireland, Catholic and Puritan. Dublin: 1910. Bibliog., pp. viii–ix.

8480 O'GRADY, HUGH. Strafford and Ireland: the history of his vice-royalty with an account of his trial. Dublin: 1923. 2 vols. Bibliog., vol. 1, pp. xi–xiii.

8481 O'DOMHNAILL, SEAN. Sir Niall Gerbh O'Donnell and the rebellion of Sir Cahir O'Doherty. *Ir. Hist. Stud.,* 3, 1942, 34–8.

8482 PERCEVAL-MAXWELL, M. Strafford, the Ulster-Scots and the covenanters. *Ir. Hist. Stud.*, vol. 18, no. 72, 1973, 524–551.

8483 PETRIE, *Sir* CHARLES. The great Tyrconnel [Richard Talbot]: a chapter in Anglo-Irish relations. Cork and Dublin [1973]. Bibliog., [p. 260].

8484 POVEY, KENNETH. The sources for a bibliography of Irish history, 1500–1700. *Ir. Hist. Stud.*, 1, 1939, 393–403.

8485 PRENDERGAST, JOHN P. The Cromwellian settlement of Ireland. 3rd ed. Dublin: 1922. Reprinted, Dublin: 1977.

8486 SARSFIELD, PATRICK. Patrick Sarsfield, by Alice Curtayne. Dublin: 1934. Bibliog., pp. 179–80.

8487 SEYMOUR, ST. JOHN D. The Puritans in Ireland, 1647–1661. [Reprinted]. Oxford; 1969. First published 1922.

8488 SIMINGTON, R.C., and MACLELLAN, JOHN. Oireachtas Library: list of outlaws, 1641–1647. *Anal. Hib.*, 23, 1966, 319–367.

8489 SIMMS, J.G. Cromwell at Drogheda, 1649. *Ir. Sword*, vol. 11, no. 45, 1974, 212–221.

8490 — Irish Jacobites: lists [with indexes] from TCD. Ms. N. 1. 3. *Anal. Hib.*, 22, 1960, 13–230.

8491 — Jacobite Ireland, 1685–91. London and Toronto: 1969. *(Studies in Irish History. 2nd ser. vol. 5)*. Bibliog., pp. 270–280.

8492 — Remembering 1690. *Studies*, 63, 1974, 231–242.

8493 — Report on the compilation of a bibliography of source material for the history of Ireland, 1685–1702. *Anal. Hib.*, 22, 1960, 3–10.

8494 — The Treaty of Limerick. Dundalk, Dublin Historical Association, 1961. *(Irish history ser.,* no. 2.)

8495 — The Williamite confiscation in Ireland, 1609–1703. London: 1956. Bibliog., pp. 163–73.

8496 SYNNOTT, P.N.N. Oliver Cromwell in Ireland. *Ir. Def. J.*, 34, 1974, 412–5.

8497 THORPE, THOMAS. Original tracts, illustrative of Irish history, collected by Thomas Thorpe, bookseller. London: 12 vols. In National Library, Dublin; period covered 1629–1758.

8498 WALTON, CLIFFORD. History of the British standing army, A.D. 1660 to 1700. London: 1894. Bibliog., pp. 859–866. Covers campaign of 1689–91.

Eighteenth Century Ireland

8499 BECKETT, J.C. Anglo-Irish constitutional relations in the later eighteenth century. *Ir. Hist. Stud.*, 14, 1964–65, 20–38.

8500 BERESFORD, MARCUS. Francois Thurot and the French attack at Carrickfergus, 1759–60. *Ir. Sword,* vol. 10, no. 41, 1972, 255–274.

8501 BOLTON, G.C. The passing of the Irish Act of Union: a study in parliamentary politics. London: 1966. Bibliog., pp. 223–230.

8502 BRADLEY, P. BRENDAN. Bantry Bay: Ireland in the days of Napoleon and Wolfe Tone. London: 1931. Bibliog., pp. 249–51.

8503 BROCK, FRANCOIS VAN. Captain [Bernard] MacSheehy's mission. *Ir. Sword,* vol. 10, no. 40, 1972, 215–228.

8504 BROWN, LUCY M., and CHRISTIE, IAN R. *eds*. Bibliography of British History, 1789–1851; issued under the direction of the American Historical Association and the Royal Historical Society of Great Britain. Oxford: 1977. Ireland, pp. 500–530.

8505 A CATALOGUE OF POLITICAL PAMPHLETS written in defence of the principles and proceedings of the patriots of Ireland, and mostly published during the administration of his Grace the Duke of Dorset, in the memorable years 1751 to 1755. [1755].

8506 DOWLING, P.J., *ed*. Calendar of Mss. relating to Ireland, 1715–82, in the House of Lords Record Office. In preparation for Irish Manuscripts Commission.

8507 DUNLOP, ROBERT. Ireland, 1792–1815. *Camb. Mod. Hist.,* 9, 1906. Bibliog., pp. 881–2.

8508 — Ireland in the eighteenth century. *ibid.* Bibliog., pp. 913–24.

8509 ENGLISH HISTORICAL DOCUMENTS; general editor, David C. Douglas. 12 vols. Wol. 10. 1714–83. London: 1957. Bibliog., pp. 679–81.

8510 FALKNER, C. LITTON. Studies in Irish history and biography, mainly of the eighteenth century. London: 1902. Bibliog., pp. 343–50.

8511 GRIFFIN, WILLIAM D. General Charles O'Hara (1740–1802). *Ir. Sword,* vol. 10, no. 40, 1972, 179–187.

8512 JACOB, ROSAMOND. The rise of the United Irishmen, 1791–94. London: 1937.

8513 JAMES, FRANCIS GODWIN. Ireland in the Empire, 1688–1770: a history of Ireland from the Williamite Wars to the eve of the American Revolution. Cambridge (Mass.): 1973. Bibliog., pp. 319–335.

8514 JOHNSTON, EDITH MARY. Ireland in the eighteenth century. Dublin: 1974. *(Gill History of Ireland, 8)*. Bibliog., pp. 196–204.

8515 JONES, E.H. STUART. An invasion that failed: the French expedition to Ireland, 1796. Oxford: 1950. Bibliog., pp. 243–6.

8516 JUPP, PETER. Earl Temple's vice-royalty and the question of renunciation, 1782–3. *Ir. Hist. Stud.*, vol. 17, no. 68, 1971, 499–520.

8517 KENNEDY, DENIS. The Irish Whigs, administrative reform, and responsible government, 1782–1800. *Eire-Ir.*, vol. 8, no. 4, 1973, 55–69.

8518 LECKY, WILLIAM EDWARD HARTPOLE. History of Ireland in the eighteenth century. London: 1892. 5 vols. Abridged ed. London: University of Chicago Press, 1972.

8519 LYLE, J.V. List of volumes of the state papers relating to Great Britain and Ireland, including the records of the Home Office from 1782 to 1837. London: Public Record Office, 1914. (*Lists and indexes*, no. xliii.)

8520 MCCABE, LEO. Wolfe Tone and the United Irishmen – for or against Christ? (1791–8). London: 1937. Bibliog., pp. 7–8.

8521 MCCARTNEY, DONAL. Lecky's *Leaders of public opinion in Ireland. Ir. Hist. Stud.*, 14, 1964, 119–141.

8522 MCCLELLAND, AIKEN. Thomas Ledlie Birch, United Irishman. *Belfast Nat. Hist. Phil. Soc. Proc., 2nd ser.*, 7, 1961–64, 24–35.

8523 MACDERMOT, FRANK. Arthur O'Connor. *Ir. Hist. Stud.* 15, 1966, 48–69. One of the leaders of the United Irishmen.

8524 MCDOWELL, ROBERT BRENDAN. Irish public opinion, 1750–1800. London: 1944. *(Studies in Irish history ser.)* Bibliog., pp. 261–93. Includes an excellent list of pamphlets.

8525 — The Fitzwilliam episode. *Ir. Hist. Stud.*, vol. 16, no. 58, 1966, 115–130.

8526 — Ireland in the eighteenth century British Empire. *Ir. Hist. Stud.*, 9, 1974, 49–63.

8527 — Proceedings of the Dublin Society of United Irishmen. *Anal. Hib.*, 17, 1949, 3–143. *Analecta Hibernica* 19, (1957) includes index to above.

8528 MADDEN, RICHARD ROBERT. The United Irishmen, their lives and times. Newly edited with notes, bibliography and index by Vincent Fleming O'Reilly. New York, Catholic Publication Society of America, [1916]. 12 vols. *(The Shamrock edition)*. Bibliog., vol. 12, pp. 202–35.

8529 MAXWELL, CONSTANTIA. Country and town in Ireland under the Georges. London: 1940. Bibliog., pp. 363–84.

8530 MORGAN, WILLIAM THOMAS. A bibliography of British history (1700–15): with special reference to the reign of Queen Anne. Bloomington, Indiana, 1934–42. 5 pts.

8531 MORRIS, H.F. Announcements in *Impartial Occurrences*, Jan. 1705–Feb. 1706. *Ir. Geneal.*, vol. 5, no. 2, 1975, 186–189.

8532 MURRAY, ROBERT H. Ireland, 1714–1829. London: 1920. *(Helps for students of history,* no. 35).

8533 NORTHERN IRELAND, Public Record Office. Aspects of Irish social history, 1750–1800: documents selected and edited by W.H. Crawford and B. Trainor, and with an introduction by J.C. Beckett. Belfast: 1969. Bibliog. note. p. 193.

8534 — Eighteenth-century Irish official papers in Great Britain: private collections. Vol. 1, Belfast: 1973. Includes Somers papers, Aswarby papers, Sackville papers, Stopford-Sackville letter, Henry Pelham papers, Clifden papers, Portland papers, Spenser Bernard papers, Ashbourne (Bolton) papers, Melville papers and Liverpool papers.

8535 O'CONNELL, MAURICE R. Irish politics and social conflict in the age of the American Revolution. Philadelphia and London: 1965. Bibliog., pp. 404–413.

8536 O'NEILL, J.J. The volunteers of 1782. *Ir. Book Lov.*, 6, 1915, 123–4, 144–5. List of pamphlets in the Haliday collection of the Royal Irish Academy.

8537 PARGELLIS, STANLEY, and MEDLEY, D.J., *eds*. Bibliography of British history: the eighteenth century, 1714–89. Oxford: 1951. Reprinted, London: 1977.

8538 PITTON, J.P. 'A Literary Journal' (Dublin, 1744–9): reflections on the role of French culture in eighteenth-century Ireland. *Hermathena*, 121, 1976, 129–141.

8539 ROGERS, PATRICK. The Irish volunteers and Catholic Emancipation (1778–93): a neglected phase of Ireland's history. London: 1934. Bibliog., pp. 315–17.

8540 ROWAN, ARCHIBALD HAMILTON. The autobiography of Archibald Hamilton Rowan, edited by William H. Drummond [1st ed. reprinted with a new] introduction by R.B. McDowell. Shannon: 1972. Facsimile reprint of 1st ed. Dublin: 1840.

8541 SIMMS, SAMUEL. A select bibliography of the United Irishmen, 1791–8. *Ir. Hist. Stud.*, 1, 1938, 158–80.

8542 TERRY, CHARLES SANDFORD. The Rising of 1745, with a bibliography of Jacobite history, 1689–1788. London: 1900. 2nd ed., 1903, with enlarged bibliog.

8543 WALL, MAUREEN. The Penal laws, 1691–1760: Church and State from the Treaty of Limerick to the Accession of George III. Dundalk, Dublin Historical Association, 1961. *(Irish History ser.*, no. 1.) Bibliog., pp. 70–2.

8544 — The United Irish movement. *Hist. Stud.*, 5, 1965, 122–140.

8545 WYATT, ANNE. Froude, Lecky and 'the humblest Irishman'. *Ir. Hist. Stud.*, vol. 19, no. 75, 1975, 261–285.

Insurrectionary Period, 1798–1803

8546 BOURKE, F.S. The Rebellion of 1803: an essay in bibliography. *Bibliog. Soc. Ir.*, vol. 5, no. 1, 1933.

8547 BROCK, FRANCOIS VAN. Dilemma at Killala. *Ir. Sword.,* 8, 1967–8, 261–73.

8548 CARTY, JAMES. The books of 1798. *Ir. Lib. Bull., new ser.*, 9, 1948, 120–2.

8549 CHINNEIDE, SILE NI. Napper Tandy and the European crisis of 1798–1803. Dublin: 1962.

8550 COLEMAN, JAMES. Bibliography of the 1798 rebellion; paper read before the Bibliographical Society of Ireland, March 31, 1932. Ms. 8 p. in National Library, Dublin.

8551 COUGHLAN, RUPERT J. Napper Tandy. Dublin: 1976. Bibliog., pp. 261–4.

8552 DE MONTFORT, SIMON L.M. Mrs. [Alice] Pounden's experiences during the 1798 rising in Co. Wexford. *Ir. Ancest.*, 8, 1976, 4–8.

8553 DICKSON, CHARLES. Revolt in the North: Antrim and Down in 1798. Dublin and London: 1960. Bibliog., pp 252–4.

8554 — The Wexford rising in 1798: its causes and its course. Tralee: 1956. Bibliog., pp. 215–24.

8555 FITZHENRY, EDNA C. Henry Joy McCracken. Dublin: 1936. Bibliog., pp. 160–4.

8556 GILBERT, JOHN T. Documents relating to Ireland, 1795–1804. [Facsimile reprint with] Introduction by Maureen Wall. Shannon: 1970. 1st ed., 1893.

8557 GRIBAYEDOFF, VALERIAN. The French invasion of Ireland in '98. New York: 1890. Bibliog., pp 7–8.

8558 HADDEN, VICTOR. The trial and death of Sir Edward Crosbie, '98. *Carloviana*, new series, vol. 1, no. 12, 1963, 8–11, 33–36.

8559 KENNEDY, W. BENJAMIN. The Irish Jacobins. *Stud. Hib.*, 16, 1976, 109–121.

8560 MCANALLY, HENRY W. The Irish militia, 1793–1816. Dublin and London: 1949. Bibliog., pp. 291–7.

8561 MACSUIBHNE, PEADAR. '98 in Carlow. Carlow: 1974.

8562 PAKENHAM, THOMAS. Humbert's raid on Ireland, 1798. *Hist. Today*, 19, 1969, 688–695.

8563 — The year of liberty: the story of the great Irish Rebellion of 1798. London: 1969. Select bibliog., pp. 356–365.

8564 ROGERS, *The Rev.* PATRICK, *ed.* Ireland in '98 as illustrated from contemporary writings. *Bonaventura*, vol. 3, no. 3, 1939–40, 45–74; *ibid.*, vol. 3, no. 4, 1940, 119–140; vol. 4, no. 1, 1940, 78–86.

8565 RYNEHART, J.G. The 1798 Rebellion – Edward Hay v Sir Richard Musgrave. *Ir. Booklore*, vol. 1, no. 2, 1971, 253. On a pamphlet entitled *Authentic Detail of the extravagant and inconsistent conduct of Sir Richard Musgrave, Baronet . . .*

8566 SAMPSON, D. The French expedition to Ireland in 1798. *Dublin Rev.,* vol. 121, no. 23, 1897, 60–79.

8567 SYNNOTT, P.N.N. 1798 Rising – some records from County Kildare. *Kildare Arch. Soc. J.*, vol. 15, no. 5, 1975–6, 448–467.

8568 TEELING, CHARLES HAMILTON. History of the Irish rebellion of 1798, and Sequel to the History of the Irish rebellion of 1798. [1st ed. reprinted with a new] introduction by Richard Grenfell Morton. Shannon: 1972. *(Irish Revolutionaries)*. 1st ed. Glasgow: 1876.

TONE, THEOBALD WOLFE.

8569 MACCAULEY, J.A. Wolfe Tone – the last phase. *Ir. Sword.* vol. 11, no. 44, 1974, 185–192.

8570 MACDERMOT, FRANK. Theobald Wolfe Tone: a biographical study. London: 1939. Bibliog., pp. 321–5.

8571 MACMANUS, M.J. Bibliography of Theobald Wolfe Tone. *Dublin Mag., new ser.,* vol. 15, no. 3, 1940, 52–64.

8572 ST. MARK, JOSEPH JAMES. Wolfe Tone letter, 1795. *Eire-Ir.*, vol. 6, no. 4, 1971, 15–16.

8573 — Wolfe Tone's diplomacy in America, August – December, 1795. *Eire-Ir.*, vol. 7, no. 4, 1972, 3–11.

8574 WHEELER, H.F.B. and BROADLEY, A.M. The war in Wexford: an account of the rebellion in the south of Ireland in 1798. London: 1910. Bibliog., pp. 327–32.

Nineteenth Century Ireland

8575 ADAMS, WILLIAM FORBES. Ireland and Irish emigration to the new world from 1815 to the famine. New Haven and London: 1932. *(Yale Hist. pub. miscell.*, no. 23). Bibliog., pp. 429–38.

8576 BRODERICK, JOHN F. The Holy See and the Irish movement for the repeal of the union with England, 1829–47. Rome: 1951. *(Analecta Gregoriana ... vol. 55, series facultatis historiae ecclesiasticae, sectio B.*, no. 9.) Bibliog., pp. xxi–xxvii.

8577 BROWN, LUCY M. and CHRISTIE, IAN R. *ed*. Bibliography of British history, 1789–1851, issued under the direction of the American Historical Association and the Royal Historical Society of Great Britain. Oxford: 1977. Ireland, pp. 500–530.

8578 BROWN, MALCOLM. The politics of Irish literature: from Thomas Davis to W.B. Yeats. London: 1972. Bibliog. note, pp. 412–415.

8579 BROWN, THOMAS N. Irish-American nationalism, 1870–1890. Philadelphia and New York: 1966. *(Critical periods of history)*. Bibliog., pp. 189–200.

8580 BRYNN, EDWARD. Crown and Castle: British rule in Ireland, 1800–1830. Dublin: 1978. Bibliog., pp. 160–6.

8581 BUCKLEY, MARY. John Mitchel, Ulster and Irish nationality, (1842–1848). *Studies*, 65, 1976, 30–44.

8582 CARTY, JAMES. Bibliography of Irish history, 1870–1911. Dublin: 1940.

8583 — *compiler*. Ireland from Grattan's parliament to the Great Famine (1783–1850): a documentary record. Dublin: 1949.

8584 — *compiler*. Ireland from the Great Famine to the Treaty (1851–1921): a documentary record. Dublin: 1951.

8585 CASAIDE, SEAMUS UA. Five Young Ireland pamphlets. *Ir. Book Lov.*, 18, 1930, 86.

8586 CHRISTIANSON, GALE EDWARD. Population, the potato and depression in Ireland, 1800–1830. *Eire-Ir.*, vol. 7, no. 4, 1972, 70–95.

8587 COLBURN, GEORGE A. Imagination and reality: T.M. Healy's role in Parnellite politics. *Eire-Ir.*, vol. 10, no. 1, 1975, 85–90.

8588 CORFE, T.H. The troubles of Captain Boycott. *Hist. Today*, 14, 1964, 758–764, 854–862.

8589 — The Phoenix Park murders: conflict, compromise and tragedy in Ireland, 1879–1882. London: 1968. Bibliog., pp. 266–76. The murder of the Chief Secretary for Ireland, Lord Frederick Cavendish, and the Under-Secretary, Thomas Henry Burke.

8590 CRONIN, SEAN. 'The country did not turn out': the Young Ireland rising of 1848. *Eire-Ir.*, vol. 11, no. 2, 1976, 3–17.

8591 CULLEN, L.M. Six generations: life and work in Ireland from 1790. Cork: 1970.

8592 CURRAN, CHARLES. The spy behind the Speaker's chair. *Hist. Today*, 18, 1968, 745–754. Major Henry le Caron (*i.e.* Thomas B. Beach), who was author of *Twenty-five years in the secret service*, London: 1892.

8593 CURTIS, L.P. *Jr*. Coercion and conciliation in Ireland, 1880–1892: a study in conservative unionism. Princeton and London: 1963. Bibliog. note, pp. 443–5.

8594 — Government policy and the Irish party crisis, 1890–92. *Ir. Hist. Stud.*, 13, 1962–63, 295–315.

8595 D'ANGELO, GIOVANNI. Italy and Ireland in the 19th century: contacts and misunderstandings between two national movements. Athlone: 1975.

8596 DANGERFIELD, GEORGE. The damnable question: a study in Anglo-Irish relations. London: 1977. Bibliog., p. 371.

8597 D'ARCY, F.A. The artisans of Dublin and Daniel O'Connell, 1830–1847: an unquiet liaison. *Ir. Hist. Stud.*, vol. 17, no. 66, 1970, 221–43.

8598 DE BLAGHD, EARNAN P. Tim Kelly, guilty or not guilty. *Dublin Hist. Rec.*, vol. 25, no. 1, 1971, 12–24. Kelly was one of the accused in the Phoenix Park murders.

8599 DUNLOP, ROBERT. Ireland and the Home Rule movement. *Camb. Mod. Hist.*, vol. 12, 1910. Bibliog., pp. 856–62.

8600 — Great Britain and Ireland, 1832–41. *ibid.*, vol. 10, 1907. Bibliog., pp. 867–70.

8601 DWYER, T. RYLE. Americans and the great Irish famine: a story of human concern. *Cap. Ann.*, 1974, 270–278.

8602 EDWARDS, R. DUDLEY, and WILLIAMS, T. DESMOND, *eds*. The Great Famine: studies in Irish history, 1845–52 [Facsimile reprint]. New York: 1976. 1st pub. Dublin: 1956. Select [updated] bibliog., pp. 499–509.

8603 FLANAGAN, THOMAS. Rebellion and style: John Mitchel and the *Jail Journal*. *Ir. Univ. Rev.,* vol. 1, no. 1, 1970, 1–29.

8604 FRENCH BOOKS ON IRISH SUBJECTS, 1801–1900. *Ir. Book Lov.,* 16, 1928, 42–3, 59–61. Lists 129 items.

8605 GREENE, THOMAS F. The English Catholic press and the Home Rule Bill, 1885–86. *Eire-Ir.*, vol. 10, no. 3, 1975, 18–37.

8606 GRIFFITHS, A.R.G. The Irish Board of Works in the famine years. *Hist. J.*, 13, 1970, 634–652.

8607 GWYNN, DENIS. Young Ireland and 1848. Cork and Oxford: 1949.

8608 HAMER, D.A. The Irish question and liberal politics, 1886–1894. *Hist. J.*, 12, 1969, 511–532.

8609 HAMMOND, J.L. Gladstone and the Irish nation. [Reprint of 1st ed.]. London: 1964. Originally published 1938.

8610 HANHAM, H.J. *compiler*. Bibliography of British history, 1851–1914. Issued under the direction of the American Historical Association and the Royal Historical Society of Great Britain. Oxford: 1976. Ireland, pp. 1173–1238.

8611 HERNON, JOSEPH M., *Jr.* The Historian as politician: G.O. Trevelyan as Irish Chief Secretary. *Eire-Ir.*, vol. 8, no. 3, 1973, 3–15.

8612 HOWARD, C.H.D. Documents relating to the Irish 'Central Board' scheme, 1884–5. *Ir. Hist. Stud.*, 8, 1952–3, 237–63, 324–61.

8613 — 'The man on a tricycle': W.H. Duignan and Ireland, 1881–5. *ibid.*, vol. 14, no. 55, 1965, 246–260.

8614 HURST, MICHAEL. Parnell and Irish nationalism. London: 1968. Bibliog., pp. 108–110.

8615 LARKIN, EMMET. The Roman Catholic Church and the creation of the modern Irish state, 1878–1886. Philadelphia and Dublin: 1975.

8616 LEE, JOSEPH. The modernisation of Irish society, 1848–1918. Dublin, 1973. *(The Gill History of Ireland).*

8617 LYNE, D.C. Irish-Canadian financial contributions to the Home Rule movement in the 1890s. *Stud. Hib.*, 7, 1967, 182–206.

8618 LYONS, F.S.L. Ireland in the famine: 1830 to the present day. London: 1971.

8619 MCCAFFREY, LAWRENCE J. Daniel O'Connell and the Repeal Year. Lexington: 1966.

8620 — Irish federalism in the 1870s: a study in conservative nationalism. [with bibliog.]. *Amer. Phil. Soc. Trans.*, *new ser.*, vol. 52, pt. 6, 1962, 1–58.

8621 MCCARTNEY, DONAL. James Anthony Froude and Ireland: a historiographical controversy of the nineteenth century. *Hist. Stud.*, 8, 1971, 171–190; also contained in *Ir. Univ. Rev.*, vol. 1, no. 2, 1971, 238–257.

8622 MCCARTNEY, DONALD. The writings of history in Ireland, 1800–30. *Ir. Hist. Stud.*, 10, 1957, 347–62.

8623 MCDOWELL, ROBERT BRENDAN. Public opinion and government policy in Ireland, 1801–46. London: 1952. Bibliog., pp. 261–92.

8624 MACGRATH, KEVIN M. Writers in 'The Nation', 1842–5. *Ir. Hist. Stud.*, 6, 1948–9, 189–223.

8625 MACHIN, G.I.T. The Catholic question in English politics, 1820–1830. Oxford: 1964. Bibliog., pp. 196–213.

8626 MACINTYRE, ANGUS. The Liberator: Daniel O'Connell and the Irish Party, 1830–1847. London: 1965. Bibliog., pp. 311–329.

8627 MACMANUS, M.J. *ed.* Thomas Davis and Young Ireland. Dublin: 1945. Bibliography of Young Ireland, by *Bibliophile* [*i.e.*, M.J. MacManus], pp. 125–7, including bibliographies of Thomas Davis, John Mitchel, Thomas Francis Meagher, William Smith O'Brien, Thomas D'Arcy McGee, and James Clarence Mangan.

8628 MARLOW, JOYCE. Captain Boycott and the Irish. London: 1973. Bibliog., pp. 303–308.

8629 MOODY, T.W. and O'BROIN, LEON. Select documents: XXXII: The I.R.B. Supreme Council, 1868–78. *Ir. Hist. Stud*., vol. 19, no. 75, 1975, 286–332.

8630 NORMAN, EDWARD. A history of modern Ireland. London: 1971. Bibliog., pp. 315–322. From 1800 to the present day.

8631 NORTHERN IRELAND, Public Record Office. The Ashbourne papers, 1869–1913: a calendar of the papers of Edward Gibson, 1st Lord Ashbourne, compiled by A.B. Cooke and A.P.W. Malcolmson. Belfast: 1974. Ashbourne was Lord Chancellor of Ireland.

8632 NOWLAN, KEVIN B. Charles Gavan Duffy and the Repeal Movement. Dublin: 1963. *(O'Donnell Lectures series no. 7).*

8633 — The meaning of repeal in Irish history. *Hist. Stud.*, 1963, 1–17.

8634 — The politics of repeal: a study in the relations between Great Britain and Ireland, 1841–50. London and Toronto: 1965. *(Studies in Irish history, second series, vol. 3).* Bibliog., pp. 232–241.

8635 O'BRIEN, JOSEPH V. William O'Brien and the course of Irish politics, 1881–1918. Berkeley and London: 1976. Bibliog., pp. 259–267.

8636 O'BROIN, LEON. Revolutionary underground: the story of the Irish Republican Brotherhood, 1858–1924. Dublin: 1976.

8637 O'CONNELL, MAURICE R. Daniel O'Connell: income, expenditure and despair. *Ir. Hist. Stud.*, vol. 17, no. 66, 1970, 200–220.

8638 O'DEA, LAURENCE. Thomas Drummond. *Dublin Hist. Rec.*, 24, 1970–1, 112–123. Lord Lieutenant for Ireland, 1835–40.

8639 O'DONOVAN ROSSA, DIARMUID. Rossa's Recollections. [Facsimile reprint with] introduction by Sean O'Luing and a new index. Shannon: 1972. First ed. New York: 1898.

8640 O'FARRELL, PATRICK. England and Ireland since 1800. London: 1975. Bibliog., pp. 181–190.

8641 O'LUANAIGH, DONAL. Ireland and the Franco-Prussian war. *Eire-Ir.*, vol. 9, no. 1, 1974, 3–13.

8642 — Ireland and the Paris Commune, 1871. *Cap. Ann.*, 1972, 233–246.

8643 O'NEILL, THOMAS P. A bibliography of the Great Irish Famine. Not published, but forms part of thesis for M.A., National University of Ireland: 1946.

8644 — Notes on Irish radical journals [1848–9]. *An Leab.*, 12, 1954, 139–44.

8645 O'SULLIVAN, THOMAS F. The Young Irelanders. 2nd ed. Tralee, 1945. Bibliog., pp. 663–70. First published 1944.

8646 O'TUATHAIGH, GEAROID. Ireland before the famine, 1798–1848. Dublin and London: 1972. *(Gill History of Ireland vol. 9.)*

8647 PALMER, NORMAN DUNBAR. The Irish land league crisis. New Haven: 1940. *(Yale Hist. Pub. Miscell.,* no. 37.) Bibliog., pp. 313–23.

8648 REYNOLDS, JAMES A. The Catholic emancipation crisis in Ireland, 1823–9. New Haven: 1954. *(Yale Hist. Pub. Miscell.*, no. 60). Bibliog., pp. 177–87.

8649 ROSSI, JOHN PATRICK. Home Rule and the Liverpool by-election of 1880. *Ir. Hist. Stud.*, 19, 1974, 156–168.

8650 SAVAGE, DONALD C. The Irish Unionists: 1867–1886. *Eire-Ir.*, vol. 2, no. 3, 1967, 86–101.

8651 SELECT LIST OF REFERENCES ON HOME RULE IN IRELAND. Washington, Library of Congress, 1912.

8652 SILLARD, P.A. The life and letters of John Martin (*i.e.* John Mitchel) with sketches of Thomas Devin Reilly, Father John Kenyon, and other 'Young Irelanders'. 2nd ed. Dublin: 1901. Bibliog. of John Mitchel's writings, pp. 283–285.

8653 SINNOTT, NIGEL H. Charles Bradlaugh and Ireland. *Cork Hist. Arch. Soc. J.*, vol. 77, no. 225, 1972, 1–24.

8654 STEELE, E.D. Gladstone and Ireland. *Ir. Hist. Stud.*, 17, 1970, 58–88.

8655 — Gladstone and Ireland: the ultimate triumph of morality. *Leeds Phil. Lit. Soc. Proc., Lit. Hist. Sec.*, vol. 14, pt. 1, 1970, 1–26.

8656 — Ireland and the Empire in the 1860s: imperial precedents for Gladstone's first Irish Land Act. *Hist. J.*, 11, 1968, 64–83.

8657 STRAUSS, E. Irish nationalism and British democracy. [Facsimile reprint]. Westport (Connecticut): 1975. 1st pub. London: 1951. Bibliog., pp. 293–8.

8658 TANSILL, CHARLES CALLAN. America and the fight for Irish freedom, 1866–1922: an old story based upon new data. New York: 1957. Bibliog., pp. 451–9.

8659 TIERNEY, MARK. Dr. Croke, the Irish bishops and the Parnell crisis: 18 November

1890 – 21 April 1891: some unpublished correspondence. *Coll. Hib.*, 11, 1968, 11–148. Dr. T.W. Croke, Archbishop of Cashel, 1875–1902.

8660 WHYTE, J.H. The Independent Irish party, 1850–9. London: 1958. *(Oxford historical ser.)* Bibliog., pp. 184–90.

8661 WOODHAM-SMITH, CECIL. The Great hunger: Ireland, 1845–9. London: 1962. Bibliog., pp. 419–498.

8662 YOUNG IRELAND BIBLIOGRAPHY. *Ir. Book Lov.,* 15, 1925, 48.

Fenian Movement

8663 BATEMAN, ROBERT J. Captain Timothy Deasy, Fenian. *Ir. Sword,* vol. 8, no. 31, 1967, 130–137.

8664 BOURKE, MARCUS. John O'Leary: a study in Irish separatism. Tralee: 1967. Sources and notes, pp. 236–244.

8665 — John O'Leary's place in the Fenian movement. *Nth. Munster Antiq. J.,* 10, 1966–67, 148–156.

8666 D'ARCY, WILLIAM. The Fenian movement in the United States, 1858–1886. New York: 1971. Reprint of 1947 ed. Bibliog., pp. 412–28.

8667 DE COURCY IRELAND, JOHN. Fenianism and naval affairs. *Ir. Sword.*, vol. 8, no. 30, 1967, 10–22.

8668 — A preliminary study of the Fenians and the sea. *Eire-Ir.*, vol. 2, no. 2, 1967, 36–54.

8669 DEVOY, JOHN. Recollections of an Irish rebel [1st ed. reprinted with an introduction by Sean O'Luing]. Shannon: 1969. Originally published New York: 1929.

8670 DUGGAN, G.C. The Fenians in Canada: a British officer's impressions. *Ir. Sword,* vol. 8, no. 31, 1967, 88–91.

8671 GUPTILL, PATRICIA F. A popular bibliography of the Fenian movement. *Eire-Ir.*, vol. 4, no. 2, 1969, 18–25.

8672 HURST, JAMES W. The Fenians: a bibliography. *Eire-Ir.*, vol. 4, no. 4, 1969, 90–106.

8673 JENKINS, BRIAN. Fenians and Anglo-American relations during reconstruction. Ithaca and London: 1969. Bibliog., pp.329–340.

8674 KEANE, EDWARD. Active Fenians in Co. Limerick as listed in the Crown Solicitor's brief. *Nth. Munster Antiq. J.*, 10, 1966–67, 169–172.

8675 LYNE, D.C., and TONER, PETER M. Fenianism in Canada, 1874–84. *Stud. Hib.*, 12, 1972, 27–76.

8676 MACGIOLLA CHOILLE, BREANDAN. Fenian documents in the State Paper Office. *Ir. Hist. Stud.*, 16, 1968–69, 258–284.

8677 — Mourning the martyrs: a study of a demonstration in Limerick City, 8.12.1867. *Nth. Munster Antiq. J.*, 10, 1966–67, 173–205.

8678 MITCHELL, ARTHUR. The Fenian movement in America. *Eire-Ir.*, vol. 2, no. 4, 1967, 6–10.

8679 MOODY, T.W., *ed.* The Fenian movement. Cork [1968]. The Fenian movement: a select bibliography, pp. 113–126.

8680 NEIDHARDT, W.S. Fenianism in North America. University Park and London: 1975. Bibliog., pp. 152–159.

8681 NOLAN, PETER. Fariola, Massey and the Fenian Rising. *Cork Hist. Arch. Soc. J.*, 75, 1970, 1–11.

8682 O'BROIN, LEON. A Charles J. Kickham correspondence. *Studies,* 63, 1974, 251–258. Kickham was President of the Irish Republican Brotherhood.

8683 — Fenian fever: an Anglo-American dilemma. London: 1971. Bibliog., pp 259–260.

8683a — Revolutionary underground: the story of the Irish Republican Brotherhood. Dublin: 1976.

8684 O'CATHAOIR, BRENDAN. American Fenianism and Canada, 1865–1871. *Ir. Sword.*, vol. 8, no. 31, 1967, 77–87.

8685 O'FIAICH, THOMAS. The Clergy and Fenianism, 1860–70. *Ir. Eccles. Rec.,* 109, 1968, 81–103.

8686 O'KELLY, SEAMUS G. The bold Fenian men. Dublin: 1967.

8687 O'LUING, SEAN. Aspects of the Fenian rising in Kerry, 1867. *Kerry Arch. Hist. Soc. J.*, 3, 1970, 131–153; 4, 1971, 139–164; 5, 1972, 103–132; 6, 1973, 172–194; 7, 1974, 107–133.

8688 PENDER, SEAMUS. Fenian papers in the Catholic University of America; a preliminary report. *Cork Hist. Arch. Soc. J.*, 74, 1969, 130–140; 75, 1970, 36–53; 76, 1971, 25–47, 137–149; 77, 1972, 45–59, 124–136; 78, 1973, 14–26; 79, 1974, 1–13; 80, 1975, 61–73; 81, 1976, 120–133; 82, 1977, 127–138.

8689 ROSE, PAUL. The Manchester martyrs: the story of a Fenian tragedy. London: 1970. Bibliog., pp. 137–140. William Phillip Allen, Michael Larkin and Michael O'Brien.

8690 RYAN, DESMOND. The historians and Fenianism. *Ir. Comm. Hist. Sci. Bull., new ser.*, vol. 6, no. 79, 1957–8, 3–4.

8691 — The Fenian Chief: a biography of James Stephens, with an introductory memoir, by Patrick Lynch. Dublin and Sydney: 1967. Bibliog., pp. ix–x.

8692 SEOIGHE, MAINCHIN. The Fenian attack on Kilmallock public barracks. *Nth. Munster Antiq., J.*, 10, 1966–67, 157–168.

8693 UNIVERSITY REVIEW, vol. 4, no. 3, 1967. Issue devoted to Fenianism.

Twentieth Century

General

8694 CARTY, JAMES. Bibliography of Irish history, 1870–1911. Dublin: 1940.

8695 — Bibliography of Irish history, 1912–21. Dublin: 1936.

8696 CRONIN, SEAN. The McGarrity papers. Tralee: 1972.

8697 FOX, R.M. Green banners: the story of the Irish struggle. London: 1938. Bibliog., pp. 341–3.

8698 KING, CLIFFORD. The Orange and the green. London: 1965. Bibliog., pp. 182–3.

8699 MACARDLE, DOROTHY. The Irish republic: a documented chronicle of the Anglo-Irish conflict and the partitioning of Ireland, with a detailed account of the period. 4th ed. Dublin: 1951. Bibliog., pp. 993–1002.

8700 O'MAHONY, T.P. The politics of dishonour: Ireland, 1916–1977. Dublin: 1977.

8701 TARPEY, MARIE V. Joseph McGarrity, fighter for Irish freedom. *Stud. Hib.*, 11, 1971, 164–180.

8702 THORNLEY, DAVID. Ireland: the end of an era? *Studies*, 53, 1964, 1–17.

Early Period

8703 BAYLEN, J.O. 'What Mr. Redmond thought': an unpublished interview by W.T. Stead with John Redmond, December 1906. *Ir. Hist. Stud.*, 19, 1974, 169–189.

8704 BUCKLAND, P.J. The Southern Irish unionists, the Irish question, and British politics, 1906–14. *Ir. Hist. Stud.,* vol. 15, no. 59, 1967, 228–255.

8705 DAVIS, RICHARD P. Arthur Griffith and non-violent Sinn Fein. Dublin: 1974. Bibliog., pp. 208–217.

8706 DEUTSCH-BRADY, CHANTAL. The King's visit and the People's Protection Committee, 1903. *Eire-Ir.*, vol. 10, no. 3, 1975, 3–10.

8707 FAIR, JOHN D. The King, the constitution and Ulster: interparty negotiations of 1913 and 1914. *Eire-Ir.*, vol. 6, no. 1, 1971, 35–52.

8708 FANNING, J.R. The Unionist Party and Ireland, 1906–10. *Ir. Hist. Stud.*, 15, 1966–7, 147–171.

8709 FERGUSSON, *Sir* JAMES. The Curragh incident. London: 1964. Bibliog., pp. 230–232.

8710 HEPBURN, A.C. The Irish council bill and the fall of Sir Anthony MacDonnell, 1906–7. *Ir. Hist. Rec.*, vol. 17, no. 68, 1971, 470–498.

8711 MCCREADY, H.W. Home rule and the Liberal Party, 1899–1906. *Ir. Hist. Stud.*, 13, 1962–63, 316–348.

8712 MCEVATT, R.M. Arthur Griffith and his early Sinn Fein politics. *Cap. Ann.*, 1971, 232–238.

8713 — Thomas Martin and the founding of Sinn Fein. *Cap. Ann.*, 1970, 97–113.

8714 Martin, F.X., *ed*. The Howth gun-running and the Kilcoole gun-running, 1914: recollections and documents. Dublin: 1964.

8715 O'Broin, Leon. The Chief Secretary: Augustine Birrell in Ireland. London: 1969. Bibliog., pp. 226–228.

8716 O'Connor, Ulick. A terrible beauty is born: the Irish troubles, 1912–1922. London: 1975. Bibliog., pp. 171–5.

8717 O'Donoghue, Florence. A checklist of sources for Irish history, 1913–23. *Eire-Ir.*, vol. 1, no. 4, 1966, 104–106.

8718 Powell, John Stocks. Dividing Ireland, 1912–1914. *Hist. Today*, 27, 1977, 658–666.

8719 Ryan, A.P. Mutiny at the Curragh. London: 1956. Bibliog., pp. 213–5.

8720 Snoddy, Oliver. The Midland Volunteer Force, 1913. *Old Athlone Soc. J.*, vol. 1, no. 1, 1969, 39–44.

8721 The Times. Ireland of today; reprinted, with some additions, from *The Times*. London: 1913. Bibliog., pp. 403–5.

8722 Ward, Alan J. Ireland and Anglo-American relations, 1899–1921. London: 1969. Bibliog., pp. 269–274.

World War I Period

8723 Boyce, D.G. British conservative opinion, the Ulster question and the partition of Ireland, 1912–21. *Ir. Hist. Stud.*, 17, 1970, 89–112.

8724 — British opinion, Ireland and the War, 1916–1918. *Hist. J.*, vol. 17, no. 3, 1974, 575–593.

8725 — and Hazelhurst, Cameron. The Unknown Chief Secretary: H.E. Duke and Ireland, 1916–18. *Ir. Hist. Stud.* vol. 20, no. 79, 1977, 286–311.

8726 British Museum. Subject index of the books relating to the European War, 1914–18, acquired by the British Museum, 1914–20. London: 1922.

8727 Fitzpatrick, David. Politics and Irish life, 1913–1921: provincial experience of war and revolution. Dublin: 1977.

8728 Harris, Henry. The Irish regiments in the first world war. Cork: 1968.

8729 Irish National War Memorial. Ireland's memorial records, 1914–1918; being the names of Irishmen who fell in the great European War, 1914–1918, compiled by the Committee of the Irish National War Memorial, with decorative borders by Harry Clarke. Dublin: 1923. 8 vols. Privately printed for the Committee . . . by Maunsel and Roberts Ltd. Ed. limited to 100 copies.

8730 Ward, Alan J. Lloyd George and the 1918 Irish conscription crisis. *Hist. J.*, vol. 17, no. 1, 1974, 107–129.

The Rising

8731 Bell, J. Bowyer. The secret army: a history of the I.R.A., 1916–1970. London: 1970.

Bibliographies of 1916 and the Irish Revolution, by P.S. O'Hegarty.

8732 1. P.H. Pearse. *Dublin Mag., new series,* vol. 6, no. 5, 1931, 44–9.

8733 2–3. Thomas MacDonagh [and] Joseph Mary Plunkett. *ibid.*, vol. 7, no. 1, 1932, 26–30.

8734 4. Seumas O'Kelly. *ibid.*, vol. 9, no. 4, 1934, 47–51.

8735 5. James Connolly. *ibid.*, vol. 11, no. 2, 1936, 62–4.

8736 6–9. The O'Rahilly, Thomas J. Clarke, Constance Gore-Booth, Countess de Markievicz, Micheal ua hAnnrachain (Michael O'Hanrahan). *ibid.*, vol. 11, no. 3, 1936, 57–9.

8737 10–11. Terence MacSwiney and F. Sheehy Skeffington. *ibid.*, vol. 11, no. 4, 1936, 74–8.

8738 12–14. Arthur Griffith, Michael Collins, Kevin O'Higgins. *ibid.*, vol. 12, no. 1, 1937, 61–7.

8739 15. Darrell Figgis. *ibid.*, vol. 12, no. 3, 1937, 47–54.

8740 16. Erskine Childers. *ibid.*, vol. 23, no. 2, 1948, 40–3.

8741 17. Roger Casement. *ibid.*, vol. 24, no. 2, 1949, 31–4.

8742 Bouch, Joseph J. The Republican proclamation of Easter Monday, 1916. *Bibliog. Soc. Ir.,* 3, 1933–8, 43–52.

8743 Bourke, Marcus. The O'Rahilly. Tralee: 1967.

8744 CAULFIELD, MAX. The Easter rebellion. London: 1964. Bibliog., pp. 371–373.

8745 COFFEY, THOMAS M. Agony at Easter: the 1916 Irish uprising. London: 1970. Bibliog., pp. vii–ix.

8746 DAVIS, RICHARD. The advocacy of passive resistance in Ireland, 1916–1922. *Anglo-Irish Stud.*, 3, 1977, 35–55.

8747 DUGGAN, *Comdt.* J.P. German arms and the 1916 rising. *Ir. Def. J.*, 30, 1970, 97–104.

8748 FITZGIBBON, CONSTANTINE, Out of the lion's paw: Ireland wins her freedom. London: 1969.

8749 GOODSPEED, D.J. The conspirators: a study of the *coup d'état*. London: 1962. Chapter 2: Dublin, 1916. Bibliog., pp. 239–44.

8750 GREAVES, C. DESMOND, Liam Mellows and the Irish revolution. London: 1971.

8751 HEUSTON, JOHN M. Headquarters Battalion, army of the Irish Republic, Easter Week, 1916. [Dublin]: 1966.

8752 HOLT, EDGAR. Protest in arms: the Irish troubles, 1916–23. London: 1960. Bibliog., pp. 310–15.

8753 LIEBERSON, GODDARD. The Irish Uprising, 1916–1922. Foreword by Eamon de Valera. New York: 1966.

8754 MACGIOLLA CHOILLE, BREANDAN. Intelligence notes, 1913–16, Chief Secretary's Office, Dublin Castle, preserved in State Paper Office. Baile Atha Cliath: 1966.

8755 MCHUGH, ROGER, *ed.* Dublin: 1916: an illustrated anthology. London: 1976.

8756 MACLOCHLAINN, PIARAS F. Last words: letters and statements of the leaders executed after the Rising at Easter, 1916. Dublin: 1971.

8757 MARTIN, F.X. Eoin MacNeill on the 1916 rising. *Ir. Hist. Stud.,* vol. 12, no. 47, 1961, 226–71.

8758 — Leaders and men of the Easter rising: Dublin, 1916. London: 1967. (*Thomas Davis lectures*).

8759 — The 1916 Rising – a *coup d'état* or a 'bloody protest'? *Stud. Hib.*, 8, 1968, 106–137.

8760 — The Easter Rising, 1916, and University College, Dublin: 1966. Contents: Introduction by J.J. Hogan. Eoin MacNeill and the Easter Rising preparations, by F.X. Martin. Thomas MacDonagh and the Rising, by Michael Hayes. An tEiri Amach mar do chonnacsa e, by An tOllamh Liam O'Briain. In the G.P.O.: the medical unit, by Dr. James Ryan. Insan G.P.O.: Cumann na mBan, by Luise Ghabhanach Ni Dhubhthaigh. In the G.P.O.: the fighting men, by Joseph A Sweeney. Appendix 1. Contribution of University College, Dublin, to the national struggle, 1916–1921, by Michael Hayes. Appendix 2. Contribution of University College, Dublin, to the building of the new state, 1919–1935, by Michael Hayes.

8761 NATIONAL GALLERY OF IRELAND. Cuimhneachan, 1916: a commemorative exhibition of the Irish rebellion, 1916. Dublin: 1966.

8762 O'BROIN, LEON. Dublin Castle and the 1916 rising. Rev. ed., London: 1970. Bibliog., pp. 186–188.

8763 O'CALLAGHAN, EDWARD P. Correspondence between Bishop O'Dwyer and Bishop Foley on the Dublin Rising, 1916–17. *Coll. Hib.*, 18–19, 1976–77, 184–212.

8764 O'CATHASAIGH, P. [Sean O'Casey]. The story of the Irish Citizen Army. Dublin: 1971. Facsimile reprint of 1st ed. Dublin: 1919.

8765 O'DONOGHUE, FLORENCE. Plans for the 1916 Rising. *Univ. Rev.,* vol. 3, no. 1, 1962, 3–21.

8766 O'HIGGINS, BRIAN. The Soldiers story of Easter week: poems of 1916 [and] Prison letters, 1917–20, of Brian O'Higgins [hitherto unpublished] with sketches of the leaders, by Liam C. Martin. Dublin: 1966.

8767 ROBBINS, FRANK. Under the starry plough: recollections of the Irish Citizen Army. Dublin: 1977. Appendix: The Shelling of Liberty Hall in 1916, pp. 239–244.

8768 ROLLINS, RONALD G. O'Casey, Yeats and Behan: a prismatic view of the 1916 Easter week rising. *S.O'C. Rev.*, vol. 2, 1976, 196–207.

8769 RYAN, A.P. The Easter Rising, 1916. *Hist. Today*, 16, 1966, 234–242.

8770 SAVAGE, DAVID W. The attempted Home Rule settlement of 1916. *Eire-Ir.*, vol. 2, no. 3, 1967, 132–145.

8771 SNODDY, OLIVER. 1916 Government propaganda. *Old Athlone Soc. J.*, vol. 1, no. 3, 1972–3, 204–5.

8772 THOMPSON, WILLIAM IRWIN. The imagination of an insurrection: Dublin, Easter 1916: a study of an ideological movement. New York: 1967. Bibliog., pp. 245–250.

Aftermath and Civil War

8773 AKENSON, D.H. and FALLIN, J.F. The Irish Civil War and the drafting of the Free State Constitution: 'The drafting process'. *Eire-Ir.*, vol. 5, no. 2, 1970, 42–93.

8774 — The Irish Civil War and the drafting of the Free State Constitution: Collins, De Valera and the pact: a new interpretation. *ibid.*, 4, 1970, 28–70.

8775 BENNETT, RICHARD. The Black and Tans. Rev. ed. London: 1976. Bibliog., pp. 223–4. 1st published 1959.

8776 BOYCE, GEORGE. An encounter with Michael Collins: 1921. *Cork Hist. Arch. Soc. J.*, 80, 1975, 49–58.

8777 BROMAGE, MARY C. Consolidation of the Irish revolution, 1921–22: De Valera's plan. *Univ. Rev.,* vol. 5, no. 1, 1968, 23–35.

8778 BUTLER, EWAN. Barry's flying column. London: 1971. The story of the I.R.A.'s Cork no. 3 Brigade, 1919–21.

8779 COOGAN, TIM PAT. The I.R.A. London: 1970. Bibliog., pp. 357–8.

8780 — Ireland since the Rising. London: 1966. Bibliog., pp. 341–345.

8781 COSTIGAN, GIOVANNI. The Anglo-Irish conflict, 1919–1922: a war of independence or systematized murder? *Univ. Rev.*, vol. 5, no. 1, 1968, 64–86.

8782 CRONIN, SEAN. Ireland since the treaty. Dublin: 1971.

8783 — The story of Kevin Barry. Cork: 1965.

8784 CURRAN, JOSEPH M. The Consolidation of the Irish Revolution, 1921–1923: the Free Staters. *Univ. Rev.,* vol. 5, no. 1, 1968, 36–50.

8785 — The decline and fall of the IRB. *Eire-Ir.*, vol. 10, no. 1, 1975, 14–23.

8786 — Ireland since 1916. *Eire-Ir.*, vol. 1, no. 3, 1966, 14–28.

8787 — Lloyd George and the Irish settlement, 1921–1922. *Eire-Ir.*, vol. 7, no. 2, 1972, 14–46.

8788 DEASY, LIAM. The Beara Peninsula campaign. *Eire-Ir.*, vol. 1, no. 3, 1966, 63–78.

8789 — The Schull Peninsula in the War of Independence. *Eire-Ir.,* vol. 1, no. 2, 1966, 5–18.

8790 — Towards Ireland free: the West Cork brigade in the War of Independence, 1917–1921. Dublin and Cork: 1973. Bibliog., pp. 358–9. Reprinted 1977.

8791 GALLAGHER, FRANK. The indivisible island: the history of the partition of Ireland. London: 1957. Bibliog., pp. 307–8.

8792 GREAT BRITAIN. Parliament. Documents relative to the Sinn Fein movement. London: 1921. *(Command,* no. 1108, vol. 29.)

8793 — Intercourse between Bolshevism and Sinn Fein. London: 1921. *(Command,* no. 1326.)

8794 HAND, G.J. The last fifty years: what did Dublin Governments do [in relation to Partition]. *Soc. Stud.*, vol. 1, no. 3, 1972, 278–288.

8795 HAWKINS, JOHN. The Irish question today: the problems and dangers of partition. London: 1941. *(Fabian Society research ser.,* no. 54.) Bibliog., pp. 51–2.

8796 HAYES, MICHAEL. Dail Eireann and the Irish Civil War. *Studies*, 58, 1969, 1–23.

8797 KAVANAGH, SEAN. The Irish volunteers intelligence organisation. *Cap. Ann.*, 1969, 354–367.

8798 KIELY, BENEDICT. Counties of contention: a study of the origins and implications of the partition of Ireland. Cork: 1945. Bibliog., pp. 187–8.

8799 LAFFAN, MICHAEL. The unification of Sinn Fein in 1917. *Ir. Hist. Stud.*, 17, 1970–1, 355–379.

8800 MACAULAY, AMBROSE. The Government of Ireland Act, 1920: the origins of partition. *Cap. Ann.*, 1971, 289–296.

8801 McDonnell, Kathleen Keyes. There is a bridge at Bandon: a personal account of the Irish War of Independence. Cork and Dublin: 1972.

8802 McDowell, R.B. The Irish Convention, 1917–18. London and Toronto: 1970. *(Studies in Irish history, 2nd ser. vol. 6)*. Bibliog., pp. 228–231.

8803 MacEoin, Gary. The Irish Republican Army. *Eire-Ir.*, vol. 9, no. 2, 1974, 3–29.

8804 Martin, Ged. The Irish Free State and the evolution of the Commonwealth, 1921–49. *In* Reappraisals in British imperial history, by Ronald Hyam and Ged Martin. London: 1975.

8805 Mitchell, Arthur. Labour and the national struggle, 1919–1921. *Cap. Ann.*, 1971, 261–288.

8806 Mulcahy, Richard. Chief of Staff, 1919. *Cap. Ann.*, 1969, 340–352.

8807 — Michael Collins and the making of a new Ireland. *Studies*, 67, 1978, 187–200.

8808 Neeson, Eoin. The Civil war in Ireland, 1922–23. Rev. ed. Cork: 1969. *(Mercier paperback ser.)* Bibliog., pp. 345–348.

8809 Neligan, David. The spy in the castle. London: 1968. The author served with Michael Collins at the time of the Black and Tans.

8810 O'Beirne-Ranelagh, John. The I.R.B. from the Treaty to 1924. *Ir. Hist. Stud.,* 20, 1976, 26–39.

8811 O'Connor, Frank. The Big Fellow: Michael Collins and the Irish Revolution. Rev. ed., Dublin: 1965. First pub. 1937.

8812 O'Muraile, Nollaig. Aspects of the Anglo-Irish struggle, 1919–1921. *Zenith,* 2, 1972, 69–78.

8813 O'Neill, Thomas P. In search of a political path: Irish republicanism, 1922 to 1927. *Hist. Stud.,* 10, 1976, 147–171.

8814 Pyne, Peter. The new Irish state and the decline of the Republican Sinn Fein Party, 1923–1926. *Eire-Ir.*, vol. 11, no. 3, 1976, 33–65.

8815 Skinner, Liam C. Politicians by accident. Dublin: 1946. Includes biographical sketches of Eamon de Valera, Sean F. Lemass, Sean MacEntee, Dr. James Ryan, Frank Aiken, Thomas Derrig, Gerald Boland, Patrick J. Little, Oscar Traynor, Eamon Kissane, Sean O'Grady, Patrick Smith, Erskine H. Childers.

8816 Snoddy, Oliver. Ireland and the Paris Peace Conference, 1919. *Cap. Ann.*, 1969, 389–400.

8817 Taylor, Rex. Assassination: the death of Sir Henry Wilson and the tragedy of Ireland. London: 1961. Bibliog., p. 220.

8818 Townshend, Charles. The British campaign in Ireland, 1919–1921: the development of political and military politics. London: 1975. Bibliog., pp. 224–232.

8819 Whyte, John H. Whitehall, Belfast and Dublin: new light on the treaty and the border. *Studies*, 60, 1971, 233–242. Review article of Thomas Jones's *Whitehall diary*, vol. 3.

8820 Younger, Carlton. A state of disunion: Arthur Griffith, Michael Collins, James Craig [Lord Craigavon], Eamon de Valera. London: 1972. Bibliog., pp. 338–340.

Nineteen-Thirties

8821 Bell, J. Bowyer. Ireland and the Spanish Civil War, 1936–1939. *Stud. Hib.,* 9, 1969, 137–163.

8822 Gilmore, George. 1934 Republican congress. Dublin [1970].

8823 MacManus, Francis. *ed*. The years of the great test [1926–39]. Cork: 1967. *(Thomas Davis lectures series)*.

8824 Manning, Maurice. The Blueshirts. Dublin [1971]. Bibliog., pp. 251–254.

8825 White, Terence de Vere. Social life in Ireland, 1927–1937. *Studies*, 54, 1965, 74–82.

World War II Period

8826 Bromage, Mary C. Churchill and Ireland. Notre Dame: 1964.

8827 Burdick, Charles. 'Gruen', German military plans and Ireland, 1940. *Ir. Def. J.*, 34, 1974, 77–80.

8828 CARROLL, JOSEPH T. Ireland in the war years. Newton Abbot and New York: 1975. Bibliog., pp. 184–5.

8829 CARTER, CAROLLE J. The spy who brought his lunch [Gunther Schutz]. *Eire-Ir.*, vol. 10, no. 1, 1975, 3–13.

8830 COX, COLM. Militar geographische angaben uber Irland. *Ir. Def. J.*, vol. 35, no. 3, 1975, 83–96. An account of the handbook on Irish military geographical data issued in Germany during the two world wars.

8831 DWYER, T. RYLE. American efforts to discredit De Valera during World War II. *Eire-Ir.*, vol. 8, no. 2, 1973, 20–33.

8832 — David Gray and the Axis representatives to Ireland during World War II. *Cap. Ann.*, 1973, 108–117.

8833 HOGAN, VINCENT PAUL. The neutrality of Ireland in World War II. 1953. *(University microfilms, Ann Arbor, Mich., pub.* 5272.)

8834 KEARNS, A.P. Off course landings and crashes – World War II. [German aircraft]. *Ir. Def. J.*, 37, 1977, 173–7.

8835 NOWLAN, KEVIN B. and WILLIAMS, T. DESMOND. Ireland in the war years and after, 1939–51. Dublin: 1969.

8836 SHARE, BERNARD. The emergency: neutral Ireland, 1939–45. Dublin: 1978. Bibliog., pp. 144–6.

8837 STEPHAN, ENNO. Spies in Ireland. Translated from the German . . . London: 1963. Bibliog., pp. 300–2. Originally published Hamburg: 1961.

Republic of Ireland

8838 FITZGERALD, GARRET. Towards a new Ireland. London and Dublin: 1972.

8839 LYSAGHT, D.R. O'CONNOR. The Republic of Ireland: an hypothesis in eight chapters and two intermissions. Cork: 1970. Bibliog., pp. 235–255.

8840 O'BRIEN, CONOR CRUISE. States of Ireland. London: 1972.

8841 SWEETMAN, ROSITA. 'On our knees': Ireland, 1972. London: 1972.

ULSTER

8842 ARCHER, CANON. Lough Neagh in legend and history. *Belfast Nat. Hist. Phil. Soc. Proc.,* 1923–4, 19–26.

8843 ARTHUR, PAUL. The people's democracy, 1968–1973. Belfast: 1974. Bibliog., pp. 150–2.

8844 BARRITT, DENIS P. and CARTER, CHARLES F. The Northern Ireland problem: a study in group relations. 2nd ed., London: 1972.

8845 BELFAST PUBLIC LIBRARIES. Northern Ireland, 1920–50: a selected list of books and pamphlets in the Belfast Public Libraries. Belfast: 1950.

8846 — Selected from the exhibition of Northern Ireland books and manuscripts. Belfast Museum and Art Gallery, May 3 to June 2, 1951. Belfast: 1951.

8847 BELL, SAM HANNA, *compiler*. Within our province: a miscellany of Ulster writing. Belfast: 1972.

8848 BLAKE, JOHN W. Northern Ireland in the Second World War. Belfast: 1956.

8849 BOEHRINGER, G.H. Beyond Hunt: a police policy for Northern Ireland of the future. *Soc. Stud.*, vol. 2, no. 4, 1973, 399–414.

8850 BOLAND, EAVAN. The Ulster experience. *Studies*, 63, 1974, 397–401.

8851 BOYD, ANDREW. Brian Faulkner. Tralee: 1972.

8852 — Holy war in Belfast. Tralee: 1969. Bibliog., p. 204.

8853 BRYANS, ROBIN. Ulster: a journey through the Six Counties. London: 1964.

8854 CAHILL, GILBERT A. Some nineteenth-century roots of the Ulster problem, 1829–1848. *Ir. Univ. Rev.*, vol. 1, no. 2, 1971, 215–237.

8855 CALLAGHAN, JAMES. A house divided: the dilemma of Northern Ireland. London: 1973.

8856 CARSON, WILLIAM ARTHUR. Ulster and the Irish Republic. Belfast: 1957. Includes introduction by David Gray, United States Minister to Eire, 1940–7.

8857 CLARK, DENNIS J. Irish blood: Northern Ireland and the American conscience. London and Port Washington: 1977. Bibliog., pp. 91–93.

8858 — and BOSERUP, ANDERS. The passion of protracted conflict. *Transaction*, vol. 7, no. 5, 1970, 14–31. Religion and politics in Northern Ireland.

8859 COLE, FRANCIS J. John Wesley and his Ulster contacts. *Belfast Nat. Hist. Phil. Soc. Proc., 2nd ser.,* vol. 2, pt. 5, 1944–5, 199–215.

8860 COSTELLO, M.A. De Annatis Hiberniae: a calendar of the first fruits levied on papal appointments to benefices in Ireland, A.D. 1400 to 1535. St. Patrick's College, Catholic Record Society. Maynooth: 1912. vol. 1, Ulster. No further volumes published.

8861 DARBY, JOHN. Conflict in Northern Ireland: the development of a polarised community. Dublin and New York: 1976. Bibliog., pp. 198–242.

8862 — Register of research into the Irish conflict. [Belfast]: Northern Ireland Community Relations Commission, [1972].

8863 DE PAOR, LIAM. Divided Ulster. London: 1970.

8864 DEUTSCH, RICHARD R. Northern Ireland, 1921–1974: a select bibliography. New York and London: 1975.

8865 — and MAGOWAN, VIVIEN. Northern Ireland, 1968–73: a chronology of events. Belfast.
Vol. 1. 1968–71. 1973.
Vol. 2. 1972–73. 1974.
Vol. 3. 1974. 1975.

8866 DILLON, MARTIN, and LEHANE, DENIS. Political murder in Northern Ireland. Harmondsworth: 1973.

8867 EDWARDS, OWEN DUDLEY. The sins of our fathers: roots of conflict in Northern Ireland. Dublin and London: 1970.

8868 FALLS, CYRIL. The Birth of Ulster [1st ed. reprinted.] London and New York: 1973. Bibliog., pp. 260–1.

8869 FARRELL, MICHAEL. Northern Ireland: the Orange state. London: 1976.

8870 FAULKNER, BRIAN. Memoirs of a statesman, edited by John Houston. London: 1978.

8871 FIELDS, RONA M. A society on the run: a psychology of Northern Ireland. Harmondsworth: 1973. Bibliog., pp. 214–16. Study of the long-term effects of stress on the population.

8872 GRACEY, J.W., and HOWARD, P. Northern Ireland political literature, 1968–1970: a catalogue of the collection in the Linen Hall Library. *Ir. Book*, vol. 1, no. 1, 1971, 44–82.

8873 GREAVES, C. DESMOND. The Irish crisis. London: 1972.

8874 HASTINGS, MAX. Ulster, 1969: the fight for civil rights in Northern Ireland. London: 1970.

8875 HEALY, T.M. Stolen waters: a page in the conquest of Ulster. London: 1913. Bibliog., pp. ix–x.

8876 HEATLEY, E., *and others*. Register of archives for Northern Ireland. *Ir. Comm. Hist. Sci. Bull., new series.,* vol. 3, no. 68, 1954, 4–6.

8877 HOBART, ANN E.L. A list of periodical references relating to Northern Ireland, 1921–59. [1959]. Typescript, compiled for competition held by Northern Ireland Branch of the Library Association.

8878 HULL, ROGER H. The Irish triangle: conflict in Northern Ireland. Princeton: 1976. Bibliog., pp. 273–305.

8879 KELLY, HENRY. How Stormont fell. Dublin and London: 1972.

8880 — Northern Ireland: so far. *Eire-Ir.*, vol. 6, no. 4, 1971, 6–14.

8881 KINGSTON, WILLIAM. Northern Ireland – if reason fails. *Pol. Qtr.,* 44, 1973, 22–32.

8882 LEAVY, JAMES. Structure or process?: new approaches to the problem of Northern Ireland. *Studies*, 62, 1973, 107–122.

8883 MACAULAY, AMBROSE. 'Britain's New Irish State' based on illegality and treason. *Cap. Ann.*, 1972, 351–361.

8884 MCGUIRE, MARIA. To take arms: a year in the Provisional IRA. London: 1973.

8885 MARRINAN, PATRICK. Paisley: a man of worth. Tralee: 1973.

8886 MARSHALL, JOHN J. Lough Neagh in legend and in history, with notices of its surrounding territories and clans. Dungannon: 1934.

8887 **Marshall**, W.F. Ulster sails west: the story of the great emigration from Ulster to North America in the eighteenth century . . . 3rd ed. Belfast: 1950. Bibliog., pp. 58–61.

8888 **Mawhinney, Brian**, and **Wells, Ronald**. Conflict and Christianity in Northern Ireland. Berkhamsted: 1975.

8889 **Miller, David** W. Queen's rebels: Ulster loyalism in historical perspective. Dublin and New York: 1978.

8890 **Moody**, T.W. The Ulster question, 1603–1973. 3rd ed. Dublin and Cork: 1978. Bibliog., pp. 112–23.

8891 — and **Beckett**, J.C. Ulster since 1800: a political and economic survey. London: B.B.C. (1st series) 1954. (2nd series), 1957.

8892 **Murphy, Dervla**. A place apart. London: 1978. Bibliog., pp. 289–290.

8893 **National Library of Ireland**. Books on Ireland. Dublin: Cultural Relations Committee, 1953. Ulster question, pp. 30–2.

8894 **Northern Bibliography**. *Hibernia,* vol. 37, no. 1, 1973, 22. List of titles, mainly political.

8895 **Northern Friends Peace Board**. Orange and green: a Quaker study of community relations in Northern Ireland. Sedbergh (Yorkshire): 1969.

8896 **Northern Ireland**. Ministry of Finance. Guide to periodical official publications. Belfast. [1925].

8897 — Stationery Office. List of Parliamentary and Stationery Office publicatons of the government of Northern Ireland. Belfast, 1923–. Supplements issued at frequent intervals.

8898 **Northern Ireland**, Public Record Office. Sources for the study of local history in Northern Ireland: a catalogue for an exhibition, January–July, 1968. Belfast: 1968.

8899 **O'Ceallaigh, Seamus**. Gleanings from Ulster history. Cork and Oxford: 1951.

8900 **O'Leary, Cornelius**. Northern Ireland: the politics of 'illusion'. *Pol. Qtr.,* 40, 1969, 307–315.

8901 **Oliver, John**. Ulster today and tomorrow. London: P.E.P., 1978. *(Broadsheet no. 574.)*

8902 **O'Neill, Terence**. The autobiography of Terence O'Neill. London: 1972.

8903 — Ulster at the crossroads; with an introduction by John Cole. London: 1969.

8904 **P.E.N., Belfast**. Ulster writings: a short Northern Ireland book list. Belfast: 1955.

8905 **Perceval-Maxwell**, M. The Scottish migration to Ulster in the reign of James I. London: 1973. Bibliog., pp. 374–394.

8906 **Probert, Belinda**. Beyond orange and green: the political economy of the Northern Ireland crisis. London: 1978. Bibliog., pp. 161–4.

8907 **Report on Transcripts of Hearth money Rolls**. Co. Antrim, 1669; Co. Londonderry, 1663; Co. Tyrone, 1666; and Subsidy Rolls, Co. Down, 1663. *Rep. D.K. Pub. Rec. Office, Nth. Ir.,* 1, 1924, 27–9.

8908 **Riddell, Patrick**. Fire over Ulster. London: 1970. Bibliog., pp. 207–208.

8909 **Rose, Richard**. Governing without consensus: an Irish perspective. London: 1971.

8910 — Northern Ireland: a time of choice. London: 1976.

8911 **Roth, Arthur**. Marching to different drummers: the passion for parades in Northern Ireland. *Harper's Mag.*, vol. 244, no. 1463, 1972, 32–42.

8912 **Russell, Hugh**, *ed*. Northern Ireland local history: a checklist of books and articles on Northern Ireland. Belfast: Belfast Public Libraries. Vol. 1, Cumulation. [1971].

8913 **Shearman, Hugh**. Ulster. London: 1949. *(County books ser.)* Includes short bibliogs. for the counties of Antrim, Londonderry, Down, Armagh, Tyrone, Fermanagh, Donegal, Monaghan and Cavan.

8914 **Stetler, Russell**. The Battle of the Bogside: the politics of violence in Northern Ireland. London: 1970. Bibliog. on CS [Gas] pp. 203–208; Sources pp. 209–212.

8915 **Stewart**, A.T.Q. The narrow ground: aspects of Ulster, 1609–1969. London: 1977. Bibliog., pp. 195–8.

8916 — The Ulster crisis. London: 1967. Bibliog., pp. 250–3. The first full account of 'Carson's army'.

8917 ULSTER BOOKS AND AUTHORS, 1900–53. *Rann,* 20, 1953, 55–73.

8918 ULSTER JOURNAL OF ARCHAEOLOGY. Belfast, vol. 1–, 1853–.

8919 ULSTER YEAR BOOK: official yearbook of Northern Ireland. Belfast: 1926–. Normally published at intervals of three years. A short bibliography is appended to each chapter.

8920 WALLACE, MARTIN. Drums and guns: revolution in Ulster. London: 1970.

8921 — Northern Ireland: 50 years of self-government. Newton Abbot: 1971. Bibliog., pp. 183–187.

8922 WINCHESTER, SIMON. In holy terror: reporting the Ulster troubles. London: 1974.

8923 WITHEROW, THOMAS. Derry and Enniskillen in the year 1689: the story of some famous battlefields in Ulster. 4th ed. Belfast: 1913. Bibliog., pp. xi–xiii.

8924 WOODBURN, JAMES BARKLEY. The Ulster Scot: his history and religion. London: 1914. Bibliog., pp. 11–15.

Antrim

8925 ANTRIM COUNTY LIBRARY. A subject catalogue of books and some other material relating to County Antrim. 2nd ed. Ballymena: 1969. Prev. ed. 1966. Typescript.

8926 BEBBINGTON, JOHN. Belfast in literature. *Belfast Nat. Hist. Phil. Soc. Proc., 2nd ser.,* 4, 1955, 5–16.

8927 BECKETT, J.C. and GLASSCOCK, R.E. Belfast: the origin and growth of an individual city. London: 1967. Bibliog., pp. 199–204.

8928 BOYD, HUGH ALEXANDER. Rathlin Island, north of Antrim. Ballycastle: 1947. Bibliog., pp. 60–1.

8929 BRITISH ASSOCIATION FOR THE ADVANCEMENT OF SCIENCE. Belfast in its regional setting: a scientific survey, prepared for the meeting held in Belfast, September 3–10, 1952. Belfast: 1952. Bibliogs. appended to each chapter.

8930 BUDGE, IAN, and O'LEARY, CORNELIUS. Belfast, approach to crisis: a study of Belfast politics, 1613–1970. London: 1973.

8931 CLARK, WALLACE, Rathlin – disputed island. Portlaw (Co. Waterford): 1971. Bibliog., p. 132.

8932 DOWLIN, AVY, *compiler*. Ballycarry in olden days. Belfast: 1963.

8933 DUBOURDIEU, JOHN. Statistical survey of the county of Antrim with observations, on the means of improvement . . . Dublin: Dublin Society, 1812.

8934 FEDDEN, ROBIN. The Giant's Causeway: an illustrated account. London: 1971.

8935 THE GLYNNS: journal of the Glens of Antrim Historical Society. vol. 1–, 1973–.

8936 HAYWARD, RICHARD. Belfast through the ages. Dundalk: 1952.

8937 HILL, GEORGE. An historical account of the MacDonnels of Antrim. [Facsimile reprint of 1st edition, with an introduction by E.R.R. Green]. Antrim: 1976. 1st ed. Belfast: 1873.

8938 HUME, A. Origin and characteristics of the people of the counties of Antrim and Down. Belfast: 1874.

8939 IRELAND, DENIS. From the jungle of Belfast: footnotes to history, 1904–1972. Belfast: 1973.

8940 JONES, EMRYS. A social geography of Belfast. London: 1960.

8941 KIELY, BENEDICT. The Giant's Causeway. *Ir. Wel.*, vol. 15, no. 2, 1966, 6–9.

8942 LOWRY, MARY. The story of Belfast and its surroundings. London: 1913. Bibliog., p. [191].

8943 MCCAUGHAN, MICHAEL, *ed*. An account of life in late nineteenth century East Belfast. *Ulster Folk,* 19, 1973, 3–12.

8944 MALCOMSON, A.P.W. Election politics in the borough of Antrim, 1750–1800. *Ir. Hist. Stud.,* 17, 1970, 32–57.

8945 MILLIN, S. SHANNON. Sidelights on Belfast history. Belfast and London: 1932.

8946 — Additional sidelights on Belfast history. Belfast and London: 1938.

8947 O'BYRNE, CATHAL. As I roved out in Belfast and district. 2nd ed. reprinted, with a new foreword by J.J. Campbell. East Ardsley: 1970. 1st published, 1946.

8948 O'HANLON, JOHN. Index of materials for the history and topography of the county of Antrim in the Irish Ordnance Survey Office. *Kilkenny S.E. Ir. Arch. Soc. J.*, 7, 1862–3, 238–45.

8949 OWEN, D.J. History of Belfast. Belfast and London: 1921. Bibliog., pp. xiii–xvi.

8950 PILSON, JAMES A. History of the rise and progress of Belfast, and annals of the county Antrim from the earliest period . . . Belfast: 1846.

8951 PRIOR, D.B., and BETTS, N.L. Flooding in Belfast. *Ir. Geog.*, 7, 1974, 1–18.

8952 ST. J. CLARKE, H.J. Thirty centuries in south-east Antrim: the parish of Coole or Carnmoney. Belfast: 1938. Bibliog., pp. 304–7.

8953 SHARKIE, R.B. A bibliography of printed material relating to the County of Antrim. Thesis accepted by Library Association [London] 1971–2, for Fellowship.

8954 SIMMS, S. Brief sketches of some forty authors of Belfast birth. *Belfast Nat. Hist. Phil. Soc. Proc.*, Session 1932–3, pp. 58–77.

8955 SMITH, W.S. Historical gleanings in Antrim and neighbourhood. Belfast: 1888.

8956 STEVENSON, NORAGH. Belfast before 1820: a bibliography of printed material. Belfast: The Belfast Library and Society for Promoting Knowledge (Linen Hall library): 1967. Contains 618 entries.

8957 YOUNG, R.M., *ed*. Historical notices of old Belfast and its vicinity: a selection from the Mss. collected by William Pinkerton, for his intended history of Belfast. Belfast: 1896.

8958 — Notes on the ancient deeds of Carrickfergus. *R. Soc. Antiq. Ir. J., 5th ser.*, 3, 1893, 64–8.

Derry

8959 BOYLE, E.M.F.G. Records of the town of Limavady, 1609–1808. Londonderry: 1912. Bibliog., p. 150.

8960 CARSON, W.R.H. A bibliography of printed material relating to the county and county borough of Londonderry. Thesis approved for Fellowship of the Library Association, 1968; Xerox copies available from University Microfilms International Ltd.

8961 COLBY, THOMAS. Ordnance survey of the county of Londonderry. Dublin: 1837. Unpaginated copy in Royal Dublin Society struck off previous to final revision for the purpose of being laid before the British Association, on its meeting in Dublin. [1835]. Dublin: 1835.

8962 LONDONDERRY COUNTY LIBRARY. The North Coast, Antrim and Londonderry [a bibliography, compiled by Keith Burridge and Phillip Reid]. 2nd ed. Coleraine [1973]. Typescript.

8963 MCKEE, JOHN. Co. Londonderry: a bibliography. 1959. Typescript, compiled for competition held by Northern Ireland branch of the Library Association.

8964 MARTIN, SAM. Historical gleanings from Co. Derry (and some from Fermanagh): traditions, superstitions and legends. Dublin: [1955].

8965 MILLIGAN, CECIL DAVIS. History of the siege of Londonderry. Belfast: 1951. Bibliog., pp. 381–9.

8966 — The walls of Derry: their building, defending and preserving. Londonderry: 1948–50. 2 pts. Bibliogs., pt. 1, pp. 89–91; pt. 2, 137–42.

8967 MOODY, T.W. The Londonderry plantation, 1609–41: the city of London and the plantation of Ulster. Belfast: 1939. Bibliog., pp. 418–39.

8968 MULLIN, *The Rev.* T.H. Coleraine in bygone centuries. Belfast: 1976.

8969 — Coleraine in Georgian times. Belfast: 1977.

8970 O'DONOVAN, JOHN. Letters containing information relative to the antiquities of Co. Londonderry, collected during the progress of the Ordnance Survey in 1834. [Dublin, 1926]. Typed copy in National Library, Dublin.

8971 O'HANLON, JOHN. Index of materials for the history and topography of the county of Londonderry in the Irish Ordnance Survey records and in the Royal Irish Academy. *Kilkenny S.E. Ir. Arch. Soc. J.*, 7, 1862–3, 313–15.

8972 PHILLIPS, THOMAS. Londonderry and the London companies, 1609–29; being a survey and other documents submitted to King

Charles I, by Sir Thomas Phillips. Belfast: 1928.

8973 SAMPSON, G. VAUGHAN. Statistical survey of the county of Londonderry, with observations on the means of improvement . . . Dublin: Dublin Society, 1802.

8974 SIMPSON, ROBERT. The annals of Derry, showing the rise and progress of the town from the earliest accounts on record to the plantation under James I – 1613, and thence of the city of Londonderry to the present time. Londonderry: 1847.

8975 UNPUBLISHED HISTORICAL MSS. COLLECTIONS relating to the county of Derry: a bibliographical note. *Ulster J. Arch.*, 15, 1909, 185.

8976 WALKER, GEORGE. The siege of Londonderry in 1689, edited by P. Dwyer, with a new introduction by E.E.R. Green. Wakefield: 1971. Facsimile reprint of 1893 ed. London. First published 1689.

Donegal

8977 ALLINGHAM, HUGH. Ballyshannon: its history and antiquities, with some account of the surrounding neighbourhood. Londonderry: 1879.

8978 CO. DONEGAL HISTORICAL SOCIETY JOURNAL. Vol. 1–, 1947–. (From vol. 2 *Donegal Annual.*)

8979 DOHERTY, WILLIAM JAMES. Inis-Owen and Tirconnel; being some account of antiquities and writers of the county of Donegal. 2nd ser. Dublin: 1895.

8980 GRAHAM, JEAN M. South-west Donegal in the seventeenth century. *Ir. Geog.*, vol. 6, no. 2, 1970, 136–152.

8981 IRISH MANUSCRIPTS COMMISSION. The civil survey, A.D. 1654–6. Vol. 3. Counties of Donegal, Londonderry and Tyrone: with the returns of church lands for the three counties, prepared for publication, with introductory notes by Robert C. Simington. Dublin: 1937.

8982 MACDONAGH, J.C.T., and MACINTYRE, EDWARD. Bibliography of Co. Donegal. *Donegal Hist. Soc. J.*, 1, 1947–50, 49–80, 152–64.

8983 MCKERROW, RAY E. The Legend of Bonnie Prince Charlie's travels in Donegal in 1746. *Eire-Ir.*, vol. 10, no. 4, 1975, 48–61.

8984 MCNAMARA, G. Notes towards a recent bibliography of County Donegal. *Donegal Ann.*, vol. 6, no. 2, 1965, 175–184.

8985 M'PARLAN, JAMES. Statistical survey of the county of Donegal, with observations on the means of improvement . . . Dublin: Dublin Society, 1802.

8986 O'CNAIMHSI, C.P. An historical geography of South Donegal. *Donegal Ann.*, vol. 10, no. 1, 1971, 36–61.

8987 O'DOMHNAILL, NIALL. Leabhraisneis ar Thir Chonaill. *Donegal Hist. Soc. J.*, 1, 1947–50, 217–30.

8988 O'DONNELL, *Fr.* TERENCE. Rosses: from the earliest times to 1640. *Donegal Ann.*, vol. 10, no. 1, 1971, 62–82; vol. 11, nos. 2–3, 1975–6, 131–153.

8989 O'DONOVAN, JOHN. Letters containing information relative to the antiquities of Co. Donegal, collected during the progress of the Ordnance Survey in 1834. [Dublin, 1926]. Typed copy in National Library, Dublin.

8990 O'GALLACHAIR, P. An early list of county Donegal parishes. *Donegal Ann.*, vol. 11, no. 1, 1974, 66–70.

8991 O'HANLON, JOHN. Index of materials for the history and topography of the county of Donegal in the Irish Ordnance Survey Office. *Kilkenny S.E. Ir. Arch. Soc. J.*, 7, 1862–3, 316–7.

8992 O'HANRAHAN, BRENDA. Contribution to bibliography of Donegal born writers. Completed for Fellowship of the Library Association of Ireland.

8993 SIMMS, J.G. Donegal in the Ulster plantation. *Ir. Geog.*, vol. 6, no. 4, 1972, 386–393.

8994 — The Ulster Plantation in County Donegal. *Donegal Ann.*, vol. 10, no. 1, 1971, 3–14.

Tyrone

8995 DILLON, MICHAEL Coalisland: the evolution of an individual landscape. *Stud. Hib.*, 8, 1968, 79–95.

8996 HUTCHISON, W.R. Tyrone precinct: a history of the plantation settlement of Dungannon and Mountjoy to modern times. Belfast: 1851. Bibliog., pp. 215–24.

8997 McEvoy, John. Statistical survey of the county of Tyrone, with observations on the means of improvement . . . Dublin: Dublin Society, 1802.

8998 Marshall, John J. Clocher na Righ (Clogher of the Kings); being a history of the town and district of Clogher, in the county of Tyrone. Also some account of the parish of Errigal Keeroge, in the county of Tyrone, and of the parish of Errigal Truagh in the county of Monaghan. Dungannon: 1930.

8999 — History of Dungannon . . . and bibliography of Dungannon printing. Dungannon: 1929. Bibliog., pp. 129–37.

9000 O'Daly, Bernard. Material for a history of the parish of Kilskeery. *Clogher Rec.*, vol. 1, no. 1, 1953, 4–17; vol. 1, no. 2, 1954, 8–13; vol. 1, no. 3, 1955, 88–110.

9001 O'Doibhlin, Eamon. Domhnach Mor (Donaghmore): an outline of parish history. An Omaigh, Clolann na Struaile, 1969. Bibliog., pp. 255–6.

9002 O'Gallachair, P. The Parish of Donaghcavey. *Clogher Rec.*, vol. 7, no. 2, 1970, 251–320.

9003 O'Hanlon, John. Index of materials for the history and topography of the county of Tyrone in the Irish Ordnance Survey records, and in the Royal Irish Academy. *Kilkenny S.E. Ir. Arch. Soc. J.*, 8, 1864–6, 20–27.

Down

9004 Barry, John. Hillsborough: a parish in the Ulster Plantation. Belfast: 1962.

9005 Crowe, W. Haughton. The Ring of Mourne. Dundalk: 1968.

9006 Dubourdieu, John. Statistical survey of the county of Down, with observations on the means of improvement . . . Dublin: Dublin Society, 1802.

9007 Garner, M.A.K. North Down as displayed in the Clanbrassil Lease and Rent Book. *Belfast Nat. Hist. Phil. Soc. Proc.*, 8, 1964–70, 19–27.

9008 Hamilton, James. The Hamilton manuscripts containing some account of the settlement of the territories of the Upper Clandeboye, Great Ardes and Dufferin in the county of Down . . . in the reigns of James I and Charles I . . . edited by T.K. Lowry. Belfast [1867].

9009 Harris, Walter. The ancient and present state of the County of Down . . . [Facsimile reprint, Ballynahinch (Co. Down) 1977]. 1st published Dublin: 1744.

9010 O'Donovan, John. Letters containing information relative to the antiquities of Co. Down, collected during the progress of the Ordnance Survey in 1834. [Dublin, 1926]. Typed copy in National Library, Dublin. Also printed as supplement to *An Leab.*, vol. 3, no. 1, 1909.

9011 O'Hanlon, John. Index of materials for the history and topography of the county of Down in the Irish Ordnance Survey records. *Kilkenny S.E. Ir. Arch Soc. J.,* 7, 1862–3, 14–36.

9012 Parkinson, Edward. The city of Downe from its earliest days, edited by R.E. Parkinson. [Facsimile ed.]. Bangor, (Co. Down): 1972. 1st pub. Belfast: 1927. Traces the history of Downpatrick from early Celtic times to the beginning of the 20th century.

9013 Parkinson, R.C. Downpatrick, the medieval city. *Belfast Nat. Hist. Phil. Soc. Proc.,* 8, 1964–70, 28–37.

9014 Pollock, W.G. Six miles from Bangor: the story of Donaghadee. Belfast: 1975.

9015 Stevenson, John. Two centuries of life in Down, 1600–1800. Belfast: 1920.

Armagh

9016 Coote, Charles. Statistical survey of the county of Armagh, with observations on the means of improvement . . . Dublin: Dublin Society, 1804.

9017 Garstin, John R. List of documents transferred from Armagh Diocesan Registry to the Public Record Office, Dublin. *Louth Arch. J.,* vol. 3, 1915, 347–56.

9018 Gwynn, Aubrey. The medieval province of Armagh, 1470–1545. Dundalk: 1946. Bibliog., pp. ix–xi.

9019 O'HANLON, JOHN. Index of materials for the history and topography of the county of Armagh in the Irish Ordnance Survey records. *Kilkenny S.E. Ir. Arch. Soc. J.*, 7, 1862–3, 310–13.

9020 PATERSON, T.G.F. The Armagh Manor Court Rolls, period 1625–7, and incidental notes on seventeenth century sources for Irish surnames in Co. Armagh. *Seanchas Ard.*, vol. 2, no. 2, 1957, 295–322.

9021 — Harvest home: the last sheaf: a selection from the writings of T.G.F. Paterson relating to County Armagh, edited, with an introduction, by E. Estyn Evans. Armagh: [1976].

9022 — An unpublished early 17th century census of the men and arms on the estates of the English and Scotch settlers in Co. Armagh. *Sean. Ard.*, vol. 5, no. 2, 1970, 401–417.

9023 SEANCHAS ARDMHACHA: journal of the Armagh Diocesan History Society. [Armagh.] vol. 1–, 1954–.

9024 STUART, JAMES. Historical memoirs of the city of Armagh; new ed. rev. corrected and largely re-written by the Rev. Ambrose Coleman. Dublin: 1900.

Monaghan

9025 COOTE, CHARLES. Statistical survey of the county of Monaghan, with observations on the means of improvement . . . Dublin: Dublin Society, 1801.

9026 O'HANLON, JOHN. Index of materials for the history and topography of the county of Monaghan in the Irish Ordnance Survey records and in the Royal Irish Academy. *Kilkenny S.E. Ir. Arch. Soc. J.*, 8, 1864–6, 20–7.

9027 O'MORDHA, PILIP. Some notes on Monaghan history, 1692–1866. *Clogher Rec.*, vol. 9, no. 1, 1976, 17–63.

9028 RUSHE, DENIS CAROLAN. Monaghan in the eighteenth century. Dublin and Dundalk: 1916.

9029 — History of Monaghan for two hundred years, 1660–1860. Dundalk: 1921.

Fermanagh

9030 DUNDAS, W.H. Enniskillen, parish and town. Dundalk and Enniskillen: 1913. Bibliog., pp. viii–ix.

9031 LIVINGSTONE, PEADAR. The Fermanagh story: a documented history of the county of Fermanagh from the earliest times to the present day. Enniskillen: 1969. Bibliog., pp. 501–519; printing and newspapers, pp. 520–3.

9032 O'DONOVAN, JOHN. Letters containing information relative to the antiquities of the county of Fermanagh, collected during the progress of the Ordnance Survey in 1834–5. [Dublin, 1926]. Typed copy in National Library, Dublin.

9033 O'HANLON, JOHN. Index of materials for the history and topography of the county of Fermanagh in the Irish Ordnance Survey records. *Kilkenny S.E. Ir. Arch. Soc. J.*, 8, 1864–6, 20–7.

9034 ROGERS, MARY. Prospect of Erne: a study of the islands and shores of Lough Erne, Co. Fermanagh, Ulster's first national park. Belfast: 1967. Bibliog., pp. 247–53.

Cavan

9035 COOTE, CHARLES. Statistical survey of the county of Cavan, with observations on the means of improvement . . . Dublin: Dublin Society, 1802.

9036 CULLEN, SARA. Books and authors of County Cavan: a bibliography and an essay. Cavan: 1965. *See also* Sources for Cavan local history, by Sara Cullen, *Breifne*, vol. 5, no. 18, 1977–8, 185–205.

9037 GAELIC SOURCES FOR CAVAN HISTORY. In *A Genealogical history of the O'Reillys written in the eighteenth century,* edited by James Carney. Cavan: 1959, pp. 7–24.

9038 O'DONOVAN, JOHN. Letters containing information relative to the antiquities of the counties of Cavan and Leitrim, collected during the progress of the Ordnance Survey in 1836. [Dublin, 1926]. Typed copy in National Library, Dublin.

9039 O'HANLON, JOHN. Index of materials for the history and topography of the county of Cavan in the Irish Ordnance Survey records. *Kilkenny S.E. Ir. Arch. Soc. J.*, 8, 1864–6, 20–7.

9040 SMYTH, T.S. The civic history of the town of Cavan. Cavan: 1934.

9041 — Municipal charters of the town of Cavan. *Admin.,* 10, 1962, 310–317.

9042 SOURCES OF INFORMATION ON THE ANTIQUITIES AND HISTORY OF CAVAN AND LEITRIM: suggestions. *Breifny Antiq. Soc. J.,* 1, 1920–2, 3–6, 53.

CONNAUGHT

9043 ANNALA CONNACHT: the annals of Connacht. (A.D. 1224–1544), edited by A. Martin Freeman. Dublin: 1944.

9044 COLEMAN, JAMES. Bibliographia Conaciensis: a list of the topographical and other works relating to Connaught and each of its five counties. *Galway Arch. Hist. Soc. J.,* 5, 1907–8, 28–34, 239.

9045 IRISH MANUSCRIPTS COMMISSION. Index to *The Compossicion Booke of Conought, 1585*, prepared by G.A. Hayes-McCoy. Dublin: 1942. Is a source of exceptional value for the history of Connaught and Clare families and place names.

Leitrim

9046 COLEMAN, JAMES. See no. 9044.

9047 M'PARLAN, JAMES. Statistical survey of the county of Leitrim with observations on the means of improvement . . . Dublin: Dublin Society, 1802.

9048 O'DONOVAN, JOHN. See no. 9038.

9049 O'HANLON, JOHN. List of materials for the history and topography of the county of Leitrim in the Ordnance Survey records. *Kilkenny S.E. Ir. Arch. Soc. J.,* 9, 1867, 218–20.

Sligo

9050 COLEMAN, JAMES. See no. 9044.

9051 IRISH FIELD CLUB UNION. Report of the fourth triennial conference and excursion held at Sligo, July 12–18, 1904. [with bibliogs.]. *Ir. Nat.,* 13, 1904, 173–224.

9052 KILGANNON, TADHG, *compiler*. Sligo and its surroundings: a descriptive and pictorial guide to the history, scenery, antiquities, and places of interest in and around Sligo. Sligo: 1926.

9053 MACDONAGH, JAMES CHRISTOPHER. History of Ballymote and the parish of Emlaghfad. Dublin: 1936. Bibliog., pp. [vii–viii].

9054 MACLYSAGHT, E. Seventeenth century Hearth money rolls, with full transcript relating to Co. Sligo. *Anal. Hib.*, 24, 1967, 1–89.

9055 M'PARLAN, JAMES. Statistical survey of the county of Sligo, with observations on the means of improvement . . . Dublin: Dublin Society: 1802.

9056 MCTERNAN, JOHN C. Here's to their memory: profiles of distinguished Sligonians of bygone days. Dublin and Cork: 1977.

9057 — Historic Sligo: a bibliographical introduction to the antiquities and history, maps and surveys, Mss. and newspapers, historical families and notable individuals of County Sligo. Sligo: 1965.

9058 O'DONOVAN, JOHN. Letters containing information relative to the antiquities of Sligo, collected during the progress of the Ordnance Survey in 1836. [Dublin, 1926]. Typed copy in National Library, Dublin.

9059 O'HANLON, JOHN. List of materials for the history and topography of the county of Sligo in the Ordnance Survey records. *Kilkenny S.E. Ir. Arch. Soc. J.,* 9, 1867, 103–6.

9060 O'RORKE, T. The history of Sligo: town and county. Dublin: [1889]. 2 vols.

9061 WOOD-MARTIN, W.G. History of Sligo, county and town . . . to 1668. Dublin: 1882–9. 2 vols.

Mayo

9062 BENNETT, JIM. Ireland's largest Island: Achill, Co. Mayo. *Country Life,* vol. 155, no. 4012, 1974, 1296–8.

9063 COLEMAN, JAMES. See no. 9044.

9064 IRISH MANUSCRIPTS COMMISSION. Books of survey and distribution; being abstracts of various surveys and instruments of title, 1636–1703: vol. 2. County of Mayo, with maps of the county from Petty's Atlas, 1683, and of Tirawley barony from the Down Survey, 1657, with introductory notes by Robert C. Simington. Dublin: 1956.

9065 — The Strafford Inquisition of Co. Mayo. *(R.I.A. MS.* 24 5 15), edited by William O'Sullivan. Dublin: 1958.

9066 KNOX, HUBERT THOMAS. The history of Mayo to the close of the sixteenth century. Dublin: 1908. Bibliog., p. vii.

9067 MCNALLY, KENNETH. Achill. Newton Abbot: 1973. Bibliog., pp. 229–231.

9068 M'PARLAN, JAMES. Statistical survey of the county of Mayo, with observations on the means of improvement . . . Dublin: Dublin Society, 1802.

9069 MULLOY, SHEILA. Mayo musings. *Cap. Ann.*, 1974, 305–311.

9070 O'DONOVAN, JOHN. Letters containing information relative to the antiquities of Co. Mayo, collected during the progress of the Ordnance Survey in 1838. [Dublin, 1926.] 2 vols. Typed copy in National Library, Dublin.

9071 O'FARRELL, MICHAEL. Achill. *Cap. Ann.*, 1972, 214–220.

9072 O'HANLON, JOHN. Index of materials for the history and topography of the county of Mayo in the Irish Ordnance Survey records, and in the Royal Irish Academy. *Kilkenny S.E. Ir. Arch. Soc. J.*, 9, 1867, 212–15.

Galway

9073 COLEMAN, JAMES. See no. 9044.

9074 CREERY, OLIVE. Index to the references to national and ancient monuments in Co. Galway, contained in the *Annual Reports of the Office of Public Works, Ireland,* between the years 1875–1909. *Galway Arch. Hist. Soc. J.*, 7, 1911, 120–5.

9075 CURRICULUM DEVELOPMENT UNIT. A world of stone. Dublin: [1977].

9076 D'ALTON, JOHN. History of the archdiocese of Tuam. Dublin: 1928. 2 vols. Writers of the archdiocese, vol. 2, pp. 340–67.

9077 DUTTON, HELY. A statistical and agricultural survey of the county of Galway, with observations on the means of improvement . . . Dublin: Dublin Society, 1824.

9078 EAGLE, JUDITH. Aran: islands of changing light. *Country Life,* vol. 159, no. 4114, 1976, 1162–4.

9079 EGAN, PATRICK K. The parish of Ballinasloe: its history from the earliest times to the present day. Dublin: 1960. Bibliog., pp. 322–8.

9080 FAHEY, J. The Galway historical manuscripts and how they were discovered. *Galway Arch. Hist. Soc. J.,* 1, 1900–1, 85–9.

9081 FALKINER, C. LITTON. Some suggestions towards a county history. Appendix: A list of books and documents relating to Ireland which contain information relative to the history of the county or city of Galway. *Galway Arch. Hist. Soc. J.*, 2, 1902, 91–102.

9082 GALVIA: irisleabhar chumann seandaluiochta is staire na Gaillimhe. Galway, vol. 1–, 1954–.

9083 GALWAY ARCHAEOLOGICAL AND HISTORICAL SOCIETY JOURNAL. Galway, vol. 1–, 1900–1–. Index to volumes 1–7, compiled by M. Bradshaw and J. Dowie. Dublin: 1913.

9084 GALWAY COUNTY COUNCIL PUBLIC LIBRARIES. The Galway Reader incorporating quarterly notes. 1–4, 1948–54.

9085 HARDIMAN, JAMES. History of the town and county of Galway, from the earliest period to the present time, 1820 . . . to which is added a copious appendix containing the principal charters and other original documents. Galway: 1958. First published, Dublin: 1820. Hardiman was librarian of Queen's College, Galway, from 1849 to 1855.

9086 IRISH MANUSCRIPTS COMMISSION. Books of survey and distribution, being abstracts of various surveys and instruments of title, 1636–1703. vol. 3. County of Galway, with map of the county from Petty's Atlas, 1683. Prepared for publication by Brendan MacGiolla Choille. Introductions by Robert C. Simington. Dublin: 1962.

9087 KAVANAGH, MARY. A bibliography of the County Galway. Galway: 1965.

9088 KEARNS, KEVIN C. The Aran Islands: an imperiled Irish outpost. *Amer. Phil. Soc. Proc.*, vol. 120, no. 6, 1976, 421–438.

9089 MACLYSAGHT, EDWARD, *and others*. Report on documents relating to the Wardenship of Galway. *Anal. Hib.*,no. 14, 1944.

9090 MAHER, HELEN. Galway authors: a contribution towards a biographical and bibliographical index, with an essay on the history and literature in Galway. Galway: 1976.

9091 MOULD, D.C. POCHIN. The Aran islands. Newton Abbot: 1972. Bibliog., pp. 161–165.

9092 MURTAGH, HARMAN. Galway and the Jacobite war. *Ir. Sword,* vol. 12, no. 46, 1975, 1–14.

9093 NOLAN, J.P. The references for political changes of property, Co. Galway. *Galway Arch. Hist. Soc. J.,* 3, 1903, 37–43.

9094 O'DONOVAN, JOHN. Letters containing information relative to the antiquities of the county of Galway, collected during the progress of the Ordnance Survey in 1839. [Dublin: 1927]. Typed copy in National Library, Dublin.

9095 O'HANLON, JOHN. Index of materials for the history and topography of the county of Galway in the Irish Ordnance Survey records. *Kilkenny S.E. Ir. Arch. Soc. J.*, 9, 1867, 215–18.

9096 O'SULLIVAN, M.D. Old Galway: the history of a Norman colony in Ireland. Cambridge: 1942. Bibliog., pp. 468–74.

9097 REDINGTON, M. Catalogue of the exhibit of the Galway Archaeological and Historical Society in the archaeological section of the Galway exhibition, 1908. *Galway Arch. Hist. Soc. J.,* 5, 1908, 178–92.

9098 SEMPLE, MAURICE. Reflections on Lough Corrib. Galway: 1974.

9099 THOMAS, VERONICA. The Arans, Ireland's invincible isles. *Nat. Geog.,* 139, 1971, 545–572.

9100 TOWNLEY, C. Writings on the town and county of Galway. *Galway Reader,* vol. 4, nos. 2–3, 1954, 109–115.

Roscommon

9101 THE ANNALS OF LOCH CE: a chronicle of Irish affairs from A.D. 1014 to 1590, edited with a translation by William M. Hennessy. London: 1871. 2 vols. *(Rolls series)*.

9102 BURKE, FRANCIS. Loch Ce and its annals: North Roscommon and the diocese of Elphin in times of old. Dublin: 1895.

9103 COLEMAN, JAMES. See no. 9044.

9104 FREEMAN, T.W. The town and district of Roscommon: *Ir. Geog.*, vol. 2, no. 2, 1950, 61–76.

9105 IRISH MANUSCRIPTS COMMISSION. Books of survey and distribution; being abstracts of various surveys and instruments of title, 1636–1703: vol. 1. County Roscommon, with maps c. 1636 of the baronies of Athlone and Moycarnan and of parishes in Ballintober . . . with introductory notes by Robert C. Simington. Dublin: 1949.

9106 O'CALLAGHAN, MICHAEL. For Ireland and freedom: Roscommon's contributions to the fight for independence, 1917–1921. Boyle: 1964.

9107 O'DONOVAN, JOHN. Letters containing information relative to the antiquities of Roscommon, collected during the progress of the Ordnance Survey in 1837. [Dublin: 1926]. 2 vols. Typed copy in National Library, Dublin.

9108 O'HANLON, JOHN. Index of materials for the history and topography of the county of Roscommon in the Ordnance Survey records. *Kilkenny S.E. Ir. Arch. Soc. J.*, 9, 1867, 106–9.

9109 WELD, ISAAC. Statistical survey of the county of Roscommon . . . Dublin: Dublin Society, 1832.

LEINSTER

9110 CARRIGAN, WILLIAM. The history and antiquities of the diocese of Ossory. Dublin: 1905. 4 vols. Bibliog., vol. 1, pp. xxi–xxv.

9111 COLEMAN, JAMES. Bibliography of the counties of Kilkenny, Carlow and Wicklow. *Waterford S.E. Ir. Arch. Soc. J.*, 11, 1907–8, 126–33.

9112 — Bibliography of the counties of Louth, Meath, Westmeath and Longford. *Louth Arch. J.*, 2, 1908, 24–6.

9113 WHITE, TERENCE DE VERE. Leinster. London: 1968.

Longford and Westmeath

9114 ARDAGH AND CLONMACNOIS ANTIQUARIAN SOCIETY, Longford. Journal. vols. 1–2, 1926–51.

9115 CLARKE, DESMOND. Athlone: a bibliographical study. *An. Leab.,* 10, 1952, 138–9.

9116 COLEMAN, JAMES. See no. 9112.

9117 COX, LIAM. Westmeath in 1798 period. *Ir. Sword*, vol. 9, no. 14, 1969, 1–15.

9118 FARRELL, JAMES P. History of the county of Longford, illustrated. Dublin: 1891.

9119 KEANEY, MARIAN, *compiler*. Westmeath authors: a bibliographical and biographical study. Mullingar: 1969.

9120 KIERNAN, KATHLEEN M. A bibliography of the history of the county of Westmeath (in printed books). [1959]. Typewritten copy, for Fellowship of the Library Association of Ireland.

9121 MURRAY, MARIE CELINE. A bibliography of County Longford: 1961. Typescript copy in Longford-Westmeath County Library.

9122 O'CONNOR, S. Short list of books from the special collection of the Longford-Westmeath County Library, dealing with or having reference to the diocese of Meath. *Riocht na Midhe,* vol. 1, no. 1, 1955, 62. *ibid.* vol. 2, no. 2, 1960, 66–8.

9123 O'DONOVAN, JOHN. Letters containing information relative to the antiquities of Co. Longford, collected during the progress of the Ordnance Survey in 1837. [Dublin, 1926]. Typewritten copy in National Library, Dublin.

9124 — Letters containing information relative to the antiquities of Co. Westmeath, collected during the progress of the Ordnance Survey in 1837. ₅Dublin, 1926]. 2 vols. Typewritten copy in National Library, Dublin.

9125 O'HANLON, JOHN. Index of materials for the history and topography of the county of Longford in the Irish Ordnance Survey records, and in the Royal Irish Academy. *Kilkenny S.E. Ir. Arch. Soc. J.*, 6, 1861, 321–3.

9126 — Index of materials for the history and topography of Westmeath in the Irish Ordnance Survey records and in the Royal Irish Academy. *Kilkenny S.E. Ir. Arch. Soc. J.,* 6, 1860, 193–5.

9127 O'SUILLEABHAIN, SEAN. Longford authors: a biographical and bibliographical dictionary. Mullingar: 1978.

9128 STOKES, GEORGE THOMAS. Athlone, the Shannon and Lough Ree: a guide book . . . with a local directory, edited by John Burgess. Dublin and Athlone [1897].

9129 WOODS, JAMES. Annals of Westmeath, ancient and modern. Dublin: 1907. Bibliog., p. [xvi].

Meath

9130 COLEMAN, JAMES. See no. 9112

9131 IRISH MANUSCRIPTS COMMISSION. The Civil Survey, A.D. 1654–6. vol. 5. County of Meath with returns of tithes for the Meath baronies . . . with introductory notes and appendices by Robert C. Simington. Dublin: 1940.

9132 MEATH COUNTY LIBRARY. Bibliography of articles written by Rev. John Brady, diocesan historian, Co. Meath. *Riocht na Midhe,* vol. 2, no. 2, 1960, 64–6.

9133 — Books of archaeological interest in Meath County Library, compiled by M.K. McGurl. *Riocht na Midhe*, vol. 1, no.1, 1955, 61; *ibid.*., vol. 2, no. 2, 1960, 66–8. The County Librarian maintains a bibliography of Co. Meath on cards.

9134 MILLS, JAMES, and MCENERY, M.J., *eds*. Calendar of the Gormanston register . . . 1175–1397. Dublin: 1916. *(R. Soc. Antiq. Ir.*, extra volume).

9135 O'CONNOR, S. See no. 9122.

9136 O'DONOVAN, JOHN. Letters containing information relative to the antiquities of Co. Meath, collected during the progress of the Ordnance Survey in 1836. [Dublin: 1927]. Typed copy in National Library, Dublin.

9137 O'HANLON, JOHN. Index of materials for the history and topography of Meath in the Irish Ordnance Survey records, and in the Royal Irish Academy. *Kilkenny S.E. Ir. Arch. Soc. J.*, 5, 1858, 42–8.

9138 O'MEACHAIR, DONNCHADH. A short history of Co. Meath. Meath. [1928].

9139 RIOCHT NA MIDHE: records of Meath Archaeological and Historical Society. vol. 1–. 1955–.

9140 **Thompson, Robert.** Statistical survey of the county of Meath, with observations on the means of improvement . . . Dublin: Dublin Society, 1802.

Louth

9141 **Coleman, James.** See no. 9112.

9142 **County Louth Archaeological Journal.** vol. 1, 1904–. Alphabetical list of articles, plates and illustrations, and contributors, vols. 1–13, in vol. 14, no. 4, 1960, 232–78.

9143 **D'Alton, John.** The history of Drogheda . . . Dublin: 1844. 2 vols.

9144 — The history of Dundalk, and its environs . . . Dublin: 1864.

9145 **Leslie, James** B. History of Kilsaran. Dundalk: 1908. Bibliog., pp. xi–xiv.

9146 **MacAlister,** R.A.S. Robert Downing's *History of Louth. R. Ir. Acad. Proc., Sec. C,* 33, 1916–17, 499–504.

9147 **MacCarte, James.** John D'Alton's Ms. materials for a history of Co. Louth. *Louth. Arch. J.,* vol. 1, no. 1, 1904, 60.

9148 — On the Ordnance Survey papers relating to Co. Louth. *ibid.*, vol. 1, 1904–7, 74–6; vol. 2, 1908–11, 442; vol. 3, 1912–15, 110.

9149 **MacIomhair,** *The Rev.* **Diarmuid.** Primate [Nicholas] Mac Maoiliosa and County Louth. *Sean Ard.*, vol. 6, no. 1, 1971, 70–93.

9150 **Moynagh,** S.H. Notes on some of the old Dundalk charters. *R. Soc. Antiq. Ir. J.,* 38, 1908, 232–5.

9151 **O'Donovan, John.** Letters containing information relative to the antiquities of Co. Louth, collected during the progress of the Ordnance Survey in 1835–6. [Dublin: 1927]. Typed copy in National Library, Dublin.

9152 **O'Hanlon, John.** Index of materials for the history and topography of the county of Louth in the Irish Ordnance Survey records, and in the Royal Irish Academy. *Kilkenny S.E. Ir. Arch. Soc. J.*, 5, 1858, 97–105.

9153 **Tempest's Centenary Dundalk Annual,** 1959. Edited by H.G. Tempest. Dundalk: 1959. Includes biographical notes and portraits of Dundalk people, 1859–1959.

Dublin

9154 **Adams, Benjamin William.** History and description of Santry and Cloghran parishes, Co. Dublin. London: 1883. Bibliog., pp. 138–41.

9155 **Archer, Joseph** Statistical survey of the county of Dublin, with observations on the means of improvement . . . Dublin: Dublin Society, 1801.

9156 **Arnold,** L.J. The Cromwellian settlement of County Dublin, 1652–1660. *R. Soc. Antiq. Ir. J.*, 101, 1971, 146–153.

9157 **Ball, Francis Elrington.** A history of the county of Dublin. Dublin: 1902–20. 6 vols. Reprinted Dublin: 1979.
Pt. 1: Being a history of that portion of the county comprised within the parishes of Monkstown, Kill-of-the-Grange, Dalkey, Killiney, Tully, Stillorgan, and Kilmacud.
Pt. 2: . . .Donnybrook, Booterstown, St. Bartholomew, St. Mark, Taney, St. Peter, and Rathfarnham.
Pt. 3: . . . Tallaght, Cruagh, Whitechurch, Kilgobbin, Kiltiernan, Rathmichael, Old Connaught, Saggart, Rathcoole, and Newcastle.
Pt. 4: . . . Clonsilla, Leixlip, Lucan, Aderrig, Kilmactalway, Kilbride, Kilmahuddrick, Esker, Palmerston, Ballyfermot, Clondalkin, Drimnagh, Crumlin, St. Catherine, St. Nicholas Without, St. James, St. Jude, and Chapelizod, as well as within the Phoenix Park.
Pt. 5: Howth and its owners.
Pt. 6: Southern Fingal [Castleknock, Mulhuddart, Cloghran, Ward, St. Margaret, Finglas, Glasnevin, Grangegorman, St. George, Clonturk].

9158 — and **Hamilton, Everard.** The parish of Taney: a history of Dundrum, near Dublin, and its neighbourhood. Dublin: 1895.

9159 **Berry, Henry** F. Minute Book of the Corporation of Dublin, known as *The Friday Book,* 1567–1611. *R. Ir. Acad. Proc., Sec. C,* 30, 1912–13, 477–514.

9160 **Burke, Nuala** T. An early modern Dublin suburb: the estate of Francis Aungier, Earl of Longford. *Ir. Geog.*, vol. 6, no. 4, 1972, 365–385.

9161 **Campion, Maud.** Skerries. *Dublin Hist. Rec.*, vol. 23, no. 1, 1969, 36–43.

9162 CARY, G.S. Hearth money roll for Co. Dublin: 1664. *Kildare Arch. Soc. J.*, 10, 1922–28, 245–254; 11, 1930–33, 386–466.

9163 CHART, D.A. The story of Dublin. Rev. ed. London: 1932.

9164 COSGRAVE, DILLON. North Dublin. Dublin: 1977. First published 1909; does not include index found in previous edition.

9165 CRAIG, MAURICE J. Dublin, 1660–1860. London: 1952. Bibliog., pp. 342–52. Reprinted Dublin: 1969.

9166 D'ALTON, JOHN. The history of County Dublin. [Facsimile reprint]. Cork: 1976. First published Dublin: 1838.

9167 DUBLIN HISTORICAL RECORD. Dublin, vol. 1–, 1938–. Vol. 10, 1948–9, pp. 115–24, lists contents of vols. 1–10. Subject index . . .vols. 1–17, Vol. 17, 1962, 133–40. Index of contributors, compiled by G. Lennox Barrow. vols. 1–30, 1938–77.

9168 DUTTON, HELY. Observations on Mr. Archer's Statistical Survey of the county of Dublin. Dublin: Dublin Society, 1802.

9169 FITZPATRICK, SAMUEL A. OSSORY. Dublin: a historical and topographical account of the city. [Facsimile reprint]. Cork: 1977. 1st published 1907.

9170 GILBERT, JOHN T. A history of the city of Dublin [1st ed. reprinted]; introduction by F.E. Dixon; index compiled by Diarmuid Breathnach. Shannon: 1972. 3 vols. 1st ed. Dublin: 1854–1859.

9171 — and GILBERT, *Lady*. Calendar of ancient records of Dublin in the possession of the municipal corporation of that city. Dublin: 1889–1944. 19 vols. Covers period 1171–1831; there is an index to the first volume in manuscript, the property of Mr. Patrick Meehan, which may be consulted at the Old Dublin Society's premises, 58 South William Street, Dublin.

9172 GILLESPIE, ELGY, *ed*. The Liberties of Dublin. Dublin: 1973. Area of the city, bounded by the Castle, the Quays, Saint James's Gate and Blackpitts.

9173 HALIDAY, CHARLES. The Scandinavian kingdom of Dublin. Shannon, Ir. Univ. Press: 1969. Reprint of 2nd ed. 1884, with introduction by Breandan O'Riordain.

9174 HANDCOCK, WILLIAM DOMVILLE. The history and antiquities of Tallaght in the county of Dublin. Cork: 1976. Facsimile reprint of 2nd rev. and enl. ed. Dublin: 1899.

9175 HARVEY, JOHN. Dublin: a study in environment, with a new chapter and postscript by the author. East Ardsley: 1972. 1st ed. London: 1949.

9176 IRISH MANUSCRIPTS COMMISSION. The Civil Survey, A.D. 1654–6. vol. 7, County of Dublin, with introductory notes and appendices by Robert C. Simington. Dublin: 1945.

9177 LYON, JOHN. Original autograph collections for the history of Dublin, with topographical, historical and other notices in reference to other parts of Ireland. 6 vols. sm.4to. 1 vol. fol. Monck Mason collection sale catalogue no. 508, and Phillipps Mss. 17725, 17577, 17579–82, 23089. In National Library, Dublin, *Mss. collection*, nos. 100–6.

9178 MACCOIL, LIAM. The book of Blackrock: the story of the town of Blackrock, Co. Dublin through the ages. Blackrock: 1977. Bibliog., pp. 121–4.

9179 M'CREADY, C.T. Dublin bibliography, historical and topographical. Dublin: 1892. Reprint of the appendix to M'Cready's *Dublin street names, dated and explained*, 1892.

9180 MAXWELL, CONSTANTIA. Dublin under the Georges, 1714–1830. 2nd ed. rev., London: 1956. Bibliog., pp. 323–35. First published 1936.

9181 NATIONAL BOOK LEAGUE, LONDON. County of Dublin: selected books published during the last 100 years. 1956. *(Book information bureau book list.)*

9182 O'DONOVAN, JOHN. Letters containing information relative to the antiquities of Co. Dublin, collected during the progress of the Ordnance Survey in 1837. [Dublin, 1926]. Typed copy in National Library, Dublin.

9183 O'HANLON, JOHN. Index of materials for the history and topography of the county of Dublin in the Irish Ordnance Survey records, and in the Royal Irish Academy. *Kilkenny S.E. Ir. Arch. Soc. J.*, 5, 1858–9, 12–15.

9184 WALSH, ROISIN. A short list of books dealing with Dublin, with some notes on early printing and book production in Dublin. In *Dublin Civic Week, 1929, Official Handbook*. Dublin: 1929, pp. 48–56.

9185 WARBURTON, J., *and others*. History of the city of Dublin . . . by J. Warburton, *the Rev*. J. Whitelaw, and *the Rev*. Robert Walsh. London: 1818. 2 vols.

Wicklow

9186 COLEMAN, JAMES. See no. 9111.

9187 FRASER, ROBERT. General view of the agriculture and mineralogy, present state and circumstances of the county of Wicklow, with observations on the means of their improvement . . . Dublin: Dublin Society, 1801.

9188 O'DONOVAN, JOHN. Letters containing information relative to the antiquities of Co. Wicklow, collected during the progress of the Ordnance Survey in 1838. [Dublin, 1927]. Typed copy in National Library, Dublin.

9189 O'HANLON, JOHN. Index of materials for the history and topography of Wicklow in the Irish Ordnance Survey records and in the Royal Irish Academy. *Kilkenny S.E. Ir. Arch. Soc. J.,* 4, 1856–7, 424–7.

9190 SCOTT, GEORGE DIGBY. The stones of Bray, and the stories they can tell of ancient times in the barony of Rathdown. Dublin: 1913. Bibliog., pp. xiii–xv.

9191 WICKLOW COUNTY LIBRARY. [Wicklow bibliography, compiled by Brigid Redmond, 1956.] Typescript, 13 p. including sections on topography, literary associations, history and antiquities, Glendalough, 1798 in Wicklow, place names, Charles Stewart Parnell, geology, economics, folk-lore, sport and forestry.

Kildare

9192 CARY, GEORGE SYDNEY, *compiler*. Index to the intestate administrations of the diocese of Kildare, in the Republic of Ireland [1678–1857]. *Kildare Arch. Soc. J.,* 5, 1906–8, 185–92.

9193 COUNTY KILDARE ARCHAEOLOGICAL SOCIETY JOURNAL. Vol. 1–, 1891–.

9194 IRISH MANUSCRIPTS COMMISSION. The Civil Survey, A.D. 1654–6. vol. 8. County of Kildare, with introductory notes and appendices by Robert C. Simington. Dublin: 1952.

9195 KAVANAGH, MICHAEL V. *compiler*. A contribution towards a bibliography of the history of County Kildare in printed books. Newbridge: [1977].

9196 THE LEADBEATER PAPERS. The Annals of Ballitore, by Mary Leadbeater, with a memoir of the author: letters from Edmund Burke, heretofore unpublished, and the correspondence of Mrs. R. Trench and Rev. George Crabbe with Mary Leadbeater. London: 1862. 2 vols.

9197 O'DONOVAN, JOHN. Letters containing information relative to the antiquities of Co. Kildare, collected during the progress of the Ordnance Survey in 1837. [Dublin 1927]. 2 vols. Typed copy in National Library, Dublin.

9198 O'HANLON, JOHN. Index of materials for the history and topography of Kildare in the Irish Ordnance Survey records and in the Royal Irish Academy. *Kilkenny S.E. Ir. Arch. Soc. J.,* 4, 1856–7, 293–8.

9199 RAWSON, THOMAS JAMES. Statistical survey of the county of Kildare, with observations on the means of improvement . . . Dublin: Dublin Society, 1807.

9200 SOME AUTHORITIES FOR KILDARE COUNTY HISTORY. *Kildare Arch. Soc. J.* 10, 1922–8, 155–60.

Offaly

9201 BYRNE, MICHAEL. Sources for Offaly history. 2nd ed., Tullamore: 1978. 1st ed. 1977.

9202 COOKE, JOHN. A bibliography of County Offaly, 1976. Typescript: available at Offaly County Library.

9203 COOTE, CHARLES. General view of the agriculture and manufactures of the King's County, with observations on the means of their improvement . . . Dublin: Dublin Society, 1801.

9204 COUGHLAN, ANNE. Catalogue of the contents of the Offaly County Library local history collection, 1976. Typescript.

9205 CURTIS, E. The Survey of Offaly in 1550. *Hermathena,* 45, 1930, 312–52.

9206 MACALISTER, R.A.S. The memorial slabs of Clonmacnois, King's County, with an appendix on the materials for a history of the monastery. Dublin: 1909. *(R. Soc. Antiq. Ir.,* extra volume.) Bibliog., pp. 157–8.

9207 O'DONOVAN, JOHN. Letters containing information relative to the antiquities of King's County, collected during the progress of the Ordnance Survey in 1837–8. [Dublin, 1926]. 2 vols. Typed copy in National Library, Dublin.

9208 O'HANLON, JOHN. Index of materials for the history and antiquities of King's County in the Irish Ordnance Survey records, and in the Royal Irish Academy. *Kilkenny S.E. Ir. Arch. Soc. J.*, 4, 1856–7, 250–4.

Leix

9209 COOTE, CHARLES. General view of the agriculture and manufactures of the Queen's County with observations on the means of their improvement . . . Dublin: Dublin Society, 1801.

9210 MACCABA, SEOSAMH. Historical notes on Laois, and place names of Ballyroan. Portlaoise. [1962.]

9211 O'BYRNE, DANIEL. The history of Queen's County . . . Dublin: 1856.

9212 O'DONOVAN, JOHN. Letters containing information relative to the antiquities of Queen's County, collected during the progress of the Ordnance Survey in 1838. [Dublin, 1926]. 2 vols. Typed copy in National Library, Dublin.

9213 O'FAOLAIN, EAMONN. A bibliography of the history of the county of Laois, in printed books. 1960. Typescript.

9214 O'HANLON, JOHN. Index of materials for the history and topography of Queen's County in the Irish Ordnance Survey records and in the Royal Irish Academy. *Kilkenny S.E. Ir. Arch. Soc. J.,* 4, 1856–7, 192–4.

9215 — and O'LEARY, EDWARD. History of the Queen's County. Dublin: 1907–14. 2 vols.

9216 WALSH, HILARY D. Borris-in-Ossory, Co. Laois: an Irish rural parish and its people. Kilkenny: [1970]. Bibliog., pp. 231–236.

Carlow

9217 CARLOVIANA: Journal of the Old Carlow Society. Carlow, vol. 1–, 1947–.

9218 COLEMAN, JAMES. See no. 9111.

9219 MACLEOD, IONA. Bibliography of articles relating to Carlow and district. *Carloviana*, vol. 1, no. 1, 1947, 33–36.

9220 O'DONOVAN, JOHN. Letters containing information relative to the antiquities of the county of Carlow, collected during the progress of the Ordnance Survey in 1839. [Dublin: 1927]. Typed copy in National Library, Dublin.

9221 O'HANLON, JOHN. Index of materials for the history and topography of the county of Carlow in the Irish Ordnance Survey records. *Kilkenny S.E. Ir. Arch. Soc. J.*, 4, 1856–7, 321–4.

9222 O'MALLEY, *Miss* B. A bibliography of Carlow. In preparation for Fellowship of the Library Association of Ireland.

9223 RYAN, JOHN. The history and antiquities of the county of Carlow. Dublin: 1833.

9224 SNODDY, O. Writers in Irish from County Carlow. *Ir. Booklore,* vol. 1, no. 2, 1971, 260.

Wexford

9225 COLEMAN, JAMES. See no. 9256

9226 FRASER, ROBERT. Statistical survey of the county of Wexford. Dublin: Dublin Society, 1807.

9227 GRIFFITHS, GEORGE. Chronicles of the County Wexford, being a record of memorable incidents, disasters, social occurrences, and crimes; also biographies of eminent persons, etc., etc., brought down to the year 1877. Enniscorthy [1890].

9228 HORE, HERBERT F. and HORE, PHILIP HERBERT. List of Mss. original and copies, bound manuscripts, pedigrees, and papers on historical subjects principally relating to the county of Wexford, and its past and present landed gentry, compiled and collected by the author and his son Philip . . . Wexford, n.d.

9229 — Bibliographical note on the collectins of Herbert Hore, of Pole-Hore, Co. Wexford, relating to Irish history and to Co. Wexford. *R. Soc. Antiq. Ir. J.,* 23, 1893, 213.

9230 HORE, PHILIP HERBERT, *ed*. History of the town and county of Wexford, compiled principally from the state papers, the public records, and Mss. of the late Herbert F. Hore. London: 1900–11. 6 vols.

9231 **Irish Manuscripts Commission.** The Civil Survey, A.D. 1654–6. vol. 9. County of Wexford, with introductory notes and appendices by Robert C. Simington. Dublin: 1953. Appendix B: Hore collection, list of Mss., pp. 315–21.

9232 **List of Wexford Municipal Records Printed.** *N and Q., series.* 11, vol. 6, 1912, 91.

9233 **O'Donovan, John.** Letters containing information relative to the antiquities of Co. Wexford collected during the progress of the Ordnance Survey in 1840. [Dublin, 1927]. 2 vols. Typed copy in National Library, Dublin.

9234 **O'Hanlon, John.** Index of materials for the history and topography of Wexford in the Irish Ordnance Survey records and in the Royal Irish Academy. *Kilkenny S.E. Ir. Arch. Soc. J.,* 4, 1856–7, 392–7.

9235 **Old Wexford Society,** Wexford. Journal, no. 1–, 1968–.

9236 **Roche, Richard.** Saltees: islands of birds and legends; with a section on the bird life, by Oscar Merne. Dublin: 1977. Bibliog., p. 148: list of shipwrecks pp. 75–78.

Kilkenny

9237 **Bence-Jones, Mark.** A town of medieval form: Kilkenny. *Country Life,* 139, 1966, 1170–3, 1254–7.

9238 **Butler, Hubert.** Kilkenny in the days of the dukes. *J. Butler Soc.,* vol. 1, no. 5, 1973–4, 339–347.

9239 **Coleman, James.** See no. 9111.

9240 **Empey, C.A.** The Cantreds of the medieval county of Kilkenny. *R. Soc. Antiq. Ir. J.,* 101, 1971, 128–134.

9241 **Healy, William.** History and antiquities of Kilkenny (county and city), with illustrations and appendix, compiled from inquisitions, deeds, wills, funeral entries, family records, and other historical and authentic sources. Kilkenny: 1893. vol. 1. No more published.

9242 **Hogan, John.** Kilkenny: the ancient city of Ossory, the seat of its kings, the see of its bishops, and the site of its cathedral. Kilkenny: 1884.

9243 **Irish Manuscripts Commission.** Kilkenny city records: Liber Primus Kilkenniensis. The earliest of the books of the corporation of Kilkenny now extant, edited by Charles McNeill. Dublin: 1931.

9244 **Jackson, Robert Wyse.** The story of Kilkenny. Dublin and Cork: 1974. Bibliog., pp. 111–112.

9245 **O'Donovan, John.** Letters containing information relative to the antiquities of Co. Kilkenny, collected during the progress of the Ordnance Survey in 1839. [Dublin, 1928]. Typed copy in National Library, Dublin.

9246 **O'Hanlon, John.** Index of materials for the history and topography of the county of Kilkenny in the Irish Ordnance Survey records and in the Royal Irish Academy. *Kilkenny S.E. Ir. Arch. Soc. J.,* 4, 1856–7, 153–4.

9247 **O'Kelly, Owen.** A history of County Kilkenny. Kilkenny, [1970].

9248 **Old Kilkenny Review.** Kilkenny, no. 1–, 1948–. For catalogue of articles in the first twelve numbers, see no. 13, 1961, 35–39.

9249 **Otway-Ruthven, Jocelyn,** *trans.* Liber Primus Kilkenniensis. Kilkenny, 1961. For Corrigenda see *Anal. Hib.*, 26, 1970, 73–87.

9250 **Pilsworth,** W.J. History of Thomastown and district. [Thomastown, 1953].

9251 **Prim, John** G.A. Documents connected with the city of Kilkenny militia in the seventeenth and eighteenth centuries. *Kilkenny S.E. Ir. Arch. Soc. J.,* 3, 1854, 231–74.

9252 — Papers, some original, some copies, relating to the history of Kilkenny, collected or compiled by the late Mr. J.G.A. Prim . . . one time honorary secretary of the Kilkenny Archaeological Society. *Rep. D.K. Pub. Rec. Ir.*, no. 58, 1951, 50–70.

9253 **Sparks, May,** and **Bligh, Eric.** Kilkenny, pen and picture pages of its story. Kilkenny: 1926. Kilkenny's writers, pp. 107–9.

9254 **Tighe, William.** Statistical observations relative to the county of Kilkenny made in the years 1800 and 1801. Dublin: Dublin Society, 1802.

9255 **Walton, Julian** C. The Hearth money rolls of Co. Kilkenny, extracted from the Carrigan Mss. *Ir. Geneal.*, 5, 1974–5, 33–47, 169–180.

MUNSTER

9256 COLEMAN, JAMES. Bibliography of the counties of Waterford, Tipperary, and Wexford. *Waterford S.E. Ir. Arch. Soc. J.,* 10, 1907, 323–8.

9257 CROKER, THOMAS CROFTON. Researches in the South of Ireland illustrative of the scenery, architectural remains and the manners and superstitions of the peasantry, with an appendix containing a private narrative of the Rebellion of 1798. Introduction by Kevin Danaher. Shannon: 1969. Photolithographic facsimile of 1st ed. London: 1824.

9258 FFOLLIOTT, ROSEMARY. Provincial town life in Munster. *Ir. Ancest.*, vol. 5, no. 1, 1973, 34–37.

9259 NORTH MUNSTER ANTIQUARIAN JOURNAL. Vol. 1–, 1936–.

9260 NORTH MUNSTER ARCHAEOLOGICAL SOCIETY (*Incorp.* Limerick Field Club, 1897–1908). Index to journal, 1897–1919, compiled by Dermot Foley. [1958].

9261 O'BUACHALLA, LIAM. Contributions towards the political history of Munster, A.D. 450–800. *Cork Hist. Arch. Soc. J., 2nd ser.* 56, 1951, 87–90; 57, 1952, 67–86; 59, 1954,111–26; 61, 1956, 89–102.

9262 O'CORRAIN, DONNCHA. Studies in West Munster history. *Kerry Arch. Hist. Soc. J.*, 1, 1968, 46–55.

9263 O'HANLON, JOHN. Index of materials for the history and topography of Munster in the Irish Ordnance Survey records, and in the Royal Irish Academy. *Kilkenny S.E. Ir. Arch. Soc. J.* 8, 1864–6, 418–24.

9264 RYNNE, ETIENNE, *ed.* North Munster studies: essays in commemoration of Monsignor Michael Moloney. Limerick: 1967. Published work of the late Monsignor Michael Moloney, by Roisin de Nais, pp. 5–7. Includes material on archaeology, numismatics, and folklife.

9265 SEYMOUR, ST. JOHN D. The diocese of Emly. Dublin: 1913. Bibliog., pp. 15–17.

Waterford

9266 COLEMAN, JAMES. See no. 9256.

9267 DOWNEY, EDMUND. The story of Waterford from the foundation of the city to the middle of the eighteenth century. Waterford: 1914. Bibliog., pp. viii–x.

9268 EGAN, P.M. History, guide and directory of county and city of Waterford. Kilkenny: 1891. Waterford in literature, including bibliographical and biographical notes on local writers, local ballads, histories of Waterford, etc., pp. 243–86.

9269 IRISH MANUSCRIPTS COMMISSION. The Civil Survey, A.D. 1654–6. vol. 6. County of Waterford. With appendices: Muskerry barony, Co. Cork; Kilkenny city and liberties (part); also valuations, c. 1663–4, for Waterford and Cork cities. With introductory notes by Robert C. Simington. Dublin: 1942.

9270 — Council books of the Corporation of Waterford, 1662–1700, together with nine documents of 1580–82. Edited by Seamus Pender. Dublin: 1964.

9271 O'DONOVAN, JOHN. Letters containing information relative to the antiquities of Waterford, collected during the progress of the Ordnance Survey in 1841. [Dublin, 1926]. Typed copy in National Library, Dublin.

9272 O'HANLON, JOHN. List of materials for the history and topography of the county of Waterford in the Ordnance Survey records. *Kilkenny S.E. Ir. Arch. Soc. J.,* 8, 1864–6, 129–31.

9273 PENDER, SEAMUS. Studies in Waterford history. *Cork Hist. Arch. Soc. J.*, 51, 1946, 10–26, 108–125; 52, 1947, 18–29, 149–177; 53, 1948, 39–59, 104–114; 54, 1949, 25–30; 55, 1950, 31–45; 58, 1953, 14–19, 67–76; 59, 1954, 11–21, 89–100; 60, 1955, 33–46; 61, 1956, 123–127; 70, 1965, 99–107; 72, 1967, 1–9; 73, 1968, 137–143.

9274 RYLAND, R.H. The history, topography and antiquities of the county and city of Waterford; with an account of the present state of the peasantry of that part of the south of Ireland. London: 1824.

9275 SMITH, CHARLES. The ancient and present state of the county and city of Waterford, containing a natural, civil, ecclesiastical, historical and topographical description thereof. 2nd ed. with additions. Dublin: 1774. 1st ed. 1746.

9276 WALSH, JOSEPH J. *compiler*. Waterford's yesterdays and tomorrows; and an outline of Waterford history. Waterford: 1960.

9277 WATERFORD COUNTY LIBRARY. A card catalogue of books is maintained covering the county and city, also an index listing articles and items dealing with the county contained in books in stock.

9278 WATERFORD PUBLIC LIBRARY. Catalogue of books, compiled by John P. Morrin. Waterford: 1899.

Tipperary

9279 BURKE, WILLIAM P. History of Clonmel. Waterford: 1907.

9280 COLEMAN, JAMES. See no. 9256.

9281 COTTER, JAMES H. Tipperary. New York: 1929. Bibliog., pp. 191–2.

9282 FLYNN, PAUL J. The Book of the Galtees and the Golden vein: a border history of Tipperary, Limerick and Cork. Dublin: 1926.

9283 HAYES, *The Rev.* W.J. *ed.* Tipperary remembers. Thurles: 1976.

9284 IRISH MANUSCRIPTS COMMISSION. The Civil Survey, A.D. 1654–6. vols. 1–2. County of Tipperary. Introductory notes by Robert C. Simington. Dublin: 1931–34.

9285 MCLOUGHNEY, MARY. A bibliography of Tipperary history and antiquities, 1972. Typescript, for Fellowship of the Library Association of Ireland.

9286 O'DONOVAN, JOHN. Letters containing information relative to the antiquities of Co. Tipperary, collected during the progress of the Ordnance Survey in 1840. [Dublin, 1928]. 3 vols. Typed copy in National Library, Dublin.

9287 O'HANLON, JOHN. List of materials for the history and topography of the county of Tipperary in the Ordnance Survey records. *Kilkenny S.E. Ir. Arch. Soc. J.*, 8, 1864–6, 124–31.

9288 POWER, PATRICK C. Carrick-on-Suir and its people. Dun Laoghaire: 1976.

Clare

9289 CLANCY, JOHN. Gleanings in seventeenth century Kilrush. *Nth. Munster Antiq. J.*, 3, 1942–3, 203–13.

9290 CLARE COUNTY LIBRARY. Catalogue of local literature on the Co. Clare, compiled by Dermot Foley, 1937. Typescript, 8 p.

9291 COLEMAN, JAMES. Limerick and Clare bibliography: a list of the topographical and historical works relating to the counties of Limerick and Clare. *Limerick Fld. Cl. J.*, 3, 1907, 139–42.

9292 DUTTON, HELY. Statistical survey of the county of Clare, with observations on the means of improvement . . . Dublin: Dublin Society, 1808.

9293 FLYNN, MAURICE. A bibliography of Clare history and antiquities in printed books, 1967. Typescript, for Fellowship of the Library Association of Ireland.

9294 FROST, JAMES. The history and topography of the county of Clare, from the earliest times to the beginning of the eighteenth century. Dublin: 1893.

9295 HEWSON, MICHAEL. The diaries of John Singleton of Quinville, Co. Clare. *Nth. Munster Antiq. J.*, 17, 1975, 103–109. Covers period 1816–17 and 1845–51.

9296 — A source for nineteenth century Clare history. *ibid.*, 9, 1962–5, 194–5. Description of 140 volumes of newspaper cuttings, compiled by Theobald Butler, in the National Library.

9297 IRISH MANUSCRIPTS COMMISSION. Books of survey and distribution, being abstracts of various surveys and instruments of title, 1636–1703. Vol. 4. County of Clare. Reproduced from the manuscript in the Public Record Office of Ireland. Introduction, by R.C. Simington; index of persons, places and subjects, by Brendan MacGiolla Choille. Dublin: 1967.

9298 MACLOCHLAINN, ALF. Social life in County Clare, 1800–1850. *Ir. Univ. Rev.*, vol. 2, no. 1, 1972, 55–78.

9299 MACMATHUNA, SEOSAMH. Kilfarboy [a history of a west Clare parish]. [1974] Published privately by the author.

9300 O'DONOVAN, JOHN. Letters and extracts relative to ancient territories in Thomond. 1841. [Dublin, 1928].

9301 — Letters containing information relative to the antiquities of Co. Clare, collected during the progress of the Ordnance Survey in 1839. [Dublin, 1926]. 2 vols. Typed copies in National Library, Dublin.

9302 O'GORMAN and STEELE's Ms. collections chiefly relating to the county of Clare. See Catalogue of the library of Thomas Crofton Croker, sold by Puttick and Simpson, December 19, 1854.

9303 O'HANLON, JOHN. List of materials for the history and topography of the county of Clare in the Ordnance Survey records. *Kilkenny S.E. Ir. Arch. Soc. J.,* 8, 1864–6, 418–22.

Limerick

9304 BRADSHAW, BRENDAN. Fr. [David] Wolfe's description of Limerick city, 1574. *Nth. Munster Antiq. J.*, 17, 1975, 47–53.

9305 COISTE OIDEACHAIS MUINTEOIRI LUIMNIGH. Limerick: a handbook of local history. [1971].

9306 COLEMAN, JAMES. Limerick's historical documents: bibliographical note. *Limerick Fld. Cl. J.,* vol. 1, no. 3, 1899, 38–9. See also no. 9291 for Limerick bibliography.

9307 DE NAIS, ROISIN. A bibliography of Limerick history and antiquities. Limerick: [1962].

9308 FERRAR'S LIMERICK DIRECTORY, 1769: containing merchants, traders, and others, etc. *Ir. Geneal.,* vol. 3, no. 9, 1964, 329–340. Only 3 copies are known to exist of this directory which appears to be the first ever printed for Limerick.

9309 FITZGERALD, P. and MCGREGOR. J.J. The history, topography, and antiquities of the county and city of Limerick; with a preliminary view of the history and antiquities of Ireland. Dublin: 1826–7. 2 vols.

9310 HAMILTON, G.F. Records of Ballingarry, Limerick diocese. Limerick: 1930. Bibliog., pp. 115–7.

9311 HERBERT, ROBERT. City of Limerick Public Library: catalogue of the museum and reference library. Limerick: 1940. Reprinted from *Nth. Munster Antiq. J.*, 2, 1940–1, 76–81. Lists works on Irish history chronologically, also archaeology and local history.

9312 — Worthies of Thomond: a compendium of short lives of the most famous men and women of Limerick and Clare to the present day. Limerick: 1944. 1st series. No more published.

9313 IRISH MANUSCRIPTS COMMISSION. The Civil Survey, A.D. 1654–6. vol. 4, County of Limerick, with a selection of Clanmaurice barony, Co. Kerry . . . with introductory notes and appendices by Robert C. Simington. Dublin: 1938.

9314 IRISH PROVINCIAL DIRECTORIES. A general directory of the Kingdom of Ireland, 1788, by Richard Lucas. Limerick, County of Limerick. *Ir. Geneal.*, vol. 3, no. 12, 1967, 529–537.

9315 LENIHAN, MAURICE. Limerick, its history and antiquities, ecclesiastical and military . . . Dublin: 1866. Bibliog., pp. x–xi; list of charters, pp. 739–40.

9316 MISCELLANEOUS PAPERS, chiefly relating to the city and county of Limerick, fifteenth to nineteenth century. *British Museum Add. Ms.,* no. 31888.

9317 O'DONOVAN, JOHN. Letters containing information relative to the antiquities of Co. Limerick, collected during the progress of the Ordnance Survey in 1840. [Dublin, 1926.]. 2 vols. Typed copy in National Library, Dublin.

9318 O'HANLON, JOHN. Index of materials for the history and topography of the county of Limerick in the Irish Ordnance Survey records, and in the Royal Irish Academy. *Kilkenny S.E. Ir. Arch. Soc. J.*, 8, 1864–6, 422–4.

9319 TIERNEY, MARK. Murroe and Boher: the history of an Irish county parish. Dublin: 1966. Bibliog., pp. 239–244.

9320 WESTROPP, T.J., *and others*. The antiquities of Limerick and its neighbourhood [with bibliogs.], by T.J. Westropp, R.A.S. Macalister, and G.V. MacNamara. Dublin: 1916. *(R. Soc. Antiq. Ir. antiquarian handbook ser.*, no. 7).

Cork

9321 **Alexander the Coppersmith**. Remarks upon the religion, trade, government, police, customs, manners, and maladys of the city of Corke, [new ed.]Cork: 1974. 1st pub. Cork: 1737. Includes a critical review of the foregoing work of Alexander the Coppersmith, by William Boles.

9322 **Barnby, Henry**. The Sack of Baltimore. *Cork Hist. Arch. Soc. J.*, 74, 1969, 101–129.

9323 **Beecher, Sean**. The story of Cork. Cork: 1971.

9324 **Bennett, George**. The history of Bandon and the principal towns in the West Riding of Co. Cork. Enl. ed. Cork: 1869.

9325 **Bolster, Evelyn**. A history of Mallow. Cork: 1971.

9326 — A landgable roll of Cork city. *Coll. Hib.*, 13, 1970, 8–20. The importance of this roll lies in it being a quasi directory of leading Cork citizens for the period 1377–1413.

9327 **Cody, Bryan A**. The River Lee, Cork, and the Corkonians. [Reprint of 1st edition] Cork: 1974. Originally published London: 1859.

9328 **Coleman, James**. Historical Mss. relating to the county of Cork, by J. Coleman and W.A. Copinger. *Cork Hist. Arch. Soc. J.,* 1, 1892, 169–70, 207–9.

9329 — The three *Cork Remembrancer's* and their authors, by J.C. *ibid., 2nd ser.,* 15, 1909, 154–5.

9330 **Collins, John T**. Legal documents relating to Fermoy, Castlelyons, and other parts of East Cork. *Cork Hist. Arch. Soc. J., 2nd ser.,* 52, 1947, 178–85; 53, 1948, 13–18.

9331 — Unpublished Cork inquisitions in the Royal Irish Academy. *ibid.,* 65, 1960, 76–82, 127–9. Deal mostly with early seventeenth century.

9332 — Gleanings from old Cork [news] papers. [1738–66]. *Cork Hist. Arch. Soc. J.,* 62, 1957, 95–101; 63, 1958, 95–102; 68, 1963, 96–101; 69, 1964, 56–59, 132–5; 70, 1965, 66–70, 140–2; 72, 1967, 72–4.

9333 **Coombes, James**. A history of Timoleague and Barryroe. Timoleague: 1969.

9334 **Cork County Library**. The library maintains manuscript lists covering Cork printing, Cork writers, Cork twentieth century writers, and printing in Irish, which are comprehensive in scope.

9335 **Cork Historical and Archaeological Society Journal**. Cork. vol. 1–, 1892–, Indexes, 1892–1940, 1941–1960, 1961–1970, compiled by Denis J. O'Donoghue. Cork: 1943–1970.

9336 **Donnelly, James S.,** *Jr.* The land and the people of nineteenth-century Cork. London and Boston: 1975. *(Studies in Irish History, 2nd ser.* vol. 9) Bibliog., pp. 385–417.

9337 **Doran, C.G**. Local bibliography. *Cork Hist. Arch. Soc. J.*, 1, 1892, 60, 83–4, 107–8, 151–2, 171–2.

9338 **Feehan, Sean**. The scenery and character of Cork. Cork: 1974.

9339 **Gaughan, J. Anthony**. Doneraile. 2nd ed. Dublin: 1970. First published 1968.

9340 **Gibson, C.B**. The history of the county and city of Cork. London: 1861. 2 vols.

9341 **Gilbert, John**. A record of the authors, artists and musical composers born in the county of Cork. *Cork Hist. Arch. Soc. J., 2nd ser.,* 19, 1913, 168–81.

9342 **Hartnett, P.J.,** *ed.* Cork city, its history and antiquities. Cork [1944]. Reprinted from *Cork Hist. Arch. Soc. J.,* vol. 48, no. 167, 1943. Includes bibliogs., also paper by Eugene Carberry, *The Development of Cork city,* which lists maps chronologically for the period 1545–1834.

9343 **Milner, Liam**. The River Lee and its tributaries. Cork: 1975.

9344 **Mulcahy, Michael**. A short history of Kinsale. [Cork], 1966. Bibliog., p. 68.

9345 **O'Hanlon, John**. List of materials for the history and topography of the county of Cork in the Ordnance Survey records. *Kilkenny S.E. Ir. Arch. Soc. J.,* 8, 1864–6, 452–7.

9346 **O'Murchadha, Diarmuid**. History of Crosshaven and the parish of Templebreedy. Cork: 1967.

9347 **Orme, A.R**. Youghal, county Cork – growth, decay, resurgence. *Ir. Geog.*, vol. 5, no. 3, 1966, 121–149.

9348 O'SULLIVAN, FLORENCE. The history of Kinsale. Cork: 1976. 1st published, 1916.

9349 O'SULLIVAN, WILLIAM. The economic history of Cork city from the earliest times to the Act of Union. Dublin: 1937. Bibliog., pp. 363–82.

9350 PETTIT, S.F. The Royal Cork Institution: a reflection of the cultural life of a city. *Cork Hist. Arch. Soc. J.,* 81, 1976, 70–90.

9351 — This city of Cork, 1700–1900. Cork: 1977. Bibliog., pp. 302–3.

9352 SHEEHAN, R.A. Notes on the literary history of Cork. *Cork Hist. Arch. Soc. J.,* 1, 1892, 4–10.

9353 SMITH, CHARLES. The ancient and present state of the county and city of Cork. Dublin: 1750. 2 vols. 2nd ed., 1774. Reprinted as a supplement to the Journal of the Cork Historical and Archaeological Society, Cork: 1893–4.

9354 SOMERVILLE-LARGE, PETER. The coast of West Cork. London: 1972. Bibliog., pp. 215–217.

9355 SULLIVAN, T.D. Bantry, Berehaven and the O'Sullivan sept. [Facsimile reprint]. Cork: 1978. First published 1908.

9356 TOWNSEND, HORATIO. Statistical survey of the county of Cork, with observations on the means of improvement . . . Dublin: Dublin Society, 1810.

9357 WAIN, H. The history of Youghal. Cork: 1965.

9358 WEBSTER, CHARLES A. The diocese of Cork. Cork: 1920. Bibliog., pp. xvii–xxxii.

9359 WINDELE, JOHN. Cork, historical and descriptive notices of the city of Cork from its foundation to the middle of the nineteenth century; revised, abridged and annotated by James Coleman. Cork: 1910. Bibliog., p. 87.

9360 WRITERS AND PRINTERS OF YOUGHAL. *Cork Hist. Arch. Soc. J., 2nd ser.,* 5, 1899, 133–46.

Kerry

9361 BARRINGTON, T.J. Discovering Kerry: its history, heritage, and topography. Dublin: 1976. Bibliog., pp. 307–316.

9362 BOURKE, F.S. A handlist of books on Killarney. *Bibliog. Soc. Ir.,* vol. 6, no. 2, 1953.

9363 COLEMAN, J.C. The mountains of Killarney. Dundalk: 1948. Includes reading list.

9364 COLEMAN, JAMES. Bibliographia Kerriensis: a list of topographical and other separately published works relating to the county of Kerry. *Kerry Arch. Mag.,* 1, 1908, 38–44.

9365 COURT OF EXCHEQUER RECORDS RELATING TO KERRY. *Kerry Arch. Mag.*, 4, 1917, 124–46.

9366 FEEHAN, SEAN. The Scenery and character of Kerry: illustrated by Gladys Leach. Cork: 1975.

9367 GAUGHAN, J. ANTHONY. Listowel and its vicinity. 2nd ed. Cork: 1974. Bibliog., pp. 558–586.

9368 HALL, S.C., and HALL, A.M. Killarney and the South of Ireland. [Facsimile ed.] Cork: 1976. 1st pub. London: 1865.

9369 HODGSON, BRYAN. Irish ways live on in Dingle. *Nat. Geog.*, 149, 1976, 551–576.

9370 HUNTER, R.J. Fragments of the Civil Survey of Counties Kerry, Longford and Armagh. *Anal. Hib.*, 24, 1967, 227–231.

9371 IRISH MANUSCRIPTS COMMISSION. The Kenmare manuscripts, edited by Edward MacLysaght. Dublin: 1942. Period covered: seventeenth and eighteenth centuries.

9372 JOURNAL OF THE KERRY ARCHAEOLOGICAL AND HISTORICAL SOCIETY. Tralee. no. 1–. 1968–.

9373 KERRY COUNTY LIBRARY. Local history [a bibliography]. 1956. Typescript, 7 p., which includes topography, geology, archaeology, and biography.

9374 KING, JEREMIAH. Co. Kerry, past and present: a handbook to the local and family history of the county. Dublin: 1931. Bibliog., pp. 27–8.

9375 — History of Kerry. Liverpool: 1908.

9376 — Kerry bibliography. See his *Irish Bibliography*, vol. 1, pp. 121–5.

9377 LAVELLE, DES. Skellig: island outpost of Europe. Dublin: 1976. Bibliog., p. 103.

9378 MOULD, D.C. POCHIN. Valentia: portrait of an island. Dublin: 1978. Bibliog., pp. 142–3.

9379 O'DONOVAN, JOHN. Letters containing information relative to the antiquities of Co. Kerry, collected during the progress of the Ordnance Survey in 1841. [Dublin, 1928.] Typed copy in National Library, Dublin.

9380 O'HANLON, JOHN. Index of materials for the history and topography of the county of Kerry in the Irish Ordnance Survey office. *Kilkenny S.E. Ir. Arch. Soc. J.,* 8, 1864–6, 486–90.

9381 O'SULLIVAN, THOMAS F. Romantic hidden Kerry: legendary, antiquarian and historical associations, political, economic and social conditions and scenic attractions of the barony of Corkaguiny. Tralee: 1931. Bibliog., notes. pp. 586–636.

9382 O'SULLIVAN, WILLIAM. William Molyneux's geographical collections for Kerry. *Kerry Arch. Hist. Soc. J.*, 4, 1971, 28–47.

9383 PETTY-FITZMAURICE, HENRY W.E., *6th Marquis of Lansdowne.* Glanerought and the Petty-Fitzmaurices. London: 1937. Bibliog., pp. xvii–xxviii.

9384 SMITH, CHARLES. The ancient and present state of the County of Kerry. [Facsimile reprint] Cork: 1969. Reprint of Dublin 1756 ed.

THE IRISH ABROAD

9385 BANE, MARTIN J. Catholic pioneers in West Africa. Dublin: 1956. Bibliog., pp. 213–14.

9386 BAYOR, RONALD H. Neighbors in conflict: the Irish, Germans, Jews and Italians of New York City, 1929–1941. Baltimore and London: 1978. (*Johns Hopkins Univ. Stud. Hist. Pol. Sci. 96th ser.*, 1978, no. 1)

9387 BERKELEY, G.F.H. The Irish battalion in the Papal army of 1860. Dublin: 1929. Bibliog., pp. xix–xxii.

9388 BRENNAN, THOMAS A. Brennans and Brannans in American military and naval life, 1745–1918. *Ir. Sword*, vol. 12, no. 48, 1976, 239–245.

9389 CLARK, BRIAN, *trans*. Napoleon's Irish legion, 1803–15: the historical record. *Ir. Sword*, vol. 12, no. 48, 1976, 165–172.

9390 CLARK, DENNIS. The Irish in Philadelphia: ten generations of urban experience. Philadelphia: 1973. Bibliog., pp. 237–242.

9391 CLEARY, PATRICK SCOTT. Australia's debt to Irish nation-builders. Sydney: 1933. Contains information about Irish Australians and their publications.

9392 CLISSOLD, STEPHEN. Bernardo O'Higgins and the independence of Chile. London: 1968. Bibliog., pp. 247–8.

9393 COSTELLO, CON. Ireland and the Holy Land: an account of Irish links with the Levant from the earliest times. Alcester and Dublin: [1974]

9394 — Nineteenth-century Irish explorers in the Levant. *Ir. Geog.*, 7, 1974, 88–96.

9395 DAVIN, NICHOLAS FLOOD. The Irishman in Canada. [Facsimile reprint] With an introduction by Daniel C. Lyne. Shannon: 1969. 1st ed. Toronto, 1877.

9396 DAVIS, RICHARD P. Irish issues in New Zealand politics, 1868–1922. Dunedin: 1974.

9397 DUFFY, CHRISTOPHER. The Irish at Hochkirch, 14th October 1758. *Ir. Sword.* vol. 12, no. 48, 1976, 212–220.

9398 DUNAWAY, WAYLAND F. The Scotch-Irish of colonial Pennsylvania. London: 1962. Bibliog., pp. 233–257. First published Philadelphia: 1944.

9399 EVANS, E. ESTYN. Cultural relics of the Ulster Scots in the Old West of North America. *Ulster Folk.*, 11, 1965, 33–38.

9400 — The Scotch-Irish in the new world: an Atlantic heritage. *R. Soc. Antiq. Ir. J.*, 95, 1965, 39–49.

9401 FFOLLIOTT, ROSEMARY. The Irish passengers aboard *The New World,* Liverpool-New York, October-December 1853. *Ir. Ancest.,* vol. 7, no. 1, 1975, 6–10.

9402 FORDE, FRANK. The Irish regiment of Canada. *Ir. Def. J.* 27, 1967, 489–493.

9403 FUNCHION, MICHAEL F. Irish nationalists and Chicago politics in the 1880s. *Eire-Ir.*, vol. 10, no. 2, 1975, 3–18.

9404 GREELEY, ANDREW M. and MCCREADY, WILLIAM C. An ethnic group which vanished: the strange case of the American Irish. *Soc. Stud.*, vol. 1, no. 1, 1972, 38–50.

9405 GRIMES, MARILLA R. Some newspaper references to Irish immigrants in Oneida Co., New York. *Ir. Ancest.*, vol. 6, no. 2, 1974, 97–8.

9406 GWYNN, AUBREY. An Irish settlement on the Amazon (1612–29). *R. Ir. Acad. Proc. Sec. C.*, 41, 1932–4, 1–54.

9407 HANDLEY, JAMES EDMUND. Irish in Scotland, 1798–1845. 2nd ed. Cork: 1945. Bibliog., pp. 325–37.

9408 — The Irish in modern Scotland. Cork: 1947. Bibliog., pp. 328–37.

9409 HANNA, CHARLES A. The Scotch-Irish, or the Scot in North Britain, North Ireland, and North America. New York and London: 1902. 2 vols. Scotch-Irish bibliography, vol. 2, pp. 531–51.

9410 HAYES, RICHARD. Biographical dictionary of Irishmen in France. Dublin: 1949. Bibliog., pp. 319–26.

9411 — Old Irish links with France: some echoes of exiled Ireland. Dublin: 1940.

9412 HAYES-MCCOY, G.A. Captain Myles Walter Keogh, United States Army, 1840–1876. Dublin [1966].

9413 HENNESSY, MAURICE. The Wild Geese: the Irish soldier in exile. London: 1973. Bibliog., pp. 214–16.

9414 IRISH BORN RECIPIENTS OF THE U.S. CONGRESSIONAL MEDAL OF HONOUR. *Ir. Sword,* vol. 12, no. 47, 1975, 149–151.

9415 JACKSON, JOHN ARCHER. The Irish in Britain. London: 1963.

9416 JAMES, DAVID. An Irish visitor to the court of the Shah of Peria in 1835: extract from the unpublished diary of Sir Francis Hopkins of Athboy. *Studies*, 60, 1971, 139–154.

9417 JENNER, HENRY. The Irish immigrations into Cornwall in the late fifth and early sixth centuries. *84th Annual Report of the Royal Cornwall Polytechnic Society, new ser*. vol. 3, pt. III, 1917, 38–85.

9418 JENNINGS, BRENDAN, *ed*. Wild Geese in Spanish Flanders, 1582–1700: documents, relating chiefly to Irish regiments, from the Archives générales du Royaume, Brussels, and other sources. Dublin: Irish Manuscripts Commission: 1964. Sources, pp. 58–63.

9419 JONES, PAUL. The Irish brigade. Washington: 1969. This book revolves around the figure of Company Commander Thomas F. 'Meagher of the Sword.'

9420 KELLY, E.T. A bridge of fish: the Irish connection with Newfoundland, 1500–1630. *Eire-Ir.*, vol. 4, no. 2, 1969, 37–51.

9421 KELLY, JOSEPH F. Irish influence in England after the Synod of Whitby: some new literary evidence. *Eire-Ir.*, vol. 10, no. 4, 1975, 35–47.

9422 KIERNAN, T.J. The Irish exiles in Australia. Dublin: 1954. Bibliog., pp. 192–3.

9423 KILKENNY, JOHN F. Shamrocks and shepherds: the Irish of Morrow County. Portland: 1969.

9424 LAMBERT, ERIC. General [Daniel] O'Leary and South America. *Ir. Sword*, vol. 11, no. 43, 1973, 57–74.

9425 — Irish soldiers in South America, 1818–30. *Studies*, 58, 1969, 376–395.

9426 LEESON, FRANCIS. Records of Irish emigrants to Canada in Sussex archives, 1839–1847. *Ir. Ancest.*, vol. 6, no. 1, 1974, 31–42.

9427 LEVINE, EDWARD M. The Irish and Irish politicians: a study of cultural and social alienation. Notre Dame and London: 1966.

9428 LOBBAN, R.D. The Irish in Greenock [Scotland] in the nineteenth century. *Ir. Geog.*, vol. 6, no. 3, 1971, 270–281.

9429 LONDON, HERBERT. The Irish and American nativism in New York city, 1843–7. *Dublin Rev.*, 510, 1966–67, 378–394.

9430 MCCAFFREY, LAWRENCE J. The Irish diaspora in America. Bloomington and London: 1976. Bibliog., pp. 179–187.

9431 MACDONAGH, OLIVER. The Irish in Victoria, 1851–91: a demographic essay. *Hist. Stud.*, 8, 1971, 67–92.

9432 MCDONALD, GRACE. History of the Irish in Wisconsin in the nineteenth century. Washington: 1954. Bibliog., pp. 299–308.

9433 MCNEILL, CHARLES. Publications of Irish interest published by Irish authors on the continent of Europe prior to the eighteenth century. With index compiled by Rosalind M. Elmes. *Bibliog. Soc. Ir.,* vol. 4, nos. 1–2, 1930.

9434 MAGUIRE, JOHN FRANCIS. The Irish in America [1st ed. reprinted]. New York: 1969. Orig. pub. London: 1868.

9435 MANNION, JOHN. J. Irish settlements in Eastern Canada: a study of cultural transfer and adaptation. Toronto and Buffalo: 1974. *(Univ. of Toronto, Dept. Geog. Res. Pub. no. 12.)*.

9436 MITCHELL, ARTHUR H. Irishmen and the American Revolution. *Cap. Ann.*, 1977, 70–88.

9437 — A view of the Irish in America: 1887. *Eire-Ir.*, vol. 4, no. 1, 1969, 7–12.

9438 MITCHELL, N.C. Katikati: an Ulster settlement in New Zealand. *Ulster Folk.,* 15–16, 1970, 203–215.

9439 MOLLOY, DOROTHY. In search of the Wild Geese. *Eire-Ir.*, vol. 5, no. 3, 1970, 3–14.

9440 MORTON, GRENFELL, Ulster emigrants to Australia, 1850–1890. *Ulster Folk.,* 18, 1972, 111–120.

9441 MURPHY, J.J.W. Kipling and the Irish soldier in India. *Ir. Sword,* 9, 1969–70, 318–329.

9442 MURRAY, JOHN. The Irish and others in Argentina. *Studies*, 38, 1949, 375–388.

9443 NATIONAL LIBRARY OF IRELAND. Books on Ireland. Dublin: Cultural Relations Committee, 1953. The Irish abroad, pp. 32–6.

9444 NIEHAUS, EARL F. The Irish in New Orleans, 1800–1860. Baton Rouge, Louisiana: 1965.

9445 O'BRIEN, MICHAEL J. The Irish at Bunker Hill: evidence of Irish participation in the battle of 17th June, 1775. Edited by Catherine Sullivan with an introduction by A.M. Sullivan. Shannon: 1968.

9446 — Pioneer Irish in New England. New York: 1937.

9447 O'CALLAGHAN, JOHN C. History of the Irish brigades in the service of France. [Facsimile reprint] with an introduction by Patrick J. Hally. Shannon: 1969. First published 1870.

9448 O'CONNOR, KEVIN. The Irish in Britain. London: 1972. Bibliog., pp. 181–2.

9449 O'DONNELL, ELLIOT. The Irish abroad: a record of the achievements of wanderers from Ireland. London: 1915.

9450 O'FIAICH, TOMAS. Irish Peregrini on the continent: recent research in Germany. *Ir. Eccles. Rec.,* 103, 1965, 233–240.

9451 O'GORMAN, EDMUND. Our islands and Rome. Alcester and Dublin: 1974. The Irish in Rome, pp. 162–171.

9452 O'GRADY, JOSEPH P. How the Irish became Americans. New York: 1973. Bibliog., pp. 179–182.

9453 O'LUANAIG, DONALL. Irishmen and the Franco-German war, 1870–71. *Cap. Ann.*, 1971, 155–163.

9454 O'RAHILLY, CECILE. Ireland and Wales: their historical and literary relations. London: 1924.

9455 O'RYAN, WILLIAM D. and GAYNOR, ROBERT M. Irish recipients of awards for bravery in the United States armed forces, 1863–1963. *Ir. Sword,* 8, 1967–8, 274–6.

9456 PROUDFOOT, BRUCE. Irish settlers in Alberta. *Ulster Folk.*, 15–16, 1970, 216–223.

9457 PUNCH, TERENCE M. Some Irish immigrant weddings in Nova Scotia, 1801–1817. *Ir. Ancest.,* 6, 1974, 101–112; 7, 1975, 39–54, 105–20.

9458 READY, WILLIAM B. The Irish and South America. *Eire-Ir.*, vol. 1, no. 1, 1965–66, 50–63.

9459 RUDA, RICHARD. The Irish Transvaal brigades. *Ir. Sword,* vol. 11, no. 45, 1974, 201–211.

9460 SELECT LIST OF REFERENCES on the Scotch-Irish in the South and the Ohio Valley, with special reference to Kentucky. Washington: Library of Congress, 1913.

9461 — Additional references. 1918. Typescript.

9462 SHANNON, WILLIAM V. The American Irish. New York and London: 1963.

9463 SMITH, RAYMOND. The fighting Irish in the Congo. Dublin: 1962.

9464 SMYTH, WILLIAM J. The Irish in mid nineteenth-century Ontario. *Ulster Folk.*, 23, 1977, 97–105.

9465 THOMAS, CHARLES. The Irish settlements in post-Roman Western Britain: a survey of the evidence. *R. Inst. Cornwall J., new ser.*, vol. 6, pt. 4, 1972, 251–274.

9466 WALSH, JAMES P. American-Irish: West and East. *Eire-Ir.*, vol. 6, no. 2, 1971, 25–32.

9467 WALSH, MICHELINE. Notes towards a biographical dictionary of the Irish in Spain: some O'Neills. *Ir. Sword.*, vol. 4, no. 14, 1959, 5–15.

9468 — The Hadsors and some other Louth exiles in France and Spain. *Louth Arch. Hist. J.*, vol. 18, no. 4, 1976, 263–271.

9469 — Spanish knights of Irish origin: documents from Continental archives. Dublin: 1960–70. 3 vols.

9470 WANNAN, BILL, *ed*. The wearing of the green: the lore, literature, legend and balladry of the Irish in Australia. Melbourne: 1966.

9471 WERLY, JOHN M. The Irish in Manchester, 1832–49. *Ir. Hist. Stud.*, vol. 18, no. 71, 1973, 345–358.

9472 WILLIAMS, HAROLD A. History of the Hibernian Society of Baltimore, 1803–1957. Baltimore: 1957.

9473 WILLIAMS, JOSEPH J. Whence the 'Black Irish' of Jamaica? New York: 1932. Bibliog. pp. 76–90.

9474 WITTKE, CARL. The Irish in America. Louisiana: 1956. Bibliog., pp. 295–306.

SUPPLEMENTARY

9475 BAPTIST HISTORICAL SOCIETY. Association records of the Particular Baptists of England, Wales and Ireland to 1660, edited by B.R. White; indexes compiled by K.W. Howard. London: 1977.

9476 BELL, J. BOWYER. A time of terror: how democratic societies respond to revolutionary violence. New York: 1978. The Irish experience: democracy and armed conspiracy, 1922–1977, pp. 204–233.

9477 BENSON, CIARAN. The place of the arts in Irish education: report of the Working Party appointed by the Arts Council. [Dublin]. 1979. Bibliog., pp. 176–9.

9478 BERLETH, RICHARD. The twilight lords. London: 1979. Struggle of the last feudal lords of Ireland against the England of Elizabeth I.

9479 BRADY, JOHN. Catholics and Catholicism in the eighteenth-century press. Maynooth, 1965.

9480 BURNS, D. THORBURN, and MACDAEID, D.A. Three hundred years of Irish contributions to analytical chemistry. *Orbital*, 2, 1978, 14–30. Includes lists of references for Robert Boyle, Richard Kirwan, Charles Alexander Cameron, James Emerson Reynolds, Walter Noel Hartley and Cecil Leeburn Wilson.

9481 BUTLER, PATRICIA. A guide to art galleries in Ireland. Dublin: 1978.

9482 CARDOZO, NANCY. Maud Gonne: lucky eyes and a high heart. London: 1978.

9483 COX, RONALD C., *compiler*. Engineering Ireland, 1778–1878: exhibition catalogue. Dublin: 1978.

9484 CRAIG, MAURICE. Architecture in Ireland. Dublin: 1978. Bibliog., p. 57.

9485 CURL, JAMES STEVENS. Mausolea in Ulster. Belfast: 1978. Bibliog., p. 20.

9486 DAVIES, G.L. HERRIES, and STEPHENS, NICHOLAS. Ireland; with contributions on the Pleistocene history from Francis M. Synge. London: 1978. *(The Geomorphology of the British Isles)*. Bibliog., pp. 222–242.

9487 ENGLEFIELD, DERMOT J.T. The printed records of the parliament of Ireland, 1613–1800: a survey and bibliographical guide. London: Lemon Tree Press, 1978. Prepared in connection with the microfilm edition of the *Printed records of the Parliament of Ireland*, 1613–1800, published by the Trans-Media Pub. Co., Dobbs Ferry, New York: 10522.

9488 DOSSENBACH, MONIQUE *and others*. Great stud farms of the world, by Monique and Hans D. Dossenbach [and] Hans Joachim Kohler. London: 1978. Includes the National Stud, Ardenode, Moyglare, Gilltown, Balreask, and Tulira Castle.

9489 FANNING, RONAN. The Irish Department of Finance, 1922–58. Dublin: 1978. Bibliog., pp. 690–695.

9490 FAULKNER, ANSELM. Liber Dubliniensis: chapter documents of the Irish Franciscans, 1719–1875. Killiney: Franciscan Friars, 1978.

9491 FOX, ROBIN. The Tory Islanders: a people of the Celtic fringe. Cambridge: 1978.

9492 GAUGHAN, J. ANTHONY. Austin Stack: portrait of a separatist. Dublin: 1973.

9493 GRAVER, LAWRENCE, and FEDERMAN, RAYMOND, *ed*. Samuel Beckett. London: 1979. *(Critical heritage series.)*

9494 HADFIELD, CHARLES, and SKEMPTON, A.W. William Jessop, engineer, Newton Abbot: 1979. Jessop in Ireland, pp. 86–109.

9495 HARMON, MAURICE, *ed*. Irish poetry after Yeats: seven poets. Austin Clarke; Richard Murphy; Patrick Kavanagh; Thomas Kinsella; Denis Devlin; John Montague; Seamus Heaney. Portmarnock (Co. Dublin): 1979. Select bibliog. of twentieth century Irish poetry, pp. 227–231.

9496 HART, IAN. Dublin Simon Community, 1971–1976: an exploration. Dublin: 1978. *(Economic and Social Research Institute, Broadsheet no. 15*)

9497 HIBERNIAN SPECIALISED CATALOGUE OF THE POSTAGE STAMPS OF IRELAND, 1922–1978. 2nd ed. Dublin: 1979.

9498 HOOD, A.B.E., *ed*. St. Patrick: his writings and Muirchu's Life, edited and translated by A.B.E. Hood. London: 1978. *(History from the sources)*.

9499 JEFFREY, D.W., *gen. ed*. North Bull Island, Dublin Bay: a modern coastal natural history, edited by D.W. Jeffrey, R.N. Goodwillie, B. Healy, C.H. Holland, J.S. Jackson and J.J. Moore. Dublin: Royal Dublin Society, 1977. Bibliog., pp. 125–9.

9500 KEYNES, GEOFFREY. A bibliography of George Berkeley, bishop of Cloyne: his works and his critics in the eighteenth century. Oxford: 1976. *(Soho bibliographies, 18)*.

9501 LUCAS, A.T. Irish ploughing practices. *Tools and Tillage*, 2, 1972–5, 52–62, 67–83, 149–160, 195–210.

9502 LUKE, PETER. *ed*. Enter certain players: Edwards-MacLiammoir and the Gate, 1928–1978. Dublin: 1978. Productions, compiled by Patricia Turner, pp. [93–104].

9503 LYONS, J.B. Brief lives of Irish doctors. Dublin: 1978. Bibliog., pp. 167–175.

9504 MACCURTAIN, MARGARET, and O'CORRAIN, DONNCHA, *ed*. Women in Irish society: the historical dimension. Baldoyle (Dublin): 1978.

9505 MITCHELL, LILLIAS. Irish spinning, dyeing and weaving: an anthology, from original documents. Dundalk: 1978.

9506 NATIONAL FILM INSTITUTE OF IRELAND. Catalogue: 16mm. educational films. Dublin: 1978.

9507 NATIONAL LIBRARY OF IRELAND. A select list of books on Ireland. Dublin: 1978.

9508 O'DANACHAIR, CAOIMHIN. A bibliography of Irish ethnology and folk tradition. Dublin and Cork: 1978.

9509 O'DRISCOLL, ROBERT, and REYNOLDS, LORNA, *ed*. Yeats and the theatre. London and Basingstoke: 1975. *(Yeats Studies series)*. Bibliographical appendices: Suggested guidelines for catalogue of Yeats manuscripts, 278–281; Catalogue of Yeats manuscripts in the Olin Library, Cornell University, by Phillip Marcus, 282–284; A note on some of Yeats's revisions for *The Land of Heart's Desire*, by Colin Smythe, 285–6.

9510 PENNIMAN, HOWARD R. *ed*. Ireland at the polls: the Dail elections of 1977. Washington: 1978.

9511 PRONE, TERRY. Write – and get paid for it. Dublin: 1979. Includes well compiled lists of book publishers, newspapers (national and provincial), magazines, and useful information on markets for plays, songwriting, etc.

9512 ROBERTS, JANICE. The Irish setter. London: 1978. Bibliog., pp. 183–4.

9513 ROTHERY, SEAN. The shops of Ireland. Dublin: 1978. Bibliog., pp. 118–19.

9514 SWORDS, LIAM, *ed*. The Irish-French connection, 1578–1978. Paris: The Irish College: 1978. Bibliog., pp. 166–9. A history of the Irish College, Paris.

9515 A SYMPOSIUM ON 'THE INTERIM REPORT ON EQUAL PAY OF THE COMMISSION ON THE STATUS OF WOMEN.' Contributions: A trade union viewpoint, by Evelyn Ownes.– The Economics of equal pay, by P.J. Geary and B.M. Walsh – Some practical considerations, by John Gogarty. *Stat. Social Inq. Soc. Ir. J.*, vol. 22, pt. 4, 1971–72, 106–143.

9516 **Webb, Arthur**. The clean sweep: the story of the Irish Hospitals Sweepstake. London: 1968.

9517 **Went**, A.E.J. List of some historical papers, etc. on Irish fish, fishing and fisheries, 1940–1974. Dublin: 1978. *(Fishery leaflet, no. 97.)*.

AUTHOR INDEX

Numerals refer to individual numbered entries and not to pagination

SUBJECT INDEX

Numerals refer to individual numbered entries and not to pagination